P9-CAL-726

OTHER A TO Z GUIDES FROM THE SCARECROW PRESS, INC.

Edited by Jon Woronoff

1. *The A to Z of Buddhism* by Charles S. Prebish, 2001.
2. *The A to Z of Catholicism* by William J. Collinge, 2001.
3. *The A to Z of Hinduism* by Bruce M. Sullivan, 2001.
4. *The A to Z of Islam* by Ludwig W. Adamec, 2002.
5. *The A to Z of Slavery & Abolition* by Martin A. Klein, 2002.
6. *Terrorism: Assassins to Zealots* by Sean Kendall Anderson and Stephen Sloan, 2003.
7. *The A to Z of the Korean War* by Paul M. Edwards, 2005.
8. *The A to Z of the Cold War* by Joseph Smith and Simon Davis, 2005.
9. *The A to Z of the Vietnam War* by Edwin E. Moise, 2005.
10. *The A to Z of Science Fiction Literature* by Brian Stableford, 2005.
11. *The A to Z of the Holocaust* by Jack R. Fischel, 2005.
12. *The A to Z of Washington, D.C.* by Robert Benedetto, Jane Donovan, and Kathleen DuVall, 2005.
13. *The A to Z of Taoism* by Julian F. Pas, 2006.
14. *The A to Z of the Renaissance* by Charles G. Nauert, 2006.
15. *The A to Z of Shinto* by Stuart D.B. Picken, 2006.
16. *The A to Z of Byzantium* by John H. Rosser, 2006.
17. *The A to Z of the Civil War* by Terry L. Jones, 2006.
18. *The A to Z of the Friends (Quakers)* by Margery Post Abbott, Mary Ellen Chijioke, Pink Dandelion, and John William Oliver JR., 2006
19. *The A to Z of Feminism* by Janet K. Boles and Diane Long Hoeveler, 2006.
20. *The A to Z of New Religious Movements* by George D. Chryssides, 2006.
21. *The A to Z of Multinational Peacekeeping* by Terry M. Mays, 2006.

The A to Z of the Civil War

Volume 2
M–Z

Terry L. Jones

The A to Z Guide Series, No. 17

The Scarecrow Press, Inc.
Lanham, Maryland • Toronto • Oxford
2006

SCARECROW PRESS, INC.

Published in the United States of America
by Scarecrow Press, Inc.
A wholly owned subsidary of
The Rowman & Littlefield Publishing Group, Inc.
4501 Forbes Boulevard, Suite 200, Lanham, Maryland 20706
www.scarecrowpress.com

PO Box 317
Oxford
OX2 9RU, UK

Copyright © 2006 by Terry L. Jones

All rights reserved. No part of this publication may be reproduced,
stored in a retrieval system, or transmitted in any form or by any
means, electronic, mechanical, photocopying, recording, or otherwise,
without the prior permission of the publisher.

British Library Cataloguing in Publication Information Available

Library of Congress Cataloging-in-Publication Data

Jones, Terry L., 1952–
    Historical dictionary of the Civil War / Terry L. Jones.
        p. cm. — (Historical dictionaries of war, revolution, and civil unrest ; no. 18)
    Includes bibliographical references (p.).
    Contents: v. 1.A–L — v. 2. M–Z.
    ISBN 0-8108-4112-6 (alk. paper)
        1. United States—History—Civil War, 1861–1865—Dictionaries. I. Title. II.
Series.
    E468 .J777 2002
    973.7'03—dc21   20010491616

ISBN-13: 978-0-8108-5386-7 (pbk. : alk.paper)
ISBN-10: 0-8108-5386-8 (pbk. : alk. paper)

⊗™ The paper used in this publication meets the minimum requirements of
American National Standard for Information Sciences—Permanence of
Paper for Printed Library Materials, ANSI/NISO Z39.48-1992.
Manufactured in the United States of America.

Contents

THE DICTIONARY

– M –

McARTHUR, JOHN (1826–1906) USA. A native of Scotland, McArthur worked as a blacksmith before immigrating to the United States at age 23. Settling in **Illinois**, he opened a prosperous ironworks and rose to captain in the state militia.

McArthur entered Union service in May 1861 as colonel of the 12th Illinois and was given a **brigade** command in **Charles F. Smith's** division in February 1862. After leading the brigade at **Fort Donelson**, he was promoted to brigadier general of volunteers in March. McArthur saw heavy combat near the "Hornets' Nest" during the **Battle of Shiloh**, and one of his **regiments** suffered the highest percentage of losses (59 percent) of any Union regiment in the battle. He also was wounded in the foot but assumed command of **W. H. L. Wallace's division** when Wallace was mortally wounded. As a division commander, McArthur fought at **Iuka** and **Corinth, Mississippi**, under **E. O. C. Ord** and in the **Vicksburg Campaign** as part of **James B. McPherson's corps** in the **Army of the Tennessee**. After **Vicksburg** was captured, he also commanded the city for a time.

In August 1864, McArthur's division was sent to northern **Georgia**, where it protected **William T. Sherman's** supply line during the **Atlanta Campaign**. He later briefly served in **Missouri** and brought the XVI Corps' 1st Division back to **Tennessee** in time to fight at the **Battle of Nashville**. McArthur won praise and a **brevet** to major general of volunteers at the battle when his division crushed the Confederate left flank. His last military service was participating in the **Mobile Campaign** in the spring of 1865.

McArthur was mustered out of service in August 1865 and returned to Illinois. He was commissioner of public works during the Great Chicago Fire of 1871, and later as postmaster was held liable for the loss of $73,000 of postal funds during a bank failure.

McCALL, GEORGE ARCHIBALD (1802–1868) USA. A native of **Pennsylvania**, McCall graduated from **West Point** in 1822 and served mostly in **Florida** over the next 20 years. As a captain of infantry, he fought in the **Mexican War** and won two **brevets** for gallantry at Palo Alto and Resaca de la Palma. After the war, McCall was promoted to major and in 1850 was named one of the **U.S. Army's** two inspectors general with the rank of colonel. He then retired from the **army** in 1853.

McCall entered Union service in May 1861 when he was appointed major general of Pennsylvania troops and was given command of the **Pennsylvania Reserves**. When these reserves were accepted into Federal service in July, he was appointed brigadier general of volunteers and was placed in command of the **division**. The Pennsylvania Reserves Division was assigned to the **Army of the Potomac** in October. Afterward, McCall planned the operation at **Dranesville, Virginia**, and part of his division saw combat there in December.

McCall fought in the **Peninsula Campaign** and then played a key role during the **Seven Days Campaign** when his V Corps division became the first unit attacked by the Confederates at **Mechanicsville**. After fighting at **Gaines' Mill**, he was captured at **Frayser's Farm** when he mistakenly rode into the Confederate lines during a **reconnaissance**. McCall was imprisoned at **Libby Prison** until **exchanged** in August 1862 for Confederate Brig. Gen. **Simon B. Buckner**. Taking sick leave upon his release, he resigned his commission in March 1863 and retired to become a Pennsylvania farmer.

McCAULEY, CHARLES STEWART (1793–1869) USA. A native of **Pennsylvania**, McCauley entered the **U.S. Navy** as a midshipman at age 15 and served in the War of 1812. A career naval officer, he served all over the world before being promoted to captain in 1839. During the antebellum period, McCauley also commanded the Washington Navy Yard, the Pacific Squadron, and the South Atlantic Squadron.

During the **secession** crisis, McCauley was in command of the Gosport Navy Yard at **Norfolk, Virginia**. Under orders not to take any action that might encourage **Virginia** to secede, he did not even defend his command. McCauley later was ordered to withdraw the *Merrimac* and other ships and supplies, but he failed to act in time. After the fall of **Fort Sumter**, Virginia seceded, and on April 20, 1861, the secessionists seized Norfolk. Faced with an attack, McCauley then burned the government buildings and supplies and burned or scuttled eight of the 11 ships in the navy yard, including the *Merrimac*, before evacuating his post. The Confederates salvaged the *Merrimac* (which was rechristened the *Virginia*) and secured many valuable supplies and cannons that had escaped destruction. McCauley was criticized for his actions, and a Senate investigative committee found that he had been irresponsible. Faced with such censure, McCauley retired from the navy in 1862.

McCAUSLAND, JOHN (1836–1927) CSA. A native of **Missouri**, as a boy, McCausland moved to **Virginia** with his family. He graduated first in the **Virginia Military Institute** class of 1857 and returned a year later to teach mathematics there.

When Virginia seceded, McCausland organized the Rockbridge Artillery but declined his election as its captain because the governor already had offered him a commission of lieutenant colonel. Sent to the Kanawha Valley to recruit, he raised the 36th Virginia and was elected its colonel. McCausland's **regiment** served under **John B. Floyd** during his operations in western Virginia and fought at **Carnifex Ferry**. Afterward, he and his men were sent to **Kentucky**.

In February 1862, McCausland was given command of a **brigade** in Floyd's **division**. He fought with it at **Fort Donelson** and led his men to freedom before the doomed fort surrendered. In the spring of 1862, McCausland returned to Virginia with his regiment and for the next two years served in the western part of the state under a number of different commanders. When **Albert Jenkins** was killed at **Cloyd's Mountain** in May 1864, McCausland assumed command of Jenkins's cavalry and was promoted to brigadier general.

McCausland's cavalry helped oppose **David Hunter's Shenandoah Valley Campaign** and then accompanied **Jubal A. Early's Washington Raid**. During the raid, McCausland collected a $20,000 ransom from the citizens of Hagerstown, Maryland (he demanded $200,000) and was praised by Early for his service at the **Battle of the Monocacy**. After the raid, Early ordered McCausland and **Bradley Johnson** to raid **Pennsylvania** and to demand $100,000 in gold or $500,000 in **greenbacks** from the citizens of **Chambersburg**. If refused, they were to burn the town in retaliation for Hunter's destruction of the **Shenandoah Valley**. When the citizens refused, the Confederates burned more than 400 buildings. While returning to Virginia, McCausland and Johnson were surprised and defeated by **William W. Averell** at **Moorefield, West Virginia**. The burning of Chambersburg became one of the war's great controversies, and McCausland and Johnson feuded over who was to blame for their defeat at Moorefield. After the burning of **Chambersburg**, McCausland served with Early during **Philip Sheridan's Shenandoah Valley Campaign** and then participated in the **Petersburg Campaign**. He fought at

Five Forks and, in the **Appomattox Campaign**, led his cavalry through the enemy lines and escaped capture at Appomattox.

McCausland left the country after the war and lived for a while in Europe and Mexico as an unreconstructed **Rebel**. He finally returned to **West Virginia** and farmed for the next 60 years but was a rather unpopular figure in the mostly pro-Union area and remained largely a recluse. McCausland was the penultimate Confederate general to die.

McCLELLAN, GEORGE BRINTON (1826–1885) USA. A native of **Pennsylvania**, McClellan came from a very prominent family and was a first cousin of **J .E. B. Stuart's** chief of staff, Henry B. McClellan. He attended preparatory schools and the University of Pennsylvania before entering **West Point** and graduating second in the class of 1846. McClellan was assigned to the **engineers** and earned much recognition (and two **brevets**) during the **Mexican War** while serving under **Winfield Scott**. After the war, he taught at the academy, translated into English a French treatise on **bayonet** exercises, participated in several western exploration expeditions, and served as an observer in the Crimean War. McClellan also designed a lightweight saddle, known as the McClellan Saddle, which was adopted by the **U.S. Army** and remained in use until World War II. When he resigned his captain's commission in 1857, McClellan was one of the best known and most respected officers in the **army**. He then became chief engineer of the Illinois Central Railroad and later was made president of the Ohio & Mississippi Railroad.

When the Civil War began in April 1861, McClellan was appointed major general of **Ohio** troops. Given command of all of the state's military forces, he quickly organized a well trained and **disciplined** force. Impressed with McClellan's ability, **Abraham Lincoln appointed** him major general in the regular army in May and made him the second-ranking general behind Scott. That same month McClellan assumed command of Union forces operating in western **Virginia**. His victories at **Rich Mountain** and **Carrick's Ford** in July earned him the **Thanks of Congress** and made him the only successful Union general at the time. When the Union army was defeated at **First Manassas**, McClellan was the obvious choice to assume command of the troops around **Washington, D.C.**

Arriving in the capital with much fanfare just days after the defeat, McClellan quickly demonstrated that he was unsurpassed in administrative ability, enforcing **discipline**, and improving morale. He created the **Army of the Potomac**, replaced the aging Scott as general-in-chief in November, and developed a bond with his soldiers that was never broken. Known as "Little Mac" and "the Young Napoleon," McClellan was the most popular commander the Army of the Potomac ever had. Unfortunately, he also demonstrated that he was vain, slow, overly cautious, and unable to work with the Lincoln administration. A **Democrat**, McClellan was very conservative and clashed with the **Radical Republicans** by insisting that the restoration of the Union, not the abolition of **slavery**, was the war's goal. His support in the government quickly eroded over the next year because he was slow to engage the enemy, always greatly overestimated the opposing force, and never was able to move swiftly enough to win a great victory.

Frustrated by McClellan's failure to take action, Lincoln finally ordered him to advance against the Confederates at Manassas by February 22, 1862. McClellan then reluctantly shared with Lincoln his own plan to capture **Richmond, Virginia**. Referred to as the **Urbanna Plan**, it called for placing the army on ships and moving it to Chesapeake Bay and then up the Rappahannock River to Urbanna, Virginia. This would put McClellan behind the Confederates' right flank only 50 miles east of Richmond. Lincoln reluctantly approved the plan, but in March the Confederates ruined things by abandoning Manassas and falling back behind the Rappahannock. McClellan then revised his **strategy** and decided to take the army by ship to **Fort Monroe, Virginia**, at the tip of the Virginia Peninsula. By moving up the peninsula to Richmond, his flanks would be protected by the James and York Rivers and his supply line would be secured. Lincoln approved this plan, as well, but then angered McClellan by withholding thousands of troops to guard the capital.

As the **Peninsula Campaign** was beginning in March 1862, Lincoln removed McClellan as general-in-chief so he could concentrate on the campaign. Once on the peninsula, McClellan was convinced by **Allan Pinkerton**, who headed his intelligence service, that he was greatly outnumbered by **John B. Magruder's** small Confederate force. As a result, he used slow siege **tactics** he had learned in the Crimean War to crawl up the peninsula and gave **Joseph E. Johnston** time to shift his Confederate army from the Rappahannock to the peninsula. As the Confederates slowly retreated, battles were fought at **Yorktown**, **Williamsburg**, and **Seven Pines**, with Johnston being wounded in the latter. **Robert E. Lee** took over the **Army of Northern Virginia** and in June embarrassed McClellan by sending Stuart's cavalry on a ride completely around the Union army. Lee learned from **Stuart's Ride** that McClellan's right flank was "in the air" and decided to counterattack. In the **Seven Days Campaign**, Lee battered McClellan and forced him to retreat back down the peninsula to **Harrison's Landing**. McClellan showed little leadership during the retreat and many times was not even on the battlefield. Claiming he was badly outnumbered (when actually he had a much superior force), he accused Lincoln of withholding crucial reinforcements and blamed him for the defeat.

Disappointed with McClellan, Lincoln ordered him to send his men to reinforce **John Pope's Army of Virginia** for operations in Northern Virginia. McClellan dragged his feet, and Pope was defeated by Lee in the **Second Manassas Campaign**, largely because of his own ineptness but partly because he never received all the reinforcements from McClellan that were ordered. Lincoln was furious at McClellan's behavior but gave him command of the defeated forces straggling back to Washington because he knew no one was equal to McClellan in restoring an army's morale and fighting ability. McClellan did an admirable job in rebuilding the army in time to pursue Lee during the **Antietam Campaign**. However, once again he greatly overestimated the enemy, and even after discovering Lee's campaign plans in the **Lost Order**, he squandered precious hours before pursuing the Confederates. McClellan's "slows" allowed Lee time to concentrate his scattered army and fight the Federals at Antietam. McClellan's battle plan was sound, but he again remained in the rear and failed to coordinate his attacks, thus enabling the Confederates to shift units to threatened areas and prevent defeat. After the stalemate, McClellan did not pursue Lee back into Virginia, and shortly afterward, Stuart's cavalry again rode around his army. Lincoln replaced McClellan in November 1862 with **Ambrose Burnside** as commander of the Army of the Potomac.

At his home in **New Jersey**, McClellan awaited new orders that never came. In 1864, he became the Democratic nominee for president but was hampered by the party's strong peace platform. Although McClellan renounced the peace platform and made it clear he would not negotiate with the Confederates, he carried only three states and suffered a stinging defeat. He resigned his military commission on election day and after the war served as New Jersey's governor from 1878 to 1881.

McCLERNAND, JOHN ALEXANDER (1812–1890) USA. A native of **Kentucky**, as a child, McClernand moved to **Illinois** with his family. His antebellum life closely resembled **Abraham Lincoln's**, whom he came to know quite well, after opening a Springfield law practice. McClernand was largely self-educated, served in the Black Hawk War as a private, and became active in **Democratic** politics. As an **abolitionist** who was a moderate on **secession**, he served in the state legislature from 1836 to

1843 and twice in the **U.S. Congress** from 1843 to 1851 and 1859 to 1861. McClernand was a very popular politician in southern Illinois, where many people had close ties to the South. Although disagreeing with him on many issues, Lincoln admired McClernand because he supported the Union when secession did occur.

In August 1861, Lincoln appointed McClernand brigadier general of volunteers to gain the political support of Democrats in the Midwest. Although a skilled politician, McClernand proved to be a difficult general, and he frequently quarreled with fellow officers, was self-promoting, and became involved in political intrigue within the military. He also had few battlefield victories. McClernand resigned his congressional seat in October 1861 to accept a **brigade** command under **U. S. Grant**. Despite his inexperience, he fought well at **Belmont** and was given command of a **division** in February 1862 for operations against **Forts Henry and Donelson**. Grant criticized McClernand for being too reckless after he launched a premature attack at Fort Donelson, but McClernand was promoted to major general in March and fought at **Shiloh**. After the **siege of Corinth, Mississippi**, he was sent on recruitment duty in the Midwest.

Because of his political ties with Lincoln, McClernand received permission to lead the attack against **Vicksburg, Mississippi**, in late 1862. He successfully raised a large number of troops and sent them to Memphis, Tennessee, in preparation for the operation. Grant and General-in-Chief **Henry Halleck** disliked and distrusted McClernand, so Grant ordered **William T. Sherman** to take McClernand's men downriver to Vicksburg in December before McClernand could arrive in Memphis. Sherman did so, but he was badly defeated at **Chickasaw Bayou**. A furious McClernand then came downriver in January 1863 to reclaim the **Army of the Mississippi** and led it against **Arkansas Post**. Although successful in capturing the position, he was criticized by Grant for wasting resources against an insignificant objective. In turn, McClernand bristled at the slight and became forever resentful of **West Point** graduates.

Lincoln finally put Grant in charge of the **Vicksburg Campaign**, and in January 1863 Grant reduced McClernand to command the **Army of the Tennessee's** XIII Corps. When Grant launched his first unsuccessful attack against Vicksburg in May 1863, McClernand claimed that he had made good progress and could break the enemy lines if properly supported. Based on that claim, Grant ordered another attack a few days later, but it only led to more heavy casualties. Grant accused McClernand of misleading him and was further outraged when, without permission, McClernand released stories to the press, praising his men and criticizing the efforts of the other **corps**. As a result, Grant relieved McClernand of command in June and sent him home.

McClernand returned to duty in February 1864 and briefly led the XIII Corps in the **Department of the Gulf**. After contracting malaria there, he resigned his commission for health reasons in November and returned to Illinois, where he became a judge.

McCOMB, WILLIAM (1831?–1918) CSA. A native of **Pennsylvania**, McComb's exact date of birth is unknown, and little is known of his early life. He moved to **Tennessee** in the 1850s and was living there when the Civil War began.

McComb entered Confederate service in early 1861 as a private in the 14th Tennessee and was elected 2nd lieutenant in May. He soon was appointed regimental adjutant and accompanied the **regiment** to **Virginia**. As part of the Tennessee Brigade, McComb served in western Virginia during the winter of 1861–62 and in the **Peninsula Campaign** in early 1862. He was elected major in May 1862, fought in the **Seven Days Campaign** with the **Army of Northern Virginia**, and in August was promoted to lieutenant colonel to replace the officer who was mortally wounded at **Cedar Mountain**. A few weeks later, the colonel was mortally wounded at **Second Manassas**, and McComb was promoted to take his place. McComb was seriously wounded at **Antietam** and **Chancellorsville** and missed the **Battle of Gettysburg**, but after returning to duty in late summer 1863, he often commanded the **brigade** when **James J. Archer** was absent sick. He fought throughout the **Overland Campaign**, and during the **Petersburg Campaign**, was recommended to replace Archer permanently when that officer died in October 1864. McComb was promoted to brigadier general in February 1865 and **surrendered** with the **army** at **Appomattox**.

After the war, McComb lived in **Alabama** and **Mississippi** before settling on a Virginia plantation. He was active in veterans' affairs and served as a deacon and Sunday school superintendent in his Baptist church.

McCOOK, ALEXANDER McDOWELL (1831–1903) USA. One of the **"Fighting McCooks,"** McCook was a native of **Ohio** and the brother of **Daniel McCook Jr.** and **Robert McCook** and a first cousin of **Edward M. McCook**. He graduated from **West Point** in 1852 (taking five years to finish) and served with the infantry on the frontier. In 1858, McCook became an instructor of infantry **tactics** at the academy and was teaching there when the Civil War began.

In April 1861, McCook was commissioned colonel of the 1st Ohio. After fighting at **First Manassas**, he was **brevetted** major in the regular

army and was promoted to brigadier general of volunteers in September. Sent to **Kentucky**, McCook was placed in command of the **Army of the Ohio's** 2nd Division in December. He led it in the capture of Nashville, Tennessee; at the **Battle of Shiloh**; and during the **siege of Corinth, Mississippi**; and earned two more brevets for Nashville and Shiloh. Promoted to major general in July 1862, McCook commanded the army's I Corps at **Perryville** (for which he later was brevetted brigadier general of regulars) and the **Army of the Cumberland's** XIV Corps at **Stones River** and XX Corps during the **Tullahoma** and **Chickamauga Campaigns**. The latter campaign ruined McCook's career. After the Confederates broke his line at Chickamauga, he retreated to Chattanooga, Tennessee, with army commander **William S. Rosecrans**. McCook and Maj. Gen. **Thomas L. Crittenden** were blamed for the defeat, but a court of inquiry ultimately cleared them. His reputation was ruined, however, and McCook never again held a major field command, ending the war commanding a **district** in **Arkansas**. Nonetheless, he was brevetted major general of regulars at war's end.

McCook remained in the army after the war and was promoted to lieutenant colonel of the 26th U.S. Infantry in 1867. He retired in 1895 as a major general.

McCOOK, DANIEL, JR. (1834–1864) USA. One of the **"Fighting McCooks,"** McCook was a native of **Ohio** and was the brother of **Alexander M.** and **Robert L. McCook** and a cousin of **Edward M. McCook**. He reportedly graduated from an **Alabama** university before studying law in Ohio, and before the Civil War practiced law in **Kansas** with **Thomas Ewing** and **William T. Sherman**.

McCook entered Union service in May 1861 as a captain in the 1st Kansas and fought at **Wilson's Creek** before becoming **George H. Thomas's** chief of staff in November. After serving at **Shiloh** (although not seeing any combat), he was commissioned colonel of the 52nd Ohio in July 1862. McCook briefly was put in command of a **brigade** in Sherman's **division**, but he eventually was assigned to **Philip Sheridan's** division. His brigade fought at **Perryville** with the **Army of the Ohio** but guarded wagons while with the **Army of the Cumberland** at the **Battle of Stones River** and was only lightly engaged at **Chickamauga**. After participating in the **Chattanooga Campaign**, McCook's brigade participated in the **Knoxville Campaign** when it was sent to relieve the siege of Knoxville, Tennessee. In the **Atlanta Campaign**, his brigade was placed in **Jefferson C. Davis's** division of the Army of the Cumberland's XIV Corps. At **Kennesaw Mountain**, Sherman chose McCook's brigade to lead the disastrous assault, and McCook was mortally wounded just as he reached the Confederate works. He was appointed a brigadier general of volunteers on July 16, 1864, but died in Ohio the next day.

McCOOK, EDWARD MOODY (1833–1909) USA. One of the **"Fighting McCooks,"** McCook was a native of **Ohio** and a first cousin of **Alexander A.** and **Robert L. McCook.** As a young man, he moved to the **Kansas** Territory, became a lawyer, and was elected a territorial representative in 1859.

When the Civil War began, McCook traveled to **Washington, D.C.,** and in May 1861 was commissioned a 2nd lieutenant in the 1st U.S. Cavalry. He was appointed major of the 2nd Indiana Cavalry in September and was promoted to lieutenant colonel in February 1862. McCook commanded the **regiment** at **Shiloh** but did not see any combat (although he was **brevetted** for his service there). In late April, he was promoted to colonel and in September was given command of a cavalry **brigade** in the **Army of the Ohio.** McCook won another brevet for his service at **Perryville,** but he missed the **Battle of Stones River.**

In January 1863, McCook was given command of a cavalry brigade in the **Army of the Cumberland.** After leading it in the **Tullahoma Campaign,** he was promoted to a **division** command in September. McCook won his third brevet at **Chickamauga** and a fourth for his service in eastern **Tennessee.** Promoted to brigadier general of volunteers in April 1864, he fought through the **Atlanta Campaign** and suffered heavy casualties while on **Stoneman's and McCook's Raid** south of Atlanta with **George Stoneman.** After the fall of Atlanta, McCook accompanied **George H. Thomas** back to Tennessee for the **Franklin and Nashville Campaign.** His last campaign was **James H. Wilson's Selma, Alabama, Raid,** for which he received his fifth brevet.

When McCook left the service in January 1866, he had received brevets to major general of volunteers and brigadier general of regulars. After the war, he served as the U.S. minister to Hawaii for three years and from 1869 to 1875 as the territorial governor of **Colorado.**

McCOOK, ROBERT LATIMER (1827–1862) USA. One of the **"Fighting McCooks,"** McCook was a native of **Ohio** and was the brother of **Alexander M.** and **Daniel McCook** and a first cousin of **Edward M. McCook.** He worked as a lawyer before the Civil War and entered Union service in May 1861, when he was commissioned colonel of the 9th Ohio.

McCook first served under **George B. McClellan** in western **Virginia** and then led a **brigade** at **Carnifex Ferry** and **Mill Springs,** where he was wounded in the leg and had a horse shot from under him. Promoted to brigadier general of volunteers in March 1862, he commanded a brigade in the **siege of Corinth, Mississippi**, and in the **Kentucky Campaign**. In the latter campaign, McCook was riding in an ambulance because of illness when Confederate guerrillas under Frank B. Gurley attacked him near Decherd, Tennessee, on August 5, 1862. McCook was whipping his horses to run faster when Gurley mortally wounded him in the stomach. McCook spoke with Gurley before dying the next day and said he held no ill will toward him, but friends accused the Confederate of murder. Gurley actually was found guilty of murder twice—once during the war after being captured and once after the war—but he was punished neither time.

McCOWN, JOHN PORTER (1815–1879) CSA. A native of **Tennessee**, McCown graduated from **West Point** in 1840 and served with the **artillery** at various posts before fighting in the **Mexican War** and winning one **brevet** for gallantry. Afterward, he fought in the **Seminole Wars** and served in the **Utah Expedition**. When the Civil War began, McCown was a captain, but he resigned that commission in May 1861 and joined the Confederacy as a lieutenant colonel of artillery. Later that month, he was appointed colonel of Tennessee's artillery **corps**.

In October 1861, McCown was appointed brigadier general and was given first a **brigade** and then a **division** in the **Confederate army** at Columbus, Kentucky. When Columbus was evacuated, he was sent to reinforce **New Madrid and Island No. 10** and was promoted to major general in March 1862. When the Federals advanced against him, McCown abandoned New Madrid and placed his troops in a precarious position on a peninsula, where they later were trapped and captured. He was relieved of command at the end of March, and after Island No. 10 was lost, he was blamed for the defeat. McCown was given command of a division under **Earl Van Dorn** in April 1862 and took over the **Army of the West** when Van Dorn was sent to **Vicksburg, Mississippi**, in June. In July, his division reinforced **Edmund Kirby Smith** in east Tennessee, and after being placed in command of the **Department of East Tennessee** he joined **Braxton Bragg** for the **Kentucky Campaign**. Bragg believed McCown was his weakest division commander in the **Army of Tennessee** but still chose him to lead the attack at **Stones River**. He then blamed McCown for his defeat and charged him with disobedience of orders in February 1863. McCown, in turn, believed Bragg should be relieved and stated that he would grow potatoes on his Tennessee farm if Bragg remained in command. Found guilty of disobedience in March, McCown was suspended from duty for six months. Becoming very bitter over the incident, he began publicly criticizing the government and the **army**. These outbursts kept McCown from regaining any significant command until April 1865, when he led a small group of defenders on **North Carolina's** Catawba River.

After the war, McCown taught school in Tennessee and then moved to **Arkansas** to farm.

McCULLAGH, JOSEPH BURBRIDGE (1842–1896) USA. A native of Ireland, McCullagh immigrated alone to the United States when he was 11. He became a printer in **New York** before moving to **Missouri** in 1858 to work for the St. Louis *Advocate*. Afterward, McCullagh worked for the St. Louis *Democrat* and became the state legislature's stenographer before moving to **Ohio** to become a reporter for the Cincinnati *Daily Gazette*.

McCullagh became one of the best-known **war correspondents** in the western theater. He first covered **John C. Frémont's** campaign in Missouri, but his dislike for the general led him to join **U. S. Grant** for the **Forts Henry and Donelson Campaign**. Writing from **Andrew Foote's** gunboat *St. Louis*, McCullagh served as a volunteer secretary to the commodore and was praised for continuing to write while the ship was hit 65 times by Confederate **artillery** fire. He later covered the **Battle of Shiloh**, but his editors thought his story was too harsh on the **army** and refused to publish it. McCullagh then quit the *Daily Gazette* and joined its rival, the Cincinnati *Daily Commercial*. He covered the **Vicksburg Campaign** and the 1863 Ohio gubernatorial race for the *Daily Commercial* before becoming the paper's **Washington, D.C.**, correspondent. Assuming the pen name "Mack," McCullagh was well known for publishing interviews with notable persons and briefly covered **William T. Sherman's** campaigns in **Georgia**.

After the war, McCullagh worked for the *Daily Commercial* and the Associated Press until 1868. He continued to serve as editor for various newspapers until he died in an accidental fall from one of his house windows during an illness.

McCULLOCH, BEN (1811–1862) CSA. A native of **Tennessee**, McCulloch was the brother of **Henry McCulloch**. Davy Crockett was a friend and neighbor, whom McCulloch followed to **Texas**, but measles prevented him from joining Crockett at the Alamo. Joining **Sam Houston**, instead, McCulloch commanded an **artillery** piece at San Jacinto and won a commission as 1st lieutenant. After the Texas Revolution, he worked as a surveyor and Texas Ranger and won much praise as an **Indian** fighter.

While running for the Texas House of Representatives in 1839, McCulloch fought a **rifle** duel with political rival Ruben Ross and was severely wounded in the right arm, which remained partially paralyzed. McCulloch won the election, and later in the year, he killed Ross with a pistol in another duel. McCulloch did not run for reelection and returned to his surveying and Indian fighting. He won recognition for his role as a scout against the Comanches and for driving out the Mexican army that seized San Antonio in 1842. After turning back a second Mexican column later in the year, McCulloch participated in a planned invasion of Mexico but left his comrades shortly before they were captured by the Mexicans.

During the **Mexican War**, McCulloch led a **company** in Jack Hays's 1st Regiment, Texas Mounted Volunteers. He served as Zachary Taylor's chief of scouts and became a national hero after some of his men (who were journalists) publicized his escapades. Taylor much appreciated McCulloch's service and commissioned him a major of volunteers. Moving to **California** after the war, he was elected sheriff of Sacramento during the Gold Rush. McCulloch was considered for command of the 2nd U.S. Cavalry in the 1850s, was appointed U.S. marshal for Texas, and became one of the peace commissioners who helped prevent violence during the **Utah Expedition**.

After Texas seceded, McCulloch was appointed colonel of state troops in February 1861. He led the troops that seized the U.S. arsenal at San Antonio from **David Twiggs** and was appointed brigadier general in the **Confederate army** in May, becoming the second-ranking Confederate brigadier and the first civilian to be so appointed. During his tenure as a general, McCulloch never owned a **uniform**. Given command of the **Indian Territory**, he established his headquarters at **Little Rock, Arkansas**, and raised the **Army of the West**. Although he and Missouri's **Sterling Price** failed to cooperate, **Albert Pike** aided McCulloch in securing a number of crucial Indian allies, and McCulloch authorized **Stand Watie** to organize a Confederate Cherokee unit. McCulloch's **army** won the **Battle of Wilson's Creek** in August 1861, and he personally led a charge that captured five cannons. However, McCulloch's inability to cooperate with Price forced **Jefferson Davis** to place **Earl Van Dorn** over both officers in January 1862. McCulloch bitterly protested Van Dorn's advance toward **Missouri** but provided valuable service, nonetheless. At **Pea Ridge**, he commanded the Confederate right wing and initially drove back the enemy. At mid-morning, however, McCulloch mistakenly rode into a Union position while scouting and was killed by a shot to the chest. His death led to a breakdown in command and contributed to the Confederate defeat.

McCULLOCH, HENRY EUSTACE (1816–1895) CSA. A native of **Tennessee**, McCulloch was the younger brother of **Ben McCulloch** and followed him to **Texas** in 1837. Henry was elected county assessor and sheriff, frequently fought **Indians** on the frontier, and served as a **company** captain in the 1st Texas Rifles during the **Mexican War**. In the 1850s, he briefly served as a company captain in the Texas Rangers and was elected to both the state assembly and senate. When the Civil War began, McCulloch was serving as U.S. marshal in east Texas.

In February 1861, McCulloch was commissioned colonel of state cavalry and successfully negotiated the surrender of several frontier forts from Capt. **Edmund Kirby Smith** of the 2nd U.S. Cavalry. He then was given command of the Texas troops along the Red River in March and was appointed colonel in the **Confederate army** and commander of the 1st Texas Mounted Rifles the following month. In September, McCulloch briefly was placed in command of the **Department of Texas** and created some controversy when he refused to recognize **Paul O. Hébert's** authority when that officer relieved him a few weeks later. No official action was taken against McCulloch, however, and in February 1862 he was put in command of the District of the Rio Grande.

McCulloch was promoted to brigadier general in March 1862 and was assigned to coordinate troop movements in east Texas. He performed well in this position and forwarded more than 20,000 men to **Arkansas** before joining them in September as commander of a **division** under **Theophilus H. Holmes**. In December, McCulloch was replaced by **John G. Walker** and was reduced to a **brigade** command in Walker's division. McCulloch performed poorly at the **Battle of Milliken's Bend**, and his superior, **Richard Taylor**, criticized him for failing to handle his men well. As a result, he was sent back to Texas. McCulloch failed to regain a field command, but in 1863, he refused the gubernatorial nomination and remained in the army. For the rest of the war, he commanded a subdistrict in northern Texas where he fought Indians, tried to control Confederate guerrillas, and hunted **deserters** and draft dodgers.

After the war, McCulloch worked in the cattle and **railroad** industries and was appointed superintendent of the Texas Asylum for the Deaf and Dumb.

McCULLOCH, HUGH (1808–1895) USA. A native of **Maine**, McCulloch attended Bowdoin College for a year and taught school and became a lawyer before moving to **Indiana** in 1833. There he became a successful state bank president and kept the bank solvent through the 1857 economic panic. McCulloch lobbied against an 1862 national bank bill because he believed it would hurt state banks, but the following year, he agreed to be appointed U.S. comptroller of the currency, with the responsibility of enforcing the bank bill he had opposed. He also supervised the issuing of large amounts of **greenbacks** authorized by the **Legal Tender Acts**, even though he had opposed those acts, as well.

During his tenure as comptroller of the currency, McCulloch strongly supported the gold standard even though the Union had resorted to greenbacks to help **finance** the war. In March 1865, **Abraham Lincoln** appointed him secretary of the treasury after **William P. Fessenden** was elected to the Senate. In the cabinet, McCulloch tried unsuccessfully to retire the greenbacks in circulation, restore the United States to the gold standard, and retire the national debt. He stepped down as secretary of the treasury in 1869 and resumed his banking interests but returned to the treasury position in the latter months of President Chester A. Arthur's administration.

McDOWELL, IRVIN (1818–1885) USA. A native of **Ohio**, McDowell was educated in France before receiving an appointment to **West Point**. He graduated in 1838 and taught **tactics** at the academy from 1841 to 1845 before serving as Brig. Gen. **John E. Wool's** aide during the **Mexican War** and winning one **brevet** for gallantry. McDowell remained in the **U.S. Army** after the war and served in the adjutant general's office, making many valuable political contacts that would be useful during the Civil War.

In May 1861, Secretary of the Treasury **Salmon P. Chase**, one of McDowell's supporters, secured his promotion from major to brigadier general of regulars, even though he had never led men in the field. Given command of the Union troops south of the Potomac River, McDowell was pressured by **Abraham Lincoln** to attack the Confederates at Manassas before McDowell thought the troops were ready. McDowell drew up a good tactical plan, but timely Confederate reinforcements led to his defeat at **First Manassas**, and he was replaced in July by **George B. McClellan**.

In March 1862, McDowell was promoted to major general of volunteers and was given command of the **Army of the Potomac's** I Corps. When McClellan departed for his **Peninsula Campaign**, Lincoln withheld McDowell's **corps** to protect **Washington, D.C.** His corps remained in northern **Virginia** because of the threat posed by **Stonewall Jackson's Shenandoah Valley Campaign** and thus missed the **Peninsula** and **Seven Days Campaigns.** In the summer of 1862, McDowell was given command of the III Corps in **John Pope's Army of Virginia.** His actions at **Cedar Mountain** won him a brevet of major general of volunteers in 1865, but his later actions at **Second Manassas** were severely criticized. Both McDowell and **Fitz John Porter** were investigated for misconduct, with Porter being formally court-martialed. Officers then criticized McDowell for being a witness against Porter, even though he was being investigated on the same charges. Because of his political connections—and perhaps in payment for his testimony—he never was court-martialed for the errors he made at Second Manassas. The stigma of Second Manassas haunted McDowell, and he never again had a significant field command. He was placed in command of the **Department of the Pacific** in July 1864 and remained there until war's end.

McDowell remained in the **army** after the war and rose to major general of regulars in 1872. He was serving in **California** as commander of the Division of the Pacific when he retired in 1882.

McDOWELL, VIRGINIA, BATTLE OF (MAY 8, 1862). In the spring of 1862, **Thomas J. "Stonewall" Jackson** was ordered to occupy Union troops in the **Shenandoah Valley** so they could not reinforce **George B. McClellan's Army of the Potomac** then threatening **Richmond, Virginia**, in the **Peninsula Campaign. Nathaniel P. Banks's** 15,000 men were already in the lower Valley, while **John C. Frémont** was approaching the Valley from the west with 20,000 more. Frémont's advance guard under **Robert H. Milroy** was at McDowell, about 30 miles west of Staunton, while Brig. Gen. **Robert C. Schenck** was not far behind.

Leaving **Richard S. Ewell's division** at Swift Run Gap to block Banks's advance to Staunton, Jackson deceived the enemy on April 30 by marching his 9,000 men over the Blue Ridge Mountains as if he was heading for Richmond. After a harrowing march through driving rain (covering 92 miles in four marching days), Jackson placed his men on **railroad** cars at Mechum's Station and quickly reentered the Valley, reaching Staunton on May 6. He then attacked Milroy at McDowell before Frémont could reinforce him.

Jackson made contact on May 7 and drove Milroy across the Bull Pasture River. Milroy informed Schenck of the encounter, and Schenck marched 34 miles in 23 hours to join him and assume command. By day-light of May 8, Schenck had 6,000 men around McDowell. Jackson approached town that morning from the southeast and seized dominating high ground on Setlinger's Hill. Schenck attacked Jackson in mid-afternoon to delay the Confederates long enough for him to evacuate McDowell safely. As the Federals fought their way up the hill through thick woods, Confederate Brig. Gen. **Edward "Allegheny" Johnson** was severely wounded in the foot, and Jackson was forced to call for reinforcements. **William B. Taliaferro's brigade** counterattacked on Jackson's right and stopped the Union advance. Fighting was intense and casualties were heavy, but the Federals were unable to force Jackson off the ridge. By nightfall, Schenck had retreated, but he had suffered only 256 casualties to Jackson's approximately 500.

Jackson entered McDowell the next day and on May 10 began a pursuit. He finally called it off and returned to the Valley to continue his famous **Stonewall Jackson's Shenandoah Valley Campaign**.

McGINNIS, GEORGE FRANCIS (1826–1910) USA. A native of **Massachusetts**, when he was 11, McGinnis moved to **Ohio** with his father. After fighting in the **Mexican War** with the 2nd Ohio and rising to the rank of captain, he moved to **Indiana** and became a hatter like his father.

McGinnis entered Union service in April 1861 as a private in **Lew Wallace's** 11th Indiana. Within days he rose to captain and then to lieutenant colonel. When this 90-day **regiment** was reorganized in August, McGinnis was elected colonel. The regiment originally served in western **Virginia**, but its first serious combat was at **Fort Donelson**, where Wallace commended McGinnis. McGinnis then was placed temporarily in command of a **brigade** at **Shiloh** and led it in the **siege of Corinth, Mississippi**.

Promoted to brigadier general of volunteers in April 1863, McGinnis led a brigade in **John A. McClernand's** XIII Corps of the **Army of the Tennessee** during the **Yazoo Pass Expedition** and the **Vicksburg Campaign**. Unfortunately for McGinnis, neither Wallace nor McClernand were popular among the army's **West Point** graduates, and his association with them probably hurt his career. After the fall of **Vicksburg, Mississippi**, he was assigned to the **Department of the Gulf**, where he held relatively unimportant brigade and **division** commands. McGinnis ended the war in command of a mixed force defending the mouth of **Arkansas's** White River.

McGinnis was mustered out of the volunteer service in August 1865 and did not receive the customary **brevet** for wartime service. He returned to

Indiana and served in various state and county offices before being appointed postmaster of Indianapolis in 1900.

McGOWAN, SAMUEL (1819–1897) CSA. A native of **South Carolina**, McGowan graduated from South Carolina College in 1841 and became a lawyer and state legislator. When the **Mexican War** began, he left his legislative seat and volunteered as a private in the Palmetto Regiment. McGowan rose to the rank of captain and was commended for his actions at Chapultepec. Returning to South Carolina after the war, he resumed his legislative career and became a major general in the state militia.

McGowan was commissioned a brigadier general of state troops when South Carolina seceded in 1860 and commanded a **brigade** during the bombardment of **Fort Sumter**. He then joined Brig. Gen. **Milledge Bonham's** staff as an aide-de-camp and served at **First Manassas**. Returning to South Carolina, McGowan was commissioned lieutenant colonel of the 14th South Carolina in September 1861 and became colonel in April 1862 after the commander resigned. Assigned to **Maxcy Gregg's** brigade of **A. P. Hill's division**, he fought well with the **Army of Northern Virginia** through the **Seven Days Campaign** and was wounded at **Gaines' Mill**. McGowan went on to fight at **Cedar Mountain** and **Second Manassas** and led a counterattack on **Stonewall Jackson's** far left in the latter fight that helped hold the line against Union assaults. Wounded again in this battle, he missed the **Antietam Campaign**. McGowan returned to duty in time for **Fredericksburg** and was promoted to brigadier general in April 1863 after Gregg was killed.

McGowan's first battle as a brigade commander was **Chancellorsville**, where he was severely wounded in the leg. When he returned to duty in February 1864, he still required a cane to walk. At the **Wilderness**, McGowan's brigade was routed by a massive Union assault on the second day of fighting, but it then was praised for leading a counterattack at **Spotsylvania's** "Bloody Angle" that helped restore the Confederate line. McGowan received his fourth wound (in the right arm) at Spotsylvania and after returning to duty in August 1864 fought in the **Petersburg** and **Appomattox Campaigns**.

After the war, McGowan was elected to the **U.S. Congress** from South Carolina but was refused his seat because of **Reconstruction** politics. He strongly opposed the **Radical Republicans** and finally was re-elected to the state legislature in 1878. The following year, McGowan was elected to the state supreme court, a position he held until defeated for reelection in 1893.

McGUIRE, HUNTER HOLMES (1835–1900) CSA. A native of **Virginia**, McGuire graduated from both the Winchester Medical College and the Medical College of Virginia. He briefly taught at the University of Louisiana but returned to Virginia when it seceded and joined the 2nd Virginia as a private. McGuire became a close friend of his colonel, **Stonewall Jackson**, and was commissioned regimental surgeon in May 1861. Becoming **brigade** surgeon for the **Stonewall Brigade**, he remained with Jackson from **First Manassas** through Jackson's wounding at **Chancellorsville**. McGuire also served as medical director for Jackson's **Valley District** and later for the **Army of Northern Virginia's** II Corps. It was McGuire who amputated Jackson's arm after he was wounded at Chancellorsville. After Jackson's death, McGuire continued to serve as the **corps'** medical director under **Richard S. Ewell** and for **Jubal A. Early's Valley Army**. Two of his greatest accomplishments were helping to establish an **ambulance corps** for the **army** and creating a system of reserve hospitals. McGuire was captured in March 1865 but was quickly released.

After the war, McGuire was one of the veterans who actively promoted Jackson's image as a **Lost Cause** martyr and helped start the Richmond University College of Medicine, serving as its president.

McINTOSH, JAMES McQUEEN (1828–1862) CSA. A native of **Florida**, McIntosh was the son of a **U.S. Army** colonel who was killed during the **Mexican War** and the brother of Union Brig. Gen. **John B. McIntosh**. He graduated last in the **West Point** class of 1849 and was assigned to the infantry, but he later transferred to the cavalry. After serving on the frontier, McIntosh resigned his captain's commission in May 1861 to join the Confederacy, an act his brother claimed was "a blot on his family honor" (Davis, ed., *The Confederate General*, vol. 4, p. 124).

McIntosh entered Confederate service as a captain of cavalry in May 1861 and was sent to **Arkansas**, where he joined Gov. **Henry M. Rector's** staff. He was commissioned colonel of the 2nd Arkansas Mounted Rifles in July and led it at **Wilson's Creek**. There, McIntosh showed great bravery and leadership and was lavishly praised by numerous officers. After the battle, he temporarily was placed in command of **Ben McCulloch's division** and led it to **Indian Territory** to help defeat a band of Creeks that had joined the Union. After fighting at **Chustenahlah** in late 1861, McIntosh returned to Arkansas and was appointed a brigadier general in March 1862.

In the spring of 1862, **Earl Van Dorn** placed McIntosh in command of a cavalry **brigade**. When **Ben McCulloch** was killed at **Pea Ridge**,

McIntosh assumed command of the Confederates and was killed instantly when he was shot through the heart while leading his men in a charge against the enemy. His death was much lamented, and it was generally believed that he would have been an important figure in the war if he had lived.

McINTOSH, JOHN BAILLIE (1829–1888) USA. A native of **Florida** and the son of a **U.S. Army** colonel who was killed in the **Mexican War**, McIntosh was the brother of Confederate Brig. Gen. **James M. McIntosh**. Joining the **U.S. Navy** as a midshipman, he served in the Mexican War aboard the USS *Saratoga* but then resigned his position and became a **New Jersey** businessman.

When the Civil War began, McIntosh was horrified that his brother joined the Confederacy, calling it a "blot on his family honor" (Davis, ed., *The Confederate General*, vol. 4, p. 124). He entered Union service in June 1861 as a 2nd lieutenant in the 2nd U.S. Cavalry. The **regiment** was redesignated the 5th U.S. Cavalry in August, and McIntosh accompanied it to **Virginia**. He won a **brevet** for gallantry while serving in the **Seven Days Campaign** with the **Army of the Potomac** and was promoted to 1st lieutenant in late June 1862. After fighting at **South Mountain** and **Antietam**, McIntosh was appointed colonel of the 3rd Pennsylvania Cavalry in November.

In February 1863, McIntosh was placed in command of a cavalry **brigade** in **Alfred Pleasonton's** 2nd Division of the Army of the Potomac's Cavalry Corps. He led his brigade at **Kelly's Ford**, in **George Stoneman's Raid** during the **Chancellorsville Campaign**, and at **Gettysburg** (where he won a second brevet). McIntosh's service during these campaigns led Brig. Gen. **William W. Averell** to declare that he was one of the **army's** best cavalry commanders. Following Gettysburg, McIntosh was badly injured in a fall from his horse and temporarily was placed in command of the cavalry in the **Washington, D.C.**, defenses. He rejoined his brigade for the **Overland Campaign** and received a third brevet for his actions at Ashland. After fighting in the early part of the **Petersburg Campaign**, McIntosh was promoted to brigadier general of volunteers in July 1864 and was transferred to the **Shenandoah Valley** with his brigade. There he received a severe wound at **Third Winchester** that cost him his right leg and ended his field service. McIntosh received brevets to brigadier general of regulars and major general of volunteers for Third Winchester and was mustered out of the service in April 1866.

McIntosh remained in the regular army with the rank of captain and was promoted to lieutenant colonel in 1866. He retired from the army in 1870 as a brigadier general.

McKEAN, THOMAS JEFFERSON (1810–1870) USA. A native of **Pennsylvania**, McKean graduated from **West Point** in 1831 but resigned his commission in 1834 to become a civil engineer. After serving in the **Seminole Wars** as a 1st lieutenant and adjutant of the 1st Pennsylvania, he moved to **Iowa** in 1840 and in 1844 served as a delegate to the Iowa constitutional convention. McKean volunteered for service in the **Mexican War** (where he was wounded at Churubusco) and served throughout the conflict as a private and sergeant major of the 15th U.S. Infantry, even though his West Point education and experience should have earned him a commission.

McKean entered Union service in June 1861 as a paymaster of volunteers. He was promoted to brigadier general of volunteers in November and during the war commanded numerous **districts** in **Missouri**, Nebraska, **Kansas**, **Florida**, **Louisiana**, and **Mississippi** because he was too old for field service. His only field command was leading a **division** at the **Battle of Corinth** and commanding briefly the cavalry in the **Department of the Gulf**. McKean was **brevetted** major general of volunteers for his war service and was mustered out of the volunteers in August 1865.

Returning to Iowa after the war, McKean was elected mayor of Marion and farmed. After serving as a delegate to the 1868 **Republican** National Convention, he was appointed a district pension agent in Iowa by President **U. S. Grant**, but McKean declined the position.

McKEAN, WILLIAM WISTER (1800–1865) USA. A native of **Pennsylvania**, McKean entered the **U.S. Navy** as an acting midshipman in 1814. He was a captain in command of the USS *Niagara* when the Civil War began and steamed back to the United States from the Far East. While his vessel was being refitted in **Massachusetts**, McKean eliminated those officers favoring the South by requiring all of his officers to take a **loyalty oath**.

Appointed flag officer in September 1861, McKean was placed in command of the **Gulf Blockading Squadron** and participated in the shelling of Fort McRee, the **Pensacola** Navy Yard, and Warrington, Florida. In January 1862, he was given command of the Eastern Gulf Blockading Squadron and was promoted to commodore. Illness forced him to retire from the navy in June.

McKINSTRY, JUSTUS (1814–1897) USA. A native of **New York**, as a boy, McKinstry moved to **Michigan** with his family. He graduated near the bottom of the 1838 **West Point** class but performed well and won a

brevet for gallantry in the **Mexican War** while a captain in the Quarter-master Department. After the war, McKinstry continued to serve in the Quartermaster Department at various posts. McKinstry was serving as a major and chief quartermaster for the **Department of the West** when the Civil War began. Stationed in **Missouri**, he was promoted to brigadier general of volunteers in September 1861 and briefly led a **division** under **John C. Frémont**. As quartermaster, McKinstry routinely padded the payroll, demanded bribes from contractors, and once was presented a $3,000 silver service for his wife. He also was involved in a scheme wherby contractors sold products to one firm, and the goods then were resold to the **army** at exorbitant prices. One contractor made $280,000 profit on $800,000 worth of goods he sold to the army.

When **David Hunter** took over the **department**, he had McKinstry investigated and arrested. After being detained for a year, McKinstry was cashiered from the service in January 1863 for "neglect and violation of duty" (Warner, *Generals in Blue*, 304), thus becoming the only Union general dismissed for criminal activities during the war. Afterward, McKinstry worked as a stockbroker and in real estate.

McLAWS, LAFAYETTE (1821–1897) CSA. A native of **Georgia**, McLaws attended the University of Virginia before entering **West Point** in 1838. After graduating near the bottom of his 1842 class, he was assigned to the infantry and served mostly in the South before entering the **Mexican War** as a 1st lieutenant. McLaws served under both Zachary Taylor and **Winfield Scott** and after the war married one of Taylor's nieces, making him Confederate Lt. Gen. **Richard Taylor's** first cousin by marriage.

After serving at numerous frontier outposts, McLaws resigned his captain's commission in March 1861 and entered Confederate service in May as a major of infantry. He first served in the quartermaster department and was an adjutant in Georgia before being promoted to colonel in June and taking command of the 10th Georgia. After taking his **regiment** to **Virginia**, McLaws was promoted to brigadier general in September and was given a **brigade** command. In April 1862, he was given a **division** under **John B. Magruder** during the **Peninsula Campaign**, with a promotion to major general coming the next month. Because of the early date of his commission, McLaws was one of the senior major generals in the Virginia theater.

McLaws led his division through the Peninsula and **Seven Days Campaigns** and performed good service with the **Army of Northern Vir-**

ginia during the **Antietam Campaign** by occupying Maryland Heights and helping force the surrender of **Harpers Ferry, Virginia**. His division then fought well in Antietam's West Woods. Although not a brilliant commander, McLaws was a capable officer. At **Fredericksburg** he helped defend Marye's Heights and was credited for having carefully prepared his position for the battle. During the **Chancellorsville Campaign**, however, McLaws disappointed **Robert E. Lee** by not handling his division at **Salem Church** as well as Lee expected. His career was damaged further after the **Gettysburg Campaign** when he and his **corps** commander, **James Longstreet**, began feuding. Longstreet had been a close friend of McLaws previously and had actively promoted his career, but McLaws disliked Longstreet's performance at Gettysburg and began criticizing him.

The ill will between the two generals came to a head during the **Knoxville Campaign**. When Longstreet failed to capture the town, he relieved McLaws and preferred charges against him and two other generals for mismanaging the attack on **Fort Sanders**. The incident largely backfired, however, and hurt Longstreet when it was proven that McLaws was innocent of most of the charges. Although McLaws was found guilty of some of the charges in May 1864, President **Jefferson Davis** disagreed with the court and returned him to duty. Placed in command of **Savannah, Georgia**, McLaws was forced to abandon the city when it was attacked by **William T. Sherman** in December 1864. He then participated in the **Carolinas Campaign**.

McLaws returned to Georgia after the war and was appointed tax collector and postmaster by his friend President **U. S. Grant**. He also was active in veterans' organizations and wrote several articles about the war.

McLEAN, NATHANIEL COLLINS (1815–1905) USA. A native of **Ohio**, McLean was the son of Congressman, Postmaster-General, and Supreme Court justice John McLean. He graduated from **Kentucky's** Augusta College in 1834 and from Harvard Law School in 1838.

McLean left his Ohio law practice in September 1861 to enter Union service as colonel of the 75th Ohio. He led his **regiment** at **McDowell** and **Cross Keys** and commanded a **brigade** in the **Army of Virginia's** I Corps at **Second Manassas**. Promoted to brigadier general of volunteers in November 1862, McLean took command of a brigade in **Charles Devens's** XI Corps **division**. At **Chancellorsville**, he temporarily took command of the division after Devens was wounded but was unable to rally the brigades that had been shattered by **Stonewall Jackson's** flank attack until he reached **Joseph Hooker's** headquarters. His failure earned him the displeasure of **corps** commander **Oliver O. Howard**, who had McLean transferred to the **Department of the Ohio** soon afterward.

Serving under **Ambrose Burnside**, McLean became **department provost marshal** for a year but then was given a brigade in **John Schofield's** XXIII Corps for the **Atlanta Campaign**. At **New Hope Church**, Howard again criticized McLean for poor leadership, and he was transferred again to a division command in **Kentucky**. McLean rejoined Schofield as a brigade, and later division, commander for the **Carolinas Campaign** in March 1865, but he resigned his commission for unknown reasons in April.

After the war, McLean resumed his Ohio law practice and then farmed in **Minnesota** before moving to **New York**.

McLEAN, WILMER (1814–?) CSA. Although little is known of McLean, his Civil War experience was unusual. Living on Bull Run near Manassas, Virginia, he scouted for **P. G. T. Beauregard** prior to the **First Battle of Manassas**, and his house was used as Beauregard's headquarters during the fight at **Blackburn's Ford**. On July 21, 1861, during the opening phase of the First Battle of Manassas, a shell is said to have hit the house while Beauregard was having breakfast. After the battle, McLean worked as a volunteer in the Confederate quartermaster department, but he became disenchanted by 1862 because of waste and mismanagement. He then sold his home in March 1862 and traveled across the South as a sugar speculator.

In late 1863, McLean settled his family at **Appomattox Court House, Virginia**, west of **Richmond**, in hopes of avoiding the war. On April 9, 1865, however, the conflict returned to his family. On that day, **Robert E. Lee's** aide Col. Charles Marshall was looking for a place where Lee and **U. S. Grant** could meet to discuss the **surrender** of the **Army of Northern Virginia**. McLean first suggested an abandoned house, but when Marshall decided it was unsuitable, he offered his own house for the meeting. After the surrender, souvenir hunters carried away furniture and other memorabilia, often without paying for it.

McLEMORE'S COVE, GEORGIA, BATTLE OF (SEPTEMBER 10–11, 1863). After **Braxton Bragg's Army of Tennessee** evacuated Chattanooga, Tennessee, in September 1863 and retreated into **Georgia, William S. Rosecrans's Army of the Cumberland** was widely scattered as it moved into the rugged country. Taking advantage of Rosecrans's tactical error, Bragg halted his retreat and on September 9 ordered **Thomas Hindman's** and **Patrick Cleburne's divisions** to attack **George H. Thomas's** isolated XIV Corps at McLemore's Cove. On September 10, the Confederates hit **James S. Negley's** division, but coordination among the units was poor, and Negley withdrew to Davis' Cross Roads to await reinforcements. Angered at the lost opportunity, Bragg ordered another attack for the following day, but by then Negley had been joined by **Absalom Baird's** division, and the two retired to Bailey's Cross Roads behind a strong rear guard. **Skirmishing** continued as the Federals withdrew to Stevens Gap at **Lookout Mountain**, but the Confederates were unable to inflict any further damage on the enemy. The number of casualties for the day's fighting is unknown. Afterward, both armies began consolidating to fight the upcoming **Battle of Chickamauga**.

McMILLAN, JAMES WINNING (1825–1903) USA. A native of **Kentucky**, McMillan moved often while growing up. He fought in the **Mexican War** with two different units and afterward settled in **Indiana** to become a businessman.

McMillan entered Union service in July 1861 when he was appointed colonel of the 21st Indiana, a **regiment** he organized. Sent to **Louisiana**, he helped garrison **New Orleans** in the spring of 1862 and fought at **Baton Rouge** in August. McMillan's regiment then was dispatched to guard Berwick Bay, Louisiana, and remained there until February, when it was redesignated the 1st Indiana Heavy Artillery.

Promoted to brigadier general of volunteers in April 1863, McMillan was given command of a XIX Corps **brigade** and sometimes commanded a **division**. He led a brigade with skill during the **Red River Campaign** and was praised for helping stem the Federal rout at **Mansfield**. After fighting at **Pleasant Hill** and **Monett's Ferry**, McMillan led the division in the campaign's closing days. After the campaign, the XIX Corps was sent to join **Philip Sheridan's 1864 Shenandoah Valley Campaign** in July 1864. Commanding a division, McMillan fought well at **Third Winchester**, and at **Cedar Creek** he placed his division in a strong position that allowed the defeated **corps** to rally. After the campaign, he was put in command of a division in the **Department of West Virginia** until war's end. McMillan was **brevetted** major general of volunteers in March 1865 and resigned his commission two months later.

After living in **Kansas** for a time after the war, McMillan was appointed to the pension office's board of review in 1875 and kept that position until his death.

McNAIR, EVANDER (1820–1902) CSA. A native of **North Carolina**, McNair moved with his family to **Mississippi** as a child. He was working as a merchant when the **Mexican War** began and became a 1st sergeant in **Jefferson Davis's** 1st Mississippi Rifles. After the war, he moved to **Arkansas** and became a merchant there.

When the Civil War began, McNair organized McNair's Arkansas Battalion and was appointed its lieutenant colonel. Other **companies** were added to the battalion, and in August 1861 it was redesignated the 4th Arkansas, with McNair being appointed its colonel. He fought at **Wilson's Creek** and **Pea Ridge** in **Louis Hébert's brigade** and assumed command of the brigade in the latter fight when Hébert was captured. Afterward, McNair led the brigade in the **Kentucky Campaign** as part of **Thomas Churchill's division**.

McNair was given command of his own brigade in **John P. McCown's** division in October 1862 and was promoted to brigadier general the following month. While with the **Army of Tennessee**, he was commended for his leadership at **Stones River** and may have been wounded there. During the **Vicksburg Campaign**, McNair's brigade served in **Samuel G. French's** division under **Joseph E. Johnston's** command around Jackson, Mississippi. His brigade later fought at **Chickamauga**, where McNair was seriously wounded while leading his men in an attack that captured two Union batteries. After service in the **Atlanta Campaign**, he was sent to Arkansas, where he commanded another brigade and may have participated in **Sterling Price's Missouri Raid**. McNair remained in Arkansas for the remainder of the war.

After the war, McNair became a businessman in **Louisiana** and Mississippi.

McNEIL, JOHN (1813–1891) USA. A native of Canada, McNeil moved to **Massachusetts** as a boy and became a hatter. He eventually moved to **Missouri**, served in the state legislature from 1844 to 1845, and became president of an insurance company in 1855.

McNeil entered Union service in May 1861 when he was appointed colonel of the 90-day 3rd Missouri (Union). He led it in a successful Missouri **skirmish** but then was mustered out of service in August. In June 1862, McNeil was appointed colonel of the 2nd Missouri Militia Cavalry (Union) and was given command of the District of Northern Missouri. For the next several months he was occupied in the frustrating duty of fighting guerrillas.

Promotion to brigadier general of volunteers came in November 1862, and McNeil commanded various **districts** in Missouri and **Louisiana**.

He was in command of a Missouri district during **Sterling Price's 1864 Missouri Raid**. McNeil's failure to carry out an ordered attack at the **Battle of Westport** angered his superior, **Alfred Pleasonton**, and resulted in McNeil's being relieved of command. He was returned to a Missouri district command in February 1865 and kept that position until his resignation was accepted in April (he was **brevetted** major general of volunteers on the same day).

After the war, McNeil remained in Missouri. There he twice served as clerk of the St. Louis criminal court, was elected county sheriff, became an inspector in the Indian Bureau, and served as superintendent of a St. Louis post office.

McNEILL, JOHN HANSON (1815–1864) CSA. A native of western **Virginia**, "Hanse" McNeill moved to **Kentucky** early in life, but he finally settled in **Missouri** and became a well-known cattle breeder. In 1861, he sided with the secessionists and became a militia **company** captain. McNeill fought at **Carthage**, **Wilson's Creek**, and **Lexington**, where he was wounded. When his company's enlistment expired in December, he returned home to raise a new unit. Captured in the attempt, McNeill escaped from **prison** and returned to Virginia with his three sons. There he raised a new company that became part of the 18th Virginia Cavalry in September 1862. McNeill was commissioned captain, and the company became known as **McNeill's Rangers**.

Although part of a **regiment**, McNeill's Rangers acted independently and cooperated with **John D. Imboden's** 1st Virginia **Partisan Rangers**, and sometimes with **John S. Mosby**, in **West Virginia** and the **Shenandoah Valley**. McNeill was so effective in raiding the Baltimore & Ohio Railroad and harassing Union troops that his wife and two children were imprisoned briefly in **Ohio** to intimidate him. Besides his guerrilla activity, he also participated in **Jones's and Imboden's Raid** into western Virginia, the **Gettysburg Campaign**, and the **Battle of New Market**. Despite McNeill's effectiveness, Imboden disliked his **tactics** and court-martialed him in the spring of 1864 for accepting Confederate **deserters** into his command. McNeill was acquitted, however, and remained on duty. In October 1864, he was shot accidentally and badly wounded by one of his own men in a raid against Mount Jackson. Left behind on his own orders, McNeill was captured and interrogated by **Philip Sheridan**. A few days later, his comrades rescued him in a daring raid, but he died about a month later.

McNEILL'S RANGERS. While this Confederate **partisan rangers** command is less well known than **John S. Mosby's** unit, it proved to be very effective against Union soldiers in **West Virginia** and the **Shenandoah Valley**. **John Hanson McNeill**, a native of western **Virginia** who first fought in **Missouri**, organized the command in Hardy County, Virginia, in September 1862. Officially designated Company E of the 18th Virginia Cavalry, the **company** actually operated independently as partisans but under the overall direction of Col. **John D. Imboden**.

Based at Moorefield, West Virginia, the rangers were very successful in raiding the Baltimore & Ohio Railroad, as well as Union supply bases and outposts. They also participated in **Jones's and Imboden's Raid** into West Virginia, saw some service during the **Gettysburg Campaign**, and fought at **New Market**. Two of the rangers' more famous exploits under McNeill were the capture of the entire 1st West Virginia (Union) at **Moorefield** in September 1863 and 60 members of the 6th West Virginia Cavalry (Union) who were bathing in a river in the summer of 1864.

During a raid on Mount Jackson in October 1864, McNeill was shot accidentally by one of his own men and mortally wounded. Left behind on his own orders, he was captured and interrogated by **Philip Sheridan** but then was rescued a few days later. After McNeill died in November, his son, 1st Lt. Jesse McNeill, took command of the rangers and led them on a raid into West Virginia with **Thomas L. Rosser**. Under Jesse McNeill the rangers also accomplished their most famous feat when they captured Union generals **George Crook** and **Benjamin F. Kelley** from a Cumberland, Maryland, hotel. McNeill finally surrendered his command to Brig. Gen. **Rutherford B. Hayes** at New Creek, West Virginia, in late April 1865.

McPHERSON, JAMES BIRDSEYE (1828–1864) USA. A native of **Ohio**, McPherson (muk-FUR-sun) was forced to start working in a country store when he was 13 to support his family (his father was mentally unstable). The storeowner became his sponsor and helped him get an education at a local academy and an appointment to **West Point**. He graduated first in the class of 1853, and his classmates included **John Bell Hood**, whose Confederate **Army of Tennessee** would kill him 11 years later. Assigned to the **engineers**, McPherson taught at the academy and worked on various coastal projects and fortifications, including supervising the fortifications on Alcatraz Island in San Francisco, California.

When the Civil War began, McPherson was a 1st lieutenant, but he quickly was promoted through the ranks to lieutenant colonel by November 1861. He first served as Maj. Gen. **Henry W. Halleck's** aide in the **Department of the Missouri**, but in February 1862 he was made **U. S. Grant's** chief engineer. McPherson served at **Forts Henry and Donelson**, **Shiloh**, and the **siege of Corinth, Mississippi**. Promoted to colonel in April and to brigadier general of volunteers in August, he also participated in the **Battle of Iuka** and afterward was made superintendent of **railroads** for western **Tennessee**.

After sending forward troops to pursue the enemy after the **Battle of Corinth**, McPherson was promoted to major general of volunteers in October 1862 (only 14 months earlier, he had been a 1st lieutenant). He commanded the **Army of the Tennessee's** right wing during **Grant's Overland Vicksburg Campaign** and was given command of the XVII Corps the following month. McPherson served skillfully during the **Vicksburg Campaign** (playing the key role in the victory at **Champion Hill**), became one of Grant's most dependable subordinates, and was appointed brigadier general of regulars in August. He also impressed **William T. Sherman** during the Vicksburg and **Meridian Campaigns**. Thus, when Sherman was placed in command of the Union's western forces in March 1864, McPherson was chosen to replace him in command of the Army of the Tennessee.

During the **Atlanta Campaign**, McPherson had an inauspicious start. During operations at **Resaca**, Sherman sent him to **Snake Creek Gap** to get behind the Confederates to cut their line of retreat. McPherson successfully reached the gap but then met light resistance and failed to push into the enemy's rear. Sherman was very disappointed in his lieutenant and admonished McPherson that he had missed an opportunity of a lifetime. During the rest of the campaign, McPherson often was used to make **turning movements** to force the Confederates out of strong defensive positions.

When Hood's army attacked McPherson at the **Battle of Atlanta** on July 22, 1864, McPherson was at Sherman's headquarters, but he quickly rode through the woods to rally his men. Accompanied by an orderly, he blundered into Confederate soldiers who demanded his surrender. Wheeling his horse, McPherson attempted to escape but was shot and killed. Sherman later broke down and wept when the body was brought to his headquarters. McPherson was engaged to a Baltimore woman, and Sherman earlier had denied his request for leave to get married. McPherson was the only Union **army** commander to be killed during the war.

McRAE, CSS. This 830-ton ship originally was the Mexican vessel *Marquis de la Habana*. It was seized initially as a pirate vessel by the U.S. government but subsequently became part of the small **Confederate**

navy in 1861. Armed with eight guns and renamed the *McRae*, it was captained by George N. Hollis as part of the **New Orleans, Louisiana**, river defenses. The gunboat played a key role in routing Union ships that tried to come up the Mississippi River in October 1861. After spending the winter at New Madrid, Missouri, the *McRae* was sent back to New Orleans in early 1862 and was stationed near **Forts Jackson and St. Philip**.

When **David G. Farragut** ran past the forts in April 1862, the *McRae* (now under 1st Lt. Thomas B. Huger) was one of the few Confederate gunboats that actively engaged the Union fleet. Huger was mortally wounded during the fight and was replaced by Lt. Charles W. Read. Badly damaged during the battle, the gunboat was run aground near Fort St. Philip and after the forts' surrender was used to take wounded men to New Orleans. On its way back downriver, the *McRae* struck an underwater object and sank.

McRAE, DANDRIDGE (1829–1899) CSA. A native of **Alabama**, McRae graduated from South Carolina College in 1849 and moved to **Arkansas** to become a lawyer and a county and circuit court clerk. He was serving on the governor's staff when the Civil War began but in May 1861 was appointed special state mustering officer. While serving on this recruitment duty in June, McRae was placed in command of several hundred men at Fayetteville and made a successful **demonstration** toward Springfield, Missouri.

McRae was appointed lieutenant colonel of the 3rd Arkansas Battalion in July 1861 and was commended for his service at **Wilson's Creek**. After being promoted to colonel of the 21st (McRae's) Arkansas in December, he again fought with distinction at **Pea Ridge**. In May 1862, McRae declined reelection as the **regiment's** colonel and instead was appointed colonel of the 28th (McRae's) Arkansas the following month. He led this regiment in Arkansas until commissioned brigadier general in November 1862.

Given a **brigade** command, McRae fought at **Prairie Grove** and **Helena**, but at the latter, he was criticized by his superior, **Theophilus H. Holmes**. Holmes earlier had accused McRae's brigade of being poorly **disciplined** and trained. After Helena, he claimed McRae had followed **Sterling Price's** orders instead of his own and had failed to aid Brig. Gen. **James F. Fagan**. Holmes also claimed it was McRae's failure that forced him to retreat, but both Price and Fagan defended McRae's actions. McRae demanded a court of inquiry to clear himself, but was forced to fight at **Little Rock** before one could be convened. Holmes then relieved him of his brigade command in October 1863 and assigned him to Price. In March 1864, McRae was placed in command of north-eastern Arkansas and reportedly fought at **Marks' Mill** and **Jenkins' Ferry**. He finally was cleared of wrongdoing at Helena by a court of inquiry in June 1864 but resigned his commission anyhow and returned home.

McRae resumed his law practice and after the war served as Arkansas's deputy secretary of state and on the state's chamber of commerce.

MACKALL, WILLIAM WHANN (1817–1891) CSA. A native of **Maryland**, Mackall (MAKE-awl) graduated from **West Point** in 1837 and was assigned to the **artillery**. He was severely wounded in the foot while fighting in the **Seminole Wars**. During the **Mexican War**, Mackall was promoted to captain, was wounded again, and received two **brevets** for gallantry. After Mexico, he transferred to the Adjutant General's Department and remained with it until the outbreak of civil war.

In May 1861, Mackall declined a commission as lieutenant colonel and, instead, resigned his major's commission in July and joined the Confederacy as a lieutenant colonel and assistant adjutant general on **Albert Sidney Johnston's** staff. In March 1862, he was promoted to brigadier general and was placed in command of the defenses at **New Madrid, Missouri, and Island No. 10.** Mackall took command of the troops after **John P. McCown**, the previous commander, had already placed them in a precarious position on a peninsula. As a result of his poor position, Mackall was forced to surrender only a week after assuming command.

After being **exchanged** in October 1862, Mackall briefly commanded the District of the Gulf until he was replaced by **Simon B. Buckner** and was given a **division** command within the **department**. Between April and October 1863, he served as chief of staff for **Braxton Bragg's Army of Tennessee**, but he disliked serving under Bragg and asked for a new assignment. Mackall then led an infantry **brigade** in **Mississippi** until January 1864, when he became **Joseph E. Johnston's** chief of staff for the Army of Tennessee. He remained in that position until Johnston was replaced by **John Bell Hood** in July. A strong Johnston supporter, Mackall was relieved of his position at his own request and spent the rest of the war in **Georgia** awaiting orders.

After the war, Mackall farmed in **Virginia**.

MACKENZIE, RANALD SLIDELL (1840–1889) USA. A native of **New York**, Mackenzie's father (who took on the surname of Mackenzie to honor a maternal uncle) was a brother of Confederate diplomat **John Slidell** and as a navy officer hanged Philip Spencer, son of the secretary of the navy, in a mysterious 1842 mutiny episode. Mackenzie also was related by marriage to **P. G. T. Beauregard**, who married the sister of Slidell's wife.

Mackenzie dropped out of Williams College to accept an appointment to **West Point** and attended the academy while Beauregard was superintendent. Graduating first in the class of 1862, he was appointed an assistant **engineer** of the **Army of Virginia's** IX Corps and was wounded at **Second Manassas**. Mackenzie recovered in time to serve with the **Army of the Potomac** in the **Antietam Campaign** and then was chief engineer for **Edwin V. Sumner's** II Corps at **Fredericksburg, Chancellorsville**, and **Gettysburg** (winning two **brevets** for the latter two battles). During this time, he was promoted to 1st lieutenant in March 1863. Promoted to captain in November 1863, Mackenzie led an engineering battalion during the **Overland Campaign** and in the early part of the **Petersburg Campaign**. During the latter, he was wounded and brevetted again. In July 1864, Mackenzie was appointed colonel of the 2nd Connecticut Heavy Artillery and served in the **Washington, D.C.**, defenses before being sent to participate in **Philip Sheridan's Shenandoah Valley Campaign**. He fought at **Third Winchester, Fisher's Hill**, and **Cedar Creek** and received yet another wound and brevet for the latter battle.

Promoted to brigadier general of volunteers in October 1864, Mackenzie led a **brigade** in the VI Corps' 1st Division at the end of Sheridan's Shenandoah Valley Campaign before returning to Petersburg. In March 1865, he was given command of the cavalry in the **Army of the James** and led it so well at **Five Forks** and in the **Appomattox Campaign** that U. S. **Grant** declared he was the most promising young officer in the **army**.

Mackenzie was mustered out of the volunteer service in January 1866 after receiving brevets of brigadier general of regulars and major general of volunteers for his war service. After the war, he became colonel of the 41st U.S. Infantry and the 4th U.S. Cavalry and earned great fame as an **Indian** fighter. He invaded Mexico illegally (although with Sheridan's permission) and defeated the Apaches, before suppressing the Cheyennes. During these Indian campaigns, Mackenzie suffered his seventh combat wound, which pained him the rest of his life, and a severe head injury after falling from a wagon. His mind was affected by these injuries, and he briefly was committed to an asylum. Displaying signs of irrational behavior, Mackenzie finally was forced to retire in 1884 with the rank of brigadier general.

MacRAE, WILLIAM (1834–1882) CSA. A native of **North Carolina**, MacRae worked as a civil engineer during the antebellum period. He entered Confederate service in June 1861 as a captain in the 5th North Carolina, redesignated the 15th North Carolina in November. After serving in **Virginia** and North Carolina, MacRae saw his first combat during the **Peninsula Campaign** and was elected lieutenant colonel of the **regiment** when it was reorganized in May 1862. At **Malvern Hill** with the **Army of Northern Virginia**, MacRae took command when the regiment's colonel was wounded.

As part of **Howell Cobb's brigade**, MacRae led the 15th North Carolina at **Crampton's Gap** and **Antietam** and took temporary command of the brigade in the latter fight. In November 1862, the regiment was transferred to **John R. Cooke's** brigade, where it remained until war's end. After **Fredericksburg**, MacRae's brigade was sent to southeast Virginia, where it engaged in several small **skirmishes**. Promoted to colonel in February 1863, he and the brigade returned to the Army of Northern Virginia in October and participated in the **Battle of Bristoe Station**. Cooke was severely wounded there, and when the senior colonel resigned in December, MacRae led the brigade in the 1864 **Overland Campaign**. When Brig. Gen. **William W. Kirkland** was wounded near **Cold Harbor** in June 1864, MacRae was placed in command of his brigade in **Henry Heth's division** and was promoted temporarily to brigadier general.

A strict disciplinarian, MacRae soon made the brigade one of the **army's** best, and he performed well at **Weldon Railroad**, **Reams' Station**, and **Burgess' Mill**. He was given the permanent rank of brigadier general in November 1864, becoming one of only two temporary Confederate generals to receive permanent appointments (the other was **David Weisiger**). MacRae continued to lead the brigade through the **Petersburg Campaign** and **surrendered** with the army at **Appomattox**.

After the war, MacRae was a **railroad** superintendent in North Carolina and **Georgia**.

MAFFITT, JOHN NEWLAND (1819–1886) CSA. Appropriately, this Confederate naval officer was born at sea but was raised by a **North Carolina** uncle because his minister father was too impoverished to provide for him. After attending school in **New York**, Maffitt joined the **U.S.**

Navy as a midshipman at age 13 and served at sea until he was assigned to the U.S. Coastal Survey in 1842. He then surveyed and charted the Atlantic coast until returning to sea in 1857. In April 1861, Maffitt resigned his lieutenant's commission and entered Confederate service the next month as a navy lieutenant.

Maffitt was stationed first at Hilton Head, South Carolina, but soon was given command of the CSS *Savannah* and helped defend **Port Royal, South Carolina**. In January 1862, he was promoted to captain and became a highly successful **blockade runner**. Maffitt sailed to Nassau in May and took command of a ship that became the **commerce raider CSS** *Florida*. He boldly disguised it as a British vessel and ran the **blockade** in daytime to enter Mobile Bay, Alabama. After being refitted, the *Florida* began a successful raiding voyage in January 1863. Maffitt took 47 prizes, but he was weakened by yellow fever and in August sailed to France and asked to be relieved. After recovering from his illness, he returned to blockade running and in 1864 briefly commanded the ram *Albemarle*. Maffitt's superiors believed his aggressiveness might lead to the loss of the valuable **ram** and soon relieved him. He then returned to blockade running with the *Owl*.

After the war, Maffitt commanded a British merchant ship chartered to Brazil and briefly was involved with Cuban revolutionaries while commanding one of their vessels. He finally retired to a North Carolina farm and wrote a novel, as well as articles about the sea and his military service.

MAGOFFIN, BERIAH (1815–1885) CSA. A native of **Kentucky**, Magoffin graduated from Centre College and studied law at Transylvania University. Active in **Democratic** politics, he was elected to the state senate in 1850, lost an 1844 gubernatorial race, and was elected governor in 1859. Magoffin believed in **secession** but hoped it could be avoided. When the South began seceding after the **election of 1860**, he favored convening a Kentucky secession convention, but the pro-Union legislature refused. When war began, Magoffin turned down **Abraham Lincoln's** call for volunteers, refused to support the Confederacy, and declared Kentucky's neutrality in May 1861.

During the war, Magoffin remained friendly to the Confederacy and was constantly opposed by the legislature. The Confederates invaded Kentucky in September 1861, and the Union followed suit, but the legislature passed a bill calling for him to order only the Confederates out. Magoffin's veto was overridden, and he complied with the measure, although he made it clear that he did not agree with it. Despite his pro-Confederate tendencies, Magoffin denounced the Kentucky Confederate government that was established in November. The governor's influence waned as the legislature stripped him of authority. He considered resigning, but the lieutenant governor had died, and Magoffin would not accept the speaker of the house as governor. As a compromise, the speaker resigned in August 1862 and was replaced by **James F. Robinson**. Magoffin then resigned and was replaced by Robinson.

Magoffin resumed his farming and law career and during **Reconstruction** urged voters to ratify the **13th Amendment** freeing the slaves and to extend civil rights to the **freedmen**. He also served in the state legislature from 1867 to 1869.

MAGRATH, ANDREW GORDON (1813–1893) CSA. A native of **South Carolina**, Magrath (muh-GRAW) graduated first in the South Carolina College class of 1831 and attended Harvard Law School. Becoming a lawyer, he was elected to the state legislature in 1840 and 1842. A moderate on **secession**, Magrath was appointed a U.S. district judge in 1856 and held that position until **Abraham Lincoln** was elected in 1860. Declaring that Lincoln's **election** had destroyed constitutional government, he then resigned his judgeship and was elected to the state secession convention.

After secession, Magrath became the state's secretary of state and served on the Executive Council until he was appointed Confederate district judge for South Carolina in 1862. As judge, he generally supported **states rights** and became increasingly unpopular with **Jefferson Davis**. In December 1864, Magrath was elected governor by the legislature and immediately was faced with **William T. Sherman's** invasion during the **Carolinas Campaign**.

Governor Magrath tried to protect the state from both the Union and Confederate governments. He was given authority to exempt from **conscription** citizens he deemed necessary for state defense and took measures to restrict the Confederate authorities' **impressment** of slaves. Despite his efforts, South Carolina was overrun by the enemy, and Magrath had to move the capital from Columbia in February 1865 to Winnsboro, Union, and Spartanburg. When faced with inevitable defeat, he returned to Columbia in April.

In May 1865, Magrath was arrested for treason and was imprisoned at **Fort Pulaski, Georgia**. Released in November on orders from President **Andrew Johnson**, he resumed his law practice.

MAGRUDER, JOHN BANKHEAD (1807–1871) CSA. A native of **Virginia**, Magruder graduated from **West Point** in 1830. He was assigned to the infantry but after one year of service transferred to the **artillery**. After serving in the **Seminole Wars**, Magruder fought in the **Mexican War** and won a promotion to captain and two **brevets** for gallantry. After the war, he served at posts in **Maryland**, **California**, **Kansas**, and **Rhode Island** and earned the nickname "Prince John" because of his fondness for fancy **uniforms**, pomp, and the theater. Magruder's rather haughty attitude was made comical by his speaking with a lisp, especially when cursing.

Magruder resigned his commission in April 1861 and entered Confederate service the following month as a colonel of infantry. Placed in command of the **Department of the Peninsula**, he was promoted to brigadier general in June and to major general in October. Magruder was praised when his men won the first battle of the war at **Big Bethel** and when his greatly outnumbered force slowed **George B. McClellan's** advance on **Richmond, Virginia**, during the 1862 **Peninsula Campaign**. His shrewd use of **Quaker guns**, empty trains, and bands gave the appearance of a much larger force than really existed and kept McClellan at bay until **Joseph E. Johnston** arrived with the main **Confederate army**. Magruder's reputation was damaged when he led an **Army of Northern Virginia division** during the **Seven Days Campaign**. He largely failed in his responsibilities during the campaign and was rumored to have been drunk at **Malvern Hill**. Magruder was transferred to the **Trans-Mississippi Department** after the Seven Days, but he soon returned to Richmond, where he finally was cleared of the Malvern Hill accusations. In October 1862, he was sent to **Texas**, and on New Year's Day, 1863, he led a daring attack against Union forces at **Galveston** that successfully recaptured that important port from the enemy. Magruder remained in Texas for the rest of the war holding various positions, including command of the District of Texas, New Mexico, and Arizona.

After the war, Magruder moved to Mexico and served in **Emperor Maximilian's army**. After the emperor was deposed, Magruder returned to the United States and went on a lecturing tour before settling in Texas.

MAHAN, DENNIS HART (1802–1871) USA. A native of **New York**, Mahan (muh-HAHN) graduated first in the **West Point** class of 1824. He taught mathematics and engineering at the academy for two years before being sent to Europe for four years to study European military and construction practices. After studying under some of Napoleon's former officers, Mahan returned to the United States in 1830 to resume his teaching career at West Point.

Mahan became the most influential professor at the academy because of his extensive knowledge of military **tactics** and **strategy**. He taught most of the cadets who later became leading Civil War generals and thus had a large impact on how the war was fought. Mahan's classes stressed the use of strong defensive fortifications to stop an attack and using direct counterattacks and **turning movements** to defeat the enemy. His work *A Treatise of Field Fortification* was used by both sides during the Civil War. Mahan continued at West Point until 1871, when he drowned after accidentally walking off the side of ship in New York City harbor. His son, Alfred Thayer Mahan, taught at the **U.S. Naval Academy** and became the leading American naval theorist with his classic work, *The Influence of Sea Power upon History*.

MAHONE, WILLIAM (1826–1895) CSA. "Billie" Mahone (or "Little Billie" since he reportedly weighed less than 100 lbs.) was a **Virginia** native, who, as a boy, worked as a mail carrier. After graduating from the **Virginia Military Institute** in 1847, he taught at the Rappahannock Military Academy and studied engineering. After teaching at the academy for two years, Mahone became a **railroad** engineer and remained associated with railroads as an engineer, president, and superintendent until 1861.

When Virginia seceded in April 1861, Mahone was appointed state quartermaster general, but he quickly was elected lieutenant colonel of the 4th Virginia Artillery. The following month, he was appointed colonel of the 6th Virginia and was assigned to **Norfolk, Virginia**. Placed in command of a **brigade** in October, Mahone was promoted to brigadier general the following month. When Norfolk was evacuated in May 1862, he first took command of the defenses at **Drewry's Bluff**, but his brigade then was assigned to **Benjamin Huger's** division and saw heavy combat at **Seven Pines** and during the **Seven Days Campaign**.

In July 1862, Mahone was assigned to **Richard H. Anderson's** division in the **Army of Northern Virginia**. He was badly wounded at **Second Manassas** but returned to his men in time to lead them at **Fredericksburg** and **Chancellorsville**, receiving a commendation for his leadership at **Salem Church** during the latter campaign. Kept in reserve at **Gettysburg**, the brigade saw little combat there and suffered the fewest casualties of the entire **army**. Mahone made his greatest contribution to the war during the last year of fighting. At the **Wilderness**, he led **James Longstreet's** flank attack that temporarily routed the Union left flank. In the reorganization that followed Longstreet's wounding, Mahone took command of Anderson's **division** and led it with skill at

Spotsylvania, North Anna River, and **Cold Harbor**. During the **Petersburg Campaign**, he captured hundreds of **prisoners** and four cannons in fighting along the Jerusalem Plank Road. Mahone's devastating counterattack at the **Crater** earned him much praise and a promotion to major general in August 1864. He continued to fight well at **Weldon Railroad, Reams' Station**, and **Hatcher's Run** until he surrendered with the Army of Northern Virginia at **Appomattox**.

After the war, Mahone became a Virginia railroad tycoon but lost much of his popularity when he supported the Republican governor during **Reconstruction** and became a powerful political lobbyist. After losing his railroad empire in the Panic of 1873, he was elected to the U.S. Senate in 1880 and for a time was the leader of Virginia's **Republican Party**.

MAINE. A center of **abolitionism** and native state of **Abraham Lincoln's** Vice President **Hannibal Hamlin**, Maine strongly supported the Union war effort. Although one of the weaker Northern **industrial** states, it gave generously of its manpower. Out of an 1860 population of 628,279, approximately 67,000 Maine men served in the Union armed forces, with nearly 9,000 becoming fatalities. Two of its most famous military units were the 1st Maine Heavy Artillery and the 20th Maine. Among the officers Maine produced were **Oliver O. Howard, Joshua L. Chamberlain**, and **Adelbert Ames**. The only military action in the state was an 1862 raid on Portland harbor by a detachment from the **CSS** *Florida,* which tried unsuccessfully to seize a revenue cutter.

MAJOR, JAMES PATRICK (1836–1877) CSA. A native of **Missouri**, Major graduated from **West Point** in 1856 and fought **Indians** in **Texas** with the 2nd U.S. Cavalry before joining Maj. **Earl Van Dorn's** staff. While in Texas, he also married the sister of future Confederate general **Thomas Green**.

Major resigned his 2nd lieutenant's commission in March 1861 and again joined Van Dorn's staff, this time in the **Confederate army**. After a few months, he returned to Missouri and was appointed lieutenant of cavalry in the state forces. Major quickly was promoted to lieutenant colonel of the 1st Cavalry, Missouri State Guard, and was commended for his service at **Wilson's Creek**. Returning to Texas to raise a **regiment** of lancers, he clashed with Gov. **Francis Lubbock**, who claimed he was interfering with the governor's own recruitment efforts. Now a colonel in the Missouri State Guard, Major failed to organize his regiment and returned to **Arkansas** in March 1862. That summer, he was appointed Van Dorn's acting chief of **artillery** and helped him repulse the Union fleet that attacked **Vicksburg, Mississippi**, later that spring. When Van Dorn was murdered in May, Major was given a cavalry **brigade** under **Richard Taylor** in **Louisiana**. Serving under his brother-in-law, Tom Green, he fought in the 1863 **Bayou Teche Campaign** and earned Taylor's respect and praise. In numerous raids and **skirmishes**, Major showed great skill as a cavalryman, and Taylor enthusiastically recommended him for promotion.

In July 1863, Major was appointed brigadier general and accompanied Green to defend the Texas Gulf coast. The two returned to Taylor for the 1864 **Red River Campaign** and skillfully opposed the advancing enemy. After fighting at **Mansfield** and **Pleasant Hill**, Major was with Green when he was killed at **Blair's Landing**. He then harassed the Union navy as it retreated down the Red River and captured a transport loaded with 270 men of the 120th Ohio. After the campaign, Major's brigade was assigned to **John A. Wharton's division** in Arkansas for the remainder of the war.

After the war, Major lived in France for a while but returned to the United States and farmed in Texas and Louisiana. After his first wife died, he married the sister of Confederate general **Paul O. Hébert**.

MALLORY, STEPHEN RUSSELL (1813–1873) CSA. A native of Trinidad, Mallory settled in Key West, Florida, as a boy. There he became a lawyer, customs inspector, port collector, and judge and served in the **Seminole Wars** as the commander of a small ship. Elected to the U.S. Senate in 1850 and 1856, Mallory served on the Committee on Naval Affairs and served as its chairman from 1855 to 1861. In that position, he strongly advocated expanding and strengthening the **U.S. Navy**. Although opposing **secession**, Mallory resigned his Senate seat in early 1861 after **Florida** seceded. Not wanting war, he tried to prevent a clash between secessionists and Union troops at **Fort Pickens** at **Pensacola, Florida**, by convincing President **James Buchanan** not to land reinforcements.

In February 1861, **Jefferson Davis** appointed Mallory Confederate secretary of the navy. With no knowledge of and little interest in naval affairs, Davis largely allowed Mallory to run his department without interference (he and Postmaster General **John H. Reagan** were the only two Confederate cabinet members to keep their positions throughout the war). Mallory immediately began building a small **Confederate navy** from scratch. Raising money by first selling cotton bonds in Europe and then cotton itself through the **blockade**, he sent such agents as **James D. Bulloch** to purchase ships in the North, Canada, and Europe. Some powerful **commerce raiders** were acquired from Great Britain, although

Bulloch failed to receive the so-called **Laird rams**. Mallory's department also oversaw the building of a number of **ironclads** in the Confederacy and actively sought out new technologies in **torpedoes** and **submarines** (like the *H. L. Hunley*).

One of Mallory's failures was that he contributed to the poor command system on the Mississippi River by not taking control of the **River Defense Fleet**. He also believed the enemy would attack **New Orleans, Louisiana**, from upriver and did not take adequate precautions to strengthen **Forts Jackson and St. Philip** downstream, because he believed they could stop any Union thrust from the Gulf of Mexico. As a result, Mallory was criticized for the loss of New Orleans and Memphis, Tennessee, as well as for the abandonment of **Norfolk, Virginia**, and the destruction of the **CSS *Virginia***. He was investigated by the **Confederate Congress** for these defeats but was cleared of any wrongdoing. Modern historians give Mallory credit for performing competently under very trying conditions.

Mallory joined Davis on his flight to **Georgia** at war's end, but he left the president shortly before he was captured. He was captured by the Federals and was kept a **prisoner** for 10 months. After being released, Mallory returned to Florida and resumed his law practice.

MALTBY, JASPER ADALMORN (1826–1868) USA. A native of **Ohio**, Maltby served in the **Mexican War** as a private in the 15th U.S. Infantry and was badly wounded at Chapultepec. Afterward, he moved to **Illinois** and became a gunsmith and storeowner.

Maltby entered Union service in December 1861 as lieutenant colonel of the 45th Illinois. He served with the **regiment** at **Forts Henry and Donelson** and was wounded in the leg at the latter battle. Promoted to colonel in March 1863, Maltby served well through the **Vicksburg Campaign** with the **Army of the Tennessee** and was promoted to brigadier general of volunteers in August. He was given command of a **brigade** in the XVII Corps' 3rd Division in April 1863 and served around **Vicksburg, Mississippi**, for the rest of the war, sometimes in command of the city's garrison. Maltby never saw combat after becoming a brigadier general and was not given the customary **brevet** of major general after the war, even though he was from **U. S. Grant's** hometown.

After being mustered out of service in January 1866, Maltby settled in Vicksburg and became a merchant. He was appointed mayor in 1867 but died three months later.

MALVERN HILL, VIRGINIA, BATTLE OF (JULY 1, 1862). Also known as the Battle of Crew's Farm or Poindexter's Farm, this was the last battle of the **Seven Days Campaign**. In very heavy fighting, **Robert E. Lee's Army of Northern Virginia** forced **George B. McClellan's Army of the Potomac** down the Virginia Peninsula away from **Richmond, Virginia** during the 1862 campaign. After the **Battle of Frayser's Farm**, McClellan retreated to Malvern Hill, a 150-foot high hill located on the James River about five miles from **Harrison's Landing**. **Fitz John Porter's** V Corps first reached the hill on June 30, 1862, and began preparing a defense. The position was nearly impregnable, with deep ravines protecting McClellan's flanks, forcing the Confederates to make a **frontal attack** across open ground that was covered by approximately 100 cannons. Union Chief of Artillery **Henry J. Hunt** had another 150 guns in reserve. Lee, however, believed the Federals were demoralized and that one final assault would crush them. Thus, he ordered what turned out to be a disastrous attack.

Lee's **army** filed into position on July 1, 1862. **Stonewall Jackson** was on the left with the **divisions** of **Richard S. Ewell**, **W. H. C. Whiting**, and **Daniel H. Hill**. When **John B. Magruder** arrived, his division was to form on Jackson's right, with **James Longstreet** and **A. P. Hill** to form the reserve. Magruder, confused by two roads bearing the name of Quaker Road, took the wrong road and did not arrive at his designated position. Instead, **Benjamin Huger** was placed on Jackson's right, and when Magruder finally arrived at 4:00 P.M., he was placed behind Huger.

Lee's plan was to mass his **artillery** for a preliminary bombardment, and when the Union guns were silenced **Lewis Armistead's brigade** of Huger's division was to attack with a loud shout to signal the other brigades to follow. However, the Confederate artillery was poorly handled, and few guns actually got into action. Those that did were completely overwhelmed by the more numerous and better placed Union batteries, which began bombarding the Confederate line at about 1:00 P.M.

When Armistead attacked at 3:30 P.M., he soon was pinned down by **George W. Morell's** V Corps division. Lee then ordered Magruder to send in all of his 15,000 men, but confusion and poor staff work led to only about one-third being actually engaged, and they were quickly repulsed. When Daniel H. Hill heard Magruder attack, he believed it was the signal for the general advance and reluctantly sent his men forward against **Darius Couch's** IV Corps division at about 6:45 P.M. He quickly was crushed by the Union artillery, as were eight other Confederate brigades that trickled forward in uncoordinated attacks. Afterward, Hill commented that Malvern Hill "was not war—it was murder" (Sears, *To the Gates of Richmond*, p. 335)

Lee lost 5,355 men in the battle, while McClellan counted 3,314 casualties. Recognizing that they had won a great tactical victory, some of

McClellan's generals wanted to counterattack. McClellan, however, ordered a retreat and fell back to Harrison's Landing that night, ending the Seven Days Campaign.

MANASSAS, VIRGINIA, FIRST CAMPAIGN AND BATTLE OF (JULY 16–22, 1861). By July 1861, there were two Confederate forces in northern **Virginia. P. G. T. Beauregard** had 22,000 men defending a line along Bull Run, near Manassas, while **Joseph E. Johnston** had another 12,000 men in the **Shenandoah Valley**. **Abraham Lincoln** was eager for a quick victory and was impatient for Federal forces to engage these Confederates and push "On to Richmond." Lincoln had two armies to oppose the enemy—the 33,000 men assembled at **Washington, D.C.**, under Brig. Gen. **Irvin McDowell** and about 18,000 men under **Robert Patterson** who were in the Shenandoah Valley to prevent Johnston from reinforcing Beauregard. Although McDowell protested against a hasty advance because his troops were untrained, Lincoln argued that the Confederates were just as unready and pressured McDowell to advance toward Manassas on July 16, 1861.

It took the inexperienced Union soldiers two days to march the few miles to Centreville, and the **army** was accompanied by numerous politicians and onlookers who wished to see the battle. From Centreville on July 18, McDowell ordered Brig. Gen. **Daniel Tyler's division** to make a **reconnaissance in force** to Bull Run. Tyler encountered **James Longstreet's brigade** guarding **Blackburn's Ford**, and a sharp fight erupted. Reinforced by **Jubal A. Early's** brigade, Longstreet held the ford, and Tyler retreated. The clash at Blackburn's Ford convinced McDowell that the main creek fords were too heavily defended for a **frontal attack**.

For the next two days both sides prepared for battle. On July 18, Johnston used a cavalry screen to hide his movement and began transferring his men from the Shenandoah Valley to Manassas by **railroad** without Patterson's knowledge. It was the first time in history that railroads were used to make such a **strategic** military move. These troops, which began arriving at Manassas on July 19, would play a crucial role in the coming battle.

By July 20, both McDowell and Beauregard had developed similar **tactical** plans. Both intended to fix their opponent in place along Bull Run and make a **turning movement** around the enemy's left flank. Although Johnston was the senior officer, he allowed Beauregard to exercise tactical command of the Confederates because of his familiarity with the ground, while Johnston directed the flow of reinforcements from the Valley.

At daylight, July 21, the Federals moved first against the six-mile-long Confederate line along Bull Run. Placing Tyler's division near the Stone Bridge on the Warrenton Turnpike, McDowell opened **artillery** fire on Beauregard's left flank to fix it in place, while the divisions of **David Hunter** and **Samuel P. Heintzelman** marched upstream beyond the Confederate left and crossed Bull Run at Sudley Ford. Confederate signalmen detected this movement and warned Brig. Gen. **Nathan G. Evans**, who was holding Beauregard's left flank. Evans shifted part of his brigade to the left and encountered Hunter's division at Matthew's Hill about mid-morning. The battle raged throughout that Sunday morning as both sides rushed in reinforcements. McDowell had the upper hand, however, and in hard fighting pushed back the Confederate brigades of Evans, **Barnard E. Bee**, and **Francis S. Bartow**.

The battle next moved to Henry House Hill, a key hill just south of the Warrenton Turnpike. One of Johnston's newly arrived brigades from the Valley was that of Brig. Gen. **Thomas J. Jackson**. Recognizing the hill's importance, Jackson occupied it and provided a place for the Confederates to rally on. Fighting desperately in the valley below, Bee saw Jackson and called out to his men, "Look! There is Jackson standing like a stone wall! Rally behind the Virginians!" Bee soon was mortally wounded, but Jackson and his brigade had been given their nom de guerre.

The battle raged up and down Henry House Hill, with both sides sometimes mistakenly firing into their own men because standard **uniforms** had not yet been adopted. Both armies were exhausted, but Johnston's fresh troops from the Valley kept arriving, giving the Confederates an advantage. At about 4:00 P.M., Early's brigade launched a crushing attack against McDowell's right flank, and the entire Union line quickly came unhinged and began retreating. When a Confederate shell wrecked a wagon and blocked the bridge across Cub Run, the Federals panicked, and the retreat became a rout. Numerous Northern spectators, including one congressman, were captured in the disaster.

In this first large-scale battle of the war, McDowell lost 2,896 men and 27 cannons to the Confederates' 1,982 casualties. **Jefferson Davis** arrived on the field just as the Federals began their retreat and discussed pursuing the beaten foe with his generals. Exhaustion and confusion, however, prevented the Confederates from exploiting their success. Later, Davis and Beauregard bitterly feuded over who was to blame for this lack of pursuit.

MANASSAS, VIRGINIA, SECOND CAMPAIGN AND BATTLE OF (AUGUST 25–SEPTEMBER 1, 1862). Following **Robert E. Lee's**

victory in the **Seven Days Campaign**, the Confederates in **Virginia** quickly were threatened again by Union Maj. Gen. **John Pope's Army of Virginia**. Pope's 63,000-man **army** had been created in late June 1862 to protect **Washington, D.C.**, and the **Shenandoah Valley** and to assist **George B. McClellan's** advance on **Richmond, Virginia**, by threatening Charlottesville and diverting enemy attention away from the Virginia Peninsula. After McClellan's defeat in the Seven Days Campaign, he was ordered to send his **Army of the Potomac** to Washington to reinforce Pope. Lee realized that if McClellan joined Pope, the combined force would be too large for his **Army of Northern Virginia** to stop. His only hope was to move north and defeat Pope before McClellan could reinforce him.

When Pope marched for Gordonsville on July 14, Lee sent **Stonewall Jackson's** command to confront him. Jackson defeated Pope's advance in a poorly managed battle at **Cedar Mountain** on August 9, 1862. By this time, Lee had confirmed that McClellan was transferring all of his army to Washington and moved the rest of the Army of Northern Virginia to join Jackson. He then planned to make a **turning movement** against Pope's left flank to cut him off from the Rappahannock River, but Pope realized the danger he was in and withdrew across the river. In the maneuvers that followed, Confederate cavalryman **Fitzhugh Lee** raided Pope's headquarters near **Catlett's Station** on August 22 and gathered intelligence indicating that McClellan's troops were beginning to join Pope. In a bold plan, Lee divided his army into two wings under Jackson and **James Longstreet**. Leaving Longstreet to pin down Pope on the river, he sent Jackson and **J. E. B. Stuart's** cavalry upstream to move around Pope's right flank and into his rear. Jackson was to cut off Pope from Washington and force him to withdraw from the Rappahannock line. Lee and Longstreet then would follow Jackson's route, join him, and together fight the decisive battle.

Jackson began his march on August 25 and quickly covered 54 miles in 36 hours. He captured Pope's supply base at Manassas Junction on the night of August 26 and burned it the next night before moving to nearby **Groveton** and taking a hidden position near the Warrenton Turnpike. Thinking the Confederates were simply a cavalry raid, Pope sent units to the rear to drive them off. So intent was he on destroying the Confederates in his rear that Pope failed to take adequate steps to block Lee, and Lee followed Jackson's route and joined him later. With his 75,000 men positioned between the separated enemy wings, Pope missed an excellent opportunity to hold Lee at bay and **defeat in detail** the two Confederate forces.

Late in the afternoon of August 28, **Rufus King's** division marched past the hidden Jackson at Groveton. Jackson attacked, and a vicious fight erupted around Brawner's Farm with the soldiers slugging it out at close range in an open field until well after dark. Groveton was one of the fiercest battles of the war, and it was the Union **Iron Brigade's** initiation into combat. While the battle raged, Lee and Longstreet moved through **Thoroughfare Gap** and closed the distance to Jackson.

Still ignoring Lee, Pope ordered his army to concentrate against Jackson, who had assumed a defensive position on the old Manassas battlefield along the cuts and embankments of an unfinished **railroad**. Reinforced by some of McClellan's **divisions**, Pope sent **Samuel P. Heintzelman's** III Corps and **Franz Sigel's** I Corps against Jackson's left and center on August 29. On several occasions, the Federals briefly broke through the Confederate line, but Pope failed to support the attacks sufficiently, and all were finally repulsed in vicious, sometimes hand-to-hand, fighting. The most critical moment came on Jackson's far left late in the afternoon when **Philip Kearny's** division broke through and was repulsed only after very bloody fighting. Throughout the day, Pope outnumbered Jackson 62,000 to 20,000, but he unwisely committed his men piecemeal and was unable to overwhelm the stubborn Confederate defense.

Lee arrived on the field about noon and placed Longstreet on the right at nearly right angles to Jackson, poising the army much like a trap ready to spring shut against the Federals. Pope continually ignored warnings that Lee had arrived, and during the fighting on August 29 he ordered **Fitz John Porter's** V Corps to move against Jackson's right flank. In doing so, Porter encountered Longstreet's line and informed the commander of its presence. Pope, however, refused to believe it and later charged Porter with disobeying orders by failing to make the attack.

On August 30, Pope confused a realignment of the Confederate line for a general withdrawal and ordered a pursuit. After some light **skirmishing**, the Federals made a massive **frontal attack** in mid-afternoon against a deep ravine in the Confederate right center where the railroad embankment was cut by a gully. At the cut, **William E. Starke's Louisiana Tigers** held the line and threw rocks at the enemy after running out of ammunition until Confederate **artillery** massed on Jackson's right finally repulsed the attacks. During the fighting, Lee ordered Longstreet to counterattack, but Longstreet did not believe the time was yet right and convinced Lee to wait. When the artillery broke up the enemy assault, Longstreet finally advanced, crushed Pope's left wing, and sent the Union army reeling back to Chinn Ridge. There in intense fighting the Federals made a stand but after about an hour were forced back to Henry House Hill on the old Manassas battlefield. Longstreet continued to pound this new Union line before darkness finally ended the fight. The Second Battle of Manassas was a disaster for the Federals and cost Pope 13,826 men to Lee's 8,353.

Pope retreated to Centreville, and on August 31 Lee sent Jackson north and east to cut off the fleeing enemy from Washington. Following the Little River Turnpike, Jackson hoped to intercept Pope where that road intersected the Warrenton Turnpike at Chantilly. Pope realized the Confederate plan, however, and positioned his men to cover the crossroads. There during an intense thunderstorm on September 1, he attacked Jackson near **Chantilly** at Ox Hill. The Federals drove off some of Jackson's units, but the battle ended in a stalemate, and Pope continued his retreat to Washington. The successful campaign gave Lee the initiative in Virginia and allowed him to launch the **Antietam Campaign** shortly afterward.

Pope bitterly blamed his subordinates, particularly Porter, for his defeat at Second Manassas and accused McClellan of trying to regain army command by deliberately withholding timely reinforcements so he would be defeated. These accusations perhaps were true, for two Union **corps** did not join Pope until the fight was over. McClellan went unpunished for his slowness in forwarding reinforcements and actually regained command of the Union forces around Washington. McClellan's supporter, Fitz John Porter, became the army's scapegoat. Relieved of command, he was convicted in a court-martial for disobeying orders and was discharged from the service (he later was exonerated in 1878). As for Pope, he never again led troops against the Confederacy and was sent to **Minnesota** to put down the **Sioux uprising**.

MANASSAS GAP, VIRGINIA, BATTLE OF (JULY 23, 1863). After the **Battle of Gettysburg**, **Robert E. Lee's Army of Northern Virginia** retreated up the **Shenandoah Valley**, while **George G. Meade's Army of the Potomac** paralleled it along the east side of the Blue Ridge Mountains. On July 23, 1863, Meade sent **William H. French's** III Corps to attack the Confederates at Manassas Gap. In poorly coordinated attacks, French forced **Richard Anderson's division** to withdraw toward the mountain crest, but there the Federals were stopped after **Robert Rodes's** division reinforced Anderson. French disengaged, the Confederates retreated into the Luray Valley, and the following day French occupied Front Royal. Total casualties for both sides in the small battle were approximately 440.

MANEY, GEORGE EARL (1826–1901) CSA. A native of **Tennessee**, Maney (MAY-nee) graduated from the University of Nashville in 1845. He entered the **Mexican War** as a 2nd lieutenant but was given a medical discharge before his **regiment** left the state. In 1847, Maney was commissioned a 1st lieutenant in the 3rd U.S. Dragoons and served in it for just over a year. Upon his discharge in 1848, he became a Tennessee lawyer.

Maney entered Confederate service in May 1861 as a captain in the 11th Tennessee. Days later, he was elected colonel of the 1st Tennessee and led the regiment to **Virginia**, where it served at **Cheat Mountain** in **Samuel R. Anderson's brigade.** Transferred to **Stonewall Jackson's** command, Maney served in Jackson's expedition to Romney in early 1862 and then took the regiment back to Tennessee after the fall of **Fort Donelson**. At **Shiloh**, he led a small brigade in **Benjamin F. Cheatham's division** and was highly praised for leading attacks on both days of battle.

Promoted to brigadier general in April 1862, Maney led his Tennessee brigade at **Perryville**, **Stones River**, **Chickamauga**, and **Missionary Ridge**. Serving in **W. H. T. Walker's** division of the **Army of Tennessee** at the latter battle, he was wounded in the right arm while supporting **Patrick Cleburne**. During the **Atlanta Campaign**, Maney served in both Cheatham's and **Alexander P. Stewart's** divisions and again earned accolades for his tenacious defense at **Kennesaw Mountain's** "Dead Angle." He temporarily commanded Cheatham's division at the **Battles of Atlanta** and **Jonesboro** and was wounded in the latter fight. Maney was given a surgeon's certificate of disability after Jonesboro and does not appear to have performed any field duty for the rest of the war.

After the war, Maney became a **railroad** president in Tennessee and was active in **Republican** politics. He served in the state legislature and in the 1880s and 1890s was the U.S. minister to Colombia, Bolivia, Paraguay, and Uruguay.

MANIGAULT, ARTHUR MIDDLETON (1824–1886) CSA. A member of a prominent **South Carolina** family, Manigault (MAN-i-GOH) dropped out of the College of Charleston in 1841 to enter the export business. After serving as a sergeant major in a local militia unit, he fought in the **Mexican War** as a 1st lieutenant in the Palmetto Regiment and was wounded three times. After the war, he returned to South Carolina, where he worked as a commission merchant and rice planter and became captain of a local militia **company**.

In April 1861, Manigault was commissioned lieutenant colonel and joined **P. G. T. Beauregard's** staff as adjutant and inspector general. After serving at **Fort Sumter**, he was appointed colonel of the 10th South Carolina in May and served as commander of the District of South Carolina under **Robert E. Lee**. In April 1862, the **regiment** was sent west and became part of **Jones M. Withers's brigade**. Manigault served in the **siege of Corinth, Mississippi,** and temporarily commanded the brigade when the town was evacuated. He also participated in the **Kentucky Campaign** but saw no combat other than some **skirmishing**. Manigault's first real battle was at **Stones River** with the **Army of Tennessee**, where he commanded **James Patton Anderson's** brigade and served as the "hinge" for **Braxton Bragg's** swinging maneuver on the first day. Although suffering heavy casualties (more than 500 men), Manigault pushed back the enemy and captured a battery of **artillery**. His bravery and leadership won him promotion to brigadier general in April 1863.

At **Chickamauga**, Manigault saw very hard fighting on the second day and later estimated that 300 of his men were shot down within three minutes. Taking a position on **Missionary Ridge** at Chattanooga, Tennessee, his brigade was among those Confederate units that were routed when the Federals attacked during the **Chattanooga Campaign**. Manigault barely escaped capture by riding through a hail of bullets. Serving in Anderson's **division** during the **Atlanta Campaign**, he fought in nearly all of the campaign's major battles and was wounded in the hand at **Resaca**. At **Peachtree Creek**, Manigault's and another brigade overran 16 Union cannons but were able to bring back only six, at a cost of 400 of Manigault's men. During the campaign, he became bitter over such wasteful **tactics** and, outside Atlanta, became outraged when he received orders to attack a strongly fortified Union position with only his brigade. Manigault reluctantly did so—twice—but failed. Such experiences made him quite critical of his superiors in his postwar memoirs. After fighting at **Jonesboro**, Manigault participated in the **Franklin and Nashville Campaign** and was wounded at Franklin by a bullet that clipped his ear and cut a groove across the side of his face. Although not initially appearing serious, the wound kept him off duty for the rest of the war.

After the war, Manigault lived in South Carolina as a rice planter and was elected state adjutant and inspector general in 1880. He died in 1886 as a result of complications from his head wound.

MANN, AMBROSE DUDLEY (1801–1889) CSA. A native of **Virginia**, Mann dropped out of **West Point** and became a lawyer. In 1842, he was appointed U.S. consul to the German states and in 1849 was a special agent to Hungary's Louis Kossuth. Mann returned to the United States after this second mission and served as the assistant secretary of state from 1853 to 1856.

When the Civil War began, Mann proposed that the Confederacy become economically self-sufficient and develop direct trade with Europe. As a result, **Jefferson Davis** appointed him, **William Lowndes Yancey**, and **Pierre A. Rost** special commissioners to Europe. Mann traveled to Great Britain in April 1861 and met with Foreign Secretary Lord Russell, but he failed to secure recognition for the Confederacy. Assigned to Belgium in September, he unsuccessfully lobbied King Leopold for two years to pressure Great Britain and France to recognize the Confederacy. Transferred to the Vatican in September 1863, Mann again enjoyed little success, except to convince the pope to oppose the Union's efforts to enlist European Catholics into its **army**. Although he had some success in gaining support for the Confederacy in European newspapers, Mann was a complete failure as a diplomat.

When Mann left for Europe in 1861, he vowed never to return to the South until the Confederacy won its independence. When the war ended, he kept his word and lived in Paris until his death.

MANSFIELD, JOSEPH KING FENNO (1803–1862) USA. A native of **Connecticut**, Mansfield entered **West Point** when he was 13 and graduated second in the class of 1822. As an **engineer**, he worked on defense fortifications and during the **Mexican War** served as Zachary Taylor's chief engineer and won three **brevets** for gallantry. In 1853, Secretary of War **Jefferson Davis** appointed Mansfield to the Inspector General's department with the staff rank of colonel.

Mansfield was the **U.S. Army's** inspector general when the Civil War began. In April 1861, he was placed in command of the **Department of Washington, D.C.**, and was promoted to brigadier general of regulars the following month. Putting his engineering skills to good use, Mansfield occupied **Virginia** along the Potomac River and began establishing strong fortifications around the capital. In March 1862, he was sent to **Fort Monroe, Virginia**, to serve under Maj. Gen. **John E. Wool**. Mansfield also led a **division** in the VII Corps at **Suffolk, Virginia**, before being placed in command of the **Army of the Potomac's** XII Corps in September 1862.

Mansfield joined his **corps** in **Maryland** while the **army** was pursuing **Robert E. Lee** during the **Antietam Campaign**. Five days later at Antietam, he was ordered to advance against the Confederate left wing. Mansfield marched through the East Woods to the edge of the famous cornfield and came under heavy fire. Ignoring protests from the men, he believed Union troops were mistakenly firing on his position and ordered the corps to cease firing. Mansfield then was shot in the stomach. Taken from the field, he died the next day. In March 1863, Mansfield was promoted to major general of volunteers posthumously.

MANSFIELD, LOUISIANA, BATTLE OF (APRIL 8, 1864). Also known as the Battle of Sabine Cross Roads, this clash turned back the Union's invasion of northwest Louisiana during the **Red River Campaign**. In March 1864, Union Maj. Gen. **Nathaniel P. Banks**, with approximately 30,000 men and **David D. Porter's** fleet, advanced up the Red River to Natchitoches (NAK-uh-tish), Louisiana. There he made the crucial mistake of leaving the gunboats and their supporting cannons and troops and marching toward Shreveport on a narrow road that traversed dense pine timber. During the march, Banks made another mistake by putting only part of his infantry at the head of his column, while the rest was left in the rear of a long wagon train.

Near Sabine Cross Roads, about three miles southeast of Mansfield, a small 8,800-man Confederate **army** under **Richard Taylor** blocked the road on the edge of a large field. When Banks's vanguard crossed the field shortly after noon, it took heavy fire from the Confederates and fell back to a defensive position on a hill behind a rail fence. By late afternoon, two **brigades** of William J. Landram's **division** were positioned there under the command of **Thomas E. G. Ransom**. In all, only 5,700 Federals were on the line; the rest were to the rear struggling to pass the wagon train.

Around 4:00 P.M., Taylor attacked before the enemy could finish defensive preparations. **J. J. Alfred Mouton's** division began the attack on the left, followed by **John G. Walker's** division on the right, and **Thomas Green's** cavalry on the flanks. Mouton was killed, but Brig. Gen. **Camille Polignac** kept the advance going. After suffering heavy casualties, the Confederates finally overran Ransom's position and forced him to fall back to a second line held by **Robert A. Cameron's** division. Cameron resisted for about an hour, but then he, too, was forced back. Panic soon gripped the Union soldiers, and the retreat turned into rout. Near dark, **William H. Emory's** division finally stopped the Confederates three miles from where the battle began.

In addition to inflicting 2,235 casualties on Banks, Taylor also captured 20 cannons, hundreds of **rifles**, and nearly 200 wagons filled with supplies. Confederate losses are estimated to have been about 1,000. Banks retreated during the night to **Pleasant Hill**, where he repulsed Taylor's attacks the next day and then abandoned the campaign.

MANSON, MAHLON DICKERSON (1820–1895) USA. A native of **Ohio**, Manson moved to **Indiana**, where he became a teacher. He also studied medicine (and became a druggist), served as a captain in the 5th Indiana during the **Mexican War,** and as a **Democrat** was elected to the state legislature in the 1850s.

Manson entered Union service in April 1861 as a captain in the 10th Indiana, but a week later he was commissioned its major. He became the **regiment's** colonel in May and later in the summer led it at the **Battle of Rich Mountain**. The regiment was mustered out of service afterward, but Manson reorganized it and reentered the **army** about six weeks later. In November, he was given a **brigade** command in the **Army of the Ohio**. Manson fought with it at **Mill Springs** in January 1862 and won a promotion to brigadier general of volunteers in March. During the 1862 **Kentucky Campaign**, he was wounded and captured at **Richmond**. After being **exchanged** in December, Manson fought against **John Pegram's** Confederate raiders in **Tennessee** during the summer of 1863. In late 1863, he sometimes temporarily commanded his **division** and even the XXIII Corps, but he returned to his brigade command in **Jacob D. Cox's** division for the 1864 **Atlanta Campaign**. At the **Battle of Resaca**, Manson was seriously wounded by a shell, and the injury forced him to resign his commission in December 1864 (he ran unsuccessfully for Indiana's lieutenant governor that autumn).

Returning to Indiana, Manson served in the **U.S. Congress** from 1871 to 1873 and became the state auditor, lieutenant governor, and a collector for the internal revenue service.

MARAIS DES CYGNES RIVER, KANSAS, BATTLE OF (OCTOBER 25, 1864). *See* MINE CREEK AND MARAIS DES CYGNES RIVER, KANSAS, BATTLES OF.

MARCH TO THE SEA (NOVEMBER 15–DECEMBER 21, 1864). This epic march by **William T. Sherman's** armies in **Georgia** proved the Confederacy was rapidly weakening in late 1864 and unable even to protect its vital interior. After the 1864 **Atlanta Campaign**, Confederate Gen. **John Bell Hood** tried to lure Sherman away from Atlanta by moving north with his **Army of Tennessee** and attacking Sherman's supply line. Sherman briefly gave chase but then decided a better **strategy** was to leave **George H. Thomas** to stop Hood while he took the bulk of his **armies** back to Atlanta to prepare his next move.

Sherman proposed to General-in-Chief **U. S. Grant** that he march his command from Atlanta through the Georgia interior to the Atlantic coast,

foraging off the land as he advanced. Besides destroying war-related **industries** and supplies, the raid would greatly demoralize Southern civilians and soldiers by demonstrating that the Confederacy was unable to protect even its heartland. Sherman promised to "make Georgia howl," (Marszalek, *Sherman*, p. 295) and Grant reluctantly approved the audacious plan. Picking only the fittest soldiers, Sherman led 62,000 men out of Atlanta on November 15, 1864. His command consisted of the **Army of Georgia's** XIV and XX Corps under **Henry W. Slocum**, the **Army of the Tennessee's** XV and XVII Corps under **Oliver O. Howard**, and **H. Judson Kilpatrick's** cavalry **division**. For the next five weeks, the Federals cut a swath from Atlanta to Savannah. The only Confederates facing them were about 8,000 men in **Gustavus W. Smith's** Georgia militia and **Joseph Wheeler's** small cavalry **corps**. By placing his men in separate columns on roughly parallel roads, Sherman often advanced on a 60-mile-wide front and forced the Confederates to spread thin their troops. Sherman skillfully kept the Confederates off guard until the last possible minute before converging on a particular target. Because of the Federals' overwhelming numbers, there were no major battles in the campaign (**Griswoldville** being the largest), but there were frequent small clashes at such places as **Buck Head Creek** and **Waynesborough**.

Forced to live off the land, Sherman had regularly appointed commissary officers who took needed supplies, but they usually left enough food behind to feed the civilians through the winter. Excessive confiscation, however, did come from **bummers**, or unauthorized soldiers, who left the ranks and frequently took everything they could carry. Destruction was widespread during the march, but the number of private homes torched has probably been exaggerated. Public property and buildings (such as at the state capitol of Milledgeville) were routinely destroyed, as were **railroads** (which were turned into "**Sherman's neckties**" and many barns and warehouses. Private houses were rarely burned, although they were often vandalized by the bummers. Personal violence, including rape—another evil associated with the march—was rare and was aimed more at slaves than at whites.

Sherman disappeared from Atlanta in mid-November and was not heard from again until he reached the coast at **Savannah** on December 9. There he began encircling the 18,000 Confederates under **William J. Hardee** and captured **Fort McAllister**, but Hardee escaped by moving north on the night of December 20. The following day when Sherman entered the city, he jubilantly wired **Abraham Lincoln** that he was presenting him Savannah as a Christmas present. The March to the Sea was a huge success. With a loss of approximately 2,200 men, Sherman destroyed much of the Confederacy's ability to wage war and greatly demoralized Southern civilians and soldiers by demonstrating that Union armies could raid with impunity deep inside the Confederacy.

MARCY, RANDOLPH BARNES (1812–1887) USA. A native of **Massachusetts**, Marcy graduated from **West Point** in 1832 and served with the infantry in **Michigan** and **Wisconsin** before fighting in the **Mexican War** as a captain. Afterward, he was posted to the southwestern frontier, where he escorted settlers and explored. Marcy also participated in the **Utah Expedition** and served as Utah's acting inspector general. His voluminous exploration notes, which were written during his frontier service, were published by the War Department in 1859 under the title *The Prairie Traveler*. That same year, Marcy was appointed paymaster for the Pacific Northwest with the staff rank of major.

In 1860, Marcy's subordinate, **George B. McClellan**, married his daughter. Because of this connection, Marcy was brought east when the Civil War began, and in August 1861 he was appointed senior colonel and head of the Inspector General's office. In that capacity, he served as McClellan's chief of staff during the **Peninsula**, **Seven Days**, and **Antietam Campaigns**. Marcy was promoted to brigadier general of volunteers in late September 1862, but the Senate failed to confirm the appointment (perhaps because of his close ties to McClellan), and the commission expired in March 1863. For the rest of the war, he served on inspection duty in various **departments** and at army headquarters in **Washington, D.C.** For his war service, Marcy was **brevetted** brigadier general of regulars and major general of volunteers.

Marcy remained in the **army** after the war, and in 1878 was appointed inspector general with the staff rank of brigadier general. He remained in that position until retiring in 1881.

MARINE CORPS, CONFEDERATE STATES. The Confederate Marine Corps was authorized in March 1861, by the same legislation that created the **Confederate navy**. The corps originally was to consist of six **companies** and be commanded by a major, but this was amended in May to 10 companies and a colonel. The corps also was to operate under all **U.S. Marine Corps** laws and regulations that did not conflict with the two acts creating the Confederate Corps. Although eventually authorized to include 46 officers and 944 men, the corps never was that large.

In May 1861, former **U.S. Army** paymaster **Lloyd J. Beall** was appointed the corps' colonel, and he commanded the corps for its entire existence. Of the 56 officers appointed to the corps during the war, 19 were former U.S. Marine officers. The Marines served onboard many of the Confederacy's warships, including the *Virginia* and *Alabama*. Its companies also manned **artillery** pieces at **Drewry's Bluff, Virginia**; **Pensacola, Florida**; Hilton Head, South Carolina; and **Fort Fisher, North Carolina**; and garrisoned the naval stations at **Mobile, Alabama**; **Savannah, Georgia**; **Charleston, South Carolina**; Charlotte and **Wilmington, North Carolina**; and **Richmond, Virginia**. Besides serving as guards onboard ships, the corps also participated in numerous coastal actions, such as **First** and **Second Drewry's Bluff, Mobile Bay**, and **Spanish Fort**. At war's end, displaced Marines and sailors were organized into a battalion at Richmond under **Richard S. Ewell**. This combined battalion fought at **Sailor's Creek**, where most of the Marines were killed or captured, and the survivors **surrendered** at **Appomattox**. The last organized Confederate Marine unit surrendered at Mobile in May 1865.

MARINE CORPS, UNITED STATES. Originally formed in 1775, the U.S. Marine Corps was expanded to include 93 officers and 3,074 men when the Civil War began in 1861. During the war, however, its efficiency suffered because some of its best officers joined the Confederacy, and patronage was used extensively to appoint new junior officers.

Marines participated in the first large battle at **First Manassas**, but commandant Col. John C. Harris worked hard to maintain the corps' separate identity by generally avoiding participation in **U.S. Army** operations. He largely was successful, and in 1863 Corps supporters defeated a congressional resolution that would have placed it under **army** control. When Harris died in 1864, he was replaced by Maj. Jacob Zeilin, who continued Harris's policy. Except for several hundred Marines who participated in the January 1865 assault on **Fort Fisher, North Carolina**, the Marines largely confined themselves to serving on ships and manning coastal batteries. During the war, 17 Marines earned the **Medal of Honor**, 148 were killed in action, and 312 died from other causes.

MARION, VIRGINIA, BATTLE OF (DECEMBER 16–18, 1864). On December 1, 1864, Union cavalryman Maj. Gen. **George Stoneman** left Knoxville, Tennessee, with 5,500 troopers on a raid against **Saltville, Virginia**. He brushed away light Confederate opposition and occupied Bristol, Virginia, on the night of December 13. On December 16, Stoneman continued toward Saltville, where Confederate Maj. Gen. **John C.**

Breckinridge was concentrating his 2,100 men, while **Alvan C. Gillem's brigade** advanced on Marion, 12 miles to the southwest. Gillem drove Brig. Gen. **John C. Vaughn's** small Confederate force out of Marion and beyond Wytheville and then destroyed the area's lead mines and **railroad**. That same evening, Breckinridge left a few men to face Stoneman at Saltville, while he took the rest of his command to Marion. On December 17, Breckinridge attacked **Stephen G. Burbridge's** Union brigade, which was guarding a covered bridge across the Holston River near Marion. Stoneman soon arrived to assist Burbridge and recalled Gillem, who was moving on Saltville. Stoneman attacked Breckinridge throughout December 18, and the Confederates finally withdrew toward Wytheville that night after running low on ammunition. In the fighting around Marion, both sides together lost an estimated 300 men. After the battle, Stoneman rode to Saltville and captured it on December 21.

MARKS' MILLS, ARKANSAS, BATTLE OF (APRIL 25, 1864). In the spring of 1864, Union Maj. Gen. **Frederick Steele** launched the **Camden Expedition** in **Arkansas** to threaten Shreveport, Louisiana, from the north, while **Nathaniel P. Banks** advanced on the city from **Louisiana** in the **Red River Campaign**. Steele reached Camden, Arkansas, in April, but he suffered from a lack of supplies and was confronted by Gen. **Edmund Kirby Smith**, who had brought thousands of Confederate troops to Arkansas after Banks had been defeated at **Mansfield, Louisiana**. On April 24, Confederate cavalryman **Joseph O. Shelby** learned that a Union supply train was returning to **Pine Bluff** from Camden. Riding 45 miles that night, he attacked the 240 wagons and their approximately 1,700-man escort at Marks' Mills at dawn, April 25. In fierce fighting, Union commander Col. Francis M. Drake was wounded, and the Union defense collapsed. All of the empty wagons and 1,300 of Drake's men were captured, while the Confederates lost only 293 men. When Steele learned of this disaster and that Banks was retreating on the Red River, he withdrew from Camden on the night of April 26 and retreated to **Little Rock**.

MARMADUKE, JOHN SAPPINGTON (1833–1887) CSA. A native of **Missouri**, Marmaduke attended Lexington's Masonic College and Yale and Harvard Universities before receiving an appointment to **West Point** in 1853. He graduated near the bottom of his class in 1857 and went on to serve with the infantry in **Kansas** and the **Utah Expedition**.

On garrison duty in **New Mexico** during the **secession** crisis, Marmaduke returned home on furlough to discuss his future plans with his father, a former Missouri governor. Although his father opposed the Confederacy, Marmaduke resigned his 1st lieutenant's commission in April 1861 and entered Confederate service as a colonel in the Missouri State Guard. After the guard was defeated at Booneville in June, he became disgusted with state service and resigned his commission. Traveling to **Richmond, Virginia**, Marmaduke received an appointment in the **Confederate army** as a 1st lieutenant.

Marmaduke returned west and joined Brig. Gen. **William J. Hardee's** staff for a short time before being appointed lieutenant colonel and commander of the 1st Arkansas Infantry Battalion in the summer of 1861. Sent to **Kentucky**, the battalion was redesignated the 3rd Confederate Infantry, and Marmaduke was appointed its colonel. After winning praise and receiving a wound at **Shiloh**, he was given command of his own **brigade** in Hardee's corps and led it during the **siege of Corinth, Mississippi**. Marmaduke was transferred to the **Trans-Mississippi Department** in September 1862 and was put in command of Maj. Gen. **Thomas C. Hindman's** cavalry **division** with the rank of acting brigadier general. He again earned much praise for his leadership at **Cane Hill** and **Prairie Grove**, and his appointment was made permanent in November.

In 1863, Marmaduke led his cavalry division on two Missouri raids, fought at the **Battle of Helena**, and opposed the Federal advance from Helena to **Little Rock, Arkansas**. After he questioned Brig. Gen. **L. Marshall Walker's** courage at Helena, he was challenged to a duel in September and mortally wounded Walker. **Sterling Price** arrested Marmaduke but then returned him to duty when almost all of Marmaduke's officers requested he do so. After the Federals captured Little Rock in September, Marmaduke officially was released from arrest and the following month led his division in an unsuccessful attack on **Pine Bluff**.

During the **Camden Expedition**, Marmaduke fought at Elkins' Ferry **Prairie d'Ane**, **Poison Spring**, and **Jenkins' Ferry**. Afterward, he took one brigade to Lake Village, Arkansas, where he harassed shipping on the Mississippi River and fought the Federals at **Ditch Bayou**. Marmaduke's last service was in **Price's Missouri Raid**. During the retreat, he was captured in fighting near **Marais des Cygnes River, Kansas**, and was imprisoned at **Fort Warren, Massachusetts**, until war's end. While being held captive, Marmaduke was promoted to major general in March 1865.

Marmaduke was released from **prison** in August 1865 and briefly lived in Europe. Returning to Missouri, he became a commission merchant, an insurance agent, editor of the *Journal of Agriculture*, and a member of the Missouri Railway Commission. Marmaduke was elected governor in 1884 and died in office.

MARR, JOHN QUINCY (1825–1861) CSA. A native of **Virginia** and an 1846 **Virginia Military Institute** graduate, Marr taught at his alma mater and became his county's treasurer and sheriff. He organized a local militia **company** just before the **secession** crisis and was a delegate to the Virginia secession convention. Marr entered Confederate service as a captain in May 1861 and took his company to garrison Fairfax Court House. In the predawn hours of June 1, Fairfax was attacked by Union cavalry, and Marr was killed. He generally is recognized as the first Confederate killed in the war.

MARSHALL, HUMPHREY (1812–1872) CSA. A native of **Kentucky**, Marshall graduated from **West Point** near the bottom of the 1832 class. After cavalry service in the Black Hawk War, he resigned his 2nd lieutenant's commission less than a year later and became a successful lawyer. Marshall also became active in the state militia and served as colonel of the 1st Kentucky Cavalry in the **Mexican War**. Entering **Whig** politics after the war, he was elected to the **U.S. Congress** in 1848 and 1850 and became a U.S. commissioner to China in 1852. Upon his return to Kentucky, Marshall was elected to Congress again as a **Know-Nothing** in 1854 and 1856.

When the Civil War began, Marshall supported Kentucky's neutrality. When the Confederates invaded, however, he feared arrest by Federal authorities and fled to **Richmond, Virginia**, where he was commissioned a Confederate brigadier general in October 1861. Marshall was given command of the **Army of Southwest Virginia and Eastern Kentucky** and campaigned in the rugged mountains of that region. He claimed that **Jefferson Davis** had given him an independent command and promised him enough men and support to liberate Kentucky. Nothing came of Marshall's claim, and he was reduced mainly to **skirmishing** and fighting guerrillas. This belief that he had a special agreement with the government made him argumentative and difficult.

After skirmishing in Kentucky in January 1862, Marshall was elected to the **Confederate Congress** in February, but he declined to take his seat at that time. After **Edmund Kirby Smith** was put in command of Knoxville, Tennessee, in March 1862, Marshall submitted his resignation in June. To participate in the **Kentucky Campaign**, he asked for reinstatement and resumed his command. During the invasion, Marshall's 4,500 men advanced along the mountains to attack the Union garrison at Cumberland Gap, Tennessee, but the Federals escaped, and he failed to reach the main **army** in time to fight at **Perryville**. Marshall remained in Kentucky for a while after the Confederates retreated but then withdrew to southwestern **Virginia**. After being relieved of command in April 1863 and ordered to report to **Joseph E. Johnston** in Chattanooga, Tennessee, he resigned for the second time, in June. For the rest of the war, Marshall served in Congress as a member of the influential Military Affairs Committee and generally supported **conscription**, while opposing many **taxes** and the **suspension of the writ of habeas corpus**.

When the war ended, Marshall fled to **Texas**, but he eventually settled in **Louisiana**. He practiced law there before returning to his native Kentucky and starting a practice there.

MARSTON, GILMAN (1811–1890) USA. A native of **New Hampshire**, Marston taught school to put himself through Dartmouth College. After graduating in 1837, he served as a headmaster in **Indiana** for a time and then entered Harvard Law School. Marston graduated in 1840, became a New Hampshire lawyer, and entered politics. He was elected to the state legislature in 1845 (serving 13 terms by the time of his death), was a delegate at the 1850 constitutional convention, and served in the **U.S. Congress** from 1859 to 1863 (although his military duties kept him frequently absent).

When the Civil War began, Marston raised the 2nd New Hampshire while still a congressman and was appointed its colonel in June 1861. As part of **Ambrose Burnside's brigade**, he was wounded leading his **regiment** at **First Manassas** and then went on to fight in the **Peninsula** and **Seven Days Campaigns** with the **Army of the Potomac**. In the autumn of 1862, Marston assumed command of the garrison at Centreville, Virginia, protecting the Orange & Alexandria Railroad.

Promoted to brigadier general of volunteers in November, Marston rejoined his regiment and fought at **Fredericksburg**. Afterward, he was transferred to **Washington, D.C.**, and in the summer of 1863 established the **prison** at **Point Lookout**. Marston served as prison commandant until May 1864, when he was given a brigade command in the 1st Division of the **Army of the James's** XVIII Corps. After leading the brigade in the disastrous charge at **Cold Harbor**, he at times commanded the **division** during the early part of the **Petersburg Campaign**. Marston received the Thanks of the New Hampshire legislature for his war service but, oddly, did not receive any **brevets**, despite his political influence. He was discharged from the volunteers in April 1865.

After the war, Marston returned to his political career in New Hampshire. He again served several terms in the state legislature, was a delegate to the 1876 constitutional convention, served in the U.S. House of Representatives from 1865 to 1867, and for a few months in 1889 was in the U.S. Senate.

MARTIN, JAMES GREEN (1819–1878) CSA. A native of **North Carolina**, Martin graduated from **West Point** in 1840 and served with the **artillery** in New England. During the **Mexican War**, he rose to the rank of captain, lost his right arm at Churubusco, and received one **brevet** for gallantry. Because of the loss of his limb, Martin came to be known as "Old One Wing." After Mexico, he served at numerous posts and was on staff duty in **Kansas** when the Civil War began.

Martin resigned his commission in June 1861 and was appointed captain and adjutant general of North Carolina troops. As adjutant, he had great influence with Gov. **John W. Ellis** and convinced him to employ **blockade runners** to bring needed supplies into the state. Martin was placed in command of all North Carolina troops in September with the rank of major general. Faced with an invasion from the sea and responding to the Union threat to **Richmond, Virginia**, he raised 12,000 troops above the state's quota and sent many of the men to **Virginia**. Martin's excellent service probably made North Carolina soldiers the Confederacy's best equipped and best trained troops.

Desiring a field command, Martin was appointed a Confederate brigadier general in May 1862. He resigned in July believing the appointment conflicted with his state duties, but he was reappointed in August. Placed in command of the District of North Carolina, Martin did not see any combat for months. In October 1863, he raised an infantry **brigade** and led it in the campaign against **New Bern, North Carolina**, in February 1864. When the enemy threatened Richmond in the May 1864 **Bermuda Hundred Campaign**, Martin's brigade was rushed to Virginia. After successfully attacking the enemy's forward positions, the men hoisted Martin onto their shoulders and cried out, "Three cheers for Old One Wing" (Davis, *The Confederate General*, vol. 4 p.161).

Martin remained in Virginia and became part of **Robert Hoke's division** of the **Army of Northern Virginia**. He fought at **Cold Harbor** and correctly predicted to **Robert E. Lee** that **U. S. Grant** would withdraw and move to Petersburg (Lee came to respect Martin highly and once said, "General Martin is one to whom North Carolina owes a debt she can never repay" [Davis, ed., *The Confederate General,* vol. 4, 161]). After fighting in the early stages of the **Petersburg Campaign**, Martin was relieved of his brigade command in late June because of poor health and was charged with protecting the Southside and the Richmond & Danville **railroads**. He was transferred again in mid-July to command the District of Western North Carolina and remained there until war's end. After the war, Martin remained in his native state, became a lawyer, and was active in the Episcopal Church.

MARTIN, WILLIAM THOMPSON (1823–1910) CSA. A native of **Kentucky**, Martin graduated from Centre College in 1840 and became a Unionist **Mississippi** lawyer and district attorney. When Mississippi seceded, he joined his adopted state and raised the Adams County Cavalry Company. Sent to **Virginia** in the spring of 1861, the **company** became part of the Jeff Davis Legion, and Martin was promoted to major.

After participating in some **skirmishes** and raids, Martin was promoted to lieutenant colonel in February 1862. He participated in **J. E. B. Stuart's Ride** around the **Army of the Potomac** that June and earned a promotion to colonel. Martin remained with the Jeff Davis Legion and fought with the **Army of Northern Virginia** through the **Seven Days** and **Antietam Campaigns**. When he was appointed brigadier general in December 1862, he was transferred west.

In March 1863, Martin was given command of a cavalry **division** under **Joseph Wheeler** in the **Army of Tennessee** and led it through the **Kentucky, Tullahoma, Chickamauga**, and **Knoxville Campaigns**. Promoted to major general in November, he continued to serve in Wheeler's cavalry **corps** through the 1864 **Atlanta Campaign** and in **Wheeler's Raid** into **Tennessee** during the latter part of the campaign. After resisting **William T. Sherman's March to the Sea** in late 1864, Martin and Wheeler parted company. Martin complained that his commander did not keep him supplied, and Wheeler was angry that Martin did not follow orders to participate in an attack in August. Wheeler relieved Martin of command, and he was transferred to command the District of Northwest Mississippi in early 1865.

After the war, Martin remained in Mississippi and became involved in **Democratic** politics. He served 12 years in the state senate and attended Democratic national conventions for 32 years. Martin also served as a trustee of the University of Mississippi and Jefferson College and became president of a company that was involved in **railroad** construction.

MARTINDALE, JOHN HENRY (1815–1881) USA. A native of **New York**, Martindale was the son of a **Whig** congressman. He graduated third in the **West Point** class of 1835 but resigned from the **U.S. Army**

the next year when he was not assigned to the **engineers**. Martindale then became a lawyer and served two terms as a district attorney.

Martindale entered Union service in August 1861 when he was commissioned a brigadier general of volunteers. Given command of a **brigade** in the **Army of the Potomac**, he fought in the **Peninsula Campaign** as part of the III Corps' 1st Division. Afterward, Martindale's brigade was assigned to the 1st Division of **Fitz John Porter's** V Corps. Porter and Martindale clashed at the **Battle of Malvern Hill**. When Martindale declared he would surrender before abandoning his wounded, Porter relieved him of command and ordered an investigation into Martindale's behavior. A court of inquiry cleared Martindale in October 1862, but he was transferred in February 1863 to take command of the District of Washington, D.C.

In May 1864, Martindale was given command of an XVIII Corps **division**. He fought at **Cold Harbor** and in the **Bermuda Hundred** and **Petersburg Campaigns** and even briefly commanded the **corps** in July. Poor health forced Martindale to resign his commission in September. At war's end, he was **brevetted** major general of volunteers to rank, ironically, from the Battle of Malvern Hill.

After the war, Martindale resumed his New York law practice. He served as the state's attorney general from 1867 to 1869 and became vice president of the National Asylum for Disabled Volunteer Soldiers.

MARYLAND. Maryland was one of the **border states** whose loyalties were divided during the Civil War. With slaves representing about 13 percent of the 1860 population of 687,049, many eastern Marylanders were pro-Confederate, while most western Marylanders had strong family and business connections to the North that made them loyal to the Union. During the **election of 1860**, Maryland's southern sympathies were evidenced when **John C. Breckinridge** carried the state. Baltimore, particularly, had a large pro-Confederate population, and there the first violence erupted after the fall of **Fort Sumter**. When **Benjamin Butler's Massachusetts** soldiers marched through the city on April 17, 1861, they were attacked by a secessionist mob. The **Baltimore Riot** killed and wounded a number of people and led to the song "Maryland, My Maryland."

Abraham Lincoln had to keep Maryland in the Union because if it seceded, **Washington, D.C.**, would be surrounded by Confederate territory. Secessionists dominated the legislature, but Gov. **Thomas H. Hicks** was a moderate Unionist and prevented **secession** by delaying calling the legislature into session until the Union gained control of the state. When Hicks finally did convene the legislature, it condemned the war effort but did not call for a secession convention. Lincoln used Butler's troops to maintain control of Baltimore and **suspended the writ of habeas corpus** to fight disloyalty. Federal authorities even arrested Baltimore's mayor and 19 members of the legislature for suspicion of disloyalty. The state supplied soldiers to both sides, although Governor Hicks officially ignored Lincoln's 1861 call for volunteers. About a third of the white Marylanders who fought in the war joined the Confederacy. Maryland's soldiers sometimes had the misfortune of fighting each other, as happened at **Front Royal, Virginia**, in 1862. The war swept over the state on several occasions. **Robert E. Lee** hoped to gain Maryland for the Confederacy in 1862 by launching the **Antietam Campaign**, which resulted in the bloodiest single day of the war at the Battle of Antietam. Lee's **army** also crossed and recrossed Maryland during the **Gettysburg Campaign**, and **Jubal A. Early** entered it and fought at the **Monocacy** during **Early's 1864 Washington Raid**. Besides these campaigns, frequent Confederate cavalry raids also disrupted life in the state. *See also* BATTLE OF FALLING WATERS; BATTLE OF SOUTH MOUNTAIN, MARYLAND.

MARYLAND CAMPAIGN. *See* ANTIETAM, MARYLAND, CAMPAIGN AND BATTLE OF.

MASON, JAMES MURRAY (1798–1871) CSA. Born in **Washington, D.C.**, Mason was the grandson of Revolutionary War and Constitutional Convention figure George Mason. After graduating from the University of Pennsylvania, he studied law at the College of William and Mary and became a **Virginia** lawyer and politician. Arrogant and confident, Mason gained the support of the western Virginia back country and became a powerful political figure. He served in the state legislature in the 1820s, was a delegate to the 1829–30 constitutional convention, and was elected to the U.S. House of Representatives in 1838 and to the U.S. Senate in 1847. A close ally of **John C. Calhoun**, Mason supported **states rights**, served as chairman of the Foreign Relations Committee, and drafted the **Fugitive Slave Act** in 1850. After **Abraham Lincoln** was elected president in 1860, Mason resigned from the Senate in March 1861 (before Virginia seceded) and entered the Provisional **Confederate Congress** in July, where he chaired the Foreign Relations Committee.

   Jefferson Davis appointed Mason an envoy to Great Britain to win British recognition of the Confederacy. Along with fellow diplomat **John Slidell**, he was captured aboard the British steamer *Trent* in November 1861 and was held **prisoner** in **Fort Warren, Massachusetts**. The *Trent* **Affair** touched off an international incident, and the Lincoln administration finally was forced to release the two envoys after Britain threatened to intervene in the war. Upon his release from **prison**, Mason traveled to Great Britain and tried to gain recognition through **Cotton Diplomacy** but never was successful. Abandoning that mission in late 1862, he concentrated on selling bonds, securing loans for the Confederacy, and improving trade. Davis ended Mason's mission a year later, but Mason remained in Europe as a Confederate commissioner and divided his time between London and Paris.

When the war ended, Mason moved to Canada in 1866, but he took advantage of President **Andrew Johnson's** amnesty offer and returned to Virginia in 1869.

MASON, JOHN SANFORD (1824–1897) USA. A native of **Ohio**, Mason graduated from **West Point** in 1847. He was on garrison duty in Mexico during the **Mexican War** and then served at various posts across the country. When the Civil War began, Mason was a captain in the 11th U.S. Infantry at Fort Vancouver, Washington Territory.

In October 1861, Mason was appointed colonel of the 4th Ohio. He led it in **James Shields's** operations in western **Virginia** that autumn and winter and in **Stonewall Jackson's 1862 Shenandoah Valley Campaign**. Sent to the **Army of the Potomac**, Mason served under **George B. McClellan** at **Harrison's Landing** and at **Antietam**, where he was **brevetted** for gallantry. At **Fredericksburg**, he took command of **Nathan Kimball's** brigade in the II Corps' 3rd Division after Kimball was wounded, but then Mason was severely wounded while attacking Marye's Heights. This wound kept Mason off duty until April 1863. Sometime after Fredericksburg, he was appointed brigadier general of volunteers, effective from November 1862. Upon returning to duty, Mason recruited in Ohio, served on staff duty in **California**, and was appointed commander of the District of Arizona. He was mustered out of the volunteers in April 1866 with **brevets** through the rank of brigadier general of volunteers.

After the war, Mason remained in the **army** as a major, and after serving on the frontier, he retired in 1888 as colonel of the 9th U.S. Infantry.

MASSACHUSETTS. Massachusetts played a major role in Civil War history as the center of **abolitionism** and a powerful **industrial** state that was key to the Union victory. It also was the home state of such figures as **Joseph Hooker**, **Nathaniel P. Banks**, **Darius Couch**, **Charles Sumner**, **Benjamin F. Butler**, **Charles Francis Adams**, **Gustavus V. Fox**, **William Lloyd Garrison**, **Julia Ward Howe**, and **Robert Gould Shaw**.

Under war governor **John A. Andrews**, Massachusetts was the first state to answer **Abraham Lincoln's** 1861 call for volunteers when Butler led a detachment of soldiers to **Washington, D.C.**, and was attacked in the **Baltimore Riot**. Out of an 1860 population of 1,231,066, the state contributed 152,048 men to the Union cause (this was many more than the state's quota). One of its most famous units was the **54th Massachusetts**, which was one of the Union's first **regiments** of **black troops**. Massachusetts's **Springfield Armory** also helped arm the Union by producing nearly 800,000 **Springfield Rifles**.

MASSACHUSETTS 54TH REGIMENT. Having always been a hotbed of **abolitionism**, **Massachusetts** formed one of the first **regiments** of **black troops** in the Union **army**. In 1863, Gov. **John A. Andrews** received permission from the federal government to organize a regiment of free Massachusetts blacks. Native-son **Robert Gould Shaw**, whose father was a renowned abolitionist, was chosen to command the regiment, and the regiment's officers were to be white. When it became obvious that there were not enough interested free blacks in the state to form the regiment, blacks from other states were allowed to join. The 54th Massachusetts finally was mustered into service in May 1863.

Sent to the **Department of the South**, the regiment fought **skirmishes** in **South Carolina**, **Georgia**, and **Florida**. At first, the men suffered from intense discrimination from white comrades, and the men of the 54th once refused any pay until the pay of black soldiers was made equal to that of whites. Gradually, the regiment earned the respect of its fellow soldiers. Its most famous battle was in July 1863, when it participated in the attack on **Fort Wagner, North Carolina**. Among the leading assault troops, the men gallantly went forward but were slaughtered by the Confederates. Shaw was killed in the unsuccessful attack, and the regiment lost 272 out of 650 men engaged. Sergeant William H. Carney was awarded the **Medal of Honor** for planting the regiment's colors on the enemy works. When his comrades attempted later to retrieve Shaw's body, the Confederates sneered, "We have buried him with his niggers!" (McPherson, *Battle Cry of Freedom,* 687). Rather than taking this as an insult, Shaw's family saw it as a point of honor and refused to have the body moved afterward. Colonel Edward N. Hallowell took command of the regiment after Shaw's death and led it until it was recalled to Massachusetts to receive a hero's welcome in 1864.

MASSACRES. *See* BAXTER SPRINGS, KANSAS; BUCK HEAD CREEK, GEORGIA; CENTRALIA, MISSOURI; FORT PILLOW,

TENNESSEE; LAWRENCE, KANSAS; NUECES RIVER, TEXAS; POISON SPRING, ARKANSAS; SALTVILLE, VIRGINIA; SAND CREEK, COLORADO; SHELTON LAUREL, NORTH CAROLINA.

MATAMOROS, MEXICO. This Mexican town, located at the mouth of the Rio Grande, served as an important port of entry for the Confederates as the **blockade** became increasingly effective. Thousands of bales of cotton were sent to the town from **Texas** to be shipped to Europe on neutral European ships or on **blockade runners**. Because Matamoros was foreign territory, the **U.S. Navy** could not interfere with this trade, except to catch Confederate blockade runners outside the port. Matamoros was sometimes controlled by forces loyal to French-imposed **Emperor Maximilian** and sometimes by rebel forces under Benito Juárez. No matter which side occupied it, however, they both accommodated the Confederates because of the money to be made in running cotton and supplies for the South.

MATTHIES, CHARLES (OR KARL) LEOPOLD (1824–1868) USA. A native of Prussia, Matthies was a university-educated former Prussian soldier who immigrated to the United States in 1849 and opened a liquor business in **Iowa**. During the **secession** crisis, he supposedly was the first person to offer a military **company** to the Union **army** when he offered one he had raised to Gov. **Samuel J. Kirkwood** in January 1861.

Matthies entered Union service in May 1861 as a captain in the 1st Iowa. After being promoted to lieutenant colonel in July and fighting at **Island No. 10**, he was promoted to colonel while participating in the **siege of Corinth, Mississippi**, after the **Battle of Shiloh**. Matthies fought at **Iuka** (where he lost nearly half of his men) and **Corinth**, and then commanded various **brigades** in different **corps** over the next several months.

Matthies was promoted to brigadier general in April 1863 and led a brigade in the 3rd Division of the **Army of the Tennessee's** XV Corps during the **Vicksburg Campaign**. Later in 1863, he was dispatched to reinforce Chattanooga, Tennessee, and was wounded in the head while fighting at **Missionary Ridge** during the **Chattanooga Campaign**. When he returned to duty, Matthies temporarily led a XV Corps **division**, but he resigned his commission in May 1864 because of poor health.

After leaving the army, Matthies returned to Iowa and served in the state senate.

MAURY, DABNEY HERNDON (1822–1900) CSA. A native of **Virginia**, Maury (MAW-ree) was raised by his uncle **Matthew Fontaine**

Maury after his father died. After graduating from the University of Virginia in 1842, he entered **West Point** and graduated in 1846. Maury served in the **Mexican War** and received a crippling wound to his left arm and a **brevet** for gallantry. After the war, he taught a variety of subjects at the academy from 1847 to 1852 and then spent four years on duty in **Texas**. From 1856 to 1860, Maury was superintendent of the cavalry school at Carlisle Barracks, Pennsylvania.

Maury was serving in the **New Mexico Territory** as a 1st lieutenant and adjutant general during the **secession** crisis. He submitted his resignation in May 1861, but it was refused. Maury was later dismissed from the **U.S. Army** in June 1861 for apparently speaking out in favor of the Confederacy. He received a Confederate commission as captain of cavalry in July and for the rest of the year served as adjutant general for **Joseph E. Johnston** and **Theophilus H. Holmes** in **Virginia**. In February 1862, Maury was promoted to colonel and was made **Earl Van Dorn's** chief of staff in the **Trans-Mississippi Department**. Van Dorn highly praised his conduct at **Pea Ridge**, and Maury won promotion to brigadier general in March 1862.

Accompanying the **Army of the West** to **Mississippi**, Maury led a **brigade** in **Samuel Jones's** division during the **siege of Corinth** and commanded the rear guard when the city was evacuated in the spring of 1862. Taking command of a **division** in June, he at first was resented by the men because of his strict **discipline**, but they came to respect his ability and nicknamed him "Little Dab" (small in stature, Maury also was referred to as "Puss in Boots"). Maury led the division at the **Battles of Iuka** and **Corinth** and was promoted to major general in November.

In early 1863, Maury's division helped defend **Vicksburg, Mississippi**, at **Snyder's Bluff** and Fort Pemberton. He briefly commanded the **Department of East Tennessee** in April, but in May **Jefferson Davis** specifically picked him to take over the District of the Gulf at Mobile, Alabama. Maury held this position until war's end, and Davis made sure no officers his senior were placed in the area. He served well at Mobile, building up its defenses and helping support other areas with his men. Maury also briefly commanded the **Department of Alabama, Mississippi, and East Louisiana** in the summer of 1864 but soon resumed his post at Mobile. It was during his absence that **David G. Farragut** won the **Battle of Mobile Bay**. Unable to prevent the capture of **Spanish Fort** and **Fort Blakely** in April 1865 during the **Mobile Campaign**, Maury finally was forced to evacuate Mobile. His men then formed a division in **Richard Taylor's** command at Meridian, Mississippi, and were surrendered in May.

After the war, Maury moved to Virginia and opened the Classical and Mathematical Academy at Fredericksburg. He then settled in **Louisiana** and worked as an express agent and naval stores manufacturer. Maury founded the Southern Historical Society in 1868 and chaired its executive committee until 1886. Retaining his strong sense of honor, he refused an offer by the corrupt Louisiana Lottery Company to work for $30,000 a year, and when a yellow fever epidemic struck **New Orleans** in 1868, he remained in the city and volunteered as a nurse. After serving as U.S. minister to Colombia from 1885 to 1889, Maury moved to **Illinois**.

MAURY, MATTHEW FONTAINE (1806–1873) CSA. A native of **Virginia**, Maury (MAW-ree) was the uncle of **Dabney Herndon Maury** and raised him and his brother after their father died. Maury entered the **U.S. Navy** as a midshipman in 1825 and rose to the rank of lieutenant in 1836. After publishing the influential *A New Theoretical and Practical Treatise on Navigation*, he suffered a crippling leg injury that ended his seafaring career. Maury was transferred to the navy's Depot of Charts and Instruments and devoted himself to navigation, hydrography, and meteorology. He published several influential works, most notably *The Physical Geography of the Sea,* and became known as the "Pathfinder of the Seas." In 1853, Maury was promoted to commander, and an international conference was held in Belgium because of his publications. He was placed on the retired list against his will in 1855 and blamed **Florida** Sen. **Stephen R. Mallory**, who headed the navy committee and became the future Confederate secretary of the navy.

When Virginia seceded in the spring of 1861, Maury resigned his commission and was appointed by Gov. **John Letcher** to a council to help prepare the state's defenses. He was commissioned a commander in the state navy in April and retained that rank when it was incorporated into the **Confederate navy** in June. Maury first served on court-martial duty but then was placed in charge of defending **Richmond, Virginia**, from attack up the James River. In carrying out these duties, he invented the electric **torpedo** (or mine) and used it in the river. While in Richmond, Maury and Mallory clashed over the types of ships best suited for defense. Mallory preferred large **ironclads** since the **CSS** *Virginia* had been so successful, while Maury recommended small, maneuverable gunboats with large guns because the Confederacy could produce more of them. Because of his outstanding reputation, Maury was sent to Europe in late summer 1862 to serve as an agent to acquire ships and supplies. He helped promote the Confederate cause, continued improving the electronic torpedo, and secured the **commerce raider CSS *Georgia***. Maury remained in London until May 1865, when he sailed for **Texas** with $40,000 of torpedo equipment to forestall final defeat, but he learned the war was over when he reached Cuba.

After the war, Maury lived in Mexico (where he served on **Maximilian's** cabinet) and Great Britain. He returned to the United States in 1868 and taught meteorology at the **Virginia Military Institute**.

MAXEY, SAMUEL BELL (1825–1895) CSA. A native of **Kentucky**, Maxey graduated next to last in his **West Point** class of 1846 (**George E. Pickett** was last) and was awarded two **brevets** for gallantry while fighting in the **Mexican War** with the 7th U.S. Infantry. He resigned his commission in 1849 and became a law partner with his father, first in Kentucky and then in **Texas**. Maxey served as district attorney for two years and was elected to the Texas senate in 1861, but then he resigned his seat so he could serve in the military (his father replaced him in the senate).

Maxey organized a Confederate volunteer **company** in 1861 that became part of the 9th Texas. Commissioned its colonel in September, he first served under **Albert Sidney Johnston** in Kentucky and was promoted to brigadier general in March 1862. Maxey was sent to Chattanooga, Tennessee, to raise troops and to harass the Union garrisons in northern **Alabama**. In the spring of 1863, he helped defend Port Hudson, Louisiana, but was transferred before the **Port Hudson Campaign** began and served under **Joseph E. Johnston** at Jackson, Mississippi, during the **Vicksburg Campaign**. In August 1863, Maxey was transferred to the **Trans-Mississippi Department**, where in December his friend **Edmund Kirby Smith** appointed him to command the **Indian Territory**. He performed good service in the area and won the respect of the **Indians** by treating them fairly and by insisting that race not be used to determine the ranking of officers. In April 1864, Maxey resisted the **Camden Expedition** but arrived at **Poison Spring** after the Federals had been defeated and **massacred** and called off the pursuit. This decision undoubtedly stopped further atrocities, but many men criticized Maxey for failing to win a more complete victory.

Maxey resumed command of the Indian Territory in May 1864 and was appointed major general by Kirby Smith, although the Senate never confirmed the appointment. When the War Department appointed **Douglas Cooper** to command the Indian Territory in July, Kirby Smith unsuccessfully tried to get the government to reconsider. He even delayed carrying out the orders for a while, but Maxey was finally replaced in February 1865. Maxey then took command of a dismounted cavalry **division** in April but resigned his commission in May and returned to his Texas law practice.

After the war, Maxey held several political positions and served two terms in the U.S. Senate in the 1870s and 1880s.

MAXIMILIAN, EMPEROR ARCHDUKE FERDINAND (1832– 1867). In 1863, Napoleon III of France took advantage of the American Civil War to reestablish the French empire in America. He invaded Mexico in June, overthrew Benito Juárez's government, and installed Austrian Archduke Ferdinand Maximilian as Mexico's emperor. This violated the Monroe Doctrine, but **Abraham Lincoln's** preoccupation with the Civil War prevented him from taking action.

With the support of French troops, Maximilian stayed in power throughout the war and allowed the Confederates to use **Matamoros** as a port. In turn, the Confederates supported his regime in hopes of gaining recognition from Napoleon. The United States refused to recognize the Maximilian government, however, and even adjusted its military **strategy** because of it. Expeditions to **Sabine Pass, Texas**, and the **Red River Campaign** were launched partially to establish a Union presence in **Texas** as a means of countering the French in Mexico.

Union pressure and European politics finally forced Napoleon to reduce his support of Maximilian, and he never recognized the Confederacy. When the war ended, the United States made a concerted effort to have Maximilian removed. **Philip Sheridan** took 50,000 men to the Rio Grande to threaten the emperor, while **John Schofield** met with Napoleon in France, and **William T. Sherman** talked with Mexican revolutionary Juarez. Because of this pressure, in May 1866 Napoleon withdrew the French troops that were keeping Maximilian in power. The revolutionaries then overthrew Maximilian and executed him in 1867.

MAYNARD CARBINE. This carbine was invented by Dr. Edward Maynard, a dentist in **Washington, D.C.** The breech-loader fired an unprimed brass cartridge that was loaded when the trigger guard was pulled down to expose the breech. Another of Maynard's inventions, the Maynard tape, was used to prime the cartridge. The tape resembled modern-day caps used in toy guns and had bits of fulminate of mercury fixed onto a long roll of tape that coiled up into the carbine's magazine. When the carbine was cocked for loading, the next primer on the tape advanced into position to fire the cartridge. The Maynard carbine was the first firearm that checked the blow-back of explosive gasses by causing the brass cartridge to expand when fired. Used by Union troops, just over 20,000 carbines were bought by the government.

MAYNARD TAPE. *See* MAYNARD CARBINE.

MEADE, GEORGE GORDON (1815–1872) USA. Born in Spain, Meade was the son of a wealthy **Pennsylvania** businessman and U.S. naval agent who was ruined financially by the Napoleonic Wars. The family returned to Pennsylvania, and in 1831 Meade received an appointment to **West Point**. Graduating in the middle of his 1835 class, he resigned his commission the next year after brief service in the **artillery** during the **Seminole Wars** and became a **railroad** and civil engineer. Meade reentered the **U.S. Army** in 1842 as a 2nd lieutenant of **engineers**. He won a **brevet** for gallantry in the **Mexican War** while serving under Zachary Taylor and then rose to the rank of captain while working on lighthouses and Great Lakes surveys.

Meade was promoted to brigadier general of volunteers in August 1861 and was given command of a Pennsylvania **brigade** in the **Army of the Potomac**. He first served in the **Washington, D.C.**, defenses but then fought under **George B. McClellan** in the **Peninsula** and **Seven Days Campaigns**. At **Frayser's Farm**, while with the V Corps' 3rd Division, Meade received two severe wounds to his hip and arm almost simultaneously but recovered in time to lead his brigade at **Second Manassas**. In September 1862, he was given command of the I Corps' 3rd Division and led it at both **South Mountain** and **Antietam**. Meade also temporarily assumed command of the entire **corps** after **Joseph Hooker** was wounded at Antietam.

Promoted to major general in November, Meade enjoyed the Army of the Potomac's only success at **Fredericksburg** when his men temporarily broke through **Stonewall Jackson's** line on the Confederate right. On Christmas Day 1862, he assumed command of the V Corps and led it through the horrid **Mud March** and **Chancellorsville Campaign**. Throughout his Civil War service, Meade was a steady and dependable, if not brilliant, general. He held the respect of both his officers and men, although his temper and use of profanity were legendary. When Hooker was removed from command of the Army of the Potomac in late June 1863, the men approved when Meade was named his replacement.

Meade took command on June 28, 1863, after **Robert E. Lee** had already launched the **Gettysburg Campaign**. This placed him in a difficult position, but he rose to the occasion and fought the Battle of Gettysburg with great skill. Meade did not reach the field until the night after the first day's battle, but he made the decision to stay and fight and defeated the Confederates by taking advantage of his **interior line** and skillfully shifting troops to defend the high ground. Despite his important victory, Meade was criticized by **Abraham Lincoln** and others for failing to pursue Lee vigorously enough. Stung by the rebuke, Meade tendered his resignation, but the administration quickly smoothed over the insult by promoting him to brigadier general of regulars in early July (he had been promoted to major of engineers in June 1862). In January 1863, he also received the **Thanks of Congress** for his victory at Gettysburg.

In the autumn of 1863, Meade was forced to retreat into northern **Virginia** during the **Bristoe Station Campaign** but then took the offensive in the **Mine Run Campaign**. When **U. S. Grant** was appointed general-in-chief of the Union armies in March 1864, he decided to direct the war while accompanying the Army of the Potomac. Meade graciously offered to step aside as commander, believing Grant would prefer one of his western officers in the position. Grant, however, was impressed by the selfless offer and kept him as **army** commander for the rest of the war. In his memoirs, Grant wrote of Meade: "He was brave and conscientious, and commanded the respect of all who knew him. He was unfortunately of a temper that would get beyond his control, at times. . . ." (Grant U.S., *Personal Memoirs*, vol. 2, 538).

The last year of war was difficult for Meade. His relationship with Grant was often strained because Grant took control of **strategy** and **tactics**, leaving Meade simply to follow his orders. Meade also had a poor relationship with **Philip Sheridan**, whom Grant had made commander of the cavalry, and **war correspondents** intentionally avoided mentioning Meade's name in articles to punish him for his contemptuous treatment of reporters. Largely as a result of the reporters' conspiracy of silence, Meade never attained the fame that he deserved.

Meade served Grant well through the bloody **Overland** and **Petersburg Campaigns**. As a reward, Grant promoted him to major general of regulars in August 1864 but only after Grant's protégés, Sheridan and **William T. Sherman**, had been given that rank. Also, Grant came to rely more on Sheridan during the last days of the Petersburg Campaign and through the **Appomattox Campaign** than he did Meade.

After the war, Meade remained in the army and commanded various **departments** and **districts** in the east and south during **Reconstruction**. He was commanding the Division of the Atlantic when he died.

MEAGHER, THOMAS FRANCIS (1823–1867) USA. A native of Ireland, Meagher (MARR) was banished to Tasmania by the British in 1849 after becoming involved in Ireland's independence movement. Escaping in 1852, he made his way to New York City by way of **California**. Meagher became a well-known lawyer and lecturer and was very popular with the New York Irish community because of his speaking ability and support of Irish independence.

When the Civil War began, Meagher raised an Irish **Zouave company** that became part of the 69th New York in April 1861. Appointed major, he fought at **First Manassas** in **William T. Sherman's brigade** before his **regiment** was mustered out of service in August. That autumn, Meagher raised the famous **Irish Brigade** in the **Army of the Potomac** and was appointed brigadier general of volunteers in February 1862. As part of the I Corps' 2nd Division, he fought in the **Peninsula, Seven Days**, and **Antietam Campaigns** and was injured in the latter battle when his horse fell on him. Meagher's and the brigade's most famous moment came at **Fredericksburg** when he launched a dramatic, but doomed, assault against Marye's Heights.

After fighting at **Chancellorsville**, Meagher became involved in a bitter dispute with his superiors. As a **Democrat**, he had always been overly vocal about **army** politics and had made few friends in **Abraham Lincoln's** administration. When Meagher's request to recruit new men for his brigade was refused, it was proposed that the unit be abolished by dispersing its undersized regiments to other brigades. As a result, Meagher resigned his commission in May 1863, but it was not accepted, and in December he returned to service. For the rest of the war, he commanded minor rear areas in the west and finally resigned while in Savannah, Georgia, in May 1865.

After the war, Meagher was appointed Montana's territorial secretary and served as acting governor when the governor was out of the territory. While drinking, he drowned in 1867 after falling from a Missouri River steamboat. The circumstances of his death were rather mysterious, and his body was never discovered.

MECHANICSVILLE, VIRGINIA, BATTLE OF (JUNE 26, 1862). Also known as Beaver Dam Creek and Ellerson's Mill, this was the first large battle of the 1862 **Seven Days Campaign** when **Robert E. Lee's Army of Northern Virginia** drove **George B. McClellan's Army of the Potomac** away from **Richmond, Virginia**. Lee massed most of his **army** north of the Chickahominy River to crush **Fitz John Porter's** isolated Union V Corps. **Stonewall Jackson's Valley Army** was to advance on Porter from the north from the **Shenandoah Valley** and attack his right flank. The sound of Jackson's attack would be the signal for the **divisions** of **James Longstreet**, **Daniel H. Hill**, and **A. P. Hill** to move against Porter from the west. It was agreed that Jackson would launch his attack early on the morning of June 26.

At Mechanicsville, A. P. Hill anxiously waited in vain throughout the morning for Jackson's attack. At about 3:00 P.M., he finally attacked on his own initiative, fearing the day would pass without any action being taken. Hill's men charged into Porter's position along Beaver Dam Creek and suffered heavy losses without penetrating the formidable defenses. Near dark, Lee sent in part of Daniel H. Hill's division as well, but it, too, was repulsed by Porter's entrenched infantry and 36 well-placed cannons. In one of the war's most controversial episodes, Jackson failed to get into position on time and actually camped for the day within earshot of the battle. He complained that the Federals had slowed his advance by felling trees in the road, but he was strangely lethargic throughout the Seven Days. It is speculated that this odd behavior was caused by total exhaustion from **Jackson's Shenandoah Valley Campaign**.

While Porter had fought an outstanding defensive battle, McClellan ordered him to withdraw during the night and decided to change his base from the York River to the James River. For the next five days, Lee chased McClellan down the peninsula to **Harrison's Landing**. At Mechanicsville, the Confederates lost 1,484 men to Porter's 361.

MEDAL OF HONOR. This is the highest honor awarded to U.S. military personnel for bravery in battle. The **U.S. Congress** created it in December 1861 to be a medal for **U.S. Navy** and **Marine** enlisted men. **U.S. Army** enlisted men were made eligible for the medal in July 1862 and **army** officers in March 1863, with all being eligible to receive the award retroactively to the war's beginning. Oddly, navy and marine officers were not made eligible for the medal until 1915.

The medal was awarded for combat service above and beyond the call of duty, but during the Civil War its standards were more lax than they became later. For example, soldiers automatically were awarded the medal for capturing a Confederate battle **flag**. This led to abuse because some stragglers stayed out of the fight and then picked up fallen flags from the field and turned them in. In 1916, the War Department reexamined medal recipients and revoked the medals of more than 900 men. The first of approximately 1,200 Civil War soldiers to receive the Medal of Honor were the six survivors of **Andrews' Raid** in 1862.

MEDALS. *See* DECORATIONS; MEDAL OF HONOR.

MEDICINE. The Civil War was so deadly largely because medical knowledge had not kept up with technology. While modern weapons were developed to slaughter men on the battlefield, the medicine practiced to save soldiers' lives was little better than that used in the **Mexican War.** Each **regiment** usually had at least one surgeon, but the skills of these physicians varied greatly.

In the war, soldiers were much more likely to die from disease than from bullets. Overcrowded, unsanitary living conditions caused such diseases as typhoid, diarrhea, measles, and smallpox to become widespread. Surgeons held daily sick call while in camp and examined each soldier complaining of these and other illnesses. A vaccine for smallpox was available to prevent that dreaded disease, but other illnesses sometimes called for drastic measures. Blue mass (a concoction made from mercury and chalk) often was used to purge the body of unhealthy contents, while diarrhea was treated with opium or a tree-bark product. Bleeding and mustard plasters were used to treat pneumonia and other lung diseases, and quinine was given to those who suffered from malaria or other fevers. The Union usually had a large supply of medicines, many of which had alcohol as their main ingredient, but the Confederacy often had to use homemade cures or develop substitute ingredients because the **blockade** made medical supplies scarce.

The treatment of wounds generally was primitive and sometimes more harmful than the wound itself. Actual surgery was rare; thus if a soldier was shot in the head or body, little could be done for him. Porcelain probes were inserted into the wound to locate the bullet (the lead bullet would leave a mark on the probe, or one could hear the tapping noise created by the probe contacting the bullet). The surgeon might be able to extract the bullet, but if it was buried deeply, it had to be left in place. Wounds to the extremities were cleaned as well as possible and then bound with bandages. If bone was shattered, surgeons could either resect the bone and leave the limb limp and useless or amputate it. Early in the war, amputations were common, but surgeons soon recognized that the procedure had a high mortality rate. As the war progressed, resections were used more frequently, but these were time consuming and often were not possible when large numbers of patients were waiting to be treated.

Chloroform generally was used as an anesthesia, with liquor being used if chloroform was unavailable. Most surgeons had ample supplies of chloroform, but on occasion supplies did run out, and they then were forced to perform amputations with no anesthesia. Bullets clearly showing teeth marks have been found around some Civil War field hospitals, proving that surgeons did sometimes have patients bite a bullet during surgery. Infection made Civil War surgical procedures deadly. Little was known of bacteria and germs, and surgeons did not take such precautions as sterilizing their instruments or washing their hands between patients.

MEIGS, JOHN RODGERS (1842–1864) USA. A native of **Washington, D.C.**, Meigs (MEGZ) was the son of **Montgomery C. Meigs**. He entered **West Point** in 1859, took leave to serve as an aide at **First Manassas**, and then returned to graduate first in the class of 1863. Appointed to the **engineers**, Meigs first served on Brig. Gen. **Benjamin F. Kelley's** staff and fought at **New Market** and then served under **David Hunter** and **Philip Sheridan** during their **Shenandoah Valley Campaigns**. He was **brevetted** twice for his service with Sheridan, who appointed him his chief of engineers in August 1864.

On October 3, 1864, Meigs was killed in the **Shenandoah Valley** near Dayton, Virginia, when he and two men encountered three Confederates while returning from a surveying mission. One of his companions was captured, and one escaped to tell Sheridan that the Confederates had murdered Meigs. Outraged, Sheridan ordered Dayton and all homes burned within a five-mile radius of the crime scene. Probably because the Union **prisoner** was immediately **paroled**, the Federals did not burn the town, but a number of houses were torched. Montgomery Meigs believed his son was murdered and offered a $1,000 bounty for the arrest of his killer. The Confederates involved in the shooting maintained the killing was justified, and in 1914 *Confederate Veteran* magazine published an article that exonerated the men.

MEIGS, MONTGOMERY CUNNINGHAM (1816–1892) USA. A native of **Georgia**, Meigs (MEGZ) was the father of **John Rodgers Meigs**. He grew up in **Pennsylvania** and attended the University of Pennsylvania before securing an appointment to **West Point**. After graduating near the top of his class in 1836, Meigs served one year in the **artillery** before transferring to the **engineers**. He helped build the Potomac Aqueduct and supervised the construction of the Capitol's dome and its House and Senate wings.

Meigs was a captain when the Civil War began, but he was promoted to colonel in May 1861. The following day, he was promoted to brigadier general of regulars and was made the Union **army's** quartermaster general to replace **Joseph E. Johnston**, who had joined the Confederacy.

Meigs served in that capacity until he retired in 1882. In charge of keeping the Union armies' supplies, he oversaw the spending of more than one and a half billion dollars during the war, which was the U.S. government's largest expenditure up to that time. Meigs's duties also included supervising all transportation used to supply the armies and the Military Telegraph Corps. Despite some unavoidable scandals caused by corrupt contractors, he did an outstanding job and was rewarded with a **brevet** to major general of regulars in July 1864. Tragically, during the war Meigs's son was killed while serving as an army engineer.

After the war, Meigs traveled widely to study other nations' military organizations and became the architect for the Pension Office Building in **Washington, D.C.** He also served as a regent for the Smithsonian Institution.

MEMMINGER, CHRISTOPHER GUSTAVUS (1803–1888) CSA. A native of the Germanic states, Memminger immigrated to the United States as a young boy after his father was killed while serving in the army. He was orphaned soon after arriving in **South Carolina** but was raised by a prominent family. Memminger became an influential lawyer and politician, created **Charleston's** first public education system, and was elected to the state legislature in 1836 (serving almost continuously until 1860). As chairman of the Committee on Finance, he gained recognition as a competent financier. Originally a moderate on **secession**, Memminger came to embrace it after **John Brown's Raid on Harpers Ferry, Virginia**, and attended the state's secession convention.

When the Confederacy was formed, Memminger became a member of the Provisional **Confederate Congress** and chaired both the committee that wrote the provisional **Confederate Constitution** and the Committee on Commercial Affairs. **Jefferson Davis** then selected him as secretary of the treasury in February 1861, and he struggled to **finance** the Confederate war effort during most of the conflict. Faced with almost insurmountable problems, Memminger remained a loyal supporter of Davis, but he had a contentious relationship with the Congress, which often interfered in his department. From the beginning, he opposed the **Cotton Diplomacy** policy of withholding cotton from Europe to force Great Britain and France to recognize the Confederacy. Memminger believed it better to ship as much cotton as possible to Europe to build up Confederate credit before the Union **blockade** became effective. He also was forced to issue millions of dollars in treasury notes even though he had always been a firm believer in specie. Among Memminger's failures were his not pursuing vigorously enough a viable **tax** system for the

Confederacy and not securing foreign loans. He made many enemies within the cabinet and Congress and became a scapegoat for the failure of the Confederate economy. Amid growing criticism, Memminger resigned in July 1864 and was replaced by **George A. Trenholm**.

After the war, Memminger resumed his law practice and promoted free public education for blacks and whites.

MEMPHIS, TENNESSEE, FIRST BATTLE OF (JUNE 6, 1862). Although the Confederate **River Defense Fleet** sank two Union gunboats at **Plum Run Bend**, the superior Union fleet and the evacuation of **Corinth, Mississippi**, forced the Confederates to abandon **Fort Pillow, Tennessee**, in the spring of 1862. The River Defense Fleet, commanded by Capt. James E. Montgomery, then withdrew to Memphis, Tennessee, to block any Union naval attempt to capture the city.

On June 6, 1862, a Union fleet consisting of eight **rams** under Col. **Charles Ellet** and five **ironclads** under **Charles H. Davis** approached the city from upstream. In a short, decisive battle at daybreak, witnessed by thousands of spectators lining the bank, the Union fleet sank or captured all but one of the Confederate ships. Ellet was mortally wounded and was the only Union casualty in the battle, while the Confederates lost approximately 180 men. Ellet's son, Lt. Charles Rivers Ellet, and two men disembarked after the fight and raised the Union **flag** over the city's courthouse. Later that morning, the mayor officially surrendered the city to Davis. The capture of Memphis, an important economic center, was another blow to the Confederacy as it steadily lost control of the Mississippi River.

MEMPHIS, TENNESSEE, SECOND BATTLE OF (AUGUST 21, 1864). On the morning of August 21, 1864, Confederate cavalryman **Nathan Bedford Forrest** carried out a raid against Memphis, Tennessee, with 2,000 men. His goal was to capture three Union generals stationed there, free Confederate **prisoners** from a local **prison**, and force the enemy to withdraw from northern **Mississippi**. Forrest rode into Memphis before daylight and **skirmished** with the Union garrison before splitting his column to carry out the different assignments. After cutting **telegraph** lines and taking a large number of horses and prisoners, he eventually was forced to withdraw. Forrest did succeed in drawing Union forces out of northern Mississippi, but he was foiled by **Cadwallader Washburn's** Union garrison from capturing the generals or releasing the prisoners. Casualty figures for the affair are disputed, but it is estimated that the Federals lost 80 men and 400 prisoners, while Forrest suffered approximately 62 casualties.

MEMPHIS *APPEAL*. *See* DILL, BENJAMIN FRANKLIN.

MERCER, HUGH WEEDON (1808–1877) CSA. The grandson of Revolutionary War Brig. Gen. Hugh Mercer, Mercer was a native of **Virginia** who graduated near the top of his **West Point** class in 1828. After brief service in the **artillery**, he served on **Winfield Scott's** staff for two years and then at various posts before resigning his 1st lieutenant's commission in 1835. Settling in **Georgia**, Mercer worked as a bank cashier and became an officer in the state militia.

Entering Confederate service in the spring of 1861 as colonel of the 1st Georgia, Mercer was sent to Savannah, where he served for most of the war. In October, he turned down an appointment as major general of state forces and instead accepted a commission as a Confederate brigadier general. The next month, Mercer commanded about 2,000 men under **Robert E. Lee** and defended the Georgia coast near Brunswick. After briefly commanding the District of South Carolina in the spring of 1862, he took command of the District of Georgia in June with his headquarters located at Savannah.

In Savannah, Mercer became the first Confederate general to impress free blacks and slaves to work on fortifications. This eventually led him into conflict with slave owners, however, and his superiors finally revoked the right of **impressment**. In April 1864, nearly all of Mercer's troops were sent to reinforce **Joseph E. Johnston** for the **Atlanta Campaign**. His **brigade** was the largest in the **Army of Tennessee** and served well in **W. H. T. Walker's division**, especially at **Kennesaw Mountain**. When Walker was killed at the **Battle of Atlanta**, Mercer assumed command of the division. He was in poor health, however, and **John Bell Hood** apparently did not believe he was a capable division commander. In July 1864, Hood disbanded Mercer's unit and put his brigade in **Patrick R. Cleburne's** division. Mercer's health remained poor, and Cleburne noted that it had a negative effect on the brigade's effectiveness. He led the brigade for the last time at **Jonesboro** and was relieved of command that evening. Accompanying **William J. Hardee** to **Savannah, Georgia**, Mercer remained there until it was evacuated in December 1864 and then served with Hardee until war's end.

After the war, Mercer reentered the banking business in Savannah, but in 1869, he moved to **Maryland** and became a commission merchant. A few years before his death, he moved to Germany for his health and died there.

MEREDITH, SOLOMON (1810–1875) USA. A native of **North Carolina**, Meredith moved to **Indiana** when he was 19. After working as a farm laborer, he was elected sheriff when he was 24 and served two terms before being elected to the state legislature four times. Appointed U.S. marshal in 1849, Meredith became a well-known lawman.

Meredith entered Union service in July 1861 when he was appointed colonel of the 19th Indiana. At nearly 51, he was one of the oldest colonels in the Union **army**—he was also one of the largest, reportedly standing six feet, six inches tall. Meredith's three sons also served the Union, and two of them died in the war. While with the famous **Iron Brigade**, Meredith was badly wounded in the **regiment's** first fight at **Groveton**.

Promoted to brigadier general of volunteers in October 1862, Meredith took command of the Iron Brigade and led it at **Fredericksburg**, **Chancellorsville**, and **Gettysburg**, where he again was severely wounded during the first day's fighting. When he returned to duty in November 1863, Meredith's age and wounds caused him to be posted to such noncombat positions as commander of Cairo, Illinois, and Paducah, Kentucky. He was still in Paducah when he was mustered out of service in May 1865. For his war service, Meredith was **brevetted** major general of volunteers in August.

After the war, Meredith served as surveyor general of the Montana Territory from 1867 to 1869 and then retired to his Indiana farm.

MEREDITH, SULLIVAN AMORY (1816–1874) USA. A native of **Pennsylvania**, Meredith sailed to China twice on a clipper ship as a young man and then settled in **California** in 1848 as a businessman. In April 1861, he was appointed colonel of a militia unit that was designated the 10th Pennsylvania. He may have secured this appointment through the influence of his brother, a prominent state politician and former U.S. secretary of the treasury.

Meredith's military career began when he was placed in charge of training and equipping some 30,000 Pennsylvania recruits. He then served under **Robert Patterson** in the **Shenandoah Valley** just prior to **First Manassas**. After helping defend **Washington, D.C.**, Meredith raised the 56th Pennsylvania and was appointed its colonel in March 1862. Serving in **Abner Doubleday's brigade**, he was badly wounded at **Second Manassas** and was unable to return to duty until July 1863. Promoted to brigadier general of volunteers in November 1862, Meredith was in charge of **prisoner exchange** at **Fort Monroe, Virginia**, from July 1863 until January 1864. It appears that his service displeased superiors because **Benjamin F. Butler** relieved him of his duties at Fort Monroe in January 1864 and sent him to **Missouri**, where

department commander **William S. Rosecrans** failed to find him another command.

Leaving the service in August 1865, without the usual **brevet**, Meredith remained in Missouri and held the position of commissioner of exchanged prisoners until 1866. He then moved to **New York** and worked in the drug wholesale business.

MERIDIAN, MISSISSIPPI, CAMPAIGN (FEBRUARY 3–MARCH 4, 1864).

In early 1864, **William T. Sherman** planned to launch a large raid from **Vicksburg** to Meridian, Mississippi, to destroy the **railroads** that linked Meridian to Selma and Mobile, Alabama, and to weaken enemy morale by creating havoc in the Confederacy's interior. The campaign was a prelude to Sherman's much larger, but similar, **March to the Sea** later in the year. Sherman planned to take 26,000 men of the **Army of the Tennessee's** XVI and XVII Corps from Vicksburg and march eastward through Jackson to Meridian. At the same time, **William Sooy Smith** was to move with 7,000 cavalrymen from Memphis, Tennessee, to Meridian, destroying the Mobile & Ohio Railroad in the process. By destroying the area's **railroads**, Sherman would greatly hamper the Confederacy's ability to move troops in **Mississippi** or western **Tennessee** and thus secure much of the territory along the Mississippi River's east bank. This would mean that fewer Union soldiers would be required to defend the area, and he could strip the region for reinforcements for his upcoming **Atlanta Campaign**.

On February 3, 1864, Sherman left Vicksburg. The 13,500 Confederate troops in Mississippi under Lt. Gen. **Leonidas Polk** were unable to offer serious resistance to the march, and Sherman made good headway. After some **skirmishing**, he entered Jackson on February 5 and continued eastward. Through great effort, Polk transferred most of Meridian's rolling stock, supplies, and troops to Demopolis, Alabama, and abandoned Meridian on February 14. When Sherman arrived later that day, he found the Confederates, trains, and supplies already gone. To make matters worse, **Sooy Smith's Expedition** never arrived from Memphis. Longer than expected preparations had delayed his departure until February 11, and then his column was slowed by thousands of runaway slaves who joined it. After destroying 55 miles of track, he was turned back by **Nathan Bedford Forrest** at **West Point**. Smith lost 700 men in the expedition, and Sherman labeled his performance "unsatisfactory." Unable to accomplish anything more, Sherman destroyed more than 100 miles of track and began his return to Vicksburg on February 20, arriving on March 4.

The campaign largely was a failure. Sherman reported losing 170 men, while capturing 400 **prisoners** and 3,000 draft animals, liberating 5,000 slaves, and taking in 1,000 white refugees. The Confederate locomotives, rolling stock, and supplies largely escaped intact, which meant the Confederates could still operate in Mississippi. As a result, Sherman could not take the reinforcements from the area that he had planned for the Atlanta Campaign. One short-term benefit of Sherman's raid was that **Jefferson Davis** weakened **Joseph E Johnston's Army of Tennessee** in northern **Georgia** by ordering **William J. Hardee's corps** to join Polk. These troops, however, were able to rejoin Johnston for the Atlanta Campaign.

MERRIMAC, **USS.** *See VIRGINIA,* CSS.

MERRITT, WESLEY (1834–1910) USA. A native of **New York**, Merritt moved with his family to an **Illinois** farm when he was seven. He graduated from **West Point** in 1860 and served with the dragoons in Utah prior to the Civil War.

Merritt was a 1st lieutenant and adjutant of the 2nd U.S. Cavalry (formerly the 2nd Dragoons) until February 1862, when he was appointed aide-de-camp to Brig. Gen. **Philip St. George Cooke**, commander of the **Army of the Potomac's** cavalry. He served with Cooke through the **Peninsula Campaign**, earning a promotion to captain of regulars in April 1862, and then joined the staff of **George Stoneman**, Cooke's replacement.

Under Stoneman, Merritt received his first combat command when he led the Cavalry Reserve Brigade in **Stoneman's Raid** during the **Chancellorsville Campaign**. After fighting well at **Brandy Station**, he was promoted from captain to brigadier general of volunteers in June 1863, just two days before the **Battle of Gettysburg**. At Gettysburg, Merritt commanded the Reserve Cavalry Brigade in **John Buford's division** and won a **brevet** in the regular **army**. For the rest of the year, he led his **brigade**, and sometimes a cavalry division, in the **Bristoe Station** and **Mine Run Campaigns**.

Merritt led a division during much of the 1864 **Overland Campaign** and earned two more brevets, but he was back with the Reserve Brigade for **Cold Harbor** and the early part of the **Petersburg Campaign**. In August, he was given command of a division under **Philip Sheridan** and fought well at **Third Winchester**, **Fisher's Hill**, and **Cedar Creek** during **Sheridan's Shenandoah Valley Campaign**, winning a brevet of major general of volunteers for the first two battles. In January 1865,

Merritt was placed in command of Sheridan's cavalry **corps** and after leading it with skill at **Waynesboro**, he accompanied Sheridan back to Petersburg and fought well at **Five Forks** and in the **Appomattox Campaign** (where he was Sheridan's second in command). He won brevets of brigadier general and major general of regulars for this service and received an appointment to major general of volunteers in April. At Appomattox, Merritt also was appointed one of the three Union commissioners to receive formally the Confederate **surrender**. He was one of the Union's youngest and most remarkable generals of the war and had attained the rank of brigadier general just three years after graduating from West Point.

Mustered out of the volunteer service in February 1866, Merritt remained in the regular **army** as a lieutenant colonel of cavalry, fought **Indians** on the frontier, and became superintendent of West Point. As a major general and the army's second-ranking officer, he captured Guam during the Spanish-American War and then participated in operations in the Philippines. Merritt retired from the army in 1900.

MERVINE, WILLIAM (1791–1868) USA. A native of **Pennsylvania**, Mervine entered the **U.S. Navy** as a midshipman in 1809. He won some fame in both the War of 1812 and the **Mexican War** and was serving as a captain when the Civil War began.

Mervine was placed in command of the **Gulf Blockading Squadron** in May 1861 and sailed from **Massachusetts** on the USS *Mississippi*. With only 17 ships, his mission of **blockading** the Gulf Coast from Key West, Florida, to Brownsville, Texas, was nearly impossible. Secretary of the Navy **Gideon Welles** believed Mervine lacked energy and initiative and replaced him with **William W. McKean** in September 1861. Mervine then served in various administrative positions, including president of the Navy Retiring Board, even though he himself was on the retired list officially. He was promoted to commodore in 1862 and to rear admiral in 1866.

MESSES. During the Civil War, soldiers on both sides grouped themselves into informal units called messes. Each mess shared quarters, took turns cooking meals, and generally looked out for each other. Numbering perhaps five to 10 men each, the mess often included best friends and relatives.

MEXICAN WAR. In 1846, tension was great between the United States and Mexico because of America's annexation of Mexico's former province of **Texas**; a dispute over the south Texas boundary; and the philosophy of Manifest Destiny, which convinced many Americans that it was their destiny to push west and control the Mexican territory of **California** and the desert Southwest. When an American attempt to buy California was rejected by Mexico, both sides massed troops along the Rio Grande. After the Mexican army attacked an American patrol on the north side of the river, President James K. Polk asked for and received a declaration of war from the **U.S. Congress**.

Zachary Taylor's small army invaded northern Mexico and won victories at Monterrey and Buena Vista, while **John C. Frémont** and Stephen Kearny captured California and **New Mexico**, respectively. General **Winfield Scott** then led an amphibious landing at Vera Cruz and fought his way inland, defeating Santa Anna at Cerro Gordo, Churubusco, and Chapultepec. Mexico City was captured, the Mexicans surrendered, and the Treaty of Guadalupe Hidalgo was signed in 1848 ending the war. The treaty established the Rio Grande as the boundary of Texas and allowed the United States to buy California and the American Southwest.

The Mexican War is sometimes referred to as the "dress rehearsal for the Civil War" because so many Civil War personalities received their baptism of fire there. These included **U. S. Grant**, **Robert E. Lee**, **P. G. T. Beauregard**, **Jefferson Davis**, and **George B. McClellan**.

MICHIGAN. Michigan was largely a rural state when the Civil War began, with relatively few **railroads** or **industry**. It did, however, have a fairly large population (749,113 in 1860) and contributed 87,000 men and more than 70 military units to the Union war effort. Of the Michigan soldiers, 14,700 died in service.

The state's **regiments** compiled an outstanding war record and became known as very dependable units. Among its more famous regiments were the 1st Michigan, the first fully equipped Union regiment from the west; the 7th Michigan, which had 397 men killed or died of disease; the 24th Michigan, which was part of the famous **Iron Brigade**; and the 4th Michigan Cavalry, which was credited for capturing **Jefferson Davis** at war's end. Prominent Union officers hailing from Michigan included **George A. Custer**, **Henry J. Hunt**, **Henry Hastings Sibley**, **Orlando B. Willcox**, and **Elon J. Farnsworth**. Civilians **Annie Etheridge**, **Sarah E. Edmonds**, and **Bridget Divers** also played prominent roles in the nursing corps.

"MICHIGAN ANNIE." *See* ETHERIDGE, ANNA OR ANNIE.

MIDDLE BOGGY, INDIAN TERRITORY, BATTLE OF (FEBRUARY 13, 1864). In an attempt to force the Chickasaws and Choctaws in

Indian Territory to support the Union, Col. William A. Phillips led an expedition from **Fort Gibson** toward the **Texas** border in February 1864. On February 13, at Middle Boggy, a detachment of the 14th Kansas Cavalry under Maj. Charles Willette surprised Maj. John Jumper's Confederate Seminole Battalion, detachments of the 1st Choctaw and Chickasaw Cavalry, and the 20th Texas. In a short fight, the Federals killed 47 Confederates and chased away the rest, with no loss to themselves. The Confederates were gathering reinforcements from Boggy Depot when Willette withdrew. This small victory was about the only gain from Phillips's expedition. Although he killed some 250 **Indians** in the raid and laid waste to much of the countryside, Phillips failed to force the Indians to abandon the Confederate cause.

MIDDLE DEPARTMENT (UNION). Comprising **New Jersey, Pennsylvania, Delaware**, eastern **Maryland**, and the **Virginia** coast, this Union **department** was created in March 1862 under Maj. Gen. **John A. Dix**, with its headquarters at Baltimore, Maryland. In March 1863, **West Virginia** was added, but by year's end New Jersey, Pennsylvania, and most of West Virginia had been assigned to other departments. By mid-1863, most of the 50,000 men in the department's VIII Corps were on various garrison duty protecting Potomac River crossings, **railroads**, and canals. The most important garrisons were at Winchester, Virginia, and **Harpers Ferry, West Virginia**, guarding the lower **Shenandoah Valley** from Confederate invasion. When **Robert E. Lee** began the **Gettysburg Campaign**, the Union soldiers at Winchester were overwhelmed and mostly captured in the **Second Battle of Winchester** and **Stephenson's Depot**, but a year later the department was active in repelling **Jubal A. Early's Washington Raid**. In August 1864, the department became part of the larger **Middle Military Division**. Commanders of the department included Dix, **John E. Wool, Robert C. Schenck, William H. Morris, Erastus B. Tyler, Henry H. Lockwood, Lew Wallace**, and **E. O. C. Ord**.

MIDDLE MILITARY DIVISION (UNION). Confederate Lt. Gen. **Jubal A. Early's Washington Raid** in the summer of 1864 and his subsequent activities in the lower **Shenandoah Valley** showed Union officials a weakness in their military organization. Four different military **departments**—Middle, **Western Virginia**, the **Susquehanna**, and **Washington**—overlapped in the area of operations, making it difficult to coordinate efforts to defend the capital. As a result, **U. S. Grant** recommended that the four departments be consolidated into one division under the command of **Philip Sheridan**. In August 1864, this was done with the creation of the Middle Military Division. Under Sheridan, the division's **Army of the Shenandoah** defeated Early in **Sheridan's 1864 Shenandoah Valley Campaign** and then devastated the Valley. Sheridan relinquished command to **Alfred T. A. Torbert** in February 1865, and he turned over command to **Winfield S. Hancock** the following month. Hancock commanded the division until it was abolished in June 1865.

MIDDLEBURG, VIRGINIA, BATTLE OF (JUNE 17–19, 1863). While **Robert E. Lee**'s **Army of Northern Virginia** advanced toward **Maryland** through the **Shenandoah Valley** at the beginning of the **Gettysburg Campaign**, Lee had **J. E. B. Stuart's** cavalry screen the movement by guarding the Bull Run Mountain passes to the east. On June 17, 1863, Maj. Gen. **Joseph Hooker**, commander of the Union **Army of the Potomac**, sent his cavalry under **Alfred Pleasonton** to find the **Confederate army**.

The Federals first made contact with the Confederates at **Aldie**. While trying to fight through the mountain pass there, Col. **Alfred N. Duffié's** 1st Rhode Island Cavalry slipped through Thoroughfare Gap and past the guarding Confederates. Riding toward Stuart's headquarters at Middleburg, Duffié reached the town at 4:00 P.M. after some **skirmishing** and forced Stuart to withdraw since he did not know the strength of the enemy column. **Beverly Robertson's brigade** was left behind to contest the Union advance, and he attacked and drove back Duffié that afternoon. The next morning, **John R. Chambliss's** Confederate brigade cut off Duffié's escape route and captured about 200 of his men. On June 19, **David M. Gregg's** Union **division** moved forward to attack Stuart west of Middleburg at Mount Defiance. Gregg drove back Chambliss's and Robertson's brigades before Stuart took a position too strong for Gregg to attack. In this fighting, Gregg lost 99 men to Stuart's 40.

MILES, DIXON STANSBURY (? – 1862) USA. An 1824 graduate of **West Point**, Miles served with the infantry in the **Mexican War** and won two **brevets**. He attained the rank of colonel in 1859 and when the Civil War began was given command of a **brigade** under **Robert Patterson** in the **Shenandoah Valley**. Elevated to a **division** command, Miles participated in the advance on **Manassas**, Virginia, in July 1861 but did not see any combat. In treating Miles for an illness before the engagement, Miles's surgeon had prescribed small amounts of liquor, but Miles had become drunk by the time the **First Battle of Manassas** began. While stationed in a supportive position, troops complained of his drunken condition, and **Irvin McDowell** ordered Col. **Israel B. Richardson** to relieve him. When Miles argued with Richardson, the colonel preferred charges of drunkenness against him. A court of inquiry found that while Miles was, indeed, drunk, his illness was a mitigating factor and decided not to court-martial him.

In March 1862, Miles was placed in command of the 12,000-man garrison at **Harpers Ferry, Virginia**, and was there in September when **Stonewall Jackson** attacked it during the **Antietam Campaign**. As the Confederates approached, Brig. Gen. **Julius White** arrived at the post, but he allowed Miles to continue to command since he was more familiar with the **tactical** situation. Miles poorly placed his men for defense, and Jackson successfully besieged and captured the post. In the last stage of the fight, Miles was killed, rumored to have been intoxicated. He probably would have been court-martialed had he not been killed.

MILES, NELSON APPLETON (1839–1925) USA. A native of **Massachusetts**, Miles was raised on a farm and then moved to Boston when he was 17. There, he worked in a store, attended night school, and received some military training from a former French officer.

Miles entered Union service in September 1861 as a 1st lieutenant in the 22nd Massachusetts. During the **Peninsula Campaign**, he served with the **Army of the Potomac** on Brig. Gen. **Oliver O. Howard's** staff as an aide-de-camp. At **Seven Pines**, Miles was wounded in the foot while temporarily commanding part of the 81st Pennsylvania, but his actions won him an appointment as lieutenant colonel of the 61st New York in late May 1862. After fighting at **Antietam**, he was promoted to colonel in late September 1862 to replace the wounded regimental commander and took charge of both his **regiment** and the 64th New York. Miles was again wounded at **Fredericksburg** and was commended by **brigade** commander, **Winfield S. Hancock**. He recovered in time to lead his regiment at **Chancellorsville**. There, Miles received his third wound, but he performed so gallantly that in 1867 he was **brevetted** brigadier general of regulars and was awarded the **Medal of Honor** in 1892.

Miles's wound caused him to miss **Gettysburg**, but when he returned to duty the day after the battle, he was given command of a brigade in the II Corps' 1st Division. He led it through the **Bristoe Station** and **Mine Run Campaigns** and then was promoted to brigadier general of volunteers in May 1864 for his role in breaking through the Confederate lines at **Spotsylvania's** "Bloody Angle" (for which he won another brevet). In July 1864, Miles took command of the **division** during the **Petersburg Campaign**. He received a fourth wound there and was brevetted major general of volunteers for his conduct at **Reams' Station**. Miles briefly led the **corps** in February 1865 and played a key role in the **Appomattox Campaign** at **Sutherland Station**.

One of the Union's outstanding commanders, Miles remained in the **army** after the war's end and was promoted to major general of volunteers in October 1865. For a time, he served as **Jefferson Davis's** jailer at **Fort Monroe, Virginia**, and had to follow orders to place the former Confederate president in chains. Miles was commissioned colonel of the 40th U.S. Colored Infantry in 1866, married **William T. Sherman's** niece in 1868, and compiled a military record second to none. During his postwar career, he fought **Indians** on the frontier (where he was involved in the capture of the Apache leader Geronimo), rose to the rank of major general of regulars, and became general-in-chief in 1895. Miles also supervised much of the war effort in the Spanish-American War, captured Puerto Rico, and was promoted to lieutenant general in 1901. In 1902, however, he became involved in a dispute with President Theodore Roosevelt and was forced to retire the following year. When Miles died in 1925, he was the last of the Civil War's major generals.

MILES, WILLIAM PORCHER (1822–1899) CSA. A native of **South Carolina**, Miles graduated with honors from the College of Charleston in 1842. He taught mathematics at his alma mater for 12 years, was awarded a gold medal for volunteering as a nurse during a **Virginia** yellow fever epidemic, and served as **Charleston's** mayor from 1855 to 1857. Miles was elected to the **U.S. Congress** in 1857, but he resigned in 1860 when he became convinced that **secession** was necessary. After serving as a prosecession delegate at the state's secession convention, he became one of the negotiators sent to **Washington, D.C.**, to secure a peaceful surrender of federal installations. Miles also was one of the negotiators who dealt with **Robert Anderson** at **Fort Sumter**.

After war began, Miles was elected to the **Confederate Congress**, was reelected twice without opposition, and chaired the powerful Committee on Military Affairs and the committee that designed the Confederate national **flag**. He became one of the most influential members of the Confederate government and strongly supported **Jefferson Davis's** war effort. The only areas in which his opinion really differed from the president's were the government's providing **railroads** with land grants, the **suspension of the writ of habeas corpus**, and the establishment of a powerful **supreme court**.

Having married the daughter of a very wealthy man during the war, Miles spent the postwar period in luxury, living in Virginia for a time and then becoming president of the University of South Carolina in 1880. After resigning in 1882, he moved to **Louisiana** and managed his father-in-law's large plantations.

MILITARY DIVISION OF THE GULF (UNION). This name sometimes was used for the **Military Division of West Mississippi.**

MILITARY DIVISION OF THE MISSISSIPPI (UNION). In October 1863, the Union took a significant step in winning the war by unifying the western **Departments of the Ohio, the Tennessee, the Cumberland,** and **Arkansas** into one large Military Division of the Mississippi so as to coordinate the region's several **armies** under one commander, **U. S. Grant.** When Grant was promoted to general-in-chief in March 1864, **William T. Sherman** took over the division and commanded it until June 1865. Military forces within the division included the **Armies of the Ohio, the Tennessee, the Cumberland,** and **Georgia.**

MILITARY DIVISION OF THE MISSOURI (UNION). This military division was organized in January 1865 by combining the **Departments of the Missouri** and **the Northwest. John Pope** was placed in command in February with his headquarters at St. Louis, Missouri. The division originally included **Missouri, Kansas, Wisconsin, Iowa, Minnesota,** and parts of the Nebraska, Dakota, and **Colorado territories.** In February and March 1865, the Utah Territory and the **Department of Arkansas** were added to it, respectively. The territory south of the Arkansas River was removed from the division in May 1865 and was placed in the Division of the Southwest. Little fighting, except some guerrilla activity, took place in the division since the war was nearly over when it was created. Still, Confederate Brig. Gen. **Stand Watie's surrender** occurred within its confines in June 1865. The division was abolished four days later.

MILITARY DIVISION OF THE POTOMAC (UNION). This short-lived military division was created in July 1861, four days after the Union defeat at **First Manassas,** by combining the **Departments of Northeastern Virginia** and **Washington. George B. McClellan** was placed in command, but in August, the division was abolished when it merged with the **Department of the Potomac.**

MILITARY DIVISION OF THE SOUTHWEST (UNION). This military division was created in December 1861 and consisted of a part of southwestern **Missouri** that was taken from the **Department of the Missouri.** Under the command of **Samuel R. Curtis,** it had the 15,000-man

Army of the Southwest to defend it. Curtis's command fought at **Pea Ridge** before **Frederick Steele** replaced him in August 1862. In October **Eugene A. Carr** replaced Steele, but Carr served only a month before **Willis A. Gorman** replaced him. In December, the division was abolished when it was merged with the **Department of the Tennessee.**

MILITARY DIVISION OF THE WEST (CONFEDERATE). In October 1864, the Confederates tried to bring unity to the western theater by combining the **Departments of Tennessee and Georgia** and **of Alabama, Mississippi, and East Louisiana** into one Military Division of the West. This was done particularly to coordinate efforts for **John Bell Hood's Franklin and Nashville Campaign. P. G. T. Beauregard** was placed in command of the division, but he was little more than an adviser to the **armies** of Hood and **Richard Taylor.** In 1865, the division was enlarged by adding western **Georgia** to Hood's **Department of Tennessee and Georgia** and by adding to the division the Confederate troops operating in **South Carolina.** When the war ended, the division was still in existence, with Beauregard serving as **Joseph E. Johnston's** second in command in **North Carolina.**

MILITARY DIVISION OF WEST MISSISSIPPI (UNION). This military division was created in May 1864 and consisted of the **Departments of the Gulf** and **of Arkansas.** It was placed under the command of **E. R. S. Canby** and was enlarged in June to include the **Department of the Missouri.** Sometimes referred to as the Trans-Mississippi Division, it was abolished in May 1865.

MILITARY ORDER OF THE LOYAL LEGION OF THE UNITED STATES (MALLUS). When the Civil War began to end in April 1865, Union officers created an organization to ensure that the peace would last. Meeting in Philadelphia, **Pennsylvania**, that month, these officers formed the Military Order of the Loyal Legion of the United States and pledged to support the U.S. government and, if necessary, come to its aid in the future. The organization was open to all officers, and their descendants, who had served honorably in the Union military during the war. Local, state, and a national headquarters were created, but the members were never required to serve the government again since the peace did last. Instead, the organization became more of a social fraternity that supported veterans' issues, compiled histories of their participation in the Rebellion, and provided relief to war widows and orphans. The voluminous histories the members compiled are known as the MOLLUS papers and today are very valuable to historians as a primary source on the war.

MILL SPRINGS, KENTUCKY, BATTLE OF (JANUARY 19, 1862). In the autumn of 1861, small battles broke out as Union Maj. Gen. **George H. Thomas** advanced to gain control of eastern **Kentucky**. In November, Confederate Brig. Gen. **Felix Zollicoffer** moved his small force, without orders, from Cumberland Gap across the Cumberland River to near Beech Grove. Zollicoffer's superior, Maj. Gen. **George B. Crittenden**, had been ordered by **department** commander **Albert Sidney Johnston** not to cross the river, so he ordered Zollicoffer to withdraw. When Zollicoffer failed to act, Crittenden assumed command of his troops in January 1862 but found the river too swollen from recent rains to recross. Thomas was advancing toward him, as well, and Crittenden decided to fight rather than risk a difficult retreat in the face of the enemy.

Thomas's 4,000 men reached Logan's Cross Roads on January 17, 1862. Crittenden advanced his 4,000 men to meet Thomas and first made contact before daylight on January 19 during a fierce rainstorm. After daylight, Crittenden advanced Zollicoffer's **brigade** and drove the Federals back. Rain, smoke, and fog greatly confused the fighting, and the weather prevented many of the Confederates' outdated flintlock muskets from firing. In the confusion, Zollicoffer rode out to stop what he believed were Confederates firing on their own men. Riding up to the Union line by mistake, he and an aide were shot and killed. (Zollicoffer was killed by Union Col. **Speed S. Fry**.) Crittenden continued to advance with Zollicoffer's and **William H. Carroll's** brigades. Thomas, recently arrived on the field, countered with **Samuel Carter's** brigade and two additional **regiments**. After a fierce fight in the rain and fog, the Federals finally broke the Confederate line when Carter pushed back Crittenden's right, and other Union troops flanked his left. Crittenden then abandoned much of his equipment and wounded and retreated across the swollen Cumberland River in boats.

Crittenden lost 529 men and 12 cannons in the battle, while Thomas counted 262 casualties. Also known as Logan's Cross Roads, Fishing Creek, Beech Grove, and Somerset, this relatively small battle dislodged the Confederate defenses in Kentucky and helped the Union gain control of the state.

MILLER, JOHN FRANKLIN (1831–1913) USA. A native of **Indiana**, Miller received a law degree from Ballston Spa, New York, and practiced law in Indiana and **California**. He returned to Indiana from California in 1855 and was elected to the state senate in 1861.

Miller entered Union service in August 1861 as colonel of the 29th Indiana. As part of **Edward N. Kirk's brigade**, the **regiment** fought on the second day at **Shiloh**, but some question remains as to whether Miller was present. In September 1862, he was given command of a brigade in the **Army of the Ohio** and led it through the latter part of the **Kentucky Campaign**. Miller then took command of a brigade in the 2nd Division of the **Army of the Cumberland's** XIV Corps in November and was wounded while leading it at **Stones River**. He received a second, more serious, wound in June 1863 at Liberty Gap during the **Tullahoma Campaign**. This wound kept Miller off duty for months, but he was promoted to brigadier general of volunteers in April 1864 while recuperating. In June 1864, he was placed in command of Nashville, Tennessee, and led his garrison in the **Battle of Nashville** that winter, winning a **brevet** of major general of volunteers for his service.

Miller declined an appointment to colonel in the regular **army** and resigned his commission in September 1865. He returned to California and became the collector of the port of San Francisco. After serving as president of a fur trading company for 12 years, Miller was elected to the U.S. Senate in 1880 and became most famous for opposing Chinese immigration.

MILLER, STEPHEN (1816–1881) USA. A native of **Pennsylvania**, Miller received a local education and served as his county's clerk before moving to Harrisburg and becoming a prominent **Whig** newspaper editor. Moving to **Minnesota** in 1858, he then became a businessman and local **Republican** politician and served as a delegate to the 1860 Republican National Convention.

Miller entered Union service in April 1861 as lieutenant colonel of the 1st Minnesota. The regiment suffered heavy losses at **First Manassas** as part of **William B. Franklin's brigade** and served as a rear guard in the humiliating Union defeat at **Ball's Bluff**. After brief service in the **Shenandoah Valley**, Miller and his **regiment** joined the **Army of the Potomac** for the **Peninsula Campaign**. He fought at **Seven Pines** and in the **Seven Days Campaign** (where he commanded the regiment) and in August 1862 was appointed colonel of the 7th Minnesota, a regiment that was organized to fight the **Sioux uprising** in Minnesota. Taking command at Mankato, Miller played a key role in suppressing the **Indians** and in December supervised the execution of 38 Sioux warriors, whose hanging **Abraham Lincoln** had authorized.

Miller was promoted to brigadier general of volunteers in October 1863. Soon afterward, he was elected governor of Minnesota and resigned his commission a week after taking office in January 1864. Miller spent the last year of the war promoting recruitment and keeping the

Sioux pacified. He declined to run for reelection, became a **railroad** agent, and served in the Minnesota legislature in the 1870s.

MILLER, WILLIAM (1820–1909) CSA. A native of **New York**, Miller moved with his family to **Louisiana** as an infant. There he attended the University of Louisiana and then fought in the **Mexican War** as an enlisted man. Moving to **Florida** after the war, Miller opened a law practice and operated a sawmill until the Civil War.

Miller entered Confederate service in the summer of 1861 as major and commander of the 1st Florida Battalion (also known as the 3rd Florida Battalion). He rose to the rank of lieutenant colonel, and the battalion was merged a year later with the 1st Florida. Miller was appointed colonel of the **regiment** in August 1862 and led it in the **Kentucky Campaign** as part of **John C. Brown's brigade**. When Brown was wounded at **Perryville**, Miller assumed command of the brigade. At **Stones River** with the **Army of Tennessee**, he led the consolidated 1st and 3rd Florida in **William Preston's** brigade and was wounded during an attack on the battle's last day. Miller's command suffered heavy casualties, but he was praised for his leadership and for refusing to leave his men even after being wounded.

Miller returned to Florida while he recovered from his wound and was placed in charge of the Conscript Bureau for the Southern District of Florida and Alabama. He performed his duties well and in August 1864 was promoted to brigadier general. Miller was given command of Florida's reserve forces the following month and command of the District of Florida in October and succeeded in blunting Union raiding parties into his area. After being replaced as **district** commander in March 1865, he took charge of the district's troops and continued to counter Union advances.

After the war, Miller resided in Florida and became active in logging and farming. He also served in the state assembly in 1885 and was elected to the state senate in 1886 and 1903.

MILLIKEN'S BEND, LOUISIANA, BATTLE OF (JUNE 7, 1863). During the 1863 **Vicksburg Campaign**, Confederate Lt. Gen. **John C. Pemberton** was desperate for help. He asked Lt. Gen. **Edmund Kirby Smith**, commander of the **Trans-Mississippi Department**, to attack the Union supply lines on the **Louisiana** side of the Mississippi River, hoping to force Maj. Gen. **U. S. Grant** to withdraw from **Mississippi**. Kirby Smith ordered Maj. Gen. **Richard Taylor** to make such an attack with **John G. Walker's** Texas **division**, and if successful, to cross the Mississippi River and reinforce **Vicksburg**. Taylor disagreed with the plan, claiming that by the time he could attack, Grant would have already established supply depots on the Mississippi side of the river, and that Pemberton should be withdrawn from Vicksburg, not reinforced.

By early June 1863, Taylor was in northeast Louisiana with Walker's division. On the night of June 6, he sent **James M. Hawes's brigade** to attack Young's Point, across the river from Vicksburg, and **Henry Mc-Culloch's** 1,500-man brigade to attack the supply depot at Milliken's Bend, just upriver from Vicksburg. Milliken's Bend was garrisoned by about 900 untrained **black troops** in the newly formed 9th and 11th Louisiana Infantry of African Descent and the 1st Mississippi Infantry of African Descent and about 300 men from the 23rd Iowa. **Skirmishing** in the area had alerted the Federals, and the gunboats *Choctaw* and *Lexington* also had been sent to Milliken's Bend.

McCulloch attacked at daylight on June 7 and pushed the Federals away from one levee and back to another along the river. The fighting was vicious and hand-to-hand, and little quarter was given on either side. While the Confederates claimed the white Iowa soldiers fled and left the black troops to their fate, the Iowans disagreed and claimed the black troops broke first. In any case, the Federal line finally held along the river, with the assistance of the gunboats, and McCulloch realized he could do little more. After burying his dead, McCulloch retired from the field. Downstream, Hawes rather timidly approached Young's Point and disappointed Taylor by withdrawing without an attack.

In the bloody fight, the Confederates lost 175 men, while the Federals lost about 450. Of the Union casualties, 101 were killed on the field. The black troops suffered the heaviest losses, with the 9th Louisiana losing 128 dead or mortally wounded out of 285 men engaged. This 45-percent mortality rate is believed to be the highest for any Union **regiment** in a single engagement, but because black soldiers were involved, it has received little attention.

Milliken's Bend was an important turning point for black soldiers. Coming shortly after the **Louisiana Native Guards** fought in the **Port Hudson Campaign**, the victory received a great deal of media attention and helped convince authorities that blacks would make good soldiers. It also received much publicity because it was rumored afterward that the Confederates summarily executed captured black soldiers and their white officers. Grant investigated the matter and concluded there was no validity to the rumors. Modern research shows that about 60 black soldiers were captured in the battle and were sent to **Texas** for the duration of the war. While no **massacre** of black troops occurred, it does appear that two of three captured white officers were executed by their captors, but there is no evidence to suggest that Taylor was aware of it.

MILROY, ROBERT HUSTON (1816–1890) USA. A native of **Indiana**, Milroy graduated from **Vermont's** Captain Partridge's Academy in 1843 and served in the **Mexican War** as a captain in the 1st Indiana. After the war, he became a lawyer and served as a delegate at the 1850 constitutional convention and as a judge before resuming his law practice.

Milroy entered Union service in April 1861 as a captain of a volunteer **company** he had raised, but a few days later, he was commissioned colonel of the 90-day 9th Indiana. He persuaded his men to reenlist when their terms expired and then participated in **George B. McClellan's** campaign in western **Virginia**. Promoted to brigadier general of volunteers in September 1861, Milroy first commanded the area around **Cheat Mountain** before being sent to the **Shenandoah Valley** with a **brigade** in April 1862. After fighting at **McDowell**, his brigade saw combat at **Second Manassas** with the **Army of Virginia** while attached to **Franz Sigel's corps** as an independent brigade.

Promoted to major general of volunteers in March 1863, Milroy was given a **division** command at Winchester, Virginia, in January 1863. In June, he was defeated and nearly his entire division was captured at **Second Winchester** and **Stephenson's Depot** when **Richard S. Ewell** led the **Army of Northern Virginia's** vanguard in the **Gettysburg Campaign**. Milroy escaped with a few hundred soldiers but lost 4,400 men and 23 cannons. For the next 10 months, he was without a field command while the disaster was investigated. When finally cleared, Milroy was transferred in July 1864 to **Tennessee**, where he guarded **railroads**, fought guerrillas, and organized militiamen. He resigned his commission in July 1865.

After the war, Milroy was a trustee for a canal company and served as an **Indian** agent in the Pacific Northwest.

MILTON, JOHN (1807–1865) CSA. A native of **Georgia**, Milton attended Georgia's Louisville Academy and became a lawyer. He later moved to **Alabama**, where he established a prosperous law practice and fought in the **Seminole Wars** as a captain of volunteers. Over the next few years, Milton lived in **Arkansas** and **Louisiana** before settling in **Florida** in 1846. He was elected as a **Democrat** to the state senate in 1848 and became a staunch supporter of **states rights**.

After serving as a delegate at the 1860 Democratic National Convention in **Charleston, South Carolina**, Milton was elected Florida's governor in 1861. He strongly supported **secession**, signed the state's secession ordinance, and supported the seizure of federal installations within the state. Milton was inaugurated in October 1861 and became very active in the war effort. He favored planting fewer cash crops in favor of food items, opposed what he believed was unfair **conscription** (although he limited exemptions and encouraged men to volunteer), and urged **Jefferson Davis** to take control of **blockade running** to ensure vital war materials were delivered to the Confederacy. Milton turned over for Confederate service most of the troops he raised and thus frequently was forced to ask for help in defending Florida from Union raids and invasions. Depressed over looming defeat, he committed suicide in April 1865.

MINE CREEK AND MARAIS DES CYGNES RIVER, KANSAS, BATTLES OF (OCTOBER 25, 1864). During **Sterling Price's 1864 Missouri Raid**, the Confederate column was being pursued toward **Kansas** in late October by **Alfred Pleasonton's** Union cavalry. After being defeated at **Westport, Missouri**, Price continued his retreat into Kansas and camped on the north bank of the Marais des Cygnes (MAIRduh-SEEN) River. On October 25, 1864, Pleasonton drove the Confederates across the river and sent Lt. Col. Frederick W. Benteen and Col. John F. Philips after them. They caught up with the Confederates at Mine Creek later that day as the Confederate wagons were trying to cross the stream.

The Confederates deployed about 7,000 cavalrymen in **James F. Fagan's** and **John S. Marmaduke's divisions** on the north side of the creek to protect their wagons. Although outnumbered, the 2,600 Federal troopers attacked before the Confederates could dismount and used their superior repeating and breech-loading weapons to good effect. The Confederates were forced to continue their retreat after suffering about 300 casualties (including a number who were **massacred** by Union troops for wearing captured Union **uniforms**) and losing 500 **prisoners**. Among the prisoners were Confederate generals **William L. Cabell** and the wounded Marmaduke. The Federals lost about 150 men. The fight at Mine Creek was one of the war's largest cavalry clashes and was the only full-scale battle between Union and Confederate troops in Kansas.

MINE RUN, VIRGINIA, CAMPAIGN OF (NOVEMBER 26–DECEMBER 2, 1863). By the autumn of 1863, Maj. Gen. **George G. Meade's Army of the Potomac** finally had enjoyed some success against **Robert E. Lee's Army of Northern Virginia**. The battles at

Gettysburg, **Bristoe Station**, **Rappahannock Station**, and **Kelly's Ford** had demonstrated that the Federals could defeat their adversary. In November 1863, Meade, under government pressure, launched one last offensive before the campaign season ended. Lee was encamped on the south side of the Rapidan River along a 30-mile line, and Meade planned a **turning movement** by making a swift march around his right flank.

In bitterly cold weather, the Union **army** crossed the Rapidan to Lee's right on November 26, but Lee quickly learned of the move and countered it. On the next day, he sent **Jubal A. Early's** II Corps to the east to confront Meade and brought up **A. P. Hill's** III Corps from his far left (**James Longstreet's** I Corps was on detached duty in **Tennessee**). **William H. French's** III Corps poorly led Meade's army and was running a day behind schedule when it collided with **Edward Johnson's division** at **Payne's Farm**. Farther to the south (the Union left) on the Orange Turnpike, **Robert Rodes's** and **Harry T. Hays's** Confederate divisions blunted the advance of **Gouverneur K. Warren's** II Corps at Locust Grove. These unexpected clashes further delayed Meade's movement and allowed Lee time to bring up Hill and establish a strongly fortified line behind Mine Run. Lee then withdrew Early's divisions behind the earthworks and invited Meade to attack.

After heavy **skirmishing**, Meade accepted the challenge and planned to assault Lee on November 30 after a preliminary **artillery** bombardment. Most of the Union officers and men realized such an attack would be suicidal, and Meade finally canceled the assault after he was asked to reconsider. Realizing he could accomplish nothing more, Meade began withdrawing from Mine Run back across the Rapidan on the night of December 1. Lee had planned to attack the Federals' weak left flank on December 1, but he hesitated in hopes Meade would attack first. When he realized Meade was withdrawing, Lee pursued, but it was too late, and he blamed the enemy's escape on his own delay in attacking the previous day.

Both **armies** went into winter quarters and awaited the spring. During the short campaign, Meade lost 1,633 men to Lee's 795. Although many officials in **Washington, D.C.**, criticized Meade for not accomplishing more, his men appreciated him for not launching a doomed **frontal attack** that would have cost thousands of casualties needlessly.

MINIÉ BALL. The minié (MINNY) ball was a revolutionary bullet (not a ball) that provided speed of loading like a musket but gave the accuracy of a **rifle**. Improving on previous ideas, French captains Henri-Gustave Delvigne and Claude-Étienne Minié developed the bullet in the

1840s. Conical in shape, with a hollow base containing an iron or wooden plug, it was slightly smaller than the weapon's bore. Thus, the bullet could be loaded easily without a patch or hard ramming. When fired, the rifle's explosive gasses forced the plug into the bullet's hollow base, expanding it, and forcing the bullet to grip the barrel's rifling. This gave the bullet spin and greatly improved its distance and accuracy. The **U.S. Army** adopted the minié ball in 1855, but it did not use the iron plug (the British used boxwood or clay plugs), instead letting the explosive gasses alone expand the bullet's hollow base. The minié ball allowed an average marksman to hit targets at several hundred yards and accounted for nearly all of the deaths and wounds in the Civil War.

MINNESOTA. Having been admitted to the Union in 1858, Minnesota only had a population of 172,023 in 1860. Still, it played an important role during the Civil War and became the first state formally to offer troops for the Union's defense when in January 1861 the legislature passed a resolution offering the federal government both men and money. Two days before **Abraham Lincoln** called for volunteers in April, Minnesota's Gov. **Alexander Ramsey** acted upon a request by Secretary of War **Simon Cameron** and put the state's offer in writing.

During the war, Minnesota provided about 24,000 men to the Union **armies**. Although fewer in number than larger states, its **regiments** became well known for courage and steadiness. The 1st Minnesota became one of the war's best-known units when it suffered the largest number of Union casualties at **First Manassas** and then lost 215 out of 262 men at **Gettysburg** while blunting a Confederate attack. With so many of its men at war, the state largely was left defenseless during the 1862 **Sioux uprising**. More than 800 citizens were killed in the uprising, but Gov. **Henry Hastings Sibley** finally defeated the **Indians** with the state militia. Although 307 captured Sioux were sentenced to hang, Lincoln pardoned all but 38.

MISSIONARY RIDGE, TENNESSEE, BATTLE OF (NOVEMBER 25, 1863). Missionary Ridge lies on the eastern side of Chattanooga, Tennessee, and runs southwest to northeast. When Confederate Gen. **Braxton Bragg's Army of Tennessee** besieged the Union **Army of the Cumberland** inside the city in the autumn of 1863, the ridge became an important part of its line because it overlooked the Union positions. In October 1863, **U. S. Grant** was put in command of the Union forces in the west and came to Chattanooga to lift the siege. By November, he had replaced **William S. Rosecrans** with **George H. Thomas** and had approximately 70,000 men to Bragg's 40,000 (Bragg had detached **James Longstreet's** corps for the Knoxville Campaign). In the ensuing **Chattanooga Campaign**, Grant planned for **William T. Sherman** to move across the Tennessee River north of Chattanooga to attack the northern (or right) Confederate flank on Missionary Ridge. **Joseph Hooker** was to clear the Confederates off **Lookout Mountain** and then move to Rossville Gap, where he would be positioned to threaten Bragg's left flank and rear. Thomas was to attack Bragg's center, seize an advanced Confederate position at **Orchard Knob**, and then threaten Missionary Ridge to pin down the enemy.

On November 23, Thomas attacked and seized Orchard Knob. The next day, Hooker successfully drove the Confederates off Lookout Mountain, and Sherman brushed aside one Confederate **brigade** guarding the river and crossed over. On November 25, while Hooker moved slowly toward Rossville Gap, Sherman attacked Missionary Ridge's right flank at about 11:00 A.M. **Patrick Cleburne's** division of **William J. Hardee's** corps repulsed repeated Federal attacks. While the fighting raged, Sherman requested that a diversion be made against the Confederate center. Thomas sent forward the **divisions** of **Thomas J. Wood** and **Philip H. Sheridan** late in the day against the outer trenches of **John C. Breckinridge's** Confederate **corps** holding the center of the ridge. After taking the entrenchments, the Federals came under heavy fire from farther up the slope. Without orders, the men surged forward to escape the fusillade and turned the **demonstration** into a full **frontal attack**. Watching from below, Grant was astonished and promised dire punishment if the impromptu attack failed. It succeeded, however, largely because Bragg's defensive line was poorly laid out on the topographical crest of the ridge rather than the military crest. This meant that the defenders often could not see the attacking enemy while its men struggled up the slope. When Thomas's men poured over the crest, the Confederates panicked and fled. Only a stubborn rear guard led by Cleburne allowed the bulk of Bragg's **army** to fall back 25 miles to Dalton, Georgia.

The disaster at Missionary Ridge ended Bragg's field command. At his own request, he was relieved of command, and **Joseph E. Johnston** took over the Army of Tennessee. The successful operation secured Grant's position as the premier Union commander and led to his being named general-in-chief in March 1864. Neither side enumerated their losses for Missionary Ridge, instead presenting totals for the entire campaign. Grant reported losing 5,815 men around Chattanooga, while Bragg lost 6,667.

MISSISSIPPI. The home state of **Jefferson Davis**, Mississippi was the second Southern state to secede. Under Gov. **John J. Pettus**, a **secession** convention was held in January 1861, and Mississippi's delegates voted to secede on January 9. After existing briefly as the Republic of Mississippi, the state helped form the **Confederate States of America** at the **Montgomery, Alabama, Convention** in February. Besides Davis, other notable Mississippians in the war were **Lucius Q. C. Lamar**, **William Barksdale**, and **Nathan Bedford Forrest**.

Mississippi had an 1860 population of 791,305 and provided approximately 78,000 men to the **Confederate army** (which was more service-age white men than lived in the state in 1860). Of these, about 20,000 (or 26 percent) died. So many soldiers suffered amputations because of wounds that in 1866, the purchase of artificial limbs for its veterans was Mississippi's largest state budget item.

Mississippi also saw some of the worst fighting of the war and suffered tremendous physical damage. Such battles as **Vicksburg**, **Iuka**, **Corinth**, **Okolona**, **Grand Gulf**, **Brice's Cross Roads**, **Port Gibson**, **Raymond**, **Jackson**, **Meridian**, **Tupelo**, **Big Black River Bridge**, **Chickasaw Bayou**, **Snyder's Bluff**, and **Champion Hill** made Mississippi a killing ground. Cavalry raids, such as **Grierson's Raid** and **Sooy Smith's Expedition**, also destroyed much of the state's **railroads** and infrastructure.

MISSISSIPPI MARINE BRIGADE. One of the greatest nuisances facing the **U.S. Navy** in the Mississippi Valley was the harassing activity of Confederate guerrillas. To counter this, **David D. Porter** and **Alfred W. Ellet** received permission from the War Department in the summer of 1862 to form a special unit to fight guerrillas along the Mississippi River. Ellet was commissioned brigadier general of volunteers and was given command of the Mississippi Marine Brigade. He organized three units to make up the **brigade**: the 1st Battalion Mississippi Marine Brigade Infantry, 1st Battalion Mississippi Marine Brigade Cavalry (both organized in **Missouri**), and Walling's Light Artillery Battery (organized in **Pennsylvania**).

Ellet's brigade was placed on transports and arrived at Milliken's Bend, Louisiana, in March 1863. For the next 17 months, it moved up and down the Mississippi River and its tributaries, engaging Confederate guerrillas and sometimes supporting the regular **army**. The Marine Brigade served in **Louisiana**, **Mississippi**, **Arkansas**, and **Tennessee**, and fought at **Port Gibson**, **Ditch Bayou**, and in the **Red River Campaign**. The brigade's effectiveness was marginal because of personal feuds within the Ellet family (which provided the commander and three other officers) and rivalry between the army and navy (both wanting to control the brigade). Civilians also complained that the brigade's members often engaged in looting and vandalism. The brigade was disbanded in August 1864.

MISSISSIPPI RIFLE. *See* HARPERS FERRY RIFLE.

MISSOURI. Badly divided between secessionists and Unionists (who were the clear majority), Missouri suffered more internal strife during the Civil War than any other state. Out of an 1860 population of 1,182,012, it provided 109,000 men to the Union military and approximately 40,000 to the Confederates.

In early 1861, secessionist Gov. **Claiborne F. Jackson** rejected **Abraham Lincoln's** call for volunteers to suppress the rebellion and intended to use his Missouri State Guard to seize the federal arsenal at St. Louis and take the state out of the Union. He was opposed by Congressman **Francis P. Blair Jr.**, who organized a largely German force to help protect the arsenal. Jackson's militia then encamped at **Camp Jackson**, but it was surrounded and captured by Capt. **Nathaniel Lyon** in May. The bloody **St. Louis Riot** ensued when these captured men were marched through the city's streets. Afterward, Jackson openly called for volunteers to drive out the Union forces, abandoned the capital, and retreated into southwest Missouri. After **skirmishing** broke out between the two factions, **Sterling Price** led the State Guard and some Confederate forces in victories at **Wilson's Creek** in August and at **Lexington** in September.

In October, Jackson convened a legislature in Neosho that voted for **secession**, but a pro-Union government already had been organized at Jefferson City. Price was driven from the state into **Arkansas**, fought again at **Pea Ridge** with **Earl Van Dorn** in March 1862, and then enlisted his State Guard into the **Confederate army**, in which he was commissioned a major general. Over the next three years, Missourians fought on both sides throughout the west, and significant military operations took place at **Belmont** and **New Madrid and Island No. 10**. More than 1,000 skirmishes and battles also can be documented within the state as such determined guerrilla leaders as **William Quantrill**, **William Anderson**, and Charles Jennison fought a war of retribution. In 1863, Union Brig. Gen. **Thomas Ewing Jr.** jailed a number of female relatives of Confederate guerrillas to control the Confederates. Several women were killed when the building collapsed, causing Quantrill to retaliate by raiding **Lawrence, Kansas**, in August. Afterward, Ewing issued General Orders No. 11, ordering the evacuation of all disloyal civilians living within one mile of Union military outposts in four western counties. Jennison executed the order with so much violence and destruction that the evacuated region became known as the Burnt District. A year later, the Confederates showed they could be just as brutal when Anderson carried out the **Centralia Massacre**.

Union forces controlled most of Missouri during the latter half of the war, while the Confederates maintained a government in exile, first in Arkansas and then in **Texas**. **Price's Missouri Raid** in 1864 was intended to reestablish Confederate control over the state, but it failed badly. *See also* the BATTLES OF BIG BLUE RIVER, CAPE GIRARDEAU, CARTHAGE, FREDERICKTOWN, GLASGOW, HARTVILLE, INDEPENDENCE, KIRKSVILLE, LIBERTY, LITTLE BLUE RIVER, LONE JACK, MOUNT ZION CHURCH, NEWTONIA, PILOT KNOB, SPRINGFIELD, WESTPORT.

MISSOURI COMPROMISE OF 1820. When **Missouri** applied for statehood in 1819, the **slavery** issue exploded. It had been relatively quiet previously because of an uneasy balance of power in the U.S. Senate between the 11 free and the 11 slave states. Missouri's admission would upset that delicate balance. Although the territory wished to be admitted as a slave state, **New York** Congressman James Tallmadge attempted to amend Missouri's enabling act to outlaw slavery. Southerners were outraged at this attempted congressional interference and feared that if it succeeded, the **U.S. Congress** could strangle slavery by repeating the process elsewhere.

The crisis was ended when Henry Clay secured the passage of the Missouri Compromise in 1820. It simultaneously admitted Missouri as a slave state and **Maine** as a free state to maintain the balance of power. To avoid future crises every time a Louisiana Purchase territory petitioned statehood, the nation was divided along 36°30′ N. Any territory (with the exception of Missouri) admitted north of that line would automatically be free, while those south of it would be slave. The crisis was the first of many controversies that ultimately split the nation, but the Missouri Compromise kept the peace for the next quarter of a century.

MITCHEL, ORMSBY MacKNIGHT (1809–1862) USA. A native of **Kentucky**, as a child, Mitchel moved to **Ohio** with his widowed mother. After clerking in a store, he graduated from **West Point** in 1829 and taught at the academy for the next seven years. Having become a lawyer in the meantime, Mitchel resigned his 2nd lieutenant's commission in 1836 and joined the faculty at Cincinnati College as a professor of astronomy, philosophy, and mathematics. Becoming the nation's foremost astronomer and a popular speaker, he played major roles in creating the Naval, Harvard, and Cincinnati observatories and directed the Cincinnati and Dudley observatories.

Mitchel entered Union service in August 1861 when he was appointed a brigadier general of volunteers. He first was placed in command of the **Department of the Ohio** in September, but in December, he was given command of a **division** in **Don Carlos Buell's Army of the Ohio**. Under Buell, Mitchel did not see any combat but did move into northern **Alabama** in early 1862 to seize the **railroad** at Huntsville. **Andrews's Raid** that spring was carried out by some of Mitchel's men.

Mitchel's actions in northern Alabama won him promotion to major general of volunteers in April 1862. Shortly afterward, he submitted his resignation after clashing with Buell over **discipline**. The resignation was declined by the War Department, and in September 1862 he was sent to command the **Department of the South**. Before he could accomplish anything, however, Mitchel died from yellow fever the following month.

MITCHELL, JOHN GRANT (1838–1894) USA. A native of **Ohio**, Mitchell graduated from Kenyon College in 1859 and began studying law. He joined the Ohio Reserves in June 1861 and entered Union service in July as 1st lieutenant and adjutant of the 3rd Ohio. The **regiment** first served under **William S. Rosecrans** in western **Virginia** and then under **Ormsby M. Mitchel** in northern **Alabama**. Mitchell was promoted to captain in December and to lieutenant colonel of the 113th Ohio in September 1862 after spending the summer recruiting in Ohio.

Mitchell was promoted to colonel of the 113th Ohio in May 1863 and was given command of a **brigade** in **James B. Steedman's division** of the **Army of the Cumberland** just before **Chickamauga**. He fought well in the defense of **Snodgrass Hill** but was only lightly engaged in the **Chattanooga Campaign**. During the **Atlanta Campaign**, Mitchell commanded a brigade in **Jefferson C. Davis's XIV Corps** division. His brigade suffered heavy losses at **Kennesaw Mountain** and after the campaign accompanied **George H. Thomas** to meet the Confederates in the **Franklin and Nashville Campaign**. After fighting at Nashville, Mitchell was promoted to brigadier general of volunteers in January 1865 (at 26 becoming one of the Union's youngest generals) and participated in the **Carolinas Campaign**. His gallantry at **Averasboro** and **Bentonville** won him a **brevet** to major general of volunteers.

After resigning his commission in July 1865, Mitchell returned to his Ohio law practice. He served a number of times on the Columbus city council and was appointed Ohio's pension commissioner by his wife's uncle, President **Rutherford B. Hayes.**

MITCHELL, ROBERT BYINGTON (1823–1882) USA. A native of **Ohio**, Mitchell was said to have graduated from both Kenyon and Washington Colleges, but neither institution has any record of it. He became a lawyer but interrupted his practice to serve in the **Mexican War** as a lieutenant in the 2nd Ohio. After the war, Mitchell returned to Ohio and was elected mayor of Mount Gilead in 1855. Moving to **Kansas** in 1856, he became involved with the antislavery forces, served as a **Democratic** territorial legislator, and was a delegate to both the Leavenworth constitutional convention and the 1860 Democratic National Convention in **Charleston, South Carolina.**

Mitchell entered Union service in May 1861 as colonel of the 2nd Kansas. After being badly wounded at **Wilson's Creek**, he was promoted to brigadier general of volunteers in April 1862 and was given command of a **brigade**. Mitchell became a **division** commander in August and led the 9th Division in the **Army of the Ohio's** III Corps at **Perryville**. While in command of a division in the **Army of the Cumberland's** XIV Corps in November, he was stationed in Nashville, Tennessee, and thus missed the **Battle of Stones River**. In March 1863, Mitchell was given one of the **army's** cavalry divisions and led it during the **Tullahoma Campaign**. He then took command of all the army's cavalry in September led it at **Chickamauga**. When poor health, partly due to wounds, forced him to relinquish command in November, Mitchell was placed on court-martial duty. From January 1865 until war's end, he commanded various **districts** within the **Department of Kansas.**

Mitchell resigned his commission in January 1866 and became the territorial governor of **New Mexico**. He was ill-suited for that position, however, and resigned in 1869. Returning to Kansas, Mitchell ran for Congress in 1872 but was defeated.

MOBILE, ALABAMA, CAMPAIGN (MARCH 17, 1865–APRIL 12, 1865). Mobile, Alabama, was a prize much sought after by Union forces because of its importance as a Confederate port and **railroad** center. After **David Farragut** captured **Mobile Bay** in August 1864, the Federals were unable to capture the city itself because of the strong Confederate fortifications northeast of the city at **Spanish Fort** and **Fort Blakely**. It was not until March 1865 that a sufficient land and naval force had been assembled to attempt to overrun the Confederate strongholds. Supported by Adm. Henry K. Thatcher's 20 ships, Maj. Gen. E. R. S. Canby assembled 45,000 men for the operation. Defending Mobile were 10,000 Confederates and five gunboats under Maj. Gen. **Dabney H. Maury.** Canby had Maj. Gen. **Frederick Steele** march 13,000 men from **Pensacola, Florida,** to attack Fort Blakely from the north, while his 32,000 men attacked Spanish Fort from the south. Canby left **Fort Morgan** on March 17, 1865, and moved up the east side of Mobile Bay to Spanish Fort, where he assembled 90 cannons and pounded the 4,000 Confederate defenders from March 27 to April 8. On the night of April 8, he launched a successful assault that overran the fort at a cost of 657 men. The Confederate commander, Brig. Gen. **Randall L. Gibson,** reported losing 487 dead and wounded and 250 missing, but the surviving Confederates made their way to Mobile.

Five miles to the north, Steele had been engaged in siege work at Fort Blakely since April 1 and soon was reinforced by Canby's troops. The few thousand Confederate defenders under Brig. Gen. **St. John R. Liddell** held out until April 9. On that day (the same day **Robert E. Lee** surrendered at **Appomattox**), the last major battle of the Civil War occurred when Canby attacked Fort Blakely and captured it in 20 minutes. In this battle, Union **black troops** played an important role in the assault. Canby lost 629 men but captured 3,423 **prisoners** and 40 guns. Maury evacuated Mobile on April 12, and the Federals took possession of the city shortly after noon.

MOBILE BAY, ALABAMA, BATTLE OF (AUGUST 5, 1864). In the summer of 1864, Union forces began moving against the important Confederate port of Mobile, Alabama. To capture the city, the Federals first would have to gain control of Mobile Bay, which was guarded by three forts. **Fort Gaines,** located on the eastern end of Dauphin Island, protected the bay's western approaches, while **Fort Morgan,** located southeast of Gaines, protected the bay's main entrance from Mobile Point. **Fort Powell** was a third, smaller fort, that was located northwest of Fort Gaines on Grant Pass in the Mississippi Sound. All three forts were under the command of Brig. Gen. **Richard L. Page,** headquartered at Fort Morgan. Assisting Page was Adm. **Franklin Buchanan,** who commanded a small fleet of ships that included the iron **ram** *Tennessee* and the smaller wooden gunboats *Morgan*, *Gaines*, and *Selma*.

Attacking Mobile Bay was the Union fleet under Rear Adm. **David G. Farragut,** assisted by a small land force under Maj. Gen. **Gordon Granger.** On August 5, 1864, Farragut led 18 ships into the bay. Because the Confederates had placed pilings to block all the channels except the main one, Farragut's ships had to sail past Fort Morgan. The fleet's 14 wooden ships were lashed together in pairs, with the stronger ones facing the fort, while four **monitors** steamed between them and the fort to lay down covering fire. Farragut's lead ship, the monitor *Tecumseh*, struck a **torpedo** and sank. The captain of the next vessel, the *Brooklyn*, became unnerved and threatened to disrupt the formation by backing up to avoid the torpedoes. Lashed to the rigging of the ***Hartford***, Farragut supposedly yelled, "Damn the torpedoes! Full speed ahead!" and ordered his flagship to take the lead.

Farragut boldly sailed through the minefield and engaged the Confederate fleet. The Federals disabled the *Gaines* and forced the *Selma* to surrender, while the *Morgan* escaped. Onboard the *Tennessee*, Buchanan then engaged the enemy alone. In a furious one-hour engagement against the entire Union fleet, the *Tennessee* was repeatedly rammed and raked by broadsides. Finally, the ship surrendered after it was rendered helpless, and Buchanan suffered a broken leg. That night, the Confederates evacuated Fort Powell and blew it up. Fort Gaines surrendered on August 8, and on August 9 Granger began siege operations against Fort Morgan. The combined Union **army** and naval forces bombarded the fort on August 21 and forced Page to surrender on August 23. During the battle for Mobile Bay, the Confederates lost approximately 1,500 men to the Federals' 327 casualties.

The capture of Mobile Bay prevented Confederate **blockade runners** from using it and placed Union forces in position to take the city. The Union army began the **Mobile Campaign** in March 1865 and finally captured the city in April.

MONETT'S FERRY, LOUISIANA, BATTLE OF (APRIL 23, 1864). After the 1864 **Red River Campaign** had been stopped at **Mansfield** and **Pleasant Hill**, Union Maj. Gen. **Nathaniel P. Banks** retreated back down the Red River toward Alexandria, Louisiana. From Grand Ecore, his large **army** marched down the narrow strip of land between the Red and Cane Rivers. A large part of **Richard Taylor's** small **Confederate army** had been sent to **Arkansas** to stop the **Camden Expedition**, so Taylor was too weak to seriously threaten Banks's column. Between Natchitoches (NAK-uh-tish) and Alexandria, however, Taylor decided to cut off the Federal retreat at the Cane River crossing at Monett's (mah-NETS) Ferry.

Taylor sent 1,600 cavalrymen and four **artillery** batteries under **Hamilton P. Bee** to establish a defensive position on a series of hills on the south side of the river crossing. When Banks's vanguard approached on the morning of April 23, it did not try to force a crossing. Instead, **William H. Emory's division** moved upstream and forded Cane River, while the other Federal troops **demonstrated** against Bee's front. Sweeping down on Bee's left flank, Emory routed the defenders and cleared the river crossing. Bee lost approximately 400 men to Emory's 200 casualties. Taylor blamed Bee for the poor defense and later relieved him of command. Banks continued the retreat to Alexandria, where he reunited with **David Porter's** fleet.

MONITOR. After **John Ericsson** designed the USS *Monitor*, all similar **ironclad** gunboats that mounted guns in turrets in the Civil War were known as monitors.

MONITOR, **USS.** This famous ship ushered in a new type of **ironclad** gunboat. Designed by Swedish inventor **John Ericcson** to help **blockade** Southern shallow water ports, it was launched in January 1862. Unusual in shape, the *Monitor*'s exposed parts were covered in iron from 4.5 to 8 inches thick, and it had a deck that barely rose above the water line. Jutting from the low deck toward the bow was a pilothouse, and a revolving steam-driven turret located amidships mounted two 11-inch **Dahlgrens**. Above water, the ship measured 172 feet long and 41.5 feet wide, being slightly smaller below the water line. The *Monitor* displaced 1,200 tons with a 10.5-foot draft. Dubbed "Ericcson's Folly," the ship was said to resemble a cheese box on a raft. Despite its unorthodox design, the *Monitor* proved to be a valuable weapon.

Captained by **John L. Worden**, the *Monitor* left New York City in early March and was being towed to **North Carolina** when the CSS *Virginia* attacked the wooden Union blockading fleet at **Hampton Roads, Virginia**. The *Monitor* arrived on the night of March 8 and the next day engaged the *Virginia* at Hampton Roads. This historic clash was a **tactical** stalemate, but the power of ironclads was demonstrated.

The *Monitor* served in **Virginia** on the James River for most of the year and fought at **First Drewry's Bluff** in May. In late December 1862, as it was being towed to North Carolina, it foundered in a storm off Cape Hatteras shortly after midnight in the early morning of December 31 and sank with 16 officers and men. The wreck was discovered in 1973 and is now a protected historic site.

MONOCACY, MARYLAND, BATTLE OF (JULY 9, 1864). As **Jubal A. Early's** 14,000 Confederates of the **Army of Northern Virginia's** II Corps moved into **Maryland** during **Early's Washington Raid** in the summer of 1864, Union Maj. Gen. **Lew Wallace**, commander of the **Middle Department**, prepared a defense. Wallace assembled some 5,800 men from **Erastus B. Tyler's brigade** and **James B. Ricketts's division** (which had been hurried to his aid from the **Army of the Potomac's** VI Corps) along the Monocacy (muh-NOK-acy) River, just south of Frederick, Maryland. Uncertain if Early was heading for **Washington, D.C.**, or Baltimore, Maryland, Wallace had to defend two river crossings. To the north, he placed Tyler's brigade on the river's west bank to block the National Road leading to Baltimore, while Ricketts held the southern or left flank on the east bank to guard the Georgetown Pike and Baltimore & Ohio Railroad crossings. Wallace recognized he was outnumbered and did not expect to win the battle. Instead, he intended to uncover Early's plans and delay him long enough for reinforcements from the Army of the Potomac in **Virginia** to reach the capital.

In the early morning of July 9, Early's **corps** approached from the west along both roads. **Stephen D. Ramseur's** division drove Ricketts advance guard back across the river to the east side, but Ramseur decided the covered bridge on the Georgetown Pike was too heavily defended to force a crossing. Heavy **skirmishing** continued along both roads until Confederate cavalry crossed the river a short distance beyond Ricketts's left flank. Fighting increased there as both sides realized the significance of turning Wallace's left flank and sent in reinforcements. Wallace finally burned the covered road bridge about noon and moved all of Ricketts's division to the left.

Early ordered **John C. Breckinridge** to cross the river and attack Wallace's left with the divisions of **John B. Gordon** and **John A. Wharton**. While Ramseur and **Robert Rodes** kept up the pressure on the Georgetown and National Roads, respectively, Breckinridge attacked the Union left with Gordon's division at about 3:30 P.M. The fighting was bitter, with numerous attacks being made, and losses were heavy on both sides as Gordon slowly forced back the Federals. Realizing he could not hold his position, Wallace finally ordered a withdrawal and escaped to Washington.

The Battle of the Monocacy was remembered by veterans as one of the war's hardest fought engagements. Early lost 700–900 men, while Wallace counted 1,294 casualties. While the battle was a victory for Early, Wallace had accomplished his purpose and bought enough time to allow reinforcements to reach Washington from Virginia. Thus, Early was unable to take the capital a few days later and had to retreat back into Virginia.

MONROE'S CROSS ROADS, NORTH CAROLINA, BATTLE OF (MARCH 10, 1865).

On March 6, 1865, during the **Carolinas Campaign**, Union cavalry under **H. Judson Kilpatrick** entered **North Carolina** while screening **William T. Sherman's** left flank. Learning that 4,000 Confederate cavalrymen under **Wade Hampton** were to his rear, moving north to reach the safety of Fayetteville, Kilpatrick blocked Hampton's three possible routes and then camped with George E. Spencer's **brigade** at Monroe's Cross Roads. Hampton discovered the Federals and sent 1,000 men under **Matthew C. Butler** to attack Spencer, while **Joseph Wheeler** blocked the Union line of retreat with his command.

Attacking at dawn, the Confederates completely surprised the Federals and routed them. Kilpatrick was forced to flee in his nightshirt. Intervening swamps prevented Wheeler from reinforcing Butler, and Kilpatrick finally brought up reinforcements and drove off the Confederates. In the sharp clash, the Federals lost about 190 men, while Butler suffered approximately 100 casualties. Afterward, Hampton was able to reach Fayetteville safely.

MONTGOMERY, ALABAMA, CONVENTION. On February 4, 1861, the seceding Southern states met in convention in Montgomery, Alabama, to form the **Confederate States of America**. The convention decided that each state would be allowed the same number of delegates as it had previously held in the U.S. House of Representatives, plus two at-large delegates. **South Carolina, Georgia, Florida, Alabama, Mississippi, Louisiana**, and **Texas** (which arrived after the convention began) sent 50 delegates, who organized themselves into a provisional congress. Working largely in secret, by March 16 the soon-to-be Provisional **Confederate Congress** created the new government and adopted a **Confederate constitution** (largely a copy of the U.S. Constitution) and **flag**; chose **Jefferson Davis** and **Alexander Stephens** as president and vice president, respectively; authorized a **Confederate army**; issued $15 million in treasury bonds; and created a cabinet. The Confederate government made Montgomery its capital until May, when it was moved to **Richmond, Virginia**.

MONTGOMERY, WILLIAM READING (1801–1871) USA. A native of **New Jersey**, Montgomery graduated near the bottom of the 1825 **West Point** class. Posted to the infantry, he served on the Canadian border, in the **Seminole Wars**, and in **Texas**. As a captain of the 8th U.S. Infantry during the **Mexican War**, Montgomery was **brevetted** twice for gallantry and was wounded twice while serving under Zachary Taylor. Promoted to major in 1852, he was assigned to **Kansas** and there became involved in controversy when he apparently angered the proslavery faction by becoming too close to the **abolitionists**. Afterward, **slavery** supporters supposedly had Montgomery dismissed from the **U.S. Army** in 1855 on charges he had used his position to gain land for a **Free-Soil** town.

Montgomery moved to **Pennsylvania** and later entered Union service in May 1861 when he was commissioned colonel of the 1st New Jersey. He served at **First Manassas** in the reserve **division** but did not see combat. Promoted to brigadier general of volunteers in August, Montgomery spent the rest of the war in various administrative positions in **Virginia**, **Maryland**, and Pennsylvania. He resigned his commission, supposedly for health reasons, in April 1864.

After leaving the service, Montgomery returned to Pennsylvania, where he worked for a time in the wood molding business and then retired.

MOODY, YOUNG MARSHALL (1822–1866) CSA. A native of **Virginia**, Moody moved to **Alabama** when he was 20 and became a teacher, merchant, and circuit court clerk. He was serving in the latter position when the Civil War began.

Resigning his clerkship, Moody entered Confederate service in June 1861 as a captain in the 11th Alabama and served in Virginia in **Cadmus M. Wilcox's** brigade until early 1862. He then went to Mobile, Alabama, helped raise the 43rd Alabama, and was commissioned its lieutenant colonel in May. As part of **Danville Leadbetter's brigade**, the **regiment** served around Chattanooga, Tennessee, and Moody led it during the **Kentucky Campaign**, but the men did not see any serious combat. In November 1862, Moody was promoted to colonel when his commander **Archibald Gracie** took over the brigade. He and the regiment garrisoned Cumberland Gap until August 1863, at which time they reinforced the **Army of Tennessee** for the **Battle of Chickamauga**. After fighting well there, Moody participated in both the siege of **Chattanooga** and the **Knoxville Campaign** and temporarily led the brigade at **Bean's Station** after Gracie was wounded.

In May 1864, Moody commanded the brigade when it was transferred to Virginia. As part of **Robert Ransom's division**, he fought at **Second Drewry's Bluff** and was seriously wounded in the ankle but recovered in time to rejoin his regiment for the **Petersburg Campaign**. When Gracie was killed in December, Moody took permanent command of the brigade and was promoted to brigadier general in March 1865. He continued to serve at Petersburg until illness confined him to an ambulance during its evacuation. Moody was captured the day before the **surrender** at **Appomattox**. After the war, Moody became a successful Alabama businessman. He traveled to **Louisiana** in 1866 to expand his business but died from yellow fever once he got there.

MOORE, ANDREW BARRY (1807–1873) CSA. A native of **South Carolina**, Moore moved to **Alabama** as a young man, passed the bar exam, and taught school. He served as a justice of the peace for eight years and was elected to the state legislature in 1839 as a **Democrat**. Moore was defeated for reelection in 1840, but he was elected again in 1842 and served until 1847, the last four years as speaker of the house. Appointed a circuit judge in 1851, he kept that position until he resigned in 1857 to run unopposed for governor. Moore was reelected two years later.

As governor, Moore supervised the building of the state's insane asylum and the school for the blind. A moderate on the **secession** issue, he ordered elections for January 1861 to choose delegates to a secession convention and ordered the seizure of federal forts and arsenals in the state a few days before the convention met in Montgomery. The delegates supported Moore's actions, and they voted to secede on January 11.

With war approaching, Moore persuaded the legislature to authorize money and the incurring of debt to prepare the state's defenses. When fighting began, he vigorously raised troops and generally supported **Jefferson Davis's** war efforts. State law prohibited Moore from serving more than four years as governor, so in December 1861 **John G. Shorter** succeeded him. For the rest of the war, Moore served as Shorter's aide-de-camp and adviser and continued to recruit troops, gather slave labor for important construction projects, and obtain food for the poor.

At war's end, Moore was arrested in May 1865 and was imprisoned in **Fort Pulaski, Georgia**, until August. Upon his release, he resumed his law practice.

MOORE, JOHN CREED (1824–1910) CSA. A native of **Tennessee**, Moore attended **Virginia's** Emory and Henry College before graduating from **West Point** in 1849. Assigned to the **artillery**, he served in the **Seminole Wars** and on the frontier before resigning his 1st lieutenant's commission in 1855 to engage in civil engineering and railroading. Moore had been teaching at **Kentucky's** Shelby College for about a year when the Civil War began.

Moore entered Confederate service in April 1861 as a captain of Confederate artillery and was sent to organize the defenses at Galveston, Texas. With **Earl Van Dorn's** support, he raised the 2nd Texas and was commissioned its colonel in September. In April 1862, the **regiment** was sent to Corinth, Mississippi, where it became part of **John K. Jackson's brigade**. Moore saw heavy fighting at **Shiloh** and temporarily commanded a brigade on the second day. His actions were praised by his **division** commander, although **William J. Hardee** criticized him for performing poorly. Nevertheless, Moore earned a promotion to brigadier general in May.

Taking command of a brigade in **Dabney H. Maury's** division, Moore fought well at **Corinth**, where he captured several enemy positions before the Confederates were driven away. After serving under Van Dorn in northern **Mississippi** for several months, his brigade was sent to **Vicksburg, Mississippi**, in December. Moore helped turn back the **Yazoo Pass Expedition** in early 1863 and then guarded the southern approaches to Vicksburg when **U. S. Grant** crossed the Mississippi River during the **Vicksburg Campaign**. As part of **John H. Forney's** division, Moore's brigade saw heavy combat in the trenches throughout the siege of Vicksburg and was captured when the city fell.

Moore was **exchanged** in September 1863 and was sent with his brigade that autumn to reinforce **Braxton Bragg's Army of Tennessee** at Chattanooga, Tennessee. This caused some controversy, because Grant declared that Moore had not been exchanged officially and that he was in violation of his **parole**. The matter was not settled until records proving Moore's exchange were found in 1876. Assigned to John K. Jackson's division, Moore fought well on **Lookout Mountain,** and at **Missionary Ridge** he held his ground after other units fled and then helped form the rear guard. After the defeat, he was one of several officers who bitterly criticized Jackson for his lack of leadership during the fighting. In December 1863, Moore was assigned to Maury at Mobile, Alabama, and was put in command of his "eastern division." However, he resigned his commission for obscure reasons in February 1864 and returned to Galveston. After the war, Moore remained in **Texas** and worked as a teacher and writer.

MOORE, PATRICK THEODORE (1821–1883) CSA. A native of Ireland, Moore was the son of a British diplomat who went to **Massachusetts** by way of Canada. He settled in **Virginia** in 1850, became a merchant, and rose to the rank of captain in the militia.

Moore entered Confederate service in May 1861 when he was commissioned colonel of the 1st Virginia. While serving in **James Longstreet's**

brigade, he was severely wounded in the head at **Blackburn's Ford**. The wound prevented him from resuming his field command, so he joined **Joseph E. Johnston's** staff as a volunteer aide-de-camp and served in the **Peninsula Campaign**. When Johnston was wounded at **Seven Pines**, Moore joined Longstreet's staff and served with him in the **Army of Northern Virginia** during the **Seven Days Campaign**. After the Seven Days, he served on court-martial duty until 1864 and then assisted **James Kemper** in organizing Virginia's reserve forces. Moore was promoted to brigadier general in September 1864 and took command of a brigade under **Richard S. Ewell** in the **Richmond** defenses. It is not certain, but Moore probably was captured with Ewell at **Sailor's Creek**.

After the war, Moore settled in Richmond and became an insurance agent.

MOORE, THOMAS OVERTON (1804–1876) CSA. A native of **North Carolina**, Moore moved to **Louisiana** as a young man and became a prominent sugar planter. Becoming involved in **Democratic** politics, he served on his parish's police jury and was elected to the state assembly in 1848 and to the senate in 1856.

Moore was elected governor in 1859 and strongly supported **secession**. After convening a special legislative session in November 1860 to prepare for a secession convention, he mobilized the militia and began seizing federal installations even before Louisiana seceded. Two of these were the valuable **Baton Rouge** arsenal, where Moore captured 50,000 muskets and numerous cannons, and the U.S. Mint in **New Orleans**. After Louisiana seceded in January 1861, he recruited troops, encouraged merchants to accept Confederate Treasury notes, and prepared the state for defense. When Baton Rouge fell to the **U.S. Navy** in the spring of 1862, Moore moved the capital first to Opelousas and then to Shreveport. In Shreveport, he cooperated with Gen. **Edmund Kirby Smith** in defending the **Trans-Mississippi Department**, sponsored relief programs for soldiers' families, and tried to stamp out trade with the enemy. Prohibited by law from running for reelection, Moore was replaced in 1864 by **Henry Watkins Allen**.

After leaving office, Moore lived for a while in **Texas** but exiled himself to Mexico and Cuba when the war ended. He returned to Louisiana in 1866 and resumed his life as a planter.

MOOREFIELD, WEST VIRGINIA, BATTLE OF (AUGUST 7, 1864). After Confederate Brig. Gen. **John McCausland** made his **Chambersburg, Pennsylvania, Raid** in July 1864, he withdrew his and **Bradley**

T. Johnson's cavalry **brigades** to near Moorefield, West Virginia. Angered over the burning of Chambersburg, Union Maj. Gen. **David Hunter** ordered **William W. Averell** to cross the Potomac River and attack the Confederates. In a daring move, Averell took 1,600 Union cavalry across the river on August 1 in search of the enemy. After discovering McCausland's camp, the Federals captured the **pickets** and attacked with complete surprise. First striking Johnson and then McCausland, Averell routed the Confederates and forced them to abandon their wagons and four cannons. Averell also reported capturing about 420 men (mostly taken **prisoner**), while losing only 41.

MORELL, GEORGE WEBB (1815–1883) USA. A native of **New York**, Morell was the son of a state militia major general and future **Michigan** chief justice. He graduated first in the **West Point** class of 1835 and entered the **engineers** but resigned his commission two years later. Morell then worked in **railroad** construction before becoming a lawyer in 1842. He was commissioned a major during the **Mexican War**, but his regiment never obtained enough troops to be mustered into service.

In May 1861, Morell was appointed colonel and quartermaster of New York volunteers. He was commissioned brigadier general of volunteers in August and was given a **brigade** in **Fitz John Porter's** division of the **Army of the Potomac**. After fighting in the **Peninsula Campaign**, Morell took command of the **division** when Porter took over the V Corps. He fought well in the **Seven Days Campaign** and was promoted to major general of volunteers in July 1862. After serving in the **Second Manassas** and **Antietam Campaigns**, Morell's career was ruined by Porter's court-martial. Called as a witness, his testimony supported Porter and earned Morell the enmity of the government. When the Senate did not confirm his promotion to major general, he never again held a field command. For the rest of the war, Morell waited in vain for orders and served around **Washington, D.C.**, and in **Indiana**. He finally was mustered out of service in December 1864 and became a New York farmer.

MORGAN, EDWIN DENISON (1811–1883) USA. A native of **Massachusetts**, Morgan moved with his family to **Connecticut**, where he attended a private academy and became a clerk in his uncle's store. After serving on the local city council, he moved to New York City and became very wealthy from his financing and merchant interests. Morgan was elected city alderman as a **Whig** in 1849 and served two terms in the state senate from 1855 to 1858. He declined to run for a third term and, instead, served as commissioner of immigration from 1855 to 1858. Having helped organize the **Republican Party** in **New York**, Morgan also served as state party chairman from 1856 to 1862. In 1858, Morgan was elected New York's governor. A very popular politician, he was known for being honest and worked hard to improve the state's finances and canal network. Reelected in 1860, Morgan strongly supported **Abraham Lincoln's** war policies and provided more than 200,000 men for Union service. In September 1861, Lincoln appointed him a major general of volunteers and commander of the **Department of New York** as a way to increase his effectiveness.

Although a Republican, Morgan was a moderate on the **slavery** issue and eventually angered the **Radical Republicans**. As a result, he declined to run for a third term, left office, and resigned his military commission in January 1863. Just before his term expired, Morgan was elected to the U.S. Senate. When **Andrew Johnson** became president, he nominated Morgan secretary of the treasury, but Morgan refused the position (he declined a second time in 1881). As a senator, Morgan opposed most of Johnson's **Reconstruction** policies and voted to convict him during the impeachment. He was defeated for reelection and failed in several other political races, although he did serve as the state Republican chairman from 1872 to 1876. Morgan also was a generous philanthropist.

MORGAN, GEORGE WASHINGTON (1820–1893) USA. A native of **Pennsylvania**, Morgan dropped out of college when he was 16, moved to **Texas**, and was appointed a captain in the Texas army by **Sam Houston**. He then entered **West Point** in 1841 but resigned in 1843 because of poor grades. Afterward, Morgan became a lawyer and prosecutor, and he entered the **Mexican War** as colonel of the 2nd Ohio. He soon was commissioned colonel of the 15th U.S. Infantry and was wounded twice and **brevetted** brigadier general. Settling in **Ohio** after the war, Morgan first farmed and practiced law before being appointed U.S. consul to Marseilles, France, in 1856. He was serving as U.S. minister to Portugal when the **secession** crisis erupted. Resigning his post, Morgan returned to the United States and was appointed brigadier general of volunteers in November 1861.

Placed in command of a **division** in the **Army of the Ohio** in March 1862, Morgan's greatest war contribution came the next month when he captured the Cumberland Gap from the Confederates. Although he led a division under **William T. Sherman** during the **Battle of Chickasaw Bayou**, Sherman was not pleased with his leadership. When the Federals attacked **Arkansas Post** in early 1863, Morgan led the XIII Corps, but he was back in a division command with the **Army of the Tennessee** for the **Vicksburg Campaign**. After **Vicksburg** was surrounded in the spring of 1863, Morgan became disgruntled with the **army** because of his difficulties with Sherman and the increased reliance on **black troops**. He resigned his commission in June and returned home.

Morgan returned to Ohio politics and supported **George B. McClellan** for president in 1864. He was defeated for governor in 1865 but afterward served three terms in the **U.S. Congress**, where he opposed radical **Reconstruction**.

MORGAN, JAMES DADA (1810–1896) USA. A native of **Massachusetts**, Morgan went to sea in 1826. Other crewmen mutinied after only a month, and the ship was burned, but he reached South Africa after spending two weeks in a life raft. Returning to the United States, Morgan settled in **Illinois**, became a prosperous merchant, and served in the local militia during the Mormon disturbances of the mid-1840s. After serving in the **Mexican War** as a captain in the 1st Illinois, he returned to his Illinois business.

Morgan entered Union service in April 1861 as lieutenant colonel of the 90-day 10th Illinois and became colonel the following month. When the **regiment** reenlisted for three years, he was elected colonel but then was placed in command of a **brigade** in February 1862 and led it during operations at **Island No. 10** and in the **siege of Corinth, Mississippi**. Promoted to brigadier general of volunteers in July, Morgan joined the **Army of the Cumberland's** XIV Corps in November 1862 and temporarily commanded his **division** during much of 1863. That autumn, he was sent to Bridgeport, Alabama, where his brigade guarded the vital **railroad** crossing during the **Chickamauga** and **Chattanooga Campaigns**. Morgan served throughout the **Atlanta Campaign** under **Jefferson C. Davis**, but he took command of the division in August 1864 and led it during the **March to the Sea** and the **Carolinas Campaign**.

A dependable officer, Morgan was **brevetted** major general of volunteers for his war service and was mustered out of the volunteers in August 1864. He then returned to his Illinois business and banking interests and became active in veterans' affairs.

MORGAN, JOHN HUNT (1825–1864) CSA. A native of **Alabama**, as a boy, Morgan moved to **Kentucky** with his family. He entered Transylvania University in 1842 but was suspended two years later for dueling. Morgan rejected a **U.S. Marine Corps** commission in 1845, but he joined the 1st Regiment of Mounted Volunteers the following year and during the **Mexican War** was wounded and promoted to 1st lieutenant. ·After the war, he bought a Kentucky hemp factory and wool mill and became a prosperous businessman.

Morgan had been active in the militia before the Civil War and in 1857 had organized his own unit, the Kentucky Rifles. Although pro-Confederate, he initially did not become active in the war, possibly because of his invalid wife. After her death in July 1861, Morgan and his Kentucky Rifles joined the Confederate forces at Bowling Green. Although serving as his **company's** captain, he was not officially mustered into service until October. During his career, Morgan became one of the most famous Confederate officers and was seen as the epitome of the cavalry raider. Standing six feet tall and having dashing good looks, he electrified both sides with the daring **Morgan's Kentucky Raids**.

Morgan gained much recognition for carrying out successful raids against enemy outposts in Kentucky and was promoted to colonel in February 1862. His reputation helped him recruit more men for his command, and in April, he was made colonel of the new 2nd Kentucky Cavalry (Confederate). Playing only a small role at **Shiloh**, Morgan afterward continued raids in Kentucky and **Tennessee** and in August destroyed an important **railroad** bridge at **Gallatin, Tennessee**. Remaining in Kentucky when **Braxton Bragg** withdrew at the end of the **Kentucky Campaign**, Morgan doubled back through central Kentucky and exited by way of Hopkinsville. In early December, with the help of Kentucky infantry, he captured **Hartsville, Tennessee**, and some 2,000 Union soldiers.

These exploits earned Morgan promotion to brigadier general that month. That same month he launched his Christmas Raid, which resulted in the destruction of important railroad trestles near Elizabethtown, Kentucky. After this raid, Morgan's effectiveness waned. His brother-in-law and second in command, Brig. Gen. **Basil Duke**, believed he became too distracted after marrying young Martha Ready in December 1862 (Morgan also was the brother-in-law of Maj. Gen. **A. P. Hill**). Bragg also became disillusioned with Morgan because he did not serve well under others, and his command returned from raids so broken down as almost to negate any gains made.

Morgan was given a cavalry **brigade** in **Joseph Wheeler's** command and then a **division**. His most famous raid, **Morgan's Ohio Raid**, began in July 1863 when he crossed the Ohio River against orders and raised havoc in **Indiana** and **Ohio** before being captured with most of his men. Imprisoned in the Ohio Penitentiary, Morgan and six fellow officers made a daring escape in November and returned South. Returning to brigade command, he quickly launched another unauthorized raid into Kentucky seeking to recoup his reputation. This raid was marked by much plundering and a lack of **discipline**, because Duke, who had been Morgan's disciplinarian, remained in **prison**. By that time, Duke had come to be recognized as the brains behind Morgan's successful raids, and one newspaper editor noted, "Someone might hit Duke on the head and knock Morgan's brains out" (Davis, ed., *The Confederate General*, vol. 4, 189).

Despite his problems, Morgan captured 500 **prisoners** at **Cynthiana, Kentucky**, in June 1864, but the next day was attacked and defeated. Shortly afterward, he was placed in command of the **Department of Western Virginia and East Tennessee**, but he was removed in August because of growing concerns about his conduct. A court of inquiry was ordered for September, but Morgan was surprised by Union troops at Greeneville, Tennessee, on September 3 and was killed while trying to escape.

MORGAN, JOHN TYLER (1824–1907) CSA. A native of **Tennessee**, Morgan moved with his family to **Alabama** as a boy. Home-schooled, he became a prominent lawyer and served in the Alabama **secession** convention, where he voted for secession.

Morgan briefly served on militia Maj. Gen. Jeremiah Clemens's staff at **Fort Morgan, Alabama**, but entered Confederate service in May 1861 as a private in the 5th Alabama. Within a few days, he was elected major and accompanied the **regiment** to Virginia. Morgan was promoted to lieutenant colonel in November, but when his regiment's enlistment expired in May 1862, he returned to Alabama and raised the 51st Alabama Partisan Rangers in August. Appointed colonel the following month, he guarded **railroads** in northern Alabama and Middle Tennessee and briefly served under **Nathan Bedford Forrest** before being transferred to **Joseph Wheeler's** command and fighting with him and the **Army of Tennessee** at **Stones River** and in the **Tullahoma Campaign**.

Morgan was promoted to brigadier general in June 1863 and was ordered to **Virginia**, but he declined the commission to remain with the regiment when he learned that its lieutenant colonel had been killed. He soon was given command of a **brigade** in **William T. Martin's** cavalry **division** and led it at **Chickamauga** and in **Wheeler's Raid** into Tennessee. Morgan was reappointed brigadier general in November 1863, and during the **Knoxville Campaign**, he assumed command of his division when Martin took over **James Longstreet's** cavalry. After covering the retreat from Knoxville, Morgan's division was routed by Union cavalry near **Fair Garden** in January 1864, and Morgan was almost captured. Resuming command of the brigade in the spring of 1864, he was placed under arrest for drunkenness while in command of Rome, Georgia, but was released in August. Morgan then was given command of a reserve cavalry force and led it in the latter part of the **Atlanta Campaign**. After briefly serving under Wheeler during the **March to the Sea**, he was sent to Alabama to recruit. It is ironic that although he was an avowed white supremacist, Morgan was in **Mississippi** attempting to raise **black troops** from Alabama and Mississippi when the war ended.

After the war, Morgan resumed his Alabama law practice and was elected to the U.S. Senate in 1876. He served continously until his death in 1907.

MORGAN'S KENTUCKY RAIDS. Confederate cavalry raider **John Hunt Morgan** made three **Kentucky** raids during the Civil War. His first was in July 1862 when he led two **regiments** from Knoxville, Tennessee, into Kentucky to disrupt Union Maj. Gen. **Don Carlos Buell's** advance on Chattanooga, Tennessee, while **Nathan Bedford Forrest** led his cavalry on a similar raid into **Tennessee**. Leaving Knoxville on July 4 with about 800 men, Morgan captured Tomkinsville, Kentucky, and its garrison on July 9. Union supply depots at Glasgow and Lebanon fell on the 10th and 11th, respectively, before he moved to Cynthiana by way of Harrodsburg and Georgetown. After a small engagement on July 17 with Union militia at Cynthiana, the raiders destroyed a supply base at Crab Orchard. Morgan returned to Tennessee on August 1, having traveled more than 1,000 miles and captured and **paroled** 1,200 **prisoners** at a loss of fewer than 100 men. His and Forrest's raids embarrassed Union officials and helped save Chattanooga from capture.

Morgan's second Kentucky raid came in October 1862 at the end of the **Kentucky Campaign**. Morgan received permission to leave **Braxton Bragg's** retreating **Army of Tennessee** at Crab Orchard and take his 1,800-man **brigade** eastward through central Kentucky to impede the Union pursuit by attacking **railroads** and isolated garrisons. Leaving on October 17, he captured Lexington the next day and then returned to Tennessee by riding west and south through Versailles, Bardstown, and Hopkinsville, seizing small outposts and destroying railroad bridges along the way. Morgan safely reached Springfield, Tennessee, on November 1.

The so-called Christmas Raid was Morgan's third Kentucky raid. With his 4,000-man cavalry **division**, he left Alexandria, Tennessee, on

December 21, 1862, to raid Union Maj. Gen. **William S. Rosecrans's** lines of communications just before the **Battle of Stones River**. Riding north through Glasgow and Bardstown, Morgan captured Elizabethtown on December 27 and the next day destroyed the railroad that supplied Rosecrans's **Army of the Cumberland**. He was attacked while crossing the Rolling Fork River and suffered some casualties before reaching Bardstown. Morgan successfully bypassed a large Union force at Lebanon and reached Columbia, Tennessee, on January 1, 1863. During the raid, he successfully destroyed several important railroad trestles, bridges, depots, tracks, and supplies worth an estimated $2 million. He also captured 1,887 prisoners while losing only 26 men.

MORGAN'S OHIO RAID (JULY 2–26, 1863). After being forced out of Middle **Tennessee** during the 1863 **Tullahoma Campaign**, **Braxton Bragg** ordered **John Hunt Morgan** to raid behind **Williams Rosecrans's Army of the Cumberland** to disrupt his lines of communications and slow his advance toward Chattanooga, Tennessee. Morgan believed taking the war to the North would strengthen the peace movement and proposed raiding across the Ohio River, but Bragg rejected the idea and authorized a raid only into **Kentucky**.

Morgan crossed the Cumberland River near Burkesville, Kentucky, on July 2 with his 2,500-man **division**, successfully avoiding 10,000 Federals who were guarding the river to prevent such a raid. When a detachment of the 25th Michigan prevented him from crossing the Green River on July 4, he attacked Lebanon the next day and captured 400 men and a large amount of supplies. Despite Bragg's orders, Morgan then crossed the Ohio River at Brandenburg on July 7 and captured **Corydon, Indiana**, and about 350 **prisoners** on July 9.

Over the next several days, Morgan's men rode to the east destroying supplies and looting. Rather than strengthening the peace movement, the raid brought the local people together to resist the Confederates. As Morgan rode toward **Ohio**, his command began to dwindle as both men and mounts gave way to exhaustion. He crossed into Ohio at Harrison on July 13 and rode through the suburbs of Cincinnati before arriving at Pomeroy on the 18th. Having covered 90 miles in 35 hours, Morgan's raiders supposedly had made the longest continuous march by any command during the war.

By this time, authorities were concentrating forces to deal with Morgan. When the Confederates attempted to recross the Ohio River at **Buffington Island** on July 19, they were badly mauled by a waiting Union detachment. Morgan lost about 820 men (mostly taken prisoner), while the Federals suffered only 25 casualties. Left with only about 350 men, he then rode east toward **Pennsylvania** but was pursued by Union Brig. Gen. **Edward H. Hobson.** Finally caught near **Salineville**, Morgan was forced to surrender with his men on July 26 after a sharp fight. He and his officers were imprisoned in the Ohio Penitentiary, but Morgan escaped several months later.

The cavalry raid was one of the war's longest at 700 miles, and it spread panic through **Indiana** and caused temporary havoc behind Union lines. Morgan captured and **paroled** 6,000 prisoners; occupied 14,000 regulars and 120,000 militiamen; destroyed 34 bridges; cut **railroads** at more than 60 places; and destroyed large amounts of supplies.

MORMON WAR (1857–1858). *See* UTAH EXPEDITION.

MORRIS, WILLIAM HOPKINS (1827–1907) USA. The son of poet George Pope Morris, who wrote "Woodman, Spare That Tree," Morris was a native of **New York**. He graduated from **West Point** in 1851 but resigned in 1854 to join his father in publishing the *New York Home Journal.* In 1859, Morris also received a patent on a repeating carbine and published several works promoting it to the War Department.

Morris entered Union service in August 1861 as a captain and assistant adjutant general on the staff of his friend and neighbor Brig. Gen. **John J. Peck.** After serving with the **Army of the Potomac** in the **Peninsula Campaign**, he was appointed assistant adjutant general for the IV Corps' 2nd Division in June 1862. Morris resigned his position in September and was immediately appointed colonel of the 135th New York. This **regiment** was reorganized as the 6th New York Heavy Artillery the next month and was stationed around **Washington, D.C.**, and Baltimore, Maryland.

In March 1863, Morris was promoted to brigadier general of volunteers and was placed in command of a **brigade** stationed at Maryland Heights near **Harpers Ferry, Virginia**. After the **Gettysburg Campaign**, he was attached to the III Corps and served through the **Bristoe Station** and **Mine Run Campaigns**. Reassigned to **James B. Rickett's** VI Corps **division** in March 1864, Morris led his brigade in the **Overland Campaign** and won a **brevet** for the **Wilderness**. At **Spotsylvania**, he was severely wounded and was unable to return to the field. Morris then served on various commissions until mustered out of service in August 1865.

After the war, Morris wrote on military affairs and became a brigadier general and brevet major general in the New York national guard.

MORTAR. Mortars were short-barreled, squat-looking **artillery** pieces that fired exploding projectiles at a high trajectory so they could fall behind walls and fortifications. They were rated according to their bore diameter, which ran from 5.8 inches to 13 inches, and were used most often in sieges and in attacking fortifications. The huge 13-inch mortar fired a 220-pound shell approximately 2.5 miles with a 20-pound powder charge and could be fitted onto vessels and **railroad** cars. Union forces made good use of mortars at **Forts Jackson and St. Philip** and in the **Vicksburg** and **Petersburg Campaigns**. *See also* COEHORN MORTAR.

MORTON, JAMES ST. CLAIR (1829–1864) USA. A native of **Pennsylvania**, Morton entered the University of Pennsylvania at age 14, but he left after four years to accept an appointment to **West Point**. Graduating second in the class of 1851, he was assigned to the **engineers** and worked on various Atlantic coastal projects until the Civil War's second year.

Morton was promoted to captain of engineers in August 1861 and was supervising construction of Fort Jefferson, Florida, in the Dry Tortugas when he was ordered to Nashville, Tennessee, in early 1862. There he supervised the construction of the city's defenses until he was appointed chief engineer for **Don Carlos Buell's Army of the Ohio** in June 1862. After seeing service at **Perryville**, Morton became chief engineer for **William S. Rosecrans's Army of the Cumberland** in October 1862. He commanded the **army's pioneer brigade** at **Stones River** and was awarded a **brevet** for his actions.

Promoted to brigadier general of volunteers in April 1863 and major of regulars in July, Morton continued to lead the army's pioneer brigade until he was wounded, and later brevetted, at **Chickamauga**. While at Chattanooga, Tennessee, in November, he was mustered out of the volunteer service at his own request, probably because he preferred engineering work over field service. Morton improved the Nashville defenses and in January 1864 was appointed assistant to the chief engineer in **Washington, D.C.** In May, he became chief engineer for **Ambrose Burnside's** IX Corps and joined it after the **Overland Campaign** had already begun. Morton saw service at **North Anna River**, **Totopotomoy Creek**, and **Cold Harbor** before being killed in the **Petersburg Campaign** on June 17, 1864, while reconnoitering for a planned attack. He was brevetted brigadier general of regulars posthumously.

MORTON, OLIVER PERRY (1823–1877) USA. A native of **Indiana**, Morton was raised by two aunts after his mother died. He attended Miami

University, became a very successful corporate lawyer and circuit judge, and was active in **Democratic** politics, although he did not hold any elective offices before 1861. After opposing the **Kansas-Nebraska Act**, Morton helped form the **Republican Party** in Indiana and was nominated for governor in 1856. Although defeated, he was elected lieutenant governor in 1860 and became governor two days after inauguration when the governor resigned to accept the position of U.S. senator.

Taking office in January 1861, Morton became perhaps the best Union war governor. He strongly supported the war effort and provided more than twice Indiana's quota of troops (around 150,000). Morton also was tireless in his campaign against the **Copperheads**. Still, he sometimes clashed with **Abraham Lincoln** over such issues as the **suspension of the writ of habeas corpus**, **conscription**, and the freeing of slaves. Morton's relentless efforts also brought him into conflict with the state legislature, which became weary of the war. Fearful the legislature would not adequately fund his plans, he took out large loans and used profits from the state arsenal to keep the government operating instead of calling the legislature into session. Despite this opposition, Morton was reelected in 1864, largely by securing leave for thousands of soldiers to come home to vote.

Morton suffered a crippling stroke in the summer of 1865, but he remained in office and was allied with the **Radical Republicans** during **Reconstruction** until he resigned in 1867 to accept the position of U.S. senator. After helping pass the 14th Amendment, he was reelected but died in office after suffering a second stroke.

MORTON'S FORD, VIRGINIA, BATTLE OF (FEBRUARY 6–7, 1864). In February 1864, Union Maj. Gen. **Benjamin F. Butler** planned an attack against **Richmond, Virginia**, to free the Union **prisoners** held there. As a diversion, **Alexander Hays's** II Corps **division** of the **Army of the Potomac** crossed the Rapidan River at Morton's Ford on February 6, while the I Corps **demonstrated** at Raccoon Ford, and cavalry crossed at Robertson's Ford. **Alexander S. Webb's** division reinforced Hays at dusk, but Confederate Lt. Gen. **Richard S. Ewell** moved the **Army of Northern Virginia's** II Corps to Morton's Ford on February 7 and prevented the Federals from pushing any farther. After sporadic fighting, the Federals finally withdrew. It is estimated that both sides suffered a total of 723 casualties in the battle. During the fighting, the Confederates learned of Butler's planned attack from a **deserter**, and Butler was forced to cancel the operation.

MOSBY, JOHN SINGLETON (1833–1916) CSA. A native of **Virginia**, Mosby attended the University of Virginia but was jailed after killing a local bully who had threatened him. Found guilty of an "unlawful shooting," he served seven months of a one-year sentence before being pardoned by the governor. Mosby had begun reading law under his defense attorney and after being released from jail passed the bar exam and became a lawyer.

Mosby entered Confederate service in 1861 as a private in **J. E. B. Stuart's** 1st Virginia Cavalry and fought at **First Manassas**. He was promoted to 1st lieutenant in February 1862 but left the **regiment** to join Stuart as a scout after he clashed with Stuart's replacement, Col. **William E. "Grumble" Jones**. Mosby participated in **Stuart's Ride around George B. McClellan** during the **Peninsula Campaign** and, in fact, originated the idea.

In late 1862, Mosby was given permission to raise a **partisan ranger** unit in Northern Virginia. He first led a small, unorganized band of men in guerrilla operations and won acclaim in March 1863 when he captured Union Brig. Gen. **Edwin H. Stoughton** in a raid on Fairfax Court House. That same month, Mosby was elevated to captain and then to major. So many men had joined his ranks by June 1863 that he was able to form the 43rd Virginia Cavalry Battalion, better known as **Mosby's Rangers**. For the next two years, the so-called Gray Ghost terrorized Union soldiers in Fauquier and Loudoun Counties, an area that came to be known as **"Mosby's Confederacy."** Mosby's Greenback Raid against the Baltimore & Ohio Railroad near **Harpers Ferry, West Virginia**, in October 1864 became one of his most famous when he captured and burned a train and escaped with $178,000 in **greenbacks**. Frustrated by such successful **tactics**, Union officers sometimes summarily executed Mosby's men when they were captured.

A small, thin man, Mosby was fearless and often personally led his daring forays against enemy wagon trains, outposts, **railroads**, and couriers. As a result, he was wounded at least three times and was commended by **Robert E. Lee** more than any other officer. Both Lee and Stuart came to rely on Mosby for his accurate intelligence, and he was promoted to lieutenant colonel in January 1864 and to colonel in December. His command also was increased to two battalions.

After learning of Lee's **surrender** in April 1865, Mosby disbanded his battalions rather than surrendering them. He returned to his law practice and lost some of his popularity in the South when he supported **U. S. Grant** for president. Grant, in turn, appointed Mosby U.S. consul to Hong Kong.

MOSBY'S CONFEDERACY. This was the nickname given to Fauquier and Loudoun Counties, Virginia, the area that was dominated by **Mosby's Rangers.**

MOSBY'S RANGERS. Known officially as the 43rd Virginia Cavalry Battalion, this famous **partisan ranger** unit was commanded by **John S. Mosby,** who first led 15 guerrillas in Northern **Virginia** in January 1863 after being given permission to raise a partisan command. After such successful raids as the capture of Union Brig. Gen. **Edwin H. Stoughton** at Fairfax Court House in March, his ranks soon were flooded with eager recruits. By June, Mosby had enough men to form Company A, 43rd Virginia Cavalry Battalion. Over the next two years, approximately 1,900 men served in his command (in December 1864, the battalion was split into two small battalions), but there never were more than about 800 men at any one time, and the rangers usually operated in small bands.

Mosby's rangers were based in Fauquier and Loudoun Counties, an area that became known as **Mosby's Confederacy,** but they also operated in the **Shenandoah Valley** and parts of **Maryland.** The rangers were housed and fed by local civilians and easily hid in woodlots between raids. Their raids against outposts, couriers, **railroads,** and wagon trains played havoc with Union commanders and tied down thousands of Federal troops. The intelligence the battalion collected was invaluable to **Robert E. Lee.** One of the rangers' most famous raids was known as the Greenback Raid. In October 1864, Mosby and 84 rangers attacked a train on the Baltimore & Ohio Railroad near **Harpers Ferry, West Virginia.** The train was burned, and two Union paymasters were relieved of $178,000 in **greenbacks,** which were divided among the raiders.

Such activity infuriated Union commanders and led to harsh retaliation. **Philip Sheridan** created a special unit in late 1864 under Capt. Richard Blazer to destroy Mosby's command. Armed with **Spencer carbines, Blazer's Scouts** pursued the rangers, but they were annihilated by their quarry, who then took their carbines. **U. S. Grant** tried to control the rangers in November 1864 by destroying all available supplies in Loudoun County and ordering Mosby and his men to be executed without trial if captured (he also considered imprisoning their families). When **George Armstrong Custer** hanged six rangers, Mosby retaliated by hanging seven of Custer's men. The executions then stopped as neither side wished to continue the acts of retaliation.

After learning of Lee's and **Joseph E. Johnston's surrenders,** Mosby quietly disbanded his command on April 21, 1865. More than a third of his men had been killed or wounded during the war, and nearly 500 had been captured.

MOSSY CREEK, TENNESSEE, BATTLE OF (DECEMBER 29, 1863). After his failed 1863 **Knoxville Campaign**, Confederate Lt. Gen. **James Longstreet** left cavalry on the French Broad River near Dandridge, Tennessee, while the rest of his command went into winter quarters. On December 28, Union Brig. Gen. **Samuel D. Sturgis** sent his cavalry down two roads from Mossy Creek to attack the Confederate cavalry near Dandridge. While they were gone, Maj. Gen. **William T. Martin's** Confederate cavalry attacked the remaining Union garrison at Mossy Creek on the morning of December 29. At first Martin drove out the Federals under Col. Samuel R. Mott, but then Sturgis's cavalry returned and forced Martin to withdraw. The number of Confederate casualties in the battle is unknown, but the Federals lost 151 men.

MOTT, GERSHOM (1822–1884) USA. A native of **New Jersey**, Mott clerked in a store until the **Mexican War**, when he was appointed a 2nd lieutenant in the 10th U.S. Infantry. He did not serve outside the United States during the war and afterward worked as a port collector and businessman.

Mott entered Union service in August 1861 as lieutenant colonel of the 5th New Jersey. Serving with the **Army of the Potomac** in the **Peninsula Campaign**, he was promoted to colonel of the 6th New Jersey in May 1862 and led it at **Seven Pines**, in the **Seven Days Campaign**, and at **Second Manassas**, where he was wounded. Promoted to brigadier general of volunteers in September 1862, Mott was given command of a **brigade** in the III Corps' 2nd Division in February 1863. He was wounded again while leading it at **Chancellorsville** but recovered in time to command his brigade in the **Mine Run Campaign**.

In May 1864, Mott was given command of the II Corps' 4th Division and led it in the **Overland Campaign**. His **division** was broken by the enemy at the **Wilderness**, and at the **Battle of Spotsylvania** on May 10, he was accused of failing to support an attack properly. **George G. Meade** gave Mott the choice of making his small division a brigade in the 3rd Division or being mustered out of service. Mott reluctantly accepted the demotion but went on to assume command of the division in June. He led it with skill through the **Petersburg** and **Appomattox Campaigns** and was **brevetted** major general of volunteers for his service at the **Crater**.

Mott remained in the volunteers after the war and was promoted to major general in December 1865. He left the service in February 1866 and became employed by a **railroad**. In 1868, Mott declined a colonel's commission in the **U.S. Army**, but he did become commander of the New Jersey National Guard.

MOUNT ZION CHURCH, MISSOURI, BATTLE OF (DECEMBER 28, 1861). In December 1861, Union Brig. Gen. **Benjamin M. Prentiss** took seven **companies** of mounted men and **sharpshooters** into **Missouri's** Boone County to protect the **railroad** there and to subdue secessionist support in the region. Arriving at Sturgeon on December 26, he learned that the secessionist Missouri State Guard under Col. Caleb Dorsey was near Hallsville and decided to attack.

On December 27 a small fight erupted at Hallsville between one Union company and Dorsey, and the Federals were forced to retreat to Sturgeon. The next day, Prentiss advanced his entire command and routed one of Dorsey's companies on the road from Hallsville to Mount Zion. At Mount Zion Church, Prentiss engaged the main Confederate force, but in a short time, Dorsey abandoned his dead, wounded, and supplies and withdrew. In the fight, Dorsey suffered 210 casualties, while Prentiss lost 72 men. The Union victory at Mount Zion Church helped the Federals gain control over central Missouri.

MOUNTAIN DEPARTMENT (UNION). Formerly known as the **Department of Western Virginia**, this Union military **department** was created in March 1862. It included **West Virginia**, southwest **Virginia**, and eastern **Kentucky** and was commanded by **John C. Frémont** (**William S. Rosecrans** commanded the department until Frémont arrived in late March). After its troops were defeated at **McDowell** and **Cross Keys**, the Mountain Department was abolished in June, and its forces were designated the **Army of Virginia's** I Corps.

MOUTON, JEAN JACQUES ALFRED ALEXANDER (1829–1864) CSA. A native of **Louisiana**, Alfred Mouton (MOO-tahn) was the son of a future governor. After being educated at Louisiana's St. Charles College, he was admitted to **West Point** and graduated near the bottom of his 1850 class. Mouton resigned from the **U.S. Army** in a few months and returned to Louisiana to manage his father's sugar plantation. After a brief stint as a **railroad** engineer, he bought his own sugar plantation and in 1855 was appointed brigadier general of state militia.

Mouton entered Confederate service in the spring of 1861 as a captain and was placed in command of an infantry training school. In July, he began raising his own volunteer **company** and was elected lieutenant colonel of a battalion. When additional companies were added to this unit, it was designated the 18th Louisiana in October, with Mouton being appointed its colonel. After service in **Mississippi** and **Tennessee**, he led his regiment at **Shiloh**. In savage fighting on the first day, Mouton suffered heavy casualties, had his horse shot from under him, and counted a dozen bullet holes in his **uniform** and saddle. On the second day, he was painfully wounded in the face.

Two weeks after the Battle of Shiloh, Mouton was promoted to brigadier general for his service there. Returning to Louisiana to recover from an illness, he was put in command of the **Bayou Lafourche** (luh-FOOSH) region by **Richard Taylor** in October 1862. Later that month, Mouton was attacked and defeated at **Georgia Landing** and had to retreat to Bayou Teche, where he began constructing fortifications at Bisland Plantation. When **Henry H. Sibley** replaced him in command of the area, Mouton took charge of a small infantry **brigade**. He fought well in the **Bayou Teche Campaign** and was given command of the troops in south Louisiana after Sibley was dismissed in April 1863. Although he was ordered to harass Union forces in the area during the **Port Hudson Campaign**, Mouton took little action. After fighting at **Stirling's Plantation** in September, he was put in command of a **division** in December and spent the winter in northeast Louisiana.

In the spring of 1864, Mouton's division played a critical role in the **Red River Campaign**. At the **Battle of Mansfield** on April 8, Taylor ordered him to lead the attack that led to **Nathaniel P. Banks's** defeat. In the charge, Mouton was killed under uncertain circumstances. He may have been killed by Union soldiers, who, after surrendering, realized the general was alone and shot him.

MOWER, JOSEPH ANTHONY (1827–1870) USA. A native of **Vermont**, as a child, Mower moved with his family to **Massachusetts**. After attending Norwich Academy, he worked as a carpenter and then served in the **Mexican War** as a private in a regular **U.S. Army** engineering battalion. Mower left the service at war's end but in 1855 was commissioned a 2nd lieutenant in the 1st U.S. Infantry.

When the Civil War began, Mower was a 1st lieutenant serving in **Missouri**, but he was promoted to captain in the 9th U.S. Infantry in September 1861. He was appointed colonel of the 11th Missouri (Union) in May 1862 and was **brevetted** major of regulars for his service during the **siege of Corinth, Mississippi**, after the **Battle of Shiloh**. Mower also fought at the **Battles of Iuka** (for which he was brevetted again) and

Corinth. In the latter battle, he was wounded and captured but then escaped, only to be captured again before reaching his lines. After being **paroled**, Mower was promoted to brigadier general of volunteers in March 1863. He led a **brigade** in **William T. Sherman's** corps of the **Army of the Tennessee** during the **Vicksburg Campaign** and was awarded another brevet for his role in capturing **Jackson, Mississippi**. After serving in Sherman's **Meridian Campaign**, Mower commanded the two **divisions** that Sherman sent to aid **Nathaniel P. Banks** in the 1864 **Red River Campaign**. In the campaign, Mower led the attack that captured **Fort De Russy** (for which he was brevetted) and commanded the rear guard that fought at **Yellow Bayou**.

Mower was promoted to major general of volunteers in August 1864 and helped oppose **Sterling Price's Missouri Raid** before rejoining Sherman in **Georgia**. He led a division in the Army of the Tennessee's XVII Corps during the **March to the Sea** and the **Carolinas Campaign** (for which he won yet another brevet) and was given command of the XX Corps at war's end in April 1865. Through all of his service from regimental to **corps** commander, Mower exhibited great skill and came to be one of Sherman's most trusted officers. Sherman once said that he was "the boldest young soldier we have" (Warner, *Generals in Blue*, 339). Mower won five brevets in the regular **army** for his service, ending the war as a brevet major general.

Mower was mustered out of the volunteer service in February 1866, but he remained in the regular army as a captain. He soon was appointed colonel of a **regiment** of **black troops** and died in **Louisiana** while in command of the 25th U.S. Infantry.

MUD MARCH (JANUARY 20–23, 1863). After the Union's disastrous defeat at **Fredericksburg, Virginia**, in December 1862, Maj. Gen. **Ambrose Burnside** made new plans to defeat **Robert E. Lee's Army of Northern Virginia**. Burnside would take his **Army of the Potomac** up the Rappahannock River from Fredericksburg, cross over at Banks' Ford, and turn Lee's left flank. The plan was a good one, but it required stealth and speed, and the **army** was not up to the task. Most of Burnside's commanders disapproved of the **strategy**, claiming the army needed several months to recover from the recent defeat.

Burnside began his march on January 20, 1863, but heavy rains began almost immediately. The roads turned to bottomless quagmires, and the army's progress slowed to a crawl. Lee soon discovered the movement and sent troops, who called out insults to the Federals across the river, to shadow the march. After two days of continuous rain, Burnside finally accepted the inevitable and canceled the expedition on January 23. Known officially as the Mud March, the aborted expedition further weakened Union morale and led to Burnside's replacement by **Joseph Hooker**.

MUDD, SAMUEL ALEXANDER (1833–1883) USA. A native of **Maryland** and a member of a prominent slave-owning family, Mudd attended St. John's Georgetown College before receiving a medical degree from the University of Maryland in 1856. He became a physician and during the Civil War was well known for his dislike of the **Abraham Lincoln** administration.

In the predawn hours of April 15, 1865, **John Wilkes Booth** and **David Herold** stopped at Mudd's Maryland home while fleeing from authorities after **Lincoln's assassination**. The doctor set Booth's broken leg, provided food and lodging, and may have helped the pair escape into **Virginia** later that day. When questioned, Mudd admitted having treated Booth and was arrested. Although denying involvement in the assassination plot, he was convicted of conspiracy in July and was sentenced to life imprisonment. Sent to Fort Jefferson in the Dry Tortugas, Florida, Mudd was placed in irons in September after being caught trying to escape. However, after bravely treating guards and prisoners alike during an 1867 yellow fever epidemic, he was pardoned and released in 1869 by President **Andrew Johnson** upon the recommendation of prison officials. Mudd returned to his Maryland practice and died in 1883. In 1979, President Jimmy Carter issued a presidential proclamation clearing him of any involvement in Lincoln's assassination. Still, Mudd's name has entered American lexicon in the phrase, "His name is mud," when one wants to show disapproval of someone.

"MULE SHOE" AT BATTLE OF SPOTSYLVANIA, VIRGINIA (MAY 12, 1864). *See* SPOTSYLVANIA, VIRGINIA, BATTLE OF.

MUMFORD, WILLIAM B. (1820?–1862) CSA. Little is known of Mumford's early life, but he was a gambler when Union forces entered **New Orleans, Louisiana**, on April 26, 1862, and raised the U.S. **flag** over the mint building. That same day, he helped lead a mob that took down the flag, which he then tore to pieces. In his attempt to quell pro-Confederate activity, Union Maj. Gen. **Benjamin F. Butler** arrested Mumford for treason and quickly tried and convicted him. Despite pleas from his wife and friends, he was hanged publicly at the mint building on June 7. Mumford was hailed as a martyr by many citizens, and his execution helped earn Butler the nickname "Beast."

MUNFORDVILLE, KENTUCKY, CAPTURE OF (SEPTEMBER 14–17, 1862). During the 1862 **Kentucky Campaign**, the Louisville & Nashville Railroad bridge across the Green River at Munfordville, Kentucky, became an important target for the Confederates because supplies were forwarded over it to the Union troops in **Tennessee**. Colonel John T. Wilder commanded the garrison there, which held a strong defensive position centered on a blockhouse (known as Fort Craig) and earthworks on the south side of the river at Woodsonville. As **Braxton Bragg's Army of Tennessee** approached, Wilder sent for reinforcements from Louisville.

Confederate cavalry under Col. John S. Scott arrived in Munfordville on September 13 and demanded Wilder's surrender. When he refused, Scott sent to Brig. Gen. **James R. Chalmers** for help. Chalmers arrived with his **brigade** that night and rashly attacked Wilder on September 14, but he was repulsed with heavy losses. Placing his men on both sides of the river, Chalmers then demanded Wilder's surrender. Wilder declined and told Chalmers, "If you wish to avoid further bloodshed keep out of the range of my guns" (Foote, *The Civil War* vol. 1, p. 658).

On September 15, Union Col. Cyrus L. Dunham arrived with reinforcements and assumed command of the garrison. By the next day, Dunham had approximately 4,000 men and several cannons in position to defend the bridge. Bragg arrived with the main Confederate **army** on September 17 and positioned his troops and cannons to crush the Federals. When Dunham informed his superiors of his intention to surrender, he was relieved of command and replaced by Wilder. Wilder was unsure whether duty required him to hold out to the last man or save his men's lives by surrendering. He also was uncertain whether the Confederates actually outnumbered him as they claimed. Learning from civilians that Kentucky Confederate Maj. Gen. **Simon B. Buckner** was an honorable officer, Wilder entered the Confederate position under a flag of truce to discuss the situation with him. To Buckner's astonishment, Wilder asked his advice on what to do. Buckner refused to advise but did agree to let Wilder tour his position to show that he was outnumbered and outgunned. Convinced that the situation was hopeless, Wilder surrendered his men that morning. Wilder lost 4,148 men, nearly all of whom were captured and **paroled**, while the Confederates lost 285 men. Bragg burned the **railroad** bridge and continued his invasion three days later.

MURFREESBORO, TENNESSEE, BATTLE OF (DECEMBER 31, 1862–JANUARY 2, 1863). *See* STONES RIVER, TENNESSEE, BATTLE OF.

MURRAH, PENDLETON (1824–1865) CSA. A native of **South Carolina**, Murrah was probably illegitimate and for a while lived in an orphan's home. With financial aid from a Baptist charity, he graduated from Brown University in 1848 and moved to **Alabama** to read law. Tuberculosis forced Murrah to move to a healthier climate in **Texas** in 1850. There he became a lawyer and in 1857 was elected to the legislature, where he became a staunch secessionist.

In 1861, poor health caused Murrah to abandon his race for the **Confederate Congress**, but he did serve as quartermaster for the 14th Texas for a short time. He was elected governor in 1863 but clashed with Confederate authorities over **conscription** and slave **impressment** and over control of the cotton trade. Murrah accused the military of stripping Texas of its ability to guard the frontier against **Indian** attacks and allowed all draft-age citizens to join the state militia to avoid Confederate service. He and **Trans-Mississippi Department** commander **Edmund Kirby Smith** finally came to an agreement to leave the state troops in Texas unless a severe emergency required them elsewhere.

Murrah fled to Mexico at war's end, but he was in poor health and died in Monterrey on August 4, 1865.

MUSIC. Music was very important in the Civil War to both soldiers and civilians, and it is estimated that some 9,000 new songs were written during the war (perhaps the most recognizable today is **"Taps"**). Most **regiments** in both **armies** had a band that provided entertainment during camp and music for special occasions. Among the soldiers, songs of a sentimental nature were favored over those with a martial tone. Some of their favorites were "The Last Rose of Summer," "Home Sweet Home," "Annie Laurie," "Listen to the Mockingbird," and "Lorena." Of the songs that were more sectional in nature, Confederate favorites were **"Dixie"** and **"The Bonnie Blue Flag,"** while the Federals enjoyed "Hail Columbia!" and "John Brown's Body" (later renamed **"Battle Hymn of the Republic"**). Many times the opposing armies were so close that soldiers of one could enjoy the music played by the other. On a cold night at the **Battle of Stones River**, opposing bands took turns serenading the armies. *See also* DANIEL BUTTERFIELD; JULIA WARD HOWE; GEORGE F. ROOT.

MYER, ALBERT JAMES (1827–1880) USA. A native of **New York**, Myer graduated from Hobart College in 1847 and from Buffalo Medical College in 1851, where he wrote a thesis on sign language for the deaf. After practicing medicine for three years, he joined the **U.S. Army** as an assistant surgeon. While serving in the Southwest, Myer became impressed with **Indian** smoke signals. With the assistance of future Confederate general **Edward Porter Alexander**, he used a sign language he had developed to create the army's **"wigwag"** system of using flags to signal in the daytime and torches to signal at night. The **army** adopted the system in 1858, and two years later Myer was promoted to major and became the army's signal officer.

Myer's first attempt to use his system in conjunction with a **balloon** failed at **First Manassas**. He then was assigned to the **Army of the Potomac** and served as signal officer through the **Peninsula, Seven Days**, and **Antietam Campaigns**. Myer was a leading figure in the formation of the U.S. Signal Corps and was appointed its chief in March 1863 with the rank of colonel. However, he became involved in a dispute with the Military Telegraph Service over control of the **telegraph**. Myer lost the struggle and in November was relieved of duty with the Army of the Potomac, had his colonel's commission revoked, and was transferred to **Georgia**. There, Myer won some acclaim when his signalmen brought reinforcements to the beleaguered garrison of **Allatoona** in October 1864. Afterward, he saw service in the **Mobile Campaign**.

Myer was **brevetted** three times for his wartime service and remained in the army after the war. In 1870, he again was put in charge of the Signal Corps and commanded it for 10 years. Not long after being promoted to brigadier general, Myer died in 1880. Fort Myer, Virginia, is named for him. *See also* SIGNAL COMMUNICATIONS.

MYERS, ABRAHAM CHARLES (1811–1889) CSA. A native of **South Carolina**, Myers graduated near the bottom of the 1833 **West Point** class. Assigned to the infantry, he served in the **Seminole Wars** and became a captain with the quartermaster department. Myers won two **brevets** during the **Mexican War** and was serving in **Louisiana** when the Civil War began.

In January 1861, Myers surrendered his supply post to Louisiana state troops and resigned his commission on the same day. In March, he entered the **Confederate army** as a lieutenant colonel and was appointed its first quartermaster general in December. As quartermaster, Myers was responsible for providing the **armies** with everything except food and munitions. **Jefferson Davis** at first was very impressed and secured him a promotion to colonel in February 1862. But Myers quickly lost favor, partly because of the impossible task of supplying the army and partly because of rumors that Mrs. Myers had called Davis's wife, Varina, a "squaw" because of her dark complexion.

As the war continued, Myers's job became increasingly difficult even though many of his problems were beyond his control. Inflation, the **blockade**, the destruction of **railroads**, and myriad other difficulties made it virtually impossible to keep the armies supplied adequately. Critics complained that Myers did not have the skills necessary to carry out his duties. His Jewish ancestry may also have played a role in the attacks upon him. To secure him a higher rank, Myers's congressional friends passed a law that upgraded the quartermaster's position to that of brigadier general. Davis, however, appointed **Alexander R. Lawton** to the new grade, and Myers resigned in August 1863.

Myers took up residence in **Georgia**, living in poverty, and largely relying on the charity of friends to survive. He later lived in **Maryland** and **Washington, D.C.**

– N –

NAGLE, JAMES (1822–1866) USA. A native of **Pennsylvania**, Nagle worked as a painter and paperhanger and organized a militia **company**, which he led in the **Mexican War**. He entered state service in April 1861 as colonel of the 6th Pennsylvania, but after serving under **Robert Patterson** in the **Shenandoah Valley**, the **regiment** was mustered out in July. Nagle then raised the 48th Pennsylvania and was appointed its colonel in October.

Nagle was given a **brigade** command and was sent to the **North Carolina** coast, but then he was transferred to **Virginia** in July 1862 and was placed in command of a brigade in the **Army of the Potomac's** IX Corps. After suffering heavy losses at **Groveton**, he was promoted to brigadier general of volunteers in September and led his brigade at **South Mountain**, **Antietam** (where he attacked Burnside's Bridge), and **Fredericksburg**. Nagle's appointment to brigadier general expired in March 1863 after the Senate failed to confirm it. He was reappointed that month and led his brigade to **Kentucky**, but poor health forced him to resign his commission in May. Twice over the next year, Nagle organized and became colonel of short-term militia regiments to defend Pennsylvania. His 39th Pennsylvania served during the **Gettysburg Campaign** and the 194th Pennsylvania, during **Jubal A. Early's Washington Raid**. Nagle was mustered out of service for the last time in November 1864 and died less than two years later.

NAGLEE, HENRY MORRIS (1815–1886) USA. A native of **Pennsylvania**, Naglee graduated from **West Point** in 1835 but quickly resigned his commission and became a **New York** civil engineer. During the **Mexican War**, he served in **California** as a **company** commander in the 1st New York and remained there after the war to become a banker.

Naglee entered Union service in May 1861 when he was commissioned lieutenant colonel of the 16th U.S. Infantry. In January 1862, he resigned this position to accept an appointment as brigadier general of volunteers in February 1862. Sent to **Washington, D.C.**, Naglee was given a **brigade** in **Silas Casey's division**. He first served in the Washington defenses and then fought with the **Army of the Potomac** through the **Peninsula** and **Seven Days Campaigns**. Naglee remained in southeast **Virginia** and **North Carolina** after the Army of the Potomac withdrew from the Virginia Peninsula.

While in Virginia, Naglee clashed with Virginia's Union Gov. **Francis Harrison Pierpont** over individuals having to take **loyalty oaths** to the new state government to regain confiscated property. When Naglee refused to support the oaths, he was relieved of command in September 1863 and was sent to **Ohio** to await orders that never came. Mustered out of service in April 1864, he returned to his California banking interests and produced Naglee Brandy.

NAPOLEON CANNON. Named for France's Napoleon III, under whom it was developed in 1856, the Napoleon Gun Howitzer (its official name) was the most common **artillery** piece used in the Civil War. It was a smoothbore, muzzle-loading cannon that fired a 12-pound **solid shot**, **grape shot**, **canister**, spherical case, or exploding shell. Both **armies** used the model 1857, which generally was made of bronze, although the Confederacy's **Tredegar Iron Works** developed one Napoleon that was made of iron with a reinforcing band at the breech.

NASHVILLE CONVENTION. After the intense congressional debates over the **Wilmot Proviso** and the exclusion of **slavery** from the territory acquired in the **Mexican War**, **John C. Calhoun** urged the South in 1849 to hold a convention in Nashville, Tennessee, to form a plan that would uphold Southern **slavery** rights. Interest waned, however, after Henry Clay introduced what became known as the **Compromise of 1850**, and only nine slave states attended the June 1850 Nashville Convention. Moderate delegates won control of the convention from the radical **South Carolina** faction that wanted immediate **secession**. The convention passed a resolution calling for the opening of all territories to slavery but in a cooperative spirit agreed to settle for the extension of the **Missouri Compromise** Line to the Pacific Ocean. It then adjourned until November, but since the Compromise of 1850 had diffused the slavery issue, only a small number of delegates returned to Nashville. Those who did were **"fire-eaters,"** and they reiterated the right of secession. In the end, the Nashville Convention had no great impact on the country except to bring Southerners together to discuss the concept of secession and to demonstrate to the North that the South was contemplating extreme measures to protect its interests.

NASHVILLE, TENNESSEE, BATTLE OF (DECEMBER 15–16, 1864). *See* FRANKLIN AND NASHVILLE, TENNESSEE, CAMPAIGN AND BATTLES OF.

NATIONAL UNION PARTY. *See* UNION PARTY.

NATURAL BRIDGE, FLORIDA, BATTLE OF (MARCH 6, 1865). Near war's end, Union forces under Brig. Gen. **John Newton** and Lt. Comdr. William Gibson attacked a Confederate fort at the confluence of the Wakulla and St. Marks Rivers near St. Marks, Florida. Newton disembarked 1,000 men of the 2nd and 99th U.S. Colored Troops and 2nd Florida Cavalry (Union) from Gibson's ships when it was found the St. Marks River was too shallow to enter. He captured the East River Bridge, a few miles from the St. Marks lighthouse, on March 5, 1865, but was stopped by Confederates at the Newport Bridge. That night, Newton left a holding force at the bridge and then marched north to a river crossing known as the Natural Bridge. On March 6, Confederates under Brig. Gen. **William Miller** stopped Newton at the Natural Bridge, forcing him to abandon his campaign. In the operation, Newton lost 148 men, while Confederate casualties are estimated at 25.

NAVAL ACADEMY, CONFEDERATE STATES. In late 1861, the **Confederate Congress** authorized a program to train midshipmen for the **Confederate navy**. Lieutenant William H. Parker, an 1848 graduate of the **U.S. Naval Academy**, became the superintendent of the Confederate States Naval Academy and began accepting applications in April 1862. The academy itself was the **CSS *Patrick Henry***, which was anchored in **Virginia's** James River at **Drewry's Bluff**. Some 106 men were appointed midshipmen to train at the academy, although the *Patrick Henry* could accommodate only part of them at any one time. Classes began in October 1863, and the first class of 59 graduated in December 1864. The academy operated until **Richmond, Virginia**, was captured in April 1865. Parker and some of his cadets then escorted **Jefferson Davis** and the government's archives out of the city. The *Patrick Henry* was burned during the city's evacuation.

NAVAL ACADEMY, UNITED STATES. The U.S. Congress established the U.S. Naval Academy in Annapolis, Maryland, in 1845. When it appeared **Maryland** might fall under Confederate control in May 1861, the academy was moved to Newport, **Rhode Island**, for the duration of the Civil War. The Union **army** then took over the abandoned site at Annapolis and used it as a post and hospital. During the war, Superintendent George S. Blake expanded the academy's curriculum to include more math and science courses and was criticized by many career officers who believed he was doing so at the expense of seamanship training. At war's end in May 1865, Adm. **David G. Farragut** headed an investigative board that concluded the academy should return to Annapolis. It did so that summer, and Farragut's foster brother, **David Porter**, became the new superintendent.

NAVY, CONFEDERATE. When the Civil War began, the Confederates had no navy or even much **industry** with which to build ships. When its major naval yards at **New Orleans, Louisiana**, and **Norfolk, Virginia**, were captured early in the war, the Confederacy was placed at an even greater disadvantage. Still, Secretary of the Navy **Stephen Mallory** quickly began cobbling together a makeshift navy with which to defend the coast and inland waterways.

Although some formidable **ironclads** as the *Arkansas*, *Virginia*, and *Tennessee* were built, the Confederates never were able to float anything like a force comparable to the **U.S. Navy**. Most of the Confederate naval victories, with the exception of **Plum Run Bend**, were won by single ships using audacity to surprise the enemy. Generally, whenever a Confederate fleet encountered a Union fleet, it was defeated.

Such actions as took place at **Forts Jackson and St. Philip** and at **Memphis, Tennessee**, demonstrated the inability of the Confederate navy to take on the enemy in pitched battles. As a result, the Confederates resorted to **privateers** and used **commerce raiders** like the *Alabama* to disrupt Union trade. The Confederates were also more willing to experiment with novel **"infernal machines"** to make up for the numerical disadvantage. The Confederates' *Virginia* was the war's first successful ironclad, and the *H. L. Hunley* became the first **submarine** to sink a warship. **Torpedoes**, or mines, also were used to protect harbors and forts. Despite these innovations, however, the Confederates remained greatly outclassed by their Union adversaries.

NAVY, UNITED STATES. The Civil War caught the **U.S. Navy** ill prepared for such a huge conflict. With more than 3,500 miles of Confederate coastline to **blockade**, the Navy had only 42 commissioned ships when **Abraham Lincoln** took office, and most of these were on patrol far out at sea. Yet the Union had the advantage of having a large pool of trained seaman, an industrial base with which to build up its navy, numerous ports to operate from, and excellent leadership in the persons of **Gideon Welles** and **Gustavus V. Fox.**

When the war began, the navy quickly bought private ships for conversion to warships and began building new vessels. By the end of 1861, more than 260 warships were in service, with another 100 under construction, and by 1864 there were 671 warships on duty. Many of these were placed on blockade duty to cut off Confederate trade with Europe, while others hunted down Confederate **commerce raiders.** Although the capture of **blockade runners** steadily increased, the navy was unable to cut off trade completely, and the Confederates continued to bring in supplies throughout the war.

The greatest contribution the U.S. Navy made to the war effort was in capturing strategic areas and supplying the army. It was responsible for capturing **Fort Henry** and **Memphis, Tennessee**; **Mobile Bay, Alabama**; and **Forts Jackson and St. Philip** and **New Orleans, Louisiana**, and played a crucial supporting role in operations against **Richmond, Virginia**; and at **Island No. 10**; **Vicksburg, Mississippi**; **Port Hudson, Louisiana**; **Charleston, South Carolina**; **Savannah, Georgia**; and in the **Red River** and **Mobile Campaigns.**

NEGLEY, JAMES SCOTT (1826–1901) USA. A native of **Pennsylvania**, Negley graduated from the Western University of Pennsylvania in 1846 and then volunteered for service in the **Mexican War** as a private in the 1st Pennsylvania. After the war, he became a well-known horticulturalist and rose to the rank of brigadier general in the state militia.

In April 1861, Negley was appointed brigadier general of Pennsylvania Volunteers and took charge of organizing and equipping volunteers in the Pittsburgh area. After serving under **Robert Patterson** in the **Shenandoah Valley** that summer, he was sent to **Kentucky** in October and was placed in command of a **brigade** under **Don Carlos Buell**.

Appointed brigadier general of volunteers in February 1862, Negley participated in the capture of **Nashville, Tennessee**. During the **Kentucky Campaign**, he was given a **division** in Buell's **Army of the Ohio**, but he remained in **Tennessee** to guard **railroads** while Buell pursued **Braxton Bragg's Army of Tennessee**. In November 1862, Negley took over a **division** in the **Army of the Cumberland's** XIV Corps and was rewarded for his actions at **Stones River** with a promotion to major general of volunteers (effective November 1862). He also served well in the **Tullahoma Campaign**, but on the second day of **Chickamauga**, he was caught up in the Union rout and left the field. When other division commanders later accused him of cowardice, Negley was removed from command in October 1863. Although a court of inquiry cleared him of wrongdoing, he spent the rest of the war waiting in vain for new orders. Believing his mistreatment was the result of **West Point** graduates' jealousy of civilian officers, Negley resigned his commission in January 1865 and returned to Pennsylvania.

After the war, Negley was elected to the **U.S. Congress** as a **Republican** in 1868. He was reelected three times, was defeated twice, and became active in **New York railroads**.

NEGRO TROOPS, USE OF. *See* BLACK TROOPS, USE OF.

NEILL, THOMAS HEWSON (1826–1885) USA. A native of **Pennsylvania**, Neill attended the University of Pennsylvania but dropped out to accept an appointment to **West Point**. He spent most of his antebellum military career on frontier duty after graduating in 1847, but he did teach at the academy for three years.

When the Civil War began, Neill was a captain in the 5th U.S. Infantry. In the summer of 1861, he was made assistant adjutant general for **George Cadwalader's** division in the **Department of Pennsylvania**. Neill was appointed colonel of the 23rd Pennsylvania in February 1862, joined the **Army of the Potomac**, and led his men through the **Peninsula** and **Seven Days Campaigns**, winning a **brevet** for **Malvern Hill**. His **regiment** was not engaged at **Antietam**, but just prior to **Fredericksburg**, Neill was given a **brigade** in the VI Corps' 2nd Division. After leading it at Fredericksburg, he was promoted to brigadier general of volunteers in April 1863.

During the **Chancellorsville Campaign**, Neill won two brevets for his service at **Second Fredericksburg** and **Salem Church**. After being held in reserve at **Gettysburg**, his brigade saw combat at **Rappahannock Station** and in the **Mine Run Campaign**. During the **Overland Campaign**, Neill took command of the **division** after his superior was wounded in the **Wilderness** and led it through the rest of the campaign, earning a fourth brevet at **Spotsylvania**. During the 1864 **Petersburg Campaign**, he briefly served on the XVIII Corps' staff before becoming **Philip Sheridan's** acting inspector general in September. Neill served with Sheridan at **Cedar Creek**, but records do not indicate what he did after December 1864.

Neill was mustered out of the volunteers in August 1865, but he remained in the regular **army** as a major. He rose to the rank of colonel, served as commandant of cadets at West Point, and was brevetted brigadier general for his war service before retiring in 1883.

NELSON, ALLISON (1822–1862) CSA. A native of **Georgia**, Nelson became a lawyer and state politician before the Civil War. He was elected to one term in the legislature in 1848 and served as Atlanta's mayor in 1855. More interested in the military than politics, Nelson raised a volunteer **company** and served as its captain in the **Mexican War** and later was appointed a brigadier general by Narcisco Lopez in the fight for Cuban independence. Moving west in the 1850s, he served with the proslavery forces in **"Bleeding Kansas,"** fought **Indians** in **Texas**, and was elected to the Texas legislature in 1859.

After serving as a prosecession delegate at the Texas **secession** convention, Nelson helped organize the 10th Texas in 1861 and was elected its colonel. After performing an admirable job in equipping and training the men, he joined **Thomas Hindman's** command in **Arkansas**. In June 1862, Nelson was given two additional units and some **artillery** and the following month harassed Union shipping on the White River at **Devall's Bluff**. Upon Holmes's recommendation, Nelson was promoted to brigadier general in September 1862 and was given command of a **division**. However, he contracted a fever and died in camp in October before he could demonstrate his effectiveness as a division commander. Holmes wrote of Nelson, "He is an irreparable loss to me" (Davis, ed., *The Confederate General,* vol. 4, 195).

NELSON, WILLIAM "BULL" (1824–1862) USA. A member of a prominent **Kentucky** family, Nelson attended **Vermont's** Norwich Academy before being appointed a midshipman in the **U.S. Navy** in 1840. During the **Mexican War**, he participated in **Winfield Scott's** capture of Vera Cruz and afterward rose to the rank of lieutenant.

During the **secession** crisis, Nelson investigated public sentiment in Kentucky for **Abraham Lincoln** (who had appointed Nelson's brother Thomas as minister to Chile), and when the Civil War began he was ordered by Lincoln to raise Union recruits there. He established Camp Dick Robinson and in September 1861 was appointed brigadier general of volunteers. After some **skirmishing**, Nelson was given command of a **division** in the **Army of the Ohio** in December and led it at **Shiloh**. He participated in the siege of **Corinth, Mississippi**, and was promoted to major general of volunteers in July 1862 (the day before, he was promoted to lieutenant commander in the navy). Known as "Bull" because of his loud, blustery personality, Nelson was the only naval officer on either side to become a major general during the war.

In July 1862, Nelson was detached from the Army of the Ohio and was sent to Kentucky to help defend it during the **Kentucky Campaign**. He was badly defeated, and slightly wounded, at **Richmond** before moving to Louisville to prepare its defenses. During this time, Nelson and fellow general **Jefferson C. Davis** became involved in a personal feud. Davis was to assist Nelson in Louisville's defense, but Nelson found him lacking in ability and openly rebuked him. Being a regular **U.S. Army** officer, Davis demanded more respect, but Nelson relieved him of command. In a hotel altercation on September 29, the two again had words. Davis threw a wadded piece of paper into Nelson's face, and Nelson slapped Davis. A few moments later, Davis borrowed a pistol, followed Nelson upstairs, and mortally wounded him in the chest. Although arrested, Davis was never tried because it was generally believed that he was defending his honor, and officers could not be spared at that critical time to sit on a court-martial.

NEVADA. The Nevada Territory was created by the **U.S. Congress** on March 2, 1861, and became a state of the Union on October 31, 1864. Although slightly populated, it was very important to the Union because of the $45 million worth of silver it provided to the government during the war. **Abraham Lincoln** appointed James W. Nye territorial governor, and he kept Nevada firmly under Union control. Because of its small population (it did not meet federal requirements for statehood, but Lincoln pushed its admittance nevertheless), Nevada did not provide any significant number of troops to the war effort. However, 1,080 men did garrison Nevada forts and guard mail routes during the war.

NEW BERN, NORTH CAROLINA, CAPTURE OF (MARCH 14, 1862). After Union Brig. Gen. **Ambrose Burnside** captured **Roanoke Island, North Carolina**, in February 1862, he moved against New Bern on the mainland. On March 13, Burnside landed 11,000 men on the Neuse River's west bank and advanced upstream along a road that was blocked by Confederate Brig. Gen. **Lawrence O. Branch** six miles below New Bern. After a rainy night, the Federals attacked Branch's left and center on the morning of March 14. In the center, **Jesse Reno's brigade** briefly broke through the defenses, but he was driven out by a

Confederate counterattack. **John G. Parke's** brigade then renewed the Union attack on the center and pierced it again. Branch was forced to retreat to **Kinston**, leaving New Bern in Union hands. The successful operation won Burnside a promotion to major general and gave the Union a foothold on the **North Carolina** coast. The fall of New Bern also led to the resignation of Confederate Secretary of War **Judah P. Benjamin**. In the operation, Burnside lost 476 men to Branch's 609.

NEW BERN, NORTH CAROLINA, RAIDS ON (MARCH 13–15, 1863, AND FEBRUARY 1–2, 1864). In February 1863, Confederate Lt. Gen. **James Longstreet** was put in command of the **Department of Virginia and North Carolina** to gather supplies for the **Army of Northern Virginia** and to keep the Federals in their defensive positions along the **North Carolina** coast. On March 13, 1863, **Daniel H. Hill's division** advanced on New Bern, North Carolina. After driving in the Union **pickets,** Hill approached the town the next day and demanded Fort Anderson's garrison to surrender. When it refused, Hill began shelling the fort. Although unable to capture the town, Hill did gather a large amount of supplies from the surrounding countryside. When Union gunboats arrived on March 15 and began shelling the Confederate position, Hill withdrew.

In January 1864, **Robert E. Lee** dispatched **George Pickett** to North Carolina to dislodge the enemy from New Bern. Pickett had 13,000 men and advanced on the town from the southwest, northwest, and northeast, while a flotilla of small gunboats under **John Taylor Wood** came down the Neuse River. On February 1, the Confederates pushed back the Union pickets, and Wood's gunboats captured and scuttled the USS *Underwriter*. On February 2, two of Pickett's columns reported the enemy positions too strong to carry, and Pickett reluctantly withdrew. During the operation, 22 North Carolina Confederates who had joined the Union **army** were captured and were later hanged by Pickett at Kinston.

NEW HAMPSHIRE. A **Republican** stronghold, New Hampshire was one of the North's smallest states, but it enthusiastically supported the Union. Its population of 326,073 supplied more than 20 military units and 36,000 men (or half the men of military age) to the Union forces. In addition, New Hampshire's mills, farms, and shipyards supplied valuable food, ships, and equipment to the war effort.

NEW HOPE CHURCH AND DALLAS, GEORGIA, BATTLES OF (MAY 25–27, 1864). During the early part of the **Atlanta Campaign**, **William T. Sherman** repeatedly forced **Joseph E. Johnston** out of his defensive positions by pinning down the **Army of Tennessee** with part of his force while sending the rest on **turning movements** around the Confederate flanks to threaten the **railroad** supply line in the rear. When Johnston retreated to Allatoona Pass, Sherman decided it was too strong to attack and moved his armies around the Confederate left flank toward Marietta by way of Dallas. Johnston quickly realized Sherman's intentions and shifted his **army** to counter the move.

The **Army of the Cumberland's** XX Corps, under Maj. Gen. **Joseph Hooker**, led the way for Sherman and on May 25 encountered Confederate resistance on Pumpkinvine Creek. After pushing back the Confederates three miles, Hooker ran into the main enemy defenses around New Hope Church. The countryside was perfect for defense, with gullies and thick woods and brush, and both armies dug elaborate earthworks and trenches. On May 25, Hooker launched several attacks against **Alexander P. Stewart's division** of **John Bell Hood's** corps, but he was repulsed with over 1,600 casualties at a place that came to be nicknamed the "Hell Hole." Stewart lost only about 350 men.

On the night of May 25, Hooker's left was extended by **Oliver O. Howard's** IV Corps, and the following day, **John Palmer's** XIV Corps and **John Schofield's Army of the Ohio** arrived to extend the Union right and left, respectively. To counter the lengthening enemy line, Hood extended his right with **Thomas C. Hindman's** division. Throughout May 26, fighting was fierce as each side attacked and probed the other. Sherman sent **James B. McPherson's Army of the Tennessee** southwest of New Hope Church to Dallas to turn Hood's left flank. McPherson, however, encountered **William J. Hardee's** entrenched **corps** and was unable to make any progress.

On May 27, Sherman attempted to turn the Confederate right flank with Howard's corps, but he was badly defeated by **Patrick Cleburne** at **Pickett's Mill**. The last battle around New Hope Church came on May 28 when Confederate Maj. Gen. **William B. Bate** misunderstood his orders and attacked McPherson's entrenched men near Dallas. Bate was repulsed with perhaps 1,500 casualties, while McPherson lost only 380 men. Sherman finally abandoned the New Hope Church Line and on June 1 began moving back east to the railroad at Acworth. Despite repeated attacks by Johnston, the Federals reached the railroad in early June and resumed their advance toward Atlanta.

NEW IRONSIDES, USS. Built in Philadelphia, Pennsylvania, and launched in May 1862, the *New Ironsides* was a 230-foot-long steam frigate. It was clad in 4.5-inch iron plating and carried 16 11-inch

Dahlgren guns. The ship became Adm. **Samuel F. Du Pont's** flagship when it joined the **South Atlantic Blockading Squadron** in January 1863. In April, the *New Ironsides* suffered 50 hits during Du Pont's attack on **Charleston, South Carolina**, but it was not badly damaged. In October, the Confederate torpedo boat *David* exploded a spar **torpedo** against the *New Ironsides*'s hull, but the ship remained on duty until May 1864, when it returned to Philadelphia for refitting. Joining the **North Atlantic Blockading Squadron** at **Norfolk, Virginia**, in August 1864, the *New Ironsides* participated in the attacks against **Fort Fisher, North Carolina**, in December 1864 and January 1865. After the fort's capture, it served on the James River in **Virginia** until war's end. The *New Ironsides* was decommissioned in April 1865 and was destroyed by fire nine months later.

NEW JERSEY. Although a Northern state, New Jersey had enough social and economic ties to the South to make a significant portion of its 672,017 people favor **slavery**. The state had abolished slavery in 1846, but the law allowed blacks to be held as apprentices for life (although only 18 were so held in 1860). The proslavery population was mostly concentrated in northern New Jersey, while Quakers and other **abolitionists** dominated the southern part of the state.

    Abraham Lincoln carried New Jersey in the **elections of 1860** and 1864 (when resident **George B. McClellan** was the **Democratic** candidate), but his **conscription** policy and the **Emancipation Proclamation** were not popular during the Civil War. Governors **Charles S. Olden** (a **Republican**) and **Joel Parker** (a Democrat) supported the Union war effort, but the legislature was controlled by **Peace Democrats**. Despite the legislature's lukewarm support of the war, New Jersey provided 80,000 men in 48 military units to the Union cause, including the famous **1st New Jersey Brigade** in the **Army of the Potomac**. Of these, 6,200 were killed in battle. Besides McClellan, such officers as **Alfred T. A. Torbert**, **Philip Kearny**, **H. Judson Kilpatrick**, **George W. Taylor**, and **Samuel F. Du Pont**, hailed from the state, as well as Confederate generals **Samuel Cooper** and **Samuel G. French**.

NEW JERSEY 1ST BRIGADE. One of the more famous infantry **brigades** in the **Army of the Potomac** was the 1st New Jersey Brigade. Originally composed of the 1st, 2nd, and 3rd New Jersey, it fought in nearly all of the **army's** battles from **First Manassas** to **Appomattox**. In the months following First Manassas, the brigade was joined by the 4th and 10th New Jersey and by the 15th New Jersey in August 1862.

In addition, the nine-month 23rd New Jersey, the 40th New Jersey, and the dismounted 1st Delaware Cavalry also served in the brigade during part of the war. The brigade became the 1st Brigade of the VI Corps' 1st Division. It first was led by **Philip Kearny** until he was given a **division** command in May 1862. **George W. Taylor** then took over, but he was killed during the **Second Manassas Campaign**. **Alfred T. A. Torbert** next led the brigade until he took a cavalry division in April 1864, and he was followed by a succession of colonels. During the war, 900 men of the New Jersey Brigade were killed or mortally wounded in battle, and 595 died from disease, for a total of 1,495 dead.

NEW MADRID AND ISLAND NO. 10, MISSOURI, CAPTURE OF (MARCH 3–14, 1862). After the loss of **Forts Henry and Donelson, Tennessee**, and the evacuation of Columbus, Kentucky, in early 1862, the Confederates' hold on the upper Mississippi River was tenuous. The river defense hinged on New Madrid (MAD-rid), Missouri, and Island No. 10, two positions that had been prepared a year earlier to stop Union traffic on the Mississippi River. Island No. 10 was located where the river made a sharp looping turn to the west and north, while New Madrid was on the west bank where the river looped back south and east. This curve formed a peninsula on the river's east bank opposite New Madrid. Confederate Gen. **P. G. T. Beauregard** reinforced the town's 2,000-man garrison in early March with an additional 5,000 men under Brig. Gen. **John P. McCown**. In addition, there were 50 heavy cannons and Capt. **George N. Hollins's** small flotilla of gunboats to protect the area.

On February 28, 1862, Union Maj. Gen. **John Pope** left Commerce, Missouri, with 18,000 men to seize New Madrid and open the river to Memphis, Tennessee. After reaching New Madrid on March 3, he began a siege, and on March 13, Hollins ferried McCown's men to the peninsula across the river and withdrew his ships downstream. McCown had saved his troops, but he had placed them in a precarious position on the peninsula and was replaced by **William W. Mackall** for abandoning New Madrid.

Pope next planned to cross the river south of New Madrid to cut off the Confederates' line of retreat from the peninsula. He wanted **Andrew H. Foote's** fleet, which had arrived upstream from Island No. 10 on March 15, to support this movement. Pope cut a canal on the west bank across the tip of land facing Island No. 10 so the gunboats could avoid running past the enemy fortifications on the island. This was completed on April 4, and a gunboat moved downstream that night to support Pope's crossing. Two nights later, another of Foote's boats successfully made the run. On April 7, the Union infantry was ferried to the river's east bank and cut Mackall's line of retreat from the peninsula. Later that day, Mackall surrendered Island No. 10 and the approximately 6,000 men on it and the peninsula, plus numerous heavy cannons. Pope had lost approximately 50 men in the entire operation. The victories at New Madrid and Island No. 10 allowed the Union to continue downstream to **Fort Pillow** and **Memphis, Tennessee**. It also enhanced Pope's reputation and led to his being called to **Washington, D.C.**, that summer to take command of the **Army of Virginia**.

NEW MARKET, VIRGINIA, BATTLE OF (MAY 15, 1864). As part of **U. S. Grant's** overall **strategy** in the spring of 1864, Maj. Gen. **Franz Sigel** advanced into **Virginia's Shenandoah Valley** with approximately 6,500 men to deny its use to the Confederacy as a breadbasket. Protecting the Valley was Confederate Maj. Gen. **John C. Breckinridge**, who was authorized by **Robert E. Lee** to use the **Virginia Military Institute** (VMI) cadets in combat, if necessary.

On May 2, Sigel marched up the Valley from Winchester but moved slowly in the face of **John Imboden's** harassing Confederate cavalry. Breckinridge took advantage of the delay and assembled a small 5,000-man **army**, including 257 VMI cadets and six of their officers. After heavy **skirmishing** on May 14, Sigel moved some troops south of New Market toward Breckinridge on May 15, but he took up a defensive position about a mile north of town instead of attacking the Confederates. Breckinridge seized the initiative and began exchanging heavy **artillery** fire with the Federals just before noon. He then attacked and swept north through increasingly heavy rain and thunderstorms. The Confederates drove Sigel's advance line back through town (to the cheers of residents) to the main line, where Union artillery began pounding them. Up to this point, the VMI cadets (known as "Katydids" to the Confederate veterans) had been held in reserve because Breckinridge was reluctant to expose them to battle. At this critical moment, however, the Union artillery was battering his line, and Breckinridge ordered, "Put the boys in" (Faust, ed., *Historical Times Illustrated Encyclopedia of the Civil War,* 528). The cadets eagerly rushed forward, joined in a general advance, and captured one of the enemy's cannons, even though they were exposed to heavy artillery fire. Sigel, who was said to have been shouting out his orders in German, attempted a counterattack on his right, but it failed. Breckinridge continued his advance and soon put the entire Union army to flight. Sigel fell back across the Shenandoah's North Fork and burned the bridge behind him to prevent the Confederates from following.

In the short, decisive victory, Breckinridge lost 577 men, including 10 cadets killed and 47 wounded. Sigel lost 831 men. The VMI cadets became known as the "boy heroes," while Sigel was replaced by **David Hunter** on May 19. The battle temporarily saved the Shenandoah Valley for the Confederates and allowed Breckinridge to join Lee, who was engaged in the **Overland Campaign**.

NEW MARKET HEIGHTS, VIRGINIA, BATTLE OF (SEPTEMBER 29, 1864). During the **Petersburg Campaign** in late September 1864, **U. S. Grant** ordered **Benjamin F. Butler's Army of the James** to attack the **Richmond, Virginia**, defenses to prevent **Robert E. Lee** from sending further reinforcements to **Jubal A. Early** in the **Shenandoah Valley**. Butler crossed the James River in the predawn hours of September 29 with two columns. On his left, **E. O. C. Ord's** XVIII Corps moved against **Forts Harrison** and Gilmer, while on the right (or east) **David B. Birney's** X Corps crossed at Deep Bottom for an attack against New Market Heights. In all, Butler had about 20,000 men, 18,000 of those being with Birney.

New Market Heights was a high bluff manned by about 1,800 Confederates from **John Gregg's** and **Martin W. Gary's** infantry and cavalry **brigades**. At 5:00 A.M., Birney reached the position and extended his line to the left to connect with Ord's column. After Grant arrived and ordered a general assault, Birney attacked at about 3:00 P.M. with a **division** of **black troops** under **Charles Paine**. Although Paine badly scattered the division, his soldiers attacked with great valor. The Federals were stopped, however, and Confederates, who came out of their trenches to engage them, **massacred** some of the wounded. Birney then renewed the attack, adding to the assault **Alfred Terry's** division (which included a black brigade), and finally overran the enemy defenses. To the left, Ord's troops captured Fort Harrison and repulsed a Confederate counterattack the next day, but the operation did little to change the tactical situation around Richmond. During the fighting at New Market Heights and Fort Harrison, the Federals lost about 3,300 men to the Confederates' approximately 2,000.

NEW MARKET ROAD, VIRGINIA, BATTLE OF (JULY 27–29, 1864). *See* DEEP BOTTOM, VIRGINIA, FIRST BATTLE OF.

NEW MEXICO TERRITORY. Won from Mexico in the **Mexican War**, the New Mexico Territory was organized as part of the **Compromise of 1850**. It had a population of 93,516 in 1860 but was little involved in the growing **slavery** debate because its land was unsuitable for plantation agriculture, and most of its population was either Unionist or neutral.

The Confederates attempted to seize control of the territory when Col. **John R. Baylor** led his 2nd Texas Mounted Rifles on **"Baylor's Buffalo Hunt"** from San Antonio, Texas, on May 1, 1861. Moving into southern New Mexico, he captured **Fort Fillmore** and on August 1 created the Confederate Territory of Arizona, which included all the region south of the 34th parallel from **Texas** to **California**. Baylor declared himself governor, with his capital located at Mesilla, and the **Confederate Congress** formalized his actions in January 1862. When **Henry H. Sibley** arrived to take command, he attempted to expand Confederate control over the northern part of the territory and launched **Sibley's New Mexico Campaign** in early 1862. Although Sibley captured Albuquerque and Santa Fe, and his men enjoyed success at the battles of **Valverde** and **Glorieta Pass**, he was forced to abandon the territory in May after his supplies were destroyed.

In February 1863, the **U.S. Congress** created the Territory of Arizona out of the western half of New Mexico. The New Mexico Territory was quiet for the rest of the war except for some fighting between the Union **army** and **Indians**. **Christopher "Kit" Carson** made one such military expedition against the Navajos in 1864.

NEW ORLEANS, LOUISIANA. New Orleans, Louisiana, was the Confederacy's largest city, with a population of 168,000 in 1860. It also housed a U.S. Mint, from which the Confederates seized a large amount of gold in early 1861, and had considerable **industry** that produced **ironclads**, **submarines**, munitions, **uniforms**, and other military items. Although the city's population was overwhelmingly secessionist, there also was a large number of Unionists, because some families had relatives and trade ties in the North. New Orleans also included many free people of color who had earned a respected niche in society as artisans, craftsmen, and slave owners, and almost 40 percent of the population (the most of any Southern city) were foreign-born people who sometimes had little loyalty to the Confederacy.

New Orleans sent thousands of men to the **Confederate army**. The **Washington Artillery** claimed some of the city's leading aristocrats, Coppens's **Zouaves** and the Tiger Rifles wore outlandish Zouave uniforms, the 6th Louisiana was made up almost entirely of Irishmen, and the 10th Louisiana boasted men from at least 24 different nations. Such units helped create the rowdy and fierce reputation of the **Louisiana Tigers**. The city also provided several thousand men for the Union cause, most notably the **Louisiana Native Guards**, several **regiments** of **black troops**, who at first offered their services to the Confederacy.

Despite its significance, New Orleans fell to the Union early in the war when **David Farragut** ran past **Forts Jackson and St. Philip** and anchored at the city on April 25, 1862. Confederate Maj. Gen. **Mansfield Lovell** decided it was impossible to defend the city when the Union fleet arrived and withdrew his men without a fight. City officials then surrendered New Orleans on April 28, and on May 1, Maj. Gen. **Benjamin F. Butler** landed his occupation troops. Butler ruled over the city with an iron fist for less than a year and earned the nickname "Beast" because of his harsh measures. He was replaced in December 1862 by **Nathaniel P. Banks**, who organized a Unionist state government in New Orleans in 1864 as part of **Abraham Lincoln's Ten Percent Plan**. New Orleans remained the Union capital of Louisiana through the **Reconstruction** period.

NEW ORLEANS, LOUISIANA, CAPTURE OF (APRIL 25–MAY 1, 1862). *See* FORTS JACKSON AND ST. PHILIP, LOUISIANA, SIEGE OF; NEW ORLEANS, LOUISIANA.

NEWTON, JOHN (1823–1895) USA. A native of **Virginia** and the son of a 29-year veteran of the **U.S. Congress**, Newton graduated second in the **West Point** class of 1842. Assigned to the **engineers**, his antebellum career was confined to engineering projects, teaching at the academy, and serving as chief engineer on the **Utah Expedition**.

A captain of engineers when the Civil War began, Newton served as chief engineer for the **Departments of Pennsylvania** and **the Shenandoah** during the war's first months and won a promotion to major. Promoted to brigadier general of volunteers in September 1861, he commanded a **brigade** and continued engineering duties around **Washington, D.C.**, and Fredericksburg, Virginia, before being given a brigade in the 1st Division of the **Army of the Potomac's** VI Corps during the **Peninsula Campaign**. Newton fought in the **Seven Days** and **Antietam Campaigns** and won a **brevet** in the regular **army** for his service in the latter. He then was given command of a VI Corps **division** in October 1862 and led it at **Fredericksburg**. Although only slightly engaged at Fredericksburg, Newton was one of the officers who became embroiled in disputes with army commander **Ambrose Burnside** afterward. He complained of Burnside's leadership in a letter to **Abraham Lincoln**, and Burnside listed Newton as one of several officers he wanted dismissed from the service. Burnside was dismissed, instead, but Newton's testimony in a later inquiry also hurt his career.

Newton was promoted to major general of volunteers in March 1863 and led his division with great skill at **Second Fredericksburg** during the **Chancellorsville Campaign**. At **Gettysburg**, he was given command of the I Corps after **John F. Reynolds** was killed and led it through the **Bristoe Station** and **Mine Run Campaigns**. However, his earlier testimony in the Burnside affair came back to hurt him, and Newton's appointment to major general was not confirmed by the Senate. Therefore, when the army was reorganized in the spring of 1864, he reverted to brigadier general in April and was sent west. During the **Atlanta Campaign**, Newton commanded the 2nd Division in the **Army of the Cumberland's** IV Corps and was brevetted brigadier general of regulars for his service at **Peachtree Creek**. After Atlanta's fall, he was placed in command of the District of Key West and Tortugas and remained there until war's end. When Newton mustered out of the volunteer service in January 1866, he had received brevets of major general in both the regular and volunteer service and had been appointed lieutenant colonel of engineers.

Newton remained in the engineers after the war and in 1884 became the army's chief of engineers with the rank of brigadier general. He retired from the army in 1886 and became involved in **railroads** and public works.

NEWTONIA, MISSOURI, BATTLE OF (SEPTEMBER 30, 1862). In September 1862, Union Brig. Gen. **Friedrich Salomon** took 4,500 men in two **brigades** from Fort Scott, Kansas, into southwestern **Missouri**. On September 30, a small detachment under Col. Edward Lynde encountered a Confederate force of 200 men at Newtonia. Lynde attacked and forced the Confederates back into town, but the Confederates were soon reinforced by Col. **Douglas H. Cooper** and his **Indian** command. The Confederates counterattacked and drove Lynde back, but soon he was met by Salomon, who launched an unsuccessful attack of his own. By this time, Cooper had received more help from **Joseph O. Shelby's** Missouri cavalry, bringing his total up to nearly 7,000 men. Launching a massive attack with mostly his Choctaw, Chickasaw, and Cherokee Indians, Douglas broke the Union line and sent the Federals fleeing in panic. In the fight, the Confederates lost 78 men, while the Federals reported losing more than 400. Afterward, Union **district** commander **John M. Schofield** moved against the Confederates at Newtonia and engaged in **skirmishing** for several days. In early October, Cooper withdrew into **Indian Territory**, and Shelby fell back into northwestern **Arkansas**.

NEW YORK. With an 1860 population of 3,880,735 and a very strong **industrial** and financial base, New York provided more men, material, and money to the Union than any other state during the Civil War. In all, 474,701 New Yorkers served the Union, with approximately 50,000 losing their lives. Among the more famous units were **Duryée's Zouaves**, **Ellsworth's Zouaves**, the **Corcoran Legion**, and the **Irish Brigade**. Also, Secretary of State **William H. Seward**, Generals **William W. Averell**, **Francis Barlow**, **Henry Halleck**, **Philip Kearny**, **Wesley Merritt**, **John M. Schofield**, **Philip Sheridan**, **Daniel Sickles**, **Henry Slocum**, **George Stoneman**, **Emory Upton**, **Gouverneur K. Warren**, and about one hundred other Union generals hailed from the state. The only hostile act in the state was the unsuccessful November 1864 **Confederate plan to burn New York City**.

Although the vast majority of New Yorkers supported the war effort, there was a sizeable number of **Democrats** who either opposed the war or opposed the harsh measures imposed by **Abraham Lincoln**. Republican Gov. **Edwin D. Morgan** provided huge numbers of recruits and equipment to the administration, but he was defeated in 1862 by Democrat **Horatio Seymour**. Under Seymour, New York continued to play a major role in the war, but growing war weariness also set in, and many people began to resent the shift in goals from saving the Union to ending **slavery**. As a result, when **conscription** was used in 1863, the bloody **New York City Draft Riot** erupted. When the war began going better for the Union in 1864, Lincoln and the **Republicans** carried the state in that year's elections.

NEW YORK CITY, CONFEDERATE PLAN TO BURN (NOVEMBER 25, 1864). By late 1864, Confederate civilians were suffering greatly as Union **armies** ravaged **Georgia** and the **Shenandoah Valley**. In retaliation, the Confederate Secret Service sent agents into New York City to burn down its hotels. Colonel Robert M. Martin led seven men into the city on the night of November 25, 1864, and checked into various hotels with 402 bottles of Greek fire. None of the hotel fires caused serious damage, and only a blaze in Barnum's Museum could be viewed as successful. Union officials issued orders to hang the agents if caught, and one, Capt. Robert Cobb Kennedy, was captured and executed. The others managed to escape safely.

NEW YORK CITY DRAFT RIOT (JULY 13–16, 1863). By the summer of 1863, volunteers began to dwindle, and the Union was forced to rely on **conscription** to fill the **army's** ranks. Although designed mainly to encourage men to enlist voluntarily before being conscripted, the draft was unpopular with many Northerners. Poor, lower class citizens especially resented it since they were unable to avoid conscription by hiring **substitutes** or paying **commutation** fees like more wealthy men.

On July 11, 1863, New York City held its first draft at a time when politics and racism made it a powder keg. Much of the city's largely **Democratic** population bitterly opposed **Abraham Lincoln's** harsh war measures, and the Irish immigrants resented the war's new goal of ending **slavery**. When the names of those drafted were published in newspapers, a bloody three-day riot broke out on July 13. Mostly Irish mobs roamed the streets attacking **Republican** newspapers and blacks. A black-orphan home and church were burned, the office of the **New York *Tribune*** was ransacked, the provost marshal's home was attacked, and many blacks were murdered. Damages were estimated at $1.5 million. To regain control, officials called in units from the **Army of the Potomac**, which had just won the **Battle of Gettysburg**. Order was restored, and the draft was renewed in August without further trouble. The number of dead in the riot is disputed. Newspapers claimed hundreds were killed, while modern historians put the number much lower.

NEW YORK FIRE ZOUAVES. *See* ELLSWORTH'S ZOUAVES.

NEW YORK *TIMES*. Started by Henry Jarvis Raymond and George Jones in 1851 as the New York *Daily Times*, this prominent newspaper changed its name to the *Times* in 1857. By the time the Civil War began, it was the second leading daily paper in New York City and competed fiercely with the *New York Tribune* and *Herald*. Although less partisan than most other papers, the *Times* did support **Abraham Lincoln's** administration. During the war, the paper was edited by Alexander Wilson or James Spaulding and boasted some of the Union's best **war correspondents**, including Walt Whitman, who contributed as a free-lance writer.

NEW YORK *TRIBUNE*. Begun by **Horace Greeley** in 1841, the *Tribune* became one of the country's leading liberal newspapers and constantly competed with the *New York Times* and *Herald*. It had a small army of **war correspondents**, including **Charles Dana**, **George Smalley**, and **Henry Villard**, as well as some women, who covered both the war and social issues. One of its most famous correspondents was Dana, who coined the often-used phrase "Forward to Richmond!" in 1861. Greeley, himself, often wrote the editorials, and one entitled **"The Prayer of Twenty Millions"** became a classic. The *Tribune* merged with the *Herald* in 1924 and continued to be published as the *Herald-Tribune* until it went out of business in 1966.

NICHOLLS, FRANCIS REDDING TILLOU (1834–1912) CSA. A native of **Louisiana** and the son of a prominent legislator and judge, Nicholls graduated from **West Point** in 1855. He served in the **artillery** during the **Seminole Wars** and in **California** before resigning his 2nd lieutenant's commission in 1856 because of poor health. After attending the University of Louisiana, Nicholls passed the bar exam and became a lawyer.

When the Civil War began, Nicholls organized a volunteer **company** and was elected captain. When the company became part of the 8th Louisiana in June 1861, he was elected lieutenant colonel and accompanied it to **Virginia**. After serving at **First Manassas**, Nicholls's **regiment** fought in **Stonewall Jackson's 1862 Shenandoah Valley Campaign**. He was shot in the left elbow at **First Winchester** and after having his arm amputated was left behind and captured during the retreat back up the Valley.

After being **exchanged** in September, Nicholls was sent to **Texas** on temporary duty and the following month was promoted to brigadier general. Returning to Virginia, he took command of the 2nd Louisiana Brigade in the **Army of Northern Virginia** and led it during Jackson's flank attack at **Chancellorsville**. The same night Jackson was mortally wounded, Nicholls was hit by a cannon shell and lost his left foot. Unfit for further field service, he was put in command of **Lynchburg, Virginia**, in August 1863 and defended the town during **David Hunter's 1864 Shenandoah Valley Campaign**. Afterward, Nicholls was sent to the **Trans-Mississippi Department**, where he commanded the Volunteer and Conscript Bureau.

After the war, Nicholls returned to Louisiana and entered politics. In 1876, the **Democrats** nominated for governor "all that is left of General Nicholls" (Davis, ed., *The Confederate General,* vol. 4, 200). During the campaign, he sometimes wore his **uniform** and asked voters to vote for him for governor because he was too one-sided to be a judge. In an election tainted with corruption, both candidates claimed victory, but Nicholls was declared the winner after the Compromise of 1877. After his first term, he served on the West Point Board of Visitors, was re-elected governor in 1888, and was a state supreme court justice from 1892 to 1911. Nicholls State University at Thibodaux, Louisiana, is named for him.

NICKERSON, FRANKLIN STILLMAN (OR STEBIN) (1826–1917)
USA. A native of **Maine**, Nickerson studied law and became a U.S. Customs official before the Civil War. He entered Union service in June

1861 as major of the 4th Maine and was commended for his service at **First Manassas**. Nickerson was promoted to lieutenant colonel in September and in November was appointed colonel of the 14th Maine.

Sent to the **Department of the Gulf** with **Benjamin F. Butler**, Nickerson again was commended for his actions at the **Battle of Baton Rouge**. He was given command of a **brigade** in the XIX Corps in January 1863 and was promoted to brigadier general of volunteers in March 1863. Nickerson briefly commanded his **division** during the **Port Hudson Campaign** and led his brigade during the 1864 **Red River Campaign**. In late June 1864, he was ordered to report to the adjutant general's office in **Washington, D.C.** There is no further record of Nickerson's service after that, and he resigned his commission in May 1865.

Nickerson settled in **Massachusetts** after the war and practiced law. He was one of the last Union generals to die.

NICOLAY, JOHN GEORGE (1832–1901) USA. A native of Bavaria, Nicolay immigrated to the United States with his family in 1838. He eventually settled in **Illinois** and was employed by a newspaper after being orphaned. It was during this time that Nicolay became friends with **John M. Hay**. Nicolay eventually became owner of the newspaper, sold it in 1856, and moved to Springfield, where he worked as a state clerk and **Abraham Lincoln's** personal secretary. In 1860, Nicolay was able to get his friend Hay hired as Lincoln's assistant secretary and both accompanied him to **Washington, D.C.**, when he became president in 1861. For the next four years, Nicolay essentially served as Lincoln's chief of staff. In the spring of 1865, Lincoln appointed him consul to Paris, a position Nicolay kept until 1869. He was appointed marshal of the **U.S. Supreme Court** in 1872 and served in that capacity until retiring in 1887.

Nicolay devoted the rest of his life to writing. He wrote *The Outbreak of Rebellion* (1881) and *A Short Life of Abraham Lincoln* (1902) and edited *Abraham Lincoln: Complete Works* (1894). His best-known publication was the 10-volume *Abraham Lincoln: A History,* which he coauthored with Hay in 1890.

NITER AND MINING BUREAU, CONFEDERATE. To improve the Confederacy's ability to provide munitions to its **armies**, Chief of Ordnance **Josiah Gorgas** convinced the **Confederate Congress** to create a niter corps in April 1862. Placed under **Isaac M. St. John** (who was replaced in February 1865 by Richard Morton), the corps provided the

Ordnance Department with niter (or saltpeter), an essential ingredient in gunpowder. In April 1863, Congress redesignated the corps the Niter and Mining Bureau and made it independent from the Ordnance Department. Working directly under the War Department, this new unit was responsible for gathering niter, iron, copper, lead, coal, and zinc for the military. The Confederacy was divided into approximately 14 districts, each with a head who was responsible for the department's activities in his district. By September 1864, the department had provided almost 3.5 million pounds of niter, with about half coming from overseas and half produced domestically; nearly 5 million pounds of lead; and 24,355 tons of iron. By late 1863, at least 775,000 pounds of copper had also been mined. In September 1864, the department employed 2,783 white men and 4,557 slaves.

NORFOLK, VIRGINIA. The site of the important Gosport Shipyard (also known as the Norfolk Navy Yard), Norfolk was abandoned by its Union garrison on April 20, 1861, just three days after **Virginia** seceded. Ten Union vessels were burned or scuttled as the Federals withdrew, including the USS *Merrimac*, which was raised by the Confederates and renamed *Virginia*. Much of the shipyard's facilities also were destroyed but not its important dry dock and 1,200 heavy cannons. Thus, when the Confederates seized Norfolk on April 21, they gained a valuable navy yard and much-needed ordnance. In May 1862, **Abraham Lincoln** accompanied Brig. Gen. **John Wool** and his command from **Fort Monroe, Virginia**, across Hampton Roads to Ocean View. This movement forced the Confederates to abandon Norfolk and allowed Wool to occupy the city on May 10. The city remained in Union hands for the rest of the war.

NORTH ANNA RIVER, VIRGINIA BATTLE OF (MAY 23–26, 1864). After more than a week of bloody fighting at **Spotsylvania** during the 1864 **Overland Campaign**, U. S. Grant once again withdrew the **Army of the Potomac** from **Robert E. Lee's** front and moved to the southeast to turn Lee's right flank. Grant began his march on the night of May 20, 1864, and headed for the important crossroads at Hanover Junction. Lee countered the move the next morning and on the morning of May 22 had his **Army of Northern Virginia** in a blocking position at North Anna River. When Grant arrived on the morning of May 23, he expected to push through the exhausted Confederates' position.

Marching south, Grant sent **Winfield Scott Hancock's** II Corps straight down the Telegraph Road to cross the river by bridge. Upstream, to Hancock's right, **Gouverneur K. Warren's** V Corps was to ford the river at Jericho Mill. Lee mistakenly believed the advancing Union forces were mere scouting parties and left only one **brigade** on the north bank of the river to guard the bridge on Telegraph Road. After a preliminary **artillery** bombardment, Hancock attacked the bridge with two brigades at about 6:00 P.M., drove the Confederates back, and captured the vital bridge intact. Upstream, Warren's **corps** crossed the North Anna at Jericho Mill with little trouble. **A. P. Hill's** corps launched a counterattack against Warren late in the afternoon but was unable to drive him back across the river.

That night Lee made plans to assume the offensive. He withdrew from Jericho Mill and the Telegraph Road bridge and placed his army in a position resembling an inverted *V*, with the angle resting on Ox Ford (about the Union center). Hill held the left wing, **James Longstreet's** I Corps the center, and **Richard Ewell's** II Corps the right wing. If Grant continued as before, he would split his army at the angle and place his two flanks on opposite sides of the inverted *V*, where they would be unable to support each other. By entrenching, Lee planned to hold one of his wings with a small force while concentrating his men on the other side and **defeating** Grant **in detail**.

On May 24, Grant resumed his advance. Finding no Confederates at the two river crossings, he assumed Lee was retreating and moved into the trap. A IX Corps brigade was mauled when it tried crossing at Ox Ford, and **John Gibbon's** II Corps **division** was bloodied on Grant's left when it encountered **Robert Rodes's** division. Late in the day, Grant realized the danger he faced and ordered his men to entrench. The two armies **skirmished** heavily until May 26, but Lee never delivered the knockout blow he had planned, probably because he fell ill on May 24 and was confined to his tent. During the fighting on the North Anna River, Grant lost 2,623 men to Lee's 2,517. On May 26, Grant abandoned his works and again moved to the southeast to **Cold Harbor**.

NORTH ATLANTIC BLOCKADING SQUADRON. To carry out the naval **blockade** against the Confederacy, the **U.S. Navy** created the North Atlantic Blockading Squadron in July 1861 to patrol the Atlantic coast north of the **North** and **South Carolina** state line. Captain **Louis M. Goldsborough** assumed command in September and saw the squadron increase from 13 to more than 50 ships by February 1862. By October 1864, there were more than 100 ships in the squadron. Rear Admiral **Samuel P. Lee** took command in September 1862, followed by

David D. Porter in October 1864. Besides blockading ports and chasing **blockade runners**, the squadron also cooperated with the **army** in the capturing of **Roanoke Island**, **New Bern**, and **Fort Fisher, North Carolina**; and in the **Peninsula** and **Seven Days Campaigns**. In July 1865, the squadron was consolidated with the **South Atlantic Blockading Squadron** to form the Atlantic Squadron.

NORTH CAROLINA. With only about one-fourth of its families owning slaves in 1860 and having a large number of Unionists living in the western mountainous regions, North Carolina was more moderate than most other Southern states during the **secession** crisis. As a result, it was the next to the last state to secede on May 20, 1861. Yet North Carolina suffered about one-fourth of all Confederate casualties (more than one-fourth of **Robert E. Lee's** casualties at **Gettysburg** were North Carolinians), while supplying only one-sixth the soldiers. With an 1860 population of 661,563, the state provided approximately 120,000 men to the Confederacy, including **Theophilus H. Holmes, Daniel H. Hill, William D. Pender, Stephen D. Ramseur**, and 32 other generals. With 40,275 of the state's soldiers losing their lives and 23,694 deserting, North Carolina suffered the largest number of deaths and **deserters** of all the Confederate states. While Gov. **Zebulon Vance** often clashed with **Jefferson Davis** over **conscription**, the **suspension of the writ of habeas corpus**, and various **states rights** issues, he made great efforts to support his troops. By ordering all of North Carolina's cotton mills to produce **uniforms**, Vance kept the men well clothed throughout the war while other states suffered uniform shortages.

During most of the war, military operations were confined to such coastal areas as **Roanoke Island, New Bern**, and **Wilmington**. Not until March 1865 was North Carolina faced with a massive invasion. When **William T. Sherman** crossed into the state during the **Carolinas Campaign**, his men recognized North Carolina's reluctant **secession** and did not inflict the same amount of destruction on it as they did to **South Carolina**. Major battles were fought in the war's closing days between Sherman and **Joseph E. Johnston** at **Averasboro** and **Bentonville** before Johnston finally surrendered in April 1865 near **Durham Station**. *See also* ALBEMARLE SOUND; FORT FISHER; FORT MACON; GOLDSBORO BRIDGE; HATTERAS INLET; MONROE'S CROSS ROADS; PLYMOUTH; SOUTH MILLS; WASHINGTON; WHITE HALL; WYSE FORK; NORTH CAROLINA.

NORTHERN DEMOCRATIC PARTY. *See* DEMOCRATIC PARTY.

NORTHERN DEPARTMENT (UNION). Organized in January 1864, this military **department** consisted of **Michigan, Ohio, Indiana,** and **Illinois,** with headquarters at Columbus, Ohio. Over the course of its existence, small parts of Indiana, Illinois, and **Kentucky** either were taken out or added to it. Major General **Samuel P. Heintzelman** was the department's original commander, but he was replaced in October 1864 by Maj. Gen. **Joseph Hooker,** who led it until war's end. The main responsibilities of the two generals were to guard **prison** camps, enforce **conscription,** and guard against Confederate spies and military incursions. The department was abolished in June 1865 when it was merged with the **Department of the Ohio.**

NORTHRUP, LUCIUS BELLINGER (1811–1894) CSA. A native of **South Carolina,** Northrup graduated from **West Point** in 1831 and was assigned to the dragoons after two years in the infantry. During this service, he became close friends with future Confederate president **Jefferson Davis.** Not an especially conscientious officer, Northrup once was charged with negligence of duty but remained in the **U.S. Army.** He was severely wounded in the **Seminole Wars** when his pistol accidentally discharged and shot him in the knee, and he spent several years on leave. During his lengthy convalescence, Northrup studied medicine and was dismissed from the **army** in 1848 for practicing a profession. When Davis became secretary of war in 1853, Northrup was reinstated and promoted to captain, but he remained on sick leave—practicing medicine—until 1861.

Northrup resigned his commission in January 1861 and in March was appointed by Davis to Confederate lieutenant colonel and acting commissary general. He was promoted to colonel in June and was made permanent commissary general. Having little talent for his position, Northrup did not perform particularly well and was criticized because of his close association with Davis. He also faced such overwhelming problems as poor transportation, loss of valuable food-producing areas, and strangling red tape of his own design. Blamed for the poor performance of his department, Northrup became one of the most hated officers in the Confederacy. Davis stood by his friend through constant criticism and congressional inquiries and even promoted him to brigadier general in November 1864 (but he never sought Senate confirmation). By early 1865, however, even **Robert E. Lee** was demanding Northrup's removal, and Davis's support was waning. When **John C. Breckinridge** was appointed secretary of war in February 1865, he made Northrup's removal a condition of his acceptance. Northrup was relieved that month and was replaced by **Isaac M. St. John.**

Northrup accompanied the fleeing government after the fall of **Richmond, Virginia**, but was arrested in June 1865. Imprisoned, he was charged with deliberately starving Union **prisoners**, but the case was never pursued, and he was released in October. Northrup then retired to **Virginia** and became a farmer.

NORTHWEST CONSPIRACY. **Copperheads** and **Sons of Liberty** members in the old northwest states of **Indiana** and **Illinois** opposed the Union war effort. In 1864, Confederate agents in Canada hoped to use this to their advantage and made contact with Sons of Liberty members to organize an uprising, during which Confederate **prisoners** of war would be freed from **Camp Douglas, Illinois**. The freed prisoners then would aid the Sons of Liberty in taking control of the state governments and creating a Northwest Confederation that would support the Confederacy and force the Union to end the war.

Some Confederate agents did infiltrate Chicago, Illinois, in late summer 1864, but they had to postpone the planned uprising twice because local support was lacking. A final date for the uprising was set for August during the **Democratic** National Convention at Chicago. Just before the deadline, however, the Camp Douglas commandant and a Chicago newspaper editor uncovered the plan. Several arrests were made, but evidence of a large-scale conspiracy was lacking.

Indiana's Gov. **Oliver P. Morton** also feared a similar conspiracy in his state. In the autumn of 1864, a raid on a leading Sons of Liberty member uncovered papers that then were somewhat falsely manipulated to show such a conspiracy existed. Soon afterward, a shipment of pistols sent to the man's business was also seized. He and a Democratic newspaper editor were arrested, and Morton declared that a "Northwestern conspiracy" had been foiled.

Late in the war, many Confederates hoped such a Northwest Conspiracy would bring about a peace, but they were disappointed. While there were some Confederate agents and **Peace Democrats** involved in such plots, their numbers were small, and there probably never was any real danger of such a thing happening.

NORWOOD'S PLANTATION, LOUISIANA, BATTLE OF (MAY 18, 1864). *See* YELLOW BAYOU, LOUISIANA, BATTLE OF.

NUECES RIVER, TEXAS, BATTLE OF (AUGUST 10, 1862). Many German settlers in **Texas** remained loyal to the Union during the Civil War. In the summer of 1862, Fritz Teneger led approximately 65 Unionists from their homes near Fredericksburg toward Mexico, where they hoped to secure passage to **Louisiana** to join the Union **army**. Learning of the plan, 94 Confederates under Lt. C. D. McRae gave chase and caught up with the party at the Nueces (noo-AY-sis) River near the Mexican border. On the morning of August 10, 1862, McRae attacked the Germans' camp and killed 19 of the men. The Confederates later executed nine of the wounded Germans. The Texans lost two dead and 18 wounded. *See also* MASSACRES.

NULLIFICATION CRISIS. John C. Calhoun popularized the theory of nullification during the antebellum period and touched off the first real crisis between the North and South. After the **U.S. Congress** passed the 1828 Tariff (or as it was known in the South, the Tariff of Abomination) Vice President Calhoun wrote his *South Carolina Exposition and Protest*. Many Southerners viewed such tariffs as discriminatory and unconstitutional since they forced the South to pay tariffs that protected Northern **industry**. In his protest, Calhoun argued that since each state had voluntarily ratified the Constitution, each state had the right to decide for itself which federal laws were constitutional. If a state decided to "nullify" a federal law, Congress then would either have to abolish the law or secure an amendment to make it constitutional. If that occurred, Calhoun believed the state could decide either to obey the law or pass an ordinance of **secession**.

In 1832, another tariff bill was passed. This time **South Carolina** sparked the Nullification Crisis when it voted to nullify the tariff. Tension rose as President Andrew Jackson had Congress pass the Force Act, authorizing him to use military force to collect the tariff. Neither side wanted war, and South Carolina and the federal government accepted a compromise tariff proposed by Henry Clay that provided for a declining tariff rate over a number of years. South Carolina rescinded its nullification act but in defiance nullified the Force Act. Civil war was avoided, but Southern **"fire-eaters"** maintained that states had the right to nullify unconstitutional laws, and to such radicals secession increasingly became an acceptable solution to their growing political problems.

– O –

OAK GROVE, VIRGINIA, BATTLE OF (JUNE 25, 1862). *See* KING'S SCHOOL HOUSE, VIRGINIA, BATTLE OF.

OAK HILLS, MISSOURI, BATTLE OF (AUGUST 10, 1861). *See* WILSON'S CREEK, MISSOURI, BATTLE OF.

OATH OF ALLEGIANCE. When large numbers of U.S. officers and government employees began resigning to join the Confederacy in early 1861, the federal government ordered all military personnel to take an oath of allegiance beginning in April. In August, the **U.S. Congress** passed a law requiring civilian government employees also to take such an oath. To simplify matters, the **Ironclad Oath** was introduced in 1862 for military and civilian personnel. The Ironclad Oath's requirement that one had never supported the Rebellion prevented former Confederates from participating in politics during **Reconstruction** unless they received a presidential pardon. In 1884, Congress passed a new Oath of Allegiance, which removed these restrictive measures and only demanded an oath of loyalty to the Constitution.

Besides government officials, the Union also used oaths of allegiance to ensure the loyalty of Southern civilians during the war. Often an oath had to be taken to protect one's property, receive aid, conduct business with the government, receive a **parole** after being captured, or to be compensated for property losses. In December 1863, **Abraham Lincoln's** Proclamation of Amnesty and Reconstruction required Southerners (excluding high-ranking Confederates) to take an oath of allegiance to gain amnesty and a pardon.

OBLIQUE ATTACK. Also known as attacking in **echelon**, this **tactical** maneuver was made by first attacking with one's flank unit, followed in order by the others down the line so they strike the enemy like a wave washing ashore. Its goal was to knock loose the enemy's flank first, and then his entire line would come unhinged and be "rolled up" as the succeeding attacking units hit it. The maneuver was praised by military theorist **Baron Antoine Henri Jomini** and had been used successfully in ancient times and by Frederick the Great. The Confederates employed it in such battles as **Seven Pines**, **Gaines' Mill**, and **Gettysburg**.

OCEAN POND, FLORIDA, BATTLE OF (FEBRUARY 20, 1864). *See* OLUSTEE, FLORIDA, BATTLE OF.

ODELL, MOSES FOWLER (1818–1866) USA. A native of **New York**, Odell worked in business before becoming active in **Democratic** politics and winning patronage jobs in the customs department and as a public appraiser. He was elected to the **U.S. Congress** in 1860 and served on the Indian Affairs Committee and as chairman of the Treasury Department Committee.

Odell's most important congressional position was on the **Committee on the Conduct of the War**, to which he was appointed in December

1861. As a Democrat on the mostly **Republican** committee, he looked out for Democratic interests. Reelected in 1862, Odell also served on the Military Affairs Committee. He declined to run for a third term and became the naval agent for the port of New York.

OFFICIAL RECORDS. *See WAR OF THE REBELLION: A COMPILATION OF THE OFFICIAL RECORDS OF THE UNION AND CONFEDERATE ARMIES.*

OGLESBY, RICHARD JAMES (1824–1899) USA. A native of **Kentucky**, Oglesby was orphaned when he was nine and later claimed that the selling of the family slaves at that time made him an **abolitionist**. Raised in **Illinois** by an uncle, he worked as a farmer, rope maker, and carpenter and saved his money to study law. After passing the bar exam, Oglesby served in the **Mexican War** as a lieutenant of Illinois volunteers. He then practiced law and participated in the **California** Gold Rush before spending two years abroad. When he returned to Illinois, Oglesby became one of the state's first **Republicans** and won a seat in the state senate in 1860 after running unsuccessfully for the U.S. House of Representatives in 1858.

Oglesby entered Union service in April 1861 as colonel of the 8th Illinois and resigned his senate seat a few months later. Known to his men as "Uncle Dick," he was given command of a **brigade** in October and served at **Forts Henry and Donelson** and in the **siege of Corinth, Mississippi**. Promoted to brigadier general of volunteers in March 1862, Oglesby was severely wounded at the **Battle of Corinth** while leading a brigade in what became the **Army of the Tennessee's** 2nd Division.

Oglesby's wound kept him off duty for months, but he was promoted to major general of volunteers in November 1862. He was given command of a **division** and sometimes led the XVI Corps' left wing in western **Tennessee** and northern **Mississippi** until he resigned his commission in May 1864 to enter the Illinois gubernatorial race. Elected in November, Oglesby strongly supported **Abraham Lincoln**, succeeded in ratifying a number of **Reconstruction** constitutional amendments, and repealed some anti-black legislation. He also supported the **Radical Republicans** against President **Andrew Johnson** during Reconstruction.

After leaving the governor's office in 1869, Oglesby practiced law and was elected governor again in 1872 under a political agreement that had him resign the seat immediately so the lieutenant governor could take over and Oglesby could be appointed U.S. Senator. He declined to run for reelection in 1879 but was elected governor a third time in 1884, making him the first person ever elected Illinois governor three times. Oglesby retired after failing to be elected to the Senate in 1891.

OHIO. Out of an 1860 population of 2,339,511, Ohio provided more than 340,000 men to the Union cause, with nearly 25,000 becoming fatalities. The state also was invaluable to the Union war effort because of its rich farms, good **railroad** network (2,900 miles), and industrial base, and it was the home of such notable Union figures as **William T. Sherman, U. S. Grant**, the **"Fighting McCooks," Philip Sheridan, George B. McClellan, George A. Custer, Irvin McDowell, Rutherford B. Hayes, James A. Garfield, Edwin M. Stanton, Salmon P. Chase, Benjamin F. Wade**, and **John Sherman**.

Despite this strong Union support, Ohio had a large number of **Copperheads** who opposed the war and sometimes resisted **conscription**. Most notable of the antiwar figures was Congressman **Clement L. Vallandigham**, who was so vocal in his protests that he was branded a traitor by the government and finally was banished into Confederate territory.

No large military activities occurred in Ohio, although **John Hunt Morgan's Ohio Raid** in the summer of 1863 crossed the southern part of the state and ended at **Buffington Island** and **Salineville**.

OKOLONA, MISSISSIPPI, BATTLE OF (FEBRUARY 22, 1864). On February 20, 1864, Union Brig. Gen. **William Sooy Smith's Expedition** had reached **West Point, Mississippi. Nathan Bedford Forrest** initially opposed Smith with 2,500 Confederate cavalry, but after some **skirmishing**, he was reinforced to about 4,000 men. On the morning of February 21, Forrest attacked the Federals just south of West Point.

Believing he was outnumbered and convinced the raid already was a success, Smith ordered a retreat. Throughout the day, Forrest pursued the Federals as they fell back to within about four miles of Okolona (OH-kuh-LON-uh). At dawn of February 22, Forrest attacked again and pushed Smith back 11 miles in a running battle. Twice the Federals tried to make defensive stands, but each time they were overwhelmed. After losing six cannons, Smith made a final stand a few miles north of Okolona. In fierce fighting, the Confederates moved against his front and flank, and Forrest's brother Jeffrey was killed. After making two unsuccessful counterattacks, Smith renewed his retreat, and Forrest ordered a halt because of his men's exhaustion and a lack of ammunition.

Smith, who was supposed to join forces with **William T. Sherman** in his **Meridian Campaign**, withdrew all the way to **Tennessee**. In the fighting around West Point and Okolona, Forrest reported losing 144 men. Smith reported losing 700 men, but neither commander gave their casualties for the individual battles.

O'LAUGHLIN, MICHAEL (1840–1867) CSA. A native of **Maryland** and the childhood friend of **John Wilkes Booth**, O'Laughlin briefly served in the **Confederate army**. He became one of Booth's original conspirators in the plan to kidnap **Abraham Lincoln** and **exchange** him for Confederate **prisoners**. O'Laughlin at first thought the plan was impractical, but Booth convinced him to participate. When Booth changed the plan to murder, however, O'Laughlin quit. He turned himself in to Federal authorities on April 17, 1865, and was convicted of participating in the murder with seven other conspirators on June 30. Sentenced to life imprisonment, O'Laughlin was sent to Dry Tortugas, Florida, with co-conspirator Dr. **Samuel Mudd** and died there during the 1867 yellow fever epidemic.

"OLD ABE." In addition to being a nickname for **Abraham Lincoln**, this also was the name of the 8th Wisconsin's eagle mascot. The eagle was captured by **Indians** as a chick and was traded to a white settler, who eventually offered him to the **regiment's** Company C as a mascot. Soon, the entire regiment adopted "Old Abe" and became known as the Eagle Regiment. The men built a perch, which was carried much like a **flag**, and the eagle sat on it during marches. Flying high overhead and screeching during battles, "Old Abe" would return to his perch when the shooting stopped. He was said to have survived 42 battles and **skirmishes** during his three years with the regiment. The Confederates dubbed him the "Yankee buzzard" and tried unsuccessfully to shoot him down. The **company** gave the eagle to the state of **Wisconsin** in September 1864, and he was put on display at the state capitol. "Old Abe" died of smoke inhalation in 1881 when the capitol burned. He was mounted and put on display again but then was destroyed in another fire in 1904. Today, replicas of "Old Abe" sit in the capitol's Memorial Hall and in the Assembly Chamber.

OLD CAPITOL PRISON. This Union **prison** was located in **Washington, D.C.**, and was originally constructed to house the capitol after the British burned the city in the War of 1812. Becoming worn and dilapidated, it also had been used as a hotel before being pressed into service as a prison. Used to house **prisoners** of war, Union **deserters**, spies, and suspected disloyalists, the Old Capitol Prison was a harsh place. It had poor food, vermin, and a draftiness that was very unhealthy. Among its more illustrious inmates were **Belle Boyd**, **Rose O'Neal Greenhow**, and **Henry Wirz**.

OLD FORT WAYNE, INDIAN TERRITORY, BATTLE OF (OCTOBER 22, 1862). After the Union defeat at **Newtonia, Missouri**, in September 1862, **John Schofield's Army of the Frontier** advanced on the town and defeated the Confederates there on October 4. The Confederate **Indians** under **Douglas H. Cooper** and **Stand Watie** then retreated into **Indian Territory**. On the morning of October 22, Union Brig. Gen. **James G. Blunt's division** attacked Cooper's Confederates just inside Indian Territory near Old Fort Wayne. After a brief fight, Cooper abandoned some **artillery** and equipment and retreated across the Arkansas River. Cooper lost about 150 men in the clash to Blunt's 14.

"OLD GENTLEMEN'S CONVENTION." *See* WASHINGTON PEACE CONFERENCE.

OLDEN, CHARLES SMITH (1799–1876) USA. A native of **New Jersey**, Olden worked in his father's store before becoming a clerk in **Pennsylvania**. He moved to **Louisiana** in 1826, became a prosperous businessman, and retired to New Jersey eight years later. After farming and serving as Princeton University's treasurer and as a bank director, Olden served as a state senator from 1845 to 1851 and in 1859 was elected governor on the **Republican** ticket.

When the **secession** crisis deepened, Olden wanted a compromise settlement and attended the **Washington Peace Conference**. Once Southern states began seceding, however, he fully supported the Union war effort. Olden already had expanded the state militia as a precaution, and he raised $500,000 from state banks to **finance** his war efforts. He also denounced those he viewed as being disloyal and began raising troops. Although a strong supporter of **Abraham Lincoln**, Olden did oppose the **suspension of the writ of habeas corpus**.

Olden was prohibited by the state constitution from running for reelection and left office in January 1863. He then served as a judge on the Court of Errors and Appeals and as a member of the Court of Pardons.

OLIVER, JOHN MORRISON (1828–1872) USA. A native of **New York**, Oliver attended St. John's College before moving to **Michigan** and becoming a druggist and court reporter. He entered Union service in April 1861 as a private in the 4th Michigan but was promoted to 1st lieutenant in June. Although with the Union **army** during the **First Battle of**

Manassas, Oliver was not engaged. After being promoted to captain in September, he was appointed colonel of the 15th Michigan in March 1862.

Oliver was commended for his gallantry at **Shiloh** and shortly afterward was given command of a **brigade**, which he led in the **siege of Corinth, Mississippi.** He commanded another brigade at the **Battle of Corinth** before returning to his **regiment** in the **Army of the Tennessee** for the **Vicksburg Campaign.** After participating in the siege of **Jackson, Mississippi,** in July 1863, Oliver was given a brigade in the XV Corps' 4th Division in August. He led this brigade through the **Atlanta Campaign** but then took over a 2nd Division brigade and commanded it through the **March to the Sea** and siege of **Savannah, Georgia.** In January 1865, Oliver was promoted to brigadier general and served through the **Carolinas Campaign. Brevetted** major general for his war service, he took command of his **division** in May, but he was mustered out of service in August while serving in **Arkansas.**

Oliver remained in Arkansas and practiced law before becoming state assessor of internal revenue. He later was appointed superintendent of postal service for the Southwest and eventually moved to **Washington, D.C.**

OLUSTEE, **CSS.** *See TALLAHASSEE,* CSS.

OLUSTEE, FLORIDA, BATTLE OF (FEBRUARY 20, 1864). Northern **Florida** had a significant number of Unionists, and in February 1864, **Abraham Lincoln** wanted to use such areas to form loyal governments as part of his **Reconstruction** policy. Major General **Quincy A. Gillmore,** commander of the **Department of the South,** received permission to invade north Florida to liberate these Unionists, cut Confederate supply lines, and recruit **black troops** among the slaves there.

Gillmore and Brig. Gen. **Truman Seymour's division** left **South Carolina** and landed at Jacksonville, Florida, on February 7. Gillmore then returned to South Carolina after ordering Seymour to protect Jacksonville and not to push beyond Baldwin. When Seymour's cavalry reported that the Confederates were massing beyond Baldwin near Lake City, however, he ignored orders and planned to advance past Lake City with his 5,500 men to destroy the Florida, Atlantic & Gulf Railroad crossing over the Suwannee River.

Confederate **district** commander **Joseph Finegan** was reinforced from South Carolina and had about 5,100 men around the depot of

Olustee (oh-LUS-tee). On February 20, Seymour engaged Finegan outside Olustee near Ocean Pond on a narrow neck of land between two swamps. The limited field prevented Seymour from fully utilizing his men, but he attacked **Alfred H. Colquitt's** Confederate **brigade** that afternoon. The Federals were driven back with the loss of two cannons, but heavy **skirmishing** continued for some time. Colquitt finally received reinforcements and turned Seymour's right flank, capturing three more cannons. Seymour brought up the **54th Massachusetts** to reinforce the threatened line and then began withdrawing to Jacksonville at dusk. In the battle, Seymour lost 1,861 men to Finegan's 946. The Federals returned safely to Jacksonville and held it for the rest of the war. The Confederate victory at Olustee stopped the only large-scale Union invasion of Florida and prevented the Union from establishing control over north Florida.

O'NEAL, EDWARD ASBURY (1818–1890) CSA. A native of **Alabama**, O'Neal graduated first in his class from La Grange College in 1836 and became a lawyer in 1840. During the antebellum period, he participated in local politics and became a strong supporter of **secession**.

O'Neal entered Confederate service in June 1861 as major of the 9th Alabama. He was promoted to lieutenant colonel in October and to colonel of the 26th Alabama in March 1862. Serving in **Robert Rodes's brigade**, O'Neal led his **regiment** in the **Peninsula Campaign** and during the **Battle of Seven Pines** had his horse killed under him and was wounded by a shell fragment. He temporarily led the brigade in the **Army of Northern Virginia** during the early part of the **Antietam Campaign**, but he then returned to his regiment and suffered another wound at Boonsboro, during the fighting at **South Mountain**. In January 1863, O'Neal again assumed command of the brigade and received his third wound while fighting at **Chancellorsville**.

Upon **Robert E. Lee's** recommendation, O'Neal was promoted to brigadier general in June 1863 and was given permanent command of Rodes's brigade (Rodes having been promoted to **division** command). On the first day at **Gettysburg**, he did not accompany his brigade into the fight, did not place it where Rodes ordered, and kept a large portion of the men out of the battle. As a result, the brigade was driven back, and Rodes's entire line was threatened. Because of this poor performance, Lee withdrew his recommendation, and **Jefferson Davis** canceled O'Neal's promotion. O'Neal returned to his regiment and served in the **Mine Run Campaign** before being sent to recruit in Alabama. He was assigned to **James Cantey's** brigade for the **Atlanta Campaign** and took command of it in May 1864 when Cantey was promoted to division command. After Atlanta fell, O'Neal was removed from command of both the brigade and his regiment in September for unknown reasons. Afterward, he was sent to northern Alabama to collect **deserters**.

After the war, O'Neal resumed his Alabama law practice and served in various state offices. He was elected governor in 1882 and won re-election two years later.

OPEQUON CREEK, VIRGINIA, BATTLE OF (SEPTEMBER 19, 1864). *See* WINCHESTER, VIRGINIA, THIRD BATTLE OF.

ORCHARD, THE, VIRGINIA, BATTLE OF (JUNE 25, 1862). *See* KING'S SCHOOL HOUSE, VIRGINIA, BATTLE OF.

ORCHARD KNOB, TENNESSEE, BATTLE OF (NOVEMBER 23, 1863). In preparation for the main assault on **Missionary Ridge** during the **Chattanooga Campaign**, **U. S. Grant** ordered **Gordon Granger's** IV Corps, of the **Army of the Cumberland**, to make a **reconnaissance in force** to Orchard Knob. This 100-foot hill was located between the opposing lines and was the forward position of **Braxton Bragg's Army of Tennessee**.

For an hour on November 23, 1863, Granger misled the Confederates by having **Philip Sheridan's** and **Thomas J. Wood's** divisions march as if on parade. The Confederates came out of their trenches to watch silently, unaware that Granger was positioning for an attack. At 1:30 P.M., a signal cannon was fired, and the two **divisions** moved against the surprised Confederates. The Federals drove the enemy off the hill, and the entire Union line advanced to protect Granger's flanks. Neither side reported casualties for the operation, but Granger's success caused Grant to change his plans for the main attack against Missionary Ridge. Instead of having **Joseph Hooker** simply **demonstrate** against **Lookout Mountain** on the Confederate left flank, Grant ordered him to push on to Rossville and threaten Bragg's rear, if possible. The next day, the Federals resumed the offensive and pushed Bragg off Missionary Ridge.

ORD, EDWARD OTHO CRESAP (1818–1883) USA. A native of **Maryland**, as a child, Ord moved with his family to **Washington, D.C.** He graduated from **West Point** in 1839 and served with the **artillery** in the **Seminole** and **Mexican Wars**. After Mexico, Ord was stationed in the Pacific Northwest and at **Fort Monroe, Virginia**. As a captain, he was sent to **Harpers Ferry, Virginia**, following **John Brown's Raid** in 1859 and then was stationed in **California**.

In September 1861, Ord was appointed brigadier general of volunteers and was brought to Washington, where he was given a **brigade** in the city's defenses the following month. After defeating **J. E. B. Stuart** at **Dranesville**, he was promoted to major general of volunteers in May 1862 and was given command of a **division**. In June, Ord was transferred west, where he took command of a division in what became the **Army of the Tennessee** and was **brevetted** colonel of regulars for his service at **Iuka** (even though he did not participate in the battle). Shortly afterward, he fought at the **Battle of Corinth, Mississippi**, and was wounded.

Ord was unable to return to duty until June 1863, by which time **U. S. Grant** had relieved **John A. McClernand** from command of the XIII Corps. Grant gave the **corps** to Ord, and he led it for the remainder of the **Vicksburg Campaign** and during **William T. Sherman's** siege of **Jackson, Mississippi**. After service in the **Department of the Gulf**, Ord was transferred to **Virginia** in 1864. He briefly served in the **Shenandoah Valley** before taking command of the **Army of the James's** XVIII Corps in July. Ord was wounded in the attack on **Fort Harrison** during the **Petersburg Campaign** and, upon returning to duty in January 1865, was chosen by Grant to replace **Benjamin F. Butler** in command of the Army of the James and the **Department of North Carolina**. He led the **army** for the rest of the war and was present when **Robert E. Lee** surrendered at **Appomattox**.

Ord was appointed brigadier general of regulars in July 1866 and was mustered out of the volunteers in September 1866 after being brevetted major general of regulars. He remained in the army until his retirement in 1881 as a major general.

ORDER OF AMERICAN KNIGHTS. Along with the **Knights of the Golden Circle** and **Sons of Liberty**, this organization was part of the Northern **Copperhead** movement. Founded by Phineas C. Wright in St. Louis, Missouri, in 1863, the American Knights opposed the **Emancipation Proclamation**, the **suspension of the writ of habeas corpus,** and other harsh Union war measures. Although some Union officials believed the order was pervasive and had a Northern branch led by **Clement L. Vallandigham** and a Southern branch led by **Sterling Price**, the group actually existed largely on paper only.

ORDER OF BATTLE. This military term usually means a list of military units participating in a battle or campaign, but in the Civil War it meant how units were positioned in preparation for a battle or campaign.

ORDNANCE RIFLE. Developed by the Union in 1863, this **artillery** piece also was referred to as the 3-inch **Rodman rifle**. It had a long range of more than 4,000 yards and was often used by the **horse artillery**.

OREGON. Admitted as a state in 1859, Oregon did not play a significant role in the **secession** crisis or the Civil War, although some of its citizens did. In 1860, Oregon's Sen. Joseph Lane ran for vice president on the Southern **Democratic** ticket with **John C. Breckinridge**, but **Abraham Lincoln** and **Stephen A. Douglas** together carried more than twice as many votes in the state. With an 1860 population of only 52,465, Oregon was so remote that few of its men served in the war. One who did was former senator and Lincoln friend **Edward D. Baker**, who was killed at **Ball's Bluff**. During the war, the state was mostly concerned with protecting itself against **Indian** attack.

ORETO, CSS. *See FLORIDA*, CSS.

ORME, WILLIAM WARD (1832–1866) USA. A native of **Washington, D.C.**, Orme attended **Maryland's** Mount St. Mary's College before moving west. After briefly working as a bank messenger in **Illinois**, he became a law partner of Leonard Swett, one of **Abraham Lincoln's** close associates. Over the years, Lincoln came to regard Orme as the most promising young lawyer in Illinois.

After serving as a delegate at the 1861 state constitutional convention, Orme entered Union service in August 1862 as colonel of the 94th Illinois. In October, he was given command of a **brigade** in the **Army of the Frontier's** 3rd Division and was highly commended while leading it at the **Battle of Prairie Grove**. Promoted to brigadier general of volunteers in March 1863, Orme led a brigade in **Francis J. Herron's division** of the **Army of the Tennessee** in the 1863 **Vicksburg Campaign**. It was in the trenches at **Vicksburg, Mississippi**, that he contracted tuberculosis. Afterward, Orme briefly served in the **Department of the Gulf**, but he was forced to resign his field command because of poor health and became an inspector of **prison** camps. He was in command of **Camp Douglas** by December 1863, but he was forced to resign his commission in April 1864 because of his health. Lincoln appointed Orme a supervising special Treasury agent in **Tennessee**, but his poor health forced him to resign that position in November 1865. Returning to Illinois, he died in 1866.

"ORPHAN BRIGADE." Officially known as the 1st Kentucky Brigade, the Orphan Brigade became one of the most famous Confederate military units. The brigade's nickname apparently derived from its unique origin and situation. **Kentucky's** neutrality early in the war forced the **regiments** to organize at **Tennessee's** Camp Boone, and the **brigade** was unable to return home after the state fell under Union control. While fighting at **Stones River**, the brigade suffered heavy losses, and former commander **John C. Breckinridge** cried out in anguish, "My poor Orphans! My poor Orphans!" (Current, ed., *Encyclopedia of the Confederacy*, vol. 3, 1170).

After some initial shifting of units, the Confederate 2nd, 4th, 5th, 6th, and 9th Kentucky were formed into a brigade with Robert Cobb's and Rice E. Grave's **artillery** batteries (**John Hunt Morgan's** 1st Kentucky Cavalry and the batteries of Edward Byrne and **Hylan B. Lyon** also briefly served in the brigade). The Orphan brigade had numerous commanders. **Simon Bolivar Buckner** was its first, but **John C. Breckinridge** replaced him in November 1861. In March 1862, Col. **Roger W. Hanson** assumed command, but he was captured at **Fort Donelson**, along with the 2nd Kentucky. Colonel Robert P. Trabue led the brigade at **Shiloh** and **Baton Rouge**, but Hanson replaced him after he was **exchanged**. Hanson then was mortally wounded at Stones River and was replaced by **Ben Hardin Helm**. Helm was mortally wounded at **Chickamauga** and was replaced by **Joseph Lewis**, who led the brigade until war's end.

As part of the **Army of Tennessee**, the Orphan Brigade compiled an outstanding combat record. It was highly commended at Shiloh for helping capture the "Hornets' Nest" and for covering the **army's** retreat. It helped defend **Vicksburg, Mississippi**, in the summer of 1862 and then fought at Baton Rouge. At Stones River, the brigade suffered heavy losses while participating in the last day's doomed attack, which was opposed by both Hanson and Breckinridge. The Orphans also served in the **Vicksburg, Chickamauga**, and **Atlanta Campaigns** and was almost destroyed at **Jonesboro**. Afterward, many of the survivors were allowed to acquire horses and become mounted infantry. When the brigade surrendered in **Georgia** in May 1865, only about 600 men were left out of the 4,000 who had served during the war.

ORR, JAMES L. (1822–1873) CSA. A native of **South Carolina**, Orr studied law at the University of Virginia and became a lawyer at age 21. After editing a South Carolina newspaper for two years, he began practicing law and entered politics. Elected to the state legislature in 1844, Orr served two terms before becoming a U.S. congressman in 1849. Although agreeing with the right of **secession**, he was a moderate congressman and believed Southern rights could be protected within the Union. After becoming Speaker of the House in 1856, Orr retired from the **U.S. Congress** in 1859 because of poor health.

After **Abraham Lincoln's** election, Orr was appointed president of South Carolina's secession convention and decided secession was the only way the South could defend its rights. Afterward, he was one of three state commissioners who met with President **James Buchanan** to negotiate the fate of federal installations in South Carolina. In July 1861, Orr was commissioned colonel of the 1st South Carolina Rifles (Orr's Rifles), a **regiment** he had raised, and served at **Charleston, South Carolina**, until February 1861. At that time, he resigned his commission to accept a Confederate Senate seat to which he had been elected.

Orr served as a senator for the rest of the war. He chaired the Committees on Foreign Affairs and on Rules and served on the Committees on Commerce, Flag and Seal, Pay and Mileage, and Finance and Printing. Orr at first supported **Jefferson Davis**, but he eventually took a stronger **states rights** stance and began opposing such measures as **conscription**, **impressment**, and the **suspension of the writ of habeas corpus**. By war's end, he was promoting a negotiated peace with the Union.

After the war, Orr was supported by President **Andrew Johnson** in setting up a provisional state government and was elected governor in October 1865. While in office, he joined the **Republican Party** and was appointed a circuit judge when he vacated the position in 1868. President **U. S. Grant** appointed Orr minister to Russia in 1872, but he died shortly after reaching his post.

OSTERHAUS, PETER JOSEPH (1823–1917) USA. A native of Prussia, Osterhaus received a military education in Berlin and participated in the European revolutions of 1848. Forced to leave Europe because of his revolutionary activities, he immigrated to the United States in 1849 and settled first in **Illinois** and then in **Missouri**. There, Osterhaus became a popular figure with the large population of Germans in St. Louis.

Osterhaus entered Union service in April 1861 as major of Osterhaus's Missouri Battalion, a unit he had raised. After participating in the capture of **Camp Jackson** and fighting at **Wilson's Creek**, he was appointed colonel of the 12th Missouri (Union) in December and the following month was given a **brigade** command. At the **Battle of Pea Ridge**, Osterhaus temporarily led a **division**, and he was given a permanent division command in the **Army of Southwest Missouri** in May 1862.

In June 1862, Osterhaus was promoted to brigadier general of volunteers, but he returned to a brigade command in September. Serving with the **Army of the Tennessee**, he led the XIII Corps' 9th Division during the **Vicksburg Campaign** and was slightly wounded by a shell fragment at the **Big Black River Bridge**. After the fall of **Vicksburg, Mississippi**, Osterhaus accompanied **William T. Sherman** for the siege of **Jackson, Mississippi**. Placed in command of the XV Corps' 1st Division in September 1863, he reinforced Chattanooga, Tennessee, in the autumn of 1863 and played a key role at **Lookout Mountain** during the **Chattanooga Campaign**. After leading his division through the **Atlanta Campaign**, Osterhaus was promoted to major general of volunteers in July 1864 (over the objection of Sherman, who accused him of leaving his command to politick for promotion). He was put in command of the **corps** in September and led it during the **March to the Sea** and in the early part of the **Carolinas Campaign**. In January 1865, Osterhaus was made **E. R. S. Canby's** chief of staff, a position he held during the **Mobile Campaign** and until war's end. In May 1865, **Simon B. Buckner** surrendered the Confederate **Trans-Mississippi Department** to Osterhaus.

Osterhaus was mustered out of the volunteer service in January 1866. During the postwar period, he divided his time between France and St. Louis and served as a diplomat in France and Germany. Osterhaus was placed on the retired list as a brigadier general of regulars in 1905 and was receiving a military pension when he died in Germany, just weeks before the United States entered World War I. Of the 12 German-born men to become Union generals, Osterhaus was the most competent and popular with his superiors.

O'SULLIVAN, TIMOTHY (1840?–1882) USA. Although the exact date and place of his birth are unknown, O'Sullivan was born in Ireland and, as a child, immigrated to **New York** with his family. As a boy, he became acquainted with future photographer **Mathew Brady** and may have learned the photography trade from him. By 1850, O'Sullivan was working with Brady in his New York City gallery.

By the Civil War, O'Sullivan was employed by Brady associate **Alexander Gardner** in **Washington, D.C.** At the beginning of the war, he worked with the Union topographical **engineers** and held the honorary rank of 1st lieutenant. Becoming perhaps Brady's best photographer, O'Sullivan photographed war activities on the **South Carolina** coast in late 1861 and early 1862 before returning to Washington and photographing the **Manassas**, **Antietam**, and **Fredericksburg** battlefields. In 1863, Gardner left Brady's employ to open his own photographic studio and lured O'Sullivan away from Brady to become his chief photographer. Unlike his experience with Brady, O'Sullivan was given full credit for the photographs he took while working for Gardner. His photographs of the **Chancellorsville**, **Gettysburg**, **Overland**, **Fort Fisher**, and **Petersburg Campaigns** are among the war's best known and graphic. When **Richmond, Virginia**, was evacuated, O'Sullivan entered it and photographed the destroyed city.

O'Sullivan continued to work in photography after the war and documented expeditions to the west and Panama. Returning to New York, he was appointed official photographer for the U.S. Treasury Department in 1880 but died from tuberculosis two years later.

OULD, ROBERT (1820–1881) CSA. A native of **Washington, D.C.**, Ould was a prominent lawyer before the Civil War. He resigned his position as U.S. district attorney and joined the Confederacy when the war began. Ould served as assistant secretary of war in early 1862, but he then was named chief of the Bureau of Exchange of Prisoners. For the next two years, he represented the Confederacy in **paroling** and **exchanging prisoners** of war. When the exchange system broke down in 1864, Ould was given a position in the military court system. After the war, he was jailed for eight weeks on suspicion of misappropriating funds of captured Union prisoners but eventually was cleared and opened a **Virginia** law practice.

OUR AMERICAN COUSIN. Written by Tom Taylor and starring Laura Keene, this was the play **Abraham Lincoln** was watching in **Ford's Theater** the night of **Lincoln's assassination**.

OVERLAND CAMPAIGN (MAY 4–JUNE 12, 1864). In March 1864, **U. S. Grant** was promoted to lieutenant general and was made general-in-chief of the Union armies. That spring he devised a **strategy** to overwhelm the Confederacy by making simultaneous advances on numerous fronts. Since **Robert E. Lee's Army of Northern Virginia** was the main Confederate force, Grant accompanied **George G. Meade's Army of the Potomac** for an advance against **Richmond, Virginia**. With approximately 120,000 men, Grant believed he could bring Lee to battle and destroy his 60,000 veterans.

On May 4, 1864, Grant crossed the Rapidan River and headed south. The next day, Lee confronted him in the **Wilderness**, where the thick woods largely negated Grant's superior numbers and **artillery**. Meade's V Corps attacked Lee's left flank on May 5 and made some headway against **Richard Ewell's** II Corps before being pushed back. On the right there was vicious fighting between **A. P. Hill's** Confederate III Corps and the Union II and VI **Corps** that left the Confederates exhausted and disorganized. When **Winfield S.** Hancock's II Corps renewed the assault on the morning of May 6, only the timely arrival of **James Longstreet's** I Corps saved Lee from destruction. Just as Longstreet was making a successful flank attack about noon, he was accidentally shot by his own men and was put out of action for months. When the fighting ended, Grant had lost as many as 20,000 men, while Lee had suffered perhaps 11,000 casualties.

Grant withdrew on the night of May 7, but instead of retreating, he moved south to turn Lee's right flank at Spotsylvania Court House. Union morale soared as the soldiers realized they were marching forward instead of retreating. Correctly guessing Grant's plan, Lee sent **Richard Anderson** and the I Corps to hold **Spotsylvania**. Union confusion and Anderson's rapid march allowed the Confederates to reach the crucial crossroads first and hold it on May 8 against repeated Union assaults. Lee's entrenched works were nearly impregnable except for the "Mule Shoe," a **salient** that jutted out toward the Union lines.

On May 10, Grant attacked the western side of the salient and temporarily broke through using **Emory Upton's tactic** of advancing a massed column instead of a battle line. Impressed, he ordered a larger attack against the "Mule Shoe's" center on May 12. Led by Hancock's II Corps in a pouring rain, the assault at first succeeded, and much of Ewell's corps was captured. The Confederates counterattack, however, and drove the Federals back. For the next 20 hours some of the war's most horrific combat took place at the "Bloody Angle," as the opposing armies fought from either side of the contested breastworks. Not until long after dark were the Confederates allowed to withdraw to a new line. Fighting continued at Spotsylvania for days. Grant launched another attack on May 18 but was repulsed with heavy losses. The following day, Lee sent Ewell's corps against the Union right flank, but it, too, was repulsed. It was not until May 20 that Grant acknowledged the futility of his attacks and withdrew the **army** to turn Lee's right flank again. During the two weeks at Spotsylvania, Grant lost an additional 18,000 men to Lee's approximately 10,000.

During the fighting at Spotsylvania, Union cavalry commander **Philip Sheridan** launched **Sheridan's Richmond Raid** to draw out and destroy **J. E. B. Stuart's** cavalry. Leaving on May 9, Sheridan destroyed a considerable amount of **railroad** stock, freed some **prisoners**, and generally raised havoc, but he failed to destroy the Confederate cavalry. In the raid's major battle at **Yellow Tavern** on May 11, Stuart was mortally wounded.

On May 20, Grant began withdrawing from Spotsylvania to move again around Lee's right, but Lee successfully intercepted the Federals at the **North Anna River**. Lee positioned his army between Grant's two separated wings and prepared a clever trap to **defeat in detail** the Federals, but Grant realized the danger and reunited his forces before Lee could attack. Finally realizing he could not fight his way through Lee's defenses, Grant withdrew on May 26.

Once again moving toward Lee's right, Grant next headed for **Cold Harbor**, but the Confederates beat him there and entrenched. Frustrated at finding his path blocked again, Grant launched a disastrous **frontal attack** on June 3. In what was little more than a suicide charge, the Federals lost approximately 7,000 men in less than 30 minutes, while Lee suffered fewer than 1,500 casualties. This battle more than any other earned Grant the nickname "Butcher." While at Cold Harbor, Sheridan launched a second cavalry raid that was defeated at **Trevilian Station**, but there was little more fighting in the Overland Campaign.

Realizing the futility of continuing his flanking maneuvers, Grant settled on a bold plan. By withdrawing from Lee's front and crossing the James River by **pontoon bridge**, he believed he could swiftly march south and capture the important **railroad** center of Petersburg before Lee could react. If successful, the supply line to Richmond largely would be severed, and the Confederates would probably have to evacuate the city. Grant moved out on the night of June 12 and began the **Petersburg Campaign**.

The Overland Campaign saw some of the bloodiest fighting of the war. The opposing armies were in nearly constant combat for some six weeks, and Grant and Meade lost an average of 2,000 men per day. Although Lee lost considerably fewer men, he was unable to replace them all. As a result, the Army of Northern Virginia was bled to exhaustion and became unable to continue offensive operations. Although the Federals were able to replace their losses, the new recruits were poorly trained, and the fighting effectiveness of the Army of the Potomac suffered significantly. *See also* BATTLES OF HAW'S SHOP; SAMARIA CHURCH; TOTOPOTOMOY CREEK; WILSON'S WHARF.

OWEN, JOSHUA THOMAS (1821–1887) USA. A native of Wales, as a boy, Owen immigrated to the United States with his family. Known as "Paddy," he graduated from **Pennsylvania's** Jefferson College in 1845 and became a teacher and lawyer. Owen also enlisted as a private in the state militia and served in the state legislature from 1857 to 1859.

When the Civil War began, Owen raised the 90-day 24th Pennsylvania and was commissioned its colonel in May 1861. He served under

Robert Patterson in the **Shenandoah Valley** during the **First Manassas Campaign**, and when the **regiment's** enlistment expired, he was commissioned colonel of the 69th Pennsylvania. Owen led his regiment in the **Army of the Potomac** through the **Peninsula** and **Seven Days Campaigns** (performing particularly well at **Frayser's Farm**) and in July 1862 was given command of the **Philadelphia Brigade** in the II Corps' 2nd Division. After leading the **brigade** at **Antietam**, he was rewarded for his earlier performance at Frayser's Farm with a promotion to brigadier general of volunteers in November 1862.

After fighting at **Fredericksburg**, Owen's promotion was not confirmed by the Senate, and he had to be reappointed brigadier general in March 1863. He led his brigade at **Chancellorsville** but for unknown reasons was placed under arrest during the **Gettysburg Campaign**. **Alexander S. Webb** took over the brigade, but Owen regained his command in August and served in the **Bristoe Station** and **Mine Run Campaigns**. Over the next six months, he also frequently commanded the **division**. Owen's military career came to an end during the 1864 **Overland Campaign**. After the **Battle of Cold Harbor**, division commander **John Gibbon** charged Owen with disobedience for failing to support the brigade on his right. The charges were dropped when Owen was mustered out of the service, apparently at his own request, in July 1864.

Owen returned to his Pennsylvania law practice and in 1871 founded a law journal entitled the *New York Daily Register*. This journal became the official publication of **New York** courts in 1873, and Owen worked as one of its editors until his death.

OX HILL, VIRGINIA, BATTLE OF (SEPTEMBER 1, 1862). *See* CHANTILLY, VIRGINIA, BATTLE OF.

– P –

PADUCAH, KENTUCKY, BATTLE OF (MARCH 25, 1864). After turning back **William Sooy Smith's Expedition** at **Okolona, Mississippi**, in February 1864, 3,000 Confederate cavalrymen participated in one of **Nathan Bedford Forrest's Raids** from Columbus, Mississippi, into western **Tennessee** and **Kentucky**. Forrest's goals were to gather recruits and mounts, recover **deserters**, and to prevent the Federals from reinforcing **William T. Sherman** in Chattanooga, Tennessee, for the upcoming **Atlanta Campaign**.

Forrest reached Paducah, Kentucky, on March 25 and demanded the surrender of the 650-man garrison under Col. Stephen G. Hicks. Having a strong position inside Fort Anderson and with the support of two gunboats in the Ohio River, Hicks refused. Forrest did not plan to attack the fort, but Col. Albert P. Thompson did so against orders with the 3rd and 7th Kentucky Cavalry (Confederate). Thompson was killed within sight of his home, and his men were repulsed. After gathering supplies and destroying military property for 10 hours, Forrest finally withdrew to Tennessee. He lost 50 men in the battle, while Hicks lost 60. When Union newspapers later reported that Forrest had failed to find 140 horses that had been hidden, he sent **Abraham Buford** back in April to seize them.

PAGE, CHARLES ANDERSON (1807–1901) USA. A native of **Illinois** and a college graduate, Page was a newspaper reporter and active **Republican** before the Civil War. He went to **Washington, D.C.**, in 1861 to attend **Abraham Lincoln's inauguration** and received a clerk's appointment in the Treasury Department. In early 1862, Page took a leave of absence from that position when the **New York** *Tribune* hired him as a **war correspondent**.

Page joined the **Army of the Potomac** on the Virginia Peninsula and filed a story on the **Battle of Gaines' Mill** in June 1862. Publisher **Horace Greeley** was so impressed, he eventually allowed Page to write under the byline "C.A.P." After covering the **Seven Days Campaign**, Page joined the **Army of Virginia** just prior to the **Second Battle of Manassas**. When **John Pope** banned reporters from the **army**, Page managed to stay on by becoming a hospital assistant. Following the battle, he scooped all other reporters by writing an account of the fight while traveling to New York City to deliver it to his paper. For the rest of the war, Page worked at his Treasury Department job and covered the Army of the Potomac during leaves of absence. Late in the war, he often wrote articles attacking **Democratic** presidential candidate **George B. McClellan**, and he accompanied the army during the **Overland** and **Petersburg Campaigns**. Page also covered Lincoln's entry into **Richmond, Virginia**, in April 1865.

Later in 1865, President **Andrew Johnson** appointed Page U.S. consul to Switzerland. While there he began an evaporated milk business that became known as the Nestlé Company.

PAGE, RICHARD LUCIEN (1807–1901) CSA. A native of **Virginia** and a first cousin of **Robert E. Lee**, Page entered the **U.S. Navy** as a midshipman in 1824. Becoming a lieutenant in 1834, he served in the Pacific Squadron during the **Mexican War** and later was assistant inspector of ordnance and the executive officer at Virginia's Norfolk Navy Yard. A strict disciplinarian, Page's sailors referred to him as "Ramrod Page" or "Bombast Page."

Page was promoted to commander in 1855 and was serving as ordnance officer at **Norfolk** when Virginia seceded in April 1861. He resigned his commission, became Gov. **John Letcher's** aide, and began organizing a state navy and preparing defenses for the James and Nansemond Rivers. In June, Page was commissioned a commander in the **Confederate navy** and again was made ordnance officer at Norfolk. He was sent to **South Carolina** later in the year and served as second in command to **Josiah Tattnall** during the **Battle of Port Royal**. Returning to Norfolk, Page commanded several **artillery** batteries in the area and helped serve a gun at Sewell's Point during the **Battle of Hampton Roads**. Promoted to captain in the spring of 1862, he helped remove valuable machinery and stores from Norfolk before it was abandoned. Page accompanied the machinery to Charlotte, North Carolina, where he created the Charlotte Naval Works to manufacture munitions and other naval equipment. He commanded the Naval Works until early 1864, except for a few months in the spring of 1863 when he commanded the Savannah, Georgia, squadron.

Page was appointed brigadier general in March 1864 and was placed in command of the outer defenses of Mobile Bay, Alabama, including **Forts Morgan**, **Gaines**, and **Powell**. Having little faith in the Confederate navy, he became worried and depressed as evidence mounted of an impending Union attack. His superior, **Dabney H. Maury**, apparently thought of replacing him, but the enemy attacked in early August. After Fort Powell was evacuated, Page went to Fort Gaines to stop it from surrendering but was too late. He held out in Fort Morgan through a Union bombardment and refused to give it up. After bravely enduring a two-week bombardment, he finally capitulated on August 23, 1864.

Page was held **prisoner** in **Fort Delaware** and was not released until July 1865. He then returned to Norfolk, where he became superintendent of schools.

PAINE, CHARLES JACKSON (1833–1916) USA. A native of **Massachusetts**, Paine was the great-great grandson of a signer of the Declaration of Independence. He attended the Boston Latin School, graduated from Harvard University in 1853, and became a successful Boston lawyer.

Paine entered Union service in October 1861 when he became captain of a **company** he recruited for the 22nd Massachusetts. Sent to **Washington, D.C.**, he was appointed major of the 30th Massachusetts in January 1862 and apparently accompanied it to the **Department of the Gulf.** Paine was mustered out of the service in March but in October was commissioned colonel of the 2nd Louisiana (Union). This **regiment** is sometimes identified as a unit of **black troops**, but it actually was composed of white Unionists. Paine led his regiment in the **Port Hudson Campaign**, and in May 1863, he was elevated to **brigade** command in the XIX Corps' 1st Division. In November, he was given command of a cavalry brigade and led it until he was mustered out of service in March 1864.

Through **Benjamin F. Butler's** efforts, Paine was appointed brigadier general of volunteers in July 1864 and joined Butler in **Virginia**. There in August he was given command of the XVIII Corps' 3rd Division, a unit of black troops, which he led at **New Market Heights**. Paine also led **divisions** of black troops in Butler's attack on **Fort Fisher, North Carolina**, and in **Alfred Terry's** X Corps during the **Carolinas Campaign**. He was mustered out of service in January 1866 with a **brevet** of major general of volunteers.

Paine became very successful in **railroads** after the war, serving as director of the Atchison, Topeka, & Santa Fe; the Chicago, Burlington & Quincy; and the Mexican Central Railroads. He also served on an 1897 international commission on silver monetary reform. A wealthy man, he became an active yachtsman and defended "America's Cup" several times.

PAINE, ELEAZER ARTHUR (1815–1882) USA. A native of **Ohio**, Paine was a cousin of Union general **Halbert Eleazer Paine**. He graduated from **West Point** in 1839 and briefly served on Zachary Taylor's staff during the **Seminole Wars**. Paine resigned his commission in 1840 and became an Ohio lawyer and militia brigadier general. He moved to **Illinois** in 1848 and was practicing law there when the Civil War began.

Paine entered Union service in July 1861 as colonel of the 9th Illinois. He was promoted to brigadier general of volunteers in September and was given command of a **brigade** at Paducah, Kentucky. Paine led a **division** at **New Madrid and Island No. 10**, at **Shiloh**, and during the **siege of Corinth, Mississippi**. Apparently, his service was less than impressive, for in August 1862 he was sent to the rear to guard **railroads** in the **Department of the Ohio**. He briefly commanded the District of Western Kentucky in late summer 1864, but after going six months without a command, he resigned his commission in April 1865. Paine then resumed his Illinois law practice.

PAINE, HALBERT ELEAZER (1826–1905) USA. A native of **Ohio**, Paine was a cousin of Union general **Eleazer Arthur Paine**. After graduating from Western Reserve University in 1845, he taught school in **Mississippi** before returning to Ohio and becoming a lawyer in 1848. Paine later moved to **Wisconsin** and became **Carl Schurz's** law partner.

Paine entered Union service in July 1861 as colonel of the 4th Wisconsin Cavalry. After briefly serving in **Washington, D.C.**, he joined **Benjamin F. Butler's** command for the capture of **New Orleans, Louisiana**. Paine then was stationed in **Baton Rouge** as part of **Thomas Williams's** brigade. He and Williams clashed when Paine, an **abolitionist**, refused to follow Williams's orders to return fugitive slaves to their masters. Thomas placed Paine under arrest, and Paine in turn filed charges against Thomas. Thomas's death at the **Battle of Baton Rouge** elevated Paine to **brigade** command and ended the controversy. When he was ordered by Butler to evacuate and burn Baton Rouge soon afterward, Paine refused to burn the city, although his men thoroughly pillaged it.

Paine was promoted to brigadier general of volunteers in March 1863 and led first his brigade and then a **division** in the **Port Hudson Campaign**. He was severely wounded during one attack and lost his leg to amputation. **Brevetted** major general of volunteers, Paine was transferred to Washington, where in 1864 he helped defend the city against **Jubal A. Early's Washington Raid**. He ended the war stationed in **Illinois** and resigned his commission in May 1865.

After the war, Paine was elected to the **U.S. Congress** in 1865. Reelected twice, he chaired the Committee on Elections during his last term. After leaving Congress, Paine practiced law in Washington, served as U.S. commissioner of patents from 1878 to 1880, and in 1888 wrote a treatise on election law.

PAINE, LEWIS (1844–1865) CSA. *See* POWELL, LEWIS.

PALMER, INNIS NEWTON (1824–1900) USA. A native of **New York**, Palmer graduated from **West Point** in 1846. He served with the Mounted Rifles in the **Mexican War**, was wounded at Chapultepec, and was **brevetted** twice. After the war, Palmer served on the frontier and became a captain in the 2nd U.S. Cavalry in 1855.

In April 1861, Palmer was promoted to major and was given a provisional cavalry battalion. He led his men at **First Manassas** and won a brevet for commanding the only Union cavalry on the field. Promoted to brigadier general of volunteers in September, Palmer was given command of a **brigade** in **Darius Couch's division** in December and fought with it and the **Army of the Potomac** through the **Peninsula** and **Seven Days Campaigns**. Afterward, he was sent to recruit in **New Jersey** and **Delaware** and to supervise the draft in Philadelphia, Pennsylvania. In December 1862, Palmer began a lengthy tour of duty in **North Carolina**. For the rest of the war, he held various commands there, including brief periods as **corps** and **department** commander. During this time, Palmer was promoted to lieutenant colonel of regulars in September 1863. He was mustered out of the volunteers in January 1866 with brevets of major general of volunteers and through all ranks to brigadier general of regulars.

Palmer remained in the **army** after the war and served mostly on the frontier. After taking three years of sick leave, he retired in 1879 as colonel of the 2nd U.S. Cavalry.

PALMER, JOHN McCAULEY (1817–1900) USA. A **Kentucky** native, as a teenager, Palmer moved to **Illinois** with his father. He attended Shurtleff College for two years, then read the law and passed the bar exam. Becoming involved in **Democratic** politics, Palmer served as a county judge and in the state senate. Opposed to **slavery**, he helped organize the Illinois **Republican Party** in 1856 and unsuccessfully ran for the **U.S. Congress** in 1859. In 1860, Palmer served as a delegate at the Republican National Convention and in 1861 attended the **Washington Peace Conference**.

Palmer entered Union service in May 1861 as colonel of the 14th Illinois. He was promoted to brigadier general of volunteers in December and was given command of a **division** in the **Army of the Mississippi**. Palmer led this division against **Island No. 10** but was demoted to a **brigade** command during the **siege of Corinth, Mississippi**. He was returned to division command in August 1862 and led the 2nd Division in the **Army of the Cumberland's** XIV Corps at **Stones River**. Promoted to major general of volunteers in March 1863, Palmer led a division in the **Tullahoma** and **Chickamauga Campaigns** and the XIV Corps in the **Chattanooga Campaign** and in the early part of the **Atlanta Campaign**. During the latter, he became involved in a dispute with **John M. Schofield** over rank and asked to be relieved in August 1864. Palmer's request was granted, and in February 1865 he was placed in command of the **Department of Kentucky**.

Palmer was mustered out of service in September 1866, returned to Illinois, and was elected governor in 1868. Having always been a moderate, he supported **Horace Greeley** for president in 1872 and returned to the Democratic Party. After serving as a delegate at the 1884 Democratic National Convention, Palmer was defeated for governor in 1888 but won a U.S. Senate seat in 1891. In 1896, he and former Confederate general **Simon B. Buckner** ran for president and vice president, respectively, on the unsuccessful Gold Democrats ticket.

PALMER, JOSEPH BENJAMIN (1825–1890) CSA. A Tennessee native, Palmer was raised by his grandparents after being orphaned. He graduated from Tennessee's Union University, became a lawyer in 1848, and in 1849 was elected to the legislature as a **Whig**. Palmer was reelected in 1851 and then served as Murfreesboro's mayor from 1855 to 1859. Although a Unionist, he remained loyal to his state and in April 1861 became captain of a volunteer **company** he had raised. When the company became part of the 18th Tennessee in June, Palmer was elected colonel.

Sent to **Kentucky**, Palmer's **regiment** became part of **John C. Brown's brigade**. The brigade reinforced **Fort Donelson** in February 1862 and was captured there when the fort fell. After being **exchanged** in August, Palmer was reelected colonel and in October was given command of a brigade in **John C. Breckinridge's** division of the **Army of Tennessee**. He led it at **Stones River** until the last day of battle, when **Gideon Pillow** assumed command. In Breckinridge's doomed charge on the last day of battle, Palmer was wounded three times but refused to leave the front until dark. His wounds kept him off duty for months.

Returning to the regiment in the summer of 1863, Palmer led his men in the **Tullahoma Campaign**. Afterward, the regiment again was assigned to Brown's brigade and saw heavy combat at **Chickamauga**, where Palmer received a second severe wound on the first day of fighting and again was put of action for months. When he returned to duty in July 1864, he assumed command of Brown's brigade and led it through the rest of the **Atlanta Campaign**, suffering yet another wound at **Jonesboro**. During the **Franklin and Nashville Campaign**, Palmer commanded a consolidated brigade composed of his and **Alexander W. Reynolds's** brigades. He arrived too late to participate in the Battle of Franklin, and in early December 1864 was sent with **Nathan Bedford Forrest** to attack the **railroad** at Murfreesboro. The day after they left, Palmer was promoted to brigadier general, but he soon felt Forrest's wrath when his brigade panicked while fighting at Murfreesboro. He returned with Forrest to the **army** after the defeat at Nashville and helped him form the rear guard while in command of a small **division**. Palmer served under **Joseph E. Johnston** during the **Carolinas Campaign** in command of a brigade that was made up of all the surviving Tennessee infantry from the Army of Tennessee. After fighting well at **Bentonville**, he was **surrendered** with the rest of Johnston's troops in April 1865.

After the war, Palmer resumed his Tennessee law practice, became active in the Southern Historical Society, and declined several requests to run for governor. *See also* SOUTHERN HISTORICAL SOCIETY PAPERS

PALMETTO ARMORY. After the 1832 **Nullification Crisis**, **South Carolina** took steps to provide its own arms to the state militia rather than relying on the federal government. In 1850, the state legislature passed an act to strengthen the militia and to purchase arms. About that same year, William Glaze, James Boatwright, and Benjamin Flagg founded the Palmetto Armory in Columbia to take advantage of the act. The state contracted with the armory in 1851 to buy 6,000 muskets with **bayonets**; 1,000 **rifles**; 1,000 pistols; and 2,000 **sabers**. The firearms' lock plates were stamped with "Palmetto Armory SC," while the sabers were stamped with either "W. G. & Co." or "Wm. Glaze & Co." After filling the state contract, the armory became the Palmetto Iron Works and made engines, boilers, and assorted other iron and machine works. When the Civil War began, the company was contracted to make **artillery** ordnance and bayonets, and to rifle several thousand smoothbore muskets. **William T. Sherman** destroyed the ironworks in February 1865 during the **Carolinas Campaign**.

PALMETTO STATE*, CSS.** This **ironclad ram** was built by Cameron & Co. in **Charleston, South Carolina**, in January 1862. It was armed with several 7-inch **rifles**, was 150 feet long, had a draft of 14 feet, and was covered in four inches of iron, with 22 inches of wood backing. With the **CSS *Chicora, the *Palmetto State* attacked the Union fleet at Charleston on January 3, 1863. It rammed and forced the surrender of the USS *Mercedita*, while the *Chicora* damaged the USS *Keystone State* and forced it to be towed away. The *Palmetto State* continued to protect Charleston until it was destroyed when the city was evacuated in February 1865.

PALMITO RANCH, TEXAS, BATTLE OF (MAY 12–13, 1865). As the Civil War was ending in the spring of 1865, the opposing forces around Brownsville, Texas, agreed to an informal truce. This truce was broken when Union Col. Theodore H. Barrett assumed command of the garrison on Brazos Santiago Island, at the mouth of the Rio Grande. On May 12, he took 800 men of the 62nd U.S. Colored Troops and part of the 2nd Texas Cavalry (Union) to the mainland and attacked a Confederate camp at Palmito Ranch, located about 12 miles from Brownsville. The next day, former Texas Ranger Col. John S. "RIP" Ford's 350 Confederate cavalrymen and six cannons attacked Barrett's front and right flank. Although denied by Ford, some Union soldiers accused the Texans of **massacring** the **black troops** and Texas Unionists as they tried to surrender. Barrett was forced to retreat back to the coast that evening and then on to Brazos Santiago Island. This last documented battle of the Civil War was a Confederate victory. Barrett lost 143 men to Ford's five. Thirteen days later, Ford disbanded his cavalry.

PANADA. Different recipes were used to make this hot gruel which first became popular with American soldiers in the **Mexican War**. A typical concoction was made by mixing mashed **hardtack** with corn meal, boiling water, ginger, and wine. Also called "ginger panada" or"bully soup," it largely was associated with such Union nurses and **U.S. Sanitation Commission** employees as **Mary Ann Bickerdyke** and **Eliza Harris**.

PARKE, JOHN GRUBB (1827–1900) USA. A native of **Pennsylvania**, Parke attended the University of Pennsylvania before graduating second in the **West Point** class of 1849. Assigned to the **engineers**, he surveyed the northwestern boundary with Canada and was in the Washington Territory as a 1st lieutenant when the Civil War began.

Promoted to captain in September 1861, Parke returned east the following month and was promoted to brigadier general of volunteers in November (rising from 1st lieutenant to general in less than three months). The following month, he was given a **brigade** in **Ambrose Burnside's** expedition to **North Carolina** and fought at **Roanoke Island** and **New Bern**. In April 1862, Parke was given command of the 3rd Division and led it at **Fort Macon** (for which he was **brevetted** in the regular **army**).

Promoted to major general of volunteers in August 1862, Parke accompanied Burnside's IX Corps to **Virginia** but missed the **Second Battle of Manassas**. He then served as Burnside's chief of staff at **South Mountain**, but when **Isaac P. Rodman** was killed at **Antietam**, he resumed command of the 3rd Division. Parke next served as the **Army of the Potomac's** chief of staff when Burnside took command in November. After **Fredericksburg**, he went west with Burnside and commanded the IX Corps in **Kentucky** during the **Vicksburg Campaign** and while Burnside commanded the **Department of the Ohio**. When Burnside was sent to defend Knoxville, Tennessee, Parke resumed his duties as chief of staff and received two more brevets for his actions in the **Knoxville**

Campaign. Parke continued to serve as Burnside's chief of staff during the 1864 **Overland Campaign** and in the early part of the **Petersburg Campaign**. When Burnside was relieved of command after the **Battle of the Crater**, Parke took over the **corps** in August and temporarily commanded the Army of the Potomac from December 1864 to January 1865 when **George G. Meade** was on leave. After returning to the IX Corps, he played a key role in repulsing the Confederate attack at **Fort Stedman** and was brevetted major general of regulars. Parke garrisoned Petersburg, Virginia, during the **Appomattox Campaign** and then was stationed around **Washington, D.C.**

Parke was mustered out of the volunteers in January 1866, but he remained in the army engineers. He had been promoted to major during the war and rose to the rank of lieutenant colonel and superintendent of West Point. Parke retired in 1889 as a colonel and assistant chief of engineers.

PARKER, ELY SAMUEL (1828–1895) USA. A native of **New York**, Parker was a full-blooded Seneca **Indian**, whose given name was Donehogawa. He studied law but was unable to become a lawyer because Indians were not U.S. citizens. Parker then studied engineering and met **U. S. Grant** while Grant was clerking in his father's **Illinois** store.

When the Civil War began, Parker at first was denied a Union commission because he was an Indian. With Grant's help, he finally was appointed captain and assistant adjutant general in May 1863 for Grant's friend Brig. Gen. **John E. Smith**. Becoming chief **engineer** for the XVII Corps' 7th Division in the **Army of the Tennessee**, Parker served in the **Vicksburg** and **Chattanooga Campaigns**. In August 1864, he was promoted to lieutenant colonel and became Grant's military secretary in the **Petersburg Campaign**. Parker was introduced to **Robert E. Lee** when Lee met with Grant at **Appomattox** to **surrender** the **Army of Northern Virginia**. Lee at first took Parker to be black and was somewhat taken aback. When he realized Parker was Indian, he remarked that he was glad to see that one "real American" was there. Parker replied that they now all were Americans. It was Parker who then wrote out copies of the surrender for each general.

Parker eventually was **brevetted** brigadier general in both the volunteer and regular services and remained in the **army** as Grant's secretary until resigning his colonel's commission in 1869. President Grant then appointed Parker Commissioner of Indian Affairs, but he was surrounded by corruption and was investigated by the **U.S. Congress**. Although cleared of wrongdoing, Parker resigned his position and afterward often lived in near poverty as he worked as a businessman.

PARKER, JOEL (1816–1888) USA. A native of **New Jersey**, Parker was the son of a state treasurer. He graduated from the College of New Jersey in (now Princeton University) 1839 and became a lawyer and **Democratic** politician. Parker was elected to the legislature in 1847, served one term as county prosecutor, and became a major general in the state militia. After serving as a **Stephen A. Douglas** delegate at the 1860 Democratic National Convention in **Charleston, South Carolina**, he at first opposed **Abraham Lincoln's** policies but then supported the war effort after the firing on **Fort Sumter**. In 1862, Parker became a compromise gubernatorial candidate and won the election, largely by criticizing the administration's **suspension of the writ of habeas corpus**.

As New Jersey's governor, Parker opposed **abolitionism**, emancipation, and the suspension of the writ of habeas corpus but strongly supported the war to save the Union. He succeeded in meeting the state's quota of recruits without having to resort to **conscription** and sent the militia to help defend **Pennsylvania** during the **Gettysburg Campaign**. Parker's term was made more difficult when the **Peace Democrats** won control of the legislature.

After being defeated for reelection in 1865, Parker won back the governor's seat in 1873. He also served as state attorney general and as a justice on the state supreme court.

PARKER'S CROSS ROADS, TENNESSEE, BATTLE OF (DECEMBER 31, 1862). During **Nathan Bedford Forrest's Raid** into western **Tennessee** in December 1862, he destroyed the Mobile & Ohio Railroad track between Union City and Jackson before riding southeast with his 2,000 troopers to recross the Tennessee River. To trap him, Union gunboats guarded the river crossing and Maj. Gen. **Jeremiah Sullivan** mobilized his 10,000 cavalrymen for pursuit. On December 31, Colonel Cyrus L. Dunham's **brigade** was sent to Parker's Cross Roads, at Red Mound, to cut off the Confederate escape route.

When Forrest approached, he used his **artillery** to blast the Federals from their original position one mile north of the crossroads and forced them to retire to a position just south of it. He then sent two detachments to strike Dunham's rear while another attacked his front. Just as Dunham refused a surrender demand, Forrest was surprised when Col. **John W. Fuller's** brigade, accompanied by Sullivan, arrived from Huntingdon and attacked his rear. Forrest was forced to fight on two fronts and supposedly called on his men to "charge them both ways" (Kennedy, ed., *The Civil War Battlefield Guide,* 150). He abandoned some captured cannons (as well as six of his own) and ammunition but successfully cut his way out of the trap. Forrest escaped with most of his men and safely recrossed the Tennessee River on January 1, 1863. In the clash, he reported losing only 160 men, but his loss probably was more like 500 since Sullivan claimed to have captured more than 400 **prisoners**. The Federals counted 237 casualties.

PAROLE. During the Civil War, neither side had the capacity to handle the large number of **prisoners** that often were taken in battle. The parole was one way to keep the captured men from returning to the fight, while not having to feed and house them in **prison** camps. Soon after capture, a prisoner could be released after taking an oath and signing a parole paper promising that he would not fight again until he had been **exchanged** for an enemy prisoner. The prisoner kept a copy of the parole paper to prove that he was on parole and not a **deserter**. Some parolees went home until exchanged, while others were kept in parole camps administered by their own government. The parole system largely was abandoned in 1864 after the Union stopped most of the exchanges to deny the Confederacy manpower.

PARROTT RIFLE. Developed by **Robert Parker Parrott** in 1861 at the **West Point Foundry**, this cast-iron muzzle-loading **rifled** cannon came in 3-inch (10-pound) to 10-inch (250-pound) models. The Parrott's breech was reinforced by shrinking an iron band around it to allow the piece to withstand the higher gaseous pressures of a rifled gun. Although sometimes lacking in accuracy and having a tendency to burst when fired, Parrotts were used by both sides in the Civil War. They were particularly useful for battering down masonry walls and were much superior to the smoothbore **Napoleons**. The 30-pound model had a range of 4,400 yards, although most were effective to about 2,500 yards. When the 3-inch model was found to be unreliable, it was replaced with the 3-inch **Ordnance rifle**.

PARROTT, ROBERT PARKER (1804–1877) USA. A native of **New Hampshire**, Parrott graduated third in the **West Point** class of 1824 and was assigned to the **artillery**. After fighting Creek **Indians**, he first became assistant to the chief of the Ordnance Bureau and then was assigned as inspector of ordnance at the **West Point Foundry**. Parrott resigned his captain's commission in 1836 to become the foundry's superintendent and eventually leased the facility and ran it himself. He experimented with artillery for 41 years and developed the **Parrott rifle** and the **Parrott shell**, sight, and **fuse**. During the Civil War, Parrott's foundry stopped making other types of guns and began producing only

Parrott rifles. He left the foundry in 1867 but continued to experiment with artillery and ordnance.

PARROTT SHELL. Designed by **Robert Parker Parrott** to be used in his **Parrott rifle**, this **artillery** shell was designed to be fired from a **rifled** barrel. The shell had a brass ring around its base, which was expanded by the exploding gases when the piece was fired. The ring then gripped the rifling and gave the projectile the spin needed for accuracy and distance.

PARSONS, LEWIS BALDWIN (1818–1907) USA. A native of **New York**, Parsons graduated from Yale University in 1840 and ran a **Mississippi** school for a while before studying law at Harvard University. Becoming a lawyer, he first practiced in **Illinois** but settled in **Missouri** in 1854. There, Parsons became executive officer of the Ohio & Mississippi Railroad.

A Unionist, Parsons's first Civil War service came when he served as a volunteer aide to **Francis Blair Jr.** during the 1861 affair at **Camp Jackson**. In October, he was appointed captain and assistant quartermaster. Recognizing Parsons's talent for running **railroads**, the federal government made him chief of rail and river transportation for the **Department of the Missouri** in December. He shipped men and material with great success and was rewarded in February 1862 with a promotion to colonel. Parsons was put in charge of rail and river transportation in the **Department of the Mississippi** the following month and finally for the entire western theater. He did such an outstanding job that in August 1864 he was sent to **Washington, D.C.,** to coordinate river and rail transportation for all of the Union **armies**. One of Parsons's most successful missions was in the transportation of the entire **Army of the Ohio** from Mississippi to near Washington in only 17 days. He was promoted to brigadier general of volunteers in May 1865 and remained at his post until April 1866, when he was mustered out of service with a **brevet** of major general of volunteers.

After taking a much-needed two-year vacation, Parsons resumed his railroading career and became involved in banking. One of the Union's unsung heroes, his work was invaluable in winning the war.

PARSONS, MOSBY MONROE (1822–1865) CSA. A native of **Virginia**, Parsons settled in **Missouri** as a boy. There he became a lawyer and served with distinction in the **Mexican War** as a captain in the 1st Missouri Mounted Infantry. After the war, Parsons served as Missouri's attorney general from 1853 to 1857 and was elected to the state senate in 1857 as a **Democrat**.

During the **secession** crisis, Parsons strongly supported Gov. **Claiborne F. Jackson** and raised the Missouri State Guard's 6th Division. Appointed brigadier general, he led the **division** at **Carthage**, **Wilson's Creek**, and **Lexington**. Transferred to **Mississippi**, Parsons missed the **Battle of Shiloh** but two days later was put in command of all of the Missouri State Guard in **Earl Van Dorn's Army of the West**. After the **siege of Corinth, Mississippi**, he and his men were sent to **Arkansas**, and by September, he was in command of a **brigade** posted at Yellville.

Parsons was appointed brigadier general of Confederate troops in November 1862 and joined **Daniel M. Frost's** division. After being commended for his part in the **Battle of Prairie Grove**, he became part of **Sterling Price's** division in April 1863. Parsons's brigade suffered heavy casualties at **Helena** but saw no combat during the Union advance on **Little Rock** later that year. In April 1864, he assumed command of a small division and led it at **Pleasant Hill** during the **Red River Campaign**. When **Nathaniel P. Banks** retreated, Parsons's division was sent back to Arkansas, where it helped defeat **Frederick Steele's** Union **army** at **Jenkins' Ferry** during the **Camden Expedition**. **Edmund Kirby Smith** assigned Parsons the duties of a major general in May, but he never was confirmed at that rank. For the rest of the war, he served at various posts in Arkansas and **Louisiana**.

When Kirby Smith surrendered the **Trans-Mississippi Department** in May 1865, Parsons refused to sign a **parole** and moved to Mexico. There he joined **Maximilian's** forces and was killed by rebels, probably on August 15, 1865.

PARTISAN RANGERS. Partisan rangers were officially sanctioned guerrilla fighters during the Civil War. They were authorized by the **Confederate Congress** in April 1862 through the Partisan Ranger Law and were used to harass Union forces behind the lines. The partisans were supposed to wear military **uniforms**, received pay for captured enemy equipment, and were recognized as being part of the **Confederate army**. Some, like **John S. Mosby** and **John H. McNeill** were very effective against Union regulars. Others, most notably **William Quantrill** and **William "Bloody Bill" Anderson**, were little more than bandits and murderers. Many officers disliked the partisans because of their independent style and notorious lack of **discipline**. As a result, the Confederate Congress repealed the law authorizing them, but the secretary of war was allowed to authorize any such units he deemed worthy. The effectiveness of partisan rangers varied greatly, but they often did occupy large numbers of Union soldiers guarding supply lines and rear areas.

PATRICK HENRY, CSS. This Confederate wooden side-wheeler was built in 1859 as a commercial vessel and was originally named the *Yorktown.* It was 250 feet long, displaced 1,300 tons, and had a crew of 150 men. **Virginia** authorities seized the ship on the James River in April 1861 and sold it to the Confederate government. Converted into a warship, it was covered with 2–3.75 inches of iron plating and armed with ten 32-pounders, one 10-inch gun, and one 8-inch gun. Under the command of Cmdr. **John R. Tucker**, the *Patrick Henry* served as the flagship for the James River Squadron and fought at **Hampton Roads** and in the **Peninsula Campaign**. As the Union **Army of the Potomac** approached **Richmond, Virginia**, in the spring of 1862, the ship's guns were taken ashore, and its crew served in the **First Battle of Drewry's Bluff**. The *Patrick Henry* remained docked at **Drewry's Bluff** and became the **Confederate States Naval Academy** in July 1863. The ship served in that capacity and in the defense of Richmond until it was destroyed in April 1865 during the city's evacuation.

PATRICK, MARSENA RUDOLPH (1811–1888) USA. A native of **New York**, Patrick ran away from home as a boy and worked at a number of jobs before Gen. Stephen van Renssalaer secured him an appointment to **West Point**. Graduating near the bottom of his class in 1835, he served with the infantry in the **Seminole** and **Mexican Wars** and won one **brevet** in the latter, while serving as Gen. **John E. Wool's** chief quartermaster. Patrick resigned his captain's commission in 1850, became a well-known agricultural leader in New York, and helped found the New York Agricultural Society and the New York State Agricultural College (the forerunner of Cornell University).

Patrick entered Union service in April 1861 when he was appointed brigadier general and inspector general for New York troops. He held this position and served on **George B. McClellan's** staff until McClellan secured him an appointment to brigadier general of volunteers in March 1862. Patrick was given a **brigade** command in **Rufus King's division** of the III Corps and led it at **Second Manassas**. His division then was assigned to **Joseph Hooker's** I Corps in the **Army of the Potomac** and fought at **South Mountain** and **Antietam**. During this service, Patrick became known as a strict disciplinarian, although he personally had a very kind personality. Recognizing these strengths, McClellan appointed him the Army of the Potomac's provost marshal in October 1862. Patrick remained in this position under all of the **army's** successive commanders, and late in the war **U. S. Grant** made him provost marshal of all the armies besieging **Richmond, Virginia**. During his tenure, Patrick did an outstanding job policing the soldiers, guarding **prisoners**, and protecting property. In recognition of this service, he was brevetted major general of volunteers in March 1865.

After the war, Patrick served as commander of **Virginia's** District of Henrico, but he soon was removed because of his **Democratic** politics, sympathy toward the poor Southern whites, and dislike for **Radical Republicans**. He resigned his commission in June 1865 and returned to his New York farm. Patrick eventually moved to **Ohio** and was serving as governor of the Dayton Soldiers' Home when he died.

PATTERSON, FRANCIS ENGLE (1821–1862) USA. A native of **Pennsylvania**, Patterson was the son of Maj. Gen. **Robert Patterson** and the brother-in-law of Brig. Gen. **John J. Abercrombie**. He fought in the **Mexican War** as a 2nd lieutenant in the 1st U.S. Artillery and remained in the **U.S. Army** until he resigned his infantry captain's commission in 1857.

Patterson entered Union service in April 1861 as colonel of the 17th Pennsylvania. This 90-day **regiment** served under Patterson's father in western **Virginia** before being mustered out in August. Patterson was appointed brigadier general of volunteers in April 1862 and commanded a **brigade** in **Joseph Hooker's division** of the **Army of the Potomac** during the **Peninsula Campaign**. He fought at **Williamsburg** and **Seven Pines**, but illness forced him to relinquish command during the latter battle. After missing the **Second Manassas** and **Antietam Campaigns**, Patterson's career was affected in November 1862 when he withdrew his brigade from its position at **Catlett's Station, Virginia**, because of a false rumor that Confederates were approaching. The incident was to be investigated, but Patterson was found dead in his tent near Fairfax Court House on November 22 from what was ruled an accidental pistol discharge.

PATTERSON, ROBERT (1792–1881) USA. A native of Ireland, Patterson was the father of Brig. Gen. **Francis E. Patterson**. As a boy, he immigrated to **Pennsylvania** with his father, when the rebellious elder Patterson was banished from Ireland. Robert worked as a banker and served in the War of 1812, becoming a colonel in the Pennsylvania militia and a captain in the 32nd U.S. Infantry. Over the next decades, he became a successful businessman, an influential **Democrat**, and an important state politician. During the **Mexican War**, Patterson was commissioned a major general of volunteers and was praised by **Winfield Scott** for his actions during the advance on Mexico City. He ended the war serving on

Scott's staff. Afterward, Patterson expanded his business interests to include a **Louisiana** sugar plantation and 30 Pennsylvania cotton mills.

Patterson reentered the service in April 1861 as a 90-day major general of Pennsylvania volunteers and commander of the **Department of Pennsylvania**. In May, he was ordered to recapture **Harpers Ferry, Virginia**, and to prevent the Confederates under **Joseph E. Johnston** from leaving the **Shenandoah Valley** to reinforce **P. G. T. Beauregard** at Manassas. At the advanced age of 69, however, Patterson moved too slowly. He did not leave Pennsylvania until mid-June, took Harpers Ferry only after the Confederates had burned everything of value, and then allowed Johnston to reinforce Beauregard for the **First Battle of Manassas**. Scott relieved Patterson of command, and he received an honorable discharge when his 90-day enlistment expired.

After leaving the service, Patterson requested a court of inquiry to clear his name but never received one. He then resumed his Pennsylvania business interests.

PAUL, GABRIEL RENÉ (1813–1886) USA. A native of **Missouri**, Paul graduated from **West Point** in 1834 and served in the Southwest and in the **Seminole Wars**. As a captain during the **Mexican War**, he won a **brevet** for storming Chapultepec and was presented a ceremonial sword by the citizens of St. Louis, Missouri. After the war, Paul served again in the Southwest and in the **Department of New Mexico** and was an inspector general when the Civil War began.

Paul was promoted to major of the 8th U.S. Infantry in April 1861 and to colonel of the 4th New Mexico (later merged into the 1st New Mexico Cavalry) in December. He was in command of Fort Union during **Henry H. Sibley's New Mexico Campaign** and supported the troops in the field. Paul was promoted to lieutenant colonel of the 8th U.S. Infantry in April 1862 and reverted to that rank when the 4th New Mexico's term of enlistment expired.

In August 1862, Paul's wife successfully lobbied **Abraham Lincoln** for his promotion. He was appointed brigadier general of volunteers in September and was given command of the 1st Division's 3rd Brigade in the **Army of the Potomac's** I Corps. Paul missed the **Battle of Fredericksburg**, and the Senate failed to confirm his appointment to general. He was reappointed in April 1863 and led a **New Jersey brigade** during the **Chancellorsville Campaign**. When his brigade was mustered out of service, Paul was given command of another one in the **corps'** 2nd Division. At **Gettysburg**, he was wounded on the first day of battle by a bullet that entered his right temple and exited his left eye. Paul initially was believed to have been mortally wounded, but he survived (although he was blinded and lost much of his sense of smell and hearing) and was given administrative duties until he retired in February 1865.

Paul was brevetted brigadier general of regulars for his actions at Gettysburg and received a jeweled sword from New Jersey. He was placed on the retired list as a brigadier general of regulars after the war, and in 1870 the **U.S. Congress** authorized him full pay.

PAULDING, HIRAM (1797–1878) USA. A native of **New York**, Paulding entered the **U.S. Navy** as a midshipman in 1811 and served under Oliver Hazard Perry as an acting lieutenant during the Battle of Lake Erie in the War of 1812. Becoming a career naval officer, he served on missions to China and Europe and participated in the capture of filibusterer William Walker. Paulding was promoted to captain in 1844 and in 1861 was appointed chief of the Bureau of Detail.

In April 1861, Paulding was put in command of an expedition to defend **Virginia's** Norfolk Navy Yard from secessionists. After arriving, he decided the base could not be defended and on April 20 ordered the ships and machinery destroyed before evacuating **Norfolk**. In August, Paulding was assigned to a three-man board to choose the best **ironclad** design for use by the navy. This board eventually adopted **John Ericsson's monitor** design. That autumn, Paulding assumed command of the New York Navy Yard and remained there until war's end, supplying and repairing vessels on **blockade** duty and continuing to work even after being officially retired in December 1861. He was placed on the retired list as a rear admiral in July 1862 but continued to run the navy yard. The following year, Paulding sent warships to New York City to help quell the **New York City Draft Riot**, and in 1864 he dispatched three of his ships to help hunt the **commerce raider CSS *Tallahassee***.

After the war, Paulding was put in charge of Philadelphia's Naval Asylum in 1866. He kept that position until 1870, when he became port admiral for Boston, Massachusetts.

PAXTON, ELISHA FRANKLIN (1828–1863) CSA. A distant cousin of **Sam Houston**, Paxton was a native of **Virginia**. He attended Washington College, Yale University, and the University of Virginia and graduated at the top of his class from the latter's law school in 1849. Paxton at first practiced law in **Ohio** but returned to Virginia in 1854, where he opened a law practice and became a bank president. Living in Lexington, he became acquainted with **Stonewall Jackson**, **Alexander "Sandie" Pendleton**, and other future Confederate personalities associated with the **Virginia Military Institute**. Known as "Bull" (because of his strong physique) or "Frank," Paxton was forced to quit his law practice in 1860 because of poor eyesight.

Paxton entered Confederate service as a 1st lieutenant in the 5th Virginia in April 1861 and fought with the **regiment** at **First Manassas** in the famed **Stonewall Brigade**. There he won much praise by charging forward with a **flag** and planting it inside an enemy battery. Impressed with his bravery, Jackson assigned Paxton to his staff in August. He rose to major of the 27th Virginia in October and served with it during the Romney Expedition and part of **Jackson's 1862 Shenandoah Valley Campaign**. When Paxton's regiment failed to reelect him major in the spring of 1862, Jackson appointed him his assistant adjutant general.

In November 1862, Paxton was appointed brigadier general upon Jackson's recommendation and was appointed commander of the Stonewall Brigade. This leap of three grades over senior **brigade** colonels was very unpopular with brigade members and some officers in the **Army of Northern Virginia**. After leading his brigade at **Fredericksburg**, Paxton was placed under arrest by Brig. Gen. **William B. Taliaferro** for disrespect, but nothing came of the incident. After being lightly engaged at **Chancellorsville** during Jackson's flank attack, Paxton began speaking openly of his imminent death. He was killed the next day, May 3, 1863, while leading his brigade in an attack.

PAYNE, WILLIAM HENRY FITZHUGH (1830–1904) CSA. A member of a prominent **Virginia** family, Payne graduated from the **Virginia Military Institute** in 1849. Afterward, he studied law at the University of Virginia, opened a practice, and in 1859 became a commonwealth attorney.

Payne entered Confederate service in April 1861 as a private but within days was appointed captain in the Black Horse Cavalry. After earning great fame at **First Manassas**, the **company** became part of the 4th Virginia Cavalry in September, and Payne was commissioned the **regiment's** major. As part of **J. E. B. Stuart's brigade**, the 4th Virginia Cavalry fought in the **Peninsula Campaign**, and Payne was wounded and captured while temporarily commanding the regiment at **Williamsburg**. After being **exchanged** three months later, he was promoted to lieutenant colonel in August 1862 and was given temporary command of the 2nd North Carolina Cavalry in September. Payne led the regiment in the **Antietam**, **Fredericksburg**, and **Chancellorsville Campaigns** and then returned to his old regiment in February 1863. He commanded it until Col. Sol Williams returned to duty in June, but Williams was killed the next day at **Brandy Station**, and Payne resumed command. As part of **W. H. F. "Rooney" Lee's** brigade, the regiment next saw heavy combat during the **Gettysburg Campaign**. At **Hanover**, Payne again was captured after he received 11 **saber** wounds and was turned a dark brown color, when he was dumped into a vat of dye when his horse was killed under him.

After being exchanged that autumn, Payne commanded **Lynchburg, Virginia**, while recuperating in a hospital there. He was given command of a cavalry brigade in the summer of 1864 and, during **Philip Sheridan's 1864 Shenandoah Valley Campaign**, led **Jubal A. Early's** attack at **Cedar Creek**. Payne was promoted to brigadier general in November and led a brigade during the **Petersburg Campaign**, receiving yet another wound at **Five Forks**. Returning home to recuperate from the wound, he was captured at his house. Payne was sent to **Johnson's Island** (where he had been held previously) and finally was released in late May 1865.

After being released from **prison**, Payne resumed his law practice and served as commonwealth attorney until 1869. In 1879, he was elected to one term in the state legislature and then moved to **Washington, D.C.**, where he became lead counsel for the Southern Railway.

PAYNE'S FARM, VIRGINIA, BATTLE OF (NOVEMBER 27, 1863). On November 26, 1863, Maj. Gen. **George G. Meade** pushed the **Army of the Potomac** across the Rapidan River in **Virginia** to turn **Robert E. Lee's** right flank in what became known as the **Mine Run Campaign**. Speed was essential if Meade hoped to outflank the enemy's 30-mile-long defensive line before Lee realized what was happening. The advance was plagued by slowness and confusion, and the **army** was barely across the river at the end of the day. Meade largely blamed **William H. French's** III Corps for the delay but allowed him to lead the advance on November 27.

Lee reacted quickly and sent the **Army of Northern Virginia's** II Corps, temporarily under the command of **Jubal A. Early**, to block Meade's advance, while **A. P. Hill's** III Corps came up in support (**James Longstreet's** I Corps was in **Tennessee** engaged in the **Knoxville Campaign**). Early positioned his **corps** across French's front, with **Edward Johnson's division** on the left and his other two divisions on the right. French's column was slowed by taking a wrong road, and it was afternoon before contact was made. **Skirmishing** erupted around Locust Grove as Johnson moved his division down a road to get into position. When his wagon train unexpectedly came under fire, he put his men into line and moved left off the road to drive away what he thought was Union cavalry. Advancing through thick woods, Johnson instead ran into **Joseph Carr's** III Corps division, which was positioned behind a rail fence across a field at Payne's Farm. In a confusing fight, the Confederates made several attacks but were unable to dislodge the stubborn enemy before darkness finally ended the battle.

Johnson reported losing 545 men at Payne's Farm, with Gens. **George H. Steuart** and **John M. Jones** among the wounded, but the Federals did not list their casualties. The fight was the largest battle of the Mine Run Campaign. With Lee fully alerted, Meade was unable to turn the Confederate flank and blamed French's slowness for allowing the enemy to block his advance. The campaign ended a few days later.

PEA RIDGE, ARKANSAS, BATTLE OF (MARCH 7–8, 1862). In December 1861, Confederate Maj. Gen. **Sterling Price** remained in a threatening position in southwestern **Missouri**, and the state's fate was still in doubt. Union Brig. Gen. **Samuel R. Curtis** advanced his **Army of the Southwest** against the Confederates in February 1862 and forced Price to withdraw into northwestern **Arkansas**, where he joined forces with Brig. Gen. **Ben. McCulloch**. Curtis then took up a defensive position near Pea Ridge, Arkansas, with his 10,250 men to block any move the Confederates might make against Missouri.

Confederate Maj. Gen. **Earl Van Dorn**, the newly appointed commander of the **Trans-Mississippi Department**, joined Price and McCulloch in early March. He combined their 16,500 men into the **Army of the West** and advanced toward Missouri on March 4 in a thick, wet snowstorm. The ill Van Dorn directed the advance and coming battle from an ambulance. When Curtis discovered the Confederate movement, he took up a fortified position along a creek just south of Pea Ridge around Elkhorn Tavern (for which the battle also is named).

After a minor clash with the Union rear guard on March 6, Van Dorn approached Curtis's position from the west that evening. That night he was joined by **Albert Pike**, whose command included several hundred **Indians** under **Stand Watie**. Rather than attacking Curtis's front, Van Dorn attempted to deceive the enemy by keeping his campfires burning that night and secretly moving his **army** to the north around the Union right flank to attack from the rear. Price led the way, but when McCulloch fell behind, Van Dorn sent him to the southeast toward Elkhorn Tavern. Thus, the Confederate army was split in two, with Curtis positioned between the separated wings. Curtis discovered Price's maneuver and turned his army to the north at Elkhorn Tavern to face the approaching

Confederates. At the same time, he sent the **divisions** of **Peter J. Oster-haus** and **Jefferson C. Davis** to the west to intercept McCulloch just north of Leetown. The resultant Battle of Pea Ridge was actually two distinct clashes nearly two miles apart.

To the west, the Confederates at first drove the Federals back on the morning of March 7, but as Union resistance stiffened about mid-morning, McCulloch rode ahead to reconnoiter and was killed. Brigadier General **James McIntosh** took over, but he too was killed while leading the men forward to recover McCulloch's body. Colonel **Louis Hébert** then attacked with his **brigade** and pushed the Federals back before being stopped and repulsed by a counterattack. Hébert was captured in the close-quarter fighting, and the Confederates finally were repulsed when **Franz Sigel** arrived with Union reinforcements. After the battle, the Federals claimed to have found numerous Union bodies that had been scalped by Stand Watie's Indians.

At Elkhorn Tavern that morning, Van Dorn and Price encountered Col. **Eugene A. Carr's** well-placed division on top of a plateau. Van Dorn shelled the enemy for several hours before finally ordering Price to attack. In very heavy fighting, the Confederates pushed Carr back almost a mile and seized the plateau, but darkness then ended the fight.

That night both Curtis and Van Dorn concentrated their forces around Elkhorn Tavern. Van Dorn took up a defensive position around the tavern, while Curtis prepared to attack. On the morning of March 8, Curtis pounded Van Dorn with **artillery** fire for several hours before advancing the divisions of Sigel and Carr against the Confederate right center and left, respectively. The Confederates were exhausted, and poor staff work had left the ammunition train too far distant to resupply the artillery. When the Federals attacked, the Confederates broke and retreated in a haphazard fashion. Van Dorn took part of the army to the southeast around Curtis's right flank, while other units fled to the north and west. The Confederates did not reassemble until several days later at Van Buren.

During the two-day battle, Van Dorn lost approximately 2,000 men, while Curtis suffered 1,384 casualties. The victory was decisive, for it ended the Confederate threat to Missouri and led to the Union occupation of much of Arkansas.

PEACE AND CONSTITUTIONAL SOCIETY. One of several Southern peace societies, this group was organized by Unionists in Union City, Arkansas, in 1861. Its goals were to help the Union **army** when it entered **Arkansas** and to encourage Confederate soldiers to **desert**. Confederate authorities discovered the society in the autumn of 1861 when 27 men were arrested for refusing to support the Confederacy.

PEACE DEMOCRATS. This was a faction of the Northern **Democratic Party** that opposed **Abraham Lincoln's** harsh war measures and believed the Civil War's cost in blood and money was too great to save the Union and preferred a negotiated settlement with the Confederates. These politicians succeeded in adding a plank to the 1864 platform calling for such a settlement, but candidate **George B. McClellan** repudiated it. *See also* COPPERHEADS.

PEACE SOCIETIES, CONFEDERATE. In the South, there was opposition to **secession** from the beginning. Mostly former **Whigs**, these people operated clandestinely to oppose Confederate **conscription** and other harsh war measures and strove to return the South to the Union. Some of the more famous peace societies were the **Peace Society**, Heroes of America (founded by William Woods Holden), and the **Peace and Constitutional Society**. Operating largely in **North Carolina, Alabama, Tennessee, Texas,** and **Arkansas,** they encouraged **deserters,** aided Union forces, and called for a peace settlement and the restoration of the Union. In October 1862, Confederates hanged a large number of Texas Unionists in the "**Great Gainesville, Texas, Hanging.**"

PEACE SOCIETY. One of several **Confederate peace societies,** this organization was probably created within Union lines in 1862 and was active in **Alabama,** east **Tennessee, Mississippi, Georgia,** and perhaps **Florida.** The society had its greatest success in August 1863 when it helped elect to the **Confederate Congress** six candidates who advocated an end to the war and the restoration of the Union. The organization also had some success in infiltrating the **army.** In December 1863, 60 society members in **James H. Clanton's brigade** were discovered after they attempted to mutiny and go home for Christmas.

PEACH ORCHARD, AT BATTLE OF GETTYSBURG, PENNSYLVANIA (JULY 2, 1863). Located between Cemetery and Seminary Ridges, **Gettysburg's** Peach Orchard bordered the east side of the Emmitsburg Road. On July 2, 1863, Union Maj. Gen. **Daniel Sickles** disliked the ground he held on the **Army of the Potomac's** left and without orders advanced his III Corps beyond Cemetery Ridge to higher ground along the Emmitsburg Road. His new line ran south along the road to the orchard and then southeast through the **Wheatfield** and **Devil's Den** to Little Round Top, forming a weak angle, or **salient,** at the orchard itself. That afternoon **James**

Longstreet's I Corps of the **Army of Northern Virginia** attacked Sickles, with **Lafayette McLaws's division** moving against the Peach Orchard. In prolonged, vicious fighting, the Confederates finally overwhelmed Union Brig. Gen. **Charles Graham's brigade** and broke Sickles's line. The fighting then shifted to the Wheatfield and Devil's Den. Casualties are uncertain, although Graham and about 250 of his men were captured.

PEACH ORCHARD AT BATTLE OF SHILOH, TENNESSEE (APRIL 6, 1862). *See* SHILOH, TENNESSEE, CAMPAIGN AND BATTLE OF.

PEACHTREE CREEK, GEORGIA, BATTLE OF (JULY 20, 1864). When **Joseph E. Johnston** was relieved of command of the **Army of Tennessee** during the 1864 **Atlanta Campaign**, he was preparing an offensive. **William T. Sherman** had allowed his Union armies to cover a broad front as they approached Atlanta, Georgia. **George H. Thomas's Army of the Cumberland** was advancing in the center toward Peachtree Creek, just five miles north of the city, while **James B. McPherson's Army of the Tennessee** and **John Schofield's Army of the Ohio** were about three miles to the east moving toward Decatur. This left Thomas isolated and vulnerable, and Johnston planned to mass his **army** to strike Thomas on July 20 as he crossed the creek.

After **John Bell Hood** took command of the **Confederate army** on July 17, he carried out Johnston's plan and positioned the **corps** of **William J. Hardee** and **Alexander P. Stewart** to attack Thomas. Before Hood could advance, however, **Joseph Wheeler** informed him that McPherson was moving toward Atlanta from Decatur. This forced Hood to delay his attack for three hours while he shifted troops to his right to block McPherson. By the time Hardee and Stewart attacked at 4:00 P.M. with their 19,000 men, Thomas already had the 20,000 men of **Joseph Hooker's** XX Corps across Peachtree Creek on higher ground and somewhat prepared to meet the assault.

Hardee advanced on the right and Stewart on the left, but heavy timber and deep ravines broke up their lines. The Confederates charged with enthusiasm, and the battle raged for two hours as they repeatedly attacked Hooker. Each assault failed, however, and by the time Hood called off the fight, he had lost approximately 2,500 men (some sources incorrectly place the number in excess of 4,000) to Thomas's 1,779. Having failed to destroy Thomas, Hood next massed his army to the east of Atlanta and attacked McPherson two days later in the **Battle of Atlanta**.

PECK, JOHN JAMES (1821–1878) USA. A native of **New York**, Peck graduated from **West Point** in 1843. He served with distinction in the

artillery during the **Mexican War** and won two **brevets** for gallantry. Resigning his 1st lieutenant's commission in 1853, Peck returned to New York, became successful in banking and **railroads**, and served as president of the local board of education. He also unsuccessfully ran twice for the **U.S. Congress** and served as a delegate at the 1856 and 1860 **Democratic** National Conventions.

Peck entered Union service in August 1861 as a brigadier general of volunteers. He was given command of a **brigade** in the **Army of the Potomac**, and in the **Peninsula Campaign** fought with the IV Corps' 1st Division. Just days before the **Seven Days Campaign**, Peck took command of the **corps'** 2nd Division and was promoted to major general of volunteers in July 1862 shortly after the campaign ended. He remained in southeastern **Virginia** after the **army** was withdrawn from the peninsula and was wounded while playing a key role in defending **Suffolk** against **James Longstreet's** siege in the spring of 1863. In August 1863, Peck was placed in command of the District of North Carolina and served there for nearly a year. He was transferred to New York in July and served as second in command of the **Department of the East** until war's end.

After being mustered out of service in August 1865, Peck remained in New York, where in 1867 he founded the New York State Life Insurance Company. He served as its president for the rest of his life.

PECK, WILLIAM RAINE (1818–1871) CSA. A native of **Tennessee,** Peck moved to **Louisiana** as a young man and became a planter. He entered Confederate service in July 1861 as a private in the 9th Louisiana but by April 1862 was serving as a **company** captain. A huge man at six feet, six inches in height and weighing 300 pounds, Peck became known in the **army** as "Big Peck." Promoted to lieutenant colonel in April 1862, he fought in **Stonewall Jackson's 1862 Shenandoah Valley Campaign** as part of **Richard Taylor's brigade.** Peck helped capture an enemy battery at **Port Republic** by having his men kill the horses so the Federals could not retake the guns. He went on to serve with the **Army of Northern Virginia** in the **Seven Days, Second Manassas, Antietam, Fredericksburg, Chancellorsville,** and **Gettysburg Campaigns** before being promoted to colonel in October 1863. At **Rappahannock Station,** Peck barely escaped capture by riding his horse across a **pontoon bridge** through a hail of bullets. After fighting through the **Overland Campaign**, he commanded the 1st Louisiana Brigade at the **Battle of the Monocacy** and was commended by his superior. At **Third Winchester,** Peck was slightly wounded and was given command of the two consolidated brigades of **Louisiana Tigers** after **Zebulon York** was wounded. He served in the **Petersburg Campaign** in late 1864 and led his brigade in three attacks at **Hatcher's Run** in early 1865. Peck was appointed brigadier general in February 1865 and was credited by **John B. Gordon** with leading the Army of Northern Virginia's last offensive when the Louisiana Tigers made an attack at **Appomattox**. This may be in error, however, for Peck was not with the brigade at **Fort Stedman** in March, and he received his **parole** in May at **Vicksburg, Mississippi**, not Appomattox.

After the war, Peck returned to his Louisiana plantation.

PEEBLES' FARM, VIRGINIA, BATTLE OF (SEPTEMBER 30–OCTOBER 2, 1864). After Union forces captured **Fort Harrison**, outside **Richmond, Virginia**, in September 1864 during the **Petersburg Campaign**, **Robert E. Lee** rushed thousands of reinforcements from his Petersburg line to retake it. **U. S. Grant** took advantage of this Confederate redeployment and extended his lines to the west to cut the Southside Railroad, one of Lee's most important supply lines.

On September 30, elements of **Gouverneur K. Warren's** V Corps, **John G. Parke's** IX Corps, and **David M. Gregg's** cavalry moved westward. Warren advanced west of Poplar Spring Church, while Parke and Gregg protected his southern, or left, flank. Contact with **Wade Hampton's** Confederate cavalry was made that morning near Poplar Spring Church. Shortly after noon, **Charles Griffin's** V Corps **division** attacked the Confederate position along Squirrel Level Road at Fort Archer, north of Peebles' farm, and forced the Confederates to fall back to an inner defensive line protecting the Boydton Plank Road. **A. P. Hill** rushed in reinforcements from his Confederate III Corps, and that afternoon he used the divisions of **Henry Heth** and **Cadmus M. Wilcox** to repel an attack by **Robert Potter's** IX Corps division, which had advanced to the left of Griffin. Potter fell back to Peebles' farm and with the help of Griffin repulsed a Confederate attack later in the day. That night, Warren also withdrew his **corps** back to Peebles' farm and entrenched.

Hill attacked Warren the next morning but was repulsed by **Romeyn B. Ayres's** V Corps division. Hampton's cavalry then tried to turn the Union left flank but was blocked by **Henry E. Davies's** entrenched cavalry **brigade**. On October 2, Warren received a II Corps division as reinforcements and put some pressure on the Confederate line, but no general assault was made. Hill's quick reaction had blunted the Union offensive and had saved Lee's western supply line. During the battle, the Federals lost 2,869 men, while Confederate losses are estimated at 1,300.

PEGRAM, JOHN (1832–1865) CSA. A native of **Virginia**, Pegram (PEE-grum) graduated from **West Point** in 1854. He served with the dragoons in **California**, was a cavalry instructor at the academy, participated in the **Utah Expedition**, was an unofficial observer of the 1859 Italian War, and fought **Indians** in the Southwest.

Pegram resigned his 1st lieutenant's commission in May 1861 and became the first U.S. officer from Virginia to offer his services to his native state. He entered Confederate service that spring as lieutenant colonel of the 10th Virginia. While serving under **Robert S. Garnett** at **Rich Mountain**, Pegram was surrounded and forced to surrender to **George B. McClellan**. Some believed he surrendered too quickly, and the event forever haunted him. Released from **prison** in January 1862, Pegram was not officially **exchanged** until April. He then became **P. G. T. Beauregard's** chief **engineer** for the **Army of Tennessee** with the temporary rank of colonel. Pegram remained in that position under **Braxton Bragg**, but he was serving as **Edmund Kirby Smith's** chief of staff by late summer and saw combat at **Richmond** during the **Kentucky Campaign**.

Pegram was given command of a cavalry **brigade** in late October 1862 and was promoted to brigadier general the following month. Bragg criticized him at **Stones River** for providing faulty intelligence that caused Bragg to keep part of his **army** out of the battle. Afterward, Pegram led a raid into **Kentucky** and in August 1863 was given a cavalry **division** under **Nathan Bedford Forrest**. His division was involved in the opening clash at **Chickamauga** and then protected the army's right flank during the remainder of the battle.

In October 1863, Pegram was transferred to the **Army of Northern Virginia**, where he took a brigade in **Jubal Early's** II Corps division. He may have requested this transfer to get closer to Hetty Cary, a woman he loved, or there may have been friction with his cavalry subordinates. Pegram participated in the **Mine Run Campaign** and later was badly wounded while leading a charge in the **Wilderness**. Returning to duty in August 1864, he fought at **Third Winchester** and took command of the division when **Stephen D. Ramseur** replaced the slain **Robert Rodes**. After leading the division at **Fisher's Hill** and **Cedar Creek**, Pegram accompanied the **corps** back to Petersburg, Virginia. He never was promoted to major general, but he continued to lead the division during the **Petersburg Campaign**. Pegram married Cary in January 1865 in what was described as the social event of the winter. Barely three weeks later, on February 6, he was shot through the heart and killed while trying to rally his men at **Hatcher's Run**. Pegram's younger brother, Col. William "Willie" Pegram, was an artillerist in the Army of Northern Virginia who was killed at **Five Forks**.

PEIRPOINT, FRANCIS HARRISON (1814–1899) USA. *See* PIERPONT, FRANCIS HARRISON.

PELHAM, JOHN (1838–1863) CSA. A native of **Alabama**, Pelham entered **West Point** in 1856, but he dropped out just weeks before graduation and joined the Confederacy as an ordnance lieutenant. After gaining recognition while serving with the **artillery** at **First Manassas**, he was promoted to captain in March 1862 and became commander of one of **J. E. B. Stuart's horse artillery** batteries. Pelham became good friends with Stuart and served him through the **Peninsula** and **Seven Days Campaigns**. He was promoted to major in August 1862, took command of all of Stuart's horse artillery, and fought through the **Second Manassas** and **Antietam Campaigns** with the **Army of Northern Virginia**. At **Fredericksburg**, Pelham took one cannon and positioned himself on the Confederate right to harass the advancing Union infantry. So effective was his fire that the entire Union assault on that wing was thrown into disarray. Pelham refused several orders to disengage and only withdrew after running out of ammunition. Because of his bravery, he was dubbed the "Gallant Pelham" and became one of the **army's** most popular officers.

On March 17, 1863, Pelham was away from his unit and on an impulse joined in the cavalry attack at **Kelly's Ford**. He was struck on the neck by a shell fragment and was thought to have been killed. Thrown over a horse, Pelham was taken to the rear, where he was discovered to be alive, but he died later that day at the home of his fiancée.

PEMBER, PHOEBE YATES LEVY (1823–1913) CSA. A member of a prominent **South Carolina** Jewish family, Miss Levy moved to **Georgia** and married Thomas Pember. They moved to **Massachusetts**, but she returned to Georgia after he died in 1861. In late 1862, Pember used her friendship with the wife of Confederate Secretary of War **George W. Randolph** to become chief matron of Hospital No. 2 in **Richmond, Virginia's, Chimborazo Hospital**. She spent the rest of the war caring for sick and wounded soldiers and in 1879 published her memoir, *A Southern Woman's Story*. The book is considered to be the best first-person account available on Confederate hospitals.

PEMBERTON, JOHN CLIFFORD (1814–1881) CSA. A native of **Pennsylvania**, Pemberton was educated by private tutors and learned to speak Hebrew, Greek, and Latin. He entered **West Point** in 1833, became friends with some Southern cadets, and adopted their views on national issues. After graduating in 1837, Pemberton served in the **artillery** during the **Seminole Wars** and married a member of a prominent **Virginia** family. As a 1st lieutenant, he served in the **Mexican War** on Gen. William J. Worth's staff. Pemberton was wounded twice in the war and received two **brevets** and a ceremonial sword from the citizens of Philadelphia, Pennsylvania. After the war, he rose to the rank of captain, participated in the **Utah Expedition**, and served in the Pacific Northwest.

During the **secession** crisis, Pemberton brought troops from **Minnesota** to **Washington, D.C.** There he turned down a colonel's commission and resigned from the **U.S. Army** in April 1861. Even though two of his brothers served the Union, Pemberton was appointed a lieutenant colonel of Virginia troops. He was promoted to colonel in May and was sent to train artillerists at **Norfolk**. In June, Pemberton was appointed major of Confederate artillery, but he was commissioned a brigadier general two days later. After joining **Robert E. Lee** in **South Carolina** in November, he was promoted to major general in February and assumed command of the **Department of South Carolina, Georgia, and Florida** in March. Pemberton defended **Charleston** until October 1863, when he was promoted to lieutenant general and was put in command of the **Department of Mississippi and East Louisiana**.

Pemberton was responsible for defending **Vicksburg, Mississippi**, and **Port Hudson, Louisiana**, but proved incapable of saving either. Although outnumbering **U. S. Grant's** army at the beginning of the **Vicksburg Campaign**, he was indecisive and unable to devise a winning **strategy**. Pemberton also was under conflicting orders—**Jefferson Davis** ordered him to defend Vicksburg at all costs, while his superior, **Joseph E. Johnston**, ordered him to leave the city's defenses and strike Grant before he reached Vicksburg. Pemberton remained in Vicksburg while Grant marched on **Jackson**, and then fought Grant at **Champion Hill** and was defeated. Finding himself trapped inside Vicksburg, he waged a stubborn defense for 47 days. Running short of food, medicine, and ammunition, Pemberton finally surrendered on July 4, 1863. Many Confederates branded the northern-born officer a traitor, but Pemberton stated he surrendered on Independence Day because he believed Grant would give more generous surrender terms on that day.

After being **exchanged** a few weeks later, Pemberton found himself the target of much criticism, and virtually no one would serve under him.

He resigned his commission in May 1864 but asked to reenter the service as a private. Davis refused and reappointed him lieutenant colonel of artillery. Pemberton served until war's end in command of an artillery battery defending **Richmond, Virginia**, and as an ordnance inspector. Although a poor **army** commander, he was a dedicated Confederate who devoted himself to the cause.

After the war, Pemberton worked as a Virginia farmer until moving to Pennsylvania in 1875 to live with his brothers and sisters.

PENDER, WILLIAM DORSEY (1834–1863) CSA. A native of **North Carolina**, Pender graduated from **West Point** in 1850. He served with the **artillery** in **Florida** and with the dragoons in the southwest and northwest. Rising to the rank of 1st lieutenant, Pender was involved in several **Indian** fights during this time.

Pender resigned his commission in March 1861 and entered Confederate service as a captain of artillery. He was elected colonel of the 3rd North Carolina (later designated the 13th North Carolina) in May but left that **regiment** in August to become colonel of the 6th North Carolina. At **Seven Pines**, **Jefferson Davis** was so impressed with a particularly difficult battlefield maneuver conducted by Pender, he called out, "General Pender, I salute you" (Davis, ed., *The Confederate General,* vol. 5, 10).

Promoted to brigadier general in July 1862, Pender took command of a **brigade** in **A. P. Hill's Light Division** and saw heavy combat with the **Army of Northern Virginia** in the **Seven Days**, **Second Manassas**, **Antietam**, and **Fredericksburg Campaigns**. He was wounded numerous times but never seriously. Despite a good combat record, Pender was not popular with either his men or officers because of his strict **discipline**. Hill, however, called him "one of the very best officers I know" (Davis, ed., *The Confederate General,* vol. 5, 11), and lobbied for his promotion. After fighting well at **Chancellorsville**, Pender was promoted to major general in May 1863 and took command of the **division**. He led it well on **Gettysburg's** first day but was wounded in the leg by a shell fragment on the second day of fighting. After Pender was removed to **Virginia**, an artery ruptured in his leg, forcing surgeons to amputate it on July 18. He died within hours.

PENDLETON, ALEXANDER SWIFT "SANDIE" (1840–1864) CSA. A native of **Virginia**, Pendleton was the son of Confederate Brig. Gen. **William N. Pendleton** and the brother-in-law of **Edwin G. Lee**. Raised in **Maryland**, he graduated from Virginia's Lexington College (where he became acquainted with **Stonewall Jackson**) and taught at Washington

College for two years before beginning work on a master's degree at the University of Virginia.

Pendleton dropped out of school after he was appointed a 2nd lieutenant of Virginia troops in May 1861. He joined Jackson's staff that month and served on it until Jackson's death. Pendleton was a religious, well-liked, and very capable officer and was commissioned a 1st lieutenant in the **Confederate army** in November. While serving with Jackson in the **Shenandoah Valley**, he was praised for manning an **artillery** piece at **Kernstown** when he saw the gun crew had been killed. Pendleton was promoted to captain in June 1862, and Jackson came to depend on his great administrative ability to run the **corps**. After temporarily serving as assistant adjutant general for the **Army of Northern Virginia's** II Corps, Pendleton was promoted to major and was given the position permanently in December 1862. He wrote most of Jackson's reports, prepared his body for burial, and served as a pallbearer at his funeral. In July 1863, Pendleton was appointed lieutenant colonel and **Richard S. Ewell's** chief of staff. He remained with the II Corps after **Jubal A. Early** took command but was mortally wounded in the stomach at **Fisher's Hill** and died on September 22, 1864.

PENDLETON, WILLIAM NELSON (1809–1883) CSA. A native of **Virginia**, Pendleton was the father of **Alexander Swift "Sandie" Pendleton** and the father-in-law of Confederate Gen. **Edwin G. Lee**. He attended **West Point**, where he became close friends with **Jefferson Davis** and graduated near the top of his class in 1830. Pendleton served with the **artillery** at several posts and was a mathematics professor at the academy for one year before resigning his commission in 1833. After becoming a math professor at **Pennsylvania's** Bristol College, Pendleton entered the Episcopal ministry in 1837. For the next 24 years, he held various educational and religious positions in **Delaware, Maryland**, and Virginia.

Pendleton entered Virginia state service in April 1861 when he was elected captain of the Rockbridge Artillery. Naming his four cannons Matthew, Mark, Luke, and John, he served at **Harpers Ferry** before being promoted to colonel in July and appointed **Joseph E. Johnston's** chief of artillery. Pendleton saw some service at **First Manassas** and prayed aloud, "Lord, have mercy on their souls" (Davis, ed., *The Confederate General,* vol. 5, 13) before opening fire on the enemy.

Promoted to brigadier general in March 1862, Pendleton served as chief of artillery for both Johnston and **Robert E. Lee** (for whom he was sometimes mistaken). One of his accomplishments was reorganizing the

Army of Northern Virginia's artillery in the spring of 1863 by placing the artillery in more effective massed battalions attached to each **corps** rather than being scattered among the different infantry **brigades**. After this reorganization, Pendleton was left mainly with only administrative responsibilities. Many officers did not think he possessed much knowledge of **tactics** and believed his assignment to administrative duties might have been intentional. Except for a brief inspection assignment with the **Army of Tennessee**, Pendleton remained with the **Army of Northern Virginia** for the entire war.

On the battlefield, Pendleton performed poorly at **Malvern Hill** when he failed to concentrate the Confederate artillery, and at **Shepherdstown** he was accused of panicking and abandoning his guns by rushing to Lee to report that the entire artillery reserve had been captured, when actually only four pieces were lost. Pendleton fought well at **Gettysburg**, however, and, at the end of the **Petersburg Campaign**, he helped withdraw most of the army's cannons from the fortifications. He also performed good service during the **Appomattox Campaign** by using his artillery to cover the army's retreat. When Lee finally surrendered, he appointed Pendleton, **James Longstreet**, and **John B. Gordon** to arrange the details. Besides all of these military activities, Pendleton also preached often to the soldiers and provided other spiritual services.

After the war, Pendleton resumed his Virginia ministry in Lexington (where his friendship with Lee continued) and was awarded the degree of doctor of divinity in 1868.

PENINSULA CAMPAIGN (MARCH 17–JUNE 24, 1862). In March 1862, **George B. McClellan** was forced to abandon his **Urbanna Plan** to capture **Richmond, Virginia**, when **Joseph E. Johnston's** Confederates evacuated Manassas, Virginia. He then decided to move his **Army of the Potomac** by sea to **Fort Monroe, Virginia**, located southeast of Richmond on the tip of the Virginia Peninsula. From there, McClellan could march up the Virginia Peninsula toward the city and have his flanks protected by the York and James Rivers and his waterborne supply line secured. **Abraham Lincoln**, however, preferred an overland march toward Richmond to keep **Washington, D.C.**, protected, but he finally approved the plan on the condition McClellan leave enough troops behind to protect the capital. Still unsure of success, Lincoln also removed McClellan from his position as general-in-chief so he could concentrate on the campaign and ordered 35,000 men be left behind to defend Washington against any surprise Confederate attack.

McClellan departed Washington for Fort Monroe on March 17 with more than 100,000 men. By April 4, his **army** was ashore, and he began moving up the peninsula toward Richmond. Facing McClellan were Maj. Gen. **John B. Magruder** and about 17,000 Confederates strongly entrenched along the Warwick River in a line running across the peninsula from Yorktown to the James River. Magruder performed admirably, using such ruses as marching men, playing music, and running trains back and forth behind the lines to give the appearance of steadily arriving reinforcements. Overly cautious, largely because of faulty intelligence provided by **Allan Pinkerton**, McClellan decided the line was too strong to assault and began a methodical siege that took a month. During that time, Johnston arrived with his **Army of the Potomac (Confederate)**, giving the Confederates approximately 60,000 men.

After besieging **Yorktown**, McClellan finally advanced on May 4, but Johnston had already retreated. McClellan caught up with the Confederate rear guard at **Williamsburg** on May 5, and a sharp battle erupted in wet, muddy conditions, but Johnston extracted his army successfully. During the fight, the Confederates lost approximately 1,700 men to the Federals' 2,200 casualties. Johnston's retreat left **Norfolk** undefended and forced the Confederates to destroy the **CSS *Virginia***. The **U.S. Navy** then moved up the James River, but in a few days, it was stopped at the **First Battle of Drewry's Bluff**.

Johnston retreated to the outskirts of Richmond and prepared a defense, while McClellan followed up and roughly paralleled the Confederate line. In doing so, McClellan split his army across the Chickahominy River, leaving two **corps** on the south side, while three corps remained to the north. With heavy rains swelling the river, it would be difficult for him to reinforce either flank if attacked. Johnston took advantage of this tactical error and on May 31 attacked the two southern Union corps at **Seven Pines**. Confusing orders and poor Confederate staff work prevented a victory, however, and Johnston was severely wounded in the fighting. **Jefferson Davis** placed **Gustavus Smith** in command of the Confederate army, but renewed attacks the next day failed to defeat McClellan. Seven Pines cost the Confederates approximately 6,100 men to the Federals' 5,000 casualties. Davis replaced Smith with **Robert E. Lee** on June 1, and the two armies remained in their respective positions until the **Seven Days Campaign** began on June 25. Although a separate campaign, the Seven Days sometimes is considered to have been a part of the Peninsula Campaign.

PENNSYLVANIA. With an 1860 population of 2,906,215, a strong agricultural and **industrial** base, and 2,442 miles of **railroads**, Pennsylvania played a key role in the Union victory. Led by Gov. **Andrew G. Curtin**, the state provided much needed food, equipment, horses, and, most importantly, men. When **Abraham Lincoln** called for volunteers after the loss of **Fort Sumter**, Pennsylvania responded by sending five unarmed **companies** to **Washington, D.C.** By war's end, the state had furnished the Union 270 **regiments** and 427,000 men. Among its more famous units were the **Philadelphia Brigade, Pennsylvania Reserves,** and the **"Pennsylvania Bucktails."** Pennsylvania also provided the Union with 66 generals, including **George B. McClellan, George G. Meade, John F. Reynolds, Winfield S. Hancock, John Gibbon, Herman Haupt, Andrew J. Smith,** and **David M. Gregg.** Confederate Lt. Gen. **John C. Pemberton** also hailed from Pennsylvania.

Pennsylvania escaped widespread destruction during the war, except for cavalry clashes at **Chambersburg** (which was burned in another raid) and **Hanover,** and of course, the war's largest battle at **Gettysburg.** During the Gettysburg Campaign, much of south-central Pennsylvania also was stripped of horses, grain, and supplies by the invading **Confederate army.**

"PENNSYLVANIA BUCKTAILS." Officially designated the 13th **Pennsylvania Reserves**, this **regiment** was organized in April 1861 out of **companies** that exceeded the state's quota. It also was referred to as the 1st Pennsylvania Rifles and later was designated the 42nd Pennsylvania when the state's reserve regiments were given volunteer numbers. Mostly woodsmen and hunters, each man demonstrated his marksmanship by wearing on his hat a tail from a buck deer he had killed. This distinctive headgear gave the regiment its nickname. Part of the regiment fought in **Stonewall Jackson's 1862 Shenandoah Valley Campaign**, while the rest served in the **Army of the Potomac's** I and V Corps during the **Peninsula** and **Seven Days Campaigns**. The Bucktails were reunited in the summer of 1862 and fought in the **Second Manassas, Antietam, Fredericksburg, Gettysburg,** and **Overland Campaigns**. During its existence, 252 of the regiment's men were killed or died of disease.

The Bucktails originally were commanded by Charles J. Biddle, but he was replaced by Hugh W. McNeil, who was killed at **Antietam**. McNeil was followed by Charles F. Taylor, who was killed at **Gettysburg**. W. R. Hartshorn then took command and led the regiment until it was mustered out of service in June 1864. Those soldiers whose enlistments were not expired at the time were transferred to the 190th Pennsylvania.

PENNSYLVANIA CAMPAIGN (JUNE 3–JULY 14, 1863). *See* GETTYSBURG, PENNSYLVANIA, CAMPAIGN AND BATTLE OF.

6TH PENNSYLVANIA CAVALRY. *See* RUSH'S LANCERS.

PENNSYLVANIA RESERVES. When **Abraham Lincoln** called for 75,000 volunteers in April 1861 to suppress the rebellion, more of **Pennsylvania's** men responded than were numbered in its quota, and Gov. **Andrew G. Curtin** organized the excess into 13 reserve **regiments**. These originally were designated the 1st–13th Pennsylvania Reserves, but they later were named the 30th–42nd Pennsylvania Volunteers. The regiments were organized into a **division** known as the Pennsylvania Reserves and served in the **Army of the Potomac's** I Corps until 1863. During the **Gettysburg Campaign**, two of the **brigades** became part of the V Corps' 3rd Division and fought with it until the men were mustered out in June 1864. At that time, those men who had enlistment time remaining were formed into the 190th and 191st Pennsylvania. During the war, the division's commanders were **George A. McCall**, **John F. Reynolds**, **George G. Meade**, and **Samuel W. Crawford**. *See also* PENNSYLVANIA BUCKTAILS

PENNYPACKER, GALUSHA (1844–1916) USA. A native of **Pennsylvania**, Pennypacker was educated in private schools and entered Union service as a private at age 16 when he joined the 90-day 9th Pennsylvania in April 1861. He declined an appointment to 1st lieutenant because of his young age but did become the **regiment's** quartermaster sergeant that same month. When the regiment's enlistment expired, Pennypacker raised a **company** for the 97th Pennsylvania in August and was appointed its captain. He was promoted to major in October (when he was only 17), served with the regiment in the **Department of the South**, and fought at **Secessionville** and **Fort Wagner**. Joining **Benjamin F. Butler's Army of the James** in **Virginia** in the spring of 1864, Pennypacker was promoted to lieutenant colonel in April and fought at **Swift Creek**, **Second Drewry's Bluff**, and **Chester Station**. In a clash at Green Plains, he was wounded three times and was put out of action for three months. When he returned to duty, Pennypacker was promoted to colonel in August and was given command of a **brigade** in the X Corps' 2nd Division the following month.

Pennypacker led his brigade at **Fort Harrison** and **New Market Heights**, where again he was wounded and had his horse killed under him. He remained in command and fought at **Darbytown Road** and **Fort Fisher, North Carolina**. In the latter battle, Pennypacker was in **Adelbert Ames's division** and received his eighth wound in seven months when he mounted the wall in a successful attack. **Corps** commander **Alfred Terry** stated that Pennypacker was "the real hero of Fort

Fisher" (Warner, *Generals in Blue,* 366) and claimed the fort would not have been captured had it not been for his heroism. For his actions there, Pennypacker was awarded the **Medal of Honor** and was **brevetted** brigadier general of volunteers.

In April 1865, Pennypacker was promoted to brigadier general of volunteers. At age 20, not only was he the youngest general ever to serve in the **U.S. Army** (not **George A. Custer**, as is sometimes claimed), he could not even vote yet. Unable to return to duty because of his wounds, Pennypacker resigned his commission in April 1866 after being brevetted major general of volunteers. A few months later, he reentered the regular **army** as colonel of the 34th U.S. Infantry, becoming the youngest regimental colonel ever in the U.S. Army. After being brevetted brigadier general and major general of regulars for Fort Fisher, Pennypacker retired in 1883.

PENSACOLA, FLORIDA. Pensacola, Florida, was not an important port during the antebellum period because of the area's poor transportation system, but it did have perhaps the best harbor on the Gulf Coast and was the sight of a **U.S. Navy** yard. Forts McRee and Barrancas guarded the bay from the mainland and **Fort Pickens** from Santa Rosa Island. During the **secession** crisis, Pensacola became a major point of confrontation between the North and South.

In January 1861, Union troops abandoned Forts McRee and Barrancas and took up a strong position at Fort Pickens. Secessionists seized the navy yard in April 1861, but the Union troops in Fort Pickens refused to surrender their post. Reinforcements soon arrived, and the fort became an irritant to **Braxton Bragg**, the Confederate commander of Pensacola. In September, Union Col. Harvey Brown launched raids that destroyed Bragg's dry dock and burned the CSS *Judah.* The next month, Bragg retaliated with a night attack against **Santa Rosa Island**. Harvey then responded by heavily bombarding Bragg's position in November 1861 and January 1862. Bragg began evacuating Pensacola in March 1862 to reinforce **Albert Sidney Johnston** for the upcoming **Battle of Shiloh**. When the evacuation was completed on May 9, the Confederates burned Fort McRee, the navy yard, and a large amount of mills, boats, and cotton. The next day, Union forces from Fort Pickens occupied the town.

PERCUSSION CAPS. First invented in 1805 by a Scotsman, the Rev. Alexander John Forsyth, percussion caps were used to fire most Civil War shoulder arms. They were made of small copper caps filled with fulminate of mercury. Once the musket was loaded, the cap was placed on the nipple below the hammer. When the hammer struck the cap, it exploded and sent fire into the barrel to set off the powder charge. Percussion caps were adopted by the **U.S. Army** in 1840 and were much superior to the flintlock system because they would fire in wet conditions.

PERRIN, ABNER MONROE (1827–1864) CSA. A native of **South Carolina**, Perrin fought in the **Mexican War** and rose to the rank of 1st lieutenant in the **U.S. Army**. After the war, he returned to his native state and became a lawyer.

Perrin entered Confederate service in the summer of 1861 as a captain in the 14th South Carolina. After in-state service, his **regiment** was sent to **Virginia**, where it fought with distinction in the **Seven Days Campaign** as part of **Maxcy Gregg's brigade** in the **Army of Northern Virginia**. The brigade earned more respect for its service at **Cedar Mountain**, **Second Manassas**, **Antietam**, and **Fredericksburg**. In the latter battle, Perrin was slightly wounded, and Gregg was killed. In January 1863, Perrin was promoted to colonel and led his regiment at **Chancellorsville** and assumed command of the brigade on May 3 when its commander and all the senior colonels were wounded. He then led the brigade skillfully during the first day's battle at **Gettysburg**, where he lost nearly half his men.

Perrin was promoted to brigadier general in September 1863 and led the South Carolina brigade until the wounded **Samuel McGowan** returned to duty in February 1864. At that time, Perrin was given command of **Cadmus Wilcox's** brigade. He led it well in the **Wilderness** and while approaching **Spotsylvania** reportedly remarked, "I shall come out of this fight a live major general or a dead brigadier" (Davis, ed., *The Confederate General,* vol. 5, 19). On May 12, 1864, while leading his brigade in a counterattack at the "Mule Shoe," Perrin was mortally wounded by seven bullets.

PERRY, EDWARD AYLESWORTH (1831–1889) CSA. A native of **Massachusetts**, Perry dropped out of Yale University in 1850 to become a teacher at **Alabama's** Greenville Academy. He also studied law while there and opened a **Florida** law practice in 1857.

Despite his Northern birth, Perry supported **secession**, raised a volunteer **company**, and entered Confederate service in July 1861 as its captain. He took the company to **Virginia**, where it became part of the 2nd Florida. The **regiment** first guarded **prisoners** in **Richmond** and in September was sent to the Virginia Peninsula. During the **Peninsula Campaign**, Perry fought at **Yorktown** and **Williamsburg** and was elected regimental colonel in May 1862. Becoming part of **Samuel Garland Jr.**'s brigade, the regiment captured an enemy **artillery** battery and battle **flag** at **Seven Pines**, but it lost 10 of its 12 captains and nearly half of its men. Transferred to **Roger A. Pryor's** brigade, Perry led the regiment at **Gaines' Mill** and **Frayser's Farm** and was severely wounded in the latter battle.

Upon returning to duty in September 1862, Perry was promoted to brigadier general and took command of the **Army of Northern Virginia's** Florida **brigade**. As part of **Richard H. Anderson's division**, he fought at **Fredericksburg** and suffered more losses there while assisting **William Barksdale** contest the enemy's river crossing than the rest of the division combined. Afterward, Perry was commended for his actions at **Chancellorsville**, but a bout of yellow fever prevented him from accompanying the brigade to **Gettysburg**. He returned to duty in September and led his men into action at **Bristoe Station** the following month. While fighting in the **Wilderness** in May 1864, Perry received a severe wound that kept him off duty for months. When he returned to duty, he served with Alabama's reserve forces until war's end.

Perry returned to Florida after the war and became a well-known lawyer. He opposed **Reconstruction** and was elected governor on the **Democratic** ticket in 1884.

PERRY, MADISON STARKE (1814–1865) CSA. A native of **South Carolina**, Perry moved to **Florida** as a young man and became a prosperous planter. Becoming involved in **Democratic** politics, he was elected to the state assembly in 1849, to the state senate in 1850, and governor in 1856. As governor, Perry greatly increased **railroad** mileage within the state and opened up the interior for settlement.

A secessionist, Perry urged the legislature to strengthen the state militia following **John Brown's Raid on Harpers Ferry, Virginia**, in 1859 and prepared the state for **secession** during the 1860 **election**. After **Abraham Lincoln's** election, he oversaw the state's secession, seized Federal installations, raised troops for the Confederacy, and strengthened coastal defenses. Perry served as governor until **John Milton** took over in October 1861 and then was elected colonel of the 7th Florida in April 1862. He contracted a fever while serving in **Tennessee** and was forced to resign his commission in June 1863. Returning to Florida, he died in March 1865.

PERRY, WILLIAM FLANK (1823–1901) CSA. A native of **Georgia**, Perry moved to **Alabama** as a boy. Becoming involved in education, he served as the first state superintendent of education from 1854 to 1858 and then became president of the East Alabama Female College. Perry did not join the **Confederate army** until May 1862, when he volunteered as a private in the 44th Alabama. He was elected major that same month and accompanied the **regiment** to **Virginia**, where it became part of **Ambrose R. Wright's brigade** in the **Army of Northern Virginia**. After serving at **Second Manassas** and **Antietam**, Perry took command of the regiment in September 1862 after the colonel was killed. Although he was appointed lieutenant colonel and colonel in September 1862, the appointments were not made official until April 1863 and September 1864, respectively. As part of **Evander Law's** brigade, Perry saw no combat at **Fredericksburg**, but afterward two of his **companies** were captured during the siege of **Suffolk**. The regiment saw hard service at **Gettysburg's Devil's Den** and Little Round Top and at **Chickamauga**. In the latter battle, Perry assumed command of the brigade after Law took over the **division**. After fighting at **Wauhatchie** and in the **Knoxville Campaign**, he again took command of the brigade when Law resigned his commission in a dispute with other officers.

Perry's superiors recommended his promotion to brigadier general in January 1864, but Law withdrew his resignation and returned to the brigade. Over the next few months, Law and Perry frequently traded brigade command as Law feuded with **James Longstreet** and **Micah Jenkins**. Perry led the brigade in the **Wilderness** and at **Spotsylvania**, but he returned to the 44th Alabama when Law resumed command. When Law was wounded at **Cold Harbor**, Perry returned to brigade command during the early part of the **Petersburg Campaign**. He finally received his appointment to brigadier general in March 1865, becoming the last general appointed in the Army of Northern Virginia. Perry surrendered with the **army** at **Appomattox**.

After the war, Perry farmed in Alabama and taught college in **Kentucky**.

PERRYVILLE, KENTUCKY, BATTLE OF (OCTOBER 8, 1862). By October 1862, the **Kentucky Campaign** had reached its climax. **Braxton Bragg's** Confederate **Army of Mississippi** was positioned at Bardstown and Frankfort, while **Don Carlos Buell's** Union **Army of the Ohio** was in Louisville. Under pressure from his superiors to confront the Confederates, Buell moved out of Louisville on October 1 and headed southeast in three columns toward Bardstown and Harrodsburg. As a diversion, two **divisions** also marched toward Frankfort, where Bragg was installing a Confederate state government. Bragg believed the diversion was Buell's main force and deployed **Edmund Kirby Smith** to attack it. Unaware of Buell's other columns heading for Bardstown, Bragg also ordered **Leonidas Polk** to attack the Federals from the south. Gaining an accurate picture of the enemy's movements from his cavalry, Polk disobeyed orders. After informing Bragg of his intentions, he retreated southeast to Harrodsburg while sending **William J. Hardee's corps** southwest to Perryville.

On October 7, Buell approached Perryville from the west on three roads, with **Thomas L. Crittenden's** II Corps on the right following the Lebanon Pike, **Charles C. Gilbert's** III Corps in the center on the Springfield Pike, and **Alexander McCook's** I Corps on the left on the Mackville Pike. After **Joseph Wheeler's** Confederate cavalry began **skirmishing** with the approaching Federals, Hardee positioned **Simon B. Buckner's** division to block Gilbert, who was leading the Union advance. Polk soon arrived with a division of reinforcements and decided to let the enemy make the first move, even though Bragg had ordered him to attack immediately.

In the early morning of October 8, the Battle of Perryville began northwest of town when **Philip Sheridan's** Union division made contact with **St. John R. Liddell's brigade** on the Springfield Pike. Sheridan pushed back Liddell but then was ordered by the cautious Gilbert to fall back to Peters Hill and assume a defensive position. During this brisk fight, Buell was only two miles to the rear, but he was unaware the battle had begun because of a rare **acoustic shadow** and did not ride to the battlefield until about 4:00 P.M.

Bragg arrived at Perryville by mid-morning and decided to attack Buell's left flank and left center. He positioned **Benjamin F. Cheatham's** division on the far right near the Chaplin River, while Buckner's division held the center, and **James P. Anderson's** division was on the left. Learning that the Union right was farther north than expected, Cheatham moved his division farther north and attacked McCook at about 2:00 P.M. He had planned to attack the enemy flank but found himself advancing against McCook's strong center. Bloody fighting erupted and spread southward across Buckner's and Anderson's fronts. McCook slowly fell back under the relentless pressure and lost Brig. Gens. **James Jackson** and **William Terrill** mortally wounded. In the center, the Confederate brigades of **Patrick Cleburne** and **Daniel Adams** drove back **James Jackson's** Union division along the Mackville Pike. Although the Federals made a final desperate stand and inflicted heavy casualties on the Confederates, they finally were forced to withdraw along the pike.

During the heavy fighting on Buell's left and center, Gilbert largely kept his corps out of the battle because of orders from Buell to be cautious. Realizing the danger McCook was in, however, Buell finally sent part of Gilbert's corps to the left as reinforcements late in the day. Michael Gooding's brigade made a valiant stand at a Mackville Pike intersection and stopped the Confederate advance until a final Confederate attack forced it back about dark. During the fighting, Polk narrowly escaped capture when he mistakenly rode up to a Union line and ordered it to stop firing on a Confederate brigade. That afternoon on Gilbert's front, Sheridan's and **Robert Mitchell's** divisions stopped an attack by Samuel Powell's brigade. A counterattack by **William Carlin's** brigade then drove the Confederates through Perryville and across the Chaplin River.

Tactically, the Confederates had won the battle. They had badly mauled McCook's corps, captured 11 cannons, and mortally wounded two Union generals. That night, however, Buell ordered up the rest of his **army** and made plans to attack on October 9. As a result, Bragg withdrew during the night and joined Kirby Smith's command near Harrodsburg. With water scarce because of a drought, supplies running low, and now outnumbered, Bragg ended the campaign and withdrew back to **Tennessee**. Thus, the Battle of Perryville became a **strategic** Union victory, but Buell was removed from command shortly afterward for failing to follow up and destroy Bragg. In the fighting at Perryville, Bragg lost over 3,000 men out of approximately 16,000 engaged, while Buell suffered approximately 4,200 casualties out of approximately 22,000 men engaged. For the numbers involved, Perryville was one of the bloodiest battles of the war.

PETERSBURG, VIRGINIA, CAMPAIGN (JUNE 12, 1864–APRIL 2, 1865).

After weeks of bloody fighting in the **Overland Campaign**, **U. S. Grant** made a bold move to break the stalemate. He withdrew the **Army of the Potomac** from **Cold Harbor, Virginia**, on the night of June 12, 1864, and made a sweeping march to the south toward Petersburg. Petersburg was a major **railroad** center and through it came much of the supplies feeding **Robert E. Lee's Army of Northern Virginia**. **Benjamin F. Butler's Army of the James** had attacked the city earlier in the **Bermuda Hundred Campaign**, but it had been defeated by **P. G. T. Beauregard** and now was bottled up on Bermuda Hundred. Grant believed that by moving swiftly, he could capture Petersburg before Lee could react. With his supply line cut, Lee then would have to attack at a disadvantage or abandon **Richmond**.

Grant's plan worked well at first. He disappeared from Lee's front, crossed the James River by transports and **pontoon bridge** on June

14–15, and attacked Petersburg on June 15 before Lee determined what had happened. The attack was badly handled, however. **William F. Smith's** XVIII Corps did not advance aggressively because of a rumor that Lee had arrived, and **Winfield S. Hancock** failed to support the attack adequately with his II Corps. **Ambrose Burnside's** IX Corps joined in the attack on June 17 and forced Beauregard back a short distance, but Beauregard and his 5,400 men held back the Federals until Lee arrived with the bulk of his **army** on June 18. That same day, Burnside renewed his attack and was joined by **Gouverneur K. Warren's** V Corps, but little headway was made against **A. P. Hill's** and **Richard H. Anderson's** Confederate **corps**. At a cost of more than 10,000 men, Grant had captured only a few forward positions, while inflicting an estimated 3,000–5,000 Confederate casualties.

Grant made his headquarters at **City Point** and working through **George G. Meade**, the commander of the Army of the Potomac, slowly extended his lines to the west over the next 10 months to cut the roads and railroads supplying Lee's army. Lee countered by stretching his lines thinner and thinner to block Grant. Soon there were miles of trenches, fortifications, **abatis**, and other obstructions ringing the eastern and southern sides of Richmond and Petersburg. The war became one of trench warfare as maneuverability was lost. Despite the dangerous and dreary duty, the Union soldiers were kept supplied by the James River, while the Confederates slowly ran out of supplies as Grant began cutting the remaining supply lines.

On June 22–24, Grant stretched his left southward to cut the vital **Weldon Railroad**, but in heavy fighting along the railroad and the Jerusalem Plank Road, Lee defended his supply line and inflicted nearly 3,000 casualties on the Federals at a cost of fewer than 600 men. From June 21–30, the Federal cavalry again attacked the railroads in the **Wilson-Kautz Raid** and fought at **Staunton River Bridge** and **Reams' Station**, but the Confederates quickly repaired the damage inflicted. One of the bloodiest episodes of the campaign came on July 30 when elements of Burnside's IX Corps dug a mineshaft under the Confederate defenses and exploded a mine. In the resultant **Battle of the Crater**, Union troops stormed into the crater, but were trapped and slaughtered by a Confederate counterattack, and many **black troops** were **massacred**. Burnside lost nearly 4,000 men in the battle to the Confederates' 1,500.

Operations also were launched north of the James River near Richmond to force Lee to weaken his Petersburg lines to protect the capital. On June 27–29, Grant attacked the Confederates at **First Deep Bottom** to support Burnside's mine project. After learning Lee had sent reinforcements to the

Shenandoah Valley, he attacked again August 13–20 in the **Second Battle of Deep Bottom**. Both attacks failed, and Grant lost more than 3,000 men, while Lee suffered about 1,500 casualties.

Over the next eight months, combat was nearly constant with daily **artillery** and **sharpshooter** fire, probes, and occasional major operations. Larger fights erupted at the Weldon Railroad, **Fort Harrison**, **New Market Heights**, **Peebles' Farm**, **Darbytown Road**, **Burgess' Mill**, and **Hatcher's Run** as the Federals extended their lines westward or attacked Richmond's defenses north of the James River. By March 1865, most of Lee's supply lines were cut, the army was weak from hunger and disease, and thousands of soldiers had **deserted**. Desperate, he planned to attack the Union line at **Fort Stedman** and escape to **North Carolina** to join forces with **Joseph E. Johnston**. On March 25, Lee attacked, but the Federals sealed the breakthrough and forced the Confederates to retreat back into their lines. Lee lost nearly 4,000 men in the failed breakout to Grant's 1,500.

Realizing Lee's army was on the verge of collapse, Grant launched a massive attack at **Dinwiddie Court House** and **Five Forks** on the Confederate right on March 29–April 1. The Confederate flank was crushed, and Grant launched a general attack all along the Petersburg front the next day. Lee was forced to evacuate Richmond and Petersburg on the night of April 2, 1865, and begin the long retreat known as the **Appomattox Campaign**. The Petersburg Campaign lasted 10 months and cost Grant approximately 42,000 men (to Lee's estimated 28,000 casualties), but it ended in the capture of Richmond and Petersburg and led to the Army of Northern Virginia's **surrender** at Appomattox.

PETTIGREW, JAMES JOHNSTON (1828–1863) CSA. Pettigrew, who usually went by his middle name, was a native of **North Carolina** and a member of a prominent planter family. An outstanding student, he graduated first in the University of North Carolina class of 1847 at age 18. Pettigrew then served briefly as an assistant professor at the Washington Naval Observatory before settling in **South Carolina**. He became a lawyer, legislator, and militia colonel and traveled extensively in Europe.

In 1860, Pettigrew was colonel of the 1st South Carolina Rifles. During the **secession** crisis, he seized **Castle Pinckney** and later served at **Fort Sumter**. With the outbreak of war, Pettigrew volunteered as a private in the **Hampton Legion** and accompanied it to **Virginia**. Just hours before the **First Battle of Manassas**, he accepted an appointment as colonel of the 22nd North Carolina (originally designated the 12th North Carolina).

When **Jefferson Davis** appointed Pettigrew brigadier general in early 1862, he at first declined the commission on the grounds he had not yet led troops in combat but finally accepted the promotion in February. His first battle was at **Seven Pines**, where he was severely wounded by a bullet to the neck. Left behind when the Confederates retreated, Pettigrew received another gunshot wound and a **bayonet** cut to his leg and was captured. Originally thought to be dead, he was **exchanged** in August 1862 and the following month took command of a **brigade** in the **Department of North Carolina**. Pettigrew fought at **New Bern** in early 1863 and then returned to Virginia to join **Henry Heth's** division in the **Army of Northern Virginia**. He missed the **Chancellorsville Campaign** but rejoined the **army** in time for **Gettysburg**. Pettigrew's brigade suffered very heavy casualties on the first day of battle, and he took command of the **division** when Heth was wounded. While leading his men in **Pickett's Charge**, his horse was killed under him, and he was wounded in the right hand by **canister** but was one of the last soldiers to leave the field. Pettigrew led the division in the retreat and formed the rear guard as the army crossed the Potomac River on July 13–14. In a clash with Union cavalry at **Falling Waters**, he was mortally wounded in the stomach while searching for an enemy cavalryman who was hiding in a garden. Pettigrew died three days later.

PETTUS, EDMUND WINSTON (1821–1907) CSA. A native of **Alabama**, Pettus attended **Tennessee's** Clinton College and became an Alabama lawyer in 1842. He was elected district solicitor in 1844, served in the **Mexican War** as a lieutenant, and then lived in **California** for two years before returning to Alabama.

During the **secession** crisis, Pettus was sent to **Mississippi** as a commissioner to discuss Mississippi's secession plans with his brother, Gov. **John J. Pettus**. He then returned home, helped raise the 20th Alabama, and in September 1861 was elected its major. Pettus was elected lieutenant colonel the next month and served the remainder of the year with **Edmund Kirby Smith** in eastern Tennessee. The **regiment** was sent to reinforce **Vicksburg, Mississippi**, in early 1863. At the **Battle of Port Gibson** during the **Vicksburg Campaign**, Pettus fought well and was captured but managed to escape. He was commended for his service at **Champion Hill** and during the siege of Vicksburg where he personally led a counterattack that recaptured an important position. When his regiment's commander was killed in June 1863, Pettus was promoted to colonel.

Captured when Vicksburg fell, Pettus soon was **exchanged** and was promoted to brigadier general in September 1863. During the **Chattanooga**

Campaign, his **brigade** fought well with the **Army of Tennessee** at **Lookout Mountain** and **Missionary Ridge**. During the **Atlanta Campaign**, Pettus defended **Rocky Face Ridge** and fought in most of the campaign's major battles. Afterward, he accompanied **John Bell Hood** on the **Franklin and Nashville Campaign** and secured the Duck River crossing in November 1864. Although Pettus's brigade was not engaged at Franklin, it was heavily attacked at Nashville on the first day and stopped an enemy cavalry charge on the second. After the failed campaign, he was sent to the Carolinas to reinforce **Joseph E. Johnston**. During the **Carolinas Campaign**, Pettus was praised for holding his ground at **Wyse Fork** and was wounded at **Bentonville**.

After the war, Pettus resumed his Alabama law practice and became active in state **Democratic** politics. He served as a delegate to all of the Democratic National Conventions from 1876 to 1896 and was elected to the U.S. Senate in 1896. Pettus was reelected in 1902 and died while in office. He was the last Confederate general to serve in the Senate.

PETTUS, JOHN JAMES (1813–1867) CSA. The brother of Confederate general **Edmund Winston Pettus**, Pettus was a native of **Tennessee,** but he moved with his family to **Alabama** as a child. He then moved to **Mississippi** as a young man and became a prosperous planter. Becoming active in **Democratic** politics, Pettus served in the state assembly from 1844 to 1846 and in the state senate from 1848 to 1858. While serving as president of the senate in 1854, he became governor for five days when **Henry S. Foote** resigned the position. A secessionist, Pettus was elected governor in 1859.

As war approached, Pettus prepared Mississippi by strengthening the militia and increasing defense spending. He led the state in its **secession** movement in January 1861 and became a staunch Confederate. Pettus raised troops and tried to restrict cotton planting to create a cotton shortage to pressure foreign governments to recognize the Confederacy. Although a state military board sometimes opposed him, he easily won reelection in November 1861. During the war, Pettus generally supported **Jefferson Davis's** war measures, but he believed the state should have more control over the use of **conscripts**. He became more distrustful of Davis as **Vicksburg** became threatened, and the national government did not supply the troops he thought necessary for its defense. Pettus prepared Vicksburg's defenses the best he could but was forced to flee with the state government when Union troops captured **Jackson** during the **Vicksburg Campaign**. Prevented by the state constitution from running for a third time, he was succeeded in office by **Charles Clark** in November 1863.

Pettus then joined the 1st Mississippi as a private in the summer of 1864, but he rose to the rank of colonel on staff duty by war's end.

A few months after the war, Pettus fled to **Arkansas** when he heard he was to be arrested. He died there in 1867, having failed in his attempt to secure a pardon from President **Andrew Johnson**.

PHELPS, JOHN SMITH (1814–1886) USA. A native of **Connecticut**, Phelps attended Washington College (present-day Trinity College) and then became a lawyer in 1835. He moved to **Missouri** in 1837, began a prosperous law practice, and entered **Democratic** politics. Phelps was elected to the state legislature in 1840 and to the **U.S. Congress** in 1844. Over the next 18 years, he supported the building of **railroads**, establishing an overland mail route, and the admission of **California** and **Oregon** as free states.

After the Civil War began in 1861, Phelps returned to Missouri, recruited the six-month "Phelps' Regiment" in October, and was appointed its lieutenant colonel. He was promoted to colonel in December and a few months later was wounded while leading his men at **Pea Ridge**. The **regiment** was mustered out in May 1862, but **Abraham Lincoln** appointed Phelps military governor of **Arkansas** in July. In November, Lincoln appointed him brigadier general of volunteers so he would have the necessary military rank to accomplish his duties. The Senate did not confirm this appointment, and Phelps's Civil War career came to an end in early 1863. He had decided not to run for reelection to Congress in 1862, and his term expired in early 1863, about the same time his military commission did. Phelps then resigned as military governor because of poor health and returned to Missouri in 1864.

Phelps resumed his law practice and was defeated for governor in 1868 but then won in 1876 and became a popular governor who was able to unite the northern and southern factions of the Democratic Party. He resumed his law practice after leaving office in 1881.

PHELPS, JOHN WOLCOTT (1813–1885) USA. A native of **Vermont**, Phelps graduated from **West Point** in 1836. He served with the **artillery** in the **Seminole Wars**, along the Canadian border, and in the **Mexican War**. In Mexico, Phelps took the unusual action of declining a **brevet** for his war service, but it is speculated he may have done so because the war was unpopular in **abolitionist** Vermont. He then served the next 10 years on the frontier before resigning his commission in 1859. For the next two years, Phelps dedicated himself to writing tracts condemning **slavery** and the Masons.

Phelps entered Union service in May 1861 as colonel of the 1st Vermont. He commanded the troops that occupied Newport News, Virginia, later that month and was promoted to brigadier general in August. In December, Phelps was assigned to **Benjamin F. Butler's Department of the Gulf** and commanded the expedition that seized Ship Island on the Gulf Coast. He then accompanied Butler to **New Orleans, Louisiana**, and was given command of the **department's** 1st Brigade. While in New Orleans, Phelps began to recruit **black troops** without War Department authorization. He resigned his commission in protest in August 1862 when **Abraham Lincoln's** administration disavowed the action and on the same day was declared an outlaw by the Confederate government for organizing black units. Later, Phelps apparently was vindicated when the administration offered him a major general's commission to command black troops, but he declined the appointment.

Phelps returned to Vermont and continued to work in social crusades. He was active in the Vermont Historical Society and the Vermont teachers' association and ran for president in 1880 on the Anti-mason ticket.

PHILADELPHIA BRIGADE. This Union **brigade** was formed around the 1st California, a **regiment** sponsored by **California** Sens. James A. McDougall and **Edward D. Baker**. Although recruited in Philadelphia, Pennsylvania, in early 1861, the 1st California was equipped by McDougall and so named because he did not want his state to be unrepresented in the Union **army**. Baker was named its colonel. By October, the 1st California was joined by the 2nd, 3rd, and 5th California, all raised from Philadelphia, and a brigade was formed under Baker's command.

After Baker was killed at **Ball's Bluff**, the brigade was named the Philadelphia Brigade (the only Union brigade named for its city of origin), and the regiments were redesignated the 71st Pennsylvania (1st California), 72nd Pennsylvania (2nd California), 69th Pennsylvania (3rd California), and 106th Pennsylvania (5th California). **William W. Burns** took command of the brigade in March 1862, and it was assigned to the 2nd Division of the **Army of the Potomac's** II Corps. The brigade fought in the **Seven Days Campaign** and then suffered heavy casualties in **Antietam's** cornfield. After fighting at **Fredericksburg**, the Philadelphia Brigade earned its greatest fame at **Gettysburg**. There it fought **James Longstreet's** Confederate **corps** on the second day and suffered heavy casualties while repulsing **Pickett's Charge** on the third day. During the battle, the brigade captured 750 **prisoners** and three battle **flags**. Gettysburg was the brigade's last battle. The 71st and 72nd Pennsylvania were mustered out of service in April 1864, and the 69th and 106th Pennsylvania were merged with other regiments for the rest of the war.

PHILIPPI, WESTERN VIRGINIA, BATTLE OF (JUNE 3, 1861). When **Virginia** seceded in April 1861, much of the state's western mountainous area opposed the action. This region remained loyal to the Union and posed problems for the Confederacy because it controlled the important Baltimore & Ohio Railroad and three turnpikes. In late spring, Virginia authorities sent Col. **Thomas J. Jackson** to seize **Harpers Ferry**, disrupt the **railroad**, and extend Confederate control over the turnpikes.

Union authorities put **George B. McClellan** in command of the **Department of the Ohio,** which included western Virginia. When McClellan advanced into the region, Confederates under Col. George A. Porterfield withdrew to Philippi (FIL-uh-pee). On June 2, Union Brig. Gen. Thomas A. Morris advanced against Philippi with five **regiments** in two columns. He attacked Porterfield's 775 men at dawn on June 3 and completely routed them. The Confederates fled after firing only one volley and ran away in such a panic that the Federals called it the "Philippi Races." This was one of the war's first battles, and it received much attention, although it had little significance. In the clash, Morris lost two men wounded while Porterfield suffered 15 casualties.

PHILLIPS' LEGION. This Confederate unit from **Georgia** was one of several **legions** to be formed during the Civil War. Attorney William Phillips was put in charge of raising recruits around Marietta by his friend Gov. **Joseph Brown**. In the spring of 1861, Phillips organized approximately 1,000 men into three separate infantry, cavalry, and **artillery** battalions, which collectively were called Phillips' Legion. Brown accepted the legion into state service in July, and Phillips was appointed its colonel in August.

Phillips' Legion first was assigned to the **Army of the Kanawha** in western **Virginia**, but the artillery battalion was broken up into different batteries and was scattered throughout the **Confederate army**. Phillips lost an eye that autumn while fighting in the Kanawha Valley, and the legion was transferred to the **Department of South Carolina, Georgia, and Florida** in December. It protected **railroads** in **South Carolina** until joining the **Army of Northern Virginia** in late 1862. At that time, the infantry and cavalry battalions were separated and assigned to different **brigades**. At **Fredericksburg**, the cavalry served under **J. E. B. Stuart** and the infantry was in **Thomas R. R. Cobb's** brigade. Phillips resigned his commission in February 1863 because of "paralysis," but the legion continued to serve in the Army of Northern Virginia under a series of officers. The infantry and cavalry of Phillips' Legion remained separated for the remainder of the war and were active in all of the **army's** battles. The cavalry served first under Stuart, and then **Wade Hampton**, and distinguished itself at the **Battle of Trevilian Station** before participating in the **Carolinas Campaign** in January 1865. The infantry remained in **Lafayette McLaws's division** of **James Longstreet's corps** and fought with it for the remainder of the war.

PHILLIPS, WENDELL (1811–1884) USA. A native of **Massachusetts** and the son of Boston's first mayor, Phillips graduated from Harvard University and briefly practiced law. He soon became involved in the **abolitionist** movement, and became a disciple of **William Lloyd Garrison** and Elijah P. Lovejoy and was active in the **American Anti-Slavery Society**. After Lovejoy's murder in 1837, Phillips turned more radical and became a popular lecturer condemning not only **slavery** but also the Constitution for sanctioning it and any form of compromise that allowed it to survive. Unlike Garrison, Phillips believed in violent resistance to slavery and during the Civil War thought **Abraham Lincoln** was too conservative on emancipation. At war's end, he became president of the American Anti-Slavery Society and continued to campaign for **freedmen**, women's rights, **prison** reform, labor unions, **Indian** rights, and prohibition.

PIATT, ABRAM (OR ABRAHAM) SANDERS (1821–1908) USA. A native of **Ohio**, Piatt farmed, studied law, and edited a newspaper before the Civil War. He entered Union service in April 1861 when he was made colonel of the 90-day 13th Ohio, but the **regiment** never left the state, and in September Piatt was appointed colonel of the 34th Ohio. Sent to western **Virginia**, his regiment served in the rear areas under **William S. Rosecrans**.

Piatt was promoted to brigadier general of volunteers in April 1862 and was given command of a **brigade** in **Samuel Sturgis's** division. His was the only brigade of the **division** to fight at **Second Manassas**, and he was commended by **John Pope**. Piatt defended **Washington, D.C.**, in the months after the battle and thus missed the **Antietam Campaign**. At **Fredericksburg**, he was in the 3rd Division of the **Army of the Potomac's** III Corps and seriously injured his back when his horse fell on him. This injury apparently forced Piatt to resign his commission in February 1863.

Piatt returned to his Ohio farm and in 1879 unsuccessfully ran for governor on the Greenback-Labor Party ticket. He also was very active in the Granger movement.

PICKENS, FRANCIS WILKINSON (1805–1869) CSA. A native of **South Carolina**, Pickens was the son of Gov. Andrew Pickens Jr. and the grandson of Revolutionary War Gen. Andrew Pickens. He came from a very wealthy family and was arrogant, sometimes rude, and generally overbearing. Pickens attended South Carolina College and passed the bar exam, but he preferred spending his time politicking and managing his six plantations and 417 slaves to practicing law. He served in the state assembly from 1832 to 1834, in the **U.S. Congress** from 1834 to 1843, and in the state senate from 1844 to 1846. During his time in **Washington, D.C.**, Pickens was a spokesman for **John C. Calhoun** and **nullification**. Pickens also served as President **James Buchanan's** minister to Russia from 1858 to 1860.

Pickens returned to South Carolina from Russia in 1860 and was elected governor in December 1860, just two days before the state seceded. Earlier, he had been a moderate on **secession**, but in late 1860, Pickens believed it was the only way to protect states rights. He spent the next several months trying to find a peaceful way to remove the Union garrison from **Fort Sumter**, although he did approve the firing on the supply ship *Star of the West*. Once Fort Sumter was fired upon and war began, Pickens began raising troops, but he preferred using 12-month recruits rather than enlisting men for the war's duration. He was unpopular with the people because of his heavy-handed **conscription** and **impressment** of slaves, and he often clashed with the Executive Council over war measures.

Pickens's term expired in December 1862, and he retired to his plantation. Ruined financially by the war, he advised cooperating with the **Republicans** during **Reconstruction**.

PICKET. A picket was a guard who was posted beyond an encampment to give warning of any approaching enemy and to regulate the comings and goings from camp. The picket line was a string of such guards. Picket duty was rotated among **regiments** and while it sometimes provided an enjoyable break from dull camp life, it also could be dangerous because of marauding cavalry, guerrillas, and **sharpshooters**.

PICKETT, GEORGE EDWARD (1825–1875) CSA. A native of **Virginia**, Pickett graduated at the bottom of his 1846 **West Point** class, largely because of demerits received for flaunting the dress and personal code by wearing fine clothing and perfuming his hair. Assigned to the infantry, he served well during the **Mexican War**, and at Chapultepec he took the **flag** from a wounded **James Longstreet** and carried it over the wall. Pickett's bravery won him two **brevets** and Longstreet's permanent loyalty. After the war, Pickett served in **Texas** and the Washington Territory (where he again won recognition for preventing the British from capturing San Juan Island) and rose to the rank of captain in 1855.

Pickett resigned his commission in June 1861 and entered Confederate service as a major of **artillery**. Commissioned a colonel of Virginia troops the following month, he served on the lower Rappahannock River until February 1862, when he was appointed brigadier general and was transferred to Longstreet's command. Pickett led a **brigade** in Longstreet's **division** and fought well at **Williamsburg** and **Seven Pines**. He then was wounded in the shoulder at **Gaines' Mill** and missed the battles of **Second Manassas** and **Antietam**.

When he returned to the **Army of Northern Virginia**, Pickett was promoted to major general in October 1862 and assumed command of one of Longstreet's divisions. He was not heavily engaged at **Fredericksburg** or during the siege of **Suffolk**. Pickett's next battle, at **Gettysburg,** was his most famous. He had only three of his five brigades present and was not engaged until the last day, when his division participated in the attack that became known as **Pickett's Charge**, even though his men made up only part of the attacking force. Although eager to make the charge, Pickett afterward blamed **Robert E. Lee** for the defeat and never forgave his commander for having his men "massacred." Some writers have called into question Pickett's bravery during the charge, but there is no evidence that he behaved in any but a professional manner.

After Gettysburg, Pickett's reputation began to suffer. Although well liked personally, he did not have the **discipline** or ability to manage a division successfully, and it was said among Longstreet's staff that Longstreet had to look after Pickett to see that orders were carried out properly. While the rest of Longstreet's **corps** went west in the autumn of 1863, Pickett was sent to **North Carolina**. Pickett launched an unsuccessful raid against **New Bern** and afterward became embroiled in controversy when he hanged 22 North Carolina **deserters** who had been captured in Union **uniforms**. Brought back to Virginia, he fought at **Second Drewry's Bluff** and **Cold Harbor** in May 1864 and participated in the **Petersburg Campaign**. During the latter, he became so enamored with his 16-year-old wife, LaSalle Corbell (whom he had married in September 1863), that he ignored the division's welfare and was sometimes absent without leave, forcing Lee to warn Longstreet "to correct the evils" (Davis, ed., *The Confederate General,* vol. 5, 34) in the division. Pickett's last battle was at **Five Forks** in April 1865. While the Federals crushed his division, Pickett was at a shad bake in the rear with **Fitzhugh Lee**. He rode to the front but was too late to salvage the situation. Lee relieved Pickett of duty, but he remained with the **army** unassigned until the **surrender** at **Appomattox**.

After the war, Pickett briefly lived in Canada but soon returned to Virginia and worked for a life insurance company. After he died, he came to be seen as the epitome of the romantic Confederate officer. This largely was due to his wife's tireless efforts to promote his memory and publishing his greatly altered wartime letters.

PICKETT PAPERS. These papers were the Confederate State Department papers that were removed from **Richmond, Virginia,** in March 1865 and later sold to the U.S. government. As the fall of Richmond seemed imminent in the latter days of the **Petersburg Campaign,** Confederate Secretary of State **Judah P. Benjamin** entrusted his department's papers to William J. Bromwell for transfer to **North Carolina.** At war's end, Bromwell took personal possession of the papers and in 1868 anonymously offered to sell them to the government through attorney John T. Pickett. After a government commissioner verified the papers' authenticity, Bromwell was paid $75,000 for the collection in 1872. The collection became known as the Pickett Papers after the attorney who handled their sale.

PICKETT'S CHARGE AT GETTYSBURG, PENNSYLVANIA (JULY 3, 1863). After pounding the **Army of the Potomac** at **Gettysburg** for two days, **Robert E. Lee** decided one massive attack against the Union center would crack the enemy line. He ordered **James Longstreet** to organize an attack force, but Longstreet disagreed with the **tactic** and argued that the **Army of Northern Virginia** should withdraw and make a **turning movement** to force the enemy out of its position. Lee insisted on the attack, however, and Longstreet assembled approximately 13,000 men (estimates range from 12,000 to 15,000). **George E. Pickett's division** and **Cadmus Wilcox's** brigade were positioned on the right, while **James Pettigrew's** division was on the left, and **Isaac Trimble's** two **brigades** supported Pettigrew. While Pickett was responsible for getting the units into position, Longstreet was in overall command, and Pickett led only one wing. The attack more accurately should be called the Pickett-Pettigrew-Trimble Charge, but it came to be known for Pickett and his **Virginians**, even though troops from **North Carolina, Alabama, Tennessee**, and **Mississippi** also were involved.

The attack was preceded by a two-hour **artillery** barrage beginning at about 1:00 P.M., July 3, 1863, to knock out the enemy's cannons on Cemetery Ridge, but the barrage was largely ineffective because most of the shells overshot their targets. The infantry then advanced toward a small copse of trees located in the Union center. The attack was one of the war's most dramatic moments as the nearly one-mile-long battle line marched in precision over a mile-wide field. When Union artillery tore holes in the line, the Confederates impressed their enemy by periodically stopping to dress the line as if on parade. As the Confederates neared the Union position, **Winfield S. Hancock's** II Corps **divisions** of **John Gibbon** and **Alexander Hays** opened fire and shot down hundreds of men. A deadly **enfilade** fire broke the attackers' left flank, and the line became disorganized. All organization was gone by the time the Confederates approached the copse of trees. While a mob of soldiers managed to break through temporarily, the Federals quickly sealed the gap in vicious hand-to-hand fighting and drove the Confederates back. As the survivors limped back to Seminary Ridge, the Union soldiers began chanting "**Fredericksburg!**" in revenge for the bloody defeat they had suffered seven months earlier.

Dismayed at the carnage and defeat, Lee met the survivors and took responsibility for the failed attack. Nearly half of the force was lost. Brigadier General **Richard Garnett** was dead, Brig. Gen. **Lewis Armistead** was mortally wounded, Brig. Gen. **James Kemper** and Pettigrew were wounded, Trimble was wounded and captured, and all 13 regimental colonels in Pickett's division were casualties. Total Confederate losses may have reached as many 7,500. Hancock, who was wounded in the groin, lost about 1,500 men.

PICKETT'S MILL, GEORGIA, BATTLE OF (MAY 27, 1864). After **Joseph E. Johnston's Army of Tennessee** fell back to Allatoona Pass, Georgia, during the 1864 **Atlanta Campaign, William T. Sherman** moved his **armies** to the south toward **New Hope Church and Dallas** to turn him out of the strong position. Johnston quickly countered the move and entrenched in the Federals' path. On May 25–26, 1864, heavy fighting broke out at New Hope Church as **Joseph Hooker's** XX Corps tried to fight its way through the Confederate position.

On May 27, **Oliver O. Howard** took 14,000 men of his IV Corps to Hooker's left to attack the Confederate right flank at Pickett's Mill. Moving through very thick and broken terrain, **Thomas J. Wood's division** attacked at about 4:30 P.M., but it encountered **Patrick Cleburne's** division, which had just extended the Confederate line into that area. The fighting was close and bloody with the Confederates having the advantage of strong entrenchments. The Union **brigades** of **William B. Hazen** and William H. Gibson were shot to pieces as they attacked through the dense woods. After dark, Wood finally withdrew. The Federals lost about 1,600 men in the futile attacks, while Cleburne suffered approximately 450 casualties. **Ambrose Bierce** was a member of Hazen's staff and later based one of his short stories on the battle.

PIEDMONT, VIRGINIA, BATTLE OF (JUNE 5, 1864). On May 26, 1864, **David Hunter's Shenandoah Valley Campaign** was launched to destroy the Valley's supplies and the vital **railroad** at Staunton, Virginia, that supplied **Robert E. Lee's Army of Northern Virginia**. To defend this strategic region, the Confederates reinforced **John D. Imboden's** cavalry with Brig. Gen. **William E. "Grumble" Jones's brigade**. With approximately 5,600 men, Jones took up a defensive position at Piedmont, about seven miles south of **Port Republic**. Jones's infantry blocked the main road, with his left flank anchored on the Middle River, while Imboden's cavalry was placed over a mile to the southeast to guard against Hunter moving around Jones's right flank. This left a large gap between Jones and Imboden, which no one on the Confederate side seemed to notice.

Early on the morning of June 5, Hunter's nearly 20,000 men made contact with the Confederate cavalry and effectively used their superior **artillery** to push them slowly south toward Piedmont. At about noon, Hunter arrived at Jones's position. Augustus Moor's brigade made repeated **frontal attacks** to fix Jones in position, while Joseph Thoburn's brigade moved around his right flank and took advantage of the gap between Jones and Imboden. Hunter's cavalry, under **Julius Stahel**, also rode to the southeast toward Imboden, forcing him to remain in position. The Federals kept relentless pressure on the entire Confederate line, and the fighting sometimes was hand-to-hand. When Jones was shot in the head and killed, his line crumbled. The Confederate infantry and cavalry withdrew to the south to Fisherville, but their rear guard prevented Hunter from making a vigorous pursuit. Hunter entered Staunton the next day. The Confederates lost about 1,600 men in the battle, while Hunter lost 780.

PIERCE, BYRON ROOT (1829–1924) USA. A native of **New York**, Pierce worked in a wool mill before becoming a dentist. He moved to

Michigan in 1856 and was practicing there and serving as a militia captain when the Civil War began.

Pierce entered Union service in June 1861 when he was appointed captain in the 3rd Michigan. After fighting at **First Manassas**, he was promoted to major in October. Pierce's **regiment** fought with the **Army of the Potomac** in the **Peninsula** and **Seven Days Campaigns**, and he was promoted to lieutenant colonel in July 1862. After seeing combat at **Groveton**, **Chantilly**, and **Fredericksburg** (where he commanded the regiment), he was promoted to colonel in January 1863. Pierce was wounded in his next battle at **Chancellorsville**, but he also received a commendation from his superior. He went on to lead the regiment at **Gettysburg**, where he suffered his third wound of the war and had to have his leg amputated. During the **Overland Campaign**, Pierce commanded a II Corps **brigade** and was promoted to brigadier general of volunteers in June 1864. He remained on duty through the **Petersburg Campaign** and performed valuable service at **Sailor's Creek**, for which he was **brevetted** major general of volunteers.

Pierce was mustered out of service in August 1865. He returned to Michigan, where he worked in the postal service, was active in veterans' organizations, directed the Michigan Soldiers' Home, and operated a hotel.

PIERPONT, FRANCIS HARRISON (1814–1899) USA. A native of western **Virginia**, Pierpont (also spelled Peirpoint) graduated from **Pennsylvania's** Allegheny College and taught school in **Virginia** and **Mississippi**. He eventually settled in Virginia and became a prosperous **railroad** and coal-mining lawyer. Although he did not become active in politics before the Civil War, other than serving as a **Whig** elector, Pierpont fiercely opposed the slave-owning aristocrats and supported the Union.

Most of the people who lived in mountainous western Virginia opposed **secession** in 1861. When the state did secede in April, Pierpont helped organize a pro-Union legislature that met in Wheeling in June. Made up of representatives from the western counties, the legislature formed a loyal state government with Pierpont as governor and set in motion the creation of a new, loyal state. In November 1861, a constitutional convention met in Wheeling, and the state of **West Virginia** was organized by 1862. When the state was admitted to the Union in 1863, **Arthur I. Boreman** was elected governor, and Pierpont continued as the Union governor of Virginia with his headquarters at Alexandria. For his role in creating the new state, Pierpont became known as the "Father of West Virginia."

Pierpont remained Virginia's governor until 1868, when he was replaced by a military governor under the Military **Reconstruction** Act. He then moved to West Virginia, resumed his law practice, served one term in the legislature, and worked as an internal revenue collector.

PIGEON'S RANCH, NEW MEXICO TERRITORY, BATTLE OF (MARCH 26–28, 1862). *See* GLORIETA PASS, NEW MEXICO TERRITORY, BATTLE OF.

PIKE, ALBERT (1809–1891) CSA. A native of **Massachusetts**, Pike was admitted to Harvard University but was unable to attend because of a lack of money. Becoming a poet, instead, he moved west in 1831 and joined hunting and trading parties to **New Mexico** and **Texas**. Pike settled in **Arkansas** in 1832 and over the years managed the Little Rock *Advocate*, became involved in politics, and worked as a lawyer. In the latter field, Pike was very successful and once argued a case before the **U.S. Supreme Court**. He also commanded a militia **company** and led it during the **Mexican War**. A dispute with Col. **John S. Roane** over conduct at Buena Vista led to two duels, one in Mexico and one later in Arkansas. Neither duelist was shot (although both fired two shots in the second duel), and they agreed never again to discuss the matter. After the war, Pike became a well-known poet and lawyer, representing the Creeks and other **Indians** in disputes with the U.S. government.

Although a reluctant secessionist, Pike was appointed the Confederate Commissioner of Indian Affairs in 1861 with orders to sign treaties with the various tribes in **Indian Territory** and to recruit Indian troops. He was successful in gaining the loyalty of most of the Five Civilized Tribes because of the trust he had gained by representing the Indians in lawsuits against the government. Pike then was commissioned a brigadier general in August 1861 and was given command of the **Department of the Indian Territory**. He led an Indian **brigade** at **Pea Ridge** but was criticized when they murdered some wounded Federals, scalped the dead, and then fled in the face of a counterattack and never reentered the fight. These incidents embarrassed and angered Pike, and he took steps to correct them, but the Union held him responsible for the atrocities and the Confederates blamed him for contributing to the defeat.

Pike became bitter when his superior, **Earl Van Dorn**, did not support him in the Pea Ridge controversy as he thought he should. Afterward, he was sent back to the Indian Territory and there feuded again with Roane and **Thomas C. Hindman**. The dispute with Hindman was over money and material, and Hindman ordered Pike's arrest. Pike fled to the hills, instead, and then resigned his commission in July 1862. Afterward, he made matters worse by accusing other commanders of stealing his supplies and the Confederate government of mistreating the Indians. Some officers believed he had gone insane, and **Jefferson Davis** accepted his resignation in November.

After the war, Pike was pardoned by President **Andrew Johnson** in 1866 and lived in **Tennessee** before moving to **Washington, D.C.**, in 1868. He continued to be a popular poet and author.

PILE, WILLIAM ANDERSON (1829–1889) USA. A native of **Indiana**, as a child, Pile moved with his family to **Missouri** and became an Episcopal minister. He entered Union service in June 1861 as chaplain of the 1st Missouri Light Artillery. After serving with the **regiment** at **Fort Donelson** (and perhaps **Shiloh**) and in the **siege of Corinth, Mississippi**, Pile was appointed captain in July 1862.

In September 1862, Pile was appointed lieutenant colonel of the 33rd Missouri (Union). After being promoted to colonel in December, he led his **regiment** in the **Yazoo Pass Expedition** during the **Vicksburg Campaign** and then was placed on garrison duty in **Arkansas**. Pile was promoted to brigadier general of volunteers in December 1863 and was given command of a **brigade** of **black troops** in Missouri. He next commanded Port Hudson, Louisiana, from December 1864 to February 1865 and then led a brigade of black soldiers in the **Mobile Campaign**. Pile was **brevetted** major general of volunteers for his service at **Fort Blakely** and was mustered out of service in August 1865.

Returning to Missouri, Pile was elected to the **U.S. Congress** in 1866 as a **Radical Republican**. After being defeated for reelection in 1868, he was appointed territorial governor of **New Mexico** and served there until he was named U.S. minister to Venezuela in 1871. Settling in **Pennsylvania** in 1876, Pile worked as a Venezuelan agent before moving to **California**.

PILLOW, GIDEON JOHNSON (1806–1878) CSA. A native of **Tennessee**, Pillow graduated from the University of Nashville in 1827 and became a law partner of future president James K. Polk. He became very active in backroom politicking within the **Democratic Party** (some people claimed he won Polk the 1844 presidential nomination), but he never held any office himself. Because of his association with Polk, Pillow was appointed a brigadier general and then major general during the **Mexican War** and suffered two wounds. Difficult and vain, he feuded with **Winfield Scott** and was investigated twice on allegations he had written newspaper articles praising himself and criticizing Scott. Polk, however, stood by Pillow, and he was honorably discharged in 1848. After the war, Pillow continued to be active in politics. He played a key role in securing the 1852 presidential nomination for Franklin Pierce but failed to win the vice presidential nomination for himself in 1852 and 1856.

During the **secession** crisis, Pillow was a moderate and did not favor secession until after **Fort Sumter** surrendered. He was appointed Tennessee's senior major general in May 1861 but was angered when he was made only a brigadier general when he mustered into the **Confederate army** in July. Pillow fought at **Belmont** in November and in February 1862 was made second in command at **Fort Donelson**. He led the attempted breakout during the siege but then became too cautious and withdrew just as escape was possible. That night, **John B. Floyd** gave Pillow command of the fort so that he could escape. Pillow then relinquished command to **Simon B. Buckner** and also escaped the doomed fort. Because of his actions at Fort Donelson, Pillow was relieved of duty, but a letter from **Albert S. Johnston** praising him and Floyd partially revived his career. He led a **brigade** in **John C. Breckinridge's division** of the **Army of Tennessee** at **Stones River**, but some men accused him of hiding behind a tree when his command went into action. After the battle, Pillow spent two years recruiting in Tennessee and in February 1865 became commissary general of **prisoners**. While in that position, he tried to protect **prison** camps in **Georgia** from being overrun by Union cavalry.

After the war, Pillow failed as a planter and then practiced law in Tennessee with former governor **Isham Harris**. He was ruined financially when a coal company he had seized for Tennessee at the beginning of the war won a $38,500 lawsuit against him.

PILOT KNOB, MISSOURI, BATTLE OF (SEPTEMBER 26–28, 1864). Early in **Sterling Price's 1864 Missouri Raid**, the Confederates learned of a 1,500-man Union garrison at Pilot Knob, Missouri, defending the St. Louis & Iron Mountain Railroad. On September 26, 1864, Price dispatched **Joseph O. Shelby's** division to cut the **railroad** north of Pilot Knob while he advanced on the town with the rest of the **army**.

The Union garrison was commanded by Brig. Gen. **Thomas Ewing Jr.**, who decided to hold his position and delay the Confederate advance on St. Louis as long as possible. On the evening of September 26, Ewing engaged Price's lead **division** under **James F. Fagan** at Arcadia, just south of Pilot Knob. The Federals drove back Fagan, but they then retreated in the face of superior numbers and took up a position at Fort

Davidson on the south side of Pilot Knob. The fort was formidable, protected by 11 cannons and a deep ditch, but Price took the advice of Fagan and Maj. Gen. **John S. Marmaduke** and decided to take it by assault. Moving over rugged terrain, he positioned his force to attack the fort from the north, south, and east. When Ewing refused a demand to surrender, Price made ready to attack at dawn.

The Confederates advanced at dawn on September 27 and drove Ewing's cavalry **videttes** back toward town. After some shelling, **John B. Clark's** and **William L. Cabell's** brigades attacked from the south at 2:00 P.M. Ewing's men raked the two **brigades** with shot and shell, and only Cabell reached the fort, but he soon had to withdraw. Price then ordered Shelby to rejoin the army and began constructing scaling ladders for another assault next morning. Before Price could attack on September 28, Ewing evacuated Pilot Knob at 3:00 A.M. and moved undetected past a Confederate brigade that was supposed to block his escape route. Price did not realize the enemy had fled until after dawn and then made an unsuccessful pursuit. The battle was a poor beginning for Price's Raid and was a harbinger of things to come. Price lost nearly 1,000 men in the fight, while Ewing suffered 213 casualties.

PINE BLUFF, ARKANSAS, BATTLE OF (OCTOBER 25, 1863). After Union troops captured **Little Rock, Arkansas**, and other towns on the White River in August 1863, Confederate Maj. Gen. **John S. Marmaduke** probed their position at Pine Bluff on October 25. With about 2,000 cavalrymen, Marmaduke entered the town from three sides and encountered 550 Union soldiers and 300 freed slaves barricaded in the courthouse square with nine cannons. Despite several charges and an attempt to burn down the courthouse, Marmaduke failed to dislodge the Federals and finally withdrew after looting the town. In the fight, he lost about 40 men while the Federals and former slaves lost 73.

PINKERTON, ALLAN (1819–1884) USA. A native of Scotland, Pinkerton immigrated to the United States in 1842 and became a cooper in Chicago, Illinois. Moonlighting as a detective, he won acclaim for breaking a counterfeiting ring and was appointed Cook County's deputy sheriff. Pinkerton organized the Pinkerton National Detective Agency in 1850 and became successful as America's first private detective. His motto "We Never Sleep," coupled with the image of an open eye, led to the term *private eye*. Pinkerton worked for the Illinois Central Railroad and came to know its lawyer, **Abraham Lincoln**. As an **abolitionist**, he also helped the **Underground Railroad** and at times worked with **John Brown**.

Because of his renown as a detective, Pinkerton escorted Lincoln to **Washington, D.C.**, in 1861 for **Lincoln's inauguration**. He uncovered what was believed to be an assassination plot in Baltimore, Maryland, and had Lincoln avoid danger by slipping into Washington unannounced. Although Pinkerton may have saved Lincoln's life, the president became much chagrined when the press perceived it as a cowardly entrance.

When **George B. McClellan** became commander of the **Department of the Ohio**, he had Pinkerton set up the first Secret Service to gather military intelligence. Pinkerton followed McClellan to Washington and performed the same duty for the **Army of the Potomac** during the **Peninsula Campaign**. Using spies, infiltrators, slaves, and other sources, he used the code name Maj. E. J. Allen and attempted to keep McClellan apprised of the Confederates' strength. The system was flawed, however, for Pinkerton often relied on uneducated slaves who did not have a good concept of numbers. As a result, he then overestimated the enemy's strength two- and threefold and caused the cautious McClellan to be even more timid.

Pinkerton served McClellan until he was relieved of command after **Antietam**. He then returned to Chicago and resumed working with his agency. After the war, the Pinkertons became infamous for breaking up labor strikes and for fighting Western outlaws who preyed on **railroads**.

PIONEER, CSS. Although the *H. L. Hunley* was more famous, the CSS *Pioneer* was one of the Confederacy's first **submarines**. Built in **New Orleans, Louisiana**, in 1861–62 by John McClintock and Baxter Watson, it was 34 feet long, 6 feet high, and 4 feet wide. The *Pioneer* had one hatch for the two-man crew to enter and was powered by a hand-cranked propeller. It towed a powder charge on a long rope and attacked its target by submerging under it and dragging the **torpedo** into the ship's side. One trial run against a barge was successful, but New Orleans was captured before the submarine could be put into combat. To keep it out of enemy hands, the *Pioneer* was sunk in the New Basin Canal but soon was recovered and examined by Union officers. It was sold as scrap metal in 1868 for $43. Another submarine was discovered in waters around New Orleans in 1868 and eventually was given to the Louisiana State Museum. Although claimed to be the *Pioneer*, this is almost certainly a case of mistaken identity.

PIONEERS. Pioneers were units of construction soldiers who opened blocked roads, cut new roads, built bridges and fortifications, and performed many other engineering-type jobs. Although similar to **engineers**, the pioneers generally moved with the **army**, while engineers were used more in rear areas. Many times the pioneers simply were ordinary soldiers who were taken from the ranks as the situation warranted, but often they were separate battalions or other units. The Union **Army of the Cumberland** had a 3,000-man Pioneer Corps made up of men from each **regiment**.

PITCHER, THOMAS GAMBLE (1824–1895) USA. A native of **Indiana**, Pitcher graduated next to last in his **West Point** class of 1845. He won one **brevet** for gallantry in the **Mexican War** and afterward rose to the rank of captain in the 8th U.S. Infantry. When the Civil War began, Pitcher was serving as a depot commissary in **Texas**.

Pitcher was sent east and for a time commanded a battalion made up of **companies** from the 8th and 12th U.S. Infantry at **Harpers Ferry, Virginia**. He led this unit at **Cedar Mountain**, his only Civil War combat experience, and was severely wounded in the knee. When he returned to duty in January 1863, Pitcher performed commissary duties and was promoted from captain to brigadier general of volunteers in March. In June, he became **Vermont's** provost marshal to enforce **conscription**, and his men once were driven out of town by a mob. Afterward, Pitcher served in Indiana's conscription bureau until war's end.

Pitcher was mustered out of the volunteers in April 1866 and received a brevet of brigadier general of regulars. He remained in the **army** and served as superintendent of West Point from 1866 to 1871 and director of the Washington Soldiers' Home before retiring in 1878 as a colonel.

PITTSBURG LANDING, TENNESSEE, BATTLE OF (APRIL 6–7, 1862). *See* SHILOH, TENNESSEE, CAMPAIGN AND BATTLE OF.

PLAINS STORE, LOUISIANA, BATTLE OF (MAY 21, 1863). In May 1863, Maj. Gen. **Nathaniel P. Banks** began the **Port Hudson Campaign** when he attempted to surround the Confederate fortifications at Port Hudson, Louisiana. He moved his three **divisions** toward the stronghold from the north, while **Christopher C. Augur's** division came up from the south from **Baton Rouge**. To prevent the two columns from uniting and surrounding him, Confederate Maj. Gen. **Franklin Gardner** sent Col. Frank P. Powers with 600 men to Plains Store, a vital crossroads northeast of Port Hudson.

Skirmishing broke out at the crossroads on the morning of May 21 as Powers encountered Nathan A. M. Dudley's **brigade**. Low on ammunition, Powers withdrew but then attacked late in the day after receiving 400 reinforcements under Col. William R. Miles. At first Powers successfully drove back one Union **regiment** and captured a cannon. Augur then forced the Confederates back in a counterattack and recaptured the gun. Powers withdrew to Port Hudson, and Banks united with Augur the next day and completed the encirclement of Gardner's garrison. Powers lost approximately 100 men in the fight, while Augur lost about 150.

PLANK ROAD. This was a road that usually ran through low or swampy ground and had wooden planks on its surface to keep wagons from sinking in the mud.

PLEASANT HILL, LOUISIANA, BATTLE OF (APRIL 9, 1864). On April 8, 1864, **Richard Taylor's** small Confederate **army** stopped **Nathanial P. Banks's** advance in the **Red River Campaign** at **Mansfield, Louisiana,** and Banks withdrew during the night to Pleasant Hill. Unnerved by the battle, Banks sent his wagon train and part of his cavalry back to Natchitoches (NAK-uh-tish) while the rest of the army spent April 9 preparing a defense at Pleasant Hill. By the afternoon of April 9, he had about 12,000 men from **Andrew Jackson Smith's** and **William H. Emory's** divisions in a line stretching across and to the left of the Mansfield Road through mostly thick pine forest. Wide gaps, however, were scattered throughout the line, and Banks made no effort to close them.

Taylor was reinforced by **Thomas J. Churchill's** 4,000-man **division** on the night of April 8 and approached Pleasant Hill the next day with about 12,000 men. In a somewhat complicated **tactical** plan, he sent Churchill on a sweep to the right to hit the Federal left flank. **John G. Walker's** division was placed on the right of the road with orders to attack and link up with Churchill when he heard the assault begin. Two cavalry **brigades** were stationed astride the road to charge Pleasant Hill when the Union flank was crushed, and two more were to ride around Banks's right flank and cut his line of retreat.

Because of his men's exhaustion, Taylor was unable to deploy until mid-afternoon. Then Churchill took a wrong road and hit the Union left center instead of the left flank. Heavy fighting broke out at about 5:00 P.M. as Churchill drove one of Emory's brigades out of a deep ravine and back almost to town. Emory counterattacked and drove the Confederates back. Fighting spread down the line toward the road, but the Confederates were unable to make any headway without Churchill dislodging the enemy flank. Fighting finally broke off after dark.

Although Banks could claim a tactical victory, he threw it away by ordering a retreat to Natchitoches that night. Strategically, the Battle of

Pleasant Hill was a Confederate victory because it turned back Banks's invasion. At Pleasant Hill, Banks lost 1,369 men to Taylor's 1,626. Taylor was prepared to follow up the Federals and attack again, but **Edmund Kirby Smith** ordered him to send much of his force to **Arkansas** to stop Union Maj. Gen. **Frederick Steele's Camden Expedition.** As a result, Taylor could do little more than follow Banks and harass his retreat.

PLEASONTON, ALFRED (1824–1897) USA. A native of **Washington, D.C.,** Pleasonton graduated from **West Point** in 1844. He was **brevetted** for gallantry while serving in the **Mexican War** and afterward fought **Indians** on the frontier and in the **Seminole Wars.**

When the Civil War began, Pleasonton was in Utah serving as a captain in the 2nd Dragoons (later named the 2nd U.S. Cavalry). He led the **regiment** to **Washington, D.C.,** in the autumn of 1861 and served in the city's defenses that winter. Promoted to major in February 1862, Pleasonton commanded the regiment in the **Army of the Potomac** during the **Peninsula** and **Seven Days Campaigns** when it was attached to **George B. McClellan's** headquarters. McClellan was impressed with Pleasonton and had him promoted to brigadier general of volunteers in July 1862.

Pleasonton at first was given command of a cavalry **brigade** in the Army of the Potomac, but he quickly rose to command a **division**, which he led in the **Antietam, Fredericksburg,** and **Chancellorsville Campaigns.** In none of these campaigns did he perform particularly well, and he never was successful at gathering useful intelligence on enemy movements. At Antietam, Pleasonton won a **brevet** for **skirmishing** and guarding the **army's** wagon train, but then he failed to prevent **J. E. B. Stuart's** Confederate cavalry from riding around the army afterward. Because of personal competition, cavalry commander **George Stoneman** left Pleasonton behind with a single brigade to serve the army during the **Chancellorsville Campaign** while he made his raid toward **Richmond, Virginia. Stoneman's Raid** failed, and when Pleasonton's role in holding the Union line at Hazel Grove became exaggerated, he was named to replace Stoneman in May 1863. He was promoted to major general of volunteers the following month.

Some of Pleasonton's finest moments came in 1863 when his cavalry finally began to fight on equal terms with the Confederates. His troopers' performance at **Brandy Station, Aldie, Middleburg,** and **Upperville** brought Pleasonton accolades, but during the **Gettysburg Campaign,** he did not lead his men much in the field and failed to gather the vital intelligence needed by **George G. Meade.** Pleasonton's position was weakened further in early 1864 when he opposed the **Kilpatrick-Dahlgren Raid**, which was supported by the administration. When **U. S. Grant** reorganized the Union armies in March 1864, Pleasonton was replaced by **Philip H. Sheridan**. Sent west, he was put in command of the District of Central Missouri in July and performed well in resisting **Sterling Price's 1864 Missouri Raid**, particularly at **Westport** and **Marais des Cygnes River**, and received another brevet.

Pleasonton remained in the **army** after the war. He left the volunteers in January 1866 and reverted to his regular rank of major, although he had been brevetted major general of regulars. Unhappy that so many officers he had commanded during the war now outranked him, Pleasonton resigned his commission in 1868. He served in the Internal Revenue Service and at other minor government posts before being placed on the army's retired list in 1888—as a major.

PLUM POINT BEND, TENNESSEE, BATTLE OF (MAY 10, 1862). *See* PLUM RUN BEND, TENNESSEE, BATTLE OF.

PLUM RUN BEND, TENNESSEE, BATTLE OF (MAY 10, 1862). After the Union captured **New Madrid and Island No. 10** in early 1862, plans were made to move down the Mississippi River, force the Confederates out of **Fort Pillow, Tennessee,** and capture Memphis, Tennessee. Before any operation could be launched, Maj. Gen. **John Pope** was transferred to **Virginia** and Flag Officer **Andrew H. Foote** went on sick leave. This left the Union fleet commanded by Capt. **Charles H. Davis**.

The Confederate's **River Defense Fleet** was commanded by James E. Montgomery, who decided to strike the enemy first. With an assortment of eight lightly armed **cottonclads** and **rams**, he attacked Davis's 24 ships on May 10, 1862, at Plum Run Bend (also known as Plum Point Bend), Tennessee. The attack caught the Federals by surprise, and the USS *Cincinnati* and *Mound City* were sunk after being rammed by the Confederates. After this initial success, Montgomery withdrew when the rest of the Union fleet arrived. The battle had no lasting effect on operations on the Mississippi River. The two Union ships were refloated and put back into service, and the next day the Federals effectively destroyed the Confederate River Defense Fleet at the **First Battle of Memphis**.

PLUMMER, JOSEPH BENNETT (1816–1862) USA. A native of **Massachusetts**, Plummer taught school before entering **West Point** in 1837. After graduating in 1841, he had a routine antebellum career serving at various outposts and was a captain in the 1st U.S. Infantry when the Civil War began.

Plummer was wounded while leading four **companies** at **Wilson's Creek** in August 1861 and was appointed colonel of the 11th Missouri (Union) in September while recuperating. He returned to duty in time to lead his **regiment** at **Fredericktown** in October. In February 1862, Plummer was given command of a **brigade** in the **Army of the Mississippi's** 1st Division, and the following month he took command of the 5th Division. He was promoted to brigadier general of volunteers that same month and led the **division** during operations against **New Madrid and Island No. 10.** In April 1862, Plummer at times commanded a brigade and a division during the **siege of Corinth, Mississippi.** His health broke, perhaps from returning to duty too soon after being wounded, and he had to be relieved of duty in June. Plummer died in camp on August 9.

PLYMOUTH, NORTH CAROLINA, BATTLE OF (APRIL 17–20, 1864). In April 1864, Confederate Gen. **Braxton Bragg** ordered the **CSS Albemarle** on the Roanoke River and **Robert F. Hoke's** three infantry **brigades** to capture Union-held Plymouth, North Carolina. When Hoke began bombarding and probing the Union defenses on April 17, Union Brig. Gen. **Henry W. Wessells** unsuccessfully appealed for reinforcements to support his four infantry **regiments** and small force of cavalry and **artillery.**

On April 19, the *Albemarle* attacked the Union ships in the river, ramming and sinking the *Southfield,* damaging the *Miami,* and forcing the others to withdraw. The next day, Hoke attacked the city from its undefended east side with **Matt W. Ransom's brigade,** while he **demonstrated** against the main Union position of Fort Williams from the west. Caught between the two forces and bombarded by the *Albemarle,* Wessells was forced to surrender. In the action, Hoke captured nearly 3,000 **prisoners,** while losing only 300 men.

POE, ORLANDO METCALFE (1832–1895) USA. A native of **Ohio,** Poe graduated from **West Point** in 1856. Assigned to the **engineers,** he helped survey the Great Lakes and was a 1st lieutenant when the Civil War began.

Poe first served as one of **George B. McClellan's** engineers in the western **Virginia** operations and then was assigned to the **Washington, D.C.,** defenses. He was appointed colonel of the 2nd Michigan in September 1861 and led it during the **Peninsula Campaign.** Poe was on sick leave during the **Seven Days Campaign,** but upon his return in August 1862 he was named commander of a **brigade** in the 1st Division of the **Army of** the Potomac's III Corps. He led this brigade at **Second Manassas** but served in Washington during the **Antietam Campaign**. Poe then was promoted to brigadier general of volunteers in November and was given command of a brigade in the IX Corps' 1st Division. After fighting at **Fredericksburg**, he accompanied the IX Corps to the west, but his brigadier's appointment expired in March 1863 after the Senate failed to confirm it. Poe reverted to captain of engineers (to which he had been promoted in March 1863) in the regular **army**. In that capacity, he served in the west under **Ambrose Burnside** and **William T. Sherman** and won four **brevets** for his service as chief engineer in the **Knoxville, Atlanta, March to the Sea**, and **Carolinas Campaigns**. At war's end, Poe was brevetted brigadier general of regulars for his wartime service.

Poe remained in the engineers after the war and served as Sherman's aide from 1873 to 1884 with the staff rank of colonel. Afterward, he worked on numerous national projects as an engineer until being injured while working on Michigan's Soo locks in 1895. This injury forced Poe's retirement and ultimate death.

POINDEXTER'S FARM, VIRGINIA, BATTLE OF (JULY 1, 1862). *See* MALVERN HILL, VIRGINIA, BATTLE OF.

POINT D'APPUI. A French term, *point d'appui* (pwan-da-PWEE) means a "support" or "fulcrum." In military terms, it refers to a strong or fortified position that gives one control over a particular area.

POINT LOOKOUT, MARYLAND. Located on a peninsula where the Potomac River enters Chesapeake Bay, this Union **prison** camp was begun in August 1863 to house the large number of Confederate enlisted men taken **prisoner** at **Gettysburg**. Officially known as Camp Hoffman, after Commissary General of Prisoners William Hoffman, it covered about 40 acres of low, sandy ground and was divided into two walled pens. The prison was notorious for having bad water and overcrowded, unsanitary living conditions. Officially, 3,584 deaths were recorded at Point Lookout, but the total may have exceeded 4,000. By May 1865, nearly 20,000 prisoners were housed in tents, suffering from intense winter cold and summer mosquitoes. Housing approximately 52,000 prisoners during its existence, Point Lookout probably was the largest prison camp of the Civil War. It closed in July 1865.

POISON SPRING, ARKANSAS, BATTLE OF (APRIL 18, 1864). While **Nathanial P. Banks** advanced on Shreveport, **Louisiana**, in the 1864 **Red River Campaign**, Maj. Gen. **Frederick Steele** launched the

Camden Expedition in **Arkansas.** After fighting a small battle at **Prairie D'Ane** in early April, Steele finally reached Camden after suffering severe supply shortages, owing to the poor land he traveled over. On April 17, 1864, Steele dispatched a 700-man **foraging** expedition into the countryside under Col. James M. Williams. After filling 200 wagons with supplies, Williams was returning to Camden on April 18 when he was reinforced by nearly 500 more men. At about mid-morning, his train was attacked at Poison Spring by 3,600 Confederate cavalrymen under **John S. Marmaduke** and **Samuel B. Maxey.** Williams at first held his ground and even pushed back the enemy with a counterattack. But then he was attacked from the rear, and his line crumbled. Williams's survivors fled back to Camden without their wagons and four guns.

During the battle, the Confederates probably **massacred** a number of **black troops** in the **1st Kansas Colored Volunteers** who were wounded or trying to surrender. This one **regiment** suffered most of the Union casualties, losing 117 dead and 65 wounded. The Confederates, however, denied the murder charges and claimed the blacks simply fought to the death. For the entire battle, Williams lost 301 men to the Confederates' 114. The losses could have been worse, but Maxey assumed command after Marmaduke had fought the battle and prevented him from pursuing the beaten enemy. Soon after the battle, Steele learned of Banks's retreat from **Mansfield** and **Pleasant Hill,** and he began withdrawing to **Little Rock** a few days later.

POLIGNAC, CAMILLE ARMAND JULES MARIE, PRINCE DE (1832–1913) CSA. A native of France, Polignac's (Poe-leen-YAK) mother was British and his father had served as president of Charles X's council of ministers. After graduating from St. Stanislaus College, where he won first place in a European-wide math competition, he joined the French army in 1853 and fought in the Crimean War as a lieutenant. Polignac then resigned his commission in 1859 and took a research trip to Central America to study botany.

Polignac was still in Central America when the Civil War began. He had become acquainted with **P. G. T. Beauregard** while traveling through the United States and wrote him to offer his services to the Confederacy. As a result, Polignac was appointed lieutenant colonel of infantry in July 1861 and was made Beauregard's chief of staff. The small Frenchman became a colorful member of the **Confederate army.** He had black hair, white teeth, and waxed moustache; spoke fluent English; drank like a sailor; and cursed "like a trooper" (Davis, ed., *The Confederate General,* vol. 5, 41). Polignac served Beauregard at **Shiloh** and

Corinth, and then was on **Braxton Bragg's** staff for the **Kentucky Campaign**. He was commended for the **Battle of Richmond**, where he picked up a **regiment's** fallen **flag** and exhorted the men to stand fast. Polignac's bravery won him promotion to brigadier general in January 1863.

Assigned to the **Trans-Mississippi Department** in March 1863, Polignac was given command of a **brigade** of Texans in **Richard Taylor's army** in **Louisiana**. The Texans at first disliked their commander and called him "a damn frog-eating Frenchman" (Davis, ed., *The Confederate General*, vol. 5, 41). They also had trouble pronouncing his name and referred to him as "General Polecat," holding their noses when he passed by. Polignac won them over, however, when he led an expedition into central **Louisiana** in early 1864 to rout out **Jayhawkers**, capture needed mounts, and break up Union lessee plantations. He also engaged some Union gunboats on the Ouachita (WASH-hi-taw) River.

During the 1864 **Red River Campaign**, Polignac's brigade served in **Alfred Mouton's division**. At **Mansfield**, he was praised for taking over the division when Mouton was killed and keeping the attack going. One soldier also claimed the general was slightly wounded, but there is no official record of it. The next day, Polignac saw more combat at **Pleasant Hill**. Retaining command of the division, he **skirmished** with the retreating enemy and led his men in the campaign's last battle at **Yellow Bayou**. Promoted to major general in June 1864, Polignac was given permanent command of the division. (Polignac and **Patrick Cleburne** were the only two foreign-born officers to become Confederate major generals.) When he was ordered across the Mississippi River to reinforce **Mobile, Alabama**, many of his men **deserted**, and others refused to leave Louisiana. As a result, Polignac was ordered to remain in the Trans-Mississippi Department. His last service to the Confederacy was in early 1865 when he volunteered to travel to France to seek aid from Napoleon III. Polignac was in Spain on this mission when the war ended.

Polignac returned to his French estate and resumed his academic career, studying math and political economy and writing several articles on the war. Rejoining the French army as a major general in 1870, he saw service in the Franco-Prussian War as commander of the 1st French Division and won the Legion of Honor. Polignac was the last surviving Confederate major general before his death in 1913. As late as the 1990s, his son was still alive in France.

POLK, LEONIDAS (1806–1864) CSA. A native of **North Carolina**, Polk was the uncle of Confederate general **Lucius E. Polk**. He attended the University of North Carolina before entering **West Point** in 1823. While there, Polk became friends with fellow cadet **Jefferson Davis** and accepted Christianity. He resigned his commission shortly after graduating in 1827 and attended the Virginia Theological Seminary. Polk then was ordained an Episcopal minister and for a time was an assistant rector of a **Richmond, Virginia**, church. He resigned his position because of poor health, and eventually moved to **Tennessee**, where he worked as a minister and planter. Although Polk had little experience, he was named Missionary Bishop of the Southwest in 1838 and the bishop of **Louisiana** in 1841. He failed as a Louisiana planter and was starting the University of the South at Sewanee, Tennessee, when the war intervened.

Polk welcomed Louisiana's **secession** and even seceded his Louisiana diocese from the church. Davis appointed his friend major general in June 1861 and allowed him to command **Department No. 2** from July to September, even though Polk had no real military experience. Later, he was put in command of a **division** within the **department**, but in September 1861, he made one of the Confederacy's gravest errors when he violated **Kentucky's** neutrality without orders and occupied the strategic town of Columbus. Polk then persuaded Davis to let him stay in Columbus and thus turned many Kentuckians against the Confederacy and gave the Union an excuse to enter the state with a larger force.

Polk commanded the Confederate troops at the small **Battle of Belmont**, but afterward he was put out of action for a few weeks when he was injured when a cannon accidentally exploded. During his tenure in Kentucky, he quarreled with **Gideon J. Pillow** and resented being under the command of **Albert Sidney Johnston**, his former West Point roommate. Polk even submitted his resignation, but Davis refused to accept it. In late March 1862, he was given command of a **corps** in Johnston's **Army of Mississippi**. He led it at **Shiloh** and then commanded **Braxton Bragg's** Right Wing during the **Kentucky Campaign**. Polk did not serve particularly well in Kentucky, once disobeying Bragg's orders to strike the enemy advancing on Frankfort and later disobeying orders by delaying his attack at **Perryville**. At Perryville, Polk barely escaped death or capture when he mistakenly rode up to what he thought was a Confederate line and began barking out orders to the Federals to stop firing on a Confederate unit.

After the Kentucky Campaign, Polk was one of the officers who schemed unsuccessfully to have Bragg relieved of command. He was promoted to lieutenant general in October 1862 and led his corps in the **Stones River**, **Tullahoma**, and **Chickamauga Campaigns**. In the days preceding this last battle, Polk again disobeyed Bragg's orders and prevented him from attacking. When on the second day of Chickamauga, he delayed the right wing's attack, a furious Bragg finally relieved him of command after the battle. Davis tried to resolve the matter, but failing that he transferred Polk in December 1863 and put him in command of the **Department of Mississippi and East Louisiana**. While serving in this capacity, Polk faced **William T. Sherman** in the **Meridian Campaign** and succeeded in saving most of the important **railroad** stock.

In May 1864, Polk was made a corps commander in **Joseph E. Johnston's Army of Tennessee** for the **Atlanta Campaign**. While atop Pine Mountain on June 14 with other officers, he was killed by a direct hit from an **artillery** shell. Although well-liked by his men, Polk proved to be too independent-minded and uncooperative to be a good corps commander.

POLK, LUCIUS EUGENE (1833–1892) CSA. A native of **North Carolina**, Polk was the nephew of Confederate general **Leonidas Polk**. As a child, he moved to **Tennessee** with his family and attended the University of Virginia for one year. Moving to **Arkansas**, Polk was a prosperous planter when the Civil War began.

In early 1861, Polk entered Confederate service as a private in **Patrick Cleburne's** Yell Rifles of the 1st Arkansas (changed to the 15th Arkansas in December 1861), but he quickly was elected a 2nd lieutenant. The **regiment** first served west of the Mississippi River but then was transferred to **Mississippi** in early 1862. At **Shiloh**, Polk was wounded in the face while commanding his **company**, but a few days later, he was elected regimental colonel. As part of Cleburne's **brigade**, he helped form the rear guard during the retreat from the **siege of Corinth, Mississippi**. He then participated in the **Kentucky Campaign** and received a second wound to the head at **Richmond**. Polk was back on duty in time for the **Battle of Perryville**, where he received his third wound.

In December 1862, Polk was promoted to brigadier general and took command of Cleburne's brigade in the **Army of Tennessee** when Cleburne was made **division** commander. He led the brigade well in the **Stones River, Tullahoma**, and **Chickamauga Campaigns**. Polk played a key role in breaking the Union line on the second day of Chickamauga and then received high praise for fighting with Cleburne at **Missionary Ridge** during the **Chattanooga Campaign** and for helping form the rear guard at **Ringgold Gap, Georgia**. During the **Atlanta Campaign**, he was severely wounded by a shell at **Kennesaw Mountain**. Polk never recovered completely from this wound and was forced to retire from the **army**.

After the war, Polk became a Tennessee planter. He opposed the Ku Klux Klan during **Reconstruction**, once intervening on the behalf of a

freedman who was to be whipped, served as a delegate at the 1884 **Democratic** National Convention, and was elected a state senator in 1887.

POLLARD, EDWARD ALFRED (1832–1872) CSA. A native of **Virginia**, Pollard attended Virginia's Hampden-Sydney College and the University of Virginia but was expelled from the William and Mary law school for misconduct. He then participated in the **California** Gold Rush and became a journalist there. After a trip to Asia, Pollard returned to the East Coast and resumed his journalism career by becoming a spokesman for Southern causes.

Pollard was living in **Washington, D.C.**, when the Civil War began and immediately supported the Confederacy. He and his brother, H. Rivers Pollard, moved to **Richmond, Virginia**, and joined the staff of the **Richmond** *Examiner*. Pollard served as the paper's acting editor in the summer of 1862 while editor John Moncure Daniel was absent and wrote first drafts of editorials, which Daniel then edited and published. Pollard also began publishing yearly volumes on the war's history, beginning in 1862. In all of his writings, Pollard followed Daniel's lead and strongly criticized **Jefferson Davis**. In 1864, he was captured by the **U.S. Navy** while trying to run the **blockade** to Europe and was kept a **prisoner** until **exchanged** in January 1865.

After the war, Pollard became one of the best known Southern writers on the **Lost Cause**. His *Southern History of the War* was published in an 1866 abridged edition entitled *The Lost Cause,* in which he coined the popular phrase "Lost Cause" and harshly blamed Davis for losing the war. Pollard left the *Examiner* in 1867 and edited two newspaper of his own. He eventually became reconciled to the South's defeat, softened his writings, and began advocating reconciliation.

POMEROY CIRCULAR. Union Secretary of the Treasury **Salmon P. Chase** never believed **Abraham Lincoln** deserved the presidency and schemed to win the 1864 election himself. In the months preceding the election, he secretly began courting leading **Republican** figures who believed the Lincoln administration was unable to win the war. One of these was **Kansas** Sen. Samuel C. Pomeroy. Pomeroy wrote, or had written, a letter for private circulation that criticized Lincoln and praised Chase. Unfortunately for Chase, the letter was made public when it was published in **Washington, D.C.**, newspapers in February 1864. Horrified that his hand had been exposed, Chase denied any knowledge of the Pomeroy Circular and offered to resign. Lincoln refused it, and a chastised Chase stopped his maneuvering when leading Republicans came to Lincoln's support.

PONTOON BRIDGE. A pontoon bridge was a rapidly deployed, temporary floating bridge that was made by anchoring special wooden or canvas boats called pontoons in a line across a river. Bridging material then was laid across the boats. Three of the longest pontoon bridges in American history up to that time were constructed during the Civil War. In late 1863, Confederate forces in **Louisiana** laid a bridge across the Atchafalaya (uh-CHAF-uh-LIE-uh) River, followed in May 1864 by one built by **Nathaniel P. Banks's** Union **army** at the end of the **Red River Campaign**. These bridges were eclipsed in June 1864 by a 2,200-foot-long pontoon bridge on the James River that allowed **U. S. Grant's armies** to cross the river at the end of the **Overland Campaign** and advance on **Petersburg, Virginia**.

POOK TURTLES. When James B. Eads was contracted by the U.S. government in August 1861 to construct **ironclads** for use on the western rivers, he hired Samuel M. Pook and Thomas Merritt to design the ships. This collaboration led to the construction at St. Louis, Missouri, and Mound City, Illinois, of seven so-called city class ships—the *Cairo, Carondelet, Cincinnati, Louisville, Mound City, Pittsburg,* and *St. Louis* (later renamed the *Baron De Kalb*). Known as Pook Turtles, the ships were 175 feet long, displaced 512 tons, and had a draft of six feet. Each also had sloping sides covered in iron plating and an assortment of **rifled** and smoothbore guns.

POPE, JOHN (1822–1892) USA. A native of **Kentucky**, Pope was a distant descendant of George Washington, the son of a prominent territorial secretary and federal judge, and a nephew of a U.S. senator, as well as being related by marriage to **Mary Todd Lincoln**. After graduating from **West Point** in 1842, he was assigned to the **engineers** and won two **brevets** for gallantry in the **Mexican War**. When the Civil War began, Pope was still serving in the engineers as a captain.

Pope was a highly respected officer in 1861, not to mention well connected. He was appointed brigadier general of volunteers in June and was placed under **John C. Frémont** in the **Western Department**. Pope performed well and finally was put in charge of capturing the upper Mississippi River. After skillfully seizing **New Madrid** in March 1862, he was promoted to major general of volunteers. Pope then captured **Island No. 10**, as well, and participated in the **siege of Corinth, Mississippi**, in command of **Henry W. Halleck's** left wing. Afterward, he was brought to **Virginia** and was put in command of the **Army of Virginia** after **George B. McClellan** was defeated in the **Seven Days Campaign**. In July, Pope was appointed to brigadier general of regulars.

Pope's reputation was ruined in Virginia. His quick rise to prominence angered some generals (former commander Frémont refused to serve under him in Virginia) and his arrogant, tactless demeanor won no friends. One of Pope's first steps was to issue a greeting to his new soldiers in which he unintentionally insulted them by saying he came from the west where his men were used to seeing only the backside of Confederates. When one signed dispatch bore the heading "Headquarters in the Saddle," men quipped that his headquarters were where his hindquarters should be. The classic response to Pope came from Brig. Gen. **Samuel Sturgis**, who reportedly said, "I don't care for John Pope one pinch of owl dung" (Warner, *Generals in Blue,* 487). Pope also became hated by Confederates, because his destructive advance in northern Virginia left many private homes destroyed and the countryside ravaged. It was said that he was the only Union general for whom **Robert E. Lee** developed an intense personal dislike.

In the **Second Manassas Campaign,** Pope was completely outmaneuvered by Lee and **Stonewall Jackson.** When Jackson raided the Union supply base at Manassas Junction, Pope unwisely turned his back on Lee and the rest of the **Army of Northern Virginia** to deal with Jackson. During fighting at **Groveton** and **Second Manassas,** he seemed to have forgotten about Lee and allowed the Confederates to reunite and win a stunning victory. Afterward, Pope blamed his subordinates for the defeat and preferred charges against **Fitz John Porter,** which led to Porter being cashiered from the **army.** He also believed, perhaps correctly, that McClellan intentionally delayed sending him reinforcements as part of a plan to have him defeated so McClellan could retake command.

Pope ultimately was held responsible for the defeat, was relieved of command in September 1862, and was given command of the **Department of the Northwest.** There, he put down **Minnesota's Sioux uprising** and performed well overall. At the end of the war, Pope was brevetted major general of regulars before being mustered out of the volunteers in September 1866. Remaining in the regulars, he held various **department** commands and was promoted to major general before his retirement in 1886.

POPLAR SPRING CHURCH, VIRGINIA, BATTLE OF (SEPTEMBER 30–OCTOBER 2, 1864). *See* PEEBLES' FARM, VIRGINIA, BATTLE OF.

POPULAR SOVEREIGNTY. Popular sovereignty was the belief that the voters of a territory should decide for themselves whether or not to allow **slavery** and not have it dictated to them by the **U.S. Congress**. Although the theory was made popular by **Stephen A. Douglas** in his 1854 **Kansas-Nebraska Act**, it had been around since the 1840s. Lewis Cass even espoused popular sovereignty when he ran for president on the **Democratic** ticket in 1848. Although both North and South liked the idea, they argued over when it could be used. Southerners believed slavery had to be allowed in the territory first so proslavery voters could have a chance to establish themselves before action was taken, while Northerners believed the territorial legislature could act on the issue at any time. In effect, the **U.S. Supreme Court** declared popular sovereignty unconstitutional in the 1857 **Dred Scott case**, when it ruled that territories could not outlaw slavery within their boundaries.

PORT GIBSON, MISSISSIPPI, BATTLE OF (MAY 1, 1863). On April 30, 1863, Maj. Gen. **U. S. Grant** crossed the Mississippi River at Bruinsburg, Mississippi, with his **Army of the Tennessee** to begin the **Vicksburg Campaign** in earnest. Confederate Brig. Gen. **John S. Bowen**, who was stationed at **Grand Gulf, Mississippi**, received reinforcements from **John C. Pemberton** at **Vicksburg** and sent troops to contest the crossing. On May 1, two Confederate **brigades** were deployed just west of Port Gibson, Mississippi, in a position to block the Federals as they marched inland from Bruinsburg. **Martin E. Green's** brigade was on the Rodney Road, while **Edward Dorr Tracy's** brigade blocked the roughly parallel Bruinsburg Road to the north. This left a wide gap separating the two Confederate wings, but Bowen believed the rough, thick terrain would minimize the danger.

Grant began marching inland along the Rodney Road on the night of April 30. **Skirmishing** broke out after midnight around the Shaifer House, located near an intersection where a short north-south road connected the Rodney Road with the Bruinsburg Road. At sunrise, May 1, Grant had about 23,000 men on hand, with **John A. McClernand's corps** in the front. McClernand sent **Peter J. Osterhaus's** division north along the intersecting road toward the Bruinsburg Road and Tracy's position, while the rest of the corps advanced on the Rodney Road against Green. Bowen arrived that morning to assume command of the Confederates after the fighting had already begun. The badly outnumbered Confederates fought desperately along the Rodney Road around Magnolia Church against the **divisions** of **Eugene A. Carr** and **Alvin P. Hovey**. At mid-morning, they fell back toward Port Gibson and took up a position behind the newly arrived brigades of **William E. Baldwin** and **Francis M. Cockrell**.

To the north, Tracy was killed by a bullet to the chest, but his brigade fought well under **Isham W. Garrott** as it was forced back slowly. Bowen sent Green's brigade as reinforcements, but nothing could stop the Union advance. Even though a Confederate counterattack along the Rodney Road briefly pushed back the Federals, the Confederates ultimately were forced back on both roads as **John A. Logan's** division of **James B. McPherson's** corps entered the fight.

Bowen urgently called for reinforcements from Pemberton and warned him that Grant's advance could threaten **Jackson, Mississippi** and cut off Vicksburg and **Port Hudson, Louisiana**, from the east. It was too late, however, and Bowen was forced to withdraw that night toward Vicksburg. In less than three weeks, Grant would have Vicksburg surrounded. In the Battle of Port Gibson, Bowen lost four cannons and 787 men out of approximately 8,000 engaged, while Grant suffered 875 casualties.

PORT HUDSON, LOUISIANA, CAMPAIGN (MAY 14–JULY 8, 1863). While **U. S. Grant** carried out the **Vicksburg Campaign**, **Nathanial P. Banks's Army of the Gulf** besieged Port Hudson, Louisiana. Port Hudson was located about 25 miles north of **Baton Rouge** and was the only other Confederate stronghold on the Mississippi River. If both **Vicksburg** and Port Hudson were captured, the Union would have complete control of the river. Recognizing the importance of Port Hudson, the Confederates had spent a year preparing its defenses, which included 4.5 miles of earthworks, and by the spring of 1863, it was as well defended as Vicksburg. Within its perimeter were about 7,000 Confederate troops under Maj. Gen. **Franklin Gardner**.

On March 14, 1863, Adm. **David G. Farragut** attempted to run his fleet upstream past Port Hudson to cut off Confederate supplies coming down the Red River from the west. Only two ships made it, however, and he was unable to stop the flow of material. Banks then decided to accomplish with his **army** what Farragut had failed to do with the **U.S. Navy**. First, he cleared **Richard Taylor's** small Confederate army out of south Louisiana in the **Bayou Teche Campaign** to deny the Port Hudson garrison supplies from the region and to make certain his rear would not be threatened once he besieged Gardner. After pushing Taylor north of Alexandria, Banks moved down the Red River with three **divisions** on May 14 to begin his attack on Port Hudson. Another two divisions marched north from Baton Rouge toward Port Hudson. On May 21, Gardner engaged the Federals at **Plains Store** in an unsuccessful attempt to prevent the two columns from uniting. Banks then successfully surrounded the garrison with approximately 30,000 men, while Farragut maintained a naval presence on the river.

Seeking to avoid a long siege, Banks ordered a general assault on May 27. The attack was poorly executed and was hampered by the rough terrain. The piecemeal assaults allowed Gardner to take advantage of his **interior line** and skillfully shift troops to defend threatened positions. Banks hit the Confederate left first and was repulsed. This attack included the 1st and 3rd **Louisiana Native Guards**, two of the Union's first **regiments** of **black troops**. The black soldiers fought bravely and advanced as far as their white counterparts but ultimately failed. Banks's attack on the Confederate left was already repulsed by the time he attacked the center. When this second assault was made, the Confederates were ready and inflicted heavy casualties on the Federals. In these futile attacks, Banks lost approximately 2,000 men, while Gardner counted fewer than 500 casualties.

For the next two weeks, Banks gathered reinforcements (eventually having about 40,000 men), brought up more guns, and began siege operations. When Gardner refused a surrender demand on June 13, Banks launched a second attack on Gardner's center the next day, with diversionary attacks being made against the Confederate right flank. **Halbert E. Paine's** division bore the brunt of the main assault, which failed by mid-morning. Banks lost another 1,805 men to Gardner's 200 or less.

After this second failed attack, Banks settled into siege work. For several weeks there was constant **artillery** and **sharpshooter** fire. Gardner's men suffered from malnutrition and were forced to eat rats, while Banks men suffered tremendously from exposure and disease. Still, the Confederates held out until learning of Vicksburg's surrender on July 7. Realizing it was hopeless for him to continue, Gardner agreed to surrender his garrison on July 8 and did so the following day. The siege of Port Hudson was the longest true siege in American history and cost Banks nearly 10,000 casualties (about evenly divided between battle and disease). Gardner lost approximately 1,000 dead and wounded and 6,500 captured. With Port Hudson's capture, **Abraham Lincoln** claimed that the Mississippi River flowed "unvexed" to the sea.

PORT REPUBLIC, VIRGINIA, BATTLE OF (JUNE 9, 1862). By early June 1862, Maj. Gen. **Thomas "Stonewall" Jackson's 1862 Shenandoah Valley Campaign** had routed the Federals from the **Shenandoah Valley**, but he was in danger of being trapped by converging enemy forces. Racing back up the Valley, he was pressed from the rear by Union Maj. Gen. **John C. Frémont**, while **James Shields** moved on a parallel course to the east through the Luray Valley. Jackson had destroyed all of the bridges across the South Fork, which separated him from Shields, and thus prevented Shields and Frémont from uniting. The nearest standing bridges across the river that would allow Jackson to escape eastward across the Blue Ridge Mountains were at Port Republic, where the North and South Rivers joined to form the South Fork of the Shenandoah. On June 8, **Richard Ewell's** division defeated Frémont at **Cross Keys** while Jackson engaged Shields's advance guard four miles to the southwest at Port Republic. Jackson barely escaped capture but held on to the river crossings. The next morning, he left Ewell's **division** at Cross Keys to make sure Frémont posed no further threat and sent **Charles Winder's brigade** across the South River to attack Shields. The commander of Shields's advance, Brig. Gen. **Erastus B. Tyler**, had taken up a strong position with 3,000 men about two miles east of Port Republic. He had anchored his left on the Blue Ridge Mountains, and his line stretched half a mile westward across an elevated plateau to the South Fork. A key position in the line was on the mountainside at the Lewiston Coaling, where Tyler had positioned a seven-gun **artillery** battery.

Advancing across an open field, the Confederates were raked by Union infantry and the artillery at the Coaling. Soon **Richard Taylor's** brigade crossed the river to support Winder. Jackson took one of Taylor's **regiments** to reinforce Winder and sent the rest to attack the deadly battery. Winder was repulsed again, but he ordered a near suicide charge to buy time for Taylor to get into position for his attack. Winder was being forced from the field, when Ewell arrived with two regiments on the left flank and helped stabilize the line. At about the same time, Taylor finally launched his surprise attack and vicious hand-to-hand fighting broke out at the battery, which changed hands several times before Taylor, with help from Ewell, managed to capture six of the guns. With his left flank broken, Shields withdrew from the field and was pursued five miles by Jackson.

In the bloody fighting, which ended Jackson's Shenandoah Valley Campaign, the Confederates lost 800 men, while Shields counted some 1,000 casualties, half of whom were taken **prisoner**. Jackson then escaped by burning the bridge across the river and marching to the Blue Ridge Mountains. A few weeks later, he joined **Robert E. Lee** outside **Richmond, Virginia**, for the **Seven Days Campaign**.

PORT ROYAL, SOUTH CAROLINA, BATTLE OF (NOVEMBER 7, 1861). As the Union began its **blockade** of the Confederacy in 1861, an expedition was launched to capture Port Royal, South Carolina, to serve as a coaling and supply station for ships on blockade duty. With 77 ships and the support of 12,000 infantrymen under **Thomas W. Sherman**, Flag Officer **Samuel F. Du Pont** left Hampton Roads, Virginia, on October 29, 1861. The entrance to Port Royal Sound was defended by poorly trained Confederates, at Hilton Head, who had 41 guns in Forts Beauregard and Walker. Du Pont attacked on the morning of November 7. Placing his ships in a continuously moving circle between the forts, he kept both under constant bombardment. The garrisons held out until afternoon but finally abandoned Fort Walker after running out of ammunition. Ninety minutes later, Fort Beauregard also was abandoned, and Port Royal was captured. At a cost of only 31 men, Du Pont had secured for the **U.S. Navy** a vital base for its blockading operations. The Confederates lost 66 men in the two forts. Two days later, Du Pont attacked and captured Beaufort, South Carolina.

PORT WALTHALL JUNCTION, VIRGINIA, BATTLE OF (MAY 6–7, 1864). As part of **U. S. Grant's strategy** to end the war in the spring of 1864, Maj. Gen. **Benjamin F. Butler** was to attack **Petersburg, Virginia**, with his **Army of the James** to cut the Richmond & Petersburg Railroad, which brought supplies to **Robert E. Lee's Army of Northern Virginia**. While Grant and Lee battled it out in the **Wilderness**, Butler landed his 39,000 men at Bermuda Hundred on May 5 and began the **Bermuda Hundred Campaign**.

Petersburg was defended by Gen. **P. G. T. Beauregard**, but he was greatly outnumbered. Butler, however, entrenched on May 6 after advancing only a short distance and gave Beauregard and his subordinate, **George E. Pickett**, time to prepare a defense. That afternoon, Butler sent **Charles Heckman's** XVIII Corps **brigade** to cut the **railroad** at Port Walthall Junction. Heckman attacked **Bushrod R. Johnson's** brigade at the junction, but he quickly broke off the engagement for fear of being outnumbered. After dark, **Johnson Hagood's** brigade arrived to reinforce Johnson, along with **Daniel H. Hill**, who simply acted as an adviser to the two Confederate brigadiers. On May 7, Butler sent Brig. Gen. **William T. H. Brooks's division** back to the junction. Brooks overwhelmed Johnson's brigade and tore up some track before withdrawing that afternoon, but the railroad was later repaired. Butler lost 289 men in the operation, while the Confederates counted 184 casualties.

PORTER, ANDREW (1820–1872) USA. Porter was a native of **Pennsylvania** and the first cousin of both **Mary Todd Lincoln's** mother and **U. S. Grant's** aide, Horace Porter. Entering **West Point** in 1836, Porter dropped out after only six months, but he was commissioned a 1st lieutenant in the **U.S. Army** during the **Mexican War**. He was promoted to captain during the war and won two **brevets** for gallantry. Porter remained in the **army** afterward and served on the **Texas** frontier and in the Southwest.

In May 1861, Porter was appointed colonel of the 16th U.S. Infantry. Later that month, he took command of a **brigade** in northeastern **Virginia** and led it at **First Manassas**. When his superior, **David Hunter**, was wounded, Porter assumed command of the **division**. He was appointed provost martial of **Washington, D.C.**, at the end of July 1861 and was promoted to brigadier general of volunteers the following month. In October, Porter was named provost martial for the **Army of the Potomac** and served in that capacity until August 1862. Afterward, he enforced **conscription** and served in Washington, but he was often sick. Porter resigned his volunteer and regular commissions in April 1864 and moved to France.

PORTER, DAVID DIXON (1813–1891) USA. A native of **Pennsylvania** and the son of a prominent **U.S. Navy** officer, Porter was the brother of **William D. Porter**, the foster brother of **David G. Farragut**, and a cousin of **Fitz John Porter**. Porter went to sea with his father when he was 10, saw combat against pirates in the Caribbean, and was captured by the Spanish while serving in the Mexican navy in the 1820s. He then joined the **U.S. Navy** in 1829 and served in the **Mexican War**.

In April 1861, Porter was promoted to commander and was given command of the USS *Powhatan*. He led the expedition that relieved **Fort Pickens, Florida**, that spring and then served on **blockade** duty on the Gulf Coast. During this service, Porter unsuccessfully chased the Confederate **commerce raider CSS *Sumter***. In early 1862, he was picked to command the **mortar** flotilla that accompanied Farragut to **Forts Jackson and St. Philip, Louisiana,** for the attack on **New Orleans**. Porter bombarded the forts before Farragut ran past them and then remained behind and accepted the forts' surrender several days later.

Porter was given command of the Mississippi River Squadron in September 1862 with the acting rank of rear admiral and earned a reputation for cooperating well with the **army** in joint operations. He participated in the capture of **Arkansas Post** in early 1863 and then joined **U. S. Grant** for the **Vicksburg Campaign**. During the campaign, Porter bravely ran his ships past the Confederate batteries at **Vicksburg, Mississippi,** to get into position to ferry Grant's troops across the Mississippi River. He then participated in the siege by continuously bombarding the city. In recognition of these important actions, Porter's rank of rear admiral was made permanent in July 1863.

In the spring of 1864, Porter cooperated with **Nathaniel P. Banks** in the **Red River Campaign**. He helped capture **Fort De Russy** but was prevented from reaching Shreveport, Louisiana, by low water and a blocked river channel. The falling water nearly trapped Porter's fleet, but he finally escaped through **Joseph Bailey's** Dam. In October 1864, he was given command of the **North Atlantic Blockading Squadron** and participated in the attacks on **Fort Fisher, North Carolina**. When the war ended, Porter was serving on **Virginia's** James River and accompanied **Abraham Lincoln** when he entered **Richmond** in April 1865.

Porter remained in the navy after the war, served as commandant of the **U.S. Naval Academy**, and in 1870 became the navy's senior officer when he was promoted to admiral. Although arrogant, ambitious, and scheming, he was one of the most successful Union navy commanders and played a pivotal role in several important campaigns, earning the **Thanks of Congress** three times.

PORTER, FITZ JOHN (1822–1901) USA. A native of **New Hampshire**, Porter was the son of a **U.S. Navy** officer and a cousin of **David D. Porter** and **William D. Porter**. Although his immediate family had a naval heritage, Porter graduated from **West Point** in 1845. He served with the **artillery** in the **Mexican War**, was wounded at Chapultepec, and won two **brevets** for gallantry. Afterward, Porter served as an artillery instructor at the academy and was **Albert Sidney Johnston's** adjutant during the **Utah Expedition**.

In May 1861, Porter was promoted from 1st lieutenant of artillery to colonel of the 15th U.S. Infantry. That summer he was made **Robert Patterson's** chief of staff but in August was promoted to brigadier general of volunteers and joined **George B. McClellan's Army of the Potomac**. Given a **division** command in October, Porter remained a McClellan supporter for the remainder of the war. He led a III Corps division at the beginning of the **Peninsula Campaign** and rose to command the V Corps in May 1862. Porter fought very well at **Mechanicsville** and **Gaines' Mill** during the **Seven Days Campaign** and covered the **army's** retreat from **Malvern Hill**. His actions in the campaign won him promotion to major general of volunteers and brevet brigadier general of regulars in July.

After the Seven Days Campaign, Porter's **corps** was sent to reinforce **John Pope's Army of Virginia**, but he was open with his dislike of Pope and continued to be loyal to McClellan. At **Second Manassas**,

Pope ordered Porter to attack the Confederate right flank, unaware that **James Longstreet's** corps had arrived on the field and extended the Confederate flank to block such a movement. Porter failed to carry out the order, and Pope blamed him and other officers for the defeat and preferred charges of disloyalty, disobedience, and misconduct against him. After being held in reserve at **Antietam**, Porter was relieved of command in November 1862 and was court-martialed. His loyalty to the now-relieved McClellan doomed him in the politically charged trial that was overseen by anti-McClellan officers. Porter was found guilty in January 1863 and was cashiered from the service. Afterward, he worked in mining, construction, and business and was New York City's police, fire, and public works commissioner.

Porter spent the rest of his life trying to clear his name. In 1878, after passions had cooled, a board headed by **John M. Schofield** reopened the Second Manassas case and ruled that not only had Porter acted properly, he probably had saved the army from destruction by not attacking Longstreet's front. In 1882, President Chester A. Arthur remitted the sentence, and in 1886 the **U.S. Congress** reinstated Porter as a colonel of regulars (although without back pay). He then was retired from the army two days later.

PORTER, JOHN LUKE (1813–1893) CSA. A native of **Virginia**, Porter was the son of a shipwright. During the antebellum period he worked for the **U.S. Navy** as a superintendent of ship construction and developed an **ironclad** design that he would use during the Civil War. Porter was appointed a U.S. naval constructor in 1859, but in 1860 he was tried and acquitted of neglect of duty in connection with the construction of the USS *Seminole*.

Porter resigned his U.S. Navy position in May 1861 and was appointed a naval constructor for the **Confederate navy**. Along with **John M. Brooke** and William P. Williamson, he designed the **CSS Virginia** and then supervised naval construction at Rocketts Navy Yard. Porter became an adviser to Confederate Secretary of the Navy **Stephen R. Mallory** after the *Virginia*'s success and was named the Confederacy's unofficial chief naval constructor in April 1863. This latter position was made formal in January 1864. During the time he supervised naval construction, Porter designed virtually all of the Confederate ironclads, including the ***Albemarle, Arkansas, Columbia, Richmond,*** and ***Tennessee***.

After the war, Porter worked at two Virginia shipyards and became superintendent of the Norfolk County, Virginia, ferries in 1883.

PORTER, WILLIAM DAVID "DIRTY BILL" (1809–1864) USA. A native of **Louisiana**, Porter was the brother of **David D. Porter**, the foster brother of **David G. Farragut**, and a cousin of **Fitz John Porter**. The son of a prominent naval officer, Porter joined the **U.S. Navy** as a midshipman in 1823 and during the antebellum period established a system of lighthouses, designed an exploding shell, and served in the **Mexican War**. Nicknamed "Dirty Bill," he was court-martialed on various charges and was placed in retirement in 1855. Restored to duty in 1859, Porter was commanding a ship in the Pacific when the Civil War began.

Although born in Louisiana, Porter remained loyal to the Union (and even divorced his Louisiana wife to prove it), but his two sons joined the Confederacy. In October 1861, he was sent to Paducah, Kentucky, to take command of the USS *New Era*, soon to be renamed the *Essex*. Porter participated in the attack on **Fort Henry, Tennessee**, but he was forced to jump overboard when an enemy shell penetrated his boiler. Although scalded, he remained on duty and saw further action at **Fort Donelson**. After the *Essex* was repaired, Porter participated in the bombardment of **Vicksburg, Mississippi**, in July 1862, engaged the **CSS *Arkansas*** when it entered the Mississippi River, and fought at the **Battle of Baton Rouge**. During his service, Porter was short-tempered and quarrelsome and feuded with most officers—including his brother and foster brother.

Porter was promoted to commodore in July 1862, but in September, he was ordered to New York City to face accusations made against him by a fellow officer and to explain a highly critical letter he had written about the Navy Department to Secretary of the Navy **Gideon Welles**. He served at various administrative posts afterward and died from heart disease in 1864.

POSEY, CARNOT (1818–1863) CSA. A native of **Mississippi**, Posey attended the College of Louisiana and the University of Virginia before becoming a lawyer and planter in his native state. He served as a 1st lieutenant in **Jefferson Davis's** Mississippi Rifles in the **Mexican War** and was wounded at Buena Vista. After the war, Posey was appointed U.S. District Attorney for southern Mississippi by President **James Buchanan**.

When the Civil War began, Posey organized a volunteer **company** and was elected its captain. The company became part of the 16th Mississippi in June 1861, and he was elected colonel. Sent to **Virginia**, the **regiment** did not see any combat until **Stonewall Jackson's 1862 Shenandoah Valley Campaign**. As part of **Isaac Trimble's** brigade, it fought at **First Winchester** and **Cross Keys**, where Posey was slightly wounded and received a commendation from Trimble. After serving through the **Seven Days Campaign** with the **Army of Northern Virginia**, the regiment became part of **Winfield S. Featherston's brigade**. Posey again won commendations while temporarily commanding the brigade at **Second Manassas** and **Antietam**.

Posey was promoted to brigadier general in November 1862, but he led only his regiment at **Fredericksburg**. When Featherston was transferred west in January 1863, Posey took command of the brigade. Although present during the **Chancellorsville Campaign**, the brigade saw little combat. Placed in **Richard H. Anderson's** III Corps **division**, Posey did not manage his men very well at **Gettysburg** and was repulsed in a piecemeal attack on the second day. On October 14, 1863, he was hit in the leg by a spherical case shot at **Bristoe Station**, but the wound was not considered to be serious. Infection set in, however, and Posey died on November 14.

POTOMAC DEPARTMENT, CONFEDERATE. *See* DEPARTMENT OF ALEXANDRIA (CONFEDERATE).

POTTER, EDWARD ELMER (1823–1889) USA. A native of **New York**, Potter graduated from Columbia University in 1842 and studied law before going to **California** during the Gold Rush. He returned to New York afterward and was a farmer when the Civil War began.

Potter entered Union service in February 1862 when he was commissioned a captain in the commissary department. After serving as chief commissary for **John G. Foster's brigade** in **Ambrose Burnside's** 1862 expedition to **North Carolina**, he was authorized to raise the 1st North Carolina (Union) and was appointed its lieutenant colonel and acting commander in October. In December 1862, Potter was commissioned brigadier general of volunteers. For the rest of the war, he served either as Foster's chief of staff or commander of various posts and commands in the **Departments of Virginia and North Carolina** and **of the South**. He was **brevetted** major general of volunteers for his war service and resigned his commission in July 1865.

After the war, Potter lived in New York and **New Jersey**.

POTTER, ROBERT BROWN (1829–1887) USA. A native of **New York**, Potter was the son of an Episcopal bishop and attended Union College. He left before graduating, and after studying law, opened a practice in New York City.

Potter entered Union service in early 1861 when he joined the state militia as a private. He soon was promoted to lieutenant but in October was appointed major of the 51st New York. Assigned to **Ambrose Burnside's** IX Corps, Potter was promoted to lieutenant colonel in November. During Burnside's 1862 **North Carolina** Expedition, he was commended for his actions at **Roanoke Island** and was wounded at **New Bern**. Transferred to **Virginia**, Potter fought at **Cedar Mountain** and led the **regiment** at **Second Manassas** before being promoted to colonel in early September. His regiment fought at **South Mountain** with the **Army of the Potomac** and was one of the units that successfully stormed **Antietam's** Burnside's Bridge.

After serving at **Fredericksburg**, Potter accompanied Burnside west and was appointed brigadier general of volunteers in March 1863. Given command of the IX Corps' 2nd Division, he served in the **Vicksburg Campaign** and commanded the **corps** during the **Knoxville Campaign**. Returning to Virginia, Potter returned to his **division** and served through the **Overland** and **Petersburg Campaigns**. It was one of his regiments that dug the mine that led to the **Battle of the Crater** at Petersburg, and Potter was the only one of Burnside's division commanders who was present with his men during the assault. His actions early in the Petersburg Campaign won him a **brevet** of major general of volunteers in August 1864. In April 1865, Potter was wounded in the final assault on Petersburg. He was promoted to major general of volunteers in September 1865 and then was mustered out of the service in January 1866.

After the war, Potter worked for a **railroad** and lived for a while in Great Britain.

POTTS, BENJAMIN FRANKLIN (1836–1887) USA. A native of **Ohio**, Potts worked as a store clerk, attended a **Pennsylvania** college for a year, and taught school before becoming a lawyer in 1859. He also served as a delegate at both 1860 **Democratic** National Conventions.

When the Civil War began, Potts raised a volunteer **company** and entered Union service in August 1861 as a captain in the 32nd Ohio. He served in western **Virginia** and fought at **McDowell** and **Cross Keys** under **John C. Frémont**. In November, Potts was promoted to lieutenant colonel and to colonel the following month. Shortly afterward, the **regiment** was transferred west. After fighting in the **Vicksburg Campaign** with the **Army of the Tennessee**, he was given command of a **brigade** in the XVII Corps' 3rd Division in November 1863 and led it in the **Meridian Campaign**. In July 1864, during the **Atlanta Campaign**, Potts was given command of a brigade in the **corps'** 4th Division and led it for the rest of the war. After the **March to the Sea**, he was promoted to brigadier general of volunteers in January 1865 and served through the

Carolinas Campaign. Potts was **brevetted** major general of volunteers for his war service and was mustered out of the **army** in January 1866. Unsuccessful in obtaining a regular colonel's commission, Potts resumed his Ohio law practice and became involved in politics. He served in the state legislature and was governor of the Montana Territory from 1870 to 1883. Afterward, Potts became a rancher and territorial legislator.

POWELL, LEWIS (1844–1865) CSA. Powell was a native of **Florida** who served with the **Army of Northern Virginia**. He was captured at **Gettysburg** but escaped from **prison** and served with **John S. Mosby** in **Virginia** before becoming a courier known as Wood. In this position, Powell met **John Wilkes Booth** and, using the alias Lewis Paine, became part of Booth's conspiracy to kidnap **Abraham Lincoln**. Later, in **Lincoln's assassination** plot, Booth assigned Powell to murder Secretary of State **William Seward**.

On the night of April 14, 1865, Powell went to Seward's house on the pretense of bringing the secretary medicine (Seward had been involved in a serious carriage accident). When he was refused entrance, Powell forced his way into the house, attacked Seward's son and slashed several others before assaulting Seward in his bed with a knife. A neck brace saved Seward from death, but he was badly cut. Powell then ran from the house and escaped, but he was captured at **Mary Surratt's** boarding house on April 17. Found guilty with the other conspirators, he was hanged on July 7, 1865.

POWELL, WILLIAM HENRY (1825–1904) USA. A native of Wales, as a child, Powell immigrated to the United States with his parents and attended schools in **Tennessee**. He became a prominent ironworks engineer and was managing an **Ohio** ironworks when the Civil War began.

Powell entered Union service in November 1861 when a volunteer cavalry **company** he organized became part of the 2nd Virginia Cavalry (Union). Serving as company captain, he participated in raids and **skirmishes** in western **Virginia** and was promoted to major in June 1862. After being promoted to lieutenant colonel in October, Powell led 20 men the following month on a daring raid that captured 500 enemy **prisoners**. For this feat, he was awarded the **Medal of Honor** in 1890.

Promoted to colonel in May 1863, Powell was wounded and captured at Wytheville, Virginia, in July. Held in **Libby Prison**, he was **exchanged** in February 1864 and led a cavalry **brigade** in **David Hunter's Shenandoah Valley Campaign** late that spring. Powell also led a cavalry brigade in **Philip H. Sheridan's Shenandoah Valley Campaign** and fought at **Third Winchester** and **Fisher's Hill**. He then took command of **William Averell's division** at the end of September and led it at **Cedar Creek**. Powell's service there earned him a promotion to brigadier general of volunteers in October 1864. After the battle, he was mostly involved in fighting guerrillas and earned a reputation for summarily executing his captives. Powell resigned his commission in January 1865, perhaps because his superiors disliked his reputation for brutality. Nevertheless, he was later **brevetted** major general of volunteers.

Powell returned to work in Ohio's ironworks, but then he lived in numerous places while building nail factories. He became active in veterans' activities, served as a department commander of the **Grand Army of the Republic**, and was appointed collector of internal revenue by President William McKinley.

PRAIRIE D'ANE, ARKANSAS, BATTLE OF (APRIL 10–13, 1864). In April 1864, Maj. Gen. **Frederick Steele** was advancing through **Arkansas** toward Shreveport, Louisiana, in the **Camden Expedition**. Confederate Maj. Gen. **Sterling Price** took his 5,000 men from Camden in early April and moved northwest to protect Washington. He reached Prairie D'Ane on April 7 and entrenched, and **skirmishing** began as the Federals approached on April 10. After some maneuvering by Steele on April 11, Price withdrew most of his men toward Washington and left only a small force in the entrenchments. On April 12, Steele moved toward Camden in search of food and **forage**, but the next day his rear guard was attacked by the Confederates at Prairie D'Ane. **John M. Thayer**, who commanded the rear guard, repulsed the Confederates and then rejoined Steele for the march to Camden. In the small action at Prairie D'Ane, Steele and Thayer lost about 100 men, while Price suffered about 50 casualties.

PRAIRIE GROVE, ARKANSAS, BATTLE OF (DECEMBER 7, 1862). After **John M. Schofield's Army of the Frontier** forced the Confederates out of southwest **Missouri** in the autumn of 1862, the Union forces were left widely scattered. **James G. Blunt's** 5,000-man **division** was posted in northwestern **Arkansas** near **Indian Territory**, while **Francis J. Herron's** two divisions were more than 70 miles away near Springfield, Missouri. When Schofield took sick leave and left Blunt in command, Blunt advanced deeper into Arkansas, defeated the enemy at **Cane Hill**, and encamped there. Thirty miles south of Cane Hill was the 11,000-man Confederate **Army of the Trans-Mississippi** under

Thomas C. Hindman. Hindman planned to attack Blunt by first fixing him in position with his cavalry and then sending the infantry to the east to get into his rear. If all went well, Blunt would be destroyed before Herron could come to his aid. Suspecting such a move, Blunt ordered Herron to come quickly with his 7,000 men. Herron advanced on December 3, the same day Hindman began his move from Van Buren.

The Confederates spent the next three days marching through the rugged Boston Mountains, while Herron quickly covered the 110 miles from Missouri in an extraordinary march. Learning of Herron's approach on December 6, Hindman abandoned his plan to strike Blunt and instead marched north to attack Herron. By the morning of December 7, Herron's vanguard was at Fayetteville, only 18 miles from Cane Hill.

Hindman and Herron met on the morning of December 7 between Fayetteville and Cane Hill. Hindman fell back to a hill on which the Prairie Grove Church was located and deployed his men in a defensive line around the hill's crest. Herron believed Hindman was simply a blocking force to prevent him from reaching Cane Hill. Determined to cut his way through, he massed his 3,500 men (the rest were straggling behind) against Hindman's right wing and opened a heavy **artillery** bombardment at 10:00 A.M. Herron then attacked, but he encountered two full Confederate divisions under **John S. Marmaduke** and **Francis A. Shoup.** The Federals were overwhelmed and forced back down the hill to the protection of their massed cannons. The Confederates pursued but were driven back by the 24 guns.

To the south at Cane Hill, Blunt heard the battle raging and quickly moved his men to join Herron. Located between Blunt and Herron, Hindman was in an excellent position to **defeat in detail** the Federal forces, but by assuming the defensive, he had relinquished the initiative and thus allowed the enemy to unite. Realizing that he outnumbered Herron, Hindman advanced his left wing to drive the enemy back into the Illinois River. The attack was slow in coming, however, and by the time it began, Blunt's vanguard had arrived and was in position on Herron's right to block Hindman's advance. Blunt massed 30 guns and repulsed the attack with artillery fire. The fighting finally died out after dark.

That night, Blunt's force grew as stragglers and cavalrymen reached his position. Hindman saw his force dwindle as men deserted. Because of the **desertions** and a lack of ammunition and sufficient cannons, Hindman retreated to the Boston Mountains. Blunt followed and captured Van Buren the next day. Tactically, the battle was a stalemate, but Blunt won a strategic victory by breaking up Hindman's **army** and preventing the Confederates from recapturing northwest Arkansas. Out of approximately 9,000 men engaged, Blunt lost 1,251. Hindman had about 11,000 men on the field and lost 1,317.

PRATT, CALVIN EDWARD (1828–1896) USA. A native of **Massachusetts**, Pratt taught school and joined the state militia before being elected justice of the peace in 1853. When the Civil War began, he was practicing law in New York City.

Pratt and a friend organized the 31st New York, which was mustered into Union service in August 1861 with Pratt as colonel. Before being officially accepted into the **army**, the **regiment** served in reserve at **First Manassas**. Pratt fought in the **Peninsula Campaign** with the **Army of the Potomac** and was wounded in the face at **Mechanicsville** during the **Seven Days Campaign**. He was appointed brigadier general of volunteers in September 1862 and led a **brigade** in the VI Corps's 3rd Division at **Fredericksburg**.

Pratt resigned his commission for unknown reasons in April 1863 and resumed his **New York** law practice. He also served as a collector of internal revenue and was elected to the appellate court. Thirty years after being wounding at Mechanicsville, Pratt finally had the bullet removed from his face.

"PRAYER OF TWENTY MILLIONS, THE." During the first half of the Civil War, **New York** *Tribune* editor **Horace Greeley** was one of the most outspoken proponents of emancipation. By mid-1862, he was impatient for **Abraham Lincoln** to take some step toward freeing the slaves, especially after the **U.S. Congress** passed the Second **Confiscation Act** that summer. On August 20, 1862, Greeley published an editorial entitled "The Prayer of Twenty Millions." Claiming to be speaking for the Northern people, he urged Lincoln to be more vigorous in enforcing the Confiscation Act, freeing slaves that came into Union lines, and punishing slave owners. Hurt by the editorial, Lincoln replied in a letter published by Greeley on August 25 that his sworn duty was to preserve the Union and not to free the slaves. Although he did not mention it, Lincoln had already written the **Emancipation Proclamation** and was waiting for a battlefield victory to issue it.

PRENTISS, BENJAMIN MAYBERRY (1819–1901) USA. A native of western **Virginia**, as a teenager, Prentiss moved with his parents to **Missouri**. There he manufactured ropes for several years before moving to **Illinois**. Prentiss served in the militia during the Mormon disturbances and was a **company** captain in the 1st Illinois during the **Mexican War**.

Returning to Illinois after the war, he became a lawyer and unsuccessfully ran for the **U.S. Congress** as a **Republican** in 1860. Prentiss was a militia officer when the Civil War began and entered Union service in April 1861 when he was commissioned colonel of the 10th Illinois. He was promoted to brigadier general of volunteers in August and was given command of northern Missouri, where he fought guerrillas. In March 1862, Prentiss was given a **division** command under **U. S. Grant** and led it at **Shiloh**, where his men fought tenaciously at the "Hornets' Nest" and slowed the Confederate attack before finally being overwhelmed and captured. **Exchanged** in October 1862, Prentiss was a member of the court-martial that tried **Fitz John Porter** and then was put in command of the District of Eastern Arkansas. He was promoted to major general of volunteers in March 1863 and in July successfully defended **Helena** against a Confederate attack. Citing health and family reasons, Prentiss resigned his commission in October 1863, but his true motivation may have been a belief that his military career was over since he had been assigned to an unimportant area.

Prentiss resumed practicing law in Illinois and Missouri and served as a pension agent and postmaster.

PRESIDENT'S (LINCOLN'S) GENERAL WAR ORDERS NO. 1. Although an excellent administrator and organizer, Union Maj. Gen. **George B. McClellan** was slow and unaggressive. When he was appointed general-in-chief and took command of the **Army of the Potomac** in the summer of 1861, **Abraham Lincoln** expected him to take offensive action before the campaign season ended. However, McClellan kept giving excuses for not moving against the Confederates in **Virginia** and refused to reveal any plans he had for such action. Under intense political pressure to act, Lincoln became impatient and finally issued President's General War Orders No. 1 on January 27, 1862, to prod McClellan into action. The order stipulated that by February 22, 1862, Union forces would move against the Confederates in Northern Virginia, the Virginia Peninsula, western Virginia, southern **Kentucky**, and along the Mississippi River—in effect an advance on all fronts. Although unrealistic and never obeyed, the order did stir McClellan from his malaise and forced him to reveal his **Urbanna Plan** to Lincoln.

PRESTON, JOHN SMITH (1809–1881) CSA. A native of **Virginia**, Preston graduated from Hampden-Sydney College in 1824, attended the University of Virginia, and studied law at Harvard University. He began a Virginia law practice but then moved to **South Carolina** in 1840. Preston

PRESTON, WILLIAM (1816–1887) CSA • 1125

then became a successful **Louisiana** sugar planter, but he returned to South Carolina in 1848 and served eight years in the state senate before living in Europe from 1856 to 1860. In 1860, he was strongly prosecession and led the state delegation at the **Democratic** National Convention in **Charleston, South Carolina**.

After South Carolina seceded, Preston was sent to Virginia in February 1861 to convince Virginia to secede. He was appointed lieutenant colonel and assistant adjutant general shortly afterward and was assigned to **P. G. T. Beauregard's** staff. After seeing service at **Fort Sumter** and **First Manassas**, Preston joined **Jefferson Davis's** staff in August 1861 as assistant adjutant general. In October 1861, Davis sent Preston to South Carolina, where he took command of the **prison** camp at Columbia and later a **conscript** camp, as well. Promoted to colonel in April 1863, he was made superintendent of the Bureau of Conscription in July. Preston's lack of tact and independent spirit made him particularly unpopular in this thankless position, but he worked with zeal and was so successful that Davis extended his authority to the previously independent western Confederacy. Preston was promoted to brigadier general in June 1864 and served as the superintendent until war's end.

After the war, Preston lived in Great Britain until 1868, at which time he returned to South Carolina. He remained an unreconstructed **Rebel** and became a popular speaker in defense of the **Lost Cause**.

PRESTON, WILLIAM (1816–1887) CSA. A native of **Kentucky**, Preston was the brother-in-law of **Albert Sidney Johnston**. He attended **Kentucky's** Augusta and St. Joseph's Colleges before graduating from Harvard University in 1838. After practicing law and serving as a militia officer, Preston served in the **Mexican War** as a lieutenant colonel, but he arrived too late in Mexico to see any combat. Returning home, he became a delegate at the state constitutional convention, served in both houses of the legislature, and in 1852 was elected to the first of two terms in the **U.S. Congress** as a **Whig**. Joining the **Democratic Party**, Preston helped nominate **James Buchanan** for president in 1856 and was rewarded with an appointment as U.S. minister to Spain. He resigned from that position in late 1860 during the **secession** crisis.

Returning to Kentucky, Preston fled south with **John C. Breckinridge** in September 1861. Both joined the Confederacy, although Preston received only a colonel's commission on the staff of his brother-in-law Johnston, while Breckinridge was appointed brigadier general. Preston served with Johnston at **Shiloh** and was present with the general when he bled to death.

Preston was appointed brigadier general in April 1862, perhaps because of **Jefferson Davis's** fondness for the slain Johnston. He led a **brigade** in Breckinridge's **division** in the **siege of Corinth, Mississippi**, but he missed the **Battle of Baton Rouge** because of sickness and arrived too late to see any combat at **Perryville** during the **Kentucky Campaign.** Preston did fight well at **Stones River** with the **Army of Tennessee** and in May 1863 was placed in command of **Virginia's** District of Abingdon. In September 1863, he led a division from his **district** to reinforce **Braxton Bragg** at **Chickamauga.** During all of this time, Preston proved to be a schemer and used his connections with Davis to carp constantly about his fellow generals and to criticize Beauregard and Bragg.

In October 1863, Preston was sent back to his Virginia district. When Bragg was relieved of command and brought to **Richmond, Virginia,** Preston was transferred to the **Trans-Mississippi Department.** Before he could resume duties, however, he was appointed Confederate minister to **Maximilian's** Mexico in January 1864. Preston traveled to Europe, but he was unable to make any contact with the emperor. He ultimately returned to the Trans-Mississippi Department by way of **Matamoros, Mexico,** just as the war ended. Some sources claim that Preston was promoted to major general in January 1865, but there is no official record of it.

After the **surrender,** Preston joined other Confederates in exile in Mexico. From there, he eventually traveled to Europe and then back to Kentucky by way of Canada. Preston resumed his law practice in 1866 and served in the state legislature from 1868 to 1869.

PRICE, STERLING (1809–1867) CSA. A native of **Virginia**, Price attended Hampden-Sydney College and studied law before moving to **Missouri** in 1830. There he became a prosperous merchant and planter and as a **Democrat** served in the state legislature from 1836 to 1838 and 1840 to 1844 (he was speaker twice). Price then was elected to the **U.S. Congress** in 1844. He resigned his seat during the **Mexican War** and became colonel of the 2nd Missouri. Sent to **New Mexico,** Price put down an anti-American uprising and then invaded Mexico and captured Chihuahua. **Brevetted** brigadier general for his exploits, he returned to Missouri after the war and served two terms as governor from 1852 to 1856. Afterward, Price served as a state bank commissioner.

Although originally opposed to **secession** (he presided over the Missouri state convention that rejected secession), Price joined the secessionists after the attack on **Camp Jackson** and the **St. Louis Riot.** Governor **Claiborne F. Jackson** appointed him major general and commander of the Missouri State Guard in May 1861. A very personable man, Price (known to his men as "Old Pap") proved to be one of the most popular Confederate commanders and a fairly capable **division** commander. He at first tried to remain neutral, but he felt he had to fight when Brig. Gen. **Nathaniel Lyon** ordered the guard disbanded in June. Withdrawing to southwestern Missouri, Price raised more troops and with **Ben McCulloch** moved against Springfield in August. The Confederates defeated Lyon at **Wilson's Creek**, and Price captured **Lexington**, but he eventually was forced to retreat into **Arkansas**. Joining forces with **Earl Van Dorn**, his men fought well at **Pea Ridge**, but the Confederates were defeated and forced to retreat again.

Price was appointed major general of Confederate troops in March 1862 and the following month took his men across the Mississippi River. He participated in the siege of **Corinth, Mississippi**, that spring and then fought and lost the **Battle of Iuka** before joining Van Dorn in an unsuccessful attack on **Corinth** that autumn. After much pleading, Price finally was sent back to the **Trans-Mississippi Department** in December 1862, but he was not allowed to take his men with him. Instead, he was given command of a division under **Theophilus H. Holmes** and fought at **Helena, Arkansas**, that July. When Holmes went on sick leave, Price assumed command of the Confederate forces in Arkansas and evacuated **Little Rock** when it was threatened by **Frederick Steele**.

In the spring of 1864, Price was ordered by **Edmund Kirby Smith** to confront Steele in the **Camden Expedition**. Throughout April, he **skirmished** and delayed the Federals until **Nathaniel P. Banks's army** was defeated in the **Red River Campaign**, and Price received reinforcements from **Louisiana**. Serving under Kirby Smith, he joined in the attack against Steele at **Jenkins' Ferry**, but the enemy escaped. In late summer 1864, Kirby Smith authorized **Price's Missouri Raid** to relieve some of the Union pressure on **Atlanta, Georgia**. With 12,000 poorly armed mounted infantry, Price entered Missouri in September. The raid, however, was a failure, and the Confederates suffered several defeats, including **Pilot Knob**, **Westport**, and **Mine Creek and Marais des Cygnes**.

When the war ended, Price moved to Mexico and led a colony of Confederate exiles until 1867. He then returned to Missouri and began a commission business but died from cholera shortly afterward.

PRICE'S MISSOURI RAID (AUGUST 28–DECEMBER 2, 1864). Missouri's Confederate Maj. Gen. **Sterling Price** was always eager to operate against the enemy in his home state and thus was agreeable when exiled

Missouri Gov. **Thomas C. Reynolds** proposed such a raid in July 1864. Price secured permission from Gen. **Edmund Kirby Smith**, commander of the **Trans-Mississippi Department,** to enter Missouri, capture St. Louis, and then cross the Mississippi River to carry the war into **Illinois.** Price left Camden, Arkansas, on August 28 and the next day joined with his force of 14 cannons and 12,000 mounted men, only some of whom were armed. Splitting his **Army of Missouri** into two columns, he sent **Joseph O. Shelby's** cavalry to the east of **Little Rock** to attack **De-Vall's Bluff** as a diversion, while he accompanied **John S. Marmaduke's** and **James F. Fagan's** divisions to the west of the city. The two columns reunited at Pocahontas on September 13. Price crossed into southeastern Missouri on September 19 and reached Fredericktown five days later.

At Fredericktown, Price learned that a Union garrison was 20 miles to the west at Ironton and that **Andrew Jackson Smith's** Union **corps** had been transferred from **Mississippi** to the St. Louis area. He sent Shelby's **division** north to Mineral Springs to destroy the **railroad** between Ironton and St. Louis to keep Smith from reinforcing Ironton. On September 26, Price took his other two divisions toward Ironton and launched a bloody, but unsuccessful, attack against **Pilot Knob**. The Union garrison withdrew during the night. Price sent his two divisions after them, but the Confederates withdrew after learning that **Alfred Pleasonton** was on his way from St. Louis with 4,500 Union cavalrymen. With a growing enemy force in his front and Smith's corps at St. Louis, Price abandoned the original goal of seizing St. Louis. He would continue the raid, however, in the belief he could gather thousands of recruits and perhaps demoralize the North enough to cause **Abraham Lincoln's** defeat in the November election.

On September 30, Price sent Shelby toward St. Louis as a diversion while he took the rest of the troops up the Missouri River toward Jefferson City. The Confederates **foraged** off the land and destroyed railroad tracks and bridges, but the large number of expected recruits never materialized. Price reached Hermann on October 5, but he bypassed Jefferson City because it was now heavily defended, and Pleasonton's cavalry was putting pressure on the Confederate rear. Skirting south of Jefferson City and then turning northwest, Price captured Boonville on October 9. From there he sent Shelby north to **Glasgow** on October 14 to seize muskets that were reportedly there, and **M. Jeff Thompson** southwest to raid Sedalia. Shelby captured Glasgow and 500 **prisoners**, but the Federals destroyed the weapons he sought. Thompson also was successful in capturing a militia force at Sedalia.

While Shelby and Thompson were on their raids, Price left Boonville on October 14 and headed northwest toward Waverly, but his progress was slowed by a long 500-wagon supply train and Pleasonton's harassing cavalry. This slowness allowed Union **department** commander **William S. Rosecrans** to bring together scattered forces to trap Price. While Pleasonton pressured the Confederate rear, Smith's corps was brought from St. Louis to Sedalia, and another force under Maj. Gen. **Joseph A. Mower** was ordered north from **Arkansas**. Independently of Rosecrans, **Samuel Curtis**, commander of the **Department of Kansas**, also had assembled more than 15,000 men on the Missouri-Kansas border. On October 15, Curtis sent 2,000 men under **James G. Blunt** to **Lexington, Missouri**, just west of Price's position. Very rapidly, Price was being surrounded by thousands of Federals.

Price moved through Waverly on October 18 and on to Lexington the next day. When he pushed back Blunt's vanguard, Price became aware that Smith and Blunt might unite and trap him. Turning southwest, he hoped to **defeat in detail** the two enemy forces by getting between them. On October 21, the Confederates encountered Blunt's 400-man vanguard at the **Little Blue River**. The bulk of Blunt's force was with Curtis a few miles to the southwest on the west bank of the **Big Blue River**. Price attacked the small Union force and was pushing it back when Blunt arrived with reinforcements. A fierce fight erupted between the numerically superior Confederates and the Federals with their rapid-firing breech-loading **rifles**. The greater numbers finally prevailed, and Blunt retreated back to Curtis on the Big Blue River.

On October 22, Price attempted to force a crossing of the Big Blue. While Marmaduke's division held off Pleasonton in the rear, and one of Shelby's **brigades demonstrated** against Curtis's front, Price sent two brigades to force a crossing at Byram's Ford. This attack failed, but one Confederate **regiment** crossed the river at an unguarded ford farther upstream and turned Curtis's right flank. Price then attacked at Byram's Ford and forced Curtis to withdraw, but darkness prevented him from winning a complete victory. The successful river crossing was marred by Price's rear guard being defeated. Pleasonton's cavalry had driven back **William L. Cabell's** brigade at the Little Blue River and at **Independence** and forced Marmaduke to retreat behind the Big Blue River that night. When Marmaduke informed Price of the desperate situation, Price decided to head south.

Curtis had withdrawn to a position just south of **Westport**. On October 23, Price sent Shelby's reinforced division to attack Curtis at dawn, but Pleasonton also launched a strong attack against Marmaduke at Byram's Ford. After numerous cavalry charges and counterattacks, both Union forces won out. At Byram's Ford, Pleasonton crushed Marmaduke and captured hundreds of prisoners about noon after the Confederates ran short of ammunition. At almost the same time, Blunt attacked Shelby's right wing at Westport and nearly broke through. Learning of Marmaduke's defeat, Price ordered Shelby to fight a delaying action while the rest of the **army** headed south. Confederate morale was shattered, and only Shelby's skillful rear guard action prevented the withdrawal from becoming a rout. Curtis helped by not pursuing for 12 hours and thus allowing Price time to escape the closing trap. Still, the cumbersome wagon train slowed Price and allowed Blunt and Pleasonton to catch up with the Confederates and defeat them at **Mine Creek and Marais des Cygnes, Kansas**, on October 25. In this fighting, Marmaduke, Cabell, and a large number of Confederates were captured. Price burned many of his wagons, but the fighting retreat continued for several days, with a last rear guard action occurring at Newtonia on October 28.

After Newtonia, Rosecrans recalled his troops, leaving Curtis too few men to continue the pursuit. Price crossed the **Indian Territory** and reached Bonham, Texas, on November 23. He then returned to Laynesport, Arkansas, on December 2, having fought 43 engagements, ridden 1,488 miles, and suffered approximately 4,000 casualties (mostly **deserters**). Although Price did gather a few thousand recruits and captured some prisoners, the raid had been a failure. He did not liberate Missouri or inflict any serious damage on the Union army or its vital railroads. In addition, many of the recruits Price did gain were violent guerrillas, and their lawless activities caused many Missourians to turn away from the Confederate cause. Governor Reynolds, who went on the raid, greatly criticized Price's generalship, and Confederate authorities held an inquiry into the raid's failure. Price's Missouri Raid ended organized Confederate resistance in the Trans-Mississippi Department.

PRINCE, HENRY (1811–1892) USA. A native of **Maine**, Prince graduated from **West Point** in 1835 and was assigned to the infantry. After being wounded while fighting in the **Seminole Wars**, he was wounded again and won two **brevets** in the **Mexican War**. This second wound kept Prince off duty for three years. He was appointed major and paymaster in 1855 and then served on the frontier and in **Washington, D.C.**

Prince was promoted to brigadier general of volunteers in April 1862 and was given command of a **brigade** in the 2nd Division of the

Army of **Virginia's** II Corps. When **Christopher C. Augur** was wounded at **Cedar Mountain**, Prince took command of the **division**, but he then was captured. After being **exchanged** in December 1862, he was sent to **North Carolina**, where he first commanded a division in the XVIII Corps and then the District of Pamlico. Shortly after **Gettysburg**, Prince was given command the 2nd Division in the **Army of the Potomac's** III Corps. He served in the **Bristoe Station** and **Mine Run Campaigns** but was criticized in the latter for being too slow in his movements. In April 1864, Prince was transferred west and for the remainder of the war held various **district** commands in **Tennessee**, **Alabama**, and **South Carolina**.

After the war, Prince was brevetted brigadier general in the regular **army** and returned to his paymaster duties. He rose to the rank of lieutenant colonel and deputy paymaster general by the time he retired in 1879. Prince committed suicide in 1892, perhaps partly because of pain and ill health caused by his wounds.

PRISONERS. The number of prisoners taken by both sides during the Civil War is uncertain. It is estimated that 211,411 Union soldiers were captured, and 30,218 died in captivity. Not counting those who were surrendered at war's end, approximately 220,000 Confederates were captured, with 25,976 dying in captivity. Since neither side had made any plans to handle large numbers of prisoners when the war began, releasing captives on **parole** was a common practice. For those who were sent to **prisons**, an **exchange** system was agreed to in July 1862. For two years, prisoners were swapped, although problems frequently arose over such issues as the exchange of **black troops** in the Union **army**. This system, however, benefited the Confederates since they suffered the most from manpower shortages. As a result, **U. S. Grant** stopped virtually all exchanges in 1864.

PRISONS. Since neither side anticipated taking large numbers of **prisoners** when the Civil War began, the housing of captives presented a huge problem. In all, more than 150 places served as prisons during the war, including warehouses, state prisons, forts, and open enclosures. Most were horrid places, with overcrowded, unsanitary conditions, and prisoners suffered from exposure, disease, and hunger. From 1862 to 1864, prisoners could look forward to relatively short periods of confinement because of the **exchange** system. But when the system broke down in 1864, prisoners were forced to spend the rest of the war in captivity. Some prisons, like **Andersonville** and **Point Lookout**, became known for cruel guards and scant food, but in most cases abuse was not purposeful. In the case of Confederate prisons, especially, a general lack of supplies and a dismal transportation system prevented the Confederates from providing adequate food. *See also* ALTON PRISON; BELLE ISLE; CAHABA CAMP CHASE; CAMP DOUGLAS; CAMP FORD; CAMP GROCE; CAMP MORTON; CASTLE PINCKNEY; CASTLE THUNDER; ELMIRA PRISON; FORT DELAWARE; FORT LAFAYETTE; FORT WARREN; JOHNSON'S ISLAND; LIBBY PRISON; OLD CAPITOL PRISON; ROCK ISLAND PRISON; SALISBURY PRISON.

PRIVATEERS. Privateers were privately owned ships that received permission, or letters of marque, from one country to attack the shipping of another. The United States made good use of privateers in the Revolutionary War and the War of 1812. The Declaration of Paris in 1856 abolished the practice, however, and the United States abided by the agreement but never signed the declaration. Thus, when **Jefferson Davis** publicly offered letters of marque in April 1861, the Union could make little protest. The Confederacy issued letters of marque to 52 ships, but probably less than half of them actually were active. Confederate **commerce raiders** inflicted far more damage on Union shipping than privateers. **Abraham Lincoln** announced in 1861 that captured crews of privateers would be treated as pirates and executed, but in the *Enchantress* **Affair**, he backed away from the threat, and captured privateers were treated as **prisoners** of war.

PROCTOR'S CREEK, VIRGINIA, BATTLE OF (MAY 16, 1864). *See* DREWRY'S BLUFF, VIRGINIA, SECOND BATTLE OF.

PROLONGE. This was an 18-foot rope that was laced between two hooks located on the top of a cannon's carriage trail. It was used to maneuver a gun when it was unlimbered.

PROVISIONAL ARMY OF THE CONFEDERATE STATES. *See* CONFEDERATE ARMY.

PROVISIONAL CONFEDERATE CONGRESS. *See* CONFEDERATE CONGRESS.

PRYOR, ROGER ATKINSON (1828–1919) CSA. A native of **Virginia**, Pryor attended Petersburg's Classical Academy, graduated first in his class from Hampden-Sydney College in 1845, and then studied law at the University of Virginia. After practicing law for a few years, he left the practice for health reasons and became a journalist. Pryor became a newspaper editor in 1849 and joined the **Richmond** *Enquirer* in 1853 as editor. This profession was interrupted in 1855 when President Franklin Pierce sent him on a diplomatic mission to Greece. Upon his return, Pryor settled in **Washington, D.C.**, and published the sectional newspaper, *The South.* Pryor was chosen to fill a congressional vacancy in 1859 and was re-elected to the **U.S. Congress** in 1860. He also attended the **South Carolina secession** convention and openly called for the state to secede. Pryor then joined **P. G. T. Beauregard's** staff as a volunteer aide and encouraged authorities to fire on **Fort Sumter**. Resigning his congressional seat in March 1861, he was one member of the party that carried Beauregard's final surrender demand to **Robert Anderson** in April. Pryor then declined an offer to fire the first shot at Fort Sumter.

In 1861, Pryor was elected to both the Provisional **Confederate Congress** and the first regular Congress and was also appointed colonel of the 3rd Virginia. He chose a military career over politics, however, and accompanied his men on active duty, finally resigning his congressional seat in April 1862. Pryor was stationed on the Virginia Peninsula and during the **Peninsula Campaign** was given command of a **brigade** in **James Longstreet's** division. He fought well at **Williamsburg** in May and won promotion to brigadier general. Afterward, Pryor was commended for his actions at **Seven Pines**, and during the **Seven Days Campaign** he fought particularly well at **Frayser's Farm**. Joining **Cadmus M. Wilcox's** division in the **Army of Northern Virginia** after the Seven Days, Pryor fought in the **Second Manassas** and **Antietam Campaigns** and assumed command of the **division** at Antietam. He lost so many men in these battles, however, that his brigade was disbanded. Pryor also had apparently fallen out of favor with Longstreet and **Robert E. Lee**, for he was sent to command a small brigade in southeastern Virginia. He remained there until Longstreet began the siege of **Suffolk** in early 1863, but then Longstreet replaced him in March. Pryor never regained a brigade command and resigned his commission in August 1863. In 1864, he served as a volunteer courier for **Fitzhugh Lee** and was captured in November. Pryor was released just before Lee's **surrender**, but he performed no other military duty.

Pryor moved to New York City after the war and wrote for the New York *Daily News*. He also practiced law, served as a judge, and sat on the state supreme court. For the last 20 years of his life, Pryor served as a special arbitrator for the state supreme court's appellate division.

PUMPKINVINE CREEK, GEORGIA, BATTLE OF (JUNE 25–27, 1864). *See* NEW HOPE CHURCH AND DALLAS, GEORGIA, BATTLES OF.

– Q –

QUAKER GUNS. This was the name given to fake cannons made by painting logs black and mounting them in defensive positions to deceive the enemy as to one's real strength. Quaker guns were used effectively by the Confederates during the **Peninsula Campaign**.

QUAKER ROAD, VIRGINIA, BATTLE OF (MARCH 29, 1865). After **Robert E. Lee** failed to cut his way out of Petersburg, Virginia, at **Fort Stedman** on March 25, 1865, **U. S. Grant** extended his **army's** left wing to the west on March 29 to cut the Southside Railroad and turn Lee's flank. **Charles Griffin's division** of the **Army of the Potomac's** V Corps began pushing back Confederate **skirmishers** early that morning and by noon had reached the point where the Quaker Road crossed Gravelly Run. Griffin fought his way across the creek at about noon and soon was joined by **Samuel W. Crawford's** division on his left. After advancing some way, the Federals were attacked near Lewis's Farm and driven back by **Bushrod Johnson's** division of the **Army of Northern Virginia**, but they soon were reinforced and continued forward. The Federals finally reached the intersection of the Quaker and Boydton Plank Roads and entrenched. The Union V Corps lost 370 men in the action. Confederate losses are unknown, but the Federals reported capturing 200 **prisoners** and burying 130 of the enemy. The **Petersburg Campaign** ended a few days later when the Federals crushed Lee's right flank at **Five Forks**.

QUANTRILL, WILLIAM CLARKE (1837–1865) CSA. A native of **Ohio**, Quantrill taught school before settling in **Kansas**. After being driven out of town as a thief, he joined an **army** expedition to Utah as a teamster. Late in 1858, Quantrill also joined a gold mining party to **Colorado**, but 12 of the 19 men died of exposure. Returning to Kansas, he assumed the name of Charley Hart and became a gambler and outlaw and during the days of **"Bleeding Kansas"** was active with the proslavery "border ruffians."

When the Civil War began, Quantrill enlisted in the **Confederate army** and served at **Wilson's Creek**, but he then became a guerrilla fighter in 1862. After capturing **Independence, Missouri**, that August, he was commissioned a captain but was not given a position with a regular military unit. Instead, Quantrill organized about 150 guerrillas and began fighting in **Missouri**. This group came to include such notorious men as **William "Bloody Bill" Anderson**, the Younger brothers, and Frank James. In November 1862, Quantrill captured a wagon train and murdered 12 of its teamsters. He went to **Richmond, Virginia**, that same month to seek command of a regularly sanctioned military unit under the **Partisan Ranger** Law. Publicity of his atrocities prevented him getting the command he wanted, but he was promoted to colonel.

Quantrill returned to Missouri in early 1863. In August, he carried out his most famous **massacre** when his men raided **Lawrence, Kansas**, looted the town, and killed about 150 boys and men. The raid supposedly was to avenge some of Quantrill's female relatives who died when a **prison** collapsed on them in Kansas City, Missouri. After the Lawrence raid, Quantrill's men dispersed after bickering among themselves. He raised another smaller group, including future outlaw Jesse James, and headed to **Kentucky** as the war was ending. On May 10, 1865, Quantrill was mortally wounded and captured at Bloomfield. Paralyzed, he died in Union captivity on June 6.

QUARLES, WILLIAM ANDREW (1825–1893) CSA. A native of **Virginia**, as a child, Quarles moved with his family to **Kentucky**. He was later forced to drop out of the University of Virginia to manage the family farm after his father died. Becoming a lawyer, Quarles opened a practice in **Tennessee** and became active in politics. He served as a delegate to the 1856 and 1860 **Democratic** National Conventions, became a **railroad** president and state banking supervisor, and filled in for a sick judge for one year on the circuit court.

After the Civil War began, Quarles organized the 42nd Tennessee and was elected its colonel in November 1861. He reinforced **Fort Donelson** early in 1862 and was praised for his leadership during the attempted breakout. Captured when the fort surrendered, Quarles was **exchanged** in September. He then was given command of several consolidated Tennessee **regiments** and served in northern **Mississippi** before being sent to Meridian, Mississippi, to reorganize **paroled prisoners**. Quarles's consolidated regiments then served at Port Hudson, Louisiana, in **Samuel B. Maxey's brigade** from January to May 1863, but they reinforced **Joseph E. Johnston** at Jackson, Mississippi, before the **Port Hudson Campaign** began. After **Vicksburg** fell, Quarles helped defend **Jackson** against **William T. Sherman** in July.

Maxey's brigade was sent to Mobile, Alabama, in August 1863. When he left the unit, Quarles was promoted to brigadier general in September and took command. That autumn, he reinforced **Braxton Bragg** at Chattanooga, Tennessee, but returned to Mobile in January 1864 without seeing any combat in the **Chattanooga Campaign**. In May, he reinforced Johnston's **Army of Tennessee** for the **Atlanta Campaign** and fought at

Pickett's Mill, Kennesaw Mountain, and **Ezra Church**. After Atlanta fell, Quarles participated in the **Franklin and Nashville Campaign** and was wounded while leading his men at Franklin. He was captured in December while recuperating in a nearby home.

Paroled in May 1865, Quarles returned to his Tennessee law practice and entered politics. He served in the state senate from 1875 to 1877 and 1887 to 1889 and was a delegate to the 1880 and 1884 Democratic National Conventions.

QUEEN OF THE WEST. This Union warship originally was a privately owned merchant vessel known for its great speed, but it was acquired by **Charles Ellet** in 1862 and was converted into a Union **ram**. Ellet used it as his flagship during the **First Battle of Memphis**, but he was mortally wounded in the fight. His brother, Alfred W. Ellet, then took command of the Ellet rams and steamed to **Vicksburg, Mississippi**. The *Queen of the West* was among those ships scattered by the **CSS *Arkansas*** in July 1862 when it came down the Yazoo River and anchored at Vicksburg. Ellet attacked the *Arkansas* a week later, but the *Queen of the West* was badly damaged in the fight and had to be taken upstream for repairs.

In February 1863, the *Queen of the West* returned to duty, ran past the Vicksburg batteries, and began a successful mission destroying Confederate shipping on the river. After destroying four enemy ships, it ran aground while in the Red River and was captured. The Confederates quickly put it back into action and used it to capture the *Indianola*. On April 14, 1863, however, the *Queen of the West* was trapped on **Louisiana's** Grand Lake by three Union warships and was destroyed during the **Bayou Teche Campaign**.

QUINBY, ISAAC FERDINAND (1821–1891) USA. A native of **New Jersey**, Quinby graduated from **West Point** in 1843. He performed routine garrison duty and taught natural philosophy at the academy before resigning his commission in 1852 to teach mathematics and science at the University of Rochester, **New York**.

Quinby entered Union service in May 1861 when he raised the 90-day 13th New York and was named its colonel. After fighting at **First Manassas** in **William T. Sherman's brigade**, he resigned his commission and resumed teaching but returned to the **army** in March 1862 when he was appointed brigadier general of volunteers. Quinby first was given command of the District of Mississippi, but in September, he took command of a **division** under **U. S. Grant**. During the **Vicksburg Campaign**, he commanded a division in the **Army of the Tennessee's** XVII

Corps. Although sick much of the time, Quinby participated in the **Yazoo Pass Expedition**, the **Battles of Champion Hill** and **Big Black River Bridge**, and in the early assaults on **Vicksburg, Mississippi**. Apparently because of poor health, Quinby resigned his commission again in December 1863 and returned to the University of Rochester. He later served as a New York provost marshal, a U.S. marshal, and city surveyor for Rochester.

– R –

RADFORD, WILLIAM (1809–1890) USA. A native of **Virginia**, Radford entered the **U.S. Navy** in 1825 as a midshipman. He rose through the ranks to become commander in 1855 and was commanding the *Dacotah* in the Far East when the Civil War began. Because of Radford's Southern origin, Secretary of the Navy **Gideon Welles** relieved him of command and ordered him back to the United States.

Radford served as a lighthouse inspector until he was returned to sea duty in February 1862. Given command of the *Cumberland*, he was absent from the ship on court-martial duty when it was attacked and sunk by the **CSS** *Virginia* at **Hampton Roads**. Radford tried to return to the *Cumberland* in time to fight but arrived only to watch her sink. Promoted to captain in July 1862 and to commodore in April 1863, he commanded the New York Navy Yard until given the **USS** *New Ironsides* in March 1864. Radford served well as an acting flag officer in the operations that finally captured **Fort Fisher, North Carolina**, in early 1865. He then was put in command of the James River Squadron and cooperated with the **army** during the **Petersburg Campaign** in the war's final months.

Radford remained in the navy after the war and served as commander of the Atlantic Squadron. In October 1865, he was put in command of the Washington Navy Yard. Promoted to admiral in 1866, Radford later commanded the European Squadron before retiring in 1870.

RADICAL REPUBLICANS. Those **Republicans** who supported a vigorous prosecution of the war, immediate emancipation of the slaves, and punishing the former Confederates after war's end were known as the Radical Republicans. Their influence far outweighed their numbers because they held key positions in the government, including the cabinet, and dominated the **Committee on the Conduct of the War**. During the war, the Radicals were able to adopt such measures as the **confiscation acts** and the recruitment of **black troops** and pressured **Abraham Lincoln** to issue the

Emancipation Proclamation. After the war, they believed **Reconstruction** should be controlled by the U.S. **Congress** and not the president, and they impeached President **Andrew Johnson** because of his moderate policies and opposition to them. Among the Radicals were **Thaddeus Stevens, Charles Sumner, Henry Wilson, Zachariah Chandler, Benjamin Wade, Salmon P. Chase**, and **Edwin M. Stanton**.

RAILROADS. The Civil War was the first war in which railroads played a vital role. In virtually all of the major campaigns, the **armies** depended on railroads to bring supplies and men to the front and to evacuate the wounded. In many cases, the location and condition of the railroads themselves dictated how campaigns were fought, and in the **First Manassas** and **Chickamauga Campaigns**, they played key roles in determining final victory.

When the war began, the Union had a great advantage in railroads with approximately 20,000 miles of track, with **Ohio** and **Illinois** each boasting about 2,900 miles. The Union also used its track wisely. At first, the railroad companies overcharged the government to make quick profits, but fearing regulation they finally agreed on uniform government rates. The U.S. **Congress** also passed the Railways and Telegraph Act in January 1862, creating the United States Military Railroads system. This act essentially placed all Northern railroads and **telegraphs** under government control and gave the president the authority to **impress** railroad and telegraph systems for the war effort, to regulate their maintenance and security, and to place them under military authority. During the war, the United States Military Railroads oversaw 16 railroads in the east and 19 in the west. David C. McCallum was put in charge of the system, with **Herman Haupt** being named chief of construction and maintenance. When the war ended, McCallum slowly returned the lines to private control and repaired wartime damage.

The Confederates had about 9,000 miles of track when the war began. **Arkansas** had only 38 miles, while **Virginia** had the most of any Confederate state, with 1,771 miles. In addition to a shortage of track, many of the Confederates' lines were of different gauge, and tracks in and out of some towns did not actually connect. This was the case in the strategic city of **Petersburg, Virginia**. It meant that trains frequently had to stop and transfer their loads to another train, which caused great delays. The Confederacy's small **industrial** base made it difficult to build new tracks (although some were constructed in **Alabama, Florida, North Carolina**, and Virginia), and the Confederates could do little to straighten out rails twisted into **"Sherman's neckties."** The government also did little to gain control over what track it did have. Unlike the Union, the Confederates never took steps to place the railroads under government control to facilitate their war use. By war's end, the Confederate railway system lay in shambles from enemy raids and a lack of rails and rolling stock. Despite there being plenty of food in the countryside late in the war, the lack of a working rail system prevented the government from getting it to the armies.

RAINS, GABRIEL JAMES (1803–1881) CSA. A native of **North Carolina**, Rains graduated from **West Point** in 1827. Assigned to the infantry, he served in **Indian Territory**, on the court-martial of **Jefferson Davis**, and in the **Seminole Wars**. In the Seminole Wars, Rains was wounded and invented a **torpedo**, or land mine, to protect camps against **Indian** ambushes. Afterward, he served in the **Mexican War** and garrisoned numerous posts before being appointed lieutenant colonel of the 5th U.S. Infantry in June 1860.

Rains resigned his commission in July 1861 and was commissioned a Confederate brigadier general in September. Assigned to the Virginia Peninsula, he commanded a **division** there until the spring of 1862, when he was given a **brigade** in **Daniel H. Hill's** division during the **Peninsula Campaign**. While serving on the peninsula, Rains outraged the Federals by using his land torpedoes to slow their pursuit, and **James Longstreet** finally ordered him to cease.

Rains was severely criticized by Hill for failing to attack at **Seven Pines**, but afterward he was given a special assignment by **Robert E. Lee**. Taking advantage of Rains's specialty, Lee released him from his brigade and had him mine the Appomattox and James Rivers in June 1862 to stop the **U.S. Navy's** advance. After serving a time as commander of the District of Cape Fear, he was named superintendent of the Bureau of Conscription in December, but he also continued to design imaginative explosives and showed his work to Davis. Impressed, Davis sent Rains to **Vicksburg, Mississippi**, with orders to use his mines to protect an important position there.

For the next year Rains was on "special service," working around the Confederacy placing his mines at strategic points. He worked at **Charleston, South Carolina**; **Mobile, Alabama**; **Richmond, Virginia**; and, **Savannah, Georgia**, mostly mining waterways. Rains was made superintendent of the Torpedo Bureau in June 1864 and spent his time designing **"infernal machines."** In this work, he was incidentally helped by his brother, **George W. Rains**, who provided powder from the **Augusta (Georgia), Powder Works**. Among Rains's successes was the sabotage of the huge Union supply depot at **City Point, Virginia**, in August 1864 when his agents used explosives disguised as coal to set off a devastating explosion onboard a ship there. Near war's end, he mined the main roads and other positions around Richmond, but his efforts failed to save the city, and he fled with the other government officials in April 1865.

After the war, Rains worked as a chemist in **Georgia**, patented a safety valve, offered to teach a course on mine warfare at West Point, and served as a clerk in the U.S. Quartermaster Department in **South Carolina**.

RAINS, GEORGE WASHINGTON (1817–1898) CSA. A native of **North Carolina** and the brother of **Gabriel J. Rains**, Rains graduated near the top of his **West Point** class in 1842. He was assigned to the **engineers** but requested **artillery** duty a year later. After teaching chemistry at the academy, Rains fought in the **Mexican War** and won two **brevets** for gallantry. Afterwards, he fought in the **Seminole Wars** and served at numerous posts before resigning his captain's commission in 1856 to become president of New York's Washington Iron Works.

Rains quit his position when war erupted in 1861 and returned south. He entered Confederate service in July 1861 as a major of artillery and was assigned to the Ordnance Bureau, where he procured gunpowder for the military and built the Confederacy's **Augusta (Georgia), Powder Works**. Rains also created the **Niter and Mining Bureau** to gather niter for making gunpowder. Promoted to lieutenant colonel in May 1862 and to colonel in July 1863, he spent most of the war supervising the Augusta Powder Works and supplied the Confederacy with 2,750,000 pounds of gunpowder.

After the war, Rains taught chemistry at the Medical College of Georgia and became its dean in 1867. After retiring, he moved to **New York**.

RAINS, JAMES EDWARDS (1833–1863) CSA. A native of **Tennessee**, Rains graduated from Yale Law School in 1854 and opened a Tennessee law practice. While working under **Felix K. Zollicoffer** as associate editor of the Nashville *Banner* in 1858, he was elected city attorney. Two years later, Rains was elected district attorney for the Nashville area.

Rains entered Confederate service in early 1861 as a private in the 11th Tennessee but quickly was made captain in May. A week later, he was elected colonel and was assigned to Zollicoffer's brigade in east Tennessee. Given command of Cumberland Gap in November, Rains engaged in some **skirmishing** with the enemy over the next several months and often rode out on night patrols into **Kentucky** to gather intelligence. After being forced to withdraw from Cumberland Gap in June 1862, his command became part of **Carter L. Stevenson's brigade**. When Stevenson was given a **division**, Rains took over the brigade in July 1862. At the beginning of the **Kentucky Campaign**, Stevenson's division was left behind to threaten Cumberland Gap and later marched into Kentucky. Although Rains saw no combat in Kentucky, he performed well enough to win promotion to brigadier general in November.

After the Kentucky Campaign, Rains was transferred to **John P. Mc-Cown's** division in the **Army of Tennessee**. At the **Battle of Stones River**, he led his men in the initial attack on the Confederate left and captured one enemy brigade and a battery. Just at his moment of triumph, however, Rains was hit in the heart by a bullet and was killed nearly instantly. The Confederates received permission from **William S. Rosecrans** to pass Rains's body through the lines for burial in Nashville. To the Federals' dismay, the funeral was a large event, and Rains for a time was seen as one of the Confederacy's most popular martyrs.

RAMS. Since ancient times, warships known as rams sank enemy vessels by ramming them with a strong prow made for that purpose. Civil War rams usually were **ironclads** with iron rams mounted on the bow to strike an enemy ship below the water line. Confederate rams included the *Virginia*, *Arkansas*, and *Tennessee*. The Union had such rams as the *Carondelet* and *Queen of the West* and the rams built by **Charles Ellet**. Rams saw action at **Hampton Roads**, **Memphis**, **Forts Jackson and St. Philip**, **Plymouth**, **Galveston**, **Charleston**, and **Mobile Bay**.

RAMSAY, GEORGE DOUGLAS (1802–1882) USA. A native of **Virginia**, Ramsay graduated from **West Point** in 1820 and was assigned to the **artillery**. In 1835, he was given the staff rank of captain and was transferred to the Ordnance Department. Ramsay served as Zachary Taylor's chief of ordnance during the **Mexican War** and won a **brevet** for gallantry at Monterrey. He remained with the Ordnance Department until the outbreak of the Civil War and was promoted to major in April 1861.

Promoted to lieutenant colonel in August 1861, Ramsay proved to be a modern thinker in the otherwise conservative Ordnance Department. He commanded the Washington Arsenal from 1861 to 1863, during which time **Abraham Lincoln** came to admire him because of his integrity, experience, and energy. Ramsay was promoted to colonel in June 1863 and became Lincoln's choice to replace retiring Chief of Ordnance **James W. Ripley**. Secretary of War **Edwin Stanton** preferred another officer, so he and Lincoln compromised by promoting Ramsay to brigadier general of regulars and chief of ordnance in September but allowing Stanton's candidate actually to run the department. Ramsay served in this intolerable situation until he retired in September 1864, but during that time, he nearly doubled the number of breech-loading **rifles** purchased by the **army** and increased the number of repeating weapons in the arsenal.

Ramsay continued to work for the government after retiring from the army and from 1864 to 1870 acted as a special agent inspecting arsenals and performing other duties. For his long army service, he was brevetted major general of regulars in March 1865.

RAMSEUR, STEPHEN DODSON (1837–1864) CSA. A native of **North Carolina**, Ramseur (ram-SOOR) attended Davidson College before entering **West Point** in 1855. After graduating in 1860, he was assigned to the **artillery** but resigned his 2nd lieutenant's commission in April 1861 to join the Confederacy.

Ramseur entered Confederate service in April 1861 as a 1st lieutenant of **artillery** but was elected captain in the 1st North Carolina Artillery that same month. He was promoted to major the next month and was sent to **Virginia**, where he took command of an artillery battalion under **John B. Magruder**. After seeing combat in the **Peninsula Campaign**, Ramseur was appointed colonel of the 49th North Carolina in April 1862. Joining **Robert Ransom's brigade** in the **Army of Northern Virginia**, he led his **regiment** in the **Seven Days Campaign** and was badly wounded in the right arm at **Malvern Hill**.

Promoted to brigadier general in November 1862, Ramseur was given command of a brigade in **Robert Rodes's division** in January 1863 and quickly earned a reputation as one of the best brigade commanders in the **army**. At **Chancellorsville**, **Robert E. Lee** praised him after he was wounded while leading his men in an attack that reunited the separated Confederate wings. At **Gettysburg**, Ramseur again fought well, helping rout the Union army on the first day. During the 1864 **Overland Campaign**, he played a key role at the **Wilderness** by again uniting the army's divided wings. A short time later, Ramseur received his fourth wound of the war while leading a counterattack that helped seal the Union breakthrough at **Spotsylvania's** "Bloody Angle."

Because of his excellent service, Ramseur was given temporary command of **Jubal A. Early's** division in late May 1864 and was promoted to major general in June. Just one day past his 27th birthday, he was the youngest officer to be appointed a Confederate major general. In September, Ramseur was given permanent command of Rodes's old division, but as a division commander, he had a checkered record. He did not perform well at **Rutherford's Farm** or **Fisher's Hill**, but he did earn accolades for his defensive stand at **Third Winchester** and for successfully attacking the enemy at **Cedar Creek**. Late in the day of the latter battle, Ramseur was mortally wounded while trying to repel a Union attack. Wearing a flower in his lapel in honor of the daughter he learned had been born the previous day, he was shot through the lungs. Captured, Ramseur was taken to **Philip Sheridan's** headquarters and died the next day.

RAMSEY, ALEXANDER (1815–1903) USA. A native of **Pennsylvania**, Ramsey was orphaned at age 10 and later attended Lafayette College but dropped out to read law. After becoming a lawyer, he entered **Whig** politics and served in the U.S. House of Representativs from 1843 to 1847. Ramsey then served as **Minnesota's** territorial governor from 1849 to 1853; was mayor of St. Paul, Minnesota, in 1855; and was elected the state's **Republican** governor in 1859 and 1861 after losing his first bid in 1857.

Ramsey was in **Washington, D.C.**, when **Fort Sumter** was fired on and became the first Northern governor to offer state troops for the Union's defense. Returning to Minnesota, he organized 20 **regiments** for service but then was faced with the 1862 **Sioux uprising**. During this **Indian** war, Ramsey raised additional militia forces but had to request federal troops to put down the Sioux. The uprising killed many people and hurt the state's economy, but Ramsey still won election to the U.S. Senate in 1863. He served there for the rest of the Civil War but did not play a major role in national politics.

Ramsey served in the Senate until 1875. He was President **Rutherford B. Hayes's** secretary of war from 1879 to 1881 and a member of the 1882 Edmunds Commission to investigate Mormon polygamy. He became successful in real estate, and twice served as president of Minnesota's historical society.

RANDALL, ALEXANDER WILLIAMS (1819–1872) USA. A native of **New York**, Randall practiced law for a while but moved to **Wisconsin** in 1840. Becoming involved in politics, he often switched parties, joining the **Whigs**, **Democrats**, and **Free-Soil** Parties before finally settling on the **Republicans**. Randall's offices included postmaster, district attorney, and judge, with one unsuccessful bid for state attorney general.

Randall was elected Republican governor of Wisconsin in 1857. He attacked corruption and **slavery** and quickly raised troops to defend the

Union after the fall of **Fort Sumter**. Although the state's quota was only one **regiment**, Randall raised four. After leaving office in 1862, he hoped to be appointed a Union general but, instead, **Abraham Lincoln** appointed him minister to the Vatican. When he returned to the United States less than a year later, Randall again failed to win a military commission. This time, he was appointed assistant postmaster general, and he later served as postmaster general under President **Andrew Johnson**. After leaving the latter position in 1869, Randall returned to New York and practiced law.

RANDOLPH, GEORGE WYTHE (1818–1867) CSA. A native of **Virginia**, Randolph was Thomas Jefferson's grandson and the son of Virginia Gov. Thomas Randolph. He grew up at Jefferson's Monticello and in **Massachusetts** and **Washington, D.C.** Randolph entered the **U.S.** Navy in 1831 as a midshipman and for a time served aboard the USS *Constitution*. After six years of service, he took an extended leave and then resigned his commission in 1839. Randolph attended the University of Virginia, became a lawyer, and helped organize the Richmond Howitzers, which he led to **Harpers Ferry, Virginia**, after **John Brown's Raid**.

During the 1861 **secession** crisis, Randolph served on a commission to strengthen the state's armory, was a delegate at the secession convention, and was among convention delegates who met with **Abraham Lincoln** on the day **Fort Sumter** was bombarded. After Fort Sumter's surrender, he voted for secession and entered Confederate service as major of his **artillery** unit. Sent to the Virginia Peninsula, Randolph saw combat at **Big Bethel**. He was appointed colonel of the 1st Virginia Artillery in September 1861 and became commander of **John B. Magruder's** artillery shortly afterward. Sickness kept Randolph off duty for several months, but in early 1862, he was placed in command of the forces defending Suffolk, Virginia.

In February 1862, Randolph was appointed brigadier general, but instead of receiving a field command, he was appointed secretary of war by **Jefferson Davis** in March. In that position, he tried to strengthen the western forces and enforce **conscription**, but he did not work well with Davis because of the president's slow decision making and continual meddling in his department. When Davis countermanded one of Randolph's orders concerning a troop movement, Randolph resigned his position in November 1862. For the next year, he was sick with tuberculosis. Randolph traveled to Great Britain in 1864 to seek medical treatment, resigned his military commission in December, and was still in Europe when the war ended. He took the **loyalty oath** while overseas and returned home in August 1866 but died eight months later.

RANSOM, MATTHEW WHITAKER (1826–1904) CSA. A native of **North Carolina**, "Matt" Ransom was the brother of **Robert Ransom Jr.** and a relative of Union general **George H. Thomas.** He graduated from the University of North Carolina and became a lawyer before entering politics and serving as the state attorney general and a legislator. In 1861, before North Carolina seceded, Ransom also served as a state commissioner to the Confederacy.

After North Carolina seceded, Ransom entered Confederate service as a private, but he was appointed lieutenant colonel of the 1st North Carolina in July 1861. The **regiment** served for a time in **Virginia** on the Potomac River but soon returned to North Carolina. In May 1862, he was appointed colonel of the 35th North Carolina, a regiment that belonged to his younger brother's **brigade**. Ransom led the regiment at **King's School House** and **Malvern Hill** and was wounded in the right arm and right side at the latter battle. Despite his wounds, Ransom went on to fight with the **Army of Northern Virginia** at **Antietam**, but afterward he took leave to recover fully and thus missed the **Battle of Fredericksburg**. After returning to duty, he spent much of early 1863 on court-martial duty in North Carolina. When his brother was promoted to major general in May 1863, Ransom was promoted to brigadier general and took command of the brigade.

Although at first skeptical of his ability, Ransom's men soon came to have great respect for him. He led the brigade in several small actions in North Carolina through 1863 and in 1864 fought at **New Bern**, **Suffolk**, and **Plymouth** (where he led the charge that captured the town). Sent back to Virginia, Ransom fought at **Second Drewry's Bluff** in May where his left arm was severely broken by a bullet. This wound kept him off duty until October. Ransom then led his brigade through the latter part of the **Petersburg Campaign**, fought at **Fort Stedman** and **Quaker Road**, and commanded a small **division** under **George E. Pickett** at **Dinwiddie Court House** and **Five Forks**. In the latter battle, he was injured when his horse was killed under him, and he did not hold another field command before he surrendered at **Appomattox**.

Returning to North Carolina, Ransom advised the Confederates there to keep fighting despite the war's apparent end. He then resumed his law practice and farmed before reentering politics and serving as a U.S. Senator from 1872 to 1895 and ambassador to Mexico from 1895 to 1897.

RANSOM, ROBERT, JR. (1828–1892) CSA. A native of **North Carolina**, Ransom was the brother of **Matthew Ransom** and a relative of

Union general **George H. Thomas.** After graduating from **West Point** in 1850, he was assigned to the cavalry and served several years in the Southwest. Ransom returned to the academy as a cavalry instructor in 1854–55 and then was promoted to 1st lieutenant and regimental adjutant in the 1st U.S. Cavalry. After being promoted to captain in January 1861, he resigned his commission in May to join his native state.

Ransom entered Confederate service in the spring of 1861 as a captain of cavalry and was appointed colonel of the 1st North Carolina Cavalry in October. His strict **discipline** made him unpopular with the men, but he led the **regiment** to **Virginia**, where it engaged in some **skirmishes**. After being promoted to brigadier general in March 1862, Ransom served for a time in North Carolina before returning to Virginia. There he was given command of a **brigade** in **Benjamin Huger's division** of the **Army of Northern Virginia** and earned a reputation for being one of the **army's** best combat leaders. Ransom led the brigade well in bloody fighting at **Malvern Hill**, participated in the capture of **Harpers Ferry, Virginia**, and fought at **Antietam** with **John G. Walker's** division. At **Fredericksburg**, he commanded a demi-division and suffered heavy losses while successfully defending the stone wall on Marye's Heights.

Ransom's demi-division was transferred to North Carolina in January 1863. After being promoted to major general in May, he defended the Weldon Railroad and part of southeastern Virginia until being transferred to **Tennessee** near year's end. In March 1864, Ransom took command of **James Longstreet's** cavalry in East Tennessee but was sent back to Virginia in May. There he commanded the **Department of Richmond** and led an infantry brigade in fighting at **Second Drewry's Bluff**, but his leadership in the battle was criticized by **P. G. T. Beauregard**, who blamed him for the enemy's escape to Bermuda Hundred. In June, Ransom again was transferred, this time to command the **Valley District's** cavalry. After leading his command at the **Monocacy** during **Jubal A. Early's Washington Raid**, Ransom had to relinquish his field command in August because of illness. Afterward, he commanded a **district** in **South Carolina**.

Returning to North Carolina, Ransom spent the postwar years farming and working as an express agent, Wilmington's city marshal, and a civil engineer.

RANSOM, THOMAS EDWARD GREENFIELD (1834–1864) USA. A native of **Vermont**, Ransom was the son of Norwich University's president, who was killed in the **Mexican War** while colonel of the 9th U.S.

Infantry. After graduating from the university in 1851, he became a civil engineer and real estate agent in **Illinois**.

When the Civil War began, Ransom raised a volunteer **company** and entered Union service in April 1861 as a captain in the 11th Illinois. He was promoted to major and lieutenant colonel that summer and to colonel in February 1862. Ransom first was sent to **Missouri**, where he was wounded in August during a hand-to-hand fight at Charleston. He then fought at **Fort Donelson** and **Shiloh** and was wounded in both battles but refused to leave the field. In all three of these fights, Ransom earned praise from his superiors. Appointed **John A. McClernand's** chief of staff and inspector general after Shiloh, Ransom participated in the **siege of Corinth, Mississippi**, that spring. In January 1863, he was given command of a **brigade** in the 6th Division of the **Army of the Tennessee's** XVII Corps. Ransom won much praise while leading it in the **Vicksburg Campaign** and was promoted to brigadier general of volunteers in April 1863. He won more accolades later in the year for leading a successful **foraging** expedition to Natchez, Mississippi, that netted 5,000 cattle. **U. S. Grant** called Ransom "the best man I ever had to send on expeditions" (Warner, *Generals in Blue,* 390).

In December 1863, Ransom was transferred to the **Department of the Gulf**, where in early 1864, he commanded first a brigade and then a **division**. During the **Red River Campaign**, he commanded the XIII Corps until he was badly wounded in the leg at **Mansfield**. When he returned to duty, Ransom took command of a division in the Army of the Tennessee's XVI Corps for the latter part of the **Atlanta Campaign**. He fought particularly well at **Jonesboro**, for which he was posthumously **brevetted** major general of volunteers. When **John Bell Hood's** Confederates moved into northern **Georgia** and **Alabama** after the fall of Atlanta, Ransom was given command of the XVII Corps and was sent in pursuit. He returned to Atlanta on a stretcher in October suffering from typhoid and unhealed wounds, and he died on October 29.

RAPPAHANNOCK, **CSS.** This Confederate **commerce raider** was a ship built in 1856 for the British Royal Navy and originally was named the *Victor*. The ship had three masts and a steam-powered single screw, was 193 feet long, 30 feet wide, and displaced 850 tons. It served two years in the Royal Navy but then was placed in dock. Confederate agent **Matthew Fontaine Maury** purchased it in September 1863 through a British firm. Although the British government suspected the ship might violate its neutrality and threatened to seize it, she was refitted as the *Scylla* and escaped to sea unfinished in November.

Renamed the CSS *Rappahannock*, the ship was placed under the command of Charles M. Fauntleroy. After the engines burned out, the ship limped into a French harbor for repairs and to recruit a full crew, but the French impounded it when repairs dragged on too long. Although not allowed to leave port, the *Rappahannock* did serve as a secret floating supply depot for other Confederate ships and as an assembly point for naval recruits. It was decommissioned and sold to a private citizen in March 1865, but through the efforts of **Charles Francis Adams Sr.**, the U.S. minister to Great Britain, the *Rappahannock* was turned over to the United States in 1866.

RAPPAHANNOCK STATION, VIRGINIA, BATTLE OF (NOVEMBER 7, 1863). After the **Bristoe Station Campaign** ended in October 1863, **Robert E. Lee's Army of Northern Virginia** took up a position on the south bank of the Rappahannock River. Hoping to draw **George G. Meade's Army of the Potomac** into battle, Lee had **Jubal A. Early's** division guard the **pontoon bridge** at Rappahannock Station but left only a token force to defend Kelly's Ford, four miles downstream. Positioning the bulk of his army near Kelly's Ford, Lee hoped to entice Meade to cross there so as to destroy him while he was halfway across the river.

On November 7, 1863, Meade began an offensive to capture the land between the Rappahannock and Rapidan Rivers. He sent his left wing under **William H. French** against Kelly's Ford and **John Sedgwick's** right wing against Rappahannock Station. French attacked **Robert Rodes's** division at Kelly's Ford at about noon, seized the ford, and inflicted 349 casualties (mostly **prisoners** taken) on Rodes. At Rappahannock Station, Brig. Gen. **Harry T. Hays's brigade** of **Louisiana Tigers** was manning earthworks on the river's north bank when Sedgwick approached that afternoon. Early sent **Robert Hoke's** brigade, under **Archibald C. Godwin**, to reinforce Hays, but Lee downplayed the danger and claimed the Union buildup was only a **demonstration**. Just at dark, Sedgwick advanced two VI Corps brigades, totaling 2,100 men, towards Hays's right by screening the movement behind a **railroad** embankment. He then launched a surprise **bayonet** attack that overran Hays's position after a brief hand-to-hand struggle. Hays and some of his command escaped across the bridge through a hail of gunfire, but Sedgwick took 1,673 prisoners at a cost of only 461 casualties.

For once, Lee had been caught off guard. He had planned on Meade crossing at Kelly's Ford so he could destroy him in a counterattack, but he did not think Meade also would seize the crossing at Rappahannock Station. With his left flank now threatened, Lee was forced to cancel his attack at Kelly's Ford and withdraw from the river. Many Confederates held Lee responsible for the defeat at Rappahannock Station since he had dismissed the danger and neither reinforced nor withdrew Hays.

RATION. A ration is a day's supply of food for one soldier or one animal. When the Civil War began, the Union ration was a 16-ounce biscuit (or 22 ounces of bread or flour) and a pound and a quarter of fresh or salt meat (or three-quarters of a pound of bacon). In addition, for every 100 men there was supplied eight gallons of beans, 10 pounds of rice or hominy, 10 pounds of coffee, 15 pounds of sugar, 4 gallons of vinegar, and 2 pounds of salt. The **Confederate army** adopted the same ration at the beginning of the war but was forced to cut it drastically as its transportation system collapsed. Often soldiers failed to get their full ration, particularly during a campaign when **armies** were on the move, and the meat and bread often were moldy, rancid, or filled with worms.

RAUM, GREEN BERRY (1829–1909) USA. A native of **Illinois**, Raum was the son of a prominent state politician and soldier. He became a lawyer in 1853 and served as an alternate delegate at the 1860 **Democratic** National Convention in **Charleston, South Carolina**.

Raum entered Union service in September 1861 as major of the 56th Illinois. He served in the **siege of Corinth, Mississippi**, in early 1862 and that summer was promoted to lieutenant colonel and colonel. After leading the **regiment** at the **Battle of Corinth**, Raum served with **U. S. Grant** in **Grant's Overland Vicksburg Campaign** and with the **Army of the Tennessee** in the **Vicksburg Campaign**. In June 1863, he took command of the **brigade**, which was part of the XVII Corps' 7th Division. Afterward, Raum was badly wounded while leading it at **Missionary Ridge**. When he returned to duty, he was given a brigade in the XV Corps' 3rd Division but was left behind in northern **Georgia** to guard the supply line during the **Atlanta Campaign**. He did serve in the **March to the Sea** but went on extended leave in January 1865. Raum was promoted to brigadier general of volunteers in February 1865 and apparently worked with **Winfield S. Hancock** in the unsuccessful effort to raise a **Veteran Volunteer Corps**.

Raum resigned his commission in May and worked for a **railroad**. Becoming active in **Republican** politics, he served in the **U.S. Congress** from 1867 to 1869, and was an internal revenue commissioner (1876–83) and Pension Bureau commissioner (1889–93). In this latter position, Raum was accused of corruption and returned to his Illinois law practice.

RAWLINS, JOHN AARON (1831–1869) USA. A native of **Illinois**, Rawlins became head of his household as a teenager when his father went to **California** in search of gold. He became a lawyer in 1854 and was city attorney of Galena in 1857.

When the Civil War began, Rawlins agreed to become aide-de-camp to fellow Galena resident **U. S. Grant** and was commissioned captain and assistant adjutant general in August 1861. Until his death, he was closely allied with Grant, serving as his friend, military aide, adviser, defender, and secretary of war. Rawlins was a teetotaler because drink had ruined his father, and many people claimed that one of his duties was to keep Grant sober, although this story probably is apocryphal. Grant did come to describe him as being "indispensable."

Rawlins's stature in the **army** rose with Grant's. He was promoted to major in May 1862, lieutenant colonel in November, brigadier general of volunteers in August 1863, and brigadier general of regulars and army chief of staff (a position created for him) in March 1865. He also was **brevetted** major general of volunteers and regulars for his war service. Rawlins served Grant at **Belmont** and in the **Forts Henry and Donelson, Shiloh, Vicksburg, Chattanooga, Overland, Petersburg**, and **Appomattox Campaigns**.

After the war, Rawlins began suffering from tuberculosis, which had killed his first wife, and tried unsuccessfully to regain his health by traveling in the west. In March 1869, President Grant appointed him secretary of war, but Rawlins died six months later.

RAYMOND, MISSISSIPPI, BATTLE OF (MAY 12, 1863). After winning the **Battle of Port Gibson, Mississippi**, in the **Vicksburg Campaign**, U. S. Grant headed northeast on May 8, 1863, with the **Army of the Tennessee** to cut the Southern Railroad between **Vicksburg** and Jackson. As **James B. McPherson's** 12,000-man XVII Corps marched toward Raymond on May 11, Confederate Brig. Gen. **John Gregg's brigade** arrived in Jackson from Port Hudson, Louisiana. Informed of the Union advance, Gregg headed for Raymond before daylight on May 12. Unaware he was outnumbered three to one, he placed most of his brigade southwest of town to guard the Utica Road crossing of Fourteen Mile Creek while sending the rest of his men to the left on the Gallatin Road. From there, they possibly could attack and turn the Federal right flank as it advanced.

When **John A. Logan's division** approached on the morning of May 12 and deployed in thick woods along the creek, Gregg attacked. The Confederates forced back part of Logan's line, but the Federals repulsed two of Gregg's **regiments** that crossed over the creek. The battle was indecisive until Logan was reinforced by part of **Marcellus M. Crocker's** division. Supported by 22 cannons, he then counterattacked. The fighting was furious and confused in the thick woods and smoke, but Gregg's line finally began unraveling, and he ordered a withdrawal to **Jackson**. McPherson lost 442 men in the battle, while Gregg counted 514 casualties.

Raymond was McPherson's first battle as a **corps** commander, and he did not perform particularly well. Although greatly outnumbering the enemy, he was surprised by Gregg's aggressiveness and sent his men into the fight piecemeal. After the battle, Grant was convinced there was a large Confederate force in Jackson that could threaten his rear if he advanced toward Vicksburg. Therefore, instead of moving directly against Vicksburg, he changed his plans and attacked and captured Jackson two days later.

REAGAN, JOHN HENNINGER (1818–1905) CSA. A native of **Tennessee**, Reagan moved to **Texas** in 1839 and became an **Indian** fighter, farmer, surveyor, lawyer, legislator, and judge. After being elected district judge twice, he resigned his position in 1857 to accept a seat in the U.S. House of Representatives.

Reagan was a delegate to the Texas **secession** convention in 1861. Although a moderate, he voted for secession and then resigned his congressional seat to enter the Provisional **Confederate Congress**. Twice, Reagan turned down the position of postmaster general, but he finally accepted the appointment from **Jefferson Davis** in March 1861 and became one of Davis's strongest supporters. Despite enormous difficulties, Reagan created a functioning postal system by using captured Federal equipment and supplies and hiring former U.S. postal employees. He also met a constitutional requirement to be self-sufficient after March 1, 1863, by increasing rates and cutting routes. However, Reagan was never able to operate the postal system as efficiently as the United States operated its system, and he had many critics. He and Secretary of War **James A. Seddon** fought over **conscription**, with Seddon needing military manpower and Reagan wanting to exempt his postal employees.

Reagan accompanied Davis when he fled **Richmond, Virginia**, in April 1865 and was captured with him in **Georgia**. Held **prisoner** in **Fort Warren, Massachusetts**, for months, he advised President **Andrew Johnson** to be lenient with the South and for Texans to accept **Reconstruction** and civil rights for **freedmen**. After being released in December, Reagan returned to Texas. He was a delegate at the 1875 constitutional convention, a congressman from 1875 to 1877, and a U.S.

senator from 1887 to 1891 (in the Senate, he helped create the Interstate Commerce Commission). He and was appointed head of the Texas Railroad Commission in 1891.

REAMS' STATION, VIRGINIA, BATTLE OF (AUGUST 25, 1864).

During the **Petersburg Campaign**, in August 1864, U. S. Grant succeeded in cutting the vital **Weldon Railroad** that brought much needed supplies to **Robert E. Lee's Army of Northern Virginia**. From August 22–24, Maj. Gen. **Winfield Scott Hancock's** II Corps of the **Army of the Potomac** tore up track from Globe Tavern to Rowanty Creek, while the cavalrymen of **David M. Gregg's division** and Samuel Spears's **brigade** protected its front and flanks.

On August 25, the Confederate III Corps, temporarily commanded by **Henry Heth**, advanced toward Hancock from the west with nearly 10,000 men. Hancock took up a defensive position around Reams' Station in some poorly constructed breastworks that ran parallel to the track. **Wade Hampton's** Confederate cavalry supported Gregg, who was positioned south of Hancock, and Heth drove in Hancock's **pickets** from the west. At about 2:00 P.M., Heth attacked Hancock's main line with **Cadmus Wilcox's** division and Hampton's cavalry. Wilcox fought his way up to the breastworks held by the divisions of **John Gibbon** and **Nelson Miles**, but he was unable to capture them. Reinforced by Heth's and Mahone's divisions, the Confederates advanced again after bombarding the Federal position with **artillery** fire. This time they broke through Hancock's right at an angle where the line had been **refused**. Miles contained the breakthrough, but on Hancock's left, Hampton's cavalry broke through Gibbon's position at an angle where the line was refused on that flank. Only Hancock's personal efforts and a heavy rain at dark prevented the Federals from being routed. They withdrew that night to the Jerusalem Plank Road. Hancock lost nine cannons and 2,742 men, mostly taken **prisoner**, while the Confederates's lost 814 men. The Federals blamed the defeat on their exhausted condition after marching and tearing up track and the large number of new recruits in the ranks. Heth's and Hampton's victory temporarily gave the Confederates the use of that section of the Weldon Railroad.

REBEL YELL. All Union and Confederate soldiers yelled and shouted in the heat of battle, but their styles were different. Union soldiers were said to use a deep-throated "huzzah!" while the Confederates developed the famous Rebel Yell. Some soldiers believed the yell originated at **First Manassas**, while others claimed to have heard it first when the **Louisiana Tigers** attacked at **First Winchester**. The yell was described as being a high-pitched yelping sound, almost like an **Indian** war whoop, and may have derived from a similar cry Southerners used to encourage their dogs while hunting. Some recordings of it were made in the early 20th century, but by that time the veterans were elderly men and no doubt had lost much of their zeal. Whatever its origin, the Rebel Yell was a terrifying sound and was unnerving to those on its receiving end.

REBELS. Along with other such names as Johnny Rebs, secesh (secessionists), and Butternuts, this was a nickname given to Confederate soldiers by their Union counterparts.

RECONNAISSANCE. A reconnaissance was a small probe against an enemy's position to gather such intelligence as strength, location, and intentions.

RECONNAISSANCE IN FORCE. While a **reconnaissance** was a mere probe against an enemy position, a reconnaissance in force was made by a large force (usually a **brigade** or **division**). It actually attacked the enemy and attempted to drive in his **pickets** to reach the main line to gather definite intelligence as to its location, strength, and so on.

RECONSTRUCTION (1863–1877). *Reconstruction* was the name given to the post–Civil War period when the nation was put back together and civil rights were granted to the **freedmen**. The process actually began during the war when **Abraham Lincoln** began reconstructing Union-occupied territory with his **Ten Percent Plan**, but it was not completed until 1877. Reconstruction was a time of great political turmoil and violence, as Northern politicians fought to control it, and most Southerners fought against it.

In the North, moderate **Republicans** and **Radical Republicans** fought over Reconstruction. Moderates like Lincoln believed the South was still part of the Union since **secession** was illegal and, therefore, could regain its former position in the **U.S. Congress** through presidential action. The Radicals believed the South had committed "state suicide" through secession and now was simply conquered territory, requiring congressional action to be readmitted to the Union. The moderates and Radicals also had different views on how to treat the former Confederates, the former being more forgiving, while the Radicals wanted to punish them and strip them of their political rights. The Radicals also wanted to protect the freedmen and grant them some civil and political rights.

Lincoln began Reconstruction in **Louisiana** and **Arkansas** during the war by having citizens take an **oath of allegiance** to gain a pardon and the restoration of confiscated property (except slaves). When 10 percent of a state's 1860 voters did so and agreed to abolish **slavery**, they could establish a loyal government and be readmitted to Congress. Lincoln vetoed the Radical's harsh **Wade-Davis Bill** in 1864, but he was assassinated before he could complete his own Reconstruction plan. President **Andrew Johnson** followed a moderate plan similar to Lincoln's. He pardoned most former Confederates and required the South simply to repeal the secession ordinances, take an oath of allegiance, disavow the Confederate debt, and ratify the **13th Amendment** to be readmitted. Johnson lost nearly all of his support in the North and finally was impeached. The Radicals then took over Reconstruction in 1867 when they passed, over Johnson's veto, the Military Reconstruction Act. This act divided the South into military districts, with military governors over each, and disenfranchised most former Confederates. When a majority of the loyal voters (including freedmen) approved a new constitution and ratified the 14th Amendment, the state could be readmitted.

In the South, most former Confederates opposed Reconstruction and the Radicals, **carpetbaggers**, **scalawags**, and freedmen who supported it. When most Southern whites were disenfranchised, they often resorted to violence through such secret societies as the Ku Klux Klan.

By the 1870s, much of the sectional hatred had passed, and nearly all of the former Confederates were granted amnesty and had their political rights restored. This allowed the white Southerners to regain control of their states. Reconstruction finally ended in 1877 when the last federal troops supporting the Radical governments were removed as a result of the Compromise of 1877.

RECTOR, HENRY MASSEY (1816–1899) CSA. A native of **Kentucky**, as a youngster Rector moved to **Missouri** with his family. He was educated by his mother and worked as a teamster for his stepfather before moving to **Arkansas** in 1835. There Rector worked in a bank, farmed, and became a lawyer. Becoming active in politics, he served as a U.S. marshal from 1842 to 1843 and was elected to the state senate in 1848, to the legislature in 1855, and to the state supreme court in 1859. Rector also served as the state's U.S. surveyor general and in 1860 was elected governor by a large majority.

Rector seized the federal arsenal at **Little Rock** in February 1861 and called a **secession** convention the following month, but the delegates refused to secede. Disappointed at the convention's lack of action, he refused **Abraham Lincoln's** call for troops to suppress the Rebellion and took control of **Fort Smith**. The convention finally did secede on May 6 but then tried to direct the war effort. Rector was forced to cooperate with the convention in managing the state's affairs, but the relationship was strained. He also clashed with Confederate authorities over the removal of Arkansas troops from the state and the imposition of martial law by military commanders. When a new constitution was written, it did not recognize Rector as governor. The state supreme court ruled the position was vacant, and Rector was forced to vacate his seat in November 1862.

Rector practiced law until war's end and then worked as a planter and served in two constitutional conventions.

RED RIVER CAMPAIGN (MARCH 12–MAY 20, 1864). When U. S. **Grant** adopted the **strategy** of advancing on several fronts simultaneously in the spring of 1864, one of his main objectives was Mobile, Alabama. He was forced to alter his plans, however, because **Abraham Lincoln** wanted to establish a Union presence in **Texas** to counter **Maximilian's** French-supported regime in Mexico. Thus, **Nathaniel P. Banks** was placed in command of an expedition to move up **Louisiana's** Red River to capture Shreveport, the headquarters of **Edmund Kirby Smith's** Confederate **Trans-Mississippi Department** and the Confederate state capital. From Shreveport, the Federals could then invade Texas. Banks also hoped to secure his political future in **Massachusetts** by confiscating cotton in the Red River Valley to supply the textile mills back home. To assist Banks, **William T. Sherman** lent Brig. Gen. **Andrew J. Smith** and 10,000 men from his XVI and XVII Corps with the agreement they would be returned in time to join him for the **Atlanta Campaign.** This gave Banks about 30,000 men for the expedition. Admiral **David D. Porter's** fleet would transport Smith's troops from **Vicksburg, Mississippi**, and provide additional firepower for the expedition. To stop this massive invasion, Kirby Smith had only **Richard Taylor's** small 7,000-man **army**.

On March 12, 1864, Smith and Porter arrived at Simmesport, Louisiana, from Vicksburg. Disembarking, Smith marched 30 miles up the Red River and on March 14 attacked **Fort De Russy,** while Porter bombarded it from the river. After a short fight, the fort was taken, and Porter and Smith continued upriver and reached Alexandria on March 16. During this time, Banks left south Louisiana's Berwick Bay with the XIII and XIX Corps and marched for Alexandria. By the time Banks reached the town on March 25, Porter had already stripped the countryside of cotton, and Smith's men had captured a number of Confederate **prisoners** in a surprise night attack at **Henderson's Hill.**

While at Alexandria, Banks received a message from Grant ordering him to return Smith's men by April 25, even if he had not taken Shreveport, and for him to return to **New Orleans** as soon as possible to participate in operations against **Mobile**. Now pressed for time, Banks quickly held elections for a loyal constitutional convention and moved northwest from Alexandria toward Natchitoches (NAK-uh-tish). Due to an unusually dry spring, the Red River was very low, and Porter spent several days dragging his vessels above the shallow rapids at Alexandria. It was not until April 3 that he had all 30 transports and 12 gunboats above the rapids. That same day, Banks's and Porter's leading vessels reached Grand Ecore, a small river landing a few miles outside Natchitoches. There, Banks blundered by taking a narrow road that snaked west and north to Shreveport rather than staying on the river road. This decision took him away from the river and Porter's supporting gunboats. Banks then made matters worse by placing his long wagon train in the middle of his column, making it impossible to adequately support his vanguard.

Outnumbered and outgunned, Taylor had steadily retreated before the Union juggernaut, but reinforcements finally increased his army to about 8,800 men. On April 8, he made a stand near Sabine Crossroads, just outside **Mansfield**, and attacked Banks's vanguard. Although Brig. Gen. **J. J. Alfred Mouton** was killed, the Confederates pushed back the Federals three miles in a stunning victory that also netted 20 cannons, nearly 200 wagons, and hundreds of **prisoners**. Badly shocked by the unexpected encounter, Banks retreated to **Pleasant Hill**, where Taylor attacked again the next day after receiving substantial reinforcements. This time, however, Banks held his ground and repulsed the Confederates. Despite his victory at Pleasant Hill, Banks abandoned his wounded and withdrew to Natchitoches. Although most of his generals supported the decision, it was a great mistake, for the Confederates were exhausted, and Banks probably could have pushed on to Shreveport. Taylor intended to launch a vigorous pursuit and attack again but was outraged when Kirby Smith ordered him to send nearly all of his infantry to **Arkansas** to stop **Frederick Steele's Camden Expedition**, a second Union advance on Shreveport. Taylor then was left with only about 5,000 men and was unable to inflict any serious damage on the retreating Federals.

On the Red River, Porter had continued toward Shreveport from Grand Ecore, but he was greatly hampered by the steadily falling water level. He finally was stopped near the mouth of Loggy Bayou when he found the channel blocked by a steamboat the Confederates had sunk in the river. Unable to proceed farther and learning of Banks's defeat, Porter withdrew as well. Confederate cavalry constantly harassed his ships with **artillery** and **rifle** fire and even made an unsuccessful attack at **Blair's Landing**, where Confederate Brig. Gen. **Thomas Green** was killed. When Banks left Natchitoches on April 21, the retreat became a frenzy of burning and looting. Union soldiers torched buildings in Natchitoches, Grand Ecore, and Cloutierville (CLOO-chee-ville), as well as numerous plantation houses and outbuildings. Taylor blocked the Federals' route at **Monett's Ferry**, but the small Confederate force was unable to hold its ground, and Banks reached Alexandria on April 25. Porter continued to struggle in the low water against Confederate **sharp-shooters** and **torpedoes** and lost several ships in the retreat, including the **USS *Eastport***, which sank after striking a torpedo. At Alexandria, Porter could not float his ships over the rapids and was planning to destroy the fleet rather than have it fall into enemy hands. Lieutenant Colonel **Joseph Bailey**, however, put the army to work for two weeks constructing Bailey's Dam, a series of wing dams that raised the water level and saved the ships. When Banks retreated from Alexandria on May 13, soldiers in Smith's command torched the town and completely destroyed it.

Taylor continued to follow Banks and fought a minor engagement at Mansura but was unable to inflict any serious casualties. When the Federals reached the Atchafalaya (uh-CHAF-uh-LIE-uh) River, they found themselves trapped without a bridge. Colonel Bailey again went to work and supervised the construction of a long **pontoon bridge**, but he needed time to complete it. Banks left Smith in the rear, where he delayed Taylor at **Yellow Bayou** until the bridge was completed. The Federals then completed crossing the river on May 20, the bridge was taken up, and the campaign ended.

The Red River Campaign was a disaster for the Union. Banks failed to capture Shreveport, retreated unnecessarily, and did not return Smith's 10,000 men in time to participate in the Atlanta Campaign. In addition, by concentrating on Louisiana rather than Mobile, the Federals allowed the Confederates to move 15,000 men to reinforce **Joseph E. Johnston** for the defense of Atlanta, Georgia.

RED ROVER, USS. After the capture of **Island No. 10**, in May 1862, Union forces raised a transport that had been sunk by Confederate gunfire. It was sent to St. Louis, Missouri, where, with financial aid from the Western Sanitation Association, it was converted into the hospital ship *Red Rover*. The side-wheeler was one of the largest and best hospital ships in the **U.S. Navy**, able to sustain 200 men for three months and having bathrooms, a laundry, kitchen, elevator, ice box, and operating room. The *Red Rover* served only the seriously ill and was used by the Mississippi Squadron until war's end. In November 1865, it was sold at auction for $4,500.

REDOUBT. Usually made of earth and logs, a redoubt was a fortified, enclosed earthwork used to support a fort or defensive line.

REDWOOD, ALLEN CHRISTIAN (1844–1922) CSA. A native of **Virginia**, Redwood became one of the Confederacy's best-known artists. He was educated at a **Maryland** academy and was attending **New York's** Polytechnic Institute of Brooklyn when the Civil War began. Returning home, Redwood joined the 55th Virginia, but he later transferred to the 1st Maryland Cavalry (Confederate) and even briefly served on Brig. Gen. **Lunsford L. Lomax's** staff. He fought in numerous battles with the **Army of Northern Virginia**, including **Mechanicsville**, **Second Manassas** (where he was captured and **exchanged**), **Chancellorsville** (where he witnessed the last meeting between **Stonewall Jackson** and **Robert E. Lee**), and **Gettysburg**. Redwood received wounds at Mechanicsville, Chancellorsville, and Gettysburg's **Pickett's Charge** and was captured a second time at Somerton, Virginia, in April 1865 while trying to secure a new mount.

After the war, Redwood began an artistic career depicting the common Confederate soldier in camp and battle. Although his works were used in *Harper's Monthly Magazine* and to illustrate numerous veterans' memoirs and reminiscences, they were best known for being used in *Century Magazine's* four-volume work *Battles and Leaders*. Based on Redwood's own observations, or from wartime photographs, the illustrations were vividly real and greatly praised by veterans. Besides depicting the Civil War, Redwood also witnessed the Franco-Prussian War in Europe and drew some illustrations of it. When he died in 1922, his works were donated to the Museum of the Confederacy in **Richmond, Virginia**.

REED PROJECTILE. This was a Confederate **artillery** shell developed by Dr. John Braham Reed of **Alabama.** It was first designed for **Parrott rifles**, but it later was adopted for other **rifled** cannons. It had a soft copper base that expanded and gripped the rifling when the piece was fired.

REFUSE. To protect against flank attacks, a line sometimes was "refused." This meant the flank was turned back toward the rear so it faced perpendicular to the line's front.

REGIMENT. A regiment was one of the basic organizational units in both **armies** and was the unit to which soldiers had their strongest loyalties. The infantry regiment usually had 10 **companies** and numbered approximately 1,000 men (although they never went into combat full strength because of casualties, illness, **desertion**, and detached duty), while heavy **artillery** and cavalry regiments had 12 companies. State volunteer regiments were numbered according to their acceptance into service, and their members at first were allowed to elect all officers and noncommissioned officers. Regiments were commanded by a colonel, who was assisted by a lieutenant colonel and major. Each company was designated by a letter (except *J*, because in cursive record-keeping it could be confused with *I*) and was commanded by a captain, who was assisted by lieutenants and noncommissioned officers. Usually, four or six regiments made up a **brigade**. During the war, the Union organized 2,144 regiments of infantry, 272 of cavalry, 61 of heavy artillery, and 13 of **engineers**. The Confederates had 642 regiments of infantry, 137 of cavalry, and 16 of artillery.

REID, HUGH THOMPSON (1811–1874) USA. A native of **Indiana**, Reid graduated from Bloomington College and became a lawyer. He moved to **Iowa** in 1839, where he practiced law, served as a public prosecutor from 1840 to 1842, and became a **railroad** president.

Reid entered Union service in February 1862 as colonel of the 15th Iowa, a **regiment** he raised. He was badly wounded at **Shiloh** while trying to keep stragglers from leaving the field but returned to duty in time to participate in the **siege of Corinth, Mississippi**. He then was forced on sick leave. Reid temporarily commanded his **brigade** twice in the months after he returned to duty and was promoted to brigadier general of volunteers in April 1863. During the **Vicksburg Campaign**, he commanded a brigade of **black troops** in the **Army of the Tennessee's** XVII Corps in northeast **Louisiana**. Reid did not accept the command for **abolitionist** reasons but because "every colored soldier who stops a rebel bullet saves a white man's life" (Warner, *Generals in Blue*, 393). In October 1863, he was placed in command of the District of Cairo but then resigned his commission in April 1864.

Returning to Iowa, Reid resumed his railroad career and was instrumental in building the railroad bridge over the Mississippi River at his hometown of Keokuk, Iowa.

REILLY, JAMES WILLIAM (1828–1905) USA. A native of **Ohio**, Reilly attended **Maryland's** Mount St. Mary's College and became a lawyer. He was elected to the state legislature in 1861 but in August 1862 accepted an appointment as colonel of the 104th Ohio. Reilly served on garrison duty in **Kentucky** before joining **Ambrose E. Burnside** in east **Tennessee** in the summer of 1863. He commanded a **brigade** in the 3rd Division of the **Army of the Ohio's** XXIII Corps during the **Knoxville** and **Atlanta Campaigns**. For short periods of time in early 1864, Reilly also temporarily commanded the **division**.

Promoted to brigadier general of volunteers in July 1864, Reilly accompanied **George H. Thomas** to Tennessee during the **Franklin and Nashville Campaign**. He temporarily commanded the division during the Battle of Franklin and performed very well, but he missed the Battle of Nashville. Reilly then went to **North Carolina** and led the division during the **Carolinas Campaign**, but he resigned his commission in April 1865 just before the Confederates surrendered in **North Carolina**. This probably is why he never was **brevetted** for his war services.

Reilly returned to his Iowa law practice, served as a delegate to the 1873 constitutional convention, was a trustee of the state's Soldiers' Home, and served as a bank president.

REMINGTON ARMS COMPANY. Founded in Ilion, New York, in 1816, the Remington Arms Company was one of the Union's most important weapons manufacturing companies. During the Civil War, it produced 15,000 **Remington carbines**; 125,314 **Remington revolvers**; 39,000 Model 1863 **rifle muskets** (**Zouave rifles**); 10,000 1855 **saber bayonets**; and 2,814 Beals revolvers.

REMINGTON CARBINE. Produced by the **Remington Arms Company**, this was a single-shot, rolling-block .50-caliber carbine that used the **Spencer** rim fire cartridge. The weapon was not developed until late 1863 and did not see a lot of combat in the war, but the **U.S. Army** used it extensively afterward. During the war, the Union government contracted 15,000 carbines.

REMINGTON REVOLVERS. Although the **Remington Arms Company** provided **bayonets** and **rifle muskets** to the Union **army**, its main product was revolvers. When the Civil War began, Remington produced a Model 1861 revolver in both .44 and .36 calibers for the **U.S. Army** and **Navy**, respectively. This pistol was modeled after an earlier Beals-Remington revolver and was a six-shot, single-action **percussion cap** weapon. It evolved into the New Model 1863, which had a slightly different frame and some improvements. The heavy 2-pound, 14-ounce frame easily handled the powerful .44 loads and was very dependable.

The New Model 1863 became the second most popular Union revolver (behind the **Colt**), and between 1863 and 1875, the federal government purchased 126,000 Army models and approximately 6,000 Navy models.

RENO, JESSE LEE (1823–1862) USA. Born Jesse Lee Renault, Reno's family changed its surname from the original French spelling. He was a native of western **Virginia** but moved to **Pennsylvania** with his family as a boy. Reno graduated from **West Point** in 1846 and won two **brevets** for gallantry while fighting in the **Mexican War** as an ordnance officer. After the war, he taught mathematics at the academy, participated in topographical surveys, served in the **Utah Expedition** as chief ordnance officer, and commanded the Mount Vernon, Alabama, arsenal.

During the **secession** crisis, Reno was a captain and was forced to surrender the arsenal to secessionists in January 1861. He then served as an ordnance officer in **Missouri** until promoted to brigadier general of volunteers in November. Given a **brigade** under **Ambrose Burnside**, Reno led it at **Roanoke Island** and **New Bern, North Carolina**. He was given a **division** command in April 1862 and led it in **North Carolina** until he was promoted to major general of volunteers in July and was transferred to Virginia.

At the **Second Battle of Manassas** and the **Battle of Chantilly**, Reno temporarily commanded Burnside's IX Corps while Burnside led the right wing of **John Pope's Army of Virginia**. He fought very well in both battles and was recognized as one of the **army's** better combat commanders. Reno then led the **corps** in the **Army of the Potomac** at the beginning of the **Antietam Campaign** and was presented a homemade **flag** by **Barbara Fritchie** in Frederick, Maryland. On September 14, 1862, he was mortally wounded while encouraging his men in an attack at **South Mountain's** Fox's Gap. When he was buried in Boston, Massachusetts, the Fritchie flag was used to cover the casket. Reno, Nevada, later was named for him.

REPUBLICAN PARTY. This political party was formed in 1854 in opposition to the **Kansas-Nebraska Act** and was the main Northern party that opposed **slavery**. Made up of former members of the **Whig, Democratic, Free-Soil**, and Liberty Parties, the Republicans were a fractious group who often quarreled among themselves. Some were **abolitionists** who wanted to free the slaves and grant **freedmen** certain rights. Others were racists who did not care if the South had slaves but wanted to stop the spread of **slavery** into areas where they might live. The party quickly gained support in the North and in only its second attempt won the **election of 1860** (**John C.**

Frémont was the unsuccessful candidate in 1856). Southerners viewed all Republicans as abolitionists and saw **Abraham Lincoln's** 1860 election as the first step in creating a tyrannical government that ultimately would lead to the destruction of slavery, the establishment of ruinous, high tariffs, and the usurpation of **states rights.** To protect their minority rights, the Southern states seceded.

During the Civil War, the Republicans were most associated with the Union war effort even though millions of Northern Democrats also played a major role. The party soon split between moderates and the **Radical Republicans.** The Radicals wanted not only to preserve the Union but also to free the slaves, destroy the Confederacy, and punish the **Rebels.** The moderates were more forgiving and stressed saving the Union—questions of emancipation and rights for freedmen were secondary. Lincoln headed a fragile alliance during the war and ran for reelection in 1864 under the **Union Party** banner, rather than the Republican Party, to broaden his appeal. After **Lincoln's assassination,** however, the Radicals took control of the Republican Party during **Reconstruction,** impeached moderate President **Andrew Johnson,** and imposed the Military Reconstruction Act on the South. The Republicans continued to dominate national politics until the early 20th century, mainly by blaming the Civil War on the Democrats in a tactic known as waving the bloody shirt.

RESACA, GEORGIA, BATTLE OF (MAY 14–15, 1864). As the **Atlanta Campaign** began in early May 1864, **Joseph E. Johnston's Army of Tennessee** was strongly entrenched in northern **Georgia** at **Rocky Face Ridge.** When **William T. Sherman** attempted a **turning movement** through **Snake Creek Gap** on Johnston's far left, Johnston retreated to Resaca (rih-SOK-uh). The Confederates entered strong entrenchments on a north-south line, with the left (or southern) flank anchored at Resaca, on the Oostanaula River, while the right flank was positioned near the river farther north on the Western & Atlantic Railroad. **Leonidas Polk's corps** held the left, **William J. Hardee** the center, and **John Bell Hood** the right. Johnston had about 70,000 men at Resaca to face Sherman's 100,000.

Sherman approached the Confederate works on May 14 with **James B. McPherson's Army of the Tennessee** on the right, **John M. Schofield's Army of the Ohio** in the center, and **George H. Thomas's Army of the Cumberland** on the left at about noon, **John M. Palmer's** XIV Corps attacked the Confederate center in an attempt to reach the **railroad.** Schofield and **Oliver O. Howard's** IV Corps joined in the attack and managed to push the Confederates into their main works, but Palmer suffered heavy casualties while facing **Patrick Cleburne's division**. Late in the day, the Federals enjoyed some success on their left center when **Jacob D. Cox's** division of Schofield's **army** drove back the Confederates on that part of the line. More gains were made on the Union right by elements of the XV Corps that captured a strategic hill from which they could shell the river's railroad bridge. At about 6:00 P.M., Hood counterattacked on the Confederate right and made some headway against the Union flank before being stopped by **Alpheus S. Williams's** division.

Sherman planned to renew the battle on May 15 by attacking with his left, but the rough terrain slowed his movements. Finally, the divisions of **Daniel Butterfield** and **John W. Geary** attacked **Carter L. Stevenson's** Confederate division on the far Union left. In fierce fighting, the Federals made some headway and then repulsed a counterattack by **Alexander P. Stewart's** Confederate division. During the day, Union forces laid two **pontoon bridges** across the Oostanaula River downstream from Resaca at Lays's Ferry. Part of the XVI Corps crossed over, and when a Confederate attempt to turn it back failed, Johnston's position at Resaca became untenable. He abandoned his works that night, burned the railroad bridge behind him, and retreated to Calhoun and **Adairsville**. Sherman lost an estimated 4,000 men at Resaca, while Johnston counted about 3,000 casualties. In the weeks that followed, this pattern of battle and turning movements continued through the Atlanta Campaign.

REVERE, JOSEPH WARREN (1812–1880) USA. A native of **Massachusetts**, Revere was the grandson of Paul Revere. He joined the **U.S. Navy** as a midshipman when he was 16 and served around the world before resigning his lieutenant's commission in 1850. Revere then moved to **California** and later served as a colonel in the Mexican army organizing its **artillery**. During this service, he was wounded in a local rebellion.

Revere had been living in **New Jersey** since 1852. When the Civil War began, he at first offered his services to the navy, but when it did not respond quickly enough, he joined the Union **army** in September 1861 as colonel of the 7th New Jersey. The **regiment** was sent to the Virginia Peninsula with the **Army of the Potomac**, but Revere apparently was not present during the **Peninsula Campaign**. After fighting in the **Seven Days** and **Second Manassas Campaigns**, he was promoted to brigadier general of volunteers in October 1862 and was given command of a **brigade** in **Daniel Sickles's division** of the III Corps.

Revere was only slightly engaged at **Fredericksburg** and then had his career ruined at **Chancellorsville** when he took over the division after his commander, **Hiram G. Berry**, was mortally wounded. When ordered to stop **Stonewall Jackson's** onslaught against the Union right flank, Revere instead took his men to the rear for "reorganizing." He was court-martialed and ordered dismissed from the service, but **Abraham Lincoln** allowed him to resign in August 1863. Revere returned to New Jersey but suffered from poor health and spent his time traveling abroad and writing his memoirs.

REVETMENT. This was a wall or some type of bracing that was used to support the sides of trenches, gun emplacements, or other fortifications. Materials generally used were sandbags, **gabions**, wooden posts or boards, and **fascines**.

REYNOLDS, ALEXANDER WELCH (1816–1876) CSA. A native of **Virginia**, Reynolds graduated from **West Point** in 1838 and was assigned to the infantry, in which he became a regimental adjutant. After serving in the **Seminole Wars** with the Quartermaster Department, he rose to the rank of captain in 1847. Unable to account for money missing from one of his accounts, Reynolds was dismissed from the service in 1855, but he was reinstated at the same rank and seniority three years later. Afterward, he mainly served on the frontier.

While Reynolds was serving as the **Department of Texas's** quartermaster during the 1861 **secession** crisis, state authorities seized some of his funds. He was appointed captain in the **Confederate army** in March without having resigned his federal commission, and the **U.S. Army** dropped him from its rolls in October. Reynolds returned to **Virginia** and in July was appointed colonel of the 50th Virginia, a **regiment** he raised. Sent to western Virginia, he fought at **Carnifex Ferry** and earned the nickname "Old Gauley" because of his service on the Gauley River. After serving for months in that region, Reynolds was transferred to **Tennessee**, where he was given command of a **brigade** in April 1862 and spent the next several months **skirmishing** with the enemy. He participated in the **Kentucky Campaign** that autumn as part of **Henry Heth's division** but did not see any major combat. Given a new brigade in **Carter L. Stevenson's** division, Reynolds helped defend **Vicksburg, Mississippi**, in December and spent months garrisoning Warrenton, Mississippi. During the **Vicksburg Campaign**, his brigade guarded the Big Black River and the **army's** wagon train during the **Battle of Champion Hill**. After the siege began, Reynolds skillfully defended a portion of the Confederate line.

Captured and **paroled** at **Vicksburg**, Reynolds was promoted to brigadier general in September 1863 and in November was given a brigade in **Simon B. Buckner's** division of the **Army of Tennessee**. Temporarily assigned to **J. Patton Anderson's** division at **Missionary Ridge**, he fought well, but **Braxton Bragg** mistakenly blamed him for the Confederate defeat. During the **Atlanta Campaign**, Reynolds's brigade was in Stevenson's division and fought at **Resaca** and **New Hope Church**, where Reynolds was wounded. While recovering, he was placed in command of the District of Northeast Georgia, but he did not perform well and was replaced in January 1865 by **William T. Wofford**. Reynolds apparently spent the rest of the war awaiting a new assignment.

After the war, Reynolds lived for a time in **Pennsylvania** and then moved to Egypt in 1869. He was made a colonel in the Egyptian army; served as its quartermaster, commissary, and paymaster; and died while in Egyptian service.

REYNOLDS, DANIEL HARRIS (1832–1902) CSA. A native of **Ohio**, Reynolds moved to **Tennessee** in 1856 after attending Ohio Wesleyan University. After graduating from a Tennessee law school in 1858, he became a lawyer and moved to **Arkansas**.

When the Civil War began, Reynolds raised a volunteer **company**, was elected its captain, and entered Confederate service in June 1861 as a captain in the 1st Arkansas Mounted Rifles. After fighting at **Wilson's Creek** and **Pea Ridge**, he was ordered to **Mississippi** in March 1862. During this movement, Reynolds was promoted to major in April and to lieutenant colonel in May. The **regiment** served as infantry in **Thomas J. Churchill's brigade** during the **siege of Corinth, Mississippi**, and then fought at **Richmond** during the **Kentucky Campaign**. After serving in the **Tullahoma Campaign** with the **Army of Tennessee**, Reynolds apparently missed the **Battle of Stones River**, but he temporarily took command of his and another regiment in early 1863. During the **Vicksburg Campaign**, the regiment served under **Joseph E. Johnston** around **Jackson, Mississippi**, and fought well when the Federals attacked the city after the surrender of **Vicksburg, Mississippi**. At **Chickamauga**, Reynolds took command of the regiment when his commander was killed and earned lavish praise from **division** commander **Bushrod R. Johnson**. After the battle, he was promoted to colonel and was given permanent command.

Reynolds was promoted to brigadier general in March 1864 and took command of **Evander McNair's** old brigade. During the **Atlanta Campaign**, as part of **Edward C. Walthall's** division, he was praised for his service at **Kennesaw Mountain, Peachtree Creek, Ezra Church**, and **Lovejoy's Station**. After fighting in the **Franklin and Nashville Campaign**, Reynolds was given an additional brigade and helped **Nathan Bedford Forrest** cover the **army's** retreat from Nashville. His last battle was at **Bentonville** during the **Carolinas Campaign**, where he lost a leg to amputation after being wounded by a shell fragment.

After the war, Reynolds resumed his Arkansas law practice and served in the state senate from 1866 to 1867.

REYNOLDS, JOHN FULTON (1820–1863) USA. A native of **Pennsylvania**, Reynolds graduated from **West Point** in 1841 and was assigned to the **artillery**. After serving on garrison duty in the east, he was sent to **Texas** and then fought in the **Mexican War**, where he won two **brevets** for gallantry. Afterward, Reynolds served on various garrison duty and in 1860 was made commandment of cadets and a **tactics** instructor at West Point.

Reynolds was appointed lieutenant colonel of the newly formed 14th U.S. Infantry in May 1861. In August, he was commissioned brigadier general of volunteers and in October was given command of a **brigade** of **Pennsylvania Reserves** in **George A. McCall's** division of the **Army of the Potomac**. After training his men in **Washington, D.C.**, and serving for a time as military governor of Fredericksburg, Virginia, Reynolds was sent to the Virginia Peninsula. During the **Seven Days Campaign**, he fought well at **Mechanicsville**, but at the **Battle of Gaines' Mill**, he became separated from his men and was captured the next morning.

After being held a **prisoner** for weeks in **Libby Prison**, Reynolds was **exchanged** in August 1862 and was given command of the 3rd Division of Pennsylvania Reserves. He led it in the **Second Manassas Campaign**, but at the request of Pennsylvania's governor, he was put in charge of all the state's militia during the **Antietam Campaign** and thus missed the Battle of Antietam. At the end of September, Reynolds was put in command of the Army of the Potomac's I Corps and was promoted to major general of volunteers in November. He led the **corps** at **Fredericksburg** and temporarily broke through **Stonewall Jackson's** line on the Confederate right. After seeing minor service at **Chancellorsville**, Reynolds was considered as a replacement for **army** commander **Joseph Hooker**, but he met with **Abraham Lincoln** and told him he would not accept the position unless he was given more freedom of action than previous commanders. As a result, fellow Pennsylvanian **George G. Meade** was named the new army commander.

During the **Gettysburg Campaign**, Reynolds commanded the three **corps** making up Meade's left wing and was ordered to occupy Gettysburg. When he arrived on July 1, 1863, the Union cavalry was being hard pressed by the Confederates. Reynolds was rushing troops into position and turned in his saddle to look for more when he was hit in the neck and killed either by a **sharpshooter** or a stray bullet. He was viewed as one of the **army's** most promising officers, and his death was a heavy blow to the Army of the Potomac.

REYNOLDS, JOSEPH JONES (1822–1899) USA. A native of **Kentucky**, as a boy, Reynolds moved to **Indiana** with his family. After attending Wabash College, he entered **West Point** (where he met his lifelong friend **U. S. Grant**) and graduated in 1843. Assigned to the **artillery**, Reynolds performed various garrison duties before being assigned to the academy as an instructor. After teaching at West Point for eight years, he returned to field duty in **Indian Territory** before resigning his 1st lieutenant's commission in 1857. Reynolds then taught engineering at **Missouri's** Washington University and worked in the grocery business.

Reynolds entered Union service in April 1861 as colonel of the 10th Indiana. Afterward, he was made a brigadier general in the Indiana militia and in June was appointed brigadier general of volunteers. Sent to western **Virginia**, Reynolds was put in command of the Cheat Mountain District in September and commanded the Union troops that won the **Battle of Cheat Mountain** that same month. When he learned that his brother and business partner had died, he resigned his commission in January 1862 and returned to Indiana to get his business affairs in order. While there, Reynolds helped organize new recruits and was reappointed brigadier general in September 1862. This appointment was followed by a promotion to major general of volunteers in November.

Reynolds commanded a **division** in the **Army of the Cumberland's** XIV Corps during the **Tullahoma** and **Chickamauga Campaigns** and won a **brevet** of brigadier general of regulars in the latter. In October 1863, he was made **George H. Thomas's** chief of staff and performed so well in the **Chattanooga Campaign** that he was brevetted major general of regulars. In January 1864, Reynolds was transferred to the **Department of the Gulf**, where he defended **New Orleans, Louisiana**. In July, he was given command of the XIX Corps and assisted **E. R. S. Canby** in planning the **Mobile Campaign**. Reynolds was put in charge of the **Department of Arkansas** in December 1864 and remained there until war's end.

Reynolds was mustered out of the volunteers in September 1866, but he continued to serve in the regular **army** as a colonel. He commanded several different **regiments** and posts and in 1871 was elected a U.S. senator from **Texas**, but the election was contested, and he lost the seat. Reynolds's military career was ruined in the 1877 Powder River Indian Campaign. After successfully attacking an **Indian** village, he withdrew for no apparent reason, leaving behind his dead and one wounded man who was tortured to death by the Indians. Court-martialed, Reynolds was allowed to resign in 1877 and retired to **Washington, D.C.**

REYNOLDS, THOMAS CAUTE (1821–1887) CSA. A native of **South Carolina**, Reynolds moved with his family to **Virginia** and graduated from the University of Virginia in 1842. After traveling in Europe and learning to speak French and Spanish, he returned to the United States and became a lawyer but returned overseas again in 1846 to serve as secretary to the U.S. legation in Madrid, Spain. Afterward, Reynolds opened a **Missouri** law practice and from 1853 to 1857 served as the state's U.S. district attorney. A staunch secessionist, he supported **Claiborne F. Jackson** and was elected his lieutenant governor in 1860.

In early 1861, Reynolds published a pamphlet supporting **secession** and raised troops for the Confederacy. He then fled to Neosho, Missouri, with Jackson in May and worked with the prosecession legislature there. When Jackson died in December 1862, Reynolds became governor of the exiled Confederate government. With no state to govern, he turned over his troops to the Confederacy, supported **Joseph O. Shelby's** Missouri Raid in 1863, and accompanied **Sterling Price's 1864 Missouri Raid** as Shelby's volunteer aide. When the Confederacy was collapsing in May 1865, Reynolds was the only governor in the **Trans-Mississippi Department** who refused to recommend surrender to **department** commander **Edmund Kirby Smith.**

After the war, Reynolds fled to Mexico with Shelby and others. His knowledge of Spanish helped the exiles immensely, and after **Maximilian** refused to hire Shelby's troopers, Reynolds persuaded the Mexican government to provide money to the men to allow them to return home. He remained in Mexico as Maximilian's counselor but returned to Missouri in 1868 after the emperor was deposed. In Missouri, Reynolds was elected to the legislature for one term and in 1886 was a U.S. commissioner to Central and South America. He then returned to Missouri and practiced law until he committed suicide in 1887.

RHETT, ROBERT BARNWELL (1800–1876) CSA. A member of a prominent **South Carolina** family named Smith, Rhett and his brothers changed the family name to Rhett in 1837 to honor a distinguished ancestor. He became a lawyer in 1821 and soon entered politics. Rhett served in the state legislature from 1826 to 1832 and became a strong supporter of nullification during the **Nullification Crisis**. He also became the state attorney general in 1832 and served in the U.S. House of Representatives from 1837 to 1849. As a congressman, Rhett was one of **John C. Calhoun's** chief lieutenants and became more and more of a "**fire-eater**." When Calhoun died, Rhett was elected in 1851 to finish out his Senate term. An advocate of **secession**, he resigned his seat in 1852 when most South Carolinians refused to support his drastic plan.

In the 1850s, Rhett became owner of the radical **Charleston *Mercury*** and made his son editor. He continued to promote secession and in December 1860 was chosen to write the state's secession ordinance. Rhett also led South Carolina's delegation to the **Montgomery, Alabama, Convention** and earned the title "Father of Secession" by helping write the **Confederate Constitution**. Hoping to join the Confederate government, he was disappointed when no position in the cabinet was offered him. Rhett did serve in the Provisional **Confederate Congress**, but he was defeated in 1863 for a congressional seat, because officials and citizens simply viewed him as too radical. He also became one of **Jefferson Davis's** most vocal critics and attacked the president for being too timid, for continuing to trade with nations that did not recognize the Confederacy, for **suspending the writ of habeas corpus**, and for enlisting **black troops** late in the war.

After the war, Rhett wrote an unpublished history of the conflict, refused to ask for a pardon, and then retired from public life to his son-in-law's **Louisiana** home.

RHODE ISLAND. Out of an 1860 population of 174,620, Rhode Island provided the Union 5,000 more men than its quota. During the war, the state furnished 10 infantry **regiments**, three regiments and one battalion of cavalry, three regiments of heavy **artillery**, and 10 batteries of light artillery. A total of 23,236 men served the Union, including 1,837 **black troops** and 1,878 sailors. Of these, 1,321 died, mostly from disease. Rhode Islanders mostly served in the **Army of the Potomac** and saw combat in all of its major battles. Seven Union generals hailed from the state: **Ambrose E. Burnside, Thomas W. Sherman, George S. Greene, Silas Casey, Isaac P. Rodman, Richard Arnold,** and **Frank Wheaton**. Artillerist John Hazard also came from Rhode Island.

RICE, ELLIOTT WARREN (1835–1887) USA. A native of **Pennsylvania**, Rice was the brother of **Samuel A. Rice**. As an infant, he moved to

Ohio with his family and attended school in western **Virginia** before enrolling in Ohio's Franklin College. Rice moved to **Iowa** in 1855 to study law, graduated from the University of Albany in 1858, and was practicing law in Iowa with his brother when the Civil War began.

Rice entered Union service as a private in the 7th Iowa but was made corporal in July 1861. He was promoted to major in August and temporarily commanded the **regiment** at the **Battle of Belmont** when the colonel was wounded and the lieutenant colonel was killed. In this fight, Rice received the first of seven wounds and carried the bullet in him for the rest of his life. He also served at **Fort Donelson**, while still on crutches, and at **Shiloh**. Promoted to colonel in April 1862, Rice commanded the regiment at the **Battle of Corinth** and then was sent to guard **railroads** in **Tennessee**. During the **Atlanta Campaign**, he commanded a **brigade** in the 2nd Division of the **Army of the Tennessee's** XVI Corps. Rice fought in all of the campaign's major battles and was promoted to brigadier general of volunteers in June 1864. After the fall of Atlanta, his brigade was transferred to the XV Corps' 4th Division. It served in the **March to the Sea** and the **Carolinas Campaign**, and Rice led his men into battle for the last time at **Bentonville**.

After being **brevetted** major general of volunteers in March 1865, Rice was mustered out of volunteer service in August and opened a law practice in **Washington, D.C.** Twenty years later, he retired and moved to Iowa to live with a sister.

RICE, JAMES CLAY (1829–1864) USA. A native of **Massachusetts**, Rice graduated from Yale University in 1854 and moved to **Mississippi**, where he taught school, worked for a newspaper, and studied law. Moving to **New York** in 1855, he became a lawyer and opened a law practice there.

Rice entered Union service in May 1861 as a 1st lieutenant in the 39th New York. After serving in the reserves at **First Manassas**, he was promoted to captain in August and in September was appointed lieutenant colonel of the 44th New York. Sent to the Virginia Peninsula, Rice commanded the **regiment** during the **Seven Days Campaign**, when it was part of **Daniel Butterfield's brigade** in the 1st Division of the **Army of the Potomac's** V Corps. He was promoted to colonel in July 1862 and temporarily led the brigade at the **Second Battle of Manassas**, but he apparently was not present during the **Antietam** and **Fredericksburg Campaigns**. Rice returned to duty in late December 1862 and led the regiment in limited action at **Chancellorsville** the following spring.

Rice's best wartime service came at **Gettysburg** when his regiment was part of **Strong Vincent's** V Corps brigade. During the crucial fighting on Little Round Top, he again took temporary command of the brigade when Vincent was mortally wounded and played an important role in holding that hill for the Union. Rice's actions won him promotion to brigadier general of volunteers in August 1863 and command of a brigade in **Lysander Cutler's** I Corps **division**. After serving in the **Bristoe Station** and **Mine Run Campaigns**, he was transferred to the V Corps in March 1864 and led a brigade in its 4th Division during the **Overland Campaign**. On May 10 at **Spotsylvania**, Rice's thigh was shattered by a bullet, and he died hours after his leg was amputated. During the operation, the surgeon asked him on which side he would be most comfortable. "Turn my face to the enemy," was Rice's reply (Warner, *Generals in Blue,* 401).

RICE, SAMUEL ALLEN (1828–1864) USA. A native of **New York**, Rice was the brother of **Elliott W. Rice.** After moving with his family to **Pennsylvania** as a boy, he eventually settled in **Ohio**. Rice attended Ohio's Franklin College and graduated from New York's Union College in 1849. After studying law at Union College for a year, he moved to **Iowa** and established a law practice there with his brother. Rice had a very successful legal and political career, serving as county attorney in 1853 and two terms as state attorney general.

Rice entered Union service in October 1862 when he raised the 33rd Iowa and was commissioned its colonel. After serving in **Arkansas**, he participated in the **Yazoo Pass Expedition** during the 1863 **Vicksburg Campaign** and then returned to Arkansas, where he led a **brigade** at **Helena** in July. Promoted to brigadier general of volunteers the next month, Rice sometimes commanded a **division** during the summer and autumn of 1863, assisted **Frederick Steele** in capturing **Little Rock**, and fought in the 1864 **Camden Expedition**. At the **Battle of Jenkins' Ferry**, he was in command of a brigade when he was shot in his spur and fragments of it shattered his right ankle. Taken back to Iowa, Rice died from effects of the wound on July 6.

RICE'S STATION, VIRGINIA, BATTLE OF (APRIL 6, 1865). During **Robert E. Lee's** retreat in the **Appomattox Campaign**, Confederate Lt. Gen. **James Longstreet** commanded the **Army of Northern Virginia's** vanguard. On April 6, 1865, he entrenched at Rice's Station, Virginia, to protect the Southside Railroad. When Longstreet learned that a Union column was attacking **High Bridge** across the Appomattox River to the north, he held his position and sent cavalry to secure the vital bridge for the use of other Confederate forces. During the day, **John Gibbon's** Union XXIV Corps approached Longstreet along the **railroad**, and the opposing forces **skirmished** throughout the day. When Longstreet learned that the Confederates had successfully crossed the river at High Bridge, he withdrew to Farmville. In this action, Confederate losses are unknown, while Gibbon lost 66 men.

RICH MOUNTAIN, VIRGINIA, BATTLE OF (JULY 11, 1861). In 1861, western **Virginia** opposed **secession** because it had few slaves and strong economic and family ties to **Ohio** and **Pennsylvania**. To secure the region for the Union, Maj. Gen. **George B. McClellan** took 20,000 men there in the summer of 1861. To oppose him, the Confederates had only 4,500 men under Brig. Gen. **Robert Selden Garnett**. By early July, the Federals had forced Garnett to withdraw to Rich Mountain. There he split his command by placing 1,300 men under **John Pegram** near Beverly to block the Staunton-Parkersburg Turnpike at Buckhannon Pass, while he guarded the Grafton-Beverly Road at Laurel Hill, 10 miles to the north.

On July 6, McClellan advanced toward Beverly with 8,000 men, while Thomas A. Morris's 4,000-man **brigade** marched toward Laurel Hill. **Skirmishing** occurred on July 7–10, during which time Union Brig. Gen. **William S. Rosecrans** devised a plan to take his brigade by way of mountain paths to turn Pegram's left flank. McClellan agreed, and Rosecrans began his movement on July 11 with 2,000 men. Morris was to keep Garnett occupied at Laurel Hill, and McClellan would attack Pegram from the west when he heard Rosecrans begin his attack.

Pegram had expected a move against his right flank but was caught off guard when Rosecrans attacked his left shortly after noon on July 11. In rainy conditions, the Federals routed Pegram's flank and cut his line of retreat to Beverly. Despite the defeat, the Confederates successfully withdrew in scattered groups, largely because McClellan did not attack from the west as planned. At Laurel Hill, Garnett came under **artillery** fire on July 11 and learned that evening that Pegram had been defeated. In rainy, muddy conditions, he withdrew northeast to the Cheat River Valley on July 12. There, Garnett was mortally wounded when Morris attacked him at **Carrick's Ford** on July 13. That same day, Pegram was overtaken by the Federals and surrendered over 550 men. In the fighting at Rich Mountain, the Confederates lost 88 men while the Federals counted 74 casualties.

Although Rosecrans was responsible for the victory at Rich Mountain, McClellan received the credit. The battle helped secure western Virginia for the Union and elevated McClellan to such prominence that he was given command of the principal Union army in Virginia after its defeat at **First Manassas**.

RICHARDSON, ALBERT DEANE (1833–1869) USA. A native of **Massachusetts**, Richardson attended Holliston Academy and worked for various newspapers in **Pennsylvania** and **Ohio** and for the *Boston Journal* in **Kansas** before the Civil War. In 1859, he became friends with **Horace Greeley** while accompanying the famous newspaper editor on a trip west. Greeley hired Richardson to work for the **New York** *Tribune*, and he remained with the paper for the rest of his life.

In 1860–61, Richardson toured the South to report on the **secession** movement and survived numerous death threats while there to provide the *Tribune* many interesting stories. After war broke out, he became the newspaper's chief **war correspondent** and covered the war in **Virginia** before heading west for the **Vicksburg Campaign**. Richardson was captured at **Vicksburg, Mississippi**, in May 1863 while trying to slip past the Confederate river batteries with another reporter. The two finally escaped from **Salisbury Prison, North Carolina**, in December 1864 and safely reached Union lines in East **Tennessee** after a harrowing 400-mile trek.

After the war, Richardson wrote three books based on his Civil War adventures: *The Secret Service, the Field, the Dungeon, and the Escape; Beyond the Mississippi*; and *Personal History of Ulysses S. Grant*. He was mortally wounded by the ex-husband of his fiancée while at the *Tribune* offices in November 1869. While Richardson was on his deathbed, **Henry Ward Beecher** performed the wedding ceremony.

RICHARDSON, ISRAEL BUSH (1815–1862) USA. A native of **Vermont**, Richardson was a descendant of Revolutionary War hero Israel Putnam. He graduated from **West Point** in 1841, was assigned to the infantry, and immediately entered the **Seminole Wars**. Richardson won two **brevets** for gallantry during the **Mexican War** and then served at various posts in the Southwest. Resigning his captain's commission in 1855, he farmed in **Michigan** until the beginning of the Civil War.

Richardson, who earned the nicknames "Fighting Dick" and "Greasy Dick," entered Union service in May 1861 when he recruited the 2nd Michigan and was appointed its colonel. He was given command of a **brigade** under **Irvin McDowell** in June, led it at **First Manassas**, and was one of the few Union officers who brought his men off the field in good order. Promoted to brigadier general of volunteers in August,

Richardson was given a brigade in **Samuel P. Heintzelman's division** of the **Army of the Potomac** in October. After earning a reputation as an excellent organizer and disciplinarian, he was placed in command of a II Corps division for the **Peninsula Campaign.** Richardson fought with great bravery through the Peninsula and **Seven Days Campaigns** and was promoted to major general of volunteers in July 1862. He briefly commanded a division in the I Corps but was back with the II Corps for **Antietam**, where his division successfully drove the Confederates out of the "Bloody Lane." While directing one of his batteries, Richardson was wounded by a Confederate spherical case shot. The wound at first was not considered mortal, but he died in early November at **George B. McClellan's** headquarters.

RICHARDSON, ROBERT VINKLER (1820–1870) CSA. A native of **North Carolina**, as a child, Richardson moved with his family to **Tennessee.** Becoming a lawyer, he settled in Memphis and became a business associate of **Gideon J. Pillow** and **Nathan Bedford Forrest.**

When the Civil War began, Richardson provided the Confederacy with supplies and reportedly served under Pillow in **Missouri** and at **Shiloh**, although much of his early service is unclear. By February 1863, he had organized the 1st Tennessee **Partisan Rangers** and was elected its colonel. However, some Confederate officers claimed Richardson had acted without authorization and that his men were little more than bandits. After engaging in some **skirmishes** and raids in western Tennessee, he was notified by **John C. Pemberton** in March 1863 that his authority to raise troops had expired. Pemberton sent an officer to arrest him and to muster his men into regular Confederate service, but Richardson was routed and wounded by the enemy before the officer could act. He then escaped in a canoe to **Arkansas**, reportedly carrying with him a fortune he had made in extorting men who were to be **conscripted.**

By April 1863, Richardson was in Jackson, Mississippi, to answer charges of extortion. However, when **Grierson's Raid** tore through **Mississippi**, Pemberton sent him out with cavalry to pursue the raiders. After this unsuccessful mission, Richardson cleared up the charges against him and in August organized much of his former command into the 12th, 14th, and 15th Tennessee Cavalry, with him serving as colonel of the 12th. With this small **brigade**, he accompanied **James R. Chalmers's division** on a raid to **Collierville, Tennessee**, in November. The cavalry trapped a train carrying **William T. Sherman** but failed to capture him after Chalmers was wounded, and Richardson failed to press the attack.

The following month, Richardson was placed under Forrest's command, but his old friend was disappointed in his service. Most of Richardson's men were absent, and the rest were poorly armed, yet he was receiving pay for the absent men. Despite his weaknesses, Richardson was promoted to brigadier general in December 1863. In February 1864, **Jefferson Davis** requested the nomination be returned, apparently because of continued accusations of misconduct. Unaware of these events, Richardson served under Forrest until Forrest relieved him of command in March after one of Richardson's colonels preferred unspecified charges against him. He never rejoined his troops and was **paroled** in Mississippi in May 1865.

After the war, Richardson moved to Great Britain, but he returned to Memphis in 1867. There he again was associated with Forrest and worked in levee and **railroad** construction. Richardson was mortally wounded in January 1870 by an unknown assailant while stopping overnight at a Missouri inn.

RICHMOND *ENQUIRER*. Founded by Thomas Richie in 1804, this newspaper became one of the leading **Democratic** newspapers during the antebellum period and was one of the Confederacy's most influential publications. It was purchased in 1860 by O. Jennings Wise, Nathaniel Tyler, and W. B. Allegre. During the Civil War, the *Enquirer* was edited by Bennett M. DeWitt, Richard M. Smith, and Tyler. The first two editors supported **Jefferson Davis's** administration so strongly that the paper was seen as the government's official publication. Tyler became editor near war's end and was more critical of the government. During the Civil War, the *Enquirer* competed fiercely against the **Richmond *Examiner*,** but the two merged in 1867.

RICHMOND *EXAMINER*. Founded in 1847, the Richmond *Examiner* was an important **Democratic** newspaper during the antebellum period. John M. Daniel bought the paper in 1848 and edited it throughout most of the antebellum and Civil War periods. When Daniel was not serving as editor, he appointed **Edward A. Pollard** to run the paper for him. Although strongly supporting **secession**, Daniel was one of **Jefferson Davis's** greatest critics and fiercely competed against the rival progovernment **Richmond *Enquirer*.** Both newspapers were widely read throughout the Confederacy, and the two merged in 1867.

RICHMOND, KENTUCKY, BATTLE OF (AUGUST 29–30, 1862). When **Braxton Bragg** left Knoxville, Tennessee, in August 1862 to begin the **Kentucky Campaign**, Col. John S. Scott's cavalry led the advance. Scott **skirmished** with Union troops under Brig. Gen. **Mahlon D. Manson** at Richmond, Kentucky, on August 29 but was forced to withdraw to Kingston. There he was joined by **Patrick Cleburne's division**, which was attached to **Edmund Kirby Smith's** column. Manson notified his superior, Maj. Gen. **William Nelson**, of the fight and positioned **Charles Cruft's brigade** to guard the eastern approaches to Richmond. Kirby Smith ordered Cleburne to engage the Federals at daylight and informed him that **Thomas J. Churchill's** division was being sent as reinforcements.

Early on the morning of August 30, Cleburne led his division to Richmond and engaged Manson's troops just outside town at Rogersville. Manson ordered Cruft to his support and then positioned his troops to block the road on which the Confederates were advancing. For two hours, Cleburne probed the Union line with **artillery** and **rifle** fire. Learning that Churchill was approaching, he decided to attack the Union right, but before he could issue the orders, he was shot in the face and forced to relinquish command to **Preston Smith**. Kirby Smith soon arrived and took charge of the Confederates. He attacked the Union right flank, broke it, and drove the Federals back through Rogersville in a running battle. By this time, Nelson had arrived at Richmond and taken command of the Union forces. He rallied many of Manson's routed troops on Cemetery Hill, just southeast of Richmond, but the Confederates broke this line as well. Nelson was wounded in the leg, but he escaped to Lexington. Manson was captured while trying to make his escape, and several thousand Union soldiers were taken **prisoner**.

The Confederate victory at Richmond allowed Bragg to push northward toward Lexington and Frankfort. In the fight, the Confederates lost about 450 men out of nearly 7,000 engaged, while the Federals counted 5,353 casualties (4,300 of them taken prisoner) out of 6,500 engaged.

RICHMOND, VIRGINIA. Founded in 1737, Richmond, Virginia, was the third largest city in the South in 1861, with a population of 38,000. It also was important to the Confederacy because the capital was moved there from Montgomery, Alabama, in May 1861, and because Richmond had the vital **Chimborazo Hospital**; **Libby** and **Belle Isle prisons**; **Tredegar Iron Works**; **Richmond, Virginia, Armory and Arsenal**; and other important **industrial** sites. In addition, some 7,300 Confederate recruits were raised from in and around the city.

Placing the Confederate capital so far north was a strategic error by the Confederates because Richmond then became the focus of Union attack, and the **Army of Northern Virginia** was forced to defend the city against the **Army of the Potomac** throughout the war. Richmond was nearly captured in 1862 during the **Peninsula Campaign**, but **Robert E. Lee** saved it in the **Seven Days Campaign**. For the next two years, the war in **Virginia** raged between Richmond and **Washington, D.C.**, but Richmond was not immediately threatened except in early 1864 during the **Kilpatrick-Dahlgren Raid**. During this time, the city swelled with thousands of refugees, wounded soldiers, prostitutes, and speculators. Crime was rampant, and there were food shortages that led to the 1863 **Bread Riot**.

Union forces under **U. S. Grant** finally reached the capital's outskirts again in 1864 at the end of the **Overland Campaign**, and Richmond remained besieged for the next 10 months during the **Petersburg Campaign**. When Lee was forced to abandon his Richmond-Petersburg line on April 2, 1865, the Confederate government fled south. Confederate Lt. Gen. **Richard S. Ewell**, commander of the city's defenses, set fire to warehouses and government property during the evacuation. Mobs soon looted Richmond and helped spread the flames. By April 3, when Union troops finally marched into the city, approximately 800 buildings had been destroyed. **Abraham Lincoln** happened to be visiting his **armies** at the time and made a quick tour of the devastated city before returning to Washington.

RICHMOND, VIRGINIA, ARMORY AND ARSENAL. This weapons manufacturing complex was one of the most important in the Confederacy and grew out of the Virginia Armory that had been established in 1798. The arsenal was located on James River's Byrd Island, with a nearby laboratory and armory. The **Tredegar Iron Works**, which worked closely with the complex, was in the same vicinity. Using machinery taken from the **Harpers Ferry, Virginia**, Armory, the Richmond Armory and Arsenal produced approximately one-half of all the ordnance used by the Confederate forces. From July 1861 to January 1865, it provided the Confederacy with 341 **Columbiads** and siege guns; 1,306 other **artillery** pieces; 921,441 artillery shells; 363,372 small arms; and 72,500,000 rounds of small arms ammunition.

RICKETTS, JAMES BREWERTON (1817–1887) USA. A native of **New York**, Ricketts graduated from **West Point** in 1839. Assigned to the **artillery**, he fought in the **Mexican War** and was a captain when the Civil War began.

At **First Manassas**, Ricketts commanded a battery in the 1st U.S. Artillery and was wounded four times and captured. After being **exchanged** in January 1862, he was promoted to brigadier general of volunteers in April and briefly held a **brigade** and **division** command before being given the 2nd Division of the **Army of Virginia's** III Corps in June. Ricketts's division served as the **army's** rearguard after the defeat at **Cedar Mountain** and then fought in the **Second Manassas Campaign** before being transferred to the I Corps. Two of Ricketts's horses were killed at **Antietam**, the second of which inflicted serious injuries when it fell on him. While recuperating, he served as a member of the court-martial that convicted **Fitz John Porter**. When Ricketts returned to field duty in April 1864, he was given command of the VI Corps' 3rd Division. He led it through the **Overland Campaign**, winning a **brevet** for **Cold Harbor**, and in the early part of the **Petersburg Campaign**. Sent to defend **Washington, D.C.**, against **Jubal A. Early's Washington Raid** in July 1864, Ricketts bore the brunt of the fighting at the **Monocacy** and was awarded another brevet for delaying the Confederate advance by one day. Joining **Philip Sheridan's Shenandoah Valley Campaign**, he fought at **Third Winchester** and **Fisher's Hill** and temporarily commanded the **corps** at **Cedar Creek**. During this last battle, Ricketts suffered a chest wound that permanently disabled him. Although he officially did not return to duty until after **Appomattox**, some sources claim he was with the army at the time of the Confederate **surrender**.

Ricketts was mustered out of volunteer service in April 1866 but remained in the regular army as a major of artillery with the brevet rank of major general. Because of his war wounds, he was retired in 1867 with the rank of major general but continued to serve on court-martial duty for two more years.

RIENZI. While serving at Rienzi, Mississippi, in the spring of 1862, **Philip Sheridan** acquired a horse he named Rienzi (REN-zee). It was on this horse that he made the famous ride to join his beleaguered troops during the **Battle of Cedar Creek**. Afterward, Sheridan renamed him Winchester. When Winchester died, his body was mounted and put on display at the Smithsonian Institution in **Washington, D.C.**

RIFLE. Early cannons and firearms had smooth bores and were very inaccurate. Later, much more power and accuracy were achieved by putting spiraling grooves, or rifling, in the barrel to give the projectile spin. Although the term *rifle* generally refers to a rifled long arm, any cannon (**Parrott rifle**), pistol (**Remington** or **Colt** revolver), or long arm (**Enfield** or **Springfield**) with such barrels are considered rifled weapons.

RIFLE MUSKET. Early muskets had smooth bores and were very inaccurate. Later, much more power and accuracy were achieved by putting spiraling grooves, or rifling, in the barrel to give the bullet spin. Muskets that retained the outside characteristics of a smooth bore but had rifled barrels were known as **rifle** muskets. The **U.S. Army** adopted the rifle musket in 1855. Technically, it had a 40-inch barrel, was .58 caliber, and carried a triangular **bayonet**, but any muzzle-loading long arm that had a rifled barrel in the Civil War era was referred to as a rifle musket.

RIFLE PIT. This was the Civil War version of a foxhole, which is a simple hole in the ground in which a soldier takes cover. The rifle pit differed, in that it tended to be a shallow, elongated pit in which the soldier lay with his head toward the enemy. The dirt from the pit was piled in front to protect the soldier's head.

RINGGOLD GAP, GEORGIA, BATTLE OF (NOVEMBER 27, 1863). After its defeat in the November 1863 **Chattanooga Campaign, Braxton Bragg's Army of Tennessee** retreated into northern **Georgia**. To delay Union pursuit and protect his wagon train, Bragg positioned **Patrick Cleburne's** 4,157-man **division** at Ringgold Gap, through which passed the Western & Atlantic Railroad. **Joseph Hooker** arrived with a Union column on the morning of November 27 and believed the Confederates were so demoralized that a strong attack would capture their wagon train and **artillery.** Hooker sent forward **Charles Woods's brigade,** but he was bloodily repulsed by **Hiram Granbury's** Texans. Woods then tried to turn Cleburne's right flank on White Oak Mountain but became pinned down. **James A. Williamson** brought up his brigade to support Woods, but Cleburne used the brigades of **Lucius E. Polk** and **Mark P. Lowrey** to push the Federals down the mountain in vicious close-quarter fighting. Hooker next sent **John W. Geary's division** against the Confederate position. Cleburne repulsed an attack on his right and then pinned down Geary's troops in the center and on the left.

U. S. **Grant** reached Ringgold, Georgia, by noon and decided to break off the attack. At about the same time, Cleburne was notified that the Confederate wagon train was safe, and he could disengage. In the battle, which Grant called an "unfortunate" affair, Hooker lost 507 men to Cleburne's 221. Cleburne's outstanding effort saved Bragg's wagons and earned him the Confederate **Thanks of Congress.**

RIPLEY, JAMES WOLFE (1794–1870) USA. A native of **Connecticut,** Ripley was the uncle of Confederate general **Roswell S. Ripley.** After graduating from **West Point** in 1814 (the class was graduated after only one year of study because of the War of 1812), he was assigned to the **artillery** and served in **New York** during the War of 1812. Afterward, Ripley fought in the first of the **Seminole Wars** and commanded the Kennebec arsenal for 10 years and the **Springfield Armory** for 12 years. He then served as chief of ordnance for the **Department of the Pacific**, was **brevetted** for gallantry in the **Mexican War**, and was serving as inspector of arsenals with the rank of colonel when the Civil War began.

Ripley was overseas when the South began seceding in 1860–61. Returning to the United States, he was placed in command of the U.S. Ordnance Department in April 1861 and was brevetted brigadier general of regulars in July, with promotion to that rank coming in August. Ripley was responsible for the testing and purchasing of weapons for the Union **army**. Although a devoted, incorruptible, and talented administrator, the aged officer proved to be overly conservative in his thinking, was loath to adopt technical improvements and innovations, and had a rude, arrogant personality that made him difficult. Out of 700,000 **rifles** purchased during Ripley's tenure, only 8,271 were breech-loaders. Because of his unbending opposition to the adoption of breech-loading rifles, he was finally replaced in September 1863 by the more progressive Col. **George D. Ramsay**.

Brevetted major general of regulars in 1865, Ripley remained in the **U.S. Army** and served as an inspector of armaments in East Coast forts until 1869. His retirement that year marked the end of 55 years of continuous army service.

RIPLEY, ROSWELL SABINE (1823–1887) CSA. A native of **Ohio**, Ripley was the nephew of Union general **James W. Ripley**. After graduating from **West Point** in 1843, he served with the **artillery** before teaching mathematics at the academy from 1845 to 1846. While serving on the staffs of Zachary Taylor and **Gideon Pillow** during the **Mexican War**, Ripley won a promotion to 1st lieutenant and two **brevets** for gallantry. After the war, he published a two-volume history of the Mexican War. Ripley went on to serve in the **Seminole Wars** and on garrison duty before resigning his commission in 1853 to become a businessman and militia officer in his wife's home state of **South Carolina**.

In January 1861, Ripley was appointed lieutenant colonel of South Carolina forces and took command of Fort Moultrie. He commanded Moultrie's artillery and the **mortars** on Sullivan's Island during the bombardment of **Fort Sumter** and then took command of the fort after it surrendered. Ripley was appointed brigadier general and commander of the **Department of South Carolina** in August 1861. He performed well in organizing coastal defenses, but in November, the **department** was absorbed by **Robert E. Lee's Department of South Carolina, Georgia, and Florida**, and he was reduced to a **district** command. Ripley proved to be quarrelsome and was unable to get along with his superiors. After clashing with his new department commander, **John C. Pemberton**, he secured a transfer in May 1862 to a **brigade** command in **Daniel H. Hill's division** in **Virginia**. As part of the **Army of Northern Virginia**, the brigade suffered very heavy casualties in the **Seven Days Campaign** and fought at **South Mountain** and **Antietam**, where Ripley received a throat wound. Lee, however, was displeased with his performance and agreed to a request by Gov. **Francis W. Pickens** to put him in command of **Charleston, South Carolina**.

Ripley assumed his new position in October 1862 and remained in Charleston until 1865. He did an outstanding job defending the city against attacks by the **U.S. Navy**, and its citizens and Gov. **Milledge L. Bonham** objected when it was rumored he was to be replaced in December 1864. However, Ripley clashed with his superior, **P. G. T. Beauregard**, who wrote that he was "ambitious, cunning, and faultfinding. He complains of every commanding officer he has served under" (Davis, ed., *The Confederate General,* vol. 5, 90). Ripley requested a transfer in January 1865, but Beauregard pressed charges against him. After intense maneuvering by both officers, Ripley finally was returned to duty in February. He took command of a division under **Joseph E. Johnston** during the **Battle of Bentonville**, but afterward his division was consolidated, and Ripley was left without a command for the rest of the war.

After the war, Ripley moved to Great Britain, where he became a successful businessman. Returning to Charleston in 1868, he spent the rest of his life pursuing business interests and writing articles about the war.

RIVER DEFENSE FLEET, CONFEDERATE. When the Civil War began, the Confederates had little with which to defend the Mississippi River. After **Missouri** and **Mississippi** politicians, in particular, began demanding more action be taken, **Kentucky** boatmen James E. Montgomery and James H. Townsend proposed creating a river defensive fleet. In late 1861, Secretary of War **Judah P. Benjamin** secured a million-dollar appropriation to carry out the plan. Under the direction of Maj. Gen. **Mansfield Lovell**, and with the assistance of **M. Jeff Thompson**, the Confederates began purchasing 14 assorted ships in January 1862 to be converted into warships and used to defend the Mississippi River from its mouth to Memphis, Tennessee.

Placed under the command of **army** officers, the ships were converted into **cottonclads** and were armed with one stern gun each and heavy **rams.** Six of the boats—*Defiance, General Breckinridge, General Lovell, Resolute, Warrior,* and *Stonewall Jackson*—were lost after sinking only one Union ship in the April 1862 **siege of Forts Jackson and St. Philip, Louisiana.** The next month, the surviving eight ships—*General Bragg, General Sterling Price, General Sumter, General Van Dorn, Little Rebel, Colonel Lovell, General Thompson,* and *General Beauregard*—saw combat at **Plum Run Bend** and sank two Union vessels. In June, the fleet virtually was destroyed at the **First Battle of Memphis, Tennessee.**

RIVERS' BRIDGE, SOUTH CAROLINA, BATTLE OF (FEBRUARY 2–3, 1865). By February 1865, **William T. Sherman** was moving through **South Carolina** in the **Carolinas Campaign.** In wet, rainy conditions, the Federals advanced in two columns, with **Oliver O. Howard's Army of the Tennessee** on the right and **Henry W. Slocum's** XIV and XX Corps on the left. On February 2, Howard pushed back the Confederates across Rivers' Bridge on the Salkehatchie River and prevented them from burning the span. When Confederate **artillery** under **Lafayette McLaws** opened fire on the bridge, **Joseph A. Mower** sent one of his **brigades** in an unsuccessful attack to capture the Confederate position. The next day, Mower went around McLaws's position by cutting a road through the swampy terrain, while at the same time attacking the Confederates' flanks and rear. Pressure on McLaws's right flank finally forced him to retreat toward Branchville. In the two-day battle, Mower lost 92 men, while McLaws counted 170 casualties.

ROANE, JOHN SELDEN (1817–1867) CSA. A native of **Tennessee,** Roane attended **Kentucky's** Cumberland College, but may not have graduated, and in 1837, he moved to **Arkansas** to join an elder brother who was a successful planter and politician. He was elected to the state assembly in 1842 and 1844 and became speaker of the house. During the **Mexican War,** Roane raised a volunteer **company** and defeated **Albert Pike** for the position of lieutenant colonel in Archibald Yell's **regiment.** At Buena Vista, Roane commanded several of the regiment's companies, but he performed poorly. He then took command when Yell was killed, but the regiment saw no further action in the war. Roane and Pike became involved in a dispute over Buena Vista and fought two duels, one in Mexico and one in 1847 after returning to Arkansas. In the second duel, both fired two shots, but neither was hurt. Returning to politics, Roane was elected governor in 1849 and served one term.

Roane opposed **secession** but supported his state in the Civil War. Appointed brigadier general in March 1862, he first commanded a **brigade** in **Samuel Jones's division** but in May was placed in command of all the Confederate troops in Arkansas. When Union Maj. Gen. **Samuel R. Curtis** invaded the state, Roane declared martial law, vigorously gathered together troops, and successfully defended **Little Rock**. Despite this good service, he was replaced by **Thomas C. Hindman** at the end of May, and in September 1862 he was put in command in the District of Missouri, Arkansas, and the **Indian Territory**. After briefly serving as the Confederate Superintendent of Indian Affairs and commanding a demi-division, Roane led a brigade at the **Battle of Prairie Grove**. This brigade was broken up the following month, however, because its high **desertion** rate made it ineffective. Roane finally received another brigade command in **Thomas J. Churchill's** division in November 1864 and led it until war's end.

After the war, Roane settled in Arkansas, but he died two years later.

ROANOKE ISLAND, NORTH CAROLINA, BATTLE OF (FEBRU-ARY 7–8, 1862). To establish suitable coaling stations for the **North Atlantic Blockading Station** and to gain footholds on enemy soil, the Union launched one of its first offensive operations against Roanoke Island, North Carolina, in February 1862. On January 2, Flag Officer **Louis M. Goldsborough** used 80 transports and 26 warships to move 15,000 men under Brig. Gen. **Ambrose E. Burnside** from **Fort Monroe, Virginia**, to the **North Carolina** coast.

Roanoke Island was the key to the region because it controlled the entrance to Pamlico and **Albemarle Sounds** and connected the Outer Banks with the mainland. The Confederates had fewer than 3,000 men under Col. Henry M. Shaw defending Forts Huger, Forrest, Blanchard, and Bartow on the island's western side. In addition, a small seven-vessel "mosquito fleet" under William F. Lynch also defended the area. Confederate **district** commander **Henry A. Wise** requested reinforcements from his superior, **Benjamin Huger**, but none came.

After leaving part of their force at **Hatteras Inlet**, Goldsborough and Burnside attacked Roanoke with 13,000 men and 19 warships. On February 7, Goldsborough scattered Lynch's fleet and bombarded Fort Bartow, while Burnside landed 10,000 men virtually unopposed three miles south of the fort. The Confederate defenders fell back to earthworks on Suple's Hill, and the next day Burnside attacked their center and both flanks. Although the Union troops in the center became pinned down, those on the flanks were successful. The Confederate line was broken, and the defenders retreated to the island's northern end, where they became trapped. With no hope of escape, Shaw surrendered his 2,500 men. The capture of Roanoke Island gave the Union a foothold on the North Carolina coast, boosted Northern morale, and led to the successful capture of **New Bern** and **Fort Macon** in the weeks that followed. The victory cost the Federals 264 men, while the Confederates lost 2,643.

ROBERTS, BENJAMIN STONE (1810–1875) USA. A native of **Vermont**, Roberts graduated near the bottom of the 1835 **West Point** class and after serving with the dragoons resigned his commission in 1839 to become a **New York railroad** engineer. He was appointed the state's geologist in 1841, and in 1842 helped build the railroad from St. Petersburg to Moscow, Russia. Upon his return to the United States, Roberts became a lawyer and opened an **Iowa** practice, but he then rejoined the **U.S. Army** as a 1st lieutenant in the Mounted Rifles during the **Mexican War**. During the war, he was appointed captain and won two **brevets** and a presentation sword from Iowa for gallantry. Remaining in the **army**, Roberts served in the Southwest until the Civil War.

Roberts was promoted to major of the Mounted Rifles (later renamed the 3rd U.S. Cavalry) in May 1861. In December, he was appointed colonel of the 5th New Mexico and won a brevet for his service at the **Battle of Valverde** in February 1862. After helping **Edward R. S. Canby** repulse **Henry Sibley's New Mexico Campaign**, Roberts was promoted to brigadier general of volunteers in June and was transferred to **Virginia** to become inspector general and chief of cavalry for **John Pope's Army of Virginia**. After serving Pope at **Second Manassas**, he personally wrote the charges Pope preferred against **Fitz John Porter**. Roberts was brevetted brigadier general and major general of regulars for **Cedar Mountain** and Second Manassas, respectively, but he also shared Pope's fate for the failure at Second Manassas and accompanied his superior to **Minnesota**. There he served as Pope's inspector general, helped put down the **Sioux uprising**, and led a successful expedition against the Chippewas. Roberts was transferred to **Washington, D.C.**, in February 1863 and briefly commanded part of the city's defenses. He also held **brigade** and **division** commands and tried unsuccessfully to stop **Jones's and Imboden's Raid** into **West Virginia** in the spring of 1863. Sent to the **Department of the Gulf** in June 1864, Roberts led first an infantry division and then a cavalry division before being transferred to the District of West Tennessee and serving there until war's end.

Roberts was mustered out of the volunteer service in January 1866 and resumed his rank of major of regulars. He remained in the army and was appointed professor of military science at Yale University in 1868. Roberts retired in 1870 as a lieutenant colonel of the 3rd U.S. Cavalry and then worked as a lawyer and firearms inventor and manufacturer.

ROBERTS, WILLIAM PAUL (1841–1910) CSA. A native of **North Carolina**, Roberts taught school before the Civil War. He entered state service in June 1861 as a private in the 19th North Carolina but was appointed orderly sergeant a week later. In August, the **regiment** was redesignated the 2nd North Carolina Cavalry, and Roberts was appointed 3rd lieutenant, with a promotion to 1st lieutenant coming a month later.

Roberts served on the North Carolina coast until September 1862, but his only combat was in **skirmishes** around **New Bern** and an unsuccessful attack on **Washington**. Sent to southeastern **Virginia**, his regiment next served with **James Longstreet's** command in the siege of **Suffolk**. After joining the **Army of Northern Virginia** in May 1863, Roberts fought very well at **Brandy Station**, **Hanover**, and **Gettysburg** and earned a promotion to captain in August. He then served in the **Bristoe Station** and **Mine Run Campaigns** and was rewarded with another promotion to major in February 1864. After helping repel the **Kilpatrick-Dahlgren Raid**, Roberts fought at the **Wilderness** and in numerous battles during the **Overland Campaign**. His horse was killed under him in one clash, and he received a slight head wound at **Haw's Shop**. Roberts assumed command of the **regiment** when his colonel was killed in June, and he was promoted to colonel in August 1864. He skillfully led the regiment at **Reams' Station**, **Second Deep Bottom**, **Weldon Railroad**, the **"Beefsteak Raid,"** and **Hatcher's Run**.

Roberts's outstanding service earned him a promotion to brigadier general in February 1865, making him at age 23 the youngest Confederate brigadier (it was claimed that **Robert E. Lee** presented Roberts his own gauntlets in recognition of the promotion). In March, he was given command of a cavalry **brigade** in **William H. F. Lee's division**. Roberts was defeated a month later at **Five Forks**, but he served very well during the **Appomattox Campaign**, and on the morning Lee surrendered he led a cavalry charge that captured two Union cannons. Roberts then escaped from Appomattox, but he disbanded his men when he learned of Lee's **surrender** and returned to Appomattox to receive his **parole**.

Returning to North Carolina after the war, Roberts later served as a state legislator, state auditor, and the U.S. consul to Victoria, British Columbia.

ROBERTSON, BEVERLY HOLCOMBE (1826–1910) CSA. A native of **Virginia**, Robertson graduated from **West Point** in 1849 and served in **Pennsylvania** before joining the 2nd Dragoons on the frontier. He served at several western and southwestern posts fighting Sioux and Apache **Indians** and became the **regiment's** assistant adjutant general. During the **secession** crisis, Robertson was promoted to captain in March 1861, but two weeks later, he was commissioned a captain in the **Confederate army**. He accepted the latter position without resigning his U.S. commission, and federal authorities dismissed him from the service in August for disloyalty. Robertson was elected colonel of the 4th Virginia Cavalry in September and was assigned to **J. E. B. Stuart**, with whom he clashed.

After serving in the **Peninsula Campaign**, Robertson was promoted to brigadier general in June 1862 and replaced the slain **Turner Ashby** in command of **Stonewall Jackson's** cavalry in the **Shenandoah Valley**. He remained in the Valley when Jackson participated in the **Seven Days Campaign**, but he rejoined Jackson in time to fight at **Cedar Mountain**. After Robertson moved too slowly in that battle, Jackson had his **brigade** transferred back to Stuart's command, where it fought effectively at **Second Manassas**. In September 1862, Robertson was sent to **North Carolina** to organize and train cavalry. He served under **Daniel H. Hill** until the spring of 1863, but Hill was not impressed with him and called his brigade a "wonderfully inefficient brigade" (Davis, ed., *The Confederate General*, vol. 5, 97). Robertson returned to the **Army of Northern Virginia** in May 1863, but he performed poorly. At **Brandy Station**, he was driven back from Kelly's Ford and then failed to reenter the fight. When Stuart began his raid behind the **Army of the Potomac** at the beginning of the **Gettysburg Campaign**, he left Robertson's brigade behind with **Robert E. Lee**. In command of his own and **William E. Jones's** brigade, Robertson guarded passes in the Blue Ridge Mountains, but he failed Lee by not rejoining him soon enough in Pennsylvania. During the retreat, he failed again by not following Stuart's orders to hold a pass through South Mountain. Lee was spared the necessity of relieving Robertson of command when Robertson requested a transfer to **South Carolina**. He was given command of a **district** there in October 1863 and helped defend **Charleston**. When Confederate forces evacuated the city in February 1865, Robertson's cavalry formed the rear guard. He served in the **Carolinas Campaign** until war's end and surrendered with **Joseph E. Johnston** in April.

After the war, Robertson settled in **Washington, D.C.**, and worked in the insurance business.

ROBERTSON, FELIX HUSTON (1839–1928) CSA. A native of **Texas**, Robertson was the son of Confederate general **Jerome B. Robertson**. After attending Baylor University, he entered **West Point** in 1857 but left the academy in January 1861 during the **secession** crisis.

Robertson entered Confederate service in March 1861 as a 2nd lieutenant of **artillery** and served with a **mortar** battery during the bombardment of **Fort Sumter**. Sent to **Pensacola, Florida**, he was promoted to captain in October and served on **Adley H. Gladden's** staff. Robertson became close to **Braxton Bragg** while at Pensacola and accompanied him to the **Army of Mississippi** before the **Battle of Shiloh**. He then commanded an artillery battery at Shiloh and Farmington and participated in the **Kentucky Campaign**. Robertson's service through the Kentucky Campaign seems to have been admirable, but his career took a turn at **Stones River** while he was with the **Army of Tennessee**. There his battery supported **John C. Breckinridge's** assault on the Union left on January 2, 1863. Since Robertson was not in Breckinridge's command, he refused to follow the general's orders in the placement of his guns and failed even to engage the enemy until after the attack had been repulsed. He later falsely claimed he captured 30 Union guns during the fight and admitted submitting a false report to help Bragg blame Breckinridge and other officers for his defeat. After being promoted to major in July 1863, Robertson commanded the **army's** reserve artillery in the **Chickamauga** and **Chattanooga Campaigns**. Promoted to lieutenant colonel in January 1864, he was given command of **Joseph Wheeler's horse artillery** and fought with him during the **Atlanta Campaign** until he was promoted to brigadier general in July. It is possible that Robertson's close relationship with Bragg, who now served as **Jefferson Davis's** adviser, led to this promotion.

Robertson was given command of a cavalry **brigade** and participated in **Wheeler's Raid** on **William T. Sherman's** supply line in late summer 1864. He then joined **John S. Williams's** command in southwest **Virginia** to stop **Stephen Burbridge's** Union raid against Saltville. After fighting well at **First Saltville**, Robertson supervised the **massacre** of a number of wounded **black troops**, as well as a few white soldiers, until Breckinridge arrived on the scene and stopped the murders. When Breckinridge reported the incident to **Robert E. Lee**, Lee ordered Robertson's arrest, but he fled the area and rejoined Wheeler. In the **Battle of Buck Head Creek, Georgia**, Robertson was wounded in the arm and again permitted his men to murder captured Union soldiers. When Breckinridge became Confederate secretary of war, he ordered a court of inquiry in early 1865 to investigate Robertson's role in the murders at Saltville and Buck Head Creek. Robertson never appeared before the court, but the Senate rejected his nomination to brigadier general in February. In fact, the Senate failed to confirm any of his military grades except his first one as 2nd lieutenant. Therefore, Robertson reverted back to the rank of 2nd lieutenant, but the war ended before the court of inquiry could take any action against him. On sick leave in Macon, Georgia, when **James H. Wilson's** Union cavalry arrived, he personally surrendered the city. Robertson was **paroled** as a brigadier general although he no longer held that rank.

After the war, Robertson returned to Texas, where he practiced law and supported the Ku Klux Klan. At the time of his death in 1928, he was the last surviving Confederate general.

ROBERTSON, JEROME BONAPARTE (1815–1891) CSA. A native of **Kentucky**, Robertson was the father of Confederate general **Felix H. Robertson**. After being apprenticed to a hatter, he graduated from Transylvania University's medical school in 1835. Robertson moved to **Texas** in 1836, where he fought in the Texas Revolution and in **Indian** campaigns and opened a medical practice. Becoming involved in politics, he was elected to the state assembly in 1848, the state senate in 1850, and was a secessionist delegate in the 1861 **secession** convention.

When the Civil War began, Robertson raised a volunteer **company** that became part of the 5th Texas. He entered Confederate service in early 1861 as the company's captain and accompanied the **regiment** to **Virginia**, where it became part of **John Bell Hood's Texas Brigade** in the **Army of Northern Virginia**. Promoted to lieutenant colonel in October, Robertson was said to have been a "brave and capable" officer, but he lacked charisma, and his men referred to him as "Aunt Polly" or "Old Bob." After being promoted to colonel in June 1862, he led the 5th Texas at **Gaines' Mill** and was wounded when Hood's **brigade** broke through the Union lines there. At **Second Manassas**, Robertson was wounded again, and the regiment suffered more casualties than any other regiment in the **army**. He recovered in time to fight at **South Mountain** but afterward collapsed from exhaustion and missed **Antietam**.

Robertson was promoted to brigadier general in November 1862 and replaced Hood as commander of the Texas Brigade. He saw little combat at **Fredericksburg** and missed **Chancellorsville** while serving with **James Longstreet** at **Suffolk**. At **Gettysburg**, Robertson was wounded and lost nearly 600 men while fighting around Little Round Top and **Devil's Den**. In September, his brigade accompanied Longstreet to

Chickamauga and was the first of the **corps'** units to arrive. Robertson saw heavy fighting at Chickamauga and was talking with Hood when Hood received the wound that led to the amputation of his right leg. After Chickamauga, Robertson began to quarrel with Longstreet. In November, he temporarily was relieved of command because Longstreet disliked his performance at **Wauhatchie**, and in December he was charged with criticizing fellow Brig. Gen. **Micah Jenkins's** leadership. A court-martial reprimanded Robertson for his conduct and relieved him of command. This greatly angered the Texas Brigade and nearly led to mutiny before Robertson personally quieted the men. He then returned to Texas in April 1864, took command of the state's reserve forces in June, and remained in that position until war's end.

After the war, Robertson returned to his Texas medical practice and in 1874 became superintendent of the state's Bureau of Immigration. He also became active in **railroad** construction.

ROBINSON, CHARLES (1818–1894) USA. A native of **Massachusetts**, Robinson attended private schools and became a physician. He established a private practice and opened a hospital in Massachusetts before moving to **California** during the 1849 Gold Rush. After mining gold for a while, Robinson operated a restaurant and coedited a newspaper in Sacramento. He earned some recognition for championing settlers' land rights (and was severely wounded in a confrontation between settlers and land speculators) and served in the state senate from 1850 to 1851. Robinson then returned to Massachusetts, where he reopened his medical practice and edited another newspaper.

An **abolitionist**, Robinson moved to **Kansas** in 1854 and served as an agent for the New England Emigrant Aid Society. He was very active in the antislavery movement during **"Bleeding Kansas"** and helped found the Free-State Party. Robinson was elected governor in 1856, but he never took office because the constitution under which he was elected was rejected. Joining the **Republican Party**, he was elected again in 1859 and was sworn into office in February 1861. Robinson moved swiftly to mobilize Kansas for the Civil War, but he clashed with **James H. Lane** over control of the state's Republican Party. Lane had enough political power to have Robinson impeached on charges of irregularities in the sale of state bonds, but Robinson was acquitted.

After being defeated for reelection in 1862, Robinson became a member of the Liberal Republicans after the war and was elected to the state senate in 1874 and 1876. Switching to the **Democratic Party**, he was defeated for governor in the 1880s and 1890s. Robinson served as president of the Kansas Historical Society from 1879 to 1880, and in 1892 published *The Kansas Conflict*, a history of "Bleeding Kansas."

ROBINSON, JAMES FISHER (1800–1882) USA. A native of **Kentucky**, Robinson worked as a farmer and lawyer before entering the state assembly in 1851 as a **Whig**. He later switched to the **Democratic Party** and reentered the legislature in 1861, becoming the speaker of the house. When Gov. **Beriah Magoffin** resigned in 1862, Robinson was sworn into office on August 18.

As a war governor, Robinson saw his state invaded by the enemy during the **Kentucky Campaign** and, as a moderate Democrat, often clashed with **Abraham Lincoln**. Robinson opposed the administration's military arrest of civilians suspected of disloyalty, the recruitment of troops for the Union **army**, and the **Emancipation Proclamation**. Declining to seek reelection, he resumed his law practice and farming and became involved in education and banking.

ROBINSON, JAMES SIDNEY (1827–1892) USA. A native of **Ohio**, Robinson became a printer and edited the Kenton *Republican* from 1847 to 1861. He also participated in politics and served as the legislature's chief clerk from 1856 to 1858.

Robinson entered Union service in April 1861 as a private in the 90-day 4th Ohio, but he was elected 1st lieutenant the next day and captain two weeks later. He served at **Rich Mountain** before the **regiment** was mustered out of service, and in December he was appointed major of the 82nd Ohio. Sent to **Virginia**, Robinson was promoted to lieutenant colonel in April 1862. After fighting with **John C. Frémont** at **McDowell** and **Cross Keys**, he was promoted to colonel in August after his regimental commander was killed at **Second Manassas**. Attached to the **Army of the Potomac's** XI Corps, the regiment was routed during **Stonewall Jackson's** flank attack at **Chancellorsville**. Two months later, Robinson was severely wounded when the regiment again was routed on the first day at **Gettysburg**.

When Robinson recovered from his wound, he was sent west and in May 1864 took command of a **brigade** in the 1st Division of the **Army of the Cumberland's** XX Corps. He led it through the **Atlanta Campaign** and the **March to the Sea** and earned a **brevet** of brigadier general of volunteers in December 1864. Promoted to brigadier general of volunteers in January 1865, Robinson then participated in the **Carolinas Campaign**. He was mustered out of the volunteer service in August 1865 with a brevet of major general of volunteers.

Robinson returned to Ohio after the war and became commissioner of the state's **railroads** and **telegraphs**. He also served in the **U.S. Congress** from 1881 to 1885 and was Ohio's secretary of state from 1885 to 1889.

ROBINSON, JOHN CLEVELAND (1817–1897) USA. A native of **New York**, Robinson entered **West Point** in 1835, but he was dismissed in 1838 because of a violation of regulations. In 1839, he was commissioned directly into the 5th U.S. Infantry as a 2nd lieutenant and served in the **Mexican War** as a quartermaster. Robinson was promoted to captain in 1850 and over the next decade served in **Florida**, **Texas**, and in the **Utah Expedition**.

When the Civil War began, Robinson commanded **Maryland's** Fort McHenry, and he successfully kept secessionists away during the **Baltimore Riot** of April 1861 by making an over-exaggerated show of force with his 60 men. Afterward, he recruited in **Ohio** and **Michigan** and in September was appointed colonel of the 1st Michigan. Sent to guard **railroads** in Maryland, Robinson was promoted to major of regulars in February 1862 and to brigadier general of volunteers in April.

In June 1862, Robinson was given command of a **brigade** in the 3rd Division of the **Army of the Potomac's** III Corps. After fighting in the **Peninsula** and **Seven Days Campaigns**, he was transferred to the **corps'** 1st Division and fought with it in the **Second Manassas**, **Antietam**, and **Fredericksburg Campaigns**. In December, Robinson took command of a **division** in **John Reynolds's** I Corps. His division was not heavily engaged at **Chancellorsville**, but it did see very heavy combat on **Gettysburg's** first day. There, Robinson was on the far Union right and lost two-thirds of his men while doggedly continuing to fight after the XI Corps was routed from the field. For his tenacious stand, he was **brevetted** lieutenant colonel of regulars. In April 1864, Robinson was given command of a division in **Gouverneur K. Warren's** V Corps and the following month won another brevet for his leadership in the **Wilderness**. His was the first Union division to arrive at **Spotsylvania**, and he was ordered to attack immediately before all of his men were up. Sending in his lead brigade against Laurel Hill, Robinson received a severe knee wound that cost him his leg, but he was brevetted brigadier general of regulars and was awarded the **Medal of Honor** in 1894.

Robinson's wound kept him from retaking the field, and he served the rest of the war on various commissions and in New York **district** commands. When the war ended, he was in charge of the **Freedmen's Bureau** in **North Carolina**. Robinson was brevetted major general in both the regulars and volunteers for his wartime service and was mustered out of the volunteers in September 1866.

Remaining in the regular **army**, Robinson commanded the 43rd U.S. Infantry and the **Departments of the South** and of the Lakes before being placed on the retired list in 1869 as a major general. Afterward, he became lieutenant governor of New York, president of the Society of the Army of the Potomac, and commander in chief of the **Grand Army of the Republic**. A much respected officer, Robinson once was described as being "the hairiest general . . . in a much-bearded army" (Warner, *Generals in Blue*, 407).

ROCK ISLAND PRISON. This Union **prison** camp was located on a Mississippi River island between Rock Island, Illinois, and Davenport, Iowa. Built on a low, swampy island and having 84 crude barracks for shelter, it was one of the worst Union prisons. Each barracks had only two stoves to ward off the bitterly cold winter, and most of the water supply came directly from the river. Completed in late 1863, the prison held 5,000–8,000 **prisoners** at any one time. The last prisoners were released in July 1865, and in August the prison was turned over to the Ordnance Department, which used its barracks for storehouses, barracks, and officers' quarters. The prison hospital was used until 1909.

"ROCK OF CHICKAMAUGA." This was the nickname given to Union Maj. Gen. **George H. Thomas** after he made a successful defensive stand at **Chickamauga's Snodgrass Hill** in September 1863 that allowed the **Army of the Cumberland** to retreat safely to **Chattanooga, Tennessee**.

ROCKY FACE RIDGE, GEORGIA, BATTLE OF (MAY 7–11, 1864). When **William T. Sherman** began the **Atlanta Campaign** in early May 1864, **Joseph E. Johnston's** Confederate **Army of Tennessee** was entrenched at Rocky Face Ridge, just west of Dalton in northern **Georgia**. Rocky Face Ridge is a nearly vertical 500-foot ridge running north–south, with a gap known as Buzzard's Roost (or Mill Creek Gap) piercing it northwest of Dalton. Johnston's **army** was strongly positioned on the ridge on both sides of Buzzard's Roost. When Sherman advanced to Rocky Face Ridge, he realized the position was too strong for a **frontal attack** and sent **James B. McPherson's Army of the Tennessee** south to **Snake Creek Gap** to cut Johnston's line of retreat at **Resaca**. To distract the Confederates, **George H. Thomas's Army of the Cumberland demonstrated** against Rocky Face Ridge from the west while **John M. Schofield's Army of the Ohio** threatened it from the north.

On May 7, Thomas advanced and pushed Johnston's advance **pickets** from Tunnel Hill back to Buzzard's Roost. The next day, Thomas confronted Rocky Face Ridge with his main **army** while **John W. Geary's** XX Corps **division** moved to the south four miles to demonstrate against Dug Gap. Geary attacked the gap but was driven off by J. Warren Grigsby's Confederate cavalry, which was supported by the infantry **brigades** of **Daniel H. Reynolds** and **Hiram B. Granbury**. Meanwhile, around Buzzard's Roost, Thomas and Schofield probed Rocky Face Ridge from the west and north, respectively. The Federals renewed their pressure on Buzzard's Roost Gap on May 9, but the Confederate divisions of **Alexander P. Stewart** and **William Bate** held firm. To the north, **Charles G. Harker's** Union brigade reached the top of the ridge at a point where the Confederate line angled to the northeast at the juncture of **Benjamin Cheatham's** and **Carter L. Stevenson's** divisions. There bloody fighting raged as the Federals made five unsuccessful assaults against the strong Confederate position. That same day, **Joseph Wheeler's** cavalry defeated and inflicted heavy casualties on a brigade of Sherman's cavalry north of Dalton at Varnell's Station.

Sherman had failed to dislodge the Confederates at Rocky Face Ridge, and McPherson had withdrawn when he ran into Confederates near Resaca. Referring to Buzzard's Roost as "the door of death" (Kennedy, ed., *The Civil War Battlefield Guide*, 328), Sherman decided to make no further moves there. On May 11, he left **Oliver O. Howard's** IV Corps and two cavalry divisions to keep pressure on Rocky Face Ridge and took the rest of his force south to join McPherson at Snake Creek Gap to capture Resaca. The next day, Wheeler learned of this move from **prisoners** and informed Johnston of the threat to his rear. Johnston withdrew from Rocky Face Ridge on the night of May 12 and fell back to Resaca. The fighting around Rocky Face Ridge began the Atlanta Campaign and set a pattern of Sherman using **turning movements** rather than frontal assaults to force Johnston out of his defensive positions. During the fighting, Sherman lost 837 men, while Johnston counted about 600 casualties.

ROCKY GAP, WEST VIRGINIA, BATTLE OF (AUGUST 26, 1863).

In early August 1863, Union Brig. Gen. **William W. Averell** took 2,000 men from Winchester, Virginia, on a raid into **West Virginia** to destroy Confederate munitions works near Franklin and to engage **William L. Jackson's** Confederate cavalry at Huntersville. In an exhausting raid plagued by food and equipment shortages and punctuated by frequent **skirmishes**, Averell forced Jackson to abandon Huntersville and Warm Springs and successfully destroyed several saltpeter works.

Advancing west toward White Sulphur Springs on August 26, Averell encountered 1,900 Confederates under Col. George S. Patton who had been sent by **department** commander **Samuel Jones** to stop the raiders. Patton had taken up a strong position two miles from White Sulphur Springs at Rocky Gap. Averell launched numerous attacks against the Confederates but was unable to dislodge them from the gap. Fighting continued the next day as Averell stubbornly pounded away at Patton. By noon, Averell finally called off the attacks and withdrew toward Callaghan's Station. He had lost 218 men at Rocky Gap, while Patton lost 162. The largely unsuccessful raid ended when Averell reached Beverly on August 31.

RODDEY, PHILIP DALE (1826–1897) CSA. A native of **Alabama**, Roddey received little education growing up and worked as a tailor, as a county sheriff, and on steamboats. When the Civil War began, he organized a volunteer **company** and was elected its captain. Roddey earned a reputation as a talented scout along the Tennessee River, served with **Braxton Bragg's** escort during the **Battle of Shiloh**, and performed valuable scouting duty during the **siege of Corinth, Mississippi**. In the summer of 1862, he commanded a cavalry battalion and made numerous successful raids against the enemy in northwestern Alabama.

Given permission to raise his own **regiment**, Roddey organized the 4th Alabama Cavalry in October 1862 and was appointed its colonel. He was given command of a **brigade** in January 1863 and frequently engaged the enemy while serving with the advance guard of Bragg's **Army of Tennessee**. That spring, Roddey was put in command of the District of Northern Alabama. In April, he engaged **Grenville M. Dodge** as he advanced against Decatur, Alabama, as a diversion for **Streight's Raid**. Roddey slowed the Federals and enabled **Nathan Bedford Forrest** to arrive in time to capture the raiders.

In August 1863, Roddey was promoted to brigadier general, and his brigade was attached to **Joseph Wheeler's** cavalry. He participated in **Wheeler's Raid** that autumn to cut the Union supply lines into Chattanooga, Tennessee, and in October joined **Stephen D. Lee's** cavalry to oppose **William T. Sherman's** advance from **Mississippi** to Chattanooga. By January 1864, Roddey was known as the "Swamp Fox of the Tennessee Valley." He attacked the Union garrison at Athens, Alabama, in January and then briefly joined the Army of Tennessee in north **Georgia** before returning to Alabama in April.

Roddey formed his command into a **division** in May 1864 and sent one brigade to help Forrest win the **Battle of Brice's Cross Roads**. The reunited division then fought with Forrest at **Tupelo**. In September, Roddey was given command of the District of North Alabama, and he remained there until war's end **picketing** the Tennessee River, supervising **railroad** repairs, and raiding enemy outposts. During **John Bell Hood's** retreat after the **Battle of Nashville**, Roddey's cavalry helped form the rear guard, but in late December, he failed to stop a Union attack that captured the army's **pontoon bridge** train. Because of this defeat, he was put under Forrest's command and fought with him at **Ebenezer Church** and **Selma**. Roddey was **paroled** with the rest of Forrest's men when the war ended.

After the war, Roddey became a commission merchant and often stayed in New York City. He died while in Great Britain trying to sell the rights to a new pump he had patented.

RODES, ROBERT EMMETT (1829–1864) CSA. A native of **Virginia**, Rodes graduated from the **Virginia Military Institute** in 1848 and then taught there for two years. From 1851 to 1854, he worked as a civil engineer in Virginia and then held engineering positions with **railroads** in several states before becoming chief engineer of an **Alabama** railroad.

Rodes was traveling in Europe when the Civil War began. Returning to Alabama, he raised a volunteer **company** and was elected its captain. In May 1861, the company became part of the 5th Alabama and was sent to **Fort Morgan** at Mobile Bay, Alabama. There, Rodes was appointed colonel later in the month, and in June, he took the **regiment** to Virginia to serve at **First Manassas** in **Richard S. Ewell's brigade**.

Promoted to brigadier general in October 1861, Rodes led a brigade in **Daniel H. Hill's** division during the **Peninsula Campaign**. He was highly praised for his first combat experience at **Seven Pines**, where his brigade suffered heavy losses, and he was severely wounded. Rodes tried to return to the **Army of Northern Virginia** for the **Seven Days Campaign**, but his wound forced him from the field again. Finally rejoining the brigade during the **Antietam Campaign**, he stubbornly held his position at both **South Mountain's** Turner's Gap and at **Antietam's** "Bloody Lane," where he was wounded again. Rodes was not engaged at **Fredericksburg**, but at **Chancellorsville**, he temporarily commanded the **division** and formed the first line of **Stonewall Jackson's** famous flank attack. Ewell later claimed that next to Jackson, Rodes was the hero of the battle.

Rodes's performance at Chancellorsville won him promotion to major general only days after the battle. Taking command of a II Corps division, his performance at **Gettysburg** was less than stellar. The division was badly shot up on the battle's first day because of the ineptness of subordinate officers, and on the second day, Rodes failed to properly support **Jubal A. Early's** attack on Cemetery Hill. However, this setback did not affect his great popularity or his superiors' confidence in him, and he performed well in the **Bristoe Station, Mine Run,** and **Overland Campaigns.** In this last campaign, Rodes led a counterattack that helped contain the Union breakthrough and restore the **army's** broken line at **Spotsylvania's** "Bloody Angle." In July 1864, he accompanied **Early's Washington Raid** and fought in **Philip Sheridan's Shenandoah Valley Campaign** that autumn. At **Third Winchester** on September 19, 1864, Rodes was trying to rally his men when he was shot in the head and killed instantly. His loss was said to have "cast a gloom over the whole of this army" (Davis, ed., *The Confederate General,* vol. 5, 109).

RODGERS, JOHN (1812–1882) USA. The son of **U.S. Navy** officer John Rodgers, Rodgers was a native of **Maryland** and entered the navy as a midshipman in 1828. After serving in the Mediterranean, he attended the University of Virginia before returning to duty and serving aboard ships all over the world.

Rodgers was a commander when the Civil War began. In May 1861, he was sent to **Ohio** by **George B. McClellan** to convert river steamers into gunboats, but in October, he was replaced by **Andrew H. Foote** and returned east to assume command of the USS *Flagg.* Rodgers served in **Samuel F. Du Pont's** expedition to **Port Royal, South Carolina**; was Du Pont's aide during the fighting at Hilton Head, South Carolina; and was given the honor of raising the first Union **flag** over occupied **South Carolina.** In April 1862, he was given command of the **ironclad** *Galena,* part of the flotilla supporting McClellan's **Peninsula Campaign.** Rodgers engaged the Confederates on the James River at **First Drewry's Bluff** in May but was repulsed after suffering heavy casualties. Promoted to captain in July, he next took command of the **monitor** *Weehawken* and participated in the **blockade** of **Charleston, South Carolina.** When Du Pont attacked the city in April 1863, Rodgers was employed in removing **torpedoes** from the harbor and engaging the enemy forts. The *Weehawken* was heavily damaged in the engagement, but it was repaired in time to fight the **CSS** *Atlanta* in June. Rodgers sank the enemy vessel and won both the **Thanks of Congress** and a promotion to commodore. After serving on blockade duty, he was assigned to administrative duties until war's end.

Rodgers remained in the navy after the war and commanded a squadron off Chile in late 1865. He later commanded the Boston Navy

Yard and the Asiatic Squadron during an 1871 punitive mission against Korea. After Rodgers retired from sea duty as a rear admiral in 1872, he served on various examining boards, commanded **California's** Mare Island shipyard, and became superintendent of the Naval Observatory.

RODMAN GUN. Developed by **Thomas J. Rodman**, the Rodman gun was a large-caliber **artillery** piece that was made by a cooling process Rodman discovered. Previously, a cannon tube was cast as a solid piece of metal, which then was cooled and bored to size. Traditional methods cooled the tube's outside first, but this caused weaknesses within the metal, and the guns sometimes exploded. In 1844–45, Rodman devised a method of casting the tubes around a hollow pipe of proper bore size, through which water was circulated while molten metal was poured into the cast. This allowed the tube to cool from the inside and the interior metal to become tightly compressed as the outside metal constricted. The result was a much stronger gun tube that could withstand high pressures.

Rodman had the privately owned Fort Pitt, Pennsylvania, Foundry register his patents and cast the first Rodman guns there. When the guns were proven superior to others, the **U.S. Army** adopted the new process in 1857. Beginning in 1861, **Columbiads** were made by the Rodman method in calibers of 8-, 10-, 13-, 15-, and 20-inch and largely were used for coastal defense. The Confederates never adopted the method, although the **Tredegar Iron Works** did make two Rodman Columbiads late in the war.

RODMAN, ISAAC PEACE (1822–1862) USA. A Quaker from **Rhode Island**, Rodman was a businessman and politician before the Civil War. He served on his hometown's town council and was a member of both the state assembly and senate.

Serving as a senator when the war began, Rodman was torn between his religious beliefs and his patriotic duty. However, he accepted a captain's commission in the 2nd Rhode Island in June 1861 and saw heavy combat at **First Manassas**. Rodman then resigned from the **regiment** in October to become colonel of the 4th Rhode Island. Accompanying **Ambrose E. Burnside's** expedition to **North Carolina**, he fought at **Roanoke Island**, **New Bern**, and **Fort Macon**.

Rodman's excellent service earned him promotion to brigadier general of volunteers in April 1862. He contracted typhoid fever while serving as military governor of Beaufort, South Carolina, which kept him on sick leave for a time, but he returned to duty and at **Antietam** and led a **division** in **Jesse Reno's** IX Corps of the **Army of the Potomac**. While fighting on the Union left, Rodman took his division across Antietam Creek at a ford and was attacked by **A. P. Hill's** Confederate division arriving from **Harpers Ferry, Virginia.** Shot in the chest, he was taken from the field but died on September 30, 1862.

RODMAN, THOMAS JACKSON (1815–1871) USA. A native of **Indiana,** Rodman graduated from **West Point** in 1841 and was assigned to the Ordnance Department. In 1844–45, he began experimenting with a method to strengthen cannon tubes by circulating water within the casting core to cool the tube from the inside out. The result was stronger large-caliber guns known as **Rodman guns.** After serving at stateside arsenals during the **Mexican War,** Rodman had a private **Pennsylvania** foundry register his patents on the new cooling system and began testing the guns in 1847. The tests were successful, and the **U.S. Army** adopted his method in 1857. During the 1850s, Rodman served at numerous arsenals developing new forms of gunpowder and gun casting. In 1861, his cooling system was used to make a new **Columbiad,** the first of the Rodman guns that saw widespread service during the Civil War.

When the Civil War began in April 1861, Captain Rodman was put in command of the Watertown, New York, Arsenal. He published reports on his ordnance experiments later in the year and remained at the arsenal for the entire war. During his tenure, Rodman began using his cooling system to manufacture heavy ordnance ammunition. He was promoted to major in June 1863 and by war's end was **brevetted** through all grades to brigadier general of regulars.

After the war, Rodman remained active in the Ordnance Department, served at several arsenals, and in March 1867 was promoted to lieutenant colonel. His health then deteriorated, and he died four years later.

ROLL OF HONOR. To improve **army** morale, the **Confederate Congress** authorized the awarding of medals and badges to those soldiers who were commended in battle reports. While actual medals and badges were never awarded, a roll of honor was authorized in October 1862. Any soldier who demonstrated conspicuous bravery or conduct in battle had his name inscribed on the roll. After battles, this roll of honor was read to the troops during dress parades, published in newspapers, and filed in the offices of the adjutant and inspector generals. *See also* DECORATIONS.

ROOT, GEORGE FREDERICK (1820–1895) USA. A native of **Massachusetts,** Root was a well-known **music** teacher and composer before the Civil War. He taught at the Rutgers Female Academy and the Union

Theological Seminary before moving to **Illinois** in 1860 and becoming a partner with his brother in a music store. During the war, Root wrote 28 patriotic songs, including "We'll Rally 'round the Flag, Boys," "Tramp, Tramp, Tramp, the Boys Are Marching," "The Vacant Chair," "Just before the Battle, Mother," and "The Battle Cry of Freedom."

ROSECRANS, WILLIAM STARKE (1819–1898) USA. A native of **Ohio**, Rosecrans (ROHZ-kranz) graduated near the top of his 1842 **West Point** class and was assigned to the **engineers**. Engaged in routine assignments, he did not participate in the **Mexican War** but was promoted to 1st lieutenant in 1853. After resigning his commission the next year, Rosecrans became a businessman and in 1859 was severely burned in a fire at his Ohio kerosene plant.

When the Civil War began, Rosecrans joined **George B. McClellan's** staff in April 1861 with the rank of colonel of engineers. Accompanying McClellan to western **Virginia**, he assumed command of a **brigade** there and in June was appointed colonel of the 23rd Ohio. A few days later, Rosecrans was appointed brigadier general of regulars. He and his brigade were key to the victory at **Rich Mountain**, but McClellan was given all of the credit for the battle. When McClellan was called to **Washington, D.C.**, in July to assume command of the **army** there, Rosecrans was left in charge of the **Department of the Ohio** and in September won the **Battle of Carnifex Ferry**. In October, he was given command of the **Department of Western Virginia**, but in March 1862, it was incorporated into the new **Mountain Department** under **John C. Frémont**. Rosecrans commanded the **department** until Frémont arrived later that month but then was transferred at his own request.

Sent west, Rosecrans commanded the right wing of **John Pope's Army of the Mississippi** during the **siege of Corinth, Mississippi**. When Pope was called east to lead the **Army of Virginia**, Rosecrans was left in command of the **army**. Promoted to major general of volunteers in September 1862, he led the Army of the Mississippi at **Iuka** and successfully repelled a Confederate attack in the October **Battle of Corinth**. After the latter battle, Rosecrans complained of his lack of seniority and had his brigadier's commission reappointed to date from March 1862. In late October 1862, he replaced **Don Carlos Buell** in **Kentucky** and took charge of the troops that were designated the **Army of the Cumberland**. Although short-tempered, Rosecrans was popular with his men, who referred to him as "Old Rosey," and he proved to be a very capable organizer and strategist. He defeated **Braxton Bragg's Army of Tennessee** at **Stones River** in January 1863 and was voted the **Thanks of Congress**.

That summer, Rosecrans also skillfully maneuvered Bragg out of Middle Tennessee in the **Tullahoma Campaign** and forced him to evacuate **Chattanooga, Tennessee**, and withdraw into northern **Georgia**. He then allowed his army to scatter, however, and barely concentrated his men in time to meet the Confederate attack at **Chickamauga**.

Chickamauga was a disaster for Rosecrans. On the second day of fighting, he mistakenly believed there was a gap in his defenses and ordered a **division** off the front line to close it. This created a real gap through which the Confederates attacked. When his line was broken, Rosecrans was swept up in the rout and retreated all the way back to Chattanooga, leaving **George H. Thomas** behind to hold off the Confederates. Becoming besieged inside Chattanooga, Rosecrans took little action to relieve his situation, and **U. S. Grant** finally replaced him with Thomas in October. While transferring command, Rosecrans suggested to Grant several good plans of action, leaving Grant to wonder why he had not tried them himself. At the end of January 1864, Rosecrans was placed in command of the **Department of the Missouri**. He defended **Missouri** against **Sterling Price's 1864 Missouri Raid** but was relieved of command in December. The war ended before Rosecrans received another command.

Rosecrans was mustered out of the volunteers in January 1866 and was **brevetted** major general of regulars for Stones River. Unhappy with his treatment by the army, he resigned his commission in March 1867 and moved to **California**. There, Rosecrans declined several opportunities to run for the **U.S. Congress**, but he was appointed ambassador to Mexico. He was elected to two congressional terms in the 1880s and served as chairman of the Military Affairs Committee. Rosecrans was placed on the retired list of regular officers in 1889 with the rank of brigadier general.

ROSS, LAWRENCE SULLIVAN (1838–1898) CSA. A native of **Iowa**, as an infant, Ross moved to **Texas** with his family. While attending Baylor University in 1859, he volunteered for service under **Earl Van Dorn** in an **Indian** campaign and was severely wounded in the shoulder and chest. Impressed with the young soldier, **Winfield Scott** offered to help secure him an officer's commission, but Ross declined in order to complete his education. After graduating from **Alabama's** Wesleyan University in 1859, he was commissioned a captain in the Texas Rangers in 1860 and successfully rescued Cynthia Parker (Quanah Parker's mother) in a campaign against the Comanches.

When the Civil War began, "Sul" Ross joined the 6th Texas Cavalry as a private but was commissioned its major in September 1861. Sent to

Missouri, he was praised for successfully raiding a Union wagon train far in the Union rear prior to the **Battle of Pea Ridge**. Ross was elected the **regiment's** colonel in May 1862 and again won accolades for his rear guard actions during the Confederate evacuation after the **siege of Corinth, Mississippi**. At **Thompson's Station, Tennessee**, in early 1863, his regiment attacked a much superior Union force and helped captured 1,500 **prisoners**. Afterward, Ross was given command of his regiment and the 1st Mississippi Cavalry and was sent into **Tennessee** to raid Union Maj. Gen. **William S. Rosecrans's** supply line. After his return in December 1863, he was promoted to brigadier general in February 1864 and was given command of a Texas cavalry **brigade** under Maj. Gen. **William H. Jackson**. Ross fought extensively in **Mississippi**, capturing Yazoo City and once battling Union gunboats on the Yazoo River with pistols. In one of their many battles, Ross's Texans were accused of murder when they killed 75 out of 80 members of a **company** of **black troops**, but Ross denied the accusations.

During the **Atlanta Campaign**, Ross's brigade saw heavy combat and successfully defended **Lovejoy's Station** against a Union raid. After the fall of Atlanta, he led **John Bell Hood's** invasion during the **Franklin and Nashville Campaign** and then covered the Confederate retreat after Hood's defeat at Nashville. Returning to Mississippi, Ross went to Texas on furlough in March 1865 and was there when the war ended. During the war, he had five horses killed under him and was involved in 135 engagements.

Ross became one of Texas's most prominent citizens after the war. He served as a county sheriff from 1873 to 1874, was a member of the 1875 constitutional convention, served in the state senate from 1881 to 1885, was governor from 1887 to 1891, and served as president of Texas A&M University from 1891 to 1898. Ross died in 1898 from exposure while on a hunting trip along the Trinity River.

ROSS, LEONARD FULTON (1823–1901) USA. A native of **Illinois**, Ross attended Jacksonville College for one year and then read law. After becoming a lawyer in 1845, he served in the **Mexican War** as a private and 1st lieutenant in the 4th Illinois. Returning to Illinois, Ross became a well-known stockbreeder and was active in local **Democratic** politics, serving as a probate judge and county clerk.

Ross entered Union service in May 1861 when he raised the 17th Illinois and was commissioned its colonel. He spent the first part of the war in **Missouri** and had a horse shot from under him at **Fredericktown**. Transferred to **Kentucky**, Ross commanded a **brigade** in **John A. McClernand's** division at **Fort Donelson**. Promoted to brigadier general in April 1862, he missed **Shiloh** but did participate in the **siege of Corinth, Mississippi**. In the summer of 1862, Ross guarded **railroads** in **Tennessee** and for a time commanded the District of Jackson. Late that year, he commanded a **division** in the **Army of the Tennessee's** XIII Corps during **U. S. Grant's Overland Vicksburg Campaign**. After Grant moved his operation to the Mississippi River, Ross led the infantry in the failed **Yazoo Pass Expedition**. Afterward, he was put in command of Helena, Arkansas, and thus missed the final **Vicksburg Campaign**. When **Vicksburg, Mississippi**, was captured, Ross apparently thought the war was nearly over and resigned his commission in late July 1863 and returned to Illinois.

Having become a **Republican**, Ross was appointed an internal revenue collector in 1867, served as a delegate at three Republican National Conventions, and twice ran unsuccessfully for the **U.S. Congress**. However, he was best known as one of the country's leading stockbreeders.

ROSSER, THOMAS LAFAYETTE (1836–1910) CSA. A native of **Virginia**, as a boy, Rosser moved with his family to **Texas**. Just weeks before graduating from **West Point** (where he became close friends with **George A. Custer**), he left the academy and entered Confederate service in May 1861 as a 1st lieutenant in the **Washington Artillery**.

After commanding part of the Washington Artillery at **First Manassas**, Rosser was promoted to captain in September 1861. He fought with the **Army of Northern Virginia** in the **Seven Days Campaign** and was severely wounded at **Mechanicsville**. After numerous recommendations from other officers, Rosser was promoted to lieutenant colonel in June 1862 and was elected colonel of the 5th Virginia Cavalry later that month. As part of **J. E. B. Stuart's** cavalry, he fought at **Catlett's Station, Second Manassas, Crampton's Gap**, and **Antietam**. He served with **John Pelham's horse artillery** at **Fredericksburg** and was severely wounded at **Kelly's Ford** in March 1863. After much politicking by Stuart and Rosser, Rosser was promoted to brigadier general in October and was given command of the Laurel Brigade. While his men praised his courage, many complained that he knew little about **tactics** or administration. **Robert E. Lee** and other superiors, however, highly regarded Rosser and recommended his promotion.

After fighting through the 1864 **Overland Campaign**, Rosser was transferred to the **Shenandoah Valley** that autumn and became known as the "Savior of the Valley" while fighting with **Jubal A. Early** in **Philip Sheridan's Shenandoah Valley Campaign**. He was badly defeated at **Tom's Brook** by Custer and temporarily led the **division** at **Cedar**

Creek. Rosser was promoted to major general in November and remained in the Shenandoah Valley during the winter of 1864–65. After **Rosser's Beverly, Moorefield**, and **New Creek, West Virginia, Raids**, he led his division to Petersburg, Virginia, in March 1865 and was wounded in the arm at **White Oak Road** during the **Petersburg Campaign**. Despite his wound, Rosser hosted a shad bake on April 1, which **George E. Pickett** attended, while his men were being routed at **Five Forks**. Accompanying the Army of Northern Virginia on its retreat to **Appomattox**, Rosser won one of the last Confederate victories in a small battle at **High Bridge**. He then escaped with his command but surrendered a month later.

After the war, Rosser worked at numerous jobs. He farmed, became director of the Southern Orphan Association, served as president of a land company, and worked as a **railroad** engineer. Rosser also was active in writing about the **Lost Cause** and frequently was involved in controversies with other former Confederate officers over wartime leadership and battles. He returned to the military during the Spanish-American War when he was appointed a brigadier general of volunteers.

ROSSER'S BEVERLY, WEST VIRGINIA, RAID (JANUARY 7–11, 1865). After suffering several defeats in **Philip H. Sheridan's 1864 Shenandoah Valley Campaign**, Confederates in the **Shenandoah Valley** were desperate for supplies in the cold winter of 1864–65. In January 1865, cavalryman **Thomas L. Rosser** raided a Union supply base at Beverly, West Virginia, to gain needed food and clothing for his command. With 300 men, Rosser left Staunton, Virginia, on January 7 in deep snow. After a bitterly cold 75-mile ride to Beverly, the Confederates attacked on the morning of January 11 and routed the still-sleeping 8th and 34th Ohio from their camps. At a loss of only one dead and a few wounded, Rosser inflicted 38 casualties on the enemy and captured the supply base, 580 **prisoners**, and 10,000 **rations**. Taking the supplies back to the Valley, he fed his men for some time on the captured supplies.

ROSSER'S MOOREFIELD, WEST VIRGINIA RAID (JANUARY 28–FEBRUARY 1, 1864). On January 28, 1864, Lt. Gen. **Jubal A. Early** led **Thomas L. Rosser's** Laurel Brigade and **Edward L. Thomas's** infantry **brigade** from New Market, Virginia, toward Moorefield, West Virginia, to gather supplies and cattle. Reaching Moorefield on January 29, Early learned of a Union wagon train to the south toward Petersburg, West Virginia, and sent Rosser's cavalry to intercept it. Rosser left Moorefield on January 30, fought his way through a mountain gap, and found the train at Medley guarded by four Union **regiments**. He sent one of his regiments into the enemy's rear while attacking with his other three dismounted. The Confederates at first were repulsed, but they then attacked the Union left flank and front simultaneously. The Federals fled and abandoned 95 wagons loaded with supplies.

On January 31, Rosser and Thomas proceeded to Petersburg and captured a large amount of supplies there. The next day, Rosser moved to Patterson's Creek, where he captured 80 **prisoners**, 1,200 cattle, and 500 sheep. Afterward, he and Thomas reunited and retreated back to the Shenandoah Valley. At a cost of only 25 men, the raid gathered much-needed supplies, boosted morale after the disastrous defeats in the **Shenandoah Valley** that autumn, and encouraged the Laurel Brigade to reenlist.

ROSSER'S NEW CREEK, WEST VIRGINIA, RAID (NOVEMBER 26–DECEMBER 2, 1864). On November 26, 1864, Confederate cavalryman Brig. Gen. **Thomas L. Rosser** led two **brigades** from the **Shenandoah Valley** on a raid against a Union supply base and the Baltimore & Ohio Railroad at New Creek, West Virginia. He routed a small number of Union troops at Moorefield, West Virginia, on November 27, but these soldiers were able to warn New Creek of his approach. Inexplicably, Union commander Col. George R. Latham took no precautions to meet the coming attack. Rosser rode all night and advanced on the outpost the next morning. With a small band of men dressed in Union **uniforms** leading the way, he surprised and captured the enemy **pickets** and then overwhelmed the Union garrison, which was eating lunch at the time. At a cost of only five men, Rosser captured about 700 of the nearly 800-man garrison, looted the supply base, and burned what he could not carry off. The successful raid was marred by Rosser's curious failure to destroy the **railroad** bridge or track. He retreated that afternoon and safely reached his Shenandoah Valley base on December 2. Latham was court-martialed and dismissed from the service for his lack of leadership, but he had his dismissal revoked after being elected to the **U.S. Congress**.

ROST, PIERRE ADOLPH (1797–1868) CSA. A native of France and veteran of Napoleon's campaigns, Rost immigrated to **Mississippi** in 1816 and read law under **Jefferson Davis's** brother, Joseph. Settling in **Louisiana**, he became a wealthy planter, served in the state senate, and sat on the state supreme court in 1839 and from 1846 to 1853.

In February 1861, Davis appointed Rost, **William L. Yancey**, and **A. Dudley Mann** as the Confederacy's first European diplomats. After arriving in Great Britain in April, Rost traveled to France to secure recognition of the Confederacy but utterly failed to impress his hosts. He had no diplomatic experience, was less than fluent in the language (even though he was a native), and was completely out of touch with the war's realities. When asked how the war was progressing, Rost always replied, "All goes well" (Current, ed., *Encyclopedia of the Confederacy*, vol. 3, 1347)—even after the Federals confiscated his own Louisiana plantation. After becoming something of a comic figure in France, Rost was transferred to Spain in August 1861, but he had no better success there. He resigned in May 1862 but remained in France until the war was over. Rost returned to Louisiana at the end of hostilities and died in 1868.

ROUSSEAU, LOVELL HARRISON (1818–1869) USA. A native of **Kentucky**, Rousseau worked as a laborer before reading law and moving to **Indiana** in 1840. There he became a lawyer, was elected to the state assembly in 1844, and served as a captain in the 2nd Indiana during the **Mexican War**. Returning to Indiana after the war, Rousseau served in the state senate from 1847 to 1849 and then moved his law practice to Kentucky. He was elected to the Kentucky senate in 1860 but resigned his seat in 1861 to recruit volunteers for the Union.

Because of Kentucky's neutrality early in the war, Rousseau's recruiting efforts were necessarily discreet, but he finally entered Union service in September 1861 as colonel of the 3rd Kentucky (Union). He was promoted to brigadier general of volunteers the following month and was given command of an infantry **brigade**. After serving at **Shiloh** in the **Army of the Ohio's** 2nd Division, Rousseau was given command of a **division** in **Alexander McCook's corps** and led it at **Perryville**.

Rousseau was promoted to major general of volunteers in October 1862 and the following month took command of a division in the **Army of the Cumberland's** XIV Corps. He fought well at **Stones River** and then participated in the **Tullahoma Campaign**. After missing the **Battle of Chickamauga**, Rousseau was put in command of the District of Nashville in November 1863. While there, he carried out a number of cavalry raids, including the highly successful **Rousseau's Alabama Raid** in the summer of 1864. In March 1865, the District of Middle Tennessee also was added to Rousseau's command.

Having been elected to the **U.S. Congress** from Kentucky in 1865, Rousseau resigned his commission in November 1865 to take his seat. Although elected as a **Radical Republican**, he quickly became a moderate and supported the **Reconstruction** policies of President **Andrew Johnson**. Rousseau resigned his seat in 1866 after being censured for attacking Radical Republican Josiah B. Grinnell with a cane in the capitol building, but his constituents reelected him. Johnson then appointed him a brigadier general of regulars in March 1867, with **brevet** rank of major general, and dispatched him to Alaska to take charge of that territory from Russia. Rousseau was made military commander of **Louisiana** in 1868 and died the following year in **New Orleans**.

ROUSSEAU'S ALABAMA RAID (JULY 9–22, 1864). During the **Atlanta Campaign**, **William T. Sherman** ordered **Lovell H. Rousseau**, commander of the District of Nashville, to raid the Montgomery & West Point Railroad in **Alabama** to disrupt Confederate transportation between **Mississippi**, Alabama, and **Georgia**. Rousseau decided to destroy the track between Montgomery and Opelika, and, if possible, join Sherman in Georgia. He led 2,500 cavalrymen from Decatur, Alabama, on July 9, 1864, and reached the **railroad** near Opelika on July 17. There, Rousseau destroyed miles of track before riding on to Marietta, Georgia. Confederate cavalry under **Stephen D. Lee** pursued him for days but were unable to catch the Union raiders. At a cost of only 42 men and one lost cannon, Rousseau traveled 400 miles, destroyed the vital Montgomery & West Point Railroad, captured or destroyed valuable Confederate supplies (42,000 lbs. of food at Opelika alone), and severely damaged Confederate morale.

ROWAN, STEPHEN CLEGG (1808–1890) USA. A native of Ireland, Rowan immigrated to **Ohio** as a boy and entered the **U.S. Navy** in 1826 as a midshipman. After serving around the world, he was promoted to lieutenant in 1837. During the **Mexican War**, Rowan was executive officer of the USS *Cyane* and led a number of raids in **California** while commanding a battalion of sailors and **U.S. Marines**.

Promoted to commander in 1855, Rowan was in command of the USS *Pawnee* in 1861 and participated in the attempted relief of **Fort Sumter** and in the evacuation of the **Norfolk, Virginia**, Navy Yard. He was credited with firing the first naval shots of the Civil War when he opened fire on a Confederate battery at Aquia Creek that was blockading the Potomac River. In May, Rowan led an amphibious assault that captured Alexandria, Virginia, and in August he participated in the expedition against **Hatteras Inlet, North Carolina**. In February 1862, Rowan was placed in command of the Naval Division of the **North Atlantic Blockading Squadron**. After supporting **Ambrose E. Burnside's** expedition to **Roanoke Island** and **New Bern, North Carolina**, he was promoted to captain and commodore on the same day in July 1862. Put in command of the **USS *New Ironsides*** of the **South Atlantic Blockading Squadron**, Rowan fought in several engagements at **Charleston, South Carolina**, from July to September 1863. In the autumn of 1864, he was placed in charge of all naval forces in **North Carolina** waters.

After the war, Rowan was promoted to rear admiral in 1866 and to vice admiral in 1870. He then served on shore duty until his retirement in 1889.

ROWLETT'S STATION, KENTUCKY, BATTLE OF (DECEMBER 17, 1861). In November 1861, Union Brig. Gen. **Don Carlos Buell**, commander of the **Department of the Ohio**, sent Brig. Gen. **Alexander McCook's division** to attack the Confederates on the Green River near Munfordville, Kentucky. McCook attacked on December 10 and gained a foothold on the south bank, but the Confederates partially destroyed the **railroad** bridge across the river. A **pontoon bridge** was completed on December 17, and the 32nd Indiana crossed over and advanced toward Rowlett's Station. Confederate cavalry under **Thomas C. Hindman** then attacked Col. **August Willich's Indiana regiment** and forced it to withdraw to a defensive position. When McCook advanced with reinforcements, Hindman withdrew and left the area to the Federals. In the engagement, Hindman lost 91 men, while Willich suffered 40 casualties.

ROWLEY, THOMAS ALGEO (1808–1892) USA. A native of **Pennsylvania**, Rowley worked as a cabinetmaker before being elected justice of the peace. After serving in the **Mexican War** as captain of a state volunteer **company**, he returned to Pennsylvania and worked as a contractor and clerk of court.

Rowley entered Union service in April 1861 as colonel of the 90-day 13th Pennsylvania. The **regiment** first guarded the Potomac River under **Robert Patterson** and was designated the 102nd Pennsylvania when the men reenlisted. Rowley's regiment was assigned to **John J. Peck's brigade** in **Darius Couch's** division of the **Army of the Potomac's** IV Corps. During the **Peninsula Campaign**, Rowley was wounded at **Seven Pines**, but he recovered in time to lead the regiment in the **Seven Days Campaign**. He helped cover the **Army of Virginia's** retreat after **Second Manassas** and supported an **artillery** battery at **Chantilly**. After being held in reserve at **Antietam**, Rowley's regiment was transferred to the VI Corps, and he was promoted to brigadier general of volunteers in November 1862.

At **Fredericksburg**, Rowley temporarily commanded a brigade in **John Newton's** division. In March 1863, he was transferred to the I Corps and led a brigade in **Abner Doubleday's** division at **Chancellorsville**. When Doubleday temporarily took command of the **corps** at **Gettysburg**, Rowley assumed command of the **division** on the battle's first day. He returned to his brigade on the last two days of battle but was accused of being drunk during the fighting. Just days after the Battle of Gettysburg, Rowley was transferred to supervise **conscription** in **Maine**. He returned to **Virginia** in early 1864 but was court-martialed in April for his behavior at Gettysburg and was ordered dismissed from the service after being found guilty of conduct unbecoming an officer. Secretary of War **Edwin Stanton**, however, restored Rowley to duty and ordered him to report to **U. S. Grant**. Grant refused to give him a command and returned him to **Washington, D.C.**, where Rowley finally was given command of the District of the Monongahela in late 1864. He remained there until he resigned his commission in December.

Rowley practiced law in Pennsylvania after his resignation and served as a U.S. marshal from 1866 to 1870.

RUCKER, DANIEL HENRY (1812–1910) USA. A native of **New Jersey**, Rucker moved to **Michigan** as a young man. He was commissioned directly into the 1st U.S. Dragoons as a 2nd lieutenant in 1837 and rose to the rank of captain by 1847. After winning a **brevet** for gallantry in the **Mexican War**, Rucker transferred to the Quartermaster Department and served with it for the rest of his military career.

Throughout the Civil War, Rucker commanded the important Union Quartermaster Depot in **Washington, D.C.** He was promoted to major in August 1861, to colonel the following month, and to brigadier general of volunteers in May 1863. Although his work was unglamorous, Rucker played a vital role in keeping the Union armies supplied throughout the war.

Rucker was mustered out of the volunteer service in September 1866, but he remained in the regular **army** as a colonel and assistant quartermaster general. Ten days before he retired in 1882, he was promoted to the staff rank of brigadier general and was put in command of the army's Quartermaster Department. Rucker lived another 28 years in retirement in Washington.

RUFFIN, EDMUND (1794–1865) CSA. A native of **Virginia**, Ruffin (RUF-un) was educated by private tutors and attended the College of William and Mary for one semester. He left college in 1810 to run the plantation he inherited when his father died that year. Ruffin became the leading Southern agricultural expert, promoted crop rotation, and was one of the first planters to use such scientific methods as fertilizer to increase crop yields. He became editor of the *Farmer's Register* and served as president of the Virginia Agricultural Society. Ruffin also staunchly defended **slavery** and **secession** and became one of the South's leading "**fire-eaters**." He retired from farming in 1856 and traveled the South giving speeches and publishing articles promoting secession. Before the Civil War, Ruffin was as well known for his prosecession stance as for his agricultural knowledge.

After witnessing the hanging of **John Brown**, Ruffin attended three state secession conventions and became disappointed that his native state refused to secede as well. This disappointment caused him to move to **South Carolina** in early 1861. There he joined the Palmetto Guards and supposedly was given the honor of firing the first shot at **Fort Sumter** in April. Ruffin returned to Virginia when it finally seceded and served with the Palmetto Guards at **First Manassas** but did not see any combat. He remained in the **Richmond** area for the war's duration and returned to his plantation after the Confederate **surrender**.

Ruffin's hatred for the Union remained strong, and he was disappointed that federal authorities did not arrest him at war's end. Refusing to live under the **flag** he despised, he committed suicide at his home in June 1865.

RUGER, THOMAS HOWARD (1833–1907) USA. A native of **New York**, as a boy, Ruger moved to **Wisconsin** with his family. He graduated near the top of the 1854 **West Point** class but resigned his commission after only a year's service to become a lawyer.

Ruger entered Union service in June 1861 when he was appointed lieutenant colonel of the 3rd Wisconsin. Sent to **Maryland**, he was promoted to colonel in September and was said to have prevented a **secession** legislature from convening at Frederick that autumn. Ruger then fought under **Nathaniel P. Banks** in Stonewall Jackson's 1862 **Shenandoah Valley Campaign** and at **Cedar Mountain**. Afterward, at **Antietam**, he was given temporary command of a **brigade** in the XII Corps' 1st Division and was wounded in the battle.

Ruger was promoted to brigadier general of volunteers in November 1862 and fought at **Chancellorsville** and **Gettysburg** with the **Army of the Potomac**. Because of Ruger's valuable service in stemming the XI Corps' rout at Chancellorsville, **Alpheus Williams** turned **division** command over to him at Gettysburg when Williams took temporary command of the **corps**. Ruger later was **brevetted** brigadier general of regulars for his actions at Gettysburg's Culp's Hill. After the battle, he was among those troops sent to New York City to restore order after the **New York City Draft Riot**. Ruger then was transferred west and guarded the supply lines into Chattanooga, Tennessee. He led a brigade in Williams's division of the **Army of the Cumberland's** XX Corps during the **Atlanta Campaign** and then joined **George H. Thomas's** command in **Tennessee** after the capture of Atlanta. After leading a XXIII Corps division at **Franklin**, Ruger missed the **Battle of Nashville** but then participated in the **Carolinas Campaign**. For his service at Franklin, he was brevetted major general of volunteers.

After the war, Ruger commanded the **Department of North Carolina** from June 1865 to July 1866. He was mustered out of the volunteer service in September 1866 but remained in the regular **army** as colonel of the 33rd U.S. Infantry. Ruger served as superintendent of West Point from 1871 to 1876, was commander of the **Department of the South** from 1876 to 1878, and commanded the District of Montana from 1878 to 1885. He also was promoted to brigadier general in 1886 and to major general in 1895. Ruger was retired in 1895 because he had reached the mandatory retirement age.

RUGGLES, DANIEL (1810–1897) CSA. A native of **Massachusetts**, Ruggles graduated from **West Point** in 1833 and was assigned to the infantry. He served in the **Seminole Wars** and on various garrison duty before winning two **brevets** while fighting in the **Mexican War** as a captain. After the war, Ruggles served in **Texas** and on the **Utah Expedition** before taking sick leave in 1859. While in his wife's native **Virginia**, he invented a breech-loading rifle and the first steamboat propeller.

Ruggles was still in Virginia on sick leave when that state seceded in April 1861. Deciding to support his wife's home state, he offered his services to Virginia two days before resigning his U.S. commission. Ruggles was appointed brigadier general of state troops in April and was put in command of the troops on the lower Potomac River. He successfully repulsed a Union attack against Aquia Creek, but then his command was abolished. Ruggles was mustered into Confederate service as a colonel and was promoted to brigadier general in August 1861.

Transferred to **Pensacola, Florida**, Ruggles commanded a **brigade** under **Braxton Bragg** before moving to **New Orleans, Louisiana**, in December and assuming command of a brigade under **Mansfield Lovell**. In February 1862, he was transferred to Corinth, Mississippi, and then briefly commanded the District of Northern Alabama before being given a **division** in Bragg's II Corps of the **Army of Mississippi**. Ruggles fought at **Shiloh** and claimed to have been responsible for assembling the **artillery** that bombarded the "Hornets' Nest" before its successful capture. After participating in the **siege of Corinth, Mississippi**, he guarded the **army's** supply depots in May 1862 before being given command of a **district** in **Louisiana**. Ruggles commanded a small division at the **Battle of Baton Rouge** and then briefly commanded Port Hudson, Louisiana, before taking charge of the Jackson, Mississippi, area. He remained there until January 1863, when he moved his headquarters to Columbus, Mississippi, to protect that region. In March 1864, Ruggles relinquished his **Mississippi** command and spent the next year moving about **Alabama** and **Georgia** searching for a suitable position. In March 1865, he finally was appointed commissary general of **prisoners** and served in that position until war's end.

After the war, Ruggles returned to Virginia. Except for four years as a **Texas** rancher, he remained there working as a farmer and in real estate and serving as a member of the West Point Board of Visitors.

RUSH'S LANCERS. An anachronism of the Civil War, Rush's Lancers, or the 6th Pennsylvania Cavalry, was the only Union lancer unit that actually saw combat. Colonel Richard H. Rush formed the **regiment** in the summer of 1861 out of Philadelphia's leading citizens. The men were armed with nine-foot-long lances, which were decorated with yellow pennants. Attached to the **Army of the Potomac** during the **Peninsula Campaign**, the lancers generally served well. At **Hanover Court House** they captured a number of **prisoners** and proved to be effective scouts and couriers. At **Gaines' Mill,** however, the regiment was defeated and routed from the field. In June 1863, Rush's Lancers finally gave up their lances for modern carbines. They fought well at **Brandy Station** and in the **Overland Campaign** at **Cold Harbor** and **Trevilian Station**. During the war, the regiment suffered 522 casualties.

RUSSELL, DAVID ALLEN (1820–1864) USA. A native of **New York**, Russell was the son of a congressman who appointed him to **West Point** in 1841. After graduating near the bottom of his 1845 class, he fought in the **Mexican War** with the infantry and won a **brevet** for gallantry. After the war, Russell served on various garrison duty and in the Pacific Northwest before being promoted to captain in 1854.

When the Civil War began, Russell was transferred to **Washington, D.C.**, where he served in the city's defenses through the winter of 1861–62. In January 1862, he was appointed colonel of the 7th Massachusetts and led the **regiment** in the **Peninsula** and **Seven Days Campaigns** as part of **Darius Couch's division** of the **Army of the Potomac's** IV Corps.

After serving in reserve at **Antietam,** Russell was promoted to brigadier general of volunteers in November 1862 and led a **brigade** in the VI Corps' 1st Division at **Fredericksburg.** His brigade suffered heavy casualties at **Second Fredericksburg** during the **Chancellorsville Campaign** but was only lightly engaged at **Gettysburg.** In November 1863, Russell temporarily commanded the division and was wounded while personally leading the attack that overran the Confederate position at **Rappahannock Station.** To honor his role in the victory, **army** commander **George G. Meade** gave Russell the privilege of taking eight captured enemy **flags** to Washington and made him the division's permanent commander. He skillfully commanded the division during the **Overland Campaign** and, at **Spotsylvania,** forwarded through the chain of command a plan by his brigadier **Emory Upton** to break through the enemy's line. After **Cold Harbor,** Russell was among the troops rushed to defend the capital during **Jubal A. Early's Washington Raid.** In the autumn of 1864, he fought in **Philip Sheridan's 1864 Shenandoah Valley Campaign** and was badly wounded in the chest at **Third Winchester** but remained on the field. Russell then was killed instantly by a shell fragment to the heart while leading one of his brigades. Earlier in the war, he had been promoted to major of regulars and had been brevetted brigadier general of regulars for his service at the **Wilderness.** Russell was brevetted major general in both the volunteers and regulars posthumously.

RUSSELL, WILLIAM HOWARD (1820–1907). A native of Ireland, Russell attended Trinity College Dublin before becoming a noted journalist with the London *Times.* As a special **war correspondent**, he earned great fame and knighthood for covering conflicts in Denmark, the Crimea, and India during the 1850s.

During the **secession** crisis, Russell came to the United States to cover the coming Civil War. After arriving in New York City in March 1861, he spent a month in **Washington, D.C.**, before traveling through the Confederacy for two months and angering Southerners by writing condemning reports about **slavery.** Russell then joined the Union **army** for the **First Battle of Manassas** and angered Northerners for his criticism of their soldiers' conduct there. By the spring of 1862, Russell had completely alienated all Americans and received numerous death threats and warnings not to appear in public unarmed. When government officials refused to allow him to accompany the **Army of the Potomac**, he returned to Great Britain. Russell described his American experience in *My*

Diary North and South, a classic in Civil War literature. After the Civil War, he covered the Franco-Prussian and Zulu Wars, served on the Prince of Wales's staff, and edited the *Army and Navy Gazette.*

RUST, ALBERT (1818–1870) CSA. A native of **Virginia,** Rust settled in **Arkansas** as a young man and became a prominent planter, lawyer, state legislator (1842–48 and 1852–54), and congressman (1855–57 and 1859–61). Although he was a Unionist, he eventually accepted Arkansas's **secession** and resigned his congressional seat in March 1861. Rust then was elected to the Provisional **Confederate Congress** and served on the Postal Affairs Committee.

In July 1861, Rust raised the 3rd Arkansas and was commissioned its colonel. Sent to western Virginia, he commanded **Robert E. Lee's** left wing at **Cheat Mountain** but failed to launch a planned attack for fear he was outnumbered. Rust remained in Virginia and served under **Stonewall Jackson** during his expedition to Romney and was praised by Jackson for a small victory at Big Cacapon Bridge.

Rust was promoted to brigadier general in March 1862 and was given command of the lower Arkansas River in the **Trans-Mississippi Department.** He raised a **brigade** there but in May was placed in command of the **department's** cavalry. After engaging in a number of **skirmishes,** Rust was given command of an infantry brigade in **Mansfield Lovell's division.** He opposed **Earl Van Dorn's** attack on **Corinth, Mississippi,** in October, and the entire division fought poorly in the battle. When Van Dorn was court-martialed as a result of the defeat, Rust testified he thought the attack was "madness," but that he was beginning to change his mind by the second day of fighting. After Corinth, Rust saw no further important field service. He was sent with a brigade to reinforce Port Hudson, Louisiana, in March 1863, but the next month returned to the Trans-Mississippi Department. That autumn, Rust was stripped of all duties because his devotion to the cause was questioned. By March 1865, he still was without a command and not only had become highly critical of the Confederate government but also was expressing pro-Union sentiments.

After the war, Rust returned to his Arkansas farm and served in the U.S. House of Representatives during **Reconstruction** and joined the **Republican Party.** He also ran for the U.S. Senate in 1869 but eventually dropped out of the race.

RUTHERFORD'S FARM, VIRGINIA, BATTLE OF (JULY 20, 1864). After **Jubal A. Early's Washington Raid** in July 1864, the Confederates encamped at Berryville, Virginia. Later that month, Maj. Gen. **David**

Hunter supported the Union forces at **Cool Spring, Virginia,** by sending **William W. Averell's** cavalry **division** to **demonstrate** against Early. Early withdrew from Berryville and sent **Stephen D. Ramseur's** division to engage Averell. On July 20, the two columns collided three miles north of Winchester at Rutherford's Farm, near Stephenson's Depot. Averell attacked Ramseur's left flank before it was completely deployed, threw the Confederates back in confusion, and captured four cannons and nearly 300 **prisoners** as Ramseur retreated toward Winchester. Ramseur lost about 500 men in the clash, while Averell lost 242. After the battle, Early withdrew his **army** to Fisher's Hill, and the Federals began transferring the VI and XIX Corps back to **Washington, D.C.,** to join **U. S. Grant** in the **Petersburg Campaign.** Only **George Crook** and four Union divisions were left to guard the **Shenandoah Valley.**

– S –

SABER. A saber is a sword with a curved blade that was used mostly by cavalry during the Civil War. Carried by both sides, it had become largely obsolete by 1861 because of the adoption of modern firearms. Although sabers were used in such battles as **Brandy Station,** both sides began increasingly relying on firearms as the war progressed. Confederate cavalrymen preferred pistols or even shotguns for close-quarter combat, while Union cavalrymen became armed with such repeating weapons as the **Spencer carbine.**

SABINE CROSS ROADS, LOUISIANA, BATTLE OF (APRIL 8, 1864). *See* MANSFIELD, LOUISIANA, BATTLE OF.

SABINE PASS, TEXAS, BATTLE OF (SEPTEMBER 8, 1863). Early in the Civil War, the Confederates fortified Sabine (suh-BEEN or SAB-been) Pass, Texas, on the **Louisiana-Texas** border, to guard against incursions by the **U.S. Navy.** Union gunboats drove them out of their position on September 24, 1862, but the Confederates later returned and on January 21, 1863, attacked the Federals with two **cottonclads** and captured two Union ships and more than 100 **prisoners.** The Confederates also reoccupied their defensive position at Fort Griffin and began blocking the entrance to the Sabine River.

On September 5, 1863, Union Maj. Gen. **Nathaniel P. Banks** dispatched **William B. Franklin** from **New Orleans, Louisiana,** with part of the XIX Corps, four gunboats, and seven transports to capture Sabine Pass and begin an invasion of Texas. The Federals hoped by establishing a presence in Texas, they could stop Confederate trade with **Maximilian's** Mexico and prevent the French from recognizing the Confederacy. Defending Sabine Pass were Lt. **Richard "Dick" Dowling** and 44 members of the Davis Guards, 1st Texas Heavy Artillery. These Confederates were not considered first-rate soldiers, but Dowling dutifully honed their skills by placing white poles in the pass to serve as range markers and engaging in regular **artillery** practice with their six cannons.

Franklin arrived at Sabine Pass on September 7 and was joined by four additional gunboats. On the morning of September 8, the *Clifton*, *Sachem*, *Arizona*, and *Granite City* entered the pass and engaged Fort Griffin. Using his range markers effectively, Dowling riddled the *Clifton* and *Sachem* and forced their surrender. The **army** commanders on the transports then threw overboard 200,000 **rations** and 200 mules and withdrew to the Gulf of Mexico. Dowling's 44 men had defeated a small fleet and 4,000 soldiers and had inflicted about 400 casualties (mostly taken prisoner) on the enemy without suffering a single casualty. **Jefferson Davis** was so impressed with the victory, he later referred to the battle as the "Thermopylae of the Civil War." The **Davis Guard Medal**, the only official Confederate medal issued in the war, was awarded the defenders.

SABOT. A sabot (sah-BO) was a block of wood used in the **artillery** to attach the projectile to the powder charge, thus forming a single piece of ammunition. In **rifles**, it was a detachable plug at the bullet's base that expanded the bullet and allowed it to grip the barrel's rifling when fired.

SAFFORD, MARY JANE (1831?–1891) USA. A native of **Vermont**, as a child, Safford moved with her family to **Illinois**. She was educated at a private Vermont academy and learned French and some German while traveling in Canada and working as a governess.

When the Civil War began, Safford was living in Illinois with a brother. In the summer of 1861, she volunteered to serve with **Mary Ann Bickerdyke** and became a nurse. Working out of the Union hospital at Cairo, Illinois, Safford visited nearby camps to attend sick soldiers and personally searched the **Belmont** battlefield under her own flag of truce to search for the wounded. After the **Battle of Fort Donelson**, she worked continuously for 10 days and so exhausted herself she had to take a leave of absence to recuperate. After returning to duty, Safford nursed the wounded from **Shiloh** onboard the hospital ship *Hazel Dell* and earned the nickname the "Angel of Cairo." Once again, however, she ruined her health and was forced to take leave to recover. This time Safford traveled with her family to Europe and did not return to the United States until 1866.

Safford graduated from the New York Medical College for Women in 1869 and then studied surgery in Austria and Germany. In Germany she performed the first ovariotomy by a female surgeon. After returning to Illinois in 1872, Safford opened a practice in Chicago and married. The marriage proved unhappy, and she accepted a position on the faculty of the Boston University School of Medicine. Safford divorced her husband in 1880 and retired from the university in 1886.

SAILOR'S CREEK, VIRGINIA, BATTLE OF (APRIL 6, 1865). At the end of the **Petersburg Campaign, U. S. Grant** forced **Robert E. Lee** to abandon **Richmond** and Petersburg, Virginia, on April 2, 1865. In the **Appomattox Campaign,** Lee then led the **Army of Northern Virginia** to the southwest in an attempt to join forces with **Joseph E. Johnston** in **North Carolina.** When Lee learned on April 5 that Union cavalry blocked his path at Jetersburg, he made a night march around the Union's left flank toward Farmville, where he could obtain supplies on the South Side Railroad. **James Longstreet** led the march, followed by **Richard H. Anderson, Richard S. Ewell,** the wagon train, and **John B. Gordon.** On April 6, **George A. Custer's** Union cavalry took advantage of a gap that developed between Longstreet and Anderson and cut the Confederate column in two. To save the wagon train, Ewell sent it northward around the enemy. Gordon then simply followed the wagon train as he had been doing and became separated from Ewell's command.

Ewell positioned his 5,200 men along a ridge southwest of Little Sailor's Creek to confront **Horatio G. Wright's** Union VI Corps approaching from the northeast. Wright took up a position across the creek and opened fire on Ewell with **artillery** at about 5:00 P.M. After 30 minutes, the Federals waded across the rain-swollen creek and attacked. The Confederates repulsed the first assault and then launched an unsuccessful counterattack. Wright attacked again and overwhelmed the Confederates, capturing Ewell, five other generals, and more than 3,000 men. In all, Ewell lost about 3,400 men to Wright's 440.

To the north, Gordon had to stop and protect the wagon train with his 7,000 men when it got bogged down at Double Bridges, located at the juncture of Big and Little Sailor's Creeks. Gordon positioned his men on high ground near the crossing and soon was attacked by **Andrew A. Humphreys's** 16,500-man II Corps. The Federals pushed Gordon back to the wagon train near Double Bridges. There the Confederates made a determined stand but soon were forced to retreat across the creek when the enemy crossed the creek farther upstream in a **turning movement.**

Gordon lost 1,700 men and more than 200 wagons in this action, while Humphreys counted 536 casualties.

A mile southwest of the Little Sailor's Creek Road crossing, a third battle erupted when Anderson's 6,300 Confederates made a stand against Brig. Gen. **Wesley Merritt's** 10,000 Union troopers. The Union cavalry overwhelmed the Confederate **divisions** of **George E. Pickett** and **Bushrod Johnson** and captured 2,600 men (including two generals) at a cost of only 172 casualties.

Arriving on a hill overlooking the area as the surviving Confederates streamed westward, Lee exclaimed, "My God! Has the army been dissolved?" (Thomas, *Robert E. Lee,* 358). Approximately 7,700 of his men had been lost—or nearly one-fourth of the **army**—while the Union **Army of the Potomac** suffered only 1,148 casualties. The Confederates came to call this day "Black Thursday." Lee continued to Farmville that night, where he found supplies at the **railroad**, but he soon was forced to **surrender** at **Appomattox Court House.**

ST. ALBANS, VERMONT, RAID ON (OCTOBER 19, 1864). By the autumn of 1864, the war was going very badly for the Confederates. In a desperate attempt to relieve pressure from their armies and to hurt Union morale, Confederate officials approved a plan by Bennett H. Young to raid St. Albans, Vermont. Young gathered 20 men from among escaped Confederate **prisoners** living in Canada and assembled them at St. Albans over several days in October so as not to arouse suspicion.

On the afternoon of October 19, the raiders sprang into action. They herded citizens into the town common, collected horses, and robbed three banks of $20,000. Two civilians were shot and wounded in the raid, and a Southern sympathizer was killed when he stepped into the line of fire. Young's men then rode for the Canadian border, pursued by a hastily arranged posse. The posse crossed into Canada and apprehended several of the raiders, but Canadian officials soon took custody of them and all of the other Confederates who were captured later. Despite protests by Union officials, Canadian authorities ruled that Young and his men were soldiers, not criminals, and released them after they posted a bond to guarantee their good behavior as internees. The raid had no effect on the war and actually made many Northerners more determined than ever to defeat the Confederacy.

ST. CHARLES, ARKANSAS, BATTLE OF (JUNE 17, 1862). After the Confederate defeat at **Pea Ridge, Arkansas**, in March 1862, most of the

Confederate **Army of the West** was transferred to **Mississippi** to oppose **U. S. Grant**. **Thomas C. Hindman** was left behind to defend the state against **Samuel R. Curtis's** Union **army**, which was advancing into north central Arkansas. Hindman established an **artillery** position atop a bluff at St. Charles to block Curtis's White River supply line. When a Union flotilla steamed up the river on the morning of June 17, Confederate Capt. Joseph Fry opened fire with his two heavy guns and killed 105 sailors when he pierced the *Mound City's* boiler. The 46th Indiana then disembarked downstream, marched up the river, and captured the bluff and St. Charles. In the day's action, the Federals lost 160 men to the Confederate's 40 casualties. Despite their success, however, the Federals were unable to supply Curtis by the White River because the water level fell too low for ships to navigate beyond **DeVall's Bluff**.

SAINT EMMA PLANTATION, LOUISIANA, BATTLE OF (JULY 13, 1863). *See* BAYOU LAFOURCHE, LOUISIANA, BATTLE OF.

ST. JOHN, ISAAC MUNROE (1827–1880) CSA. A native of **Georgia**, St. John moved to **New York** as a boy, attended Poughkeepsie Collegiate School, and received a law degree from Yale University in 1845. He then moved to **Maryland** and was a newspaper publisher before becoming a civil engineer and working for several different **railroads**.

Despite his Northern upbringing, St. John sided with the Confederacy and in early 1861 joined a **South Carolina** volunteer **company** as a private. After being sent to the Virginia Peninsula, he joined **John Bankhead Magruder's** staff as chief **engineer** but held no official rank until Magruder finally secured him a captain's commission in February 1862. In April 1862, St. John was put in command of the newly created Niter Corps to help manufacture gunpowder. After he was promoted to major in October, the corps was redesignated the **Niter and Mining Bureau**. St. John was promoted to lieutenant colonel in May and to colonel in June. With few natural sources of niter, he created niter "beds" and collected urine to produce the valuable mineral. When St. John quadrupled the Confederacy's niter production within a few months, he also was put in charge of collecting iron, lead, copper, and coal.

Despite his success, St. John was criticized by some people because of the large number of men his bureau exempted from the draft. Incensed, he submitted his resignation, but the War Department wisely refused to accept it. St. John continued at his post until February 1865 when Secretary of War **John C. Breckinridge** appointed him to take over the inefficient Commissary Department from the unpopular **Lucius**

B. Northrop. A promotion to brigadier general came the next day. Again, St. John performed outstanding work and quickly began providing the **armies** with more supplies than they had received in months. When **Robert E. Lee** surrendered in April 1865, St. John still had several million **rations** ready to be distributed to the soldiers. St. John fled **Richmond, Virginia**, with the government in April 1865, but he left the entourage in Georgia the following month.

After being **paroled**, St. John resumed his civil engineering and railroad work and became involved in mining.

ST. LOUIS, MISSOURI, RIOT (MAY 10, 1861). Missouri's loyalties were deeply divided when the Civil War began. Governor **Claiborne F. Jackson** favored **secession** and had the support of the Missouri State Guard, while Union Capt. **Nathaniel Lyon** was determined to keep the state in the Union. When Jackson assembled a large secessionist force outside St. Louis at **Camp Jackson** in May 1861, Lyon surrounded and captured the camp on May 10. In a questionable move, Lyon then paraded his captives through the streets of St. Louis. Secessionists were outraged and attacked the column, sparking a deadly riot that led to 28 deaths. Lyon drove off the rioters, but the damage was done, and Missouri split between the secessionist and Unionist factions.

ST. LOUIS, **USS.** This Union gunboat was one of the **"Pook Turtles"** built by James B. Eads at Carondelet, Missouri. Completed in October 1861, it was 175 feet long, 51 feet in beam, and carried four 42-pounders and seven 32-pounders. As part of the Western Gunboat Fleet, it participated in the attacks on **Forts Henry and Donelson**, rammed and sank a Confederate ship at **Fort Pillow**, and fought at **Memphis**. The ship was renamed the *Baron De Kalb* in September 1862 and was transferred the following month to **David Porter's** command. It then fought at **Arkansas Post** and in the **Vicksburg Campaign**. On July 13, 1863, the *Baron De Kalb* was sunk by **torpedoes** in the Yazoo River while on a mission with three other vessels to destroy a reported Confederate battery in the area.

SALEM CHURCH, VIRGINIA, BATTLE OF (MAY 3–4, 1863). When Union Maj. Gen. **Joseph Hooker** began the **Chancellorsville Campaign** in the spring of 1863, he left **John Sedgwick** in command of approximately 40,000 men across the Rappahannock River from Fredericksburg, Virginia. Sedgwick was to keep **Robert E. Lee** focused on the Fredericksburg area while Hooker took the rest of the **Army of the Potomac** upstream to cross the river and move into Lee's rear. Lee discovered Hooker's plan, however, and left 10,000 men at Fredericksburg under

Jubal A. Early while the rest of the **Army of Northern Virginia** attacked Hooker at Chancellorsville. After being pummeled by **Stonewall Jackson** on May 2, Hooker ordered Sedgwick to attack Early and advance against Lee's rear to relieve the pressure at Chancellorsville.

On May 3, Sedgwick attacked Early's position on Marye's Heights in the **Second Battle of Fredericksburg** and forced him to retreat. Early then made a tactical error by withdrawing to the southwest instead of west along the road to Chancellorsville. Only **Cadmus M. Wilcox's** brigade was positioned to contest Sedgwick's advance. To assist Early, Lee again split his **army** and sent **Lafayette McLaws** with four **brigades** to help stop Sedgwick. By the time he arrived, Wilcox had been forced back but was making a stubborn stand at Salem Church, six miles east of Chancellorsville. There, McLaws and Wilcox formed a defensive line along a ridge. The Confederates were attacked that afternoon by the **divisions** of **William T. H. Brooks** and **John Newton**, but they successfully held their position and then repulsed the Federals with a counterattack.

Realizing that Hooker no longer posed a threat at Chancellorsville, Lee concentrated against Sedgwick. He sent **Richard H. Anderson's** division to Salem Church and by the afternoon of May 4 had Sedgwick trapped on three sides with his back to the Rappahannock River. Anderson, McLaws, and Early launched furious attacks late that afternoon but were unable to dislodge the Federals from their strong position atop rugged ridges and hills. Sedgwick's men skillfully held their lines and then retreated successfully across the river that night. Casualties for the fighting are unknown since they were reported as part of the Chancellorsville Campaign's total figure, but it is estimated that Sedgwick lost approximately 5,000 men in the two days. Salem Church, which was used as a field hospital during the battle, is still standing.

SALIENT. A salient is part of a defensive line that protrudes toward the enemy, usually to incorporate an important feature such as high ground. **Spotsylvania's** "Mule Shoe" was a salient.

SALINEVILLE, OHIO, BATTLE OF (JULY 26, 1863). During **John H. Morgan's Ohio Raid** in July 1863, most of the Confederates were captured at **Buffington Island, Ohio**, while attempting to cross the Ohio River into **West Virginia**. Morgan escaped with a few men and continued northward to find another crossing. After passing through Salineville, the Confederates were cut off from Smith's Ford on July 26 by **Edward H. Hobson's** Union cavalry. Morgan tried to cut his way through to the ford but failed. With escape impossible, he surrendered his 364 men.

SALISBURY PRISON, NORTH CAROLINA. To care for the growing number of Union **prisoners**, Confederate officials bought an old cotton factory and 16 acres of land at Salisbury, North Carolina, in November 1861 to use as a **prison**. The three-and-a-half-story brick factory, with a well and some of its outbuildings, was fenced in and held not only prisoners of war but also Confederate **deserters** and political prisoners.

The prison was designed to hold 2,500 prisoners, and Salisbury's inmates at first had ample food, water, recreation, and housing. It never was overly crowded until October 1864 when the number of prisoners began to increase greatly after the breakdown of the **exchange** system. By November, the prison housed 8,740 inmates (mostly enlisted men), including several hundred **black troops**. This huge increase turned Salisbury from a relatively comfortable prison into a crowded, unhealthy hellhole. Inmates began suffering from poor water, unsanitary conditions, food shortages (prompting many inmates to eat acorns), and cold. There were not enough tents to house the men, and many soldiers dug holes to live in. Some prisoners robbed their comrades, while others attempted to escape. Approximately 1,700 (mostly **foreign-born soldiers**) even accepted an offer to join the **Confederate army** as a way out of Salisbury.

The overcrowding was relieved in February 1865 when the exchange was resumed. When **George Stoneman's** Union cavalry liberated, and then burned, the prison on April 12, 1865, there were only a few hundred inmates left. Of approximately 15,000 prisoners housed at Salisbury, 3,955 were buried in unmarked graves. This death rate was comparable to that of the more notorious **Andersonville Prison**. Major John Henry Gee, the commander of the Confederate guards, was tried after the war for mistreating prisoners, but he convinced a military court that he was not to blame for the miserable conditions and was released after six months' imprisonment.

SALM-SALM, AGNES ELISABETH WINONA LECLERQ JOY, PRINCESS (1840–1912) USA. A native of either **Vermont** or Canada, Agnes Joy moved to **Washington, D.C.**, when the Civil War began and married the German officer **Felix Constantin Alexander Johann Nepomuk, Prince Salm-Salm** (ZAHM-ZAHM) in 1862. An ambitious and capable woman, Salm-Salm actively promoted her husband's career and worked as a nurse while staying with the **Army of the Potomac**. Her activities in the hospitals and other relief work made her very popular with the soldiers, and **Illinois** commissioned her an honorary captain.

After the war, Salm-Salm's husband served as Emperor **Maximilian's** aide-de-camp and was condemned to death along with the emperor. She failed in a plot to help the two escape but did win her husband's release by making a dramatic plea to Benito Juárez for their lives. Before he was executed, Maximilian presented Princess Salm-Salm the Grand Cordon of the Order of San Carlos for her efforts on his behalf, and Austria later gave her a pension. The couple returned to Europe, where she again became active in relief work during the Franco-Prussian War and was awarded the Prussian Medal of Honor. Prince Salm-Salm was killed in the war, and the princess later remarried. She also published *Ten Years of My Life* in 1876, which details some of her Civil War experiences. At the turn of the 20th century, Princess Salm-Salm was still active in relief work and helped raise money for the Boer ambulance corps during the Boer War.

SALM-SALM, FELIX CONSTANTIN ALEXANDER JOHANN NEPOMUK, PRINCE (1828–1870) USA. A native of Prussia, Salm-Salm (ZAHM-ZAHM) became a cavalry officer after attending Berlin's Cadet School. During the Schleswig-Holstein War, he was wounded seven times, was taken prisoner, and was awarded a ceremonial sword by future Kaiser Wilhelm I. Salm-Salm then briefly served in the Austrian army, but when the Civil War began he came to the United States and offered his services to the Union, even though he spoke no English.

Salm-Salm's credentials gained him an audience with **Abraham Lincoln**, who appointed him a colonel and Brig. Gen. **Louis Blenker's** chief of staff. In the summer of 1862, Salm-Salm married, and his wife, **Agnes Elisabeth Winona Leclerq Joy, Princess Salm-Salm**, actively promoted his career. He was appointed colonel of the 8th New York in October 1862, but the **regiment** was disbanded the following April. The prince then was appointed colonel of the 68th New York in June 1864 and fought at the **Battle of Nashville**.

As the war came to an end, Salm-Salm was **brevetted** brigadier general of volunteers in April 1865 and later was made military governor of Atlanta, Georgia. After being mustered out of service in November 1865, he moved to Mexico and became aide-de-camp to Emperor **Maximilian**. Taken prisoner along with Maximilian, Salm-Salm was sentenced to death. His wife tried unsuccessfully to help the two escape and then made an impassioned plea to Benito Juárez for their release. Salm-Salm was released, but Maximilian was executed. The couple returned to Europe, where Salm-Salm volunteered to fight the French in the 1870 Franco-Prussian War. As a major of the Grenadier Guards, he was killed on August 18 at the Battle of Gravelotte.

SALOMON, EDWARD (1828–1909) USA. A native of Prussia, Salomon was the brother of Union Brig. Gen. **Friedrich Salomon**. After graduating from the University of Berlin in 1849, he immigrated to **Wisconsin** because of the turmoil caused by the 1848 European revolutions. There, Salomon taught school, became involved in local Democratic politics, opened a successful law practice, and served on the University of Wisconsin's board of regents. Although a **Democrat**, he supported **Abraham Lincoln** in the **election of 1860**. Thus, when the **Republicans** held their state convention in 1861, they chose Salomon to run for lieutenant governor with **Louis P. Harvey**. They were elected in January 1862, but in April, Governor Harvey drowned while visiting state troops following the **Battle of Shiloh**.

As governor, Salomon took steps to protect Wisconsin from **Indian** attack after **Minnesota's** 1862 **Sioux uprising**. He also had great difficulties enforcing **conscription**, which had become increasingly unpopular among Wisconsin's large population of naturalized citizens. When the draft was violently resisted, he arrested more than 100 people. Salomon became so unpopular for the way he enforced conscription that the party decided not to run him for reelection in 1863.

After leaving office, Salomon performed relief work for Wisconsin soldiers and campaigned for Lincoln's reelection. After losing a U.S. Senate race in 1869, he moved first to **New York** and then back to Germany.

SALOMON, FRIEDRICH (1826–1897) USA. A native of Prussia, Salomon was the brother of **Wisconsin** Gov. **Edward Salomon** and worked as a surveyor before serving as a lieutenant in the Prussian army. He was studying architecture in Berlin when the 1848 revolution began and immigrated to the United States with three brothers the following year. Settling in Wisconsin, Salomon worked as a surveyor, registrar of deeds, and **railroad** engineer.

Salomon entered Union service in April 1861 as a captain in the 90-day 5th Missouri (Union), which was commanded by one of his brothers. After fighting at **Wilson's Creek**, he was appointed colonel of the 9th Wisconsin in November and led the regiment in **Missouri** and **Arkansas** before being promoted to brigadier general of volunteers in July 1862. Given command of a brigade in August 1862, Salomon served in **Kansas** and Arkansas. Then, in May 1863, he was put in command of a **division** in the **Army of the Tennessee's** XIII Corps and successfully defended **Helena, Arkansas**, in July. Transferred in January 1864 to a division in the VII Corps, Salomon also played a key role at **Jenkins' Ferry** by holding the rear guard and allowing **Frederick Steele's army** to cross the Saline River safely. He remained in Arkansas until war's end and was **brevetted** major general of volunteers for his war service.

After being mustered out of the volunteers in August 1865, Salomon became surveyor general of Missouri and of the Utah Territory.

SALT BEEF. A part of the standard diet for soldiers on both sides was salt beef, or beef preserved in a salty brine solution. The daily **ration** for Union soldiers was 1 pound, 4 ounces, but it could not be eaten unless it was first soaked in fresh water to rid it of the brine.

SALTVILLE, VIRGINIA, MASSACRE, OR FIRST BATTLE OF (OCTOBER 2, 1864). In late September 1864, Union cavalryman Brig. Gen. **Stephen G. Burbridge** raided the vital Confederate saltworks and Virginia & Tennessee Railroad at Saltville, Virginia. A Confederate delaying action by **John C. Vaughn** at Clinch Mountain and Laurel Gap slowed Burbridge's 5,200 troopers and gave Confederate Brig. Gen. **Felix H. Robertson** time to gather 2,800 men to defend Saltville.

The Federals reached the town on October 1 and attacked the following day. The Confederates were strongly posted behind a barricade and inflicted 350 casualties on Burbridge's force while losing 108 men. On October 3, Burbridge broke off the engagement and retreated, leaving his wounded men behind. Confederate troops and guerrillas under Champ Ferguson then murdered some of the wounded Federals. Although more than 100 **black troops** of the 5th U.S. Colored Troops were claimed to have been murdered, the number probably was closer to a dozen. When Maj. Gen. **John C. Breckinridge** arrived, he arrested Ferguson for the "Saltville Massacre." After the war, Ferguson was hanged by federal authorities on October 20, 1865, for the murder of 53 people, 14 of whom were killed at Saltville. Some evidence indicates that Robertson also was personally responsible for the **massacre**, but he escaped judgment and lived to be the last surviving Confederate general.

SALTVILLE, VIRGINIA, SECOND BATTLE OF (DECEMBER 20–21, 1864). On December 1, 1864, Union Maj. Gen. **George Stoneman** began a cavalry raid from Knoxville, Tennessee, into southwestern **Virginia**. Confederate Maj. Gen. **John C. Breckinridge** had only about 2,100 men to defend the area. After riding through Bristol and Wytheville, Virginia, Stoneman drove back Breckinridge at **Marion** and headed for the vital saltworks and Virginia & Tennessee Railroad at Saltville. Breckinridge had positioned 400 men to defend Saltville. They were surrounded by Stoneman's cavalry on December 20 and were forced to surrender the following day after some **skirmishing**. Besides the 400 **prisoners**, Stoneman also seized 19 cannons, 3,000 horses, 3,000 **rifles**, 25,000 rounds of **artillery** ammunition, and thousands of bushels of salt. After damaging the saltworks and **railroad**, Stoneman withdrew. When Breckinridge returned to Saltville later that day, he reopened the saltworks in a short time, but the railroad remained out of service for two months.

SAMARIA CHURCH, VIRGINIA, BATTLE OF (JUNE 24, 1864). After Union Maj. Gen. **Philip Sheridan's** cavalry was defeated by Confederate cavalry under **Wade Hampton** and **Fitzhugh Lee** at **Trevilian Station, Virginia**, on June 12, 1864, he abandoned his raid and retreated. During the retreat, Hampton and Lee chased after Sheridan, and there were numerous clashes as the Federals rode east and south toward Bermuda Hundred. On June 24, the Confederates launched frequent attacks against **David M. Gregg's division**, which was covering Sheridan's withdrawal from a position north of Samaria Church (or Saint Mary's Church). Gregg held for a while, but the line collapsed under the relentless pressure, and he withdrew in disorder. Sheridan finally crossed the James River on June 26–28 and safely reached **U. S. Grant's** lines. In the clash at Samaria Church, the Confederates lost about 250 men, while Gregg suffered approximately 350 casualties.

SAN JACINTO, **USS.** Known as "Saucy Jack" by its crew, the *San Jacinto* was built in 1850 at the New York Navy Yard. It displaced 1,567 tons and originally was armed with one 11-inch and ten 9-inch **Dahlgrens** and one **Parrott rifle**. Commanded by Capt. **Charles Wilkes**, the *San Jacinto* became famous as the ship that intercepted the British mail carrier *Trent* in 1861 and captured Confederate envoys **James Mason** and **John Slidell** in the *Trent* **Affair**. After the incident, the *San Jacinto* was decommissioned, overhauled, and recommissioned in March 1862. It then served off the coast of **Florida** and captured a number of Confederate **blockade runners**. The *San Jacinto* ran onto a reef in the Bahamas on January 1, 1865, and sank. Although all hands were saved, Capt. Richard W. Meade was found guilty of negligence.

SANBORN, JOHN BENJAMIN (1826–1904) USA. A native of **New Hampshire**, Sanborn attended Dartmouth College but dropped out after one year to study law. After being admitted to the bar in 1854, he moved to **Minnesota**, opened a practice, and became the state's quartermaster general.

When the Civil War began in April 1861, Sanborn was made Minnesota's quartermaster and adjutant general. He organized the state's recruits into units and in December was appointed colonel of the 4th Minnesota. Sent to **Mississippi**, Sanborn commanded a **brigade**, which participated in the **siege of Corinth, Mississippi**, in the spring of 1862 After his brigade suffered heavy casualties at **Iuka**, Sanborn returned to his **regiment** for the **Battle of Corinth**. In February 1863, Sanborn was given command of a brigade in the 7th Division of the **Army of the Tennessee's** XVII Corps. After fighting through the

Vicksburg Campaign, he was given the honor of leading the Union advance into **Vicksburg, Mississippi**, after it was captured. Sanborn was promoted to brigadier general of volunteers in August 1863 and was given command of the District of Southwest Missouri in October. After fighting well at **Second Independence**, during **Sterling Price's 1864 Missouri Raid**, he was **brevetted** major general of volunteers in February 1865. Afterward, Sanborn led his men in a successful campaign against **Indians** in the Southwest and continued to serve on the frontier after the Civil War.

After being mustered out of the volunteers in April 1866, Sanford returned to his Minnesota law practice. He also served in the state assembly and senate.

SAND CREEK MASSACRE, COLORADO TERRITORY (NOVEMBER 29, 1864). Unlike those of **Indian Territory**, the **Indians** of **Colorado Territory** were not involved in the Civil War. Still, territorial officials who were trying to attain statehood saw them as a threat. Colonel **John M. Chivington**, the commander of the Military District of Colorado, particularly hated Indians and in April 1863 had ordered the shooting on sight of all Cheyennes. Such policies caused the Indians to fight back in mid-1863 and to cut the Overland Trail to Denver. To restore peace, Chiefs Black Kettle of the Southern Cheyennes and Left Hand of the Southern Arapahos released their white captives and began negotiating with Chivington and Gov. John Evans. The chiefs believed a peace had been achieved and agreed to encamp at Sand Creek. Secretly, however, Evans and Chivington were planning to exterminate them.

With two cannons and nearly 1,000 men from the 3rd Colorado Cavalry and 1st Colorado, Chivington attacked the Sand Creek encampment on the morning of November 29, 1864, after ordering his men to take no **prisoners**. A large number of Indians were killed, including many women and children, and their bodies often were mutilated. The soldiers also destroyed the village and all of the Indians' supplies. The **massacre** occurred even though Black Kettle had a U.S. **flag** and a white flag flying next to his tepee. The number of Indians involved in the massacre is uncertain. Estimates range from 500 to 1,000 and the number of dead, from 150 to 600. Chivington lost almost 50 men.

Chivington returned to Denver, where he placed Indian scalps on public display. With winter approaching, Black Kettle led his survivors north without proper food or clothing. A congressional investigation condemned Chivington, and **Henry Halleck** ordered his arrest, but the colonel simply was mustered out of service in January 1865. Evans later resigned upon the request of President **Andrew Johnson**.

SANDERS, JOHN CALDWELL CALHOUN (1840–1864) CSA. A native of **Alabama**, Sanders was a cadet at the University of Alabama when the Civil War began. He left school and raised a volunteer **company** that became part of the 11th Alabama. Sanders then entered Confederate service in June 1861 as the company's captain.

Sent to **Virginia**, Sanders became part of **Cadmus M. Wilcox's brigade** and fought with it through the **Peninsula** and **Seven Days Campaigns**. At **Frayser's Farm**, he received a serious leg wound that kept him off duty for a month. When all of the field officers were killed or wounded, Sanders was made acting major in late summer 1862 and led the **regiment** through the **Second Manassas** and **Antietam Campaigns** with the **Army of Northern Virginia**. He was wounded in the face in the latter battle. Promoted to colonel in September, Sanders saw no combat at **Fredericksburg**, but he was praised for his leadership at **Salem Church** in May 1863. In heavy fighting at **Gettysburg**, he received his third wound of the war when he was shot in the knee. Following Gettysburg, Sanders served on court-martial duty before being given temporary command of the brigade in August. After leading it in the **Bristoe Station** and **Mine Run Campaigns**, he resumed his regimental command in February 1864 when **Abner Perrin** took over the brigade. When Perrin was killed at **Spotsylvania**, Sanders again took command of the brigade and led it skillfully through the rest of the **Overland Campaign**.

Finally promoted to brigadier general in June 1864, Sanders led his men in the early part of the **Petersburg Campaign**. He fought particularly well at the **Crater** when he personally led a counterattack that recaptured the position. Sanders continued to see heavy combat around Petersburg until he was shot through both thighs at the **Weldon Railroad** on August 21. With both of his femoral arteries severed, the popular officer bled to death almost immediately.

SANDERS, WILLIAM PRICE (1833–1863) USA. A native of **Kentucky**, as a boy, Sanders moved with his family to **Mississippi**. His father was a prominent lawyer, and Sanders was awarded an appointment to **West Point** in 1852. He later was saved from being expelled for academic deficiencies by the intercession of Secretary of War **Jefferson Davis**. After graduating in 1856, Sanders served on the frontier with the dragoons and in the **Utah Expedition**.

When the Civil War began, Sanders was a 2nd lieutenant in the 2nd U.S. Dragoons. He was promoted to 1st lieutenant in May 1861 and to captain in the 6th U.S. Cavalry in August. Sanders spent the war's first winter in the **Washington, D.C.**, defenses but then fought in the **Penin-**

sula, **Seven Days**, and **Antietam Campaigns** with the **Army of the Potomac**, serving as regimental commander in the latter. After Antietam, he went on extended sick leave and did not return to duty until February 1863, at which time he was appointed colonel of the 5th Kentucky (Union). In the summer of 1863, Sanders helped chase down **John Hunt Morgan's** Confederate raiders.

Promoted to brigadier general of volunteers in October 1863, Sanders was given command of the cavalry in the **Department of the Ohio**. In early November, he was put in command of a cavalry **division** under **Ambrose E. Burnside** and led it in the **Knoxville Campaign**. After fighting at **Campbell's Station**, Sanders was mortally wounded on November 18 at Knoxville's Fort Loudon and died the next day. The fort was renamed **Fort Sanders** in his honor.

SANITARY COMMISSION, U.S. Unable to care adequately for all of its sick and wounded soldiers, the U.S. government authorized the creation of the United States Sanitary Commission in June 1861. The commission was patterned after the British Sanitary Commission, which was so effective in the Crimean War. Placed under a prominent minister, Dr. Henry W. Bellows, the commission served a vital role in providing services to the soldiers, which the government would not or could not undertake. Not only did the Sanitary Commission provide nurses, hospitals, food, supplies, and ambulances, but it also helped soldiers collect pensions, made camps more sanitary, provided lodging for discharged or furloughed soldiers, and assisted soldiers in keeping in touch with home by supplying them with paper and pencils and even writing letters for illiterate or incapacitated men. Money to operate the huge budget came from donations and **sanitary fairs**, while a large part of the supplies was donated. At its peak, the commission had approximately 500 agents and 10 branches in major Northern cities. During the war it spent more than $7 million and provided $15 million worth of supplies. *See also* HOGE, JANE; LIVERMORE, MARY A.

SANITARY FAIRS. Sanitary fairs were used by the Union to raise money for the **U.S. Sanitary Commission**. Commission agents **Mary A. Livermore** and **Jane Hoge** formed the first fair in the autumn of 1863 in Chicago, **Illinois**, to assist the northwestern branch of the Sanitary Commission. The fair had a parade, booths to sell donated goods, and entertainment, and raised more than $75,000. One item that sold for $3,000 was **Abraham Lincoln's** original draft of the **Emancipation Proclamation**. The idea of fairs soon spread, and other major cities with Sanitary Commission branches followed suit. The fairs raised at least $4.4 million, with $2.7 million actually going into the commission's treasury.

SANTA ROSA ISLAND, FLORIDA, BATTLE OF (OCTOBER 9, 1861). From April to October 1861, the opposing forces at **Pensacola, Florida**, held their respective positions. Confederate Brig. Gen. **Braxton Bragg's** 8,000-man **Army of Pensacola** occupied the town, Navy Yard, and Forts McRee and Barrancas. Union Col. Harvey Brown occupied **Fort Pickens** and the western end of Santa Rosa Island with about 1,800 men, and several Union warships were positioned offshore.

After the Federals successfully raided the Pensacola Navy Yard on September 14, 1861, Bragg took action against Santa Rosa Island. On the night of October 8, Brig. Gen. **Richard H. Anderson** landed 1,200 men a few miles east of Fort Pickens. Dividing into three columns to cover the south and north beaches and the center, the Confederates advanced down the island toward the fort in the predawn hours. Anderson's men successfully surprised the 6th New York's **pickets** and overran its camp, but they then stopped to loot and burn the Union camp. This gave Col. William Wilson time to rally his men and begin resisting the advance. Alerted by the flames and gunfire, Union reinforcements were sent from Fort Pickens to counterattack the Confederates. Anderson, who was wounded in the elbow, then retreated under heavy pressure to his boats and withdrew from the island. In the raid, the Confederates lost 87 men while the Federals lost 67.

SAP ROLLER. A sap was another name for a trench. When digging saps while in the presence of the enemy, soldiers constructed a sap roller. This was a long, cylindrical, basket-like object filled with rocks, logs, or other material that was rolled ahead of the men to protect them from enemy small-arms fire.

SAVAGE'S STATION, VIRGINIA, BATTLE OF (JUNE 29, 1862). On the fifth day of the **Seven Days Campaign**, **George B. McClellan's Army of the Potomac** was in headlong retreat down the Virginia Peninsula after being attacked by **Robert E. Lee's Army of Northern Virginia** at **Mechanicsville** and **Gaines' Mill**. By June 29, 1862, McClellan had successfully withdrawn that part of his **army** isolated on the north side of the Chickahominy River and was retreating toward the James River. Seeking a complete victory, Lee planned to strike and destroy the Union army while it was strung out in retreat.

Both sides were hampered by poor planning on June 29. McClellan left the front without designating an officer to command in his absence and simply ordered the rear guard to continue toward the James River.

As a result, Maj. Gen. **Samuel Heintzelman** believed there were enough troops to guard the rear and, without informing anyone, continued to retreat with his III Corps. This left Maj. Gen. **Edwin V. Sumner's** II Corps alone at Savage's Station to destroy the supplies there, move a hospital and wagon train, and guard the rear. On the Confederate side, Lee planned to destroy the Union army by having **John B. Magruder's** and **Benjamin Huger's divisions**, which had been guarding **Richmond**, move against the enemy's western flank while **Stonewall Jackson** pushed the Federals' rear guard from the north. Jackson, however, was slow and did not cross the Chickahominy River in a timely fashion to carry out his orders. South of the Chickahominy, Huger also was slow and did not keep up with Magruder on his left.

Magruder encountered Sumner's 26,000-man **corps** at Allen's Farm about 9:00 A.M., June 29, and fought until Sumner withdrew toward Savage's Station two hours later. Believing he was about to be attacked, Magruder then went on the defensive until Lee finally ordered him to continue east along the Richmond & York River Railroad and the Williamsburg Road. Sometime after 4:00 P.M., Magruder's 14,000 men encountered Sumner near Savage's Station. Magruder only committed about one-third of his force (Sumner committed less than half of his), but intense fighting broke out as **Lafayette McLaws's division** attacked Union Maj. Gen. **John Sedgwick's** division. The fighting, which oftentimes was close-quartered, did not end until darkness enveloped the battlefield and a strong thunderstorm broke. The battle was a stalemate, and Lee was much chagrined at the way his plan had gone awry.

In the battle, Sumner lost 919 men (plus 2,500 wounded Federals captured in the hospital) to Magruder's 444. Including the casualties suffered at Allen's Farm, the Federals lost 1,038 during the day and the Confederates 473. After Savage's Station, the Federals continued their retreat, and the two armies clashed again the next day at **Frayser's Farm**.

SAVANNAH, GEORGIA, CAPTURE OF (DECEMBER 9–21, 1864).

In December 1864, **William T. Sherman's** 62,000 men approached Savannah, Georgia, at the end of their **March to the Sea**. The vital Confederate port was protected by Lt. Gen. **William J. Hardee's** 10,000 men, who were positioned in strong fortifications ringing the city. After surrounding Savannah on the north, west, and south on December 9–10, Sherman sent **William B. Hazen's** division on December 12 to attack **Fort McAllister**, located south of the city on the south bank of the Ogeechee River. Hazen captured the fort, and Union vessels positioned offshore were able to run needed supplies and ordnance to Sherman by way of the river. After Hardee refused a surrender demand on December 17, Sherman arranged for **John G. Foster**, commander of the **Department of the South**, to position his troops on the east side of Savannah to cut the Confederates' last avenue of escape into **South Carolina**. Before Foster could act, Hardee escaped to the east, crossing the Savannah River on a **pontoon bridge** on December 20. The next day, Sherman's men occupied Savannah.

"SAVIOUR OF THE VALLEY." *See* ROSSER, THOMAS LAFAYETTE.

SAWYER GUN AND SHELL. The Sawyer gun, invented in the 1850s by Sylvanus Sawyer, was a **rifled** cannon made in 6-, 24-, and 30-pounder models. It fired an awkward shell that was coated in lead, with six rectangular ribs attached to it to fit into the cannon tube's rifling. When fired, the shell was given spin by the ribs gripping and the lead expanding into the rifling. The guns were never popular because they were difficult to load and sometimes exploded when fired. Sawyer guns were most often used for coastal defense.

SAXTON, RUFUS (1824–1908) USA. A native of **Massachusetts**, Saxton graduated from **West Point** in 1849. Assigned to the **artillery**, he fought in the **Seminole Wars**, served on a western surveying expedition, taught artillery **tactics** at West Point, served in Europe as an observer, and designed and patented a self-registering thermometer used for deep-sea soundings.

When the Civil War began, Saxton was a 1st lieutenant of artillery serving at the St. Louis Arsenal. After helping **Nathaniel Lyon** capture the secessionist Missouri State Guard at **Camp Jackson**, he was promoted to captain in May 1861 and was appointed chief quartermaster for Lyon's **Army of Southwest Missouri**. Later in the year, Saxton served as **George B. McClellan's** chief quartermaster in western **Virginia** and for the expedition that captured **Port Royal, South Carolina**.

Appointed brigadier general of volunteers in April 1862, Saxton commanded **Harpers Ferry, Virginia**, during **Stonewall Jackson's 1862 Shenandoah Valley Campaign**. For his efforts in defending his post, he was awarded the **Medal of Honor** more than 30 years later. In February 1863, Saxton was transferred to the **Department of the South**, where he held various posts and **district** commands until war's end. His main duty in the **department** was recruiting and organizing such **black troops** as the 1st South Carolina Colored Volunteers, the first full-strength black **regiment** to be accepted officially by the Union **army**. Saxton also supervised putting runaway slaves to work on abandoned Sea Islands plantations.

For his war service, Saxton was **brevetted** major general of volunteers and brigadier general of regulars. Just before hostilities ended, he joined the **Freedmen's Bureau** and served as assistant commissioner for **South Carolina, Georgia**, and **Florida**. In that position, Saxton angered President **Andrew Johnson** and was removed for supporting a plan to confiscate Southern plantations and turn them over to **freedmen**. After being mustered out of the volunteer service in January 1866, he remained in the regular army's quartermaster's department as a major. Saxton rose to the rank of colonel and assistant quartermaster general in 1882 and retired from the army in 1888.

SAYLER'S CREEK, VIRGINIA, BATTLE OF (APRIL 6, 1865). *See* SAILOR'S CREEK, VIRGINIA, BATTLE OF.

SCALAWAGS. This was the slang term used by former Confederates during **Reconstruction** to describe other native white Southerners who supported the **Republican Party**. Some scalawags cooperated with the Republicans to gain favors and to reap monetary and political profit. Others genuinely believed it was in the South's best interest to put the war behind it, cooperate in the Reconstruction process, and start rebuilding their shattered region. **James Longstreet** was one former Confederate general who was considered a scalawag.

SCALES, ALFRED MOORE (1827–1892) CSA. A native of **North Carolina**, Scales graduated from the University of North Carolina and became a lawyer and politician. He served as a county solicitor, was a four-term state legislator, and was elected to one term in the **U.S. Congress** during the antebellum period. A secessionist, Scales also attended North Carolina's **secession** convention.

When the Civil War began, Scales joined a local volunteer **company** in April 1861 as a private, but he was elected captain the following month. Becoming part of **William D. Pender's** 3rd North Carolina, the company was sent to **Virginia**. In October, Scales was elected colonel when Pender was transferred, and the following month the **regiment** was redesignated the 13th North Carolina. The regiment then became part of **Raleigh Colston's brigade**, and during the **Peninsula Campaign** it was heavily engaged at **Williamsburg** and **Seven Pines**. Transferred to **Samuel Garland's** brigade, Scales was highly praised for his actions in the **Seven Days Campaign**, particularly for **Gaines' Mill**, but he collapsed from exhaustion after the **Battle of Malvern Hill** and was off duty until November. When he returned to duty, the regiment had been attached to Pender's brigade. During the **Battle of Fredericksburg**,

Pender was slightly wounded, and Scales temporarily took command of the brigade. After taking leave to marry a woman half his age, he returned to the **Army of Northern Virginia** in time to fight at **Chancellorsville**. There his regiment performed well and captured Union Brig. Gen. **William Hays**, but Scales was severely wounded in the thigh.

Scales was promoted to brigadier general in June 1863 and took command of the brigade after Pender was promoted to **division** command. In the bloody fighting on **Gettysburg's** first day, he lost all but one of his field officers and suffered a severe leg wound from a shell fragment. Scales was taken back to Virginia in the same ambulance that transported the mortally wounded Pender. Returning to duty in August, Scales saw little combat in the **Bristoe Station** and **Mine Run Campaigns** but was heavily engaged and suffered many casualties in the **Overland** and **Petersburg Campaigns** as part of **Cadmus Wilcox's** division. In February 1865, Scales traveled to North Carolina on sick leave and was there when the war ended.

After the war, Scales had an active political career in North Carolina. He served in the legislature from 1866 to 1869, in Congress from 1875 to 1884, and was governor from 1884 to 1888. After leaving the governor's office, Scales worked as a bank president.

SCAMMON, ELIAKIM PARKER (1816–1894) USA. A native of **Maine**, Scammon graduated from **West Point** in 1837 and was assigned to the **artillery** for one year before transferring to the **engineers**. He served at West Point, in the **Seminole** and **Mexican Wars**, in the Great Lakes region, and in the **New Mexico Territory** before being dismissed from the service in 1856 for misconduct and disobedience of orders. Afterward, Scammon taught parochial school in **Ohio**.

Scammon entered Union service in June 1861 when he was commissioned colonel of the 23rd Ohio. Sent to western **Virginia**, he fought at **Carnifex Ferry** and in October was given a **brigade** command in the **Kanawha Division**. After participating in some **skirmishing** in early 1862, the **division** reinforced **John Pope's Army of Virginia** during the **Second Manassas Campaign**. Scammon's unit then became part of **Ambrose E. Burnside's** IX Corps during the **Antietam Campaign**. His brigade fought particularly well at **South Mountain**, and he temporarily led the Kanawha Division at Antietam.

Promoted to brigadier general of volunteers in October 1862, Scammon was put in command of the District of Kanawha, but in February 1864, he was captured by Confederate guerrillas while sleeping onboard a steamer. After being **exchanged** in August, he was given command of a brigade in the **Department of the South**. While serving there in operations against **Charleston, South Carolina**, Scammon was captured again in October 1864 but was quickly released. In the war's last months, he commanded the District of **Florida**.

After Scammon was mustered out of service in August 1865, he served as the U.S. consul on Prince Edward Island from 1866 to 1870. Afterward, he served as a federal engineer at New York City, but in 1875, he accepted a position as mathematics professor at Seaton Hall College and taught there for a number of years.

SCHENCK, ROBERT CUMMING (1809–1890) USA. A native of **Ohio**, Schenck graduated from Ohio's Miami University in 1827 and became a lawyer. As a **Whig**, he was elected to the state legislature in 1840 and to the **U.S. Congress** in 1842. After four terms in Congress, Schenck resigned his seat in 1851 to become the U.S. minister to Brazil, a post he kept until 1853. By 1860, he had switched to the **Republican Party** and strongly supported **Abraham Lincoln** for president.

Lincoln appointed Schenck a brigadier general of volunteers in June 1861. Given a **brigade** in **Daniel Tyler's division**, he fought at **First Manassas**, directed the Union forces at the **Battle of McDowell**, and commanded **John C. Frémont's** right wing at **Cross Keys**. In June 1862, Schenck was given command of the 1st Division in the **Army of Virginia's** I Corps. He was so severely wounded in the arm at **Second Manassas** that he became unfit for further field duty. Promoted to major general of volunteers in August 1862, Schenck was given command of the **Middle Department**. He kept that position until resigning from the service in December 1863 to accept a seat in Congress.

For the next eight years Schenck was chairman of the Committee on Military Affairs and for a time chaired the Committee on Ways and Means. After failing to be reelected in 1870, he was appointed U.S. minister to Great Britain by President **U. S. Grant** and helped settle the *Alabama* **Claims**. In 1876, Schenck became embroiled in the Emma Mine scandal and was forced to resign when he used his position to sell stock in this fraudulent silver mine. Returning to the United States, he practiced law and became known as an authority on draw poker.

SCHENKL SHELL. This shell, designed by John P. Schenkl of Boston, Massachusetts, was one of the many shells designed for rifled **artillery**. The Schenkl shell was made of cast iron and had a cone-shaped base with a papier-mâché **sabot**. When the gun was fired, the sabot expanded to grip the tube's **rifling** and gave the shell spin. The sabot was designed to fall off the shell when it left the tube. The shell was never very reliable, however, because the sabots sometimes failed to work properly.

SCHIMMELFENNIG, ALEXANDER (1824–1865) USA. A native of Prussia, Schimmelfennig (SHIM-uhl-fenig) served as a Prussian engineering officer in the Schleswig-Holstein War and as a revolutionary in the Baden Revolution. After immigrating to **Pennsylvania** in 1853, he wrote a book that accurately predicted the Crimean War and made a living as an engineer and draftsman.

When the Civil War began, Schimmelfennig apparently was employed by the U.S. War Department. He offered his services to the Union and in September 1861 was appointed colonel of the 74th Pennsylvania. Schimmelfennig was incapacitated for months afterward from an injury suffered when his horse fell on him and from a case of smallpox. His first combat was at Freeman's Ford during the **Second Manassas Campaign**. There, Schimmelfennig took command of the **brigade** in **Carl Schurz's division** when his commander was killed. He led the brigade through the remainder of the campaign and then was given a brigade command in the 3rd Division of the **Army of the Potomac's** XI Corps.

In November 1862, Schimmelfennig was promoted to brigadier general of volunteers, reportedly because **Abraham Lincoln** wanted another German general for political reasons and particularly liked Schimmelfennig's name. His career as a general was less than stellar. At **Chancellorsville**, Schimmelfennig's brigade and the rest of the **corps** were stampeded by **Stonewall Jackson's** flank attack. Then at **Gettysburg**, he temporarily commanded the division on the first day, but during the corps' rout, he was injured when he was accidentally hit in the head by a musket butt. Schimmelfennig was forced to hide in a pigsty for two days to avoid capture. After Gettysburg, he wanted to transfer out of the XI Corps but instead was sent with the division to **Charleston, South Carolina**. Schimmelfennig held several commands in the **Department of the South**, including commanding Charleston, but he often was on sick leave suffering from malaria. Toward war's end, he also developed tuberculosis and was forced to take an extended sick leave. Schimmelfennig died in September 1865 while seeking treatment for his illness.

SCHOEPF, ALBIN FRANCISCO (1822–1886) USA. A native of Poland, Schoepf (SHEPF) served as a captain in the Austrian army before joining the Hungarian revolutionaries in 1848. After the revolt was put down, he was exiled and immigrated to the United States in 1851 by way of Syria and Turkey (where he helped train the Ottoman army). Schoepf first worked as a porter in a **Washington, D.C.**, hotel, but Commissioner of Patents **Joseph Holt** took a liking to him and secured him a position as patent clerk. When Holt was appointed secretary of war in 1859, Schoepf went with him and worked in the War Department until the Civil War.

Schoepf entered Union service in September 1861 when his political connections secured him an appointment to brigadier general of volunteers. Although a competent officer, his rigid Austrian views on **discipline** and duty often made him unpopular and brought him into conflict with Secretary of War **Edwin Stanton**. He first was given a **brigade** command in the **Army of the Ohio** and was sent to **Kentucky**, where he and Confederate Brig. Gen. **Felix K. Zollicoffer** traded victories in some small **skirmishes**. After fighting at **Mill Springs**, Schoepf was given a **division** command in the **Army of the Ohio's** III Corps in September 1862. He fought at **Perryville** but apparently was linked with **corps** commander **Charles C. Gilbert's** failure to properly support other troops. Gilbert was relieved of command, but Schoepf requested to be replaced. He was put in charge of the **prison** camp at **Fort Delaware** from April 1863 to January 1866. Without receiving any **brevets** for his wartime service, he was mustered out of the volunteers in January 1866.

Schoepf returned to a clerkship in the patent office and eventually became the office's chief examiner. He held that position until his death in 1886.

SCHOFIELD, JOHN McALLISTER (1831–1906) USA. A native of **New York**, as a boy, Schofield (SCOE-field) moved to **Illinois** with his father. As a teenager, he worked as a surveyor and teacher before entering **West Point** in 1849. After graduating in 1853, Schofield was assigned to the **artillery** and served in **Florida** and taught at the academy before taking a leave of absence in 1860 to accept a position as professor of physics at **Missouri's** Washington University.

When the Civil War began, Schofield served as Missouri's mustering officer before becoming major of the 1st Missouri (Union) (later designated the 1st Missouri Light Artillery) and assistant adjutant general for the **Department of the West**. As **Nathaniel Lyon's** chief of staff, he participated in the capture of **Camp Jackson** and fought at **Wilson's Creek**, for which he later was awarded the **Medal of Honor**.

In November 1861, Schofield was appointed brigadier general of volunteers and was given command of all the Union militia in Missouri.

Over the next year, he held various **district** commands in Missouri, but in October 1862, he was put in command of the **Army of the Frontier**. Promotion to major general of volunteers came the following month, but the Senate never confirmed the promotion because of some controversial measures Schofield took to control strife-torn Missouri. As a result, he reverted to brigadier general in March 1863 and was given command of a **division** in the **Army of the Cumberland's** XIV Corps. Schofield was reappointed major general of volunteers in May 1863 and was put in command of the **Department of the Missouri**. There he again had difficulty establishing peace over the badly divided population and was replaced in early 1864. Sent to the **Department of the Ohio**, Schofield took command of the **Army of the Ohio** in April 1864 and led it throughout the **Atlanta Campaign**.

After Atlanta, Georgia, was captured, Schofield was sent to **Tennessee** to aid **George H. Thomas** in the **Franklin and Nashville Campaign**. While serving there, he was accused of scheming to take away Thomas's command. Whether this was true or not, Schofield served very well in the campaign. In the Spring Hill Incident, he slipped past the Confederate **Army of Tennessee** and took up a strong position at Franklin. In a vicious battle, Schofield defeated the Confederates and withdrew to Nashville. For this victory, he was promoted from captain to brigadier general of regulars in late November 1864. After helping defeat **John Bell Hood** at Nashville, Schofield was transferred and commanded the **Department of North Carolina** from February 1865 until war's end. In that position, he joined **William T. Sherman** at Goldsboro during the **Carolinas Campaign** and was with him at the Confederate **surrender** at **Durham Station**.

Schofield skillfully served the Union during the war and went on to hold many important positions. At war's end, he was **brevetted** major general of regulars and was sent to France, where he negotiated the withdrawal of the French troops that were supporting Mexico's Emperor **Maximilian**. After serving as secretary of war under Presidents **Andrew Johnson** and **U. S. Grant** in 1868–69, he was promoted to major general. Schofield was the officer who recommended that Pearl Harbor, Hawaii, be used as a **U.S. Navy** base and served as superintendent of West Point from 1876 to 1881 before presiding over the board that exonerated **Fitz John Porter** for his actions at **Second Manassas**. When **Philip H. Sheridan** died in 1888, Schofield replaced him as the **U.S. Army's** commanding general. He was promoted to lieutenant general in 1895 and retired later that year.

SCHURZ, CARL (1829–1906) USA. A native of Prussia, Schurz (SHURTS) was well educated at Cologne and at the University of Bonn.

After participating in the 1848 revolutions, he moved first to Switzerland and then to France. When France expelled him, Schurz lived in Great Britain for a year before immigrating to the United States in 1852. Settling in **Pennsylvania**, he became a popular public speaker and an **abolitionist**. Schurz moved to **Wisconsin** in 1856 and became active in **Republican Party** politics. He campaigned for **John C. Frémont** in 1856 and in 1860 headed the state's delegation to the Republican National Convention. There, Schurz first supported Frémont's nomination, but he then campaigned for **Abraham Lincoln**. He was instrumental in winning Lincoln the German vote, and the president appointed him U.S. minister to Spain in July 1861.

Schurz returned from Spain in 1862 to pressure Lincoln for immediate emancipation and to seek a military appointment. Lincoln refused his plea on emancipation, but in April 1862, he did appoint Schurz brigadier general of volunteers to gain support from German-Americans. In June, Schurz was given a **division** command in the **Army of Virginia's** I Corps. After fighting well at **Second Manassas**, he was given a division in the **Army of the Potomac's** XI Corps and sometimes temporarily commanded the **corps** in early 1863.

Schurz was promoted to major general of volunteers in March 1863. His division was among those routed at **Chancellorsville** and **Gettysburg**, and many Union soldiers began to hold in contempt the "Dutch" soldiers in Schurz's command. After Gettysburg, the division went west with the XI and XII Corps under **Joseph Hooker**. Schurz participated in the **Chattanooga Campaign**, but he and Hooker clashed, and by early 1864 Schurz was reduced to commanding a recruiting depot in Nashville, Tennessee. After actively campaigning for Lincoln's reelection in 1864, Schurz helped **Winfield S. Hancock** recruit for the **Veteran Volunteer Corps** before being appointed the **Army of Georgia's** chief of staff in April 1865.

Schurz resigned from the **army** in May 1865. He then devoted his life to writing and to such liberal causes as racial equality, a civil service system, and anti-imperialism. Schurz served one term (1869–75) in the U.S. Senate from **Missouri** and advocated protecting the public domain while serving as secretary of the interior in 1877. During the postwar period, he also edited five national publications, became actively involved in presidential elections, and became one of America's most respected figures. Schurz's memoirs, *The Reminiscences of Carl Schurz*, is a classic of the Civil War period.

SCOTT, THOMAS MOORE (1829–1876) CSA. Little is known of the early life of this **Georgia** native. Scott worked as a farmer, lived in several different places, and was residing in **Louisiana** when the Civil War began. In 1861, he organized the 12th Louisiana and was elected its colonel. Scott was present at, but not engaged in, the **Battle of Belmont** and helped garrison both Island No. 10 and Fort Pillow, Tennessee. Afterward, his **regiment** served at Corinth, Mississippi, and Port Hudson, Louisiana.

Scott's regiment was a part of **William Loring's division** during the 1863 **Vicksburg Campaign**. It fought well at **Champion Hill** and afterward accompanied the division to Jackson, Mississippi, where it formed part of **Joseph E. Johnston's** army. Scott remained in **Mississippi** after **Vicksburg** fell and in March 1864 was given command of a **brigade** in Loring's division. Scott was an excellent drill instructor, his was recognized as one of the best-trained brigades in the **army**. Scott's brigade joined the **Army of Tennessee** for the 1864 **Atlanta Campaign**. In May 1864, he was promoted to brigadier general and during the campaign was praised for fighting well at **Resaca**, **New Hope Church**, **Kennesaw Mountain**, and **Peachtree Creek** (where he lost 390 men). Scott also participated in the **Franklin and Nashville Campaign**. While fighting at Franklin, he was temporarily paralyzed by an exploding shell and was forced to relinquish his command for the rest of the war.

After the war, Scott returned to Louisiana and became a farmer and planter.

SCOTT, WINFIELD (1786–1866) USA. A native of **Virginia**, Scott attended the College of William and Mary and studied law before President Thomas Jefferson granted him a captain's commission in the **U.S. Army** in 1808. As a brigadier general, Scott was praised highly for his service in the War of 1812 and became one of the nation's most popular heroes after fighting on the Canadian frontier (where he was captured) and winning the Battle of Lundy's Lane. He also was badly wounded at Lundy's Lane and received a **brevet** of major general for his service there. Besides being a skilled soldier, Scott also was a capable diplomat and helped settle the Black Hawk War, the **Nullification Crisis**, Canadian border disputes, and the removal of the Five Civilized Tribes. His position as America's greatest living general was secured in 1841 when he was appointed general-in-chief of the U.S. armies.

Scott's finest service was in the **Mexican War**, where he made a successful amphibious landing at Vera Cruz and forced the Mexicans' surrender by capturing Mexico City with an outnumbered army. Many future Civil War generals served under Scott in Mexico and later put to good use the **tactics** learned from him. As a reward, Scott received the **Thanks of Congress** and was brevetted lieutenant general in 1847. Although recognized as one of the nation's most brilliant strategists and tacticians, "Old Fuss and Feathers" sometimes was difficult to get along with and often clashed with President James K. Polk because of Scott's **Whig** politics. After running unsuccessfully for president on the Whig ticket in 1852, he continued to serve as the army's general-in-chief in the years leading up to the Civil War.

During the **secession** crisis, Scott unsuccessfully urged President **James Buchanan** to reinforce the federal installations in the South. When the Civil War began, the Confederates vilified him for abandoning his native state and remaining loyal to the Union. Scott tried to ensure the loyalty of fellow Virginian **Robert E. Lee** by offering Lee command of the Union armies, but Lee refused. Scott was one of the few officers on either side who believed the war might last longer than a few weeks, and at **Abraham Lincoln's** request he devised the **Anaconda Plan** as the Union's war **strategy**.

Scott's service to the Union was short lived. His mind remained sharp at age 75, but his body had deteriorated greatly. Standing six feet, five inches tall, Scott was grossly overweight, suffered from dropsy, and could no longer mount a horse. He was partially blamed for the defeats at **First Manassas** and **Ball's Bluff** and was snubbed by **George B. McClellan** when McClellan became commander of the **Army of the Potomac**. When it became impossible to work with McClellan, Scott requested to be retired in October 1861 and was replaced by McClellan. After traveling for a while in Europe, he returned to the United States and spent the Civil War years in retirement.

SCURRY, WILLIAM READ (1821–1864) CSA. A native of **Tennessee**, Scurry moved to **Texas** as a teenager and fought in the **Mexican War** with the 2nd Texas, rising in rank from private to major. In 1859, he served on the commission that settled the Texas–New Mexico boundary dispute and in 1861 was a delegate at the state's **secession** convention.

Scurry entered Confederate service in early 1861 as lieutenant colonel of the 4th Texas Mounted Volunteers. Accompanying **Henry H. Sibley's New Mexico Expedition** in 1862, he fought at **Valverde** and then directed the Confederate forces at the **Battle of Glorieta Pass**. Scurry's performance in the expedition won him a promotion to brigadier general in September 1862. He commanded the infantry that participated in **John B. Magruder's** successful assault on **Galveston, Texas**, in January 1863, and afterward was recommended by Magruder for promotion to major general. The promotion was not made, but Scurry was put in command of east Texas in February 1863. When Union Maj. Gen. **Nathaniel P. Banks** launched the **Texas Overland Expedition** in the autumn of 1863, Scurry was transferred to **Louisiana** and was put in command of a **brigade** in **John G. Walker's division**. He remained in Louisiana and fought well throughout the 1864 **Red River Campaign**. After the **Battle of Pleasant Hill**, Scurry accompanied the division to **Arkansas** to stop **Frederick Steele's Camden Expedition**. At **Jenkins' Ferry**, he was severely wounded but refused to leave the field and subsequently bled to death.

SEARS, CLAUDIUS WISTAR (1817–1891) CSA. A native of **Massachusetts**, Sears graduated from **West Point** in 1841 and briefly served in the infantry before resigning his commission in 1842. He then moved to **Mississippi** and taught at St. Thomas' Hall, but in 1845, he accepted a position as a mathematics and engineering professor at the University of Louisiana. In 1859, Sears returned to St. Thomas' Hall as its president and remained there until the Civil War began.

Sears entered Confederate service in May 1861 as captain of a volunteer **company** he recruited. Assigned to the 17th Mississippi, the company was sent to **Virginia** and became part of **Daniel R. Jones's brigade**. Over the next year, Sears saw combat at **Blackburn's Ford, First Manassas, Ball's Bluff**, and in the **Peninsula, Seven Days**, and **Antietam Campaigns**. In December 1862, he was appointed colonel of the 46th Mississippi and returned to Mississippi in January 1863 to take command. At first his men resented him as an interloper and petitioned for his removal, but in time they came to like and respect him.

As part of **William E. Baldwin's** brigade, Sears fought in the 1863 **Vicksburg Campaign**. He was held in reserve during the **Battle of Port Gibson** and manned the trenches in **Vicksburg, Mississippi**, until its surrender in July 1863. After being **exchanged**, the brigade was transferred to the **Army of Tennessee** in late November, but it then was sent to Mobile, Alabama, in January 1864. When Baldwin died in February, Sears was promoted to brigadier general the following month and was given command of the brigade.

Sears rejoined the Army of Tennessee for the **Atlanta Campaign,** but he saw little combat. He was slightly wounded in the foot by a shell fragment at Cassville and went on sick leave until August 1864. After Atlanta, Georgia, fell, Sears accompanied the **army** north and lost 425 men in the attack against **Allatoona, Georgia**. During the **Franklin and Nashville Campaign**, his brigade fought at Franklin, but it appears Sears was not commanding it at the time. In December, however, he did participate in operations against Murfreesboro, Tennessee, under **Nathan Bedford Forrest**. Sears was placed in temporary command of the division the day before the Battle of Nashville. On the first day of the fight while sitting on his horse watching the enemy advance, a **solid shot** tore through the animal and ripped off Sears's leg just below the knee. Apparently unaware of his wound, he reportedly stood up briefly and cried for the favorite horse he had ridden throughout the war. While recovering from this traumatic wound, Sears was captured at a private residence later in the month.

Sears returned to Mississippi after the war, became a professor of mathematics at the University of Mississippi in late 1865, and taught there until his retirement in 1889.

SECESSION. At the heart of the Civil War were **states rights**, constitutional interpretation, and the philosophy of **secession**. Southerners viewed the Union as a confederation of sovereign states that voluntarily joined in an association in which the national government was given certain limited powers, but the individual states retained complete sovereignty. This basically was the original Union created during the Revolutionary War, when the term *united states* was used more as a description than a proper name. Southerners, therefore, viewed themselves as struggling to keep alive the original intent of the Founding Fathers. They also believed that a state had the right to leave or secede from the Union any time it felt its sovereignty was threatened. Northerners, however, viewed the Union as indivisible and the national government as sovereign, with each state perpetually surrendering its sovereignty when it was admitted to the Union. They argued that the Founding Fathers would never have envisioned a union in which each state could arbitrarily leap in and out at will. To do so would be unworkable, since some states likely would secede every time their political party or presidential candidate lost an election. Secession, therefore, was illegal and to allow it would mean the destruction of the nation. They viewed the "United States" as one nation, not as united states working in a cooperative arrangement. What made this debate so acrimonious was that the Founding Fathers did not address secession when they drew up the Constitution, and without a definitive guide, the sections became polarized around their own interpretation of what the Founding Fathers intended. Ironically, both sides believed they were protecting the Founders' intent and were the true torchbearers of liberty and freedom.

Although the South finally did secede, it was not the first section of the country to threaten it. New England twice debated secession—once at the time of the Louisiana Purchase when the small states were fearful of being dominated by the increasing number of new states that would result from the purchase, and once during the War of 1812 when the Hartford Convention prepared to give the **U.S. Congress** an ultimatum to protect New England from disastrous embargoes and an unpopular war. Gradually, some Southerners adopted secession as a way to protect themselves from Northern domination. Realizing that the South's political power was waning as the North's advantage in population and states grew, Southerners feared that the North's growing majority at the polls and in Congress would lead to its complete supremacy. The North could at will force upon the South protective tariffs, stop the expansion of **slavery** into the territories, or even abolish slavery. By the **election of 1860**, Southern **Democrats** feared a **Republican** victory would usher in this repressive period and saw secession as the last desperate measure that would protect them against tyranny by the majority. When **Abraham Lincoln** won the election, **South Carolina** carried out the threat of secession on December 20, 1860. The other Deep South states soon followed.

SECESSIONVILLE, SOUTH CAROLINA, BATTLE OF (JUNE 16, 1862). By early 1862, Union forces had captured **Port Royal, South Carolina**, and were concentrating against **Charleston**. When officials learned that **John C. Pemberton's** Confederates had abandoned Cole's Island, guarding the mouth of the Stono River, **Samuel F. Du Pont's** warships were sent into the river to secure a beachhead on James Island. On June 2, Maj. Gen. **David Hunter** put ashore 10,000 men under Brig. Gen. **Henry W. Benham** to attack the Confederate defenses farther up the island. Deciding the enemy was too strong to attack with the men at hand, Hunter ordered Benham not to attack without receiving reinforcements or gaining approval from him and then left the island on June 12.

Pemberton had 6,500 men on James Island under Brig. Gen. **Nathan G. Evans**. Most of the troops were stationed northeast of Benham, but about 600 men under Col. Thomas Lamar manned strong earthworks near Secessionville, a few miles east of the Federals' camp. The earthworks mounted four large cannons and blocked a narrow peninsula leading to Secessionville. While these cannons traded shots with Benham's **artillery**, another 2,500 Confederates under Col. **Johnson Hagood skirmished** with the Federals near their camps.

Despite Hunter's orders, Benham decided to silence the Confederate cannons near Secessionville. With covering fire from Union gunboats and the support of **Horatio Wright's division**, he attacked the Secessionville earthworks with 3,500 men from Brig. Gen. **Isaac Stevens's** division in the early morning of June 16. Stevens attacked several times and sometimes reached the earthworks, but he was repulsed by the Confederate defenders. During the attacks, Evans arrived with strong reinforcements that brought the defenders' numbers up to about 2,000. When Stevens's attacks stalled, Wright moved one **brigade** to the Confederates' right flank and began **enfilading** their position with **rifle** fire. Lamar was wounded, but Confederate reinforcements arrived before the Federals could take advantage of the situation. One battalion pressured Wright from the front, while Hagood's men attacked his rear, and Confederate siege guns pounded the entire area. Benham finally was forced to withdraw at midmorning.

In the short, sharp battle, the Federals lost 683 men out of 4,500 engaged, while the Confederates lost 204 men out of 3,100. Afterward, Hunter arrested Benham. His commission was revoked, but **Abraham Lincoln** later reinstated him. Lamar was voted the **Thanks of Congress** for his successful defense, and the earthworks were renamed Fort Lamar in his honor. The Federals abandoned James Island in early July, but they continued their efforts to take Charleston.

SEDDON, JAMES ALEXANDER (1815–1880) CSA. A native of **Virginia**, Seddon graduated from the University of Virginia's law school and served in the state legislature from 1845 to 1847 and from 1849 to 1851 before retiring because of poor health. An ardent secessionist, he participated in the **Washington Peace Conference** in early 1861 but afterward urged Virginia to secede. In July, Seddon won a seat in the Provisional **Confederate Congress**, but he was never assigned to any committees. After his term expired, he unsuccessfully ran for a vacant congressional seat in April 1862.

In November 1862, **Jefferson Davis** (an old friend) appointed Seddon to replace **George W. Randolph** as secretary of war. Seddon was Davis's fifth secretary, but he served longer than any other. Unlike his predecessors who chafed at Davis's interference, Seddon accepted Davis's leadership style and deferred to him in most matters concerning **strategy** and personnel. His unquestioning loyalty to Davis and acquiescence in the removal of **Joseph E. Johnston** from **army** command during the **Atlanta Campaign** earned Seddon many critics. By early 1865, the Confederate Congress was dissatisfied with Davis's government and began pressuring him to replace the cabinet. Although Davis advised Seddon to remain at his post, he tendered his resignation in February 1865.

Braxton Bragg. Source: Library of Congress

Philip H. Sheridan. *Source:* Library of Congress

Monitor v. Virginia at Battle of Hampton Roads, Virginia. *Battles and Leaders of the Civil War*

Union artillery and mortar park. *Source:* Library of Congress

Confederate fortifications around Atlanta, Georgia. *Source:* Library of Congress

Union soldiers outside Petersburg, Virginia. *Source:* National Archives

Cavalry clash. *Source: Battles and Leaders of the Civil War*

Louisiana Tigers at Second Battle of Manassas Virginia. *Source: Battles and Leaders of the Civil War*

After the war, Seddon was arrested by Union officials and was imprisoned for several months in **Fort Monroe, Virginia**. After being released, he retired to his Virginia farm.

SEDGWICK, JOHN (1813–1864) USA. A native of **Connecticut**, Sedgwick graduated from **West Point** in 1837. Assigned to the **artillery**, he fought in the **Seminole Wars**, participated in the removal of Cherokee **Indians**, and won two **brevets** for gallantry in the **Mexican War** while serving under both Zachary Taylor and **Winfield Scott**. In 1855, Sedgwick was promoted to major of the 1st U.S. Cavalry.

During the **secession** crisis, Sedgwick was promoted to lieutenant colonel in March 1861. When his colonel, **Robert E. Lee**, resigned his commission in April to join **Virginia**, Sedgwick was promoted to colonel and command of the 1st Cavalry. In August, he was appointed brigadier general of volunteers and was given command of a **brigade** in **Samuel Heintzelman's division** in the **Army of the Potomac**. When **Charles P. Stone** was relieved of command for the **Ball's Bluff** disaster, Sedgwick took over his division in February 1862. This division was assigned to the II Corps and was led by Sedgwick through the **Peninsula** and **Seven Days Campaigns** until he was wounded at **Frayser's Farm**.

After recovering from his wound, Sedgwick was promoted to major general of volunteers in July 1862 and rejoined his division in time for the **Antietam Campaign**. At Antietam, he was wounded three times and was taken from the field unconscious after his division was ambushed and cut to pieces in the West Woods. When Sedgwick returned to duty in late December, he briefly commanded the II and IX Corps before being given permanent command of the VI Corps in February 1863. He played a key role in the **Chancellorsville Campaign** when he was left behind at the **Second Battle of Fredericksburg** with 40,000 men to pin down the Confederates while **Joseph Hooker** crossed the Rappahannock River upstream. In the fighting that ensued, Sedgwick captured Marye's Heights, fought the Confederates stubbornly at **Salem Church**, and successfully withdrew his men across the river while being pressed by a large enemy force. His command was held in reserve at **Gettysburg**, but it again fought well at **Rappahannock Station** in November 1863 and captured a large number of **prisoners**.

By 1864, Sedgwick was known to his men as "Uncle John" and was one of the most popular commanders in the Army of the Potomac. When the **army** was reorganized that spring and was reduced from five **corps** to three, he retained his command. After leading his corps through the **Battle of the Wilderness**, Sedgwick was killed on May 9, 1864, at **Spotsylvania**.

While inspecting an artillery battery, he chastised the men for attempting to dodge Confederate **sharpshooters'** fire. After stating, "they couldn't hit an elephant at this distance" (Warner, *Generals in Blue,* 431), he was killed by a bullet that struck him below the left eye.

SELMA, ALABAMA, BATTLE OF (APRIL 2, 1865). *See* WILSON'S SELMA, ALABAMA, RAID.

SEMINOLE WARS. The U.S. **Army** fought **Florida's** Seminole **Indians** three times during the antebellum period and gave many future Civil War officers their first combat experience. In the early 19th century, the Seminoles frequently left the safety of Spanish Florida and raided Americans living in **Georgia** and **Alabama.** In 1817–18, Andrew Jackson invaded Florida and defeated the Indians, but he touched off an international incident that ended when Spain sold Florida to the United States in 1821. When the **U.S. Congress** ordered all Indians east of the Mississippi River to be moved west in 1830, the Seminoles under Osceola refused and again went to war from 1835 to 1842. In this bloody conflict, hundreds of American soldiers were killed, but most of the Seminoles (including Osceola) finally were captured. With only a few hundred Indians remaining free in the deep swamps, the army unilaterally abandoned its campaign. When Florida became a state in 1845, it tried to expel the few remaining Seminoles and started a third war in 1855–58. Most of the remaining Indians eventually were captured and sent west, but a little more than one hundred remained in hiding.

SEMMES, PAUL JONES (1815–1863) CSA. A native of **Georgia,** Semmes (SEMZ) was the brother of Confederate admiral **Raphael Semmes.** He briefly attended the University of Virginia in 1833 but then returned to Georgia, where he became a brigadier general in the state militia, a wealthy planter and bank agent, served on the **West Point** Board of Visitors, and commanded a prestigious militia company.

A strong supporter of **secession,** Semmes purchased arms and ammunition for Georgia in November 1860 and was named the state's quartermaster general after it seceded in January 1861. After commanding the state troops at **Jefferson Davis's** inauguration, he resigned his state commission in May to accept an appointment to colonel of the 2nd Georgia. Semmes was sent to **Virginia** and frequently requested leave for various reasons. After being turned down repeatedly, he resigned his commission in February 1862, but **Joseph E. Johnston** refused to accept the resignation. Instead, Semmes was promoted to brigadier general in March and was given command of a **brigade** in **Lafayette McLaws's division.**

Semmes led his brigade through the **Peninsula** and **Seven Days Campaigns**. After barely escaping injury by an exploding shell that shredded his clothing at **Malvern Hill**, he collapsed from exhaustion on the field and had to be carried off. Semmes was on sick leave during the **Second Manassas Campaign** but returned to duty with the **Army of Northern Virginia** in September and won great praise for his bravery at **Crampton's Gap** and **Antietam**. After fighting at **Fredericksburg's** Marye's Heights and later at **Salem Church** during the **Chancellorsville Campaign**, he was mortally wounded in the thigh at **Gettysburg's Wheatfield** on July 2, 1863. Semmes was transported back to Virginia in a wagon, but he died at a private residence on July 10, 1863.

SEMMES, RAPHAEL (1809–1877) CSA. A native of **Maryland**, Semmes (SEMZ) was the brother of Confederate general **Paul J. Semmes**. He entered the **U.S. Navy** as a midshipman in 1826 and studied law between sea duty. Semmes passed the bar exam in 1834 and was promoted to lieutenant in 1837. During the **Mexican War**, he commanded the USS *Somers* on blockade duty off Vera Cruz, but the ship sank in a storm. Barely escaping alive, Semmes was praised for his actions in the tragedy and went on to serve as a naval observer during **Winfield Scott's** advance on Mexico City. After the war, he rose to the rank of commander in 1855 and often used his legal expertise to defend fellow officers against unfair treatment by the navy.

Semmes was living in Mobile, **Alabama**, in 1861. He resigned his naval commission in February and was appointed by **Jefferson Davis** to be a naval purchasing agent in the North. After considerable success, Semmes was commissioned a commander in the **Confederate navy** in April and briefly commanded the Lighthouse Bureau before converting the steamer *Havana* into the Confederacy's first **commerce raider**. He renamed the ship the *Sumter* and commanded it on a successful six-month cruise that accounted for 18 prizes before the Union navy trapped the vessel at Gibraltar.

After abandoning the *Sumter* at Gibraltar, Semmes was promoted to captain and was given command of the *Alabama*. From September 1862 to June 1864, the *Alabama* was the most feared Confederate commerce raider. Semmes sailed from the Atlantic Ocean to the South China Sea and accounted for 66 Union ships, including the **USS *Hatteras*,** which he sank off the **Texas** coast. In June 1864, however, the *Alabama* was confronted at Cherbourg, France, by the **USS *Kearsarge***. Semmes engaged the enemy ship on June 19, but he was defeated, and the *Alabama* was sunk in the English Channel. Semmes was rescued by a British yacht and returned to the Confederacy by way of Great Britain.

Semmes was promoted to rear admiral and in February 1865 was placed in command of the James River Squadron. He destroyed his vessels when **Richmond, Virginia**, was evacuated in April and led his men to **North Carolina** in hope of joining **Joseph E. Johnston**. Davis appointed Semmes brigadier general during the evacuation, but the Senate never had a chance to confirm the appointment. Semmes subsequently surrendered with Johnston's **army** in North Carolina.

In December 1865, Semmes was imprisoned and was threatened with prosecution for treason and piracy. Federal officials finally released him after four months, and he returned to Mobile. There, Semmes at first had a difficult time supporting himself because of federal persecution. Authorities removed him from an elected judgeship and drove him from positions in education and journalism. Semmes finally established a successful law practice and wrote *Memoirs of Service Afloat, during the War between the States. See also ALABAMA* CLAIMS.

SEVEN DAYS CAMPAIGN (JUNE 25–JULY 2, 1862). After the wounding of Confederate Gen. **Joseph E. Johnston** at **Seven Pines** in May 1862, **Robert E. Lee** was put in command of the **army** defending **Richmond, Virginia**, in the **Peninsula Campaign**. George B. McClellan's 100,000-man **Army of the Potomac** was only a few miles east of the Confederate capital. Expecting reinforcements from **Irvin McDowell** at Fredericksburg, McClellan stretched his right flank north to meet them and unwisely split his army across the Chickahominy River. **Fitz John Porter's** 30,000-man V Corps was isolated on the north side of the river, while the bulk of the army was on the south side. **J. E. B. Stuart's Ride around McClellan** in June brought Lee intelligence that the Union right flank was "in the air" and vulnerable.

Lee ordered **Thomas J. "Stonewall" Jackson's Valley Army** to Richmond to reinforce his **Army of Northern Virginia** for offensive operations. Lee left only 25,000 men on the south side of the Chickahominy to defend Richmond against McClellan's 70,000 and massed nearly 50,000 on the north side of the river to destroy Porter. Jackson was to position his troops north of Porter's exposed flank and attack on the morning of June 26. Lee's other **divisions**, massed west of Porter near Mechanicsville, were to attack when they heard Jackson begin his assault. Since Jackson had miles to travel to get into position, it was risky to base the entire battle plan on his movement, but his ability was unquestioned after his **1862 Shenandoah Valley Campaign**, and he assured Lee he would be in place on time. The plan was audacious, but Lee took into account McClellan's habitual slowness and cautiousness.

The Seven Days Campaign began on June 25 when McClellan unexpectedly advanced toward Richmond to seize some high ground in his front. The resultant **Battle of King's School House** startled Lee, and he feared McClellan might have discovered his plan. But the advance was only a **reconnaissance in force**, and the Confederates continued their preparations.

On the morning of June 26, the Confederate divisions of **A. P. Hill**, **James Longstreet**, and **Daniel H. Hill** waited near **Mechanicsville** for Jackson to begin the battle. When Jackson failed to act by afternoon, A. P. Hill attacked Porter on his own, for fear the Confederates were losing the element of surprise. Intense fighting raged through the afternoon, but Hill (supported by part of Daniel H. Hill's division) was unable to break Porter's strong defenses along Beaver Dam Creek. The Confederates lost 1,484 men in the battle, while Porter lost only 361. Jackson's absence at Mechanicsville was conspicuous, and historians still debate why he failed to arrive at the appointed place on time. He was uncharacteristically slow and went into camp within hearing distance of the battle raging only a few miles away. It is generally believed that Jackson was exhausted from the Shenandoah Valley Campaign and that his fatigue caused him to be strangely lethargic.

On the night of June 26, Porter withdrew from Beaver Dam Creek and retreated across Boatswain's Swamp to near **Gaines' Mill**. There he positioned his infantry on high ground, with numerous **artillery** batteries in support. On the morning of June 27, Lee attacked again, and the battle raged for hours. This time Jackson joined in the fighting, but the Confederates made no headway against the formidable Union defenses until late afternoon when **John Bell Hood's Texas Brigade** broke through Porter's center. Lee then launched a general attack and forced the Federals to retreat. The vicious fighting around Gaines' Mill was the heaviest of the campaign and cost Lee 8,750 men. Porter suffered 6,837 casualties.

Completely unnerved by the two days of fighting, McClellan was convinced he was greatly outnumbered and began a general retreat. He claimed he was simply changing his base from the York River to the James River, but the movement was, in fact, a "great skedaddle" (Faust, ed., *Historical Times Illustrated Encyclopedia of the Civil War,* 667). Since McClellan outnumbered the Confederates and had good defensible ground, the withdrawal was a mistake, and he compounded the error by virtually abandoning his army and providing little leadership during the retreat.

June 28 was spent largely in maneuver. McClellan reunited his command south of the Chickahominy River, while Lee became frustrated at his army's inability to catch and destroy the Federals as they withdrew. On June 29, Lee hoped to crush the enemy at **Savage's Station** by having Jackson attack the Union rear guard from the north while **John B. Magruder's** and **Benjamin Huger's** divisions attacked from the west. For the second time in the campaign, Jackson moved slowly and did not aggressively press the Federals. Huger also failed to keep up with the advance, and Magruder had to attack **Edwin V. Sumner's** II Corps at Savage's Station alone. On the Federal side, McClellan left the area without appointing anyone to command the rear guard, and Sumner committed less than half of his troops to the battle. At Savage's Station, Lee lost 444 men to Sumner's 919.

On June 30, Lee tried to destroy the fleeing Federal army while it was crossing White Oak Swamp. Sending Jackson to press McClellan's rear, he ordered Longstreet, Magruder, A. P. Hill, and Huger against the Federal column from the west. For the third time, Jackson was slow and did not keep sufficient pressure on the Union rear. To the west, Magruder and Huger did not arrive in time either, and only Longstreet and Hill attacked **William B. Franklin's** VI Corps at **Frayser's Farm**. The Confederates made some temporary breakthroughs, but reinforcements from the Union II and III **Corps** sealed the Union line. In the intense fighting, Lee lost a little over 3,600 men to McClellan's over 2,700. Once again, McClellan was not on the battlefield (he was onboard a gunboat searching for suitable campsites), and he had not left anyone in command during his absence.

By July 1, McClellan had positioned his army in a very strong position at **Malvern Hill**, near the James River. There his artillery was massed to cover a deadly killing field, and the Union gunboats were near enough to provide supporting fire. Believing the Federals were demoralized and that one more attack would finish them, Lee unwisely ordered his infantry to attack the nearly impregnable position. In a series of disjointed **frontal attacks**, the Confederates were slaughtered by the Union artillery. This last battle of the Seven Days Campaign cost Lee another 5,355 men to McClellan's more than 3,000. The next day, McClellan fell back to **Harrison's Landing** on the James River, and Lee wisely decided not to attack him there. The campaign was over.

The Seven Days Campaign was Lee's first experience commanding the army he would make famous. In one week, he pushed the enemy back down the peninsula from the outskirts of Richmond. Although the campaign was marred by a lack of coordination, poor staff work, and slowness on the part of several generals, it was a great Confederate victory and marked Lee's rise to prominence. As for the Federals, the Union soldiers fought very well, and the army carried out a skillful retreat. Yet

McClellan exercised little command during the campaign and at times virtually abandoned his responsibilities. Convinced he was greatly outnumbered, he blamed the defeat on **Abraham Lincoln's** failure to reinforce him properly. During the week, Lee lost a staggering 20,141 men to McClellan's 15,849 casualties. McClellan took no action to resume the offensive afterward, and in August federal authorities began stripping his men from Harrison's Landing to reinforce **John Pope's Army of Virginia** in northern Virginia. The last of McClellan's troops left the peninsula on August 26.

SEVEN PINES, VIRGINIA, BATTLE OF (MAY 31–JUNE 1, 1862).
By late May 1862, the **Peninsula Campaign** was more than two months old, and **George B. McClellan's Army of the Potomac** had pushed **Joseph E. Johnston's** Confederate **army** up the Virginia Peninsula to the outskirts of **Richmond**. In doing so, McClellan made the tactical error of splitting his command across the Chickahominy River. **Samuel P. Heintzelman's** and **Erasmus D. Keyes's** III and IV Corps, respectively, were positioned south of the river near Seven Pines, while the other three **corps** were north of the river to link up with expected reinforcements from **Irvin McDowell** at Fredericksburg. When heavy rain on May 30 flooded the Chickahominy and isolated the 33,000 Union soldiers on its south side, Johnston made plans to attack and destroy them. Leaving only two **divisions** to counter the enemy north of the river, he massed approximately 50,000 men for a three-pronged attack against the two isolated Union corps around Seven Pines. **James Longstreet's** command was to march on the Nine Mile Road to hit the Union right flank, while **Daniel H. Hill** used the Williamsburg Road to hit the Union center, and **Benjamin Huger** marched down the Charles City Road to attack the Union left.

The Confederate offensive did not go well. Instead of issuing written orders, Johnston gave verbal ones, and the movement became confused. Longstreet was placed in overall command of the operation, but he put his men on the same roads as Huger and Hill and thus clogged them. In addition, Huger did not start his column on time. As a result of these blunders, the attack ran five hours behind schedule. At about 1:00 P.M., Hill became impatient and attacked **Silas Casey's** IV Corps across low, swampy ground. In heavy fighting, the Federals were forced back to a second line at Seven Pines. Heintzelman sent **Philip Kearny's** division as reinforcements, and Kearny and **Darius Couch's** IV Corps division carried on the fight. When **Micah Jenkins's** Confederate **brigade** crushed the Union right flank, some of the Federals marched north to

Fair Oaks, while others fell back to a third defensive position east of Seven Pines.

Despite the swollen river, II Corps commander **Edwin V. Sumner** successfully crossed **John Sedgwick's** division on the Grapevine Bridge and reinforced the battered Union line at Fair Oaks. When the fighting began, an **acoustic shadow** covered Johnston's headquarters, and he was unaware of the battle's intensity until several hours after it began. That afternoon, he personally led forward a column under **William H. C. Whiting** and attacked Fair Oaks. The battle was fierce as the Confederates attacked the Union position relentlessly, but little headway was made. While watching the action from the rear late in the day, Johnston was unhorsed and severely injured when he received almost simultaneous wounds to the shoulder and chest from a bullet and a shell fragment, respectively.

Jefferson Davis appointed **Gustavus W. Smith** to take command of the army. Longstreet was to renew the attack the next day, but he believed he was about to be attacked himself and thus did not go forward aggressively. By the time the Confederates advanced, the Federals had consolidated their position and repulsed the attack. **Robert E. Lee** arrived on the field to take command of the Confederates at about 2:00 P.M. and ordered a withdrawal. When the fighting ended, the opposing armies were about where they had been when the battle began.

The Confederate effort at Seven Pines was carried out poorly. The attacks were made piecemeal, and the commanders committed only a fraction of their available troops. Losses were heavy, with the Confederates losing approximately 6,100 men, while the Federals suffered 5,000 casualties. Although the battle did not greatly change the opposing armies' positions, it did have a great impact on the war, for Davis put Lee in charge of the army. Lee named his new command the **Army of Northern Virginia** and led it for the rest of the war. As a result of Seven Pines, McClellan concentrated the Army of the Potomac south of the Chickahominy River, leaving only **Fitz John Porter's** V Corps on the north side. This led Lee to attack McClellan a few weeks later in the **Seven Days Campaign**.

XVII CORPS MEDAL. In October 1863, Maj. Gen. **James B. McPherson**, commander of the Union XVII Corps, had New York's Tiffany and Company make a special medal to be awarded to members of his command who exhibited gallant conduct during combat. The medal came in the classes of gold and silver and included a star bearing "17th." A U.S. shield and a wreath were also part of the **decoration**, and it was pinned on the **uniform** in front of a red, white, and blue ribbon. The battle and date for which the honor was awarded were also inscribed on the medal.

79TH U.S. COLORED TROOPS. *See* 1ST KANSAS COLORED VOLUNTEERS.

SEWARD, WILLIAM HENRY (1801–1872) USA. A native of **New York**, Seward was the father of Union general **William Henry Seward Jr.** After graduating from Union College in 1820, he became a lawyer and was active in **Whig** politics. Seward served as a state senator from 1830 to 1834, ran unsuccessfully for governor in 1834, and then was elected in 1838 and 1840. A supporter of internal improvements, protective tariffs, and a national banking system, he was a reformer who also advocated education reform and stronger civil rights for blacks and whites.

Seward was elected to the U.S. Senate in 1849 and 1855 and became nationally known for his opposition to the spread of **slavery**. He also was seen as a radical, and perhaps even dangerous, when he called for Americans to follow a "higher law" than the Constitution on the slavery issue and warned that an "irrepressible conflict" was brewing between the North and South. Switching to the **Republican Party** in 1856, Seward was a leading contender at the 1856 and 1860 Republican National Conventions, but his earlier inflammatory statements cost him the nominations.

In return for supporting **Abraham Lincoln** in 1860, Seward was promised the position of secretary of state. Accepting the post reluctantly, he at first viewed himself as the leader of the administration and tried unsuccessfully to dominate Lincoln in matters of policy. Seward suggested Lincoln defer to him on making important decisions and became embroiled in the **Seward-Meigs-Porter Affair** during the **Fort Sumter** crisis. He also alarmed Lincoln with a dangerous scheme to bring the seceding states back into the Union. Seward proposed creating a common enemy threatening the North and South by initiating a war with Europe over France's presence in Mexico.

As Lincoln took charge of his administration and the war effort, however, Seward settled into his position as secretary of state and provided valuable service. He skillfully defused the 1862 *Trent* **Affair** crisis with Great Britain, successfully convinced the British not to release the **Laird rams** to the Confederacy, and helped prevent foreign nations from recognizing the Confederacy. In April 1865, Seward was targeted for murder by **John Wilkes Booth** in the **Lincoln assassination** plot, but conspirator **Lewis Powell** only wounded Seward as he lay in bed recovering from a carriage accident.

After the war, Seward supported President **Andrew Johnson's** lenient **Reconstruction** policy, negotiated with Great Britain on the *Alabama Claims*, worked to get the French out of Mexico, and oversaw the purchase of Alaska ("Seward's Folly") from Russia in 1867. Leaving office in 1869, he took a world tour before returning to New York.

SEWARD, WILLIAM HENRY, JR. (1839–1920) USA. A native of **New York**, Seward was the son of Union Secretary of State **William H. Seward**. After clerking in a store, he became his father's private secretary in 1859 while the elder Seward was a U.S. senator. A year later, Seward left **Washington, D.C.**, and began his own New York banking house.

After the Civil War began, Seward served as secretary for his congressional district's war committee and was active in recruiting troops. In August 1862, he was commissioned lieutenant colonel of the 138th New York, redesignated the 9th New York Heavy Artillery in December. While stationed with the **regiment** in the Washington defenses, Seward accepted a mysterious "delicate secret mission" from **Abraham Lincoln** to Maj. Gen. **Nathaniel P. Banks** in **Louisiana**.

In the spring of 1864, Seward's regiment reinforced the **Army of the Potomac** during the **Overland Campaign** and fought at **Cold Harbor** in **James Ricketts's** VI Corps **division**. After being promoted to colonel in June, Seward defended Washington during **Jubal Early's Washington Raid**. At the **Monocacy**, he was wounded in the arm and had his leg broken when his horse was shot from under him. While recovering from these injuries, Seward became one of the Union's youngest generals when he was promoted to brigadier general of volunteers in September. Sent to **West Virginia** in January 1865, he commanded an infantry **brigade** under **George Crook** and took temporary command of the division when Crook was captured by partisans.

Seward resigned his commission in June 1865 and returned to his New York banking house. He became one of western New York's leading citizens and was very active in politics, charities, and patriotic and historical organizations.

SEWARD-MEIGS-PORTER AFFAIR (APRIL 1861). In April 1861, U.S. Secretary of the Navy **Gideon Welles** planned to relieve beleaguered **Fort Sumter, South Carolina**, with a naval expedition. Unknown to Welles, Secretary of State **William H. Seward** proposed another expedition to relieve **Fort Pickens, Florida**. Both officials planned to use the USS *Powhatan*, and **Abraham Lincoln** made the mistake of authorizing both plans. When Seward sent Capt. **Montgomery Meigs** to **New York** to outfit his expedition, Meigs discovered that Welles also had authority to use the *Powhatan*. After Meigs informed Seward of the confusion on April 5, Seward and Welles met with Lincoln to straighten out the matter. Lincoln sided with Welles, and Seward was forced to confine his future activities to the State Department. Lieutenant **David D. Porter** set sail with the *Powhatan* before Seward changed his orders and then refused to obey them when they were delivered on the way to Fort Pickens. Porter believed Lincoln's initial authorization superseded a cabinet member's order. Thus the *Powhatan* helped relieve Fort Pickens instead of sailing to Fort Sumter.

SEYMOUR, HORATIO (1810–1886) USA. A native of **New York**, Seymour attended Alden Partridge's military academy before passing the bar in 1832. He became the secretary of politician William L. Marcy the following year and quickly became active in **Democratic Party** politics. Seymour served in the state legislature in 1841, 1844, and 1845, and was mayor of Utica in 1842. As a legislator, he served as speaker of the state assembly and became famous both for his persuasive speaking ability and for helping settle disputes between the Democratic Barnburners and Hunkers factions.

Seymour ran unsuccessfully for governor in 1850, but he then was elected in 1852 after promising to oppose **abolitionism**, prohibition, and nativism. After serving one term, he briefly retired from politics but became active again in 1860 when he supported **Stephen A. Douglas** for president. As a conservative, Seymour believed in avoiding **secession** by compromising with the South, and when the Civil War began, he opposed most of **Abraham Lincoln's** war policies. Yet in 1862, he was elected governor again on a platform calling for defending the Constitution and supporting the war effort. As governor, Seymour quickly reverted back to his anti-administration stance. During the war, he opposed as unconstitutional such measures as **conscription**, the **Emancipation Proclamation**, and the suspension of the writ of **habeas corpus**. Although he did try to fill New York's recruitment quota, Seymour opposed using state troops to enforce the draft. He became a leader of the Northern **states rights** movement but ensured New York shouldered its fair share of the war effort.

Seymour's rigid stance on states rights and his refusal to allow New York soldiers to vote by absentee ballot led to his defeat for reelection in 1864. Returning home, he remained an influential New York figure and was the unsuccessful Democratic nominee for president in 1868. Seymour continued his interest in politics and helped rid New York City of the corrupt Tammany Hall in the 1870s.

SEYMOUR, TRUMAN (1824–1891) USA. A native of **Vermont**, Seymour attended Norwich University before being admitted to **West Point** in 1842. After graduating in 1846, he was assigned to the **artillery** and won two **brevets** for gallantry in the **Mexican War**. After the war, Seymour served as a drawing instructor at the academy and fought in the **Seminole Wars**.

In April 1861, Seymour was a captain in command of an artillery **company** at **Fort Sumter, South Carolina**. After the fort's surrender, he was brevetted for gallantry and recruited before being assigned to the **Washington, D.C.**, defenses. Promoted to brigadier general of volunteers in April 1862, Seymour was given a **brigade** command in **George A. McCall's** V Corps **division** in the **Army of the Potomac**. He fought in the **Peninsula** and **Seven Days Campaigns** and temporarily took command of the division when McCall was captured at **Frayser's Farm**. After being returned to his brigade, Seymour fought in the **Second Manassas Campaign** and won two more brevets for successfully capturing Turner's Gap in the **Battle of South Mountain** and for heroic action at **Antietam**.

In November 1862, Seymour was transferred to **Charleston, South Carolina**, where he was severely wounded while commanding the land forces that unsuccessfully attacked **Fort Wagner** in July 1863. When he returned to duty, he briefly commanded the District of Hilton Head before taking command of the District of Florida in February 1864. After being defeated at **Olustee** that month, Seymour was relieved of command in March and returned to **Virginia**. Placed in command of a brigade in the VI Corps' 3rd Division, he was captured in the **Wilderness** on May 6, 1864, and was placed under fire from Union guns while imprisoned at Charleston. After begin **exchanged**, Seymour was given command of the VI Corps' 3rd Division and led it during **Philip Sheridan's 1864 Shenandoah Valley Campaign** and in the **Petersburg** and **Appomattox Campaigns**.

At the end of the war, Seymour was brevetted major general in both the volunteer and regular services. He remained in the **army** as a captain of artillery and was promoted to major in 1866. Seymour kept that rank until retiring from service in 1876.

SHACKELFORD, JAMES MURRELL (1827–1909) USA. A native of **Kentucky**, Shackelford served in the **Mexican War** as a private and 1st lieutenant in the 4th Kentucky. After the war, he became a lawyer and practiced in Kentucky until the Civil War began.

Shackelford raised the 25th Kentucky (Union) and entered Union service as its colonel in January 1862. His first combat was at **Fort Donelson**, where he fought in **Charles Cruft's brigade** of **Lew Wallace's** division. Despite some accounts to the contrary, Shackelford resigned his commission in March 1862 because of poor health and did not serve at **Shiloh**. He returned to Kentucky to raise the 8th Kentucky Cavalry (Union) and reentered service as its colonel in September 1862.

Shackelford was promoted to brigadier general of volunteers in March 1863 and, as commander of a brigade in the XXIII Corps' 2nd Division, helped pursue **John Hunt Morgan's** raiders that summer. It was to Shackelford that Morgan surrendered when finally cornered at **Salineville, Ohio**, in July. In September, Shackelford was slightly wounded in the foot during a **skirmish** with Confederate cavalry in Kentucky. At the head of a cavalry **division** in the XXIII Corps, he helped capture Cumberland Gap that autumn and was put in command of **Ambrose E. Burnside's** cavalry **corps** during the **Knoxville Campaign**. In October and December 1863, Shackelford was heavily engaged with Confederate cavalry at **Blue Springs** and **Bean's Station**.

Because of his wife's death, Shackelford resigned his commission in January 1864 and returned to his Kentucky law practice. He was appointed territorial judge for the **Indian Territory** in 1889 and settled there as attorney for the Choctaw nation.

SHALER, ALEXANDER (1827–1911) USA. A native of **Connecticut**, Shaler moved to New York City as a boy. After apparently inheriting a sizeable fortune, he became active in the state militia and was serving as major of the 7th New York Militia when the Civil War began.

Shaler's **regiment** was sent to defend **Washington, D.C.**, after the fall of **Fort Sumter**. In June 1861, he was commissioned lieutenant colonel of the 65th New York and fought with it and the **Army of the Potomac** in the **Peninsula** and **Seven Days Campaigns**. During the campaigns, Shaler served as the temporary regimental commander at **Williamsburg** and won promotion to colonel after the **Battle of Malvern Hill**. His regiment was not engaged at **Antietam**, but it did serve at **Fredericksburg**. Shaler temporarily commanded a **brigade** that stormed the Confederate position on Marye's Heights during the **Second Battle of Fredericksburg**, for which he was awarded the **Medal of Honor** in 1893.

Promoted to brigadier general of volunteers in May 1863, Shaler's brigade was held in reserve at the **Battle of Gettysburg**. After serving in the **Bristoe Station** and **Mine Run Campaigns**, he was put in command of the **prison** camp at **Johnson's Island** in early 1864. The following spring, Shaler rejoined the **army** but was captured during the **Wilderness**. After being **exchanged**, he was transferred to **Edward R. S. Canby's** command in **New Orleans, Louisiana**, and was given a brigade in the XIX Corps. When the war ended, Shaler was in command of **Arkansas's** White River District.

Shaler was **brevetted** major general of volunteers for his war service and was mustered out of the volunteers in August 1865. He returned to New York City and continued to be active in public service. Shaler served as president of the city's fire and health departments, was active in both veterans' and social clubs, and helped found and serve as president of the National Rifle Association.

SHARP, JACOB HUNTER (1833–1907) CSA. A native of **Alabama**, Sharp moved to **Mississippi** with his family as an infant. After attending the University of Alabama in 1850–51, he returned to Mississippi and opened a law practice.

When the Civil War began, Sharp enlisted in the 1st Battalion Mississippi Infantry as a private, but he quickly was elected captain. As part of the 44th Mississippi, he garrisoned Columbus, Kentucky, early in the war and played a role in shipping reinforcements across the river to fight at **Belmont, Missouri**, in November 1861. Later, Sharp was praised for his actions at **Shiloh, Perryville**, and **Stones River**, and in the **Tullahoma Campaign**. By September 1863, he was colonel of the 44th Mississippi. At **Chickamauga**, Sharp's men fought well early in the battle as part of **James Patton Anderson's brigade**, and he temporarily took command of the brigade when Anderson took over the **division**. Afterward, the **regiment** participated in the **Chattanooga Campaign**, but sources claim Sharp was "incapacitated" during that time.

During the **Atlanta Campaign**, Sharp served in **William F. Tucker's** brigade and took command of that unit when Tucker was wounded at **Resaca**. After leading the brigade all the way to Atlanta, he was promoted to brigadier general in July 1864. Sharp learned of his promotion just minutes before leading the brigade into bloody combat at **Ezra Church**. After suffering heavy casualties there, his brigade returned to the Atlanta trenches and was praised when its **skirmishers** single-handedly repulsed an enemy attack. Afterward, Sharp again was praised for his leadership in the unsuccessful attack at **Jonesboro**.

Sharp's brigade led the **Army of Tennessee** across the Tennessee River in October 1864 to start the **Franklin and Nashville Campaign** and fought well at Franklin. Following the campaign, Sharp was also given command of **William F. Brantley's** brigade. He suffered very heavy **desertions** while on his way to reinforce **Joseph E. Johnston** in **North Carolina** in March 1865 but still arrived in time to fight at **Bentonville**. Sharp surrendered with the rest of Johnston's **army** in North Carolina the following month.

After the war, Sharp returned to his Mississippi law practice. He bought a newspaper, as well, and became president of the Mississippi Press Association. Sharp also resisted **Reconstruction** and served in the state legislature from 1886 to 1890. For part of that time, he was speaker of the house.

SHARPS RIFLE. This breech-loading **rifle** was invented by Christian Sharp in 1848 and came in both rifle and carbine models. Both were usually .52 caliber and fired a paper or linen cartridge (metal cartridges for this weapon were used after the Civil War). The weapon was loaded by pulling down on the lever/trigger guard, which lowered the breech and allowed the insertion of a cartridge. When the breech was closed, a sharp edge cut off the end of the cartridge to allow the **Maynard** tape or Lawrence (spring-loaded caps) priming system to ignite the powder. The Sharps was an extremely accurate and fast-firing weapon, capable of firing 10 rounds per minute and shooting 24-inch groups of 20 shots at 300 yards. The rifle was primarily used by **sharpshooters** (such as **Berdan's Sharpshooters**), while cavalrymen carried the carbine. It is estimated that 100,000 Sharps were used during the war, with the Union government purchasing 9,141 rifles and 80,512 carbines.

SHARPSBURG, MARYLAND, BATTLE OF (SEPTEMBER 17, 1862). *See* ANTIETAM, MARYLAND, CAMPAIGN AND BATTLE OF.

SHARPSHOOTERS. Sharpshooters were the snipers of the Civil War. Some entire **regiments**, such as **Berdan's Sharpshooters**, were designated as sharpshooters, but this proved to be an inefficient use of such skilled soldiers. As the war progressed, contests were held to pick the best marksmen to be deployed as sharpshooters. These soldiers were organized into a small unit and were attached to the **brigade** or regiment. During combat, sharpshooters were placed either on the **skirmish line** or in advantageous positions to shoot such key enemy personnel as officers and **artillery** crews or simply to harass the enemy's frontline troops. When armed with scoped **Whitworth rifles, Sharps rifles**, or other accurate weapons, sharpshooters were known to hit targets at a thousand yards or more. Sharpshooters were particularly active at **Gettysburg** and

Vicksburg and in the **Atlanta** and **Petersburg Campaigns**. Union Maj. Gen. **John Sedgwick** was killed by a Confederate sharpshooter at **Spotsylvania**.

SHARPSHOOTERS, 1ST AND 2ND U.S. *See* BERDAN'S SHARPSHOOTERS.

SHAW, ROBERT GOULD (1837–1863) USA. A native of **Massachusetts**, Shaw was the son of a prominent **abolitionist**. He attended Harvard University for three years but dropped out in 1859 and moved to **New York**. There, Shaw joined the 7th New York National Guard, but when the Civil War began, he accepted a 2nd lieutenant's commission in the 2nd Massachusetts. Rising to the rank of captain, he served with the **regiment** until early 1863. At that time, Gov. **John A. Andrews** received permission from the War Department to raise a regiment of **black troops** for the Union **army**. Since Shaw came from a prominent abolitionist family, and the young officer believed in the fighting ability of blacks, Andrews picked him to raise the regiment.

Shaw left the 2nd Massachusetts, returned to Massachusetts, and raised the **54th Massachusetts**. Appointed colonel in May 1863, he then led his men to **Charleston, South Carolina**, where they engaged in routine duties until engaging in their first combat on James Island in July 1863. On July 18, Shaw was given the honor of leading the attack on **Fort Wagner**. Charging the Confederate position, he reached the top of the parapet and turned to yell, "Onward, Fifth-fourth" (Faust, ed., *Historical Times Illustrated Encyclopedia of the Civil War,* 673), when he was killed by a bullet to the chest. After the failed attack, the Confederates buried Shaw in a mass grave along with the other dead. When asked about his body, the Confederates sneered, "We have buried him with his niggers!" (Glatthaar, *Forged in Battle,* 140). Rather than taking the remark as an insult, the family viewed it as a point of honor and left Shaw's body with his men.

SHELBY, JOSEPH ORVILLE "JO" (1830–1897) CSA. A native of **Kentucky**, Shelby was a member of a wealthy and prominent family. After attending Transylvania University, he worked as a rope manufacturer before inheriting a large amount of money and moving to **Missouri** in 1852. There, Shelby became successful as a hemp producer and steamboat operator and supported the proslavery faction during the days of **"Bleeding Kansas."**

When the Civil War began, "Jo" Shelby turned down a Union commission and instead organized and became captain of Shelby's Ranger

Company. As part of the secessionist Missouri State Guard, he fought at **Wilson's Creek**, **Lexington**, and **Pea Ridge**. After briefly serving east of the Mississippi River, Shelby returned to Missouri to raise a **regiment**. In the spring of 1862, he recruited an entire cavalry regiment and was appointed colonel of the new 5th Missouri Cavalry (Confederate). Shortly afterward, Shelby was placed in command of a cavalry **brigade** under **John S. Marmaduke**. After fighting at **Prairie Grove** and being wounded in the unsuccessful attack on **Helena, Arkansas**, he led the war's longest cavalry raid into central Missouri in the autumn of 1863. From September 22 to November 3, Shelby covered 1,500 miles, destroyed $2 million of supplies, inflicted more than 1,000 Union casualties, recruited several hundred men, and equipped his command from captured material.

Shelby's Missouri Raid won him promotion to brigadier general in February 1864. After fighting well in the 1864 **Camden Expedition**, he was sent by **Sterling Price** to collect **deserters** and recruits in northeast **Arkansas** in preparation for **Price's 1864 Missouri Raid**. Shelby raised several thousand new men and was put in command of a cavalry **division** in September. **Shelby's Iron Brigade** saw hard service in Price's Missouri Raid, and after the disaster at **Mine Creek** it was the only effective Confederate command left to form a rear guard for the retreat back to Arkansas.

By the time the war ended in the summer of 1865, Shelby was recognized as one of the Confederacy's most skilled cavalrymen. His reputation as a cavalier was enhanced by his wearing a black ostrich plume pinned to one side of his upturned hat. Shelby refused to accept the **surrender** and led several hundred men to Mexico. There he offered their services to **Maximilian** but was refused. Shelby then operated a wagon freight company in Mexico before returning to Missouri in 1867. He farmed, became active in railroading and coal mining, and was viewed as a local legend. In 1893, Shelby was appointed a U.S. marshal by President Grover Cleveland and held that position when he died.

SHELBY'S IRON BRIGADE. In the spring of 1862, Confederate Capt. **Joseph O. "Jo" Shelby** was authorized to raise a new **regiment** in his home state of **Missouri**, with the understanding he would be appointed its colonel if successful. Recruiting around Waverly, he raised about 1,000 men. These recruits were organized into the 5th Missouri Cavalry (Confederate) in June 1862, with Shelby as their colonel. Shortly afterward, the 2,500 men of the 5th, 6th (Col. John T. Coffee), and 12th Missouri Cavalry (Col. Upton Hays), along with Richard A. Collins's

artillery battery, were organized into the 4th Missouri Cavalry **brigade** under Shelby's command.

Attached to **John S. Marmaduke's** cavalry **division**, Shelby's brigade became one of the war's outstanding cavalry units. Known as Shelby's Iron Brigade, its members wore red sumac in their hats and were excellent guerrilla fighters, if not well-**disciplined** soldiers. At **Cane Hill**, the brigade was outnumbered five-to-one but successfully defended Marmaduke's rear and allowed him to retreat safely. It fought at **Prairie Grove**, participated in Marmaduke's Missouri Raid in late 1862, and made the war's longest cavalry raid when it operated in Missouri from September 22 to November 3, 1863. In that raid, Shelby's Iron Brigade covered 1,500 miles, inflicted some 1,000 Union casualties, destroyed approximately $2 million worth of supplies, gathered several hundred new recruits, and completely equipped itself from captured material. Some of the brigade's hardest service came during **Sterling Price's 1864 Missouri Raid**, when it was part of Shelby's cavalry division. Under the command of Col. David Shanks, who was killed at Moreau Creek and replaced by Col. **M. Jeff Thompson**, the brigade fought in numerous battles and was the only organized Confederate unit left to form a rear guard after the disaster at **Mine Creek**.

When the war ended, several hundred of the men agreed with Shelby's refusal to surrender and accompanied him to Mexico. When **Maximilian** refused their offer to serve his government, the brigade was disbanded, and most of the men returned to the United States, using travel money that the emperor had presented to them in honor of their wartime accomplishments.

SHELLEY, CHARLES MILLER (1833–1907) CSA. A native of **Tennessee**, as a child, Shelley moved to **Alabama** with his family. There he studied architecture under his father and ran a construction company.

Shelley entered state service in February 1861 as a lieutenant in the Alabama Militia Artillery and served at Mobile's **Fort Morgan**. After war broke out, he was mustered into Confederate service as a captain in the 5th Alabama and was sent to **Virginia**. The regiment saw no combat at **First Manassas**, but **P. G. T. Beauregard** praised Shelley for his service in a **skirmish** at Parr's Cross Roads. In January 1862, he returned to Alabama to raise a new regiment, organized the 30th Alabama, and was appointed its colonel in March.

Sent to East Tennessee, Shelley's regiment became part of **Carter L. Stevenson's brigade**. After participating in the **Kentucky Campaign**, it was transferred to **Edward D. Tracy's** brigade and was sent to **Vicks-**

burg, Mississippi, late in 1862. Shelley's first major combat was at **Port Gibson** during the **Vicksburg Campaign**, where he was highly praised for holding the line against repeated Union attacks. He went on to fight at **Champion Hill** and in the siege of Vicksburg (where he was captured), receiving commendations in both actions.

After being **exchanged**, Shelley and his men were sent to Chattanooga, Tennessee, where they became part of **Edmund W. Pettus's** brigade. Beginning with **Missionary Ridge**, Shelley participated in every major engagement of the **Army of Tennessee** until war's end. During the **Atlanta Campaign**, **John Bell Hood** frequently recommended his promotion and in September 1864 placed him in command of **Alfred Cumming's** brigade. Shelley was given the temporary rank of brigadier general (which was officially confirmed by the Senate in February 1865). After leading Cumming's brigade for a few weeks, he assumed command of **James Cantey's** brigade in October. At Franklin, the brigade lost nearly half of its men, and Shelley had his horse killed under him and his **uniform** riddled by seven bullets. After the retreat from Nashville, the brigade was sent to **North Carolina**, where it fought at **Bentonville**. When the war ended, Shelley was in command of all the troops in Danville, North Carolina.

After the war, Shelley lived in **Louisiana** for a while before returning to Alabama and resuming his construction business. He was elected county sheriff in 1874 but resigned in 1876 when he was elected to the **U.S. Congress**. Shelley was reelected three more times but decided not to seek a fifth term. He then served as an auditor for the Treasury Department before returning to Alabama to promote industrial interests. Shelley was very active in the New South movement, chaired the 1892 **Democratic** Campaign Committee, and became a law partner in **Washington, D.C.**, with former Confederate general **Matthew C. Butler**.

SHELTON LAUREL, NORTH CAROLINA, MASSACRE OF (JANUARY 18, 1863). Western **North Carolina** suffered from divided loyalties during the Civil War much like East **Tennessee** and **Missouri**. Raids and atrocities were inflicted on both sides, but none compared with the **massacre** at Shelton Laurel. In January 1863, about 50 pro-Union men raided Shelton Laurel, a valley in the western mountains. Some of the raiders were **deserters** from the 64th North Carolina, and that **regiment's** commander was ordered to clear the area of all such guerrillas. Brigadier General **Henry Heth** told Col. Lawrence M. Allen, "I do not want to be troubled with any **prisoners** and the last one of them should be killed" (Faust, ed., *Historical Times Illustrated Encyclopedia of the*

Civil War, 675). Since Allen's house was one of those looted by the Unionists, he carried out his orders with enthusiasm.

The 64th North Carolina moved into Shelton Laurel; looted the houses of Unionists; beat Unionist men, women, and children; and took 15 men and boys prisoner (at least eight of whom had not been involved in the previous raid). On January 18, 13 of the prisoners were murdered while they were on their knees begging for mercy (two men had previously escaped) and were buried in a mass grave. Although Confederate officials were outraged when they heard of the massacre and demanded that those responsible be punished, only Lt. Col. James A. Keith and four other officers suffered any punishment when they were forced to resign their commissions.

SHENANDOAH, CSS. This Confederate **commerce raider** was built in Scotland in 1864. It was 220 feet long, displaced 1,018 tons, and had a steam-powered propeller that could be raised out of the water when under sail. The ship was purchased for the Confederacy by **James D. Bulloch** and was put under the command of Lt. **James I. Waddell**. The vessel slipped out of Great Britain on October 8, 1864, disguised as the British merchant ship *Sea King*. At Madeira, off the coast of North Africa, it was armed with six 68-pounders and two 32-pounders and was christened the *Shenandoah*.

The *Shenandoah* left Madeira on October 19 and began a 58,000-mile around-the-world cruise. Arriving in the Arctic Ocean by way of the Cape of Good Hope and Australia, it devastated the Union whaling fleet. The cruiser accounted for close to 40 Union vessels, two-thirds of which were taken after the war had ended. Waddell at first ignored reports that the war was over, but he finally accepted the fact when told by the crew of a British vessel in August 1865. Disguising his ship as a British merchant, he made his way back to Great Britain and **surrendered** the *Shenandoah* there on November 6, 1865. It was the last Confederate surrender of the war. The British sold the ship, and it was used as a merchant vessel until it sank in the Indian Ocean in 1879 while in the service of the sultan of Zanzibar.

SHENANDOAH VALLEY, VIRGINIA. Virginia's Shenandoah Valley played a key role in the Civil War. The 150-mile-long valley is drained by the Shenandoah River, which flows northward into the Potomac River at **Harpers Ferry, West Virginia**, and is flanked on the west and east by the Allegheny and Blue Ridge Mountains, respectively. During the war, it was one of the South's richest agricultural and livestock areas and provided tons of food and thousands of animals to the Confederates, particularly to the **Army of Northern Virginia**. The Valley also was a valuable strategic area. Running southwest to northeast, it pointed like a dagger into **Maryland**. A Confederate **army** entering the Valley could easily invade the North and have its flanks protected by the mountains. This was done by **Robert E. Lee** in the **Gettysburg Campaign** and by **Jubal A. Early** in **Early's Washington Raid**. Conversely, the Valley was useless as a Union invasion route because following it southward led one farther and farther away from **Richmond, Virginia**.

The Shenandoah Valley was the scene of much fighting. In 1862, **Stonewall Jackson's Shenandoah Valley Campaign** humiliated the Union and prevented thousands of Federals from joining the **Peninsula Campaign** against Richmond. A year later, Lee moved down the Valley on his way to Gettysburg and defeated the Federals at **Second Winchester** and **Stephenson's Depot**. Union Maj. Gen. **Franz Sigel** invaded the Valley in the spring of 1864, but he was defeated at **New Market**. **David Hunter's Shenandoah Valley Campaign** then was launched by the Union to cut the vital Virginia Central Railroad, but Hunter was driven out by Early. Early then used the Valley in the summer of 1864 to make his raid on Washington and afterward defended it against **Philip H. Sheridan's 1864 Shenandoah Valley Campaign**. Sheridan virtually destroyed Early's army and then laid waste to the Valley to deny the Confederates its vital supplies. In addition to these major campaigns, the Valley also was the scene of innumerable raids and **skirmishes**. Winchester, the main town in the lower Valley, changed hands more than 70 times during the war. Among the larger battles were **McDowell**, **Kernstown**, the three battles of **Winchester**, Harpers Ferry, Stephenson's Depot, New Market, **Cedar Creek**, and **Fisher's Hill**.

SHENANDOAH VALLEY CAMPAIGN, DAVID HUNTER'S (MAY 26–JUNE 18, 1864). On May 21, 1864, Union Maj. Gen. **David Hunter** replaced **Franz Sigel** in command of the **Department of West Virginia** following Sigel's defeat at **New Market**. Hunter invaded the **Shenandoah Valley** to destroy its supplies and **industry**, the Virginia Central Railroad at Staunton, and the James River Canal, and to cross the Blue Ridge Mountains to attack Gordonsville or Charlottesville. If possible, Lt. Gen. **U. S. Grant** also wanted Hunter to reinforce his armies then engaged in the **Overland Campaign**. Union Maj. Gen. **George Crook**, who was stationed in **West Virginia's** Allegheny Mountains, was to join Hunter in the Valley.

On May 26, Hunter left Cedar Creek, Virginia, with 8,500 men and moved up the Valley toward Staunton. **Robert E. Lee** believed the threat to the Valley had ended after Sigel's defeat and had withdrawn **John C. Breckinridge's** command to **Richmond**. This left the region defended by only about 5,600 men under **William E. "Grumble" Jones**. Jones attacked Hunter at **Piedmont** on June 5, but he was killed, and his **army** was defeated. Hunter reached Staunton on June 6 and was joined there on June 8 by Crook. The 18,000 Federals then wrecked the Virginia Central Railroad, factories, stores, and other property before moving on to Lexington on June 11. There they burned the **Virginia Military Institute** and the home of Gov. **John Letcher**, looted Washington College, and plundered and burned the entire area.

Outside Richmond, Lee was alarmed at the attack on his crucial supply line and was outraged at Hunter's wholesale destruction. He had sent Breckinridge with two **brigades** toward Charlottesville on June 6 with orders to resume command of the **Department of Western Virginia**. When Breckinridge called for more reinforcements, Lee dispatched **Jubal A. Early's** II Corps from **Cold Harbor** on June 13. The opposing forces headed for **Lynchburg**. When Hunter arrived there on June 17, he found Breckinridge already in a defensive position. Hunter attacked the next day but was driven back by Breckinridge and part of Early's **corps** that had just arrived. Learning that Early's entire corps was at hand, Hunter withdrew on the night of June 18 and began a rapid retreat to **West Virginia**. Early pursued for three days and fought Hunter at Liberty and Hanging Rock but was unable to inflict any serious damage. With the Valley momentarily safe, Early then began **Early's Washington Raid**. Because of his failure, Hunter was removed from command and was replaced on August 6 by **Philip H. Sheridan**.

SHENANDOAH VALLEY CAMPAIGN, PHILIP SHERIDAN'S (AUGUST 7, 1864–MARCH 2, 1865). The **Shenandoah Valley** was a valley of humiliation for Union forces in the spring and summer of 1864. First, **Franz Sigel** was defeated at **New Market**, then **David Hunter's Shenandoah Valley Campaign** failed, and, finally, **Jubal Early's Washington Raid** greatly embarrassed Union officials. Union General-in-Chief **U. S. Grant** took firm measures in early August to rectify the situation. Four Union **departments** that shared responsibility for the Valley were consolidated into one **Middle Military Division**, and it was placed under the command of Maj. Gen. **Philip Sheridan** on August 7. Using troops within his **district** and reinforcements supplied by Grant, Sheridan created the 40,000-man **Army of the Shenandoah** to attack and defeat Early's **Valley Army**. Grant was relying on the aggressive nature of the 33-year-old Sheridan to deny the Confederates the Valley's vital supplies and its use as an invasion corridor.

Sheridan left his base at **Harpers Ferry, West Virginia**, on August 10 and moved up the Valley toward Early. For the next few weeks the two armies maneuvered up and down the lower Valley seeking advantageous positions and skirmishing at **Guard Hill**, **Summit Point and Cameron's Depot**, **Smithfield Crossing**, and **Berryville**. During this time, **Richard H. Anderson** arrived with Confederate reinforcements. In this early phase of the campaign, Sheridan was cautious because his superiors made it clear that another defeat could not be tolerated so soon before the 1864 presidential election. When the **Atlanta Campaign** was successful in early September, Union morale was strengthened, and Sheridan felt confident to go on the offensive.

Because of Sheridan's lack of aggressiveness, Lee ordered the return of Anderson's infantry about this time. Anderson began his march back to **Richmond, Virginia**, on September 14, leaving Early with about 18,000 infantry and cavalry. When Sheridan learned of Anderson's departure and that Early had sent two **divisions** to raid the Baltimore & Ohio Railroad at Martinsburg, he received Grant's permission to attack and destroy Early's remaining two divisions north of Winchester.

Marching west from Berryville on the morning of September 19, Sheridan crossed Opequon Creek and defeated Early in very heavy fighting at the **Third Battle of Winchester**. Early lost approximately 3,500 men and retreated to the south, while Sheridan suffered about 5,000 casualties. Early next took up a very strong position at **Fisher's Hill**. After two days of probes and **skirmishes**, Sheridan attacked his left flank on September 22, crushed it, and sent the Confederates in headlong flight. Here, Early lost another 1,250 men to Sheridan's 525. Sheridan pursued Early to Staunton but then withdrew after assuming the Confederates' offensive capability was destroyed. From October 6 to 8, the Federals retreated to Strasburg, destroying everything that could be of use to the enemy. Livestock was killed or carried off, and hundreds of houses, barns, and mills were destroyed along the 92-mile march in what became known in the Valley as "The Burning." When he finished, Sheridan boasted that a crow flying over the region would have to carry its **rations**. Early sent **Thomas L. Rosser's** cavalry after the Federals, but he was routed by **Alfred T. A. Torbert's** Union cavalry at **Tom's Brook** on October 9.

Confident that Early no longer posed a threat, Sheridan encamped his **army** behind **Cedar Creek**, near Middletown, and went to **Washington,**

D.C., to confer with officials on future operations. In an audacious move, Early launched a surprise attack against the Union army at dawn of October 19. The Confederates broke the Union left flank at Cedar Creek and sent the Federals streaming in retreat, but the attack then lost momentum as Early's men stopped to plunder the enemy camps. Early also failed to press the enemy and allowed them time to reorganize. Sheridan, who was on his way back from Washington, rode furiously to reach the battlefield, skillfully organized a counterattack, and crushed Early that afternoon. Early lost approximately 5,700 men in the battle to Sheridan's 2,900.

After the Battle of Cedar Creek, the campaign largely ceased. Both sides sent the bulk of their forces to participate in the **Petersburg Campaign** and went into winter camps, with Early staying southeast of Staunton and Sheridan near Winchester. On March 2, 1865, Sheridan nearly annihilated Early's remaining 2,000 men at **Waynesboro** with his cavalry. Losing only 30 troopers, he inflicted 1,600 casualties and virtually eliminated the Confederate presence in the Valley. Afterward, Sheridan took his cavalry to join Grant at Petersburg. His success in the Shenandoah Valley denied Lee's army vital supplies and hastened the war's end. Sheridan's victories elevated him to a position of prominence, and Grant came to rely on him heavily during the **Petersburg** and **Appomattox Campaigns**.

SHENANDOAH VALLEY CAMPAIGN, STONEWALL JACKSON'S (MAY 3–JUNE 9, 1862).

In late April 1862, Union Maj. Gen. **George B. McClellan's** huge **Army of the Potomac** was threatening **Richmond, Virginia**, in the **Peninsula Campaign**. To divert Union efforts away from the capital, **Jefferson Davis's** military adviser, **Robert E. Lee**, suggested to **Thomas J. "Stonewall" Jackson** that he begin offensive operations in the **Shenandoah Valley**. Earlier in March, Jackson had carried out a similar mission when he attacked **Kernstown** and was defeated. Afterward, he was reinforced by **Richard S. Ewell's division** and had approximately 17,000 men in his **Valley Army**. Jackson eagerly followed Lee's suggestion and quickly began his offensive.

On May 3, Jackson put his division aboard train cars and moved east over the Blue Ridge Mountains as if he were reinforcing Richmond. Ewell's division was left encamped at Conrad's Store in the Luray Valley on the western edge of the Blue Ridge. Jackson's movement was a ruse, however, for once he was over the mountains, he turned around near Charlottesville and secretly shipped his men back into the Valley to surprise the enemy. Detraining at Staunton, he swiftly marched to the Allegheny Mountains, where he attacked and defeated Brig. Gen. **Robert H. Milroy** at **McDowell** on May 8 and sent him reeling back to **John C. Frémont's** army in **West Virginia**. In this battle, Jackson lost 500 men, while Milroy suffered 256 casualties.

Jackson then returned to the Shenandoah Valley and marched down it to strike **Nathaniel P. Banks's** position in the lower Valley. Near New Market, Jackson suddenly crossed over Massanutten Mountain to the east and joined Ewell in the Luray Valley. With his **army** now united, he attacked one of Banks's forward positions at **Front Royal** on May 23 and captured nearly 900 **prisoners** at a cost of only 56 men. With Jackson on his eastern flank and in a position to move into his rear, Banks quickly retreated back down the Valley toward Winchester.

On May 24, Jackson roughly paralleled the Union retreat and personally took a small force to intercept Banks at Middletown. He broke the Union column there and forced Banks's rear guard to march westward out of the Valley, but the main Union army had already passed. On May 25, Jackson attacked Banks and defeated him at the **First Battle of Winchester**, inflicting 2,019 casualties while losing 400 men. However, he was unable to pursue rapidly because the infantry was exhausted, and **Turner Ashby's** cavalry stopped to loot the enemy camps. Banks retreated across the Potomac River into **Maryland**, and Jackson halted in the lower Valley.

Jackson had virtually cleared the Shenandoah Valley of the enemy, but he now was in danger of being trapped. Banks's command was just to the north across the Potomac River, Frémont's army was in his rear to the west, and a third Union force under **Irvin McDowell** was east of the Blue Ridge Mountains at **Fredericksburg** in a position to cut his line of retreat. **Abraham Lincoln** understood that Jackson was in a precarious position and could be destroyed. He ordered Banks and Frémont to converge on the enemy and had McDowell halt his advance on Richmond and send 20,000 men under **James Shields** to help trap Jackson.

Jackson ordered his men on a rapid retreat back up the Valley and sent cavalry ahead to burn the bridges across the Shenandoah River as far as **Port Republic** to prevent Shields from crossing the river. In an exhausting march, punctuated by frequent **skirmishing** (in which Ashby was killed on June 6), Jackson reached **Cross Keys** just ahead of the pursuing enemy. On June 8, Ewell defeated Frémont there while Jackson held the vital Port Republic bridge against a weak attack by Shields. At Cross Keys, Ewell lost 288 men, while inflicting 684 casualties on Frémont. The next day, Jackson and Ewell united and defeated Shields at **Port Republic** after very bitter fighting. In the clash, Jackson lost about 800 men and Shields approximately 1,000. With this victory, Jackson was safe. He burned the bridge at Port Republic, bivouacked at Brown's Gap in the Blue Ridge Mountains, and later joined Lee for the **Seven Days Campaign**.

Jackson's Shenandoah Valley Campaign was one of the most brilliant of the war and made him the Confederacy's foremost hero. Relying on surprise, aggressiveness, and swift marching (his men became known as **"foot cavalry"** because of their marching ability), he marched 350 miles in just over 30 days, defeated three different Union commands in five battles, inflicted twice as many casualties as he sustained, captured tons of needed supplies, and succeeded in his primary mission of diverting Union attention away from Richmond by occupying some 60,000 enemy troops.

SHEPARD, ISAAC FITZGERALD (1816–1889) USA. A native of **Massachusetts**, Shepard graduated from Harvard University in 1842 and served as a grammar school principal from 1844 to 1857. He also was a newspaper editor from 1846 to 1848 and served in the state legislature from 1859 to 1860.

In 1861, Shepard moved to **Missouri**. Being a staunch **abolitionist**, he secured a position as major on **Nathaniel Lyon's** staff in June and served as assistant adjutant general for the state militia. After fighting at **Wilson's Creek**, Shepard was appointed lieutenant colonel of the 19th Missouri (Union) in late August and colonel of the 3rd Missouri (Union) in January 1862 after the two **regiments** were consolidated. He was highly praised for his actions at **Arkansas Post** in early 1863 and in May accepted command of the 1st Mississippi Infantry of African Descent, a regiment raised largely from runaway slaves along the Mississippi River. That same month, Shepard was given command of the African Brigade in northeastern **Louisiana** and in July was put in charge of the District of Northeastern Louisiana. After being promoted to brigadier general of volunteers in November 1863, he commanded a **brigade** of **black troops** in **John P. Hawkins's division** at **Vicksburg, Mississippi**. The Senate, however, failed to confirm Shepard's commission, and in July 1864, he left the service.

Returning to Missouri, Shepard had a long, distinguished political career. He served as Missouri's adjutant general, chaired the state **Republican** Committee, commanded the local **Grand Army of the Republic** chapter, edited two newspapers, and served as U.S. consul to China. After returning from China, Shepard retired to his native Massachusetts.

SHEPHERDSTOWN, VIRGINIA, BATTLE OF (SEPTEMBER 19–20, 1862).

When **Robert E. Lee** retreated across the Potomac River from **Maryland** after the **Battle of Antietam**, he left Brig. Gen. **William N. Pendleton** in command of two infantry **brigades** and 42 cannons to guard Boteler's Ford near Shepherdstown, Virginia. On September 19, 1862, Union Maj. Gen. **Fitz John Porter** engaged Pendleton with **artillery** from across the river and after dark sent **Charles Griffin's** brigade rushing across the ford. The Federals routed the Confederate infantry and captured four cannons. Pendleton panicked and raced back to Lee claiming that all of the guns had been lost. Lee was greatly alarmed, and **Stonewall Jackson** hurried his command to the ford.

On the morning of September 20, Porter sent parts of two **divisions** from his V Corps across the river, but he later ordered them withdrawn. While doing so, the Federals were attacked and routed by **A. P. Hill's** division at about 9:00 A.M. In this, (also known as the Battle of Blackford's Ford) the last clash of the Antietam Campaign, Porter lost 363 men (many of whom drowned during the retreat) while the Confederates lost 291. Disappointed in Pendleton's leadership, Lee used him for mostly administrative duties for the rest of the war.

SHEPLEY, GEORGE FOSTER (1819–1878) USA.

A native of **Maine**, Shepley was the son of a prominent politician who served as a U.S. senator and chief justice of the **U.S. Supreme Court** during his career. After graduating from Dartmouth College, Shepley became a lawyer and served twice as the state's U.S. district attorney. During his second term (1853–61), he served as a delegate to the 1860 **Democratic** National Convention in **Charleston, South Carolina**, and became friends with **Benjamin F. Butler**.

Shepley entered Union service in November 1861 when he was appointed colonel of the 12th Maine. In March 1862, he was given command of a **brigade** under his friend Butler for the expedition to **New Orleans, Louisiana**. During Butler's occupation of the city, Shepley became his most trusted subordinate. He at first served as post commander and in June was appointed **Louisiana's** military governor. While in New Orleans, Butler became hated as the "Beast" for his harsh rule, but it was Shepley who often carried out his orders. Promoted to brigadier general of volunteers in July 1862, Shepley continued to serve as Louisiana's military governor until a loyal civilian government was established in March 1864 under **Michael Hahn**. Afterward, he was placed in command of the District of Eastern Virginia within Butler's **Department of Virginia and North Carolina**. Shepley remained in this position until July 1864. In the spring of 1865, he became **Godfrey Weitzel's** chief of staff and served him until **Richmond, Virginia**, was captured. Shepley then served as military governor of Richmond from early April 1865 until he resigned from the **army** in July.

Shepley returned to his law practice after the war and in 1869 was appointed Maine's U.S. circuit judge.

SHERIDAN, PHILIP HENRY (1831–1888) USA. Sheridan's date and place of birth is uncertain since he gave different accounts on several occasions, but he is believed to have been born in **New York** in 1831. He moved with his family to **Ohio** as a child and was admitted to **West Point** in 1848. Sheridan did not graduate with his class because he was suspended for one year for chasing future Union general **William R. Terrill** with a **bayonet**. After graduating in the bottom of the 1853 class, he was assigned to the infantry and served on the frontier until the Civil War began. During this time, Sheridan married the daughter of future Union Brig. Gen. **Daniel H. Rucker.**

Sheridan was still a 2nd lieutenant in the 4th U.S. Infantry when the **secession** crisis began, but in March 1861, he was promoted to 1st lieutenant. Another promotion to captain followed in May, and in December, he was appointed chief quartermaster and commissary for the **Army of the Southwest**. In the spring of 1862, Sheridan served as quartermaster for **Henry Halleck's Department of the Mississippi** during the **siege of Corinth, Mississippi**. This duty came to an end in May 1862 when he was appointed colonel of the 2nd Michigan Cavalry upon the recommendation of **Gordon Granger**.

Sheridan's subsequent rise in rank was spectacular. He was put in command of a cavalry **brigade** in the **Army of the Mississippi** in May 1862 and was promoted to brigadier general of volunteers in September after engaging the Confederates in northern **Mississippi**. Given command of an **Army of the Ohio** division in September, Sheridan fought well at **Perryville**, and his stubborn defensive stand at **Stones River** helped save **William S. Rosecrans's Army of the Cumberland**. These actions earned him another promotion to major general of volunteers in March 1863. After suffering heavy casualties at **Chickamauga**, Sheridan took charge of a **division** in the Army of the Cumberland's IV Corps. During the **Chattanooga Campaign**, it was Sheridan's men who, without orders, led the heroic charge that captured **Missionary Ridge**. By this time, **U. S. Grant** had taken notice of him and when Grant was made general-in-chief in March 1864, he brought Sheridan to **Virginia** and put him in command of the **Army of the Potomac's** cavalry **corps** in April 1864.

As a cavalryman Sheridan was extremely aggressive, but he compiled a checkered record. During the **Overland Campaign**, he and **army** commander **George G. Meade** clashed over the proper use of cavalry, and Sheridan did not perform particularly well in screening the army or in providing intelligence. He did get his wish to engage **J. E. B. Stuart's** Confederate cavalry in **Sheridan's Richmond Raid**, however, and his troopers mortally wounded Stuart at **Yellow Tavern**. Sheridan also was defeated at **Haw's Shop** and **Trevilian Station**.

Grant admired the aggressive nature of "Little Phil" and in August put him in command of the **Middle Military Division** and the **Army of the Shenandoah** with orders to rid the **Shenandoah Valley** of **Jubal A. Early's** Confederates and to destroy the Valley's usefulness to the enemy. In **Sheridan's 1864 Shenandoah Valley Campaign**, the Confederates were decisively defeated at **Third Winchester**, **Fisher's Hill**, **Cedar Creek**, and **Waynesboro**, and the Valley was ruined in what became known as "The Burning." Sheridan's dramatic late arrival at Cedar Creek also turned the tide of battle there and made him a prominent Union hero. He received the **Thanks of Congress** for his Valley victories and was promoted to brigadier general of regulars, to rank from September 1864, and to major general of regulars, to rank from November.

In February 1865, **Sheridan's Virginia Raid** began, in which he defeated Early at Waynesboro and then led his command to Petersburg, Virginia. In the waning days of the **Petersburg Campaign**, Grant came to increasingly rely on Sheridan. After the failed Confederate breakout at **Fort Stedman**, he sent Sheridan with a large force to attack **Robert E. Lee's** right flank. In early April, Sheridan shattered the Confederate line at **Five Forks** (but was criticized by some for his summary dismissal of **Gouverneur K. Warren**) and caused the Confederates to evacuate **Richmond** and Petersburg. During the **Appomattox Campaign**, he led a large part of the **Army of the Potomac** and destroyed a significant portion of Lee's army at **Sailor's Creek**. Finally, it was Sheridan who cut off Lee's advance at Appomattox and forced his **surrender**.

After the war, Sheridan was put in command of the **Military Division of the Gulf** to counter the presence of **Maximilian** in Mexico. In 1867, he was appointed military governor of **Texas** and **Louisiana** during **Reconstruction**, but his harsh actions forced President **Andrew Johnson** to remove him after only six months. When Grant became president in 1869, Sheridan was promoted to lieutenant general when **William T. Sherman** was appointed full general to replace Grant. Sheridan commanded the **Military Division of the Missouri** during much of the **Indian** wars of the 1870s, was an observer of the

Franco-Prussian War, and was elevated to general-in-chief when Sherman retired in 1884. In 1888, just a few months before his death, Sheridan was promoted to full general.

SHERIDAN'S RICHMOND RAID (MAY 9–24, 1864). When **Philip H. Sheridan** was put in command of the **Army of the Potomac's** cavalry **corps** in April 1864, he and **army** commander **George G. Meade** clashed over the proper use of cavalry. Meade wanted the cavalry to guard the wagon trains, screen the army, and provide intelligence, while Sheridan wanted to engage **J. E. B. Stuart's** Confederate cavalry. **U. S. Grant** supported Sheridan and at the beginning of the **Overland Campaign** gave him permission to seek out and destroy Stuart. Sheridan left **Spotsylvania** Court House on May 9 with 12,000 men in three **divisions** under **Wesley Merritt, David M. Gregg**, and **James H. Wilson** and headed for the rear of **Robert E. Lee's Army of Northern Virginia**. His intentions were to ride slowly toward **Richmond, Virginia**, destroy as much of Lee's line of communication as possible, and draw Stuart into battle so the Union cavalry could destroy him.

On the evening of May 9, Sheridan reached the North Anna River and Beaver Dam Station and forced the Confederates to burn their supply base at the latter. The Federals destroyed **railroad** stock and rescued approximately 400 **prisoners** there, as well, before continuing to the South Anna River the following day. During this time, Stuart rode hard with 4,500 troopers from **Fitzhugh Lee's** division and **James B. Gordon's brigade** to cut off Sheridan. On May 11, the two columns clashed at **Yellow Tavern**, just outside Richmond. Stuart was mortally wounded in the battle, and Gordon was killed, but Sheridan broke off the engagement and rode around Richmond after deciding it was too strongly defended to be taken. Moving east across the Virginia Peninsula, the Federals reached safety within **Benjamin F. Butler's** lines at Haxall's Landing on May 14 and returned to the Army of the Potomac on the North Anna River on May 24.

The raid had mixed results. Although Stuart was killed and Sheridan did destroy some valuable property and rode around the Confederate army, the raid failed to destroy the Confederate cavalry. Sheridan lost approximately 625 men in the raid.

SHERIDAN'S VIRGINIA RAID (FEBRUARY 27–MARCH 28, 1865). After **Philip H. Sheridan** defeated **Jubal A. Early's** Confederates at **Third Winchester, Fisher's Hill**, and **Cedar Creek** in **Sheridan's Shenandoah Valley Campaign**, active campaigning in the Valley slowed for the winter of 1864–65. On orders from **U. S. Grant**, Sheridan took 10,000 cavalrymen from Winchester on February 27, 1865, and rode up the Valley to destroy the Virginia Central Railroad and the James River and Kanawha canals near Lynchburg, Virginia. He then was to join Grant in the **Petersburg Campaign**.

After **skirmishing** with Early's 1,800 men, burning bridges, and capturing supplies, Sheridan reached Staunton on March 1. Early withdrew to the east and made a stand at **Waynesboro**, near Rockfish Gap in the Blue Ridge Mountains. On March 2, Sheridan crushed his left flank and virtually destroyed his **army**. In the rout, Sheridan captured 1,600 **prisoners**, 200 wagons, and 14 cannons. Only Early and a handful of men escaped the disaster.

After his victory, Sheridan moved on to Charlottesville but decided not to attack the more heavily defended **Lynchburg**. He spent the next few weeks destroying the Virginia Central Railroad, the James River and Kanawha Canals, barns, and mills. Sheridan then moved down the **railroad** to Ashland Station, destroying it as he went. There, he learned that a large Confederate force under **James Longstreet** was moving to intercept him. To avoid the enemy, Sheridan moved north across the North Anna River and then to White House. He joined Grant south of Petersburg on March 28 and within days was back in combat at **Five Forks**.

SHERMAN, JOHN (1823–1900) USA. The younger brother of **William T. Sherman**, John Sherman was a native of **Ohio** and, like his brother, was raised by relatives after the 1829 death of his father, a state supreme court justice. He first worked as a laborer for a canal company but after being fired for his **Whig** politics, he studied law under another brother and passed the bar exam in 1844. Sherman became a successful lawyer, served as a Whig delegate at the party's 1848 and 1852 national conventions, and in 1854 successfully ran for the U.S. House of Representatives on a platform opposing the **Kansas-Nebraska Act**. Like the majority of his constituents, he was a conservative and opposed the spread of **slavery** into the territories. Switching to the **Republican Party**, Sherman was reelected and strongly supported **Abraham Lincoln** in the **election of 1860**. After the election, Lincoln and others advised Sherman to seek a Senate seat, and in March 1861, he filled the unexpired seat of the newly appointed Secretary of Treasury **Salmon P. Chase**.

As a wartime senator, Sherman helped promote his brother's military career and supported such measures as the **Legal Tender Acts**, the **income tax**, a national banking system, and emancipation. Always a moderate, he supported President **Andrew Johnson** during **Reconstruction**, but he resigned his Senate seat in 1877 to become President **Rutherford B. Hayes's** secretary of the treasury. Sherman again was elected to the Senate in 1880 and assumed his seat when Hayes's term expired. He tried three times unsuccessfully to win the Republican presidential nomination, and in the 1890s sponsored bills that became famous as the Sherman Anti-Trust Act and the Sherman Silver Purchase Act. In 1897, Sherman resigned his Senate seat to become President William McKinley's secretary of state from 1897 to 1898. He died two years after resigning his position for health reasons.

SHERMAN, THOMAS WEST (1813–1879) USA. A native of **Rhode Island**, Sherman secured an appointment to **West Point** in 1832 after walking to **Washington, D.C.**, and personally appealing to President Andrew Jackson. After graduating in 1836, he was assigned to the **artillery** and served in the removal of the Cherokee **Indians** and in the **Seminole** and **Mexican Wars**, winning a **brevet** for gallantry in the latter. After Mexico, Sherman was posted to **Minnesota** (where he fought the Sioux Indians), **"Bleeding Kansas,"** and the Dakota Territory.

Sherman was a major in the 3rd U.S. Artillery when the Civil War began. He was promoted to lieutenant colonel of the 5th U.S. Artillery in May 1861 and to brigadier general of volunteers in August. Sherman commanded the Union troops that successfully captured **Port Royal, South Carolina**, in early 1862 and was appointed commander of the **Department of the South** in March. This appointment was short lived, because the following month he was transferred to a **division** command in the **Army of the Tennessee** for the **siege of Corinth, Mississippi**. Sherman clashed with **Henry Halleck** while in this position and was relieved of command in June. Sent to the **Department of the Gulf**, he commanded a small **Louisiana** garrison from September 1862 to January 1863 before taking charge of the XIX Corps' 2nd division and the **New Orleans** defenses. At **Port Hudson**, Sherman was severely wounded and lost his right leg while leading his division. He was brevetted brigadier general of regulars for his service there but was unable to return to duty until November 1864. Sherman then resumed his position at New Orleans until war's end.

Sherman was mustered out of the volunteers in April 1866 with brevets of major general in both the volunteer and regular service. He remained in the **U.S. Army** as a colonel of artillery and served on the East Coast until he was advanced to major general for pension purposes and retired in 1870.

SHERMAN, WILLIAM TECUMSEH (1820–1891) USA. Next to **U. S. Grant**, Sherman is the second best-known Union general. The older brother of **John Sherman**, he was a native of **Ohio**. When his father, a state supreme court justice, died in 1829, the family was left destitute, and Sherman and his 10 siblings were raised by friends and relatives. Sherman lived with Thomas Ewing, a U.S. senator and cabinetmember, and later married his daughter (making Sherman the brother-in-law of Union generals **Charles**, **Hugh**, and **Thomas Ewing Jr.**). Known to his friends as "Cump," he possessed a brilliant intellect and an abundance of nervous, restless energy. Sherman's strong political connections won him an 1836 appointment to **West Point**, from which he graduated sixth in the 1840 class. During the **Mexican War**, he was disappointed not to have fought in Mexico, but he did serve as Stephen Kearny's aide and won a **brevet** for his service in **California**. Sherman resigned his captain's commission in 1853 and engaged in a number of failing business ventures. He worked unsuccessfully as a California banker and a **Missouri** lawyer before becoming superintendent of the Louisiana Seminary of Learning and Military Academy in 1859. In this position, Sherman found his calling. He was an excellent administrator, was popular with both the cadets and professors, and fit comfortably into Southern society because of his belief in **slavery** and white supremacy. However, Sherman's support of the Union was paramount, and he sadly resigned his position and returned North when **Louisiana** seceded in January 1861.

After leaving Louisiana, Sherman worked in St. Louis, Missouri, for a streetcar company before entering Union service in May 1861 as colonel of the newly created 13th U.S. Infantry. Sent to **Washington, D.C.**, he was placed in command of a **brigade** in June and led it at **First Manassas**. Sherman was promoted to brigadier general of volunteers in August (his date of commission placed him 11 names above Grant in seniority). Sent to **Kentucky**, he was made second in command of the **Department of the Cumberland** and was appointed **department** commander in October. It was during this time that Sherman's natural nervousness was overwhelmed by fatigue, discontent over the quality of his volunteers, clashes with inquisitive reporters, and the knowledge that the Confederates were becoming stronger every day while the Union did little to win the war. This combination caused him to become more erratic and outspoken, and he claimed the Confederates were amassing a huge **army**. Offended reporters began writing that Sherman was insane, and the uproar led to his being relieved of command in November 1861.

Sherman began to mend his reputation in February 1862 when he was put in charge of the District of Cairo and forwarded troops to Grant during his **Forts Henry and Donelson Campaign**. Grant was impressed, and when Sherman offered to waive his superior rank and serve under him, Grant secured a **division** command for Sherman in his **Army of the Tennessee** in March. At **Shiloh,** both Sherman and Grant were surprised by the Confederates, and Sherman was slightly wounded in the hand when his camps were overrun early on the first day. Grant triumphed in the end, however, and praised his subordinate's fighting ability. As a result, Sherman was promoted to major general of volunteers in May 1862. The two officers became close companions, and when Grant threatened to resign after clashing with **Henry Halleck** during the **siege of Corinth, Mississippi**, it was Sherman who convinced him to stay in the army.

In December 1862, Sherman led a force downriver from Memphis, Tennessee, against **Vicksburg, Mississippi**, during **Grant's Overland Vicksburg Campaign**. He was decisively defeated at **Chickasaw Bayou,** and Grant was forced to retreat after Confederate cavalry destroyed his supply base. Before Grant could take command of the troops on the Mississippi River, **John A. McClernand** assumed that position. Sherman suggested that McClernand capture **Arkansas Post**, which was successfully accomplished in January 1863. During the **Vicksburg Campaign**, Sherman and his XV Corps were back under Grant. He participated in the construction of Grant's Canals and in the **Steele's Bayou, Mississippi, Expedition** before accompanying Grant across the river below Vicksburg. Sherman saw little combat during the march to Vicksburg, but he did participate in the capture of **Jackson, Mississippi**. He served well during the siege of **Vicksburg**, and after the city fell he was promoted to brigadier general of regulars effective July 1863.

After Vicksburg's surrender, Sherman led an expedition in the siege of Jackson, and in October 1863, he was put in command of the **Army** and **Department of the Tennessee**. He reinforced the Union garrison at Chattanooga, Tennessee, and fought at **Missionary Ridge** during the **Chattanooga Campaign**, but his attacks failed. After helping relieve the Confederate siege of Knoxville, Tennessee, at the end of the **Knoxville Campaign**, Sherman returned to **Mississippi** and in early 1864 launched his **Meridian Campaign**. When Grant was made general-in-chief in March 1864, Sherman was appointed commander of the **Military Division of the West** and remained in that position until war's end.

As part of Grant's 1864 **strategy**, Sherman led the **Armies of** the Tennessee, **the Ohio**, and **the Cumberland** against Atlanta, Georgia, in May

1864 to destroy Confederate Gen. **Joseph E. Johnston's Army of Tennessee.** The **Atlanta Campaign** was a five-week campaign of maneuver, punctuated by vicious battles, in which Sherman forced the Confederates back to Atlanta. When **John Bell Hood** replaced Johnston in July 1864, Hood launched costly **frontal attacks** that only further weakened the Confederates. When Atlanta fell on September 2, Sherman was hailed as a great hero, for his victory helped ensure **Abraham Lincoln's** reelection and ultimate Union victory. As a reward, he was promoted to major general of regulars effective August 1864.

In the last year of conflict, Sherman began targeting the civilian population as a way to destroy the enemy's ability to wage war and to break down Confederate morale. After the capture of Atlanta, he forced its evacuation to make the enemy care for the refugees and further strain their resources. Sherman briefly chased Hood's army when it attacked his lines of communications that autumn, but he then appointed **George H. Thomas** to defeat Hood and devoted himself to his **March to the Sea.** With 62,000 handpicked men, Sherman left Atlanta in mid-November 1864 and cut a swath through **Georgia** to Savannah, destroying enemy supplies, barns, mills, factories, and everything of value. It was one of the great expeditions of the war and seriously hurt Confederate morale.

After capturing **Savannah** in December 1864, Sherman began the **Carolinas Campaign** in February 1865 and repeated in the Carolinas the destruction carried out in Georgia. He defeated Johnston in several battles and finally forced his surrender at **Durham Station** in April 1865. Sherman's **surrender** terms allowed the Confederate state governments to continue to function and were rebuked by Secretary of War **Edwin Stanton**. As a result, he was forced to renegotiate and offer the same terms Grant had given **Robert E. Lee.** Despite the controversy, Sherman emerged from the war with a military reputation second only to Grant's. Twice he received the **Thanks of Congress**, once for his actions at Chattanooga and once for the capture of Atlanta and Savannah. Yet Sherman became the target of Southern hatred because of the widespread havoc and destruction during the March to the Sea and the Carolinas Campaign, and particularly for the burning of **Columbia, South Carolina**.

Sherman remained in the army after the war and in 1866 was appointed lieutenant general. When Grant became president in 1869, Sherman was made a full general and was appointed general-in-chief to replace his former commander. He commanded the army during the **Indian** campaigns of the 1870s and helped modernize the service by establishing the Command School at Fort Leavenworth, Kansas. After retiring in 1884, Sherman remained a very popular figure, but he declined all entreaties to enter politics. When Sherman died in 1891, Joseph E. Johnston walked in the funeral procession bareheaded and died a few weeks later from heart failure.

"SHERMAN'S NECKTIES." Also known as "Sherman's hairpins" and "Sherman's bowties," this was a nickname given by Union soldiers to **railroad** iron that was destroyed in a certain way during the **Atlanta Campaign**, the **March to the Sea**, and the **Carolinas Campaign**. To destroy a Confederate railroad, **William T. Sherman's** men made a huge fire from crossties and laid the railroad iron across it. After the iron had heated sufficiently to make it pliable, the soldiers grabbed each end and wrapped it around a tree or pole, twisting it as they did so. This left the iron in the twisted shape of a necktie or hairpin and made it useless since the Confederates had no machinery to straighten it out again.

SHIELDS, JAMES (1810–1879) USA. A native of Ireland, Shields received a good education there and became fluent in three foreign languages. He immigrated to the United States in 1826 and settled in **Illinois**, where he became a lawyer and active in **Democratic Party** politics. After participating in the Black Hawk War, Shields was elected to the state legislature in 1836, served as the state auditor, sat on the state supreme court, and became the commissioner of the federal land office. While serving as auditor, he nearly fought a duel with **Abraham Lincoln** after Lincoln criticized Shields's job performance in the press, but the two later became close friends. Shields fought in the **Mexican War** as an Illinois brigadier general, won a **brevet** for Cerro Gordo, and was commended by **Winfield Scott**. After the war, he served as a U.S. senator from 1849 to 1855 but was defeated for reelection. Returning from **Washington, D.C.**, Shields moved to **Minnesota** and served as its U.S. senator for a one-year special term.

Shields entered Union service in August 1861 when Lincoln appointed him a brigadier general of volunteers, probably to gain the support of the large Irish-American population. In the spring of 1862, he held **division** commands in western **Virginia**, the **Army of the Potomac's** V Corps, and in the **Departments of the Shenandoah** and **the Rappahannock**. Shields's arm was broken by a shell fragment during **skirmishing** the day before the **Battle of Kernstown**, and he missed his division's victory in the battle. Afterward, he was sent into the **Shenandoah Valley** to help trap **Stonewall Jackson** during **Jackson's Shenan-**

doah Valley Campaign. Shields at first fought well at the **Battle of Port Republic**, but he eventually was defeated by Jackson and forced to retreat. Afterward, he apparently waited in vain for a new assignment and finally resigned his commission in March 1863.

Shields lived in **California** for a time, but by 1866, he was residing in **Missouri**, where he reentered politics. After losing an 1872 race for a congressional seat, he was picked to fill an unfulfilled U.S. Senate term in 1879, thus becoming the only person to have served as a U.S. senator from three states. Shields declined to run for reelection because of poor health and died later that year.

SHILOH, TENNESSEE, CAMPAIGN AND BATTLE OF (APRIL 3–8, 1862). Following the loss of **Forts Henry and Donelson** in February 1862, Confederate forces under Gen. **Albert Sidney Johnston** abandoned Middle **Tennessee** and retreated to the important **railroad** junction of Corinth, Mississippi. Union forces under Maj. Gen. **U. S. Grant** then advanced to Pittsburg Landing on the west bank of the Tennessee River, just a few miles north of the Tennessee–Mississippi state line. There Grant's 49,000-man **army** (later to become the **Army of the Tennessee**) encamped in thick woods around the landing and Shiloh Church, sandwiched between the Tennessee River on the east and Owl Creek on the west. Meanwhile, Maj. Gen. **Don Carlos Buell** and his 36,000-man **Army of the Ohio** had occupied Nashville, Tennessee, and were preparing to join Grant at Shiloh for an advance against Corinth.

Johnston decided his only hope of avoiding defeat was to strike Grant before Buell could reinforce him. Calling in reinforcements from around his **department**, he increased his **Army of Mississippi** to 44,000 men and departed Corinth for Shiloh on April 3. Secrecy and surprise were absolutely essential, but the inexperienced soldiers moved slowly along muddy roads, singing and cheering and firing their guns to check their powder. The march should have been an easy one-day movement, but Johnston did not reach Shiloh until April 5. Convinced that the element of surprise was lost, second in command **P. G. T. Beauregard** advised canceling the operation, but Johnston declared, "I would fight them if they were a million" (Hattaway, *Shades of Blue and Gray*, 69).

Johnston's complicated battle plan had been drawn up by Beauregard. Four battle lines of one **corps** each were arranged under **William J. Hardee**, **Braxton Bragg**, **Leonidas Polk**, and **John C. Breckinridge**. The army's right wing was to push along the Tennessee River toward Pittsburg Landing to cut off Grant from his navy support and isolate him from the approaching Buell. The enemy then would be driven to the northwest, away from the river and into Owl Creek bottom where they could be destroyed. This plan, however, proved to be impractical because the battle line of each corps was so long the commanders could not properly supervise their men, and the wooded, rugged terrain made maneuvers difficult.

On the afternoon and night of April 5, Union **pickets** and scouts warned their superiors of a large enemy force to the southwest, but the warnings were ignored. When Johnston's advanced units encountered the enemy pickets at about 5:45 A.M., Sunday, April 6, however, the **skirmishing** alerted some Union commanders, who began putting their men into line. At first, the Confederates overran the Union camps and plundered them. But as the battle continued, the momentum slowed as commanders lost control of their men in the thick woods, and pockets of stubborn Union resistance began forming. Johnston's elaborate battle plan broke down, and the fight deteriorated into a slugfest, or **"soldiers' battle."**

After being pushed back a mile in some places, the Union line began holding, and in the center, **Benjamin Prentiss's** division took up a strong position along a sunken road. Grant, who had rushed to the battlefield from his headquarters upriver at Savannah, desperately tried to form a defense and ordered Prentiss to hold his position at all costs. For hours, Prentiss held his ground against numerous enemy attacks, and the bloodied Confederates soon dubbed the sunken road the "Hornets' Nest."

On the eastern edge of the Hornets' Nest was Sarah Bell's farm, the scene of some of the heaviest fighting. Late in the morning, Johnston sent **Jones Withers's** division to the right to attack the enemy along the Hamburg Road. Withers drove out one Union **brigade** but then ran into stubborn resistance by **Stephen A. Hurlbut's** and **William H. L. Wallace's** divisions north of the road. About noon, Johnston brought up **Breckinridge's** corps and attacked the Federals positioned at Bell's cotton field and Peach Orchard. Several assaults were repulsed, but Johnston finally massed troops against Hurlbut's division at the Peach Orchard and personally led an attack in mid-afternoon. The position was overrun, but Johnston was shot in the leg and quickly bled to death. Wallace also was mortally wounded in the fight for the Peach Orchard. Another famous battlefield landmark on the Union left was a small pond located just north of the Peach Orchard. So many wounded men washed, drank, and died there, that the pond turned red from blood and became known as "Bloody Pond." It can still be seen on the battlefield today.

While the Federals held the Hornets' Nest and Peach Orchard, the **divisions** of **William T. Sherman** and **John C. McClernand** held the Union right against Polk and Hardee. Sherman was forced to retreat at mid-morning, however, when his left flank was broken by Hardee's and Bragg's corps. By now, the Confederates were badly confused, so Hardee assumed command of the left, Polk the center, and Bragg the right.

Beauregard took command of the army after Johnston's death and massed 62 cannons to blast the Hornets' Nest. After enduring a two-hour bombardment, Prentiss finally surrendered his 2,200 survivors at about 5:30 P.M., but his valiant stand had stalled the enemy advance for six hours and bought Grant crucial time. By the time Beauregard was able to press forward, Grant had formed a strong defensive line around Pittsburg Landing with 54 guns and the support of two gunboats in the river. Beauregard launched one last attack on his right toward Pittsburg Landing at sunset, but it was repulsed, and the battle died out.

The day's fighting had been brutal, and both sides had suffered heavy losses. Although enjoying initial success, the Confederates were slowed by the stubborn Union defenders and the thick woods. A major error committed by the Confederates was their attacking piecemeal with individual brigades instead of concentrating troops for a massive attack. Instead of forcing back the Union left as planned, the Confederates also had pushed back the enemy right and allowed Grant to form a strong defensive line around Pittsburg Landing. Although surprised and driven back a considerable distance, the Federals had fought well and had survived the day battered, but intact.

That night, Grant was reinforced by **Lew Wallace's** division and by Buell's army. Beauregard was unaware of these reinforcements and intended to attack the next morning, but Grant counterattacked at dawn first. The fighting again was bloody, but the exhausted Confederates were slowly forced back until Beauregard ordered a withdrawal back to Corinth late in the afternoon. **Nathan Bedford Forrest's** cavalry formed the rear guard and stopped the Union pursuit on April 8.

The two-day Battle of Shiloh was the war's first massive clash and the first battle for most of the soldiers involved. Grant lost 13,047 men to the Confederates' 10,694, and the total casualties exceeded all of America's combined war losses up to the Civil War. The battle did not enhance either Grant's or Beauregard's careers. Grant was criticized for being surprised (and falsely rumored to have been drunk) and was replaced in command by his superior, **Henry W. Halleck**, who began the methodical siege of **Corinth**. Beauregard later was criticized for halting the attacks at the end of the first day, and he earned **Jefferson Davis's** wrath by first misleading him with a report that a great victory had been won and by later evacuating Corinth. He was replaced in command by **Braxton Bragg**.

SHINPLASTERS. During the Civil War, *shinplasters* was a generic term for certain types of paper **Confederate money**. It generally referred to paper money that was in very small denominations (such as 25 cents) or larger denominations that had become virtually worthless because of inflation.

SHODDY. Shoddy was the name of the poor quality woolen cloth that was used to make Union **uniforms** early in the Civil War. The material was so inferior that it generally fell apart soon after being issued.

SHORTER, JOHN GILL (1818–1872) CSA. A member of a wealthy **Georgia** family, Shorter graduated from Franklin College (later called the University of Georgia) in 1837. After becoming a lawyer the following year, he moved to **Alabama**, began his practice, and entered politics. Shorter served as his district's solicitor and served in both houses of the legislature before being elected a judge in 1852. A secessionist, he was a delegate to the state **secession** convention in 1861 and was elected to the Provisional **Confederate Congress**.

As a congressman, Shorter helped write the **Confederate Constitution**, served as chairman of the Committee on Engrossment, and was a strong supporter of **Jefferson Davis**. Elected governor of Alabama in August 1861, he at first was immensely popular as he improved Mobile's defenses and provided care for soldiers' families. However, Shorter's popularity dropped dramatically when Union raids penetrated into the northern part of the state, and he increased **taxes**, **impressed** slaves for military projects, and enforced **conscription**. His support of the increasingly unpopular Davis administration also hurt him politically.

Shorter was badly defeated for reelection in August 1863 and returned to his law practice after leaving office that December. Briefly imprisoned by Union authorities after the war, he resumed his practice after being released and never reentered politics.

SHOUP, FRANCIS ASBURY (1834–1896) CSA. The son of a prominent state politician, Shoup was a native of **Indiana**. After attending Asbury College, he entered **West Point** and was assigned to the **artillery** after graduating in 1855. Shoup saw service in the **Seminole Wars** and served at Fort Moultrie, South Carolina, before resigning his 1st lieutenant's commission in 1860. Returning to Indiana, he became a lawyer and captain of a militia **company**, but he soon moved to **Florida** and started a law practice there.

Despite his Northern birth, Shoup entered Confederate service in March 1861 as a lieutenant of artillery. Assigned to Col. **William J. Hardee**, he served at **Fort Morgan, Alabama**, and in **Arkansas** before being promoted to major in November. Shoup commanded an artillery battalion in **Kentucky**, was promoted to lieutenant colonel later that year, and served as Hardee's chief of artillery at **Shiloh**. At Shiloh, Shoup helped organize the artillery barrage that finally led to the capture of the "Hornets' Nest."

P. G. T. Beauregard appointed Shoup his chief of artillery during the **siege of Corinth, Mississippi**, in the spring of 1862. In June, Shoup was transferred to Arkansas, where he led an artillery battalion before being placed in command of an infantry **brigade**. At **Prairie Grove**, he was commended by his superior, **Thomas C. Hindman** (for whom he also served as adjutant), for his skillful handling of a small **division**. Shoup's military talent won him promotion to brigadier general in April 1863 and command of a **Louisiana** brigade in the **Vicksburg Campaign** that spring. His brigade fought well during the siege and played a key role in repulsing the two major Union attacks in May.

After being **exchanged** following **Vicksburg's** surrender, Shoup took command of a brigade under **Dabney H. Maury** in Mobile, Alabama. In April 1864, however, **Joseph E. Johnston** brought him to **Georgia** and appointed him chief of artillery for the **Army of Tennessee**. He served Johnston well by reorganizing the artillery to make it more efficient and by supervising the construction of defensive lines on the Chattahoochee River during the **Atlanta Campaign**. When **John Bell Hood** replaced Johnston in July, he appointed Shoup chief of staff. Shoup served Hood until after the fall of Atlanta and then asked to be relieved. He did not return to duty until February 1865, when he was ordered to join Johnston during the **Carolinas Campaign**. Before doing so, Shoup took command of the **black troops** that had just been authorized for Confederate service. He never carried out these duties, however, because he was surrendered with the rest of Johnston's troops in **North Carolina**.

After the war, Shoup became a mathematics professor at the University of Mississippi and in 1868 was ordained an Episcopal minister. In

1869, he accepted a teaching position at the University of the South and became the university's chaplain. Shoup later left the university to serve as rector for several parishes but returned to the University of the South as a professor in 1883. Besides being a soldier, minister, and professor, he also was the author of two Civil War–era military texts and two postwar works on mathematics and metaphysics. His great-grandson, David M. Shoup, was awarded the **Medal of Honor** in World War II and served as the commander of the **U.S. Marines** from 1960–1963.

SHRAPNEL. This type of **artillery** ammunition was invented by British Gen. Henry Shrapnel during the Napoleonic Wars. It consisted of a fused, hollow shell filled with explosives and lead or iron balls that continued forward in shotgun fashion when the shell exploded. Although similar to **grape shot** and **canister**, shrapnel was developed as a way to extend the range of such multishot projectiles. In the Civil War, shrapnel more often was referred to as **case shot** or spherical case shot and was often used in **Napoleon cannons**.

SIBLEY, HENRY HASTINGS (1811–1891) USA. A native of **Michigan**, Sibley was a distant cousin of Confederate general **Henry Hopkins Sibley**. He became involved in the fur trade and by 1835 had settled in what became the **Minnesota** Territory. Entering politics, Sibley served as a nonvoting congressional delegate for the **Wisconsin** Territory in 1848, helped create the Territory of Minnesota in 1849, served in its territorial legislature, and was elected Minnesota's first state governor in 1858.

Sibley chose not to run for reelection in 1859 and remained a private citizen until after the Civil War began. When the 1862 **Sioux uprising** began in Minnesota, he was appointed colonel of state militia and successfully defeated the **Indians** in the September Battle of Wood Lake. For his service, Sibley was commissioned a brigadier general of volunteers in September 1862 and was charged with suppressing the Indians. The Senate did not confirm his commission, however, and he had to be reappointed in March 1863 (this time being confirmed). Sibley's entire Civil War military career was spent fighting the Sioux, and he probably never saw a Confederate soldier except perhaps **prisoners** of war. In the courts-martial that followed his battlefield victory, Sibley condemned 307 Indians to death, but **Abraham Lincoln** commuted all but 38 of the sentences. In 1865–66, Sibley also helped negotiate peace treaties with the hostile tribes. After being **brevetted** major general of volunteers in November 1865, he was mustered out of service in April 1866.

After the war, Sibley worked with a gas company, in insurance, and as a banker. He was elected to the state legislature in 1871 and played a key role in persuading the state not to repudiate its debts. Sibley also served as president of the St. Paul Chamber of Commerce, was a member of the University of Minnesota's board of regents, served as president of the state's historical society, and in 1888 received an honorary doctorate from Princeton University.

SIBLEY, HENRY HOPKINS (1816–1886) CSA. A native of **Louisiana**, Sibley was a distant cousin of Union general **Henry Hastings Sibley**. He graduated near the bottom of his 1838 **West Point** class and was assigned to the dragoons. Sibley fought in the **Seminole** and **Mexican Wars** and won a **brevet** for gallantry in the latter. Remaining in the **U.S. Army** after the Mexican War, he developed and patented the **Sibley Tent** in 1856, which was patterned after **Indian** tepees and which was used by both sides in the Civil War. Sibley also served in **"Bleeding Kansas"** and in the **Utah Expedition**.

Sibley was serving in the **New Mexico Territory** when the Civil War began. He resigned his commission in April 1861, and it was accepted on the same day in May that he was promoted to major. After meeting with **Jefferson Davis** in **Richmond, Virginia**, to urge an invasion of New Mexico, Sibley was commissioned a Confederate brigadier general in June and was placed in command of the **Army of New Mexico**. **Sibley's New Mexico Campaign** in early 1862 started successfully with a victory at **Valverde** and the occupation of Santa Fe and Albuquerque, but he finally was forced to retreat after the **Battle of Glorieta Pass**. Sibley was largely to blame for the failed campaign because of his poor **tactics**, alcohol addiction, and lack of leadership. When his ragged army reached San Antonio, Texas, in July, one of his officers brought charges of drunkenness, cowardice, misappropriation of goods, and mistreatment of the sick and wounded against him. Instead of being court-martialed, however, Sibley met with Davis in Richmond and got the charges dismissed.

Sibley next was sent to south Louisiana in December 1862 to serve under **Richard Taylor**. His command guarded against Union forays out of **Baton Rouge** and Plaquemine until February 1863, when he was put in command of all Confederate forces south of the Red River. Taylor was greatly disappointed by Sibley during the **Bayou Teche Campaign** that spring. When Union forces landed in the rear and threatened to cut off Taylor's forces at **Fort Bisland**, he ordered Sibley to attack the Federals. Sibley failed to do so, and the Confederates had to retreat. Taylor then placed him in command of the retreating column, but after taking a wrong road, Sibley relinquished command on account of illness. In the campaign, Sibley had failed to obey orders, at times was far away from the action, and was accused by some of being drunk. Taylor offered to let him resign rather than be court-martialed, but Sibley refused, and Taylor pressed charges against him. In his court-martial, Sibley was found not guilty of disobeying orders, but he was censured for being less than prompt in carrying out those orders. He was ordered back to Richmond but never again held a position of responsibility because the War Department could find no officer willing to have him in his command. Ordered to return to the **Trans-Mississippi Department** in the spring of 1864, Sibley sailed from Mobile, **Alabama**, to Mexico by way of Cuba, and reached Shreveport, Louisiana, that summer. He was **paroled** there in June 1865.

After the war, Sibley moved to **New York**, but in 1869, he accepted a position with the Khedive of Egypt to help reorganize his army. Sibley served as the Khedive's inspector general of **artillery** but was dismissed in 1873 because of his alcoholism and heavy debt. He returned to the United States and lived the rest of his life in **Virginia** with his daughter.

SIBLEY TENT. Patented in 1856 by Maj. **Henry Hopkins Sibley**, this **U.S. Army** tent was used by both sides during the Civil War. Patterned after the Western **Indians'** tepees, the tent was formed around an iron tripod and was conical in shape, measuring 12 feet in height and 18.5 feet in diameter. Well ventilated with two door flaps and an adjustable opening at the top, the Sibley tent could house 12 soldiers. Despite its comfort and size, the tent was cumbersome and weighed 73 pounds, making it unsuitable for active campaigning. Still, the U.S. Army continued to use the Sibley tent into the 1890s.

SIBLEY'S NEW MEXICO CAMPAIGN (DECEMBER 14, 1861–MAY 4, 1862). After resigning his commission in the **U.S. Army** in May 1861, **Henry Hopkins Sibley** left his post in **New Mexico** and met with **Jefferson Davis** in **Richmond, Virginia**, to discuss a Confederate invasion of the Southwest. Sibley proposed raising an **army** in **Texas** with which he would march through New Mexico to **California**, gaining recruits from the supposedly pro-Confederate population and adding the mineral- and cattle-rich Southwest to the Confederacy. Davis was impressed with Sibley's plan and authorized him to undertake the operation with the rank of brigadier general.

By the time Sibley arrived in Texas in August 1861, preliminary steps had already been taken for the invasion. Lieutenant Colonel **John Bay-**

lor's **"Buffalo Hunt"** had captured the Union garrison of **Fort Fillmore, New Mexico**, on July 26. He then established the Confederate Territory of Arizona on August 1 and appointed himself governor. Sibley raised the **Army of New Mexico** and joined Baylor at Fort Bliss (El Paso), Texas, by December 14. There on December 20, he issued a proclamation to the people of Arizona and New Mexico stating that he was there to liberate them and, in effect, claimed the Southwest for the Confederacy.

Sibley moved up the Rio Grande into New Mexico in early January 1862 with 2,600 men. Bypassing Fort Craig, the Confederates were attacked by the 3,800-man Union garrison a few miles north of the fort at **Valverde** on February 21 but won the battle. Sibley continued toward Albuquerque and Santa Fe, where he planned to capture much-needed supplies. The Federals, however, removed or destroyed the supplies, and Sibley found scant provisions when he occupied Albuquerque on March 5 and Santa Fe on March 10. While remaining with the occupation troops in Albuquerque, Sibley then sent part of his command 150 miles to the northeast to attack Fort Union. On March 28, this column won a tactical victory at **Glorieta Pass** but was forced to retreat when the enemy destroyed its wagon train. Glorieta Pass turned out to a strategic Union victory because it blunted the Confederate invasion.

By now, Sibley was nearly out of supplies, and the Federals were closing in on him. Union Brig. Gen. **Edward R. S. Canby**, commanding the **Department of New Mexico**, led approximately 1,200 men north from Fort Craig to unite with the Fort Union garrison and attack the Confederates. Canby arrived outside Albuquerque on April 8 and began **skirmishing** with Sibley. Out of supplies and facing a formidable enemy, Sibley retreated on April 12 and successfully reached Fort Bliss on May 4 after a dreadful, exhausting march, because Canby failed to use his superior force aggressively. He then continued to San Antonio after learning the Union **California Column** was approaching his position. The campaign cost Sibley 1,700 men, mostly soldiers who fell out on the horrific retreat, and his survivors were ragged and half-starved by the time they reached San Antonio. The Confederates never again made a serious attempt to seize the Southwest.

SICKLES, DANIEL EDGAR (1819–1914) USA. A native of **New York**, Sickles was one of the most controversial Civil War officers. He attended New York University and studied law before entering New York City's Tammany Hall politics. Sickles resigned after serving one year as New York City's corporation counsel to accept the position of secretary of legation in Great Britain. Upon his return to New York, he served in the state senate and in the **U.S. Congress** from 1857 to 1861. While a **Democratic** congressman, Sickles earned national recognition when he murdered Philip Barton Key, Francis Scott Key's son and the lover of Sickles's wife, in **Washington, D.C.** Defended by **Edwin M. Stanton**, Sickles reportedly was the first defendant to use the temporary insanity defense successfully in the United States. After being acquitted, Sickles then angered much of the nation by reconciling with his wife, for many people viewed her as the guilty party and believed the shooting had been justified.

It appeared the scandal had ruined Sickles's political career, but the Civil War allowed him the opportunity to redeem himself. Authorized to raise a **regiment** of volunteers, he soon had enough men to form the **Excelsior Brigade**. Sickles first entered the Union **army** in June 1861 as colonel of the 70th New York, but in September, he was appointed brigadier general of volunteers and **brigade** commander because **Abraham Lincoln** wanted to gain Democratic support for the war effort. During his military career, Sickles often was accused of being a womanizer and heavy drinker and was viewed by many officers as less than a gentleman; his bravery in battle, however, was never questioned. Although he spent much of his time in Washington politicking for a higher command, Sickles did see combat with **Joseph Hooker's division** in the **Army of the Potomac** during the **Peninsula** and **Seven Days Campaigns**.

After the Seven Days, Sickles assumed command of the division in September 1862 and was promoted to major general of volunteers in November. At **Fredericksburg**, he saw heavy combat and after the war was **brevetted** brigadier general of regulars for his actions there. When Hooker took command of the army in early 1863, he appointed his friend and supporter Sickles to lead the III Corps in February. At **Chancellorsville**, Sickles was criticized for advancing his **corps** to pursue what he thought was a retreating **Stonewall Jackson**, thus leaving the XI Corps isolated and vulnerable to Jackson's crushing flank attack.

Sickles's most controversial moment was at **Gettysburg**, where he still commanded the III Corps. On the second day of battle, **George G. Meade** ordered him to hold the army's left flank along Cemetery Ridge and Little Round Top. Not liking the ground he occupied, Sickles moved his men forward to the **Peach Orchard** without permission, thus abandoning Little Round Top and placing his corps in an isolated position. Before Meade could correct the move, **James Longstreet's** Confederates attacked. The corps was mauled, and Sickles lost his right leg to amputation after being hit by a shell fragment. Hard fighting and quick action by other officers saved the day, but Sickles's movement became one of Gettysburg's great controversies. His critics believed he should have been court-martialed, while others argued that his actions actually absorbed the impact of the enemy attack in advance of the main Union position and saved the army from destruction. Hero or villain, Sickles's actions won him a brevet of major general of regulars and the **Medal of Honor** after the war. Ever the showman, he donated his amputated leg to the army's medical museum and was said to have visited it often.

Gettysburg ended Sickles's active military career. His controversial actions and an ongoing feud with Meade over Meade's generalship prevented him from receiving another field command. For the remainder of the war, Sickles performed various administrative duties for the War Department.

Sickles remained in the army after the war and was appointed colonel of the 42nd U.S. Infantry in 1866. He was mustered out of the volunteers in January 1868 and was retired the following year with the advanced rank of major general of regulars. Afterward, Sickles served as President **U. S. Grant's** minister to Spain from 1869 to 1875 (where he reportedly became intimate with the former queen), served in Congress from 1893 to 1895, and then chaired the New York State Monument Commission for 26 years before being forced out of office after being accused of misappropriating funds.

SIGEL, FRANZ (1824–1902) USA. A native of the Grand Duchy of Baden (Germany), Sigel graduated from a German military academy in 1843 and became a lieutenant in the Grand Duke's army. After serving as the revolutionary minister of war in the failed 1848 revolution against Prussia, he fled to the United States by way of Switzerland and Great Britain and became a teacher in **New York** and a major in the state militia. Sigel then moved to St. Louis, **Missouri**, where he became a leader of the antislavery German population while serving as the city's director of schools.

Sigel entered Union service in May 1861 as colonel of the 3rd Missouri (Union) and helped **Nathaniel Lyon** capture the secessionist militia at **Camp Jackson**. He then was given command of a **brigade** in the **Army of Southwest Missouri** that summer and fought at **Carthage**. To gain the support of St. Louis's large German population, **Abraham Lincoln** appointed Sigel brigadier general of volunteers in August. After fighting at **Wilson's Creek**, he was given a **division** command in early 1862. At **Pea Ridge** in March, Sigel played a key role in the Union victory while commanding two divisions and was promoted to major general of volunteers later that month.

Sigel was transferred to the east and in June 1862 was put in command of a division under **John C. Frémont** in the **Shenandoah Valley**. In **Virginia**, his military reputation became tarnished, but Sigel never lost the support or devotion of his largely German command. "I fights mit Sigel!" was the proud declaration of his immigrant soldiers. When Frémont refused to serve under **John Pope**, Sigel was placed in command of the **Army of Virginia's** I Corps in late June 1862. After **Second Manassas**, the **corps** was redesignated the XI Corps of the **Army of the Potomac**, but it saw no significant combat in the **Antietam** or **Fredericksburg Campaigns**. Sigel was forced to relinquish command in early 1863 because of illness and thus missed **Chancellorsville** and **Gettysburg**. When he returned to duty, he was given command of the **Department of West Virginia** in March 1864, but after being defeated by a smaller enemy force at **New Market**, he was removed and put in charge of the **department's** reserve division. After this command was taken away in July 1864, Sigel was left without a position, and he finally resigned his commission in May 1865.

After the war, Sigel served as a federal pension agent and ran for several public offices after switching from the **Republican** to the **Democratic Party**.

SIGNAL COMMUNICATIONS. Among its many "firsts," the Civil War was the first conflict to make extensive use of the **telegraph**. The Union had an advantage over the Confederacy because of its more extensive system of telegraph wires and because it had created the U.S. Signal Corps under **Albert J. Myer** in 1860 to supervise all military communications. Also, Secretary of War **Edwin M. Stanton** was a former telegraph company director and recognized the usefulness of a well-organized system. For the first year of the war, the Signal Corps used such visual communications as **"wigwag" signal** flags, rockets, and fires to communicate short distances and the American Telegraph Company and the Western Union Telegraph Company to transmit its electronic military communications. Myer also created the **Flying Telegraph Trains** to maintain telegraph communications between armies and within an **army**.

In February 1862, the U.S. Military Telegraph Corps was created under **Anson Stager** to operate all of the Union's telegraph lines. Soon, conflict over control of the telegraph lines erupted between the Military Telegraph Corps and Myer's Signal Corps. Myer believed the Signal Corps should be in charge of all battlefield or **tactical** communications, while Stager's organization should deal only with administrative or **strategic** communications. Besides clashing over authority, the two organizations also used different communication systems, with the Military Telegraph Corps using Morse Code and the Signal Corps using the **Beardslee Telegraph**. In November 1863, Stanton supported Stager and removed Myer from the Signal Corps. Afterward, the Military Telegraph Corps was solely responsible for military telegraph communications and answered only to Stanton, not to military officers. The Signal Corps was reduced to using only short-range visual signals. During the war, the Military Telegraph Corps used approximately 12,000 telegraphers; strung 15,000 miles of wire; and averaged more than 5,000 (mostly coded) messages a day.

The Confederates never had as elaborate a communications system as the Union, but they did create the first effective signal corps. **Edward Porter Alexander**, who had helped Myer create the **U.S. Army's** wigwag system, was put in charge of a signal corps that was used effectively at **First Manassas**. In April 1862, the Confederates created a Signal Corps within the Adjutant General's Office to operate all visual (flags, rockets, and torches) and telegraphic signals, as well as to perform secret service operations. Not only did small teams of signalmen operate with the armies, but they also were used aboard **blockade runners** to communicate with shore defenses while running into and out of ports. Because of a less-developed telegraph system, the Confederates never employed as many signalmen as the Union, using only about 1,500 during the war. The Confederates also never created a nationwide military telegraph system as the Union's.

SILL, JOSHUA WOODROW (1831–1862) USA. A native of **Ohio**, Sill graduated near the top of his 1853 **West Point** class and was assigned to the ordnance department. He served at various arsenals and was an instructor at the academy before resigning his commission in January 1861 to accept a position as a mathematics and engineering professor at the Brooklyn Collegiate and Polytechnic Institute.

When the Civil War began, Sill offered his services to his native Ohio and was appointed state assistant adjutant general. After serving with the 33rd Ohio at **Rich Mountain**, he was appointed the **regiment's** colonel in August 1861. Sill fought in numerous **skirmishes** in **Kentucky** and was given command of a **brigade** in the **Army of the Ohio's** 3rd Division in November. Sent to northern **Alabama**, he continued to skirmish with the enemy, and part of his command conducted **Andrews' Raid** in April 1862, resulting in the "Great Locomotive Chase."

Sill was promoted to brigadier general of volunteers in July 1862 and commanded a **division** in the Army of the Ohio's I Corps during the

Kentucky Campaign, although he did not see any combat. After the campaign, he briefly commanded a division in the **Army of the Cumberland's** XIV Corps but was back in brigade command in **William T. Sherman's** division at **Stones River**. Sill's brigade was heavily engaged on the battle's first day and was forced back with the rest of the division. While leading his men in the repulse of one Confederate attack, Sill was killed instantly. After the war, his friend Maj. Gen. **Philip H. Sheridan** named Fort Sill, Oklahoma, in his honor.

SIMMS, JAMES PHILLIP (1837–1887) CSA. Simms was a native of **Georgia**, but little is known of his antebellum life other than he became a lawyer. It also is uncertain when he actually entered Confederate service. Simms seems to have been serving as assistant quartermaster for the **Army of Northern Virginia's** 42nd Georgia in August 1862 and by September was a major in the 53rd Georgia. Although it does not appear that he was with the **regiment** at **Antietam**, he was appointed its colonel in October.

Simms's regiment was kept in reserve at **Fredericksburg**, but he afterward fought well with **Paul Jones Semmes's brigade** in the **Chancellorsville Campaign** and captured an enemy **flag** at **Salem Church**. Simms led the regiment in the **Gettysburg** and **Knoxville Campaigns** and was wounded at **Fort Sanders**. After fighting through much of the **Overland Campaign** in **Goode Bryan's** brigade, he took temporary command of the brigade when Bryan relinquished it in June 1864. The brigade reinforced **Jubal A. Early** during **Philip Sheridan's Shenandoah Valley Campaign** in October 1864. As part of **Joseph Kershaw's division**, Simms led the division's attack at **Cedar Creek** and helped capture an enemy battery. After Kershaw's division returned to the Army of Northern Virginia during the **Petersburg Campaign**, Simms was promoted to brigadier general in February 1865. He led a brigade throughout the remainder of the siege and was captured at **Sailor's Creek** on April 6.

After being released from **Fort Warren, Massachusetts**, in July 1865, Simms returned to his Georgia law practice and was elected to the state legislature in 1865 and 1866.

SIOUX UPRISING OF 1862. Taking advantage of the withdrawal of U.S. troops from **Minnesota** to fight the Civil War, the Santee Sioux attacked the state's white settlers in the summer of 1862 to win back their homeland. Led by Chief Little Crow, the Sioux killed approximately 800 settlers in the Minnesota River Valley that summer and drove the survivors into Fort Ridgely, which was unsuccessfully attacked, as well. After his defeat at **Second Manassas, John Pope** was sent to Minnesota to lead the **army** against the **Indians**. **Henry Hastings Sibley** was appointed colonel of the state militia and led 1,400 men against the Sioux. He defeated the Indians at the Battle of Wood Lake on September 23 and forced Little Crow and his survivors to flee to the west. Of the approximately 1,500 Sioux taken prisoner, 307 were tried and sentenced to death, but **Abraham Lincoln** pardoned all but 38. The 38 Indians were hanged publicly in December.

SKIRMISH. A skirmish was the smallest combat encounter between Civil War **armies**. It usually occurred between opposing **pickets** or **skirmish lines** and consisted of probing and taking shots at each other to feel out the enemy's position.

SKIRMISH LINE. Both **armies** used a skirmish line to lead a force against an enemy position and to provide flank protection. During campaigns, **skirmishers** spread out several yards apart in a skirmish line and advanced before the main body of troops. The skirmish line was the first to make contact with the enemy and was to give warning of their proximity and probe and feel out the enemy's strength and position before the main bodies became engaged. Drill manuals provided instructions on the placement of the skirmish line and the **tactics** to be used in confronting the enemy.

SKIRMISHERS. Skirmishers were the soldiers who manned the **skirmish line**. The **companies** of a **regiment** usually took turns in providing skirmishers.

SLACK, JAMES RICHARD (1818–1881) USA. A native of **Pennsylvania**, as a young man, Slack moved with his family to **Indiana**. There he worked on the family farm, taught school, and became a lawyer when he was 22. After starting his practice, Slack was elected county auditor in 1842 and after a nine-year tenure began the first of seven terms in the state legislature.

Slack entered Union service in December 1861 when he was commissioned colonel of the 47th Indiana. In February 1862, he was given a **brigade** command in the **Army of the Mississippi's** 2nd Division and led it at **New Madrid and Island No. 10**. Afterward, Slack garrisoned **Arkansas** until the 1863 **Vicksburg Campaign**. Placed in command of a brigade in the 12th Division of the **Army of the Tennessee's** XIII Corps in February 1863, he served in the **Yazoo Pass Expedition** and in operations against **Vicksburg, Mississippi.** After the city's surrender, Slack participated in the siege of **Jackson, Mississippi**, before being transferred to the **Department of the Gulf** in August 1863. After serving a minor role in the 1864 **Red River Campaign**, he was promoted to brigadier general in November 1864. In early 1865, Slack was given a brigade command in the XIII Corps' 1st Division and played a major role in the **Mobile Campaign** while fighting at **Spanish Fort** and **Fort Blakely.** For his role in the city's capture, he was **brevetted** major general of volunteers to rank from March 1865.

Slack was mustered out of service in early 1866 and returned to his Indiana law practice. He later was appointed a circuit judge by the governor and was reelected in 1872 and 1878.

SLACK, WILLIAM YARNELL (1816–1862) CSA. A native of **Kentucky**, Slack moved to **Missouri** as a child. There he became a lawyer and served in the **Mexican War** as a captain in the 2nd Missouri Mounted Volunteers.

When the Civil War began, Gov. **Claiborne F. Jackson** appointed Slack a brigadier general in the Missouri State Guard, and in June 1861, he organized the State Guard's 4th Division. Slack commanded a cavalry **regiment** and infantry battalion at **Carthage** and played a key role in forcing the Federals to retreat. At **Wilson's Creek**, he was highly praised by his superiors but was severely wounded in the groin while leading his **division** in an attack. In January 1862, **Sterling Price** reorganized his **army** and placed Slack in command of a brigade. While leading his men in an attack at **Pea Ridge**, Slack's groin "was fearfully lacerated by a musket-ball" (Davis, ed., *The Confederate General,* vol. 5, 159) in nearly the same place he was wounded at Wilson's Creek. He was carried from the field but died from his wound on March 21. In April, Slack was promoted to brigadier general posthumously.

SLAUGHTER, JAMES EDWIN (1827–1901) CSA. A native of **Virginia**, Slaughter was the great-nephew of President James Madison. He entered the **Virginia Military Institute** in 1845 but left his studies the following year to accept a 2nd lieutenant's commission in the **U.S. Army** during the **Mexican War**. Slaughter remained in the **army** after the war and in 1852 was commissioned a 1st lieutenant of **artillery**.

After being dismissed from the service in May 1861, Slaughter joined the Confederacy as a captain of artillery. He was assigned to **Braxton Bragg's** staff at **Pensacola, Florida**, and was promoted to major in November. Slaughter impressed his superiors with his administrative and training skills and was commissioned a brigadier general in March 1862. Appointed assistant inspector general for the **Army of Mississippi**, he served Gen. **Albert Sidney Johnston** at **Shiloh** and then **P. G. T. Beauregard**. After serving Bragg in the **Kentucky Campaign**, Slaughter was put in command of the Mobile, Alabama, defenses until April 1863, when he was sent to Galveston, Texas, to become **John B. Magruder's** acting chief of staff and chief of artillery. Magruder put Slaughter in command of the West Subdistrict of Texas in late 1863, and there he participated in the war's last engagement at **Palmito Ranch** in May 1865.

After the war, Slaughter accompanied several other Confederate generals to Mexico and ran a sawmill before returning to the United States in 1867. He then worked as a civil engineer and served as Mobile's postmaster before settling in **Louisiana**. Slaughter died in Mexico City while on a visit and was buried there.

SLAUGHTER MOUNTAIN, VIRGINIA, BATTLE OF (AUGUST 9, 1862). *See* CEDAR MOUNTAIN, VIRGINIA, BATTLE OF.

SLAVERY. Although the Civil War was fought over the constitutional right of **secession**, the nation's nearly four million slaves were at the root of the conflict. African slaves were introduced into the American colonies in the early 17th century and became the South's main labor source. The Northern colonies never became dependent on slave labor because they were not suited to cash crop agriculture and had larger populations of Quakers and others who opposed slavery. Whereas some Northerners were **abolitionists** who opposed slavery on moral grounds, most Northerners opposed it for economic reasons. This majority believed in white supremacy and for the most part did not care if the South had slaves; however, they feared their wage labor system could not compete with slavery and thus did not want slavery to spread outside the South.

Slavery was a source of contention between the North and South from the nation's birth, but it did not become an important divisive issue until the early 19th century. Until then, there was an uneasy balance of power in the U.S. Senate between the slave and free states. When **Missouri** petitioned to be admitted as a slave state in 1819, this balance of power was threatened, and a bitter political battle ensued. The 1820 **Missouri Compromise** settled the issue temporarily and led to a shaky truce by admitting **Maine** as a free state and Missouri as a slave state to maintain the balance of power and partitioning the Louisiana Purchase between free and slave areas. Such abolitionists as **William Lloyd Garrison** kept pressure on slavery afterward, but it was not until new western territory was won in the **Mexican War** that the issue exploded again. Southern agricultural lands were becoming exhausted and world competition more threatening, and many planters were facing an uncertain financial future. They saw the West as an area of opportunity, either to move there themselves to start over or as a profitable market for slaves they would provide.

Such Northerners as the **Free-Soilers** bitterly opposed the spread of slavery westward because it would threaten their plans for establishing **homesteads**, family farms, and wage labor there. At the heart of the issue were the constitutional questions concerning the status of slaves and whether or not the **U.S. Congress** had the right to restrict the spread of slavery into territories. Southerners argued that since slaves were property and property was protected by the Constitution, Congress could not pass laws interfering with someone's right to carry his property into the territories. Northerners argued that territories were common property owned by all of the people, and as the people's representative government, Congress regulated territories and thus did have the right to restrict slavery in them. It should be noted that both sides recognized that states held special status in the Union that the territories did not, and no one debated the right of a state to allow or forbid slavery as it saw fit. Of course, the crucial point was whether slave owners would be given the opportunity to populate a territory before it achieved statehood and thus have a chance to affect its decision.

The Mexican War marked the beginning of the road to civil war. When the North introduced the **Wilmot Proviso** to forbid slavery in any territory won from Mexico, the South felt it was being deprived the spoils of victory. Soon afterward, the debate over slavery in the West was aggravated by the more emotional issues of the slave trade in **Washington, D.C.**, and runaway slaves. The **Compromise of 1850** provided a temporary settlement of these issues, but the antislavery faction gained significant support in 1852 when **Harriet Beecher Stowe** published her powerful *Uncle Tom's Cabin* and in 1854 when the Ostend Manifesto revealed that some Southern politicians were willing to plunge the nation into war with Spain to gain Cuba as additional slave territory. Also in 1854, Sen. **Stephen A. Douglas** got the **Kansas-Nebraska Act** passed, which abolished the Missouri Compromise Line and replaced it with **popular sovereignty** as a means of determining slavery in the territories. Douglas, who believed slavery could never survive on the arid Great Plains, was vehemently criticized by Northerners for opening the way for slavery there. As a result of the Kansas-Nebraska Act, the **Republican Party** was formed to oppose the spread of slavery, and fighting broke out in **"Bleeding Kansas."** By 1856, emotions over slavery had escalated to the point that violence erupted on the Senate floor in the Brooks-**Sumner** Affair.

The 1857 **Dred Scott decision** seemed to vindicate the Southern position on slavery when the **U.S. Supreme Court** ruled that slaves were property and could not be denied entry into territories. While Southerners rejoiced in the legal victory, Northerners criticized the decision by noting that the justices simply voted along sectional lines, and that the Southern justices formed a majority. Just when it appeared the North had no way to fight the spread of slavery legally, Douglas proposed his Freeport Doctrine during the 1858 **Lincoln-Douglas Debates**. In it, he noted that while territories could not outlaw slavery, they could still keep slavery out by requiring slave owners to pay taxes or post bonds on all slaves and thus make it too expensive to bring them in.

John Brown's Raid on Harpers Ferry, Virginia, in 1859 was the last major event involving slavery before the **1860 presidential election**. Southerners viewed Brown as a typical abolitionist who was willing to engage in murder and treason to free slaves. While most Northerners opposed Brown's methods, they admired his goals. Thus by 1860, the North and South were completely polarized over the slavery issue. Most Southerners wanted to find a peaceful compromise but were determined not to accept what they saw as tyranny by the majority. A mistaken belief that **Abraham Lincoln** and the Republicans secretly were out to destroy slavery and thus bring down the Southern socioeconomic system led the South to threaten secession if Lincoln was elected. Lincoln's victory set in motion secession and ultimately civil war.

When the Civil War began, Lincoln's goal was to restore the Union, not to destroy slavery (even though he personally opposed it). It was not until mid-1862, when the Union was struggling on the battlefield, that he began to view emancipation as a military measure that could help win the war. By expanding the war's goals to abolish slavery, the Union could disrupt the Confederacy's labor supply by encouraging slaves to run away and hopefully prevent antislavery European powers from recognizing the Confederacy. Thus, in September 1862, Lincoln issued the **Emancipation Proclamation** and changed the Civil War from a war to restore the Union to a war to restore the Union without slavery.

Historians still debate the role slavery had in causing the war. Some argue that it was the main cause, while others claim the war was strictly

over constitutional issues of **states rights**. While some Confederate officials (such as Vice President **Alexander Stephens**) and newspapers
clearly indicated the war was to defend slavery rights, the vast majority
of Confederate soldiers fought either to defend their homes against invasion or to defend their state's sovereign rights. Slavery was rarely
mentioned in their letters and diaries. It would be fair to say that while
the issue of slavery led to secession and war, most Confederates did not
feel they were fighting to defend the "peculiar institution." *See also* UN-
DERGROUND RAILROAD.

SLEMMER, ADAM JACOBY (1829–1868) USA. A native of **Pennsylvania**, Slemmer graduated from **West Point** in 1850. His antebellum career included combat in the **Seminole Wars**, garrison duty in **California**,
and a teaching position at the academy. When the Civil War began,
Slemmer was a 1st lieutenant of **artillery** in command of the Union
troops at Fort Barrancas, Florida.

After **Florida** seceded in January 1861, Slemmer evacuated Fort Barrancas and moved his small command to a more defensible position at
Fort Pickens. There he held the fort against the secessionists and ensured
that Fort Pickens remained in Union hands for the war's duration. That
spring, Slemmer helped recruit the new 16th U.S. Infantry and in May
was appointed its major. Later that year, he was made acting inspector
general for the **Department of the Ohio** and served on **Don Carlos
Buell's** staff during the **siege of Corinth, Mississippi**, and in the **Kentucky Campaign**. At **Stones River** with the **Army of the Cumberland**,
Slemmer was severely wounded while in command of part of his **regiment** and a battalion. The battle ended his active military career but won
him a promotion to brigadier general in April 1863. For the remainder of
the war, Slemmer served as president of a board that examined sick and
wounded officers. He was appointed lieutenant colonel of regulars in February 1864 and was **brevetted** brigadier general of regulars in 1865.

Slemmer was mustered out of the volunteers in August 1865, but he
remained in the regular **army**. After serving in various administrative
positions, he was put in command of Fort Laramie, Dakota Territory
(Wyoming), in 1867 and died there the following year.

SLIDELL, JOHN (1793–1871) CSA. A native of **New York**, Slidell graduated from Columbia College in 1810 and became a lawyer and businessman. After his mercantile business failed during the War of 1812 and
he was involved in a rather scandalous duel over a woman, he moved to
Louisiana in 1819. There, Slidell established a successful law practice

and became involved in **Democratic** politics. He served as a federal attorney and was elected to the state legislature in 1838 after failing to win a U.S. Senate seat. Slidell was elected to the **U.S. Congress** in 1843 and helped carry Louisiana for James K. Polk in the 1844 presidential election. In 1845, Polk sent him to Mexico on an unsuccessful mission to negotiate peacefully the issues that were drawing the two countries toward war. Slidell reached the pinnacle of his antebellum influence in 1853 when he was appointed to the U.S. Senate. During the turbulent 1850s, he was a moderate and became a strong influence on President **James Buchanan**. As the nation began to polarize over the spread of **slavery**, however, many moderates were forced to choose sides, and Slidell finally joined the Southern **"fire-eaters."**

Slidell supported **John C. Breckinridge** in the **election of 1860**, and when **Abraham Lincoln** won, he resigned his senate seat and returned to Louisiana. In 1861, he accepted the position of Confederate minister to France and sailed for Europe with **James Mason**. Their capture by the **U.S. Navy** in the November 1861 *Trent* **Affair** caused a diplomatic crisis between the United States and Great Britain, but the pair finally was released and continued their mission.

In France, Slidell was a popular figure, but he had little success in gaining support for the Confederacy since Napoleon III tended to follow Great Britain's lead. His attempt to secure **commerce raiders** also proved unsuccessful when the few ships he managed to obtain were detained in port because of Union pressure on the French government. Slidell did arrange the **Erlanger Loan** by using Confederate cotton as collateral, but it failed to provide any significant funds for the Confederacy.

When the war ended, a bitter Slidell refused to ask for a pardon or return to the United States and remained in Europe until his death.

SLOCUM, HENRY WARNER (1827–1894) USA. A native of **New York**, Slocum attended Cazenovia Seminary and taught school before entering **West Point** in 1848 (and becoming **Philip Sheridan's** roommate). After graduating in 1852, he was assigned to the **artillery** and served in the **Seminole Wars** and on garrison duty before resigning his 2nd lieutenant's commission in 1856. Returning to New York, Slocum became a lawyer, served as county treasurer and in the state legislature, and was appointed colonel in the state militia.

Slocum entered Union service in May 1861 when he was appointed colonel of the 27th New York. He fought at **First Manassas** in **Andrew Porter's brigade** and was wounded in the thigh. Slocum was promoted to brigadier general of volunteers in August 1861 and in October was given a brigade command in **William B. Franklin's division** of the **Army of the Potomac**. After fighting in the **Peninsula Campaign**, he was given command of Franklin's division in May 1862 when that officer was promoted to command the VI Corps. Slocum performed well during the **Seven Days Campaign** and earned a promotion to major general of volunteers in July, at the time becoming the second youngest major general in the Union **army**.

Slocum's division fought well at **Second Manassas**, where it helped cover the army's retreat and saw combat at **South Mountain** and **Antietam**. In October 1862, he was given command of the XII Corps but missed **Fredericksburg**. At **Chancellorsville**, Slocum played a major role while commanding three **corps** early in the battle and losing nearly 3,000 men in his own corps. Afterward, he was one of the officers who highly criticized **Joseph Hooker's** generalship. At **Gettysburg**, Slocum commanded the army's right wing, and his corps successfully defended Culp's Hill.

Following the Union defeat at **Chickamauga** in September 1863, the Army of the Potomac's XI and XII Corps were placed under Hooker's command and were sent to reinforce the besieged Union **Army of the Cumberland** at **Chattanooga, Tennessee**. Slocum tendered his resignation rather than serve under Hooker, but the resignation was refused. Instead, it was agreed that Slocum would command one of Hooker's divisions and protect the **railroad** in **Tennessee**, while Hooker went to Chattanooga. In April 1864, Slocum was placed in command of the District of **Vicksburg**. When Hooker resigned command of the XX Corps in a dispute over rank, Slocum was placed at its head in August and led it for the remainder of the **Atlanta Campaign**. After the city's capture, he served as Atlanta's military governor and then commanded the army's left wing during the **March to the Sea**. Slocum continued leading the left wing, which came to be known as the **Army of Georgia**, during the **Carolinas Campaign** and fought at **Averasboro** and **Bentonville**.

Slocum resigned his commission in September 1865 and returned to New York, where he practiced law and turned down a colonel's commission in the regular army. He served on the Gettysburg Monument Commission, was a **Democratic** presidential elector in 1868, and served in the **U.S. Congress** from 1869 to 1873 and from 1883 to 1885, where he supported **Fitz John Porter's** bid to reverse his court-martial conviction.

SLOUGH, JOHN POTTS (1829–1867) USA. A native of **Ohio**, Slough (SLOW) entered **Democratic** politics at an early age and was elected to the state legislature when he was 21. Later that year, however, a fistfight with a fellow legislator over a political issue resulted in his expulsion. Two years later, Slough was appointed secretary of the state's Democratic committee, but he left that position to migrate to **Kansas** and later to **Colorado**.

Slough entered Union service in May 1861 as captain of a **company** he raised for the 1st Colorado. There initially was some question as to his loyalty because of his strong Democratic background, but in August he was appointed regimental colonel. Slough trained his **regiment** well before it joined **Edward R. S. Canby's** command in **New Mexico**. There he blunted **Henry H. Sibley's New Mexico Campaign** when he disobeyed Canby's orders and attacked and defeated the Confederates at **Glorieta Pass** in March 1862. Afterward, he was briefly given a **brigade** command in the **Army of Virginia** in the **Shenandoah Valley**. Appointed brigadier general of volunteers in August 1862, Slough served the rest of the war as military governor of Alexandria, Virginia, and was a member of the court-martial that convicted **Fitz John Porter**.

After being mustered out of the service in August 1865, Slough was appointed chief justice for the New Mexico Territory. However, as had happened before in his political career, the hot-tempered Slough proved difficult to work with, and the legislature attempted to remove him. After one legislator introduced a resolution censuring him for unprofessional conduct, Slough was mortally wounded in an altercation the two had in a billiard hall.

SMALLEY, GEORGE WASHBURN (1833–1916) USA. A native of **Massachusetts**, Smalley graduated from Yale University in 1854 and then attended Harvard Law School. He became a leading Boston attorney and was a close associate of fellow **abolitionists William Lloyd Garrison** and **Wendell Phillips** (whose adopted daughter he married). When the Civil War began, Smalley's poor eyesight made him ineligible for military service.

Through Phillips, Smalley became known to **New York *Tribune*** editor Sydney Howard Gray and was hired as a **war correspondent** in late 1861. Taking advantage of Smalley's abolitionism, Gray first had him report on the lifestyle of blacks in newly captured **Port Royal, South Carolina**. Afterward, Smalley joined **John C. Frémont's** army in the **Shenandoah Valley** and accompanied it during **Stonewall Jackson's 1862 Shenandoah Valley Campaign**. When Smalley blamed Maj. Gen. **James Shields** for the Union defeat at **Port Republic**, Shields and his supporters began to attack him in the press. Joining the **Army of the**

Potomac, Smalley next rode with **George B. McClellan** to watch the **Battle of South Mountain** and served as **Joseph Hooker's** volunteer aide at **Antietam**. In the thick of the fighting at Antietam, he was with Hooker when the general was wounded, and afterward provided the first news accounts of the battle. Smalley's initial story was delayed on the wires, so he caught a train to **New York** and submitted a more detailed story to his home office. For his outstanding reporting of Antietam, Smalley was rewarded with an editor's position at the *Tribune*. For the most part, he remained in New York for the rest of the war but did visit the **army** after **Chancellorsville** and wrote a scathing article about its poor condition. The authorities, however, refused to let it be printed. During the **New York City Draft Riot** in July 1863, Smalley had to arm some of his employees and guard the paper's office from rioters.

Smalley remained with the *Tribune* after the war. He covered the Austro-Prussian War of 1866, opened the paper's London bureau, helped cover the 1870 Franco-Prussian War, and served as the *Tribune's* European bureau chief until 1895. At that time, Smalley was hired by the London *Times* to be its American correspondent, and he divided his time between New York and London until retiring in 1905.

SMITH, ANDREW JACKSON (1815–1897) USA. A native of **Pennsylvania**, Smith graduated from **West Point** in 1838 and was assigned to the dragoons. He served at numerous frontier outposts and in the **Mexican War** and had attained the rank of captain by the time the Civil War began.

Smith was serving in **California** in 1861 and was promoted to major in May. In October, he was appointed colonel of the 2nd California Cavalry, but he resigned a month later to become Maj. Gen. **Henry W. Halleck's** chief of cavalry. Smith served Halleck during the **siege of Corinth, Mississippi**, and in March 1862 was promoted to brigadier general of volunteers. In October 1862, Smith was given a **division** command in the **Army of Kentucky**, but the following month he was transferred to a division command in the **Army of the Tennessee's** XIII Corps. He led this division at **Chickasaw Bayou, Arkansas Post**, and in the **Vicksburg Campaign** and earned a reputation for being one of the Union's most dependable commanders. In the spring of 1864, Smith was given command of elements of the XVI and XVII Corps and was lent to **Nathaniel P. Banks** for the **Red River Campaign**. His self-proclaimed "Smith's Gorillas" captured **Fort De Russy** and fought hard at **Pleasant Hill** (for which Smith received a **brevet**), but the men tarnished their reputation by engaging in widespread vandalism and perhaps burning Alexandria, Louisiana.

Smith was promoted to major general of volunteers in May 1864 and returned to **Mississippi**. There he won acclaim, and a regular army brevet of brigadier general, by defeating **Stephen D. Lee** at **Tupelo** in July. After service in **Missouri**, Smith brought his wing of the XVI Corps back to **Tennessee** and joined **George H. Thomas** for the **Battle of Nashville** in December. In February 1865, he was given command of the **corps** and was sent to the **Department of the Gulf**, where he participated in the **Mobile Campaign**. During the war, Smith was promoted to lieutenant colonel of regulars, and at war's end was brevetted major general of regulars.

Remaining in the regular **army** after the war, Smith was appointed colonel of the 7th U.S. Cavalry in 1866. He resigned his commission in 1869 to accept the position of postmaster of St. Louis, Missouri. Smith also served as the city's auditor from 1877 to 1889 and led a brigade of state militia during the railroad strike of 1877.

SMITH, CALEB BLOOD (1808–1864) USA. A native of **Massachusetts**, as a boy, Smith moved to **Ohio** with his family. After attending Cincinnati College and Miami University, he established an **Indiana** law practice in 1828 and founded a **Whig** newspaper in 1832. Entering politics, Smith was elected to the state legislature in 1833 and to the **U.S. Congress** in 1843. After serving in Congress for seven years, he resumed his law practice and became a **railroad** manager.

Having become a **Republican**, Smith was a powerful member of the state's delegation at the 1860 National Convention. There, **Abraham Lincoln's** campaign manager, David Davis, promised him a cabinet position in return for his support of Lincoln. Although Lincoln was not aware of the promise, he honored it, and appointed Smith secretary of the interior in early 1861. He did not play a major role in the government but did irritate Lincoln by appointing his son to a position within his own department and for being rather blatantly self-serving in his patronage. Smith also seemed to be on the wrong side of most major issues, advising against resupplying **Fort Sumter**, lobbying for the dismissal of **George B. McClellan**, and supporting **John Pope** before the disaster at **Second Manassas**.

In December 1862, Smith resigned his cabinet position because of poor health but then accepted a federal judgeship in Indiana. He died in 1864 while holding that position.

SMITH, CHARLES FERGUSON (1807–1862) USA. A native of **Pennsylvania**, Smith graduated from **West Point** in 1825. After routine duty, he returned to the academy in 1829 and for the next 13 years held various positions there, including commandant. During the **Mexican War**, Smith fought under both Zachary Taylor and **Winfield Scott** and won three **brevets** for gallantry. After the war, he served on the frontier exploring northern Idaho and participated in the **Utah Expedition**. During this time, Smith rose to the rank of lieutenant colonel.

When the **secession** crisis began in late 1860, Smith was commanding the **Department of Utah**. He later briefly commanded the **Department of Washington** in April 1861 before being brought back to **Washington, D.C.** There Smith's outspokenness earned him the enmity of some politicians, and he was sent to recruit in **New York** until **John C. Frémont** used his influence to secure him a promotion to brigadier general of volunteers in August. Smith joined Frémont and in September was promoted to colonel in the regular **army**. He commanded the District of Western Kentucky from September 1861 to January 1862. In February, Smith was given a **division** command and accompanied his former pupil **U. S. Grant** on the expedition to **Forts Henry and Donelson**. Grant had revered Smith at West Point and at times found it difficult to issue orders to his former professor. At Fort Donelson, Smith won Grant's further admiration by personally leading an attack that penetrated the Confederates' defenses and forced them to surrender. It also was Smith who suggested to Grant that he demand unconditional surrender of the forts.

In March 1862, Smith was promoted to major general of volunteers. Because of Maj. Gen. **Henry W. Halleck's** jealousy of Grant, Smith was given command of the Union troops that advanced up the Tennessee River to Pittsburg Landing after the capture of Fort Donelson. When jumping into a boat, however, Smith badly scraped his shin and had to relinquish command to Grant when infection set in. Smith was bedridden during the **Battle of Shiloh** and died shortly afterward.

SMITH, EDMUND KIRBY (1824–1893) CSA. *See* KIRBY SMITH, EDMUND.

SMITH, GILES ALEXANDER (1829–1876) USA. A native of **New York**, Smith was the brother of Union general **Morgan L. Smith**. He moved to **Ohio** as a young man and lived there for 10 years before settling in **Illinois** and buying a hotel.

Smith entered Union service in June 1861 as a captain in his brother's 8th Missouri (Union). He fought well at **Fort Donelson** and **Shiloh** and participated in the **siege of Corinth, Mississippi**. Smith replaced his brother as colonel of the **regiment** in June 1862. Beginning in November, he commanded various **brigades** that saw combat at **Chickasaw Bayou**, **Arkansas Post**, and in the **Vicksburg Campaign**. In the latter campaign, his brigade was in the 2nd Division of **William T. Sherman's** XV Corps of the **Army of the Tennessee**. During the **Steele's Bayou Expedition**, Smith played a prominent role in rescuing the trapped Union gunboats. After participating in the siege of **Jackson, Mississippi**, he was promoted to brigadier general in August 1863. Smith accompanied the **corps** to reinforce **Chattanooga, Tennessee**, that autumn and was badly wounded **Missionary Ridge**.

During the **Atlanta Campaign**, Smith was put in command of a XVII Corps **division** in July 1864 and helped repulse the Confederate attacks on **James B. McPherson's** left wing at the **Battle of Atlanta**. For his role in the campaign, he was **brevetted** major general of volunteers in September. Smith led his division through the **March to the Sea** and the **Carolinas Campaign** and was promoted to major general of volunteers in November 1865. Based on the date from which his commission was effective, he was the last-appointed major general of volunteers of the Civil War era. Smith ended his military career in command of the XXV Corps, a unit of **black troops**, on the Texas-Mexico border.

Smith was mustered out of the volunteer service in 1866 and returned to Illinois. He served as a postmaster from 1869 to 1872 and then moved to **California** in 1874 to restore his failing health. Unsuccessful, Smith returned to Illinois in 1876 and died two months later.

SMITH, GREEN CLAY (1826–1895) USA. A native of **Kentucky**, Smith was the nephew of Union general **Cassius M. Clay** and the son of a congressman. After graduating from Transylvania University, he served in the **Mexican War** as a 2nd lieutenant in the 1st Kentucky and after the war graduated from Lexington Law School. Smith was a member of his father's law practice for a while but soon moved away and began his own political career. As a **Republican** member of the state legislature in 1860, he was a staunch Unionist.

Smith reportedly first entered Union service as a private, but in March 1862, he was appointed colonel of the 4th Kentucky Cavalry (Union). In May, he helped defeat Confederate raider **John Hunt Morgan** and was promoted to brigadier general of volunteers in June. In October, Smith was put in command of the **Army of Kentucky's** 2nd Division, but later in the month, he was reduced to a **brigade** command. Despite his impressive early service, he disappointed his superiors, and they wished to rid themselves of him. Smith was removed from his brigade command in January 1863 and does not seem to have held another position. Having been elected to the **U.S. Congress**, he resigned his commission in December 1863 to accept his seat. Although his military career was less than notable, Smith was **brevetted** major general of volunteers for his service.

Smith served in Congress until 1866, at which time he resigned to become Montana's territorial governor. In 1869, he became an ordained Baptist minister and moved back to Kentucky to pastor a church. Smith became active in the temperance movement and was the National Prohibition Party's presidential candidate in 1876.

SMITH, GUSTAVUS ADOLPHUS (1820–1885) USA. A native of **Pennsylvania**, Smith settled in **Illinois** in 1837 after living for a time in **Maryland** and **Ohio**. There he established a very lucrative carriage manufacturing business.

Smith first entered Union service as a drillmaster, but in September 1861, he was appointed colonel of the 35th Illinois. In his first battle at **Pea Ridge**, he was caught in a hail of bullets. In moments, Smith's horse was shot from under him, his sword was struck while in his hand, his belt was shot from his waist, he received a bullet wound to the right shoulder, and he was hit on the head by a shell fragment that fractured his skull. Believed to be mortally wounded, Smith was taken from the field, but he survived (although he did not fully recover until 1868).

Although not fully recovered from his wounds, Smith was authorized to raise a **brigade** in July 1862 and was appointed brigadier general of volunteers in September. His wounds, however, prevented him from taking the field, so the Senate did not confirm his appointment. Smith returned to his position as colonel of the 35th Illinois and was dismissed from the service in September 1863 for having practiced unlawful recruiting practices. He reentered the **army** in February 1863 as colonel of the 155th Illinois and served on **railroad** guard duty in **Tennessee** until war's end.

After being **brevetted** brigadier general of volunteers, Smith was mustered out of the service in December 1865. He lived for a while in **Alabama** and then was appointed internal revenue collector for **New Mexico** in 1870. Smith also was very active in the Odd Fellows lodge.

SMITH, GUSTAVUS WOODSON (1821–1896) CSA. A native of **Kentucky**, Smith graduated from **West Point** in 1842 and was assigned to the **engineers**. He taught at the academy and worked on various construction projects before entering the **Mexican War**, where he won three **brevets** for gallantry. After the war, Smith returned to teach at West Point but resigned his 1st lieutenant's commission in 1854 to become a civil engineer in **Louisiana** and **New York**. When the Civil War began, Smith was New York City's street commissioner, with his close friend **Mansfield Lovell** serving as his assistant.

A loyal **Democrat**, Smith hoped armed conflict between the sections would be avoided, and his acquaintances were unsure which side he would support. He was highly regarded by officials on both sides and each wanted his services. When Smith finally decided to support the Confederacy, he and Lovell left New York and made their way south amidst much publicity. In September 1861, Smith was appointed major general in the **Confederate army** and was given command of a **division** in **Virginia** under **Joseph E. Johnston**. There, Smith became a strong supporter of **P. G. T. Beauregard**, Johnston's second in command, and united with the general to dominate Johnston. When Beauregard was sent west after **First Manassas**, Smith became Johnston's second in command by virtue of seniority.

During the **Peninsula Campaign**, Smith commanded one wing of Johnston's **army**, but he failed to live up to his vaunted reputation. His performance on the field was weak, and he frequently was absent sick at crucial moments, leading some officers to believe he was reluctant to make command decisions or take responsibility. Smith's performance at **Seven Pines** was disappointing, but he replaced Johnston at the head of the army after Johnston was wounded. The following day, **Jefferson Davis** found Smith in a near state of physical and mental collapse and replaced him with **Robert E. Lee**. Davis apparently concluded that Smith's reputation was undeserved and never again placed him in a field position of importance. In September 1862, he was put in command of the **Department of North Carolina and Southern Virginia**, and Davis named him interim secretary of war for a few days in November 1862 after **George W. Randolph** resigned. In February 1863, Smith resigned his commission in protest of less senior officers being promoted over him. He went to **Georgia** and in 1864 was appointed major general of state troops. There he served competently as a division commander during the **Atlanta Campaign** and the **March to the Sea** before surrendering his command at Macon, Georgia, in April 1865.

After the war, Smith resumed engineering, operated a **Tennessee** iron foundry, and served as Kentucky's state insurance commissioner. He finally returned to New York City, where he published a number of articles and books on the war and continued a diatribe against Davis and Johnston that was begun during the war.

SMITH, JAMES ARGYLE (1831–1901) CSA. A native of **Tennessee**, Smith graduated near the bottom of his 1853 **West Point** class. Assigned to the infantry, he was posted at various Western forts, fought **Indians**, and served in **"Bleeding Kansas"** and the **Utah Expedition**. When the **secession** crisis began in December 1860, Smith was away from the **U.S. Army** on extended leave.

Smith resigned his 1st lieutenant's commission in May 1861 and entered Confederate service as a lieutenant of infantry. He soon rose to the rank of captain and joined **Leonidas Polk's** staff. In March 1862, Smith was promoted to major and was made Polk's assistant adjutant general, but almost immediately, he was appointed lieutenant colonel of the 2nd Tennessee. After seeing heavy combat at **Shiloh**, the **regiment** was converted into a four-company battalion, with Smith serving as commander. In July, the battalion was consolidated with another **regiment** to form the 5th Confederate, and Smith was appointed its colonel. As part of **Bushrod R. Johnson's brigade**, the regiment participated in the **Kentucky Campaign**, where it helped capture Fort Dunham at **Munfordville** and performed well at **Perryville**. Just prior to **Stones River**, Smith's regiment was transferred to **Lucius E. Polk's** brigade in **Patrick Cleburne's division** of the **Army of Tennessee**. At Stones River, Smith was commended for helping rout the enemy and capturing four cannons.

In the spring of 1863, Smith's regiment was consolidated with the 3rd Confederate, but Smith remained in command. His leadership during heavy fighting at **Chickamauga** won him a promotion to brigadier general in October. Assigned to command the late **James Deshler's** Texas brigade, Smith helped Cleburne defend **Missionary Ridge** during the **Chattanooga Campaign**, and his brigade captured many **prisoners** and four **flags**. When he finally was ordered to retreat, he was severely wounded by a bullet through both thighs. Smith returned to his brigade in July 1864, and at the **Battle of Atlanta,** he led it in an attack that captured an enemy brigade commander, 15 cannons, two flags, and hundreds of prisoners. A counterattack drove him back, however, and he again was severely wounded. When Smith returned to the **army** in November, he was given command of **Hugh W. Mercer's** former brigade in Cleburne's division. He guarded the army's wagon train during the **Battle of Franklin** but took command of the division (after Cleburne's death) when he reached Nashville in early December. At **Nashville**, Smith's division held its ground the first day but was routed on the second. After retreating from Tennessee, the division joined **Joseph E. Johnston's** command for the **Carolinas Campaign**. Smith fought his last battle at **Bentonville** before surrendering his men at Greensboro, North Carolina, a few days after Johnston's **surrender**.

After the war, Smith became a **Mississippi** farmer and served as the state's superintendent of instruction from 1877 to 1886.

SMITH, JAMES YOUNGS (1809–1876) USA. A native of **Connecticut**, Smith worked as a store clerk before opening his own **Rhode Island** lumber business. He became a wealthy man and expanded his interests into cotton milling and manufacturing. Politically active, Smith became head of the state's **Republican Party**, was elected mayor of Providence in 1855, and served in the state legislature.

After losing a gubernatorial bid in 1861, Smith won the seat in 1863. As Rhode Island's war governor, he became controversial with **War Democrats** because he opposed **conscription** and used agents and a **bounty** system to raise recruits. Despite some political opposition, Smith remained popular with the voters (largely because of his opposition to the draft) and won reelection in 1864 and 1865. Although an investigation cleared him of any wrongdoing in recruiting practices, he declined to run for reelection in 1866. After leaving office, Smith retired from politics, returned to his business interests, and became active in education and charities.

SMITH, JOHN EUGENE (1816–1897) USA. A native of Switzerland, Smith was the son of a Napoleonic officer who fought at Waterloo. He immigrated to **Pennsylvania** with his family as a child and became a jeweler and goldsmith. After living in **Missouri** for a while, Smith finally settled in **Illinois** in 1836. There he became a somewhat prominent citizen and in 1860 was elected county treasurer.

When the Civil War began, Smith recommended his fellow townsman **U. S. Grant** to the governor for a military position and thus shares some of the credit for making the war's leading general. Smith then served on Gov. **Richard Yates's** staff for a time before raising the 45th Illinois and becoming its colonel in July 1861. He fought at **Fort Donelson** and **Shiloh** and served in the **siege of Corinth, Mississippi**, before being promoted to brigadier general of volunteers in November 1862.

Over the next several months, Smith held **brigade** commands in the **Army of the Tennessee's** XIII and XVI Corps before being assigned a brigade in **James B. McPherson's** XVII Corps in April 1863. He fought in the **Vicksburg Campaign** and in June took command of the **division** during the siege. After the fall of **Vicksburg**, Smith served in the **Chattanooga Campaign** and led the division at **Missionary Ridge**.

In December 1863, he was given a division command in the XV Corps. It guarded the rear area during the **Atlanta Campaign** but did participate in the **March to the Sea**. After playing a major role in the capture of **Savannah, Georgia**, Smith went on to participate in the **Carolinas Campaign**. For his war service, he was **brevetted** major general of volunteers and in late 1865 was placed in command of the District of Western Tennessee.

Smith was mustered out of the volunteers in April 1866, but he returned to the regular **army** in July as colonel of the 27th U.S. Infantry. He was brevetted brigadier general and major general of regulars, and before his retirement in 1881, served at several frontier outposts during the **Indian** uprisings.

SMITH, MARTIN LUTHER (1819–1866) CSA. A native of **New York**, Smith graduated from **West Point** in 1842 and was assigned to the **engineers**. After routine duty in the South, he served in the **Mexican War** and was awarded one **brevet** for his service in the months after the war. After supervising the construction of a drainage system for Mexico City, Smith returned to routine engineering duty in the South and served as chief engineer for a **Florida railroad** from 1856 to 1861.

Married to a Southern woman, Smith supported the South and resigned his captain's commission in April 1861, two weeks after being appointed a Confederate major of engineers. Sent to **New Orleans, Louisiana**, he supervised the construction of the city's defenses and became **Mansfield Lovell's** chief engineer and ordnance officer. Lovell frequently recommended Smith's promotion, but there were no higher engineer ranks available. Thus in February 1862, Lovell secured his appointment as colonel of the 22nd Louisiana (not the 21st as is sometimes reported). Promotion to brigadier general followed in April.

Lovell retained Smith as his chief engineer and put him in command of New Orleans's inner defenses. When the **U.S. Navy** approached the city in late April 1862, Smith briefly battled **David G. Farragut's** gunboats from batteries below New Orleans. After the city was evacuated, he took command of **Vicksburg, Mississippi**, in May and began strengthening defenses there. Smith also supervised the batteries' fire against the Union gunboats that attacked the city in May–July. Remaining in Vicksburg under the command of **John C. Pemberton**, Smith was promoted to major general in November and was highly praised in December when his men repulsed the enemy at **Chickasaw Bayou**. In April 1863, he was given command of one of Pemberton's **divisions** and the following month also was made Pemberton's chief engineer. Smith carried out these dual duties throughout the **Vicksburg Campaign**, defending the **army's** left flank during the siege, and was captured when the city fell on July 4, 1863.

Smith was **paroled** after his capture but was not **exchanged** until February 1864. In March, he was appointed chief of the Engineer Bureau in **Richmond, Virginia**, but the following month was made chief engineer for the **Army of Northern Virginia**. At the **Wilderness**, it was Smith who first discovered the abandoned **railroad** grade on the Confederate right that allowed **James Longstreet** to make his devastating flank attack on the second day of battle. After pushing back the enemy, Smith found another way to flank them and was given command of three **brigades** to carry out the attack.

Smith remained with the Army of Northern Virginia until July 1864, when he was transferred to **Georgia** to become chief engineer for **John Bell Hood's Army of Tennessee**. He served Hood during the remainder of the **Atlanta Campaign** and in October became **P. G. T. Beauregard's** chief engineer for the **Military Division of the West**. The following month, Smith was assigned to **Dabney H. Maury** at Mobile, Alabama, and became his acting chief engineer. He served in that capacity until January 1865 and constructed the formidable defenses at **Spanish Fort** and **Fort Blakely**. Even after returning to Beauregard that January, Smith occasionally traveled to Mobile to inspect the defenses. He was paroled in May at Athens, Georgia.

After the war, Smith worked as a civil engineer in Georgia.

SMITH, MORGAN LEWIS (1821–1874) USA. A native of **New York**, Smith was the brother of Union general **Giles A. Smith**. His antebellum career was a varied one, working as a schoolteacher and serving five years in the **U.S. Army** under an assumed name before becoming a river boatman in 1850.

When the Civil War began, Smith recruited the 8th Missouri (Union) from among the St. Louis boatmen and was appointed its colonel in July 1861. In February 1862, he was placed in command of a small two-regiment **brigade** in **Charles F. Smith's division** and led it at **Fort Donelson**. Later that month, Smith became a brigade commander in **Lew Wallace's** division and led it through fierce fighting on the second day at **Shiloh** and in the **siege of Corinth, Mississippi**.

Promoted to brigadier general in July 1862, Smith led his brigade until November, when he was put in command of a XIII Corps division. He was badly wounded at **Chickasaw Bayou** the following month and was unable to return to duty until October 1863. At that time, Smith took command of a XV Corps division in the **Army of the Tennessee** and led it in the **Chattanooga** and **Atlanta Campaigns**. When **John A. Logan** assumed command of the **army** in July 1864 after **James B. McPherson's** death, Smith was elevated to **corps** command. This position lasted only a few days, however, because he was soon incapacitated by his old wound. When Smith returned to duty in September, he was put in command of **Vicksburg, Mississippi**, and held that position until war's end.

After resigning his commission in July 1865, Smith was appointed U.S. consul to Hawaii. He held that position until removed when **U. S. Grant** became president in 1869 and then became a businessman in **Washington, D.C.**

SMITH, PRESTON (1823–1863) CSA. A native of **Tennessee**, Smith graduated from Jackson College and became a prominent lawyer. He entered Confederate service in May 1861 as colonel of the 154th Tennessee Senior Regiment (made up of militia **companies**, the **regiment** was designated "Senior" to show its seniority over other regiments). Under **Leonidas Polk**, the regiment was sent to Columbus, Kentucky, where it became part of **Benjamin F. Cheatham's brigade**. Smith impressed his superiors, and in October became one Cheatham's brigade commanders when Cheatham was given a **division**. His first battle was **Belmont**, where he sent reinforcements across the Mississippi River before taking his own brigade across and engaging the enemy. After the battle, Smith was displaced as brigade commander by the arrival of the more senior **Bushrod R. Johnson**. At **Shiloh**, Johnson was wounded on the first day, and Smith resumed command of the brigade. He, too, was wounded on the second day but earned Cheatham's commendation.

After temporarily leading a brigade through much of the **siege of Corinth, Mississippi**, Smith was given his own brigade in July 1862. That summer, the brigade was sent with another to join **Edmund Kirby Smith** at Knoxville, Tennessee. Assigned to **Patrick Cleburne's** division, Smith won the **Thanks of Congress** at **Richmond, Kentucky**, when he assumed command and won the battle after Cleburne was wounded. He remained in command of the division until Cleburne returned in September. Following the **Kentucky Campaign**, Smith's brigade returned to Cheatham, and Smith was promoted to brigadier general in October 1862. Illness forced him from the field in November, but when he learned that the **Battle of Stones River** was raging, he left his sickbed, reached the battlefield by train on the last day of fighting, and assumed command of the brigade shortly after the fighting ended. After guarding Rossville Gap and the Chattanooga Valley in early September 1863, Smith rejoined the **Army of Tennessee** for **Chickamauga**. On the night of September 19, his brigade supported a night attack made by Cleburne's division. When the attack stalled, Smith brought his brigade to the front, but he mistakenly rode into the Union line in the dark and was mortally wounded. Although removed from the field, he died within an hour.

SMITH, THOMAS BENTON (1838–1923) CSA. A native of **Tennessee**, Smith worked for a **railroad** after graduating from the Nashville Military Institute. He entered Confederate service in June 1861 as a 2nd lieutenant in the 20th Tennessee but soon was promoted to captain. The **regiment** became part of **Felix Zollicoffer's** command and fought with him at **Mill Springs**. After seeing heavy fighting at **Shiloh**, the regiment was reorganized in May 1862, and Smith was elected its colonel.

In August 1862, Smith was given temporary command of one of **John C. Breckinridge's brigades** and at **Baton Rouge** assumed command of the **division** when the commander was wounded and captured. Breckinridge commended Smith for his actions, but after the battle, Smith resumed his regimental command. Sent back to Tennessee, the regiment became part of **William Preston's** brigade in Breckinridge's **Army of Tennessee** division. At **Stones River**, it saw heavy fighting, and Smith was severely wounded. When he rejoined the **army** in January 1863, he temporarily commanded the brigade for a time. Transferred to **William Bate's** brigade of **Alexander P. Stewart's** division in June, Smith saw combat in the **Tullahoma Campaign** at **Hoover's Gap** and was severely wounded while attacking the enemy at **Chickamauga**.

When he rejoined the army after the **Chattanooga Campaign**, Smith assumed command of Bate's brigade, which now was back in Breckinridge's (later Bate's) division. He led the brigade through the **Atlanta Campaign** and performed so well that he was promoted to brigadier general in July. During the **Franklin and Nashville Campaign**, Smith fought at Franklin and then at Murfreesboro in early December. Rejoining the army for the Battle of Nashville, he was overwhelmed on the second day and was captured by Col. William L. McMillen's Union brigade. While being escorted to the rear, Smith repeatedly was struck on the head by the saber-wielding McMillen (who apparently was enraged by the determined stand made by Smith's brigade) and was nearly killed. Although his skull was fractured and his brain exposed, Smith survived and was sent to **Fort Warren, Massachusetts**. The injury affected him permanently, and afterward he was described by one fellow **prisoner** as acting slow-witted.

After being released from **prison**, Smith returned to Tennessee and worked as a railroad conductor. He unsuccessfully ran for the **U.S. Congress** in 1870 and in 1876 was committed to the Tennessee State Hospital for the Insane (no doubt because of his wound), where he remained for the next 47 years.

SMITH, THOMAS CHURCH HASKELL (1819–1897) USA. A native of **Massachusetts**, Smith graduated second in his class from Harvard University in 1841. He then moved to **Ohio** to begin a law practice and later helped connect the North and South by **telegraph**.

Smith entered Union service in September 1861 as lieutenant colonel of the 1st Ohio Cavalry. He joined **John Pope's** staff in the spring of 1862 and participated in the **siege of Corinth, Mississippi**, before being appointed Pope's aide-de-camp in July. Smith accompanied Pope to **Virginia** when the general took command of the **Army of Virginia** and served under him during the **Second Manassas Campaign**. After the campaign, he was a key witness against **Fitz John Porter** in his celebrated court-martial. Although much of Smith's testimony was inaccurate, he was rewarded by being promoted to brigadier general of volunteers in March 1863. Smith accompanied Pope to **Minnesota** and in 1863 took command of the District of Wisconsin, where he had to suppress draft riots. He followed Pope to the **Department of the Missouri** at war's end and served as his inspector general before being mustered out of service in January 1866.

After leaving the **army**, Smith raised livestock in **Missouri**, but the 1871 Chicago Fire ruined him financially. He then accepted a government position in the Treasury Department and from 1878 to 1883 served as an army paymaster with the rank of major.

SMITH, THOMAS KILBY (1820–1887) USA. A native of **Massachusetts**, Smith moved to **Ohio** as a boy. After graduating from Cincinnati College in 1837, he began a law career by studying under **Salmon P. Chase**. During the antebellum period, Smith also worked as a Post Office Department clerk in **Washington, D.C.**, and as a U.S. marshal in Ohio.

Smith entered Union service in September 1861 as lieutenant colonel of the 54th Ohio and the following month was promoted to colonel. He fought at **Shiloh** in **David Stuart's** brigade of **William T. Sherman's division** and assumed **brigade** command when Stuart was wounded on the first day of battle. Smith remained in brigade command during part of the **siege of Corinth, Mississippi**. In December 1862, he again led a brigade in Sherman's failed attack at **Chickasaw Bayou** and afterward in the capture of **Arkansas Post**. Smith led a brigade in Sherman's **Army of the Tennessee** XV Corps early in the **Vicksburg Campaign**, but in May 1863, he became Maj. Gen. **U. S. Grant's** aide.

Smith served Grant until after **Vicksburg** fell. Then in August 1863, he was promoted to brigadier general of volunteers and was given a brigade in the XVII Corps. When a "Provisional Division" was detached from the **corps** to participate in the 1864 **Red River Campaign**, Smith was chosen to lead it. Ordered to defend **David D. Porter's** gunboats, he performed his duties well. After the failed campaign, Smith was sent with the remnants of his command to **Tennessee**, where he pursued Confederate raider **Nathan Bedford Forrest**. After illness forced him to give up his command late in the war, Smith was **brevetted** major general of volunteers for his service.

Smith was mustered out of the service in January 1866 and briefly served as the U.S. consul to Panama. He lived in **Pennsylvania** before moving to **New York** and joining the business staff of the New York *Star*.

SMITH, WILLIAM "EXTRA BILLY"(1797–1887) CSA. A native of **Virginia**, Smith was educated at local schools and at **Connecticut's** Plainfield Academy. He became a lawyer but began an interstate overland mail business in 1827 and shrewdly won government mail contracts. Smith's ability to earn extra bonuses gained him the famous nickname of "Extra Billy." In 1836, he was elected to the first of five state senate terms and from 1841 to 1843 served in the U.S. House of Representatives. After serving as a **Democratic** presidential elector in 1844, he was elected governor in 1846. While governor, Smith lost a race for the U.S. Senate, and when his term expired he moved to **California** to participate in the Gold Rush. He then returned to Virginia and served again in Congress from 1853 to 1861.

When the Civil War began, Smith organized the 49th Virginia and led a few of its **companies** with distinction at **First Manassas**. When he was commissioned the **regiment's** colonel in August 1861, he became one of the Confederacy's oldest commissioned officers. Despite being in the **army**, Smith also was elected to the **Confederate Congress** in November and served in it supporting **Jefferson Davis** when the army was inactive. He fought in the **Peninsula**, **Seven Days**, and **Second Manassas Campaigns** (receiving two wounds at **Seven Pines**), and temporarily led **Jubal A. Early's** brigade at **Antietam**, where he received three wounds. During these battles, Smith became one of the **Army of Northern Virginia's** most recognizable officers, as the old man wore a tall beaver hat to shield himself from the sun and carried a worn blue umbrella to ward off rain.

Smith was promoted to brigadier general in April 1863 after resigning from Congress earlier in the month. He took command of Early's **brigade** in the spring of 1863 and led it at **Gettysburg**. Smith was promoted to major general in August, but having been elected governor, he left the army to assume his new position in January 1864. Remaining a strong administration supporter, he stayed in office until war's end. During his tenure, Smith worked hard to recruit new soldiers and supported the recruitment of **black troops** near war's end. When **Richmond, Virginia**, fell in April 1865, he transferred the state government to Danville and finally surrendered in May.

After the war, Smith farmed before being elected to the state legislature in 1877 at the age of 80. He narrowly lost a bid for the U.S. Senate the following year.

SMITH, WILLIAM DUNCAN (1825–1862) CSA. A native of **Georgia**, Smith graduated from **West Point** in 1846 and was assigned to the dragoons. After being severely wounded in the **Mexican War**, he performed routine garrison duty and rose to the rank of captain. In 1859, Smith received leave from the **U.S. Army** and went to Europe, but he returned in January 1861 and resigned his commission.

Smith entered Confederate service in March 1861 as major of the 1st Georgia Regulars and in May became acting assistant adjutant general to Brig. Gen. **Alexander R. Lawton** in Georgia. In July, he was commissioned a captain of Confederate cavalry but was placed in command of a Georgia infantry battalion. Sent to **Virginia**, the battalion was expanded to become the 20th Georgia in August, and Smith was appointed its colonel.

After serving in **Jubal A. Early's brigade**, Smith was promoted to brigadier general in March 1862 and was put in command of a brigade under Lawton in the District of Georgia. He was sent to James Island at **Charleston, South Carolina**, in June to take command of all the troops defending it. After becoming commander of the 1st Military District of South Carolina in June, Smith fought a small, unsuccessful battle at Grimball's Landing after being ordered by **department** commander **John C. Pemberton** to establish a battery there. Smith apparently then became embroiled in an argument with Pemberton over the wisdom of such a move and briefly was placed under arrest. When Pemberton was replaced in command by **Nathan G. Evans** in June, Smith served as his second in command. At **Secessionville**, he apparently commanded the

Confederate right wing, but his actions there are unclear. At least one officer gave Smith, not Evans, credit for winning the fight. After the battle, he resumed command of the troops on the island and in July took command of the 1st Military District. While preparing defenses for the Stono and Folly Rivers, Smith contracted yellow fever and died in October 1862.

SMITH, WILLIAM "BALDY" FARRAR (1824–1903) USA. A native of **Vermont**, Smith graduated near the top of his 1845 **West Point** class. Because of his thinning hair, he was given the nickname "Baldy," which he kept throughout his career. Assigned to the **engineers**, Smith's antebellum career included various surveys, exploration expeditions, and time spent as an instructor at the academy.

When the Civil War began, Smith was a captain of engineers. He was appointed colonel of the 3rd Vermont in July 1861 but served at **First Manassas** a few days later as one of **Irvin McDowell's** staff officers. Smith was promoted to brigadier general of volunteers in August and was given command of a **brigade** and then a **division** in the **Army of the Potomac**. His division served first with the IV and then the VI Corps during the **Peninsula** and **Seven Days Campaigns**, and he earned a **brevet** for gallantry at **Frayser's Farm**. Smith remained with the VI Corps and led his division at **South Mountain** and **Antietam**, winning a promotion to major general of volunteers. In November 1862, he took command of the **corps** and led it at **Fredericksburg** but did not see heavy combat. Smith remained in command of the VI Corps until February 1863, when he took over the IX Corps.

After Fredericksburg, Smith became involved in **army** politics. A strong supporter of **George B. McClellan**, he joined **William B. Franklin** in writing a letter to **Abraham Lincoln** harshly criticizing the generalship of army commander **Ambrose Burnside** and promoting their own talents. The blatantly self-serving letter backfired, however, partly because of Smith's friendship with McClellan. Although Smith was put in command of the IX Corps in February 1863, the Senate refused to confirm his appointment to major general, and in March his rank reverted to brigadier general.

In June 1863, Smith was given the relatively unimportant duty of commanding a division of **Pennsylvania** militia during the **Gettysburg Campaign**. Later that summer, he was transferred west, where he was made the **Army of the Cumberland's** chief engineer. It largely was Smith who laid out the famous "Cracker Line," which brought a trickle of food to the starving garrison at Chattanooga, Tennessee. Smith's sagging military career was revived in October 1863 when his friend **U. S. Grant** was put in command of the **Military Division of the Mississippi**. Grant made Smith his chief engineer, and Smith served well in the successful attack against **Missionary Ridge** during the **Chattanooga Campaign**. In March 1864, the same month Grant was made general-in-chief, Smith was reappointed major general of volunteers and was sent back to **Virginia**, where, in May, he was given command of the **Army of the James's** XVIII Corps.

During the Union offensives against **Richmond, Virginia**, in the spring of 1864, Smith first served under **Benjamin F. Butler** in the **Bermuda Hundred Campaign**. In June, his corps was transferred to Grant, under whom he fought at **Cold Harbor**. When Smith returned to Butler, he performed poorly in the attack on **Petersburg** on June 15. He perhaps could have taken the city from the outnumbered Confederates and ended the war quickly, but he acted too cautiously, failed to press his advantage, and allowed **Robert E. Lee** time to arrive and reinforce the garrison. It is possible that Smith's lack of aggression at Petersburg was caused by weakness brought on by an attack of malaria.

Having incurred the ill will of the well-connected Butler, Smith was relieved in July 1864 and never again held a field command. He resigned his volunteer commission in November 1865 and his regular major's commission (to which he had been promoted during the war) in 1867. Smith was a talented engineer and mediocre field commander, but his friendship with McClellan and his short temper earned him many enemies. During the war, he feuded with Burnside over the Fredericksburg defeat, with **William B. Rosecrans** over credit for opening the "Cracker Line," with **George G. Meade** over Cold Harbor, and with Butler and **Winfield S. Hancock** over the failure at Petersburg. Despite all this, he still was **brevetted** major general of volunteers for his war service.

After the war, Smith worked as a civil engineer and served as president of a **telegraph** company and of New York City's board of police commissioners. He also wrote numerous articles about the war, including several for the series *Battles and Leaders of the Civil War.*

SMITH, WILLIAM SOOY (1830–1916) USA. A native of **Ohio**, Smith graduated from the University of Ohio in 1849 and from **West Point** in 1853. He served only one year in the **artillery** before resigning his 2nd lieutenant's commission to become a **railroad** engineer. Poor health plagued him, however, and Smith eventually was forced to give up this job. After teaching for two years, he helped found a private engineering firm and earned some recognition while working on the International

Bridge at Niagara Falls, New York, and a railroad bridge at Savannah, Georgia.

Smith entered Union service in June 1861 as colonel of the 13th Ohio. After service in western **Virginia**, where he fought at **Carnifex Ferry**, he was given a **brigade** command in the **Army of the Ohio's** 5th Division in December. Smith led this brigade on the second day of **Shiloh** and won promotion to brigadier general of volunteers later that April 1862. In August 1862, he took command of a **division** that became part of the **army's** II Corps. Smith led it in the **Kentucky Campaign** but did not see any serious combat. That November, he commanded a division in the **Army of the Cumberland's** XIV Corps, but he relinquished it three weeks before the **Battle of Stones River**. Smith returned to the field in March 1863 when he was given a division in the **Army of the Tennessee's** XVI Corps. With this command, he joined the rest of the army in June during the **Vicksburg Campaign** and served in the trenches until **Vicksburg** fell. After participating in the march on **Jackson, Mississippi**, Smith was appointed the army's chief of cavalry by **U. S. Grant**.

When Grant became head of the **Military Division of the Mississippi**, he appointed Smith his chief of cavalry. Smith first led the Union cavalry in the **Chattanooga Campaign** in November 1863 and then was sent to Knoxville, Tennessee, to help lift the siege there at the end of the **Knoxville Campaign**. In February 1864, his reputation was dealt a severe blow when **Sooy Smith's Expedition** failed to aid **William T. Sherman** in the **Meridian Campaign**. Smith took a column from **Tennessee** to join Sherman at Meridian, Mississippi, but an outnumbered Confederate force under **Nathan Bedford Forrest** defeated and turned him back at **Okolona**. After the embarrassing defeat, he performed administrative duties in Nashville, Tennessee.

Because of poor health, Smith resigned his commission in July 1864 and became an **Illinois** farmer. After a year, he became involved in engineering once again and contributed greatly to the engineering science of bridges and skyscrapers. One of Smith's accomplishments was the construction of the world's first all-steel bridge, located on the Missouri River at Glasgow, Missouri. He also helped build nearly all of the skyscrapers constructed in Chicago, Illinois, before his death. In recognition of his groundbreaking work, Smith was awarded an 1876 American Centennial Exposition prize.

SMITHFIELD CROSSING, WEST VIRGINIA, BATTLE OF (AUGUST 28–29, 1864). When Confederate Lt. Gen. **Jubal A. Early** returned to **Virginia** after **Early's Washington Raid** in the summer of 1864, he and **Philip H. Sheridan** skirmished frequently in the **Shenandoah Valley**. In late August, the two forces were probing each other in the lower Valley along Opequon (oh-PECK-un) Creek. After **skirmishing** heavily on August 28 at Smithfield Crossing, Union cavalryman **Wesley Merritt** pushed a **brigade** over the Opequon at the crossing the next day. Early sent in the **divisions** of **John B. Gordon** and **Stephen Ramseur** to force back the Federals, but they were unable to stand up against the cavalrymen's repeating carbines. When Gordon finally crossed upstream and flanked Merritt, the cavalrymen began a fighting retreat back to Charles Town. The Union VI Corps was sent to support Merritt, and by the end of the day, the Confederates had withdrawn, and the Federals reoccupied the crossing. It is estimated that the Federals lost about 100 men in the engagement, while the Confederates lost about 200.

SMYTH, THOMAS ALFRED (1832–1865) USA. A native of Ireland, Smyth immigrated to the United States as a young man and became a wood carver in **Pennsylvania**. After serving with William Walker's filibustering expedition to Nicaragua, he settled in **Delaware** in 1858 and worked as a coach maker.

When the Civil War began, Smyth became a member of a volunteer **company** whose service was rejected by the state. Undaunted, the volunteers went to Pennsylvania and were mustered into service as part of the all-Irish 24th Pennsylvania, a 90-day **regiment**. When the regiment was disbanded, Smyth was appointed major of the 1st Delaware in October 1861. After service in southeastern **Virginia**, the regiment fought at **Antietam** in a **brigade** in the 3rd Division of the **Army of the Potomac's** II Corps and lost nearly one-third of its men. Smyth temporarily commanded the unit at **Fredericksburg** and in late December 1862 was promoted to lieutenant colonel. Promoted to colonel in February 1863, he received permanent command of the regiment and led it at **Chancellorsville**. Shortly after the battle, Smyth was elevated to a brigade command in the II Corps' 3rd Division. In his first battle as a brigade commander, he was wounded on the last day of **Gettysburg** while helping repulse **Pickett's Charge**. Smyth returned to duty the next day, however, and led the brigade through the **Bristoe Station** and **Mine Run Campaigns**. In March 1864, he was given command of the famed **Irish Brigade** and led it through the opening battles of the **Overland Campaign**. At **Spotsylvania**, Smyth was transferred to a different brigade in the same **division**. He led this unit, and sometimes the division, through heavy fighting in the **Petersburg Campaign**.

Smyth was promoted to brigadier general of volunteers in October 1864. In April 1865, he again served as a division commander as **U. S. Grant** chased **Robert E. Lee's Army of Northern Virginia** during the **Appomattox Campaign**. On April 7, while inspecting his **skirmish line** at Farmville, Smyth was mortally wounded when he was shot through the mouth and spine. He died two days later, on the same day as the Appomattox **surrender**, and was the last Union general to be killed in the war. Smyth was promoted to major general of volunteers posthumously.

SNAKE CREEK GAP, GEORGIA (MAY 7–13, 1864). When Maj. Gen. **William T. Sherman** began the **Atlanta Campaign** in May 1864, his **armies** immediately ran into the formidable Confederate defensive position at **Rocky Face Ridge**, where Gen. **Joseph E. Johnston's Army of Tennessee** was strongly entrenched. Rather than make a **frontal attack**, Sherman decided to use the **Armies of the Cumberland** and **of the Ohio** to pin down the Confederates at the ridge while **James B. McPherson's Army of the Tennessee** moved southward by the right flank to Snake Creek Gap. By marching rapidly, it was hoped McPherson could push through the gap to **Resaca** and cut the Confederate line of retreat.

McPherson began his move on May 7 while the two armies were engaged at Rocky Face Ridge. At dawn of May 9, he was completing his passage through Snake Creek Gap when he encountered a Confederate mounted **brigade** under Col. J. Warren Grigsby. McPherson pushed aside the small enemy force and that afternoon sent part of **Grenville M. Dodge's** XVI Corps, supported by **John A. Logan's** XV Corps, ahead to cut the vital **railroad** north of Resaca. At this critical moment, when it appeared success was at hand, McPherson became overly cautious. Surprised to learn that Confederate infantry were in Resaca, he was afraid of being attacked and cut off, and on May 10 withdrew into Snake Creek Gap and entrenched. The Confederates at Resaca actually were only **James Cantey's** brigade, which was being brought up from Mobile, Alabama, as reinforcements.

Sherman was very disappointed at McPherson's failure and remarked to his friend that he had lost the opportunity of a lifetime. Unable to penetrate Rocky Face Ridge, Sherman left a small force there to occupy Johnston and took the rest of his men to Snake Creek Gap on May 11. He hoped he could still push through the gap and cut off Johnston at Resaca, but the movement was slow, and the Federals did not begin passing through the gap until May 13. By that time, Johnston had learned of the maneuver. He evacuated Rocky Face Ridge on May 12 and retreated to a strong position around Resaca, where the next battle of the Atlanta Campaign was waged.

SNODGRASS HILL AT BATTLE OF CHICKAMAUGA, GEORGIA (SEPTEMBER 20, 1863). On September 20, 1863, the second day of the **Battle of Chickamauga**, Confederate troops under **James Longstreet** poured through the Union lines where a gap had mistakenly been created. **William S. Rosecrans's Army of the Cumberland** collapsed, and most of it and Rosecrans retreated to **Chattanooga, Tennessee**. Major General **George H. Thomas**, commanding the XIV Corps, remained on the field and began rallying units on Snodgrass Hill (after the war, the area became known as Horseshoe Ridge). Thomas received much-needed help from **Gordon Granger**, who brought his Reserve Corps to the sound of battle without orders. In vicious fighting throughout the afternoon, the Federals repulsed repeated enemy attacks, although their own line was bent back nearly upon itself. At dusk, Thomas began a withdrawal. Three of Granger's **regiments**—the 22nd Michigan and the 21st and 89th Ohio—were left behind to hold Snodgrass Hill until the **army** retired. These regiments did so, without any ammunition, and then surrendered. Thomas's heroic stand saved the army, and he became nicknamed the **"Rock of Chickamauga."**

SNYDER'S BLUFF, MISSISSIPPI, BATTLE OF (APRIL 29–MAY 1, 1863). In April 1863, during the **Vicksburg Campaign**, **U. S. Grant** began his march down the **Louisiana** side of the Mississippi River to position his **army** to cross the river below **Vicksburg, Mississippi**. To prevent the Confederate defenders from discovering the movement, Grant left **William T. Sherman's** XV Corps to cooperate with **David Porter's** fleet in a **demonstration** against the city's defenses. On April 29, Sherman put **Francis P. Blair Jr.'s division** aboard transports and sent it up the Yazoo River with eight gunboats under naval Lt. Cmdr. K. Randolph Breese. Blair and Breese demonstrated against the Confederate batteries at Snyder's Bluff and Drumgould's Bluffs for three days before Grant successfully crossed the river and sent word they could return to their base.

"SOLDIERS' BATTLE." This term refers to a hard-fought battle in which the courage and skill of the individual soldiers, not the **tactics** of the generals, determine the fight's outcome. Among numerous "soldiers' battles" in the Civil War were **Shiloh**, **Groveton**, **Missionary Ridge**, and the **Wilderness**.

SOLID SHOT. This was solid iron **artillery** ammunition that was designed to batter down walls and other obstacles through force rather than explosion. Solid shot for smoothbores were spherical, while those for **rifled** guns were oblong.

SOMERSET, KENTUCKY, BATTLE OF (JANUARY 19, 1862). *See* MILL SPRINGS, KENTUCKY, BATTLE OF.

SONS OF LIBERTY. Along with the **Knights of the Golden Circle** and the **Order of American Knights**, the Sons of Liberty made up the Northern antiwar movement that was referred to as the **Copperheads.** The Sons of Liberty were organized in Indianapolis, **Indiana**, in early 1864 by Harrison H. Dodd to protect individuals' constitutional rights and **states rights**. However, Dodd was implicated in a plot to ship weapons to his organization to start a "revolution." Federal authorities made some arrests and held two treason trials in Indianapolis that damaged the Sons of Liberty's image. The organization was never very influential, and there is no evidence it existed outside Indianapolis.

SOOY SMITH EXPEDITION (FEBRUARY 11–26, 1864). When Union Maj. Gen. **William T. Sherman** launched his **Meridian Campaign** in February 1864, Brig. Gen. **William Sooy Smith** was to cooperate with him. As Sherman marched east from **Vicksburg, Mississippi**, toward the vital **railroad** center of **Meridian, Mississippi**, Smith was to lead a column of cavalrymen from Tennessee to wreck the Memphis & Ohio Railroad in north **Mississippi** and move south through Okolona to join Sherman at Meridian. Smith was ordered to begin his movement on February 1, but he waited for reinforcements and did not depart Collierville, Tennessee, until February 11.

With 7,000 cavalrymen, Smith rode southwest to Pontotoc, Mississippi, and destroyed railroad track, cotton, and Confederate supplies after easily dispersing a few militiamen. Confederate cavalryman **Nathan Bedford Forrest** rode north from Meridian to engage Smith and made contact with the Federals north of **West Point** on February 20. Smith became apprehensive. Unsure how many men Forrest had and ever mindful of the cavalryman's fierce reputation, he moved cautiously through West Point on February 21 in the face of stiffening Confederate resistance led by Forrest's brother, Jeffrey. After Forrest reinforced his brother south of West Point, Smith decided he was being lured into a trap and ordered a retreat.

A running fight occurred as Smith retreated back through West Point. On the morning of February 22, Forrest attacked Smith near **Okolona** and pushed him back several miles until Smith made a defensive stand several miles northwest of town. There, fierce charges and counter-charges were made, and Jeffrey Forrest was killed, before Smith broke off the engagement and continued his retreat to Pontotoc. The Federal column was harassed by Confederate militia until it finally returned to Collierville on February 26. The expedition had been an embarrassing failure, and Smith never again participated in any major field service. He lost 700 men in the operation, while Forrest reported losing 144.

SORREL, GILBERT MOXLEY (1838–1901) CSA. A native of **Georgia**, Sorrel (sor-REL) was the brother-in-law of Confederate general **William W. Mackall** and became a banking clerk for a **railroad** company after attending Chatham Academy. After Georgia's **secession**, he joined a militia **company** as a private and participated in the capture of **Fort Pulaski**. Afterward, the company was sent to **Charleston, South Carolina**, where it witnessed the bombardment of **Fort Sumter**.

With the outbreak of war, Sorrel left his company and went to **Virginia** to seek a better appointment. Through his father's influence, he became Brig. Gen. **James Longstreet's** volunteer aide. After impressing Longstreet with his service at **First Manassas**, Sorrel was commissioned a captain in September 1861 and was made Longstreet's assistant adjutant general. He served Longstreet's **division** well through the **Peninsula** and **Seven Days Campaigns** and earned another promotion to major. An excellent officer and aide, Sorrel remained with Longstreet after he became commander of the **Army of Northern Virginia's** I Corps. Not only did he write orders and attend to other mundane administrative duties, he also served on the battlefield delivering orders and placing troops into position. During this service, Sorrel was wounded by shell fragments at **Antietam** and **Gettysburg**. His skillful service won him a promotion to lieutenant colonel in June 1863.

After serving with Longstreet at **Chickamauga** and **Knoxville**, Sorrel returned with his commander to Virginia for the 1864 **Overland Campaign**. At the **Wilderness**, he led three Confederate **brigades** along an unfinished railroad grade on the Confederate right flank to get into position to attack the Union left flank. Although not officially given credit for it, Sorrel also claimed later to have led the attack. Later that day, he was with Longstreet when the general was accidentally wounded by his own men. In October 1864, Sorrel was promoted to brigadier general and was given command of **Ambrose R. Wright's** old brigade in **William Mahone's** division. He led the brigade through the **Petersburg Campaign** and suffered two more wounds. One of these was a bullet through the right lung at **Hatcher's Run**, and it resulted in rumors of his death. By the time Sorrel recovered from this second wound and was returning to his men, the **army** surrendered at **Appomattox**.

After the war, Sorrel returned to Georgia and became manager of a steamship company. He also served on the Savannah city council from 1873 to 1875 and was an officer of the Georgia Historical Society. Sorrel's war memoir, *Recollections of a Confederate Staff Officer*, is considered to be a classic.

SOUTH ATLANTIC BLOCKADING SQUADRON. This **U.S. Navy** squadron was created to maintain the **blockade** against the Confederacy along the Atlantic coast south of the **North Carolina** border. In September 1861, Capt. **Samuel F. Du Pont** was put in command, and he successfully captured **Port Royal, South Carolina**, in November and used it as his main base for the remainder of the war. Besides blockading Confederate ports and chasing **blockade runners**, the squadron also frequently cooperated with the **army** in such coastal operations as **Roanoke Island** and **Fort Wagner** and performed valuable service in the capture of **Charleston, South Carolina**, and **Savannah, Georgia**. The number of ships in the squadron grew to approximately 70 by the time **John A. Dahlgren** took command from Du Pont in July 1863. After the war ended, the South Atlantic Blockading Squadron was consolidated with the **North Atlantic Blockading Squadron** in July 1865 to form the Atlantic Squadron.

SOUTH CAROLINA. South Carolina played a crucial role in the coming of the Civil War and the war itself. The state's economy was perhaps more tied to **slavery** than other Southern states, and slaves accounted for approximately 57 percent of the 1860 population of 703,708. South Carolina was at the forefront of the antebellum **states rights** and **secession** movements and was home to such Southern leaders as **John C. Calhoun** and **Robert Barnwell Rhett**. It also was the scene of great national tension during the 1832 **Nullification Crisis** and became the first Southern state to secede on December 20, 1860. When war finally came between North and South, it began in **Charleston, South Carolina**, at **Fort Sumter**.

South Carolina was very important to the Confederacy in terms of supplies, trade, **industry**, and manpower, and its three wartime governors (**Francis W. Pickens, Milledge L. Bonham**, and **Andrew G. Magrath**) worked hard to support the war effort. Charleston, the Confederacy's second largest city, was also its third greatest industrial center and an important trade center until the Union **blockade** greatly curtailed its activities. **Columbia**, the state capital, was the site of the important **Palmetto Armory**. The state provided approximately 75,000 soldiers to Confederate service, plus another 10,000 to the state militia. Of these, some 40,000 were killed or seriously wounded, giving South Carolina one of the highest mortality rates in the Confederacy.

For most of the war, only the coastal area of South Carolina was the scene of combat. Union forces captured **Hilton Head Island**, Beaufort, and **Port Royal** early in the war and often attacked Charleston, with **Forts Wagner** and Sumter being frequently bombarded. In early 1865, **William T. Sherman** began the **Carolinas Campaign** and finally brought the war to the state's interior. Because it was the cradle of secession, South Carolina suffered great destruction at the hands of the Federals, including the burning of Columbia. With the Union **army** threatening the rear, Confederate forces defending Charleston were forced to abandon the city in February. *See also* BATTLES OF HONEY HILL; RIVERS' BRIDGE; SECESSIONVILLE.

SOUTH CAROLINA EXPOSITION AND PROTEST. Written anonymously by **John C. Calhoun** in 1828 to protest the Tariff of 1828, this document set forth the theory of nullification and helped lead to the 1832 **Nullification Crisis**. Southerners opposed protective tariffs on the grounds they drove up the price of manufactured goods and did nothing to help the Southern economy (because there was little manufacturing in the South). Since protective tariffs were discriminatory, Southerners viewed them as unconstitutional. In his *Exposition and Protest*, Calhoun argued that through a statewide convention, such as used to ratify the Constitution, a state could decide for itself if a federal law was constitutional. If it decided the law was not constitutional, the state could nullify it within its border. The **U.S. Congress** then would either have to abolish the law or secure an amendment to make it constitutional. If the latter was done and the state continued to view the law as unconstitutional, the state had the right to secede. Although Calhoun's *Exposition and Protest* has been viewed as a radical proposition, it actually was his intention to weaken the growing **secession** movement by providing the Southern states a course of action short of secession.

SOUTH MILLS, NORTH CAROLINA, BATTLE OF (APRIL 19, 1862). After capturing **Roanoke Island, North Carolina**, in February 1862, Union Maj. Gen. **Ambrose E. Burnside** sent Brig. Gen. **Jesse L.**

Reno inland to destroy the Dismal Swamp Canal's South Mills lock to prevent the Confederates from moving gunboats from **Norfolk, Virginia**, to Albemarle Sound. On the night of April 18, Reno's 3,000 men moved to Elizabeth City by transport and then marched that night to the lock. At about noon on April 19, Reno encountered 900 Confederates under Col. **Ambrose R. Wright** just outside South Mills. Wright held off the Federals for several hours before a flanking maneuver forced him to retire. Reno did not pursue because of his substantial casualties, his men's exhaustion, and rumors of arriving Confederate reinforcements. He withdrew to Elizabeth City that night without destroying the lock and returned to New Bern. In the clash, Reno suffered 114 casualties, while Wright counted about 25.

SOUTH MOUNTAIN, MARYLAND, BATTLE OF (SEPTEMBER 14, 1862). Not long after **Robert E. Lee's Army of Northern Virginia** entered **Maryland** in the 1862 **Antietam Campaign**, Union Maj. Gen. **George B. McClellan** came into possession of Lee's Special Order No. 191, or the **Lost Order**, on September 13. Realizing that Lee's **army** was scattered and that a substantial part of it was attacking **Harpers Ferry, Virginia**, McClellan planned to push his **Army of the Potomac** through the South Mountain gaps to place himself between Lee's divided army. He then would be in a position to save the Harpers Ferry garrison and **defeat in detail** Lee's army.

Despite the need for speed, McClellan did not move against the South Mountain gaps until September 14. He then made his main effort at Turner's Gap, the northernmost pass, while **William B. Franklin's** 12,000-man VI Corps seized **Crampton's Gap**. Franklin was to destroy the 8,000 Confederates under **Lafayette McLaws** who lay beyond the gap and rescue Harpers Ferry. McLaws, who was moving his men into position to cut off Harpers Ferry from the north, left more than 1,000 men under William A. Parham and **Thomas T. Munford** to defend the gap in his rear.

Franklin advanced on Crampton's Gap at dawn, but he spent several hours deploying his men in front of the small Confederate force positioned behind a stone wall on the eastern slope. Realizing the danger to his rear, McLaws sent **Howell Cobb's brigade** to reinforce Parham. The Union **divisions** of **Henry W. Slocum** and **William F. Smith** advanced at about 3:00 P.M. and quickly overran the Confederate position, with Slocum bearing the brunt of the fighting. The head of Cobb's brigade was just arriving at the time, and about 400 of its men were captured. Approximately 500 other Confederates were killed or wounded. Franklin lost 531 men, almost all members of Slocum's division. With the way now open to McLaws's rear, Franklin timidly refused to advance farther without reinforcements because he believed the Confederates in his front outnumbered him. This decision doomed the Harpers Ferry garrison.

To the north, **Ambrose E. Burnside** directed the advance against Turner's Gap and found it defended by **Daniel H. Hill's** Confederate division. Rather than make a **frontal attack**, he moved against the Confederates' flanks, with **Jesse L. Reno's** IX Corps marching one mile to the south to force its way through Fox's Gap, while **Joseph Hooker's** I Corps moved north beyond the Confederate left flank. **Jacob D. Cox's** IX Corps brigade attacked Fox's Gap at about 9:00 A.M. and forced back the Confederate brigade of **Samuel Garland Jr.**, after Garland was killed. Instead of pushing on through the gap, the Federals waited for the rest of the IX Corps to arrive and allowed Lee time to bring up **John Bell Hood's** and **David R. Jones's** divisions. When the Union troops renewed their advance, they found the way blocked again. Fighting lasted until after dark, and Reno was mortally wounded, but the Confederates held firm.

To the north, Hooker had a little more success. He attacked the Confederate left flank and slowly drove back Jones's division, but by the time the Federals reached the top of the mountain it was nightfall. Hooker was unable to press on in the confusing darkness and halted. To Hooker's right, the Union brigade of **John Gibbon** had spent the day attacking Turner's Gap, but it had no success against **Alfred H. Colquitt's** Confederate brigade. The day's fighting had cost McClellan 1,813 men and the Confederates approximately 2,685.

With the enemy having gained control of Crampton's Gap to the south, Lee's men could not remain at Fox's and Turner's gaps. Therefore, they evacuated their positions that night and withdrew toward Sharpsburg. The daylong series of battles kept McClellan at bay long enough for **Stonewall Jackson** to get into position to capture Harpers Ferry and for Lee to bring his scattered army together at Sharpsburg. Three days later, the two armies fought the campaign's climatic battle at Antietam.

SOUTHERN BIVOUAC: A MONTHLY LITERARY AND HISTORICAL MAGAZINE. This was one of several magazines published after the Civil War to promote the Southern side of the conflict. It began publication in Louisville, Kentucky, in September 1882 and was acquired by several different publishers before it printed its final issue in May 1887. At first the magazine concentrated on publishing war-related memoirs and articles, but it came to include more and more literary articles on Southern life in general.

SOUTHERN DEMOCRATIC PARTY. *See* DEMOCRATIC PARTY.

SOUTHERN HISTORICAL SOCIETY PAPERS. After the Civil War, Southerners became concerned that their side of the conflict would never be known to future Americans. This fear was deepened when the federal government bought the **Pickett Papers** in 1871 and refused to give Southerners access to Confederate papers confiscated at the war's conclusion. When the government announced its intentions to publish wartime military records (in what became the *War of the Rebellion: A Compilation of the Official Records of the Union and Confederate Armies* and *Official Records of the Union and Confederate Navies in the War of the Rebellion)*, Southerners became concerned that the project would only venerate the Union cause and condemn the Confederacy. To make sure the South's point of view was presented, the Southern Historical Society began publishing the *Southern Historical Society Papers* in 1876. Included in the publication were articles by former Confederate soldiers, previously unpublished Confederate military and government reports, memoirs, diaries, correspondence, and other valuable material. The papers were published monthly at first, but they gradually became less and less frequent. Today, they are among the most important primary sources for the Civil War. In 1953, the society's last surviving member turned over to the Virginia Historical Society all of the society's remaining papers.

SOUTHERN MANIFESTO. After the **election of 1860** many Southerners believed **secession** was the only option available to protect Southern rights from **Abraham Lincoln**. On December 14, 1860, six days before **South Carolina** seceded, **Texas** Sen. **Louis T. Wigfall** and **Alabama** Sen. James L. Pugh coauthored the Southern Manifesto. It declared that there no longer was hope of the South having its rights protected in the Union and that honor and security demanded that the South create its own confederacy. Signed by six senators and 23 congressmen, the manifesto was widely read in the South and helped persuade moderates that the time for secession had come.

SPANGLER, EDWARD (?–1875) CSA. Little is known of Edward (also known as Edman) Spangler before his arrest in **Abraham Lincoln's assassination**. A native of **Maryland**, he worked as a stagehand in **Ford's Theater** and held **John Wilkes Booth's** horse in the alley the night Booth shot Lincoln. Arrested afterward, Spangler was sentenced to six years at Dry Tortugas, Florida. After surviving a yellow fever epidemic, he was pardoned in 1869 along with fellow conspiracy **prisoners** held there. *See also* MUDD, SAMUEL ALEXANDER.

SPANISH FORT, ALABAMA, BATTLE OF (MARCH 27–APRIL 8, 1865). After capturing **Forts Gaines** and **Morgan** and gaining control of **Mobile Bay, Alabama**, in August 1864, Union forces had to seize Spanish Fort and **Fort Blakely** east of Mobile before they could capture the city itself. On March 17, 1865, Maj. Gen. **Edward R. S. Canby** moved up the eastern side of the bay toward Spanish Fort with his XIII and XVI Corps to join Maj. Gen. **Frederick Steele**, who was marching west from **Pensacola, Florida**.

When Canby and Steele united at Danly's Ferry, the Federals had 45,000 men to use against the Confederates. Canby sent Steele to lay siege to Fort Blakely, three miles to the north, while he concentrated against **Randall L. Gibson's** 4,000 Confederates at Spanish Fort. The siege of Spanish Fort began on March 27, and for nearly two weeks the Federals pounded the fort with **artillery** and small arms fire. On April 8, Canby employed 90 guns and six gunboats under Adm. Henry K. Thatcher to deliver a devastating bombardment against the Confederates, and then he attacked. Late in the afternoon, the 8th Iowa pierced the Confederate line on the northern flank, but a determined defensive stand and darkness prevented the Union soldiers from capturing the fort. That night, Gibson abandoned 50 guns, evacuated his garrison, and withdrew across a long, narrow treadway bridge to Mobile. He had lost 741 men to Canby's 657. The following day, Canby attacked and captured Fort Blakely and forced the Confederates to evacuate Mobile on April 12.

SPEARS, JAMES GALLANT (1816–1869) USA. A native of **Tennessee**, Spears became a slave-owning lawyer who was elected clerk of the circuit court in 1848. A Unionist **Democrat**, he attended two pro-Union conventions in the spring of 1861 before fleeing the state when he learned that Confederate authorities were about to arrest him.

Settling in **Kentucky**, Spears entered Union service in September 1861 when he organized the 1st Tennessee (Union) and was appointed its lieutenant colonel. He led the unit at **Camp Wildcat** and **Mill Springs**. Promoted to brigadier general of volunteers in March 1862, Spears was given a **brigade** command in the **Army of the Ohio's** 7th Division and participated in the capture of Cumberland Gap and in the **Kentucky Campaign** before receiving another brigade command in the **Army of the Cumberland**. He saw combat at **Stones River** but at **Chickamauga** was held in reserve. Spears also participated in the relief of Knoxville, Tennessee, in late 1863 at the end of the **Knoxville Campaign**.

Although a staunch Unionist, Spears also strongly supported **slavery** and was incensed at the **Emancipation Proclamation**, which he believed was unconstitutional. His very vocal criticism led to an investigation (approved by **Abraham Lincoln**) and his arrest in February 1864. Spears refused an opportunity to resign his commission and was dismissed from the service in August 1864. Returning to Tennessee, he resumed his law practice.

SPECIAL ORDERS NO. 191. *See* LOST ORDER.

SPEED, JAMES (1812–1887) USA. A native of **Kentucky**, Speed attended St. Joseph's College and Transylvania University before becoming a lawyer in 1833. He was elected to the state assembly in 1847, but his opposition to **slavery** apparently cost him reelection. In 1861, Speed opposed **secession** and believed Kentucky should remain neutral in the crisis. When war began, however, he abandoned his neutrality and fully supported the Union. After being elected to the state senate in 1861, Speed worked with **Abraham Lincoln** to arm Kentucky Unionists and supported emancipation and the **confiscation acts**.

After Speed left office in July 1863, Lincoln appointed him his adviser on Kentucky matters. When Attorney General **Edward Bates** resigned in November 1864, Lincoln appointed Speed to the position the following month. Speed supported Lincoln's wartime and **Reconstruction** policies and won the president's admiration. After Lincoln's death, however, he became more radical and joined the **Radical Republicans** in calling for harsher treatment of the defeated South and voting rights for the **freedmen**. Speed's growing radicalism brought him into conflict with President **Andrew Johnson**, and he resigned his position in July 1866 after Johnson vetoed the Freedmen's Bill.

Speed resumed his Kentucky law practice and attempted to reenter politics. He ran unsuccessfully for the U.S. Senate and U.S. House of Representatives in 1867 and 1870, respectively, but did serve as a delegate to the 1872 and 1876 Republican National Conventions. Speed also taught law at Louisville University.

SPENCER CARBINE. This breech-loading repeating carbine was patented by Christopher M. Spencer in 1860 and became a popular firearm with the Union cavalry in the Civil War. The **rifled** weapon was 39 inches long, weighed 8.25 pounds, and had a lever system attached to the trigger guard. Seven .52-caliber metallic bullets were loaded into a tube magazine that fitted into the carbine's butt stock. When the lever was pulled down, the breech opened, and a bullet was inserted when the lever was closed. The hammer was cocked manually, and the weapon then was fired. When the lever was pulled down again, the expended cartridge was ejected, and a new round was fed into the breech when the lever closed.

The Spencer was the first repeating weapon to use the metallic cartridge successfully. Its weaknesses included a lack of range because of its small powder charge, and the copper rim fire cartridges sometimes stuck in the breech after firing. Still, its rapid fire proved extremely effective in the hands of Union cavalrymen and gave them an edge in firepower. By 1864, the carbine was the Union cavalry's standard weapon. Some cavalrymen were so eager to get Spencers that they personally raised the necessary money to purchase them. A longer rifle version also was made, and it was used by some infantrymen.

SPHERICAL CASE SHOT. *See* SHRAPNEL.

SPIKING A CANNON. When an **artillery** position was overrun by the enemy or abandoned, retreating cannoneers tried to render their cannons useless to the enemy by spiking them. This involved ramming a spike or nail down the vent tube and breaking it off flush with the outside surface. With the vent thus plugged, the enemy could not fire the guns until going through the painstaking procedure of clearing them.

SPINOLA, FRANCIS BARRETTO (1821–1891) USA. A native of **New York**, Spinola became a lawyer in 1844. Active in **Democratic** politics, he served as a Brooklyn alderman, a state assemblyman, a state senator, and a delegate at the 1860 Democratic National Convention in **Charleston, South Carolina**.

After the Civil War began, Spinola raised a **brigade** of troops for the Union and was appointed brigadier general of volunteers in October 1862. His brigade was called the Empire Brigade and was stationed at Suffolk, Virginia, until late December. Afterward, Spinola was sent to **North Carolina**, where in April 1863, he took command of a brigade of **Pennsylvania** militia known as the Keystone Brigade. After **Gettysburg**, the brigade reinforced the **Army of the Potomac**, and Spinola was wounded in a small battle at **Manassas Gap, Virginia**, in July 1863. His service did not impress his superiors, and when the Army of the Potomac was reorganized in the spring of 1864, he was left without a command. Spinola was sent to recruit in New York, but he was court-martialed for working with **bounty** brokers to defraud recruits. Although ordered dismissed from the service, he was allowed to resign his commission in June 1865.

Returning to New York, Spinola worked in banking and insurance and returned to politics. Beginning in 1886, he was elected to three terms in the **U.S. Congress** and died while in office.

SPOILING ATTACK. When one **army** learned that its opponent was about to launch an attack, a spoiling attack sometimes was made to throw the enemy into confusion and disrupt his offensive plans.

SPOTSYLVANIA, VIRGINIA, BATTLE OF (MAY 7–21, 1864). At the beginning of the 1864 **Overland Campaign**, Union Lt. Gen. **U. S. Grant** and the **Army of the Potomac** engaged in a bloody slugfest with **Robert E. Lee's Army of Northern Virginia** in the dense **Wilderness**. After two days of fighting, Grant disengaged and moved to the southeast by his left flank. If he could steal a march on Lee, he could place his **army** between Lee and **Richmond, Virginia**, and force Lee to leave his works and attack at a disadvantage.

On the night of May 7, Grant withdrew from the Wilderness and sent **George G. Meade's** army south toward Spotsylvania Court House. Anticipating such a maneuver, Lee sent **J. E. B. Stuart's** cavalry and **Richard H. Anderson's corps** to Spotsylvania to block the enemy. Meade's march was slow and poorly conducted, and the Confederates barely reached Spotsylvania first on May 8. Anderson had left camp earlier than ordered and was unable to stop to rest because the Wilderness fighting had started forest fires along his route. This turned out to be fortuitous, for when he reached Spotsylvania in the morning, he found Stuart fighting **Philip Sheridan's** cavalry. Anderson pitched into the battle, and the Confederates repulsed Sheridan and began entrenching. The Union V and VI Corps soon arrived, and fighting continued northwest of Spotsylvania, but the Confederates held firm.

Both armies began concentrating around Spotsylvania on May 9 and strongly entrenched along roughly parallel lines. While inspecting his lines that day, Union Maj. Gen. **John Sedgwick** of the VI Corps was killed by a Confederate **sharpshooter**. Fighting continued the next day as the armies probed each other. Fighting was intense on Lee's left as **Henry Heth's** Confederate **division** attacked the Union II Corps divisions of **Francis Barlow** and **David Birney**. On that same wing, **Gouverneur K. Warren's** V Corps and **Winfield Scott Hancock's** II Corps unsuccessfully attacked Anderson's corps at Laurel Hill.

The only Union success on May 10 came in the Confederate center where **Richard S. Ewell's** line made a large bulge. Although this **salient**, dubbed the "Mule Shoe," was vulnerable, Lee decided to hold it because the entrenchments there took advantage of a low ridge. Union Col.

Emory Upton was given permission to try a new **tactic** on the salient's left, or western, side. Rather than attacking along a wide front, Upton massed 12 **regiments** in a narrow, compact column and sent them forward with orders not to return fire until the enemy works were taken. The attack overran **George Dole's** Confederate **brigade** and broke through the entrenchments, but a fierce counterattack and a lack of support forced Upton to withdraw. Impressed with the results, Grant decided to try the same tactic, on a larger scale, against the Mule Shoe's apex.

During the fighting at Spotsylvania, Sheridan received permission to take his cavalry on **Sheridan's Richmond Raid** to draw out Stuart's cavalry and destroy it. On May 11, they clashed at **Yellow Tavern**, and Stuart was mortally wounded, but it was the only success Sheridan enjoyed in the raid.

Grant massed Hancock's II Corps at the Mule Shoe's apex before daylight on a wet, rainy May 12. The Confederates heard the noise of moving troops, but Lee misinterpreted it to mean that Grant was withdrawing. To be better prepared to match the enemy move, he ordered Ewell's **artillery** to be withdrawn from the salient. By daylight, however, it was obvious an attack was in the making, and the artillery was ordered back. Hancock attacked at about 4:30 A.M. and completely overran and captured most of **Edward Johnson's** division, including the **Stonewall Brigade**. Ewell's missing artillery pieces (20 guns) were just arriving, and they, too, were captured. Fanning out to both sides, the Federals then began clearing out the entrenchments. Strong Confederate counterattacks, especially by **John B. Gordon's** brigade, pushed Hancock back across the entrenchments and the salient's apex. Both sides rushed in reinforcements, and for the next 20 hours the armies grappled in what was perhaps the most vicious combat of the war. In a drenching rain, the two sides shot, bayoneted, and clubbed each other, separated only by a few feet of earthworks. This small area became known as the "Bloody Angle," and was the scene of unspeakable horrors. **Rifle** fire was so heavy that an oak tree 22 inches in diameter was shot down. While fighting raged at the Bloody Angle, the Union IX Corps attacked the Mule Shoe's eastern side, but the Confederate defenders repulsed it. While the battle roared, Lee had a new line of works constructed across the base of the Mule Shoe. Finally, late that night, orders were given for Ewell's survivors to withdraw from the Bloody Angle back to the new line. During the day, Grant lost about 9,000 men to Lee's 8,000. It is estimated that approximately 12,000 of these casualties occurred at the Bloody Angle.

Grant and Meade readjusted their corps over the next few days seeking to gain an advantage over Lee, and attacks were made on May 18 without success. To ascertain the position of Grant's right flank, Lee sent Ewell on a **reconnaissance in force** on May 19. Ewell ran into heavy opposition, and a sharp clash erupted at Harris's Farm that inflicted significant casualties on both sides. By this time Grant decided to withdraw from Spotsylvania and move again around Lee's right flank to draw him out of his earthworks. He began pulling out his men on the night of May 20 and headed southeast toward the **North Anna River**. Lee followed on May 21.

The fighting around Spotsylvania had been costly to both armies. Out of approximately 63,000 men, Lee suffered about 10,000 casualties, including eight generals. Out of 111,000 men, Grant lost about 18,000, including five generals. Neither side had won any great advantage. Grant failed to destroy Lee's army but had inflicted heavy casualties that Lee could ill afford. Lee successfully blocked the enemy advance but at a staggering cost. Spotsylvania demonstrated that the conflict was developing into trench warfare and that attrition would be the **strategy** that could finally defeat the Confederates. It was at Spotsylvania on May 11 that Grant wired his famous dispatch, "I propose to fight it out on this line if it takes all summer" (Rhea, *The Battles for Spotsylvania Court House,* 213).

SPRAGUE, JOHN WILSON (1817–1893) USA. A native of **New York**, Sprague dropped out of Rensselaer Polytechnic Institute before graduating and entered business. He moved to **Ohio** in 1845 and there served as his county's treasurer from 1851 to 1852.

When the Civil War began, Sprague raised a volunteer **company** and entered Union service in April 1861 as a captain in the 7th Ohio. After serving in western **Virginia**, he was appointed colonel of the 63rd Ohio in January 1862 and was sent west. Sprague was assigned to the **Army of the Mississippi** and led his new **regiment** at **Island No. 10**, during the **Siege of Corinth, Mississippi**, and at the **battles** of **Iuka** and **Corinth**. After losing nearly half of his men at Corinth, he spent the next 18 months on garrison duty in western **Tennessee**. During this time, Sprague was promoted to a **brigade** command in the **Army of the Tennessee's** XVI Corps.

In the 1864 **Atlanta Campaign**, Sprague's brigade served with the XVI Corps' 4th Division. During the **Battle of Atlanta**, he was stationed at Decatur, Georgia, and successfully defended the **corps'** wagon train against attack. For this victory, Sprague was awarded the **Medal of Honor** posthumously in 1894. In July 1864, he was promoted to brigadier general of volunteers. After briefly commanding the 7th Division in October, he led his brigade through the **March to the Sea** and the **Carolinas Campaign**. Sprague was **brevetted** major general of volunteers in March 1865 and was mustered out of the service in September 1866.

Sprague worked in **railroad** construction after leaving the service and in 1870 became a division manager for the Northern Pacific Railroad. After helping found Tacoma, Washington, he resigned from the railroad but remained in Tacoma as a business leader.

SPRAGUE, KATE CHASE (1840–1899) USA. A native of **Ohio**, Sprague was the beautiful, educated, daughter of widowed U.S. Secretary of the Treasury **Salmon P. Chase** and became an important part of the **Washington, D.C.**, social scene when she arrived in 1861. The Chases frequently entertained the most powerful Union political and military leaders, and Kate's knowledge of and interest in politics made her something of a celebrity. She married wealthy **Rhode Island** Sen. **William Sprague** in November 1863 in what was described as one of the greatest social events of the war. Besides her social activities, Kate also was something of a political intriguer, actively promoting her father to replace **Abraham Lincoln** as president and campaigning for his nomination in 1868.

Kate's life began spiraling downward after the war. In 1873, her father died, she gave birth to a mentally handicapped daughter, and William Sprague lost much of his fortune in the Panic of 1873. She was also surrounded by scandal when it was rumored that she was involved with Republican leader Roscoe Conkling. Kate and Sprague divorced in 1882, and she lived in Europe for a time. After returning to the United States, she lived in poverty in her late father's old Washington home and earned a living selling chickens and milk.

SPRAGUE, WILLIAM (1830–1915) USA. A native of **Rhode Island**, Sprague was the son of a wealthy textile tycoon. After taking over the family business with his brothers, he became active in the **Republican Party** and was elected governor in 1859 in an election that was tainted by rumors of bribery.

Sprague also served as a militia colonel and was reelected governor in 1861. He used his personal fortune to outfit some of the state's first **regiments** and accompanied them to **Washington, D.C.**, where he served as Brig. Gen. **Ambrose E. Burnside's** aide. The governor fought at **First**

Manassas, where he had a horse shot from under him. Although dedicated to the Union cause, Sprague was immature and meddlesome and became something of a nuisance in the capital. He tried to secure an appointment to major general by offering to have the state legislature repeal a law limiting volunteers to 90 days' service. Sprague, however, never received his commission because **Abraham Lincoln** vetoed the plan, and Sprague refused an offered brigadier general's commission. He did remain in the **Army of the Potomac** as an aide for a while longer and served during part of the **Peninsula Campaign**.

Despite his faults, Sprague was reelected governor in 1862 but resigned the position the following year to accept a seat in the U.S. Senate. While in Washington, in November 1863, he married the popular **Kate Chase**, daughter of Secretary of the Treasury **Salmon P. Chase**. Sprague remained in the Senate until 1875, but he was not one of its more influential members. The Panic of 1873 nearly ruined him financially, and Kate was rumored to be romantically involved with Republican Sen. Roscoe Conkling. Sprague began drinking heavily and several years later physically attacked Conkling while drunk. He and Kate divorced in 1882. Sprague eventually remarried, moved to France with his new wife, and lived there for the rest of his life.

SPRING HILL, TENNESSEE, INCIDENT (NOVEMBER 29, 1864). *See* FRANKLIN AND NASHVILLE, TENNESSEE, CAMPAIGN AND BATTLES OF.

SPRINGFIELD ARMORY, MASSACHUSETTS. When the Civil War began, the two main Union gun-making factories were the Springfield Armory in **Massachusetts** and the **Harpers Ferry, Virginia**, Arsenal. The Springfield Armory was created in the 1790s but had an annual rifle-making capacity of only 1,200 in 1860. After secessionists took control of Harpers Ferry, Union officials quickly expanded the Springfield Armory to make the famous **Springfield Rifle Musket**. With a rifle-making capacity of 300,000 by June 1864, the armory produced 793,434 Springfield Rifles during the Civil War period.

SPRINGFIELD, MISSOURI, FIRST BATTLE OF (OCTOBER 25, 1861). After the Union defeats at **Wilson's Creek** and **Lexington, Missouri**, in late summer of 1861, Union Maj. Gen. **John C. Frémont** began an offensive in October against **Sterling Price's** Confederates. On October 12, he led 38,000 men from near Tipton, Missouri, and forced Price to retreat southwest of Springfield to Neosho. Frémont camped on the Pomme de Terre River some 50 miles from Springfield, but his bodyguard, under Maj. Charles Zagonyi, moved on to engage the Missouri State Guard at Springfield.

On October 25, Zagonyi successfully entered Springfield and drove out the state guard under Col. Julian Frazier. In the small clash, Zagonyi lost 85 men and inflicted 133 casualties on Frazier. After freeing some Union **prisoners**, Zagonyi withdrew before Frazier could organize a counterattack. On October 27, Frémont occupied Springfield, but **David Hunter** replaced him in command on November 2. At Neosho, the secessionist state government voted to secede from the Union on November 3, but it was of little importance since Union forces controlled much of the state.

SPRINGFIELD, MISSOURI, SECOND BATTLE OF (JANUARY 8, 1863). After performing well at the **Battle of Prairie Grove** in December 1862, Confederate cavalryman **John S. Marmaduke** was ordered by **Thomas C. Hindman** to make a raid into **Missouri**. Marmaduke divided his force into two columns, sending one toward Hartville, while he led 2,000 men to the Union supply base at Springfield. The small Union garrison there under Brig. Gen. **Egbert B. Brown** learned of the approaching Confederates and prepared a defense behind earthworks. When Marmaduke attacked on the morning of January 8, 1863, Brown held firm. Supported by **artillery**, he fought off Marmaduke all day but was wounded in the fight. After losing about 240 men, Marmaduke disengaged and withdrew the next day. Brown suffered 163 casualties in the battle.

SPRINGFIELD RIFLE MUSKET. One of the finest military **rifles** ever made, the Springfield Rifle Musket officially was known as the United States Rifle Musket. It was first produced at **Massachusetts's Springfield Armory** as Model 1855. This .58-caliber muzzle-loading rifle musket had a rifled barrel, fired the **minié ball**, and used Maynard tape primers, but only about 47,000 were produced by the end of 1861.

The Model 1861 replaced the **Maynard** tape with **percussion caps** and became the standard rifle used by the Union **armies** in the Civil War. The Model 1861 weighed nearly 10 pounds, used a 20-inch triangular **bayonet**, and at 56 inches was somewhat shorter than the Model 1855. Two different Model 1863 versions were made that were slight variations of the Model 1861, but the Model 1861 was by far the most common. An extremely accurate weapon, the rifle fired a 500-grain bullet (with a powder charge of 60 grains), had a maximum effective range of 500 yards, and could be fired about six times a minute. The Springfield Armory and other contractors produced approximately 1,700,000 Model 1861 (or its 1863 variations) rifle muskets. It was the most commonly used weapon of the war.

STAFFORD, LEROY AUGUSTUS (1822–1864) CSA. A native of **Louisiana**, Stafford was educated in **Kentucky** and **Tennessee** and became a wealthy Louisiana planter. He was elected parish sheriff in 1845 and served as a private in the **Mexican War**. Stafford opposed **secession**, but when war began, he organized a volunteer **company** and entered Confederate service in July 1861 as a captain in the 9th Louisiana. He then was elected lieutenant colonel and served under Col. **Richard Taylor**. The **regiment** was sent to **Virginia**, and when Taylor was promoted to brigadier general in October, Stafford was promoted to colonel.

Stafford was an excellent regimental commander and was described by Maj. Gen. **Edward Johnson** as being the bravest man he ever saw. Serving in Taylor's **brigade** of **Richard S. Ewell's division**, his service in **Stonewall Jackson's 1862 Shenandoah Valley Campaign** was commendable, and he temporarily led the brigade in the **Army of Northern Virginia** during the latter part of the **Seven Days Campaign**. After the campaign, his regiment was transferred to the other brigade of **Louisiana Tigers** under **William E. Starke**. During the **Second Manassas Campaign**, Stafford again took temporary command of the brigade when Starke was promoted to division command at **Groveton**. Under his leadership, it fought at Groveton and Second Manassas and gained fame at the latter by defending its position with rocks after running out of ammunition. Stafford again led the brigade at **Antietam** and saw heavy combat against the famed Union **Iron Brigade** (which he also had faced at Groveton). During the battle, he was painfully bruised on the foot by a shell fragment and had to relinquish command. After Antietam, Stafford's 9th Louisiana was transferred to **Harry T. Hays's** Louisiana brigade. At **Salem Church**, it successfully broke through two Union lines but was stopped at a third. When the Federals counterattacked, Stafford was too exhausted to retreat and sat on a log and was captured. Quickly **exchanged**, he returned to the regiment in time for the **Gettysburg Campaign**. There he was one of the first men to enter the Union batteries atop Cemetery Hill in **Jubal A. Early's** twilight attack on July 2, 1863.

In October 1863, Stafford was promoted to brigadier general and was put in command of the Louisiana Brigade in Edward Johnson's division. After seeing heavy combat at **Payne's Farm** during the **Mine Run Campaign**, he led the brigade into the **Wilderness** in May 1864. Positioned near the Orange Turnpike, Stafford was attempting to extricate his men from a thick wood under fire when he was shot through the spine and mortally wounded. Taken to **Richmond, Virginia**, he died on May 8.

STAGER, ANSON (1825–1885) USA. A native of **New York**, Stager worked for a newspaper until 1845. At that time he became partners with the newspaper's publisher in a venture to erect **telegraph** lines from **Pennsylvania** to the Great Lakes. Stager learned telegraphy during the construction and in 1846 began working as a telegrapher in Pennsylvania. The following year, he became manager for a large telegraph company and earned a reputation as one of the most skillful and innovative men in the business. After inventing a system that allowed several telegraph lines to be connected to one battery, Stager moved to **Ohio** and became general superintendent of the Western Union Company. While working with it, he developed contracts with **railroads** that gave his company the sole right to erect telegraph lines next to railroads.

As one of the Union's leading telegraphers, Stager found himself much valued when the Civil War began in 1861. In November, he joined Maj. Gen. **George B. McClellan's** staff as a captain in the Quartermaster Department. After serving in western **Virginia**, Stager was promoted to colonel in February 1862 and was made General-in-Chief **Henry Halleck's** aide. He also was placed in charge of the newly created U.S. Military Telegraph Corps. Stager controlled all of the Union's telegraph offices and lines and developed a secret cipher code for War Department telegrams that never was broken. His work, however, brought him into conflict with **Albert J. Myer**, who headed the U.S. Signal Corps. Besides competing for control of the military telegraph system, the two organizations used different types of equipment. Stager relied on Morse-type equipment, while Myer used the **Beardslee** system. Stager eventually won the dispute and in November 1863 was put in charge of all Union telegraph communications. For his work, he was **brevetted** brigadier general of volunteers.

After leaving the service in 1866, Stager returned to Western Union and became superintendent of its central branch. He later moved to **Illinois** and helped found Western Electric Manufacturing Company.

STAHEL, JULIUS (1825–1912) USA. A native of Hungary, Stahel's (SHTAHL) original surname was Szamvald. He joined the Austrian army as a private and rose to the rank of lieutenant but was forced to flee when he supported Hungarian revolutionaries in 1848–49. After teaching school and working as a journalist in London and Berlin, Stahel immigrated to **New York** in 1859 and began working for a German-language newspaper.

When the Civil War began, **Louis Blenker** and Stahel raised the 8th New York (1st German Rifles) and entered Union service in April 1861 as its colonel and lieutenant colonel, respectively. After participating in the **First Battle of Manassas**, where he led the **regiment** and Blenker the **brigade**, Stahel replaced Blenker as colonel in August. Three months later, he was promoted to brigadier general of volunteers and was given a brigade command in Blenker's **division**.

Assigned to **John C. Frémont** in the **Shenandoah Valley**, Stahel fought in **Stonewall Jackson's 1862 Shenandoah Valley Campaign**. Afterward, he joined the **Army of Virginia** and fought with it at **Second Manassas**. During the battle, Stahel took command of the division when **Robert C. Schenck** was wounded. Assigned to the **Army of the Potomac**, he led an XI Corps division during the **Antietam** and **Fredericksburg Campaigns** but served in the rear areas. In February 1863, Stahel was put in command of a cavalry division in the **Washington, D.C.**, defenses and was promoted to major general of volunteers the following month. In the spring of 1864, his cavalry division was assigned to **Franz Sigel** in the **Shenandoah Valley** and was defeated with him at **New Market**. When **David Hunter** took over the **army** from Sigel, he wrote that "it would be impossible to exaggerate the inefficiency of General Stahel" (Faust, ed., *Historical Times Illustrated Encyclopedia of the Civil War,* 711). Despite his superior's opinion, Stahel won some fame at the **Battle of Piedmont**, where he was severely wounded, and in 1893 was awarded the **Medal of Honor** for his service there. After recovering from his wound, he served on court-martial duty until he resigned his commission in February 1865.

After the war, Stahel joined the diplomatic service and spent nearly 20 years as a U.S. consul in Japan and China. He returned to the United States in 1885 for health reasons and worked in insurance.

STAINLESS BANNER. *See* FLAGS, CONFEDERATE.

STAND OF ARMS. This term officially referred to a complete set of equipment for one soldier, that is, **rifle**, **bayonet**, cartridge belt, and cartridge box. However, it frequently was used to refer to just the rifle and cartridge belt.

STAND OF COLORS. Although plural, this refers to one **flag** or color.

STANLEY, DAVID SLOANE (1828–1902) USA. A native of **Ohio**, Stanley was a descendant of Puritan **Massachusetts** figure Thomas Stanley. He at first studied medicine but received an appointment to **West Point** and graduated there in 1852. Assigned to the dragoons, Stanley was posted on the frontier to guard against **Indians** and served in **"Bleeding**

Kansas." He was serving in **Indian Territory** as a captain in the 1st U.S. Cavalry when the Civil War began.

Stanley turned down an offered Confederate commission in early 1861 and safely led his men from Fort Washita to **Kansas**. After leading a cavalry **company** at **Wilson's Creek**, he was commissioned a brigadier general of volunteers in September. An accidentally broken leg kept Stanley off duty for a few months, but in March 1862 he was given a **division** command in the **Army of the Mississippi**. He led it at **New Madrid and Island No. 10**, during the **siege of Corinth, Mississippi**, and at the **battles** of **Iuka** and **Corinth**.

In November 1862, Stanley took a division command in the **Army of the Tennessee's** XIII Corps. Later in the month, he was promoted to major general of volunteers and was put in charge of the cavalry in **William S. Rosecrans's Army of the Cumberland**. Stanley won a regular army **brevet** of major for his service at **Stones River** and assisted Rosecrans in driving the Confederates out of **Tennessee** in the **Tullahoma Campaign**. Illness caused him to miss the **Chickamauga Campaign**. When he returned to duty in November 1863, Stanley was given a division in the **army's** IV Corps. He led it during the first part of the **Atlanta Campaign** and won another regular army brevet for **Resaca**. In July 1864, Stanley assumed command of the **corps**, but his actions at **Jonesboro** did not please **William T. Sherman**, who believed his slowness had allowed the enemy to escape. Thus, when Sherman picked the units to accompany him on the **March to the Sea**, Stanley's corps was not among them. His IV Corps was among those units sent to Tennessee to oppose the Confederates in the **Franklin and Nashville Campaign**. Stanley was brevetted brigadier general in the regular **army** for his role in the small affair at Ruff's Station and was brevetted major general of regulars for Franklin. Although wounded, he was praised for leading a counterattack that helped save the Union line at Franklin, and in 1893, he was awarded the **Medal of Honor**. When Stanley returned to duty, he served out the rest of the war in Tennessee.

Stanley was mustered out of the volunteer service in February 1866, but he remained in the regular army. Later that year, he was appointed colonel of the 22nd U.S. Infantry and served many years on the frontier. Stanley rose to the rank of brigadier general and commander of the **Department of Texas** before retiring in 1892.

STANNARD, GEORGE JERRISON (1820–1886) USA. A native of **Vermont**, Stannard worked as a farmer and teacher before joining a foundry as a clerk. He eventually became a partner in the business and served as a colonel in the state militia.

When the Civil War began, Stannard helped recruit and train volunteers before being commissioned lieutenant colonel of the 2nd Vermont in June 1861. Sent to **Virginia**, he fought at **First Manassas** and with the **Army of the Potomac** in the **Peninsula** and **Seven Days Campaigns**. In July 1862, Stannard was appointed colonel of the 9th Vermont and was transferred to **Harpers Ferry, Virginia**. There, he and his **regiment** were captured by **Stonewall Jackson** during the **Antietam Campaign**. After being **exchanged**, Stannard was promoted to brigadier general of volunteers in March 1863 and was given command of a **brigade** of nine-month Vermont troops around **Washington, D.C.** During the **Gettysburg Campaign**, the brigade was rushed to reinforce the Army of the Potomac and arrived at Gettysburg after the battle had begun. Assigned to the I Corps' 3rd Division, Stannard was severely wounded by a shell fragment, but he won a commendation for pushing his men into a gap in the Confederate line during **Pickett's Charge** and inflicting heavy casualties on the enemy.

When Stannard returned to duty, he was given a brigade command in the 3rd Division of the **Army of the James's** XVIII Corps. He fought in the **Bermuda Hundred Campaign** in May 1864 and then joined the Army of the Potomac at **Cold Harbor**, where he received a second wound. After Stannard was wounded a third time early in the **Petersburg Campaign**, he was given command of an XVIII Corps division. While leading it against **Fort Harrison** in September, he was wounded a fourth time and lost an arm. Stannard was **brevetted** major general of volunteers for his service at Fort Harrison and upon returning to duty was placed on garrison duty along Vermont's Canadian border to guard against they type of Confederate raid that was made against **St. Albans**.

When the war ended, Stannard served for a time with the **Freedmen's Bureau** in **Maryland**, but he then resigned his commission in June 1866. He became a customs official in Vermont and was the doorkeeper of the U.S. House of Representatives from 1881 to 1886.

STANTON, EDWIN McMASTERS (1814–1869) USA. A native of **Ohio**, Stanton received little formal education growing up because he was forced to go to work in a bookstore at age 13 after his father died. He eventually put himself through two years of schooling at Kenyon College and then studied law under his guardian. After becoming a lawyer in 1836, Stanton began to prosper. He became a respected lawyer while working as **Pennsylvania's** counsel from 1849 to 1856 and as a federal special counsel litigating fraudulent **California** land claims in 1858. This latter work, especially, led to President **James Buchanan** appointing Stanton his attorney general in December 1860.

During the antebellum period, Stanton opposed **slavery**, but politically he was a moderate. He supported the **Dred Scott decision** because he believed the Union could only be preserved if the South's rights were protected. Stanton also supported the conservative Buchanan presidency and backed Southern Democratic candidate **John C. Breckinridge** for president in 1860.

Through 1861, Stanton had been allied with the **Democrats** and was critical of the **Abraham Lincoln** administration. Despite this, his reputation was so great that he was picked by Lincoln to replace Secretary of War **Simon Cameron** when Cameron resigned the position in January 1862. The stubborn, prickly, and outspoken Stanton became one of the most controversial members of the cabinet, but he was an effective secretary of war.

Stanton began to root out the fraud that had become widespread under Cameron and efficiently organized the Union war machine. He also became a leading critic of **George B. McClellan** and urged Lincoln to remove the general. Stanton made many enemies as he censored a loose press and clashed with contractors who often tried to defraud the government. Although he frequently disagreed with Lincoln on policy and sometimes privately criticized the president, he forged a close working relationship with Lincoln, and both came to appreciate the strengths of the other. Rumors that Stanton may have been involved in **Lincoln's assassination** are utterly false. Although a man hard to like, he was crucial to the Union victory.

Stanton remained as secretary of war after Lincoln's death and became a close ally with the **Radical Republicans** as President **Andrew Johnson's Reconstruction** policy became increasingly lenient. Johnson's attempted removal of Stanton from the cabinet without Senate approval in 1867 was a major cause of his impeachment. When it became apparent that Johnson would not be convicted, Stanton resigned his position in May 1868 and returned to private life. In 1869, President **U. S. Grant** nominated him to a seat on the **U.S. Supreme Court**, but Stanton died just days after his confirmation.

STAR OF THE WEST, USS. This ship played a role in the drama at **Fort Sumter, South Carolina**, during the 1861 **secession** crisis and provoked the first shots of the war. A privately owned side-wheeler, the *Star of the West* was hired by the U.S. government to resupply the beleaguered garrison at Fort Sumter. Under the command of civilian John McGowan, the ship departed New York City on January 5, 1861, supposedly on a run to **New Orleans, Louisiana**. Unfortunately, Northern newspapers published its real mission and thus alerted the secessionists at **Charleston,**

South Carolina. Reaching Charleston on the night of January 8, the *Star of the West* attempted to enter the harbor the next day, but it was fired on by secessionist batteries on Morris Island and at Fort Moultrie. McGowan withdrew without suffering any damage.

Pressed into Union service once the war began, the *Star of the West* was captured by **Earl Van Dorn's** Confederates at Indianola, Texas, in April 1861. In March 1863, the Confederates sank the ship in the Tallahatchie River at Fort Pemberton, Mississippi, to block the river channel during the **Vicksburg Campaign**.

STARKE, PETER BURWELL (1815–1888) CSA. A native of **Virginia**, Starke was the brother of Confederate general **William E. Starke**. He and his brothers operated an overland stage line in Virginia before he moved to **Mississippi** in the early 1840s to become a planter. Becoming involved in **Whig** politics, Starke unsuccessfully ran for the **U.S. Congress** in 1846, but he won elections to the state assembly in 1850, 1852, and 1856. He was elected to the state senate in 1858 and was serving there when the Civil War began.

Starke raised a volunteer cavalry **company** for local defense when the war began but in February 1862 was appointed colonel of the 28th Mississippi Cavalry. For the rest of the year, his **regiment** helped defend **Vicksburg**, attacked Union shipping on the Mississippi River, and guarded northern Mississippi. In January 1863, Starke's regiment joined **George Cosby's brigade** and two months later participated in the **Battle of Thompson's Station** as part of **Earl Van Dorn's corps**. After **skirmishing** in Middle **Tennessee** that spring, Starke joined **Joseph E. Johnston's** command near Jackson, Mississippi, during the **Vicksburg Campaign**. After Vicksburg's surrender, he skirmished with **William T. Sherman** during the siege of **Jackson**. Starke continued to serve around Jackson until December, when he replaced Cosby in command of the brigade.

As part of **William H. Jackson's division**, Starke saw extensive combat during Sherman's **Meridian Campaign** and earned high praise from his superiors. In April 1863, he resumed command of his regiment and accompanied the brigade to **Georgia** to participate in the **Atlanta Campaign**. He again served well in several fights, but from June to September he was frequently away from the regiment because of illness. Starke recovered in time to lead the regiment in the **Franklin and Nashville Campaign**, and he saw frequent combat while serving under **Nathan Bedford Forrest**. He was promoted to brigadier general in December 1864 and in February 1865 was given a brigade command in **James R.**

Chalmers's division. Starke helped pursue the enemy during **James H. Wilson's Selma Raid** in April 1865, but he did not join Forrest in time to fight at Selma. In May, he surrendered his troops in **Alabama**.

After the war, Starke returned to Mississippi, where he served on the state's levee board from 1866 to 1872 and was elected sheriff of Bolivar County. In 1873, he returned to Virginia and lived there until his death.

STARKE, WILLIAM EDWIN (1814–1862) CSA. A native of **Virginia**, Starke was the brother of Confederate general **Peter B. Starke**. He and his brothers ran an overland stage line in Virginia before Starke moved to **Louisiana** by way of **Alabama**. He became a successful cotton broker in Louisiana but returned to his native Virginia when the Civil War began.

Starke entered Confederate service as **Robert S. Garnett's** aide, but after Garnett was killed at Carrick's Ford, he was appointed colonel of the 60th Virginia. Starke continued to serve in western Virginia until assigned to **Charles W. Field's brigade** in the **Army of Northern Virginia**. He was commended twice for his service in the **Seven Days Campaign** and was promoted to brigadier general in August 1862. Placed in command of a brigade of **Louisiana Tigers** in **Stonewall Jackson's** old **division**, Starke was lightly engaged at **Cedar Mountain**, but he saw heavy combat at **Groveton** in August 1862. When **William Taliaferro** was wounded there, he assumed command of the division. Starke continued in that position through the **Second Battle of Manassas**. In that fight, Starke took up a **flag** and personally led a counterattack that captured two enemy cannons.

Starke resumed his brigade command for the **Antietam Campaign**, but Jackson placed him under arrest for refusing to bring his men back to Frederick, **Maryland**, after they had been falsely accused of stealing from civilians. He was allowed to continue in command while under arrest and assisted in the capture of **Harpers Ferry, Virginia**. At the Battle of Antietam, Starke assumed command of the division when **John R. Jones** was wounded. Repeating his performance at Second Manassas, he grabbed a flag and was leading his men in a counterattack when he was mortally wounded when struck by three bullets. Starke died within the hour.

STARKWEATHER, JOHN CONVERSE (1830–1890) USA. A native of **New York**, Starkweather graduated from Union College in 1850 and became a lawyer. He later moved to **Wisconsin** and was practicing law there when the Civil War began.

Starkweather entered Union service in May 1861 as colonel of the 90-day 1st Wisconsin. Sent to **Virginia**, the **regiment** served under **Robert Patterson** and participated in some **skirmishes** before its enlistment expired. The men reenlisted for three years and were transferred to **Kentucky**. In September 1862, Starkweather was given a **brigade** command in the 3rd Division of the **Army of the Ohio's** I Corps and led it at **Perryville**. In December, he became a brigade commander in the 1st Division of the **Army of the Cumberland's** XIV Corps. After fighting at **Stones River**, Starkweather was promoted to brigadier general of volunteers in July 1863.

Starkweather led his brigade in the **Chickamauga** and **Chattanooga Campaigns**, but at the beginning of the **Atlanta Campaign** in May 1864, he was sent to Pulaski, Tennessee, to command the garrison there. In September, his career suffered irreparable damage when **Nathan Bedford Forrest** raided the area and captured or drove off most of his men. However, Secretary of War **Edwin Stanton** owed Starkweather a favor after the general sat on the court-martial that removed Surgeon General **William A. Hammond**. Thus, when Starkweather applied for a position with **Philip Sheridan**, Stanton urged Sheridan to grant the request. Nonetheless Sheridan flatly rejected it. When no position was offered to him, Starkweather resigned his commission in May 1865 and returned to Wisconsin.

After farming and practicing law for a while, Starkweather moved to **Washington, D.C.**, and practiced law there until his death.

STARR REVOLVER. This double-action revolver was designed by Eben T. Starr, and next to **Remingtons** and **Colts**, it was the most popular pistol with Union troops. Two six-shot 1858 models, a Navy and Army, were produced. The Navy model was .36 caliber, while the Army model was .44 caliber. Both fired combustible paper cartridges and had the unusual feature of a large trigger serving as the mechanism that rotated the cylinder and cocked the hammer. The actual firing trigger was mounted on the trigger guard behind this cocking trigger. The **U.S. Navy** rejected the Navy model, and the **U.S. Army** bought only 1,402 of the Army models. The most popular model was the 1863 Army. It was made in single-action to bring its cost more in line with that of the Remingtons and Colts, which the government favored. The government bought 31,000 of this model.

STARS AND BARS. *See* FLAGS, CONFEDERATE.

STATES RIGHTS. *States rights* was a general term that was associated with having a strict constructionist's view of the Constitution. Popular among Southerners during the antebellum period, it was the belief that federal government authority was limited to those areas that the Constitution specifically granted to it. The individual states, being sovereign entities, reserved all other powers. Thus the states, not the federal government, held authority over such areas as citizenship, voting rights, and **slavery** within their own borders.

The states rights philosophy could be traced to the beginning of the republic. Under the Articles of Confederation, the states reserved the right to print money and had the sole right to tax. Thomas Jefferson and James Madison had argued in the Virginia and Kentucky Resolutions that individual states had the right to judge for themselves the constitutionality of federal laws, a position that was strengthened by **John C. Calhoun's** *South Carolina Exposition and Protest*. States rights became increasingly important to the South as the Northern states gained a sizeable majority in population and political power. States rights came to be seen as the only way the South could protect its minority rights and not suffer from tyranny by the majority. As sectional strife grew more tense, the right of **secession** came to be viewed as the ultimate state's right.

This argument over federal versus state power was at the heart of the bitter struggle over the spread of slavery into the western territories. The South believed slavery had to expand or else it (and the Southern socioeconomic system) would die out. Since slaves were constitutionally protected property, Southerners had the right to carry them into territories, and the federal government had no right to restrict them. Most Northerners, however, believed the **U.S. Congress** was responsible for the administration of territories and therefore could pass laws restricting slavery in them. Both agreed, however, that a state had the right to decide for itself whether to allow slavery or not. The South appeared to have won this argument in 1857 with the **Dred Scott decision**.

Ironically, the philosophy of states rights helped weaken the Confederacy. Having based its existence on it, the Confederate government found itself unable for political reasons to seize the same kind of central control that **Abraham Lincoln** did in the North. Powerful governors like **Zebulon Vance** and **Joseph E. Brown** used the states rights argument as a way to retain control over **conscription** and the **impressment** of supplies in their states.

STAUNTON RIVER BRIDGE, VIRGINIA, BATTLE OF (JUNE 25, 1864). In June 1864, during the **Petersburg Campaign**, U. S. Grant ordered two of his cavalry **divisions** on what became known as the **Wilson-Kautz Raid**. The raid's objective was to cut the **railroads** that supplied **Robert E. Lee's Army of Northern Virginia** around Petersburg, Virginia. The cavalry divisions of **James H. Wilson** and **August V. Kautz** began the raid on June 22 and on the next day began destroying track of the Richmond & Danville Railroad and the Southside Railroad at Burkeville. On June 25, Kautz advanced down the Richmond & Danville Railroad, but he encountered 900 men of the Confederate Home Guard strongly positioned with six cannons in two redoubts at the Staunton (STAN-tn) River bridge. The Confederates prevented the cavalrymen from reaching and destroying the vital bridge. Having already pushed about 100 miles into enemy territory, the Federals called off the attack and withdrew back to Petersburg. In the clash, the total number of casualties is estimated to have been about 150.

STEEDMAN, JAMES BLAIR (1817–1883) USA. A native of **Pennsylvania**, Steedman had little formal education but became a printer. After service in a **Texas** unit during the **Mexican War**, he won election to the **Ohio** state assembly in 1847 and 1848, participated in the **California** Gold Rush, and became owner of an Ohio newspaper. In 1857, Steedman was appointed public printer for the federal government. Becoming involved in **Democratic** politics, he supported **Stephen A. Douglas** as a delegate at the 1860 National Convention in **Charleston, South Carolina**, and ran unsuccessfully for the **U.S. Congress** that same year.

Steedman entered Union service in April 1861 as colonel of the 90-day 14th Ohio. A very large man, he earned the respect of his men and convinced them to reenlist for three years after they saw their first combat at **Philippi**. Sent to the west, Steedman next fought at **Mill Springs** and was appointed brigadier general of volunteers in July 1862. Given a **brigade** in the **Army of the Ohio** two months later, he performed very well at **Perryville** and was given a brigade in the 3rd Division of the **Army of the Cumberland's** XIV Corps. Steedman led it at **Stones River** and from January to April 1863 commanded the **division**. During the **Tullahoma Campaign**, he was back in brigade command, but in August 1863, he was given a division in **Gordon Granger's** Reserve Corps. At **Chickamauga**, Steedmen won great praise for leading his division through heavy fire to reinforce **George H. Thomas** on **Snodgrass Hill**. During the fighting, he was painfully bruised when his horse was shot from under him. At one point, Steedmen carried a regimental **flag** and asked an officer to make sure the newspapers spelled his name correctly in his obituary. To his surprise, Steedman survived the fight and afterward was put in command of Chattanooga, Tennessee.

Steedman's Democratic affiliation twice hindered his career. **Abraham Lincoln** nominated him brigadier general in March 1862, but Congress did not confirm him until July 1863. Even after his service at Chickamauga, Congress delayed confirming him major general of volunteers until April 1864 because his newspaper had been critical of the **Emancipation Proclamation.** For the rest of the war, Steedman held administrative positions in the **Department of the Cumberland**, but at **Nashville**, he saw heavy combat while in command of a "provisional detachment" of about 11 **regiments.**

After resigning his commission in August 1866, Steedman was appointed a collector of internal revenue in **Louisiana**. He eventually moved back to Ohio, where he worked as a newspaper editor, served in the state senate, and became Toledo's chief of police.

STEELE, FREDERICK (1819–1868) USA. A native of **Connecticut**, Steele graduated from **West Point** in 1843. Assigned to the infantry, he performed routine garrison duty before winning two **brevets** for gallantry in the **Mexican War.** After the war, Steele served at numerous frontier posts and had risen to the rank of captain by 1861. When the Civil War began, he was serving at Fort Leavenworth, **Kansas**, and was promoted to major in the 11th U.S. Infantry.

After seeing some minor combat, Steele commanded a battalion of regulars at **Wilson's Creek.** He then quickly rose through the ranks, being appointed colonel of the 8th Iowa in September 1861 and promoted to brigadier general of volunteers in January 1862. Steele commanded the District of Southeast Missouri until May, at which time he was given a **division** in the **Army of the Southwest.** After participating in the capture of **Helena, Arkansas**, he briefly commanded the **army** during the late summer and autumn. In late 1862, Steele was transferred east of the Mississippi River and was given a division command under **William T. Sherman** for the December attack on **Chickasaw Bayou.** After that defeat, he took a division in **John C. McClernand's** XV Corps and participated in the capture of **Arkansas Post.** During the 1863 **Vicksburg Campaign**, Steele led a division in Sherman's XV Corps of the **Army of the Tennessee.** He was promoted to major general of volunteers in March and performed well enough during the siege to earn a brevet in the regular army. After **Vicksburg** was captured, Steele briefly commanded the **corps** and participated in Sherman's siege of **Jackson, Mississippi.**

In August 1863, Steele was sent back to **Arkansas** and was placed in command of the troops that captured **Little Rock** in September. This successful operation earned him a brevet of brigadier general of regulars. Put in command of the **Department of Arkansas** in January 1864, he was ordered to cooperate with **Nathaniel P. Banks's Red River Campaign** by advancing against Shreveport, Louisiana, from the north. Steele's **Camden Expedition** was no more successful than Banks's operation, however, and Steele suffered defeats at **Poison Spring** and **Jenkins' Ferry**. He remained in Arkansas until early 1865, when he was sent to the **Department of the Gulf**. There, Steele took command of the District of West Florida in March and led a division during the **Mobile Campaign**.

Steele was brevetted major general of regulars for his wartime service and was sent to **Texas** before mustering out of the volunteers in January 1867. He remained in the regular army as colonel of the 20th U.S. Infantry and was put in command of the Department of the Columbia. While on leave in **California**, Steele died from injuries he suffered when an apoplectic attack caused him to fall from a carriage.

STEELE, WILLIAM (1819–1885) CSA. A native of **New York**, Steele graduated from **West Point** in 1840. Assigned to the dragoons, he fought in the **Seminole Wars** and won a **brevet** for gallantry in the **Mexican War**. After Mexico, Steele served in **Texas** for a time and then fought Apaches and the Sioux on the frontier. During this service, Steele married a woman from Texas and adopted that state as his own.

By the time of the Civil War, Steele was a captain in the 2nd U.S. Dragoons. He resigned his commission in May 1861 and entered Confederate service as colonel of the 7th Texas Cavalry. After serving in **Henry H. Sibley's New Mexico Campaign**, Steele was promoted to brigadier general in October 1862. He was put in command of the **Indian Territory** in December but became frustrated there because **department** commander **Edmund Kirby Smith** frequently took away his troops without any notification and because his troops looked upon him with suspicion because of his Northern birth. The fact he had the same last name as Union general **Frederick Steele** even led to rumors that they were brothers. After a year of command, Steele was replaced at his own request in December 1863. Kirby Smith continued to have confidence in him, however, and asked that he remain in the territory to command the **Indian** troops until his replacement (**Samuel B. Maxey**) arrived. Angry at the treatment he had received, Steele refused.

In February 1864, Steele was placed under **John B. Magruder** in Texas and was given command of Galveston the following month. When the **Red River Campaign** began, he was sent to **Louisiana** to command a cavalry **division** in **Richard Taylor's** army, but he never received all of the troops he was promised and ended up supervising only William H. Parson's **brigade**. Steele received high praise from Taylor for his role at **Pleasant Hill** and for assuming command of all of the cavalry after **Thomas Green's** death and successfully harassing the Union **army** during its retreat down the Red River. After the campaign, Steele accompanied the cavalry into **Arkansas**, where he was given command of a small two-brigade cavalry **corps** in January 1865.

After the war, Steele settled in Texas, where he became a commission merchant and the state adjutant general. It was under his supervision that the Texas Rangers became an effective law enforcement organization.

STEELE'S ARKANSAS EXPEDITION (MARCH 23–MAY 3, 1864). *See* CAMDEN, ARKANSAS, EXPEDITION.

STEELE'S BAYOU, MISSISSIPPI, EXPEDITION (MARCH 14–25, 1863). In early 1863, Maj. Gen. **U. S. Grant** was frustrated in his attempts to attack **Vicksburg, Mississippi**, during the **Vicksburg Campaign**. Floodwaters and the Confederate batteries on Vicksburg's bluffs prevented him from approaching the city with his **Army of the Tennessee**. As a result, Grant searched for ways to approach the city from a direction other than the Mississippi River. This led to Grant's Canals, the **Yazoo Pass Expedition**, and the Steele's Bayou Expedition.

The Steele's Bayou Expedition actually was Adm. **David Porter's** idea. By moving ships from the Mississippi River into the Yazoo River upstream from Vicksburg, the Federals could detour into Steele's Bayou. Because of the high floodwaters, Porter believed he could steam through Steele's Bayou, Black Bayou, Deer Creek, Rolling Fork, and the Big Sunflower River to reenter the Yazoo upstream of (or behind) the Confederate batteries blocking the river at Haynes' and Drumgould's Bluffs. Porter intended for transports to follow his warships to land infantry behind the enemy strongholds and attack Vicksburg from the northeast.

Grant agreed to supply troops from **William T. Sherman's** XV Corps, and Porter began the operation with five gunboats and assorted other vessels on March 14. Porter's optimism, however, proved ill-founded. He entered Deer Creek without trouble but then found the narrow, twisting stream almost impassable. The advance slowed to a crawl, and Confederate troops began felling trees ahead of the flotilla. Porter was forced to send 300 men ahead of the ships to drive off the enemy.

Porter entered the Rolling Fork but then was stopped by thick willow trees. With the Federals' progress halted, the Confederates tried to trap the ships by felling trees behind Porter. In addition, 2,000–3,000 Confederate troops were sent from Haynes' Bluff to attack the ships. Learning of Porter's predicament, Sherman, who had been following behind, rushed troops to him overland through the boggy swamps on March 21. Three **regiments** under Col. **Giles A. Smith** reached Porter that same day and blocked the Confederate advance. The following day, Sherman arrived with more troops and began escorting Porter back downstream. Constant **skirmishing** with the Confederates took place over the next few days, but the flotilla safely reached the Mississippi River on March 25.

STEPHENS, ALEXANDER HAMILTON (1812–1883) CSA. A native of **Georgia**, Stephens was raised by an uncle after being orphaned as a boy. After graduating first in his class from Franklin College in 1832, he taught school and became a lawyer. Entering politics, Stephens served as a popular state legislator from 1836 to 1843 and as a **Whig** congressman from 1843 to 1859. A lifelong bachelor and a frail, sickly man (who became known as "Little Aleck" because he never weighed more than 90 lbs.), Stephens proved to be a great speaker and hard-working politician.

In the **U.S. Congress**, Stephens supported **slavery** and **states rights** but not at the peril of the Union. Along with fellow Georgians **Robert Toombs** and **Howell Cobb**, he became a moderate **Democrat** and tried to avoid **secession**. By 1860, however, Stephens virtually stood alone as a Southern Unionist. He supported **Stephen A. Douglas** in the **election of 1860** but also was friends with **Abraham Lincoln**. When Lincoln won and the Southern states began seceding, Stephens attended the Georgia secession convention as a Unionist. He passionately tried to avoid secession but then signed the ordinance after it was passed.

In February 1861, the reluctant secessionist served in the Provisional **Confederate Congress** as chairman of the Rules Committee and the Committee on the Executive Departments. He hoped to be chosen as the provisional president but finally accepted the position of vice president. Almost immediately, Stephens and President **Jefferson Davis** clashed. Davis tended to ignore Stephens's advice, and Stephens opposed such strong national measures as **conscription** and the suspension of the writ of **habeas corpus**. He also made a widely publicized speech in Savannah, Georgia, in which he declared that slavery was the "cornerstone" of the Confederacy. Davis believed this detracted from the main issue of states rights. Joining forces with Georgia Gov. **Joseph Brown** and Toombs, Stephens opposed nearly all of Davis's programs. So great was the split between them that Stephens returned to Georgia and essentially played no role in the government during the war. Because he was an advocate of a negotiated peace, Stephens was chosen to attend the **Hampton Roads Conference** in early 1865, but its failure forced him to recognize that negotiation was impossible.

When the war ended, Stephens was imprisoned in **Fort Warren, Massachusetts**, until **paroled** in October 1865. Returning to Georgia, he was elected to the U.S. Senate in January 1866, but the **Radical Republicans** refused to seat him. Stephens then practiced law until winning election to Congress in 1872. He also wrote *A Constitutional View of the Late War between the States* and was elected governor of Georgia in 1882. Stephens died after only a few months in office.

STEPHENSON'S DEPOT, VIRGINIA, BATTLE OF (JUNE 15, 1863). At the beginning of the **Gettysburg Campaign, Robert E. Lee's Army of Northern Virginia** advanced northward through the **Shenandoah Valley** with **Richard S. Ewell's corps** in the lead. On June 14, 1863, Ewell attacked **Robert H. Milroy's** Union garrison at **Second Winchester** and captured the main forts defending the town. Expecting Milroy to withdraw during the night, Ewell sent **Edward Johnson's division** to the rear of Winchester to cut the enemy's escape route at Stephenson's Depot.

Johnson reached the depot before dawn on June 15 and took up a position behind a stone wall to block the road. Milroy attacked at about daylight and tried to cut his way through, but the Confederates held firm. The Federals then tried to turn the Confederate flanks, but Johnson shifted his troops to counter that move. The Union force then became disorganized as it fragmented into groups and fled. Approximately 2,500 Union soldiers were taken **prisoner** in the short, fierce fight, but Milroy and about 4,000 Federals rode around Johnson and escaped. Johnson's casualties were very light.

STEPHENSON'S DEPOT, VIRGINIA, SECOND BATTLE OF (JULY 20, 1864). *See* RUTHERFORD'S FARM, VIRGINIA, BATTLE OF.

STEUART, GEORGE HUME "MARYLAND" (1828–1903) CSA. A native of **Maryland**, Steuart graduated next to last in his 1848 **West Point** class. Assigned to the cavalry, he served at various frontier posts, fought **Indians**, and was in the **Utah Expedition**.

Steuart resigned his captain's commission in April 1861 and entered Confederate service as a cavalry captain. Placed under **Joseph E. Johnston**, he was appointed lieutenant colonel of the newly formed 1st Maryland (Confederate) in June. Regimental colonel **Arnold Elzey** was placed in charge of the **brigade**, so at **First Manassas**, Steuart led the

regiment and won promotion to colonel for his outstanding service. In March 1862, "Maryland" Steuart, as he became known, was promoted to brigadier general and was given a brigade command in **Richard S. Ewell's division**. After leading his brigade through the opening phase of **Stonewall Jackson's 1862 Shenandoah Valley Campaign**, he was transferred by Jackson in May to command a two-regiment cavalry brigade. At **First Winchester**, however, Steuart angered Jackson by not pursuing the enemy. He was returned to his infantry brigade in early June and was severely wounded in the shoulder by a shell fragment at **Cross Keys**.

Steuart was unable to return to duty until May 1863. Given command of an infantry brigade in **Edward Johnson's** division of Ewell's Corps, **Army of Northern Virginia**, Steuart saw heavy fighting at **Gettysburg's** Culp's Hill. After service in the **Bristoe Station** and **Mine Run Campaigns**, he saw his brigade mauled in the **Overland Campaign**. At **Spotsylvania**, Johnson's division held the apex of the famous Confederate "Mule Shoe" and was the target of the Union attack on May 12, 1864. When the Federals overran the position, both Johnson and Steuart were captured, along with hundreds of their men. After being **exchanged**, Steuart took command of a brigade in **George Pickett's** division. He fought at **Five Forks** during the **Petersburg Campaign** and then was captured at **Sailor's Creek**.

After being released from **prison**, Steuart settled in Maryland as a farmer and became active in Confederate veterans' activities. For many years, he served as commander of the state's **United Confederate Veterans** organization.

STEVENS, CLEMENT HOFFMAN (1821–1864) CSA. Stevens was a native of **Connecticut**, but as a boy, he moved with his family to **Florida**. The family soon moved again to **South Carolina**. There, Stevens accepted a position as private secretary for two relatives who served as naval officers and spent several years traveling with them. He eventually left that position and became cashier for a **Charleston** bank. A part-time inventor, Stevens developed a new type of **ironclad artillery** fortification that was erected on Morris Island in 1861. It was perhaps the first ironclad battery ever designed and was used during the bombardment of **Fort Sumter**. It also reportedly was the forerunner of the ironclad *Virginia*. Stevens also invented a portable baking oven that later was used by his men to bake bread.

After the fall of Fort Sumter, Stevens joined the staff of brother-in-law **Barnard E. Bee** as a volunteer aide. While serving at **First Manassas**, he saw Bee killed and was seriously wounded himself. It was Stevens who claimed that Bee's reference to **Thomas J. Jackson** as a "stonewall" in the battle was made in derision because of Jackson's inaction, not as a compliment for his stubborn stand. Returning to South Carolina to recuperate, he was appointed commander of a militia **regiment** and served as Brig. Gen. **Roswell S. Ripley's** volunteer aide. After helping raise the 24th South Carolina, Stevens was commissioned its colonel in April 1862. He led it in some small actions around Charleston and was in command of the Confederate **picket line** during the **Battle of Secessionville**. For the rest of the summer and, Stevens remained on James Island and sometimes commanded all of the troops around Secessionville.

In December 1862, Stevens was given a **brigade** command and briefly served around **Wilmington, North Carolina**, before returning to James Island and his regimental command. Assigned to **States Rights Gist's** brigade in the spring of 1864, he led his men to **Mississippi**, where they served under **Joseph E. Johnston** around Jackson, Mississippi, during the **Vicksburg Campaign**. After helping defend **Jackson** in July 1863, the brigade reinforced the **Army of Tennessee** around Chattanooga, Tennessee. When the **Battle of Chickamauga** began, Stevens's regiment was at Rome, Georgia, and could not reach the battlefield because of the local **railroad** engineer's dereliction of duty. Stevens commandeered the train, threatened to shoot the engineer, and finally made it to Chickamauga in time to fight on the second day. He won commendations from his superiors in the battle, had two horses shot from under him, and again was severely wounded.

Promoted to brigadier general in February 1864, Stevens was given a brigade command in **William H. T. Walker's division**. The brigade saw little combat during the early part of the **Atlanta Campaign**, but Stevens's yeoman-like service earned him the nickname "Rock." The brigade was in the thick of battle at **Peachtree Creek** when Stevens was mortally wounded by a shell while he led his men in the attack. He died five days later.

STEVENS, ISAAC INGALLS (1818–1862) USA. A native of **Massachusetts**, Stevens graduated first in the 1839 **West Point** class. Assigned to the **engineers**, he worked on New England construction projects until the **Mexican War**. In Mexico, Stevens was severely wounded in the foot while serving under **Winfield Scott** and won two **brevets** for gallantry. After playing an active role in getting **James Buchanan** elected president in 1852, he resigned his 1st lieutenant's commission in 1853 to become governor of the Washington Territory. On his way there, Stevens also surveyed a **railroad** route to the Pacific for the Northern Pacific Railroad. His arbitrary ways and declaration of martial law during **Indian** troubles made him a controversial territorial governor, but he was popular enough to be elected the territory's nonvoting congressional representative in 1856 and 1858. Because he was a friend of Joseph Lane, the 1860 Southern **Democratic** vice presidential nominee, Stevens served as campaign chairman for **John C. Breckinridge** and the Southern Democratic ticket and caused many Northerners to suspect his loyalty.

Because of the suspicion about him, Stevens did not receive a proper military appointment until after **First Manassas**. He was appointed colonel of the 79th New York in late July 1861 and was expected to bring **discipline** to the rowdy, nearly mutinous unit. Although standing only 5 feet, 1 inch tall, Stevens maintained strict discipline and soon had the **regiment** in shape. He became so popular with the men that when he was promoted to brigadier general of volunteers in September, the 79th New York asked to be assigned to his **brigade**. Stevens served in the operation that captured **Port Royal, South Carolina**; for a time commanded Beaufort, South Carolina; and in April 1862 was given a **division** command in the **Department of the South**. After fighting at **Secessionville** in June, he was transferred to **Virginia** and was given a division command in the **Army of the Potomac's** IX Corps. At **Second Manassas**, Stevens saw heavy fighting while leading the Union attacks against the Confederate left. Two days after the battle, he was killed instantly when he was shot in the temple at **Chantilly**. Stevens was promoted posthumously to major general of volunteers in March 1863.

STEVENS, THADDEUS (1792–1868) USA. A native of **Vermont**, Stevens was raised by his widowed mother in a poor household and never forgot the plight of poor people of all races. After graduating from Dartmouth College, he moved to Gettysburg, Pennsylvania, in 1816 and became a lawyer. A radical of the first order, Stevens not only was an **abolitionist** who defended runaway slaves for free, but he also advocated a classless society and became a champion of the poor. As his law practice grew, he began purchasing land and became a prominent iron foundry owner. Because of his genuine concern for the less fortunate, Stevens continued to operate foundries at a loss just to keep his workers employed. He also donated the land on which Gettysburg College was built.

Stevens's first political position was in the state legislature from 1833 to 1842, where he advocated free public schools. He became a **Whig** in 1848 when he was elected to the **U.S. Congress**, but he later helped form the **Republican Party** in Pennsylvania and was reelected on its 1858 ticket. Although he was a leader of the Republican Party, Stevens was not appointed to a Cabinet position by **Abraham Lincoln** because his radical beliefs would alienate the **border states** and moderates. Still, Stevens strongly supported the war effort and played an important role in the ultimate Union victory through his position as chairman of the House Ways and Means Committee. He advocated total war and the complete destruction of the Southern slave-owning aristocracy and clashed with Lincoln because of the president's slowness to accept emancipation. During the war, Stevens advocated not only immediate emancipation for the slaves but also black equality and the enlistment of **black troops.** As part of this crusade, he helped pass bills that abolished **slavery** in the territories, prevented military commanders from returning runaway slaves, and put in motion the **13th Amendment.** In retaliation, Confederate troops burned his iron foundry during the **Gettysburg Campaign.**

After the war, Stevens was one of the **Radical Republicans** who bitterly opposed President **Andrew Johnson's Reconstruction** policies and largely was responsible for his impeachment. He helped get the 1865 **Freedmen's Bureau** bill and the Civil Rights Act of 1866 passed over Johnson's veto. Stevens also was a moving force behind the harsh Military Reconstruction Act of 1867, and made ratification of the 14th Amendment a condition for the readmission of Southern states.

STEVENS, WALTER HUSTED (1827–1867) CSA. A native of **New York,** Stevens graduated near the top of his 1848 **West Point** class and entered the **engineers.** He worked on various surveys, inspections, and construction projects in **Louisiana** and **Texas** and married the sister of future Confederate general **Louis Hébert.**

Because of his Southern family connections, Stevens resigned his 1st lieutenant's commission after **Texas** seceded in March 1861, but the War Department refused to accept it. Instead, the government dismissed him from service in May. Stevens then entered the **Confederate army** as a captain of engineers and joined **P. G. T. Beauregard's** staff. He helped construct defensive positions in northern **Virginia** and participated in the **First Battle of Manassas.** After the battle, Stevens was promoted to major and became chief engineer for **Joseph E. Johnston's army** in Virginia. When Johnston was wounded at **Seven Pines** in May 1862, **Robert E. Lee** promoted Stevens to colonel and assigned him to the **Richmond, Virginia,** defenses. Over the next two years, he performed excellent service supervising the construction of Richmond's defenses, and he commanded the defenses from autumn 1863 until July 1864. Stevens was appointed the **Army of Northern Virginia's** chief engineer in July 1864 and was promoted to brigadier general two months later. Throughout the **Petersburg Campaign**, he served Lee well in overseeing the fortifications and other defenses protecting the army. Stevens was said to have been the last Confederate soldier to leave Richmond and remained with Lee until the **surrender** at **Appomattox.**

After the war, Stevens moved to Mexico and worked as a **railroad** engineer for **Maximilian.** He died there in 1867.

STEVENSON, CARTER LITTLEPAGE (1817–1888) CSA. A native of **Virginia**, Stevenson graduated near the bottom of his 1838 **West Point** class. Assigned to the infantry, he served at various posts before seeing combat in the **Mexican War** as Gen. Hugh Brady's aide. Stevenson was promoted to captain during the war and afterward fought **Indians** on the frontier and served in both the **Seminole Wars** and the **Utah Expedition.**

Stevenson was in Utah when the Civil War began. He submitted his resignation in June 1861 before heading south, but it was not delivered to the War Department, and he was dismissed from the service later that month. Entering Confederate service in June as a major, Stevenson was promoted to lieutenant colonel in July and was appointed colonel of the 53rd Virginia later in the month. Upon **P. G. T. Beauregard's** recommendation, he was promoted to brigadier general in March 1862 and was transferred west.

Stevenson assumed command of the troops in eastern **Tennessee** around Knoxville and Cumberland Gap. After his men were forced out of Cumberland Gap in June 1862, he assembled them into a **brigade.** Stevenson was elevated to a **division** command for the **Kentucky Campaign** and was left behind to threaten Cumberland Gap when **Edmund Kirby Smith** invaded **Kentucky.** His presence forced the Federals to evacuate the gap, which allowed him then to join the main **army** in Kentucky. Although he did not arrive in time to participate in any of the battles during the invasion, Stevenson was promoted to major general in October before the Confederates began their withdrawal.

After the Kentucky Campaign, Stevenson was given a division in the **Army of Tennessee**, but he was ordered to take it to **Vicksburg, Mississippi**, and thus missed the **Battle of Stones River.** He arrived at **Chickasaw Bayou** in December 1862 on the afternoon **William T. Sherman** was defeated there. Stevenson then took command of the position and remained there until **U. S. Grant** crossed the Mississippi River during the **Vicksburg Campaign**. He joined the rest of **John C. Pemberton's** army at that time and saw heavy fighting at **Champion Hill**. After commanding the army during its withdrawal into the Vicksburg defenses, Stevenson was given command of Pemberton's right wing. He was captured there on July 4, 1863, but was **paroled** immediately.

In a controversial move that was protested by Union officials, Confederate authorities declared Stevenson and his men **exchanged** in September 1863. His division was sent to Chattanooga, Tennessee, later that month and took up defensive positions around **Lookout Mountain**. Stevenson was defeated there by **Joseph Hooker** in November and then accompanied the Army of Tennessee into **Georgia** after the disaster at **Missionary Ridge**. During the **Atlanta Campaign**, he served well at **Resaca** and **Kennesaw Mountain** and temporarily commanded **John Bell Hood's corps** after Hood was elevated to army command. Stevenson accompanied the army on the **Franklin and Nashville Campaign** in November 1864 but did not participate in the Battle of Franklin. He did, however, see heavy fighting at Nashville, where his division held the Confederate center. When **Stephen D. Lee** was wounded, Stevenson took temporary command of the corps and personally led the rear guard during the retreat from Tennessee. In early 1865, his division reinforced **Joseph E. Johnston** during the **Carolinas Campaign**, and it fought its last battle at **Bentonville**.

After the war, Stevenson became a **Mississippi** planter before returning to Virginia and working as a civil engineer.

STEVENSON, JOHN DUNLAP (1821–1897) USA. A native of **Virginia**, Stevenson attended South Carolina College and became a lawyer but moved to **Missouri** to open his law practice. He served in the **Mexican War** under Stephen Kearny as captain of a Missouri militia **company** he organized. Returning to Missouri after the war, Stevenson served in the state legislature before the Civil War and was president of the senate for one term.

Stevenson entered Union service in June 1861 as colonel of the 7th Missouri (Union). He first served in Missouri but then was sent to **Tennessee**, where he fought at **Shiloh**. After participating in the **Battle of Corinth**, Stevenson was given a **brigade** command in the 3rd Division of the **Army of the Tennessee's** XVII Corps in November 1862. He was promoted to brigadier general of volunteers in March 1863 and served throughout the **Vicksburg Campaign** in **John Logan's division** of **James McPherson's corps**. After the fall of **Vicksburg**, Stevenson briefly commanded the division and made an expedition into northern

Louisiana to clear it of Confederates. He missed the **Chickamauga** and **Chattanooga Campaigns** because he was left in command of the District of Corinth. When the **Atlanta Campaign** began, Stevenson was left in the rear to guard the **railroads**. Unhappy with this assignment, he resigned his commission in April 1864 but returned to the **army** in August with the rank of brigadier general of volunteers and the same seniority as when he left. Stevenson was placed in command of a reserve division and garrisoned **Harpers Ferry, West Virginia**, until war's end. A native of the **Shenandoah Valley**, he tried to advise **Philip Sheridan** on how to combat Confederate guerrillas in the area, but Sheridan generally ignored him.

Stevenson was **brevetted** major general of volunteers for his war service and was mustered out of the volunteers in January 1866. He was appointed colonel and commander of the 30th U.S. Infantry later that year and received a brevet of brigadier general of regulars in 1867. Before he asked for a discharge in 1870, Stevenson briefly commanded the 25th U.S. Infantry, a regiment of **black troops**.

STEVENSON, THOMAS GREELY (1836–1864) USA. A native of **Massachusetts**, Stevenson became active in the militia and rose to the rank of major before the Civil War. He was an excellent drillmaster, and many of his militiamen went on to become officers in Civil War **regiments**.

When the war began, Stevenson formed the 24th Massachusetts around his old militia battalion and was appointed its colonel in December 1861. As part of **John G. Foster's brigade**, the regiment participated in the capture of **Roanoke Island** and **New Bern, North Carolina**, and conducted operations within the state. Upon Foster's recommendation, Stevenson was appointed brigadier general of volunteers in December 1862. The U.S. Senate did not confirm the appointment, however, and he had to be reappointed in April 1863.

Assigned to the **Department of the South's** X Corps, Stevenson's brigade participated in operations against **Charleston, South Carolina**, and **Fort Wagner**. He contracted malaria while there and was forced off duty during the winter of 1863–64. When he returned to duty, Stevenson was given a **division** in **Ambrose E. Burnside's** IX Corps in April 1864. During the 1864 **Overland Campaign**, he was killed at **Spotsylvania** on May 10 by a Confederate **sharpshooter**.

STEWART, ALEXANDER PETER (1821–1908) CSA. A native of **Tennessee**, Stewart graduated from **West Point** in 1842. He served for a time with the **artillery** but then returned to the academy to teach mathematics. Stewart resigned his 2nd lieutenant's commission in 1845 and taught at Tennessee's Cumberland University before joining Nashville University's faculty in the 1850s.

Although an opponent of **secession**, Stewart joined the Confederacy after Tennessee seceded and became a major of artillery. Known to his men as "Old Straight" (a nickname he apparently acquired while teaching at West Point), he became a rather obscure but effective Confederate **corps** commander during the war. Brave and capable, Stewart often rode along his line before a battle shouting encouragements to his men. His first assignment was overseeing the placement of batteries at Columbus, Kentucky, to block the Mississippi River, and in November 1861, he used those batteries to support the Confederates fighting at **Belmont** across the river. This action earned Stewart a promotion to brigadier general that same month.

Stewart was given a **brigade** command in **Leonidas Polk's** corps of the **Army of the Mississippi**. His brigade was mistakenly fired on by its own comrades at **Shiloh**, but it still supported the attacks being made against the "Hornets' Nest." When **division** commander **Charles Clark** was wounded on the first day, Stewart assumed temporary command of the division for the rest of the battle. He returned to his brigade before the **Kentucky Campaign** that autumn and led it at **Perryville**. At **Stones River** with the **Army of Tennessee**, Stewart continued to show his steady dependability by playing a key role in breaking the Union right flank on the first day of battle.

Stewart was promoted to major general in June 1863 and led a division in **Simon B. Buckner's** corps in the **Chickamauga Campaign**. At Chickamauga, the division was heavily engaged on both days and participated in the Confederate breakthrough on the second day of fighting. As part of **John C. Breckinridge's** corps, Stewart's division joined in the siege of Chattanooga, Tennessee, and held the Confederate left at **Missionary Ridge** during the **Chattanooga Campaign**. During the **Atlanta Campaign**, he was back in Polk's corps. After fighting well around **New Hope Church and Dallas**, Stewart assumed command of the corps (also known as the **Army of Mississippi**) in June 1864 when Polk was killed. Promotion to lieutenant general came later that month, and he led his corps during the remainder of the Atlanta Campaign and supported **Joseph E. Johnston** in his ongoing feud with **Jefferson Davis**. When Johnston was relieved in July, Stewart unsuccessfully tried to persuade him not to relinquish command of the **army**. Despite this, the new army commander, **John Bell Hood**, thought highly of Stewart, and he served Hood well at **Peachtree Creek** and **Ezra Church**, where he was wounded. In the **Franklin and Nashville Campaign**, however, Hood's confusing orders and what Stewart believed were Hood's failures at Franklin and Nashville led to bad feelings between them. After the disastrous campaign, Stewart was given command of the Army of Tennessee and led it in the **Carolinas Campaign** under Johnston. His last battle was at **Bentonville**, where he performed his usual capable service.

After the war, Stewart returned to education. He first taught at Cumberland University but then served as the chancellor of the University of Mississippi from 1874 to 1886. While in **Mississippi**, Stewart also served on the commission that led to the creation of the Chickamauga and Chattanooga National Military Park. Prior to his death in 1908, he was the last surviving Confederate army commander.

STIRLING'S PLANTATION, LOUISIANA, BATTLE OF (SEPTEMBER 29, 1863). In September 1863, Union Maj. Gen. **Nathaniel P. Banks** was attempting to gain a foothold in **Texas**. An expedition to **Sabine Pass, Texas**, was defeated and turned back early in the month. Afterward, he launched the **Texas Overland Expedition** to move up Bayou Teche (TESH) to Vermilionville, Louisiana, and then overland to Texas. Banks prepared for the move by concentrating elements of the XIII and XIX Corps on the lower Teche and by placing **Napoleon J. T. Dana's division** at Morganza on the upper Atchafalaya (uh-CHAF-uh-LIE-uh) River to prevent the Confederates from operating in that area. Dana sent about 1,000 men under Col. J. B. Leake on a **reconnaissance** to Stirling's Plantation, located about seven miles down the road leading to the Atchafalaya.

The Confederate response was quick. On the rainy night of September 28, **Thomas Green's** Confederate cavalry moved into position to attack Dana, while Confederate infantry marched into the enemy's rear. On the morning of September 29, Green attacked the Federals at Fordoche Bridge and pushed them back. Most of Leake's men escaped the Confederate trap by withdrawing to Morganza on a secluded path, but Green's cavalry captured 462 men and two cannons, and another 61 Federals were killed or wounded. Green reported losing 121 men. In October, **William B. Franklin** began the unsuccessful Texas Overland Expedition, while Banks led an expedition to establish a Union presence around Brownsville, Texas.

STOLBRAND, CHARLES JOHN (1821–1894) USA. A native of Sweden, Stolbrand served as a cadet in the royal **artillery** and fought in the

Schleswig-Holstein war of 1848–50. He then immigrated to the United States and settled in **Illinois**, where he became a prominent member of the Swedish community.

When the Civil War began, Stolbrand organized an artillery **company** and entered Union service in October 1861 as its captain when the unit was mustered into the **army** as a battery of the 2nd Illinois Light Artillery. He was promoted to major in December and led the battery at **Island No. 10**. In the autumn of 1862, **John A. Logan** appointed Stolbrand chief of his **brigade's** artillery. He continued to serve Logan after Logan became a **division** commander and saw considerable combat in the **Vicksburg Campaign** with the **Army of the Tennessee**. Stolbrand remained with Logan in the same position during the **Chattanooga Campaign** and after Logan was given command of the Army of the Tennessee's XV Corps in December 1863.

Stolbrand was captured in May 1864 while on a **reconnaissance** near Kingston, Georgia, during the **Atlanta Campaign**. Sent to **Andersonville Prison**, he escaped and rejoined his command in October. Stolbrand served as the XV Corps chief of artillery through the **March to the Sea** and the capture of **Savannah, Georgia**, but he then asked to be mustered out of service because of his failure to be promoted. Not wanting to lose Stolbrand, **William T. Sherman** had him deliver messages to **Abraham Lincoln** on his way home in February 1865. One of the messages was a recommendation for Stolbrand's promotion, which prompted Lincoln to promote the surprised officer there in his office. Stolbrand returned to Sherman and led a XVII Corps brigade in the last weeks of war.

After some service in **Kansas**, Stolbrand was mustered out of the volunteers in January 1866 and settled in **South Carolina**. Becoming involved in **Reconstruction** politics, he served as secretary of the 1868 constitutional convention and was a delegate to that year's **Republican National Convention**. Stolbrand also served as superintendent of the state penitentiary and was appointed superintendent of the federal courthouse and post office in **Charleston**.

STONE, CHARLES POMEROY (1824–1887) USA. A native of **Massachusetts**, Stone graduated from **West Point** in 1845 and won two **brevets** for gallantry while serving in the **Mexican War** as an ordnance officer. After the war, he served as an ordnance officer in the Pacific Northwest but resigned his commission in 1856. Stone then worked for the Mexican government surveying the state of Sonora and wrote a book about his experiences there.

When the Civil War began, Stone was appointed colonel and inspector general for the District of Columbia's militia and helped maintain order in the capital during the early turbulent weeks of the **secession** crisis. In May 1861, he was commissioned colonel in the regular **army** and was given command of the 14th U.S. Infantry. He was promoted to brigadier general of volunteers in August.

Stone first was given an infantry **brigade** and served under **Robert Patterson** in the **Shenandoah Valley**. After the **First Manassas** defeat, he was given an **Army of the Potomac division** in October and was assigned to guard the upper Potomac River. That month, Stone ordered his subordinate **Edward D. Baker** to put pressure on the Confederates on his front. Baker unwisely placed his brigade in a vulnerable position at **Ball's Bluff** and was killed in a disastrous battle. Baker, who was a friend of **Abraham Lincoln's** and a popular U.S. senator, was hailed as a hero, while Stone was blamed unfairly for Baker's death. Some politicians already suspected Stone's loyalty because he had supposedly returned a runaway slave to his owner and was said to be too friendly with secessionists. As a result, he was arrested in February 1862 and was confined in **prison** for 189 days, much of the time in solitary confinement. Stone's requests for a trial were ignored, and no charges were ever brought against him. He finally was released, but his military career was virtually ruined.

After receiving no assignment for nine months, Stone was sent to the **Department of the Gulf**. He served under **Nathaniel P. Banks** in the **Port Hudson Campaign** and became Banks's chief of staff in July 1863. Secretary of War **Edwin Stanton** had Stone mustered out of the volunteer service in April 1864 while he was serving Banks in the **Red River Campaign**. He retained his regular army commission of colonel but again was left without a position until August, when he briefly was given a brigade command in the Army of the Potomac's V Corps during the **Petersburg Campaign**. Stone finally resigned his colonel's commission in September 1864.

After the war, Stone moved to Egypt and served as the Khedive's chief of staff for 13 years. When he returned to the United States, he worked as an engineer and laid the foundation for the Statue of Liberty, an ironic task, given the fact he had been held in prison incommunicado for more than six months.

"STONE FLEETS." When the **U.S. Navy** began its **blockade** of the Confederacy, it found that it had far too few ships to perform the duty adequately. A plan was adopted in July 1861 whereby the navy acquired ships, loaded them with rocks and other materials, and sank them in Southern harbor channels. The first of these so-called stone fleets was used in December when 15 ships were sunk at **Charleston, South Carolina**. They proved ineffective, because they either deteriorated or sank in the soft mud.

STONE, WILLIAM MILO (1827–1893) USA. A native of **New York**, Stone practiced law in **Ohio** before moving to **Iowa** in 1854. There, he also practiced law, became a newspaper editor and a judge, and helped found the state's **Republican Party**.

Stone entered Union service in June 1861 as a **company** captain in the 3rd Iowa. He was promoted to major later in the month and was wounded in a small clash at Blue Mills, Missouri, in September. Stone was captured in the **Battle of Shiloh** and, after being **exchanged**, was appointed colonel of the 22nd Iowa in September 1862. He was wounded again during the 1863 **Vicksburg Campaign** but recovered in time to participate in the siege of **Jackson, Mississippi**, after **Vicksburg's** surrender. During the late summer of 1863, Stone temporarily commanded a **brigade** in the 1st Division of the **Army of the Tennessee's** XIII Corps.

After being chosen the Republican Party candidate, Stone resigned his commission in August 1863 to enter Iowa's gubernatorial race. He won and was sworn into office in January 1864. Stone was a two-term governor, and his administration worked for the relief of soldiers' families, organized a militia, and got the **13th Amendment** passed. He was **brevetted** brigadier general of volunteers for his war service and later worked as a land office commissioner.

STONEMAN, GEORGE (1822–1894) USA. A native of **New York**, Stoneman graduated from **West Point** in 1846. He served in the **Mexican War** as quartermaster for the "Mormon Battalion," which helped occupy **California**. After the war, Stoneman served on the frontier in the 2nd U.S. Cavalry and had risen to the rank of captain by the outbreak of the Civil War. In command of Fort Brown, Texas, in early 1861, he refused a secessionist demand to surrender and escaped with part of his command.

Stoneman was promoted to major in May 1861 and served on **George B. McClellan's** staff during his early operations in western **Virginia**. When McClellan took command of the Union **army** in **Washington, D.C.**, after **First Manassas**, he had Stoneman appointed brigadier general of volunteers in August and gave him a cavalry **division** in the

Army of the Potomac. After serving in the **Peninsula** and **Seven Days Campaigns**, Stoneman spent the rest of 1862 alternately in command of cavalry and infantry units in the Army of the Potomac. He spent the **Antietam Campaign** in Washington with a III Corps division but assumed command of the **corps** in October and won a regular army **brevet** for leading it at **Fredericksburg**.

Joseph Hooker made Stoneman the Army of the Potomac's chief of cavalry in February 1863, and he was promoted to major general of volunteers the following month. During the **Chancellorsville Campaign**, Hooker sent the cavalry on the first of **Stoneman's Raids**. Intended to threaten **Richmond, Virginia**, and divert Confederate attention while Hooker began his offensive, the raid failed to achieve any material success and simply deprived Hooker of his cavalry at a crucial time. After the failed raid, Stoneman was replaced by **Alfred Pleasonton** and was put in command of the Cavalry Bureau. He was absent from the field until February 1864, when he was sent to the west and was put in command of the **Army of the Ohio's** XXIII Corps.

In April 1864, Stoneman was placed in command of the Army of the Ohio's cavalry. He led it in the **Atlanta Campaign** but was captured at Macon, Georgia, in late July in **Stoneman's and McCook's Raid**, while attempting to disrupt Atlanta's supply line and free Union **prisoners** at **Andersonville**. After being **exchanged** in October, Stoneman assumed command of the **Department of the Ohio** in November and the following month led his cavalry on a raid into southwestern Virginia against Confederate salt and lead mines at Saltville. He was placed in command of the District of East Tennessee in March 1865 and led his last raid into **North Carolina** to assist **William T. Sherman's Carolinas Campaign**. This raid accomplished little except capturing **Salisbury, North Carolina**.

After being brevetted through the rank of major general of regulars for his war service, Stoneman was mustered out of the volunteers in September 1866. He remained in the regular army as a colonel and became commander of the 21st U.S. Infantry and the Department of Arizona. After retiring from the army in 1871, Stoneman settled in California, where he served as a state **railroad** commissioner and was elected governor in 1882.

STONEMAN'S AND McCOOK'S RAID, ATLANTA CAMPAIGN (JULY 27–31, 1864). By mid-July 1864, **William T. Sherman** had pushed the Confederate **Army of Tennessee** back into the Atlanta, Georgia, defenses during the **Atlanta Campaign**. Hoping to force **John Bell Hood's army** to withdraw by denying it supplies, Sherman sent his cavalry to cut the remaining Confederate **railroad** to the south. The cavalrymen were to move out in two columns, ride around opposite sides of the city, and link up to destroy the Macon & Western Railroad at Lovejoy's Station south of Atlanta. Major General **George Stoneman** led 6,500 troopers to the east from Decatur, while Brig. Gen. **Edward M. McCook** took 3,500 men to the west from the Chattahoochee River. Stoneman also received permission to attack **Andersonville prison** after the railroad had been cut and release the Union **prisoners** held there.

Stoneman set out on July 27 but immediately disobeyed orders and headed for Andersonville first. Sending one **division** under **Kenner Garrard** south to draw away the Confederate cavalry, he rode toward Macon. By thus splitting the Union cavalry into three small columns, Stoneman allowed **Joseph Wheeler's** Confederate cavalry to attack and **defeat in detail** each column. Wheeler's 10,000 troopers first defeated Garrard on July 28 and forced him to withdraw to the north. Detaching one **brigade** to follow Garrard, Wheeler then attacked Stoneman near Macon on July 29. The Confederates surrounded the Federals and captured Stoneman and 700 of his men as they tried to fight their way out of the encirclement. Some of Stoneman's troopers escaped but were chased and harassed by the Confederates for several days afterward. McCook reached the railroad south of Atlanta on July 29 and destroyed part of it before heading west. On July 30, Wheeler successfully surrounded McCook at Newman, but the Federals cut their way out after losing about 500 men.

The raid cost Sherman 2,000 cavalrymen and gained nothing except McCook's temporarily severing the railroad and destroying some Confederate wagons. The failure convinced Sherman that cavalry could not or would not cut Hood's supply line. As a result, he moved the bulk of his armies south of the city to accomplish the task. For the Confederates, the raid was perhaps the high point of Wheeler's career and proved that Confederate cavalrymen still outmatched their counterparts in the west.

STONEMAN'S RAIDS. Union cavalryman Maj. Gen. **George Stoneman** led several raids during the Civil War, but few proved very successful. His first came during the 1863 **Chancellorsville Campaign** while he was serving as chief of cavalry for **Joseph Hooker's Army of the Potomac**. As a prelude to the campaign, Hooker planned to send Stoneman west from Falmouth, Virginia, and then southeast into **Robert E. Lee's** rear toward **Richmond**. The raid was to disrupt Lee's supply line, draw away **J. E. B. Stuart's** Confederate cavalry, and distract Lee while Hooker crossed the Rappahannock River beyond Lee's left flank. The raid had to be postponed from April 13 to April 29, because heavy rains made the Rappahannock unfordable. Thus, instead of being a prelude to the Chancellorsville offensive, Stoneman's 10,000 troopers crossed the river the same day as the infantry.

Stoneman split his command into two columns. The smaller one of 3,400 men under **William W. Averell** was to head west to Culpeper and then south to Gordonsville along the Orange & Alexandria Railroad to destroy the track and distract the Confederates from the main raid. Stoneman would accompany the larger column containing **John Buford's** and **David Gregg's divisions** and ride west and then south to disrupt the Virginia Central Railroad around Louisa Court House before moving southeast to break the Richmond, Fredericksburg & Potomac Railroad in Lee's rear. Averell, who was faced by only **W. H. F. "Rooney" Lee's** cavalry **brigade**, believed he was outnumbered and timidly advanced only 25 miles to Rapidan Station. Disgusted, Hooker finally ordered him back to the main **army** on May 2, and when he continued to show a lack of aggressiveness, replaced him with **Alfred Pleasonton**.

Stoneman, Buford, and Gregg crossed the river at Kelly's Ford and headed south. The Federals dispersed into separate columns and over several days destroyed a significant amount of supplies, part of the James Canal, and some **railroad** track around Louisa Court House and between Richmond and Hanover Junction, but it proved to be only temporary damage. Coming within two miles of Richmond, they also frightened government officials, but Stoneman wisely avoided attacking the city's defenses. Some of the Union troopers rode on to join Union forces on the Virginia Peninsula, some retraced their route back to Kelly's Ford, and others rode around Lee's **Army of Northern Virginia** to the east and returned to their original camps around Falmouth. In the entire raid, Stoneman lost only 92 men.

The raid was a complete failure and played a large role in Hooker's defeat at Chancellorsville. Lee failed to take the bait and kept most of Stuart's cavalry along the Rappahannock. Stuart not only made first contact with Hooker near Chancellorsville and stalled his advance until Lee arrived with the army, but he also discovered Hooker's exposed right flank, which Lee attacked. With most of his cavalry away on the raid, Hooker was virtually blind and unaware of Lee's movements.

After his Chancellorsville Raid, Stoneman was transferred west, where he took command of the **Army of the Ohio's** cavalry. In July 1864, during the **Atlanta Campaign**, he participated in **Stoneman's and McCook's Raid**, which was intended to disrupt Confederate supply lines into Atlanta and free Union **prisoners** at **Andersonville**. Stoneman disobeyed orders and headed immediately for Andersonville instead of first breaking the Confederate railroad as planned. He was defeated and captured near Macon, Georgia, on July 29.

After being **exchanged** in October 1864, Stoneman was put in command of the **Department of the Ohio**. In late November, he planned a cavalry raid into southwestern **Virginia** to destroy important Confederate salt and lead mines. On December 10, Stoneman left Knoxville, Tennessee, in cold, wet weather with 5,500 troopers and followed the East Tennessee & Virginia Railroad toward Virginia. **John C. Breckinridge** commanded Confederate troops in the area, but he was outnumbered. Stoneman defeated **Basil Duke's** small Confederate cavalry brigade near Kingsport, Tennessee, on December 14, captured 300 prisoners, and continued **skirmishing** with the enemy as he moved through Bristol, Abington, and **Marion**. Breckinridge concentrated at Wytheville, Virginia, to protect the mines there, but Stoneman captured it on December 16. With Breckinridge now confronting him, Stoneman next sent a detachment back to **Saltville**, which he had bypassed earlier, to begin destroying the saltworks there. After forcing Breckinridge to withdraw southward toward **North Carolina**, he destroyed some mines and foundries around Wytheville and then returned to Saltville with the rest of his men. After completely destroying the saltworks and salt that was stockpiled there, the Federals headed back to **Tennessee** on December 21. This raid was Stoneman's most successful. Besides destroying valuable salt and lead mines, he also destroyed miles of railroad track and up to 100,000 bushels of salt and captured 900 **prisoners**, 19 cannons, 3,000 horses, and 3,000 **rifle muskets**.

Stoneman's fourth and last raid took place in the spring of 1865. During the **Carolinas Campaign**, **William T. Sherman** wanted a cavalry raid sent into the Carolinas to threaten Columbia, South Carolina, to distract the Confederates. By the time Stoneman began the raid, however, Sherman had already captured **Columbia** and entered **North Carolina**. The raid was modified to ride into North Carolina and southwestern Virginia.

The 3,000 Union cavalrymen left Jonesboro, Tennessee, on March 20 and crossed the Blue Ridge Mountains toward Salisbury, North Carolina, before turning north into Virginia. Stoneman destroyed railroad track between Wytheville and Lynchburg, Virginia, and then rode south to cut another railroad between Danville, Virginia, and Greensboro, North Carolina. Stoneman then captured **Salisbury** on April 12 and continued to Hendersonville, where he learned that **Joseph E. Johnston** had surrendered to Sherman. The raid captured about 2,000 prisoners and succeeded in destroying Confederate railroads, but it really did not affect the war's outcome since it occurred so close to the **surrenders**.

STONES RIVER, TENNESSEE, BATTLE OF (DECEMBER 31, 1862–JANUARY 2, 1863). After the 1862 **Kentucky Campaign**, **William S. Rosecrans's Army of the Cumberland** and **Braxton Bragg's Army of Tennessee** warily watched each other in middle **Tennessee**. On December 26, Rosecrans marched 47,000 men out of Nashville to drive Bragg from his base at Murfreesboro, Tennessee. Although Bragg had sent one **division** to reinforce **Vicksburg, Mississippi**, he still had 38,000 men at Murfreesboro and decided to fight. Bragg positioned his **army** northwest of town to cover all the roads leading to Murfreesboro, but he did not entrench, and his line was split at the right center by Stones River. To disrupt Rosecrans's advance, he also sent **Joseph Wheeler's** cavalry on a successful raid behind the Federals that captured a significant number of **prisoners** and wagons. Because of the wet weather and marauding enemy cavalry, Rosecrans did not cover the 30 miles to Murfreesboro until December 30. When he failed to attack that day, Bragg seized the initiative and decided to attack with his left wing the next morning. Coincidentally, Rosecrans also planned to attack Bragg with his left the next morning. Whoever moved first would have the advantage.

At daylight on December 31, the Confederates struck first when Bragg sent his entire left wing forward in an attack that made a giant right wheel as it advanced. Bragg's plan was to crush the Union right wing, drive it back to seize Rosecrans's supply line—the **railroad** and the Nashville Pike—and then to push the enemy into Stones River. This attack was made by two divisions of **William J. Hardee's corps** on Bragg's left and **Leonidas Polk's** corps in the left center. Fighting was vicious in dense cedar thickets that broke up the Confederate lines. **Alexander McCook's** Union **corps**, which held Rosecrans's right flank, bore the brunt of the attack and was pushed back steadily by the divisions of **Patrick Cleburne**, **John P. McCown**, **Benjamin F. Cheatham**, and **Jones M. Withers**. **Philip Sheridan's** Union division and other units made a desperate stand along the Wilkinson Pike and slowed up the Confederate attack but eventually had to fall back, as well. McCook's and **George H. Thomas's** corps (on McCook's left) retreated three miles to the Nashville Pike, and there, McCook made a last desperate stand.

The Union line now resembled a *V* with **William Hazen's brigade** holding the angle at a place known as the Round Forest or Hell's Half Acre. Rosecrans stripped troops from his left wing and reinforced the defensive line running from the Round Forest northwest along the Nashville Pike. Repeatedly at midday, Polk's brigades charged Hazen's position, only to be annihilated by volleys of **rifle** fire and massed cannons. Determined to seize the pike, Bragg ordered up four fresh brigades from **John C. Breckinridge's** division, which had been detached from Hardee's corps and positioned across Stones River on the far right. When these troops arrived at about 2:00 P.M., Polk wasted them by sending them against the Round Forest piecemeal. Unable to break the stubborn Union defense, the bloody Confederate assaults finally sputtered out around dark.

Neither side attacked on January 1, 1863, but the cavalry was active in raids and **skirmishes** behind Union lines. Bragg expected Rosecrans to retreat, but, instead, the Federals remained and only withdrew from the Round Forest to straighten out the line.

By January 2, the bulk of both armies were on the west side of Stones River. Breckinridge's Confederate division remained alone east of the river, as did **Thomas L. Crittenden's** Union division under Col. **Samuel Beatty**. Bragg's main line could be **enfiladed** by the Federals east of the river, so he ordered Breckinridge to attack and drive them back. Breckinridge vehemently protested the order, claiming the Union **artillery** on the west bank would enfilade his attacking line. Bragg insisted on the attack, however, and Breckinridge finally obeyed under protest. The Confederates advanced late in the afternoon and drove Beatty back to the river. But then, as Breckinridge predicted, his men were cut down by the massed cannons on the west bank and were forced to retreat.

With their men exhausted and Stones River rising from recent rains and threatening to cut the **army** in two, Confederate generals Cheatham and Withers wrote a memorandum (endorsed by Polk) on the night of January 2 asking Bragg to retreat. Bragg at first refused but then agreed when he mistakenly believed Rosecrans was being reinforced. In a driving rain, the Confederates withdrew late on the night of January 3. Although Bragg initially enjoyed great tactical success, his retreat allowed Rosecrans to claim victory. The three-day battle had no long-term effect on the war except costing Bragg 10,266 men and Rosecrans 13,249.

STONEWALL BRIGADE. This infantry **brigade** was the most famous in the **Confederate army**. Organized in the spring of 1861, it was composed of the 2nd, 4th, 5th, 27th, and 33rd Virginia Infantry and was manned by volunteers from the **Shenandoah Valley**. Placed under the command of Brig. Gen. **Thomas J. Jackson**, the brigade earned its name at **First Manassas**, where Jackson held the high ground at Henry House Hill. When Brig. Gen. **Barnard Bee** cried out that Jackson was standing like a stone wall, both Jackson and his brigade had new identities.

The Stonewall Brigade became famous for its marching and fighting abilities and served in virtually every major battle fought by the **Army of Northern Virginia**. It suffered particularly heavy casualties at **First Manassas**, **Kernstown**, **Cedar Mountain**, **Groveton**, **Second Manassas**, **Chancellorsville**, **Gettysburg**, and **Spotsylvania**. After Jackson's death in May 1863, the War Department officially named the unit the Stonewall Brigade to honor him, making the brigade the only one in the **Confederate army** with an official nickname.

Over the course of the war, the brigade commanders also included **Richard B. Garnett**, **Charles S. Winder**, William S. H. Baylor, **Elisha F. Paxton**, **James A. Walker**, and **William Terry**. Of these, Winder, Baylor, Paxton, and Garnett were killed (Garnett after leaving the brigade), and Walker was wounded and captured. Because heavy casualties had reduced its effectiveness, the Stonewall Brigade was merged with two other brigades after Spotsylvania and lost much of its identity. Approximately 6,000 men served in the brigade, but after fighting in 39 engagements, only 210 men were left at **Appomattox**.

STONEWALL, CSS. This **ironclad ram** was built in France for the Confederate government under a contract signed in July 1863. Finished in 1864, it was 171 feet long, displaced 900 tons, and was armed with one 300-pounder and two 70-pounder **Armstrong guns**. The *Stonewall* also had both steam-powered screw propellers and square-rigged sails. Diminishing French enthusiasm for the Confederate cause because of Confederate military reversals, France's own Mexican problems, and increasing Union diplomatic pressure prevented the ram from being delivered. The ship's codesigner, Lucien Arman, sold it to Denmark, but Denmark sold it back to Arman, who arranged to turn it over to the other codesigner, Confederate naval agent **James D. Bulloch**. The ram went through several name changes but finally was named the *Stonewall* when it took on a Confederate crew off the coast of France.

Under Capt. Thomas J. Page, the ram underwent repairs in Spain and then sailed unchallenged past two blockading Union warships and headed for Havana, Cuba. There, Page learned the war was over. He sold the *Stonewall* to Spanish officials in May 1865 for $16,000, paid the crew, and dismissed them. Later, the **U.S. Navy** bought the ram for the same price and sold it to Japan. Named first the *Kotetsu* and later the *Adzuma,* it served Japan for 30 years.

STOUGHTON, EDWIN HENRY (1838–1868) USA. A native of **Vermont**, Stoughton (STOH-tun) graduated from **West Point** in 1859, but he resigned his 2nd lieutenant's commission in March 1861 after serving on routine garrison duty. In September, he was appointed colonel of the 4th Vermont, and he and his men served in the **Washington, D.C.**, defenses until early 1862. As part of **William T. H. Brooks's Army of the Potomac brigade**, the 4th Vermont saw its first combat in the **Peninsula** and **Seven Days Campaigns**. Although Stoughton was absent on leave from July to November 1862, he was promoted to brigadier general of volunteers upon his return to duty. At age 24, he was the youngest general in the Union **army** at the time.

Given a Vermont brigade, Stoughton spent the next several months on garrison duty outside Washington, where he earned a reputation for enjoying liquor and women. In March 1863, he was captured from his headquarters at Fairfax Court House, Virginia, by **John S. Mosby** in one of the war's most daring raids. The capture ruined Stoughton's career. The Senate had failed to confirm his appointment to brigadier general and refused to do so after he was **exchanged** in May. Unable to gain another command, Stoughton eventually settled in **New York** and practiced law.

STOVALL, MARCELLUS AUGUSTUS (1818–1895) CSA. Although a native of **Georgia**, Stovall was educated in **Massachusetts**. After fighting in the **Seminole Wars** with Georgia militia, he entered **West Point** but was forced to leave after only one year because of rheumatism. Stovall returned to Georgia after traveling in Europe, became a merchant, and served as captain of a local militia **artillery company**.

When the Civil War began, Stovall was appointed colonel of artillery in the Georgia militia. He entered Confederate service in October when he was commissioned lieutenant colonel of the 3rd Georgia Infantry Battalion. Stovall was an excellent administrator, and his unit became known for its **discipline** and high morale while serving on garrison duty in **Virginia**, **North Carolina**, and East **Tennessee**. As part of **James E. Rains's brigade**, Stovall saw some minor combat in the summer of 1862 in Tennessee, but he did not engage in a large battle until he fought at **Stones River** with the **Army of Tennessee**. There, Rains was killed, and Stovall was praised for his role in the attack on the Union right wing on the first day.

Stovall was promoted to brigadier general in April 1863 and was given command of **William Preston's** old brigade in **John C. Breckinridge's division**. He served around Jackson, Mississippi, during the

Vicksburg Campaign and participated in the siege of **Jackson** in July 1863. At **Chickamauga**, Stovall again was praised for leading an attack that helped turn the enemy left flank. Afterward, he was given command of a Georgia brigade in **Alexander P. Stewart's** division. During the **Atlanta Campaign**, Stovall often was absent sick, but he returned to duty in time to fight at **Jonesboro**. Although not engaged at **Franklin**, Stovall served at **Nashville** and helped form the rear guard during the retreat from Tennessee. In early 1865, Stovall served in the **Carolinas Campaign** and fought his last battle at **Bentonville**.

After the war, Stovall returned to Georgia, where he worked as a cotton broker and fertilizer manufacturer and founded the Georgia Chemical Works.

STOWE, HARRIET BEECHER (1811–1896) USA. A member of a prominent **Connecticut abolitionist** family, Stowe was the daughter of Rev. Lyman Beecher and the sister of **Henry Ward Beecher**. She moved to **Ohio** as a young woman, married Calvin Stowe in 1836, and had seven children. Stowe moved to **Maine** with her husband in 1850 when he became a professor at Bowdoin College and while there wrote her famous novel, *Uncle Tom's Cabin*, which was published in March 1852.

The novel was filled with religious overtones, condemned **slavery** as evil, and described the life of the kind, Christian slave named Uncle Tom, who died at the hands of an overseer. The novel was a huge bestseller in the North and convinced many previously ambivalent people that slavery was wrong. It also further split the nation, and **Abraham Lincoln** supposedly remarked that Stowe's book caused the Civil War when he once was introduced to her. Northerners accepted the novel as a true depiction of slavery, while outraged Southerners (one of whom sent Stowe a severed slave's ear) pointed out that most slave owners were decent people. Southerners also noted that except for a brief trip to **Kentucky**, Stowe had never seen slavery herself.

Stowe continued to write after the publication of *Uncle Tom's Cabin,* but she never again had such success.

STRAHL, OTHO FRENCH (1831–1864) CSA. A native of **Ohio**, Strahl graduated from Ohio Wesleyan University and moved to **Tennessee**, where he studied law under former classmate and future Confederate general **Daniel H. Reynolds**. After passing the bar, he opened his own Tennessee law practice.

When Tennessee seceded, Strahl supported his adopted state, was elected captain of a volunteer **company**, and entered Confederate service in May 1861 as part of the 4th Tennessee. He was elected lieutenant colonel the day of mustering and accompanied the **regiment** to the Mississippi River, where it became part of the Columbus, Kentucky, garrison. When Col. Rufus P. Neely was made **brigade** commander, Strahl took command of the regiment and participated in the **Battle of Belmont**, although he was not actively engaged. His first combat was at **Shiloh**. There the regiment fought under Neely in **Alexander P. Stewart's** brigade and lost more than half its men but captured a Union battery. Neely died shortly afterward, and Strahl was elected colonel during the **army's** reorganization in the spring of 1862.

During the **Kentucky Campaign**, Strahl was not actively engaged at **Munfordville**, but he was in the thick of battle at **Perryville** and lost nearly half the regiment. Just prior to **Stones River**, the 5th Tennessee was consolidated with Strahl's 4th Tennessee in the **Army of Tennessee**. He was praised at Stones River for helping drive **Philip Sheridan's division** away from the Wilkinson Pike. In late February 1863, Strahl took over the brigade when Stewart was promoted to division command, but he did not receive his promotion to brigadier general until July.

After fighting at **Chickamauga** in **Benjamin F. Cheatham's** division, Strahl's brigade was transferred to Stewart's division. He fought under Stewart at **Missionary Ridge** but was sent back to Cheatham for the **Atlanta Campaign**. During the campaign, Strahl saw nearly continuous fighting and was under fire 60 of the first 71 days. During the **Franklin and Nashville Campaign**, his brigade was part of **John C. Brown's** division. At Franklin on November 30, 1864, Strahl led his men up to the Union works and was handing loaded **rifles** to soldiers firing over the breastworks when he was shot. A second and then a third bullet finally killed him.

STRATEGY. In military terms, strategy generally is one's plans to achieve objectives that are large in scope (such as winning a war or campaign) as opposed to **tactics**, which are the maneuvers used to win a specific battle. In the Civil War, the Union's war strategy was the offensive **Anaconda Plan**, while the Confederacy depended largely on a defensive strategy to conserve resources. An example of campaign strategy is **William T. Sherman's** use of **turning movements** rather than **frontal attacks** to force the Confederates out of their strong defensive positions during the **Atlanta Campaign**. The Confederate strategy was to remain in strong earthworks to force the Federals to exhaust themselves in frontal attacks and then seek opportunities to counterattack.

STRAWBERRY PLAINS, VIRGINIA, BATTLE OF (JULY 27, 1864). *See* DEEP BOTTOM, VIRGINIA, FIRST BATTLE OF.

STREIGHT, ABEL D. (1828–1892) USA. A native of **New York**, Streight operated a lumber mill for a number of years before moving to **Indiana** by way of **Ohio**. He entered Union service in December 1861 as colonel of the 51st Indiana and was present at the battles of **Shiloh** and **Perryville**, although he was not actually engaged. After fighting at **Stones River** with the **Army of the Cumberland**, Streight proposed launching a mounted raid into northern **Alabama** and **Georgia** to destroy Confederate **railroads**. **William S. Rosecrans** authorized the raid as a means to force the Confederate **Army of Tennessee** to withdraw from **Tennessee** and to draw **Nathan Bedford Forrest's** cavalry away from **Grierson's Raid** in nearby **Mississippi**. **Streight's Raid** in the spring of 1863 was a failure, for Forrest's cavalry chased down Streight and forced his surrender on May 3.

After being held at **Libby Prison** for a number of months, Streight was one of more than 100 **prisoners** who tunneled their way to freedom in February 1864. Rejoining his **regiment**, he guarded railroads in Tennessee until he was given his own **brigade** in the 3rd Division of the Army of the Cumberland's IV Corps in November. After fighting at the **Battles of Franklin and Nashville**, Streight was **brevetted** brigadier general of volunteers for his war service.

Streight resigned his commission in March 1865 and returned to Indiana, where he worked as a publisher and in the lumber industry. He also became head of a chair manufacturing company and in 1876 was elected to the state senate.

STREIGHT'S RAID (APRIL 21–MAY 3, 1863). When Maj. Gen. **U. S. Grant** prepared to cross the Mississippi River and begin the **Vicksburg Campaign** in earnest in April 1863, two mounted raids were sent behind enemy lines to distract the Confederates. These were **Grierson's Raid**, ordered by Grant, and Streight's Raid, ordered by **Army of the Cumberland** commander, **William S. Rosecrans**.

Colonel **Abel D. Streight**, commander of the 51st Indiana, had proposed a raid against Confederate **railroads** in western **Georgia**. Rosecrans authorized the raid as a means to force the Confederate **Army of Tennessee** to withdraw from middle **Tennessee** and to draw **Nathan Bedford Forrest's** cavalry away from Grierson's Raid in **Mississippi**. The raid soon was plagued with problems. First, Streight was convinced by others that mules were better suited for the mountainous terrain than horses. He accepted the mules, but they proved to be too worn out and stubborn to be of much use. Streight then took his 2,000 men (plus 800 mules) to Eastport, Mississippi, by steamer to join forces with Brig. Gen. **Grenville M. Dodge**. By the time he got there, Dodge had been driven off by Confederate cavalrymen. While Streight visited Dodge's far-off camp, the Confederates raided Eastport and ran off 200 of his mules.

Streight finally left Eastport, Mississippi, on April 21, 1863, and moved to Tuscumbia, Alabama, where he received additional mules. Handpicking 1,500 men, he left Tuscumbia and entered the rugged mountains of north **Alabama**, heading for the Western & Atlantic Railroad in western Georgia. Forrest's cavalry moved faster on its horses and made an exhausting ride to catch up with the raiders at Sand Mountain on April 30. There, an attempt by Forrest to surround the raiders failed when Streight ambushed one of the Confederate columns at **Day's Gap** and captured two of Forrest's cannons. With Forrest in pursuit, Streight headed for Rome, Georgia, where he planned to cross the Oostanaula River and burn the bridge behind him. Forrest, however, again pushed his men to their limit and caught up with Streight near the Georgia state line at Cedar Bluff. Although Forrest had only 600 men, he brought Streight to bay and then marched his men in a circle through a field to make it appear he had a much larger force. Completely exhausted and believing himself outnumbered, Streight surrendered on May 3. Forrest lost only 65 men in the pursuit and capture of 1,500 Federals, but he also had been drawn out of Mississippi during a critical phase of the Vicksburg Campaign.

STRINGHAM, SILAS HORTON (1797–1876) USA. A native of **New York**, Stringham entered the **U.S. Navy** as a midshipman at age 11 and served in the War of 1812, in the Mediterranean Sea, around Africa, and in the West Indies. He was a captain serving as commandant of the New York Navy Yard when the **Mexican War** began. Stringham participated in the bombardment of Vera Cruz during the war and then commanded the Norfolk Navy Yard, the Mediterranean Squadron, and the Boston Navy Yard.

When the Civil War began, Stringham was a commodore in charge of **Massachusetts's** Boston Navy Yard. During the **Fort Sumter** crisis, he served as an adviser to President **James Buchanan** and unsuccessfully proposed reinforcing the fort. Placed in command of the **North Atlantic Blockading Squadron** in May 1861, Stringham helped plan the capture of **Hatteras Inlet, North Carolina**, and led the naval forces that were involved in the attack. Only a month later, in September, Stringham requested to be relieved of command. A feud with Assistant Secretary of the Navy **Gustavus Fox** and a lack of credit for his service at Hatteras Inlet probably were behind his request.

Stringham was placed on the retired list as an admiral in 1862, but he returned to command the Boston Navy Yard that same year and remained there until war's end. Before his death in 1876, he also served as port admiral for New York City.

STRONG, GEORGE CROCKETT (1832–1863) USA. A native of **Vermont**, Strong was raised by an uncle in **Massachusetts**. After graduating from **West Point** in 1857, he served in the ordnance department at various arsenals until the beginning of the Civil War.

As a 1st lieutenant, Strong served as **Irvin McDowell's** ordnance officer at **First Manassas** and briefly was **George B. McClellan's** assistant ordnance officer for the **Army of the Potomac**. In September 1861, he was appointed **Benjamin F. Butler's** assistant adjutant general with the rank of major. Strong helped plan Butler's expedition to **New Orleans, Louisiana**, and became Butler's chief of staff and chief of ordnance during the city's occupation. Although frequently absent sick in 1862–63, he did lead successful raids along the **Mississippi** Gulf Coast and into southeastern **Louisiana**.

Strong was promoted to brigadier general of volunteers in March 1863 and was sent to **South Carolina**. He took command of the forces on St. Helena Island in June and on July 11 led his **brigade** in an unsuccessful attack on **Fort Wagner**. Seven days later, Strong was severely wounded in the thigh during a second attack on the fort. He developed tetanus, died in New York City nearly two weeks later, and was promoted posthumously to major general of volunteers.

STRONG, WILLIAM KERLEY (1805–1867) USA. A native of **New York**, Strong was a wealthy, retired wool merchant and a prominent **Democrat** in 1861. Traveling in Egypt when the Civil War began, he went to France and helped secure weapons for the Union before returning to the United States. Impressed with pro-Union speeches made by Strong, **Abraham Lincoln** appointed him a brigadier general of volunteers in September 1861. He first commanded Benton Barracks in St. Louis, Missouri, before being put in charge of the District of Cairo in July 1862. After a few months there, Strong was sent to **New York** for unknown duty before being named to a commission to investigate the Union evacuation of **New Madrid**, Missouri. He commanded the District of St. Louis from June 1863 until his resignation in October. Just before war's end, Strong suffered a carriage accident in New York City and was paralyzed for the rest of his life.

STUART, DAVID (1816–1868) USA. A native of **New York**, Stuart moved to **Michigan** as a young man. There he became a lawyer and in 1852 was elected to the **U.S. Congress** as a **Democrat**. Defeated for re-election, Stuart became solicitor for the Illinois Central Railroad.

Stuart entered Union service in July 1861 as lieutenant colonel of the 42nd Illinois, but three months later, he was appointed colonel of the 55th Illinois. In March 1862, he was given a **brigade** command in **William T. Sherman's division** and fought well at **Shiloh**, where he was wounded while holding the extreme Union left flank. After leading his **regiment** in the **siege of Corinth, Mississippi**, Stuart was sent to **Tennessee**, where he commanded a XIII Corps brigade.

Stuart was promoted to brigadier general of volunteers in November 1862 and fought at **Chickasaw Bayou** in command of a brigade in **Morgan L. Smith's** division in the XV Corps. After Smith was wounded in the battle, Stuart assumed command of the division and led it at **Arkansas Post**. He continued to command the division in the **Army of the Tennessee** during the early part of the **Vicksburg Campaign**, but in March 1863, he was forced to relinquish it when the Senate inexplicably refused to confirm his appointment to brigadier general. In relieving him, **William T. Sherman** highly praised Stuart's performance as an officer.

After resigning from the volunteers in April 1863, Stuart returned to his Michigan law practice. He also practiced law in **Louisiana** after the war but soon returned to Michigan.

STUART, JAMES EWELL BROWN "JEB" (1833–1864) CSA. A native of **Virginia,** "Jeb" Stuart attended Emory and Henry College before entering **West Point** in 1850. After graduating in 1854, he served in **Texas** with the Mounted Rifles before being assigned to the 1st U.S. Cavalry in **Kansas**. While with the cavalry, Stuart was wounded by **Indians**, married the daughter of future Union general **Philip St. George Cooke**, and was promoted to 1st lieutenant. He also patented a **saber** hook that allowed a cavalryman to detach his saber and scabbard quickly from the belt. In 1859, Stuart was in **Washington, D.C.**, on leave to secure his patent (which he later sold to the government for $5,000) when **John Brown's Raid on Harpers Ferry, Virginia**, occurred. After serving as **Robert E. Lee's** volunteer aide during Brown's capture, he returned to Kansas. Stuart was on leave when Virginia seceded and promptly resigned his commission in May 1861.

A week after resigning his commission, Stuart entered the Virginia state **army** as a lieutenant colonel. Assigned to Col. **Thomas J. Jackson** at **Harpers Ferry**, he first commanded several cavalry **companies**, but in July 1861, he was appointed colonel of the 1st Virginia Cavalry. Less than a week later, Stuart became famous for leading a cavalry charge at **First Manassas** that routed an enemy **regiment**. Following the battle, he earned more praise from **Joseph E. Johnston** for his great skill in scouting and manning **picket** posts in Northern Virginia. As a result, Stuart was promoted to brigadier general in September and was given command of Johnston's cavalry.

Stuart continued to perform scouting and guard duty in Northern Virginia until March 1862, when he covered Johnston's withdrawal south of the Rappahannock River. His rise to prominence came on the Virginia Peninsula in June 1862. After Lee assumed command of the **Army of Northern Virginia**, Stuart received permission to make a cavalry raid behind **George B. McClellan's Army of the Potomac**. With 1,200 troopers, he made **Stuart's Ride**, a four-day raid around the enemy army that not only provided Lee with the intelligence that McClellan's right flank was unprotected, but also made Stuart a Confederate hero. During the ride, he was pursued by his father-in-law, Cooke. In the subsequent **Seven Days Campaign**, Stuart performed valuable scouting and escort duty, which won him promotion to major general in July 1862.

Only days after this promotion, Lee reorganized the cavalry into a **division** and put it under Stuart. The dashing trooper became the epitome of the romantic cavalier. Stuart was daring and brave, and his good humor and charismatic personality won him his men's loyalty. He also was a showman who enjoyed the attention his thigh-high boots and ostrich-plumed hat brought. Most importantly, Stuart was an effective cavalryman whose training and leadership made the Confederate cavalry unmatched during the first half of war. In August 1862, he embarrassed Maj. Gen. **John Pope** by stealing his **uniform** and dispatch book and capturing several hundred **prisoners** from the **Army of Virginia** headquarters during the **Catlett's Station Raid**. Over the next three months, Stuart led Jackson's march to the Federal rear in the **Second Manassas Campaign**, guarded Lee's flanks during the Second Battle of Manassas, effectively used his **horse artillery** to repulse Union attacks at **Antietam**, and made his **Chambersburg Raid** in October. In December, he again guarded Lee's flank at **Fredericksburg** and supervised **John Pelham's** horse artillery, which stalled the Union attack on the Confederate right. After the battle, Stuart led his cavalry on the **Dumfries Raid** in late December.

At **Chancellorsville**, Stuart showed that cavalry was most valuable in providing intelligence. It was his men who first learned that the Federal right flank was "in the air" and allowed **Stonewall Jackson** to make his famous flank attack. When Jackson fell mortally wounded, Stuart assumed command of his **corps** and led it during the battle's final day. Stuart was disappointed when Lee passed over him for permanent corps command, but Lee felt he was irreplaceable as cavalry chief.

Stuart's reputation was somewhat tarnished when his cavalry was surprised at **Brandy Station** in 1863 by the increasingly effective Union cavalry. Although he remained in control of the field, he was embarrassed by the fight, and his desire to make up for the surprise may have led him to ask Lee's permission to raid behind the Union army during the **Gettysburg Campaign**. Lee allowed it on the condition that Stuart keep in contact with the army and leave enough troopers behind to screen the invasion and to provide intelligence. Stuart left his weakest units with Lee, and the advancing Union Army of the Potomac trapped him and prevented him from rejoining Lee until July 2, 1863. His **Gettysburg Raid** left Lee largely blind in **Pennsylvania** and helped lead to the unwanted Battle of Gettysburg. Although Stuart rejoined the army on the battle's second day and fiercely fought the Union cavalry on July 3, the campaign was his worst performance of the war and earned him one of Lee's rare rebukes.

In September 1863, Stuart's cavalry was organized into a two-division corps, but he was never promoted to the appropriate rank of lieutenant general. During the 1864 **Overland Campaign**, he went in pursuit of **Philip Sheridan's Richmond Raid** on May 9. On May 11, Stuart engaged Sheridan at **Yellow Tavern** and was mortally wounded in the right abdomen by a pistol shot fired at close range by a Federal trooper who was retreating past him. Taken to **Richmond**, Stuart died the next day. His loss was devastating to the Confederates and led Lee to remark, "He never brought me a piece of false information" (Thomas, *Bold Dragon,* 297).

STUART'S RIDE AROUND McCLELLAN (JUNE 12–15, 1862). To gain intelligence on the right flank of Maj. Gen. **George B. McClellan's Army of the Potomac**, then threatening **Richmond, Virginia**, during the **Peninsula Campaign, Robert E. Lee** sent **J. E. B. Stuart's** cavalry on a raid around McClellan's right flank. Stuart picked 1,200 troopers and left Richmond in the predawn hours of June 12, 1862. After riding northwest for several miles, he turned to the east and headed for McClellan's right flank, located north of the Chickahominy River. Stuart continued past the unprotected flank and into McClellan's rear, facing little opposition from the Union cavalry under Stuart's father-in-law, **Philip St. George Cooke.** Thinking Cooke might be closing in on his rear, Stuart decided to return to Richmond by riding southward completely around the Union **army.** The column had some tense moments, such as having to rebuild a bridge across the Chickahominy River when the enemy was pressing the rear, but Stuart returned to Richmond on June 15 after losing only one man killed. In four days, he covered more than 100 miles, captured a number of horses and **prisoners**, and rode completely around the Army of the Potomac. Most importantly, Stuart provided Lee with the crucial intelligence that McClellan's right flank was "in the air," which led to Lee attacking the Federals in the **Seven Days Campaign**.

STUMBAUGH, FREDERICK SHEARER (1817–1897) USA. A native of **Pennsylvania**, Stumbaugh was a lawyer and militia officer before the Civil War. He entered Union service in April 1861 as colonel of the 90-day 2nd Pennsylvania. When the **regiment** was mustered out of service after guarding Potomac River fords, Stumbaugh raised the 77th Pennsylvania and was appointed its colonel in October. Sent west, he joined the **Army of the Ohio** and led his regiment on the second day of battle at **Shiloh** and in the **siege of Corinth, Mississippi.** During the **Kentucky Campaign**, Stumbaugh's regiment accompanied **Don Carlos Buell** into **Kentucky**, but he did not participate in the **Battle of Perryville**.

Stumbaugh was promoted to brigadier general of volunteers in November 1862 and commanded a **brigade** around Nashville, Tennessee, during the **Battle of Stones River**. For reasons unknown, his appointment to brigadier general was revoked in January 1863, and he returned to his regimental command. Stumbaugh then requested a discharge, which was granted in May. Returning to Pennsylvania, he practiced law until moving to **Iowa** later in life.

STURGIS, SAMUEL DAVIS (1822–1889) USA. A native of **Pennsylvania**, Sturgis graduated from **West Point** in 1846. While serving with the dragoons, he fought in the **Mexican War** and was captured and briefly held prisoner near Buena Vista. After the war, Sturgis served on the frontier fighting **Indians** and rose to the rank of captain in the 1st U.S. Cavalry.

Sturgis was stationed at **Fort Smith, Arkansas**, when the Civil War began. There a number of the **regiment's** officers resigned to join the Confederacy, and the post itself was threatened by secessionists, but

Sturgis withdrew much of the regiment safely to Fort Leavenworth, Kansas. Promoted to major in May 1861, he commanded a **brigade** at **Wilson's Creek** and took charge of the **army** when **Nathaniel Lyon** was killed. Sturgis's actions there won him one **brevet** and a promotion to brigadier general of volunteers in March 1862.

After briefly serving as **David Hunter's** chief of staff in **Missouri** in November 1861, Sturgis was transferred to the **Washington, D.C.**, defenses in May 1862 and was given command of an infantry brigade. During the **Second Manassas Campaign**, he was given command of the **Army of Virginia's** Reserve Corps and reinforced **John Pope** just prior to the Second Battle of Manassas. An admirer of **George B. McClellan**, Sturgis then uttered his famous quip, "I don't care for John Pope one pinch of owl dung" (Warner, *Generals in Blue,* 487). He won a second brevet for his service at Second Manassas and was given a **division** command in the **Army of the Potomac's** IX Corps for the **Antietam Campaign**. Sturgis led it at **South Mountain**, at Antietam's Burnside's Bridge, and at **Fredericksburg's** Marye's Heights. Sturgis later was awarded two more brevets for his service at Antietam and Fredericksburg.

In early 1863, Sturgis accompanied the IX Corps to the west, where he was made the **Department of the Ohio's** chief of cavalry in July. After some service in East **Tennessee**, he was sent to engage **Nathan Bedford Forrest** in northern **Mississippi** to prevent Forrest from interfering with the **Atlanta Campaign**. In June 1864, Sturgis's superior cavalry force fought Forrest at **Brice's Cross Roads**, but he suffered a stinging defeat that ruined his career. The battle later was investigated, and he spent the rest of the war waiting in vain for a new command.

Sturgis was mustered out of the volunteers in August 1865 with brevets of brigadier general and major general of regulars, but he remained in the army as lieutenant colonel of the 6th U.S. Cavalry. He was promoted to colonel of the 7th U.S. Cavalry in 1869 and was in command of it when his lieutenant colonel, **George A. Custer**, led the regiment and was killed at the Battle of the Little Big Horn. After serving as governor of the Washington Soldiers' Home for four years, Sturgis retired from the army in 1888.

SUBMARINES. The Civil War was the first war in which submarines were used successfully in battle. Both sides experimented with them, but the Confederates were more active because their inferior resources forced them to be more inventive and imaginative. The submarines generally were cylindrical or cigar-shaped. Some were hand powered, with the crew turning a crankshaft that ran down the center of the boat.

New Orleans, Louisiana, was the site of much experimentation with submarines. In 1861, the two-man submarine *Pioneer* was constructed there. It carried a **torpedo** on its deck that could be attached to an enemy vessel and apparently successfully sank some target vessels in Lake Pontchartrain. The *Pioneer* entered Confederate service in March 1862, but it was never used in battle. When the Federals captured New Orleans in the spring of 1862, it was scuttled to keep it out of enemy hands. For many years a submarine identified as the *Pioneer* was on display in New Orleans, but it now is believed to be another unidentified boat. Other submarines apparently were also built in New Orleans, but their design and fate are unknown.

The *Pioneer* was the prototype of the more famous **CSS *H. L. Hunley***, which became the only successful submarine of the war. Built in Mobile, Alabama, by its inventor, H. L. Hunley, the boat carried a spar torpedo and a crew of nine. Accidents during testing cost the lives of two crews, including Hunley, but a third crew successfully sank the **USS *Housatonic*** in **Charleston, South Carolina**, harbor in February 1864. However, the *Hunley* also sank for unknown reasons and the crew was lost (it was located in 1995 and was raised in 2000).

Other Confederate submarines were the *American Diver, Pioneer II*, and the *St. Patrick*. The four-man *American Diver* was built in Mobile, but foul weather prevented it from ever attacking the enemy. The five-man *Pioneer II* also was built in Mobile and attempted to attack the Union fleet in February 1864, but it was swamped in rough seas and sank without loss of life. The five-man *St. Patrick* was built in Selma, Alabama, and attacked the USS *Octorara* at **Mobile Bay** in January 1865, but its spar torpedo failed to explode.

The Union built the ***Alligator*** for use against the **CSS *Virginia***. Completed in June 1862, the submarine was powered by underwater oars and required a diver to exit the boat and physically attach the torpedo to the enemy ship. It was stationed in **Virginia's** James River but was never used in battle. In April 1863, the *Alligator* was being towed to Charleston, South Carolina, when it sank in a storm off Cape Hatteras, North Carolina. *See also* "INFERNAL MACHINES."

SUBSTITUTES. America's first **conscription**, or draft, laws were passed during the Civil War. The Confederacy passed the first draft law in 1862, followed by the Union in 1863. The purpose of conscription actually was to encourage voluntary enlistments, for being drafted carried with it the stigma of reluctant loyalty. When a man was drafted, he could either enter the service himself, pay a **commutation** fee to avoid service, or hire a substitute to serve in his place. The purpose of allowing commutation fees and substitutions was to allow vital skilled laborers to avoid military service. A draftee acquired a substitute by either contracting one himself or using the services of professional substitute brokers, and the fee paid the substitute varied as supply and demand fluctuated. Substitutes became very unpopular because they reinforced the idea that the war was a "rich man's war and a poor man's fight." Substitutes also gained a reputation for being unreliable, and they frequently **deserted** at the first opportunity in order to hire out again. Because of these abuses, the Confederacy abolished the substitute system in 1863.

SUFFOLK, VIRGINIA, SIEGE OF (APRIL 11–MAY 3, 1863). In February 1863, Lt. Gen. **James Longstreet** was detached from the **Army of Northern Virginia** and was put in command of the **Department of Virginia and North Carolina**. With the **divisions** of **John Bell Hood**, **George Pickett**, and **Daniel H. Hill**, he was to protect **Richmond, Virginia**, and gather supplies for the **Army of Northern Virginia** in southeastern **Virginia** and northeastern **North Carolina**. In March 1863, Longstreet sent Hill's division to gather supplies in North Carolina and to attack **New Bern** and **Washington**. He then sent Hood, Pickett, and **Samuel G. French** from Petersburg to Suffolk, Virginia, in early April. They were to besiege Maj. Gen. **John J. Peck's** 17,000 Federals at Suffolk, while other troops gathered supplies in southeastern Virginia.

Over the next few weeks, several clashes occurred around Suffolk as the Confederates invested it. The siege began in earnest on April 13 when a battery was established at Hill's Point on the Nansemond River, at what became known as **Fort Huger**, to harass Union shipping. The following day, another Confederate battery upriver at Norfleet House damaged the USS *Mount Washington*, but on April 15, the Federals opened fire from secretly constructed batteries and drove away the Confederates. At about dusk on April 19, a small Union force launched a surprise attack by transport against the Confederates at Fort Huger. In 10 minutes, the 270 Federals captured all five Confederate cannons and over 130 **prisoners**. On April 24, the Confederates repulsed another Union attack by Brig. Gen. **Michael Corcoran** against Pickett's right flank. The clashes ended on April 30, when **Robert E. Lee** ordered Longstreet to return to the Army of Northern Virginia at Fredericksburg, Virginia. Longstreet began his wagon trains of supplies first and then disengaged from Suffolk on the night of May 3. During the siege, the Confederates suffered about 900 casualties, while the Federals lost 260 men.

SULLIVAN, JEREMIAH CUTLER (1830–1890) USA. A native of **Indiana**, Sullivan became the son-in-law of Union general **Benjamin F. Kelley**. He entered the **U.S.** Navy as a midshipman in 1848 and served on four ships before resigning his commission in 1854 to become a lawyer. Sullivan helped raise the 90-day 6th Indiana when the Civil War began and was mustered into Union service in April 1861 as one of the **regiment's** captains. After fighting at **Philippi**, the regiment was mustered out in July, but Sullivan was commissioned colonel of the 13th Indiana.

After serving at **Rich Mountain**, Sullivan took a **brigade** command in **James Shields's** division in the **Shenandoah Valley** in January 1862. He led it at **Kernstown** and was promoted to brigadier general of volunteers in April. Transferred west, Sullivan was given a brigade command in the **Army of the Mississippi's** 3rd Division in June. He led it at **Iuka** and **Corinth** and in November was put in command of the District of Jackson, Tennessee. Sullivan remained in Jackson until the spring of 1863, at which time he became **U. S. Grant's** acting inspector general for the **Army of the Tennessee**. He remained with Grant through the **Vicksburg Campaign**, but after the city's surrender, he was appointed chief of staff for **James B. McPherson's** XV Corps.

In September 1863, Sullivan was transferred back east, where he was assigned to his father-in-law's **Department of West Virginia**. After guarding **railroads** for several months while in command of the Maryland Heights Division, he was given a **division** command in December. At its head, Sullivan participated in the 1864 Union defeats at **New Market** and **Lynchburg, Virginia**. These engagements apparently ruined Sullivan's career, for afterward no commander wanted him. He was given a brigade in the District of the Kanawha in August 1864 but resigned his commission in May 1865.

After the war, Sullivan lived in **Maryland** before moving to **California** around 1878. There he held minor clerical positions until his death.

SULLY, ALFRED (1821–1879) USA. A native of **Pennsylvania**, Sully was the son of painter Thomas Sully. After graduating from **West Point** in 1841, he was assigned to the infantry and served in both the **Seminole** and **Mexican Wars**. Sully then was stationed on the frontier, where he fought the Cheyenne **Indians**.

Sully was a captain in the 2nd U.S. Infantry when the Civil War began. He served in **Minnesota** and in the **Washington, D.C.**, defenses before being appointed colonel of the 1st Minnesota in March 1862. As part of the **Army of the Potomac**, the **regiment** fought in the **Peninsula**

Campaign, and Sully won a **brevet** for his actions at **Seven Pines**. In June 1862, he was given a **brigade** command in **John Sedgwick's** II Corps' **division** and won a second brevet for **Malvern Hill** during the **Seven Days Campaign**. Sully returned to his regiment after the Seven Days and led it at **Antietam**.

In late September 1862, Sully was promoted to brigadier general of volunteers. He returned to his brigade command and led it at **Fredericksburg** but was relieved by division commander **John Gibbon** in May 1863 because he did not move aggressively enough against a rebellious regiment. Sully was exonerated by an investigative panel he requested, but he still was transferred west. For the rest of the war, he served in **district** commands in **Iowa** and the Dakotas and fought the Sioux. For this service, Sully was brevetted brigadier general of regulars and major general of volunteers.

Sully was mustered out of the volunteers in April 1866, but he remained in the regular **army** with the rank of major. He served extensively on the frontier and died in 1879 while colonel of the 21st U.S. Infantry. During his long military career, Sully earned more fame as an Indian fighter than a Civil War general.

***SULTANA* SINKING (APRIL 27, 1865).** One of the greatest accidents in American history was the sinking of the steamship *Sultana* at the end of the Civil War. In April 1865, Mississippi River steamboats were busy transferring recently freed Union **prisoners** of war to their homes. The federal government paid the ships' owners for each soldier they carried, so it was very profitable to fill the ships beyond their safe capacity. The *Sultana* was built to carry 400 passengers, but it took aboard more than 2,000 men at **Vicksburg, Mississippi**, on April 26 and headed upstream. Above Memphis, Tennessee, her boilers exploded during the predawn hours of April 27. Estimates of the number of men who either drowned or were scalded to death run as high as 1,585.

SUMMIT POINT AND CAMERON'S DEPOT, WEST VIRGINIA, BATTLE OF (AUGUST 21, 1864). Following **Jubal A. Early's Washington Raid** in the summer of 1864, Early and Union Maj. Gen. **Philip Sheridan** maneuvered and **skirmished** in the **Shenandoah Valley**. On August 21, Early advanced in two columns from Winchester against Sheridan's command at Charles Town. Early accompanied one column approaching Charles Town from the west by way of Cameron's Depot, while **Richard H. Anderson** led the other to outflank the enemy on the south by way of Summit Point. Early drove back one Union **division** to

Cameron's Depot, but Sheridan brought up reinforcements. Early expected Anderson to turn Sheridan's left flank, but Anderson's cavalry had been blocked around Summit Point. That night, Sheridan withdrew to strong entrenchments at Halltown. Early remained in the area for a few days but finally withdrew on August 26 as his supplies ran out. In the series of clashes, Early lost approximately 400 men, while Sheridan lost about 600.

SUMNER, CHARLES (1811–1874) USA. A native of **Massachusetts**, Sumner graduated from Harvard Law School in 1833, passed the bar, and worked as a reporter for the U.S. circuit court before teaching at the Harvard Law School from 1835 to 1837. After traveling in Europe for several years, he returned to Boston in 1840 and became a prosperous lawyer and popular **abolitionist** speaker. Sumner's popularity grew after he opposed the annexation of **Texas**, the **Mexican War**, and the **Compromise of 1850**, and he was elected to the U.S. Senate in 1851.

As a **Republican** senator, Sumner became a leader of the abolitionists. He bitterly opposed the **Fugitive Slave Act**, **popular sovereignty**, the **Kansas-Nebraska Act**, and any other proposal he saw as mollifying the South. In 1856, Sumner made a speech entitled "The Crime against **Kansas**," which was especially critical of slave owners, and was attacked on the Senate floor by **South Carolina** Congressman Preston Brooks. Using a heavy cane, Brooks injured him so severely he was unable to resume regular Senate duties until December 1859. This Brooks-Sumner Affair outraged most Northerners, and Massachusetts reelected Sumner in 1857 even though his seat remained vacant for two years.

During the Civil War, Sumner was a leader of the **Radical Republicans** and chaired the Senate Foreign Relations Committee. He championed such harsh measures as the **confiscation acts** and urged **Abraham Lincoln** to emancipate the slaves immediately. In foreign relations, however, Sumner was a realist and played an important role in the release of the Confederate envoys who were captured in the 1862 *Trent* **Affair**. During **Reconstruction**, he was one of the most important political leaders and believed the South had committed "state suicide." According to Sumner, **secession** had voided any constitutional rights the Southern states had and only the **U.S. Congress** could set the requirements for readmission. He also argued for **freedmen's** equal rights and the disenfranchisement of former Confederates. This brought Sumner into conflict with Lincoln's and President **Andrew Johnson's** more lenient, presidential Reconstruction policies. Sumner was a leading force behind the harsh Military Reconstruction Act and Johnson's impeachment and frequently clashed with President **U. S. Grant**. It was said Grant could not pass by Sumner's house without shaking his fist at it. Sumner's opposition to the *Alabama* **Claims** settlement finally led to his removal as chairman of the Foreign Relations Committee.

Sumner suffered from failing health in the 1870s and suffered a heart attack in 1874 while working in the Senate chamber. He died the next day.

SUMNER, EDWIN VOSE "BULL" (1797–1863) USA. A native of **Massachusetts**, Sumner was the father-in-law of **Robert E. Lee's** secretary **Armistead Long**. He was commissioned a lieutenant in the **U.S. Army** in 1819 and served in the military the rest of his life. Sumner fought **Indians** on the frontier and, as a major of dragoons in the **Mexican War**, was wounded and won two **brevets**. During this antebellum service, he earned the nickname "Bull Head" (later becoming just "Bull"), reportedly because a musket ball once bounced off his head. Sumner served on the frontier after the war and became colonel of the 1st U.S. Cavalry in 1855. Afterward, he was acting governor of the **New Mexico Territory**; commanded Fort Leavenworth, Kansas, during the worst of the "**Bleeding Kansas**" period; and commanded the **Department of the West**.

During the 1861 **secession** crisis, Sumner was chosen by **Winfield Scott** to escort president-elect **Abraham Lincoln** from **Illinois** to **Washington, D.C.** He then was promoted to brigadier general of regulars in March to replace **David E. Twiggs**, who had resigned. The following month, Sumner was put in command of the **Department of the Pacific**, but in November, he returned east to take charge of a **division** in the **Army of the Potomac**. When he was elevated to command the II Corps in March 1862, he was the oldest **corps** commander in the Union **army**.

Sumner led his corps through the **Peninsula Campaign**, serving as **George B. McClellan's** second-in-command at **Williamsburg** and winning a brevet of major general of regulars at **Seven Pines**. After fighting in the **Seven Days Campaign**, he was promoted to major general of volunteers in July 1862. Later that summer, Sumner reinforced **John Pope's Army of Virginia** and helped cover his retreat after the defeat at **Second Manassas**. He then saw bloody combat in the **Antietam Campaign**, where he was criticized for needlessly exposing himself to danger by personally leading his men into battle at Antietam and for sending them in piecemeal. At **Fredericksburg**, Sumner commanded the army's right wing and launched the futile assaults against Marye's Heights. When **Ambrose E. Burnside** was relieved of command in early 1863, Sumner requested a change in assignment. He was appointed commander of the

Department of the Missouri but died from pneumonia before he could assume the new position.

SUMTER, **CSS**. Originally named the *Havana*, this wooden ship was built in Philadelphia, Pennsylvania, in 1859 and was used as a packet ship between **New Orleans, Louisiana**, and Havana, Cuba, before the Confederates acquired it. **Raphael Semmes** was put in command of the vessel in April 1861, and he supervised its conversion into a Confederate **commerce raider** at Algiers, Louisiana. Renamed the *Sumter*, it was powered by both sails and steam engines and had a retractable smokestack to make it more streamlined while under sail. At 184 feet long, the vessel carried four 32-pounders and one 8-inch gun.

Semmes departed New Orleans in June 1861 and outran the USS *Brooklyn* to make it to open seas and become the first Confederate vessel to show the **flag** in foreign countries. Cruising in the Gulf of Mexico, the Caribbean Sea, and the Atlantic Ocean, the *Sumter* accounted for 18 Union vessels over the next six months before being blockaded in Gibraltar by the **U.S. Navy**. There, Semmes abandoned the ship, and it was purchased at auction in December 1862 by a British merchant who renamed it the *Gibraltar*. For the rest of the war, it served as a **blockade runner**.

SUPREME COURT, CONFEDERATE. A Confederate Supreme Court, that was to be patterned after the **U.S. Supreme Court**, was authorized by the March 1861 Provisional **Confederate Constitution**, but it was never created because the **Confederate Congress** could not agree on the issue of **states rights**. Some politicians wanted the Supreme Court to have appellate jurisdiction over state courts, as did the U.S. Supreme Court. Others believed the South seceded largely on the right of **nullification** and that states had the right to interpret for themselves the constitutionality of federal laws. They wanted state court decisions to be final. Unable to agree on the matter, the Confederate Congress never took action to create the Confederate Supreme Court.

SUPREME COURT, UNITED STATES. When the Civil War began, **Roger B. Taney** was Chief Justice of the U.S. Supreme Court. When he died in October 1864, **Abraham Lincoln** nominated former Secretary of the Treasury **Salmon P. Chase** as his replacement. During the war, the Court strongly supported Lincoln's war policies, largely because he appointed four of its nine members by 1863.

The Court issued several decisions that affected the conflict. At the beginning of the war, one of the most difficult issues to be decided was the status of the Confederates. Technically, they were traitors and subject to execution if captured, but the Confederates maintained they were an independent nation and should be treated as belligerents and **prisoners** of war. Under Taney, the Court straddled this difficult issue in the case *Miller v. U.S.* It established the "double-status" principle, that the federal government held the status of being both sovereign over the Confederacy and yet also a belligerent. This allowed the government to continue to deny the legality of **secession** but at the same time, treat Confederate captives as prisoners of war and thus avoid the bloodbath of executing prisoners.

Another area the Court had to deal with was executive power. Lincoln believed the president had the emergency authority to suspend certain constitutional rights during a rebellion. However, since he also needed congressional support, he sometimes submitted his actions to the **U.S. Congress** for ratification. Because of congressional recesses, however, oftentimes the executive action was already a fait accompli by the time Congress took up the issue. An example of this was Lincoln's declaration on April 15, 1861, that the South was in rebellion and his establishing a **blockade** shortly afterward. Since Congress did not recognize the rebellion until July 13, owners of **blockade runners** captured between the two dates sued for their ships' return on the grounds that Lincoln had overstepped his constitutional authority since Congress had not yet recognized an insurrection. In what became known as the Prize Cases, the Supreme Court narrowly ruled (5–4) that the president had the responsibility to suppress a domestic rebellion when it occurred and did not have to wait for Congress to "baptize it with a name." The Court also ruled that the conflict was a legal state of war on July 13, 1861, the date Congress acted, and the president could legally assume wartime powers.

Lincoln's **suspension of the writ of habeas corpus** and use of military courts to try civilians were his most controversial wartime actions. The Supreme Court, however, never issued a ruling on these activities during the war, thus allowing the administration to continue the policies. It was not until the 1866 *Ex parte Milligan* that the Court declared it illegal for military courts to try civilians in areas where the civilian courts still functioned.

SURRATT, JOHN HARRISON (1844–1916) CSA. A native of **Maryland**, Surratt was the son of Mrs. **Mary E. J. Surratt**, who was executed for her involvement in **Abraham Lincoln's assassination**. He entered Maryland's St. Charles College, a Catholic seminary, in 1859 but dropped out in 1862 to support his widowed mother by becoming postmaster and innkeeper in the family establishment. A Southern sympathizer, Surratt worked as a secret Confederate courier during the war. Federal authorities questioned his loyalty, and he was removed as postmaster in 1863.

Surratt was recommended to **John Wilkes Booth** by another Confederate sympathizer, and the two first met in December 1864. Through Surratt, Booth also met fellow conspirator **David E. Herold**. Surratt was only a fringe member of the conspiracy to kidnap Lincoln and did not participate in the assassination. He was in New York returning from a courier mission when he learned of the murder. When federal officials identified Surratt as a conspirator, he fled to Europe by way of Canada. His mother, however, was convicted and hanged because of her relationship to Surratt and her owning the boarding house the conspirators sometimes met in.

In Italy, Surratt joined the Papal **Zouaves** under an alias and fought Giuseppe Garibaldi's forces. Incredibly, a former classmate who also was in the Zouaves, recognized him and alerted officials to gain the $25,000 reward that had been posted for his capture. The Pope assisted in having Surratt arrested in 1866, but he escaped from jail and fled to Egypt. There he was arrested again and extradited to the United States. In an 1867 trial, witnesses testified it was Surratt who had cut the spyhole in Lincoln's box seat door and that he was supposed to assassinate **U. S. Grant**. Surratt, however, maintained he was in Canada at the time of the murder. The jury deadlocked, and Surratt was released, never to be tried again. Afterward, he settled in Maryland and worked for a freight company and as a lecturer.

SURRATT, MRS. MARY ELIZABETH JENKINS (1823–1865) CSA.
A native of **Maryland**, Surratt was the mother of **John H. Surratt**, who was charged with participating in **Abraham Lincoln's assassination**. An educated woman and devout Catholic, Mary E. Jenkins married John Surratt in 1840. After living on her husband's Maryland farm, she helped manage a tavern and post office he began in 1852 in modern-day Clinton, Maryland. When Surratt died in 1862, Mary moved to a house she owned in **Washington, D.C.**, and began operating a boarding house there.

Mrs. Surratt's son John, a secret Confederate courier, became acquainted with **John Wilkes Booth** and participated in some of the early plots to kidnap Lincoln. Booth sometimes used the family's boarding house as a meeting place to plan his conspiracy. Although she probably was not involved in the assassination, Mrs. Surratt and several of her pro-Southern boarders were arrested days after the murder, and she was convicted and sentenced to hang. Her hanging became one of great controversy. Mrs. Surratt appealed for clemency and was supported by some officials who claimed to have attached the appeal to papers sent to President **Andrew Johnson**. Johnson, however, claimed he never saw any documentation supporting clemency and thus signed the death warrant. On July 7, 1865, Mrs. Surratt was hanged at the **Old Capitol Prison** in Washington, along with **Lewis Powell, David Herold**, and **George Atzerodt**. She was the first woman ever executed by the U.S. government.

SURRENDERS. The Civil War did not come to an end at one time. Instead, the Confederate **armies** surrendered from east to west over about a six-week period.

On April 9, 1865, **Robert E. Lee** surrendered his **Army of Northern Virginia** to **U. S. Grant** at **Appomattox Court House, Virginia**. After suffering through a winter of frequent battles and food shortages in the **Petersburg Campaign**, Lee was forced to evacuate Petersburg and **Richmond, Virginia**, after the Federals crushed his right flank at **Five Forks**. He fled west in the **Appomattox Campaign** but finally was surrounded at Appomattox. Realizing he was trapped, Lee asked for a meeting with Grant to discuss surrender terms. Meeting in the home of **Wilmer McLean** at about 1:30 P.M., Lee agreed to surrender the approximately 26,000 survivors of his army. The officers were allowed to keep their side arms, and officers and men were to be **paroled** and allowed to return home unmolested as long as they obeyed the law and abided by the parole terms of not taking up arms again until properly **exchanged**. All government property, including weapons, animals, **flags**, and equipment, was to be handed over to the Federals. Lee persuaded Grant also to allow soldiers who claimed to own horses or mules to take them, as well. The surrender ceremony occurred on April 11, but Lee did not attend. He issued **Lee's Farewell Address** to his troops the day before and left for Richmond on the day of the surrender.

In **North Carolina**, **Joseph E. Johnston** had been defeated at **Bentonville** during the **Carolinas Campaign**, but he was still confronting **William T. Sherman** as Sherman marched through the state. After learning of Lee's surrender and realizing there was no hope of uniting their two armies, Johnston met with fleeing president **Jefferson Davis** at Greensboro on April 12. Davis reluctantly agreed to Johnston's proposal to begin surrender negotiations with Sherman. The two generals met on April 17 at James Bennett's farmhouse near **Durham Station**. By the next day, they agreed that Johnston would surrender, but Sherman went beyond his authority and also agreed that the existing Confederate state governments would continue to function. President **Andrew Johnson's** administration rejected the surrender terms, and Grant ordered Sherman to offer only those terms he had presented to Lee. As a result, Sherman and Johnston met at the Bennett home again on April 26 and worked out the final surrender along the Appomattox terms. Johnston officially surrendered his 30,000 men on May 3.

By late April, Confederate Lt. Gen. **Richard Taylor**, commander of the **Department of Alabama, Mississippi, and East Louisiana** knew of Lee's surrender and that Johnston was negotiating with Sherman. He contacted Maj. Gen. **Edward R. S. Canby**, who had recently captured **Mobile, Alabama**, and arranged to meet on April 30 to discuss surrender. The two officers met just north of Mobile and agreed to a truce. Two days later, Taylor learned of Johnston's surrender and Davis's capture. When Canby announced he was ending the truce, Taylor decided to surrender, as well. On May 4, at Citronelle, Alabama, he surrendered his **department's** approximately 12,000 men on the same terms granted Lee and Johnston.

After some preliminary contact with Union officials about surrendering the **Trans-Mississippi Department**, Confederate Gen. **Edmund Kirby Smith** decided he would continue the fight and appealed to the civilians and soldiers to support him. In May 1865, he left his headquarters in Shreveport, Louisiana, and headed for Houston, Texas, from which he hoped to rally his troops. As knowledge of the eastern surrenders spread, however, Confederate soldiers in the department began disbanding their units or **deserting** in large numbers. Kirby Smith's army literally evaporated before he reached Houston. Acting in Kirby Smith's name, Lt. Gen. **Simon B. Buckner**, Maj. Gen. **Sterling Price**, and acting Brig. Gen. Joseph L. Brent met with Canby in **New Orleans, Louisiana**, and signed a surrender document on May 26 that allowed the soldiers to return home on parole. Kirby Smith arrived in Houston the following day and realized he had no troops. On June 2, he met with Canby in Galveston, Texas, and signed the surrender document to make it official.

The last Confederate ground forces to surrender were the **Indian** troops under Brig. Gen. **Stand Watie in Indian Territory**. In a Grand Council meeting on June 15, the leading Confederate chiefs called for their officers to surrender. Watie was the last to do so. On June 23, he surrendered his Indian battalion to Union officials at Doaksville, Indian Territory.

The last Confederate surrender was the **commerce raider CSS** *Shenandoah*. It was raiding the Union whaling fleet in the Arctic Ocean when its crew learned the war was over. Sailing to Great Britain, the *Shenandoah* surrendered to British officials on November 6, 1865.

SUTHERLAND STATION, VIRGINIA, BATTLE OF (APRIL 2, 1865). On April 1, 1865, during the **Petersburg Campaign, Philip Sheridan's** Union troops crushed **Robert E. Lee's** right flank outside Petersburg, Virginia, at **Five Forks**. At 4:30 A.M. on April 2, the **Army of the Potomac** advanced against Lee's weakened **Army of Northern Virginia** all along the Petersburg front. On the Confederate right, near Five Forks, **Andrew A. Humphreys's** II Corps moved up the Claiborne Road and engaged **Henry Heth's** Confederate **division**. The division was temporarily commanded by **John R. Cooke** and was in a defensive position at Sutherland Station protecting the Southside Railroad west of Petersburg. **Nelson A. Miles's** Union division made two unsuccessful attacks against Cooke that afternoon. At 4:00 P.M., he made a third assault against the Confederate left flank, this time supporting the infantry with heavy **artillery** fire. Cooke's men broke and retreated. At a cost of 366 casualties, Miles captured 600 **prisoners** and took control of the Southside Railroad, Lee's last **railroad**. Its loss forced Lee to withdraw to the Appomattox River's north bank that night and begin his westward retreat in the **Appomattox Campaign**.

SUTLER. A sutler was a private businessman who was authorized to sell certain goods to soldiers in camp. Both **armies** allowed each **regiment** to have one sutler, who set up shop in a tent or shack near camp. From the sutler, soldiers could buy the small consumer goods that made life more bearable. However, soldiers had little regard for the sutlers because they essentially had a monopoly on regimental business and often overcharged for their goods. Sometimes, outraged soldiers raided the sutler and looted his establishment.

"SWAMP ANGEL." This was the nickname given by Union soldiers to an 8-inch, 200-pounder **Parrott rifle** that was placed on marshy Morris Island, near **Charleston, South Carolina**, in August 1863. The battery was established by Maj. Gen. **Quincy A. Gillmore** to bombard the city, four and one-half miles across the harbor. The "Swamp Angel" fired its first shot at 1:30 A.M. on August 22. Thirty-six rounds were fired before the last shell exploded prematurely and disabled the gun on August 23. Although most of the shells were filled with Greek Fire, little damage was caused to Charleston by the brief bombardment. After the war, the gun was rescued from the scrap iron heap and is now mounted on a granite monument at Trenton, New Jersey.

SWAYNE, WAGER (1834–1902) USA. A native of **Ohio**, Swayne was the son of **U.S. Supreme Court** Justice Noah H. Swayne. After graduating from Yale University and Cincinnati Law School in 1856 and 1859, respectively, he practiced law with his father.

Swayne entered Union service in August 1861 as major of the 43rd Ohio, but he was promoted to lieutenant colonel in December. He served at **New Madrid and Island No. 10** and at **Corinth**, winning the **Medal of Honor** in 1893 for the latter battle. Promoted to regimental colonel in October 1862, Swayne performed garrison duty in **Tennessee** until the **Atlanta Campaign.** As part of the **Army of the Tennessee's** XVI Corps, he fought in most of the campaign's major battles and commanded a **brigade** in the XVII Corps' 1st Division from September to November 1864. After serving in the **March to the Sea**, Swayne lost his right leg to amputation in February 1865 after being wounded by a shell at **Rivers' Bridge** during the **Carolinas Campaign**. He was promoted to brigadier general of volunteers in March 1865 and to major general of volunteers in June. Swayne remained in the service after the war and worked for the **Freedmen's Bureau** in **Alabama**. When he retired in 1870 as colonel of the 45th U.S. Infantry, he had received **brevets** of brigadier general and major general of regulars for his wartime service. After retirement, Swayne practiced law in Ohio and **New York**.

SWEENY, THOMAS WILLIAM (1820–1892) USA. A native of Ireland, Sweeny immigrated to the United States when he was 12. Settling in **New York**, he worked in a law-publishing firm, became a militiaman, and served in the **Mexican War**. During the war, Sweeny lost his right arm at Churubusco, but he remained in the **U.S. Army** and in 1848 was promoted to 2nd lieutenant in the 2nd U.S. Infantry. He rose to 1st lieutenant in 1851 and at times fought **Indians** on the frontier.

In January 1861, Sweeny was promoted to captain, and in May he served with **Nathaniel Lyon** in the capture of **Camp Jackson, Missouri**. That same month, he was appointed brigadier general of Missouri Volunteers, and at **Carthage** two months later, he commanded the 90-day **Missouri** militia. Days after being wounded at **Wilson's Creek**, he was mustered out of the militia service. In January 1862, Sweeny was appointed colonel of the 52nd Illinois and led it at **Fort Donelson** the following month. He commanded a **brigade** in **W. H. L. Wallace's division** at **Shiloh**, in which he suffered very heavy casualties and again was wounded. Returning to his **regiment**, Sweeny fought at **Corinth** and assumed command of the brigade when his superior, **Pleasant A. Hackleman**, was killed. For the next several months, he commanded various brigades in the **Army of the Tennessee**. Sweeny was promoted to brigadier general of regulars in March 1863 and spent much of the year on garrison duty in **Tennessee** and **Mississippi** while commanding a brigade in the XVI Corps' 2nd Division. In September, he assumed command of the division and led it in the **Atlanta Campaign**.

Over the course of his career, Sweeny clashed frequently with his superior, **Grenville Dodge**, and other politician generals. The professional Sweeny resented the younger Dodge and disliked his lax **discipline** over the volunteers. Their feud came to a head at the **Battle of Atlanta**, where Sweeny served as a division commander in Dodge's XVI Corps. Sweeny became incensed that Dodge issued orders to his regiments without going through him. After the battle, he exploded in a tent and tongue-lashed Dodge and fellow division commander and politician general **John W. Fuller**. Sweeny called Dodge a liar and a coward and physically attacked him and Fuller. He also unsuccessfully challenged them to duels (he previously had unsuccessfully challenged the **corps'** surgeon in another feud). Sweeny was arrested on several charges, but he was acquitted in January 1865. Other regular **army** officers apparently protected him, but Maj. Gen. **Oliver O. Howard** refused to have him back, and he spent the rest of the war without a command.

Sweeny was dismissed from the regular army in December 1865 for being absent without leave. He then became involved in the unsuccessful Fenian plot by Irishmen in Canada and was arrested by U.S. authorities. Sweeny finally was released and even was restored to the regular army in November 1866. He was put on the retired list as a brigadier general in 1870.

SWIFT CREEK AND FORT CLIFTON, VIRGINIA, BATTLE OF (MAY 9, 1864). As part of **U. S. Grant's strategy** in the spring of 1864, Maj. Gen. **Benjamin F. Butler** and his **Army of the James** began the **Bermuda Hundred Campaign** on May 5, 1864, to cut off **Richmond, Virginia's**, supply line from Petersburg. On May 7, Butler's **army** captured **Port Walthall Junction** north of Petersburg and destroyed part of the Richmond & Petersburg Railroad before withdrawing. The Confederates under Maj. Gen. **George Pickett** withdrew behind Swift Creek.

On May 9, Butler advanced against **Petersburg** and encountered Pickett's entrenchments. After a morning of brisk **skirmishing**, Pickett attacked Butler's superior force with **Bushrod R. Johnson's division** at about 3:45 P.M., but one of its **brigades** was repulsed by **Charles Heckman's** Union brigade. Fighting along Swift Run Creek then slowed, and Butler dispatched part of his X Corps to destroy more **railroad** track. At the mouth of the creek, five Union gunboats and part of **William T. H. Brooks's** division attacked a Confederate earthwork named Fort Clifton. The Confederates sank one boat and repulsed the Union infantry. In these battles of May 9, total casualties for both sides are estimated to have been about 990.

SWINTON, WILLIAM (1833–1892) USA. A native of Scotland, Swinton immigrated to the United States and graduated from Amherst College. He then studied for the ministry for a time and taught school. Swinton joined the **New York** *Times* as a reporter in 1858 and became a **war correspondent** during the Civil War. Very knowledgeable about military affairs, he often was critical of Union military leaders. On the night after the first day's battle in the **Wilderness**, Swinton was caught hiding behind a stump eavesdropping on **U. S. Grant** and **George G. Meade**. Sometime later, he angered **Ambrose E. Burnside** with an unfavorable newspaper article. Outraged at the reporter, Grant then expelled him from the **Army of the Potomac's** camps. Afterward, Swinton wrote numerous books about the war, including the classic *Campaigns of the Army of the Potomac*.

SYKES, GEORGE (1822–1880) USA. A native of **Delaware**, Sykes graduated from **West Point** in 1842 and served with the infantry in the **Seminole** and **Mexican Wars**, winning a **brevet** for gallantry in the latter. After Mexico, he served on the frontier and rose to the rank of captain in 1855.

In May 1861, Sykes was promoted to major of the 14th U.S. Infantry. He was praised at **First Manassas** while commanding a battalion of regulars (known as "Sykes' Regulars") that helped cover the panicked retreat. Sykes was promoted to brigadier general of volunteers in September and for months commanded the regular troops that defended **Washington, D.C.** During the **Peninsula Campaign**, he first commanded a **brigade** and then a **division** in the **Army of the Potomac's** V Corps. With mostly regular **U.S. Army** units in his command, Sykes fought at **Yorktown** and won special praise at **Gaines' Mill** and **Malvern Hill** during the **Seven Days Campaign**. He saw very heavy combat at **Second Manassas** but was held in reserve at the **Battle of Antietam**.

Sykes was promoted to major general of volunteers in November 1862 and led his division the following month at **Fredericksburg**. After seeing moderate combat at **Chancellorsville**, he was placed in command of the V Corps when **George G. Meade** was elevated to **army** command in late June 1863. At **Gettysburg**, Sykes's **corps** helped support **Daniel Sickles's** fighting in the **Peach Orchard** and occupied Little Round Top. Although a tenacious fighter, Sykes became known as something of a plodder and earned the nickname "Tardy George." His habitual slowness angered Meade during the **Bristoe Station** and **Mine Run Campaigns**, and he was left without a command when the army was reorganized in the spring of 1864. Sykes was sent to command the District of South Kansas in September and remained in **Kansas** until war's end.

Sykes was mustered out of the volunteers in January 1866, but he remained in the regular army as lieutenant colonel of the 5th U.S. Infantry. He received brevets of brigadier general and major general of regulars for his war service and died on duty while serving as colonel of the 20th U.S. Infantry.

– T –

TACTICS. Tactics generally are considered the maneuvering of troops to win a battle and can be either offensive or defensive in nature. Tactics are related to **strategy**, but strategy is larger in scope, consisting of the maneuvers taken to win a war or campaign. When the Civil War began, both sides preferred the traditional tactic of massing troops in a battle line and making a **frontal attack**. The adoption of new **rifle muskets**, however, made this very costly. As the war progressed, the **armies** began using more flank attacks to dislodge an enemy and began relying on earthworks and fortifications to defend a position. **Robert E. Lee's** winning tactic at **Chancellorsville** was attacking **Joseph Hooker's** exposed right flank, while **George G. Meade** won at **Gettysburg** by holding a strong defensive position.

TALIAFERRO, WILLIAM BOOTH (1822–1898) CSA. A native of **Virginia**, Taliaferro (TAHL-i-vur) graduated from the College of William and Mary in 1841 and then studied law at Harvard University. During the **Mexican War**, he received a **U.S. Army** captain's commission and rose to the rank of major. Taliaferro left the **army** in 1848, served in the Virginia legislature from 1850 to 1853, and became a major general of state militia.

When the Civil War began in 1861, Taliaferro first occupied the **Norfolk, Virginia**, area with his militia, but in May, he was appointed colonel of the 23rd Virginia. Sent to western Virginia, he fought at **Rich Mountain** and **Carrick's Ford** with his **regiment** before being given a **brigade** command in **William W. Loring's Army of the Northwest** later in the year. Taliaferro became involved in the 1862 **Loring-Jackson feud** by personally lobbying in **Richmond, Virginia**, for the reversal of **Stonewall Jackson's** orders placing the army at Romney for the winter. Jackson never forgave Taliaferro for siding with Loring, but Taliaferro still won a promotion to brigadier general in March 1862.

Much to Jackson's dismay, Taliaferro was given a brigade in his **division** in April 1862. Taliaferro proved to be an effective fighter, but his strict **discipline** alienated his men (one soldier even physically attacked him). He served Jackson throughout **Jackson's Shenandoah Valley** and the **Seven Days Campaigns**. When **Charles Winder** was killed at **Cedar Mountain** in August 1862, Taliaferro took command of the division. Shortly afterward, he was badly wounded at **Groveton** and was put out of action for several months. Taliaferro returned to the division in time to lead it at **Fredericksburg**, where he suffered a minor wound. When he failed to be promoted to major general, he requested a transfer and in March 1863 was assigned to **P. G. T. Beauregard** at **Charleston, South Carolina**.

In July 1863, Beauregard placed Taliaferro in command of **Fort Wagner**, and he successfully defended it against Union assaults. The following month, Taliaferro assumed command of a division on James Island and led it for about six months. In February 1864, he briefly commanded the District of East Florida, but he then returned to **South Carolina**, where he held various commands for most of the year. In December, Taliaferro led a brigade in the defense of **Savannah, Georgia**, winning a division command by year's end. Promoted to major general in January 1865, he led his division in **William J. Hardee's corps** through the **Carolinas Campaign**. Taliaferro fought at **Bentonville** but appears to have lost his command when **Joseph E. Johnston's** army was reorganized in April 1865. He was **paroled** by the Federals in May 1865.

After the war, Taliaferro resumed his Virginia law practice and political career. He served in the state legislature from 1874 to 1879, was a county judge from 1891 to 1897, and sat on the boards of the **Virginia Military Institute** and the College of William and Mary.

TALLAHASSEE, CSS. This Confederate **commerce raider** was built in Great Britain in 1864 and originally was christened the *Atalanta* (not the *Atlanta* as some sources claim). It was 220 feet long, had both sails and twin steam-driven screw propellers, and displaced 500 tons. After running the **blockade** several times, the *Atalanta* was purchased by the **Confederate navy** in **Wilmington, North Carolina**, in the summer of 1864 and was renamed the *Tallahassee*. It was armed with one 100-pounder and one 32-pounder **rifles**, a 30-pounder **Parrott rifle**, and a brass **howitzer**. Placed under the command of Lt. **John Taylor Wood**, the *Tallahassee* raided the New England coast that August and accounted for over 30 Union vessels. Returning to Wilmington, the ship was renamed the *Olustee* and was taken over by Lt. William H. Ward. Ward raided the Atlantic coast in November and captured six ships. Chased back to Wilmington by the **U.S. Navy**, the *Olustee* was converted into a **blockade runner** and was renamed the *Chameleon*. Under Capt. John Wilkinson, the *Chameleon*'s blockade running career was brief, and the British government seized it in April 1865. The ship first reverted to its original name of *Atalanta,* but it then was sold at auction and was renamed the *Amelia*. In 1866, the U.S. government won possession of it in a lawsuit. The United States sold the ship at auction in Great Britain, and beginning in 1867, it engaged in trade around Japan as the *Hay Maru* until it was wrecked in 1869.

TANEY, ROGER BROOKE (1777–1864) USA. A native of **Maryland**, Taney (TAH-nee) graduated from Dickinson College in 1795 and became a lawyer. After a one-term stint in the state legislature from 1799 to 1800, he remained active in the Federalist Party and led the minority faction that supported the War of 1812. After serving again in the legislature from 1816 to 1821, Taney joined the **Democratic Party** when the Federalists faded away. He served as President Andrew Jackson's attorney general, secretary of the treasury, and acting secretary of war and strongly supported Jackson's effort to kill the Second Bank of the United States. As a reward for his support, Taney was nominated by Jackson in 1835 to replace the late John Marshall as chief justice of the **U.S. Supreme Court** and was confirmed in 1836.

Although a Southerner, Taney previously had freed his own slaves and favored protecting the rights of free blacks and slaves while serving as a lawyer and legislator. Yet, he did not believe that blacks and whites could live in harmony in the United States and came to favor compensated emancipation and the African colonization movement. As chief justice, Taney believed that **slavery** was a Southern problem in which Northerners should not interfere, and he did not believe **Congress** had any authority to prevent slave owners from taking slaves into the western territories.

In 1857, Taney wrote the majority opinion for the **Dred Scott decision**. Besides overturning a state court's decision to free Scott, he wrote that slaves were property and Negroes were not citizens of the United States, that the Founding Fathers never intended for blacks to be equal to whites, and, in effect, that territories could not pass laws forbidding the introduction of slavery. The case outraged Northerners, who accused Taney and the Southern court majority of simply voting along sectional lines.

Taney administered **Abraham Lincoln's** oath of office in the 1861 inauguration and then opposed such wartime measures as the arrest and detention of suspected disloyal citizens by the military, the **suspension of the writ of habeas corpus**, and the establishment of a **blockade** without a declaration of war. When Taney died in October 1864, many Northerners actually applauded his passing. Lincoln replaced him with **Salmon P. Chase**.

TAPPAN, JAMES CAMP (1825–1906) CSA. A native of **Tennessee**, Tappan was the great-nephew of President James Madison. After graduating with **Richard Taylor** from Yale University in 1845, Tappan studied law in **Mississippi** and became an **Arkansas** lawyer. There he became active in **Democratic Party** politics and served two terms in the state legislature (serving as speaker of the house his last term), was elected a circuit judge, and was the receiver of the Helena land office.

Tappan entered Confederate service as captain of a volunteer **company** and in May 1861 was elected colonel of the 13th Arkansas. He was praised for fighting well at **Belmont**, his first battle. When the **Battle of Shiloh** began, Tappan was absent sick, but he rejoined his **regiment** on the morning of the second day's fighting and led it during the withdrawal (some sources incorrectly claim he fought at the "Hornets' Nest" on the first day of battle).

After serving in the **Kentucky Campaign**, Tappan was promoted to brigadier general in November 1862 and was sent to Arkansas, where in February 1863, he took command of a cavalry **brigade in Sterling Price's army**. That summer he was attached to **John G. Walker's division** for a raid into northeastern **Louisiana**, but Tappan returned to Arkansas in time to participate in the unsuccessful defense of **Little Rock** in September. In the spring of 1864, he was given command of a division of Arkansas infantry and was sent to Louisiana with **Thomas J. Churchill** to reinforce Taylor during the **Red River Campaign**. After seeing heavy combat at **Pleasant Hill**, Tappan was sent back to Arkansas to stop **Frederick Steele's Camden Expedition**. He was placed back in brigade command at **Jenkins' Ferry** and in late 1864 accompanied **Price's Missouri Raid**.

After the war, Tappan resumed his Arkansas law practice and was elected to the state legislature. Although he declined twice to run for governor, he did serve as dean of the state bar association, was a delegate at the 1884 Democratic National Convention, and served on the **West Point** Board of Visitors.

"TAPS." This famous bugle call was written in July 1862 by Union Maj. Gen. **Daniel Butterfield**. Patterned after the 1835 tune "Tattoo," "Taps" became the Union **army's** unofficial end-of-the-day lights-out call during the Civil War. It was made official in 1867 and also came to be used at military funerals.

TATTNALL, JOSIAH (1795–1871) CSA. A native of **Georgia**, Tattnall attended school in Great Britain before joining the **U.S. Navy** in 1812 as a midshipman. During his long naval career, he fought in the War of 1812 and in the Barbary Pirate and **Mexican Wars**. In 1857, Tattnall was promoted to flag officer and was given command of the East India Squadron. Two years later, he created an international incident when he violated American neutrality in China and assisted the British and French navies in attacking Chinese forts. Tattnall's defense was "blood is thicker than water" (Current, ed., *Encyclopedia of the Confederacy,* vol. 4, 1568).

Although not a secessionist, Tattnall resigned his commission in February 1861 and became Georgia's senior flag officer. The following month, he was appointed captain in the **Confederate navy** and was given command of the naval defenses of Georgia and **South Carolina**. Tattnall was given few resources, and his small fleet was unable to prevent the capture of **Port Royal** in November 1861. In March 1862, he was transferred to **Virginia** to replace the wounded **Franklin Buchanan** in command of the **CSS *Virginia*** and Virginia's naval defenses. In a controversial move, Tattnall blew up the *Virginia* when **Norfolk, Virginia**, was abandoned in May 1862. A court of inquiry censored him for the action, but he demanded a court-martial and was cleared of any wrongdoing. In July, Tattnall was given command of the naval defenses of **Savannah, Georgia**, but in April 1863, he was relieved of sea duty because of his age. He then led the Confederate vessels in the Savannah River and successfully prevented the Federals from entering the river until he was forced to evacuate the city when the Confederates withdrew in December 1864. Tattnall accompanied **Joseph E. Johnston's army** through the **Carolinas Campaign** and surrendered with Johnston in April 1865.

After the war, Tattnall lived in Canada for a while before returning to Savannah and working as the inspector of the port.

TAXES, CONFEDERATE. When the Civil War began, the **Confederate Congress** had to create a system to **finance** the war. It relied mostly on loans, issuing treasury notes, and selling bonds because the government was reluctant to tax the people for fear of hurting popular support. Also, taxes were seen as less useful since much of the richest areas of the Confederacy (**Nashville, Tennessee**, and **New Orleans, Louisiana**, for example) fell into enemy hands early in the war. Thus, taxation was never used to raise large amounts of money for the Confederacy.

The Confederates did rely on import/export taxes, but the Union **blockade** seriously hurt their efforts. On August 19, 1861, Congress also authorized a direct tax on real estate, slaves, and other property. This tax, however, was largely ineffective. It was placed at only 0.5 percent, authorities were slow to implement it, and a provision was added later that allowed states to exempt their citizens and gain a 10 percent discount by having the state make direct payments to the treasury in Confederate notes or specie. Only about $17.5 million was raised by the direct tax.

As the war began going badly for the Confederacy in 1863, the people actually began demanding taxes as a way to strengthen the **armies** and turn the tide of battle. On April 24, 1863, the Confederate Congress passed a comprehensive tax bill that included taxes on certain products, income, and licenses. The products tax placed an 8 percent tax on many agricultural products (as well as liquor, salt, and naval stores). The graduated **income tax** ranged from 1 to 15 percent on incomes greater than $1,000 per year, and the $50–$500 license taxes were placed on nearly all professions (including theater and circus owners and jugglers). The most unpopular Confederate tax measure was the **tax-in-kind**, which forced farmers to pay 10 percent of their products. This tax was plagued by corrupt officials and by the wasteful rotting of food caused by the crumbling Confederate railway system, but it provided an estimated $150 million worth of supplies. The last Confederate tax, passed on March 17, 1865, placed a 25 percent tax on all coin, bullion, and foreign exchange, but it came too late in the war to raise any appreciable money.

Overall, the Confederate tax system was a failure. Fearful of losing support among its people, the government never passed taxes sufficient enough to raise the large sums of money needed to fight the war. It is estimated that taxes raised only about 7 percent of Confederate government revenue during the war, equaling approximately 1 percent of the Confederate wealth.

TAXES, UNION. Although having a well-established government and treasury, the U.S. government was ill prepared to **finance** the Civil War. During the conflict, it raised most of its money by issuing paper money, taking out loans, and selling bonds. Compared with the $2.6 billion raised by loans and treasury notes alone, taxes provided the Union with only $667 million.

When the war began, the federal government relied on borrowing money rather than levying taxes. The **U.S. Congress** was reluctant to rely on taxes because it believed the war would be short and did not want to create dissent unnecessarily. This caused concern within financial circles, and as the Union suffered military defeats, it became increasingly difficult to sell bonds or secure loans. The government did have in place a tariff when the war began, but it provided very little revenue.

On August 5, 1861, Congress passed two new tax laws. One attempted to raise $20 million through a direct tax that placed a revenue quota (based on population) on each state. Even the rebelling Southern states were included, but only $17 million was gained. The second tax was the nation's first **income tax**, which placed a flat 3 percent tax on incomes greater than $800 per year. As the war progressed, this tax was changed to range from 5 to 7.5 percent on incomes ranging from $600 to $10,000 per year and 10 percent on incomes over $10,000. During the war, the income tax raised about $55 million.

The most comprehensive Union tax was an internal tax passed on July 1, 1862. This complex law included luxury taxes, taxes on raw materials and manufacturing, property taxes, professional license fees, and taxes on corporations. It was described as a tax on everything, and the bill establishing it ran 30 pages long. In the last year of the war, the internal tax and the income tax provided the Union treasury with $209 million.

TAX-IN-KIND. As the Civil War progressed, the Confederacy became increasingly desperate to raise money and supplies. One of the steps taken to supply its **armies** was the tax-in-kind, which was proposed by Secretary of the Treasury **Christopher G. Memminger** and was passed by the **Confederate Congress** in April 1863. Designed to be an alternative to the hated **Impressment Act**, the **tax** forced farmers to donate to the government part of their crop and livestock. Such items as wheat, oats, corn, rice, potatoes, sugar, pork, and beef were placed on the tax-in-kind list. Farmers were allowed to keep a predetermined number of bushels of each crop, but they had to donate to the government 10 percent of the remainder. The government appointed agents who inventoried each farm and told the farmer what he had to donate. If the farmer believed the amount was excessive, an arbiter helped set the amount.

The tax-in-kind became perhaps the most hated act ever passed by the Confederate Congress. Farmers resented the policy because it seriously affected their income, and they often had to deal with corrupt agents who seized excessive goods. To make matters worse, there was much waste in the system as crops often rotted before the dilapidated Confederate **railroad** system could move them to the armies. Because of the opposition, Congress began amending the act in December 1863. Over the next several months, changes were made to allow payments in cash rather than in produce and meat, and some exemptions were authorized for small family farms and soldiers' families. Despite its flaws, the tax-in-kind did raise as much as $150 million in cash and supplies for the war effort.

TAYLOR, BENJAMIN FRANKLIN (1819–1887) USA. A native of **New York**, Taylor graduated from the Hamilton Literary and Theological Institute (modern-day Colgate University) in 1838 and worked as a principal in **Vermont** before moving to **Illinois** to become a reporter with the Chicago *Evening Journal* in 1845. An editor by the time of the Civil War, he joined **William S. Rosecrans's Army of the Cumberland** as a **war correspondent** in the summer of 1863 and later filed articles on **Chickamauga**, **Lookout Mountain**, and **Missionary Ridge**. In the spring of 1864, Taylor was with **William T. Sherman's** armies for the **Atlanta Campaign**, but he ran afoul of Sherman by publishing an article detailing the location of the Union defensive line. Incensed, Sherman ordered him arrested and court-martialed for espionage, but Taylor left the **army** in May and became the *Evening Journal's* **Washington, D.C.**, correspondent. There he reported on political events and **Jubal A. Early's Washington Raid**.

Taylor left the *Evening Journal* in 1865 and worked as a poet, freelance writer, and speaker. In 1872, he published a book on the Civil War entitled *Mission* [sic] *Ridge and Lookout Mountain, with Pictures of Life in Camp and Field.*

TAYLOR, GEORGE WILLIAM (1808–1862) USA. A native of **Connecticut**, Taylor joined the **U.S. Navy** as a midshipman in 1827 after graduating from Captain Partridge's Military Academy. He resigned his commission in 1831 and became a **New Jersey** farmer but then served in the **Mexican War** as a lieutenant in the 10th U.S. Infantry. After being discharged in 1848 as a captain, Taylor lived in **California** for a while, but he returned to New Jersey and worked in the mining and iron **industry**.

Taylor entered Union service in June 1861 as colonel of the 3rd New Jersey and served in the defenses of **Washington, D.C.** In early 1862, he participated in the **Peninsula Campaign** as part of **Philip Kearny's brigade** in the **Army of the Potomac**. When Kearny was elevated to a **division** command, Taylor was promoted to brigadier general of volunteers in May 1862 and took over the brigade. As part of the VI Corps' 1st Division, he led the brigade well during the **Seven Days Campaign** and then reinforced **John Pope's Army of Virginia**. During the **Second Manassas Campaign**, Taylor's brigade was sent to Pope's rear on August 27 to protect the supply line from what was believed to be Confederate raiders. Instead, Taylor encountered elements of **Stonewall Jackson's corps** near Bristoe Station. Taylor was mortally wounded in the clash at **Kettle Run**, and his brigade was shattered. He died on September 1, 1862.

TAYLOR, JOSEPH PANNELL (1796–1864) USA. A native of **Kentucky**, Taylor was the brother of President Zachary Taylor and the uncle of Confederate general **Richard Taylor** and **Jefferson Davis's** first wife, Sarah Knox Taylor. During the War of 1812, he joined the **U.S. Army** as a private but in 1813 was appointed 2nd lieutenant in the 28th U.S. Infantry. Although Taylor was mustered out of service when the war ended, he was reinstated in 1816 and became a career officer. He served in the **artillery** until he joined the commissary department in 1829. During the **Mexican War**, Taylor served as a chief quartermaster and won a **brevet** of colonel. From the war's close until the outbreak of the Civil War, he was the **army's** assistant commissary general of subsistence, rising to the rank of colonel in September 1861. In September 1863, Taylor was appointed to replace the late Col. George Gibson as the Union's commissary general. He worked to keep the Union army supplied during the war and was appointed staff brigadier general in February 1863. Taylor died on duty on June 29, 1864.

TAYLOR, NELSON (1821–1894) USA. A native of **Connecticut**, Taylor served in **California** as a volunteer captain in the **Mexican War**. He remained there when the war ended and was elected to the state senate in 1849 and county sheriff in 1855. Returning east, Taylor graduated from Harvard Law School in 1860 and made an unsuccessful bid for the **U.S. Congress** that same year.

Taylor entered Union service in July 1861 as colonel of the 72nd New York, part of **Daniel Sickles's Excelsior Brigade**. After serving in the defenses of **Washington, D.C.**, he assumed command of the **brigade** and led it in the **Peninsula Campaign** as part of the **Army of the Potomac's** III Corps. Taylor resumed his regimental command for the **Battle of Seven Pines** and the **Seven Days Campaign**, but he returned to brigade command in July 1862. After seeing heavy combat at **Second Manassas**, he was promoted to brigadier general of volunteers in early September 1862 and returned to the Washington defenses, thus missing **Antietam**. In October, Taylor was given a brigade in the I Corps' 2nd Division and led it at **Fredericksburg**. During that battle, he assumed command of the **division** when **John Gibbon** was wounded.

Although Taylor had been praised for his service at Fredericksburg, he resigned his commission for unknown reasons in January 1863 and returned to **New York** to practice law. He commanded some troops in Harlem during the **New York City Draft Riot** but never returned to active duty. Taylor served one term in Congress as a **Democrat** from 1865 to 1867 and then moved to Connecticut to practice law.

TAYLOR, RICHARD (1826–1879) CSA. A native of **Kentucky**, "Dick" Taylor was the son of President Zachary Taylor; brother of **Jefferson Davis's** first wife, Sarah Knox Taylor; nephew of Union general **Joseph P. Taylor**; brother-in-law of **Duncan F. Kenner** and **Allen Thomas**; and a cousin by marriage to Confederate generals **David R. Jones** and **Lafayette McLaws**. After graduating from Yale University in 1845, he managed the family's **Mississippi** plantation and then inherited his father's large **Louisiana** sugar plantation in 1850. Taylor became a member of the Louisiana elite, even though he was plagued by debt. He was elected to the state senate in 1855 as a **Whig** but changed his allegiance first to the **Know-Nothing Party** and then to the **Democratic Party**. Although Taylor strongly supported **slavery**, he was a political moderate. He served as a delegate to the 1860 Democratic National Convention in **Charleston, South Carolina**, and to the Louisiana **secession** convention, where he voted for secession.

Taylor entered Confederate service in July 1861 when he was elected colonel of the 9th Louisiana. Sent to **Virginia**, he arrived on the battlefield too late to participate in the **First Battle of Manassas**. To his fellow officers' surprise, Taylor was promoted to brigadier general by his former brother-in-law, Davis, in October. Some officers complained of nepotism, but he proved to be a natural leader. Placed in command of the 1st Louisiana Brigade, Taylor led his **Louisiana Tigers** through **Stonewall Jackson's 1862 Shenandoah Valley Campaign** and was recognized by Jackson and **division** commander **Richard S. Ewell** for playing a key role in winning the battles of **Front Royal**, **First Winchester**, and **Port Republic**. Promoted to major general in July 1862, he was the youngest Confederate officer at the time to attain that rank and was one of the few non-**West Point** graduates to become a major general.

Taylor was transferred to Louisiana in August 1862 and took command of the District of West Louisiana. He and **Edmund Kirby Smith**, commander of the **Trans-Mississippi Department**, clashed over **strategy**, but Taylor performed well as his small **army** frequently fought **Nathaniel P. Banks's** larger Union force in the **Bayou Teche Campaign** and the **Texas Overland Expedition**. In the spring of 1864, Banks launched the **Red River Campaign** against Shreveport, Louisiana, but Taylor stopped the invasion by attacking and defeating Banks at **Mansfield**. A second battle at **Pleasant Hill** was a tactical victory for Banks, but the Federals suffered a strategic defeat when Banks retreated. When Kirby Smith then forced Taylor to send much of his infantry to **Arkansas** to stop the **Camden Expedition**, Taylor became furious. He believed if it had been left intact, his army could have destroyed or captured Banks's army. But with the loss of his men, all Taylor could do was **skirmish** with the Federals as they retreated down Red River. He never forgave Kirby Smith and submitted his resignation in May 1864.

Instead of accepting Taylor's resignation, Davis put him in command of the **Department of Alabama, Mississippi, and East Louisiana** in July 1864 and promoted him to lieutenant general (making Taylor one of only three Confederate non-West Point graduates to make that grade). Although hampered by a lack of men and supplies, he effectively defended his **department** by relying on **Nathan Bedford Forrest's** cavalry (Taylor was one of the few high-ranking officers Forrest openly admired and praised). After briefly commanding the **Army of Tennessee** in January 1865, Taylor was unable to defend his weakening department against **James H. Wilson's Selma, Alabama, Raid** and **Edward R. S. Canby's Mobile Campaign**. He finally surrendered his department on May 4, 1865.

After the war, Taylor was faced with both personal and financial hardships. Two sons had died of scarlet fever during the war, his wife's health was broken (she died in 1875), and his plantation was ruined. Taylor continued to be active in the Democratic Party, opposed **Reconstruction** rule in Louisiana, and played a role in getting accepted the Compromise of 1877, which settled the contested 1876 presidential election and ended Reconstruction. He died at age 53 of complications from rheumatoid arthritis soon after finishing his classic memoirs, *Destruction and Reconstruction*.

TAYLOR, THOMAS HART (1825–1901) CSA. A native of **Kentucky**, Taylor graduated from Centre College in 1843 and became a lawyer. He joined the volunteers as a private during the **Mexican War** but rose to the rank of 1st lieutenant. After the war, Taylor drove two cattle herds to **California** in 1852–53 and worked as a Kentucky farmer and businessman before opening a business in **Tennessee**.

Taylor entered Confederate service in April 1861 as a captain of cavalry. During his first months of duty, he recruited in Kentucky and commanded a Tennessee depot before being sent to **Virginia**. There, **P. G. T. Beauregard** used him as a courier to carry messages through the lines from **Jefferson Davis** to **Abraham Lincoln**. In August, Taylor was appointed colonel of the 1st Kentucky (Confederate). After participating in the **Battle of Dranesville, Virginia**, he briefly commanded Orange Court House in the spring of 1862 before being sent to the Virginia Peninsula. There the **regiment** was mustered out of service in May.

In June 1862, Taylor was sent to East Tennessee, where he assumed a **brigade** command under **Edmund Kirby Smith**. His brigade was the first to enter Cumberland Gap during the opening phase of the **Kentucky Campaign**. After participating, but not fighting, in the campaign, Taylor took a brigade in **Carter Stevenson's division** and was appointed brigadier general in November 1862. He accompanied Stevenson to **Vicksburg, Mississippi**, and served in that area until March 1863. Because Davis never sent Taylor's brigadier's nomination to the Senate for confirmation, Taylor reverted to the rank of colonel in May. He was replaced as brigade commander and joined **John C. Pemberton's** staff for the **Vicksburg Campaign**. Taylor served Pemberton well at **Champion Hill** and **Big Black River Bridge** and became his inspector general and post commander during the siege of Vicksburg. After the city's surrender, he was **exchanged** and in the spring and summer of 1864, he held various commands in **Mississippi** and **Alabama**, before being named post commander of Mobile, Alabama, in November. Taylor held that position until the city was evacuated in April 1865 during the **Mobile Campaign**.

After the war, Taylor worked as an Alabama businessman before returning to Kentucky in 1870. There he served as a U.S. marshal, Louisville's chief of police, and superintendent of a canal company.

TEBE, MARIE (dates unknown) USA. Little is known about Tebe's early life, but she apparently was from Philadelphia, **Pennsylvania**. She joined the 114th Pennsylvania as a **vivandière** in August 1862 when she probably was in her mid-twenties. Tebe worked as a laundress, nurse, and cook while the **regiment** served in the **Army of the Potomac**. At **Chancellorsville,** her clothing was bullet-riddled after she carried water to the wounded while under fire. For this act, Tebe was awarded the

Kearny Cross by Maj. Gen. **David B. Birney**, but she snubbed the honor by refusing to wear it. The regiment honored Tebe with a pistol, which she wore when on parade. There is no record of her after the regiment was mustered out of service in May 1865.

TELEGRAPH. The Civil War was the first conflict that saw the extensive use of the telegraph. The near instantaneous transmission of orders and messages revolutionized warfare and helped make the Civil War one of the first modern wars.

When the war began, there were relatively few telegraph wires in the United States, with a single wire connecting **California** to the east. North and South, however, quickly began expanding their systems, with the Union's Military Telegraph Service and the U.S. Signal Corps far outstripping the Confederates in laying new wire. As the **armies** moved, the telegraph moved with them. Wagons carried the large batteries needed to power the system, and wires were laid either on poles or along the ground. By war's end, the Union had laid more than 6,500 miles of wire, while the Confederates had laid perhaps 1,000 miles. Although both the Morse Code and the **Beardslee Telegraph** system were used at the beginning of the war, the Beardslee system was largely abandoned because of its limited range.

Both armies used codes to transmit sensitive military messages. While the Union finally broke the Confederate code, the Confederates never successfully broke the Union code. However, the Confederates were successful in frequently tapping into wires and eavesdropping on uncoded Union messages. This allowed raiders such as **John H. Morgan** to evade pursuing Union soldiers and provided intelligence that made the **"Beefsteak Raid"** possible. *See also* SIGNAL COMMUNICATIONS.

TEN PERCENT PLAN, ABRAHAM LINCOLN'S. Before the Civil War was over, **Abraham Lincoln** began experimenting with ways to reconstruct the South and bring the seceded states back into the Union. On December 8, 1863, he issued his Proclamation of Amnesty and Reconstruction, offering a pardon and the restoration of property (except slaves) to any supporter of the rebellion who took an **oath of allegiance**. Lincoln also declared that a seceded state could return to the Union when 10 percent of the 1860 voters took the oath of allegiance and established a loyal state government. This so-called Ten Percent Plan reflected Lincoln's belief that most Southerners had been misled by the **"fire-eating"** slave owners and could be persuaded to abandon the rebellion. Although **Radical Republicans** opposed the plan because it was too lenient, was presidential (and not congressional) **reconstruction**, and did not provide for **freedmen's** rights, Lincoln implemented it in parts of **Louisiana**, **Arkansas**, and **Tennessee**. Continued radical opposition and **Lincoln's assassination** prevented the South from being reconstructed by the Ten Percent Plan.

TENNESSEE. Tennessee was one of the slave-owning states that hoped for compromise in the **secession** crisis. **John Bell**, the **Constitutional Union Party** candidate in the **election of 1860**, was a Tennessee senator who hoped to give the nation a noncontroversial candidate to rally behind. Tennessee's Gov. **Isham Harris**, however, supported secession and on February 9, 1861, held a secession convention referendum. It was defeated 69,357 to 56,872 and demonstrated that even after **Abraham Lincoln's** election, most Tennesseans were still looking for compromise. Not until **Fort Sumter** was fired upon and Lincoln called for volunteers to put down the rebellion did a majority of voters feel the necessity to secede and defend itself against invasion. Even then, strong opposition to secession remained in the mountainous area of East Tennessee. On April 25, the legislature voted to secede, and a referendum to ratify the action was passed on June 8 by a vote of 108,399 to 47,233.

Despite its reluctant secession, Tennessee played a vital role in the Confederacy and was the scene of much fighting. It was a leading producer of horses, mules, and agricultural products; had the third largest **railroad** system of the Confederacy; and contained considerable **industry** around Memphis and Nashville. Out of an 1860 population of 1,109,801 (of which 834,082 were white), Tennessee provided 140,000 soldiers to the Confederacy and at least 51,000 to the Union.

Tennessee was invaded by Union troops in early 1862, and much of the state remained occupied for most of the war. Among its military operations were the Campaigns of **Forts Henry and Donelson**, **Shiloh**, **Kentucky**, **Stones River**, **Tullahoma**, **Chattanooga**, **Knoxville**, and **Franklin and Nashville**. Many other battles, such as **Fort Pillow**, were fought, and Confederate cavalry under **Nathan Bedford Forrest**, **John Hunt Morgan**, and **Joseph Wheeler** often raided the state.

Since Nashville was captured in early 1862 and remained under Union control for the rest of the war, Lincoln installed Unionist governor **Andrew Johnson** early in the conflict. Johnson struggled to put down Confederate guerrillas, support the Unionist movement in East Tennessee, and bring the state back into the Union.

TENNESSEE, **CSS.** This Confederate **ironclad ram** was launched in Mobile, Alabama, in February 1864. At 209 feet long, with six-inch iron plating and six **Brooke cannons**, the *Tennessee* was one of the Confederacy's best ships. Placed under the command of Lt. James D. Johnston, it served as Adm. **Franklin Buchanan's** flagship during the August 5, 1864, **Battle of Mobile Bay**. Once Union Adm. **David Farragut** made it into the bay, Buchanan attacked and damaged six of the Federal ships, but the Union fleet continued to pound the *Tennessee* with heavy gunfire. After several hours, it became dead in the water after its smokestacks were perforated, its steering chains shot away, and three of its gun ports jammed. With Buchanan wounded and many of his crew out of action, Johnston surrendered the ship.

TERRELL'S TEXAS CAVALRY. This Confederate cavalry **regiment** originally was organized in 1862 by Lt. Col. Alexander Watkins Terrell as Terrell's Texas Cavalry Battalion. Terrell was promoted to colonel in 1863, and the battalion was expanded to become a **regiment**. It first served in **Texas**, and when it was dismounted and sent to garrison Galveston in 1863, approximately 100 of its members **deserted**. In the spring of 1864, the regiment reinforced **Richard Taylor's army** defending **Louisiana** against **Nathaniel P. Banks** in the **Red River Campaign** and saw combat at **Mansfield** and **Pleasant Hill**. Terrell was appointed brigadier general in May 1865 by Gen. **Edmund Kirby Smith**, but by then the Confederate government had collapsed, and the appointment never became official. The regiment was disbanded that same month.

TERRILL, JAMES BARBOUR (1838–1864) CSA. A native of **Virginia**, Terrill was the brother of Union general **William R. Terrill**. After graduating from the **Virginia Military Institute** in 1858, he became a lawyer.

In May 1861, Terrill entered Confederate service as major of the 13th Virginia, a **regiment** he helped raise. Under Col. **Ambrose P. Hill**, the regiment remained in a supporting role at **First Manassas**. When Hill was promoted to brigadier general in February 1862, Terrill was made lieutenant colonel. Under **James A. Walker**, the regiment fought in **Arnold Elzey's brigade** during **Stonewall Jackson's 1862 Shenandoah Valley Campaign**, and at **Cross Keys**, Terrill took command of the regiment when Walker temporarily assumed **division** command from a wounded Elzey. Terrill went on to fight with the **Army of Northern Virginia** in the **Seven Days Campaign**, at **Cedar Mountain**, and at **Second Manassas** (where he commanded half of the regiment). Terrill missed **Antietam** but commanded the regiment at **Fredericksburg** and **Chancellorsville**. Promoted to colonel in May 1863, he led the 13th Virginia at **Gettysburg**, the

Wilderness, and **Spotsylvania**. Terrill was recommended for promotion to brigadier general, but he was killed on May 30, 1864, at Bethesda Church around **Totopotomoy Creek**, during the **Overland Campaign**. That same day, **Jefferson Davis** nominated him for brigadier general, with the Senate confirming him two days later. Terrill's Unionist brother, William, also was killed in the war. The brothers' father later erected a monument to his dead sons with the inscription, "God only knows which was right" (Davis, ed., *The Confederate General*, vol. 6, p. 35).

TERRILL, WILLIAM RUFUS (1834–1862) USA. A native of **Virginia**, Terrill was the brother of Confederate general **James B. Terrill**. After graduating from **West Point** in 1853, he served with the **artillery** in the **Seminole Wars**, taught mathematics at the academy, and served in "**Bleeding Kansas.**"

When the Civil War began, Terrill decided to remain loyal to the Union as long as he did not have to serve in his native state. He was promoted to captain of the 5th U.S. Artillery in May 1861 and helped organize the unit in **Washington, D.C.**, before being shipped to **Kentucky**. There, Terrill first commanded an instructional camp at Louisville and then was appointed chief of artillery for the **Army of the Ohio's** 2nd Division in early 1862. He served very well at **Shiloh** and participated in the **siege of Corinth, Mississippi**, and in the **Kentucky Campaign**.

After fighting at **Richmond, Kentucky**, Terrill was promoted to brigadier general of volunteers in September 1862 and was given a **brigade** in **James S. Jackson's division** of **Alexander McCook's corps**. At **Perryville** on October 8, he was rallying his troops when he was mortally wounded by a shell fragment that hit him in the side. Terrill died that night. His Confederate brother, James, was also killed in the war. Their father erected a monument to his sons with the inscription, "God only knows which was right" (Davis, ed., *The Confederate General*, vol. 6, p. 35).

TERRY, ALFRED HOWE (1827–1890) USA. A native of **Connecticut**, Terry attended Yale Law School but dropped out after passing the bar in 1849. He then served as a clerk to the local superior court from 1854 to 1860 and became a militia officer.

Terry entered Union service in May 1861 when he was appointed colonel of the 90-day 2nd Connecticut. After serving at **First Manassas**, the **regiment** was mustered out, but he recruited and became colonel of the 7th Connecticut in September. As part of **Erasmus Keyes's brigade**, Terry participated in the capture of **Port Royal, South Carolina**, and **Fort Pulaski, Georgia**.

In April 1862, Terry was promoted to brigadier general of volunteers. For the next two years, he held various commands during the operations around **Charleston, South Carolina**, including commanding the troops on Hilton Head and Morris Island. In April 1864, Terry was given command of the X Corps and became part of **Benjamin F. Butler's Army of the James**. Sent to **Virginia**, he fought under Butler in the **Bermuda Hundred** and **Petersburg Campaigns**. After commanding Butler's XXIV Corps during the failed attack on **Fort Fisher, North Carolina**, in December, he was given command of a new expedition in January 1865. This time the Federals were successful. For capturing the fort and closing the vital Confederate port of **Wilmington, North Carolina**, Terry received the **Thanks of Congress**, an appointment to brigadier general of regulars, and a promotion to major general of volunteers. For the remainder of the war, he commanded the X Corps in **North Carolina** and cooperated with **William T. Sherman** in the **Carolinas Campaign** while attached to the **Army of the Ohio**.

Terry was one of those rare militia officers who earned justifiable fame during the Civil War. He also was one of the few non-West Pointers to earn a brigadier general's commission in the **U.S. Army** and was the first Civil War volunteer officer to become a major general of regulars (after the war). Terry remained in the regular **army** after the war, served as the military commander of Virginia during **Reconstruction**, and was sent west to fight **Indians**. He commanded the Department of Dakota in 1876 and was in the field leading the troops when **George A. Custer** was killed at the Battle of the Little Big Horn. Terry never commented on the controversy over whether Custer was guilty of disobeying his orders. In 1886, Terry was promoted to major general, and he retired two years later.

TERRY, HENRY DWIGHT (1812–1869) USA. A native of **Connecticut**, Terry moved to **Michigan** as a young man and became a lawyer and militiaman. When the Civil War began, he organized the 5th Michigan and was appointed its colonel in June 1861. After serving in the defenses of **Washington, D.C.**, Terry fought with the **Army of the Potomac** in the **Peninsula Campaign**. As part of **Hiram G. Berry's brigade** of **Philip Kearny's division**, his **regiment** suffered heavy casualties at **Williamsburg** and **Seven Pines**. Although Terry was absent from the **army** from June to December, he was promoted to brigadier general of volunteers in July.

Returning to duty in December 1862, Terry took a brigade command in **Michael Corcoran's** division at **Suffolk, Virginia**, and helped defend the city from **James Longstreet's** Confederates in the spring of 1863. He rejoined the Army of the Potomac in August 1863 as a division commander in the VI Corps. After participating in the **Bristoe Station** and **Mine Run Campaigns**, Terry was placed in command of the **prison** camp at **Johnson's Island** in January 1864. He was replaced there in May and apparently did not hold any other positions during the war. After Terry's resignation was accepted in February 1865, he practiced law in Washington.

TERRY, WILLIAM (1824–1888) CSA. A native of **Virginia**, Terry graduated from the University of Virginia in 1848 and briefly taught school before becoming a lawyer. He also became a newspaper editor and militia officer and helped guard the site of **John Brown's** hanging.

Terry entered Confederate service in April 1861 as a 1st lieutenant in the 4th Virginia and fought in **Stonewall Jackson's brigade** at **First Manassas**. He was promoted to major in April 1862 and served with the **Stonewall Brigade** in the **1862 Shenandoah Valley** and **Seven Days Campaigns**. Afterward, Terry was wounded at **Second Manassas**, but he returned to duty with the **Army of Northern Virginia** in time to assume command of the **regiment** at **Fredericksburg** after the lieutenant colonel was wounded. He remained in temporary command, leading the regiment at **Chancellorsville** and **Gettysburg**, and was promoted to colonel in September 1863. After fighting in the **Wilderness** in **Edward Johnson's division**, Terry's command was overrun at **Spotsylvania** on May 12, 1864, and much of the brigade was captured at the "Mule Shoe."

After the disaster at Spotsylvania, the 14 regiments of Johnson's division (including the Stonewall Brigade) were consolidated into one brigade and placed under Terry, who was promoted to brigadier general. He led the unit at **Cold Harbor** and during **Philip Sheridan's 1864 Shenandoah Valley Campaign**, in which he was wounded again at **Third Winchester**. In late 1864, Terry joined the Army of Northern Virginia in the **Petersburg Campaign**. When the Confederates tried to break out of Petersburg at **Fort Stedman** in March 1865, he was severely wounded and was unable to lead his men during the **Appomattox Campaign**.

After the war, Terry resumed his law practice and served two terms in the **U.S. Congress** from 1871 to 1873 and from 1875 to 1877. He drowned in 1888 while attempting to cross a flooded river.

TERRY, WILLIAM RICHARD (1827–1897) CSA. A native of **Virginia**, Terry graduated from the **Virginia Military Institute** in 1850 and attended the University of Virginia before becoming a merchant.

Terry entered Confederate service in April 1861 as captain of a cavalry **company** he had raised. Serving as an independent company, the cavalry **skirmished** at Fairfax Court House in June, and at the **First Battle of Manassas**, it pursued the retreating Federals and captured about 80 **prisoners**. In September, Terry was appointed colonel of the 24th Virginia Infantry. He served in the **Peninsula Campaign** as part of **Jubal A. Early's brigade** and was wounded during heavy fighting at **Williamsburg**. Terry returned to the **regiment** in time to lead it at **Second Manassas** as part of the **Army of Northern Virginia**. There he fought in **James Kemper's** brigade and temporarily took command of the brigade when acting commander **Montgomery D. Corse** was wounded. Known to his men as "Old Buck," Terry led his regiment in the siege of **Suffolk Virginia**, in the spring of 1863 and in **Gettysburg's Pickett's Charge**. During the charge, he helped save the brigade from destruction by **refusing** his regiment's right flank and protecting it from an **enfilading** fire. After Gettysburg, Terry temporarily led the brigade in the autumn of 1863 and accompanied Pickett's **division** for operations around **New Bern, North Carolina**, in early 1864.

Returning to Virginia, Terry led the brigade at the **Second Battle of Drewry's Bluff** in May 1864 and was promoted to brigadier general the following month. He commanded the brigade throughout the **Petersburg Campaign** and received what was claimed to be his seventh wound in late March 1865 at **Dinwiddie Court House**. This wound prevented Terry from being present during the **army's surrender** at **Appomattox**.

After the war, Terry served in the state senate and as superintendent of the state penitentiary and the Confederate Soldiers' Home.

TERRY'S TEXAS RANGERS (8TH TEXAS CAVALRY). This Confederate cavalry unit was organized around Houston, Texas, in September 1861 by Benjamin Franklin Terry and Thomas S. Lubbock. Sent to **Kentucky**, it was mustered into Confederate service as the 8th Texas Cavalry, with Terry and Lubbock being elected colonel and lieutenant colonel, respectively, in November. The **regiment** earned fame for its scouting and **skirmishing** prowess, but in December, Terry was killed while leading a charge during a small clash at Woodsonville, Kentucky. Lubbock assumed command, and the regiment adopted the name Terry's Texas Rangers (many of its officers had formerly been Texas Rangers). The regiment became one of the best fighting, if not **disciplined**, Confederate cavalry units. Serving under **Nathan Bedford Forrest** and **Joseph Wheeler**, it fought at **Shiloh**, **Perryville**, **Stones River**, **Chicka-**

mauga, **Knoxville**, and in the **Atlanta Campaign**. Terry's Texas Rangers were **paroled** in **North Carolina** in April 1865.

TEXAS. Although most Texans supported **secession**, the state was under the leadership of Unionist governor **Sam Houston** in early 1861. Despite heavy pressure, he at first refused to call a secession convention but finally was forced to hold an emergency legislative session in late January 1861, at which a convention and secession referendum were authorized. The convention passed an ordinance of secession on February 1 by a vote of 168–8, and voters approved it on February 23 by a vote of 46,129–14,697. The convention voted to join the Confederacy on March 5 (although the Confederacy had already admitted the state), and **Edward Clark** replaced Houston as governor when Houston refused to take a Confederate **oath of allegiance**. This secession movement was peaceful, for U.S. Brig. Gen. **David Twiggs** surrendered his posts to the Confederates and then joined their ranks.

During the war, Texas provided the Confederacy with perhaps 60,000 soldiers out of an 1860 population of 604,215 (of whom 421,649 were white). Among its more famous units were **Hood's Texas Brigade**, Neville Waul's Texas Legion, and **Terry's Texas Rangers**, with generals **Albert Sidney Johnston, John Bell Hood, Ben McCulloch, Hiram B. Granbury**, and **Thomas Green** hailing from the state. Politicians **John H. Reagan** and **Louis T. Wigfall** served in the Confederate cabinet and Senate, respectively.

Besides manpower, Texas also became increasingly important for trade as the Union **blockade** tightened. Cotton was sent through Texas to **Matamoros, Mexico**, for shipment to Europe, and needed supplies came back on the return trip. The state also supplied the Confederacy with thousands of horses and cattle.

Texas was the scene of relatively few military campaigns. **Henry Hopkins Sibley** began his **New Mexico Campaign** from west Texas, **Galveston** was the site of one battle, **Richard Dowling** stopped the Union fleet at **Sabine Pass**, and the war's last battle was fought at **Palmito Ranch**. There were other small actions along the Rio Grande and Gulf Coast, but wartime governors Clark, **Francis R. Lubbock**, and **Pendleton Murrah** spent much of the state's domestic military force fighting **Indians** on the frontier. Unionist sentiment also was seen as a threat by Texas secessionists. Although their numbers were fairly small, Unionist Germans worried the Confederates greatly and caused them to retaliate with a vengeance. Some of the Germans were killed in August 1862 at the **Nueces River** as they tried to escape to Mexico, and shortly afterward other Unionists were executed in the **"Great Gainesville Hanging."**

TEXAS 8TH. *See* TERRY'S TEXAS RANGERS.

TEXAS OVERLAND EXPEDITION (OCTOBER 3–NOVEMBER 17, 1863). After the 1863 **Port Hudson Campaign**, Union Maj. Gen. **Nathaniel P. Banks** wanted to join forces with **U. S. Grant** and **David Farragut** for an attack on Mobile, Alabama. **Abraham Lincoln's** administration, however, was eager to occupy parts of **Texas** to counter France's **Maximilian** regime in Mexico. Although General-in-Chief **Henry Halleck** preferred a move into Texas by way of the Red River, he allowed Banks the discretion of choosing his avenue of attack. Banks was convinced an invasion by sea was best and sent an expedition to **Sabine Pass**, but it was turned back on September 8, 1863, by a small Confederate force under **Richard Dowling**.

Banks next decided to move overland to Texas through south **Louisiana** by marching up Bayou Teche (TESH) to Vermilionville and then west to Texas. He picked Maj. Gen. **William B. Franklin** to lead the operation. Franklin had two **divisions** each from the XIII and XIX Corps and Brig. Gen. **Albert L. Lee's** cavalry division, about 19,500 men in all. Facing him was Maj. Gen. **Richard Taylor's** small Confederate **army**, numbering about half as many men.

Franklin left Bisland, Louisiana, on October 3, marched up Bayou Teche, and reached Opelousas and Washington after some **skirmishing**. Then, instead of moving toward Texas, he became concerned about supplies. Taylor's army had stripped the countryside of forage and fodder, and low water and muddy roads made it difficult to bring supplies up Bayou Teche. As a result, Franklin canceled the invasion and began marching back south at the end of October. Taylor followed and on November 3 attacked Brig. Gen. **Stephen G. Burbridge's** rear guard at **Bayou Bourbeau** and inflicted heavy casualties. Franklin continued the withdrawal, frequently skirmishing with the Confederates, and reached New Iberia on November 17.

Banks's Texas Expedition had failed, but he did gain a foothold on the Texas coast. On October 26, a detachment under Maj. Gen. **Napoleon J. T. Dana** sailed from **New Orleans** to Brazos Santiago, Texas, and successfully captured Brownsville, Point Isabel, and a few points inland.

THANKS OF CONGRESS. Both the Union and Confederate congresses voted Thanks of Congress during the Civil War to recognize significant acts of patriotism or service. The **Confederate Congress** issued the most and recognized both individuals and organizations. Among many others, it issued Thanks to **Alabama** for hosting the Confederate government at the **Montgomery, Alabama, Convention**, to **P. G. T. Beauregard** and his men for capturing **Fort Sumter**, and to **Raphael Semmes** and his officers on the *Alabama*. The **U.S. Congress** issued far fewer Thanks of Congress and recognized only officers and men. These included **John J. Worden** of the **USS** *Monitor* for his actions at **Hampton Roads**, **George Meade** for the **Battle of Gettysburg**, and **Philip Sheridan** for his 1864 **Shenandoah Valley Campaign**.

THAYER, JOHN MILTON (1820–1906) USA. A native of **Massachusetts**, Thayer taught school before graduating from Brown University in 1841 and becoming a lawyer and militia officer. He moved to **Nebraska** in 1854 and became a well-known **Indian** fighter after he was commissioned the territory's first militia brigadier general.

Thayer entered Union service in July 1861 as colonel of the 1st Nebraska. In early 1862, he was given a **brigade** in **Lew Wallace's division** of the **Army of the Tennessee** and fought well at **Fort Donelson** and **Shiloh** and participated in the **siege of Corinth, Mississippi**. Thayer was promoted to brigadier general of volunteers in October and participated in the ill-fated assault at **Chickasaw Bayou** with **William T. Sherman's** command. After helping capture **Arkansas Post**, he had to be reappointed brigadier general in March 1863 after the Senate failed to confirm his first nomination. Thayer led his brigade in Sherman's **corps** during the **Vicksburg Campaign**, and he temporarily commanded a division during the siege of **Jackson, Mississippi**, after **Vicksburg's** surrender. In February 1864, he was placed in command of the District of the Frontier, with headquarters at **Fort Smith, Arkansas**. Thayer participated in the **Camden Expedition** that spring and remained in **Arkansas** until war's end.

After being **brevetted** major general of volunteers for his war service, Thayer resigned his commission in July 1865 and returned to Nebraska. Becoming active in politics as a **Radical Republican**, he became one of the state's first U.S. senators in 1867 and was appointed territorial governor of Wyoming in 1871. Thayer later returned to Nebraska and was elected governor in 1886 and 1888 and remained in office until 1892 by legally challenging the citizenship of the candidate who was elected to succeed him.

13TH AMENDMENT. When the Civil War began, it was a war to save the Union; emancipation of the slaves was not a major issue. As the war dragged on much longer than anyone expected, however, increasing numbers of Northerners embraced emancipation. **Abolitionists** supported it for both moral and military reasons, while moderates saw it as a way to weaken the Confederacy. Through the congressional **confiscation acts** and **Abraham Lincoln's Emancipation Proclamation**, emancipation became an important part of the Union war effort by 1863. Abolitionists and other **Radical Republicans** remained unsatisfied, because these actions left some blacks enslaved in loyal areas. To eradicate **slavery** completely, the Radicals proposed a constitutional amendment to abolish slavery permanently in the United States. This amendment passed the Senate in April 1864 by a vote of 38–6, but it did not receive the necessary two-thirds vote in the House. A second vote was held in the House in January 1865, and the measure barely received a two-thirds approval by a vote of 119–56.

The proposed amendment created a storm of controversy because it was the first constitutional amendment that made a radical change in society rather than simply making election rule changes or limiting the power of the federal government. During **Reconstruction**, the Radicals had to receive the amendment's ratification by several former Confederate states to reach the necessary 27 votes (three-fourths of 36 states) to implement it. Even though the Radicals refused to admit some of these reorganized state governments back into Congress, they did recognize their ratification of the amendment. Thus, in December 1865, the amendment was declared ratified and was added to the Constitution as the 13th Amendment.

THOMAS, ALLEN (1830–1907) CSA. A native of **Maryland**, Thomas was the brother-in-law of **Richard Taylor** and **Duncan F. Kenner**. He graduated from Princeton University in 1850 and practiced law in Maryland before moving to **Louisiana** in 1857 to become a planter and militia officer.

When the Civil War began, Thomas was appointed major of his Louisiana Battalion, a unit he organized. After serving at **New Orleans**, the unit was expanded in May 1862 to become the 29th Louisiana (sometimes referred to as the 28th [Thomas's] Louisiana), and he was appointed colonel. The **regiment** helped defend **Vicksburg, Mississippi**, and in late 1862, Thomas sometimes temporarily commanded a small **brigade**. He earned praise from his superiors for fighting well at **Chickasaw Bayou** as part of **Stephen D. Lee's** brigade. After helping turn back the **Steele's Bayou Expedition**, Thomas's regiment served in both **Francis A. Shoup's** and **William E. Baldwin's** brigades as part of the city's defenses during the **Vicksburg Campaign**. During the siege, Thomas sometimes temporarily acted as brigade commander.

After being captured at Vicksburg, Thomas was **paroled**, and he and his men returned to Louisiana. After being **exchanged**, he served in south Louisiana to reassemble his command. Promoted to brigadier general in February 1864, Thomas was given command of a brigade that was to include all of the Louisiana units captured at Vicksburg. He had great difficulty in bringing together his new command, however, because of **desertions** and the disruptive **Red River Campaign**. Although Thomas had won much praise as a regimental commander, as a brigade leader, he was criticized by an inspector for being too lax a disciplinarian and a poor administrator. His brigade spent the rest of 1864 on non-combat duty in Louisiana and **Arkansas**. In January 1865, Thomas was given command of **Camille Polignac's** small **division** and became, according to Gen. **Edmund Kirby Smith**, a competent commander. Near war's end in April 1865, he was replaced by Brig. Gen. **Harry T. Hays** and returned to his brigade command.

After the war, Thomas worked as a Louisiana planter, was active in **Democratic Party** politics, served on the Louisiana State University board of supervisors, and taught agriculture at the university from 1882 to 1884. After serving as coiner of the U.S. Mint in New Orleans, he moved to **Florida** in 1889 and served as the U.S. consul and minister to Venezuela from 1894 to 1897.

THOMAS, BRYAN MOREL (1836–1905) CSA. A native of **Georgia**, Thomas graduated from **West Point** in 1858 and was assigned to the infantry. His antebellum career included **New York** garrison duty, fighting **Indians** on the frontier, and the **Utah Expedition**.

Thomas resigned his 2nd lieutenant's commission in April 1861 and entered Confederate service as a 2nd lieutenant of infantry. After serving as an ordnance officer at Mobile, Alabama, he joined Brig. Gen. **Jones M. Withers's** staff in March 1862 as adjutant and inspector general. At **Shiloh**, Thomas earned praise while serving as Withers's chief of ordnance and **artillery**. He quickly earned promotions to captain and major and remained on Withers's staff through the **Kentucky Campaign** and the **Battle of Stones River**. At the latter battle, Withers commended Thomas for leaving his sickbed to join the fighting on the last day.

Thomas remained with Withers in the **Army of Tennessee** until March 1864, when he was transferred to **Alabama** and was placed under Brig. Gen. **James H. Clanton**. It was intended for him to be promoted to colonel and given command of a cavalry **regiment**, but, instead, Thomas was given permission to raise a cavalry **brigade**. He only raised a small command, however, that became known as Thomas's Alabama

Reserves Cavalry Regiment. Referred to as "colonel," Thomas served in Clanton's and **Gideon J. Pillow's** brigades before joining **Dabney H. Maury** at Mobile. By this time, several superiors had recommended him for promotion, and he finally was appointed brigadier general in August 1864. The following month, Thomas was given a small command of infantry, cavalry, and artillery. He remained part of the Mobile defense for the rest of the war, except for a brief stint guarding **railroads** in **Mississippi**. Thomas's small command helped defend **Fort Blakely** in April 1865 during the **Mobile Campaign** and was captured there when Union troops seized the fort on April 9.

After the war, Thomas returned to Georgia, where he farmed and served as a U.S. marshal. He also established a private academy in 1884 and became Dalton's superintendent of schools.

THOMAS, EDWARD LLOYD (1825–1898) CSA. A native of **Georgia**, Thomas graduated with distinction from Emory College in 1846 and fought in the **Mexican War** as a 2nd lieutenant of volunteers. He declined a **U.S. Army** commission at war's end and returned to Georgia to become a prominent planter.

After the Civil War began, Thomas organized the 35th Georgia and entered Confederate service in October 1861 as its colonel. Sent to **Virginia**, his regiment became part of **James Pettigrew's brigade**. After fighting at **Seven Pines**, where Thomas temporarily took brigade command after Pettigrew was wounded and captured, the 35th Georgia was assigned to **Joseph R. Anderson's** brigade. As part of the **Army of Northern Virginia**, Thomas fought with great distinction in the **Seven Days Campaign** and was slightly wounded at **Mechanicsville**, but he remained in the field. When Anderson was wounded at **Frayser's Farm**, Thomas assumed brigade command and retained it until war's end. As part of **A. P. Hill's division**, he fought well at **Cedar Mountain** and, especially, at **Second Manassas**. Thomas was left behind at **Harpers Ferry, Virginia**, to **parole** the **prisoners** during the **Antietam Campaign** and thus missed the climactic battle at Antietam.

Thomas was promoted to brigadier general in November 1862 and led his brigade with great skill at **Fredericksburg** and **Chancellorsville**. When the **army** was reorganized in May 1863, his brigade was assigned to **William Dorsey Pender's** division. After Pender was mortally wounded at **Gettysburg**, Thomas was considered as a replacement. He was passed over in favor of **Cadmus Wilcox**, however, because Thomas's Georgia troops were a minority within the division, and it was feared his promotion would cause discontent. Thomas led his brigade through most of the major battles in the **Overland**, **Petersburg**, and **Appomattox Campaigns** and was still with his men at **Appomattox**. Although deserving a higher position, he never rose above brigade command because of army politics.

After the war, Thomas returned to his Georgia plantation. During Grover Cleveland's presidency, he served in the Land Bureau and the Indian Bureau, and when he died in 1898, he was an **Indian** agent serving in the Oklahoma Territory.

THOMAS, GEORGE HENRY (1816–1870) USA. A native of **Virginia**, Thomas was forced to hide in the woods with his family to escape murder during the 1831 Nat Turner slave rebellion. After graduating from **West Point** in 1840, he served with the **artillery** on coastal garrison duty and in the **Seminole Wars** before winning two **brevets** for gallantry in the **Mexican War**. In 1855, Thomas became a major in the 2nd U.S. Cavalry and served with it on the frontier with future Confederate generals **Albert Sidney Johnston**, **Robert E. Lee**, and **William J. Hardee** until the outbreak of civil war.

In January 1861, Thomas applied for the position of commandant of cadets at the **Virginia Military Institute** but was not chosen. When Virginia seceded, he refused an offer to become the state's chief of ordnance and instead remained loyal to the Union. This act caused his sisters and other family members to disown him permanently. When Johnston and Lee resigned their commissions to join the Confederacy, Thomas was promoted first to lieutenant colonel and then to colonel of the 2nd U.S. Cavalry in April and May, respectively. In June, he was given a **brigade** under **Robert Patterson** and served in the **Shenandoah Valley** during the **First Manassas Campaign**.

Thomas was promoted to brigadier general of volunteers in August 1861 and was sent to **Kentucky**. There he first commanded Camp Dick Robinson, but in December, he was given a **division** in the **Army of the Ohio**. Thomas commanded the troops that won the **Battle of Mill Springs**, but he arrived too late to fight at **Shiloh**. In April 1862, he was promoted to major general of volunteers and replaced **U. S. Grant** in command of the **Army of the Tennessee**. After leading the **army** in the **siege of Corinth, Mississippi**, Thomas returned to Kentucky and fought at **Perryville** that autumn as second in command to **Don Carlos Buell**. Joining the **Army of the Cumberland**, he commanded **William S. Rosecrans's** center at **Stones River** and was given command of the XIV Corps in January 1863. After leading the **corps** during the **Tullahoma Campaign**, Thomas earned great fame at **Chickamauga**. When a Confederate attack pierced the Federal line, most of the army collapsed, and Rosecrans fled to **Chattanooga**. Thomas held **Snodgrass Hill** with his corps and other scattered units and kept the enemy at bay while the bulk of the army escaped. For this service, he earned the nickname **"Rock of Chickamauga"** and was appointed brigadier general of regulars in October 1863.

When Grant relieved Rosecrans of command in October, he appointed Thomas to take over the Army and **Department of the Cumberland**. The following month, it was Thomas's men who surged up **Missionary Ridge** without orders during the **Chattanooga Campaign** and forced the Confederates to retreat. During the **Atlanta Campaign**, his army made up more than half of **William T. Sherman's** force. Although Sherman complained that Thomas was too slow and plodding, the Army of the Cumberland performed solid service during the campaign. When **John Bell Hood's Army of Tennessee** headed toward **Tennessee** in the **Franklin and Nashville Campaign** in the autumn of 1864, Sherman sent Thomas to Nashville to stop the Confederate invasion. After the Battle of Franklin, Hood's army confronted Thomas at Nashville. Thomas's slow, methodical buildup for a counterattack angered Grant, and he was taking steps to relieve him, when Thomas finally attacked in December and crushed Hood in the Battle of Nashville. In recognition of his victory, Thomas was promoted to major general of regulars in January 1865 and received the **Thanks of Congress**. He remained in Tennessee in command of the Department of the Cumberland until war's end. Along with Grant and Sherman, Thomas was one of the Union's foremost generals. Although sometimes slow, he was a solid, dependable commander who greatly contributed to the Union victory.

Thomas remained in Tennessee until 1867. While there, he became embroiled in **Reconstruction** politics when he refused to cooperate in a plan by President **Andrew Johnson** to have him supersede Grant in command of the army. At his own request, Thomas was placed in charge of the Division of the Pacific in 1869. The following year, he suffered a stroke and died in San Francisco, California.

THOMAS, HENRY GODDARD (1837–1897) USA. A native of **Maine**, Thomas graduated from Amherst College and was a lawyer before the Civil War. He entered Union service in April 1861 as a private in the 5th Maine but was appointed captain two months later. After fighting at **First Manassas**, Thomas was commissioned captain in the 11th U.S. Infantry in August and spent the next year recruiting. He eventually became involved in the recruitment of **black troops** and in March 1863 was appointed colonel of the **1st Kansas Colored Infantry**. It was claimed that Thomas was the first Union officer to accept command of a black **regiment**. Although mustered out of the regiment in July, he continued to recruit blacks and in January 1864 was appointed colonel of the 19th U.S. Colored Troops.

In May 1864, Thomas was given command of a **brigade** of black soldiers in **Edward Ferrero's** IX Corps **division** and led it through the **Overland** and **Petersburg Campaigns**, winning **brevets** for his service at **Spotsylvania** and the **Crater**. Promoted to brigadier general of volunteers in November 1864, he then was given a brigade in the **Army of the James** and served with it until war's end. When Thomas was mustered out of the volunteers in January 1866, he had received brevets through major general of volunteers and brigadier general of regulars. He reverted to his regular rank of captain and remained in the **U.S. Army** until retiring in 1891 as a major in the paymaster's department.

THOMAS, LORENZO (1804–1875) USA. A native of **Delaware**, Thomas graduated from **West Point** in 1823. He served in the **Seminole** and **Mexican Wars** and won one **brevet** during the latter while adjutant general to Maj. Gen. William O. Butler's **division**. From 1853 to 1861, Thomas served as General-in-Chief **Winfield Scott's** chief of staff with the staff rank of lieutenant colonel.

In March 1861, Thomas was promoted to colonel of regulars and was appointed the Union **army's** adjutant general to replace **Samuel Cooper**, who had resigned and joined the Confederacy. He was promoted to brigadier general in August. A conservative thinker and unenergetic officer, Thomas performed poorly in trying to master the paperwork of the huge Union war machine and ran afoul of the **Radical Republicans** when he investigated **John C. Frémont's** actions in **Missouri** in late 1861 (on **Abraham Lincoln's** orders) and issued findings critical of the general. Thomas also frequently clashed with Secretary of War **Edwin Stanton**, who sent him west in March 1863 to organize **black troops**. Although still the army's adjutant general, Thomas spent the rest of the war recruiting and organizing black soldiers in the **Military Division of the Mississippi** and performing menial inspections for Stanton. For this service, he was brevetted major general of regulars.

Thomas remained in the army after the war and served as acting secretary of war in 1868 when President **Andrew Johnson** dismissed Stanton (thus leading to Johnson's impeachment). He retired as adjutant general in 1869.

THOMPSON, FRANKLIN (1842–1898) USA. *See* EDMONDS, SARAH EMMA.

THOMPSON, JACOB (1810–1885) CSA. A native of **North Carolina**, Thompson graduated from the University of North Carolina in 1831 and became a lawyer. He soon moved to **Mississippi**, where he became a planter and was active in the **Democratic Party**. Thompson was elected to the **U.S. Congress** six times beginning in 1838, and in 1857, he was appointed President **James Buchanan's** secretary of the interior. While serving in that position, he was investigated and cleared of embezzling money from the Indian Trust Fund.

During the **secession** crisis, Thompson secretly informed **South Carolina** of the *Star of the West's* mission to resupply **Fort Sumter** and then resigned his cabinet position and joined the Confederacy. From 1861 to 1863, he served on the staffs of several generals and in 1863 was elected to the Mississippi legislature. In 1864, **Jefferson Davis** appointed Thompson the Confederate commissioner to Canada. Given at least $200,000 by the government and receiving another $330,000 from various Confederate operatives, he was supposed to work with other secret agents to devalue the Union gold market and free Confederate **prisoners** of war being held around the Great Lakes. Thompson did little, however, although he was somewhat involved in the **St. Albans Raid** and the attempt to burn **New York City**.

When the war ended, Thompson took all of his funds and moved to Europe. There he lived elegantly in a Paris hotel for four years, refusing all pleas from former Confederate officials to relinquish the money. Thompson finally did turn some of the money over to former Confederate Secretary of State **Judah P. Benjamin**, but he kept a large, but unknown, amount for himself. When he died in **Tennessee** in 1885, Thompson still was quite wealthy.

THOMPSON, MERRIWETHER JEFF (1826–1876) CSA. A native of **Virginia**, M. Jeff. Thompson (as he was better known) wanted to be a professional soldier, but both **West Point** and the **Virginia Military Institute** denied him entrance. He eventually settled in **Missouri**, where he worked as a fur trapper, surveyor, gas company owner, and real estate investor. In 1859, Thompson was elected mayor of St. Joseph.

By 1861, Thompson was a popular and prosperous citizen. A secessionist, he organized a volunteer battalion and tried to convince Missouri's citizens to secede. Joining the Missouri State Guard, Thompson rose from lieutenant colonel to brigadier general in the spring of 1861, but he never was mustered into Confederate service. His men served as a guerrilla unit and began battling Union forces in the swamps of southeastern Missouri. There they earned the nickname "Swamp Rats," while Thompson became the "Swamp Fox of the Confederacy." A popular and natural born leader, Thompson became one of the Confederacy's most colorful figures as he performed a wide variety of services. After his guerrillas were disbanded in December 1861, he and some of his **companies** joined the **River Defense Fleet** in early 1862 and fought at **Plum Run Bend**. Poor relations with the naval crews forced Thompson to take his men out of the fleet that summer and join Confederate forces operating around **New Orleans, Louisiana**. By the summer of 1863, he and his "Swamp Rats" were back in action as guerrillas in southeastern Missouri and northeastern **Arkansas**. Thompson was captured by Missouri state cavalry in Arkansas in August 1863 and was kept a **prisoner** until **exchanged** in June 1864. He then commanded **Jo Shelby's** cavalry **brigade** in **Sterling Price's 1864 Missouri Raid** and was praised for his bravery at **Westport**. After the raid, Thompson continued to operate as a guerrilla in Missouri until he surrendered in May 1865.

After the war, Thompson worked as a businessman in **Tennessee** and **Louisiana**.

THOMPSON'S STATION, TENNESSEE, BATTLE OF (MARCH 5, 1863). On March 4, 1863, Union Col. John Coburn led his infantry **brigade** from **Franklin, Tennessee**, south toward Columbia on a **reconnaissance** mission. Coburn had approximately 2,800 men, including a cavalry brigade and some **artillery** that were sent along in support. The next day, he encountered Brig. Gen. **William H. Jackson's** Confederate cavalry just north of Spring Hill. At first, Coburn forced the Confederates back, but soon Maj. Gen. **Earl Van Dorn** arrived with reinforcements, including **Nathan Bedford Forrest's** brigade. The Confederates simultaneously attacked Coburn's front and moved against his left flank. When the Union cavalry and artillery on the left gave way and fled, the Confederates quickly surrounded Coburn. After a fierce fight, the outnumbered Federals soon ran out of ammunition and were forced to surrender. Coburn lost nearly 300 dead and wounded and 1,150 captured, while Van Dorn counted 357 casualties.

THOROUGHFARE GAP, VIRGINIA, BATTLE OF (AUGUST 28, 1862). This small, but important, action took place as **Robert E. Lee** and **James Longstreet** rushed to join **Stonewall Jackson** behind enemy lines during the **Second Manassas Campaign**. **John Pope's Army of Virginia** had an opportunity to prevent the two Confederate wings from reuniting by holding Thoroughfare Gap, through which Lee's **Army of Northern Virginia** had to pass. **James Ricketts's** Union **division** guarded the pass, but on August 28, 1862, Lee outflanked him by capturing high ground to his north and south and by sending **Cadmus M. Wilcox's** division to the north to seize Hopewell Gap. After a brief **skirmish**, Ricketts abandoned Thoroughfare Gap and retreated to Manassas Junction, allowing Lee to join Jackson for the Second Battle of Manassas. If the Federals had held the gap longer, Pope perhaps could have destroyed Jackson and then turned on Lee and Longstreet. In the brief action, total casualties were approximately 100.

THRUSTON, CHARLES MYNN (1798–1873) USA. A native of **Kentucky**, Thruston graduated from **West Point** in 1814 and spent the rest of the War of 1812 working on defensive projects in **New York**. Afterward, he served with the **artillery** on garrison duty and in the **Seminole Wars**. Thruston resigned his captain's commission in 1837 and settled in **Maryland**, where he farmed, became a bank president, and was elected mayor of Cumberland.

In September 1861, Thruston entered Union service when he was appointed brigadier general of volunteers for the express purpose of commanding the troops protecting the local Baltimore & Ohio Railroad from Confederate raiders. This proved to be an impossible job, and he asked to be relieved in April 1862. Thruston's request was honored, and he returned to his farm.

TILGHMAN, LLOYD (1816–1863) CSA. A native of **Maryland**, Tilghman (TIL-mun) graduated near the bottom of his 1836 **West Point** class and served briefly with the dragoons before resigning his commission in 1836 to become a **railroad** engineer. He entered the **Mexican War** as Maj. Gen. **David Twiggs's** volunteer aide but ended the war as a captain of volunteers. Afterward, Tilghman worked as an engineer and became active in the **Kentucky** militia.

Tilghman entered Confederate service in 1861 as colonel of the 3rd Kentucky (Confederate), but in October, he was appointed brigadier general. While commanding Hopkinsville, Kentucky, he brought to Gen. **Albert Sidney Johnston's** attention the deplorable lack of defenses on the Tennessee and Cumberland Rivers. As a result, Johnston placed Tilghman in command of **Forts Henry and Donelson, Tennessee**, in November. Tilghman worked hard to prepare the two forts, but his efforts were hampered by his abrasive personality, a lack of manpower and material, and conflicting orders from his superiors.

In February 1862, Union Brig. Gen. **U. S. Grant** attacked Tilghman at Fort Henry. Tilghman remained behind with a handful of defenders to hold off the Union gunboats while the rest of the garrison escaped to Fort Donelson. He fought a brief battle with **Andrew Foote's** fleet on February 6 and then surrendered. **Exchanged** in August, Tilghman commanded the **Tennessee** camps of rendezvous and instruction for exchanged Confederate **prisoners** before being given a **brigade** in **Mansfield Lovell's** command. After participating in the **Battle of Corinth** and winning a small fight at **Coffeeville, Mississippi**, he took a brigade in **William W. Loring's division** and fought in the **Vicksburg Campaign**. At **Champion Hill** on May 16, 1863, Tilghman was killed by a shell fragment while directing the fire of his own **artillery**.

TILLSON, DAVIS (1830–1895) USA. A native of **Maine**, Tillson was forced to leave **West Point** during his third year in 1851 because of an accident that resulted in his leg being amputated. Returning to Maine, he was elected to the state legislature in 1857, was appointed state adjutant general in 1858, and became a customs collector in 1861.

After the Civil War began, Tillson resigned his legislative seat and entered Union service in November 1861 as a captain in the 2nd Maine Battery. He was promoted to major in the 1st Maine Light Artillery Battalion in May 1862 and the following month was appointed chief of **artillery** for the **Army of Virginia's** III Corps. After fighting well at **Cedar Mountain** and **Second Manassas**, Tillson was appointed the 1st Maine Light Artillery Battalion's lieutenant colonel in December.

In March 1863, Tillson was commissioned brigadier general of volunteers and was made the **Army of the Potomac's artillery** inspector. The next month, however, he was transferred west, where he was appointed the **Department of the Ohio's** chief of artillery and supervised the construction of defensive works around Cincinnati, Ohio. After a year's service, Tillson transferred to the infantry in April 1864. Given a **brigade** command in the 4th Division of the **Army of the Ohio's** XXIII Corps, he spent most of the year serving in east **Tennessee**, where he supervised the construction of defenses at Knoxville. From February 1865 until the war's end, Tillson commanded the District of East Tennessee and its infantry **division**.

After the war, Tillson remained in the **army** and worked for the **Freedmen's Bureau** in Tennessee and **Georgia**. He was **brevetted** major general of volunteers for his war service and finally was mustered out of the army in December 1866. Tillson then briefly worked as a cotton planter in Georgia before returning to Maine and entering the granite and lime business.

TIMROD, HENRY (1828–1867) CSA. A native of **South Carolina**, Timrod became known as the "Poet Laureate of the Confederacy." The son of a poet and bookbinder, he attended (but did not graduate from) Franklin College, read law for a time, and worked as a private tutor before turning to poetry. Timrod published his first works in the *Southern Literary Messenger* in 1860, but he did not become popular until 1861.

Timrod's "Ethnogenesis," published in February 1861, was a very popular patriotic piece supporting **secession**. He followed it with such works as "The Cotton Boll," "A Cry to Arms," "Carolina," "Carmen Triumphale," "The Unknown Dead," and "Charleston." Joining the **Confederate army** in March 1862, Timrod served with the 13th South Carolina and briefly was employed as a western **war correspondent** by the **Charleston *Mercury*** before receiving a medical discharge in December. He spent the rest of the war working as an editor and writer for the newspaper in South Carolina. Before dying from tuberculosis in 1867, the impoverished Timrod wrote "Ode," a eulogy to Confederate dead. A collection of his works was not published until 1884.

"TINCLADS." As opposed to heavier **ironclads**, tinclads were lightly armored Union warships that were used on the western waters. Put into service in late 1862, they often were river steamboats that were converted into warships by being covered in one-half- to three-quarter-inch iron plating and armed with two bow **howitzers**. The lighter armor gave the ships a shallow draft and allowed them to be used in small secondary streams. Tinclads saw service in the **Vicksburg** and **Red River Campaigns** and along **Arkansas's** White River. *See also* COTTONCLADS.

TISHOMINGO CREEK, MISSISSIPPI, BATTLE OF (JUNE 10, 1864). *See* BRICE'S CROSS ROADS, MISSISSIPPI, BATTLE OF.

TOD, DAVID (1805–1868) USA. A native of **Ohio** and the son of a well-known judge, Tod became a lawyer after attending Burton Academy. Becoming active in the **Democratic Party**, he was elected to the state senate in 1838, twice ran unsuccessfully for governor in the 1840s, and served as U.S. minister to Brazil from 1847 to 1857. Returning to Ohio, Tod managed his successful coal and iron business, but he failed in a bid for a congressional seat. He did, however, serve as chairman of the 1860 Democratic National Convention in **Charleston, South Carolina**.

As a **War Democrat**, Tod strongly supported the Union war effort and in late 1861 was elected Ohio's governor. He filled the state's enlistment quota by offering **bounties** to recruits, quelled antiwar sentiment by threatening to arrest dissenters, and raised money by charging high **commutation** fees to avoid **conscription**. Tod's most critical moment came in the election of 1864 when **Copperhead Clement L. Vallandigham** ran for governor. Vallandigham's arrest by Maj. Gen. **Ambrose E. Burnside** won him much sympathy and nearly got Tod removed from office. This controversy, plus Tod's sometimes arbitrary policies and his lukewarm support of the **Emancipation Proclamation**, cost him his bid for renomination.

After leaving office, Tod continued to support the war effort, and **Abraham Lincoln** offered him the position of secretary of the treasury when **Salmon P. Chase** resigned in June 1864. Tod refused on grounds of poor health and his business obligations.

TODD, JOHN BLAIR SMITH (1814–1872) USA. A native of **Kentucky**, Todd reportedly was related by marriage to both **Abraham Lincoln** and **John C. Breckinridge**. He moved to **Illinois** with his family as a boy and entered **West Point** in 1832. After graduating near the bottom of the 1837 class, Todd served in the infantry in both the **Seminole** and **Mexican Wars** and performed various frontier duties. In 1856, he resigned his captain's commission and worked as a **U.S. Army sutler** before becoming a lawyer in the Dakota Territory.

Todd entered Union service in September 1861 when he was commissioned brigadier general of volunteers. He commanded the District of North Missouri until December, when he went to **Washington, D.C.**, to serve as Dakota's first nonvoting representative. In June 1862, Todd was given command of a **division** in the **Army of the Tennessee**, but he had to relinquish it the following month after the Senate failed to confirm his commission. He was defeated for reelection to the **U.S. Congress**, but he successfully contested the election and kept his seat until March 1865. After having been defeated again for reelection, Todd returned to the Dakota Territory and served as territorial speaker of the house from 1866 to 1867. He retired after being defeated for reelection in 1868.

TOMPKINS, SALLY LOUISA (1833–1916) CSA. A native of **Virginia**, the well-to-do widow Tompkins was living in **Richmond** when the Civil War began. After **First Manassas**, she opened a private hospital to care for the wounded. Although financed by Tompkins, the hospital was known as Robertson Hospital because it was located in a house provided by Judge John Robertson. The hospital was one of the best in the city and enjoyed a reputation of returning a large percentage of its patients to duty. After the government adopted a policy requiring all hospitals to be run by military personnel, **Jefferson Davis** commissioned Tompkins a captain of cavalry in September 1861 so she could continue to operate her hospital. She was the only woman to be commissioned in the **Confederate army**. Although Tompkins never accepted any money for her work, except her military salary, she ran one of the most efficient hospitals in the Confederacy. Of 1,333 patients treated there, only 73 died. Robertson Hospital remained in service for some time after Richmond's capture, but it finally closed in June 1865. "Captain Sally" continued to be active in postwar charities and veterans' activities. Becoming impoverished, she lived for years in Richmond's Confederate Women's Home and was given a military burial when she died in 1916.

TOM'S BROOK, VIRGINIA, BATTLE OF (OCTOBER 9, 1864). After defeating Lt. Gen. **Jubal A. Early** at **Third Winchester** and **Fisher's Hill** during the **1864 Shenandoah Valley Campaign**, Maj. Gen. **Philip Sheridan** pursued the Confederates toward Staunton for a time before withdrawing his **army** back down the Valley. As he did so, Sheridan ordered Brig. Gen. **Alfred T. A. Torbert's** cavalry **division** to confiscate livestock and to burn everything that could be of use to the Confederates. From October 6 to 8, Torbert's troopers devastated the **Shenandoah Valley** in what became known as "The Burning."

Brigadier General **Thomas Rosser's** two Confederate cavalry divisions followed the Union troopers as they withdrew. When he camped south of Strasburg at Tom's Brook on October 8, Rosser was far ahead of Early's army and was completely isolated. Taking advantage of this error, Sheridan sent Torbert's 4,000 men to attack Rosser at dawn of October 9. While **Wesley Merritt's** division attacked up the Valley Pike, **George A. Custer's** division attacked the Confederate left flank. Rosser's line crumbled, and his cavalrymen panicked. The headlong rush to the rear toward Woodstock turned into a rout, which the Federals called the "Woodstock Races." Rosser lost 350 men (mostly taken **prisoner**), 11 cannons, and his baggage train. Torbert suffered only 57 casualties. The lopsided victory demonstrated how much the Union cavalry had improved in the war and how demoralized and weakened its Confederate counterpart had become.

TOOMBS, ROBERT AUGUSTUS (1810–1885) CSA. A native of **Georgia**, Toombs graduated from **New York's** Union College in 1828 and became a wealthy and influential figure in Georgia through his prosperous plantations and law practice. A member of the **Whig Party**, he served in the state legislature from 1837 to 1843 and in the **U.S. Congress** from 1844 to 1851 before entering the U.S. Senate in 1852. A powerful intellectual speaker, Toombs first served as a nationalist who opposed the **Mexican War**, but he supported the tariff. As **slavery** and **states rights** became more volatile issues, he joined the **Democratic Party** in 1855 and began advocating Southern rights.

During the **secession** crisis, Toombs did not support secession until after the **Crittenden Compromise** was rejected. He then became a leader of the secession movement and even was considered for the position of Confederate president. Toombs's heavy drinking and increasingly radical views, however, led delegates at the **Montgomery, Alabama, Convention** to choose **Jefferson Davis** instead. Although disappointed at this failure, Toombs accepted Davis's offer to become secretary of state.

Since the Confederacy had not been recognized by any nation, Toombs had little to do in his position and clashed with Davis over the president's management style. He resigned his post in July 1861 but used his political influence to obtain a brigadier general's commission. Toombs was given a **brigade** command in **Joseph E. Johnston's army**, but he gained little respect as an officer because of his drinking, constant criticisms, and poor military ability. During the **Peninsula Campaign**, he did win some acclaim for a defensive action at Dam Number One when he temporarily commanded **David R. Jones's division**. Toombs did not play a major role in any other battles on the peninsula, and at **Malvern Hill**, **Daniel H. Hill** accused him of cowardice. Outraged, Toombs challenged Hill to a duel, but religious considerations caused Hill to decline. In August 1862, Toombs was arrested for insubordination when he failed to follow orders to guard a river ford. **James Longstreet**, however, released him from arrest and allowed the contentious general to rejoin his command for the **Battle of Antietam**. There, Toombs performed his finest service to the **Army of Northern Virginia** when he tenaciously defended Burnside's Bridge for much of the day. After receiving a hand wound the following day, he returned to Georgia to recuperate.

Bitter that his battlefield performance did not win him a promotion, Toombs resigned his commission in March 1863. He remained in Georgia for the remainder of the war, becoming one of Davis's most vocal critics and running unsuccessfully for the Senate. Toombs was appointed colonel of state troops in August 1863, and during the **Atlanta Campaign**, he served as adjutant and inspector general of a militia division.

When the war ended, Toombs left the country and lived in France, but he returned in 1867. He never asked for a pardon, and thus never returned to national politics, but he did help overthrow **Reconstruction** rule in Georgia.

TOON, THOMAS FENTRESS (1840–1902) CSA. A native of **North Carolina**, Toon was near graduating from Wake Forest College when the Civil War began. He enlisted in a volunteer **company** in May 1861 but then returned to Wake Forest to graduate. Toon entered Confederate service the following month when he was elected a 1st lieutenant in the 20th North Carolina. In July, he was elected company captain.

After service in North Carolina, Toon's **regiment** was sent to **Virginia** in May 1862 and fought at **Seven Pines** as part of **Samuel Garland's brigade**. He was wounded during the battle but rejoined the regiment in time to fight at **Gaines' Mill**, where he received a slight wound. Over the next several months, Toon gained an excellent reputation while fighting with the **Army of Northern Virginia** at **Second Manassas**, **Antietam**, and **Fredericksburg**. Although he was not the senior regimental captain, he was appointed colonel in February 1863 when his fellow officers waived their rights to promotion. As part of **Alfred Iverson's** brigade, Toon led the 20th North Carolina through heavy combat at **Chancellorsville**, where he was wounded three times. He also served at **Gettysburg** and in the **Mine Run Campaign**. As part of **Robert D. Johnston's** brigade, he saw heavy combat in the **Overland Campaign**. At **Spotsylvania**, Toon received yet another wound and assumed command of the brigade when Johnston was wounded during bloody fighting at the "Mule Shoe."

In late May 1864, Toon was appointed temporary brigadier general and took command of the brigade. After service in **Jubal A. Early's Washington Raid**, he reverted to colonel when Johnston returned to the brigade. Toon led the regiment through all of the major battles of the **Philip Sheridan's 1864 Shenandoah Valley Campaign** and then rejoined the Army of Northern Virginia for the final months of the **Petersburg Campaign**. While attacking **Fort Stedman** in March 1865, he received his seventh wound and was unable to return to duty.

After the war, Toon returned to North Carolina. There he worked for a **railroad**, served as a state legislator, and taught school. When Toon died in 1902, he was serving as the state's superintendent of public instruction.

TORBERT, ALFRED THOMAS ARCHIMEDES (1833–1880) USA. A native of **Delaware**, Torbert graduated from **West Point** in 1855 and served in the **Seminole Wars** and the **Utah Expedition** before being promoted to 1st lieutenant in February 1861. Strangely, while on a leave of absence in April, he was appointed a 1st lieutenant of Confederate **artillery**—thus giving him the distinction of being an officer in both **armies** at the same time. Torbert never accepted the Confederate commission and reported back to the **U.S. Army** in April for recruiting duty.

In September 1861, Torbert was appointed colonel of the 1st New Jersey and was promoted to captain of regulars. Assigned to the **Army of the Potomac**, he led his **regiment** in the **Peninsula**, **Seven Days**, and **Second Manassas Campaigns** before being assigned a **brigade** in the VI Corps' 1st Division. After fighting in the **Antietam Campaign**, where he was wounded at **South Mountain**, Torbert was promoted to brigadier general of volunteers in November 1862 and led his brigade at **Fredericksburg**, **Chancellorsville**, and **Gettysburg**. In all of these campaigns, he frequently received high praise from his superiors.

When the Army of the Potomac was reorganized in the spring of 1864, Torbert was transferred to the cavalry and took command of a **division** under **Philip Sheridan**. After participating in **Sheridan's Richmond Raid** during the **Overland Campaign**, he was given command of the Union cavalry operating in the **Shenandoah Valley** in August 1864. During **Sheridan's 1864 Shenandoah Valley Campaign**, Torbert helped destroy the Valley in what became known as "The Burning," routed the Confederate cavalry at **Tom's Brook**, and was one of the few Union commanders who held his men together during the initial enemy onslaught at **Cedar Creek**. He assumed command of the **Army of the Shenandoah** when Sheridan launched **Sheridan's Virginia Raid** in February 1865 and led it until war's end.

For his war service, Torbert was **brevetted** through all ranks to major general in both the volunteer and regular service. When he was mustered out of the volunteers in January 1866, however, he reverted to his regular rank of captain. Receiving no further promotions, Torbert resigned from the army in October. He then served in various Latin American and French diplomatic positions from 1869 to 1878, including that of consul general in Paris. Retiring from the foreign service in 1878, Torbert was sailing to Mexico on business when he drowned in a shipwreck off the **Florida** coast.

TORPEDO. In the Civil War, a mine was referred to as a torpedo and was used mostly by the Confederates. A few torpedoes were used on land by burying **artillery** shells in a road with their percussion **fuse** exposed so as to detonate if stepped on or driven over. Confederate Brig. Gen. **Gabriel J. Rains** used land torpedoes during the **Peninsula Campaign**, but the Confederates largely abandoned the practice after they were accused of being barbaric. More common were marine torpedoes. These were containers of powder that usually were armed with either a percussion or electric fuse. They normally were suspended just under the water's surface and exploded when struck by a ship or detonated by a crew hiding nearby. The **USS** *Cairo* and *Eastport* were sunk by underwater torpedoes, while the **USS** *Housatonic* was sunk by a spar torpedo mounted on the **CSS** *H. L. Hunley.* The Confederates also lost the **CSS** *Albemarle* to a Federal torpedo. *See also* "INFERNAL MACHINES."

TOTOPOTOMOY CREEK, VIRGINIA, BATTLE OF (MAY 28–31, 1864). After engaging **Robert E. Lee** in the battles of the **Wilderness, Spotsylvania,** and **North Anna River** in the **Overland Campaign, U. S. Grant** withdrew from the North Anna River and moved toward **Cold Harbor.** He led with **Philip Sheridan's** cavalry on May 26, 1864, and the infantry followed that night. Lee shifted his forces as well, and by May 28, the Confederates were positioned along Totopotomoy (tot-tuh-POT-uh-mee) Creek, blocking the Union advance. Fighting erupted between the opposing cavalry at **Haw's Shop** on May 28 and heavy **skirmishing** continued for the next two days as Grant came into position. On May 30, heavier fighting erupted as Lee lashed out at the Federals as they attempted to flank him. **Robert E. Rodes's division** attacked **Samuel W. Crawford's** Union division at Bethesda Church, but it was repulsed in a bloody battle after some initial success. The Federals also probed Lee's position on May 30 and 31 but decided it was too strong to assault. On the night of May 31, both **armies** began shifting to Cold Harbor. In the fighting around Totopotomoy Creek, Grant lost 731 men, while Lee counted 1,159 casualties.

TOTTEN, JOSEPH GILBERT (1788–1864) USA. A native of **Connecticut,** Totten graduated with the first **West Point** class in 1805 and spent the next 59 years in the **U.S. Army,** taking only one leave of absence from 1806 to 1808 to help survey the Northwest Territory. Assigned to the **engineers,** he earned two **brevets** during the War of 1812, became the **army's** chief engineer in 1838, served as inspector of West Point, and earned another brevet in the **Mexican War** while serving as **Winfield Scott's** engineer. After the Mexican War, Totten performed great service improving navigation on the eastern seaboard, studying American harbors, and experimenting with heavy ordnance. He also helped establish the lighthouse system, wrote many scientific reports, sat on the board of regents for the Smithsonian Institution, and helped create the National Academy of Sciences.

When the Civil War began in 1861, Totten was still the army's chief engineer, holding the rank of colonel and brevet brigadier general. During the war, he supervised the construction of city and harbor defenses, improved navigation, and appointed army engineers. When the Corps of Topographical Engineers was merged into the Corps of Engineers in March 1863, Totten was appointed brigadier general and was placed in command of the corps. He died from pneumonia in April 1864 while on active duty and was brevetted major general of regulars posthumously.

TOWER, ZEALOUS BATES (1819–1900) USA. A native of **Massachusetts**, Tower graduated first in the **West Point** class of 1841 and received three **brevets** and a wound in the **Mexican War** while serving in the **engineers** under **Winfield Scott**. After the war, he performed various engineering duties on the Atlantic and Pacific coasts.

When the Civil War began, Tower was a captain of engineers. He was sent to **Fort Pickens, Florida**, in February 1861 as part of the secret relief expedition and remained there until May. Sent back north, Tower was promoted to major in August and performed routine duties until June 1862, when he was promoted to brigadier general of volunteers and was given a **brigade** command in the **Army of Virginia's** III Corps. He fought at **Cedar Mountain** and was so badly wounded at **Second Manassas** that he did not return to duty until July 1864 and even then was unfit for field command. Tower served as West Point's superintendent until September, when he was appointed inspector general of fortifications for the **Military Division of the Mississippi**. He spent the rest of the war stationed at Nashville, Tennessee.

When Tower was mustered out of service in January 1866, he had received brevets through the rank of major general of volunteers. He remained in the regular **army** as a lieutenant colonel and retired in 1883 as a colonel of engineers.

TOWNSEND, GEORGE ALFRED "GATH" (1841–1914) USA. A native of **Delaware**, Townsend was a newspaperman before the Civil War who worked as a reporter for the Philadelphia *Inquirer* and editor of the Philadelphia *Press*. In 1862, he was hired as a **war correspondent** by the New York *Herald* to cover the **Army of the Potomac** during the **Peninsula Campaign**. Townsend was an excellent writer, and his articles on the **Seven Days Campaign** and the **Battle of Cedar Mountain** became very popular. In August, he toured Great Britain as a lecturer and writer supporting the Union, but he returned to cover the Army of the Potomac for the New York *World*. Tower became a well-known figure for his articles (which were published under his initials "GAT") on **Five Forks**, the capture of **Richmond, Virginia**, and **Abraham Lincoln's assassination**.

After the Civil War, Townsend covered the 1866 Austro-Prussian War for the *World* and then returned to the United States and wrote for the Chicago *Tribune* and the Cincinnati *Enquirer*. During the postwar period, he became one of the nation's most popular writers and added the letter *H* to his byline to become known as "Gath." Besides his newspaper articles, Townsend also wrote numerous books, including *Campaigns of a Non-Combatant*. He bought land at Crampton's Gap, Maryland, in 1884 and erected a 60-foot stone arch to honor Civil War correspondents. Townsend developed an estate there that is now Gathland State Park.

TRACY, EDWARD DORR (1833–1863) CSA. A native of **Georgia**, Tracy graduated from the University of Georgia and worked as a teacher before becoming a lawyer.

Having lived in **Alabama** since 1855, Tracy entered Confederate service in May 1861 as captain of a volunteer **company** he organized. Assigned to the 4th Alabama, the **regiment** went to **Virginia** and became part of **Barnard Bee's brigade**. Four days after being promoted to major, Tracy fought at **First Manassas**, but he then left the regiment in October when he was appointed lieutenant colonel of **Joseph Wheeler's** 19th Alabama. After brief duty in Mobile, Alabama, he fought at **Shiloh's** "Hornets' Nest" in **John K. Jackson's** brigade and had a horse killed under him on the battle's second day. When Wheeler was elevated to brigade command in May, Tracy assumed command of the regiment. He joined **Edmund Kirby Smith's army** in east **Tennessee** in the summer of 1862 and participated in the **Kentucky Campaign** as part of **Franklin Gardner's** brigade. Upon Kirby Smith's recommendation, Tracy was promoted to brigadier general in August.

Given an infantry brigade, Tracy served in **John P. McCown's division** until he was transferred to **Carter L. Stevenson's** division at **Vicksburg, Mississippi**, in December 1862. During the early part of the **Vicksburg Campaign**, his brigade defended Vicksburg, but in April 1863, he reinforced **John S. Bowen's** division at **Grand Gulf, Mississippi**. On May 1, Tracy was killed instantly at **Port Gibson** when he was struck in the chest by a bullet.

TRANS-ALLEGHENY DEPARTMENT (CONFEDERATE). In November 1862, the Confederate War Department renamed the **Depart-**

ment of **Southwestern Virginia** the Trans-Allegheny Department. Placed under the command of Maj. Gen. **Samuel Jones** with headquarters at "The Narrows" on the New River, the new **department** covered the same area, except its western boundary was extended to **Kentucky** or as far west beyond the Kentucky border as possible. Jones was to protect the vital East Tennessee & Virginia Railroad and to cooperate with other Confederate forces in the area. **John C. Breckinridge** replaced him in February 1864, and **John H. Morgan** replaced him in June. When Morgan was killed in September, Breckinridge resumed command. During Breckinridge's second tenure, the department was expanded to include parts of East Tennessee and became known unofficially as the **Department of Southwestern Virginia and East Tennessee**. Under Breckinridge, the department's troops were involved in the battles of **New Market** and **Saltville, Virginia**. The department's name officially was changed to the Department of Western Tennessee and East Tennessee in 1865.

TRANS-MISSISSIPPI DEPARTMENT (CONFEDERATE). Created in May 1862, this huge **department** covered all of the Confederate territory west of the Mississippi River. It first was placed under **Thomas C. Hindman's** command, but he was replaced by **Theophilus H. Holmes** in July. In March 1863, **Edmund Kirby Smith** assumed command and led the **department** for the rest of the war from his headquarters at Shreveport, Louisiana.

After the Federals captured **Vicksburg, Mississippi**, and **Port Hudson, Louisiana**, and seized control of the Mississippi River in July 1863, the Trans-Mississippi Department was cut off from the rest of the Confederacy. Isolated from the government, Kirby Smith was forced to make his own strategic decisions, gather his own supplies and equipment, and even appoint his own officers. He retained such absolute control over his department, that the Trans-Mississippi became known as **"Kirby Smithdom."**

Numerous battles and campaigns were fought in the department, including the **Bayou Teche Campaign**, **Texas Overland Expedition**, **Red River Campaign**, **Camden Expedition**, and **Sterling Price's 1864 Missouri Raid**. Confederate forces in the department were the last ground troops to **surrender** in 1865. Kirby Smith wanted to continue the war even after the Confederacy's eastern armies had surrendered. He headed to Houston, Texas, in late May 1865 to organize his troops, but his men began disbanding their **regiments** and **deserting** by the thousands. Kirby Smith found himself a general without an **army**. On May

26, Lt. Gen. **Simon B. Buckner** signed a document in **New Orleans, Louisiana**, with **Edward R. S. Canby** to surrender the department, and Kirby Smith approved it in Galveston, Texas, on June 2. The last **surrender** in the department was Brig. Gen. **Stand Watie's Indians** in **Indian Territory** on June 23.

TRANS-MISSISSIPPI DISTRICT (CONFEDERATE). Because of friction over responsibility and authority between generals **Sterling Price**, of the Missouri State Guard, and **Ben McCulloch**, commanding **Louisiana** and **Arkansas** Confederate troops, Confederate authorities created the Trans-Mississippi District in January 1862 and placed both officers under Maj. Gen. **Earl Van Dorn's** command. As part of **Department No. 2**, this **district** included the **Indian Territory**, that part of Louisiana north of the Red River, and Arkansas and **Missouri** (except for a few eastern counties along the Mississippi River). Van Dorn created the **Army of the West** from troops within his district and fought at **Pea Ridge** before the district was absorbed by the newly created **Trans-Mississippi Department** in May 1862.

TRANS-MISSISSIPPI DIVISION (UNION). *See* MILITARY DIVISION OF WEST MISSISSIPPI (UNION).

TRAPIER, JAMES HEYWARD (1815–1865) CSA. A native of **South Carolina**, Trapier graduated near the top of his 1838 **West Point** class and was assigned to the **engineers**. He worked on various construction projects, including **Fort Pulaski, South Carolina**, and fought in the **Mexican War**. After Mexico, Trapier was appointed assistant engineer for **New York's** fortifications, but he resigned his 1st lieutenant's commission in 1848 and returned to South Carolina to become a planter and militia officer. As a militia ordnance officer, he purchased 50 heavy guns from the **Tredegar Iron Works** that later were used effectively in the bombardment of **Fort Sumter**.

In April 1861, Trapier was a major of state troops serving on **P. G. T. Beauregard's** staff at **Charleston, South Carolina**. He prepared the batteries on Morris Island for the bombardment of Fort Sumter and was praised by Beauregard for his service during the battle. After the fort's surrender, Trapier was put in command of Charleston and was promoted to brigadier general of Confederate troops in October 1861. He assumed command of the District of Eastern and Middle Florida after his promotion but was unpopular there because he kept his headquarters away from the front. In February 1862, Trapier failed to carry out orders to evacuate threatened Amelia Island on the Atlantic coast and lost 15 valuable cannons when the Federals captured the island. The Florida state convention then passed a resolution asking that he either be replaced or be forced to remain with his troops at the front. Trapier claimed he had been insulted and asked **Jefferson Davis** to replace him.

In March 1862, Trapier was transferred to **Albert Sidney Johnston's army** and was given command of a **division** in **Leonidas Polk's corps**. His service in the **siege of Corinth, Mississippi**, failed to impress his superiors, however, and in November, he was transferred again. Assuming command of a **district** in the **Department of South Carolina**, Trapier performed well at Charleston when his batteries on Sullivan's Island riddled **Samuel Du Pont's** Union ships as they attacked in April 1863. When afterward he was placed in an administrative position instead of receiving the praise he thought he deserved, Trapier sent an angry letter to his superior, **Roswell S. Ripley**, and earned the enmity of both Ripley and Beauregard. As a result, he spent the rest of the war in district command on the South Carolina coast. Trapier died in December 1865, not long after the war ended.

TRAVELLER. This famous horse belonging to **Robert E. Lee** was a native **Virginian** that Lee bought in the spring of 1862 for $200. He originally was named Jeff Davis and later Greenbrier, after the Virginia county in which he was raised. Lee was deeply attached to Traveller and once wrote a detailed description of him for an artist, stating the horse was "a Confederate grey" and handsome enough to "inspire a poet" (Boatner, *The Civil War Dictionary,* 847). Traveller outlived Lee, and his skeleton was placed on display in the Washington and Lee Museum at Lexington, Virginia.

TREATY OF WASHINGTON (MAY 24, 1871). *See ALABAMA CLAIMS.*

TREDEGAR IRON WORKS, RICHMOND, VIRGINIA. The Tredegar (TRED-de-gar) Iron Works was incorporated in **Richmond, Virginia**, in 1837 by Francis B. Deane and his partners. Named for the ironworks in Tredegar, Wales, the facility languished until **Joseph R. Anderson** became its commercial agent in 1841 and brought in new investors and increased its sales. Anderson then bought the company in 1848 for $125,000. During the 1850s, he built Tredegar into the largest industrial complex in the South and made it the only Southern facility capable of producing some types of ordnance, iron plating, and other products.

When the Civil War began, Anderson greatly expanded Tredegar to meet the tremendous demand for cannons, munitions, and other war material. By 1863, it employed 2,000 workers, about half of them slaves and free blacks. Although the Confederate government gave loans and contracts to Anderson during the war to help him expand and increase production, the mill never operated at full capacity because of a lack of raw materials and skilled labor. Still, it turned out large numbers of cannons (making almost half of the 2,200 produced for the Confederacy), iron plating for **ironclads** (including that for the **CSS Virginia**), and munitions, and even participated in some programs experimenting with **submarines** and **torpedoes**.

When Richmond was evacuated in April 1865, a militia unit made up of Tredegar workers protected the facility from mobs and fires. After the war, Anderson secured pardons for himself and his partners from President **Andrew Johnson** and put the mill back into operation. It produced much of the iron used in rebuilding the South during **Reconstruction**, but the Panic of 1873 and the growing use of steel seriously curtailed its operation. There continued to be ironwork on the site until 1958.

TRENHOLM, GEORGE ALFRED (1807–1876) CSA. A native of **South Carolina**, Trenholm (TREN-um) dropped out of school as a teenager to begin working for a **Charleston** cotton shipper. Having a keen business mind and strong charisma, he eventually became the firm's owner and made a fortune in the foreign cotton trade. Holding other business interests in banks, **railroads**, and shipping, Trenholm became known as the richest man in the South. Also active in the **Democratic Party**, he served in the state legislature from 1852 to 1856.

Trenholm strongly supported **secession**, and when the Civil War began he organized **Fraser, Trenholm, & Co.** in Great Britain to serve as a Confederate financial agent. Confederate agents **Caleb Huse** and **James Bulloch** worked out of his Liverpool office, and the company served as a depository for Confederate funds and helped secure the **Erlanger Loan**. During the war, Trenholm's company operated 60 **blockade runners** and provided the Confederacy with huge amounts of weapons, iron, munitions, and other needed goods. In doing so, of course, it also earned millions of dollars.

Having served as an adviser to Secretary of the Treasury **Christopher G. Memminger** since the war began, Trenholm was named to replace Memminger in July 1864. He tried to get the **Confederate Congress** to levy more **taxes** and issue fewer notes, but by then little could be done to salvage the collapsing Confederate financial system. To raise money to pay Confederate soldiers, Trenholm sold off government coin and cotton supplies and even personally donated $200,000. Illness forced him to be left behind when **Richmond, Virginia**, was evacuated in April 1865. Trenholm was captured by the Federals and was kept a **prisoner** at **Fort Pulaski, Georgia**, until October.

After the war, federal authorities seized Trenholm's assets to cover the wartime duties he had failed to pay. Financially ruined, he rebuilt his cotton firm in Charleston and soon recouped his fortune. Trenholm also was reelected to the legislature in 1874 and was serving there when he died two years later.

TRENT* AFFAIR (NOVEMBER 8, 1861–JANUARY 1, 1862).** When Confederate envoys **James Mason** and **John Slidell** were sent to Europe in the autumn of 1861, they had a layover in Cuba and openly talked of their destination. Hearing of their mission, Union Capt. **Charles Wilkes** of the **USS *San Jacinto decided to take action. On November 8, he intercepted the British mail packet *Trent* east of Cuba and forcibly removed Mason and Slidell. Although Wilkes acted without orders and his action violated the long-held American principle of freedom of the seas, he was seen as a hero by the Union.

Great Britain rightfully complained that her neutral rights had been violated and demanded the envoys' release. Early in the Civil War, the British were deliberating whether to recognize the Confederacy, and **Abraham Lincoln** and Secretary of State **William H. Seward** worried that this incident might push her into the Confederate camp. Yet to release the diplomats could weaken the administration politically. While negotiations continued, the British government formed a War Committee and dispatched troops to Canada in a dangerous display of saber rattling. Faced with possible conflict, Lincoln agreed to a solution proposed by Seward. The United States would release the envoys while pointing out that by demanding their freedom, the British finally were publicly recognizing America's concept of freedom of the seas. Mason and Slidell were released on January 1, 1862, and continued their mission to Europe.

TREVILIAN STATION, VIRGINIA, RAID AND BATTLE OF (JUNE 7–28, 1864). After the **Battle of Cold Harbor**, **U. S. Grant** disengaged with **Robert E. Lee** and moved his **armies** south across the James River to Petersburg, Virginia. To draw the Confederates' attention away from this bold maneuver, Grant sent **Philip H. Sheridan** and the cavalry **divisions** of **David M. Gregg** and **Alfred T. A. Torbert** on a raid toward Charlottesville to join forces with **David Hunter** from the **Shenandoah Valley** and destroy the Virginia Central Railroad and James River Canal.

Sheridan's 6,000 troopers left on June 7, moved to the northwest, and encamped near Louisa Court House on June 10. Meanwhile, Lee dispatched **Wade Hampton** and 5,000 men of his and **Fitzhugh Lee's** cavalry divisions on June 9 to stop Sheridan. On June 11, the two cavalry forces clashed two miles northeast of Trevilian Station, a depot on the Virginia Central Railroad. Early that morning Hampton's and Torbert's divisions collided first. As the battle developed, however, Hampton learned that **George A. Custer's** Union **brigade** had charged into his rear between Hampton's and Lee's divisions and captured his wagon train. Hampton was forced to disengage from Torbert to drive off Custer. In fierce fighting, Hampton recaptured his train and took a large number of **prisoners**, but Custer escaped annihilation when Torbert came to his rescue. The Federals then camped that night at Trevilian Station.

Hampton dismounted his men and entrenched. On June 12, Sheridan destroyed several miles of track and then attacked Hampton, but he was bloodily repulsed and nearly routed by a Confederate counterattack. With the Confederates now blocking his advance, Sheridan abandoned his raid and turned back toward Grant the next day, reuniting with him on June 28. **Hunter's Shenandoah Valley Campaign** also had been turned back by **John C. Breckinridge** and **Jubal A. Early** at **Lynchburg** on June 17–18, and Lee's vital supply line remained intact. Sheridan lost approximately 1,000 men on the raid, 735 of those at Trevilian Station. It is estimated that Hampton also lost about 1,000 men.

TRIMBLE, ISAAC RIDGEWAY (1802–1888) CSA. A native of **Virginia**, Trimble grew up in **Kentucky** and graduated from **West Point** in 1822. After serving 10 years in the **artillery**, he resigned his lieutenant's commission in 1832, settled in **Maryland**, and became a **railroad** engineer.

When the Civil War began, Trimble destroyed railroad bridges in northern Maryland to obstruct the arrival of Union troops. He then went to Virginia in May 1861 and was appointed lieutenant colonel of state troops. Trimble entered Confederate service in August as a brigadier general, and for the next several months, he erected artillery batteries along the Potomac River and constructed defensive works at **Norfolk**. In early 1862, he was given a **brigade** command in **Richard S. Ewell's division**. At age 60, Trimble was one of the oldest combat commanders in either **army**, but he proved to be one of the better brigade leaders. Active, with an **engineer's** eye for terrain, he always was eager for a fight.

Trimble served well in **Stonewall Jackson's 1862 Shenandoah Valley Campaign**, winning particular praise at **Cross Keys**. After fighting at **Gaines' Mill** and **Cedar Mountain**, he again won acclaim in the **Second Manassas Campaign**. Although his men were exhausted by Jackson's long flanking march, Trimble volunteered to continue while the other brigades rested and captured the Union supply base at Manassas Junction. In the Second Battle of Manassas, he was so badly wounded in the leg that soldiers speculated he had been hit by an explosive bullet.

During his long recovery, Trimble was promoted to major general in January 1863 and was placed in command of the **Valley District** in June. Desiring another field command, he accompanied the **Army of Northern Virginia** to **Gettysburg** as Ewell's volunteer aide and was given **William Dorsey Pender's** division after Pender was wounded. At its head in **Pickett's Charge**, Trimble was shot again in his injured leg and was left behind when the army retreated. Union surgeons amputated the leg, and Trimble was held **prisoner** under harsh conditions at several **prisons**. He was **exchanged** in March 1865, but the war ended before he could rejoin the army.

After the war, Trimble worked as a consulting engineer in Maryland.

TRUMBULL, LYMAN (1813–1896) USA. A native of **Connecticut**, Trumbull taught school before becoming a lawyer. Moving to **Illinois**, he was elected to the state legislature in 1840 but resigned his seat to serve as Illinois's secretary of state from 1843 to 1848. Trumbull returned to his law practice, but in 1848, he was elected to the state supreme court. After being elected to the U.S. House of Representatives in 1848, he was appointed to fill out the remainder of a U.S. Senate term before he took up his House seat. Trumbull had been a member of the **Democratic Party**, but he broke from it over the **Kansas-Nebraska Act** and joined the **Republican Party** in 1861.

As a wartime senator, Trumbull strongly opposed **slavery**, pushed for the war's vigorous prosecution, and came to support the **Radical Republicans**. He also was a leader of those politicians who wanted **Abraham Lincoln** to force **George B. McClellan** to take the offensive in the autumn of 1861, and he introduced the **Confiscation Act** in December. Once the war ended, Trumbull abandoned some of his radical ideas and became more of a moderate during **Reconstruction**. He played a key role in getting the **13th Amendment** passed and voted to acquit in President **Andrew Johnson's** impeachment trial. After supporting **Horace Greeley** for president in 1872, Trumbull resigned his Senate seat the following year and returned to his Illinois law practice. There he rejoined the Democratic Party and was its unsuccessful gubernatorial candidate in 1880.

TRUNNIONS. Trunnions are the two cylindrical protrusions from a cannon tube at its midpoint (center of gravity) that rest on the gun's carriage and allow the tube to be elevated or depressed.

TUBMAN, HARRIET (1820–1913) USA. Born on a **Maryland** plantation as Araminta, Tubman lived in brutal conditions as a slave. She took the name Harriet and married a free black named John Tubman when she was 23 but then left him in 1849 when he refused to run away with her. Escaping **slavery**, Tubman lived in **Pennsylvania** and began working with the **Underground Railroad** to help other slaves escape to freedom. After making 11 trips to the South, she moved to Canada in 1852 and was named "General Tubman" by **abolitionist John Brown**.

Tubman made 19 more secret trips to the South to help free several hundred slaves. After the Civil War began, she used **Fort Monroe, Virginia**, and Beaufort, **South Carolina**, as bases from which to continue her work. The Confederates despised her growing notoriety and offered a reward for her capture. At Beaufort, Tubman also worked as a scout and spy for Maj. Gen. **David Hunter** and served the Federals on raids that freed nearly 1,000 more slaves.

After receiving only $300 for her three years' Union service, Tubman moved to **New York** after the war and opened a Home for Indigent and Aged Negroes. She was relatively unknown when she died in 1913 and did not become a heroic figure until the modern civil rights movement popularized her wartime activities.

TUCKER, JOHN RANDOLPH (1812–1883) CSA. A native of **Virginia**, Tucker entered the **U.S. Navy** as a midshipman in 1826. After serving at the Norfolk Navy Yard, and in the East Indies, the **Mexican War**, the Mediterranean, and the Atlantic, he was promoted to commander in 1855 and was assigned to **Norfolk, Virginia**, as an ordnance officer.

Tucker resigned his commission in April 1861 and joined the Confederacy as a navy commander. Placed in charge of the James River fleet, he commanded the *Patrick Henry* and led a small flotilla of ships at **Hampton Roads** in March 1862. After sparring with the Union fleet around **Fort Monroe, Virginia**, Tucker abandoned Norfolk in May and withdrew his ships to Drewry's Bluff, where his men and guns participated in the **First Battle of Drewry's Bluff**. In August 1862, he was sent to **South Carolina**, where he first took command of the *Palmetto State* and then the *Chicora*. In January 1863, Tucker led these **ironclads** in an attack on the Union **blockade** at **Charleston, South Carolina**, and damaged two enemy ships.

Because of his effectiveness, Tucker was promoted to captain and was put in command of all of the warships defending Charleston. Among his ships was the submarine **CSS *H. L. Hunley***, which sank the **USS *Housatonic*** *in* February 1864. Tucker remained there until the Confederates evacuated the city in February 1865. With about 350 men, he went to **Richmond, Virginia**, and again took command of Drewry's Bluff. Tucker accompanied **Richard S. Ewell's** command after the city's evacuation and was captured with his men after fighting fiercely at **Sailor's Creek**.

In 1866, Tucker moved to Peru and was appointed rear admiral in that nation's navy—the third navy he served in his long career. After commanding the combined fleets of Peru and Chile in the 1866 war with Spain, he surveyed the upper Amazon River with a party of handpicked former Confederate officers. Tucker finally retired to Virginia in 1877.

TUCKER, WILLIAM FEIMSTER (1827–1881) CSA. A native of **Virginia**, Tucker graduated from Emory and Henry College in 1848. He moved to **Mississippi** that year, but it is not known what his occupation was until he was elected a probate judge in 1855. Only then did Tucker study law and pass the bar.

When Mississippi seceded in January 1861, Tucker organized a volunteer **company** and served with it at **Pensacola, Florida**. Transferred to Virginia, the company became part of the 11th Mississippi in May, with Tucker being commissioned a captain. After fighting at **First Manassas** with **Barnard Bee's brigade**, he returned to Mississippi and organized an infantry battalion that became the 41st Mississippi. Appointed colonel in May 1862, Tucker served in the **Kentucky Campaign** with **John C. Brown's** brigade and was wounded at **Perryville**. The **regiment** subsequently served with several brigades before becoming part of **James R. Chalmers's Army of Tennessee** brigade in December. Tucker fought at **Stones River** and then took temporary command of the brigade in February 1863 when Chalmers became ill. Under **J. Patton Anderson's** command, Tucker and his 41st Mississippi fought very well at **Chickamauga** and pushed farther into the enemy position than any other unit. During the **Chattanooga Campaign**, he again took temporary command of the brigade and led it during the fighting at **Missionary Ridge**.

In March 1864, Tucker was promoted to brigadier general and took permanent command of the brigade. As part of **Thomas C. Hindman's division**, he fought in the **Atlanta Campaign** and was severely wounded at **Resaca**. This wound prevented Tucker from returning to the field, but in April 1865, he was given command of the District of Southern Mississippi and East Louisiana. Although in charge of the **district** for only a few weeks, he worked with Union officials to protect civilians against **Jay-hawkers** and bandits prowling the area.

Tucker returned to his Mississippi law practice after the war. He was elected to the state legislature in 1876 and 1878 but was assassinated in 1881 by two gunmen who had been hired by a man against whom Tucker had taken legal action for misappropriating guardianship funds.

TULLAHOMA CAMPAIGN (JUNE 23–30, 1863). Following the **Battle of Stones River**, **William S. Rosecrans's** 65,000-man **Army of the Cumberland** remained in the Murfreesboro, Tennessee, area, while **Braxton Bragg's** 44,000-man **Army of Tennessee** withdrew to the south to block the approaches to Chattanooga, Tennessee. Bragg took up a strong defensive position along the Duck River between Shelbyville and Manchester, with a weaker line extending from his right as far as McMinnville. In May 1863, Union authorities feared Bragg might send reinforcements to relieve the siege of **Vicksburg, Mississippi**, and urged Rosecrans to move against the Confederates.

On June 23, 1863, Rosecrans initiated the Tullahoma Campaign by splitting his **army** into several columns to outmaneuver Bragg. He first sent **Gordon Granger's** Reserve Corps and **David S. Stanley's** cavalry in a **feint** against **Leonidas Polk's** Confederate **corps** guarding Bragg's left at Shelbyville. Rosecrans then concentrated the bulk of his **army** against Bragg's right. **Alexander M. McCook's** Union corps pushed **William J. Hardee's** advanced guard out of Liberty Gap and headed toward Hardee's main position at Wartrace. On June 24, **George H. Thomas's** Union corps marched for **Hoover's Gap**, a few miles to Mc-Cook's left, to threaten Bragg's right flank at Manchester. Colonel John T. Wilder's mounted infantry pushed the Confederates out of the gap in a heavy rain and then held it against a Confederate counterattack. Thomas's corps reinforced Wilder on June 25, brushed aside the enemy, and continued the advance toward Manchester. During this time, **Thomas L. Crittenden's** corps advanced on the far left of Rosecrans's army to threaten Bragg's right flank.

Heavy rain slowed the movement, but on June 27, Stanley's mounted infantry pushed the Confederates out of Guy's Gap and back toward Shelbyville, while Thomas crossed the Duck River and occupied Manchester. Thomas's advance placed the Federals in Polk's and Hardee's right rear and forced Bragg to abandon his Duck River line and retreat to Tullahoma. Rosecrans then concentrated his army at Manchester and on June 28 sent Wilder's mounted infantry to cut Bragg's line of retreat by destroying the Elk River **railroad** bridge in his rear. Wilder successfully reached the area but was stopped by **Nathan Bedford Forrest's** cavalry and was unable to destroy the bridge. Realizing his position was untenable, Bragg retreated from Tullahoma and crossed the Elk River on June 30, and later the Tennessee River. The campaign then ended with Bragg on the south side of the Tennessee River protecting Chattanooga and Rosecrans occupying Middle **Tennessee.**

The campaign succeeded brilliantly for Rosecrans, but it was largely overlooked because of **U. S. Grant's** successful conclusion of the **Vicksburg Campaign** a week later. With a loss of only 560 men, Rosecrans forced the Confederates out of Middle Tennessee and captured 1,634 **prisoners** and 11 cannons. However, the campaign did not seriously affect Bragg's effectiveness and simply moved the next large battle out of Tennessee to **Chickamauga, Georgia**.

TUNNEL HILL, GEORGIA, BATTLE OF (FEBRUARY 24–25, 1864). In February 1864, Maj. Gen. **George H. Thomas** sent four **divisions** from his **Army of the Cumberland** on a **reconnaissance** in northern **Georgia** to confirm reports that **Joseph E. Johnston** had sent reinforcements from his **Army of Tennessee** to **Mississippi**. Under the command of Maj. Gen. **John M. Palmer**, the Federals left their camps around Ringgold on February 22 and moved to the southeast toward Rocky Face Ridge, a mountainous ridge west of Dalton on which Johnston was positioned. On February 24, Palmer reached Tunnel Hill, located on a parallel ridge a short distance northwest of Rocky Face Ridge. A small Confederate detachment was driven off the hill by **Jefferson C. Davis's** division, but it withdrew to Rocky Face Ridge and joined **Alexander P. Stewart's** strongly posted division at Buzzard's Roost Gap.

Late in the morning of February 25, Palmer attacked Stewart. While the divisions of **Richard W. Johnson** and Davis threatened the gap from the front, **Charles Cruft's** division advanced against the northern side of Buzzard's Roost Gap. He pushed the enemy out of one position before being ordered to halt by Palmer, who was having second thoughts about his action. Cruft was left in a vulnerable position, so Palmer sent two of Davis's **brigades** toward the gap to relieve some of the pressure. These brigades were badly shot up, and Palmer finally ordered a general withdrawal. In the two-day action, Palmer suffered 345 casualties, while the Confederates lost at least 167 men. The reconnaissance was successful, for it caused Johnston to order the return of **William J. Hardee's corps**, which had been sent earlier to oppose **William T. Sherman's Meridian Campaign** in Mississippi.

TUPELO, MISSISSIPPI, BATTLE OF (JULY 14–15, 1864). In the summer of 1864, Union Maj. Gen. **Cadwallader C. Washburn**, commander of the District of West Tennessee, was under pressure from **William T. Sherman** to destroy **Nathan Bedford Forrest's** Confederate cavalry command to prevent it from raiding Sherman's supply line during the **Atlanta Campaign**. Washburn ordered Maj. Gen. **Andrew Jackson Smith** to take his 14,000-man XVI Corps from Memphis, Tennessee, to La Grange, Tennessee, and then into northeastern **Mississippi**. Not only was Smith to engage Forrest, but he also was to destroy the countryside to break Southern morale and to deny the Confederates supplies.

Smith left La Grange on July 5 and burned a swath southward as he slowly advanced toward Pontotoc, Mississippi. Confederate cavalry **skirmished** with Brig. Gen. **Benjamin Grierson's** troopers, but Forrest's superior, Lt. Gen. **Stephen D. Lee**, ordered him not to fight a general battle until he arrived with reinforcements. Smith reached Pontotoc on July 11, the same day Lee joined Forrest at **Okolona**, 22 miles to the southeast. Lee and Forrest now had about 9,500 men but were uncertain where Smith would head next. Believing he would try to break the Mobile & Ohio Railroad at Tupelo or Okolona, the Confederates massed most of their men around Okolona. On July 13, Smith decided the road to Okolona was too heavily defended and abruptly turned to the east from Pontotoc and headed for Tupelo, 17 miles away. Moving in advance of the main force, Grierson's cavalry reached Tupelo at about noon and began destroying the track. Smith's main body stopped that night at Harrisburg, one mile west of Tupelo, and fortified a strong line almost two miles long. David Moore's **division** was on the left and **Joseph A. Mower's** division on the right, with Grierson and Edward Bouton's **brigade** of **black troops** supporting Moore.

Lee and Forrest arrived on the scene by nightfall, but they disagreed as to their next move. Forrest wanted to harass the Federals while they marched and gradually weaken them before fighting a major battle. Lee, however, was under pressure to send reinforcements quickly to **Mobile**, Alabama, and decided to attack Smith immediately. By the morning of July 14, Lee had a battle line roughly paralleling Smith. **Philip D. Roddey's** division was on the Confederate right, Edward Crossland's brigade (supported by **James R. Chalmers's** and **Hylan B. Lyon's** divisions) was in the center, and **Tyree H. Bell's** and Hinchie P. Mabry's brigades were on the left. The Confederates attacked at 7:00 A.M., but the assaults were disjointed and unsuccessful against the stubborn Federal line. When Smith's troops burned Harrisburg that night and illuminated their positions, Forrest even led a rare night attack, but it, too, failed. Low on **rations**, Smith abandoned his position on July 15 and retreated back to La Grange. At Old Town Creek, Bell and Crossland unsuccessfully attacked Smith's rear guard, and Forrest was wounded in the right foot while supervising another assault. Smith continued his march and reached La Grange on July 21.

Although Smith had abandoned the field at Tupelo, he still had won a tactical victory, losing only 674 men to the Confederates' 1,326. The overall success of Smith's mission was mixed. He had kept Forrest away from Sherman's supply line and temporarily put the feared cavalryman out of action, but Forrest and his cavalry were left alive to fight another day.

TURCHIN, JOHN BASIL (1822–1901) USA. A native of Russia, Turchin's given name was Ivan Vasilovitch Turchinoff, and he was the only Russian to become a Civil War general. After graduating from the Imperial Military School, he had a distinguished career in the Russian army. Turchin became colonel of the Imperial Guard, served on the staff of future czar Alexander II during the Crimean War, and constructed the Finnish coastal defenses. He immigrated to the United States in 1856 and settled in **Illinois**, working as a **railroad** engineer.

Turchin entered Union service in June 1861 as colonel of the 19th Illinois. His Russian background proved to be a mixed blessing. Turchin's military experience helped him to train his men quickly, but his European attitudes concerning spoils of war made his command notorious for looting and harassing civilians. He was given command of a **brigade** in **Ormsby M. Mitchel's Army of the Ohio division** in February 1862. Turchin helped capture Huntsville, Alabama, in April but then became embroiled in controversy for allowing his men to rob, loot, and burn Athens, Alabama, after some civilians supposedly had shot at his men. He reportedly told his men at Athens he would shut his eyes for one hour. When nothing happened, Turchin told them he would shut his eyes for an hour and a half. The second time, the soldiers burned the town. Turchin also violated orders by allowing his wife to accompany him in the field (it was reported that she commanded the **regiment** in his absence during an 1862 **Tennessee** battle). He was convicted in a court-martial and was recommended for dismissal in July 1862, but his wife persuaded **Abraham Lincoln** not only to overrule the court but to promote Turchin to brigadier general of volunteers that same month.

Despite his controversial behavior, Turchin was given a cavalry division in the **Army of the Cumberland** in March 1863 and led it in the

Tullahoma Campaign. He then led a brigade in **Joseph J. Reynolds's** division and fought so well at **Chickamauga** that he earned the nickname "The Russian Thunderbolt." Shortly afterward, Turchin's men were the first to reach the Confederate works atop **Missionary Ridge** during the **Chattanooga Campaign**. During the **Atlanta Campaign**, he again fought well but was forced to take sick leave in July 1864 and resigned his commission in October.

Returning to Illinois, Turchin became solicitor of patents in Chicago and established a Polish community in the state. Unfortunately, he became mentally ill later in life and died while being held in a hospital for the insane.

TURNER, JOHN WESLEY (1833–1899) USA. A native of **New York**, as a boy, Turner moved to **Illinois** with his family. He graduated from **West Point** in 1855 and served in the **artillery** in **Oregon** and in the **Seminole Wars**.

When the Civil War began, Turner was a 1st lieutenant of artillery. In August 1861, he was promoted to captain and was made the **Army of Southwestern Missouri's** chief commissary. Turner joined **David Hunter's** staff in November 1861 and served as his commissary for the **Departments of Kansas** and **of the South**. In May 1862, he was promoted to colonel and was assigned to **Benjamin F. Butler** as commissary for the **Department of the Gulf**. When Butler was removed in December 1862, Turner returned to Hunter, but in June 1863, he was assigned as **Quincy A. Gillmore's** chief of staff for the Department of the South. During the operations around **Charleston, South Carolina**, that summer, including the attack on **Fort Wagner**, Turner also served as Gillmore's chief of artillery.

Turner was promoted to brigadier general of volunteers in September 1863. In June 1864, he was transferred to **Virginia**, where he was given a **division** command in the **Army of the James's** X Corps. Turner led his division during the **Petersburg Campaign** until he was made the **army's** chief of staff in November. He returned to a division command in March 1865 and led it in the final battles at Petersburg and in the **Appomattox Campaign**. After **Robert E. Lee's surrender**, Turner commanded the **army's** XXIV Corps for a time and then was in charge of the **district** that included **Richmond, Virginia**.

Although most of his wartime service was as a staff officer, Turner received **brevets** through the rank of major general in both the volunteer and regular service. He was mustered out of the volunteers in September 1866 but remained in the regular army as a colonel and served in the commissary department until resigning in 1871. Turner then became a successful Missouri businessman, serving as president of a gas company and two banks.

TURNER'S GAP, MARYLAND, BATTLE OF (SEPTEMBER 14, 1862). *See* SOUTH MOUNTAIN, MARYLAND, BATTLE OF.

TURNING MOVEMENT. A turning movement is a maneuver similar to an **envelopment**. In a turning movement, one **army** forces its opponent to abandon its position and retreat, by making a wide sweep around a flank to threaten its rear. This is a strategic maneuver and does not involve any large-scale fighting, whereas an envelopment entails maneuvering around the opponent's flank and attacking the opponent in its position. Turning movements were used by the Confederates in the **Second Manassas Campaign** and by the Federals in the **Atlanta Campaign**.

TUTTLE, JAMES MADISON (1823–1892) USA. A native of **Ohio**, Tuttle eventually settled in **Iowa**, where he became a farmer and merchant. He also was active in local politics and was elected county sheriff in 1855, county treasurer in 1857, and recorder in 1859.

Tuttle entered Union service in May 1861 as lieutenant colonel of the 2nd Iowa. He was promoted to colonel in September and led the **regiment** at **Fort Donelson**, where he was wounded. Just prior to **Shiloh**, Tuttle was given command of a **brigade** in **W. H. L. Wallace's division**. He fought well at the "Hornets' Nest" and assumed command of the division when Wallace was mortally wounded. Returning to his brigade after the battle, Tuttle participated in the **siege of Corinth, Mississippi**, in the spring of 1862 and was promoted to brigadier general of volunteers in June.

Tuttle commanded the District of Corinth until August 1862, when he was given command of the District of Cairo. He was returned to field duty in April 1863 when he was given command of a division in **William T. Sherman's** XV Corps of the **Army of the Tennessee**. Tuttle fought throughout the **Vicksburg Campaign** and in July participated in the siege of **Jackson, Mississippi**. In August, he was placed in command of Natchez, Mississippi, and remained there for a year, gaining command of the XVI Corps' 1st Division while he was there. During 1863 and 1864, Tuttle twice ran unsuccessfully for governor of Iowa on the **Democratic Party** ticket and became notorious for his conduct while at Natchez. To enrich himself, he stole government money, extorted money from area residents, accepted bribes, and even ransomed civilians he arrested on flimsy charges. Tuttle's superiors were taking action to have him arrested when he resigned his commission in June 1864.

Tuttle returned to Iowa, where he served several terms in the state legislature, farmed, and worked in real estate and the pork industry. In the 1870s, he became involved in mining and gained an interest in Arizona's Jack Rabbit Mine. Tuttle died of a stroke while at the mine in 1892.

TWENTY NEGRO LAW. This controversial and unpopular Confederate measure was part of the 1862 Conscription Act. To ensure the good behavior of slaves, the law exempted from the draft the overseer or owner of a plantation that had at least 20 slaves. Poor Confederates complained this helped make the conflict "a rich man's war and a poor man's fight." To silence opposition, the **Confederate Congress** amended the **conscription** law in May 1863 to require such exempted men pay a $500 **commutation** fee. In February 1864, another change was made when the number of required slaves was reduced to 15. To claim exemption, the owner or overseer had to have a magistrate and two witnesses swear he was needed on the plantation and provide the government with a certain amount of supplies.

TWIGGS, DAVID EMANUEL (1790–1862) CSA. A native of **Georgia**, Twiggs entered the **U.S. Army** during the War of 1812 as a captain and rose to the rank of major. Remaining in the service after the war, he had risen to the rank of colonel by the 1840s and had participated in the Black Hawk and **Seminole Wars**. Twiggs served in the **Mexican War** as a brigadier general and was awarded a ceremonial sword from the **U.S. Congress**, but **Winfield Scott** and others had little respect for his generalship. His ill temper and domineering personality made him unpopular with both officers and enlisted men.

In 1857, Twiggs was given command of the **Department of Texas**, but he clashed with Secretary of War **Jefferson Davis** and President **James Buchanan**. When he tried to circumvent a presidential opinion by establishing his own court of inquiry on a matter, he was relieved of command temporarily in 1858. Poor health that nearly killed him caused Twiggs to take a leave of absence in 1859, but he recovered and resumed his post by 1861.

When the **secession** crisis began, Twiggs was one of the **army's** four field generals. His Southern sympathies were no secret, but he remained in command of **Texas** and turned down a Georgia command after his native state seceded. Twiggs also stated clearly that he would not surrender his San Antonio command in Texas to the secessionists. Despite these assurances, he surrendered his 160 men to **Ben McCulloch's** superior force in February 1861. All other would-be Confederate officers resigned their positions or waited until being replaced before joining the South. Twiggs was the only officer to commit the treasonous act of surrendering his command before actually joining the Confederacy. The **army** dismissed him from the service in March 1861 "for his treachery."

Davis offered Twiggs a brigadier's commission in the **Confederate army**, but he declined because of his advanced age. In late May 1861, however, he changed his mind and accepted a commission as major general. Given command of **Department No. 1**, Twiggs was placed at **New Orleans, Louisiana**, and was charged with defending the important city. **Louisiana** officials quickly became dissatisfied with him, however, and asked that he be removed because his age made him unable to carry out the necessary duties. Twiggs was replaced by **Mansfield Lovell** in October and returned to Georgia, where he died the following year.

TYLER, DANIEL (1799–1882) USA. A native of **Connecticut**, Tyler was the uncle of Union general **Robert O. Tyler**. After graduating from **West Point** in 1819, he was assigned to the **artillery** and became an authority on artillery and ordnance. Tyler studied artillery in France, translated French military manuals into English, and served as the **U.S. Army's** superintendent of inspectors for privately contracted weapons. Despite his outstanding service, Tyler's honesty while serving as an inspector made him enemies, and he was still a 1st lieutenant in 1834. He resigned his commission that year, prospered in the **railroad** and canal industries, and became president of **Georgia's** Macon & Western Railroad.

Tyler entered Union service in April 1861 as colonel of the 90-day 1st Connecticut. He was promoted to brigadier general of state troops the following month and led a **division** at **Blackburn's Ford** and **First Manassas**. Tyler was mustered out of state service in August and, although he did not perform particularly well at First Manassas, he was appointed brigadier general of volunteers in March 1862. Sent west, he was given a **brigade** command in **David S. Stanley's** division of the **Army of the Mississippi** in May and participated in the **siege of Corinth, Mississippi**. Afterward, Tyler served on a commission that investigated **Don Carlos Buell's** actions during the **Kentucky Campaign,** and in early 1863 he commanded **Harpers Ferry, Virginia**, and Baltimore, Maryland. In July 1863, Tyler took command of the District of Delaware, but he resigned his commission in April 1864 after reaching age 65.

After the war, Tyler founded the town of Anniston, Alabama, which was named for his daughter-in-law. He then helped turn the town into an industrial complex for the iron and cotton industries and became president of an **Alabama** railroad.

TYLER, ERASTUS BARNARD (1822–1891) USA. A native of **New York**, as a boy, Tyler moved to **Ohio** with his family. After attending Granville College, he began working in the fur industry as a trapper and buyer.

Tyler entered Union service in April 1861 as colonel of the 7th Ohio (he was elected to the position over future president **James A. Garfield**). Sent to western **Virginia**, the **regiment** was surprised and routed in camp by the Confederates that August in its first engagement. In January 1862, Tyler was given a **brigade** command, which he led along the upper Potomac River and lower **Shenandoah Valley**. Assigned to **James Shields's division**, he fought at **Kernstown** and was promoted to brigadier general of volunteers in May 1862.

Tyler participated in **Stonewall Jackson's 1862 Shenandoah Valley Campaign** and fought with Shields at **Port Republic**. Assigned to the 3rd Division of the **Army of the Potomac's** V Corps in September, he was held in reserve at **Antietam** but saw heavy combat at **Fredericksburg** (where he was wounded) and **Chancellorsville**. When his troops' enlistments expired in 1863, Tyler was placed in command of the Baltimore, Maryland, defenses in June and remained in that area until war's end. During that service, his brigade supported **Lew Wallace** at the **Monocacy**.

After being **brevetted** major general of volunteers for his war service, Tyler was mustered out of the volunteers in August 1865. Remaining in Baltimore, he became active in the Masons and the **Grand Army of the Republic** and served as the city's postmaster in the 1870s.

TYLER, ROBERT CHARLES (1832–1865) CSA. Very little is known of this Confederate general. Tyler may have been born in **Maryland**, and he participated in William Walker's filibustering expedition to Nicaragua in 1856. Afterward, he settled in **Tennessee** and raised a **company** of volunteers when the Civil War began.

Tyler entered Confederate service in April 1861 as a private in the 15th Tennessee, but he quickly became company captain. He later was promoted to major and became quartermaster for **Gideon Pillow's** command. By November, Tyler had been promoted to lieutenant colonel of the 15th Tennessee. After leading the **regiment** at **Belmont**, he was wounded at **Shiloh** while serving in **Bushrod R. Johnson's brigade**. Tyler was promoted to colonel in June 1862 and later in the year was appointed provost for **Braxton Bragg's Army of Mississippi** (later the **Army of Tennessee**). He fought at **Perryville, Chickamauga** (where he was wounded), and **Missionary Ridge**. In this last battle, Tyler temporarily commanded **William B. Bate's** brigade and suffered a severe wound that required the amputation of his leg. While recovering from his amputation, Tyler was promoted to brigadier general in March 1864. He was unable to retake the field, however, and was put in command of West Point, Georgia, to protect the **railroad** there. On April 16, 1865, **James H. Wilson's** Union cavalry raided West Point, and Tyler was killed by a **sharpshooter** as he observed the enemy while standing on his crutches.

TYLER, ROBERT OGDEN (1831–1874) USA. A native of **New York**, Tyler grew up in **Connecticut** and was the nephew of Union general **Daniel Tyler**. After graduating from **West Point** in 1853, he was assigned to the **artillery** and served at various outposts before the Civil War.

In April 1861, Tyler was a 1st lieutenant and served in the expedition sent to relieve **Fort Sumter**. After witnessing the bombardment there, he was promoted to captain in May and was appointed depot quartermaster for Alexandria, Virginia. Appointed colonel of the 4th Connecticut in September, Tyler made the **regiment** into an effective unit. This regiment actually served as an artillery unit and was redesignated the 1st Connecticut Heavy Artillery in January 1862. In the spring of 1862, Tyler was put in command of the **Army of the Potomac's** siege train and led it through the **Peninsula** and **Seven Days Campaigns**. Despite the **army's** long, harrowing retreat in the latter campaign, he lost only one cannon.

Tyler was promoted to brigadier general of volunteers in November 1862 and was placed in command of the artillery in **Joseph Hooker's** Grand Division at **Fredericksburg**. After Hooker was given command of the army, Tyler was transferred to the army's reserve artillery, which he led in the **Chancellorsville** and **Gettysburg Campaigns**. In the latter, his guns particularly were effective in repelling **Pickett's Charge**. After Gettysburg, Tyler was placed in the defenses of **Washington, D.C.**, where he commanded a **division** from January to May 1864. His command then became one of those heavy artillery units that were converted into infantry to reinforce the Army of the Potomac during the **Overland Campaign**. Given a **brigade** in **John Gibbon's** II Corps division, Tyler fought at **Spotsylvania** and **Cold Harbor**. In the latter battle, he was shot in the ankle and never fully recovered from the wound.

Tyler ended the war with **brevets** of major general in both the regular and volunteer service. He remained in the regular army as a lieutenant colonel and deputy quartermaster general, but he suffered from declining health. When he died in 1874, Tyler still was on active duty.

***TYLER*, USS.** Purchased by the U.S. government in Cincinnati, Ohio, in May 1861, this 575-ton side-wheeler saw much service on the western waters. After extensive repairs, it entered the **U.S. Navy** and almost immediately went into action. In September, the *Tyler* engaged the CSS *Yankee* on the Mississippi River, and two months later it supported **U. S. Grant's** command at **Belmont**. It was one of three gunboats that forced the surrender of **Fort Henry** in February 1862, and then it steamed up the Tennessee River to capture the CSS *Eastport*. Two months later, the *Tyler* was heavily engaged at **Shiloh** when its guns bombarded the advancing Confederates. The gunboat also battled the **CSS** *Arkansas* when it entered the Mississippi River at **Vicksburg, Mississippi**, in July 1862, and a year later it played a key role in defending **Helena, Arkansas**, when the Confederates unsuccessfully attacked it on July 4, 1863.

TYNDALE, GEORGE HECTOR (1821–1880) USA. A native of **Pennsylvania**, Tyndale reportedly declined an appointment to **West Point** at the behest of his mother. He became an expert on ceramics while working in his father's successful glass and china import business and took over the enterprise with his brother after his father died. For charitable reasons, not political sympathy, Tyndale accompanied Mrs. **John Brown** to visit her husband in jail prior to his 1859 execution and then accompanied Brown's body home.

Tyndale was in France on business when the Civil War began, but he rushed home and entered Union service in June 1861 as major of the 28th Pennsylvania. After the **regiment** was assigned to **Nathaniel P. Banks's** command in the **Shenandoah Valley**, he was promoted to lieutenant colonel in May 1862. Tyndale fought under Banks at **Front Royal**, and at **Cedar Mountain** he commanded the regiment but was not actively engaged. After fighting at **Second Manassas** with the **Army of Virginia**, the regiment joined the **Army of the Potomac** and became part of Charles Candy's **brigade** in the XII Corps' 2nd Division. At **Antietam**, Tyndale assumed brigade command when Candy was wounded. He performed admirably, had three horses shot from under him, was wounded twice, and briefly was believed to have been killed.

Tyndale's service at Antietam won him a promotion to brigadier general of volunteers in April 1863. His next service was in July 1863 when he was put in command of a brigade in **John Geary's** XI Corps **division**. Tyndale accompanied the **corps** to **Tennessee** that autumn to reinforce the garrison at Chattanooga. After fighting at **Wauhatchie** and in the **Chat-**

tanooga Campaign, he was placed in command of the division in February 1864 and led it until April. When the XI and XII Corps were consolidated into the **Army of the Cumberland's** XX Corps in the spring of 1864, Tyndale returned to his brigade command. He took sick leave in May 1864 and resigned his commission in August for health reasons.

Tyndale returned to Pennsylvania and was **brevetted** major general of volunteers in March 1865. He resumed his import business, made an unsuccessful bid for mayor of Philadelphia, and became active in various charities.

– U –

ULLMAN, DANIEL (1810–1892) USA. A native of **Delaware**, Ullman graduated from Yale University in 1829 and became a prosperous **New York** lawyer. Entering state politics, he ran unsuccessfully for governor on the **Whig** and **Know-Nothing Party** tickets in 1851 and 1854, respectively.

Ullman entered Union service in April 1861 when he was commissioned colonel of the 78th ("Highlanders") New York, a **regiment** he helped raise. After routine garrison duty in the **Shenandoah Valley**, he became ill from typhoid fever and missed the **Battle of Cedar Mountain**. However, Ullman was captured during the retreat and was held in **Libby Prison** until **paroled** in October 1862. Promoted to brigadier general of volunteers in January 1863, he was transferred to **New Orleans, Louisiana**, where he organized five regiments of **black troops** that became the **Corps d'Afrique**. After fighting with **Nathaniel P. Banks** in the **Port Hudson Campaign**, Ullman commanded Port Hudson for a while before being given command of Morganza, Louisiana. In February 1865, he was sent to Cairo, Illinois, possibly because of a renewed bout of typhoid. After awaiting new orders, which never came, Ullman finally went home.

After being **brevetted** major general of volunteers for his war service, Ullman was mustered out of the volunteers in August 1865 and returned to New York. He traveled extensively in the postwar period and was active in scientific and literary circles.

UNCLE TOM'S CABIN. *See* STOWE, HARRIET BEECHER.

UNDERGROUND RAILROAD. This loosely knit antebellum organization, run by **abolitionists** and freed and runaway slaves, helped slaves escape from the slave states before the Civil War. Agents, such as **Harriet Tubman**, who went into the South to aid these escapes, were known as "conductors." Traveling by night, they led the runaways to safe houses known as "stations." Some slaves stopped in Northern areas where abolitionists protected them, but many were forced to continue to Canada, because many Northern states did not want blacks—free or slave—within their borders.

UNDERWOOD, ADIN BALTON (1828–1888) USA. A native of **Massachusetts**, Underwood graduated from Brown University in 1849 before studying law at Harvard University and becoming a lawyer. When the Civil War began, he helped recruit soldiers and entered Union service in May 1861 as a captain in the 2nd Massachusetts. Sent to **Virginia**, Underwood served in **Stonewall Jackson's 1862 Shenandoah Valley Campaign** and was appointed lieutenant colonel of the 33rd Massachusetts in August. In April 1863, he was promoted to colonel and served at **Chancellorsville** in **Francis C. Barlow's brigade** of the **Army of the Potomac's** XI Corps. The **corps** was routed there, but Underwood's **regiment** suffered only light losses. After fighting at **Gettysburg**, the regiment was sent west with the rest of the corps to reinforce the besieged garrison at **Chattanooga**, Tennessee. Underwood's leg was shattered by a bullet at **Wauhatchie**, and it was left four inches shorter than the other after surgeons tried to mend it. Although his wound prevented him from performing any other service, Underwood was promoted to brigadier general in November 1863. After being **brevetted** major general of volunteers, he was mustered out of the service in August 1865, and he returned to Massachusetts, where he worked as Boston's port surveyor.

UNIFORMS, CONFEDERATE. Although the opposing sides eventually adopted blue and gray uniforms for the Union and Confederate **armies**, respectively, there were no rules regulating uniforms when the Civil War began. The **U.S. Army** wore its traditional dark blue uniform from the war's beginning, but the thousands of volunteers who enlisted in the spring of 1861 had a wide variety of clothing. Some Union units wore gray, while some Confederates wore blue, and both sides had the colorful **Zouave** units. This caused so much confusion at **First Manassas** that mistaken identities caused quite a few casualties from "friendly fire." After this first large battle, the two armies began to adopt standard guidelines for the soldiers' clothing and by 1863 largely had achieved this goal.

The Confederates adopted a gray double-breasted frock coat that had buttons, collar insignia, and French-style sleeve braids known as "galons" to denote rank, and **kepis** colors and uniform trim to show branch of service. Infantry officers wore a frock coat that reached to mid-thigh, while cavalry and **artillery** officers wore a waist-length coat. Red kepis and uniform trim indicated artillery, yellow indicated cavalry, light blue indicated infantry, black indicated medical corps, and buff indicated staff. On the collar, one, two, and three gold horizontal bars identified line officers—2nd lieutenant, 1st lieutenant, and captain, respectively. Lieutenants also wore one-strand galons on the sleeve, while captains wore a two-strand galon. Field officers—major, lieutenant colonel, and colonel—had one, two, and three gold stars, respectively, on the collar and a three-strand galon on the sleeve. All officers through the rank of colonel had two rows of seven brass or gilt buttons, evenly spaced, on the frock coat. An eagle on the button denoted staff officers, while *E, A, I,* and *C* stood for **engineer**, artillery, infantry, and cavalry, respectively.

General officers had three gold stars within a wreath on the collar, with the center star being larger, and a four-strand galon on the sleeve. Brigadier generals also had two rows of eight buttons on the frock coat, positioned in pairs, while higher-ranking generals had two rows of nine buttons, positioned in threes. Line and field officers had two rows of seven buttons evenly spaced. Line officers also wore sky blue trousers, while field and general officers wore dark blue trousers. The trousers had stripes of the appropriate color running down the outside seams. Kepis also had the same galon as on the sleeve, with the appropriate number of strands.

Noncommissioned officers and enlisted men wore the same gray frock coat as officers, with sky blue trousers. The noncommissioned officers also had an appropriately colored stripe down the trousers' outside seams. Noncommissioned officers' rank was denoted by chevrons on the sleeve, point down, in the color of the appropriate branch of service. Sergeants wore three chevrons, corporals wore two, and privates had no indication of rank. Within the chevron's angle, a lozenge, star, a connecting bar, and a connecting arc denoted a first sergeant, ordnance sergeant, quartermaster sergeant, and sergeant major, respectively.

Confederate navy uniforms were patterned after the 1852 **U.S. Navy** regulations. Originally they were dark blue but were changed to gray in 1862 (white also became accepted for summer and tropical wear). Officers wore double-breasted frock coats and visored caps and had their rank insignia on the sleeves and shoulders. Sailors wore jackets or frock coats and visorless caps with their rank insignia on the sleeves. The **Confederate Marine Corps** never adopted a uniform but used a combination of army and navy styles.

Because of a lack of material, these specifications were followed less and less as the war progressed, particularly by Confederate enlisted men and noncommissioned officers. Confederate soldiers generally wore slouch hats instead of kepis and routinely used captured Union clothing. As material became scarce, more and more uniforms also became homespun and were dyed a yellowish-brown color that gave rise to the term **butternut** soldiers. *See also* UNIFORMS, UNITED STATES.

UNIFORMS, UNITED STATES. Although the **U. S. Army** had adopted a blue uniform long before the Civil War began, the hundreds of different volunteer units that streamed into service in the spring of 1861 brought with them a variety of uniform styles and colors, including gray uniforms and the colorful **Zouave** uniforms. This variety caused several cases of mistaken identity at **First Manassas** and a number of casualties from "friendly fire." As a result, the Union **army** began adopting a standard blue uniform, just as its opponent adopted a standard gray Confederate uniform.

Infantry officers and enlisted men wore a dark blue frock coat that reached to mid-thigh, while the **artillery** and cavalry wore a waist-length jacket. Officers ranking from major to general had double-breasted coats, while lieutenants and captains had single-breasted coats. An officer's rank was denoted by both insignia mounted on shoulder boards and buttons on the coat. Second lieutenants had empty shoulder boards, 1st lieutenants mounted one gold bar, and captains had two groups of two gold bars. All lieutenants and captains also had a single row of nine evenly spaced buttons. A major had two gold leaves on the shoulder board, a lieutenant colonel had two silver eagles, and a colonel had one eagle. Majors and colonels also had two rows of seven evenly spaced buttons on the frock coat. A brigadier general had one star on the shoulder board, and a major general two stars (or three stars, with the center star being largest for major generals who acted as army commanders). Brigadier generals also had, on the frock coat, two rows of eight buttons, grouped in pairs, while major generals had two rows of nine buttons grouped in threes. When **U. S. Grant** was promoted to lieutenant general in 1864, he generally wore a simple private's frock coat with three stars on his shoulder board.

Noncommissioned officers wore sleeve chevrons, point down, to denote rank. Sergeants wore three chevrons, corporals two, and privates none, except a private was allowed to wear one chevron on the lower sleeve for each five years of service. Noncommissioned officers also had symbols within the chevron to show different grades and service as did the Confederates.

Union generals, ordnance officers, and enlisted men wore dark blue trousers (except in the light artillery, where sky-blue trousers were worn). On the outside seam of the trousers was a stripe, with different colors representing the branches of service. Sky blue represented infantry, yellow cavalry, scarlet artillery, emerald green mounted riflemen, and crimson ordnance and medical corps. Head- and footgear varied, but Union soldiers generally wore **kepis** and ankle-high **Davis boots**. For cold weather, they also generally were issued dark blue overcoats that had short capes.

The **U.S. Navy** had uniforms similar to the army's. Dark blue, double-breasted frock coats and blue trousers were worn, with white trousers being acceptable for summer or tropical wear. Officers' caps had a fouled anchor displayed on them. As in the army, shoulder boards denoted rank, with the emblem for ensign, master, lieutenant, lieutenant commander, and commander matching the army rank for 2nd lieutenant, 1st lieutenant, captain, major, and lieutenant colonel (except a silver eagle was also added for the rank of master and above). The insignia for captain was a silver eagle and a fouled anchor, for commodore an eagle and a star, and for rear and full admirals a fouled anchor and two stars. Seamen and boatswain mates wore rank insignia on the sleeve and had black neckerchiefs and cloth square-rigged ribbons around the outer headband.

U.S. Marines wore uniforms that were similar to the army's except their caps had a bugle with an *M* in the center. *See also* UNIFORMS, CONFEDERATE.

UNION LEAGUE OF AMERICA. This pro-Union organization was formed in the East and Midwest in 1862 to support the war effort and to oppose **Peace Democrats** and others who were seen as disloyal. The Union League maintained some secrecy by requiring rituals, oaths, and signs, but it was closely allied with the **Republican Party**. Sometimes financially backed by the Republicans, the league encouraged military recruitment, campaigned against politicians they viewed as disloyal, and spread pro-Union propaganda.

UNION PARTY (OR NATIONAL UNION PARTY). Begun by moderate members of the **Republican Party**, the Union Party was established in 1863 as a means to bring under one banner all who supported the Union war effort. These moderate Republicans joined forces with **War Democrats** to form a bipartisan party to which all Northerners—and Southern loyalists—could belong. Despite their efforts, complete unity was never achieved. **Democrats** tended to want only to reunite the Union, and emancipation, which was important to many Republicans, was not a major issue. Working with the **Union League of America**, the Union Party helped defeat **Clement L. Vallandigham** for **Ohio's** governorship in 1863 and provided support for proadministration war governors.

In August 1864, **Abraham Lincoln** joined the Union Party and was nominated for president under its banner, along with vice presidential candidate **Andrew Johnson**, a Democrat. Lincoln defeated Democrat **George B. McClellan** in the November 1864 election, but the Union Party quickly faded away after **Lincoln's assassination**. The war's end eliminated the need for the party, and though it held a national convention in 1866, the Union Party quickly disappeared as its members returned to their respective antebellum parties.

UNITED CONFEDERATE VETERANS (UCV). This organization for veterans of the Confederate armed forces was created in **New Orleans, Louisiana**, in 1889. Under its first commander, **John B. Gordon**, the organization was structured along military lines, with local chapters being referred to as "camps," and the officers being given military rank. The UCV served as a fraternal organization, supported disabled veterans and widows, raised money for Confederate monuments, and lobbied for state pensions. It also played an important role in the **Lost Cause** movement by making sure the Confederate side of the war was published through its 12-volume *Confederate Military History* (1899) and its journal, *Confederate Veteran*. As passions cooled around the turn of the 20th century, the UCV and the **Grand Army of the Republic** began sponsoring reunions at battlefields. During its existence, the UCV had 1,855 camps and 160,000 members.

UNITED STATES ARMY. When the Civil War began, the United States Army was very small and most of its fighting force was posted on the frontier guarding against **Indian** attacks. In 1861, the army consisted of only 16,367 officers and men distributed among 19 **regiments** of infantry, cavalry, and **artillery**, and various bureaus and agencies (313 officers joined the Confederacy). This regular army was kept intact during the war and was expanded to include more units and 42,000 men (75,000 soldiers actually served in the regulars), but the vast majority of Union soldiers who fought the Confederates belonged to the huge volunteer army that was created. Thus, the Union fought the Civil War with two armies, the regulars and the volunteers. One mistake made by the Union was not distributing the trained regular officers and men among the volunteers to establish **discipline**, thereby training more quickly. Instead, the regulars remained in their separate regiments, although a number of officers were assigned to volunteer units, and the regular regiments were placed in **divisions** and **corps** that largely were composed of volunteers.

The United States volunteer army was much larger than the regular army. After the firing on **Fort Sumter** in April 1861, **Abraham Lincoln** called for 75,000 volunteers to put down the rebellion, and 300,000 recruits responded. Even this was not enough, however, and as the war continued, more volunteers were raised through **conscription** and the offer of **bounties**. During the four years of war, some 2.3 million volunteers served the Union.

During the war, the Union armies lost approximately 360,000 dead, of whom 110,000 were killed or mortally wounded in battle. Some 275,000 were wounded, and 211,411 were captured. Another 268,500 deserted, with the regulars suffering a surprisingly high **desertion** rate of 24 percent, while the volunteers' desertion rate was only 6 percent.

U.S. COLORED TROOPS 79TH. *See* 1ST KANSAS COLORED VOLUNTEERS.

UNITED STATES CONGRESS. One advantage the Union had over the Confederacy was having an established central government when the Civil War began. When the 11 Southern states seceded, the U.S. Congress was left dominated by the **Republican Party** and thus became a powerful tool in winning the war. **Abraham Lincoln** called Congress into special session on July 4, 1861, to have it sanction his wartime measures. Following the president's lead, it recognized that a state of insurrection existed and called for 500,000 volunteers to put it down. This initial cooperation between the executive and legislative branches eroded somewhat as war weariness set in, and the **Democrats** gained more strength. Still, the Republicans controlled Congress throughout the war and passed numerous important measures, including the **Confiscation Acts**, **income tax**, **conscription** act, **Legal Tender Acts**, and the **Homestead Acts**. Congress also formed the **Committee on the Conduct of the War** in December 1861, which oversaw much of the war effort.

UNITED STATES MILITARY ACADEMY. *See* WEST POINT.

UNITED STATES RIFLE. *See* HARPERS FERRY RIFLE.

UNITED STATES RIFLE MUSKET. *See* SPRINGFIELD RIFLE MUSKET.

1470 • UPPERVILLE, VIRGINIA, BATTLE OF (JUNE 21, 1863)

UPPERVILLE, VIRGINIA, BATTLE OF (JUNE 21, 1863). When **Robert E. Lee's Army of Northern Virginia** began the 1863 **Gettysburg Campaign**, cavalry from the **Army of the Potomac** tried to fight through **J. E. B. Stuart's** cavalry screen to gather intelligence on the movement. Between June 17 and 19, 1863, cavalry battles erupted at **Aldie** and **Middleburg, Virginia**, and Stuart was forced to the west toward the Blue Ridge Mountains.

On June 21, the Federal cavalry attacked Stuart's position west of Middleburg along Goose Creek. **David M. Gregg's division**, supported by part of **John Buford's** division and one infantry **brigade**, attacked **Wade Hampton's** and **Beverly Robertson's** Confederate brigades on Stuart's right. The rest of Buford's division attempted to turn Stuart's left flank, which was held by the brigades of **John Chambliss** and **William E. Jones**. The Confederates soon were forced to withdraw toward Upperville. Buford joined Gregg, and the Federals attacked again, eventually forcing the Confederates to give way. In fierce fighting, Hampton's brigade held back the Federals and gave Stuart a chance to withdraw to Ashby's Gap. Coming soon after **Brandy Station**, these clashes were additional evidence that the Union cavalry was steadily improving. In the battle, the Federals lost 209 men, while Stuart lost 180.

UPTON, EMORY (1839–1881) USA. A native of **New York**, Upton attended **Ohio's** Oberlin College for two years before entering **West Point** and graduating a month after **Fort Sumter** was fired upon in 1861. Assigned to the **artillery**, he first was sent to **Washington, D.C.**, as a 2nd lieutenant to drill recruits. A week later, Upton was promoted to 1st lieutenant, and he soon was assigned to Brig. Gen. **Daniel Tyler's** staff. After being wounded at **First Manassas**, he was given command of an artillery battery in the **Army of the Potomac** and led it through the **Peninsula** and **Seven Days Campaigns**. In September 1862, Upton was given command of the artillery in the VI Corps' 1st Division and led it at **South Mountain** and **Antietam**. A month after Antietam, he was appointed colonel of the 121st New York, and he commanded it at **Fredericksburg** and **Chancellorsville** as part of the 2nd Brigade in the VI Corps' 1st Division. Upton also commanded the **brigade** at **Gettysburg** and **Rappahannock Station** and performed so well in the latter battle that he was awarded a **brevet** in the regular **army**.

After leading his brigade at the **Wilderness** early in the **Overland Campaign**, Upton won acclaim at **Spotsylvania** when he developed a new **tactic** for breaking the Confederate line. Rather than attacking in a wide line, he assembled 12 **regiments** in a compact column and attacked the western side of the "Mule Shoe" on May 10, 1864. Not firing until they reached the Confederates, the Union soldiers pierced the line, but a lack of support and a fierce counterattack forced Upton to withdraw. Impressed, **U. S. Grant** used the same tactic two days later in the attack that led to fierce fighting at the "Bloody Angle."

In recognition of his service at Spotsylvania, Upton was promoted to brigadier general of volunteers in May 1864 and became one of the war's youngest generals at age 24. He led his brigade through the remainder of the Overland Campaign and in the early part of the **Petersburg Campaign** and in August accompanied the **corps** to participate in **Philip Sheridan's Shenandoah Valley Campaign**. At the **Third Battle of Winchester**, Upton assumed command of the **division** when **David A. Russell** was mortally wounded, but then Upton, too, was wounded. In a great display of courage, Upton continued to command the division while being carried about the field on a stretcher. When he returned to duty in December, he was given command of a cavalry division under **James H. Wilson** and served with him in **Wilson's Selma, Alabama, Raid**.

Few officers compiled as distinguished a war record as Upton. He served in all three branches of service during the war and earned brevets through the rank of major general of both regulars and volunteers by the age of 25. Mustered out of the volunteers in April 1866, Upton remained in the army and was promoted from captain of artillery to lieutenant colonel of the 25th U.S. Infantry that year. Although frequently absent sick—perhaps suffering from migraines—he had a great influence on the emergence of the modern **U.S. Army**. Upton was active in training soldiers and developing new tactics, wrote several military treatises, and served as commandant of cadets at West Point from 1870 to 1875. In 1880, he took command of the Presidio in San Francisco, **California**, and there committed suicide in 1881.

URBANNA PLAN. After spending months organizing, supplying, and training his **Army of the Potomac** following **First Manassas**, **George B. McClellan** increasingly was pressured by **Abraham Lincoln** to take the offensive against the Confederates around Manassas, Virginia. He finally decided on a plan in December 1861. Believing the Manassas defenses were too strong to attack, McClellan proposed moving the **army** by transports from **Washington, D.C.**, to the Chesapeake Bay and then up the Rappahannock River to Urbanna, Virginia, on the river's south bank. This would place the Federals only 50 miles east of **Richmond, Virginia**, and behind **Joseph E. Johnston's** Confederate army at Manassas. It also had the advantage of securing McClellan's supply line since it would be maintained by water and not be vulnerable to Confederate raiders.

McClellan, however, did not inform Lincoln of his plan. Unwilling to wait any longer, in late January 1862, Lincoln issued the **President's General War Orders No. 1**, ordering all Union armies to advance against the enemy by February 22. Unwilling to attack Manassas, McClellan then was forced to tell the president of his Urbanna Plan. Lincoln at first objected because it would leave Washington undefended, and he feared Johnston would attack the city after McClellan left. The two debated the plan after the February deadline, and McClellan received the support of his **division** commanders in early March (by a vote of 8–4). Lincoln finally approved it, but only after McClellan reluctantly agreed to leave a substantial force behind to defend the city.

Before McClellan could implement the Urbanna Plan, Johnston evacuated his Manassas line on March 9, 1862, (the day after McClellan polled his officers) and retreated to the south side of the Rappahannock River. This completely ruined the Urbanna Plan, for the **Confederate army** was now in a position to block McClellan's advance from Urbanna to Richmond. As a result, McClellan changed the plan to land his army at the tip of the Virginia Peninsula at **Fort Monroe**. He shipped out later that month and the **Peninsula Campaign** began.

USHER, JOHN PALMER (1816–1889) USA. A native of **New York**, Usher became a lawyer and opened a practice in **Indiana** in 1839. There he met and became friends with **Abraham Lincoln** while working the circuit court. Usher was elected to one term in the state legislature in 1850 and in 1856 was defeated in a bid for the **U.S. Congress** on the **Republican Party** ticket. He was appointed the state attorney general in 1861 but resigned after only months in office to accept the position of assistant secretary of the interior in Lincoln's administration. When Secretary of the Interior **Caleb Smith** resigned in December 1862, Lincoln appointed Usher to take his place.

As secretary, Usher was involved in several controversial events. He was a large stockholder in the Union Pacific **railroad** and used his position to gain it favorable rights of way, even by ordering the moving of entire **Indian** reservations. Usher also did not believe that blacks and whites could live together peacefully in the United States and became involved in attempts either to colonize blacks in Central America or to create separate reservations for them. On the positive side, Usher supported the **Homestead Act** and increased both funding for Indian reservations and taxes on mines. After **Lincoln's assassination**, he joined the **Radical Republicans**, became critical of President **Andrew Johnson**, and resigned his position in May 1865. Moving to **Kansas**, Usher became chief counsel for the Union Pacific and later moved his office to **Pennsylvania**.

UTAH EXPEDITION (1857–1858). After the Mormons settled around Salt Lake City, Utah Territory, in the 1840s, their practice of polygamy and interference with **California**-bound wagon trains (and the massacre of at least one group of pioneers) led to rumors that they were in open defiance of federal law. To gain control over Utah, the U.S. government sent troops there from Fort Leavenworth, Kansas, in the summer of 1857. This column began what was known as the Utah Expedition (or Mormon War), but it was forced to retreat by a lack of supplies and inclement weather. In November, Col. **Albert Sidney Johnston** was given command of a new column of 5,500 men (almost half the **U.S. Army**), which he led to Utah in the spring of 1858. Johnston discovered that the rumors of Mormon defiance were exaggerated, and the Mormons agreed to submit to federal authority. The expedition gave many future Civil War officers some field experience.

UTOY CREEK, GEORGIA, BATTLE OF (AUGUST 5–6, 1864). As **John Bell Hood's** Confederate **Army of Tennessee** stubbornly held on to Atlanta, Georgia, in the summer of 1864, **William T. Sherman** attempted to end the **Atlanta Campaign** by shifting his **armies** southwest of the city in late July to cut Hood's last supply line on the Macon & Western Railroad. This movement led to the fierce **Battle of Ezra Church** on July 28 as Hood successfully protected his **railroad**.

On August 3, **John Schofield's Army of the Ohio**, with **John Palmer's** XIV Corps attached, advanced on East Point, where the Macon & Western and the Atlanta & West Point railroads converged. Palmer was to lead the advance, but he moved slowly and only engaged in minor fighting because he was involved in a dispute over rank and disliked serving under Schofield. Schofield finally put his own command in front and attacked the Confederate left at Utoy (YOO-toy) Creek on August 6 with **Jacob D. Cox's** division. Cox, however, was repulsed by **William B. Bate's** well-entrenched Confederate **division**. Schofield then sent **Milo S. Hascall's** division to the right to flank Bate. Hascall gained an advantageous position on the Confederate left and forced Bate to withdraw during the night to a second position. On August 7, Schofield advanced over the abandoned earthworks but decided the second line was too strong to attack. He halted his men and entrenched along the Confederates' front. On that same day, Sherman relieved Palmer of command at his own request. In the battle along Utoy Creek, Schofield lost about 400 men, while the Confederates lost approximately 225.

– V –

VALLANDIGHAM, CLEMENT LAIRD (1820–1871) USA. A native of **Ohio**, Vallandigham (vuh-LAN-di-gum) attended the New Lisbon Academy in 1837 and then taught school in **Maryland** before entering **Pennsylvania's** Jefferson College in 1840. Returning to Ohio, he passed the bar in 1842 and began a law practice in New Lisbon. Vallandigham was elected to the state assembly in 1845 and 1846 and then edited the Dayton *Empire* until 1849. After being defeated for the **U.S. Congress** three times in the early 1850s, he was appointed a brigadier general in the state militia in 1857 and finally won a congressional seat in 1858 as a **Democrat**. Reelected in 1860, Vallandigham was a moderate who supported **states rights**, opposed radical **abolitionists**, and backed **Stephen A. Douglas** for president in 1860.

As a supporter of states rights, Vallandigham vocally opposed using force to coerce the seceding states back into the Union. He became a leading critic of **Abraham Lincoln's** war measures and opposed such actions as **conscription** and the **suspension of the writ of habeas corpus**. In doing so, Vallandigham became active in the **Copperhead** movement and angered many influential members of his own party, particularly the **War Democrats**. After Democratic leaders redrew the boundaries of his congressional district in 1862, Vallandigham lost his bid for reelection.

Vallandigham ran for governor in 1863, but he failed to win his party's nomination. In April, he tried to regain his waning support by publicly denouncing Lincoln and the war effort. Vallandigham hoped to gain sympathy by being arrested for violating an order by Maj. Gen. **Ambrose E. Burnside** (the **department's** commander) forbidding such statements. Burnside did arrest him in May, and Vallandigham was convicted in a military court without the benefit of a writ of habeas corpus and was sentenced to two years in prison. Despite his fall from political office, he was still a popular figure among **Peace**

Democrats. Torn between the need to maintain order and the desire not to make Vallandigham a martyr for peace advocates, Lincoln commuted his sentence and in late May 1863 sent him into Confederate lines south of Murfreesboro, Tennessee. Ohio's Democratic Party was outraged by the seemingly unconstitutional military arrest and trial and nominated Vallandigham for governor in June. Vallandigham did not stay in the Confederacy. He traveled to Canada in July 1863 by way of Bermuda and from Ontario ran for governor. With Lincoln's support, however, **Republican John Brough** easily won the race. In June 1864, a disguised Vallandigham slipped back into Ohio and soon was openly participating in Democratic politics. By this time, the Union was winning the war, and Lincoln chose to ignore his presence. Vallandigham actually strengthened Lincoln's position by attending the 1864 Democratic National Convention and helping create the peace platform that contributed to **George B. McClellan's** defeat in the 1864 presidential election.

After the war, Vallandigham was unable to reenter politics successfully. After being defeated in an 1867 state senate race, he resumed his law practice. Vallandigham died in a bizarre 1871 incident while demonstrating to other lawyers how a murder victim could have shot himself accidentally. While doing so, he accidentally shot himself and died the next day—but he won the case.

VALLEY ARMY AND DISTRICT, CONFEDERATE. When the Confederates established the **Department of Northern Virginia** in October 1861, the **Shenandoah Valley** fell within its boundaries and was designated the Valley District. **Thomas J. "Stonewall" Jackson** was given command of the **district**, and the soldiers under him were designated the Valley Army. The Valley Army won **Jackson's 1862 Shenandoah Valley Campaign** before being incorporated into the **Army of Northern Virginia**.

Major General **William E. "Grumble" Jones** replaced Jackson in December 1862, and he was replaced by **Isaac Trimble** in May 1863. Fighting occurred in the district at **Second Winchester** and **Stephenson's Depot** as **Robert E. Lee** began the **Gettysburg Campaign**. After Trimble was captured at Gettysburg, **John D. Imboden** took command of the district in July 1863. **Jubal A. Early** replaced Imboden in December 1863, and in June 1864 he was sent with the II Corps to defend against **David Hunter's Shenandoah Valley Campaign**. After chasing away Hunter, Early advanced through the Valley on **Early's Washing-**

ton Raid. For the remainder of 1864, the Valley Army fought frequently during **Philip Sheridan's Shenandoah Valley Campaign**. After Early was crushed at **Waynesboro** in March 1865, he was replaced by **Lunsford L. Lomax**, the last district commander. *See also* NEW MARKET, VIRGINIA, BATTLE OF.

VALVERDE, NEW MEXICO TERRITORY, BATTLE OF (FEBRUARY 21, 1862). In February 1862, Confederate Brig. Gen. **Henry H. Sibley** began **Sibley's New Mexico Campaign** with his 2,600-man **Army of New Mexico**. Leaving **Texas**, he followed the Rio Grande into **New Mexico**, where he planned to capture needed supplies at Fort Craig. Union Col. **Edward R. S. Canby** had 3,800 Federals at the fort, but Sibley hoped to cut his lines of communications to Santa Fe and force him to fight on favorable ground. On February 19, Sibley took up a defensive position east of Fort Craig on a ridge across the river. Canby sent a column across the river to drive away the Confederates, but Sibley's **artillery** forced it to withdraw.

On February 21, Sibley moved six miles north of Fort Craig to Valverde (val-VURD-ee) Ford to threaten Canby's line of communications, but Canby attacked and forced him to withdraw. Sibley then complained of illness (some said he suffered from too much heat, others said from too much liquor), and Col. **Thomas Green** assumed command of the Confederates. After an attack on the Union right drew away many of the soldiers holding Canby's center, Green attacked the Union left and center. He captured six cannons in fierce hand-to-hand fighting and forced Canby to retreat to Fort Craig. In the battle, Sibley lost 187 men to Canby's 263. The Confederates had won a **tactical** victory, but they were unable to capture the fort's needed supplies. Sibley continued toward Santa Fe and occupied it on March 10.

VAN ALEN, JAMES HENRY (1819–1886) USA. A native of **New York**, Van Alen was a member of a wealthy family and never actually had a profession. When the Civil War began, he raised and equipped at his own expense the 3rd New York Cavalry and entered Union service as its colonel in August 1861. After spending the winter in the defenses of **Washington, D.C.**, Van Alen was promoted to brigadier general of volunteers in April 1862 and was put in command of **Yorktown** and Gloucester, Virginia, during the **Peninsula Campaign**. He remained there until relieved in October 1862 and was assigned the following month to serve on the court of inquiry investigating **Irvin McDowell's** actions at **First Manassas**. In May 1863, Van Alen was appointed **Joseph Hooker's** aide-de-camp and served with the **Army of the Potomac** at **Chancellorsville**. Days after the battle was over, he was put in command of a rear area to help guard a valuable **railroad**.

Van Alen resigned his commission in July 1863 and resumed his rich lifestyle, but in 1886, he either jumped or fell overboard from a passenger ship and drowned in the Atlantic Ocean. His body was never recovered.

VANCE, ROBERT BRANK (1828–1899) CSA. A native of **North Carolina**, Vance was the brother of Gov. **Zebulon B. Vance**. After receiving a local education, he worked as a farmer and in commerce and served a number of years as his county's clerk.

Vance entered Confederate service in 1861 as captain of a volunteer **company** he raised. The company became part of the 29th North Carolina, and he was appointed its colonel in September. The **regiment** was sent to eastern **Tennessee**, where it guarded **railroads** and defended Cumberland Gap. Vance participated in the **Kentucky Campaign** with **Edmund Kirby Smith's** command, and at **Stones River** with the **Army of Tennessee**, he assumed command of **James E. Rains's brigade** when Rains was killed. After the battle, Vance was stricken with typhoid fever and was unable to resume duty for many months. During his convalescence, he was promoted to brigadier general in March 1863 and was sent to western **North Carolina** when he returned to duty in September. Having only a few hundred men, Vance was not involved in any major combat during his time there. In January 1864, he led a small cavalry raid into eastern Tennessee and was captured after he neglected to post **pickets** at an encampment. Vance remained a **prisoner** until war's end.

After the war, Vance returned to North Carolina and became a popular politician. He served one term as a state legislator and then served in the **U.S. Congress** from 1873 to 1885. After declining to run for reelection, Vance worked in **Washington, D.C.**, as assistant commissioner of patents from 1885 to 1889. He then returned to North Carolina and was elected to the state legislature in 1894 and 1896.

VANCE, ZEBULON BAIRD (1830–1894) CSA. A native of **North Carolina**, Vance was the brother of Confederate Gen. **Robert B. Vance**. After attending **Tennessee's** Washington College and the University of North Carolina Law School, he became a prosperous lawyer. Vance served as his county's solicitor in 1853 and was elected to the state legislature the following year. As a **Democrat**, he was elected to the U.S. House of Representatives in 1858 and served there during the **secession** crisis. Vance was a proslavery Unionist and supported **John Bell** in the **election of 1860**. He refused to run for a seat in the **Confederate Congress** after North Carolina seceded and instead entered Confederate service in May 1861 as a captain in the 4th North Carolina.

In August 1861, Vance was appointed colonel of the 26th North Carolina. After fighting at **New Bern, North Carolina**, and in the **Seven Days Campaign**, he was elected governor in August 1862. As a war governor, Vance strongly supported the war effort. North Carolina suffered more **Confederate Army** deaths than any other state, and led the Confederacy in number of **blockade runners**. Vance believed his primary duty was to North Carolina's soldiers and civilians and that the state's resources should support them first. He not only supplied his soldiers with adequate clothing and equipment, but he also sometimes shared resources with other states. Despite his support of the war, Vance also was a strong proponent of **states rights** and frequently clashed with **Jefferson Davis** over issues of authority. He opposed the **suspension of the writ of habeas corpus** and, although he believed in the necessity of **conscription**, frequently quarreled with Davis over the abuse of conscription officials. Vance won reelection in 1864 and continued to support the war even though more and more of his people became disillusioned, and the Unionists in the western mountains became stronger. The state finally was overrun by **William T. Sherman's armies** in the **Carolinas Campaign**, and Vance was captured in May 1865.

Vance was briefly imprisoned after the war, but he was released in July and returned to his law practice. He was elected to the U.S. Senate in 1870, but the **Radical Republicans** refused to seat him. Vance was reelected governor in 1876 and finally became a U.S. senator in 1879. He was still serving in the Senate when he died in 1894.

VAN CLEVE, HORATIO PHILLIPS (1809–1891) USA. A native of **New Jersey**, Van Cleve attended the College of New Jersey (now Princeton University) and graduated from **West Point** in 1831. After five years on garrison duty with the infantry, he resigned his 2nd lieutenant's commission in 1836 and embarked on a varied career. Van Cleve was a farmer and engineer in **Michigan**, a teacher in **Ohio**, and a surveyor and cattle rancher in **Minnesota**.

Van Cleve entered Union service in July 1861 when he was appointed colonel of the 2nd Minnesota. The regiment became part of

Robert L. McCook's brigade and fought at **Mill Springs**. Van Cleve was promoted to brigadier general of volunteers in March 1862 and assumed command of a brigade in the **Army of the Ohio** after participating in the **siege of Corinth, Mississippi**. He also participated in the **Kentucky Campaign** but was not involved in the major battles. In late September 1862, Van Cleve was given a **division** command in the Army of the Ohio, but in November, he took a division in the **Army of the Cumberland**. As part of the XIV Corps, he fought at **Stones River** and received a wound there. Transferred to a XXI Corps division in March 1863, Van Cleve's brigade participated in the **Tullahoma Campaign** and then suffered heavy casualties at **Chickamauga**. When the **corps** was disbanded in October, he failed to receive another field command and was placed in command of Murfreesboro, Tennessee. Van Cleve remained in Middle **Tennessee** until war's end.

After being **brevetted** major general of volunteers for his war service, Van Cleve was mustered out of the volunteers in August 1865. Returning to Minnesota, he served as the state's adjutant general from 1866 to 1870 and from 1876 to 1882 and was St. Anthony's postmaster from 1871 to 1873.

VAN DERVEER, FERDINAND (1823–1892) USA. A native of **Ohio**, Van Derveer received a local education and became a lawyer. He joined the volunteers during the **Mexican War** and rose in rank from 1st sergeant to **company** captain in the 1st Ohio. After the war, Van Derveer returned to his Ohio law practice and served as a county sheriff.

Van Derveer entered Union service in September 1861 when he was appointed colonel of the 35th Ohio. He participated in the **siege of Corinth, Mississippi**, in the spring of 1862 and led a **brigade** in the **Army of the Ohio's** 1st Division early in the **Kentucky Campaign**. Van Derveer was back with his **regiment** for the battles of **Perryville** and **Stones River**, although he was not actively engaged in the latter. In January 1863, he was given command of a brigade in the 3rd Division of the **Army of the Cumberland's** XIV Corps. After fighting at **Chickamauga**, Van Derveer personally led the brigade up **Missionary Ridge** during the **Chattanooga Campaign**. During the **Atlanta Campaign**, his brigade was part of **Absalom Baird's division**, and Van Derveer saw combat in all of the campaigns' battles through the end of June. He was placed on sick leave in late June 1864 and was mustered out of service in July when his men's enlistments' expired. Van Derveer was reappointed to the **army** as a brigadier general of volunteers in October and was given command of a brigade garrisoning the Huntsville, Alabama, area. When the division was reorganized in June 1865, he was left without a command and resigned his commission.

After the war, Van Derveer returned to his Ohio law practice and served a number of years as a judge.

VANDEVER, WILLIAM (1817–1893) USA. A native of **Maryland**, Vandever moved to **Illinois** but finally settled in **Iowa** in 1851. After becoming a lawyer, he was elected to the **U.S. Congress** in 1858 as a **Republican** and won reelection in 1860.

Vandever entered Union service in September 1861 when he left Congress to become colonel of the 9th Iowa. In February 1862, he was given a **brigade** command in the **Army of the Southwest's** 4th Division. Vandever fought at **Pea Ridge** and was promoted to brigadier general of volunteers in November 1862. Given a brigade command in the XIII Corps' 9th Division, he next fought at **Arkansas Post** in January 1863. After briefly commanding a **division** in the **Army of the Frontier** in the spring of 1863, Vandever took a brigade command in **Francis J. Herron's** division of the **Army of the Tennessee**. He participated in the latter part of the **Vicksburg Campaign** after he joined the besieging forces in June 1863. Vandever remained in the **Vicksburg, Mississippi**, area and on the Gulf Coast until June 1864, when he assumed command of a brigade in the Army of the Tennessee's XVI Corps. During the latter part of the **Atlanta Campaign**, he served in Rome and Marietta, Georgia, and in November 1864, he sat on the court-martial that acquitted Brig. Gen. **Thomas W. Sweeny**. Vandever retook the field in January 1865, when he was given a brigade in the XIV Corps and led it through the **Carolinas Campaign**. After being **brevetted** major general of volunteers in June, he was mustered out of the service in August 1865.

Vandever returned to his Iowa law practice and from 1873 to 1877 served as an **Indian** commissioner for President **U. S. Grant**. He moved to **California** in 1884 and served in Congress from 1887 to 1891.

VAN DORN, EARL (1820–1863) CSA. A native of **Mississippi**, Van Dorn was a great-nephew of President Andrew Jackson. He graduated near the bottom of his 1842 **West Point** class and was assigned to the infantry. Van Dorn served on garrison duty in the South before fighting in the **Mexican War** with both Zachary Taylor and **Winfield Scott**. Under

Scott, he was wounded and won two **brevets** for gallantry while serving on Brig. Gen. P. F. Smith's staff. After the war, Van Dorn served in the **Seminole Wars** and was wounded by four arrows in a battle with **Indians** on the western frontier.

By 1861, Van Dorn, known to his friends as "Buck," was a major in the **U.S. Army**. He resigned his commission after Mississippi seceded in January 1861 and was appointed brigadier general of Mississippi state troops. In early February, after **Jefferson Davis** had been elected president of the Confederacy, Van Dorn was promoted to major general and succeeded Davis in command of all of the state's troops. He entered Confederate service in March when he was appointed colonel of cavalry. Van Dorn first commanded **Forts Jackson and St. Philip** guarding **New Orleans, Louisiana**, but in April, he was given command of the **Department of Texas**. There he captured the *Star of the West* in Galveston and forced the surrender of several U.S. garrisons. As a reward for his accomplishments, Van Dorn was promoted to brigadier general in June.

Van Dorn gave up his Texas command in June 1861 and traveled to **Richmond, Virginia**. In September, he was promoted to major general and assumed a **division** command under **Joseph E. Johnston** near Manassas. Van Dorn remained in **Virginia** until January 1862, when he was sent west to take command of the **Trans-Mississippi District** to end a feud between Gens. **Ben McCulloch** and **Sterling Price**. In March, he attacked the Federals at **Pea Ridge** with his **Army of the West** but broke off the battle and retreated the next day. Crossing the Mississippi River, Van Dorn reinforced **P. G. T. Beauregard's Army of Mississippi** during the **siege of Corinth, Mississippi**, in April. After helping defend the town from the approaching Federals that spring, he was put in command of the **Department of Southern Mississippi and East Louisiana** in June (it became the District of the Mississippi in July) and successfully opposed **David G. Farragut's** fleet at **Vicksburg, Mississippi**, that summer. Despite this success, Van Dorn became very unpopular in his **district** because he declared martial law in some areas, and Davis was forced to replace him with **John C. Pemberton** in October. Before Pemberton arrived, however, Van Dorn unsuccessfully attacked **Corinth** earlier in the month with his **Army of West Tennessee**. The battle was his second major defeat, and charges (including being drunk on the field) were preferred against him. Although exonerated in a court of inquiry, Van Dorn's reputation was damaged.

In December 1862, Van Dorn was placed in command of Pemberton's cavalry. He destroyed the Federal supply base at **Holly Springs** that month and forced **U. S. Grant** to abandon his **Overland Vicksburg Campaign**. In January 1863, Van Dorn was sent to **Tennessee**, where his cavalry became part of **Braxton Bragg's Army of Tennessee**. He won other victories in March when he captured a Union column at **Thompson's Station** and a wagon train at **Brentwood**. Van Dorn proved that he was a much better cavalry leader than **army** commander, but he and **Nathan Bedford Forrest** clashed (in one confrontation they drew their swords).

While stationed at Spring Hill, Tennessee, Van Dorn's well-known reputation as a womanizer killed him. On May 7, 1863, he was shot to death in his office chair by Dr. George B. Peters, who was in a jealous rage over the general's relationship with his wife. Peters then fled safely into Union lines. Van Dorn was one of the Confederacy's more controversial generals. He was described as being a "horrible rake" and looking "more like a dandy than a general." Jefferson Davis's brother noted, "when Van Dorn was made a general, it spoiled a good captain" (Current, ed., *Encyclopedia of the Confederacy,* vol. 4, 1652).

VAN LEW, ELIZABETH (1818–?) USA. A native of **New York**, Van Lew was educated in **Pennsylvania** before settling in **Richmond, Virginia**. An avowed **abolitionist**, she was something of an oddity in Richmond, and when the Civil War began she remained staunchly loyal to the Union. To protect herself, Van Lew acted as though she was eccentric, if not insane. She dressed shabbily and muttered to herself on the street, and residents began referring to her as "Crazy Bet." In reality, Van Lew was one of the most successful Union spies of the war. She and a close circle of accomplices gathered vital intelligence for the Union and helped hide escaped Union **prisoners** from **Libby Prison**. Van Lew also openly helped the prisoners by supplying them food and clothing. Confederate officials believed she was harmless and never suspected she was involved in espionage. Her intelligence on the city's weak defenses led to the unsuccessful **Kilpatrick-Dahlgren Raid** in 1864. So elaborate was Van Lew's spy network, that during the **Overland Campaign** she sometimes smuggled flowers from her garden to place on **U. S. Grant's** table, along with her secret information. When the Federals occupied Richmond in April 1865, Grant quickly sent guards to protect Van Lew's house and soon paid her a visit himself. Only then did her neighbors realize the extent of her wartime activities.

The war ruined Van Lew financially, and the people of Richmond shunned her afterward. Grant appointed her the city's postmistress during his eight years as president, and afterward Northern friends provided her financial aid until her death.

VAN VLIET, STEWART (1815–1901) USA. A native of **Vermont**, Van Vliet (van-VLEET) graduated from **West Point** in 1840 and was assigned to the **artillery**. After serving in **Florida**, he was given the staff rank of captain in 1847 and was transferred to the Quartermaster Department, where he remained until the Civil War. After serving in the **Mexican War**, Van Vliet constructed military posts along the Oregon Trail and helped organize the **Utah Expedition**.

When the Civil War began, Van Vliet was serving at Fort Leavenworth, Kansas. He was promoted to major in August 1861 and was appointed the **Army of the Potomac's** chief quartermaster. The following month, Van Vliet was appointed brigadier general of volunteers. He helped supply the **army** during its training around **Washington, D.C.**, and in the **Peninsula Campaign**, but he clashed with **U.S. Navy** officers, whose ships transported his supplies, and asked to be relieved in July 1862.

Van Vliet's appointment to brigadier general was never confirmed by the Senate and expired in July 1862, a week after he was relieved as quartermaster. Reverting to his permanent rank of major, he was sent to **New York** and spent the remainder of the war gathering supplies and forwarding them to the army. For his war service, Van Vliet was **brevetted** through the rank of major general of regulars, and he was recommissioned brigadier general of volunteers in November 1865. After being mustered out of the volunteers in September 1866, he remained in the regular army's Quartermaster Department and retired in 1881 as a colonel.

VAUGHAN, ALFRED JEFFERSON, JR. (1830–1899) CSA. A native of **Virginia**, Vaughan graduated from the **Virginia Military Institute** in 1851. Moving to **California** by way of **Missouri**, he served as a deputy U.S. surveyor and helped negotiate **railroad** rights of way with the Plains **Indians**. Settling in **Mississippi** in 1856, Vaughan farmed until the Civil War began.

Although an opponent of **secession**, Vaughan raised a volunteer **company** that became part of the 13th Tennessee in June 1861 and entered Confederate service as its captain. He almost immediately was elected lieutenant colonel and in November fought at **Belmont**, where he was highly praised and had two horses shot from under him. When the regiment's commander was elected to the **Confederate Congress** the following month, Vaughan was promoted to colonel. Joining Robert M. Russell's **brigade**, he led the regiment at **Shiloh** and captured a Union **artillery** battery. After serving in the siege of **Corinth, Mississippi**, the regiment became part of **Preston Smith's** brigade. Vaughan participated in the **Kentucky Campaign** and saw combat at **Richmond**. He assumed command of the brigade when Smith replaced the wounded **Patrick Cleburne**, but the brigade was transferred to **Benjamin F. Cheatham's division**. Vaughan was in a supportive role at **Perryville** and served at **Stones River** with the **Army of Tennessee**. After fighting well on the first day, he returned to the regiment when Smith rejoined the brigade. In March 1863, Vaughan was put in command of the consolidated 13th and 154th Tennessee. After participating in the **Tullahoma Campaign**, he again saw fierce combat on the first day at **Chickamauga**. There his men captured several hundred **prisoners**, and Vaughan assumed command of the brigade when Smith was killed.

Vaughan was promoted to brigadier general in November 1863. He fought at **Missionary Ridge** in **Thomas C. Hindman's** division but afterward became part of Cheatham's division. During the **Atlanta Campaign**, Vaughan's brigade saw heavy combat, particularly at **Kennesaw Mountain**, where it helped defend the "Dead Angle." In early July 1864, a shell mangled his foot, and surgeons were forced to amputate it. Although he had had eight horses shot from under him, this first wound put the general out of action. Unable to retake the field, Vaughan was **paroled** in **Alabama** in May 1865.

After the war, Vaughan returned to his Mississippi farm and became leader of the state's Granger movement in the early 1870s. Moving to **Tennessee** in 1873, he operated a mercantile business until elected county clerk of criminal court in 1878 (he was reelected in 1882). In 1897, Vaughan became commander of the state's **United Confederate Veterans** division and served at that post until his death.

VAUGHN, JOHN CRAWFORD (1824–1875) CSA. A native of **Tennessee**, Vaughn served in the **Mexican War** as a captain in the 5th Tennessee Volunteers. He returned to east Tennessee after the war and became a merchant.

Vaughn was in **Charleston, South Carolina**, in the spring of 1861 and witnessed the bombardment of **Fort Sumter**. Returning home, he raised a **regiment** and entered Confederate service in July as colonel of the 3rd Tennessee. Joining **Joseph E. Johnston's** forces in **Virginia**, Vaughn earned great praise when he led his men on a forced march and burned a vital bridge on the Baltimore & Ohio Railroad. Transferred to his native east Tennessee, he served under **Edmund Kirby Smith** and was promoted to brigadier general in October 1862.

Sent to **Vicksburg, Mississippi,** Vaughn's Tennessee **brigade** successfully held the Confederate left at **Chickasaw Bayou**, but it was routed in May 1863 while contesting the advance of **U. S. Grant's army** at the **Big Black River Bridge**. Vaughn was criticized for his poor performance at the river, but he served competently during the remainder of the **Vicksburg Campaign** while in command of the city's upper defenses. After Vicksburg's surrender, he was **exchanged** in mid-July 1863 and was given command of a mounted brigade that served on **reconnaissance** duty under **James Longstreet** during the **Knoxville Campaign**. Vaughn remained in Tennessee when Longstreet returned to Virginia, and his poorly **disciplined** brigade was criticized for becoming little more than marauders. He further hurt his reputation by performing poorly at **Piedmont** in June 1864. When **Jubal A. Early** took command of the **Valley District** that summer, he requested that Vaughn be replaced. This did not occur, however, and Vaughn accompanied **Early's Washington Raid** and was wounded near Martinsburg, West Virginia. During this time, many of Vaughn's men **deserted**, and the entire brigade was sent back to southwestern **Virginia** in September 1864. That month, he succeeded **John Hunt Morgan** in command of the **Department of Western Virginia and East Tennessee** and spent the next months defending **Saltville, Virginia**, and patrolling Cumberland Gap. Learning of the **surrender** at **Appomattox**, Vaughn took his men toward **North Carolina** to join Joseph E. Johnston and became part of **Jefferson Davis's** escort as the Confederate government fled toward the **Trans-Mississippi Department**. Vaughn surrendered his brigade in **Georgia** in May 1865.

After the war, Vaughn returned to Tennessee and was elected to the state senate for one term. Moving to Georgia, he then became a planter and merchant.

VAUGHT'S HILL, TENNESSEE, BATTLE OF (MARCH 20, 1863).

On March 20, 1863, Union Col. Albert Hall's **brigade** was returning to its base at Murfreesboro, Tennessee, after conducting a two-day raid into the surrounding neighborhood. Confederate Brig. Gen. **John Hunt Morgan** pursued Hall and attacked his rear guard a mile west of Milton. Hall took up a defensive position on rocky Vaught's Hill and repulsed several Confederate attacks. When Morgan learned that Union reinforcements were coming from Murfreesboro, he broke off the attack late that afternoon and withdrew. Morgan's reputation was damaged by this defeat, in which he lost approximately 150 men to the Federals' 38.

VEATCH, JAMES CLIFFORD (1819–1895) USA. A native of **Indiana**, Veatch became a lawyer in 1840 and served as his county's auditor from 1841 to 1855. Elected to the state legislature in 1861, he left his seat to become colonel of the 25th Indiana in August.

After fighting at **Fort Donelson**, Veatch was given a **brigade** command in **Stephen Hurlbut's** division in February 1862 and led his men in fierce fighting at **Shiloh**. Promoted to brigadier general in late April, he participated in the **siege of Corinth, Mississippi**, and from July 1862 to January 1864 held **district** commands at Memphis and Jackson, Tennessee. During this time, Veatch fought a small battle at **Davis Bridge, Tennessee**, in October 1862. In January 1864, he was given command of a **division** in the **Army of the Tennessee's** XVI Corps and led it in the **Atlanta Campaign**, but he apparently did not favorably impress **Oliver O. Howard**. Veatch took sick leave in July but was ordered to remain in Memphis to await orders after he reported back to duty in September. He held some minor posts in **Tennessee, Mississippi**, and **Arkansas** until sent to the **Department of the Gulf** in February 1865. There, Veatch was given command of a XIII Corps division and fought in the **Mobile Campaign**. He was **brevetted** major general of volunteers for his service at Mobile and was mustered out of the service in August.

Veatch returned to Indiana after the war and served as state adjutant general in 1869 and as a collector of internal revenue from 1870 to 1883.

VELAZQUEZ, LORETA JANETA (1842–?) CSA. This Confederate spy claimed to have led a fascinating life, but little of it can be proved. A native of Cuba, she moved to **New Orleans, Louisiana**, with her family and married a **U.S. Army** officer in 1856. Velazquez claimed she raised a volunteer **company** under the assumed disguise of Harry Buford when her husband joined the **Confederate army** and that she eventually accompanied her husband to war as an aide and lieutenant. He subsequently was killed in an accidental shooting. Velazquez supposedly fought at **First Manassas, Ball's Bluff, Fort Donelson**, and **Shiloh** (being wounded in the latter two battles) before her true identity was discovered in 1863. She then claimed to have become a Confederate spy and mingled with many of the war's famous military and government leaders. After the war, Velazquez remarried and moved to South America. Her fantastic, and improbable, life's story is detailed in her 1876 book, *The Woman in Battle: A Narrative of the Exploits, Adventures, and Travels of Madame Loreta Janeta Velazquez, Otherwise Known as Lieutenant Harry T. Buford, Confederate States of America.*

VERMONT. Long a center of **abolitionism**, Vermont strongly supported the Union war effort. Out of an 1860 population of 315,098, the state supplied 35,262 men to the Union in 19 **regiments**, 3 **artillery** batteries, and one **company**. The **Vermont Brigade** of the **Army of the Potomac's** VI Corps became especially famous as it participated in the bloody fighting of the eastern theater. Twenty-four Union generals also hailed from Vermont, including **William B. Hazen**, **Joseph A. Mower**, and **Thomas E. G. Ransom**. Norwich University also produced 23 Union generals, one admiral, and Secretary of the Navy **Gideon Welles**. The only wartime action in the state occurred in October 1864 when Confederate agents made the **St. Albans Raid** to rob banks.

VERMONT BRIGADE. Although **Vermont** was one of the smallest Northern states, it provided the Union with one of its most famous military units. In August 1861, the 2nd and 3rd Vermont became part of a **brigade** commanded by **William F. "Baldy" Smith**. In October, Smith's command was increased to a **division** and the 4th, 5th, and 6th Vermont were added to the 2nd and 3rd Vermont to form a brigade within the division. Officially designated the 1st Vermont Brigade, this unit was one of the few Union brigades that were made up of **regiments** from one state (the nine-month 26th New Jersey served with it from October 1862 to June 1863, and the 1st Vermont Heavy Artillery was added in May 1864). It also suffered the largest number of casualties of any Union brigade. **William T. H. Brooks** commanded the brigade from October 1861 to October 1862, followed by **Lewis A. Grant** from October 1862 to June 1865. Between Brooks and Grant, a series of colonels led the unit.

As part of the **Army of the Potomac's** VI Corps, the Vermont Brigade participated in the **Peninsula**, **Seven Days**, **Antietam**, and **Chancellorsville Campaigns**. It also was sent to **New York** in the summer of 1863 to restore order after the **New York City Draft Riot**. All of the brigade's regiments reenlisted in 1864 after seeing bloody combat in the **Overland Campaign** (at the **Wilderness** and **Spotsylvania**, the brigade lost 1,646 out of 2,800 men). After helping defend **Washington, D.C.**, during **Jubal A. Early's Washington Raid**, the brigade fought in **Philip Sheridan's 1864 Shenandoah Valley Campaign** and then rejoined the Army of the Potomac for the latter part of the **Petersburg Campaign**. It led the attack that broke through the Confederate defenses on April 2, 1865, and engaged in its last battle at **Sailor's Creek**. After participating in the **Grand Review**, the brigade was disbanded in June 1865, and most of the regiments were mustered out of service in July. The 1st Vermont Heavy Artillery was mustered out in August.

VETERAN RESERVE CORPS. *See* INVALID CORPS.

VETERAN VOLUNTEER CORPS. By late 1864, the Union was searching for ways to increase its manpower. Secretary of War **Edwin M. Stanton** proposed forming a Veteran Volunteer Corps from the some 100,000 Union veterans who had been discharged from service and were exempt from **conscription** because they already had served their time. Stanton's plan was put into effect in November 1864, with discharged veterans being offered a **bounty** to reenlist in the Veteran Volunteer Corps. Major General **Winfield Scott Hancock** was appointed the **corps'** commander, and he relinquished command of the **Army of the Potomac's** II Corps to begin raising recruits for his new organization. Although some recruits reentered service with more than $1,100 in bounties, Hancock was disappointed in the response. By May 1865, only 4,422 soldiers had enlisted into the corps.

VICKSBURG, MISSISSIPPI. Vicksburg, Mississippi, was the state's second largest city in 1861 with a population of almost 5,000. It prospered because it was located on the Mississippi River in rich cotton country. The Vicksburg, Shreveport & Texas Railroad across the river in **Louisiana** and the Southern Railroad running east to Jackson brought tons of cotton to the town for transport to **New Orleans, Louisiana**. When the Civil War began, Vicksburg took on strategic importance for the Confederacy. Its **railroads** made it a vital link between the **Trans-Mississippi Department** and the eastern Confederacy, and the Confederacy's **interior line** largely depended on the ability to transport troops and supplies across the river there. Located atop high bluffs, Vicksburg also was an excellent position on which to locate batteries to block the river. Realizing one of the main goals of the Union's **Anaconda Plan** was to gain control of the Mississippi River, the Confederates began heavily fortifying the city early in the war.

By the spring of 1862, the Federals had captured the lower river at New Orleans and **Baton Rouge, Louisiana**, and the upper river down to **Memphis, Tennessee**. Vicksburg became even more important because it was the last point on the river where the Confederates had railroad heads on both banks. Recognizing the strategic importance of the city, **Abraham Lincoln** declared that Vicksburg was the key to the entire Confederacy, and the Union would not win the war until it had pocketed it.

After the fall of New Orleans, 3,000 Confederate troops under Brig. Gen. **Martin Luther Smith** were transferred from Louisiana to Vicksburg. Smith constructed seven **artillery** batteries atop the 200-foot bluffs before **David Farragut's** fleet arrived from downstream. From late May through June 1862, Farragut's fleet periodically bombarded the Vicksburg defenses, and in late June, Union infantry under Brig. Gen. **Thomas Williams** began digging a canal across the base of a peninsula on the opposite bank of the river at Louisiana's De Soto Point. It was hoped the canal would cause the river to change course and allow ships to bypass the Vicksburg batteries. During these operations, the **CSS** *Arkansas* came down the Yazoo River and engaged the Union fleet, but it was later destroyed by its own crew at the **Battle of Baton Rouge.** Falling river water and disease finally forced Williams to abandon the canal project, and Farragut steamed to the Gulf of Mexico in late July before the falling water trapped his ships in the river. Farragut's failure to take Vicksburg proved that it would take a large **army** and land operations to accomplish the task.

In June 1862, **Earl Van Dorn** took command of Vicksburg and continued working on its defenses, as well as those at Port Hudson, Louisiana, farther downstream. After Van Dorn was defeated at **Corinth, Mississippi**, that October, Lt. Gen. **John C. Pemberton** was put in command of the **department** containing Vicksburg. Major General **U. S. Grant** was made commander of the Union **Department of the Tennessee** that same month and began plans for his Vicksburg Campaigns. In December, Grant launched the **Overland Vicksburg Campaign** when he invaded north-central **Mississippi** from **Tennessee** to draw off Pemberton's defenders, while **William T. Sherman** sailed down the river to land troops at Vicksburg. Grant, however, was forced to withdraw after Confederate cavalry destroyed his supply base at **Holly Springs**, and Sherman was defeated at **Chickasaw Bayou.**

Grant began his successful **Vicksburg Campaign** in January 1863. After months attempting to bypass the stronghold with Grant's Canals and the **Yazoo Pass** and **Steele's Bayou Expeditions**, he finally moved his army downriver in April. **David Porter** ran his ships past the Vicksburg batteries and successfully ferried Grant across the river at Bruinsburg, Mississippi. In a short campaign, Grant defeated the Confederates in five battles and finally laid siege to the city. After a 47-day siege, Pemberton surrendered on July 4, 1863, and Vicksburg remained in Union hands until war's end. When the Confederates surrendered **Port Hudson** five days later, the Union had gained control of the Mississippi River. The people of Vicksburg were so humiliated by surrendering on Independence Day that they refused to celebrate the holiday until after World War II.

VICKSBURG, MISSISSIPPI, CAMPAIGN AND SIEGE OF (JANUARY 18–JULY 4, 1863). By January 1863, the Confederates held only **Vicksburg, Mississippi,** and **Port Hudson, Louisiana,** on the Mississippi River. If the Union could capture them, it would gain control of the river, split the Confederacy in two, and accomplish one of the goals of the **Anaconda Plan.** Major General **U. S. Grant,** commander of the **Department of the Tennessee,** had advanced on Vicksburg in December 1862 in **Grant's Overland Vicksburg Campaign,** but he was turned back when Confederate cavalry destroyed his supply base at **Holly Springs, Mississippi,** and **William T. Sherman** was defeated at **Chickasaw Bayou.** In January 1863, Grant assumed command of all Union forces operating against Vicksburg (including Maj. Gen. **John A. McClernand's** command, which had just captured **Arkansas Post**) and began a new campaign. On January 18, he ordered McClernand's and Sherman's corps to begin the move toward Vicksburg. Downstream, Maj. Gen. **Nathaniel P. Banks** would begin the **Port Hudson Campaign** a few months later.

Moving downriver from Memphis, Tennessee, with **David Porter's** fleet of gunboats and his own **Army of the Tennessee,** Grant was plagued by high floodwater and had to encamp his **army** along the **Louisiana** levee from Lake Providence to Young's Point. His immediate problem was how to get at the city. Vicksburg sat atop high river bluffs that were heavily defended by **artillery,** and Confederate Lt. Gen. **John C. Pemberton** had more than 40,000 Confederates at his disposal to confront Grant. Sherman's earlier unsuccessful attack at Chickasaw Bayou proved that a **frontal attack** was impossible. Also, it seemed like suicide to run the ships past the bluffs to land troops below Vicksburg.

Grant's solution to the dilemma was to bypass the bluffs with Grant's Canals. By digging a canal across the peninsula fronting Vicksburg, he hoped to straighten out the river and allow his transports to take troops below the city without having to steam past the deadly batteries. Poor canal placement and a falling river, however, doomed this project. Other canals were dug to connect the Mississippi River with inland bayous to allow ships to go from the Mississippi River through a series of Louisiana streams to reenter the Mississippi below Vicksburg. These, too, failed because of the falling river and obstructions.

At the same time Grant had his men working on the canals, he launched two other projects in **Mississippi.** In early March, he carried out the **Yazoo Pass Expedition.** Troops were put aboard transports and sent through a cut in the levee above Vicksburg at Yazoo Pass. It was believed the ships could navigate a series of waterways and enter the Ya-zoo River above Vicksburg and land troops in Pemberton's rear. This ex-pedition was stopped by the Confederates at Fort Pemberton, but Grant was undeterred. While the men on the Yazoo Pass Expedition tried to fight their way around Fort Pemberton, he began a maneuver proposed by Porter known as the **Steele's Bayou Expedition**. After steaming into the Yazoo River, Porter's boats could enter Steele's Bayou, pass through another series of waterways, and reenter the Yazoo farther upstream be-yond the Confederates' position. This expedition also failed after the Confederates concentrated troops against it and blocked the river chan-nels with felled trees.

All of these projects kept the army busy until April 1863. At that time, the floodwater receded, the land dried out, and Grant made plans to move downstream. He built a road down the Louisiana side of the river to New Carthage and convinced Porter to steam a number of ships past the Vicksburg bluffs. On the night of April 16, Porter successfully ran 11 of 12 ships past the city, proving that the passage was not as dangerous as believed. On the night of April 22, he successfully ran another 18 of 25 ships downriver. To divert the Confederates' attention away from the river during these operations, Sherman probed **Snyder's Bluff** on the Ya-zoo River, while **Grierson's** and **Streight's Raids** were launched in Mississippi and **Alabama**, respectively.

After marching McClernand's and **James P. McPherson's corps** to Hard Times, Louisiana, Grant prepared to cross the river near **Grand Gulf, Mississippi**. Porter tested the Confederate defenses there on April 29 and found them too strong to overcome. This, and intelligence gath-ered from a slave indicating there was a good road inland at Bruinsburg, Mississippi, caused Grant to change the landing site to the latter place. McClernand and McPherson were ferried across the river on April 30, and Sherman was ordered to follow.

Pemberton had been completely confused by Grant's diversions and had widely dispersed his troops to chase Grierson, defend Vicksburg, and watch Sherman on the Yazoo. As a result, there were few Confederates present to contest Grant's march inland from Bruinsburg. On May 1, McClernand and McPherson defeated a small Confederate force under **John Bowen** at **Port Gibson**. Now firmly established below Vicksburg, Grant made a fateful decision. He had been given orders to move down-river to assist Banks in capturing Port Hudson but, instead, decided to seize Jackson first. General **Joseph E. Johnston**, commander of the Con-federate **Department of the West**, was concentrating troops at Jackson,

Mississippi. Grant moved against him before turning west to attack Vicksburg so his growing army would not threaten the Union rear. By attacking Jackson, Grant also could gain control of the vital **railroad** connecting Jackson and Vicksburg, over which Pemberton received supplies and reinforcements. Such a move would make it difficult for Grant to remain in contact with his supply ships on the Mississippi River, but his failed Overland Vicksburg Campaign had shown that an army could live off the land. Against the advice of his subordinates, he left the river, marched to the northeast toward Jackson, and placed his 44,000 men deep inside Confederate territory where he was outnumbered. In his memoirs, Grant claimed he completely cut his ties with the river during this maneuver and lived off the land. This was an exaggeration, because he managed to keep some wagons hauling supplies from the river to the army during the march.

When Grant marched to the northeast from Port Gibson, Pemberton was taken by surprise, for he had expected the Federals to follow the retreating Bowen due north to Vicksburg. Sherman's corps joined Grant during the march on May 8, and on May 12, McPherson's XVII Corps defeated a small Confederate force at **Raymond**. Johnston arrived at **Jackson** the next day to take command of the Confederates there, but he was defeated on May 14 and was forced out of the city. After leaving Sherman's XV Corps to destroy the railroad and public property, Grant left Jackson and headed west toward Vicksburg.

Throughout the course of Grant's long march from Bruinsburg, Johnston had ordered Pemberton to leave Vicksburg and engage the Federals while they were on the move. Pemberton, however, had also been ordered by **Jefferson Davis** to hold the city at all costs. Faced with conflicting orders, Pemberton took no strong action to stop Grant until it was virtually too late. He finally did advance from Vicksburg and engaged Grant at **Champion Hill** on May 16. In the largest battle of the campaign, Grant defeated Pemberton in fierce fighting and forced him to retreat. The next day, he brushed aside the Confederate rear guard at the **Big Black River Bridge** and reached Vicksburg on May 18.

Grant approached the city from the east and northeast. When Sherman reached the Yazoo River north of Vicksburg, Grant finally reestablished ties with Porter's fleet and began receiving steady supplies and reinforcements. With Sherman on the right, McPherson in the center, and McClernand on the left, Grant ordered a frontal assault against the strong Confederate defenses on May 19. What he did not know was that two fresh Confederate **divisions** that had not fought at Champion Hill were now on Pemberton's line, giving the Confederates just over 30,000 men. From north to south, the Confederate line was held by the divisions of **Martin Luther Smith**, **John H. Forney**, and **Carter L. Stevenson**, while Bowen constituted the reserve. Besides the fresh enemy troops, hills, gullies, and a tangle of **abatis** also made advancing difficult, and the Confederates had spent months preparing miles of trenches, earthworks, and fortifications around the city.

When the Federals attacked on May 19, fighting was particularly heavy along the Graveyard Road and at the Confederate's Stockade Redan. Little ground was gained, and Grant lost 942 men, while Pemberton suffered fewer than 200 casualties. When McClernand claimed his men had enjoyed some success on the left and urged another attack, Grant unwisely ordered a second assault on May 22. Sherman and McPherson were repulsed, but McClernand made some gains at the Railroad Redoubt, and Grant ordered the entire line to make a second effort. Again heavy fighting took place around the Graveyard Road and at the Railroad Redoubt, but Confederate counterattacks finally repulsed the Federals. Grant lost another 3,199 men during the day, while Pemberton counted fewer than 500 casualties. In his memoirs, Grant claimed that this second attack and the one a year later at **Cold Harbor, Virginia**, were the only two he regretted making in the war. Angered over launching the attack because of McClernand's misleading claims, Grant replaced him with **Edward O. C. Ord** when McClernand had reports published praising the role his XIII Corps played in the battle at the expense of the others.

Realizing the city could not be taken by storm, Grant settled into a siege. Over the next several weeks, the Union army grew larger as reinforcements poured in, while Pemberton's men began suffering from shortages of food, medicine, and ammunition. By the end of the campaign, Grant had more than 77,000 men along the line. Artillery and **sharpshooter** fire was constant and both sides (including many civilians who remained in the city) lived in caves dug into the hillsides and endured the misery of oppressive heat, water-filled ditches, and frequent thunderstorms. At night, the Federals dug their trenches closer to the Confederates and during the day shot at everything that moved. Grant was able to rotate his men off the front line for occasional rest, but the Confederates were forced to remain in their trenches. When **rations** began running out, the Confederates ate mule meat and organized rat hunts in the trenches to supplement them. During these weeks, Johnston built up a 31,000-man army near Jackson and urged Pemberton to break out of Vicksburg and join him. Pemberton refused, however, choosing to obey Davis's orders to hold the city, and Johnston took no steps to rescue him. The only Confederate attempt to raise the siege was a small, unsuccessful Confederate attack against a Union supply base at **Milliken's Bend** in early June. As a precaution, Grant did use part of his army to construct defensive works behind him facing east in case Johnston did move against Vicksburg.

The strain of constant combat and supply shortages finally broke many of the Confederates' spirit. In early July, Pemberton received an anonymous note from his soldiers outlining the harsh conditions and stating that surrender was preferable to starvation. With the situation hopeless, he entered negotiations with Grant on the afternoon of July 3 and surrendered the city and its garrison on July 4, 1863. Pemberton was criticized for surrendering on Independence Day, but he believed he would receive better terms on that day. The only conditions he won, however, were to allow his men to be **paroled** and the officers to retain their side arms and mounts. Most of the Confederate **prisoners** soon were **exchanged** and rejoined the war, but many **deserted** and went home.

Johnston moved out of Jackson on July 1 and was marching for Vicksburg to make a diversionary attack on July 7 so Pemberton could escape. He reached the Big Black River but learned of the surrender on July 5. Sherman then marched east to confront Johnston, forced him back from the river, and carried out the successful siege of Jackson. The Confederate garrison at Port Hudson surrendered to Banks on July 9, thus finally giving the Union complete control of the Mississippi River and splitting the Confederacy in two.

In addition to capturing 29,495 prisoners at Vicksburg, Grant also seized 172 cannons, 60,000 **stands of arms**, and more than 2 million rounds of ammunition. Earlier in the campaign, the Confederates lost another 88 cannons and suffered an additional 8,000 casualties, while Grant lost a total of about 10,000 men (4,835 during the siege). The capture of Vicksburg confirmed Grant as the most successful Union general and led to his appointment as commander of the **Military Division of the Mississippi** in October. The campaign had been brilliant and showed how a smaller army could defeat a larger one through audacity and swift marching. It may also have been the turning point of the war, since the capitulation occurred on the same day **Robert E. Lee** began his retreat from **Gettysburg, Pennsylvania**. The people of Vicksburg were so humiliated at the surrender that they refused to celebrate Independence Day until after World War II.

VICKSBURG, MISSISSIPPI, CAMPAIGN, GRANT'S OVERLAND OR FIRST (NOVEMBER 26, 1862–JANUARY 2, 1863).

After Maj. Gen. U. S. **Grant** was appointed commander of the **Department of the Tennessee** on October 25, 1862, he began his campaign to capture the Confederate stronghold of **Vicksburg, Mississippi**. Grant's plan was threatened by Maj. Gen. **John A. McClernand**, a political general who had been given permission by **Abraham Lincoln** to raise an **army** to attack Vicksburg by river from Memphis, Tennessee. Moving quickly, Grant commandeered McClernand's troops before he arrived in Memphis, and in November 1862 split his **Army of the Tennessee** in two. On November 26, he led 40,000 men from Grand Junction, Tennessee, south along the Mississippi Central Railroad into northern **Mississippi** to draw Lt. Gen. **John C. Pemberton's** Confederates away from Vicksburg. Major General **William T. Sherman** was to take the other 32,000 men and move down the Mississippi River on transports to enter the Yazoo River above Vicksburg and attack the city's northern defenses. If all went well, most of the Confederates by then would be facing Grant, and Sherman could capture the city.

Grant moved through Holly Springs and Oxford, Mississippi, without trouble but was stopped by Confederate cavalry at **Coffeeville** on December 5. He then advanced toward Pemberton, who was positioned behind the Yalobusha River to protect the approaches to Grenada. On December 11, Confederate cavalry under **Nathan Bedford Forrest** raided the **railroads** that carried Grant's supplies through **Tennessee**, and on December 20, Maj. Gen. **Earl Van Dorn** destroyed his supply base at **Holly Springs**. With his supply line disrupted, Grant withdrew toward Memphis. During this retreat, he lived off the land and was surprised how many supplies came from the area. This lesson was not forgotten when he later left the Mississippi River and marched inland to Jackson, Mississippi, during the **Vicksburg Campaign**.

Sherman left Memphis the day Van Dorn attacked Holly Springs and moved toward Vicksburg with seven gunboats and 59 transports. When the **U.S. Navy** began clearing the Yazoo River of Confederate **torpedoes**, the USS *Cairo* was sunk by the **"infernal machines."** Sherman landed his troops on December 26–27, but by that time, Pemberton had sent troops from Grenada back to Vicksburg. When Sherman attacked at **Chickasaw Bayou** on December 29, he suffered a bloody repulse, losing 1,776 men to the Confederates' 207 casualties. He did not try again and reboarded his ships on January 1, 1863, to depart the next day. His curt message on the expedition read, "I reached Vicksburg at the time appointed, landed, assaulted and failed" (Kennedy, ed., *The Civil War Battlefield Guide*, 156).

When Sherman returned to Memphis, his command was attached to McClernand's **Army of the Mississippi** for the attack on Arkansas Post. After that successful operation, Grant assumed command of all the Union forces on the Mississippi River and began the Vicksburg Campaign in January 1863.

VIDETTE. A vidette was the name given to a cavalry, or mounted, **picket** or sentry.

VIELE, EGBERT LUDOVICUS (1825–1902) USA. A native of **New York**, Viele (VEE-lay) entered **West Point** after graduating from Albany Academy. Graduating in 1847, he was assigned to the infantry and performed garrison duty in Mexico City after the **Mexican War**. After some frontier duty, Viele resigned his 1st lieutenant's commission in 1853 to become a civil engineer. He was appointed **New Jersey's** topographical engineer in 1854 and later became chief engineer of New York City's Central Park. Viele was appointed chief engineer of Brooklyn's Prospect Park in 1860 and was serving in that position when the Civil War began. He published a handbook for military service in 1861 that was widely used by Union and Confederate engineering officers during the war.

Viele entered Union service in April 1861 as a captain of **engineers** with the 7th New York Militia. After serving several months in the defenses of **Washington, D.C.**, he was appointed brigadier general of volunteers in August and was given command of a **brigade** that was involved in the reduction of **Fort Pulaski, Georgia**, in April 1862. Viele was highly praised for his service during the operation and afterward was sent to **Norfolk, Virginia**, where he was appointed military governor in July. In October 1863, he was sent to recruit in **Ohio**, but he resigned his commission that month to resume his engineering career.

Viele returned to New York City and became a famous engineer there. He served as a City Park commissioner from 1883 to 1884, was elected to the **U.S. Congress** as a **Democrat** in 1884, and published treatises on the topography of Manhattan Island that were used in planning the skyscrapers that later dotted the island.

VILLARD, HENRY (1835–1900) USA. A native of Bavaria, Villard changed his name from Ferdinand Heinrich Gustav Hilgard to Henry Villard and immigrated to the United States in 1853 to escape his father's threat to put him in the military. Settling in **Illinois**, he learned English and became a correspondent for a **New York** German-language newspaper in 1858. After covering the **Lincoln-Douglas Debates**, Villard worked for several newspapers over the next few years, reporting on the Pike's Peak gold rush and the **election of 1860**.

When the Civil War began, Villard was working for the New York *Herald* and became one of its **Washington, D.C.**, correspondents and perhaps the conflict's greatest **war correspondent**. He earned some fame by establishing his own courier service during the **Baltimore Riot** and maintaining news contact with the North after the riot disrupted communications to Washington. Villard then joined **Irvin McDowell's army** and reported on the **Battles of Blackburn's Ford** and **First Manassas**, filing the Union's first story on the latter. Heading west, he covered Union operations in **Kentucky** and **Tennessee** for the Cincinnati *Commercial* and filed the story that led to rumors that **William T. Sherman** was insane. Villard arrived on the **Shiloh** battlefield late on the first day of fighting but still filed a story on the battle.

After Shiloh, Villard was hired by the **New York *Tribune*** and became its western war correspondent. After covering the **Army of the Ohio** during the **Kentucky Campaign** and the murder of Maj. Gen. **William Nelson**, he returned east and became the paper's main correspondent with the **Army of the Potomac**. Over the next three years, Villard perhaps covered more of the war than any other correspondent, witnessing and writing articles on the **Battles of Fredericksburg**, **Port Royal**, **Charleston**, **Chickamauga**, and **Chattanooga**. His story on the Fredericksburg defeat was so frank and shocking that the paper delayed publishing it until it had confirmed the details. Villard even had a private meeting with **Abraham Lincoln** to present him a true picture of the battle. After Chattanooga, he left the *Tribune* and began the Independent News Room service with fellow reporter **Adams S. Hill**. Villard was detained for two days in 1864 by Union officials who suspected him of being involved in the **Gold Hoax** but was released and resumed his war coverage.

After the war, Villard returned to the *Tribune*. He covered both the 1866 Austro-Prussian War and the 1870 Franco-Prussian War (the latter as an independent reporter). Villard then quit the newspaper business and became involved in railroading. Becoming a wealthy man, he served as president of the Northern Pacific Railroad, became the primary owner of the New York *Evening Post*, and a major stockholder in the Edison General Electric Company. Villard's wife was the daughter of **abolitionist William Lloyd Garrison**.

VILLEPIGUE, JOHN BORDENAVE (1830–1862) CSA. A native of **South Carolina**, Villepigue (VIL-ih-PIG) graduated from **West Point** in

1854 and was assigned to the dragoons. Sent to the frontier, he served against the Sioux **Indians**, in the **Utah Expedition**, and in **Pennsylvania** before resigning his 1st lieutenant's commission in March 1861.

Villepigue entered Confederate service as a captain of **artillery** soon after his resignation from the **U.S. Army**. Sent to **Pensacola, Florida**, he was appointed lieutenant colonel of the 1st Georgia Battalion and helped garrison Fort McRee. During the Union bombardment of Pensacola's fortifications in November, Villepigue was wounded in the arm by a shell fragment. **Braxton Bragg** highly praised his service during the bombardment and made him his chief of **engineers** and artillery. In January 1862, the 1st Georgia Battalion was reorganized as the 36th Georgia, and Villepigue was appointed its colonel. He then briefly commanded Pensacola before transferring to Mobile, Alabama, where he commanded the city's defenses before joining Bragg at Corinth, Mississippi.

In March 1862, Villepigue was promoted to brigadier general and was put in command of **Fort Pillow, Tennessee**. He held the fort until June, when pressure from Union gunboats forced him to destroy it and withdraw. Villepigue then was sent to northern **Mississippi** to guard the **railroad** depot at Grenada. In September, his command was organized into a **brigade** and was assigned to **Mansfield Lovell's division**. Villepigue fought at **Corinth** the following month and was praised for his role in the attack and his service in the rear guard during the withdrawal. By then, he was one of Bragg's favorite officers and had been marked for higher command. Villepigue took charge of the Port Hudson, Louisiana, area after the Battle of Corinth, but he became ill with an unidentified fever and died on November 9.

VINCENT, STRONG (1837–1863) USA. A native of **Pennsylvania**, Vincent graduated from Harvard University in 1859 and became a lawyer. He entered Union service in April 1861 as a 1st lieutenant in a 90-day state militia **regiment**. After the unit was disbanded, Vincent enlisted for three years and was appointed lieutenant colonel of the 83rd Pennsylvania in September. Becoming part of the **Army of the Potomac**, the regiment fought at **Yorktown** during the **Peninsula Campaign** before Vincent became ill with malaria. The regiment's commander was killed at **Gaines' Mill** in June 1862, and Vincent was promoted to replace him, but he apparently did not rejoin the regiment until shortly before **Fredericksburg**. He saw fierce combat there but was only lightly engaged at **Chancellorsville**.

In June 1863, Vincent was given a **brigade** command in **James Barnes's division** of the V Corps. At **Gettysburg**, **Gouverneur K. War-**

ren rushed the brigade to the top of Little Round Top on the battle's second day to defend the high ground against **James Longstreet's** attacking Confederates. While Col. **Joshua Lawrence Chamberlain** made his famous stand on the brigade's left, Vincent was mortally wounded while trying to rally the men on the right. His last words reportedly were, "Don't yield an inch!" (Foote, *The Civil War,* vol. 2, 504). Vincent was appointed brigadier general the next day, but he died on July 7.

VIRGINIA. Located in the upper South, Virginia was more moderate than some other slave states and did not secede until April 17, 1861. Most of the people in the mountainous western region actually opposed **secession** and formed the loyal state of **West Virginia** during the Civil War.

Virginia was perhaps the most important Confederate state. It had the largest population (1,105,453 in 1860); the most **railroads**, with 1,771 miles of track; and, with Richmond's **Tredegar Iron Works**, the largest **industrial** base (Virginia's industrial capacity was almost equal to that of the original seven Confederate states combined). It also produced one-third of the Confederacy's nonagricultural products, and the rich **Shenandoah Valley** provided the Confederate **Army of Northern Virginia** with much of its food, grain, and horses. Under war governors **John Letcher** and **William Smith**, Virginia provided 170,000 men to the Confederacy in 73 infantry, 49 cavalry, and 104 **artillery** units. Over one-fourth of the soldiers in the Army of Northern Virginia hailed from the state, as did one-fourth of all Confederate generals. These generals included **Robert E. Lee**, **Stonewall Jackson**, **Joseph E. Johnston**, **Jubal A. Early**, **J. E. B. Stuart**, and **A. P. Hill** (as well as **George H. Thomas**, **Winfield Scott**, and 15 other generals who served the Union). Confederate political leaders **Robert M. T. Hunter**, **George W. Randolph**, and **James A. Seddon** also were Virginians.

Virginia was devastated by some of the war's largest campaigns as the Union **Army of the Potomac** tried to capture the Confederate capital of **Richmond**. These included **First** and **Second Manassas**, the **Peninsula**, **Seven Days**, **Fredericksburg**, **Chancellorsville**, **Gettysburg**, **Bristoe Station**, **Mine Run**, **Overland**, **Petersburg**, and **Appomattox**. The Shenandoah Valley also was the scene of much fighting in **Stonewall Jackson's**, **David Hunter's**, and **Philip Sheridan's Shenandoah Valley Campaigns**.

VIRGINIA, **CSS.** When Confederate forces were poised to seize **Norfolk, Virginia**, in April 1861, the Union destroyed the Norfolk Navy Yard and burned the USS *Merrimac* to prevent its capture. After the Confederates occupied the navy yard, Secretary of the Navy **Stephen Mallory** decided to use the *Merrimac*'s hulk to build the first of many **ironclads** with which to break the Union **blockade**. The Confederates raised the ship and in July began refitting it as an ironclad named the CSS *Virginia*. Following plans by **John M. Brooke** and **John L. Porter**, the ship was finished in February 1862. It was 262 feet long and 51 feet wide, had a draft of 22 feet, carried a cast-iron ram on its bow, and was protected by a two-foot-thick sheeting of wood, covered with four inches of iron plating. The sides and ends of the vessel also were slanted at 35 degrees to deflect enemy shells. The *Virginia* was armed with six 9-inch **Dahlgrens**, two 6.4-inch **Brooke cannons**, and two 7-inch Brooke cannons and carried a crew of 320 officers and men.

The *Virginia* was put under the command of Capt. **Franklin Buchanan**, with Lt. **Catesby ap Roger Jones** serving as first officer. On March 8, 1862, Buchanan took the *Virginia* on its first sortie and engaged the enemy at **Hampton Roads**. He rammed and sank the USS *Cumberland,* set afire the USS *Congress* with **hot shot**, and forced the USS *Minnesota* to run aground trying to escape. Buchanan was wounded during the battle, and Jones took command for the next day's fight. On March 9, the *Virginia* engaged the **USS *Monitor*** in what became the first clash between ironclads. The *Virginia* outgunned the smaller vessel, but its engines were inadequate for its bulk, and Jones could not match the maneuverability of the *Monitor.* Both vessels broke off the fight at about the same time.

After the battle, Capt. **Josiah Tattnall** took command of the *Virginia*, but his tenure was short lived. When Norfolk was abandoned by the Confederates during the **Peninsula Campaign**, the *Virginia* was burned on May 11, 1862, because its deep draft prevented it from being taken up the James River to safety. After the war, parts of the vessel were salvaged on occasion, and pieces of it are now in the Museum of the Confederacy in **Richmond, Virginia**, and other repositories.

VIRGINIA MILITARY INSTITUTE (VMI). Founded in 1839 at Lexington, **Virginia**, the Virginia Military Institute (or VMI) was patterned after a French military academy and **West Point** and ranked only behind West Point as the nation's leading military school. The curriculum stressed mathematics and engineering to prepare students for civilian life, but it also had a heavy dose of **artillery** and infantry drill and other military skills. VMI was not a pure military school, however, because the curriculum did not stress military **tactics** or **strategy**.

The institute provided the Confederacy with 17 generals and 1,764 other officers and men (which was 94 percent of the students and former students alive during the war). Of these, 259 died in Confederate service. No other school provided so many field officers to the **army** that became known as the **Army of Northern Virginia**; by the end of 1861, nearly one-third of its **regiments** were commanded by VMI men. **Thomas J. Jackson**, who was a professor at VMI when Virginia seceded, was the most famous Confederate officer associated with the institute. He led most of the cadets off to war in 1861 to serve as drill instructors to train other recruits. Jackson and many of his cadets then fought at **First Manassas**, where he and his **brigade** earned the nickname "Stonewall." Other Confederate officers hailing from VMI were **Robert Rodes, Raleigh Colston, Samuel Garland**, and **James H. Lane**.

In May 1864, 257 cadets joined **John C. Breckinridge's army** at **New Market, Virginia**, and bravely charged across an open field to help defeat the enemy. During the battle, 10 cadets were killed or mortally wounded, and 45 were wounded. A ceremony is held every year at VMI to honor these boy heroes. When **David Hunter's Shenandoah Valley Campaign** ravaged the Valley later that summer, his men burned the institute on June 12. VMI was reopened in October 1865, and in 1916 it received $100,000 from the federal government to settle a claim it filed over Hunter's destruction. Today, VMI remains one of the country's most prestigious military schools.

VIVANDIÉRE. Both sides in the Civil War had women who went off to war to serve as unofficial members of **regiments**. First used by European armies, a vivandière (vee-vahn-DYAIR) washed clothes, nursed the soldiers, and performed other needed duties. These women differed from common **camp followers** in that they were accepted as members of the unit, were not prostitutes, and often had their own distinctive **uniforms**. Among the vivandières were **Kady Brownell, Bridget Divers**, Anna Etheridge and **Marie Tebe**.

VIZETELLY, FRANK (1830–1883) USA. A native of Great Britain, Vizetelly worked as a reporter and draftsman for London's *Pictorial Times* before founding *Le Monde Illustre* with his brother in 1857. After covering the 1859 Austria and Sardinia-Piedmont War and Giuseppe Garibaldi's Italian campaigns, he came to the United States in May 1861 and covered the Civil War for the *Illustrated London News*. Vizetelly reported on or sketched **First Manassas** and the **Battle of Memphis** before slipping through the lines and witnessing the **Battle of Fredericksburg** in the presence of **Robert E. Lee** and **James Longstreet**. Returning to the Union, he also covered **Samuel Du Pont's** attack on

Charleston, South Carolina; the **Vicksburg Campaign**; and operations around **Wilmington, North Carolina**. In 1863, Vizetelly again crossed the lines and accompanied **J. E. B. Stuart** in **Virginia**. After a brief trip to Great Britain, he returned to the Confederacy and covered **Philip Sheridan's 1864 Shenandoah Valley Campaign** and **Fort Fisher** before accompanying **Jefferson Davis** and the Confederate government as it fled **Richmond, Virginia**, in April 1865.

Vizetelly was one of the great **war correspondents** and illustrators, but he returned to Great Britain after the Confederate **surrenders**. He continued to work as a war correspondent in Europe and disappeared during an 1883 massacre of British troops in the Sudan. It is assumed Vizetelly was killed, but his body was never found. Of the many drawings he made during the Civil War, only a few survive today at Harvard University. Most of them were destroyed during the World War II bombing of London.

VOGDES, ISRAEL (1816–1889) USA. A native of **Pennsylvania**, Vogdes (VAH-jis) graduated from **West Point** in 1837 and taught mathematics at the academy for 12 years before serving with the **artillery** in the **Seminole Wars**. Afterward, he served at **Charleston, South Carolina**, and **Fort Monroe, Virginia**.

Vogdes was a captain of artillery when the Civil War began and was sent with the 1st U.S. Artillery to reinforce **Fort Pickens, Florida**. There he was promoted to major in May 1861. Vogdes helped defend Fort Pickens, but he was captured in October when **Braxton Bragg's** Confederates attacked **Santa Rosa Island**. After being **exchanged** in August 1862, he was promoted to brigadier general of volunteers in November. Sent to **Charleston**, Vogdes spent more than a year serving with the Union forces besieging the city. During that time, he was promoted to colonel of regulars, held various **brigade** commands, and helped erect many of the Union artillery batteries in the area. After briefly commanding a **division** in **Florida** in early 1864, Vogdes was sent to **Virginia**, where he took command of the defenses of **Norfolk** and Portsmouth in May 1864. He remained there until war's end.

After being **brevetted** brigadier general of regulars for his war service, Vogdes was mustered out of the volunteers in January 1866. He remained in the regular **army** and served on various garrison duty until he retired in 1881.

VOLTIGEUR. Like **Zouaves**, a Voltigeur (vol-ti-ZHER) was popular with both Union and Confederate troops during the heady recruiting days of

1861. A Voltigeur was the French light infantryman adopted by the French **army** in 1805 to serve as **skirmishers**. Shorter than the average soldier, the Voltigeurs were seen as elite troops who led the main battle line into action. A number of Civil War units adopted the name Voltigeurs but were used as regular infantry.

VON BORCKE, JOHANN AUGUST HEINRICH HEROS (1836–1895) CSA. A native of Prussia and a member of a prominent family, von Borcke was the son of a Prussian officer and served as a lieutenant in the Prussian dragoons. In the spring of 1862, he took a leave of absence from the dragoons and sailed to **Charleston, South Carolina**, aboard a **blockade runner** to offer his services to the Confederacy. With a letter of introduction from the Prussian consul, von Borcke was commissioned a 2nd lieutenant and joined **J. E. B. Stuart's** staff.

Von Borcke became a well-known figure in the **Army of Northern Virginia** and was a favorite of Stuart's. Besides his Prussian origins, he also was notable for carrying what was reported to be the largest sword in the **army**. Promoted to major in August 1862, von Borcke fought with Stuart in all of the major battles from **Second Manassas** to **Brandy Station**. After being badly wounded in the neck during a June 1863 engagement at **Middleburg, Virginia**, he was unable to return to the field. Voted the **Thanks of Congress**, von Borcke was promoted to lieutenant colonel and was sent on a diplomatic mission to Europe. He returned in time to visit Stuart as he lay in bed dying after being wounded at **Yellow Tavern**.

Von Borcke was promoted to colonel in December 1864, returned to Europe on a diplomatic mission to Great Britain, and was there when the war ended. Returning to Prussia, he wrote a classic memoir of the war in 1866 entitled *Memoirs of the Confederate War for Independence*. After serving on Prince Frederick Charles's staff in the Franco-Prussian War, von Borcke returned to the United States in 1884 for a visit to the battlefields.

VON STEINWEHR, BARON ADOLPH WILHELM AUGUST FRIEDRICH (1822–1877) USA. A native of the Duchy of Brunswick, von Steinwehr was the son and grandson of army officers. After attending a local military school, he was appointed a lieutenant in the duchy's army but took a leave of absence in 1847 to come to the United States to serve in the **Mexican War**. Von Steinwehr was unsuccessful in entering the service, but he did win appointment to a coastal survey and married an **Alabama** woman while in Mobile. He returned to Europe in 1849 but then immigrated to the United States in 1854 and settled in **Connecticut**.

When the Civil War began, von Steinwehr entered Union service in June 1861 as colonel of the 29th New York. After serving at **First Manassas**, but not seeing any combat, he was promoted to brigadier general of volunteers in October, and in December was given a **brigade** command in **Louis Blenker's division** of the **Army of the Potomac**. Von Steinwehr served in **Stonewall Jackson's 1862 Shenandoah Valley Campaign** and in June took command of the division. He saw heavy fighting at **Second Manassas** but remained in the defenses of **Washington, D.C.**, during the **Antietam Campaign**. Assigned to the **Army of the Potomac's** XI Corps, the division was routed at **Chancellorsville**, although von Steinwehr was one of the **corps'** few officers who took the precaution of building defensive earthworks. He also fought at **Gettysburg**, where one of his brigades was caught up in the first day's rout.

In the autumn of 1863, von Steinwehr was sent west with the corps and led his division in the **Chattanooga Campaign**. When the XI and XII Corps were consolidated into the **Army of the Cumberland's** XX Corps prior to the **Atlanta Campaign**, he was demoted to a brigade command, while a junior officer was given a division. Insulted, von Steinwehr refused the command and apparently never again held a field position during the war. He resigned his commission in July 1865.

After the war, von Steinwehr became a noted geographer and cartographer. He taught at Yale University, worked for the federal government, and published several works.

– W –

WACHUSETT, USS. This Union warship was constructed at **Massachusetts's** Boston Navy Yard and entered service in March 1862. A wooden steamer, it was 201 feet long, displaced 1,032 tons, had both sails and steam engines, and was armed with two 11-inch **Dahlgrens**, two 30-pounder **Parrott rifles**, and one 20-pounder Parrott rifle. First commanded by Cmdr. William Smith, the *Wachusett* saw service in the **Peninsula Campaign** and then captured two **blockade runners** while searching for the **CSS *Alabama*** and *Florida*. Commander Napoleon Collins assumed command of the *Wachusett* in 1864 and continued to pursue the *Florida*. Discovering the raider at Bahia, Brazil, he assured local authorities he would not violate Brazil's neutrality. On the night of October 7, however, Collins rammed the *Florida*, captured it, and towed the vessel away. Although seen as a hero by many Northerners, he created an international incident and was replaced in command by Cmdr. Robert Townsend. Under Townsend, the vessel sailed to the Pacific and was in pursuit of the **CSS** *Shenandoah* when the war ended. The *Wachusett* then became part of the East India Squadron until it was decommissioned and sold for scrap in 1887.

WADDELL, JAMES IREDELL (1824–1886) CSA. A native of **North Carolina**, Waddell walked with a permanent limp after being wounded in the leg in a duel while a cadet at the **U.S. Naval Academy**. After graduating in 1847, he served with the East India Squadron and rose to the rank of lieutenant.

When the Civil War began, Waddell tendered his resignation, but the navy took no action on it until he married into a secessionist family in December 1861. Dismissed from the service, Waddell joined the Confederacy in March 1862 as a navy lieutenant. His first assignment was to the ram CSS *Mississippi*, then being constructed in **New Orleans, Louisiana**. This vessel was destroyed at the docks, however, when New Orleans was captured that spring. Waddell then was transferred east, where he commanded the naval batteries at **Drewry's Bluff, Virginia**, and served at **Charleston, South Carolina**.

In March 1863, Waddell was sent to Europe to assume command of one of the **Laird rams** being constructed in Great Britain. These ships never entered Confederate service, however, and it was not until September 1864 that he received a vessel. Promoted to lieutenant commander, Waddell was given the *Sea King*, which was commissioned the **CSS** *Shenandoah* in October. Sailing by way of Australia, he entered the Bering Sea and Arctic Ocean and devastated the Union whaling fleet in the spring and early summer of 1865, even destroying some ships after the war had ended. In August, Waddell learned from the crew of a British vessel that the war was over. Fearing he would be considered an outlaw by Union authorities, he disguised the *Shenandoah* and sailed it nonstop to Great Britain, where he surrendered it in November 1865. After accounting for over 30 Union vessels, Waddell was the last Confederate to surrender.

Waddell finally returned to the United States and captained a ship for the Pacific Mail Company. After surviving a shipwreck off Mexico in 1877, he became commander of the **Maryland** State Fishery Force.

WADE, BENJAMIN FRANKLIN (1800–1878) USA. A native of **Massachusetts,** Wade grew up in relative poverty before moving to **Ohio** with his family in 1821. There he worked as a farmer, cattleman, laborer, and schoolteacher before becoming a lawyer. An **abolitionist**, Wade entered politics and served as his county's prosecutor, a state senator, and circuit judge. Elected to the U.S. Senate as a **Whig** in 1851, he switched to the **Republican Party** and was reelected twice. In the Senate, Wade championed the antislavery cause and once accepted a challenge from a Southerner, but his opponent backed down when Wade chose as weapons squirrel rifles at 20 steps. From this incident, Wade earned the nickname "Bluff Ben."

During the Civil War, Wade strongly supported the Union war effort and as a leading **Radical Republican** called for its vigorous prosecution. He also was one of the leading critics of Maj. Gen. **George B. McClellan** and his supporters. Wade helped create, and served as chairman of, the **Committee on the Conduct of the War** and used his position to attack inefficiency in the **army** and those officers he deemed incompetent or lacking in patriotism. He supported the **confiscation acts** and the **Emancipation Proclamation** but opposed **Abraham Lincoln's Reconstruction** policy, which he believed was too lenient. In the spring of 1864, Wade joined fellow Radical **Henry W. Davis** in writing the **Wade-Davis Bill**, a harsh Reconstruction policy that was pocket vetoed by Lincoln. Angered by this action, the two then issued the Wade-Davis Manifesto, in which they publicly denounced Lincoln for his veto and lenient policies.

After the war, Wade opposed President **Andrew Johnson's** moderate Reconstruction policy and voted to convict in the impeachment trial. After unsuccessfully seeking the 1868 Republican vice presidential nomination, he was defeated for reelection to the Senate that same year. Wade retired from politics in 1869 and resumed his Ohio law practice. He became a prosperous **railroad** attorney and in 1871 served on a committee that recommended the annexation of Santo Domingo.

WADE-DAVIS BILL. After **Abraham Lincoln** announced his moderate **Ten Percent Plan** for **Reconstruction** in December 1863, **Radical Republicans** Sen. **Benjamin F. Wade** and Repr. **Henry W. Davis** countered with a harsh plan known as the Wade-Davis Bill. This bill called for the Southern states to be provided with presidentially appointed provisionary governors after their defeat. White male citizens were required to sign an **oath of allegiance** swearing to their past loyalty to the Union, and when a majority of voters had done so, the state could hold a constitutional convention to reform its government. Former Confederate soldiers and politicians could not participate in the process or hold any state office. When the state adopted a constitution that abolished **slavery**, repudiated the Confederate debt, and barred former Confederates from ever holding significant state positions, the state's delegation would be readmitted to Congress.

Lincoln supported parts of the bill but believed overall it was too harsh. Thus, when the Wade-Davis Bill was passed on July 2, 1864, he pocket vetoed it. Wade and Davis issued a manifesto condemning the action, but the Radical Republicans were denied control of Reconstruction until after Lincoln's death. The radical Military Reconstruction Act of 1867 implemented much of the Wade-Davis goals.

WADE, MELANCTHON SMITH (1802–1868) USA. A native of **Ohio**, Wade was a retired merchant and brigadier general in the state militia when the Civil War began. He first helped recruit troops and then was appointed brigadier general of volunteers in October 1861. Wade was put in command of Ohio's Camp Dennison, the state's main recruiting depot, and from there, helped send at least 23 **regiments** to the war. Because of his advanced age and poor health, however, he resigned his commission in March 1862 and became active in fruit horticulture.

WADSWORTH, JAMES SAMUEL (1807–1864) USA. A native of **New York** and the son of a wealthy landowner, Wadsworth attended Harvard University and became a lawyer, although he never practiced his profession. He first entered politics as a **Democrat** but then helped form the **Free-Soil Party** in New York before joining the **Republican Party** in 1856.

During the **secession** crisis, Wadsworth attended the **Washington Peace Conference** and joined the Union cause when war began. After serving as **Irvin McDowell's** volunteer aide at **First Manassas**, he received an appointment as brigadier general of volunteers in August 1861 and took command of a **brigade** in McDowell's **division** of the **Army of the Potomac**. Wadsworth was put in command of the Military District of Washington in March 1862 and ran unsuccessfully for New York governor later that year. In December, he was given a division command in the Army of the Potomac's I Corps even though he had no field experience. His division saw little combat at **Chancellorsville**, but it was heavily engaged at **Gettysburg** on the first day. Wadsworth had performed well enough in battle to win command of a V Corps division when the **army** was reorganized in the spring of 1864. On the second day of fighting in the **Wilderness**, he was shot in the head while trying to repel an enemy attack. Picked up by the Confederates, Wadsworth was taken to a field hospital, but he died two days later without ever regaining consciousness. His body was returned to the Federals, and he was posthumously appointed major general of volunteers.

WAGNER, GEORGE DAY (1829–1869) USA. A native of **Ohio**, as a child, Wagner moved to **Indiana** with his parents. After growing up on a farm, he was elected to the state legislature in 1856 as a **Republican**. In 1858, Wagner was elected to the state senate and later campaigned for **Abraham Lincoln** in the **election of 1860.**

Wagner entered Union service in June 1861 as colonel of the 15th Indiana. After brief service in western **Virginia**, he was given a **brigade** command in **Thomas J. Wood's division** of the **Army of the Ohio** in February 1862. Wagner fought well at **Shiloh** and **Perryville** before taking a brigade command in the **Army of the Cumberland's** XIV Corps in November. With it, he engaged in some of the heaviest combat at the Round Forest during the **Battle of Stones River.**

In February 1863, Wagner was given a division command in the XXI Corps, and he was promoted to brigadier general of volunteers in April. Returning to a brigade command in the IV Corps in October, he was put in charge of the garrison at **Chattanooga, Tennessee**, and thus missed **Chickamauga**. At **Missionary Ridge**, however, Wagner's brigade was part of **Philip Sheridan's** division, and it suffered heavy casualties while successfully storming the Confederate position. After fighting through the **Atlanta Campaign** with the IX Corps' 2nd Division, Wagner was sent to **Tennessee** for the **Franklin and Nashville Campaign**. At Franklin, he commanded a division in **John Schofield's** IV Corps. Two of Wagner's brigades were positioned a half-mile beyond the main line with orders to fall back when the Confederates advanced. Instead, he stayed to fight and was overrun by the enemy. When Wagner finally did retreat, the Confederates followed so closely that the main Union line could not fire without hitting his men. As a result, the enemy reached the main line and almost broke it. For his role in the affair, Wagner was relieved of command two days later. In early December, he requested and received permission to retire to Indiana to care for his sick wife until receiving further orders. Wagner finally was put in charge of the District of St. Louis in April 1865, but by that time, the war essentially was over.

After being discharged from the service in August 1865, Wagner practiced law in Indiana and served as president of the state agricultural society.

WALCUTT, CHARLES CARROLL (1838–1898) USA. A native of **Ohio**, Walcutt graduated from the Kentucky Military Institute in 1858 and became a surveyor. When the Civil War began, he raised a **company** of Ohio volunteers, but the state had already filled its quota of recruits and did not accept it. Walcutt finally entered state service in June 1861 as a major and was mustered into Union service in October as major of the 46th Ohio.

After being promoted to lieutenant colonel in January 1862, Walcutt fought at **Shiloh** and was wounded in the shoulder. He then participated in the **siege of Corinth, Mississippi**, and was promoted to colonel in October. In January 1863, Walcutt was given temporary command of a **brigade** in the **Army of the Tennessee's** XVI Corps, but he was returned to his **regiment** in March. In June, he joined the **army** during the **Vicksburg Campaign** and led his regiment during the siege of **Vicksburg, Mississippi**. After participating in the siege of **Jackson, Mississippi**, that summer, Walcutt reinforced Chattanooga, Tennessee. There he participated in the **Chattanooga Campaign** as a temporary brigade commander in the XV Corps.

Walcutt led his brigade during the **Atlanta Campaign** and was promoted to brigadier general of volunteers in July 1864. At the **Battle of Atlanta**, he helped save **Francis P. Blair's** XVII Corps from destruction by refusing to obey an order to withdraw. Walcutt then participated in the **March to the Sea** and was wounded in the leg at **Griswoldville**. His actions during the battle earned him the **brevet** rank of major general of volunteers, but he was unable to return to duty until March 1865. During the latter part of the **Carolinas Campaign**, Walcutt was given a **division** command in the **Army of the Cumberland's** XIV Corps.

Walcutt was mustered out of volunteer service in January 1866 but remained in the regular army as lieutenant colonel of the 10th U.S. Cavalry, one of the regiments of **black troops** known as the Buffalo Soldiers. Resigning his commission the next year, he worked as a prison warden, tax official, and mayor of Columbus, Ohio.

WALKE, HENRY (1827–1896) USA. A native of **Virginia**, Walke entered the **U.S. Navy** as a midshipman in 1827 and spent his antebellum career cruising around the world and fighting in the **Mexican War**. In 1861, he was a lieutenant and commanded a supply ship at **Pensacola, Florida**. When secessionists captured the Navy Yard there, Walke evacuated the personnel to New York City aboard his vessel. Instead of being praised, a court-martial convicted him of leaving his post without permission, but he was only reprimanded.

Walke was promoted to commander and in late 1861 was given command of the **USS** *Tyler*, one of the Mississippi river gunboats in **Andrew H. Foote's** fleet. After covering the Union withdrawal at **Belmont** in late 1861, he took command of the **USS** *Carondelet* in February 1862 and participated in the capture of **Forts Henry and Donelson**. Steaming to the Mississippi River, Walke played a key role in the capture of **Island No. 10** in April. He was promoted to captain in July and in February 1863 took command of the USS *Lafayette*. After participating in the **Vicksburg Campaign**, Walke was given the USS *Sacramento* in June 1864 and accompanied the USS *Niagara* in search of Confederate **commerce raiders** in the Atlantic. Discovering the **CSS *Rappahannock*** at Calais, France, he spent the next 15 months blockading it there.

Walke remained in the navy after the war and was promoted to rear admiral in 1870. He retired the following year.

WALKER, HENRY HARRISON (1832–1912) CSA. A native of **Virginia**, Walker graduated near the bottom of his 1843 **West Point** class. Assigned to the infantry, he served in **Kentucky, New Mexico**, and **"Bleeding Kansas"** (as the governor's aide), before being transferred to **California**.

When the Civil War began, Walker resigned his 1st lieutenant's commission in May 1861 and entered Confederate service as a captain of infantry. He soon joined Brig. Gen. **Theophilus H. Holmes's** staff but in December was appointed lieutenant colonel of the 40th Virginia. For reasons unknown, Walker briefly commanded the 5th Alabama Battalion in April 1862, but he rejoined his Virginia **regiment** in time to fight with the **Army of Northern Virginia** in the **Seven Days Campaign** as part of **Charles W. Field's brigade**. Walker was wounded twice at **Gaines' Mill** and served in the defenses of **Richmond, Virginia**, until he recuperated.

In the summer of 1863, Walker was appointed permanent commander of his brigade after Field was wounded. The popular John M. Brockenbrough had commanded it temporarily, and Walker's appointment caused ill will within the unit. Walker was promoted to brigadier general in June, and Brockenbrough resigned. Nonetheless, the brigade soon came to respect its new commander. **James J. Archer's** brigade was joined with Walker's after **Gettysburg**, and Walker led the consolidated command through the **Bristoe Station** and **Mine Run Campaigns**. As a separate unit again, the brigade became part of **Henry Heth's division** and fought well at the **Wilderness**. In a clash near the Po River during the **Battle of Spotsylvania**, Walker's foot was shattered and had to be amputated. Unable to retake the field, he served out the remainder of the war on court-martial duty in Richmond, guarding **railroads**, and in command of Danville, Virginia.

After the war, Walker moved to New York City and worked as an investment broker. Unlike many former Confederate generals, he did not become active in the postwar veterans' organizations.

WALKER, JAMES ALEXANDER (1832–1901) CSA. A native of **Virginia**, Walker attended the **Virginia Military Institute** and was only weeks from graduating when he was expelled after becoming involved in a classroom dispute with Professor **Thomas J. Jackson**. He challenged Jackson to a duel but was refused and then missed when he tried to kill Jackson by dropping a brick on his head from a window. After leaving school, Walker worked as a teacher and **railroad** engineer before graduating from the University of Virginia and becoming a lawyer. He also raised a militia **company** and served as its captain.

Walker entered Confederate service in April 1861 when his company became part of the 4th Virginia. In May, he was appointed lieutenant colonel of **A. P. Hill's** 13th Virginia. The **regiment** was in reserve at **First Manassas**, but it saw hard service in **Stonewall Jackson's 1862 Shenandoah Valley Campaign**. Walker had been promoted to colonel in April and led the regiment (part of Hill's **brigade**) particularly well at **Cross Keys**. He went on to see heavy combat with the **Army of Northern Virginia** in the **Seven Days**, **Second Manassas**, **Antietam**, **Fredericksburg**, and **Chancellorsville Campaigns**. Walker was wounded and had his horse killed at Antietam while temporarily commanding **Isaac Trimble's** brigade, and he temporarily led **Jubal A. Early's** brigade at Fredericksburg. During these battles, he was one of the best commanders in the **army** and became known to his men as "Old Bull Dog."

After numerous officers, including Jackson, urged his promotion, Walker was appointed brigadier general in May 1863. Ironically, he assumed command of the **Stonewall Brigade** (and was nicknamed "Stonewall Jim") and ably led the brigade at **Gettysburg**, **Mine Run**, and the **Wilderness**. At **Spotsylvania**, however, Walker's command was overrun at the "Bloody Angle" on May 12, 1864. At the beginning of the battle, he was severely wounded in the elbow and was saved from capture by being taken to the rear. His elbow joint was cut out, leaving his arm disabled. After returning to duty in July, Walker defended a railroad near **Richmond, Virginia**, before rejoining the army for the **Petersburg Campaign** in February 1865 and assuming a **division** command. He played an important role in the attempted breakout at **Fort Stedman** before surrendering with the rest of the army at **Appomattox**.

After the war, Walker farmed and continued his Virginia law practice. Entering **Democratic Party** politics, he was elected to the state legislature in 1871 and lieutenant governor in 1877. Switching to the **Republican Party** because of his conservative monetary beliefs, Walker was elected to the **U.S. Congress** in 1894 and 1896. In 1899, he was badly wounded in a politically motivated courtroom shooting.

WALKER, JOHN GEORGE (1822–1893) CSA. A native of **Missouri**, Walker graduated from Missouri's Jesuit College (present-day St. Louis University). He fought in the **Mexican War** as a 1st lieutenant in the 1st Mounted Rifles and was severely wounded and earned one **brevet** for gallantry. Walker remained in the **U.S. Army** after the war and served in the Southwest and Pacific Northwest.

Walker resigned his captain's commission in July 1861 to join the Confederacy. In September, he was appointed colonel and was given command of an infantry **brigade** in **Joseph E. Johnston's** army in **Virginia**. Three months later, Walker also was appointed major of cavalry in the regular **Confederate army**, which causes him to be confused with another John G. Walker of **Terry's Texas Rangers**.

In January 1862, Walker was appointed brigadier general. After brief service in **North Carolina**, his brigade joined **Benjamin Huger's** division of the **Army of Northern Virginia** and saw some minor combat in the **Seven Days Campaign**. At the beginning of the **Second Manassas Campaign**, Walker was left on the Virginia Peninsula in command of a **division** to watch **George B. McClellan's Army of the Potomac**. When the enemy departed, he rejoined the **army** with most of his division and participated in the capture of **Harpers Ferry, Virginia**, during the **Antietam Campaign**. After fighting well at Antietam, Walker was sent to **Richmond, Virginia**, for orders. Although **Robert E. Lee** wrote that his departure would weaken the army, he made no attempt to reacquire him.

Walker was promoted to major general in November 1862 and was sent to **Arkansas**, where he took command of a **Texas** division. Walker's division was the largest unit of Texans in Confederate service and earned the nickname "Walker's Greyhounds" for its swift marching across the **Trans-Mississippi Department**. Walker was highly respected by his men and superiors and led the division in hard fighting at **Milliken's Bend**, **Mansfield**, **Pleasant Hill** (where he was wounded in the groin), and **Jenkins' Ferry**. When his superior, **Richard Taylor**, was relieved of duty in June 1864 over disputes with **department** commander **Edmund Kirby Smith**, Walker replaced him in command of the District of West Louisiana. In August, Walker was ordered to turn over his division to **John Forney** and assume command of the District of Texas, New Mexico, and Arizona. He commanded the **district** until replaced by **John B. Magruder** in April 1865. In the remaining few weeks of the war, Walker commanded a cavalry **corps** and then returned to his "Greyhounds." When the war ended, he tried to convince his men to accompany him to Mexico, but instead they dispersed without orders and went home.

After the war, Walker lived in Mexico for a time and then moved to Great Britain. After a few years, he returned to the United States and settled in Virginia, where he became a miner and worked in the **railroad** industry. In 1886, President Grover Cleveland appointed Walker consul general to Colombia.

WALKER, LEROY POPE (1817–1884) CSA. A native of **Alabama** and the son of a U.S. senator, Walker attended both the University of Alabama and the University of Virginia before becoming a lawyer in 1837. Becoming active in **Democratic Party** politics, he was elected to the state legislature in 1843 and served as speaker from 1847 to 1850. Walker became an important **states rights** figure and served as a delegate at the 1850 **Nashville Convention**. After serving as a circuit judge from 1850 to 1853, he was elected again to the legislature in 1855 but immediately left it to handle his business affairs. One of the state's wealthiest lawyers in 1860, Walker led the Alabama delegation in walking out of the 1860 Democratic National Convention at **Charleston, South Carolina**, when Northern delegates refused to accept a proslavery platform. When the party split and **Abraham Lincoln** was elected president, Walker openly called for **secession**.

In February 1861, **Jefferson Davis** appointed Walker the Confederate secretary of war even though he had no military experience. Working from scratch, he raised 200,000 recruits in six months, but he was unable to arm them all because he did not believe the war would last long and failed to order sufficient weapons from Europe. Walker proved to be a weak administrator because he lacked tact and had a quarrelsome nature. He and Davis also disagreed on **strategy**, and he tired of the president's constant meddling in his department. Walker objected to the occupation of Columbus, Kentucky, in late summer 1861, and resigned his position on September 16.

Walker was appointed brigadier general the day after he resigned and took command of a **brigade** under **Braxton Bragg**, one of his enemies. After being constantly reassigned and criticized by Bragg, he finally resigned his commission in May 1862. In June 1864, Walker was appointed colonel and served as an Alabama military court judge.

After the war, Walker received a pardon and resumed his law practice. He also served as president of the state's 1875 constitutional convention and as a delegate to the 1884 Democratic National Convention.

WALKER, LUCIUS MARSHALL (1829–1863) CSA. A native of **Tennessee**, Walker was the nephew of President James K. Polk and the brother-in-law of Confederate brigadier general **Frank C. Armstrong**. After graduating from **West Point** in 1850, he resigned his 2nd lieutenant's commission in the dragoons two years later to become a Tennessee businessman.

Walker entered Confederate service in October 1861 as lieutenant colonel of the 40th Tennessee and was promoted to colonel the following month. After commanding the post at Memphis, Tennessee, for several months, he was promoted to brigadier general in April 1862. Walker participated in the fighting at **Island No. 10**, but he fell ill about the time the island was captured. Because of his illness, he missed **Shiloh** but led a **brigade** under **John P. McCown** during the **siege of Corinth, Mississippi**. During this time, Walker's performance displeased **Braxton Bragg**, who claimed he and another officer "were not safe men to be entrusted with any command" (Davis, ed., *The Confederate General*, vol. 6, 93). Instead of facing a court of inquiry, Walker was transferred to **Arkansas** at his own request and in March 1863 was given command of a cavalry **division**. He fought at **Helena** in July and opposed the Union advance on **Little Rock** in August. In the former operation, fellow division commander **John Marmaduke** criticized Walker's performance in battle, hinting at cowardice, and requested to be transferred. Insulted, Walker challenged Marmaduke, and the two fought a duel on September 6. Both officers missed their first shots, but Marmaduke mortally wounded Walker with his second, and Walker died 13 days later. Although Marmaduke briefly was placed under arrest for the killing, he soon was released and finally was cleared of any wrongdoing.

WALKER, MARY EDWARDS (1832–1919) USA. A native of **New York**, Walker graduated from Syracuse Medical College in 1855 (the only female in the class) and became one of the few antebellum female physicians. Her gender and subsequent divorce made it difficult to maintain her **Ohio** practice, but she persevered until the Civil War.

In 1861, Walker closed her practice and offered her services to the Union as an **army** surgeon. When she was refused, she volunteered to serve as a nurse in a **Washington, D.C.**, hospital. Walker continued to serve as a nurse until September 1863, when she was appointed assistant surgeon for the 52nd Ohio by Maj. Gen. **George H. Thomas**. She was the first woman to hold such a position, and she became a well-known figure in the army. Walker wore a regulation **uniform**, but she kept her hair long so she would be recognized as a woman. While treating civilians away from camp in the spring of 1864, she was captured by the Confederates and was kept a **prisoner** for four months in **Castle Thunder**.

After being **exchanged** in August, Walker resumed her medical duties but was kept in **Kentucky** and **Tennessee** away from the front lines. She campaigned for and was awarded the **Medal of Honor** for her wartime service.

After the war, Walker was active in several reform movements, including the direct election of senators and women's rights (she eventually adopted a man's dress). Her zealous nature and radical beliefs caused many, including her own family, to oppose or shun her. Walker's creation of a women's colony known as Adamless Eden in 1897 did not help her popularity, and later in life, she was reduced to living on a small veteran's pension. In 1919, the government revoked her Medal of Honor on the grounds it was not earned in combat. Walker refused to give it back and died in poverty less than a week later. The medal was restored to her in 1977.

WALKER, REUBEN LINDSAY (1827–1890) CSA. A member of a prominent **Virginia** family, Walker graduated from the **Virginia Military Institute** in 1845 and became a civil engineer and farmer.

After serving as sergeant-at-arms at the 1861 Virginia **secession** convention, Walker entered Confederate service in April as captain of the Purcell Battery. Although his **artillery** arrived at **First Manassas** too late to engage the enemy, he did later engage Union warships on the Potomac River. In March 1862, Walker was promoted to major and was put in command of the artillery in **A. P. Hill's division** of the **Army of Northern Virginia**. Illness caused him to miss the **Seven Days Campaign** (the only campaign he missed), but he was promoted to lieutenant colonel in July. Walker received much praise for his service at **Cedar Mountain**; the capture of **Harpers Ferry, Virginia**; **Antietam**; and **Fredericksburg**. Having been highly recommended by numerous superior officers, he was promoted to colonel in April 1863. Walker's service at **Chancellorsville** again elicited praise from **Robert E. Lee** and others. In June, he was put in command of the III Corps' artillery and fought with it at **Gettysburg** and in the **Overland** and **Petersburg Campaigns**.

In February 1865, Walker was promoted to brigadier general. When Petersburg, Virginia, was evacuated, he was put in command of two **divisions** and much of the artillery and led the **army's** retreat toward **Appomattox**. Walker's last battle was on April 8 just outside Appomattox. Apparently, he left the army before the **surrender** the next day because his name does not appear on the list of soldiers **paroled**. After reportedly fighting in 63 engagements, the huge six-foot, four-inch Walker emerged from the war unscratched. It was something of a point of honor with him, and when asked about it, he would remark that it "was not my fault" (Davis, ed., *The Confederate General,* vol. 6, 97).

Walker moved to **Alabama** in 1872 and worked as a **railroad** superintendent. He returned to Virginia two years later and worked as a railroad engineer before moving to **Texas** and spending 1884–88 as construction superintendent for the Texas State Capitol. After its completion, Walker returned to Virginia to farm.

WALKER, WILLIAM HENRY TALBOT (1816–1864) CSA. A native of **Georgia**, Walker graduated near the bottom of his 1837 **West Point** class and was assigned to the infantry. He was wounded three times in one battle during the **Seminole Wars** and was forced to resign his commission in 1838 because of his injuries. Walker rejoined the **U.S. Army** in 1840 and was promoted to captain in 1845. During the **Mexican War**, he earned two **brevets** for gallantry and suffered a nearly fatal wound. Walker went on to serve as commandant of cadets and an instructor of **tactics** at West Point from 1854 to 1856.

In December 1860, Walker resigned his major's commission and four months later was appointed major general of Georgia state troops. He was commissioned a Confederate brigadier general in May 1861 and was sent to **Pensacola, Florida**, but in August, Walker was transferred to Virginia, where he took command of a **brigade** of **Louisiana Tigers** in **Joseph E. Johnston's** army. He was transferred to a Georgia brigade in October but resigned his commission almost immediately, supposedly because of poor health but perhaps from dissatisfaction at being removed from his original brigade. Governor **Joseph Brown** then appointed Walker brigadier general of state militia, but this command was dissolved when the armies were reorganized after the **Conscription** Act was passed.

Walker did not receive a new assignment until March 1863, when he was reappointed a brigadier general of Confederate troops. He led a brigade in Georgia and **South Carolina** before it was transferred to **Mississippi** in May. There, Walker was lightly engaged in the **Battle of Jackson** and remained with Johnston's **army** during much of the **Vicksburg Campaign**. He was promoted to major general in June and was given command of a **division** that defended Yazoo City, Mississippi. After participating in the siege of Jackson, Walker's division reinforced the **Army of Tennessee** in Georgia. He led the Reserve Corps under **Daniel H. Hill** at **Chickamauga** and then resumed his division command in **James Longstreet's corps**. Walker participated in the early part of the **Chattanooga Campaign** but afterward was absent sick until January 1864. When he returned to duty, he attended the **Dalton**

Conference and bitterly opposed Maj. Gen. **Patrick Cleburne's** plan to recruit **black troops**. As part of **William J. Hardee's** corps, Walker led his division through the **Atlanta Campaign** and saw heavy combat at **Peachtree Creek**. Two days later, he was killed by a Union **picket** while observing the Union line through binoculars just prior to the **Battle of Atlanta**.

WALKER, WILLIAM STEPHEN (1822–1899) CSA. A native of **Pennsylvania**, Walker was raised by his **Mississippi** uncle, Senator Robert J. Walker (who also served as President James K. Polk's secretary of the treasury). After attending school in Georgetown (**Washington, D.C.**), he was commissioned a 1st lieutenant in the **U.S. Army** in February 1847. During the **Mexican War**, Walker served as a staff officer and earned one **brevet** for gallantry. He left the **army** in 1848 but returned in 1855 as a captain in the 1st U.S. Cavalry.

Walker resigned his captain's commission in May 1861 and entered Confederate service as a captain of infantry. He was first sent to **Tennessee** to recruit but in June was assigned to **Thomas C. Hindman's** 2nd Arkansas. In March 1862, Maj. Gen. **John C. Pemberton** had Walker promoted to colonel and appointed him acting inspector general for the **Department of South Carolina**. Two months later, Pemberton gave him a **district** command near **Charleston**, and over the next several months, Walker defended his coastal area and its vital **railroad** from Union raids. His successful actions won him promotion to brigadier general in October 1862.

Walker remained in command of his district even after Pemberton was replaced by **P. G. T. Beauregard**. However, Beauregard placed him in temporary command of **Nathan G. Evans's brigade** in April 1864 when Evans was injured in an accident. Moving with his brigade to **North Carolina**, Walker commanded a district covering southern **Virginia** and northern North Carolina until May. At that time, Beauregard ordered Walker to **Petersburg, Virginia**, to help defend it. He arrived too late to fight at **Second Drewry's Bluff** but did attack **Benjamin F. Butler's** Federals in the **Bermuda Hundred Campaign** on May 20. Mistakenly riding into Union lines, Walker was badly wounded in the left arm and right leg and was captured. Union surgeons amputated his right foot and believed Walker would die, but he miraculously recovered. He was **exchanged** in October 1864 and returned to duty even though he was not completely recovered. Walker spent the war's last months in command of Weldon, North Carolina.

After the war, Walker lived in **Georgia** and worked as a businessman.

WALLACE, LEWIS "LEW" (1827–1905) USA. A native of **Indiana**, Wallace was the son of a state governor. After serving as a 1st lieutenant with the 1st Indiana in the **Mexican War**, he became a lawyer in 1849 and was elected to the state senate in 1856.

When the Civil War began in April 1861, Gov. **Oliver P. Morton** appointed Wallace Indiana's adjutant general, but he almost immediately afterward made him colonel of the 11th Indiana. Sent to western **Virginia**, he won a small engagement at Romney and was promoted to brigadier general of volunteers in September. Transferred west, Wallace was given a **division** command under Brig. Gen. **U. S. Grant** and participated in the capture of **Fort Donelson** in February 1862. This action won him a promotion to major general of volunteers in March. Wallace's rapid rise in the **army** came to a halt at **Shiloh**. His division was in the rear when the battle began and arrived on the field too late to be effective after losing its way and receiving confusing orders from Grant. Wallace's cautious attack on the second day also angered Grant. The near-defeat at Shiloh called for a scapegoat, and Wallace was a convenient target. He was relieved of command and went home to await orders. During the **Kentucky Campaign**, Wallace volunteered his services to Governor Morton, was given command of a **regiment** (even though he was a major general), and did an admirable job in preparing Cincinnati, Ohio, for defense. Afterward, he sat on the commission that investigated Maj. Gen. **Don Carlos Buell's** actions during the campaign.

In March 1864, Wallace was given command of the **Middle Department**. During **Jubal A. Early's Washington Raid** that summer, he assembled a small force and in bitter fighting at the **Monocacy** delayed the Confederate advance long enough for reinforcements to reach **Washington, D.C.** Wallace remained in **Maryland** until war's end. After **Abraham Lincoln's assassination**, he served on the court-martial that convicted the conspirators and later presided over the court that convicted **Andersonville** commandant **Henry Wirz**.

Having always been fascinated by Mexico, Wallace began raising money for the Mexican forces fighting Emperor **Maximilian** in the months following the Civil War and even accepted a commission of major general in the revolutionary army. He resigned his **U.S. Army** commission in November 1865 and led some volunteers to fight in Mexico, but he eventually returned to the United States without seeing any combat. Wallace served as the territorial governor of **New Mexico** from 1878 to 1881 and was U.S. minister to Turkey from 1881 to 1885. Although he wanted to be remembered as a great general, Wallace is most famous for writing the novel, *Ben Hur: A Tale of the Christ*, which he began researching while serving in Turkey.

WALLACE, WILLIAM HARVEY LAMB (1821–1862) USA. A native of **Ohio**, as a boy, Wallace moved with his family to **Illinois.** After becoming a lawyer in 1846, he volunteered for service in the **Mexican War** and rose from private to 1st lieutenant and adjutant in the 1st Illinois. After the war, Wallace returned to Illinois, where he served as district attorney and practiced law.

Wallace entered Union service in May 1861 as colonel of the 11th Illinois, a **regiment** he raised. He was given command of a **brigade** stationed around Cairo, Illinois, in October and led it until receiving a brigade in **John A. McClernand's division** in February 1862. After playing a major role in preventing the Confederate breakout of **Fort Donelson**, Wallace was promoted to brigadier general of volunteers in March. Just days before the **Battle of Shiloh**, he was promoted to a division command to replace **Charles F. Smith**, who had been injured in an accident. At Shiloh, Wallace helped hold the critical "Hornets' Nest" for several hours. When he finally withdrew, he was shot through the temple and eye and was left for dead. Wallace was recovered the next day and was nursed by his wife, but he died on April 10, 1862.

WALLACE, WILLIAM HENRY (1827–1901) CSA. A native of **South Carolina**, Wallace graduated from South Carolina College in 1849 and became a planter, newspaper publisher, lawyer, and state legislator. In 1860, he attended the state **secession** convention and voted for secession.

When Wallace's legislative term expired, he declined to run for reelection and entered Confederate service in late 1861 as a private in the 18th South Carolina. He soon was appointed regimental adjutant and was elected lieutenant colonel in May 1862. After serving in South Carolina during the war's first year, the **regiment** was sent to **Virginia**, where it became part of **Nathan Evans's brigade** in the **Army of Northern Virginia**. At **Second Manassas**, the regiment's colonel was killed, and Wallace assumed command. He was appointed temporary colonel but did not receive his official commission until June 1864, leading both the brigade and his regiment in the meantime. After fighting at **South Mountain** and **Antietam**, Wallace's brigade was transferred to **Mississippi**, where it served under **Joseph E. Johnston** during the **Vicksburg Campaign**. After **Vicksburg's** surrender, the brigade was sent to South Carolina in August 1863 and helped defend **Charleston** for several months.

Wallace was replaced by **Stephen Elliott Jr.** as brigade commander in the spring of 1864, and resumed his regimental command. The brigade next participated in the **Petersburg Campaign**, where it became part of **Bushrod Johnson's** division. Nearly half of Wallace's regiment was blown up in July when the Federals exploded the mine that led to the **Battle of the Crater**. When Elliott was wounded in the battle, Wallace again assumed brigade command and finally was promoted to brigadier general in September. He briefly commanded the **division** at **Five Forks** in April 1865. The brigade was virtually destroyed during that engagement, and the division was wrecked a few days later at **Sailor's Creek**. Wallace **surrendered** the survivors at **Appomattox**.

After the war, Wallace returned to his South Carolina plantation and resumed his law practice. He served three terms in the state legislature beginning in 1872. He was appointed a circuit judge in 1877 and served in that capacity until retiring in 1893.

WALNUT HILLS, MISSISSIPPI, BATTLE OF (DECEMBER 27–29, 1862). *See* CHICKASAW BAYOU, MISSISSIPPI, BATTLE OF.

WALTHALL, EDWARD CARY (1831–1898) CSA. A native of **Virginia**, as a boy, Walthall moved to **Mississippi** with his family. He studied law under his brother and served as county court clerk before becoming a lawyer in 1852. Becoming involved in local politics, Walthall was elected district attorney in 1856 and 1859.

When Mississippi seceded in January 1861, Walthall resigned as district attorney and helped raise a volunteer **company**. Elected 1st lieutenant, he entered Confederate service in June when the company became part of the 15th Mississippi. Walthall was elected lieutenant colonel in July and accompanied the **regiment** to eastern **Tennessee**, where it became part of Brig. Gen. **Felix Zollicoffer's** command. He led the regiment at **Mill Springs** and was highly praised by his superiors. In April 1862, Walthall was elected colonel of the newly organized 29th Mississippi and became part of **James R. Chalmers's brigade**. During the **Kentucky Campaign**, the regiment saw heavy combat at **Munfordville** but missed **Perryville**.

In November 1862, Walthall was given a brigade command in the **Army of Tennessee** and was promoted to brigadier general in December. Illness caused him to miss **Stones River**, but he did lead the brigade in the **Tullahoma Campaign**. Becoming part of **St. John R. Liddell's division**, the brigade saw heavy combat at **Chickamauga**, where it captured more than 400 **prisoners** and temporarily seized an **artillery** battery. During the **Chattanooga Campaign**, Walthall fought at both **Lookout Mountain** and **Missionary Ridge**. He was wounded in the foot in the latter battle but held his ground until after dark.

During the **Atlanta Campaign**, Walthall served in **Thomas C. Hindman's** division and fought very well at **Resaca**. In June 1864, he was given a division command in **Leonidas Polk's corps** and was promoted to major general the following month. Walthall led his command in very heavy fighting at **Peachtree Creek** and **Ezra Church** and lost more than one-third of his men in the latter battle. He then accompanied the **army** on the **Franklin and Nashville Campaign** and at Franklin had two horses killed under him and suffered a severe bruise. After the defeat at Nashville, Walthall was given command of eight brigades and assisted **Nathan Bedford Forrest** in forming the rear guard during the retreat. In early 1865, he reinforced **Joseph E. Johnston** for the **Carolinas Campaign** and saw his last major combat at **Bentonville**. In the last weeks of war, Walthall also commanded **Alexander P. Stewart's** corps.

After the war, Walthall returned to Mississippi and briefly practiced law with former Confederate general **Lucius Q. C. Lamar**. Becoming active in **Democratic Party** politics, he opposed **Reconstruction** and in 1885 was appointed to the U.S. Senate to replace Lamar, who had been named President Grover Cleveland's secretary of the interior. Except for a 14-month period when he was ill, Walthall remained in the Senate until his death.

WAR CORRESPONDENTS. The Civil War was the first American war in which newspapers used regular war correspondents to keep the public informed of events. Union war correspondents, who referred to themselves as the **Bohemian Brigade**, were much more numerous than Confederate correspondents. More than 300 Union reporters covered the war, while fewer than 100 Confederates did so. Such Union publications as the **New York** *Times*, **New York** *Tribune*, *Harper's Weekly*, and *Frank Leslie's Illustrated Newspaper* hired numerous artists and correspondents, including **Charles Coffin**, **Edwin Forbes**, **Adams S. Hill**, **Winslow Homer**, **Joseph Howard Jr.**, **Henry Villard**, **John Russell Young**, **George Alfred Townsend**, **Charles Anderson Page**, **Albert Deane Richardson**, **Joseph B. McCullagh**, **William Swinton**, **George Washburn Smalley**, **Alfred R. Waud**, and **Benjamin F. Taylor**. Such Confederate newspapers as the **Richmond** *Enquirer*, **Richmond** *Examiner*, Memphis *Appeal*, and **Charleston** *Mercury* also used correspondents, but they are less well known because oftentimes they were soldiers writing under pen names. **Henry Timrod** was one such correspondent, and while not an official war correspondent, **John Esten Cooke** sometimes wrote articles for Confederate newspapers. **William Howard Russell** also was a famous war correspondent writing for the London *Times*.

WAR DEMOCRATS. During the **election of 1860**, the **Democratic Party** split into Northern and Southern parties. Once **secession** began, most of the Southern Democrats (except Sen. **Andrew Johnson**) joined the Confederacy, leaving the Northern Democrats as a minority in the North and dominated by the **Republican Party**. When war began, Northern Democrats had to decide whether or not to support **Abraham Lincoln's** war policies against their former political allies. Those Northern Democrats who supported war to reunite the Union, such as Johnson and **Stephen A. Douglas**, were referred to as War Democrats. Those who believed secession was constitutional or that the cost in blood and money was too great to reunite the nation, were called **Peace Democrats,** or **Copperheads**.

WAR OF THE REBELLION: A COMPILATION OF THE OFFICIAL RECORDS OF THE UNION AND CONFEDERATE ARMIES. This U.S. government publication is the best source of primary research material on the Civil War. With the **surrender** of the Confederacy in 1865, Union **armies** came into possession of much of the surviving Confederate military records. In May 1864, the **U.S. Congress** had authorized the preservation of Union military papers, and it later was decided to include the captured Confederate documents in any publication that might be made. Work began in 1868 to assemble and sort all of the relevant Union and Confederate documents for publication in a multivolume work. Numerous individuals were involved in the project, which came under the direction of the newly created War Records Department in 1877. Because many important Confederate documents had been destroyed or were held in private, unknown, hands, the resulting publication included many more Union documents than Confederate.

The first of 128 volumes of *War of the Rebellion: A Compilation of the Official Records of the Union and Confederate Armies*, more commonly referred to as the *Official Records*, was published in 1881. The publication was arranged in four series, with each series containing numerous volumes, and some volumes containing several parts. Series I contains material relating to the military campaigns (which are arranged in chronological order), Series II covers **prisoners** of war and political prisoners, and Series III and IV relate to Union and Confederate state and national officials, respectively. The last volume, the index, was published in 1901.

Many documents, especially Confederate, were not included in the original publication because they were considered irrelevant or were held in private hands and were unavailable. In 1994, Broadfoot Publishing began a new ongoing series entitled *Supplement to the Official Records of the Union and Confederate Armies,* which includes those relevant records not found in the original publication. In 1884, the federal government began publishing *Official Records of the Union and Confederate Navies in the War of the Rebellion.* This 31-volume work was completed in 1927 and is the naval equivalent of the *Official Records. See also* PICKETT PAPERS.

WARD, JOHN HENRY HOBART (1823–1903) USA. A native of **New York,** Ward entered the **U.S. Army** as a private in 1842 and rose to the rank of sergeant major in the 7th U.S. Infantry. During the **Mexican War,** he was wounded at Monterrey and married a Mexican girl at Vera Cruz. Ward left the **army** in 1847 and returned to New York, where in the 1850s he served first as assistant to the state's commissary general and then as commissary general.

Ward entered Union service in June 1861 as colonel of the 38th New York. He fought at **First Manassas** and temporarily took command of the **brigade** in the battle. Afterward, his **regiment** became part of the **Army of the Potomac** and fought in the **Peninsula Campaign** with the II Corps' 3rd Division. At **Seven Pines,** Ward assumed command of the brigade, but after about a week, he returned to his regiment. He led it through the **Seven Days Campaign** and at **Second Manassas,** and at **Chantilly** he assumed command of **David Birney's** III Corps brigade.

Promoted to brigadier general of volunteers in October 1862, Ward led his men at **Fredericksburg, Chancellorsville,** and **Gettysburg.** At Gettysburg, he was wounded and assumed command of the **division** on the second day of battle. In the spring of 1864, Ward's division was transferred to the II Corps. He led the brigade at the **Wilderness** and **Spotsylvania** and received a second wound in the latter battle. While at Spotsylvania, Ward was relieved of command on charges of being drunk at the Wilderness and for leaving the field. He had been routinely praised for his service prior to that battle, and the accusations shocked his comrades. Ward was placed under arrest, but he was allowed to be honorably discharged in July 1864. His supporters requested he be restored and court-martialed to clear his name, but officials refused.

Ward returned to New York and began a 32-year career as clerk of the state's superior and supreme courts. While vacationing in 1903, he was struck by a train and killed.

WARD, WILLIAM THOMAS (1808–1878) USA. A native of **Virginia**, as a child, Ward moved to **Kentucky** with his family. After attending St. Mary's College, he became a lawyer and served in the **Mexican War** as major of the 4th Kentucky. Returning to Kentucky afterward, Ward served in the state legislature and from 1851 to 1853 held a seat in the **U.S. Congress** as a **Whig**. He refused to seek reelection and returned to his law practice.

When the Civil War began, Ward raised a **brigade** of volunteers for the Union and was appointed brigadier general of volunteers in September 1861. Known to his men as "Old Pap," he commanded brigades in the **Army of the Ohio** and the **Army of the Cumberland** and served on garrison duty in Kentucky and **Tennessee** for the next three years. During this time, Ward apparently served well, except when he unsuccessfully pursued **John Hunt Morgan's** raiders in 1862. In January 1864, he took command of an XI Corps **division** but in April returned to a brigade in **Daniel Butterfield's** XX Corps division. Ward fought in the **Atlanta Campaign** and was wounded twice at **Resaca**, but he remained with his men during most of the battle. In late June 1864, he assumed command of the division and led it throughout the remainder of the campaign, serving particularly well at **Peachtree Creek**. Ward went on to lead the division in the **March to the Sea** and the **Carolinas Campaign**. After being **brevetted** major general of volunteers in February 1865, he was mustered out of service in August.

After the war, Ward returned to his Kentucky law practice.

WARE BOTTOM CHURCH, VIRGINIA, BATTLE OF (MAY 20, 1864). During the 1864 **Overland Campaign**, **Benjamin F. Butler's Army of the James** launched the **Bermuda Hundred Campaign** to threaten **Richmond, Virginia**, but was checked by Confederate forces under **P. G. T. Beauregard** at **Second Drewry's Bluff**. On May 20, 1864, the Confederates attacked the right wing of Butler's defensive line near Ware Bottom Church and drove back **Quincy A. Gillmore's** X Corps **pickets** a mile to the main Union line. The Confederates then erected their own defensive line, called the Howlett Line, and effectively bottled up Butler on the Bermuda Hundred peninsula. The Federals lost 702 men in the battle, and Confederate casualties are estimated to have been about the same. The Confederate victories at Second Drewry's Bluff and Ware Bottom Church greatly reduced Butler's threat and allowed Beauregard to send reinforcements to **Robert E. Lee's Army of Northern Virginia**.

WARREN COURT OF INQUIRY. *See* WARREN, GOUVERNEUR KEMBLE.

WARREN, FITZ-HENRY (1816–1878) USA. A native of **Massachusetts**, Warren worked as a store clerk and leather manufacturer before moving to **Iowa** in 1844. There he became a newspaper editor and worked as an assistant postmaster before moving to **Washington, D.C.**, in 1861 to become a reporter for the **New York** *Tribune*.

Warren entered Union service in June 1861 as colonel of the 1st Iowa Cavalry and served his first year of duty in **Missouri** fighting guerrillas. Promoted to brigadier general of volunteers in July 1862, he commanded the post at Houston, Missouri, and briefly commanded a **brigade** in southeastern Missouri in early 1863 before being transferred east for a **division** command in the **Department of the Susquehanna** during the **Gettysburg Campaign**. In September 1863, Warren was sent to the **Department of the Gulf**, where he was given a brigade in the XIII Corps. He participated in the 1864 **Red River Campaign** and temporarily commanded the division during much of it. Afterward, Warren served at **Baton Rouge, Louisiana**, and commanded the troops on **Texas's** Rio Grande during the summer of 1864. Sickness forced him to give up the latter position, and he transferred to the **Department of the East** for administrative duty in New York City. Warren was mustered out of service in August 1865 with a **brevet** of major general of volunteers.

Warren returned to Iowa and served in the state senate in 1866, was U.S. minister to Guatemala from 1867 to 1868, and served as a **Democratic** presidential elector in 1872. He also worked for the New York *Tribune* and New York *Sun*.

WARREN, GOUVERNEUR KEMBLE (1830–1882) USA. A native of **New York**, Warren graduated second in the **West Point** class of 1850. For the next 11 years, he served on various construction projects with the **engineers**, taught mathematics at the academy, and rose to the rank of 1st lieutenant.

In May 1861, Warren was appointed lieutenant colonel of the 5th New York and fought with it at **Big Bethel** that summer. Promoted to colonel in August, he became part of the **Army of the Potomac** and led the **regiment** in the **Peninsula Campaign** before being given a **brigade** command in **George Sykes's** V Corps **division** in May 1862. Warren led this brigade through the **Seven Days** (in which he was wounded at **Gaines' Mill**), **Second Manassas**, and **Antietam Campaigns**.

Promoted to major general of volunteers in September 1862, Warren fought at **Fredericksburg** and then was appointed the **army's** chief engineer when **Joseph Hooker** took command. After serving at **Chancellorsville**, he remained chief engineer after **George G. Meade** took over the army in June 1863. Warren's finest moment came on **Gettysburg's** second day, when he realized that Little Round Top was the key to the Union line but had been left undefended when **Daniel Sickles** advanced his **corps** beyond Cemetery Ridge. Reacting swiftly, he personally sent **Strong Vincent's** and **Stephen H. Weed's** brigades to Little Round Top, and the high ground was saved, although Warren was wounded. Later, a statue of Warren was erected on Little Round Top to honor his role in the battle.

In August 1863, Warren took temporary command of the II Corps from a wounded **Winfield Scott Hancock**. He won the **Battle of Bristoe Station** in October but angered Meade in the **Mine Run Campaign** by failing to follow orders to attack the impregnable Confederate defenses. Meade later acknowledged that Warren had been correct, but friction developed between the two. When the army was reorganized in the spring of 1864, Warren was given command of the V Corps and led it in the **Overland Campaign**. He served competently but did not get along with **Philip Sheridan** and did not particularly impress **U. S. Grant**, who felt he was too cautious. During the **Petersburg Campaign**, Grant became more critical of Warren and accused him of contributing to the Union defeat at the **Crater** by not pressing the enemy troops in his front.

In March 1865, Warren's corps was put under Sheridan's command for the operation that led to the **Battle of Five Forks**. Warren was late getting into position at **Dinwiddie Court House** on March 31, and the next day he angered Sheridan at Five Forks. Sheridan told him the Confederate line extended across his front and ordered him to attack. When he advanced, Warren observed that the enemy line actually was on his left flank and not in his front. While the corps' left brigades turned to attack the Confederates, he rode after the rest of the line to turn it in the proper direction. Sheridan then arrived, and when he could not find Warren, he exploded in anger and exercised discretionary orders given him by Grant and relieved Warren of command. He later gave four reasons for his actions: that Warren had been slow on March 31, had attacked the Confederates on March 31 without orders and with only part of his corps, was inexcusably late in attacking at Five Forks, and was lacking in leadership and caused part of his corps to give way at Five Forks. The action was unfair, and Warren was left without a position just days before **Robert E. Lee's** surrender.

In May 1865, Warren was put in command of the District of Vicksburg and remained there until the last Confederate **surrender**. He resigned his volunteer commission later that month and ended the war with a **brevet** of major general of regulars for his war service. Warren remained in the army with the rank of major of engineers (later becoming a lieutenant colonel). Besides working on various construction projects (including building the Mississippi Railroad bridge at Rock Island, Illinois), he spent his postwar career trying to retrieve his reputation. The Warren Court of Inquiry finally was held in December 1879 with generals **Christopher C. Augur** and **John Newton** making up the court. After three years of irregular meetings, it finally ruled that while Warren had been slow at Five Forks, he had contributed to the victory and was innocent of Sheridan's charges. Unfortunately, Warren died a few months before the ruling was made, and he had bitterly left instructions that he was not to be buried in his uniform.

WASHBURN, CADWALLADER COLDEN (1818–1882) USA. A native of **Maine**, Washburn was the brother of Union politicians **Israel Washburn** and **Elihu B. Washburne**. Three of his brothers served either in the U.S. House of Representatives or Senate, and at one time, he, Israel, and Elihu served together in the House. Washburn moved west as a young man and in 1842 became a **Wisconsin** lawyer. Diverse business interests made him a wealthy man, and he joined the **Republican Party** in 1854 and was elected to the **U.S. Congress**. Washburn was reelected two times and was a delegate at the **Washington Peace Conference**.

Washburn entered Union service in February 1862 as colonel of the 2nd Wisconsin Cavalry. Although he seems to have been a competent officer, his career no doubt was helped by his political connections and the fact that brother Elihu was close to both **Abraham Lincoln** and **U. S. Grant**. After service in **Missouri** and **Arkansas**, Washburn was promoted to brigadier general of volunteers in July. He led one cavalry **division** in late 1862 and then took command of another in the **Army of the Tennessee's** XIII Corps in February 1863. In March 1863, Washburn was promoted to major general of volunteers and transferred to a cavalry division in the XVI Corps. During the **Vicksburg Campaign**, he commanded the **Yazoo Pass Expedition** and then led three of the **corps'** cavalry divisions to reinforce Grant during the siege of **Vicksburg, Mississippi**. After the city's surrender, Washburn was given command of the XIII Corps in late July and took it to the **Department of the Gulf** the following month. In April 1864, he was put in command of the District of West Tennessee to protect the region from **Nathan Bedford Forrest's** cavalry but largely was unsuccessful. Washburn remained in command of the **district** until war's end.

Washburn resigned his commission in May 1865 and returned to Wisconsin politics, where he served two terms in Congress (1867–71) and one term as governor (1871–73). Equally successful in business, he was one of the founders of the General Mills Corporation.

WASHBURN, ISRAEL (1813–1883) USA. A native of **Maine**, Washburn was the brother of **Cadwallader C. Washburn** and **Elihu B. Washburne**. Three of his brothers served in either the U.S. Senate or House of Representatives, and at one time, he, Cadwallader, and Elihu served together in the House. Israel became a lawyer in 1834 and served two terms in the state legislature before being elected to the **U.S. Congress** in 1851 as a **Whig**. Joining the **Republican Party**, he strongly opposed **slavery** and the **Kansas-Nebraska Act** and was reelected four times.

Washburn was elected governor in 1860 and had to resign his congressional seat to be sworn in. He was reelected easily in 1861. When the Civil War began, Washburn strongly supported **Abraham Lincoln's** war policies and began raising volunteers, forming a militia and coast guard, and strengthening coastal defenses. He also tried to convince the Federal government to erect defenses along the Canadian border to protect Maine from what he thought was growing Confederate sentiment in Canada, but the government refused. Besides supporting the war effort, Washburn also helped finance the construction of a **railroad** to Nova Scotia. He declined to run for a third term in 1862.

After leaving office, Washburn served as a customs official in Portland, but he resigned that position in 1877 to a become president of trustees for Massachusetts's Tufts College. The following year, he was also appointed president of a railroad.

WASHBURNE, ELIHU BENJAMIN (1816–1887) USA. A native of **Maine**, Washburne was the brother of **Cadwallader C. Washburn** and **Israel Washburn**. Three of his brothers served either in the U.S. House of Representative or Senate, and at one time, he, Cadwallader, and Israel served in the House together. Elihu left his home when he was 17 and adopted an old family spelling of his last name by adding an *e*. After working as a teacher and printer, he attended Maine Wesleyan Seminary and Harvard Law School and became a lawyer in 1840. Washburne then moved to **Illinois**, where he practiced law and became involved in **Whig** politics. After being defeated in an 1848 congressional race, he won the election in 1852. Washburne soon joined the **Republican Party** and remained in the **U.S. Congress** until 1869.

When the Civil War began, Washburne was serving as chairman of the House Commerce Committee. He became an adviser to **Abraham Lincoln** and was an influential **Radical Republican** who supported Secretary of the Treasury **Salmon P. Chase**. Washburne also was a powerful sponsor of such Illinois soldiers as **U. S. Grant**, who hailed from his hometown of Galena. Washburne personally took Grant to the governor's office in 1861 and secured him the colonelcy of the 21st Illinois. He also selected Grant for promotion when he was allowed to appoint one of four Illinois brigadier generals later in the year and served as a mediator between Grant and **Henry Halleck** when the two officers feuded in early 1862. Washburne even sponsored the bill that revived the rank of lieutenant general, which Grant received in 1864.

After the war, Washburne strongly opposed President **Andrew Johnson's** moderate **Reconstruction** policies and was one of the driving forces behind his impeachment. In 1868, his influence helped win Grant the presidency. Grant recognized Washburne's role in the victory by appointing him secretary of state in 1869. The appointment was an honor only, however, and Washburne resigned after one week. Within days, he was appointed U.S. minister to France and served in that position until 1877. When the revolutionary Commune took over the nation, Washburne gained some fame by offering protection to foreign nationals in the U.S. embassy. He returned to Illinois in 1877 and created ill will with Grant in 1880 by attempting to win the Republican presidential nomination. Grant believed the attempt cost him the nomination. Afterward, Washburne retired from politics and served as president of the Chicago Historical Society from 1884 until his death.

WASHINGTON ARTILLERY. This **artillery** unit from **New Orleans, Louisiana**, became one of the most famous in the **Confederate army**. Organized in 1838 as part of the state militia, it was composed of men from the most prominent New Orleans families and earned an enviable reputation while fighting in the **Mexican War**. After gaining six cannons from the Baton Rouge Arsenal when it was seized in January 1861, the artillerymen offered their services to the Confederacy, and four **companies** were mustered into the **army** on May 26.

The four Washington Artillery companies that went to **Virginia** first earned fame fighting at **First Manassas**. Afterward, they were assigned to **James Longstreet's** command and spent the rest of the war serving under him. The Washington Artillery fought with the **Army of Northern Virginia** in every major battle and particularly distinguished itself at **Fredericksburg**. These four companies were commanded successively by James B. Walton, Benjamin F. Eshleman, and William M. Owen.

A fifth company of the Washington Artillery was mustered into service on March 6, 1862, and was assigned to the western theater. It fought at **Shiloh** and then joined the **Army of Tennessee** for most of its major campaigns. After the **Battle of Franklin**, the company was sent to Mobile, Alabama, and fought there in early 1865 at **Spanish Fort**. This fifth company was commanded first by W. Irving Hodgson and then Cuthbert H. Slocumb.

After the war, the Washington Artillery returned to New Orleans. During **Reconstruction**, the veterans received permission to form a charitable and benevolent association and secretly armed themselves and drilled to oppose the **Radical Republicans**. At the 1874 Battle of Liberty Place, the artilleryman manned two small cannons against the New Orleans police under James Longstreet. After Reconstruction, the Washington Artillery resumed its state service and fought in the Spanish-American War, World War I, and World War II. It is still an active part of the Louisiana National Guard.

WASHINGTON, D.C. Located on the border of **Virginia** and **Maryland**, Washington, D.C., had a population of approximately 41,000 when the Civil War began, and its atmosphere was distinctly Southern. When Virginia seceded in 1861, and the **Baltimore Riot** indicated Maryland might follow, there was the real possibility that the Union capital would become surrounded by Confederate territory. As a result, **Abraham Lincoln** used force to ensure Maryland's loyalty and began assembling a huge garrison and building elaborate defenses to protect the capital. Lincoln's fear for the safety of Washington, located only 100 miles from the Confederate capital of **Richmond, Virginia**, greatly affected **strategy** in the east (as seen in the **Urbanna Plan** and **Peninsula Campaign**), because he insisted that a large number of soldiers be kept there permanently to protect it.

The thousands of Union soldiers who converged on Washington in the war's early months became the **Army of the Potomac**. Under Maj. Gen. **George B. McClellan**, the **army** constructed miles of elaborate defenses around the capital. McClellan detailed Maj. **John G. Barnard** to supervise this project, and by the end of 1861, some 37 miles of earthworks ringed the city. These defenses continued to be improved upon, and by war's end Washington was protected by 60 forts, 762 cannons, 74 **mortars**, and miles of trenches. The city and its defenses came under the jurisdiction of the **Department of Washington**. The only serious threat to the capital came in the summer of 1864 during **Jubal A. Early's Washington Raid**, but the Confederates were stopped on the city's outskirts at **Fort Stevens**. Washington experienced an explosion of growth during the war. With the thousands of soldiers came countless businessmen, prostitutes, criminals, speculators, gamblers, and lobbyists to take advantage of them. At its wartime peak, the city mushroomed to a population of 160,000 and largely lost its Southern identity. With its dirt streets, open sewers, crime, and oppressive summer heat and humidity, Washington was not the most comfortable city in which to live. British ambassador Lord Lyons described his tenure there as early purgatory.

Washington experienced much sadness and glory during the war. The death of Lincoln's son Willie, the frequent arrival of thousands of wounded soldiers, and **Lincoln's assassination** threw a pall over the city. But citizens also enjoyed an active social scene, including balls and the marriage of **Kate Chase** to Gov. **William Sprague**, and most of the city turned out to witness the armies' **Grand Review** in May 1865.

WASHINGTON, NORTH CAROLINA, BATTLE OF (MARCH 30–APRIL 20, 1863). After Confederate Maj. Gen. **Daniel H. Hill's** unsuccessful attack on **New Bern, North Carolina**, in March 1863, he moved north from New Bern to gather supplies around Washington, North Carolina, and to attack the 1,200 Federals there. By March 30, Hill had assumed a position on either side of the Tar River, using **Richard B. Garnett's brigade** to besiege the town on the river's north bank, while his other two brigades remained on the south bank to block any enemy reinforcements that might be sent overland from New Bern. For almost three weeks, the Confederates erected earthworks and exchanged **artillery** fire with the garrison and Union gunboats. However, they were unable to prevent Maj. Gen. **John G. Foster** from bringing ship-borne reinforcements to Washington on April 19 by way of the Pamlico and Tar Rivers. The following day, Hill ended his siege and withdrew to Goldsboro.

WASHINGTON PEACE CONFERENCE (FEBRUARY 4–27, 1861). During the 1861 **secession** crisis, **Virginia** called for a peace conference to be held in **Washington, D.C.**, to work out a compromise on **slavery** that would prevent the nation from fragmenting. While many politicians, including **Abraham Lincoln**, held out little hope for success, the **border states** strongly supported the attempt. The Washington Peace Conference opened at the Willard Hotel on February 4, 1861—the same day the Confederate **Montgomery, Alabama, Convention** began. Twenty-one states participated, but none of the six original seceding states came, nor did **Arkansas, Texas, Michigan, Wisconsin, Minnesota, California**, or **Oregon**. Presided over by former president John Tyler, the conference used the **Crittenden Compromise** as the basis for negotiations, but no one was in a mood to make any real concessions.

The conference (also known as the "Old Gentlemen's Convention") finally adopted seven recommendations to be enacted as a constitutional amendment and submitted them to the **U.S. Congress** on February 27. These recommendations included: extending the **Missouri Compromise** Line dividing free and slave territory to the Pacific Ocean; guaranteeing slavery only in territory then owned by the United States; requiring a majority vote from both the free and slave states in the House and Senate before any new territory could be acquired and prohibiting Congress from exercising any control over slavery in Washington, D.C., without the owners' and Maryland's consent; continuing to prohibit the slave trade in Washington, D.C., while protecting interstate slave trade; forbidding the foreign slave trade; providing federal compensation to slave owners for runaway slaves that were not returned; and preventing certain provisions in these recommendations and the Constitution from ever being amended or abolished without the unanimous approval of the states. Both the House and the Senate rejected the proposals, however, and this last attempt to avoid secession and war failed.

WATERHOUSE, RICHARD (1832–1876) CSA. A native of **Tennessee**, Waterhouse volunteered for service in the **Mexican War** when he was only 14. His family moved to **Texas** after the war, and he and his father opened a mercantile business.

Waterhouse entered Confederate service in May 1862 when he helped raise the 19th Texas and was appointed its colonel. Sent to **Arkansas**, the **regiment** became part of **Henry E. McCulloch's brigade** in **John G. Walker's division**. Waterhouse fought very well in his first battle at **Milliken's Bend, Louisiana**, in June 1863. Afterward, the regiment remained in **Louisiana** and saw heavy combat at **Mansfield** and **Pleasant Hill** during the 1864 **Red River Campaign**. Sent back to Arkansas, Waterhouse next fought at **Jenkins' Ferry** and, he assumed command of the brigade there when **William R. Scurry** was killed. In all of these fights, he was highly praised by his superiors.

Trans-Mississippi Department commander **Edmund Kirby Smith** appointed Waterhouse brigadier general in May 1864. For reasons unknown, the Senate did not confirm this appointment, and Kirby Smith wrote officials to secure approval of his promoting such "a good officer" (Davis, ed., *The Confederate General,* vol. 6, 109). Waterhouse continued to lead his brigade and act as a brigadier general until his commission was finally confirmed in March 1865.

After the war, Waterhouse returned to Texas and worked as a land speculator. In 1876, after being injured when he fell down a flight of stairs, he contracted pneumonia and died two days after the accident.

WATIE, STAND (1806–1871) CSA. A native of **Georgia,** Watie (or Degataga, which was his Cherokee name) was the son of a full-blooded Cherokee man and a mother who was half **Indian.** As a boy, he received an education, learned English, and became a Christian while attending a Georgia mission school. After attending **Connecticut's** Foreign Mission School, Watie returned to Georgia. There he worked as a planter, became active in tribal affairs, and helped his brother publish the *Cherokee Index.* When Georgia took steps to seize Cherokee land, Watie was among a minority of the tribe who believed it was useless to resist. In 1835, he and three other tribal leaders signed the Treaty of New Echota, which sold the Eastern Cherokee land and required the Indians to move to **Indian Territory.** Watie and his supporters migrated to Indian Territory in early 1836. The majority of the Eastern Cherokees were forced off their land in 1838–39 and were moved to Indian Territory in the infamous "Trail of Tears." These events split the Cherokees politically. Three of those who signed the Treaty of New Echota were executed in 1839 by a group of conservative Indians in accordance with a Cherokee law making it a capital offense to sell Cherokee land, but Watie escaped and became the leader of the minority faction.

By the Civil War, Watie and many other Cherokees were living as slave-owning planters and supported the South's political goals. When war began, he organized a mounted volunteer **company** in June 1861, became its captain, and patrolled Indian Territory to protect it from **Kansas Jayhawkers.** The company later fought dismounted at **Wilson's Creek** and was praised by Confederate officers for maintaining its composure under **artillery** fire. After the battle, Watie convinced John Ross and the Cherokee majority to fight for the Confederacy, and by September, his command numbered about 300 men. In October, the Confederate government appointed him colonel of the Cherokee Mounted Rifles. Watie led it against Unionist Cherokees at **Chustenahlah,** and at **Pea Ridge** it fought as part of **Albert Pike's brigade.**

For the remainder of the war, Watie served as a very effective guerrilla fighter in and around Indian Territory. He participated in more than

100 raids and **skirmishes**, including the battles at **Old Fort Wayne** and **Cabin Creek**, and was appointed brigadier general in May 1864 (he was the only Indian to become a Confederate general). The following month, Watie successfully captured and destroyed the Union supply vessel *J. R. Williams* on the Arkansas River, and later in the year, he participated in **Sterling Price's 1864 Missouri Raid**. He was the last Confederate general to quit the war, surrendering his command on June 23, 1865.

After the war, Watie resumed his life as a planter and businessman in Indian Territory.

WATTS, THOMAS HILL (1819–1892) CSA. A native of **Alabama**, Watts graduated from the University of Virginia in 1840 and became an Alabama lawyer the following year. Becoming involved in **Whig** politics, he was elected to the state legislature four times in the 1840s and to the state senate in 1853. Watts at first opposed **secession** and supported **John Bell** in the **election of 1860**, but he finally joined the secessionists after **Abraham Lincoln** was elected president. As a delegate to the state secession convention, he played an important role in the passage of a secession ordinance.

After being defeated for governor in August 1861, Watts organized the 17th Alabama and was appointed its colonel. He commanded the **regiment** at **Pensacola, Florida**, and Corinth, Mississippi, until **Jefferson Davis** appointed him Confederate attorney general in March 1862. Since the **Confederate Congress** never created a **supreme court**, it was left to state courts and the attorney general to interpret the law. Watts wrote more than 100 opinions, far more than any other Confederate attorney general. Most of his opinions, such as the one upholding **conscription**, received Davis's approval.

In August 1863, Watts was elected governor of Alabama and resigned his cabinet position in October. As governor, he opposed the **impressment** of private property and the conscription of persons whom he believed to be vital state personnel. Watts also tried desperately to defend against enemy cavalry raids in the northern part of the state and attacks on Mobile in the south. When Union troops occupied Montgomery in April 1865, he was removed from office and for a time was held under arrest in a Northern **prison**.

Watts eventually was released from custody and resumed his Alabama law practice. Joining the **Democratic Party**, he was elected to the state legislature and served as president of the state bar association.

WAUD, ALFRED RODOLPH (1828–1891) USA. A native of Great Britain, Waud studied drawing at the Royal Academy's School of Design before immigrating to the United States in 1850 and working as an illustrator for books and periodicals. When the Civil War started, he was hired by the New York *Illustrated News* as a field artist and began covering the war around **Washington, D.C.** Waud witnessed the **First Battle of Manassas** and provided the newspaper with illustrations of the fighting. After accompanying the Union forces that attacked **Hatteras Inlet, North Carolina**, in October 1861, he was hired by *Harper's Weekly* in February 1862. It was with this publication that Waud became the most prolific of all Civil War illustrators. He accompanied the **Army of the Potomac** on all of its campaigns from **Antietam** to **Appomattox** and often worked under fire. One of his last wartime sketches was of **Robert E. Lee** leaving the McLean House after his **surrender** to **U. S. Grant**.

After the war, Waud continued to work for *Harper's Weekly* as an illustrator and reporter and gained much recognition for conducting an informative tour down the Mississippi River to the defeated South. Many of his sketches were used to illustrate Century Magazine's *Battles and Leaders of the Civil War.* Waud died of a heart attack in 1891 while sketching a **Georgia** battlefield. Today, the Library of Congress has a collection of approximately 2,300 sketches made by Waud and his brother, William. *See also* WAR CORRESPONDENTS.

WAUHATCHIE, TENNESSEE, BATTLE OF (OCTOBER 28–29, 1863). By late October 1863, Maj. Gen. **U. S. Grant**, the newly appointed commander of the **Military Division of the Mississippi**, had arrived at Chattanooga, Tennessee, to raise the siege of the Union **Army of the Cumberland**. Grant had replaced **army** commander Maj. Gen. **William S. Rosecrans** with **George H. Thomas** and took steps to resupply the hungry men. This required the Federals to open a supply line from Chattanooga to Bridgeport, Alabama, the nearest station on the Nashville & Chattanooga Railroad under Union control. **Joseph Hooker's** XI and XII **Corps** were at Bridgeport, having been rushed there from **Virginia**, but **Braxton Bragg's** Confederate **Army of Tennessee** had cut the **railroad** from Bridgeport to Chattanooga.

Grant first had to gain control of Brown's Ferry, a Tennessee River crossing west of Chattanooga. Following a plan by Brig. Gen. **William F. "Baldy" Smith**, he sent one detachment down the river by boat on the night of October 26, while another marched west to the ferry across the Moccasin Bend peninsula. On the morning of October 27, these two columns surprised **Evander Law's** Confederate **brigade** at Brown's Ferry and quickly secured the crossing. The next day, Hooker brought three **divisions** from Bridgeport to link up with the Army of the Cumberland. He left **John Geary's** 1,500-man XII Corps division about three miles south of Brown's Ferry at Wauhatchie Station (located in Lookout Valley, about two miles southwest of Lookout Mountain's northern face) on the Nashville & Chattanooga Railroad to protect his lines of communication to the south and a road west to Kelley's Ferry on the Tennessee River. Hooker then took the other two divisions to Brown's Ferry.

Lieutenant General **James Longstreet** witnessed the enemy activity and received permission from Bragg to attack Geary's position that night with **Micah Jenkins's** division to capture Wauhatchie Station and isolate Hooker at the ferry. Because Union **artillery** across the Tennessee River on Moccasin Point controlled the roads needed in the operation, Longstreet was forced to make his attack at night. He moved Law's brigade from the western side of Lookout Mountain to a small hill overlooking the road from Wauhatchie to Brown's Ferry to block any enemy reinforcements sent from there. Jenkins's other three brigades were moved from the eastern side of Lookout Mountain to join Law. **Jerome Robertson's** and **Henry Benning's** brigades reinforced Law, while **John Bratton's** brigade was selected to attack Geary at Wauhatchie. Jenkins had about 3,900 men in position, with Bratton's attacking brigade numbering about 1,800 men.

Bratton's attack was made about 12:30 A.M. on October 28, making Wauhatchie one of the war's few nighttime battles. Geary's men were surprised, but they quickly formed a *V*-shaped defensive line. The battle was confused in the darkness (and just as confusing to study), but the Union brigades of **George S. Greene** and George A. Cobham repulsed several Confederate attacks with the aid of an artillery battery positioned in their rear. Hearing the firing, Hooker sent two divisions under **Oliver O. Howard** from Brown's Ferry to aid Geary. **George Hector Tyndale's** Union brigade soon encountered Law and Robertson, and a second battle began. Orland Smith's brigade then joined Tyndale, and the Federals launched several unsuccessful assaults. The two fights were vicious and often at close quarters, but after two hours, Jenkins finally ordered a withdrawal to **Lookout Mountain**. During the battle, the Federals' mule train broke free, and exaggerated claims were made later that it contributed to the Union victory by stampeding through the Confederate lines. Jenkins lost 460 men at Wauhatchie, while the Federals counted 437 casualties. Afterward, Grant established a **pontoon bridge** across the Tennessee River and opened the famous "Cracker Line" to Bridgeport.

Afterward, there was much controversy about the battle on both sides. Hooker was very critical of **Carl Schurz** because two of his brigades became lost on the way to Wauhatchie. Schurz demanded and received a court of inquiry, which cleared him of any wrongdoing. Longstreet also was displeased. He preferred charges against Law for being too timid and for ordering the withdrawal and questioned the fighting ability of Jenkins's entire division. Law insisted that he had been ordered to withdraw, and the charges finally were dropped. *See also* CHATTANOOGA, TENNESSEE, CAMPAIGN OF.

WAUL, THOMAS NEVILLE (1813–1903) CSA. A native of **South Carolina**, Waul was forced to drop out of South Carolina College because of poor health and his father's death. Moving to **Alabama**, he became a school principal at age 17 but moved to **Mississippi** a year later. There, Waul was admitted to the bar in 1835, but he soon moved to **Texas**, where he practiced law and became a planter.

Waul was defeated for the **U.S. Congress** in 1859, but in 1861, he was elected to the Provisional **Confederate Congress**. After being defeated for the Senate in 1861, he raised Waul's Texas Legion and in May 1862 was appointed its colonel. Sent to **Arkansas**, the **legion's** cavalry and **artillery** components left the command, and Waul took the remaining infantry to **Vicksburg, Mississippi**, in October. By January 1863, Waul's Legion was part of **William W. Loring's division**. Waul was placed in command of Fort Pemberton on the Yazoo River in February and received great praise from Loring for helping turn back the **Yazoo Pass Expedition**. Afterward, Waul's Legion was sent to the Vicksburg defenses, where it was captured at the end of the **Vicksburg Campaign**.

After being **exchanged**, Waul was promoted to brigadier general in September 1863 and was sent to the **Trans-Mississippi Department**, where he organized an infantry **brigade** in Texas. He was removed from command, however, and was sent to **Louisiana** in February 1864 to replace **James M. Hawes** in command of a brigade in **John G. Walker's** Texas division. Waul led the brigade with skill at **Mansfield**, **Pleasant Hill**, and **Jenkins' Ferry** and had his arm broken in the latter battle. After recuperating, he returned to brigade command until war's end.

Waul returned to Texas after the war, where he became active in **Reconstruction** politics and practiced law.

WAYNE, HENRY CONSTANTINE (1815–1883) CSA. A native of **Georgia**, Wayne attended schools in **Massachusetts**, including Harvard University, but graduated from **West Point** in 1838. After some service in the **artillery**, he taught **tactics** at the academy from 1841 to 1846. During the **Mexican War**, Wayne served as a captain in the Quartermaster Department and won two **brevets** for gallantry. He remained in the **U.S. Army** after the war, published a text on sword exercises in 1850, and was awarded a gold medal by the French Zoological Society in 1858 for his participation in Secretary of War **Jefferson Davis's** camel experiment in the American Southwest.

Wayne resigned his captain's commission in December 1860 and in early 1861 was appointed Georgia's adjutant general and inspector general. He served on Gov. **Joseph E. Brown's** staff until he was promoted to Confederate brigadier general in December 1861. However, Wayne immediately resigned his commission in January 1862 after being ordered to **Virginia**. Brown then appointed him major general and adjutant general of state troops, a position Wayne kept for the remainder of the war. After using Georgia Military Institute cadets to drill his men, he commanded two militia **brigades** during the **Atlanta Campaign** and guarded crossings on the Chattahoochee River. Wayne was relieved in the summer of 1864 and returned to his administrative duties. In November and December, he assembled a motley force of soldiers and contested the enemy at several river crossings during the **March to the Sea**. Wayne finally retreated into **Savannah, Georgia**, turned his command over to Maj. Gen. **Gustavus Smith,** and returned to his administrative duties. Although not a leading Confederate general, he discharged his wartime duties with skill and efficiency.

After the war, Wayne remained in Georgia, where he worked in the lumber industry.

WAYNESBORO, VIRGINIA, BATTLE OF (MARCH 2, 1865). After his defeat at **Cedar Creek** in October 1864, Confederate Lt. Gen. **Jubal A. Early** was ordered to send much of his command from the **Shenandoah Valley** to reinforce **Robert E. Lee** at Petersburg, Virginia. With barely 2,000 men, he then went into winter quarters near Staunton.

On February 27, 1865, Maj. Gen. **Philip Sheridan** left Winchester on **Sheridan's Virginia Raid** and advanced up the Valley with 10,000 cavalrymen. His orders from **U. S. Grant** were to destroy the Virginia Central Railroad at Staunton and to cross the Blue Ridge Mountains to destroy the James River Canal and, if possible, capture Lynchburg and cut its Virginia & Tennessee Railroad. **Skirmishing** as he went, Early retreated east from Staunton to Waynesboro to guard the Blue Ridge Mountain's Rockfish Gap, which led to Charlottesville. The Federals entered Staunton on March 1, and Sheridan sent Brig. Gen. **George A. Custer's division** in pursuit of Early the next day.

Early had 1,700 men of **Gabriel C. Wharton's** division entrench in a thin, weak line just west of Waynesboro along a north-south axis. His right extended just beyond Waynesboro, while his left was anchored on a hill near the South River. Upon reaching Early's position, Custer discovered that the Confederate left did not extend all the way to the river. At about 3:30 P.M., he attacked Early's vulnerable left flank with three dismounted **regiments**, while the rest of his division made a **frontal attack**. The Confederate line crumbled, and retreat became a rout. Custer's troopers captured virtually all of the Confederates except Early and his staff. Early lost approximately 1,600 men, 200 wagons, and 14 cannons in the battle, while Custer suffered only 30 casualties.

The victory at Waynesboro allowed Sheridan to cross the mountains at Rockfish Gap to Charlottesville. Destroying **railroad** track and canal locks as he went, he rode from Charlottesville to City Point, where he linked up with Grant for the final days of the **Petersburg Campaign**. The Battle of Waynesboro ended **Sheridan's Shenandoah Valley Campaign** and Early's career. Rejoining Lee, Early learned that the defeat had turned public opinion against him and that Lee could not put him back in command of troops.

WAYNESBOROUGH, GEORGIA, BATTLE OF (DECEMBER 4, 1864). During **William T. Sherman's March to the Sea**, Union Brig. Gen. **H. Judson Kilpatrick's** cavalry was sent to burn a **railroad** bridge between Millen and Augusta, Georgia, and to release Union **prisoners** at Millen. Confederate cavalry under Maj. Gen. **Joseph Wheeler** saved the bridge and then attacked Kilpatrick at **Buck Head Creek** on November 28. When Kilpatrick learned that the prisoners had been removed, he ended his mission. Sherman then ordered him to attack the Confederates at every opportunity and to create the impression that the Union forces were advancing toward Augusta.

Kilpatrick attacked Wheeler's cavalry at Waynesborough on December 4. Early that morning, Col. Smith D. Atkins's **brigade** drove the Confederate advance guard back into their entrenchments south of town and then outflanked that position. Wheeler's troopers fell back to a second line of defenses in Waynesborough, but this line also was broken when Kilpatrick launched a **frontal attack** with Eli H. Murray's brigade. After losing approximately 250 men, Wheeler retreated to Augusta. Kilpatrick lost 190 men and succeeded in driving the Confederate cavalry away from **Savannah**, Sherman's true target.

WEBB, ALEXANDER STEWART (1835–1911) USA. A native of **New York**, Webb was the son of newspaperman and diplomat James Watson

Webb. After graduating from **West Point** in 1855, he fought with the **artillery** in the **Seminole Wars** and then returned to the academy in 1857 to teach mathematics.

When the Civil War began in April 1861, Webb was promoted to 1st lieutenant. After helping defend **Fort Pickens, Florida**, he was promoted to captain in May and was sent to **Virginia**, where he and his artillery battery were held in reserve at **First Manassas**. Webb was appointed assistant inspector general for the **Army of the Potomac's** artillery in August and was made major of the 1st Rhode Island Light Artillery the following month. Working under chief of artillery **William F. Barry**, he participated in the **Peninsula Campaign**. In August 1862, Webb was promoted to lieutenant colonel and spent nearly a year serving as assistant inspector general and chief of staff for **Fitz John Porter's** V Corps. During this time, he served at **Antietam** and **Chancellorsville** and for a time was an artillery inspector in the **Washington, D.C.**, defenses.

In June 1863, Webb was promoted to brigadier general of volunteers and was given command of the **Philadelphia Brigade** in **John Gibbon's** II Corps **division**. During **Gettysburg's Pickett's Charge**, his **brigade** was positioned at the copse of trees that served as the attack's target. Webb was wounded while playing a key role in repulsing the attack, and his brigade lost 451 men. He won a **brevet** for his actions there and in 1891 was awarded the **Medal of Honor**. In August, Webb took temporary command of the division and led it in the **Bristoe Station** and **Mine Run Campaigns**, winning another brevet for the former. Returning to his brigade in early 1864, he fought at the **Wilderness** and at **Spotsylvania's** "Bloody Angle" (winning two more brevets) and suffered a severe wound in the latter. This wound kept Webb off duty until January 1865, when he returned to the **army** as **George G. Meade's** chief of staff. He served in that capacity through the remainder of the **Petersburg Campaign** and in the **Appomattox Campaign**.

When Webb was mustered out of the volunteers in January 1866, he held the brevet rank of major general in both the volunteers and regulars. He remained in the army until 1870, when he retired as lieutenant colonel of the 5th U.S. Infantry. Webb then became president of the City College of New York and served in that capacity for 33 years.

WEBER, MAX (1824–1901) USA. A native of the German Grand Duchy of Baden, Weber graduated from the Karlsruhe military school in 1843 (along with **Franz Sigel**) and became a lieutenant in the Grand Duchy's **army**. During the 1848 revolution, he defected to the rebels and had to immigrate to the United States when Prussia crushed the movement. Throughout the 1850s, Weber operated a hotel in New York City.

Weber entered Union service in May 1861 as colonel of the 20th New York, a **regiment** he originally organized as the "United Turner Rifles." After service at **Fort Monroe, Virginia**, and on the **North Carolina** coast, he was promoted to brigadier general of volunteers in April 1862. Weber commanded the **Department of Virginia** for a few months before being given command of a **brigade** that became part of the **Army of the Potomac's** II Corps. At **Antietam**, he fought in **Samuel French's division** and was praised for his actions, but he suffered a wound that cost him the use of his right arm. After returning to duty in late 1863, Weber served in **Washington, D.C.**, for a few months and in April 1864 was given command of **Harpers Ferry, West Virginia**, and the troops in neighboring **Maryland**. He was forced to evacuate his position temporarily during **Jubal A. Early's 1864 Washington Raid** and was never reassigned to any other duty after being replaced at Harpers Ferry in October 1864.

Weber resigned his commission in May 1865 and was appointed U.S. consul to Nantes, France, after the war. Returning to the United States, he served as a **New York** tax assessor and an internal revenue collector.

WEBSTER, JOSEPH DANA (1811–1876) USA. A native of **New Hampshire**, Webster graduated from Dartmouth College in 1832. After studying law, he became a civil engineer and worked for the government until receiving a commission with the **U.S. Army's** topographical **engineers** in 1838. After serving in the **Mexican War**, Webster resigned his captain's commission in 1854 and settled in Chicago, Illinois. There he was active in developing a sewer system and protecting the city from Lake Michigan's waters.

During the 1861 **secession** crisis, Webster opposed radicals on both sides. He served as **Illinois's** chief engineer until June, at which time he was commissioned a major of volunteers and was made a paymaster, although he continued to supervise the construction of defenses at Cairo, Illinois. Webster was promoted to colonel of the 1st Illinois Light Artillery in February 1862, but he actually served as Brig. Gen. **U. S. Grant's** chief engineer and chief of staff. He saw combat at **Belmont, Forts Henry and Donelson**, and **Shiloh**, and at this last battle was the officer who assembled the numerous cannons that formed Grant's last line of defense near the Tennessee River.

Webster was promoted to brigadier general of volunteers in November 1862 and began supervising the **railroads** that supplied Grant's

army during the **Vicksburg Campaign**. After **Vicksburg's** surrender, he served as **William T. Sherman's** chief of staff until the beginning of the **Atlanta Campaign**. Webster remained in Nashville, Tennessee, and was put in charge of the armies' supply lines. After the fall of Atlanta, he became **George H. Thomas's** chief of staff and served him during the **Franklin and Nashville Campaign**. **Brevetted** major general of volunteers for his war service, Webster resigned his commission in November 1865.

After the war, Webster returned to Chicago and worked as a city assessor from 1869 to 1872 and then as a tax collector.

WEED, STEPHEN HINSDALE (1831–1863) USA. A native of **New York**, Weed graduated from **West Point** in 1854 and served with the **artillery** in the **Seminole Wars**, "**Bleeding Kansas**," and the **Utah Expedition**.

When the Civil War began, Weed was a 1st lieutenant of artillery. He was promoted to captain of the 5th U.S. Artillery in May 1861 and spent the winter of 1861–62 on duty in **Pennsylvania**. Joining the **Army of the Potomac** in early 1862, Weed commanded a battery in the **Peninsula** and **Seven Days Campaigns**. He fought at **Second Manassas** as chief of artillery for **George Sykes's** V Corps **division** but returned to his battery for **Antietam**.

After serving as chief of artillery for the V Corps at **Fredericksburg** and **Chancellorsville**, Weed was promoted from captain of regulars to brigadier general of volunteers in June 1863 and was given command of a volunteer infantry **brigade** in **Romeyn B. Ayres's division** of regulars in the V Corps. He performed excellent service on the second day of **Gettysburg** when **Gouverneur K. Warren** sent his brigade to support **Strong Vincent's** brigade at Little Round Top. Weed helped save the Union left by stabilizing the line and then dragged six cannons to the top of the hill. While supervising their fire, he was mortally wounded in the arm and chest by a **sharpshooter's** bullet and died a few hours later.

WEISIGER, DAVID ADDISON (1818–1899) CSA. A native of **Virginia**, Weisiger worked as a businessman before serving in the **Mexican War** as a 2nd lieutenant and regimental adjutant. After the war, he resumed his business career and became active in the state militia. Weisiger became colonel of the 39th Virginia, served as officer of the day at the hanging of **John Brown**, and was commanding the 4th Virginia Battalion when the state seceded in 1861.

In April 1861, Weisiger led his battalion to **Norfolk** and spent the next two months organizing a **regiment**. He entered Confederate service in

July as colonel of the 12th Virginia and spent the winter in defense of Norfolk. Becoming part of **William Mahone's brigade**, Weisiger fought at **Seven Pines** and in the **Seven Days Campaign**. As part of the **Army of Northern Virginia**, he then served at **Second Manassas**. When Mahone was wounded there, Weisiger took temporary command of the brigade and led it in a charge until he, too, was wounded. He did not return to duty until after **Gettysburg**. At the **Wilderness**, Weisiger assumed command of the brigade when Mahone took over the **division**. He was promoted to temporary brigadier general in late May 1864 and to permanent rank in July. Weisiger led the brigade through the **Overland** and **Petersburg Campaigns**, and in the latter, he led the Confederate counterattack at the **Crater**. Wounded in the fight, he became known as the "Hero of the Crater" for his role in sealing the Union breakthrough. Weisiger continued to lead his brigade throughout the Petersburg Campaign and surrendered with the **army** at **Appomattox**.

After the war, Weisiger remained in Virginia, where he worked first as a bank cashier and then as a businessman.

WEITZEL, GODFREY (1835–1884) USA. A native of **Ohio**, Weitzel graduated second in his 1855 **West Point** class. Assigned to the **engineers**, he worked several years on the defenses of **New Orleans, Louisiana**, before returning to the academy to teach engineering from 1859 to 1861.

When the Civil War began, Weitzel was a 1st lieutenant of engineers. In the war's first months, he participated in the relief expedition to **Fort Pickens, Florida**, and supervised construction of the defenses of Cincinnati, Ohio. In December 1861, Weitzel was made chief engineer for the defenses of **Washington, D.C.**, but he was appointed chief engineer for the **Department of the Gulf** in early 1862 and accompanied **Benjamin F. Butler's** forces to New Orleans. Weitzel served as Butler's acting mayor of New Orleans and was promoted from 1st lieutenant of regulars to brigadier general of volunteers in August 1862. After commanding a **brigade** under Butler, he led a XIX Corps **division** under **Nathaniel P. Banks** during the **Bayou Teche** and **Port Hudson Campaigns** and at **Bayou Lafourche** and **Sabine Pass**. In May 1864, Weitzel was transferred to **Virginia**, where he led a division in Butler's **Army of the James** during the **Bermuda Hundred Campaign**. He then was appointed Butler's chief engineer and served in that capacity throughout much of the **Petersburg Campaign**.

After winning a **brevet** for his service at **Fort Harrison**, Weitzel was given command of the XVIII Corps in October 1864, with promotion to major general of volunteers coming the following month. In December, he was given command of the new XXV Corps, a **corps** of **black troops**, and led it for the remainder of the war. Weitzel led the corps in Butler's unsuccessful attack on **Fort Fisher, North Carolina**, and then returned to Virginia, where he commanded the first troops to enter **Richmond**. He was brevetted brigadier general of regulars for his service at Richmond and major general of regulars for his war service.

After serving under **William T. Sherman** on the U.S.–Mexico border after the war, Weitzel was mustered out of the volunteers in March 1866. He remained in the regular **army** as a captain of engineers and became highly regarded for his work on canals (including construction of the Sault Sainte Marie lock) and lighthouses. Weitzel was still on duty as a lieutenant colonel when he died in 1884.

WELDON RAILROAD, VIRGINIA, UNION OPERATIONS AGAINST (JUNE 22–AUGUST 21, 1864).

During the summer of 1864, **U. S. Grant** and the **Army of the Potomac** were heavily engaged with **Robert E. Lee's Army of Northern Virginia** in the **Petersburg Campaign**. A main objective of Grant's was to cut the Weldon Railroad, one of Lee's important supply lines connecting Petersburg, Virginia, with **North Carolina**.

When Grant's first attempt to take Petersburg by assault failed in mid-June, he settled into a siege and took action to cut the Weldon Railroad. On June 22, he launched his first attack on the vital supply line. Screened by **James H. Wilson's** cavalry, **David B. Birney's** II Corps and **Horatio G. Wrights's** VI Corps (on the left and right, respectively) marched west, but they soon became separated in the unfamiliar, wooded countryside. Reacting quickly, Confederate Lt. Gen. **A. P. Hill** sent **Cadmus Wilcox's division** to attack Wright, while **William Mahone's** and **Bushrod Johnson's** divisions hit Birney. The latter two captured 1,600 **prisoners** after mauling **John Gibbon's** Union division and bloodying **Francis Barlow's** division. On the left, Wright's **corps** also was pushed back by Wilcox. The next day, Wright and Birney advanced a little farther and secured a foothold across the Jerusalem Plank Road. Although Wilson's cavalry destroyed some track, the operation failed to cut the Weldon Railroad, and the Federals lost 2,962 men.

In August, Grant made a second move against the Weldon Railroad when he attacked the Confederate **railroads** both north and south of **Richmond**. Besides cutting the enemy's supply lines, he hoped to force the Confederates to strip the **Shenandoah Valley** of troops to reinforce their Richmond-Petersburg defenses. To the south, **Gouverneur K. Warren's**

V Corps moved off the Petersburg line on the night of August 14, marched to the Union left, and attacked the Weldon Railroad in the early morning of August 18. Easily pushing aside **James Dearing's** Confederate cavalry **brigade**, Warren captured the railroad at Globe Tavern, six miles south of Petersburg. Using one division to destroy the track, he sent another west to extend the Union line and **Romeyn Ayres's** division up the track to the north toward Petersburg. That afternoon, Confederate Maj. Gen. **Henry Heth's** division surprised Ayres when it attacked his left flank. The Confederates wrecked one brigade, but Ayres recovered, and the two divisions slugged it out in thick woods as a heavy rain fell. In this action, Warren suffered 836 casualties.

That night, both Lee and Grant sent reinforcements to Globe Tavern. Warren strengthened Ayres's position considerably on August 19 with **Samuel Crawford's** division. Hill made a second attack against Crawford's right flank that afternoon with six brigades and pushed the Federals back and captured 2,700 prisoners, but a counterattack from the east by the IX Corps stopped the Confederates and recaptured most of the lost ground. When the fighting sputtered out, Warren withdrew nearly two miles to a stronger position.

Both sides continued to reinforce the area, and heavy **skirmishing** continued along the railroad on August 20. Hill made another attack on August 21 but was repulsed by intense Union **artillery** fire. After arriving on the scene that afternoon, Lee finally ordered a halt to the fighting. This four-day battle at Globe Tavern cost the Federals 4,455 men (mostly taken prisoner) out of approximately 20,300 engaged. The Confederates lost about 1,600 men out of 14,000 engaged. Despite the high losses, Warren held on to his position, and the Federals permanently cut the Weldon Railroad on his front, although the Confederates temporarily recaptured part of it at **Reams' Station** a few days later.

WELLES, GIDEON (1802–1878) USA. A native of **Connecticut**, Welles graduated from **Vermont's** Norwich Academy. Working as a journalist, he became involved in politics and helped organize Connecticut's **Democratic Party**. Although Welles unsuccessfully ran for office three times, he did serve in the state legislature and as the state's comptroller before being appointed a postmaster by President Andrew Jackson in 1836. In 1846, Welles was put in charge of the Naval Bureau of Provisions and Clothing. As the **slavery** issue intensified, he switched political parties in 1854 and became a moderate **Republican**.

When **Abraham Lincoln** was elected president in 1860, he appointed Welles secretary of the navy. Welles had no real naval experience, but he was greatly aided by his assistant secretary, **Gustavus V. Fox**. Welles oversaw the implementation of a **blockade** against the Confederacy that became more effective as the war continued and worked to modernize the **U.S. Navy**. Although he at first did not see any great advantage in the new **ironclads**, he eventually came to appreciate them and rushed dozens into service. Welles also supported innovations in steam power and ordnance technology. His abrupt manner and frequent criticisms angered many officers and officials, but Welles made the Navy Department one of the most efficient departments in the U.S. government. He also contributed to Lincoln's administration by working as a moderate and helping offset the radical tendencies of **Edwin Stanton** and other **Radical Republicans**.

Welles continued to serve as navy secretary until 1869. After his retirement, he wrote the 1874 book *Lincoln and Seward* and edited his wartime diary, which was published in three volumes in 1911 as *Diary of Gideon Welles*. Although Welles's editing made the diary highly biased, it is considered one of the classic personal accounts of the Civil War.

WELSH, THOMAS (1824–1863) USA. A native of **Pennsylvania**, Welsh worked in the lumber industry before volunteering for the **Mexican War** as a private in the 2nd Kentucky. He fought under both Zachary Taylor and **Winfield Scott** and was badly wounded at Buena Vista. When the war was over, Welsh was commissioned a 2nd lieutenant in the 11th U.S. Infantry but was mustered out of service in 1848. Returning to Pennsylvania, he then worked as a merchant, canal boat owner, justice of the peace, and lock superintendent.

Welsh raised a **company** of volunteers in April 1861 and was mustered into Union service as a captain in the 90-day 2nd Pennsylvania. On that same day, he was elevated to lieutenant colonel. After serving with **Robert Patterson** in the **Shenandoah Valley**, the **regiment** was mustered out of service. Welsh was then appointed colonel of the 45th Pennsylvania in October. Sent to **Charleston, South Carolina**, he took a **brigade** command in **Horatio G. Wright's division** in April 1862 but was transferred back to **Virginia** that summer. Placed in command of a brigade in the 1st Division of the **Army of the Potomac's** IX Corps, Welsh led it at **South Mountain** and **Antietam**, but he reverted to his regimental command in October.

Welsh was promoted to brigadier general of volunteers in November 1862, but he led only his regiment at **Fredericksburg** because he did not receive notification of the promotion. After the battle, he accompanied the corps to the **Department of the Ohio**. Because the Senate had not confirmed Welsh's appointment to general, he had to be reappointed in March 1863. The following month, he assumed command of the division. The IX Corps joined the **Army of the Tennessee** for the **Vicksburg Campaign** in June, and Welsh led his division through the remainder of the siege of Vicksburg and the subsequent siege of **Jackson, Mississippi**. Contracting malaria soon afterward, he died in August while in **Ohio**.

WESSELLS, HENRY WALTON (1809–1889) USA. A native of **Connecticut**, Wessells graduated from **West Point** in 1833 and served with the infantry in the **Seminole Wars**. During the **Mexican War**, he was wounded at Churubusco, received a **brevet** for gallantry, and was promoted to captain. After the war, Wessells performed routine garrison duty along the Pacific coast and on the frontier.

After the Civil War began, Wessells was promoted to major of the 6th U.S. Infantry in June 1861 and in September was appointed colonel of the 8th Kansas. After serving on the Kansas-Missouri border, he resigned his commission in February 1862. Wessells then was appointed brigadier general of volunteers in April and took a **brigade** command in the 1st Division of the **Army of the Potomac's** IV Corps. He led it during the **Peninsula Campaign** and was wounded at **Seven Pines**. Wessells remained in southeastern **Virginia** later that year and led a brigade around Suffolk after the rest of the **army** was sent north. In late December 1862, he was given a **division** command in the **Department of North Carolina** and led it until being appointed commander of the District of the Albemarle in May 1863. In April 1864, Wessells's career essentially was ruined when he was forced to surrender by Confederate Brig. Gen. **Robert Hoke** at **Plymouth, North Carolina**. After being held prisoner under fire at **Charleston, South Carolina**, he was **exchanged** in August 1864. Wessells never again held a field command, but he did serve in such administrative positions as commissary of **prisoners** and supervisor of a New York **conscription** center. After being brevetted major general of volunteers for his unsuccessful defense of Plymouth and brigadier general of regulars for his war service, he was mustered out of the volunteers in January 1866.

Wessells remained in the regular army as lieutenant colonel of the 18th U.S. Infantry and served on the frontier until he retired in 1871.

WEST, JOSEPH RODMAN (1822–1898) USA. A native of **Louisiana**, West moved with his family to **Pennsylvania** as a boy. He attended the University of Pennsylvania for a year but returned to **New Orleans**,

Louisiana, in 1841. After serving as a captain of **Maryland** and **Washington, D.C.**, volunteers during the **Mexican War**, West moved to **California** in 1849 and became the owner of a San Francisco newspaper.

West entered Union service in August 1861 when he was appointed lieutenant colonel of the 1st California Volunteers. He participated in **James H. Carleton's California Column** to defend Arizona and **New Mexico** during **Henry Hopkins Sibley's New Mexico Campaign** and replaced Carleton as regimental colonel in June 1862. After being promoted to brigadier general in October, West led a successful expedition against hostile Apache **Indians** in January 1863. Apache leader Mangas Coloradas was captured during the expedition and apparently was murdered (probably with West's consent). West later commanded the District of Arizona for a time and then was transferred to **Arkansas**, where he took charge of a **division** during the 1864 **Camden Expedition**. Remaining in Arkansas, he pursued the Confederates during **Sterling Price's 1864 Missouri Raid** and ended the war in command of the **Department of the South's** cavalry.

After being **brevetted** major general of volunteers for his war service, West was mustered out of the volunteers in January 1866. Returning to New Orleans, he worked as a deputy U.S. marshal and customs auditor before being elected to the U.S. Senate as a **Republican** in 1871. When **Reconstruction** ended, West declined to run for reelection. He moved to Washington, D.C., and from 1882 to 1885 served on the District of Columbia's board of commissioners.

WEST POINT, MISSISSIPPI, BATTLE OF (FEBRUARY 21, 1864). *See* OKOLONA, MISSISSIPPI, BATTLE OF.

WEST POINT, NEW YORK (UNITED STATES MILITARY ACADEMY). The United States Military Academy at West Point, New York, had its origins in 1802 as a **U.S. Army engineering** school. This school was transformed into a military academy in 1812 for the training of officers. More commonly known as West Point, the academy was a four-year institution (with a five-year program briefly existing when the Civil War began) that stressed engineering skills and mathematics, along with infantry, cavalry, and **artillery** drill. Ironically, little attention was given to actual battlefield **tactics** or grand **strategy**. The graduates, **brevet** 2nd lieutenants, knew the intricacies of drill and perhaps some small-unit tactics, but they had little understanding of how armies operated or war was waged. **Dennis Hart Mahan** was one professor who did stress military history and strategy and thus had a large influence on future Civil War generals.

Appointments, made by members of the **U.S. Congress**, were highly prized because West Point provided young men an excellent education. Cadet life was based on the honor system and was strictly monitored and structured, with cadets being ranked in both academics and behavior. Demerits were given for even the smallest infractions, and an excessive number could get a cadet dismissed. Class ranking had a long-term effect on one's military career, for it determined the branch of service to which a graduate was assigned. Top class members were placed in the engineers, and then, in order, to the artillery, cavalry, and infantry. Oddly, matriculating at West Point did not obligate a graduate to serve in the military. Unlike today, graduates could resign their commissions immediately after graduation and return to civilian life. In the **Confederate army** 156 out of 425 generals graduated or attended the academy, while 228 out of 583 Union generals did so.

WEST POINT FOUNDRY AT COLD SPRING, NEW YORK. Also known as the Cold Spring Foundry, this private foundry was located in **New York** on the west bank of the Hudson River, across from the military academy at **West Point**. **Robert P. Parrott** served as superintendent and used the foundry to produce his superb **Parrott rifle**. During the war, the West Point Foundry reached a peak production of 25 Parrott rifles and 7,000 rounds of ammunition per week, for a war production total of over 1,700 Parrott rifles and three million rounds of ammunition.

WESTERN DEPARTMENT (CONFEDERATE). This was another name for **Confederate Department No. 2.**

WESTERN DEPARTMENT (UNION). This Union military **department** was created on July 3, 1861, by adding **Illinois** to the old **Department of the West**. The new department consisted of those states and territories lying between the Mississippi River and the Rocky Mountains (including **New Mexico)** and had its headquarters at Fort Leavenworth, Kansas. It was commanded by **John C. Frémont**, but he proved to be a poor officer. Frémont was surrounded by corruption, clashed with **Montgomery Blair's** powerful family, and angered **Abraham Lincoln** by declaring martial law and attempting to free the department's slaves. He also suffered military setbacks, and part of his command under **Nathaniel Lyon** was defeated at **Wilson's Creek** in August 1861. In early November 1861, Frémont was replaced by **David Hunter**, but on November 9, only days after Hunter assumed command, the department was merged into the **Department of Missouri and Kansas.**

WEST VIRGINIA. When **Virginia** seceded in April 1861, the majority of the mountainous western counties opposed the action because of hostility toward the rich, plantation tidewater region; the paucity of slaves in the western area; and economic and family ties the western Virginians had to **Pennsylvania** and **Ohio**. When the state's western delegates were outvoted at the **secession** convention, the western counties took steps to secede from Virginia and form a new, pro-Union state.

On June 11, 1861, delegates from 26 western counties met at Wheeling to form a new state and create a loyal government for Virginia. Ordinances were adopted two months later setting up the state of Kanawha (kan-NOW-wha) and creating a new loyal Virginia government. Kanawha, later renamed West Virginia, eventually contained 50 counties and had its capital at Wheeling. **Francis H. Pierpont** was chosen as the new governor of Virginia, along with a new loyal legislature. In November, a constitutional convention was held to finalize the new state's creation. The name West Virginia was adopted, and the constitution was ratified on April 3, 1862, by voters who had taken the **oath of allegiance**. The **U.S. Congress** approved a request made in May to admit the new state and drafted a bill to accomplish the act. One of the bill's requirements was that West Virginia had to abolish **slavery** gradually. The bill was passed on December 13, 1862, and was signed into law by **Abraham Lincoln** on April 20, 1863. West Virginia then was admitted to the Union on June 20. **Arthur I. Boreman** was elected the state's first governor.

West Virginia was important during the war because it contained the vital Baltimore & Ohio Railroad and bordered the Ohio River. When war first erupted, **George B. McClellan** led a small **army** to gain control of the mountainous region. His victories at **Philippi**, **Rich Mountain**, and **Carrick's Ford** helped secure the region for the Union and made him a popular figure. **Robert E. Lee** was then placed in command of the Confederates in the region, but he was defeated at **Carnifex Ferry** and **Cheat Mountain**. Union troops stationed in West Virginia were involved in **Stonewall Jackson's 1862 Shenandoah Valley Campaign**, and late that summer, Confederate Maj. Gen. **William W. Loring** invaded the area. For the rest of the war, the region suffered greatly because of its citizens' split loyalties, and it was the scene of frequent guerrilla warfare and such cavalry raids as **Jones's and Imboden's Raid**. West Virginia furnished approximately 25,000 soldiers to the Union cause and perhaps 15,000 to the Confederates.

WESTPORT, MISSOURI, BATTLE OF (OCTOBER 23, 1864). By October 1864, the Confederates in Maj. Gen. **Sterling Price's 1864 Missouri Raid** were struggling in western **Missouri**, a few miles south of

Kansas City near the **Kansas** border. Over several days, fights had broken out with the Federals at **Little Blue River**, **Big Blue River**, and **Independence**. Price's 9,000-man **Army of Missouri** seemingly was trapped between **Samuel Curtis's** 20,000-man **Army of the Border** to the front and **Alfred Pleasonton's** 7,000-man cavalry **division** in the rear. Rather than escaping to the south, Price adopted a plan proposed by **Jo Shelby** to attack Curtis first and then turn to defeat Pleasonton.

On October 23, Price attacked Curtis's defensive position along Brush Creek, outside Westport, while **John S. Marmaduke** delayed Pleasonton's cavalry in the rear at the Big Blue River. Sending in Shelby and **James F. Fagan**, Price at first drove back Curtis, but the Federals regrouped and successfully counterattacked. While fierce fighting raged for several hours, Pleasonton drove Marmaduke's cavalry away from the Big Blue River and began threatening Price's rear. Price then disengaged and retreated to avoid being trapped between the two enemy forces. He rapidly marched 61 miles in the next two days before fighting the campaign's last battles at **Mine Creek and Marais des Cygnes River** on October 25. The Battle of Westport was the largest Civil War battle west of the Mississippi River, in terms of numbers engaged (approximately 36,000 men). Although exact numbers of casualties are unknown, both sides lost approximately 1,500 men.

WHARTON, GABRIEL COLVIN (1824–1906) CSA. A native of **Virginia**, Wharton was the great-grandson of a British major general. After graduating second in the **Virginia Military Institute** class of 1847, he became active in mining and engineering and moved to modern-day Arizona.

When the Civil War began, Wharton joined **Albert Sidney Johnston's** band of Southerners and traveled with him to Virginia to offer his services to the Confederacy. He was appointed major of the 45th Virginia in June 1861, but the following month, he raised the 51st Virginia and was appointed its colonel. After participating in **John B. Floyd's** western Virginia Campaign later that year, Wharton's **regiment** accompanied Floyd to **Tennessee** and became part of the **Fort Donelson** garrison. He and his men avoided capture, however, by leaving the doomed fort with Floyd before the surrender. This action earned Floyd, and apparently Wharton, the enmity of **Jefferson Davis**.

After serving on Albert Sidney Johnston's staff for a while, Wharton returned to western Virginia, where he was given a **brigade** command in early 1863. Probably because of Davis's ill will, however, he was not promoted to brigadier general until September. Known to his men as "Old Gabe," Wharton was a popular officer, and he spent the rest of the war in and around **West Virginia** and East Tennessee. After defending **Saltville** against Union raids, his brigade joined **Robert Ransom's division** in late 1863 and was sent to East Tennessee to participate in **James Longstreet's Knoxville Campaign** as part of **Simon B. Buckner's** division.

Wharton's greatest service came in the spring of 1864 when his brigade was sent to the **Shenandoah Valley** to help **John C. Breckinridge** defend it against **Franz Sigel's** Union raid. Covering 187 miles in eight days, he reached Breckinridge in time to play a crucial role in the Confederate victory at **New Market**. Wharton then joined the **Army of Northern Virginia** and saw service at **Cold Harbor** before returning to the Valley to help repulse **David Hunter** at **Lynchburg**. After fighting at the **Monocacy** and participating in **Jubal A. Early's Washington Raid**, he was given command of a small division and led it at the battles of **Third Winchester**, **Fisher's Hill**, **Cedar Creek**, and **Waynesboro**. Wharton's command was virtually destroyed in the this last battle, but he escaped and finally surrendered at Lynchburg.

After the war, Wharton remained in Virginia, worked in mining and engineering and served two terms in the state legislature. When he died, he was buried with the colors of the 51st Virginia wrapped around his body.

WHARTON, JOHN AUSTIN (1828–1865) CSA. Born Edwin Waller Wharton in **Tennessee**, as an infant, Wharton moved to **Texas** with his family. There his father served as Texas's minister to the United States and renamed his son John Austin after a deceased brother. Wharton attended school and studied law in **South Carolina** and married the governor's daughter. Returning to Texas, he served as a county attorney and sheriff and became one of the state's richest men. Wharton also was a delegate at the Texas **secession** convention.

When the Civil War began, Wharton went to **Virginia** with prominent Texans Benjamin F. Terry and Thomas S. Lubbock. While his friends fought at **First Manassas** as volunteers, he missed the battle because of illness. Securing permission to raise a **regiment**, the trio returned to Texas and formed the 8th Texas Cavalry, better known as **Terry's Texas Rangers**. Wharton entered Confederate service in September 1861 as a **company** captain. Sent to Tennessee, the regiment soon lost Terry in battle and Lubbock to disease, and Wharton was made regimental colonel in early 1862. He almost missed **Shiloh** after being arrested for letting his men discharge their wet muskets on the march so they could reload with dry ammunition. In the battle, Wharton was wounded, but he remained with his men and was praised for helping form the rear guard. After brief service in East Tennessee, his regiment was placed in **Nathan**

Bedford Forrest's brigade in the summer of 1862. Wharton again won acclaim for his daring charges during a raid on Murfreesboro, Tennessee (where he again was wounded), and at **Perryville** during the **Kentucky Campaign**. Back in Texas, his friends wanted him to run for the **Confederate Congress**, but his mother's pride in his military record caused them to abandon their plans.

Wharton was promoted to brigadier general in November 1862 and performed outstanding service at **Stones River** while leading an **Army of Tennessee** brigade. He also fought very well in **Joseph Wheeler's Raid** in October 1863 and at **Chickamauga** and was promoted to major general in November. After Wharton served under Wheeler during operations around Chattanooga, Tennessee, that winter, friction developed between the two officers. Wheeler accused him of politicking for higher command and for claiming to be a better officer than his superior. At Wharton's request, he was transferred to the **Trans-Mississippi Department** in April 1864. There he took command of **Richard Taylor's** cavalry **corps** in **Louisiana** after **Thomas Green** was killed and led his troopers in pursuing the Federals in the latter part of the **Red River Campaign**. Taylor highly praised Wharton's service, and afterward Wharton took command of the cavalry corps.

On April 6, 1865, three days before **Appomattox**, Wharton was killed in an altercation with Col. George W. Baylor at Maj. Gen. **John B. Magruder's** Houston, Texas, headquarters. The two had feuded before and this time, after having a confrontation in the street concerning Baylor's lack of promotion, Wharton reportedly came into Magruder's quarters and called Baylor a liar. In an instant, Baylor shot and killed him. Baylor was not punished for killing the unarmed officer.

WHEAT, CHATHAM ROBERDEAU (1826–1862) CSA. A native of **Virginia**, Wheat graduated from the University of Nashville in 1845 and studied law before volunteering for the **Mexican War**. Rising to the rank of captain, he found great pleasure serving in the military and enjoyed the adventure of war. After Mexico, Wheat settled in **New Orleans, Louisiana**, where he practiced law and served in the state legislature. He soon returned to the military, and served in filibustering expeditions in Cuba, Mexico, and Nicaragua; was an officer in the Mexican army; and fought with Garibaldi's revolutionary army in Italy.

When the Civil War began, Wheat left Italy and returned to the United States to join the Confederacy. In New Orleans, he raised and became major of the 1st Special Battalion, Louisiana Volunteers. The battalion was largely made up of immigrants, rowdy dockworkers, and perhaps some **prisoners**, and became known for mischief, brawling, and drinking. The soldiers were described as cutthroats, thieves, and "the lowest scrapings of the Mississippi" (Jones, *Lee's Tigers*, xi). Sent to Virginia, the battalion was one of the first commands to engage the enemy at **First Manassas**, and it slowed the Federals long enough for the Confederates to bring up reinforcements. Wheat was shot through both lungs in the battle and was told by a surgeon that the wound was mortal. The major replied he did not feel like dying and astonished the surgeon by recovering.

After Manassas, Wheat's battalion became famous—partly because of its role in the battle, but also for its drinking and brawling. In December 1861, the first men executed in what became the **Army of Northern Virginia** were two of Wheat's men who attacked an officer. The most conspicuous members of the battalion belonged to the Tiger Rifles, a **Zouave company**. Because of its violent behavior, the entire battalion became known as the Tiger Battalion or Wheat's Tigers. When other Louisiana units showed similar misbehavior, all Louisiana soldiers in the Army of Northern Virginia became known as **Louisiana Tigers**. Standing six feet, four inches, and weighing some 250 pounds, "Rob" Wheat proved to be the only officer who could control his raucous battalion.

As part of **Richard Taylor's brigade**, Wheat played an important role in **Stonewall Jackson's 1862 Shenandoah Valley Campaign**. He led his men across a burning bridge under fire at **Front Royal** to save the important span for Jackson, and at **Port Republic** he used his knife to cut the throats of Union **artillery** horses to prevent the enemy from retrieving a battery the brigade had captured. In the **Seven Days Campaign**, Wheat had a premonition he would be killed. On June 27, 1862, he said good-bye to several friends and then led his men into combat at **Gaines' Mill**. Shot through the head, Wheat was killed instantly while charging the enemy line. After his death, Taylor recommended that Wheat's battalion be disbanded because it had become too small for useful service. This was done in August, and the men were assigned to the other Louisiana **regiments**.

WHEATFIELD AT BATTLE OF GETTYSBURG, PENNSYLVANIA (JULY 2, 1863).

On July 2, 1863, the second day of battle at **Gettysburg**, Maj. Gen. **Daniel Sickles** was concerned that his position on the Union left flank was weak and moved his III Corps west, several hundred yards forward, to what he thought was more defensible ground. His new position was along the Emmitsburg Road, with his left wing turning to the southeast at the **Peach Orchard** and running through a wheat field to **Devil's Den**. At about 4:00 P.M., Lt. Gen. **James Longstreet's** Confederate **corps** launched a massive attack against Sickles's position. Fighting raged for hours, with the Confederates finally pushing the Federals out of the Peach Orchard **salient**. The battle then shifted to the Wheatfield, where for several hours some of the most intense combat of the war took place. **John B. Hood's** and **Lafayette McLaws's** Confederate **divisions** repeatedly battered **David Birney's** division and finally crushed Sickles's corps. The Federals, however, rushed in as reinforcements the divisions of **John Caldwell** and **Romeyn Ayres** from the II and V Corps, respectively. The Wheatfield changed hands six times, and in one counterattack, the 1st Minnesota lost 80 percent of its men, the highest casualty rate for any Union **regiment** in one battle. Eventually, the Confederate attack stalled, and Longstreet pulled his men back toward the Emmitsburg Road. The Union line also was withdrawn back to Cemetery Ridge.

WHEATON, FRANK (1833–1903) USA. A native of **Rhode Island**, Wheaton was the son-in-law of Confederate Gen. **Samuel Cooper**, and his mother-in-law was the sister of Confederate diplomat **James Mason**. After serving in the **Mexican War**, he dropped out of Brown University and worked five years for the Mexican-American Boundary Commission. Commissioned a 1st lieutenant in the 1st U.S. Cavalry in 1855, Wheaton served on the frontier and in the **Utah Expedition**.

Wheaton was promoted to captain in March 1861 and was appointed lieutenant colonel of the 2nd Rhode Island in July. At **First Manassas**, the regimental colonel was killed, and Wheaton promoted to take his place. Becoming part of the **Army of the Potomac**, the **regiment** fought with the IV Corps in the **Peninsula** and **Seven Days Campaigns**, and he earned special praise at **Williamsburg**.

After being held in reserve at **Antietam**, Wheaton was promoted to brigadier general of volunteers in November 1862. He did not assume duties as a brigadier right away and led only his regiment at **Fredericksburg**. Two days after Fredericksburg, however, Wheaton took command of a **brigade** in the VI Corps' 3rd Division. Remaining in Fredericksburg during the **Chancellorsville Campaign**, he helped capture Marye's Heights at **Second Fredericksburg** and then fought at **Salem Church**. At **Gettysburg**, Wheaton was not engaged, but he did assume temporary command of the **division** when **John Newton** took over the I Corps. Returning to the brigade after the battle, he led his men through the **Bristoe Station** and **Mine Run Campaigns**. In 1864, Wheaton again temporarily commanded the division during the latter part of the **Battle of the Wilderness** and in the early part of the **Petersburg Campaign**, but he led his brigade at **Spotsylvania** and **Cold Harbor**.

After helping defend the capital during **Jubal A. Early's 1864 Washington Raid**, Wheaton was assigned to the **Shenandoah Valley**. During **Philip Sheridan's 1864 Shenandoah Valley Campaign**, he assumed command of the division at **Third Winchester** and led it through the fighting at **Fisher's Hill** and **Cedar Creek**. Wheaton eventually moved to Petersburg, Virginia, and served there before participating in the **Appomattox Campaign**. By war's end, he had received **brevets** through the rank of brigadier general of regulars and was brevetted major general of regulars shortly after the war ended.

Wheaton was mustered out of the volunteers in April 1866, but he remained in the regular **army** as a major. He later commanded the troops engaged in the 1873 Modoc Indian War (in which **Edward R. S. Canby** was murdered) and commanded the **Department of Texas** before retiring in 1897 as a major general.

WHEAT'S TIGERS. *See* WHEAT, CHATHAM ROBERDEAU.

WHEELER, JOSEPH "FIGHTING JOE" (1836–1906) CSA. Although a native of **Georgia**, Wheeler moved about the country with his family while growing up and attended schools in **Connecticut** and **New York**. After graduating from **West Point** in 1859, he eventually was assigned to the Mounted Rifles in the **New Mexico Territory** as a 2nd lieutenant.

In early 1861, Wheeler submitted his resignation from the **U.S. Army** and joined the Confederacy as a 1st lieutenant of **artillery** in April, a week before the **army** accepted his resignation. After serving under **Braxton Bragg** at **Pensacola, Florida**, he was promoted to colonel of the 19th Alabama in September and joined **Jones M. Withers's** command at Mobile, Alabama. At **Shiloh**, Wheeler's **regiment** saw heavy combat around the "Hornets' Nest" as part of **John K. Jackson's brigade**, and during the **siege of Corinth, Mississippi**, he was engaged in heavy **skirmishing** while temporarily in command of a brigade.

In July 1862, Bragg appointed Wheeler the **Army of the Mississippi's** chief of cavalry. After launching the first of **Wheeler's Raids** into **Tennessee** that same month, he joined Bragg for the **Kentucky Campaign**. Over a 57-day period, Wheeler was involved in 50 fights, including **Perryville**. He then was named the **Army of Tennessee's** chief of cavalry and in October was promoted to brigadier general. Known as "Fighting Joe" or "Little Joe," Wheeler became one of the Confederacy's best-known cavalry officers. At **Stones River**, his **division** raided behind the Union army destroying hundreds of wagons and capturing more than 700 **prisoners**. A second raid in January 1863 against the enemy's Cumberland River supply line destroyed three Union steamboats and captured more than 400 prisoners.

Wheeler was promoted to major general in January 1863, and the following month he was reinforced by **Nathan Bedford Forrest's** cavalry for a raid against **Dover, Tennessee**. Relations between the two cavalrymen were poor. Bragg earlier had taken away Forrest's command and given it to Wheeler, and in this raid, Wheeler was defeated at Dover. Forrest refused to serve under him again, and Bragg was forced to keep the two commands separated. After service in the **Tullahoma** and **Chickamauga Campaigns**, Wheeler's cavalry **corps** raided the precarious Union supply line into besieged Chattanooga, Tennessee. In early October, he destroyed 800–1,000 enemy supply wagons, killed or captured hundreds of draft animals, and inflicted some 2,000 casualties. A vigorous Union pursuit drove Wheeler out of Tennessee before he could accomplish more, and he suffered 2,000 casualties. The following month, he accompanied **James Longstreet** on the **Knoxville Campaign** with two of his divisions. After fighting his way to Knoxville, Wheeler returned to Chattanooga with a few men to assist Bragg in the closing days of the **Chattanooga Campaign**. He was wounded in the foot while assisting **Patrick Cleburne** form the rear guard at **Ringgold Gap**.

During the **Atlanta Campaign**, Wheeler's cavalry saw frequent combat as it guarded the **Army of Tennessee's** flanks. In July 1864, he successfully turned back **Stoneman's and McCook's Raid** against Atlanta's supply line. The following month, Wheeler made a strategic error by raiding **William T. Sherman's** supply line in northern Georgia and Tennessee. Although he succeeded in temporarily cutting some **railroads**, the raid cost him heavily in officers and men. Also because of Wheeler's absence, Sherman was able to maneuver to **Jonesboro** and force Atlanta's evacuation by cutting the last railroads into the city.

In late 1864 Wheeler's cavalry had the impossible task of confronting Sherman's **March to the Sea**. Heavily outnumbered, he engaged the enemy at **Waynesborough** and in many **skirmishes** but could do little to stop the march. By this time, Wheeler's command also had become lax in **discipline** and was accused of committing as many depredations as the Federals. Wheeler continued to lead his cavalry in early 1865 during the **Carolinas Campaign**, but his reputation was hurt badly by his men's misbehavior and his inability to stop the enemy. In March, **department** commander **P. G. T. Beauregard** replaced him with **Wade Hampton** as cavalry chief in the Carolinas. Under Hampton, Wheeler continued to lead a cavalry corps and fought at **Monroe's Cross Roads**, **Averasboro**, and **Bentonville**. As **Joseph E. Johnston** prepared to **surrender** in April, Wheeler took his men to Georgia to join fleeing President **Jefferson Davis**, but in early May, he was captured at Conyer's Station, Georgia.

After being **paroled** in June 1865, Wheeler became a merchant in **New Orleans, Louisiana**. In 1868, he moved to northern **Alabama**, where he became a planter, lawyer, and politician. Wheeler was elected to the **U.S. Congress** in 1880, but he served only a few months in 1882 before being unseated in a successful challenge of the election results. In 1883, however, he returned to Congress and served until 1900, becoming the ranking **Democrat** on the Ways and Means Committee. During the Spanish-American War, Wheeler offered his services and was appointed major general of volunteers. While fighting in Cuba, it was said he sometimes forgot himself and referred to the Spanish as "Yankees." After helping negotiate Spain's surrender, Wheeler then fought in the Philippine Insurrection and was commissioned a brigadier general of regulars in June 1900. Upon his death, he was buried in Arlington National Cemetery and is one of a few Confederates buried there.

WHEELER'S RAIDS. Confederate cavalryman **Joseph "Fighting Joe" Wheeler** made several major cavalry raids in the western theater and became one of the South's most celebrated generals. His first raid was a minor one in July 1862, soon after **Braxton Bragg** appointed him chief of cavalry for the **Army of the Mississippi**. Leaving Holly Springs, Mississippi, Wheeler rode into western **Tennessee**, destroyed a number of **railroad** bridges, and defeated the Union cavalry in eight small **skirmishes**.

Wheeler's first major raid took place during the **Chattanooga Campaign** in the autumn of 1863. After his victory at **Chickamauga**, Bragg had the Union **Army of the Cumberland** besieged in Chattanooga, Tennessee, with only a precarious 60-mile-long supply line connecting the city with Tennessee's Sequatchie Valley. Bragg ordered Wheeler to cut this lifeline, and Wheeler complied even though he believed the task was too great for his weak command. On October 1, he forced his way across the Tennessee River near Decatur, Alabama, in a sharp fight with Union Maj. Gen. **George Crook's** cavalry **division**. Reinforced by several **brigades** from **Nathan Bedford Forrest**, Wheeler advanced that night through the rain to the Sequatchie Valley. At Anderson's Cross Roads on October 2, he attacked a large supply train and captured or destroyed more than 700 supply wagons and hundreds of mules. Wheeler then divided his column, sending Brig. Gen. **John A. Wharton** to destroy a depot at McMinnville, Tennessee, while he led the rest of the men toward Murfreesboro. Union cavalry under Col. **Edward M. McCook** pursued and engaged Wheeler in the valley and recaptured a large number of wagons. Crook's Union cavalry failed to cut off the Confederates before they reached McMinnville, and on October 3, Wharton's column captured the town and several hundred **prisoners**. However, Crook did succeed in forcing Wheeler to abandon his advance on Murfreesboro. Union Maj. Gen. **Robert B. Mitchell** assumed command of Crook's and McCook's cavalry and continued to pursue Wheeler as he withdrew to the southwest in three columns. Crook caught up with **Henry B. Davidson's** brigade near Farmington and defeated it, and the Confederate rear guard was mauled on October 9 near Pulaski. Wheeler finally recrossed the Tennessee River near Rogersville on October 9.

The raid had mixed results. Wheeler caused a serious disruption in the Chattanooga supply line, inflicted 2,000 Union casualties, destroyed or captured 800–1,000 supply wagons and hundreds of draft animals, burned five bridges, and destroyed miles of railroad track and millions of dollars in supplies. However, Wheeler was driven out of Tennessee, suffered approximately 2,000 casualties, and lost six cannons.

Wheeler's second great raid occurred in August 1864 during the **Atlanta Campaign**. With **William T. Sherman** on the outskirts of Atlanta, Georgia, **John Bell Hood** attempted to break the Union stranglehold by sending Wheeler and 4,000 cavalrymen on a raid against Sherman's main supply line, the Western & Atlantic Railroad. Wheeler was first to destroy the railroad south of Chattanooga, Tennessee, and then to ride into Tennessee to attack the railroads south of Nashville. He was to leave part of his command in Tennessee to continue operations there and return to **Georgia** with the remainder and destroy the railroad between Chattanooga and Atlanta.

Wheeler began the raid from Covington, Georgia, on August 10. Between August 14 and 16, he destroyed approximately 30 miles of track in northern Georgia and unsuccessfully attacked the Union garrison at Dalton on August 14–15. The arrival of Union reinforcements forced the Confederates to ride into east Tennessee, where Wheeler destroyed the railroad bridge over the Holston River near Knoxville. Leaving two brigades behind, he then rode west to cut the railroads near McMinnville and Franklin before safely recrossing the Tennessee River at Tuscumbia, Alabama, on September 10. A few weeks later, Wheeler rode back into northern Georgia, threatened Dalton again, and on October 2 destroyed the railroad bridge at Resaca. He finally rejoined Hood at Cedartown on October 8.

These raids' hardships nearly ruined Wheeler's command and caused only temporary damage to the railroads. Also, they actually hurt Hood in the long run. Deprived of his cavalry, he was virtually blind as Sherman moved south of Atlanta to **Jonesboro** and cut the Confederates' last railroad into the city.

WHIG PARTY. This major political party was formed in the 1830s by those who opposed **Democratic** President Andrew Jackson and his destruction of the Second Bank of the United States. Its members generally represented the more elite class of Americans and supported business interests, a strong national government, tariffs, and internal improvements. In the South, Whigs tended to be the larger plantation and slave owners. Henry Clay became one of its most influential leaders, and the party won the presidential elections of 1840 and 1848, with William Henry Harrison (who was succeeded by John Tyler upon his death) and Zachary Taylor, respectively. The Whigs disintegrated in the early 1850s over the divisive issue of **slavery**.

WHIPPLE, AMIEL WEEKS (1816–1863) USA. A native of **Massachusetts**, Whipple taught school and attended Amherst College before graduating from **West Point** in 1841. Assigned to the **engineers**, he helped survey both the U.S.–Canada border and the border with Mexico. Whipple also surveyed a **railroad** route through modern-day Arizona, for which the Arizona territorial government later named its seat of government Fort Whipple.

When the Civil War began, Whipple was a captain of engineers. He was made **Irvin McDowell's** chief topographical engineer in July 1861 and saw service at **First Manassas**. Earning a **brevet** for Manassas, Whipple was promoted to major in September. He remained with McDowell and in March 1862 became his chief topographical engineer for the **Army of the Potomac's** I Corps.

In April 1862, Whipple was promoted to brigadier general of volunteers and took command of first a **brigade** and then a **division** in the **Washington, D.C.**, defenses. In November, he was given a division command in **Joseph Hooker's** III Corps, but he saw only minor combat at **Fredericksburg** (but he still was awarded a brevet). At **Chancellorsville** on May 3, 1863, Whipple was on his horse writing out an order to dislodge a Confederate **sharpshooter** when the sniper shot him through the stomach. He was taken to Washington and died there four days later. Whipple was promoted to major general of volunteers the day before he died and posthumously was brevetted brigadier general of regulars and major general of volunteers.

WHIPPLE, WILLIAM DENISON (1826–1902) USA. A native of **New York**, Whipple graduated near the bottom of his 1851 **West Point** class.

Assigned to the infantry, he fought Apaches and served on garrison duty in the **New Mexico Territory** and **Texas** before the Civil War.

When the Civil War began, Whipple was a 1st lieutenant serving on quartermaster duty in Indianola, Texas. When Texas secessionists seized the post, he escaped capture and reached **Washington, D.C.**, safely. For his entire war career, Whipple served on staff positions. Appointed adjutant general for **David Hunter's division**, he served at **First Manassas** and was promoted to captain in August 1861. Afterward, Whipple rose through the ranks to lieutenant colonel of volunteers (February 1862), major of regulars (July 1862), and brigadier general of volunteers (July 1863). During this time, he served as adjutant for the **Departments of Pennsylvania** and **of Virginia** and for the **Middle Department**. Whipple was appointed the **Army of the Cumberland's** assistant adjutant general in November 1863 and served under **George H. Thomas** during the **Chattanooga Campaign**. He then was made Thomas's chief of staff in December and remained in that position until war's end, seeing combat in the **Atlanta** and the **Franklin and Nashville Campaigns**. The Senate did not confirm Whipple's commission, and he was reappointed brigadier general of volunteers in September 1864.

When Whipple was mustered out of the volunteers in January 1866, he had received a **brevet** of major general of regulars even though he had never served in any position other than staff officer. He remained in the regular **army** as a colonel and served on Thomas's staff until Thomas's death in 1870. Whipple then served as **William T. Sherman's** aide-de-camp from 1873 to 1878 and was the adjutant general for several different **departments** and divisions from 1878 until his retirement in 1890.

"WHISTLING DICK." This famous 18-pounder banded Confederate cannon was used in the **Vicksburg, Mississippi**, defenses during the 1863 **Vicksburg Campaign** and was instrumental in sinking the USS *Cincinnati* on May 27, 1863. Originally made as a smoothbore at the **Tredegar Iron Works**, it later was **rifled**. The cannon's nickname came from the fact that its shells whistled through the air because the gun's new rifling made them unstable in flight. For many years, a **Blakely rifle** captured at Vicksburg was placed on display at **West Point** and was identified as "Whistling Dick." In the 1950s, however, it was discovered to be a different cannon. The fate of the real "Whistling Dick" is unknown.

WHITAKER, WALTER CHILES (1823–1887) USA. A native of **Kentucky**, Whitaker attended **Virginia's** Bethany College before serving in the **Mexican War** as a 2nd lieutenant in the 3rd Kentucky. After the war, he returned to Kentucky, where he farmed, practiced law, and engaged in state politics. Whitaker was serving in the state senate when the Civil War began, and after Confederate troops violated the state's neutrality, he introduced the resolution that put Kentucky on the side of the Union.

Whitaker entered Union service in December 1861 when he was appointed colonel of the 6th Kentucky (Union). As part of the **Army of the Ohio**, he fought on the second day at **Shiloh** but missed **Perryville**. After serving at **Stones River** with the **Army of the Cumberland**, Whitaker was promoted to brigadier general of volunteers in July 1863 and led a **brigade** in **James B. Steedman's division** of **Gordon Granger's** Reserve Corps at **Chickamauga**. There he participated in **George H. Thomas's** famous defense of **Snodgrass Hill**. After being wounded while leading his brigade in the **Chattanooga Campaign**, Whitaker was given command of the division and led it through the **Atlanta Campaign** as part of the IV Corps. In the autumn of 1864, he was back in command of a IV Corps brigade under Thomas in Tennessee and saw combat at the **Battles of Franklin and Nashville**.

After being **brevetted** major general of volunteers for his service in the Atlanta Campaign, Whitaker was mustered out of the volunteers in August 1865. He became a famous Kentucky criminal lawyer afterward, but heavy drinking later in life caused him to spend some time in a mental institution.

WHITE HALL, NORTH CAROLINA, BATTLE OF (DECEMBER 16, 1862). In early 1862, Union forces under **Ambrose E. Burnside** captured parts of the **North Carolina** coast, including **Roanoke Island** and **New Bern**. In July, Union Brig. Gen. **John G. Foster** took command of the **Department of North Carolina**. He led an expedition in December 1862 from New Bern to **Kinston** and captured the town. On December 15, Foster left Kinston and moved along the Neuse River toward Goldsboro. When his cavalry reached the bridge at White Hall, Confederates under Brig. Gen. **Beverly H. Robertson** fell back across the river and burned the span. The next day, Foster's **artillery** shelled the Confederates across the river while his infantry continued westward toward Goldsboro. On December 17, Foster burned the vital **Goldsboro Bridge**. Total casualties in the fighting at White Hall are estimated at 150.

WHITE, JULIUS (1816–1890) USA. A native of **New York**, White moved to **Illinois** as a young man and worked in a variety of commercial enterprises in both Illinois and **Wisconsin** before being elected to the Wisconsin legislature in 1849. He later returned to Illinois, became active in the **Republican Party**, and in 1861 was appointed Chicago's collector of customs by President **Abraham Lincoln**.

After the Civil War began, White resigned his position, raised a **regiment** of volunteers known as the "Frémont Rifles," and entered Union service in September 1861 as colonel of the 37th Illinois. Placed in command of a **brigade** in **Jefferson C. Davis's division** in February 1862, he fought at **Pea Ridge** and won promotion to brigadier general of volunteers in June 1862. Transferred east, White was put in command of **Harpers Ferry, Virginia**, in September, just as it was besieged by **Stonewall Jackson** during the **Antietam Campaign**. White allowed Col. **Dixon Miles** to remain in command of the garrison because of his familiarity with the region. Miles performed poorly and was killed, and White was forced to surrender the command. He was arrested for the fiasco, but a court cleared him of any wrongdoing and commended his bravery.

In June 1863, White was given a division command in the **Department of the Ohio's** XXIII Corps and served under **Ambrose Burnside** during the **Knoxville Campaign**. When Burnside was sent to **Virginia** in early 1864, White accompanied him as chief of staff. He served Burnside in this capacity through the **Overland Campaign** and the early part of the **Petersburg Campaign**. After the disaster at the **Crater**, Burnside was relieved of command, and White was given a IX Corps division. Within weeks, his division was broken up, and White went on sick leave and resigned his commission in November 1864. Despite his resignation, he was **brevetted** major general of volunteers in early 1865.

White returned to Illinois, became active in the **Military Order of the Loyal Legion of the United States**, and served as its state commander.

WHITE OAK ROAD, VIRGINIA, BATTLE OF (MARCH 31, 1865). On March 25, 1865, near the end of the **Petersburg Campaign, Robert E. Lee's Army of Northern Virginia** tried unsuccessfully to break out of the Petersburg, Virginia, siege at **Fort Stedman. U. S. Grant** then ordered the **Army of the Potomac** to turn the Confederates' right flank and cut Lee's last supply lines, the Richmond & Danville and the Southside Railroads. **Philip Sheridan**, who was placed in command of the operation, moved out on March 29 with three cavalry **divisions**. As he neared **Dinwiddie Court House**, he was supported by **Gouverneur K. Warren's** V Corps and **Andrew A. Humphreys's** II Corps. **Skirmishing** took place over the next two days in heavy rain as the Federals encountered 19,000 Confederate defenders under **George E. Pickett**, **Richard H. Anderson**, and **Fitzhugh Lee**.

On March 30, Sheridan pushed north with his cavalry toward Five Forks, while Warren's **corps** advanced about three miles to his right along the Quaker Road. Warren reached the intersection of the Quaker Road and Boydton Plank Road and found Anderson's Confederate corps heavily entrenched in his front along the White Oak Road. After reconnoitering, Warren received permission to push his corps across the road to prevent Confederate reinforcements from moving down it to Five Forks. **George G. Meade** later ordered Warren to suspend the operation because bad road conditions made movements difficult. Unknown to the Federals, Lee had arrived on the scene and prepared to attack Warren with the 3,800 men of the **brigades** led by **Samuel McGowan**, **Archibald Gracie** (commanded by Col. Martin L. Stansel), and **Eppa Hunton**.

At mid-morning the rain slackened, and Meade finally allowed Warren to begin his advance across White Oak Road. Brigadier General **Romeyn B. Ayres's** 4,000-man division moved forward, supported by **Samuel W. Crawford's** division. Just as he advanced, Ayres was suddenly attacked by Lee's Confederates, and his division was pushed panic-stricken back upon Crawford. Crawford's division also fell back in confusion upon **Charles Griffin's** reserve division. Warren sent **Joshua Chamberlain's** brigade across a flooded ravine in a counterattack, but Chamberlain was wounded, and the brigade was repulsed three times by the Confederates. At about 1:00 P.M., Humphreys's II Corps attacked the Confederate line farther to the east and prevented Lee from bringing up reinforcements to the White Oak Road. **Nelson Miles's** division, later joined by Ayres and Crawford, then attacked Lee and finally forced his outnumbered men back into their White Oak Road entrenchments.

Lee failed to stop the Union advance, but his line held. In the fighting, the Federals suffered 1,781 casualties (mostly in Warren's corps), while Confederate casualties were estimated at 900–1,235. That night, the Federals abandoned their hard-won position and moved to the west, where the following day they joined Sheridan's attack at **Five Forks**. Lee's right flank was finally broken there, and the Confederates were forced to evacuate **Richmond** and Petersburg.

WHITE OAK SWAMP, VIRGINIA, BATTLE OF (JUNE 30, 1862).
See FRAYSER'S FARM, VIRGINIA, BATTLE OF.

WHITE SULPHUR SPRINGS, WEST VIRGINIA, BATTLE OF (AUGUST 26, 1863).
See ROCKY GAP, WEST VIRGINIA, BATTLE OF.

WHITFIELD, JOHN WILKINS (1818–1879) CSA. A native of **Tennessee**, Whitfield served in the **Mexican War** as a captain in the 1st Tennessee and lieutenant colonel of the 2nd Tennessee. He moved to **Missouri** in the early 1850s and worked there as an **Indian** agent from 1853 to 1856 before settling in **Kansas**. Whitfield served as the territory's proslavery congressional delegate from 1854 to 1856 and when the Civil War began was serving as the registrar of the land office.

When Kansas remained in the Union, Whitfield moved to south **Texas** in 1861 and organized a cavalry unit that saw some service in **Indian Territory**. Joining forces with **Ben McCulloch** in **Arkansas**, his command was designated the 4th Texas Cavalry Battalion, and he fought as its major at **Pea Ridge**. In April 1862, Whitfield organized Whitfield's Legion (or the 1st Texas Legion) and was appointed its colonel. The command later was renamed the 27th Texas Cavalry and joined **Sterling Price** as dismounted cavalry. Assigned to **Louis Hébert's brigade**, Whitfield fought at **Iuka** and was praised for helping capture a Union battery. Wounded in the fight, he missed the **Battle of Corinth** but afterward remounted his men and joined **Lawrence S. Ross's** cavalry brigade in **Earl Van Dorn's** command. Whitfield participated in the December 1862 raid against **Holly Springs, Mississippi**, and in the Confederate victory at **Thompson's Station, Tennessee**.

Promoted to brigadier general in May 1863, Whitfield was given command of a brigade in **William H. Jackson's** cavalry **division**. After Whitfield was sent back to **Mississippi** in June, some misunderstanding occurred regarding his orders, and he was relieved of duty. **Joseph E. Johnston** apparently did not believe he was fit for command, but Johnston finally restored him to his brigade. Johnston continued to complain about Whitfield, although Whitfield's men admired him greatly, and the Federals considered his brigade to be among the best Confederate cavalry during the **Vicksburg Campaign** and siege of **Jackson, Mississippi**. In October 1863, illness forced Whitfield to take extended sick leave, and Ross assumed command of his brigade.

Returning to Texas, Whitfield did not serve again on active duty. He later served in the state legislature and was a delegate to the 1866 and 1875 constitutional conventions.

WHITING, WILLIAM HENRY CHASE (1824–1865) CSA. A native of **Mississippi**, Whiting was educated in **Massachusetts** before graduating first in the Georgetown College class of 1840. Entering **West Point**, he attained the highest grades ever recorded at the academy (until surpassed by Douglas MacArthur in 1903) and graduated first in the class of 1845.

Assigned to the **engineers**, Whiting worked on numerous river, harbor, and fortification projects on both the Atlantic and Pacific coasts before resigning his captain's commission in February 1861.

Whiting entered the Confederacy as a major of engineers and joined **P. G. T. Beauregard's** staff at **Charleston, South Carolina**, in March 1861. He participated in the bombardment of **Fort Sumter** as Beauregard's assistant adjutant general and inspector general before being placed in command of **North Carolina's** coastal defenses in May. In June, Whiting was transferred to **Virginia**, where he was appointed **Joseph E. Johnston's** adjutant and inspector general and, later, his chief engineer. There he supervised both the destruction of the arsenal at **Harpers Ferry, Virginia**, and the transfer of Johnston's troops to the **First Manassas** battlefield. For the latter accomplishment, **Jefferson Davis** gave Whiting a battlefield promotion to brigadier general.

Whiting soon angered Davis and hurt his chances at promotion by refusing to carry out the president's orders to organize Johnston's **army** into **brigades** composed of troops from one state. During the **Peninsula Campaign**, he was given command of a brigade and skillfully led it and that of **John B. Hood** at **Yorktown**. Whiting later fought well at **Seven Pines** at the head of a **division**. Some believed it was he who suggested to **Robert E. Lee** the reinforcing of **Stonewall Jackson** for **Jackson's Shenandoah Valley Campaign** and assigning Jackson the role of attacking the enemy's flank at **Mechanicsville**. Whether true or not, Lee did send Whiting's two brigades to join Jackson, and Whiting served under that officer during the **Seven Days Campaign**.

In November 1862, Lee transferred Whiting out of the **Army of Northern Virginia** to open a division command for Hood. He was put in command of the Cape Fear, North Carolina, region and turned **Fort Fisher** into a formidable bastion. By this time, Davis recognized Whiting's talents and approved his promotion to major general in April 1863. In early 1864, Johnston requested Whiting be promoted to lieutenant general and be made second in command of the **Army of Tennessee**, but Davis refused on the grounds Whiting could not be spared from North Carolina.

Whiting was placed in command of the defenses of **Petersburg, Virginia**, in May 1864 but suffered sharp criticism for his failure to attack the enemy at the **Second Battle of Drewry's Bluff**. Accused of being drunk or under the influence of drugs (when actually he may have suffered from fatigue), he requested and received a transfer back to North Carolina. When **Braxton Bragg** assumed command of the Cape Fear area, he sent Whiting to Fort Fisher, but Whiting allowed Col. William

Lamb to continue commanding the garrison and only offered advice during the December battle. He returned to the fort in January 1865 without orders and told Lamb he had come to share the colonel's fate. Whiting refused Bragg's orders to leave the fort and was mortally wounded in hand-to-hand fighting when the Federals overran Fort Fisher on January 15. Taken to **New York** as a **prisoner**, he died on March 15.

WHITWORTH GUN. This British **rifled** cannon was developed by Sir Joseph Whitworth and was used in small numbers by the Confederates, most notably in the **Army of Northern Virginia**. It came in a number of calibers, but all of the cannons had hexagonal bores and long, bolt-like projectiles that usually were **solid shot**. Extremely accurate, the larger cannons had a range of up to five miles. Those acquired by the Confederates early in the war were generally breech-loaders, but after 1863, they were muzzle-loaders. Field pieces usually were either 6- or 12-pounders, but some models fired a 70-pound shell. The Union **army** had one battery of Whitworth guns, which spent most of the war in the defenses of **Washington, D.C.**

WHITWORTH RIFLE. Developed in the mid-1850s by British **engineer** Joseph (later Sir Joseph) Whitworth, these hexagonal-bored **rifles** were very popular with Confederate **sharpshooters**. It was typical of Civil War rifles, being a single-shot, muzzle-loading weapon that used a **percussion cap**, but it fired a smaller .45-caliber bullet rather than the larger .58-caliber used by most **rifle muskets**. Resembling the **Enfield rifle**, Whitworths were fitted with a telescopic sight on the stock's left side and were accurate up to a mile. The Confederates imported the first 12 rifles in early 1863 to be evenly divided between the **Army of Northern Virginia** and the **Army of Tennessee**. Others trickled to the **armies** as the war progressed, with marksmanship contests often being held to determine which soldiers would get them. Confederate sharpshooters reportedly used Whitworths to kill Union generals **John Sedgwick** and **William H. Lytle**.

WICKHAM, WILLIAMS CARTER (1820–1888) CSA. A native of **Virginia**, Wickham studied law at the University of Virginia and passed the bar in 1842. After farming and practicing law for a while, he was elected to the state assembly in 1849 as a **Whig**, served as a county judge in the late 1850s, was active in the militia, and was elected to the state senate in 1859. As a delegate to the 1861 **secession** convention, Wickham strongly opposed secession, but afterward he led his militia **company** into Confederate service.

Wickham entered Confederate service in April 1861 as captain of the Hanover Dragoons. After fighting at **First Manassas**, he was elected lieutenant colonel of the 4th Virginia Cavalry in September. During the **Peninsula Campaign**, Wickham was wounded in the side by a **saber** at **Williamsburg** and went home to recuperate. Captured there in May 1862, he quickly was **exchanged** for his wife's relative, **Thomas L. Kane**. Promoted to colonel in August, Wickham became a prominent officer in **J. E. B. Stuart's** cavalry in the **Army of Northern Virginia**. As part of **Fitzhugh Lee's brigade**, he led his **regiment** in numerous clashes during the **Second Manassas** and **Antietam Campaigns** and in Stuart's **Chambersburg Raid**. In late October 1862, Wickham assumed command of the brigade, but he was wounded in the neck by a shell fragment during a November **skirmish**. He returned to duty in time to serve in the **Fredericksburg Campaign**.

Wickham was elected to the **Confederate Congress** in April 1863 but delayed taking his seat. He led his regiment very well at **Chancellorsville**, but in June 1863, he was badly defeated at **Kelly's Ford**. Wickham redeemed himself with excellent service at **Aldie** and in the **Gettysburg Campaign**. Promoted to brigadier general in September 1863, he took command of a brigade in **Fitzhugh Lee's division** and saw hard service in the 1864 **Overland Campaign** before joining **Jubal A. Early's** command in the **Shenandoah Valley**. There he fought at **Third Winchester**, and while in temporary command of the division, he saved Early from destruction at **Fisher's Hill** by blocking a Union column trying to cut off the Confederate retreat.

In November 1864, Wickham resigned his commission and took up his congressional seat. An advocate of peace, he served on the Military Affairs Committee and generally opposed **Jefferson Davis's** administration. Wickham worked hard to help alleviate the suffering of civilians and soldiers, to exempt men from **conscription**, and to supply cavalrymen with government horses. He also supported the **Hampton Roads Conference**.

After the war, Wickham angered many of his former comrades by joining the **Republican Party** only two weeks after **Appomattox**. He also served as president of two **railroads**, supported **U. S. Grant** for president, and in 1883 was elected to the state senate. Wickham was still in the senate when he died in 1888.

WIDOW BIXBY LETTER, ABRAHAM LINCOLN'S (NOVEMBER 21, 1864). During the autumn of 1864, **Massachusetts** Gov. **John A. Andrews** learned that Mrs. Lydia Bixby of Boston had been informed that all five of her sons had been killed in battle. Andrews forwarded the information to the War Department and requested that **Abraham Lincoln** write her a letter of condolence. After confirming the story, the War Department sent a letter to Lincoln with the information. On November 21, he wrote Bixby a short letter that included the sentences, "I feel how weak and fruitless must be any words of mine which should attempt to beguile you from grief of a loss so overwhelming. But I cannot refrain from tendering to you the consolation that may be found in the thanks of the Republic they died to save" (Faust, ed., *Historical Times Illustrated Encyclopedia of the Civil War,* 823). The letter was quoted widely in newspapers and became a famous part of Civil War lore. However, it was learned later than only two of Bixby's sons had been killed. Two had **deserted**, and one had been captured. The original letter has never been found, and some people belive that **John Hay** actually wrote it.

WIGFALL, LOUIS TREZEVANT (1816–1874) CSA. A native of **South Carolina**, Wigfall attended the University of Virginia for a year, but he graduated from South Carolina College in 1837. He became a lawyer, served in the **Seminole Wars**, and was appointed a colonel in the state militia. A hard-drinking, courageous, violent, and thin-skinned man, Wigfall made many enemies during his career. In South Carolina, he became embroiled in a political dispute that led to a brawl, two duels (and three near-duels), and a shooting. Wigfall killed a man in the shooting, missed one dueling opponent, and shot the other (Preston Brooks) in the hip, while he was wounded in the thigh. He actually used his violent reputation to cower opponents who feared angering him. In the mid-1840s, Wigfall bitterly opposed federal tariffs, supported **Texas** annexation, and became one of the South's most outspoken supporters of **secession**.

Wigfall moved to Texas in 1846 and started a struggling law practice. As a **Democrat**, he entered the state assembly in 1850, where he became a vocal critic of Unionist **Sam Houston** and helped defeat him for governor in 1857. By that time, Wigfall was the leader of the Texas **"fire-eaters"** and won election to the state senate. He supported the revival of the international slave trade and the annexation of Cuba and won election to the U.S. Senate in 1859. In the Senate, Wigfall became a leading secessionist and his intransigence helped split the Democratic Party in 1860. After **Abraham Lincoln's** election, Wigfall coauthored the **Southern Manifesto** and persuaded many Southern moderates to accept secession.

Surprisingly, Wigfall remained in the U.S. Senate even after Texas seceded in 1861. He used his position to defend the Confederacy publicly, gather intelligence, and even raise volunteers and acquire weapons. In April, Wigfall was in **Charleston, South Carolina**, where he rowed out to **Fort Sumter** to conduct unofficial negotiations with Maj. **Robert Anderson**. Becoming a popular Confederate hero, Wigfall—while still a U.S. Senator—became an aide to both **P. G. T. Beauregard** and **Jefferson Davis**, a member of the Provisional **Confederate Congress**, and a lieutenant colonel in command of a Texas battalion at **Richmond, Virginia**. The U.S. Senate finally expelled him in July.

Wigfall arrived on the field the day after the **First Battle of Manassas**. While there, he supported **Joseph E. Johnston** in his feud with Davis over rank and thus earned the president's enmity. However, Davis did support Wigfall's promotion to colonel of the 1st Texas in August 1861 and to brigadier general in October. For the next few months, Wigfall commanded the Texas **brigade** in Johnston's **army**, but he resigned his commission in February 1862 to take a seat in the Confederate Senate.

As a senator, Wigfall supported **conscription**, **impressment**, the government takeover of **railroads**, and the **suspension of the writ of habeas corpus** because he believed they were necessary for victory. However, he opposed the creation of a Confederate **supreme court**, because it conflicted with **states rights**, and Davis's military policies. Wigfall became part of the clique that believed the western theater was where the war would be won or lost, and he bitterly criticized Davis for the loss of **Vicksburg, Mississippi**, and the removal of Johnston from command of the **Army of Tennessee**. In early 1865, it was largely because of Wigfall's influence that **Robert E. Lee** finally was named the Confederate general-in-chief.

When Richmond was evacuated in April 1865, Wigfall returned to Texas with hopes of continuing the fight. Upon arrival, he found that the **Trans-Mississippi Department** had surrendered and that Federal authorities were searching for him. Wigfall eluded capture and fled to Great Britain in early 1866. He remained there until 1872, when he returned to the United States and settled in **Maryland**. Wigfall returned to Texas for a visit in 1874 and died shortly after arriving.

"WIGWAG" SIGNALS. Developed for the **U.S. Army** by **Albert J. Myer** and **Edward Porter Alexander** before the Civil War, this was a military communication system that used signal flags during the day and torches at night. Different motions made with the flags or torches represented numbers, with combinations of numbers representing letters. Although complicated and slow, such signals could be seen at long distances and were much faster than couriers. Alexander used the system at **First Manassas** to warn **P. G. T. Beauregard** that the Federals were turning his left flank.

WILCOX, CADMUS MARCELLUS (1824–1890) CSA. A native of **North Carolina**, Wilcox moved to **Tennessee** as a boy. He graduated near the bottom of his 1846 **West Point** class and fought in the **Mexican War** with the infantry, winning one **brevet** for gallantry (later in life, he wrote a history of the Mexican War). After the war, Wilcox served at West Point and other various posts, wrote a manual for rifle exercises (1859), and translated a French military manual.

Wilcox resigned his captain's commission in June 1861 and entered Confederate service the following month as colonel of the 9th Alabama. After seeing light service at **First Manassas**, he was promoted to brigadier general in October and was given a **brigade** of **Alabama** infantry. Serving in **James Longstreet's division**, Wilcox was praised for his service in several hard-fought battles during the **Peninsula** and **Seven Days Campaigns** and became one of the outstanding combat leaders in the **Army of Northern Virginia**. In August 1862, he was given command of a provisional division under Longstreet and led it at **Second Manassas**. Wilcox then returned to his brigade in **Richard H. Anderson's** division and fought with it at **Antietam, Fredericksburg**, and **Chancellorsville**. In the latter campaign, he played a key role at **Salem Church** in stopping the Union advance from Fredericksburg.

Despite his ability, Wilcox's strict **discipline** and "wicked" ways made him unpopular with some of his men, and he had a great distaste for Longstreet and wished to leave his command. His poor relationship with his superior may have delayed his promotion to major general. It was not until after fighting at **Gettysburg** that Wilcox finally was promoted in August 1863 and was given **A. P. Hill's** old **Light Division** in the III Corps. He led the division competently through the **Overland** and **Petersburg Campaigns**, had a horse killed under him at **Reams' Station**, and held the Petersburg, Virginia, line during the **army's** evacuation in April 1865.

After the war, Wilcox lived with a widowed sister-in-law in **Washington, D.C.** He declined diplomatic appointments to Egypt and Korea but late in life did accept a minor position in the federal land office.

WILD, EDWARD AUGUSTUS (1825–1891) USA. A native of **Massachusetts**, Wild graduated both from Harvard University and Jefferson Medical College. After further medical studies in France, he served as a surgeon in the Turkish army during the Crimean War and then opened a medical practice in Massachusetts.

Wild entered Union service in May 1861 as a captain in the 1st Massachusetts and became one of the **army's** most contentious officers. He was only lightly engaged at **First Manassas** but saw heavy combat and was wounded in the right hand at **Seven Pines** while serving in **Cuvier Grover's brigade** in the **Army of the Potomac**. While recuperating, Wild raised another **regiment** and was commissioned colonel of the 35th Massachusetts in August 1862. He was severely wounded in the left arm while leading it at **South Mountain**. When taken to the field hospital, Wild used his medical knowledge to evaluate his own wound and directed the surgeons to amputate the limb.

While recuperating, Wild (a staunch **abolitionist**) helped raise **black troops** in Massachusetts. He was commissioned brigadier general of volunteers in April 1863 and was sent to New Bern, North Carolina, to raise more black soldiers. "Wild's African Brigade" served around **Charleston, South Carolina**, where he became involved in controversy for hanging a Confederate guerrilla. Wild was transferred to southeastern **Virginia** late in the year and took command all of the black troops around **Norfolk** and Portsmouth. As part of **Edward W. Hincks's** XVIII Corps **division**, his brigade fought at **Cold Harbor**. Afterward, Wild dealt harshly with Southern civilians, and Hincks arrested him on charges of insubordination. Although convicted, Wild was placed back on duty by **Benjamin F. Butler** and served in the X Corps **picketing** the Appomattox River during the **Petersburg Campaign**. In January 1865, he assumed command of a division in the **Army of the James's** XXV Corps but was reduced to a brigade command in March after one of his subordinates brought more charges against him. Wild was left near **Richmond, Virginia**, during the **Appomattox Campaign**, and his African Brigade became one of the first Union units to enter the captured capital. After garrisoning the city for a time, he became embroiled in a feud with army commander **Edward O. C. Ord** and was transferred to the **Freedmen's Bureau** in **Georgia**.

Wild was mustered out of service in January 1866 and became involved in a Nevada silver mine before moving to South America. He died in Medellin, Colombia.

WILDERNESS CAMPAIGN. *See* OVERLAND CAMPAIGN.

WILDERNESS, VIRGINIA, BATTLE OF THE (MAY 5–6, 1864). In the spring of 1864, **Robert E. Lee's** 60,000-man **Army of Northern Vir-**

ginia was still in its winter camps between Gordonsville and Culpeper Court House, Virginia. Union General-in-Chief **U. S. Grant** was camped north of the Rapidan River with approximately 120,000 men in **George G. Meade's Army of the Potomac** and **Ambrose E. Burnside's** IX Corps. As part of a general offensive by all of his armies, Grant planned to lure Lee into battle by crossing the Rapidan River beyond the Confederate right (or east) flank and rapidly push toward **Richmond, Virginia**. To use his superior numbers most effectively, Grant needed to move beyond a thick tangle of woods south of the Rapidan known as the Wilderness and get into the more open country beyond it before fighting Lee. This wooded region was located around **Chancellorsville**, where **Joseph Hooker** had been decisively defeated the year before.

Grant began what became known as the **Overland Campaign** when he crossed the Rapidan at Germanna Ford in the predawn hours of May 4 and headed southeast. Lee quickly put his **army** in motion to intercept the Federals. Placing **Richard S. Ewell's** II Corps on the Orange Turnpike to the left and **A. P. Hill's** III Corps on the roughly parallel Orange Plank Road to the right, Lee moved east toward Wilderness Tavern and the heart of the Wilderness. **James Longstreet's** I Corps was farther behind with orders to join the army as quickly as possible.

On the morning of May 5, the Confederates intercepted the Federals just west of Wilderness Tavern. Lee had issued orders not to bring on a general engagement until Longstreet arrived, but the Federals were actively seeking a fight. Learning the enemy was at hand, Meade believed only a Confederate **division** was on the Orange Turnpike and at 7:30 A.M. ordered **Gouverneur K. Warren's** V Corps to attack. Warren, however, was not ready until 1:00 P.M. When he did advance, the surprise attack briefly broke Ewell's right flank, but a determined counterattack pushed back the Federals and restored the line. For the rest of the day, intense fighting occurred along and on either side of the turnpike as Warren's V and **John Sedgwick's** VI Corps traded attacks and counterattacks with Ewell's **corps**.

On Lee's right, Hill pushed forward and nearly captured the crucial Plank Road and Brock Road intersection, which would have given the Confederates an avenue into Grant's rear. **George W. Getty's** VI Corps division stopped Hill. On that front, heavy fighting continued until dark between Hill and elements of Sedgwick's VI and **Winfield S. Hancock's** II Corps. An attack by Hancock nearly broke Hill's line, but stubborn Confederate resistance and darkness put an end to the fight. That night the two armies began erecting earthworks along opposing lines that ran several miles through thick timber from below the Plank Road to beyond the turnpike. On the Confederate side, a dangerous gap existed between Ewell and Hill.

Hill's corps on Lee's right was in disarray. The men were in an exhausted, confused state, and the corps had suffered heavy casualties. Lee informed Hill that Longstreet would arrive during the night to relieve him and that he was to leave his corps in place rather than fall back to reform. Expecting to be relieved, Hill and his subordinates allowed their men to get what rest they could and did not take any significant precautions to reinforce the line. Grant was encouraged by Hancock's near success during the day and ordered a general assault for 5:00 A.M. the next day. Sedgwick and Warren were to attack Ewell, Hancock was to advance against Hill, and Burnside's IX Corps was to advance into the gap between Lee's separated wings.

At 4:30 A.M. on May 6, Ewell attacked first and touched off a bloody but indecisive fight on the Confederate left. On Lee's right, Longstreet failed to arrive as expected, and Hill's exhausted men were still on the firing line when Hancock attacked at 5:00 A.M. Hancock crushed Hill's corps and sent it fleeing down the Plank Road. At that moment, Longstreet arrived with **Hood's Texas Brigade**, under Brig. Gen. **John Gregg**, in the lead. In one of the war's most dramatic moments, Lee placed himself at the head of the **brigade** and was going to lead it into battle to restore the broken line. The Texans, however, refused to advance until Lee went to the rear. When he did so, they counterattacked and halted Hancock's advance. Longstreet then filled in the gap between Hill and Ewell (Burnside had floundered in the woods and never attacked the gap).

Later that day, the Confederates launched surprise attacks against both Union flanks. Longstreet used an unfinished **railroad** grade to conceal a movement against the Union left. Led by Lt. Col. **G. Moxley Sorrell**, the late morning attack routed Hancock's flank, and a general Confederate advance pushed the VI Corps back to the Brock Road. As Longstreet prepared to renew his attack, he was mistakenly fired upon by his own troops and was severely wounded. Lee then assumed tactical command and renewed the attack, but the Union line held. On the Confederate left, Brig. Gen. **John Gordon** discovered the Union flank was vulnerable and requested permission to attack it with his brigade. Participants disagreed over who was at fault, but the attack was delayed until nearly dark. When Gordon finally did attack, he shattered Sedgwick's flank and drove it back some distance before darkness and Federal resistance finally stopped him.

Skirmishing continued on May 7, but neither side renewed the battle. Unable to win a decisive victory in the Wilderness, Grant disengaged that night and moved toward **Spotsylvania Court House** to turn Lee's right flank. The fighting had been some of the war's heaviest, and the shooting set large woods fires that burned many wounded men alive. Because of the horrendous losses suffered by the Union army during the Overland Campaign, Grant's officers apparently underreported their Wilderness casualties for morale purposes. Officially, the Army of the Potomac lost 17,666 men, but the actual total may have been nearly 20,000. Lee's casualties also were probably higher than official records indicate. Traditional estimates place his losses at 7,500, whereas modern research indicates he suffered approximately 11,100 casualties.

WILKES, CHARLES (1798–1877) USA. A native of **New York**, Wilkes joined the **U.S. Navy** as a midshipman in 1818. He was a capable officer and excellent navigator and commanded a scientific expedition to Antarctica in 1838, but his strict **discipline** made him unpopular with both men and officers. Wilkes also was argumentative and obstinate and often clashed with his superiors. As a result, he still held the rank of captain in 1861, despite more than 40 years of service.

Wilkes's moment of fame came on November 8, 1861, while in command of the **USS San Jacinto**, when he illegally stopped the British mail steamer *Trent* and removed Confederate envoys **James Mason** and **John Slidell**. The *Trent* **Affair** caused much friction between the United States and Great Britain and threatened to spark a war between the two powers. Although the Northern people praised Wilkes's actions, the Union government was embarrassed, and **Abraham Lincoln** had no choice but to release the two diplomats.

Wilkes was promoted to commodore in July 1862 and, after commanding the James River Flotilla for a time, took command of a seven-vessel squadron in the West Indies in September to disrupt Confederate trade. However, he again overstepped his authority and illegally captured a British ship in early 1863. Unwilling to face another international incident, the navy relieved Wilkes of command, court-martialed him in March 1864, and gave him a public reprimand. He was retired in June 1864 but two years later was promoted to rear admiral on the retired list.

WILLCOX, ORLANDO BOLIVAR (1823–1907) USA. A native of **Michigan**, Willcox graduated from **West Point** in 1847 and was assigned to the **artillery**. After helping garrison Mexico City after the **Mexican War**, he served in the **Seminole Wars** and on routine garrison duty before resigning his 1st lieutenant's commission in 1857 and becoming a Michigan lawyer.

In May 1861, Willcox entered Union service as colonel of the 1st Michigan. Sent to **Virginia**, he was placed in command of a **brigade** in **Samuel Heintzelman's division** and was wounded and captured at **First Manassas**. While in Confederate hands, Willcox became one of the **prisoners** who was threatened with execution if the Union executed any captured Confederate **privateers**.

Exchanged in August 1862, Willcox was promoted to brigadier general and was given a division command in **Ambrose Burnside's** IX Corps. After fighting at **Antietam**, he took over the **corps** when Burnside was promoted to command the **Army of the Potomac** in November. Willcox led the corps at **Fredericksburg** and then accompanied Burnside to **Tennessee** in 1863. Over the next year, he sometimes led his division and sometimes the corps, but he remained with Burnside through the **Knoxville Campaign** and returned to **Virginia** with him. Willcox led the corps through all of the battles in the 1864 **Overland Campaign** and was **brevetted** for **Spotsylvania**. Afterward, he sometimes commanded the corps during the **Petersburg Campaign**. It was expected by many that Willcox would take command of the corps when Burnside was relieved after the disaster at the **Crater**, but he was passed over and remained a brigadier general in division command until war's end.

Willcox was mustered out of the **army** in January 1866 with the brevet rank of major general of both volunteers and regulars. After briefly practicing law, he returned to the **U.S. Army** in July as colonel of the 29th U.S. Infantry. Willcox held several commands over the next few decades and fought Apaches while commander of the Department of Arizona from 1878 to 1882 (for this service, the town of Willcox was named for him). After being promoted to brigadier general in 1886, he retired the following year and eventually settled in Canada. In 1895, Willcox was awarded the **Medal of Honor** for his service at First Manassas.

WILLIAMS, ALPHEUS STARKEY (1810–1878) USA. A native of **Connecticut**, Williams graduated from Yale University in 1831 and became a **Michigan** lawyer after traveling extensively at home and abroad. During the 1840s, he was a probate judge, newspaper owner, lieutenant colonel of the 1st Michigan during the **Mexican War**, and postmaster of Detroit.

In early 1861, Williams was appointed president of Michigan's military board and was made brigadier general of state militia in April. Sent east, he was given a **brigade** command under **Robert Patterson** in the **Shenandoah Valley** and was appointed brigadier general of volunteers in August. Two months later, Williams was given a brigade command in

Nathaniel P. Banks's division of the **Army of the Potomac**. He was elevated to division command in March 1862 and saw service in **Stonewall Jackson's 1862 Shenandoah Valley Campaign**. After Banks's command was designated the **Army of Virginia's** II Corps, Williams led his division at **Cedar Mountain** and **Second Manassas**. He briefly led the **corps** at the beginning of the **Antietam Campaign**, but when it was redesignated the XII Corps under **Joseph Mansfield**, he returned to the division. When Mansfield was killed at Antietam, Williams briefly took over the corps. He was back with his division at **Chancellorsville** but again took over the corps at **Gettysburg** when **Henry W. Slocum** assumed command of the **army's** right wing. Williams fought very well in both battles.

After Gettysburg, the XII Corps was sent west to reinforce the **Army of the Cumberland** at Chattanooga, Tennessee. Back in command of his division, Williams guarded the supply line during the **Chattanooga Campaign**. When the XI and XII Corps were merged to form the new XX Corps under **Joseph Hooker** in early 1864, Williams retained command of his division and led it through much of the **Atlanta Campaign**. When Hooker resigned in July, Williams was put in command of the corps. After the fall of Atlanta, he remained in command of the corps for the **March to the Sea** and most of the **Carolinas Campaign**. Known to his men as "Old Pap," Williams had an excellent war record and was **brevetted** major general of volunteers for "marked ability and energy," but he never received the regular promotion to that higher rank.

Williams was mustered out of the volunteers in January 1866 and served as the U.S. minister to El Salvador until 1869. A **Democrat**, he ran unsuccessfully for governor of Michigan in 1870 but was elected to the **U.S. Congress** in 1874. Reelected two years later, Williams died in **Washington, D.C.**, while in office. His Civil War letters were later published under the title *From the Cannon's Mouth: The Civil War Letters of General Alpheus S. Williams.*

WILLIAMS, JOHN STUART "CERRO GORDO" (1818–1898) CSA. A native of **Kentucky**, Williams graduated from **Ohio's** Miami University in 1839 and became a lawyer. He entered the **Mexican War** as a captain in the 4th Kentucky and led a scout **company** attached to the 6th U.S. Infantry before being elected colonel of the 4th Kentucky. Williams's heroics while leading a charge at Cerro Gordo led to his nickname "Cerro Gordo" Williams. He returned to his Kentucky law practice after the war and was elected to the state legislature as a **Whig** in 1851 and 1853. During the **secession** crisis, Williams first opposed secession and advocated compromise and Kentucky's neutrality, but he finally supported the Confederacy after he concluded the Union was trying to use force to coerce the South.

Williams accompanied Confederate Brig. Gen. **Humphrey Marshall** to southwest **Virginia** in 1861 to raise a command, but when that failed, he returned to eastern Kentucky and raised a **regiment** that later was designated the 5th Kentucky (Confederate). After some minor fighting, Williams withdrew into Virginia, and in November was commissioned colonel of his regiment.

After **skirmishing** with the enemy along the Virginia-Kentucky border, Williams was promoted to brigadier general in April 1862 and was given command of a Virginia **brigade**. His superiors praised his actions while scouting and skirmishing around Cumberland Gap that summer, and he participated in the **Kentucky Campaign**. In late 1862, Williams was given command of a cavalry brigade in southwestern Virginia and for a time commanded the **Departments of Southwestern Virginia** and **Western Virginia**. In late 1863, he was given command of all the cavalry in **Tennessee** east of Knoxville. In October, Williams fought with great skill and bravery at **Blue Springs**, but he was forced to retreat by a much larger force. Despite his outstanding service, he was criticized by his superiors and transferred to southwest Virginia at his own request. In early 1864, Williams took command of a Kentucky brigade in **Joseph Wheeler's** cavalry and led it through the **Atlanta Campaign**. In August, he accompanied **Wheeler's Raid** into Tennessee but was censored by his commander for failing in a mission (which Wheeler only reluctantly agreed to) to attack Strawberry Plains and for being slow to rejoin the main column. Afterward, Williams served the rest of the war in southwestern Virginia.

After the war, Williams became a Kentucky farmer. He was elected to the state legislature in 1873 and 1875 but was defeated for governor in 1875. Williams also was elected to the U.S. Senate in 1878, but he was defeated for reelection. He then returned to Kentucky and worked as a farmer.

WILLIAMS RAPID-FIRE GUN. This Confederate weapon, designed by Capt. R. S. Williams and first produced at the **Tredegar Iron Works** in September 1861, is considered to be the first rapid-fire gun used in battle. With a single barrel four feet long, the breech-loading weapon had a two-inch bore and fired one-pound projectiles at an effective range of 2,000 yards. Mounted on a carriage, it was pulled by one horse. The gun was made of steel and had a magazine mounted on top of the breech. One revolution of the hand crank dropped and fired one round of ammunition, with a rate of fire from 18 to 20 rounds per minute. The Williams Rapid-Fire Gun was first used in combat at **Seven Pines**, where Captain Williams used it while attached to **George Pickett's brigade**. Pleased with the results, the Confederate government ordered many more. By war's end, a number of Williams Rapid-Fire Guns had been made at Tredegar Iron Works; Lynchburg, Virginia; and Mobile, Alabama; and were used in both the eastern and western theaters, including the **Battle of Blue Springs, Tennessee**. One drawback to the gun was that it tended to jam because the rapid rate of fire often heated up the breech and prevented it from closing properly. Today, one of the war's captured guns is on display at **West Point**.

WILLIAMS, SETH (1822–1866) USA. A native of **Maine**, Williams graduated from **West Point** in 1842. After serving on routine garrison duty with the **artillery**, he fought in the **Mexican War** as Maj. Gen. **Robert Patterson's** aide and won one **brevet**. Remaining in the **U.S. Army** at war's end, Williams served very effectively as West Point's adjutant from 1850 to 1853. He transferred to the adjutant general's department in 1853 and served in that branch of service for the rest of his life.

Williams was a brevet captain when the Civil War began, but he was promoted to major in August 1861 and to brigadier general of volunteers in September. Appointed the **Army of the Potomac's** adjutant general, he was known for his great skill and served in that position under generals **George B. McClellan, Ambrose E. Burnside, Joseph Hooker**, and **George G. Meade**. In March 1864, Lt. Gen. **U. S. Grant** appointed Williams inspector general for all of the Union armies operating against **Richmond, Virginia**. He remained at that post until war's end.

Williams ended the war with the brevet rank of major general in both the volunteers and regulars and the regular rank of lieutenant colonel. In February 1866, he was appointed adjutant general for the Military Division of the Atlantic, but he immediately became ill and died in March from "congestion of the brain" (Warner, *Generals in Blue*, 563).

WILLIAMS, THOMAS (1815–1862) USA. Williams was a native of **New York**, but as a child, he moved to **Michigan** with his family. The son of a prominent militia general, he served under his father as a private in the Black Hawk War. After graduating from **West Point** in 1837, Williams served with the **artillery** in the **Seminole Wars** and on routine garrison duty before becoming an instructor at the academy. He was appointed **Winfield Scott's** aide-de-camp in 1844 and served with him through the **Mexican War**, winning two **brevets** for gallantry. Afterward, Williams again served in the Seminole Wars and on routine garrison duty.

When the Civil War began, Williams was a captain in the 4th U.S. Artillery, stationed at **Fort Monroe, Virginia**. He was promoted to major in May 1861 and to brigadier general of volunteers in September. After briefly serving as the **Department of Virginia's** inspector general, Williams joined **Ambrose E. Burnside's** expedition to **North Carolina** in October and was given command of the troops operating against **Hatteras Inlet**. It was during this assignment that his inability to relate to volunteer troops became apparent. Williams's strict **discipline** angered the men and made him very unpopular, and they sometimes dug pits for him to fall into.

In March 1862, Williams joined **Benjamin F. Butler's** command for operations against **New Orleans, Louisiana**. While stationed at Ship Island on the Gulf Coast, he again came into conflict with his volunteers. In May, Williams took command of the Union garrison at **Baton Rouge, Louisiana**, and that summer accompanied **U.S. Navy** forces under **David Farragut** to **Vicksburg, Mississippi**. While there, he began digging a canal across a peninsula fronting the city to straighten out the Mississippi River so ships could bypass Vicksburg. Williams's dictatorial ways again made him unpopular, and the canal attempt failed (the following year, during the **Vicksburg Campaign**, it was revived as Grant's Canal). Back in Baton Rouge, he arrested some of his officers for failing to return runaway slaves, and they retaliated by preferring charges against him.

In the August 5, 1862, **Battle of Baton Rouge**, Williams was killed while fighting skillfully against **John C. Breckinridge's** Confederates. Officially, he was shot through the heart, but Butler claimed he was decapitated by a shell. Rumors also spread that the unpopular officer was killed by his own men who held him in front of one of their own cannons.

WILLIAMSBURG, VIRGINIA, BATTLE OF (MAY 5, 1862). During the 1862 **Peninsula Campaign**, Union Maj. Gen. **George B. McClellan's** more than 100,000-man **Army of the Potomac** lumbered up the Virginia Peninsula toward **Richmond, Virginia**. With approximately 60,000 men, Confederate Gen. **Joseph E. Johnston** remained on the defensive and delayed McClellan for weeks along a defensive line at **Yorktown**. Just before McClellan planned to assault Yorktown, Johnston withdrew on May 3. Sending his **army** in pursuit, McClellan caught up with the Confederate rear guard on May 5 just east of Williamsburg.

James Longstreet's division manned a defensive line in Johnston's rear, whose center was anchored on a large earthen fortification known as Fort Magruder. On the wet, rainy morning of May 5, Longstreet was attacked by **Joseph Hooker's** division. The Confederates successfully repelled the assault and then counterattacked the Union left flank, but the arrival of **Philip Kearny's** division that afternoon strengthened the Union flank. By late morning, Johnston was on the scene and ordered up **Daniel H. Hill's** division to support Longstreet. Before Hill arrived, **Winfield S. Hancock's** Union **brigade** of **William F. Smith's** division advanced against Longstreet's left, occupied two abandoned **redoubts**, and began shelling Longstreet's flank. Soon, **Jubal A. Early's** brigade arrived at the head of Hill's column. Early and Hill led an attack against Hancock, and Early was wounded. Additional Confederate units entered the fight as they arrived, and the battle continued until dark. The disjointed Confederate attacks failed, and Johnston withdrew during the night. In the fierce battle, McClellan lost 2,283 men, while the Confederates suffered 1,560 casualties.

WILLIAMSON, JAMES ALEXANDER (1829–1902) USA. A native of **Kentucky**, Williamson grew up in **Indiana** and **Iowa**. After graduating from **Illinois's** Knox College, he opened an Iowa law practice and became active in **Democratic Party** politics. Williamson helped get the capital moved from Iowa City to Des Moines, served as chairman of the state Democratic Committee, and was a delegate to the second 1860 Democratic National Convention at Baltimore, Maryland.

Williamson entered Union service in August 1861 as a 1st lieutenant and adjutant of the 4th Iowa. Although a complete military novice, his courage and eagerness to learn marked him for rapid promotion. After fighting at **Pea Ridge**, Williamson was elected lieutenant colonel in April 1862 and was appointed colonel in July. After garrison duty in **Arkansas**, he joined **William T. Sherman's** XV Corps in the **Army of the Tennessee** and was praised for leading his **regiment** in a charge at **Chickasaw Bayou**. Although wounded, Williamson held his ground when other regiments retreated. As a result, Sherman allowed him to inscribe "First at Chickasaw Bayou" on his colors, and he was awarded the **Medal of Honor** in 1895. Williamson also participated in the capture of **Arkansas Post** and served through most of the **Vicksburg Campaign** before illness forced him on leave. When he returned to duty in August 1863, Williamson was given a **brigade** command in the XV Corps' 1st Division and led it in the **Chattanooga** and **Atlanta Campaigns** and in the **March to the Sea**. He was promoted to brigadier general of volunteers in April 1865 and ended the war in command of the District of St. Louis.

Williamson was mustered out of service in August 1865 with the **brevet** rank of major general of volunteers. He returned to Iowa and resumed his political activities, except he then was a member of the **Republican Party**. Williamson also became a **railroad** president and served as a land commissioner.

WILLIAMSPORT, MARYLAND, BATTLE OF (JULY 6, 1863). After the **Battle of Gettysburg, Robert E. Lee's Army of Northern Virginia** retreated toward Williamsport, Maryland, to recross the Potomac River into **Virginia**. High water prevented the Confederates from fording the river, and Union cavalry from **George G. Meade's Army of the Potomac** were in pursuit. On July 6, 1863, **John Buford's** Union cavalry **division** attacked the Confederate supply train at Williamsport, but it was driven off by Brig. Gen. **John D. Imboden's brigade**. Not far away at Hagerstown, Maryland, Union cavalry under **H. Judson Kilpatrick** was hotly engaged with the Confederate brigades of **John R. Chambliss, Alfred Iverson**, and **William E. "Grumble" Jones**. Kilpatrick sent two of his brigades to reinforce Buford, but he then was forced to retire when attacked by **Fitzhugh Lee's** brigade. After losing approximately 400 men in these clashes, the Union cavalry withdrew to Boonsboro. The Confederates lost 254 men and began withdrawing into Virginia on the night of July 13.

WILLICH, AUGUST (1810–1878) USA. Born August von Willich, this future Union general was a native of Prussia and the son of a Napoleonic Wars veteran. After attending two Prussian military academies, he became a captain in the Prussian army but then converted to communism. After being court-martialed, Willich was allowed to resign his commission, and he joined the rebel forces in the 1846–48 revolution. He fled Prussia after the revolt was crushed and immigrated to the United States in 1853. After working for a time as a carpenter in **New York**, Willich moved to **Ohio** in 1858, became editor of a German newspaper, and was active in the fledgling communist movement. His radical ideas made him a leader of the German community and earned him the nickname "Reddest of the Red."

When the Civil War began, Willich quickly raised hundreds of German recruits for the Union and entered service in May 1861 as 1st lieutenant and adjutant of the 9th Ohio. He was promoted to major in June and saw combat in western **Virginia** at **Rich Mountain**. In August,

Willich was appointed colonel of the German-dominated 32nd Indiana. The elderly, Prussian-accented officer was viewed as an oddity, and he perhaps was the only commander who used Prussian bugle calls for drill commands. Willich also was a strict **disciplinarian**, but his men responded well to his leadership. After fighting at **Carnifex Ferry** and **Shiloh** and participating in the **siege of Corinth, Mississippi**, he was promoted to brigadier general of volunteers in July 1862.

Given a **brigade** command in the **Army of the Ohio's** 2nd Division, Willich participated in the **Kentucky Campaign** before he was transferred to a brigade in the 2nd Division of the **Army of the Cumberland's** XIV Corps. On the first day of battle at **Stones River**, he was captured after his horse was killed. After being **exchanged** in May 1863, Willich took a brigade in the XX Corps's 2nd Division and led it through the **Tullahoma Campaign**. At **Chickamauga**, he led the **division** but was returned to brigade command during the **Chattanooga Campaign**. During the 1864 **Atlanta Campaign**, Willich's brigade was in the IV Corps' 3rd Division, but he was severely wounded in the shoulder at **Resaca** and was forced to give up field duty. He was sent to Ohio, where he performed routine duty until rejoining his brigade in **Texas** after the war was over.

Brevetted major general of volunteers for his war service, Willich was mustered out of service in January 1866. After serving three years as an Ohio county auditor, he returned to Prussia and during the Franco-Prussian War offered his services to Wilhelm I (the same monarch he had rebelled against earlier). The offer was declined because of his advanced age. After studying under Karl Marx for a while, Willich returned to the United States and settled in Ohio.

WILMINGTON, NORTH CAROLINA. Located on the Cape Fear River 28 miles upstream from the Atlantic Ocean, Wilmington, North Carolina, was the state's largest city in 1860, with a population of 9,542. With a deepwater port and three **railroads** connecting to points inland and to **Virginia** and **South Carolina**, it became one of the Confederacy's most important cities during the Civil War.

In July 1861, the **U.S. Navy** began its **blockade** of Wilmington, but the city did not become a major Confederate port until **Josiah Gorgas** based his Ordnance Bureau's **blockade runners** there in the autumn of 1862. When Union pressure on **Charleston, South Carolina**, in July 1863 effectively closed that harbor, Wilmington became the Confederacy's most important port. The Confederate government soon based government-owned blockade runners there, as did **North Carolina**, Virginia, and

Georgia. The city also became the receiving point for meat rations sent to **Robert E. Lee's Army of Northern Virginia** and thus was critical for that **army's** survival. By war's end, blockade runners had made more than 300 successful round trips from Wilmington, more than from all of the other Confederate ports combined.

As its importance grew, Wilmington's defenses increased accordingly under the watchful eye of commander Brig. Gen. **William H. C. Whiting**. Not only was the city ringed by fortifications, but its two outlets to the Atlantic were guarded by Forts Caswell and Fisher. **Fort Fisher**, under the command of Col. William Lamb, guarded New Inlet and became the more important and larger of the two since most blockade runners preferred using that inlet. By the end of 1864, Fort Fisher was manned by 1,400 troops, was protected by nearly 50 cannons, and was known as the "Gibraltar of the Confederacy." Supporting the fortifications was a small river fleet under Flag Officer William F. Lynch. The CSS *Raleigh* attacked the Union blockaders in May 1864, but it failed to sink any vessels and then was lost when it ran aground while reentering the port.

The Union had a difficult time blockading Wilmington because its two inlets divided the ships on patrol by forcing them to cover a 50-mile stretch of water. The strong fortifications—especially Fort Fisher—also kept the warships at a distance. Although Union officials had begun making plans to attack Wilmington as early as 1862, it was not until December 1864 that an operation finally set out to close this last Confederate port.

In December 1864, General-in-Chief **U. S. Grant** sent **Benjamin F. Butler** with 6,500 men of the **Army of the James** to take Fort Fisher by assault. If unsuccessful, Butler was to lay siege to the fort until it surrendered. Butler departed by ship from **Fort Monroe, Virginia**, on December 14 to join Rear Adm. **David Porter's** fleet off the North Carolina coast. Before making his attack, Butler planned to destroy Fort Fisher by exploding near it a barge loaded with 235 tons of powder. Poor communications prevented the two officers from joining forces until December 24. Porter arrived first and detonated the powder barge without waiting for Butler, but the barge ran aground too far away to inflict any damage. After a preliminary naval bombardment, Butler landed 2,200 men on December 25 and unsuccessfully attacked the fort. Rather than besieging Fort Fisher as ordered, he then returned to Fort Monroe. Grant was so incensed at Butler's behavior that he relieved the general of command.

Grant then launched a second expedition led by Brig. Gen. **Alfred H. Terry**. Terry and Porter arrived off Fort Fisher on January 13, 1865, and Terry landed an assault force. The next day, after a naval bombardment, the Federals attacked with 2,000 men. In fierce fighting, General Whiting was mortally wounded, and Terry captured the fort after dark.

The fall of Fort Fisher effectively closed Wilmington's port, but Confederate Gen. **Braxton Bragg**, commander of the **Department of North Carolina**, continued to protect Wilmington. He positioned 6,600 men under **Robert F. Hoke** in a defensive position north and northwest of Fort Fisher and withdrew scattered garrisons to help defend the city. In early February 1865, Maj. Gen. **John M. Schofield** arrived with the XXIII Corps and took command of the Union forces in the area. On February 16, he advanced **Jacob Cox's division** against Fort Anderson, a fortification protecting Wilmington. After Cox moved into the fort's rear, the Confederate troops under Brig. Gen. **Johnson Hagood** evacuated it in the predawn hours of February 19. Cox continued to push Hagood back, and by February 21, he and Terry were within reach of Wilmington. That night, Bragg destroyed supplies in the city and evacuated all of his troops. Cox's XXIII Corps entered Wilmington the next day and secured the city.

WILMOT PROVISO. This bill, sponsored by **Pennsylvania** congressman David Wilmot, was first introduced in 1846 and called for the banning of **slavery** in any territory the United States might win in the **Mexican War**. A **Democrat**, Wilmot's motivation was not **abolitionist** in nature but rather racist, since his intent was to keep the western territories open for whites only. For more than a decade, the proviso split apart the North and South because it frequently was introduced in the **U.S. Congress**. Most Northerners saw it as a means to ensure that slavery would not spread west out of the South, while Southerners bitterly opposed it as denying them the spoils of war and interfering with their constitutional rights. With a majority in the House of Representatives, the Northerners could pass the proviso there, but it always failed in the Senate. The acrimonious debate led to sectional polarization, caused many Southerners to think more about **secession**, and helped create the **Free-Soil Party**. The Wilmot Proviso was finally passed during the Civil War on June 19, 1862.

WILSON, CLAUDIUS CHARLES (1831–1863) CSA. A native of **Georgia**, Wilson graduated with honors from Emory College in 1851 and became a lawyer. Except for one year as a solicitor general, he practiced law until the Civil War.

Wilson entered Confederate service in August 1861 as captain of a volunteer **company** he raised. Elected colonel of the 25th Georgia the following month, he became part of **Hugh W. Mercer's brigade** at Savannah. Over the next year, Wilson performed routine garrison and **picket** duty around Savannah and in nearby **South Carolina**. In December 1862, he was given a brigade command and reinforced **Wilmington, North Carolina**. Placed at Masonborough, in January 1863, Wilson captured a Union warship that ran aground near there. He then took his men back to Savannah and resumed his regimental command in **William H. T. Walker's** brigade. In May 1863, the brigade reinforced **Joseph E. Johnston** during the **Vicksburg Campaign**. Wilson was only lightly engaged at **Jackson, Mississippi**, but afterward, he was promoted to brigade command when Walker took over a **division**. During the campaign, the brigade helped defend Yazoo City and afterward participated in the siege of Jackson.

In August 1863, Wilson reinforced the **Army of Tennessee** at Chattanooga, Tennessee. On the first day of fighting at **Chickamauga**, he supported **Nathan Bedford Forrest's** cavalry and won high praise from that officer. Wilson fell ill—probably with dysentery—after Chickamauga and died on November 27, 1863. His promotion to brigadier general reached the **army** shortly afterward.

WILSON, HENRY (1812–1875) USA. A native of **New Hampshire**, this leading **Radical Republican** was born to a poor family as Jeremiah Jones Colbath. He worked for a farmer under an indenture agreement for 10 years and then moved to **Massachusetts** in 1833 to become a cobbler's apprentice. Legally changing his name to Henry Wilson, he learned the cobbler trade and opened a profitable Massachusetts shoe factory. After visiting the South in 1836, Wilson became a devout **abolitionist** and was elected to the state assembly in 1841 as a **Whig**. Known for championing the poor, he was elected to the state senate in 1844 and 1852. When the Whigs failed to support the **Wilmot Proviso** at their 1848 national convention, Wilson left the party and helped form the **Free-Soil Party**. He then owned and edited one of the party's newspapers until 1851. In 1854, Wilson joined the **Know-Nothing Party**. He was defeated for the U.S. House of Representatives and for governor but in 1855 was chosen to fill out the U.S. Senate term of **Edward Everett** when he resigned. Wilson quickly abandoned the Know-Nothings, however, because they failed to oppose **slavery**, and their nativism brought criticism upon himself. He then joined the **Republican Party**, with which he would be affiliated for the rest of his life.

Wilson campaigned for **Abraham Lincoln** in 1860 and became one of the Civil War's Radical Republicans. As chairman of the powerful

Senate Committee on Military Affairs, he wielded great power in the Federal government. Wilson opposed the **Crittenden Compromise** and called for a vigorous prosecution of the war once fighting erupted. He also introduced several bills to free the slaves before the **Emancipation Proclamation** was issued and helped create the **Freedmen's Bureau**.

During **Reconstruction**, Wilson bitterly opposed President **Andrew Johnson's** moderate policies until a trip to the South showed him how devastated the region was. He then became somewhat less radical and sponsored bills to support Southern education programs and to establish a **homestead** policy there. In 1872, Wilson was elected President **U. S. Grant's** vice president, and he resigned from the Senate in 1873 to accept that position. He was serving in that capacity when he died in 1875, after completing his three-volume book *History of the Rise and Fall of the Slave Power in America*.

WILSON, JAMES HARRISON (1837–1925) USA. A native of **Illinois**, Wilson graduated in the upper ranks of his 1860 **West Point** class. Assigned to the topographical **engineers**, he was sent to Fort Vancouver in the Washington Territory.

When the Civil War began, Wilson was transferred east and was promoted to 1st lieutenant in September 1861. That autumn, he was appointed chief topographical engineer for the expedition against **Port Royal, South Carolina**. In March 1861, Wilson was made the **Department of the South's** chief topographical engineer, and the next month he helped capture **Fort Pulaski, Georgia**. In September 1862, he joined the **Army of the Potomac** as **George B. McClellan's** volunteer aide-de-camp. After participating in the **Antietam Campaign**, Wilson transferred west in October and became chief topographical engineer for **U. S. Grant's Army of the Tennessee**.

For the next year, Wilson served as Grant's topographical engineer and inspector general, and he was promoted to captain of engineers in March 1863. After serving well in the **Vicksburg Campaign**, he was promoted to brigadier general of volunteers in October. Wilson remained on Grant's staff through the **Chattanooga Campaign** and then served as **William T. Sherman's** chief engineer when he was sent to relieve Knoxville, Tennessee, at the end of the **Knoxville Campaign**.

In February 1864, Wilson was sent to **Washington, D.C.**, where he was appointed chief of the Cavalry Bureau. After all of his service as an engineering officer, he made his greatest contribution to the Union victory as a cavalryman. In April, Grant gave Wilson a **cavalry division** under **Philip Sheridan** in the Army of the Potomac. He generally fought with great skill through the **Overland**, **Petersburg**, and **Sheridan's 1864 Shenandoah Valley Campaigns**, although his service in the **Wilson-Kautz Raid** was less than stellar. While with Sheridan in the **Shenandoah Valley**, Wilson was sent back west in October 1864 to become chief of cavalry for Sherman's **Military Division of the Mississippi**.

In the war's last months, Wilson proved to be one of the most effective Union cavalry commanders. He reorganized the cavalry, trained and equipped **H. Judson Kilpatrick's** troopers for the **March to the Sea**, commanded the cavalry that helped destroy the Confederate **Army of Tennessee** during the **Franklin and Nashville Campaign**, and pursued the retreating Confederates back to the Tennessee River. In March–April 1865, **Wilson's Selma, Alabama, Raid** defeated renowned Confederate cavalryman **Nathan Bedford Forrest** and became one of the war's most successful in terms of dispersing the enemy and destroying vital Confederate infrastructure. In the war's closing days, it also was elements of Wilson's command that captured fleeing Confederate President **Jefferson Davis**.

By the time the war ended, Wilson had been **brevetted** through the ranks to major general of regulars, and he was promoted to major general of volunteers in June 1865. When the volunteer forces were mustered out of service in early 1866, he remained in the **U.S. Army** as lieutenant colonel of the 35th U.S. Infantry. However, Wilson actually served with the engineers rather than as a field officer until he was discharged at his own request in 1870. He then engaged in **railroad** activities, traveled, and became a popular writer on the war. Wilson reentered the volunteers as a major general during the 1898 Spanish-American War and served in Cuba and Puerto Rico. Remaining in the service, he also participated in China's Boxer Rebellion before being placed on the army's retired list in 1901 as a brigadier general of regulars. That same year, Wilson represented President Theodore Roosevelt at the coronation of Britain's Edward VII. When Wilson died in 1925, only three other Union generals survived him.

WILSON-KAUTZ RAID (JUNE 22–JULY 1, 1864). Early in the 1864 **Petersburg Campaign**, Union Maj. Gen. **U. S. Grant** sent Brig. Gen. **James H. Wilson** with his own and Brig. Gen. **August V. Kautz's** cavalry **division** to attack the **railroads** supplying **Robert E. Lee's** Confederate **Army of Northern Virginia** at Petersburg, Virginia. Most of Lee's cavalry was pursuing **Philip Sheridan,** who had taken the main Union cavalry force toward the **Shenandoah Valley**. Only **W. H. F.**

"Rooney" Lee's Confederate cavalry division was at Petersburg to stop the raid.

With about 5,000 men, Wilson and Kautz left Lee's Mill on June 22 and moved south along the Petersburg & Weldon Railroad, tearing up track as they advanced. They then headed west and attacked the Southside Railroad. While Wilson destroyed the railroad, Kautz rode ahead to cut the track at Burkeville Station. Lee's cavalry caught up with the raiders and got between the two Federal columns at Nottoway Station. A sharp fight occurred there as Wilson attacked the Confederates to keep them away from Kautz. Riding south, Wilson and Kautz reunited on the Richmond & Danville Railroad on June 24 and set out to destroy the **Staunton River Bridge** near Roanoke Station. While Wilson guarded the rear against Lee, Kautz reached the bridge on June 25, but he found it too strongly defended by about 900 Confederates to attack.

Unaware the Confederate cavalry had returned to the area from its brief pursuit of Sheridan, the Federals rode east to return to their lines, which they mistakenly thought had been extended to the Petersburg & Weldon Railroad. Upon reaching Stony Creek Station on June 28, Wilson and Kautz found their path blocked by **Wade Hampton's** Confederate cavalry division. Wilson engaged Hampton while Kautz tried to escape by riding north toward Reams' Station. There he unexpectedly ran into **Fitzhugh Lee's** cavalry. After fighting off Hampton, Wilson joined Kautz at Reams' Station on June 30, but he found their path was blocked by enemy cavalry and **William Mahone's** infantry division. Desperate to escape, Wilson and Kautz abandoned their **horse artillery**, wagons, and seriously wounded men and prepared to ride south toward the Nottoway River. The Confederates, however, were able to separate their two columns. Kautz took his men south, and then east, while Wilson crossed the Nottoway River and turned east, with Hampton in pursuit. Badly scattered, the last of the cavalrymen did not make it back to Union lines until July 1. Although Wilson and Kautz destroyed some 60 miles of track and a considerable amount of rolling stock, the Confederates soon had the damage repaired. The raid cost the Federals 1,500 men and 12 cannons.

WILSON'S CREEK, MISSOURI, BATTLE OF (AUGUST 10, 1861).

After **Nathaniel Lyon** captured the secessionist militia at **Camp Jackson, Missouri**, in May 1861, he was promoted to brigadier general, formed a Union **army**, and occupied Springfield. In early August, Confederate Brig. Gen. **Ben McCulloch** advanced his 12,000 men toward Lyon to win **Missouri** for the Confederacy. On the night of August 9,

McCulloch was camped along the west bank of Wilson's Creek, about 15 miles from Lyon's position. He had planned to attack the Federals, but rain-soaked ammunition caused him to postpone the advance. Not expecting an attack on their own position, the Confederates also failed to put out **pickets** that night.

Learning of the enemy's advance, Lyon decided to strike first. Leaving Springfield on the night of August 9, he split his force in two to attack the Confederate camp from two directions at once. **Franz Sigel** took one column of 1,200 men to circle around and attack the enemy camp from the south, while Lyon advanced from the north with 4,200 men. At 5:00 A.M. on August 10, Lyon attacked and drove the Confederate cavalry from Oak Hills, soon to be renamed Bloody Hill. On the east side of Wilson's Creek, Capt. William E. Woodruff's Pulaski Artillery slowed the Union advance with an **enfilading** fire and allowed Maj. Gen. **Sterling Price** time to rush his Confederate **division** into action. To the south, Sigel had attacked when he heard Lyon begin the battle. Advancing from the east side of Wilson's Creek, he drove back the Confederates, crossed the creek, and moved north to trap the enemy between the two Union forces.

On the northern part of the field, Price's division and Woodruff's **artillery** stalled Lyon atop Bloody Hill. On the east side of Wilson's Creek, Capt. **Joseph B. Plummer** had a small command protecting the Union left flank. At about 6:30 A.M., he advanced against Woodruff's artillery to silence it, but McCulloch sent Brig. Gen. **James McIntosh** with two **regiments** to meet the threat. McIntosh stopped Plummer in a cornfield and then pursued the retreating Federals until he was halted by Union artillery fire. To the south, Sigel was still advancing, but McCulloch then turned on him. Sigel mistakenly thought the advancing 3rd Louisiana was one of his gray-clad units and allowed it to advance to within 40 yards. A devastating Confederate volley riddled the Union line, and Sigel's men fled the field, with the Confederates in pursuit.

Sigel no longer was a threat to the Confederates, but fighting continued on the northern part of the battlefield. At about 7:30 A.M., militia Brig. Gen. James H. McBride led a Confederate counterattack against Lyon's right flank on Bloody Hill but finally was forced to withdraw after heavy fighting. After Sigel's rout, McCulloch concentrated against Lyon and launched a second attack on Bloody Hill at about 9:00 A.M. By that time, Lyon had reinforced his position, and the Federals repulsed this assault. A Confederate cavalry charge against Lyon's right flank and rear by Col. **Elkanah B. Greer** also was beaten back. Lyon was slightly wounded by artillery fire during this fighting, but he remained on the field. While trying to rally the men, he was shot and killed, becoming the first Union general to be killed during the war. Major **Samuel Sturgis** then assumed command of the Union army. He was struck by a third, massive enemy attack when Price was joined by the units that repulsed Sigel and sent 6,000 men against Bloody Hill. The Federals held firm in intense fighting, and by 11:00 A.M., the Confederates finally withdrew. Low on ammunition and receiving no help from Sigel, Sturgis then ordered his army to withdraw to Springfield and, later, to Rolla. Bloodied, exhausted, and low on ammunition, the Confederates declined to pursue.

In this, the war's first major battle west of the Mississippi River, the Federals lost 1,317 men, while the Confederates counted 1,222 casualties. After resting, Price advanced, occupied Springfield, and successfully besieged **Lexington** the following month.

WILSON'S SELMA, ALABAMA, RAID (MARCH 22–APRIL 20, 1865). In the spring of 1865, Union cavalryman Brig. Gen. **James H. Wilson** received permission to make a raid against the important Confederate munitions depot and manufacturing center of Selma, Alabama. He led 13,500 troopers south from Gravelly Springs, Alabama, on March 22, 1865, and traveled along three different routes to confuse Lt. Gen. **Nathan Bedford Forrest's** 7,000–8,000-man Confederate cavalry.

For the first few days there was little contact between the opposing forces. Forrest had ordered up **James R. Chalmers's** and **William H. Jackson's divisions** as reinforcements, but he could do little until they arrived. Wilson occupied Elyton (Birmingham) on March 30 and dispatched John T. Croxton's **brigade** on a raid to Tuscaloosa, Alabama (where he later burned the University of Alabama). On March 31, Wilson defeated Forrest at Montevallo, but the next day Forrest made a stand at **Ebenezer Church** with 2,000 men. In a wild, bloody melee, Forrest was wounded, but he repulsed one attack before the Federals broke his line, and the Confederates retreated.

Forrest retreated to Selma, where he was joined by **department** commander Lt. Gen. **Richard Taylor**. The Confederates had been reinforced by one of Chalmers's brigades and had approximately 5,000 men positioned in strong entrenchments to defend the city. Wilson dismounted his 9,000 men and attacked in three columns on April 2. Brigadier General **Eli Long's** division attacked the Confederate right at about 5:00 P.M., while **Emory Upton's** division attacked the left. The Federals broke through the enemy's defenses, captured the town and its vital warehouses and foundries, and forced Forrest and Taylor to flee. In the short struggle, Wilson captured 2,700 **prisoners**, 102 cannons, and a large amount of munitions and supplies.

Leaving Selma on April 9, Wilson captured Montgomery, Alabama, on April 12; Columbus, Georgia, on April 16; and Macon, Georgia, four days later. While in Macon, he learned that **Robert E. Lee** had surrendered at **Appomattox**. Wilson's Raid was one of the war's most successful. Penetrating 300 miles into Confederate territory, he lost 725 men but captured 6,820 prisoners and inflicted an estimated 1,200 casualties on the Confederates. Soon afterward, a unit of Wilson's command captured fleeing Confederate President **Jefferson Davis**.

WILSON'S WHARF, VIRGINIA, BATTLE OF (MAY 24, 1864). During his 1864 **Bermuda Hundred Campaign**, Maj. Gen. **Benjamin F. Butler** built Fort Pocahontas on the north bank of the James River at Wilson's Wharf. Commanded by Brig. Gen. **Edward Wild**, the 1,100 **black troops** there were attacked on May 24, 1864, by 2,500 Confederate cavalry under Maj. Gen. **Fitzhugh Lee**. Supported by the USS *Dawn*, Wild repulsed several attacks, and the Confederates finally withdrew. In the minor action, Wild lost 26 men while Lee is estimated to have lost 140.

WINCHESTER, VIRGINIA, FIRST BATTLE OF (MAY 25, 1862). When the Confederates captured **Front Royal, Virginia**, in **Stonewall Jackson's 1862 Shenandoah Valley Campaign**, Union Maj. Gen. **Nathaniel P. Banks** was forced to fall back from Strasburg to Winchester. Jackson intercepted Banks's column at Middletown on May 24, but the bulk of Banks's 8,500 men continued on to Winchester. Anxious to attack before the Federals could strengthen their position, Jackson marched his nearly 17,000-man **Valley Army** most of the night and reached Winchester on May 25.

Richard S. Ewell's Confederate **division** advanced on Jackson's right and began pressuring the enemy. Instead of launching a **frontal attack**, Jackson sent **Richard Taylor's brigade** of **Louisiana Tigers** to the far left to attack a key Union fort anchoring Banks's right flank. In one of the war's most dramatic moments, Taylor attacked the fort at about 7:30 A.M., just as the sun broke through a heavy fog. One soldier claimed for the first time the Valley Army heard the famous **rebel yell** as the Tigers overran the fort. The rest of the Confederate line surged forward, as well, and Banks abandoned Winchester and retreated toward **Harpers Ferry**. Jackson became furious because his cavalry failed to follow up the enemy. **Turner Ashby** was not on the scene, and **George H. Steuart** refused to obey orders to advance until they came through Ewell, his immediate superior. Banks lost 2,019 men in the debacle, while Jackson suffered about 400 casualties. Jackson advanced toward Harpers Ferry but soon had to march quickly back up the Valley when he learned that Federal forces were closing in on his rear.

WINCHESTER, VIRGINIA, SECOND BATTLE OF (JUNE 14, 1863). When **Robert E. Lee's Army of Northern Virginia** began the 1863 **Gettysburg Campaign**, **Richard S. Ewell's** II Corps led the way from near **Fredericksburg**, Virginia, into the **Shenandoah Valley**. On June 13, 1863, Ewell reached **Berryville**, about 12 miles east of Winchester. Union Maj. Gen. **Robert H. Milroy** had approximately 6,900 men at Winchester and had been warned of the approaching enemy, but he dismissed the intelligence and thus was caught unprepared.

On June 14, Ewell approached Winchester and used **Edward Johnson's division** to **demonstrate** against the town from the south and east, while **Jubal Early's** division moved to the west to attack Milroy's main fortifications north of town. Early bombarded the Federals with 20 cannons secretly positioned, and at about 6:00 P.M., **Harry T. Hays's brigade** of **Louisiana Tigers** (the same brigade that led the attack at **First Winchester**) rushed forward and captured what was called the Star Fort. The Federals made a weak attempt to recapture the position but were repulsed by Hays. Now with his line of retreat threatened, Milroy was forced to abandon Winchester. Anticipating such a move, Ewell sent Johnson's division to the north to block Milroy's escape at **Stephenson's Depot**. There the next day, Johnson captured much of Milroy's column as it tried to cut its way to safety.

At Second Winchester and Stephenson's Depot, Milroy lost approximately 4,450 men (nearly 4,000 of whom were taken **prisoner**), 23 cannons, and 300 wagons. Ewell showed great promise in this his first action as a **corps** commander. He lost only 269 men, and led the **army** across the Potomac River into Maryland on June 15. Milroy was highly criticized for his failure at Winchester, but a court of inquiry cleared him of any wrongdoing.

WINCHESTER, VIRGINIA, THIRD BATTLE OF (SEPTEMBER 19, 1864). Also known as the Battle of Opequon (oh-PEK-un) Creek, this battle began the destruction of **Jubal A. Early's Valley Army** during **Philip Sheridan's 1864 Shenandoah Valley Campaign**. In August 1864, Sheridan was put in command of the **Middle Military Division** with orders to destroy Early and to deny the Confederates the use of the

Shenandoah Valley. With his **Army of the Shenandoah,** Sheridan advanced from **Harpers Ferry, West Virginia**, and engaged Early at **Summit Point and Cameron's Depot**, **Smithfield Crossing**, and **Berryville**. In early September, he learned from a Unionist teacher in Winchester that Early had sent part of his command to reinforce **Robert E. Lee** for the **Petersburg Campaign.** Knowing that he greatly outnumbered the Confederates, Sheridan attacked.

In the early morning of September 19, Sheridan crossed Opequon Creek with about 37,000 men and advanced east toward Winchester, where Early was positioned northeast of town. Sheridan's route ran through a narrow gorge that became blocked by his long wagon train, and his advance was slowed for four hours, allowing Early time to concentrate his 12,000 men. **James H. Wilson's** Union cavalry emerged from the gorge and pushed back **Stephen D. Ramseur's** Confederate **division**. Just before noon, **Cuvier Grover's** division of **William H. Emory's** XIX Corps advanced on Sheridan's right, but by then Early had **John B. Gordon's** and **Robert E. Rodes's** divisions in place and counterattacked with Gordon. Gordon's onslaught staggered Grover's division, and when Emory sent forward another, it too was battered. On the Union left, **Horatio Wright's** VI Corps advanced against Ramseur and was driving him back when Rodes rushed his division into a gap that had formed between the two Union **corps**. Rodes drove through the Union line, but he then was stopped by a counterattack by **David A. Russell's** division. Both Rodes and Russell were mortally wounded in this phase of the fight.

After a short respite, Sheridan sent **George Crook's** VII Corps division against Gordon on the Confederate left that afternoon. Crook was driving back Gordon when **Wesley Merritt's** and **William W. Averell's** cavalry divisions attacked Early's far left flank, defended by **John C. Breckinridge** with **Fitzhugh Lee's** Confederate cavalry and **Gabriel C. Wharton's** infantry divisions. The cavalry charge shattered the Confederate flank, and Early's line came unhinged from left to right. Sheridan renewed his attack all along the line, and Early's men fled back through town. During the rout, numerous women, including Gordon's wife, blocked the streets trying unsuccessfully to get the men to make a stand. Early's **army** was defeated, and withdrew south of Winchester. In the battle, Sheridan lost about 5,000 men, while Early counted approximately 3,500 casualties. Early regrouped and made a stand at **Fisher's Hill**, but he was driven from there on September 22.

WINDER, CHARLES SIDNEY (1820–1862) CSA. Winder (WINE-dur), the grandson of two governors and the son of a **U.S. Army** officer, was a native of **Maryland**. Confederate Adm. **Franklin Buchanan** was the husband of Winder's aunt, and Winder was a distant cousin of Confederate general **John H. Winder**. Also, his mother was the sister-in-law of President **James Buchanan**. Winder attended Maryland's St. John's College, but he graduated from **West Point** in 1850. After routine garrison duty with the **artillery**, he was heading to **California** aboard the *San Francisco* in 1853 when the ship was battered by a storm. For his heroism in helping keep the ship afloat, Winder was **brevetted** captain and promoted to 1st lieutenant. Two years later, he was promoted again, reportedly becoming the youngest captain in the **U.S. Army**. Posted to the northwest, Winder fought **Indians** in several battles in the Washington Territory and became known as an excellent officer. A chronic, undiagnosed, illness then forced him on sick leave for two and a half years.

Winder resigned his commission in April 1861 and entered the **Confederate army** as a major of artillery. He participated in the bombardment of **Fort Sumter** and served as acting ordnance officer of the **Charleston, South Carolina**, arsenal. In July, Winder was appointed colonel of the 6th South Carolina and became part of **David R. Jones's brigade**. After serving in northern **Virginia** with **Joseph E. Johnston's** army, he was promoted to brigadier general in March 1862.

Sent to participate in **Stonewall Jackson's 1862 Shenandoah Valley Campaign**, Winder replaced **Richard Garnett** in command of the **Stonewall Brigade** in May 1862. The men disliked him, resenting his strict **discipline** and viewing him as an interloper, and he and Jackson often clashed. Some members of the Stonewall Brigade even talked of shooting their commander in the next battle. Winder proved to be a competent leader. He served well at **First Winchester** and helped form Jackson's rear guard during the retreat back up the **Shenandoah Valley**; his horse was shot three times at **Port Republic**. During the **Seven Days Campaign**, Winder saw heavy fighting at **Gaines' Mill** and **Malvern Hill** with the **Army of Northern Virginia**. Although very sick afterward, he accompanied his brigade to the **Battle of Cedar Mountain** and there assumed command of the **division**. While supervising the fire of his artillery, Winder was mortally wounded by a shell and died on the evening of August 9, 1862.

WINDER, JOHN HENRY (1800–1865) CSA. A native of **Maryland**, Winder (WINE-dur) was the son of War of 1812 Brig. Gen. William H. Winder and a distant cousin of Confederate general **Charles S. Winder**. After graduating from **West Point** in 1820, he served with the **artillery** and infantry before resigning his commission in 1823 to marry and become a planter. When his wife died, Winder reentered the **U.S. Army** in 1827 as a 2nd lieutenant and served in the **Seminole Wars** and as a **tactics** instructor at West Point. After winning two **brevets** for gallantry in the **Mexican War**, he served at various posts — including commanding **Fort Pickens, Florida** — before resigning his major's commission in April 1861.

Winder entered Confederate service in June 1861 as a brigadier general and was made inspector general of the camps around **Richmond, Virginia**. He also was put in charge of Union **prisoners** being held in Richmond until October, when he was placed in command of the **Department of Henrico**. In February 1862, Winder also was made Richmond's provost marshal and was responsible for enforcing the martial law declared by **Jefferson Davis**. In this position, he often was criticized for the rough, violent nature of his detectives, and the Union condemned him for the poor treatment of Union prisoners at **Libby Prison** and **Belle Isle**. From March to September 1863, Winder's duties were expanded to include the supervision of all Richmond hospitals.

Although numerous politicians recommended that Winder be promoted, he never was. In May 1864, his **department** was combined with the **Department of Richmond** and was put under **Robert Ransom**. Winder eventually was sent to **Andersonville Prison**, where he assumed command in June, but the following month, he took charge of all the **prisons** in **Georgia** and **Alabama**. In November, he was appointed commissary general of prisons and was made responsible for all Confederate prisons east of the Mississippi River. While in this position, he died of a heart attack on February 8, 1865.

After the war, the North vilified Winder because of the harsh conditions in Confederate prisons. It is believed that if he had lived, Winder — rather than **Henry Wirz** — probably would have been executed for the Andersonville horrors. In fact, he probably did as well in his position as anyone could have under the circumstances.

WINSLOW, JOHN ANCRUM (1811–1873) USA. A native of **North Carolina**, as a boy, Winslow moved to **Massachusetts**. He joined the **U.S. Navy** as a midshipman in 1827 and rose to the rank of lieutenant in 1839. During the **Mexican War**, Winslow commanded a ship on **blockade** duty. He and fellow officer **Raphael Semmes** both lost their ships during the war and then became good friends while serving on the USS *Cumberland*.

With the rank of commander, Winslow was serving as a lighthouse inspector when the Civil War began. Given command of the **USS *Benton***, he served on the Mississippi River until an injury forced him ashore in December 1861. After recovering, Winslow was sent back to the Mississippi River and was promoted to captain in July 1862. Later that year, he was given command of the **USS *Kearsarge*** in the Atlantic Ocean and began hunting the Confederate **commerce raiders** *Florida*, *Rappahannock*, and *Alabama*, the latter being under the command of his old friend, Semmes. In June 1864, Winslow learned the *Alabama* was at Cherbourg, France. Leaving the Netherlands, he sailed there and sank the *Alabama* on June 19 when Semmes left port to give battle. Hailed as a hero, Winslow was promoted to commodore.

After returning to the United States, Winslow performed administrative duty for the rest of the war, including sitting on the court-martial of **Thomas T. Craven**. After the war, he commanded the Gulf Squadron, was promoted to rear admiral in 1870, and led the Pacific fleet before retiring in 1872.

WIRE ENTANGLEMENTS. Among the many "firsts" of the Civil War was the use of wire to impede an attacking force. **Telegraph** wire often was strung low to the ground between trees or stumps to slow down and trip up an attacking enemy. It apparently was first used at **Fort Sanders, Tennessee**, during the 1863 **Knoxville Campaign**. There, the wire entanglements caused few problems for the attacking Confederates, but six months later at the **Second Battle of Drewry's Bluff, Virginia**, the Confederates were slaughtered when they became trapped in the Union wire. At Drewry's Bluff, both Maj. Gens. **Benjamin F. Butler** and **William F. Smith** claimed credit for its use.

WIRZ, HENRY (1823–1865) CSA. A native of Switzerland, Wirz was born Heinrich Hermann Wirz and became a businessman as his father insisted, even though he preferred to study medicine. Although the details are unknown, he served a short prison sentence over financial dealings in the 1840s and immigrated to the United States in 1849 upon his release. After living in **Massachusetts** and **Kentucky**, Wirz moved to **Louisiana** and was working as a physician when the Civil War began, despite never having received any medical training.

Wirz entered Confederate service in June 1861 as a private in the 4th Louisiana Battalion, but he soon was appointed lieutenant. Sent to **Virginia**, he suffered a severe wound above his right wrist, which left him partially paralyzed and in pain for the rest of his life. When he returned to duty, Wirz served under Brig. Gen. **John H. Winder**, supervisor of the **Richmond, Virginia, prisons**. Promoted to captain in August 1862, he became Winder's assistant adjutant general before being placed in charge of the prison at Tuscaloosa, Alabama. After going on a diplomatic mission to Europe in December 1863, Wirz was put in command of **Georgia's Andersonville Prison** in February 1864.

At Andersonville, Wirz was blamed for the lack of food, poor conditions, cruel guards, and high death rate, even though he only was in charge of the prison's interior and, thus, did not have much authority over food, supplies, or personnel. His German accent, violent temper, and profane manner also caused the **prisoners** to hate him. Although frequently referred to as "Major Wirz," Wirz was unsuccessful in seeking a promotion and remained a captain. After Winder died in February 1865, he became the most hated man associated with the Confederate prison system.

Wirz was arrested at Andersonville when Union troops arrived in May 1865 and was denied a request to be allowed to take his family to Europe. Instead, he was placed on trial in August 1865 at **Washington, D.C.**, for murder and the inhumane treatment of prisoners. Given little opportunity to mount a defense, Wirz was found guilty despite conflicting testimony and was hanged on November 10 at the **Old Capitol Prison**. Before the sentence was carried out, he was offered a reprieve if he would sign a document implicating **Jefferson Davis** in a conspiracy to kill Union prisoners. Wirz refused, declaring that Davis had nothing to do with what happened at Andersonville. Although it is commonly believed that Wirz was the only Civil War soldier executed for war crimes, Confederate guerrilla leader Champ Ferguson also was hanged for his role in the **Saltville, Virginia, Massacre**, but it is not clear if he was a commissioned officer.

WISCONSIN. Although most famous for providing three of the regiments that made up the famous **Iron Brigade**, Wisconsin gave the Union 52 **regiments** and a total of 91,379 servicemen out of an 1860 population of 775,881. At one soldier for every 8.5 people, this was one of the highest ratios of any state. Of these men, 11,583 died in battle or from disease. Wisconsin also provided such officers as **Alonzo H. Cushing**, **Lewis Cass Hunt**, and **Joseph Bailey** and a significant amount of lead, wool, food, and grain.

WISE, HENRY ALEXANDER (1806–1876) CSA. A native of **Virginia**, Wise graduated from **Pennsylvania's** Washington College in 1825 and became a lawyer and a staunch **states rights** supporter. Active in **Democratic Party** politics, he was as an excellent stump speaker and served in the **U.S. Congress** from 1833 to 1844. After leaving office, Wise was appointed U.S. minister to Brazil and served there until 1847. He then served as Virginia's governor from 1856 to 1860 and played an important role in the capture and hanging of **John Brown**. In 1861, Wise was a delegate to the state's **secession** convention, where he strongly supported both secession and joining the Confederacy.

After secession, Wise raised a volunteer unit known as "Wise's Legion" and led it into the Kanawha Valley. He was appointed a Confederate brigadier general in June 1861, but his men were poorly supplied and **disciplined**, and they did not serve particularly well in the western Virginia Campaign. Wise also feuded with his superior, Brig. Gen. **John B. Floyd**, and refused to reinforce him at **Carnifex Ferry**. After the Confederate defeat there, he was ordered back to **Richmond, Virginia**, where he spent most of the next several months on sick leave.

In January 1862, Wise was placed in command of a **district** in **North Carolina**. He was responsible for defending **Roanoke Island** but clashed with his superior, Maj. Gen. **Benjamin Huger**, when Huger did not send reinforcements. Wise was ill and thus not present when the Federals captured Roanoke Island in February (during which his son was mortally wounded), but he was cleared of any responsibility for the defeat. He then returned to Virginia and was put in command of a **brigade** in **Joseph E. Johnston's** army. Johnston, however, did not want him and kept Wise out of action. Wise's situation did not improve when **Robert E. Lee** assumed command of the **Army of Northern Virginia**. At **Malvern Hill**, during the **Seven Days Campaign**, fellow officers criticized Wise when he disobeyed orders and tried to take his men into action.

For more than a year after the Seven Days Campaign, Wise performed **picket** duty and led **foraging** expeditions around Richmond. In September 1863, he was sent to **South Carolina** with his brigade to take command of a district near **Charleston**. There Wise got along fairly well with his superior, **P. G. T. Beauregard**, and accompanied Beauregard back to Petersburg, Virginia, in May 1864. He fought at **Port Walthall Junction** in **W. H. C. Whiting's division** but then again clashed with his superiors when he began criticizing Confederate **strategy**. In June, Wise was placed in command of a district around **Petersburg** and served well in defending the city against enemy attacks that month. Afterward, however, he angered officers by actively seeking publicity for his actions in the Richmond newspapers. Wise was reunited with his brigade in January 1865 and served the remainder of the war in **Bushrod R. Johnson's** division. For successfully fighting his way out of the trap at **Sailor's Creek** during the **Appomattox Campaign**, he was given temporary command of Johnson's division. Wise then surrendered with the **army** at Appomattox.

After the war, Wise resumed his Virginia law practice. Although he never requested a pardon, he did advise others to work peacefully with federal officials.

WISE'S FORK, NORTH CAROLINA, BATTLE OF (MARCH 7–10, 1865). *See* WYSE FORK, NORTH CAROLINA, BATTLE OF.

WISTAR, ISAAC JONES (1827–1905) USA. A native of **Pennsylvania,** Wistar attended Haverford College and became a lawyer. When the Civil War began, he raised a volunteer **company** and entered Union service in June 1861 as a captain in the 71st Pennsylvania, also known as the California Regiment. Promoted to lieutenant colonel later in the month, Wistar received a crippling wound to his right arm in the October battle at **Ball's Bluff** while acting in command. The regiment's colonel, **Edward Baker,** was killed there, and Wistar was promoted to colonel the following month. The **regiment** then became part of the 2nd Brigade of **John Sedgwick's division** in the **Army of the Potomac's** II Corps and fought through the **Peninsula** and **Seven Days Campaigns.** It was claimed that Wistar led the regiment in these campaigns, but official records indicate junior officers were in command at the time. At **Antietam, Oliver O. Howard** led the **brigade** and noted that Wistar received another wound that crippled his left arm.

Wistar was promoted to brigadier general of volunteers in March 1863. When he returned to duty in May, he was placed in command of a reserve brigade in **George W. Getty's** division at **Suffolk, Virginia.** He remained in the area until operations began against **Richmond, Virginia,** in the spring of 1864. While in command of a brigade in **William F. Smith's** XVIII Corps of the **Army of the James,** Wistar participated in the **Second Battle of Drewry's Bluff** in May, but he performed poorly and helped cause the Union defeat. Days afterward, he was replaced in brigade command. Wistar did not receive another command and in September 1865 resigned his commission.

Wistar returned to Pennsylvania after leaving the **army.** He resumed his law practice, became active in the coal industry, and was a prominent writer and speaker on penology.

WITHERS, JONES MITCHELL (1814–1890) CSA. A native of **Alabama,** Withers graduated from **West Point** in 1835, but he only served a few months before resigning from the **U.S. Army.** Returning to Alabama, he studied law, served as the governor's private secretary, and participated in the 1836 war against the Creek **Indians**. After the war, Withers became a lawyer and prosperous cotton broker, but he reentered the army during the **Mexican War** as lieutenant colonel of the 13th U.S. Infantry. He became colonel of the 9th U.S. Infantry but again left the army when the war ended. During the 1850s, Withers practiced law and was elected to the Alabama legislature in 1855 and mayor of Mobile in 1858.

When the Civil War began, Withers resigned as mayor and entered Confederate service in April 1861 as colonel of the 3rd Alabama. Sent to **Virginia**, he assumed command of a **brigade** under **Benjamin Huger** around **Norfolk** and was promoted to brigadier general in July. Withers remained in Virginia until October, when he was assumed command of the District of Alabama. In January 1862, he took charge of Mobile's coastal defenses and led a brigade that was called the **Army of Mobile**. Withers soon joined **Albert Sidney Johnston** in northern **Mississippi** and in March was placed in command of a **division** in **Braxton Bragg's corps**. His actions at **Shiloh** earned him high praise and a promotion to major general in August.

Taking command of **Leonidas Polk's** reserve division in the **Army of Mississippi**, Withers participated in the **Kentucky Campaign**, but he missed the **Battle of Perryville**. At **Stones River** on the first day, the division served as the pivot for the **Army of Tennessee's** giant sweep to the right, and Withers lost nearly one-third of his men while attacking **Philip Sheridan's** Union division. He also was one of the generals who urged Bragg to retreat and contributed to the contention that arose between Bragg and his subordinates. During the 1863 **Tullahoma Campaign**, Withers became ill and was forced to leave the **army** in August. When he returned to duty in February 1864, he was put in command of northern Alabama. That July, Withers was put in charge of the state's reserve forces and spent the remainder of the war organizing into a home defense force those men who were too young or old for **conscription**.

After the war, Withers returned to his cotton brokerage and became editor of a Mobile newspaper. He again was elected Mobile's mayor in 1867 and served as its treasurer from 1878 to 1879.

WOFFORD, WILLIAM TATUM (1824–1884) CSA. A native of **Georgia**, Wofford became a lawyer and fought with distinction in the **Mexican War** as captain of a volunteer cavalry **company** he organized. Returning to Georgia after the war, he served in the legislature in 1849, practiced law, farmed, and worked as a newspaper editor. In 1861, Wofford was chosen as a delegate to the state **secession** convention, where he at first opposed secession but eventually changed his position and voted for it.

Wofford entered state service in April 1861 as colonel of the 1st Georgia State Troops, but this **regiment** soon was redesignated the 18th Georgia and was mustered into Confederate service. Sent to **Virginia**, he spent the winter guarding the Potomac River and in the spring of 1862 was assigned to **John Bell Hood's Texas Brigade**. Wofford fought with the **brigade** through the **Peninsula**, **Seven Days**, and **Second Manassas Campaigns**. When Hood was promoted to **division** command in September 1862, Wofford assumed command of the brigade and led it at **Antietam**. In October 1862, Wofford's regiment left the Texas Brigade and joined **Thomas R. R. Cobb's** brigade in **Lafayette McLaws'** division of the **Army of Northern Virginia's** I Corps.

When Cobb was killed at **Fredericksburg**, Wofford assumed command of the brigade and was promoted to brigadier general in April 1863. A popular officer, he personally led his men in a charge at **Chancellorsville** and fought with distinction at **Gettysburg**. Illness then forced Wofford on two months' sick leave in November 1863. When he returned to duty, he temporarily led the division through late March before rejoining his brigade for the **Overland Campaign**. Perhaps Wofford's best service was on the second day at the **Wilderness**, where he proposed and participated in **James Longstreet's** attack that routed the Union left flank. Despite numerous recommendations for promotion, he remained with his brigade through the Overland Campaign (during which he was wounded at the Wilderness and **Spotsylvania**) and the early part of the **Petersburg Campaign**. Wofford then was transferred to the **Shenandoah Valley**, where he fought with **Jubal A. Early** at **Cedar Creek**. He again went on sick leave in October 1864 and did not return to duty until late December. Wofford then requested and received command of northern Georgia in January 1865. He served there until war's end rounding up stragglers and **deserters** and breaking up illegal military organizations.

After the war, Wofford was elected to the **U.S. Congress** in 1865, but the **Radical Republicans** refused to seat him. He also served as a presidential elector in 1872 and 1876, and in the 1877 state constitutional convention.

"WOMAN'S ORDER," BENJAMIN F. BUTLER'S GENERAL ORDERS NO. 28. After **David Farragut's** Union fleet captured **New Orleans, Louisiana**, in the spring of 1862, the city was garrisoned by soldiers under Maj. Gen. **Benjamin F. Butler**. Butler's men found that the women of New Orleans were the city's staunchest **rebels**. They regularly insulted the soldiers by cursing them, spitting on their **uniforms**, turning their backs to them as they walked by, and even emptying chamber pots on their heads as they walked below bedroom windows. To bring the women under control, Butler on May 15, 1862, issued General Orders No. 28, better known as the "Woman's Order." It authorized any soldier who was insulted by a woman to treat her as a "woman of the town plying her avocation" (Winters, *Civil War in Louisiana*, 132), that is, as a prostitute. There was no sexual implication to the order; Butler simply was authorizing his men to treat an insulting woman in kind, not as a lady. If she cursed him, the soldier could curse her back.

The Woman's Order did stop the insults, but it also created a storm of controversy. The **Louisiana Tigers** in the **Army of Northern Virginia** unsuccessfully petitioned **Robert E. Lee** to allow them to return home to defend their women, and even many Northerners and Europeans believed it overstepped the bounds of civilized warfare. The order, along with Butler's hanging **William Mumford** for taking down a U.S. **flag**, led to his being nicknamed the "Beast." He also was branded a war criminal by the Confederacy, and Confederate soldiers were under orders to hang him if he ever was captured.

WOOD, JOHN TAYLOR (1830–1904) CSA. Born in the **Iowa** Territory, Wood was the grandson of Zachary Taylor, the nephew of Confederate general **Richard Taylor**, and the cousin of Confederate general **Benjamin H. Helm**. After graduating from the **U.S. Naval Academy** in 1853, he served aboard the USS *Cumberland*, was a veteran of the **Mexican War**, and taught gunnery **tactics** at the academy before the Civil War.

Wood resigned from the **U.S. Navy** in April 1861, but the navy refused to accept it and dismissed him from service, instead. Traveling to **Virginia**, he was commissioned a 2nd lieutenant in the **Confederate navy** and was assigned to the **CSS *Virginia***. Wood fought at **Hampton Roads** and then at the **First Battle of Drewry's Bluff** after the *Virginia*'s crew was put ashore. For his service at Drewry's Bluff, he was promoted to 1st lieutenant in September 1862.

Wood showed great ingenuity as an officer. Believing in small, swift, nighttime raids, he received permission from Secretary of the Navy **Stephen R. Mallory** to outfit small boats and haul them overland to attack unsuspecting Union ships. Wood used these boats to make several raids along the Atlantic Coast, and in the autumn he successfully captured the USS *Underwriter* at New Bern, North Carolina (for which he later was voted the **Thanks of Congress**) during a raid conducted by Maj. Gen. **George E. Pickett**.

In January 1863, **Jefferson Davis** appointed Wood colonel of cavalry (making him one of the few Confederates to hold commissions in both branches of service) and brought him onto the presidential staff as a liaison between the **army** and navy. He returned to naval duty in July, however, and in July 1864 was given command of the **CSS** *Tallahassee*. Raiding the Atlantic seaboard, Wood captured or destroyed over 30 Union vessels in just three weeks. He was promoted to captain in February 1865 and was in **Richmond, Virginia**, when the city was evacuated in April. Wood accompanied President Davis on his flight south and was captured with him in **Georgia**, but he bribed a guard and escaped. He then joined **John C. Breckinridge** in **Florida** and made his way to Cuba with the secretary of war. Wood eventually settled in Canada and operated a profitable merchant commercial house there.

WOOD, STERLING ALEXANDER MARTIN (1823–1891) CSA. A native of **Alabama**, Wood graduated from **Kentucky's** Jesuit College of St. Joseph's in 1841 and became a lawyer in his native state. He served as a circuit court solicitor from 1851 to 1857, was elected to the state legislature in 1857, and worked as a newspaper editor.

After Alabama seceded, Wood organized a volunteer **company** and took it to join **Braxton Bragg** at **Pensacola, Florida**, where he entered Confederate service in May 1861 as colonel of the 7th Alabama. Late that summer, Bragg put him in command of one of his **brigades**, but in November, Wood and his **regiment** were sent to Chattanooga, Tennessee. After a brief period guarding **railroads**, the regiment was sent to Kentucky in December to join **William J. Hardee's Army of Central Kentucky**.

In January 1862, Wood was appointed brigadier general and was given command of an infantry brigade. Becoming part of **Thomas C. Hindman's division**, he fought at **Shiloh** and was injured there when his horse fell on him. This injury forced Wood to leave the field temporarily, but he returned to his brigade before the battle was over. Hardee praised his actions, but Hindman brought him before a court of inquiry, which cleared Wood of any misconduct. Wood temporarily led the division during the summer of 1862, but he returned to his brigade when he was replaced in August by **Simon B. Buckner**. He participated in the **Kentucky Campaign** and fought well at **Perryville**, where he was wounded by a shell fragment, and his men helped capture a battery. In November, Wood's brigade was assigned to **Patrick Cleburne's** division in the **Army of Tennessee**. Again, he fought very well at **Stones River** (and lost nearly half of his men) and was highly praised by Cleburne. From January to March 1863, Wood commanded the District of Northern Alabama, but he returned to Cleburne in time to fight at Liberty Gap in the **Tullahoma Campaign**. Afterward, during the confused fighting at **Chickamauga**, he lost control of his brigade, and it was badly shot up. Cleburne blamed Wood for the unfortunate incident and failed to commend him in his report with the other brigadiers. As a result, Wood resigned his commission in October 1863.

Returning to Alabama, Wood resumed his law practice and reentered politics after the war. He served in the legislature from 1882 to 1883, taught law at the University of Alabama from 1889 to 1890, and worked as a **railroad** attorney.

WOOD, THOMAS JOHN (1823–1906) USA. A native of **Kentucky**, Wood was a cousin of Confederate general **Benjamin H. Helm**. After graduating near the top of his 1845 **West Point** class (where he was **U. S. Grant's** first roommate), he was assigned to the **engineers** but quickly transferred to the dragoons. Wood won a **brevet** for gallantry during the **Mexican War** and then served on the frontier fighting **Indians**. He was promoted to captain in the 1st U.S. Cavalry in 1855 but from 1859 to 1861 was on leave in Europe.

When the Civil War began, Wood was a major of cavalry and began raising recruits in **Indiana**. He was promoted to lieutenant colonel of the 1st U.S. Cavalry in May 1861 but in October was commissioned a brigadier general of volunteers (he was appointed colonel of the 2nd U.S. Cavalry the following month). After commanding a **brigade** in the **Army of the Ohio** for several months, Wood was given command of a **division** in February 1862. He fought on the second day at **Shiloh**, had part of his division engaged at **Perryville**, and in November 1862 was given a division command in **Thomas L. Crittenden's corps** of the **Army of the Cumberland**. At **Stones River**, Wood reinforced the crucial angle that developed in **William S. Rosecrans's** line after the Confederates drove back his right wing on the first day. He was wounded in the fighting but refused to leave the field until the issue was settled.

As part of the XXI Corps, Wood briefly commanded the corps in early 1863 but then returned to his division and led it through the **Tullahoma Campaign** and at **Chickamauga**. At Chickamauga, he played a crucial role that led to Rosecrans's defeat. During the confused fighting on the second day, Rosecrans mistakenly believed a gap had developed to the left of Wood's position and ordered him to fill it. Earlier that day, Rosecrans had criticized him for moving too slowly, so rather than inform the commander that no gap existed, Wood obeyed orders, moved to the left, and thus created a real gap in the Union line. The Confederates then poured through the opening and won the battle. Rosecrans was responsible for the disaster, and Wood was never punished for the mistake; in fact he was brevetted brigadier general of regulars for his service at Chickamauga.

During the **Chattanooga Campaign**, Wood's division became part of the IV Corps and reportedly was the first to rush over the Confederate line at **Missionary Ridge**. He led the division through the **Atlanta Campaign** and remained on the field at **Lovejoy's Station** even after being badly wounded in the leg. In late 1864, Wood joined **George H. Thomas** for the **Franklin and Nashville Campaign** and was given command of the corps in December. After leading it at Nashville, he was brevetted major general of regulars and in February 1865 was promoted to major general of volunteers.

After the war, Wood served on garrison duty in **Mississippi** and was recognized for his humane treatment of the citizens there. He was mustered out of the volunteers in January 1866 but remained in the regular army as a colonel. Wood was retired as a major general in 1868 because of his war wounds. Settling in **Ohio**, he later served on West Point's Board of Visitors.

WOODBURY, DANIEL PHINEAS (1812–1864) USA. A native of **New Hampshire**, Woodbury attended Dartmouth College but dropped out to enter **West Point**. After graduating in 1836, he first was assigned to the **artillery** but then joined the **engineers**. Woodbury had an outstanding antebellum career, building **Forts Warren**, Kearny, Laramie, Jefferson, and Taylor. During this time, he married into a Southern family and invested heavily in **North Carolina** property.

When the Civil War began, Woodbury was a captain of engineers. Despite pressure from family and friends to join the Confederacy, he received a special pass from **Jefferson Davis** and returned North from North Carolina to support the Union. At **First Manassas**, Woodbury served on **David Hunter's** staff and acted as a guide both for **Irvin McDowell's** advance and for the **turning movement** against the Confederate left flank. Afterward, he was promoted to major in August and to lieutenant colonel in September 1861.

Promoted to brigadier general of volunteers in March 1862, Woodbury was given command of the **Army of the Potomac's** engineering **brigade**. He served in the **Peninsula** and **Seven Days Campaigns** and laid the **pontoon bridges** across the Rappahannock River during the **Battle of Fredericksburg**. Woodbury then was given command of the District of Key West and Tortugas in March 1863. He served there for 18 months before dying of yellow fever on August 15, 1864, at Fort Taylor, which he had constructed before the war.

WOODS, CHARLES ROBERT (1827–1885) USA. A native of **Ohio**, Woods graduated from **West Point** in 1848 and served on routine garrison duty with the infantry until the Civil War.

During the **secession** crisis, Woods was a 1st lieutenant and was put in command of the reinforcements sent to **Fort Sumter** aboard the *Star of the West*. He was promoted to captain in April 1861 and served with **Robert Patterson** in the **Shenandoah Valley** and recruited in **Missouri** before being appointed colonel of the 76th Ohio in October. After participating in the western **Virginia** operations that autumn, Woods was transferred west and led his **regiment** at **Fort Donelson** and **Shiloh**. He then briefly commanded a **brigade** in **Lew Wallace's division** during the **siege of Corinth, Mississippi**. Returning to his regiment, Woods next fought at **Chickasaw Bayou** and **Arkansas Post** with **William T. Sherman's** XV Corps. In May 1863, he was given a brigade command in Sherman's 1st Division and led it through the **Vicksburg Campaign**.

In August 1863, Woods was promoted to brigadier general of volunteers. After leading his brigade at **Missionary Ridge** (for which he was **brevetted** colonel of regulars), he temporarily led a XV Corps division in early 1864 but returned to his brigade for the **Atlanta Campaign**. After fighting at **Resaca**, **New Hope Church**, and **Kennesaw Mountain**, Woods assumed command of the division and led it at **Peachtree Creek** and **Atlanta**. At the end of the campaign, he was in charge of a XVII Corps division. Returning to his XV Corps division, Woods participated in the **March to the Sea** and fought at **Bentonville** during the **Carolinas Campaign**. For his wartime service, he was brevetted major general in both the volunteers and regular **army**.

After the war, Woods was appointed lieutenant colonel of the 33rd U.S. Infantry in July 1866. He remained in the service until poor health forced his retirement in 1874 while he was colonel of the 2nd U.S. Infantry.

"WOODSTOCK RACES" (OCTOBER 9, 1864). *See* TOM'S BROOK, VIRGINIA, BATTLE OF.

WOOL, JOHN ELLIS (1784–1869) USA. A native of **New York**, Wool joined the **U.S. Army** as a captain in the War of 1812 and was wounded at Queenston Heights. He won a promotion to major and a **brevet** for gallantry and ended the war as a lieutenant colonel and the **army's** inspector general. After being brevetted brigadier general in 1826, Wool toured Europe inspecting continental armies before returning home to participate in the removal of the Cherokee **Indians** in the 1830s. After being promoted to brigadier general in 1841, he fought in the **Mexican War** and won great fame at the Battle of Buena Vista. He later received a ceremonial sword and the **Thanks of Congress** for his role in the battle and was brevetted major general. After the war, Wool commanded the Eastern Military Division from 1848 to 1853, the **Department of the Pacific** from 1854 to 1857, and the **Department of the East** from 1857 to 1861.

During the 1861 **secession** crisis, Wool performed a great service for the Union by sending reinforcements to **Fort Monroe, Virginia**, to protect it against secessionists. Given command of the **Department of Virginia** in August 1861, he was the oldest officer to hold a field command in either army. Wool disliked **George B. McClellan** and successfully kept his command separate from the **Army of the Potomac**. In May 1862, he captured **Norfolk, Virginia**, and was promoted to major general of regulars. By this time, McClellan was deeply involved in the **Peninsula Campaign** and demanded that he be given authority over Wool's **department**. As a result, Wool was transferred to the **Middle Department** the following month. He returned to command the Department of the East in January 1863 and remained there until his retirement in August 1863. At that time, Wool was the fourth ranking officer in the regular army.

WORDEN, JOHN LORIMER (1818–1897) USA. A native of **New York**, Worden joined the **U.S. Navy** as a midshipman in 1835 and spent the antebellum period serving both at sea and at the Naval Observatory. When the Civil War began, he held the rank of lieutenant.

In March 1861, Worden was sent on a secret mission to order **Fort Pickens, Florida**, not to surrender to the secessionists. While returning to the North by train, he was captured by the Confederates and was held **prisoner** for seven months. In January 1862, Worden took command of the USS *Monitor* and in March sailed it from New York to **Hampton Roads, Virginia**. There on March 9, he engaged the **CSS *Virginia*** in the first battle of **ironclads** and successfully defended the remaining blockading fleet, although he was temporarily blinded when a shell exploded in his face against the pilot house. Worden received the **Thanks of Congress** and was promoted to commander in July and to captain in

February 1863. Joining the **South Atlantic Blockading Squadron**, he was put in command of the USS *Montauk*. Worden participated in the attacks on **Fort McAllister, Georgia**, and in late February 1863, he destroyed the CSS *Nashville* on Georgia's Ogeechee River. He then served under **Samuel Du Pont** for the attack on **Charleston, South Carolina**, in April 1863. Worden left the *Montauk* in June and spent the rest of the war in New York supervising the construction of more **monitors**.

After the war, Worden served as superintendent of the **U.S. Naval Academy** from 1869 to 1874 and rose to the rank of rear admiral before retiring from the navy in 1886.

WRIGHT, AMBROSE RANSOM (1826–1872) CSA. A native of **Georgia**, "Rans" Wright became a lawyer at a young age and was active in the **Whig Party**. After supporting Georgia's **secession**, he was appointed the state's commissioner to **Maryland** in an unsuccessful attempt to persuade that state to secede.

Wright entered Confederate service in April 1861 as a private in a volunteer **company**. When the company became part of the 3rd Georgia in May, he was elected regimental colonel. Sent to the **North Carolina** coast, Wright engaged in **skirmishes** with the enemy and in one October fight single-handedly captured five Union soldiers. In April 1862, he was praised for stopping a Union raid at **South Mills**. Wright proved to be an effective fighter, but he also was harsh on his men, vain, and overly ambitious.

Promoted to brigadier general in June 1862, Wright took command of a **brigade** in **Benjamin Huger's division** of the **Army of Northern Virginia** and fought in the **Seven Days Campaign**. Afterward, the brigade became part of **Richard H. Anderson's** division of **James Longstreet's corps** and fought in the **Second Manassas** and **Antietam Campaigns**. At Antietam, Wright was severely wounded in the chest and leg, but he had himself placed on a litter and continued to advance with his men. Put out of action for months, he did not return to the brigade until just before **Chancellorsville**. In that battle, Wright's horse was hit by shell fragments, and Wright suffered a slight wound to his right knee. The brigade went on to fight on the second day at **Gettysburg**, but he was sick in a hospital and missed the battle. After the fight, Wright wrote a letter describing the battle and criticizing fellow officers, which was printed in the newspaper. Anderson placed Wright under arrest for disobedience, but he was acquitted in a court-martial.

Wright was elected to the Georgia senate in the autumn of 1863 and temporarily left the **army**. He strongly supported **Jefferson Davis's** administration in the senate but returned to the army when the session was over. Wright briefly commanded the division in February 1864, but he was absent sick for much of the year. He did fight in most of the **Overland Campaign** and at **Petersburg's Crater**. Wright was in Georgia when he was promoted to major general in November and spent the rest of the war defending **Savannah** and fighting in the **Carolinas Campaign**. He surrendered with **Joseph E. Johnston's** army in North Carolina at war's end.

After the war, Wright returned to Georgia, where he practiced law, worked as a newspaper editor, and was active in politics. He was elected to the **U.S. Congress** in 1872 but died a few weeks later.

WRIGHT, GEORGE (1801?–1865) USA. A native of **Vermont**, Wright was educated at Vermont's Norwich University. He graduated from **West Point** in 1822 and served in both the **Seminole** and **Mexican Wars**, winning one **brevet** in the former and two in the latter. Wright also was wounded while commanding the assault that overran the Mexican defenses at Molino del Rey. After serving on garrison duty, mostly in the Pacific Northwest, he became colonel of the 9th U.S. Infantry in 1855.

When the Civil War began, Wright was in command of the Department of Oregon, but in September 1861, he was transferred to command the District of Southern California. Highly regarded by his superiors, he was promoted to brigadier general of volunteers in late September and the following month was given command of the **Department of the Pacific**. Wright remained in the far west for the entire Civil War and spent his time keeping **Indians** peaceful, protecting settlers, watching the French in Mexico, and suppressing Confederate sympathizers. In July 1864, he was put in command of the District of California and remained there until war's end.

After being brevetted brigadier general of regulars in December 1864 for his faithful service, Wright was put in command of the newly created Department of the Columbia. While on his way to that post, he drowned in a shipwreck on the **California** coast on July 30, 1865.

WRIGHT, HORATIO GOUVERNEUR (1820–1899) USA. A native of **Connecticut**, Wright graduated second in his 1841 **West Point** class. Assigned to the **engineers**, he spent his antebellum career teaching at the academy and on various construction projects, including working on Forts Taylor and Jefferson in **Florida** and in the Dry Tortugas. When the Civil War began, Wright held the rank of captain and was stationed at **Norfolk, Virginia**.

After the firing on **Fort Sumter** in 1861, the Federals evacuated Norfolk. Wright tried to destroy the navy yard's dry docks beforehand, but he failed and was captured. Quickly released, he became chief engineer for **Samuel P. Heintzelman's division** and saw combat with it at **First Manassas**. Afterward, Wright was promoted to major of engineers in August 1861 and then to brigadier general of volunteers in September. He next served as chief engineer for the **Port Royal, South Carolina**, expedition in the autumn of 1861. In October, Wright was given command of a **brigade**, which he led in a raid on the Florida coast in early 1862. Given a division in April 1862, he fought at **Secessionville** that June, although he opposed making the unsuccessful attack.

In July 1862, Wright was promoted to major general of volunteers and was placed in command of the **Department of the Ohio** the following month. In March 1863, his appointment to major general expired because the Senate had not confirmed it. Wright reverted to the rank of brigadier general and in May was put in command of a division in **John Sedgwick's** VI Corps of the **Army of the Potomac**. He saw some combat at **Gettysburg** and fought at **Rappahannock Station** and in the **Mine Run Campaign**. After fighting in the **Wilderness**, Wright assumed command of the **corps** when Sedgwick was killed at **Spotsylvania**. He also was reappointed to major general of volunteers at the same time, and on this occasion, the Senate confirmed the rank.

Wright led the VI Corp until nearly war's end. He was sent to **Washington, D.C.**, in July 1864 to protect the capital against **Jubal A. Early's Washington Raid** and fought in **Philip Sheridan's 1864 Shenandoah Valley Campaign**. At **Cedar Creek**, Wright was in temporary command of Sheridan's **army** when Early launched his surprise attack. Wright was slightly wounded in the battle and was unable to restore order to the army. It was not until Sheridan arrived, that the Federals were able to counterattack and secure a victory. Wright's corps then rejoined the Army of the Potomac and fought in the latter part of the **Petersburg Campaign**. His men were the first to break through the Confederates' defensive lines at Petersburg on April 2, 1865, for which Wright was **brevetted** major general of regulars (he had earlier been awarded three brevets). His corps then pursued the enemy and was present at the final **surrender** at **Appomattox**. Through all of this service, Wright proved to be a dependable corps commander, but not a brilliant one.

When the war ended, Wright was sent to **Texas**, where he served on garrison duty for a year. He was mustered out of the volunteer service in September 1866 but remained in the regular army as a lieutenant colonel of engineers. In 1879, Wright was promoted first to colonel and then to brigadier general of engineers and became the army's chief engineer. In that position, he completed work on the Washington Monument before retiring in 1884.

WRIGHT, MARCUS JOSEPH (1831–1922) CSA. A native of **Tennessee**, Wright became a lawyer and court clerk and served as lieutenant colonel in the state militia. His militia **regiment** was mustered into state service in May 1861 as the 154th Senior Tennessee Infantry and was sent to **Kentucky**.

For a time, Wright served as military governor of Columbus, Kentucky. He led the regiment at **Belmont** and **Shiloh**, where he was wounded while serving in **Bushrod R. Johnson's brigade**. When Wright returned to duty several weeks later, he joined Maj. Gen. **Benjamin F. Cheatham's** staff as acting assistant adjutant general. He served Cheatham through the **Kentucky Campaign** and participated in the **Battle of Perryville**.

Wright was promoted to brigadier general in December 1862 and was given command of **Daniel S. Donelson's** Tennessee Brigade in the **Army of Tennessee**. As part of Cheatham's **division**, he led the brigade through the **Tullahoma Campaign** in the summer of 1863 and saw very heavy combat at **Chickamauga**. After the **army's** rout at **Missionary Ridge** during the **Chattanooga Campaign**, Wright was detached from the army and served at Atlanta and Macon, Georgia. In February 1865, he was put in command of the District of North Mississippi and West Tennessee, a position he kept until war's end.

After the war, Wright returned to his Tennessee law practice, but he later moved to **Washington, D.C.**, where he received a minor governor position at the United States Navy Yard. His greatest contribution to the Civil War came in 1878 when he was hired to collect the Confederate records that were to be included in *The War of the Rebellion: A Compilation of the Official Records of the Union and Confederate Armies*. Wright worked on this project for four decades, as well as writing numerous war-related articles for *Confederate Veteran* and his 1911 work, *General Officers of the Confederate Army*.

WYSE FORK, NORTH CAROLINA, BATTLE OF (MARCH 7–10, 1865). As **William T. Sherman** prepared for his **Carolinas Campaign** in early 1865, Union Maj. Gen. **John M. Schofield**, commanding the **Department of North Carolina**, took steps to open a supply line from New Bern to Goldsboro. In late February, Schofield ordered Brig. Gen.

Innis N. Palmer to repair the **railroad** from New Bern to Goldsboro. When Palmer failed to move quickly, Schofield placed Maj. Gen. **Jacob D. Cox** in command of Palmer's and **Samuel P. Carter's divisions** to carry out the task. A third division under **Thomas H. Ruger** was to join the others en route to Goldsboro, giving Cox about 13,000 men.

Cox left New Bern on March 1, but on March 7, he encountered Confederate Gen. **Braxton Bragg** and 6,500 men of **Robert Hoke's** division entrenched just outside Kinston at Wyse Fork (or Wise's Fork) along Southwest Creek. Bragg held off Cox that day with **artillery** fire and was reinforced on March 8 by 2,000 men under Lt. Gen. **Daniel H. Hill**. Bragg then took the offensive and advanced Hoke against the Union left flank, while Hill prepared to attack the right. Hoke crushed a small **brigade** posted in front of Cox's line and captured approximately 1,000 men, but he was unable to accomplish more. Bragg then made a tactical mistake by unsuccessfully sending Hill's command to cut off the Union brigade's retreat rather than reinforcing Hoke for a concerted push against Cox's line. Ruger's division reinforced the Federals, and Cox repelled Hoke's renewed attack on March 9.

On March 10, Bragg again sent Hoke and Hill to turn the Union flanks. Both captured some trenches, but they finally were forced to withdraw, and Bragg retreated across the Neuse River to Kinston. Cox renewed his advance, captured Kinston on March 14, and then occupied Goldsboro. In the battle, sometimes called the Second Battle of Kinston, Bragg lost 1,500 men, while Cox suffered 1,300 casualties.

– Y –

YANCEY, WILLIAM LOWNDES (1814–1863) CSA. A native of **Georgia**, Yancey moved to **New York** as a boy after his widowed mother married an antislavery minister. He attended **Massachusetts's** Williams College but dropped out and moved to **South Carolina**. There, Yancey studied law and became a newspaper editor. After passing the bar, he moved to **Alabama** in 1836, where he edited two newspapers and became active in the **Democratic Party**. Yancey was elected to the state assembly in 1841 and 1843 and to the **U.S. Congress** in 1844. Fiercely proslavery, Yancey's volatile nature caused his first debate to end in a duel with **Whig** congressman and future Confederate general **Thomas L. Clingman**. Neither was injured, but Yancey resigned his seat and returned to Alabama.

As tension built between the North and South in the 1850s, Yancey became a leader of the secessionist movement. He demanded that Southern **slavery** rights be respected in the territories and strongly supported **states rights**. Yancey labored to unify the South by corresponding with other **"fire-eaters,"** supporting states rights political candidates, and developing a sense of Southern nationalism. At the forefront of his thinking was **secession** and the creation of a unified, independent Southern nation. By the time of the **election of 1860**, Yancey was one of the South's foremost secessionists. At the Democratic National Convention in **Charleston, South Carolina**, he led the Southern delegation's walkout; helped create the Southern Democratic Party; and strongly backed **John C. Breckinridge's** nomination. Yancey hoped Breckinridge would split the Democratic vote and ensure the election of **Abraham Lincoln**, because he was certain that would lead to Southern secession. When the nation did fragment, he wrote Alabama's secession ordinance, but his radicalism prevented his selection to the Provisional **Confederate Congress** or as Confederate president. **Jefferson Davis** did appoint Yancey a commissioner to Europe with instructions to secure foreign recognition through **Cotton Diplomacy**. When his mission failed, he resigned and returned to the Confederacy to accept a seat in the Confederate Senate in March 1862.

As a senator, Yancey championed states rights and believed Davis was a failure as a president. Still, he recognized that certain strong national measures were needed to win the war and supported some of Davis's policies. Yancey agreed to both **conscription** and **impressment**, as long as the states had some control over the draft, and citizens were paid market value for their goods. He strongly opposed the creation of a **Confederate supreme court** and frequently clashed with fellow senators. Once, a senator struck Yancey in the face with one of two inkstands he threw at his head during an argument. Having played a major role in creating the Confederacy, Yancey died on July 27, 1863, before the fledgling nation was destroyed.

YANKEES. Along with other such names as "Billy Yank" and "blue bellies," this was a nickname given to Union soldiers by their Confederate counterparts.

YATES, RICHARD (1815–1873) USA. A native of **Kentucky**, as a teenager, Yates moved to **Illinois** with his family. After graduating from Illinois College, he became a lawyer in 1837 and was active in **Whig** politics. Yates was elected to the state legislature in 1842 and served in that body through most of the 1840s. He was elected to the U.S. House of Representatives in 1850 and was reelected in 1852, but he was defeated in 1854. Joining the **Republican Party**, Yates served as a delegate to the 1860 Republican National Convention and supported **Abraham Lincoln's** nomination. Later that year, he was elected governor of Illinois and assumed office in January 1861.

During the Civil War, Yates was close to Lincoln and became one of his strongest supporters. The **Democrats**, however, controlled the legislature and often opposed his wartime measures. Accusing the Democrats of being **Copperheads**, Yates took strong measures and arrested many people whom he suspected of being disloyal. This action angered the opposition and actually strengthened the antiwar movement in Illinois. When the legislature passed an 1863 resolution calling for a national reconciliation convention, an outraged Yates prorogued the assembly and ran the state for a year without a legislature. Despite this strong opposition, he filled the state's quota of recruits through **bounties** without having to resort to **conscription**.

Prevented by law from running for reelection, Yates successfully ran for the U.S. Senate in 1865, but poor health prevented him from running for reelection. After leaving the Senate, he worked as a federal **railroad** commissioner.

YAZOO PASS EXPEDITION (FEBRUARY 2–APRIL 5, 1863). During the 1863 **Vicksburg Campaign**, Union Maj. Gen. **U. S. Grant** made several attempts to attack **Vicksburg, Mississippi**, while avoiding the deadly Confederate **artillery** batteries atop the Mississippi River bluffs. In early 1863, he began Grant's Canal in **Louisiana** and the Yazoo Pass Expedition in **Mississippi**. Fifty miles downriver from Memphis, Tennessee, was Yazoo Pass, a waterway formerly connected to the Mississippi River but now cut off by a levee. By blowing up the levee there, **David Porter's** ships could enter Yazoo Pass and move through the Coldwater and Tallahatchie Rivers to the Yazoo River above Vicksburg. Using transports, Grant then could land his troops behind the enemy and attack Vicksburg from the northeast.

Engineer Lt. Col. **James H. Wilson** began assembling men at the Yazoo Pass levee on February 2. After they blew up the levee, floodwater poured through and opened the gap sufficiently to allow the ships to enter on March 7. The next several days were spent clearing the pass of logs and obstructions placed there by the Confederates. With Brig. Gen. **Leonard F. Ross's** 5,000 infantrymen, a 22-ship flotilla under Lt. Cmdr. Watson Smith entered the pass and moved down the Coldwater and Tallahatchie Rivers to the Yazoo River headwaters at the confluence of the Tallahatchie and Yalobusha Rivers.

At the confluence, Confederate Maj. Gen. **William W. Loring** had built Fort Pemberton. Under the direct command of Brig. Gen. **Lloyd Tilghman**, the fort was made largely of cotton bales, and the small garrison had only a few cannons. Although the fort did not appear very strong, it was protected from infantry assault by surrounding floodwater and contained a powerful 6.5-inch **rifled** cannon. Furthermore, the Confederates had blocked the Tallahatchie channel by sinking in it the *Star of the West*. From March 10 to 20, the Federals made numerous naval attacks and infantry probes against the small fort, but Loring and Tilghman held firm and their rifled gun battered the USS *Chillicothe* and *De Kalb*. Unable to advance farther, the fleet finally retired, but it then met reinforcements under Brig. Gen. **Isaac F. Quinby** on the Coldwater River. The infantry returned to Fort Pemberton and continued to probe the Confederates for almost two weeks before finally withdrawing on April 5.

With the failures of the Yazoo Pass Expedition, Grant's Canal, and the **Steele's Bayou Expedition** (which was carried out simultaneously with the Yazoo Pass Expedition), Grant was forced to wait until the floodwater receded before moving his **Army of the Tennessee** below Vicksburg. In mid-April, Porter finally ran his ships past the city and ferried Grant across the river to begin the campaign in earnest.

YELLOW BAYOU, LOUISIANA, BATTLE OF (MAY 18, 1864). During his retreat in the 1864 **Red River Campaign**, Union Maj. Gen. **Nathaniel P. Banks** reached the Atchafalaya (uh-CHAF-uh-LIE-uh) River near Simmesport, Louisiana, on May 17. With Confederate Maj. Gen. **Richard Taylor's** small **army** in pursuit, Banks needed time to build a **pontoon bridge** across the river to escape. While Lt. Col. **Joseph Bailey** constructed the bridge, Banks detached Maj. Gen. **Andrew J. Smith's division**, temporarily under Brig. Gen. **Joseph A. Mower**, and placed it about three miles west of the river along Yellow Bayou and Bayou De Glaize.

On May 18, 1864, Mower pushed back Taylor's **skirmishers**, but he then was driven back by a fierce Confederate counterattack. For two hours, Taylor and Mower engaged in an intense fight that largely took place in thick woods and cane breaks. When the woods caught on fire from the shooting, both sides pulled wounded men out of the fire's path and finally disengaged. By then Bailey's bridge was completed, and Banks began withdrawing over the river, completing the crossing by May 20. Although the battle at Yellow Bayou tactically was a stalemate, it is considered a Union victory because Banks accomplished his bridge-building goal. Taylor lost about 500 men in the fight (also known as Norwood's Plantation), while Mower reported 267 casualties. Yellow Bayou ended the Red River Campaign and was the last major battle of the war in **Louisiana**.

YELLOW TAVERN, VIRGINIA, BATTLE OF (MAY 11, 1864). During the 1864 **Overland Campaign, George G. Meade**, commander of the **Army of the Potomac**, and **Philip H. Sheridan**, the newly appointed cavalry chief, clashed over the proper use of the Union cavalry. Meade used Sheridan to guard his flanks, while Sheridan was eager to engage **J. E. B. Stuart's** Confederate cavalry in battle. During the **Battle of Spotsylvania**, Sheridan finally received permission from **U. S. Grant** to launch a massive cavalry raid toward **Richmond, Virginia**, to draw Stuart into battle and to disrupt the supply lines of **Robert E. Lee's Army of Northern Virginia**. The 12,000 Federal troopers began **Sheridan's Richmond Raid** on May 9.

Sheridan first cut the Virginia Central Railroad at Beaver Dam Station before continuing at a leisurely pace toward Richmond. In pursuit with 5,000 men, Stuart finally caught up with the Federals on the morning of May 11 and blocked their advance at Yellow Tavern, about six miles north of Richmond. Sheridan launched several attacks against Stuart, but he was repulsed, until **George A. Custer's brigade** broke through the Confederate line at about 4:00 P.M. Stuart sent the 1st Virginia Cavalry in a counterattack and sat on his horse by the roadside shooting at the retiring Federals with his pistol. One of Custer's men turned and fired his pistol at Stuart, hitting him in the abdomen. Sheridan finally disengaged and continued to threaten Richmond before reaching the James River on May 14 and ending his raid. In the clash at Yellow Tavern, total casualties were approximately 800. The Confederates' greatest loss was Stuart, who died in Richmond on May 12.

YORK, ZEBULON (1819–1900) CSA. A native of **Maine**, York reportedly was the only Confederate general of Polish descent, although there is no evidence to support the claim that he was Polish. After being educated at Maine's Wesleyan Seminary and **Kentucky's** Transylvania University, he moved to **Louisiana** and received a law degree from the University of New Orleans. York became a prosperous Louisiana lawyer and planter and was one of the state's richest men, co-owning six plantations and 1,700 slaves.

When the Civil War began, York raised a **company** of volunteers for a proposed "Polish Brigade." When the **brigade** failed to materialize, he entered Confederate service in June 1861 as captain of the 14th Louisiana.

York was elected major and accompanied the **regiment** to **Virginia**. The 14th Louisiana became notorious for rioting and drunkenness and played a major role in earning all of the Louisiana troops in Virginia the nickname **Louisiana Tigers**. After being promoted to lieutenant colonel in February 1862, York fought at **Williamsburg**, where he was wounded, and the regiment lost nearly 200 men. York's great bravery, which one man claimed "amounted to rashness" (Davis, ed., *The Confederate General*, vol. 6, p.166), was recognized by his men and superiors. They also noted that he was one of the most profane men in the **army**.

After serving in the **Seven Days Campaign** with **Roger Pryor's** brigade of the **Army of Northern Virginia**, York was promoted to colonel, and the regiment became part of **Harry T. Hays's** 1st Louisiana Brigade. He again was wounded at **Second Manassas** but rejoined the regiment in time to lead it at **Antietam**. After Antietam, the 14th Louisiana was attached to **Francis R. T. Nicholls's** 2nd Louisiana Brigade and served with it at **Fredericksburg**. In early 1863, York returned to Louisiana to recruit for the Louisiana Tigers and to drill conscripts. Some sources claim he returned to the 14th Louisiana in time to fight at **Gettysburg**, but there are no official records to support that claim. He did lead the regiment in heavy fighting at the **Wilderness**, after which the two Louisiana brigades were consolidated into one unit under Hays. The two brigades kept their separate identities, however, and in May 1864, York was placed in command of the 2nd Louisiana Brigade.

It appears that York was absent at **Spotsylvania**, but in early June, he was promoted to brigadier general and took command of the consolidated brigade after Hays had been wounded. He accompanied **Jubal A. Early's Washington Raid** and lost perhaps half his men in fierce fighting at the **Monocacy**. York saw more heavy combat at **Second Kernstown** and **Third Winchester**, having his wrist shattered in the latter and losing his lower arm to amputation. When he returned to duty, he was sent to **Salisbury Prison, North Carolina**, to raise recruits from the Catholic Irish and German **prisoners**. After spending some time at Salisbury, York claimed 800 Union prisoners were prepared to join the **Confederate army**.

The war ruined York financially. After the **surrender**, he settled in **Mississippi** and operated a hotel in Natchez until his death.

YORKTOWN, VIRGINIA, SIEGE OF (APRIL 5–MAY 3, 1862). Early in the 1862 **Peninsula Campaign**, Maj. Gen. **George B. McClellan's** more than 100,000-man **Army of the Potomac** was faced by only 17,000 Confederates under Maj. Gen. **John B. Magruder**. Magruder skillfully used deception, **Quaker guns,** and defensive works to slow McClellan's advance toward **Richmond, Virginia**. Believing he was outnumbered, McClellan cautiously approached Magruder's line, anchored at Yorktown, and decided against a **frontal attack**. Instead, he spent weeks bringing up large siege guns to overwhelm the enemy with **artillery** fire before sending his troops against the formidable defenses. McClellan's delay allowed **Joseph E. Johnston** time to bring his **Confederate army** from the Rappahannock River to the peninsula. On May 3, three days before McClellan planned to launch his attack, Johnston withdrew from the Yorktown-Warwick line and retreated toward **Williamsburg** to find a more defensible position. During operations around Yorktown, the Confederates lost approximately 300 men, while the Federals lost about 180.

YOUNG, JOHN RUSSELL (1840–1899) USA. A native of Ireland, as an infant, Young immigrated to the United States with his family. After living in **Pennsylvania**, he was orphaned as a boy and was raised by a **Louisiana** uncle. In 1856, Young moved back to Pennsylvania and the following year began working for the Philadelphia *Press* as a copy boy.

When the Civil War began, Young was in **Washington, D.C.**, and as a **war correspondent** he covered the **First Battle of Manassas** for the *Press*. He left the field early, thinking the Federals had won, and later had to rewrite his story when he learned of the defeat. Young's was one of the first stories printed about the battle and so impressed his employer that he appointed Young editor of the Washington, D.C., *Chronicle*. When he later published information concerning movement of the **Army of the Potomac**, Young was arrested and briefly held by authorities. He was released in time to cover the **Peninsula Campaign** but then fell ill with typhoid fever in May 1862 and returned to Philadelphia, where he became editor of the *Press*. In 1864, Young accompanied **Nathaniel P. Banks** on the **Red River Campaign** and served as both a reporter and volunteer aide. An admirer of Banks, his account of the campaign and the defeat at **Mansfield** was biased to portray the general in as favorable a manner as possible.

Young left the *Press* in early 1865 and went to work for Jay Cooke writing public relations material and advertising copy. He also started his own newspaper, New York's *The Morning Post*, but it soon failed. Young went on to become managing editor of the **New York *Tribune*** from 1866 to 1869, published the New York *Standard* from 1870 to 1872, covered the 1870 Franco-Prussian War, and worked for the New York *Herald* as a foreign correspondent. He also came to know **U. S. Grant** when he covered his world tour and, through Grant's efforts, served as U.S. minister to China from 1882 to 1885. Afterward, Young remained active in the publishing business and served as librarian of Congress from 1897 until his death.

YOUNG, PIERCE MANNING BUTLER (1836–1896) CSA. A native of **South Carolina**, as a boy, Young moved to **Georgia** with his family. After attending the Georgia Military Institute, he entered **West Point** in 1857 but resigned in March 1861 (three months before graduation) after Georgia seceded.

Young entered Confederate service in March 1861 as a 2nd lieutenant of **artillery**. He briefly served in **Pensacola, Florida**, on **Braxton Bragg's** staff but in July was appointed 1st lieutenant and adjutant of **Cobb's Legion**. Young rose to the rank of major but illness forced him to leave the unit temporarily. When he returned to duty, he was appointed lieutenant colonel in November and was put in command of the **legion's** cavalry. As part of **Wade Hampton's** cavalry **brigade**, Young fought with the **Army of Northern Virginia** in the **Seven Days** and **Second Manassas Campaigns**. He suffered two wounds during **skirmishes** in August and September 1862 and was commended for gallantry at **Antietam**. After being promoted to colonel in November 1862, Young served at **Fredericksburg** and afterward was praised for leading a charge at **Brandy Station**. He accompanied **J. E. B. Stuart's** cavalry on its **Gettysburg Raid** and suffered his third wound in an August 1863 skirmish after the **army** returned to **Virginia**.

For his Gettysburg service, Young was promoted to brigadier general in September 1863 and was given command of Hampton's former brigade. He led it in the **Bristoe Station** and **Mine Run Campaigns** that autumn and in the 1864 **Overland Campaign**. Young was wounded a fourth time in a fight at Ashland during the latter campaign and sometimes led the **division** after Hampton assumed command of the cavalry following Stuart's death. During the **Petersburg Campaign**, he also participated in the famous **"Beefsteak Raid."** In November, Young was sent to Georgia to defend the **Augusta Powder Works** during **William T. Sherman's March to the Sea** and to secure mounts and recruits for the cavalry. He was promoted to the temporary rank of major general in December and fought with Hampton as a division commander during the **Carolinas Campaign**.

After the war, Young returned to Georgia and became a farmer. He was elected to the **U.S. Congress** in 1868 and was reelected twice. After serving as a delegate to the 1872, 1876, and 1880 **Democratic** National Conventions, he was appointed consul-general to Russia by President Grover Cleveland in 1885. Young served at that post for two years and was the U.S. minister to Guatemala from 1893 until his death.

YOUNG, WILLIAM HUGH (1838–1901) CSA. A native of **Missouri**, as a child, Young moved to **Texas** with his family. After attending **Ten-**

nessee's Washington College and Texas's McKenzie College, he graduated from the University of Virginia in 1861 after the Civil War began.

After returning to Texas, Young raised a volunteer **company** and entered Confederate service in September 1861 as a captain in the 9th Texas. Becoming part of **J. Patton Anderson's brigade**, he fought at **Shiloh**, where the **regiment** broke and ran after being pounded by **artillery** fire. When the regiment was reorganized shortly after the battle, Young was elected colonel. The 9th Texas became part of **Preston Smith's** brigade and accompanied it in the **Kentucky Campaign**, but it saw only minor combat at **Perryville**. As part of the **Army of Tennessee**, Young fought very well at the Round Forest in the **Battle of Stones River**. There he had two horses shot from under him and was wounded in the shoulder. Young's superiors commended him highly for seizing the **regiment's** colors and personally leading one successful attack. In January 1863, Young's regiment was transferred to **Matthew D. Ector's** brigade. It served under **Joseph E. Johnston** around Jackson, Mississippi, during the **Vicksburg Campaign**, and Young was wounded in the right thigh during the siege of **Jackson**. He recovered in time to fight at **Chickamauga** that autumn but was wounded again in the chest. After service in **Mississippi**, Young rejoined the **army** for the 1864 **Atlanta Campaign**. When Ector was wounded outside Atlanta in July, Young assumed command of the brigade.

Young was promoted to temporary brigadier general in August 1864 and joined **Samuel G. French's division**. He had his horse shot from under him at **Allatoona**, and his foot was nearly torn off by a shell while he was leading his men dismounted. This was Young's third documented wound, and it also was claimed that he had been shot in the neck and jaw at **Kennesaw Mountain**. Left behind at Allatoona, he was captured by the Federals and was held **prisoner** until July 1865.

After the war, Young returned to Texas and became successful as a lawyer and in real estate. He also ran a freight line and edited a San Antonio newspaper.

– Z –

ZOLLICOFFER, FELIX KIRK (1812–1862) CSA. A native of **Tennessee**, Zollicoffer was of Swiss descent. After attending Tennessee's Jackson College for one year, he worked for a newspaper and became a printer. In 1834, Zollicoffer became part owner of the Columbia *Observer* and went on to become one of the state's leading newspapermen and writers. He was appointed the state printer in 1835 but the following year volunteered to fight one year as a lieutenant in the **Seminole Wars**. In the early 1840s, Zollicoffer's influence increased when he was made editor of the Nashville *Republican Banner*. He also served as campaign manager for successful **Whig** gubernatorial candidate James C. Jones. In return, Jones appointed Zollicoffer state comptroller and adjutant general from 1845 to 1849. Zollicoffer became a leader of the Whig Party, carried the state for **Winfield Scott** in the 1848 presidential election, served as a state senator from 1852 to 1854, and was elected to the **U.S. Congress** in 1852. That same year, he and a rival newspaper editor fought a duel over political issues. Zollicoffer was wounded in the hand and his opponent in the head, but both recovered and later became good friends.

Zollicoffer declined to run again for Congress in 1858. As a Unionist, he served as a delegate to the 1861 **Washington Peace Conference** and opposed Tennessee's **secession** until **Abraham Lincoln** called for troops to put down the rebellion. In April 1861, Zollicoffer was offered command of all state troops by Gov. **Isham Harris** even though he had virtually no military experience. He declined but then accepted a position as brigadier general of state troops, and in July he was commissioned a brigadier general in the **Confederate army**.

In late July 1861, Zollicoffer was put in command of the District of East Tennessee. Ordered later to take control of the Cumberland Gap, he led a small command into **Kentucky**, where units under his authority fought in some minor battles. After leaving a garrison at Cumberland Gap, Zollicoffer led his men to Beech Grove, Kentucky. On January 19, 1862, he engaged the enemy at **Mill Springs**. During the confusing fight, Zollicoffer mistakenly rode up to the enemy's line and ordered the Federals to stop shooting. Wearing a plain raincoat, he at first was not recognized as a Confederate officer, but while riding away, one of his aides galloped up and shouted, "It is the enemy, General!" (Davis, ed., *The Confederate General,* vol. 6, 195). Colonel **Speed Fry** of the 4th Kentucky (Union) then fired his pistol at Zollicoffer and ordered his men to open fire. Zollicoffer was hit several times and was killed.

ZOOK, SAMUEL KOSCIUSZKO (1821–1863) USA. A native of **Pennsylvania**, Zook became active in the militia and served as one **regiment's** adjutant. He began working for a **telegraph** company as a young man, rose to the position of superintendent, and moved to **New York**. There, Zook joined the state militia and was appointed lieutenant colonel of the 6th New York Militia in July 1861.

When the Civil War began, Zook and his regiment were sent to Annapolis, **Maryland**, where he served as military governor during the fighting at **First Manassas**. When the regiment's enlistments expired at the end of July 1861, he raised the 57th New York and was appointed its colonel in October. Becoming part of the **Army of the Potomac**, the regiment served in the **Peninsula Campaign** with **William H. French's brigade**. The brigade was not involved in the **Second Manassas Campaign**, and Zook was absent when it fought at **Antietam**. In October 1861, he was put in command of a brigade in **Winfield S. Hancock's** II Corps **division**. At **Fredericksburg**, Zook lost more than 500 men and had his horse shot from under him while attacking Marye's Heights. Hancock commended his actions, and Zook was promoted to brigadier general of volunteers.

After leading his brigade at **Chancellorsville**, Zook entered the **Gettysburg Campaign**. On the battle's second day, his brigade was rushed to reinforce the III Corps after it had been mauled by **James Longstreet's** Confederates. Zook marched his men to the front through the disorganized Union ranks, but he was mortally wounded in the abdomen as he reached the edge of the **Wheatfield**. He died shortly after midnight and was **brevetted** major general of volunteers posthumously.

ZOUAVE. During the Crimean War, the French Algerian Zouaves (ZWAHVS) gained worldwide attention for their colorful **uniforms** and bravery. Just before the Civil War, **E. Elmer Ellsworth** formed a militia unit in Chicago, Illinois, that was patterned after the Zouaves. It became very popular and toured many American cities giving drill demonstrations. The Zouaves wore colorful uniforms that included striped baggy pants, white gaiters, short jackets, and tasseled fezzes. Americans, North and South, became enamored with their uniforms and drill. Thus, when the Civil War began, numerous Union and Confederate units adopted the Zouave identity. Although their uniforms varied from unit to unit, they all were flashy and colorful, with red and blue being the preferred colors for the pants, sashes, jackets, and fezzes. Some units kept their colorful uniforms throughout the war, while others were issued standard uniforms when the original clothing wore out. Among Union Civil War Zouave units were **Ellsworth's Zouaves** (1st New York Fire Zouaves), the 9th New York (Hawkins' Zouaves), **Abram Duryée's** New York Zouaves, and the Salem (Massachusetts) Zouaves. Confederate Zouaves included the Tiger Rifles of **Chatham Roberdeau Wheat's** 1st Special Battalion, Louisiana Infantry (which originated the term **Louisiana Tigers**); the Eufaula (**Alabama**) Zouaves; and the Richmond (**Virginia**) Zouaves.

Bibliography

Abel, Annie Heloise. *The American Indian in the Civil War*. 3 Vols. Introductions by Theda Perdue and Michael D. Green. Lincoln: University of Nebraska Press, 1993.

Adams, George Worthington. *Doctors in Blue: The Medical History of the Union Army in the Civil War*. Dayton, Ohio: Morningside, 1985.

Alexander, Edward Porter. *Fighting for the Confederacy: The Personal Recollections of General Edward Porter Alexander*. Edited by Gary Gallagher. Chapel Hill: University of North Carolina Press, 1989.

Andrews, J. Cutler. *The North Reports the Civil War*. Pittsburgh: University of Pittsburgh Press, 1985.

——. *The South Reports the Civil War*. Princeton, N.J.: Princeton University Press, 1985.

Attie, Jeanie. *Patriotic Toil: Northern Women and the American Civil War*. Ithaca, N.Y.: Cornell University Press, 1998.

Ball, Douglas B. *Financial Failure and Confederate Defeat*. Urbana: University of Illinois Press, 1991.

Beers, Henry P. *Guide to the Archives of the Government of the Confederate States of America*. Washington, D.C.: National Archives, 1968.

Beringer, Richard E., Herman Hattaway, Archer Jones, and William N. Still Jr. *Why the South Lost the Civil War*. Athens: University of Georgia Press, 1986.

Billings, John D. *Hardtack and Coffee: or, The Unwritten Story of Army Life*. Edited by Richard Harwell. Chicago: Lakeside Press, 1960.

Blackett, R. J. M. *Divided Hearts: Britain and the American Civil War*. Baton Rouge: Louisiana State University Press, 2000.

Blackford, William W. *War Years with Jeb Stuart*. Baton Rouge: Louisiana State University Press, 1993.

Blanton, DeAnne, and Lauren M. Cook. *They Fought Like Demons: Women Soldiers in the American Civil War*. Baton Rouge: Louisiana State University Press, 2002.

Blight, David W. *Race and Reunion: The Civil War in American Memory*. Cambridge: Belknap Press of Harvard University Press, 2001.

Boritt, Gabor S. *Lincoln's Generals*. New York: Oxford University Press, 1994.

——, ed. *The Lincoln Enigma: The Changing Faces of an American Icon*. New York: Oxford University Press, 2001.

Brown, Campbell. *Campbell Brown's Civil War: With Ewell and the Army of Northern Virginia*. Edited by Terry L. Jones. Baton Rouge: Louisiana State University Press, 2001.

Casler, John O. *Four Years in the Stonewall Brigade*. Notes by James I. Robertson Jr. Dayton, Ohio: Morningside, 1982.

Castel, Albert. *Decision in the West: The Atlanta Campaign of 1864*. Lawrence: University Press of Kansas, 1992.

Catton, Bruce. *The Army of the Potomac*. 3 Vols. *Mr. Lincoln's Army, Glory Road*, and *A Stillness at Appomattox*. Garden City, N.Y.: Doubleday, 1951–1953.

———. *U. S. Grant and the American Military Tradition*. Boston: Little, Brown, 1954.

Chase, Salmon P. *The Salmon P. Chase Papers*. 5 Vols. Edited by John Niven. Kent, Ohio: Kent State University Press, 1993–1998.

Chesnut, Mary. *Mary Chesnut's Civil War*. Edited by C. Vann Woodward. New Haven, Conn.: Yale University Press, 1981.

Clinton, Catherine, ed. *Southern Families at War: Loyalty and Conflict in the Civil War*. New York: Oxford University Press, 2000.

Coddington, Edwin B. *The Gettysburg Campaign: A Study in Command*. New York: Scribner's, 1984.

Connelly, Thomas Lawrence. *Army of the Heartland: The Army of Tennessee, 1861–1862*. Baton Rouge: Louisiana State University Press, 1967.

———. *Autumn of Glory: The Army of Tennessee, 1862–1865*. Baton Rouge: Louisiana State University Press, 1971.

Cooling, Benjamin F. *Forts Henry and Donelson: Key to the Confederate Heartland*. Knoxville: University of Tennessee Press, 1988.

Cumming, Kate. *Kate: The Journal of a Confederate Nurse*. Edited by Richard Barksdale Harwell. Baton Rouge: Louisiana State University Press, 1959.

Cunningham, H. H. *Doctors in Gray: The Confederate Medical Service*. Baton Rouge: Louisiana State University Press, 1993.

Current, Richard Nelson. *Lincoln's Loyalists: Union Soldiers from the Confederacy*. Boston: Northeastern University Press, 1992.

Daniel, Larry J. *Soldiering in the Army of Tennessee: A Portrait of Life in a Confederate Army*. Chapel Hill: University of North Carolina Press, 1991.

Davis, Jefferson. The Papers of Jefferson Davis. Baton Rouge: Louisiana State University Press, 1971– .

Davis, William C. *The Orphan Brigade: The Kentucky Confederates Who Couldn't Go Home*. New York: Doubleday, 1980.

———. *Jefferson Davis: The Man and His Hour*. New York: HarperCollins, 1991.

———. *Look Away! A History of the Confederate States of America*. New York: The Free Press, 2002.

Dawes, Rufus R. *Service with the Sixth Wisconsin Volunteers*. Introduction by Gregory Coco. Dayton, Ohio: Morningside, 1984.

Dean, Eric T. *Shook Over Hell: Post-Traumatic Stress, Vietnam, and the Civil War*. Cambridge, Mass.: Harvard University Press, 1997.

Dew, Charles B. *Apostles of Disunion: Southern Secession Commissioners and the Causes of the Civil War*. Charlottesville: University of Virginia Press, 2001.

Donald, David, ed. *Why the North Won the Civil War*. Baton Rouge: Louisiana State University Press, 1960.

———. *Lincoln*. New York: Simon and Schuster, 1995.

Douglas, Henry Kyd. *I Rode with Stonewall*. Chapel Hill: University of North Carolina Press, 1987.

Dudley, Taylor Cornish. *The Sable Arm: Black Troops in the Union Army, 1861–1865.* Foreword by Herman Hattaway. Lawrence: University Press of Kansas, 1987.

Eicher, David J. *The Civil War in Books: An Analytical Bibliography.* Foreword by Gary W. Gallagher. Champaign: University of Illinois Press, 1996.

Fahs, Alice. *The Imagined Civil War: Popular Literature of the North & South, 1861–1865.* Chapel Hill: University of North Carolina Press, 2001.

Feis, William B. *Grant's Secret Service: The Intelligence War from Belmont to Appomattox.* Lincoln: University of Nebraska Press, 2002.

Fellman, Michael. *Inside War: The Guerrilla Conflict in Missouri during the American Civil War.* New York: Oxford University Press, 1989.

———. *The Making of Robert E. Lee.* New York: Random House, 2000.

Foote, Shelby. *The Civil War: A Narrative.* 3 Vols. New York: Vintage, 1986.

Freeling, William W. *The South vs. the South: How Anti-Confederate Southerners Shaped the Course of the Civil War.* New York: Oxford University Press, 2001.

Freeman, Douglas Southall. *R. E. Lee: A Biography.* 4 Vols. New York: Charles Scribner's Sons, 1934–1935.

Fuller, John F. C. *Grant and Lee: A Study in Personality and Generalship.* Bloomington: Indiana University Press, 1982.

Furgurson, Ernest B. *Ashes of Glory: Richmond at War.* New York: Alfred A. Knopf, 1996.

Gallagher, Gary W., and Alan T. Nolan, eds. *The Myth of the Lost Cause and Civil War History.* Bloomington: Indiana University Press, 2000.

Geary, James W. *We Need More Men: The Union Draft in the Civil War.* DeKalb: Northern Illinois University Press, 1991.

Glatthaar, Joseph T. *Forged in Battle: The Civil War Alliance of Black Soldiers and White Officers.* New York: Free Press, 1990.

Goodrich, Thomas. *War to the Knife: Bleeding Kansas, 1854–1861.* Mechanicsburg, Pa.: Stackpole, 1998.

Gordon, John B. *Reminiscences of the Civil War.* Introduction by Ralph Lowell Eckert. Baton Rouge: Louisiana State University Press, 1993.

Gorgas, Josiah. *The Journals of Josiah Gorgas, 1857–1878.* Edited by Frank E. Vandiver. University: University of Alabama Press, 1947.

Grabau, Warren E. *Ninety-Eight Days: A Geographer's View of the Vicksburg Campaign.* Knoxville: University of Tennessee Press, 2000.

Grant, Ulysses S. *Personal Memoirs of U. S. Grant.* 2 Vols. Introduction by William S. McFeely. New York: Da Capo Press, 1982.

———. *The Papers of Ulysses S. Grant.* Edited by John Y. Simon, David L. Wilson, J. Thomas Murphy, et. al. 20 Vols. Carbondale: Southern Illinois University Press, 1967–1995.

Grimsley, Mark, and Brooks D. Simpson, eds. *The Collapse of the Confederacy.* Lincoln: University of Nebraska Press, 2001.

Hanchett, William. *The Lincoln Murder Conspiracies.* Urbana: University of Illinois Press, 1983.

Hattaway, Herman. *Shades of Blue and Gray: An Introductory Military History of the Civil War.* Columbia: University of Missouri Press, 1997.

Hattaway, Herman, and Archer Jones. *How the North Won: A Military History of the Civil War.* Urbana: University of Illinois Press, 1983.

Henderson, G. F. R. *Stonewall Jackson and the American Civil War*. 2 Vols. Introduction by Thomas L. Connelly. New York: Da Capo Press, 1988.

Hennessy, John J. *Return to Bull Run: The Campaign and Battle of Second Manassas*. New York: Simon and Schuster, 1993.

Hesseltine, William Best. *Civil War Prisons: A Study in War Psychology*. Columbus: Ohio State University Press, 1930.

Hotchkiss, Jedediah. *Make Me a Map of the Valley: The Civil War Journal of Stonewall Jackson's Cartographer*. Edited by Archie P. McDonald. Dallas: Southern Methodist University, 1988.

Howard, Oliver Otis. *Autobiography of Oliver Otis Howard*. 2 Vols. Salem, N.H.: Ayer, n.d.

Jimerson, Randall C. *The Private Civil War: Popular Thought during the Sectional Conflict*. Baton Rouge: Louisiana State University Press, 1988.

Johnson, Andrew. *The Papers of Andrew Johnson*. Edited by LeRoy P. Graf, Ralph W. Haskins, and Paul H. Bergeron. 15 Vols. Knoxville: University of Tennessee Press, 1967–1999.

Johnson, Ludwell H. *Red River Campaign: Politics and Cotton in the Civil War*. Kent, Ohio: Kent State University Press, 1993.

Jones, John B. *A Rebel War Clerk's Diary at the Confederate State Capital*. Baton Rouge: Louisiana State University Press, 1993.

Jones, Terry L. *Lee's Tigers: The Louisiana Infantry in the Army of Northern Virginia*. Baton Rouge: Louisiana State University Press, 1987.

———. *Historical Dictionary of the Civil War*. Lanham, Md.: Scarecrow Press, 2002.

Kerby, Robert L. *Kirby Smith's Confederacy: The Trans-Mississippi South, 1863–1865*. Tuscaloosa: University of Alabama Press, 1991.

Klement, Frank L. *Dark Lanterns: Secret Political Societies, Conspiracies, and Treason Trials in the Civil War*. Baton Rouge: Louisiana State University Press, 1984.

Lee, Robert E. *The Wartime Papers of R. E. Lee*. Edited by Clifford Dowdey and Louis H. Manarin. New York: Da Capo Press, 1987.

Leech, Margaret. *Reveille in Washington, 1860–1865*. New York: Harper and Bros., 1941.

Leonard, Elizabeth D. *All the Daring of a Soldier: Women of the Civil War Armies*. New York: W. W. Norton, 1999.

Lincoln, Abraham. *The Collected Works of Abraham Lincoln*. Edited by Roy P. Basler. 11 Vols. New Brunswick, N.J.: Rutgers University Press, 1953–1955.

Lonn, Ella. *Foreigners in the Confederacy*. Gloucester, Mass.: P. Smith, 1965.

———. *Foreigners in the Union Army and Navy*. New York: Greenwood Press, 1979.

Lowry, Thomas P. *The Story the Soldiers Wouldn't Tell: Sex in the Civil War*. Mechanicsburg, Pa.: Stackpole, 1994.

Marszalek, John F. *Sherman: A Soldier's Passion for Order*. New York: Free Press, 1993.

Marten, James. *The Children's Civil War*. Chapel Hill: University of North Carolina Press, 1998.

Marvel, William. *Andersonville: The Last Depot*. Chapel Hill: University of North Carolina Press, 1994.

———. *Lee's Last Retreat: The Flight to Appomattox.* Chapel Hill: University of North Carolina Press, 2002.

McClellan, George B. *The Civil War Papers of George B. McClellan: Selected Correspondence, 1860–1865.* Edited by Stephen W. Sears. New York: Da Capo Press, 1992.

McMurry, Richard M. *Two Great Rebel Armies: An Essay in Confederate Military History.* Chapel Hill: University of North Carolina Press, 1989.

McPherson, James M. *Battle Cry of Freedom: The Civil War Era.* New York: Oxford University Press, 1988.

———. *For Cause and Comrades: Why Men Fought in the Civil War.* New York: Oxford University Press, 1997.

———. *Crossroads of Freedom: Antietam, the Battle that Changed the Course of the Civil War.* New York: Oxford University Press, 2002.

McWhiney, Grady. *Braxton Bragg and Confederate Defeat, Vol. 1: Field Command.* Tuscaloosa: University Press of Alabama, 1991.

Moe, Richard. *The Last Full Measure: The Life and Death of the First Minnesota Volunteers.* New York: Henry Holt, 1993.

Munden, Kenneth W., and Henry P. Beers. *Guide to Federal Archives Relating to the Civil War.* Washington, D.C.: National Archives, 1962.

Neely, Mark E., Jr. *Southern Rights: Political Prisoners and the Myth of Confederate Constitutionalism.* Charlottesville: University Press of Virginia, 1999.

Nevins, Allan. *Ordeal of the Union.* 8 Vols. New York: Charles Scribner's Sons, 1947–1971.

Nevins, Allan, James I. Robertson Jr., and Bell I. Wiley, eds. *Civil War Books: A Critical Bibliography.* 2 Vols. Baton Rouge: Louisiana State University Press, 1967–1969.

Nisbet, James Cooper. *Four Years on the Firing Line.* Edited by Bell I. Wiley. Wilmington, N.C.: Broadfoot, 1991.

Nolan, Alan. *The Iron Brigade: A Military History.* Introduction by Gary W. Gallagher. Bloomington: Indian University Press, 1994.

Oates, Stephen B. *To Purge This Land with Blood: A Biography of John Brown.* New York: Harper and Row, 1970.

Oates, William C. *The War between the Union and the Confederacy, and Its Lost Opportunities: With a History of the 15th Alabama Regiment and the Forty-eight Battles in Which It Was Engaged.* New York: Neale Publishing, 1905.

Pfanz, Donald C. *Richard S. Ewell: A Soldier's Life.* Chapel Hill: University of North Carolina Press, 1998.

Pfanz, Harry W. *Gettysburg: Culp's Hill and Cemetery Hill.* Chapel Hill: University of North Carolina Press, 1993.

Piston, William Garrett, and Richard W. Hatcher III. *Wilson's Creek: The Second Battle of the Civil War and the Men Who Fought It.* Chapel Hill: University of North Carolina Press, 2000.

Porter, Horace. *Campaigning with Grant.* Edited by Wayne C. Temple. Bloomington: Indiana University Press, 1961.

Power, J. Tracy. *Lee's Miserables: Life in the Army of Northern Virginia from the Wilderness to Appomattox.* Chapel Hill: University of North Carolina Press, 1998.

Rable, George C. *Fredericksburg! Fredericksburg!* Chapel Hill: University of North Carolina Press, 2002.

Randall, James G., and David H. Donald. *The Civil War and Reconstruction*. 2nd ed. Boston: D. C. Heath, 1969.

Rhea, Gordon C. *The Battle of the Wilderness, May 5–6, 1864*. Baton Rouge: Louisiana State University Press, 1994.

——. *The Battles for Spotsylvania Court House and the Road to Yellow Tavern, May 7–12, 1864*. Baton Rouge: Louisiana State University Press, 1997.

Rhodes, Elisha Hunt. *All for the Union: The Civil War Diary and Letters of Elisha Hunt Rhodes*. Edited by Robert Hunt Rhodes. New York: Orion Books, 1991.

Richter, William L. *Historical Dictionary of the Civil War and Reconstruction*. Lanham, Md.: Scarecrow Press, 2004.

Robertson, James I., Jr. *The Stonewall Brigade*. Baton Rouge: Louisiana State University Press, 1987.

——. *Stonewall Jackson: The Man, the Soldier, the Legend*. New York: Macmillan, 1997.

Roland, Charles P. *An American Iliad: The Story of the Civil War*. Lexington: University Press of Kentucky, 1991.

Rosen, Robert N. *The Jewish Confederates*. Columbia: University of South Carolina Press, 2000.

Sears, Stephen W. *Landscape Turned Red: The Battle of Antietam*. New Haven, Conn.: Ticknor and Fields, 1983.

——. *George B. McClellan: The Young Napoleon*. New York: Ticknor and Fields, 1988.

——. *To the Gates of Richmond: The Peninsula Campaign*. New York: Ticknor and Fields, 1992.

——. *Chancellorsville*. Boston: Houghton Mifflin, 1996.

Shaw, Robert Gould. *Blue-Eyed Child of Fortune: The Civil War Letters of Colonel Robert Gould Shaw*. Edited by Russell Duncan. Athens: University of Georgia Press, 1992.

Sherman, William Tecumseh. *Sherman's Civil War: Selected Correspondence of William T. Sherman, 1860–1865*. Edited by Brooks D. Simpson and Jean V. Berlin. Chapel Hill: University of North Carolina Press, 1998.

Sibley, Joel H. *A Respectable Minority: The Democratic Party in the Civil War Era, 1860–1868*. New York: W. W. Norton, 1977.

Simpson, Brooks D. *Let Us Have Peace: Ulysses S. Grant and the Politics of War and Reconstruction, 1861–1868*. Chapel Hill: University of North Carolina Press, 1991.

——. *Ulysses S. Grant: Triumph Over Adversity, 1822–1865*. New York: Houghton Mifflin, 2000.

Sorrel, G. Moxley. *Recollections of a Confederate Staff Officer*. Edited by Bell I. Wiley. Wilmington, N.C.: Broadfoot, 1991.

Starr, Stephen Z. *Jennison's Jayhawkers: A Civil War Cavalry Regiment and Its Commander*. Baton Rouge: Louisiana State University Press, 1973.

Stevens, Thaddeus. *The Selected Papers of Thaddeus Stevens*. 2 Vols. Edited by Beverly Wilson Palmer. Pittsburgh: University of Pittsburgh Press, 1997–1998.

Stiles, Robert. *Four Years under Marse Robert*. Introduction by Robert K. Krick. Dayton, Ohio: Morningside, 1988.

Sumner, Charles. *The Selected Letters of Charles Sumner*. Edited by Beverly Wilson Palmer. 2 Vols. Boston: Northeastern University Press, 1990.

Sword, Wiley. *Embrace an Angry Wind: The Confederacy's Last Hurrah—Spring Hill, Franklin, and Nashville.* New York: HarperCollins, 1992.
——. *Shiloh: Bloody April.* Dayton, Ohio: Morningside, 1993.
Symonds, Craig L. *Stonewall of the West: Patrick Cleburne and the Civil War.* Lawrence: University Press of Kansas, 1997.
Tanner, Robert G. *Stonewall in the Valley: Thomas J. "Stonewall" Jackson's Shenandoah Valley Campaign, Spring 1862.* Garden City, N.Y.: Doubleday, 1976.
Tap, Bruce. *Over Lincoln's Shoulder: The Committee on the Conduct of the War.* Lawrence: University Press of Kansas, 1998.
Taylor, Richard. *Destruction and Reconstruction: Personal Experiences in the Late War.* Introduction by T. Michael Parrish. New York: Da Capo Press, 1995.
Thomas, Emory M. *Bold Dragoon: The Life of J. E. B. Stuart.* New York: Harper and Row, 1986.
——. *Robert E. Lee: A Biography.* New York: W. W. Norton, 1995.
Thomas, William G., and Alice E. Carter. *The Civil War on the Web: A Guide to the Very Best Sites.* Wilmington, Del.: Scholarly Resources, 2001.
Tidwell, William A. *April '65: Confederate Covert Action in the American Civil War.* Kent, Ohio: Kent State University Press, 1995.
Trulock, Alice Rains. *In the Hands of Providence: Joshua L. Chamberlain and the American Civil War.* Chapel Hill: University of North Carolina Press, 1992.
Tunnard, William H. *A Southern Record: The History of the Third Regiment, Louisiana Infantry.* Introduction by William L. Shea. Fayetteville: University of Arkansas Press, 1997.
Turner, George Edgar. *Victory Rode the Rails: The Strategic Place of the Railroads in the Civil War.* Introduction by Gary W. Gallagher. Lincoln: University of Nebraska Press, 1992.
U.S. War Department. *The War of the Rebellion: A Compilation of the Official Records of the Union and Confederate Armies.* 128 Vols. Washington, D.C.: U.S. Government Printing Office, 1880–1901.
——. *Official Records of the Union and Confederate Navies in the War of the Rebellion.* 30 Vols. Washington, D.C.: U.S. Government Printing Office, 1894–1922.
Vance, Zebulon B. *The Papers of Zebulon Baird Vance.* 2 Vols. Edited by Frontis W. Johnston and Joe A. Mobley. Raleigh: North Carolina State Department of Archives and History, 1963–1995.
Watkins, Sam. *"Co. Aytch," Maury Grays, First Tennessee Regiment; or, A Side Show of the Big Show.* New York: Simon & Schuster, 1997.
Welles, Gideon. *The Diary of Gideon Welles.* 3 Vols. Edited by Howard K. Beale. New York: W. W. Norton, 1960.
Wert, Jeffry D. *Mosby's Rangers.* New York: Simon and Schuster, 1990.
——. *General James Longstreet, the Confederacy's Most Controversial Soldier: A Biography.* New York: Simon and Schuster, 1993.
Wilkinson, Warren. *Mother, May You Never See the Sights I Have Seen: The 57th Massachusetts Veteran Volunteers.* New York: Harper and Row, 1990.
Williams, Alpheus S. *From the Cannon's Mouth: General Alpheus S. Williams.* Edited by Milo M. Quaife and introduction by Gary W. Gallagher. Lincoln: University of Nebraska Press, 1995.
Williams, T. Harry. *Lincoln and His Generals.* New York: Alfred A. Knopf, 1952.

Wills, Brian Steel. *A Battle from the Start: The Life of Nathan Bedford Forrest*. New York: HarperCollins, 1992.

Woodworth, Steven E. *Jefferson Davis and His Generals: The Failure of Confederate Command in the West*. Lawrence: University Press of Kansas, 1990.

Worsham, John H. *One of Jackson's Foot Cavalry*. Edited by James I. Robertson Jr. Wilmington, N.C.: Broadfoot, 1991.

About the Author

Terry L. Jones is a native of Dodson, Louisiana, and received his B.A. and M.A. from Louisiana Tech University and his Ph.D. from Texas A&M University. Jones has published extensively on the American Civil War, including *Lee's Tigers: The Louisiana Infantry in the Army of Northern Virginia*, *The Civil War Memoirs of Capt. William J. Seymour: Reminiscences of a Louisiana Tiger*, and *Campbell Brown's Civil War: With Ewell and the Army of Northern Virginia*. Jones has taught for 20 years at the high school and university levels and currently is a professor of history at the University of Louisiana at Monroe.